Detective
and
Mystery
Fiction

Detective and Mystery Fiction

An International Bibliography of Secondary Sources

Walter Albert

Brownstone Books

Detective and Mystery Fiction:
An International Bibliography of Secondary Sources

Second Printing

International Standard Book Number: 0-941028-02-X

Brownstone Books
1711 Clifty Drive
Madison, IN 47250

Published 1985
Printed in the United States of America

Table of Contents

Acknowledgments vii

Preface ix

Abbreviations xi

I. Bibliographies, Dictionaries, Encyclopedias, & Checklists 1

II. General Reference Works: Historical & Critical 30

A. Books /30

B. Articles /123

III. Dime Novels, Juvenile Series & Pulps 237

A. Dime Novel & Juvenile /237

1. General References /237
2. Series /247

B. Pulps /273

1. General References /273
2. Single-character Series, Magazines & Publishers /279

IV. Authors 300

Index 733

Contributors 777

Acknowledgments

Allen J. Hubin began publishing my annual bibliography of secondary sources in The Armchair Detective in 1972, and Otto Penzler has continued to show the same commitment to bibliographic studies that Hubin considered so important to the field of crime fiction.

The annotations for this bibliography have been contributed by a dedicated team of 22 researchers. They have all shown remarkable patience with what must have seemed my constant requests for additional information, and I hope that the final version of the bibliography justifies their faith in it.

The annotations of Jacques Baudou were submitted in French, those of Renzo Cremante and Loris Rambelli in Italian, and of Hirohisa Shimpo and Toshihika Taniguchi in Japanese. Esther M. Cook provided English translations for the Italian entries and Jiro Kimura for the Japanese; translations for the French entries are by the editor.

I am also grateful for the assistance of a number of people who have sent me copies of articles and other material and answered questions on a variety of topics on which it was essential to have the most accurate and complete information possible. The following have made contributions of particular note to the project: Dee Ashliman, Jack Bales, L. Carberry, Joe R. Christopher, John Robert Colombo, Fred Cook, Bill Crider, David H. Doerrer, Norman Donaldson, Douglas G. Greene, David A. Grothe, Edward D. Hoch, Brian KenKnight, Barbara Korte, Edward S. Lauterbach, Marvin Lachman, James R. McCahery, Diana T. Mertz, Harald Mogensen, Al Nehr, Francis M. Nevins, Jr., Alan Reiland, John Roy, Jean-Jacques Schleret, Charles Shibuk, Jean and Walter Shine, and Donald A. Yates.

Permission to use material for annotations originally published in a somewhat different format has been given by the following: Gil O'Gara, editor/publisher of Yellowback Library, for excerpts from a bibliography of secondary material on the Hardy Boys written by Jack Bales and published in Yellowback Library 18 (Nov/Dec 83), pp. 5-6; Ms. Pat Browne, Editor and Business Manager of The Popular Press, Bowling Green State University, Bowling Green, Ohio, for material from "The Literature of the Subject: An Annotated Bibliography," by Robert E. Briney, published in The Mystery Story, edited by John Ball; and Ralph Carlson, Vice President, Garland Publishing Company, for material from E. F. Bleiler's annotations for Garland's catalogue, The Fiction of Popular Culture.

The camera-ready copy was prepared on the following equipment: an Eagle II computer, Spellbinder word-processing program, and a Daisywriter printer. The problems presented in adapting this equipment to the specialized needs of the bibliography were taken on generously by Margaret C. Albert, who spent days working on the often impenetrable prose of manuals and hours on the phone with equipment support technicians. The final major hurdle, the determination of codes for the printing of foreign language diacritical marks, was solved by Art Scott who spent two days with us, most of that time at the computer.

My publisher, Guy Townsend, is also a bibliographer and this made possible a working relationship that went far beyond matters of printers, binders and marketing. I want to acknowledge his editorial contributions which make of him an advisory editor as well as publisher.

And, in addition to the herculean task with the computer, my wife also advised me on essential points of punctuation and other fine points of English syntax and grammar, devised the formatting system, and handled paste-ups and headings. Any lapses are my fault and not hers, but without her this book would not have been possible.

--Walter Albert

January 1985

Preface

i

This bibliography of secondary sources is intended to be comprehensive in the areas of crime, detective, mystery, suspense and espionage fiction. It also includes the dime novel, juvenile series and the pulps, areas with which many researchers in the field are relatively unfamiliar but which constitute a vast and widely read literature that has both drawn from mystery fiction and contributed to it. In addition, the related genres of science-fiction and the western are included where crime and/or detection elements justify the term "cross-over genre." Many writers have worked in more than one genre, and the structural elements common to one are often found in others. This is particularly true of writers for the pulps and dime novels, and it is not surprising to find that these writers have been less than absolute in their observation of categorical boundaries. This bleeding into adjacent areas has been one of the most notable characteristics of the literature and reflects the tendency of the novel, that most "lawless" of genres, to put constantly to the test its conventions and to reshape its traditional configurations.

Two areas of inclusion deserve special note. This is the first international bibliography of crime fiction. The references to essays and books in several foreign languages demonstrate the extent to which English-language fiction has been translated, read and studied, but they also record the growth of indigenous national literatures of crime and detection. Much of the critical writing in the United States, Asia and Europe has appeared in fan publications and is not recorded in sources like the _Reader's Guide to Periodical Literature_, the _MLA Bibliography_ and the _Humanities Index_. Some libraries have recently begun to collect these publications, but they are not readily available for consultation. Two recent books by Michael L. Cook, _Mystery Fanfare_ (Bowling Green State University Popular Press, 1983) and _Mystery, Detective, and Espionage Magazines_ (Greenwood Press, 1983), provide information on fan publications in this country and abroad, and back issues of the magazines can sometimes be ordered from the publishers. The Popular Culture Association, more than a decade ago, began collecting data on libraries with holdings in this area, but the project was, unfortunately, abandoned almost immediately.

Some material has been excluded from this bibliography. The most extensive is the Sherlockian literature. References will be cited where they bear on more general questions (influences and literary history), but the vast literature of critical studies, already the subject of other bibliographies, will not be included. Also, since this is is a bibliography of written sources, material relating to films, radio, television and the theater will not be covered unless it bears directly on the fiction.

All annotations are based on the consultation of original sources unless the designation "not seen" is included with the reference.

ii

The bibliography is divided into four sections. The items are numbered consecutively, within sections, with internal cross references given in parentheses, where appropriate. Some numbers in the sequences are missing;

these gaps were created by the deletion of duplicate entries in the final draft when it was not feasible to renumber the entire book. Foreign-language entries are fully integrated with the English-language material, and translations of titles of books and articles are bracketed between parallel lines (|...|) immediately following the citation in the original language.

Section I includes all bibliographies, dictionaries, and checklists. These checklists do not include indices to magazines like Ellery Queen's Mystery Magazine and other digest-sized magazines that are entered in Section III with the pulps.

Critical and historical essays, articles and books are cited in Section II, with the books grouped in Part A and articles and essays in Part B. Multi-subject author entries are cited in this section and cross-referenced as necessary. Technical articles and books on the craft of writing are cited here. This material often contains comments by writers on their own work or on the work of other writers and can be a valuable source. Two magazines, The Writer and Writer's Digest, publish much of this material and are cited as main entries in II A. Contents lists are generally provided for collections of essays and for special issues of journals devoted to mystery fiction.

Section III consists of entries on the dime novel and juvenile mystery series, and on the pulps. This is the first comprehensive annotated listing of such material.

Section IV is devoted to individual authors and is the most extensive of the four categories. This listing is limited to those authors on whom critical material exists and does not constitute a dictionary of authors. If the author has used one or more pseudonyms, entries are grouped under a single heading. Every effort has been made to organize the listings under the name the author uses most frequently and with which he is most commonly identified. Where there are several pseudonyms with no one of them taking precedence (as in the case of John Creasey), entries are grouped under the author's real name. There is some cross-referencing of pseudonyms within the author section and in the Index; Hubin 2 may be consulted where there is any ambiguity.

A major feature of the author listings is a guide to biographical and critical information in standard works like Twentieth Century Crime and Mystery Writers, the Catalogue of Crime, Hubin 2, and the Author Biographies Master Index. These references are given in an abbreviated form and are not annotated.

iii

The index of names includes authors of primary and secondary material, series characters, and speciality magazines and publishing houses where those items are the subject of the entry. To distinguish between authors and fictional characters, the latter are indexed by first names or by titles (i. e., Inspector Cuff, Nero Wolfe). The designation "AR" identifies authors for whom there is general reference information in the author section but for whom there are no individually annotated sources.

Abbreviations

ABMI: Author Biographies Master Index
ABMIS: Author Biographies Master Index Supplement
ABMI(S): Author Biographies Master Index and ABMI Supplement
ADAM: Adam International Review
AHMM: Alfred Hitchcock's Mystery Magazine
AR: Author Reference
BBC: British Broadcasting Company
BFF: Benjamin F. Fisher, IV
BMJ: British Medical Journal
BoB: Bulletin of Bibliography
Breen: What About Murder? (see item A22)
CC: Catalogue of Crime (see item A10)
CC S: Catalogue of Crime Supplement
CDA: Collectors' Digest Annual
CP?: Collecting Paperbacks?
CWA: Crime Writers' Association
DAI: Dissertation Abstracts International
DFW: Detective Fiction Weekly
DJ: Deidre Johnson
DLS: Dorothy L. Sayers
DNR: Dime Novel Round-Up
DSF: Doc Savage Forum
DSM: Detective Story Magazine
DSN: Dickens Studies Newsletter
DSQ: Doc Savage Quarterly
DSR: Dickens Society Review
EFB: Everett F. Bleiler
EMD: Encyclopedia of Mystery & Detection
EQ: Ellery Queen
EQMM: Ellery Queen's Mystery Magazine
EQR: Ellery Queen Review
EWSN: Edgar Wallace Society Newsletter
FC: Fictional Character
GG: Greg Goode
HIBK: Had-I-But-Known
HS: Hirohisa Shimpo
Hubin 2: Crime Fiction, 1749-1980 (See item A83)
IH: Iwan Hedman
Int: Interview
JAmStud: Journal of American Studies
JB: Jacques Baudou
JDMB: John D. MacDonald Bibliophile
JK: Jiro Kimura
JLA: John L. Apostolou
JN: John Nieminski
JPC: Journal of Popular Culture
JRC: J. Randolph Cox
KLM: Kathleen L. Maio
KQ: Kansas Quarterly
LJ: Library Journal
LR: Loris Rambelli

M&ASR: Mystery & Adventure Series Review
MDA: Mystery & Detection Annual
MFS: Modern Fiction Studies
MLQ: Modern Languages Quarterly
MM: Mysteç127/re Magazine
MS: Mary Seeger
MSMM: Mike Shayne Mystery Magazine
MTJ: Mark Twain Journal
MWA: Mystery Writers of America
NL: Nouvelles littéraires
NYRB: New York Review of Books
NYTBR: New York Times Book Review
OULIPOPO: Ouvroir de Littérature Potentielle
PB: Paperback
PBSA: Papers of the Bibliographical Society of America
PC: Pulp Character
PCS: Popular Culture Scholar
PMLA: Publication of the Modern Language Association
Popular Press: Bowling Green University Popular Press
PQ: Paperback Quarterly
PW: Publishers' Weekly
RC: Renzo Cremante
RCSA: Robert C. S. Adey
REB: Robert E. Briney
Ref: References
RS: Robert Sampson
SAS: Steven A. Stilwell
SatEvePost: Saturday Evening Post
SFC: Science Fiction Collector
SMS: Startling Mystery Stories
SN: Série noire
SR: Saturday Review
SRL: Saturday Review of Literature
SSB: Savage Society of Bronze
TAD: The Armchair Detective
TBBC: The Boys' Book Collector
TCBG: The Comic Buyer's Guide
TCCMW: Twentieth Century Crime & Mystery Writers (see item A143)
TLS: Times (London) Literary Supplement
TMF: The Mystery FANcier
TMRN: The Mystery Readers/Lovers Newsletter
TMN: The Mystery Nook
TNSPE: The Not So Private Eye
TPP: The Poisoned Pen
TQCB: The Queen Canon Bibliophile
TRR: The Rohmer Review
TSLL: Texas Studies in Literature and Language
TSR: The Sayers Review
TT: Toshihiko Taniguchi
TTF: The Thorndyke File
UN: Unicorn Mystery Book Club News
WA: Walter Albert
WD: Writer's Digest
WLB: Wilson Library Bulletin
WM: Will Murray
WT: Weird Tales
YL: Yellowback Library

I. Bibliographies, Dictionaries, Encyclopedias, & Checklists

A1. Adey, R. C. S. "The Detective Short Story." Search and Research 1:2 (June 1974): 33-34.
Examination in a style similar to Queen's, but in more detail, of three short story collections Queen did not cover. First of a projected series that was not continued. (RCSA)

A2. ______. Locked Room Murders and Other Impossible Crimes. London: Ferret Fantasy Ltd., 1979. 190pp.
In his introduction, the author surveys locked room crime stories from Poe to the present. He then presents an annotated list of 1280 locked room short stories and novels, arranged alphabetically by author (pp. 29-133). The annotations briefly describe the impossible crime problem in each story. The rest of the book (pp. 134-187) contains the solutions to these problems. A unique and fascinating compilation (and one that requires great willpower to use without peeking!). Breen 8. (REB)

A3. ______. "The Modern Publishing Company." TPP 4:1 (Feb 81):3-7.
A brief history of a British publishing house and a checklist of titles published.

A4. Adley, Derek J.; and Lofts, W. O. G. The Thriller. Manchester (England): A. Cadwallender, 1983. Unpaged (pp. 1-25). Pictorial wraps. Edition limited to 100 copies.
The Thriller was a weekly British story paper which ran for 589 issues, 1929-1940. Two of its most prolific contributors were Leslie Charteris and Edgar Wallace. The magazine published several of the earliest stories of John Creasey, and a large number of Shadow stories by Maxwell Grant. Other familiar names appearing in its pages were Margery Allingham, Max Brand, Peter Cheyney, Agatha Christie, George Harmon Coxe, Dashiell Hammett, Talbot Mundy, E. Phillips Oppenheim, Sax Rohmer, and Roy Vickers. Adley and Lofts present an index to the fiction (and some true crime) contents of the magazine, arranged in three lists: the featured novels or novellas, the 'supporting' short stories, and the serials. (Only one point seems to have been missed: The Thriller occasionally offered supplements, such as the Sexton Blake story "Midnight Gold!" by Gilbert Chester, a separate 20-page booklet distributed with the 15 February 1930 issue.) In a four-page preface Derek Adley surveys the magazine's publishing history and discusses its editorial staff. (REB)

A5. Albert, Walter. "A Bibliography of Secondary Sources." An annual listing--from 1972--appearing in TAD. Installments have been published as follows: 1972 in TAD 7 (1973):46-47; 1973 in TAD 7 (1974): 266-269; 1974 in TAD 8 (1975):290-293, 274; 1975 in TAD 9 (1976):316-320; 1976 in TAD 11 (1978):196-202; 1977 in TAD 12 (1979):125-129, 167; 1978 in TAD 13 (1980):43-47; 1979 in TAD 13 (1980):313-318; 1980 in TAD 14 (1981):346-354; 1981 in TAD 16 (1983):29-39.

Items have been annotated since the 1976 listing and comprehensive coverage of fanzine material was introduced in the 1977 listing. In addition to the coverage of detective and mystery fiction, the bibliography has also included relevant material from films, TV, the dime novel, pulps and juvenile series. Material on Arthur Conan Doyle has, in general, been excluded from the bibliography.

A6. Allard, Yvon. Paralittératures I. Cahiers de bibliographie. Collèges, 6. Montréal: Centre de bibliographie de la Centrale des bibliothèques, 1975. 322pp. A revised and expanded version was published in 1979, as follows: Paralittératures. Sélections documentaires, 2. Montréal: La Centrale des bibliothèques. 728pp. Author and title indices.
The revised version, in addition to annotated bibliographies of secondary sources for seven categories of fiction (myth, fantasy, adventure, the sentimental novel, the historical novel, espionage and political fiction, the Western, detective fiction, science-fiction and humor), also includes biographical dictionaries of important authors, short descriptions of series like the Barzun-Taylor Fifty Classics of Crime Fiction 1900-1950 (Garland, 1979) and the Gallimard série noire in France, a selected group of novels and short stories in each category, and a list of the 100 "best" novels.

A7. Atkinson, Frank. Dictionary of Literary Pseudonyms: A Selection of Popular Modern Writers in English. 3rd ed., revised. Hamden, Conn. and London: Linnet Books and Clive Bigley, 1981.
Of limited interest. The primary resource for pseudonyms of writers in mystery and detective fiction and related categories is Hubin 2 (A83).

A8. Ballinger, John and Emily. "Biblio-Mysteries." Williamsburg, VA: The Bookpress Ltd., 1984.
A bookdealer's catalogue. 554 items are described, including some reference material (articles and pamphlets). The annotations contain short plot summaries.

A9. Barnes, Melvin. Best Detective Fiction: A Guide from Godwin to the Present. London: Clive Bingley, 1975; Hamden, Conn.: Linnet Books, 1975. 121pp. Author and title index.
An historical survey of the field, structurally similar to Queen's Quorum (A135). This is a smoothly written introductory treatment, useful mainly to beginners. (REB)

A10. Barzun, Jacques and Wendell Hertig Taylor. A Catalogue of Crime. NY: Harper & Row, 1974; Second Impression, Corrected, 1974. 1st ed: xxi, 831pp. Index by author, title and subject.
A compilation of critical opinions by the authors on some 7500 works of detective fiction and related genres, based on fifty years of appreciative and informed reading. The commentary is in the form of 3476 numbered entries, apportioned among six major sections and arranged alphabetically by author within each section. The six sections cover novels, short fiction, secondary literature, true crime, Sherlockiana, and the supernatural. Once the authors' biases as to what constitutes good detective fiction are recognized, the work can be read with great enjoyment and profit. There are, however, more errors than there should be (including that apparently indestructible assertion that Jack Vance is a pen-name for Henry Kuttner), and the bibliographical citations are sometimes incomplete or misleading (such as the listing of four Q. Patrick

short stories as Simon & Schuster hardcover novels, none of which in fact exists). Supplements to A Catalogue of Crime are a regular feature of The Armchair Detective, and a revised edition of the book has been announced. Breen 10. Reviews: Ross Macdonald, NYTBR, 16 May 71, p. 3.; TAD 4 (1971):243-5. See also comments by Bill Pronzini and Allen J. Hubin in TAD 5 (1972):114-115. (REB)

A11. ______. A Catalogue of Crime. Supplements. TAD 9 (1976):93-94, 209, 237; 271-272. TAD 10 (1977):126-7, 224-5. TAD 11 (1978):92-3, 203-4, 281, 307, 394. TAD 12 (1979):32-3, 262-3. TAD 13 (1980):208-9, 308-9. TAD 14 (1981):88-9, 142-3, 228-9, 328-9. TAD 15 (1982):76-7, 190-1, 276-7, 370-1. TAD 16 (1983):89, 211, 314-315, 440-441. N. B.: Numbered references in this bibliography to the Supplements will be preceded by the letter "S."

A12. Bates, Susannah. The Pendex. An Index of Pen Names and House Names in Fantastic, Thriller, and Series Literature. Garland Reference Library of the Humanities, Vol. 227. NY & London: Garland Publishing, Inc., 1981. vii, ix-xii, 233pp. Index.

The intended scope of the work can be inferred from the titles of its nine parts: I, Real Names; II, Pen Names; III, Collaborative Pen Names; IV, House Names; V, Stratemeyer Syndicate Names; Appendix A. Pulps & Digests: Some Working Definitions; Appendix B, Round Robin Serials; Sources & References; Index. Any compilation of pseudonyms is a battle against secrecy and confidentiality, and thus is susceptible to omissions. But the present work has some surprising gaps even in the area of well-known and publicly acknowledged pen names: there are no entries, under real name or pen name, for Michael Brett, Simon Brett, Jack Higgins (Harry Patterson), Emma Lathen, Wade Miller, Lawrence Block, Jack Vance, Dell Shannon (Elizabeth Linington), Jack Foxx (Bill Pronzini), Jack Mann (E. Charles Vivian), or Gregory Tree (John Franklin Bardin). Elizabeth Peters is not listed. Some pseudonyms of Brian Garfield and Elleston Trevor are omitted (as well as Trevor's original name). Some of these omissions may have been intentional, but there is no statement to warn the potential user that crime or mystery fiction is subject to exclusions. There are occasional errors, such as listing Jack Woodford as the real name and Josiah Pitts Woolfolk as the penname, instead of the the other way around. And there are too many misspelled names ("Salsfield" Ward, Anthony "Moreton," Gene "DeWease," Barry "Malzburg," etc.) for a book whose sole subject matter is names. (REB)

A13. Baudou, Jacques; Deloux, J.-P.; Guérif, François; and Lous, Alexandre. "54 Auteurs fichés |Dossier of 54 authors|." Magazine littéraire no. 194 (April 83), pp. 37-49. Photos.

Short critical overview of the work of 54 French and English-language writers, from "A. D. G." to Donald Westlake. Classic authors are not included; "older" contemporaries are included only if they made "significant" contributions during the 1970s.

A14. Baudou, Jacques; Deloux, J.-P.; and Guérif, François. "Polars en séries |Detective Fiction Series|." Magazine Littéraire no. 194 (April 83), pp. 56-68.

14 publishing series are profiled.

A15. "Bibliomysteries." Oak Knoll Books Catalogue Forty-Two (n. d.; circa 1982). 43pp.

An annotated listing of bibliomysteries for sale.

A16. "La Bibliothèque idéal de l'amateur de romans policiers |The ideal bibliography of the lover of detective fiction|." Enigmatika 7 (July 77):3-32.

Lists of essential works as compiled by a number of French specialists. There is also a list compiled by Borges.

A17. Bisceglia, Jacques. Trésors du roman policer, de la science fiction et du fantastique |Treasures of detective fiction, science-fiction and fantasy|. Paris: Editions de l'amateur, 1981.

An index of anthologies of detective fiction. Each collection is graded for collectors. Numerous illustrations. (JB)

A18. Bleiler, Everett F. The Checklist of Science-Fiction and Supernatural Fiction 1800-1948. Glen Rock, N.J.: Firebell Books, 1978. A revision and enlargement of the 1948 Checklist (Chicago: Shasta Books, 1948; reprinted by Fax, with additional material, 1948). An added numbering and lettering system identifies books by subject matter, including detective fiction. Books are listed by author, with a title index.

A19. _____. The Guide to Supernatural Fiction. A full description of 1,775 books from 1750 to 1960, including ghost stories, weird fiction, stories of supernatural horror, fantasy, Gothic novels, occult fiction, and similar literature. Kent, OH: Kent State University Press, 1983. Indices of authors, titles, motifs. xii, 723pp.

Plot summaries, critical comments, background, bibliography for a total of over 7,000 stories, with author and title indices and a motif index of about 40,000 entries. As the title indicates, the book is concerned with supernatural fiction, but there is an extensive overlap with crime/mystery fiction. About 100 detective stories in the limited sense are covered, and about 300 additional crime/mystery stories. The motif index classifies them in large categories: murder, portents, warnings, predictions; supernatural circumstances; supernatural discovery and/or solution; supernatural punishment; supernatural aftermaths and effects. Within these larger groups are many subdivisions. With the plot summaries the gimmicks are sometimes revealed. (EFB)

A20. Blom, K. Arne. "Vad är en procedural deckare? |What is a procedural detective novel?|." Jury 1:1 (1972):34-40.

Typology with chart and examples. (MS)

A21. Breen, Jon L. The Girl in the Pictorial Wrapper: an index to reviews of paperback original novels in the New York Times' "Criminals at Large" column, 1953-1970. Carson, CA: Library, California State College, Dominguez Hills, 1972. 46pp. Printed on recto only, stapled in decorated cover. Revised edition, with extension to subtitle: ...and The Saint Mystery Magazine's "Saint's Ratings" column, 1957-1959. Publisher as above, 1973. Dominguez Hills Bibliographic Series No. 2. pp. 1-50. Research Assistant: Rita A. Breen.

During the period 1953-1970, the New York Times' crime fiction reviewers, Anthony Boucher and his successor, Allen J. Hubin, regularly reviewed paperback original mystery novels (as few other reviewers did). It is these reviews which are listed in the present work, arranged alphabetically by the author of the book under review. The list of authors contains such now-famous names as Robert Bloch, Evan Hunter (under that name and several pseudonyms), E. Howard Hunt (also under several names), Donald Hamilton, John D. MacDonald, and Richard Stark (Donald E. Westlake). Breen's Index is a useful guide to early critical appraisals of their work and that of numerous other writers, less well known but just as worthy of attention. Breen 11. (REB)

A22. ______. What About Murder? A Guide to Books about Mystery and Detective Fiction. Foreword by Ellery Queen. Metuchen, N.J. and London: The Scarecrow Press, 1981. xviii, 157pp. Index by author, title, series and major subject.

This is an annotated bibliography of 239 books in the secondary literature of mystery and detective fiction classified under seven headings: general histories, reference books, special subjects, collected essays and reviews, technical manuals, coffee-table books, and works on individual authors. In all but a small number of cases the annotations--invariably pointed, perceptive, informative, and entertaining--are based on first-hand examination of the books. In his introduction Breen carefully states his criteria for inclusion/exclusion. (For example, books on general literary figures such as Poe, Dickens, Chesterton, etc., have been omitted, as have works on Conan Doyle and Sherlock Holmes.) This book, a cornerstone in any reference collection on mystery and detective fiction, is also prime evidence that scholarship can make enjoyable reading. (REB)

A23. Breton, Jacques. "Le Roman policier: petite bibliographie paralittéraire |The detective novel: a little paraliterary bibliography|." Paris: Ecole nationale supérieure des bibliothécaires, 1977. 19pp.

An annotated bibliography of major reference tools for detective fiction. The annotations are very full. Most of the material described is French.

A24. Briney, Robert E. "Dell Great Mystery Library...A Checklist." TMN 2:1 (15 Oct 75): 4.

A list of titles in the Dell paperback series with a short publishing history of the series.

A25. ______. "The Literature of the Subject: An Annotated Bibliography." In The Mystery Story (B15), pp. 365-390.

A bibliography of critical writing on general subjects and individual authors. Sources are limited to books and pamphlets.

A26. ______. "Subject Index to TAD's Letters Column." TAD 3 (1969/70):282-84. Volumes 1-3 are indexed.

A27. Broberg, Jan. "Spionthrillern under 1900-talet--ett försök till schematisiering |The spy novel in the 20th century--an attempt at a schematization|." Jury 4:3 (1975):4. Diagram. (MS)

A28. Brooks, Maud D.; Burtch, Arloine; and Hyatt, Ruth. "Who Done it? Detectives in Fiction." WLB 14 (1949-50): 720; 15 (1950-51): 126, 374. Lists of detectives and their authors. (KLM)

A29. Brumell, R.A. Corrections of and additions to the Queen's Quorum (A135). Letter TAD 7 (1973/74):66.

A30. Bryant, Estrella S. Bibliography of Asian Studies. Ann Arbor, MI: Association for Asian Studies, University of Michigan, 1948- . Annual. Title varies: 1948-55, Far Eastern Bibliography; 1956-present, Bibliography of Asian Studies.

Includes sections for Asia, China, Taiwan, Korea, Japan and other far Eastern countries; each section is further divided to include lists of works dealing with the fiction of that country. Each number of the Bibliography contains an author index. (GG)

A31. Carter, John, editor. Detective Fiction: A Collection of First and a Few Early Editions. Scribner's Catalogue No. 98. New York: Scribner Book Store, 1934. 78pp. Pictorial wrappers.

Much bibliographic information (and some amazing prices!). (REB)

A32. Cataio, Joseph, compiler. Mystery Checklist. Chicago, IL: Reference Books, 1978. 57pp. 5 3/4 x 3 1/2 incl, printed wrappers.

Checklists of the mystery novels of 13 leading authors. (REB)

A33. Cook, Michael L. Dime Novel Roundup. Annotated Index 1931-1981. Bowling Green, Ohio: Popular Press, 1983. 105pp.

An index of the magazine's contents by title, author and subject. Pagination is indicated by first page of entry only. The annotations consist of phrases interpolated parenthetically to clarify the subject of entries.

A34. ______. Monthly Murders. A Checklist and Chronological Listing of Fiction in the Digest-Size Mystery Magazines in the United States and England. Westport, CT & London: Greenwood Press, 1982. xvii, 1147pp. Index.

The declared scope of this checklist is indicated by the subtitle. The fiction contents of approximately 2650 issues of 110 magazines are listed. The issue-by-issue contents lists occupies the first 759 pages; pages 767-1147 are devoted to an index by author of all the story titles occurring in the main checklist. The page-count alone testifies to the enormous mass of information included in this book. Unfortunately, the arrangement of the information takes some getting used to. Each magazine has been assigned a 2-letter code, and the listings are alphabetical by code and chronological by magazine issue within each code. But the alphabetical order of the codes is not the same as the alphabetical order of the magazine titles, and one has to dig into the middle of the book (pages 761-763) in order to link magazine titles (some of which do not appear on the book's contents page) with the appropriate codes. In the author index, citations are by magazine code rather than page number, and one has to go back to the contents page to match the code to the proper pages in the checklist. The awkwardness of this back-and-forth searching could surely have been avoided without undue effort. As with any reference work of this size, there are typographical and transcription errors, missing information, and occasionally incorrect information. (For a detailed examination of all features of this book, see "Closing the Gap: A Critique" by John Nieminski in TMF 7:3 (May/June 83):6-15, 31.) Still, this is the only compilation of its kind, the result of enormous labor that no one else was willing to undertake, and it is of great value to collectors, historians and anthologists of mystery fiction. (REB)

A35. ______. Murder by Mail: Inside the Mystery Book Clubs--with Complete Checklist. Evansville, IN: Cook Publications, 1979. 109pp. Stapled in heavy paper covers. Index. Revised edition: Bowling Green, OH: Bowling Green University Popular Press, 1983. 230pp. Simultaneous clothbound and paperbound editions.

The offerings of the Detective Book Club, the Mystery Guild, and the Unicorn Mystery Book Club are listed chronologically by date of issue and cross-indexed by author. A brief history of each club is given. For the Mystery Guild, the original publication date is given for each title, with both publisher's and book club prices. A useful reference for collectors and bibliographers of mystery fiction. (REB)

A36. ______. "Murder by Mail -- Update." TPP :5/6 (Dec 81):51-55.
Detective Book Club updated through August 1981; Mystery Guild through September 1981.

A37. ______. Mystery, Detective, and Espionage Magazines. Westport, CT: Greenwood Press, 1983. xxiv, 795pp. Selected bibliography. Index by title and name.
This dictionary of popular periodicals includes pulps and digest-sized fiction magazines where the material falls largely within the categories indicated by the book's title, and fan and semiprofessional critical journals devoted to the mystery genre. The magazines in the main section (pp. 3-615) are limited to those published in the United States, Canada and Great Britain; a special section (pp. 632-73) presents "Overviews of Foreign Magazines" in which there is coverage of Scandinavian and French magazines. The journals in the main section are profiled with information sources and publication history (title changes, volume and issue data, publisher, editor, price per issue, size and pagination, and current status) provided. Cook and a number of contributors have written narrative histories for the magazines; these vary considerably in length and in coverage, but they do furnish information that is otherwise very hard to come by. There are several appendices, as follows: Magazines by Category, Key Writers in the Golden Age (with magazines to which they contributed and a table of pseudonyms), a Chronology (1882-1982; first appearance of magazines by year), American True-Detective Magazines (a list with some commencement dates of publication given), Canadian True-Detective Magazines, Sherlock Holmes Scion Society Periodicals and Other Periodicals of Interest to the Collector.

A38. ______. Mystery Fanfare. A Composite Annotated Index to Mystery and Related Fanzines 1963-1981. Bowling Green, OH: Popular Press, 1983. 441pp. Simultaneous hardcover and paperbound editions.
A composite index to 52 different magazines from The August Derleth Society Newsletter to Yellowback Library, and including Clues, several Doc Savage fanzines, JDM Bibliophile, The Mystery Fancier, The Armchair Detective, The Poisoned Pen, The Pontine Dossier, The Rohmer Review, The Thorndyke File, Xenophile, etc. There is a detailed chronology of each magazine, listing the date and physical facts about each issue published. The contents of these magazines, including letters of comment from readers, are then listed by title, by author, and by subject, all in a single alphabetical listing. There is a separate listing of book reviews, arranged alphabetically by the author of the book being reviewed. The principal aim of the Index is to assist in the location of material on specific mystery authors or topics, and in pursuit of this goal many bibliographic niceties have fallen by the wayside: titles are often quoted in abbreviated or paraphrased versions created by the compiler rather than in their original form; sometimes portions of letters or editorial material are excerpted, given titles, and listed as separate items; it is often impossible to distinguish between subtitles on the original articles and the compiler's annotations; crucial cross-references

are missing. Most of these eccentricities will not matter to anyone using this book to locate material, but they make its use as a strict bibliographical reference work very chancy. There are also occasional outright errors, such as mis-attribution or omission of items. Still, as they say, it is the only game in town, and its utility is undeniable. (REB)

A39. ______. "An Old Friend - The Detective Book Club." TAD 8 (1974/75): 77-97.
A publishing history with a listing of contents by volume. With the assistance of Don Miller, this list was partially corrected and updated in TMN 10, May 1977, pp. I1-I21. Additional material appeared in various issues of TMN and the final version was published as Murder by Mail (A35).

A40. ______. "Raven House Mysteries: Forever More!" TPP 4:5/6 (Dec 81):27-28.
A list of the first 72 titles of the Raven House paperback series.

A41. ______. "The Unicorn Mystery Book Club." TMN 12 (June 1979):I1-I14. With corrections by James L. Tinsman, Mary Groff and Don Miller.

A42. Cumulative Bibliography of Asian Studies: Subject Bibliography. Two series, 1941-65, and 1966-70. 4 vols. each series. Boston, MA: G.K.Hall.
Cumulates part of a series of studies of Asian subjects indexed as early as 1934 and subsequently updated. Sections by country, further divided into other topics, including fiction. Along with the Bibliography of Asian Studies, this is a valuable aid in locating articles and books on Oriental mystery fiction and authors. (GG)

A43. Davidson, Martha, comp. and ed. A List of Published Translations from Chinese into English, French and German. Part I: Literature, exclusive of poetry. (Tentative edition) Ann Arbor, MI: American Council of Learned Societies, 1952. xxix, 179pp.
Checklist of translations of primary sources into major Western languages, with sections on novels, stories, folktales, drama, etc. In these sections can be found, listed by Chinese title, works such as the Magistrate Pao novel, Lung-T'u Kung-An |The Cases of Judge Pao|, and citations of its translations. This was one of the first bibliographies of translations into Western languages and has been heavily relied upon by other bibliographers. Two things about this checklist are regrettable: there is no index of any kind and there was evidently no updated "non-tentative" edition. (GG)

A44. Deckar-Arsboken 79/80 |The mystery novel yearbook|. Sundyberg: Jury, 1981.
In addition to a chronicle of the mystery in books, TV, movies and radio in 1979/80, there is also a complete bibliography of every Swedish mystery novel published from 1833 to the present. (IH)

A45. "The Detection Club." Enigmatika 20 (1982):49-52.
A full listing of members for 1932 and additions, by year, through 1948.

A46. Doerrer, David. "Lachman's Reviews in TMF Volumes Two through Four." TMF 5:2 (March/April 81):6-9.
An index to Marvin Lachman's reviews.

A47. Donaldson, Norman. "In the Wake of Haycraft-Queen." TAD 5 (1972):137-144.

A 1949-51 updating of the Haycraft Cornerstone list, based on Anthony Boucher's annual Best of the Year lists in the New York Times, with annotations.

A48. East, Andy. The Cold War File. Metuchen, N. J. and London: Scarecrow Press, 1983. xiv, 362pp. Appendices on series continuations past 1969, on series publisher transitions; bibliography of secondary sources; index of secret agents.

The only booklength volume covering the spy novel of the 1960s with historical, biographical and bibliographical data on 73 authors and 4 publishers. Entries are alphabetical by author and include data on series characters and the significant novels of each author. The bibliographies extend to the pre-1960 work of authors whose primary work was in the 1960s, such as Desmond Cory and Stephen Marlowe. Post-1969 works, however, are not listed in the main body of the book but in an appendix. The authors covered are primarily the authors of series novels, such as Fleming, Deighton, le Carré, Edward S. Aarons, John Gardner and Philip McCutchan. Paperback originals are especially well covered, as are the novelizations of films and TV shows. The most serious error concerns James Dark (pseud. of James Edmond MacDonnell). Not only are five of Dark's Mark Hood books missing from the checklist, but it is concluded that Dark is most likely a penname (since the real name could not be found). This information is easily available in books such as Hubin (A83). Besides questions of inclusion and exclusion of authors, it may be objected that for some authors both British and American publication data are included, whereas for others only the American date is given. First editions in the original country of publication are usually given. The first Joe Gall books of James Atlee Phillips (Pagoda, 1951) is not listed as such. Despite these weaknesses, this one of the most painstakingly researched "special topics" bibliographies and suffers from almost none of the deficiences of the two Myron J. Smith books (A157, A158). (GG)

A49. Eck, Frank, editor. Ellery Queen's 1978 Mystery Calendar. NY: Davis Publications, Inc., 1977. 28pp, unnumbered.

In this wall calendar, each month has a full-page scene from a specific mystery story or novel. The illustrations are reprints of magazine illustrations or paperback covers. Birth and death dates of mystery writers are given as footnotes to each month's calendar. (REB)

A50. Emery, Richard. "Subject Guide to Mystery Fiction." TPP 3:1 (March/April 1980):3-15. Supplements in TPP 3:3 (May/June 1980):43-52; 3:4 (July/August 1980):41-52; 3:6 (Nov/Dec 1980):41-52.

The first installment was compiled from writer Emery's collection with additions by publisher Meyerson. The supplements have included titles furnished by other readers.

A51. Erichsson, Iwan, compiler. Register over Dast Magazine |Index to DAST magazine|. Vol. 1-XV, Sept 1968 - Dec 1982. DAST Dossier Nr. 7. Strangnas, Sweden: DAST-Magazine, 1983.

An index to articles in DAST listed by author. Material is not identified by category (review, interview, etc.) and is of limited usefulness.

A52. Frank, Frederick S. "The Gothic Novel: A Checklist of Modern Criticism." BoB 30:6 (Apr/Jun 73):45-54.

Organized under 11 headings: I. Articles and Monographs on the English

Gothic Novel and Gothic Novelists; II. Full-Length Books; III. Articles and Monographs on the American Gothic School; IV. Full-length Books on American Gothic Writers and Themes; V. Introductions to Re-editions of English and American Gothic Works; VI. Essays on Gothicism Found in Larger Critical Collections and Literary Histories; VII. Doctoral Dissertations on Gothic Types in the Twentieth Century; VIII. Books and Articles on Special Gothic Themes; IX. Books and Articles on Gothic Cinema; X. Books and Articles on the Gothic Novel's Relationship to the Gothic Revival in Architecture; XI. An Esoteric Miscellany. Includes French and German material. (REB)

A53. ______. "The Gothic Novel: A Second Bibliography of Criticism." BoB 35:1 (Jan/March 78):1-14, 52.

A54. Frank, Frederick S.; Crawford, Gary William; and Fisher, Benjamin Franklin, IV,. "The 1978 Bibliography of Gothic Studies." Gothic 1:2 (Dec 79):65-67.
An annotated bibliography, arranged in three categories: Bibliography and Textual Studies; General Studies, or broad considerations of Gothic themes involving many writers; and Authors. The first of what was intended to be an annual listing.

A55. ______. "The 1979 Bibliography of Gothic Studies." Gothic 2:2 (Dec 80):49-52.
The second and final installment published in this short-lived journal.

A56. Freeman, William, ed. Dictionary of Fictional Characters. Boston: The Writer, Inc., 1974. 579pp.
This index to characters in English and American literature of the "past six centuries" was first published in 1963 by J. M. Dent and Sons, Ltd. The present edition has been revised by Fred Urquhart, with indices of authors and titles prepared by E. N. Pennell. The original edition consisted of 20,000 characters from 2,000 books by 500 authors. Over 1500 new references were added and "selective" cuts were made in the late Victorians.

A57. Friedland, Susan, compiler. South African Detective Stories in English and Afrikaans from 1951-1971. Johannesberg: University of the Witwatersrand, Department of Bibliography, Librarianship and Typography, 1972.
A continuation of Miller, Anita (A118). A listing, by author, of detective fiction either written in Afrikaans or translated from English. There are brief notations on setting and theme, indices of titles, listings of English and Afrikaans series, and a bibliography of 18 secondary sources.

A58. Glover, Dorothy, and Greene, Graham. Victorian Detective Fiction: A Catalogue of the Collection Made by Dorothy Glover and Graham Greene. Bibliographically arranged by Eric Osborne and introduced by John Carter. Preface by Graham Greene. London: The Bodley Head, 1966. Edition limited to 500 numbered copies. xviii, 149pp. Indices of detectives, of illustrators, and of titles.
471 entries, by author, with bibliographical annotations by Dorothy Glover. Also includes a short essay by Eric Bell on the publishing history of Fergus Hume's Mystery of a Hansom Cab. Breen 14. (REB)

A59. Goode, Greg. "The Oriental in Crime Fiction and Film: A Bibliography of

Secondary Sources." TAD 15 (1982):203-211.
Subjects covered are general references, Fu Manchu, Mr. Moto, Charlie Chan, Judge Dee and Magistrate Pao. For additions to the bibliography, see TAD 16 (1983):218.

A60. Greene, Douglas G. "A Reader's Supplement to Queen's Quorum." TAD 12 (1979):228-35.
An annotated bibliography, in the style of the Quorum (A135), of 30 additional titles. There is appended a list of collections of short stories with detection elements that have been published since the Quorum.

A61. Gribbin, Lenore S. The Case of the Missing Detective Stories. Chapel Hill, NC: University of North Carolina Library, 1966. 135pp. Wraps.
A checklist of the Library's collection of detective fiction, with a one-page preface describing the rationale for the collection. (REB)

A62. ______. Who's Whodunit: A list of 3218 Detective Story Writers and Their 1100 Pseudonyms. University of North Carolina Library Studies No. 5. Chapel Hill, N. C.: University of North Carolina, 1969. ix, 174pp.
A compilation of 1100 pseudonyms used by some 3218 writers of mystery fiction. Unlike other compilations of this type in that the sources of much of the information are cited. Breen 15. CC 2953. (REB)

A63. Griffin, Lloyd W., ed. Foreign Acquisitions Newsletters. Washington, D.C.: The Association of Research Libraries, 1949- . No. 1 published March 1949. Title varies: 1-17, Farmington Plana Letter; 18-31, Farmington Plan Newsletter; 32-present, Foreign Acquisitions Newsletters.
Essentially a bibliography of bibliographies and of acquisitions in the United States of all foreign publications. Each issue contains sections for Africa, the Far East, Latin American, Southeast Asia, the Middle East, etc. In these sections can be found entries for bibliographies of foreign literature, as well as news on holdings of and acquisitions by American libraries of foreign literature. This is a handy, if remote, aid in the study of detective fiction and secondary sources in non-English languages. (GG)

A64. Gupta, Brijen Kishore. India in English Fiction. Metuchen, N. J.: Scarecrow, 1973. xiv, 296pp. Preface by George Grella, pp. vii-xiii.
An attempt at a comprehensive author bibliography of novels, tales, and short story collections written in English by Indian or foreign writers depicting some aspect of India. Although Gupta states that it was not possible to include all detective stories in which India plays a passing role, certain important mysteries set in India are missing, such as Lawrence Blochman's Bombay Mail and Red Snow at Darjeeling, as well as several of H. R. F. Keating's Inspector Ghote novels. But these omissions are far outweighed by the virtues of the book. In addition to the main author index, there are title and theme indexes. The latter is a particularly valuable inclusion, for under the heading "Mysteries" are hundreds of references to mystery and detective novels, including many by Indian authors. Mystery writers such as Tara Ali Baig, Santosh Kumar Mukherji and Kamala Sathianandhan are not included in any other Western reference book of the genre. (GG)

A65. Hagen, Ordean. Who Done It? A Guide to Detective, Mystery and Suspense Fiction. N.Y.: R. R. Bowker Co., 1969. xx, 834pp.
The first attempt at a comprehensive bibliography of mystery fiction,

together with supplementary checklists: mysteries in film and on stage, principal characters, settings, anthologies, secondary sources, etc. Although riddled with errors, many of them inevitable in such a pioneering effort, the book is still an important source of information and a starting point for further investgations. Reviews: JPC 3 (1969):372-4; TAD 3 (1970):57-8; American Scholar 39 (1969):138, 140, 142-3, 146-8 (Jacques Barzun); Mystery and Detection Annual 1972 (B2), pp. 203-211. Breen 16. CC 2954. (REB)

A66. Hancer, Kevin. The Paperback Price Guide. Cleveland, Tenn.: Overstreet Publications, 1980. 430pp. Illus. Revised edition: New York: Harmony Books, 1982. 390pp.

A price guide for the collector but useful also for the listings of imprints by number and title. The original edition was widely commented on in the fan magazines, both for the inaccuracies in the lists and for what was seen as inflationary prices for books. Hancer was assisted on the revised edition by R. Reginald and by research advisor, Rahn Kollander, and an index by author was included. The use of a greatly reduced typeface in this edition may trouble some users. Reviews: TMF 5:1 (1981):28-9; CP? 2:5 (1981):24.

A67. Hanrahan, Rita M. "Detective Fiction: An Annotated Bibliography of Critical Writing." Unpublished M. A. thesis. San Jose State University, 1976. 114pp.

Material in books and periodicals, dissertations; some foreign-language material. 383 entries. Author index.

A68. Harlequin's 30th Anniversary 1949-79. Toronto, London, NY: Harlequin Books, 1979. Wraps.

A listing of books published by Harlequin from 1949 to December 1979, with a history of the firm and other descriptive material. Review: TAD 15 (1982):156.

A69. Haycraft, Howard. "Friends and Foes. (The Critical Literature)." In his Murder for Pleasure (B143), pp. 272-97.

A bibliography of secondary material in books and magazines with an introduction in which Haycraft comments on the growth of critical interest in mystery fiction since the mid-1920s. Most of the entries were taken from the Reader's Guide to Periodical Literature and, along with the errors of transcription, there are many items which are of only marginal interest.

A70. ______. "From Poe to Hammett: A Foundation List of Detective Fiction." WLB 12 (1937/38):371-77.

An alphabetical list of authors "established before 1930-31," with annotations consisting of brief comments from critics like Dorothy L. Sayers, H. D. Thomson and E. M. Wrong, with some notations by Haycraft. Includes an index of detectives.

A71. Haycraft, Howard and Ellery Queen. "The Haycraft-Queen Definitive Library of Detective Fiction." EQMM, Oct 51, pp. 71-79.

Described by the compilers as "two centuries of cornerstones, 1748-1948." Reprinted in Haycraft, Murder for Pleasure (revised edition, Biblo & Tannen, 1968), as an appendix to an unpaginated introduction by Haycraft, "Notes on Additions to a Cornerstone Library." CC 2959.

A72. Hedman, Iwan. Dekare och Thrillers pa svenska, 1864-1973 |Detective fiction and thrillers in Swedish, 1864-1973|. DAST Dossier 3. Strangnas, Sweden, 1974. 377pp. Illustrated.

Books are listed by author; index by title. There are useful appendices listing books published in series and the contents of anthologies. CC S94.

A73. _____ Detectiver pa frimarken: en bio-bibliografi |Detectives on postage stamps: a bio-bibliography|. DAST Dossier no. 5. Introduction by Sigurd Tullberg. Strangnas, Sweden: DAST Forlag AB, 1978. 44pp. Illustrated.

In 1973, Nicaragua issued a set of 12 postage stamps commemorating the 50th anniversary of Interpol and built around the theme of the twelve most famous detectives in fiction, with each stamp picturing one of the chosen detectives: Peter Wimsey, Philip Marlowe, Sam Spade, Perry Mason, Nero Wolfe, C. Auguste Dupin, Ellery Queen, Father Brown, Charlie Chan, Inspector Maigret, Hercule Poirot, and Sherlock Holmes (in increasing order of denomination). Hedman has used this set of stamps as a framework for an interesting little book. For each of the 12 detectives (arranged now in alphabetical order), there is an enlarged photo of the stamp, a photo of the author, at least one representative book jacket, a thumbnail description of the detective, a checklist of both Swedish and English editions of works featuring the detective, and a short list of books and articles about the author and detective. There are several interesting facts about this stamp issue that the author does not mention. The selection of which detectives to depict on the stamps was made on the basis of a poll conducted among readers of EQMM. The original designs for the stamps are now part of the Guymon Collection of detective fiction at Occidental College in Los Angeles. And one curious feature of the stamps themselves is not mentioned: printed on the gummed side of each stamp is a brief statement on the importance of the detective and his creator in mystery fiction. Transcriptions and/or translations of these statements would have enhanced the value of Hedman's book. (REB)

A74. _____. "Faktaböcker om deckare/thriller-genren i Skandinavien |Fact books on the detective/thriller genre in Scandinavia|." DAST 15:3(1982):32-35.

A bibliography of 85 critical works. (MS)

A75. Hensley, Don. "Avon Classic Crime Collection." PQ 5:2 (1982):17-24.

An alphabetical index by author with publishing information and brief plot summaries.

A76. _____. "The World's Great Novels of Detection." PQ 4:4 (Winter 81):48-50. Illus.

A checklist of the paperback series edited by Anthony Boucher.

A77. Herron, Don. "San Francisco Mysteries." Mystery 3:2(1981):6-12, 57-9. Illus.

A survey with a checklist.

A78. Hetherington, John R. "Detection of Detectives." Book Collecting and Library Monthly no. 60, April 1973, pp. 110-118.

Detailed bibliographical study, with emphasis on the detective fiction items of Ward Lock's turn-of-the-century series, Copyright Novels. (RCSA)

A79. Hill, M. C. "A Crime Club Collection." CP? 2:5 (1980):14-16. Illus.
Crime Club novels in pb.

A80. ______. Paperback Checklist for Collectors. Vol I. Evansville, IN: Cook & McDowell Publications, 1980. 115pp.
A listing of titles by imprint and number for Ace (nos. 1-411), Dell (nos. 1-159), Pocketbook (nos. 1-500), Popular Library (nos. 1-835), Armed Services Editions (nos. 1-1322) and Avon (nos. 1-864).

A81. ______. "The Saint Mystery Library." 2:4(1979):4-10. Illus.
A listing of the contents, by issue. Mr. Hill also notes earlier publication information on the stories.

A82. Hubin, Allen J. The Bibliography of Crime Fiction, 1749-1975. Listing all mystery, detective, suspense, police, and gothic fiction in book form published in the English language. San Diego and Del Mar, CA: Univ. Extension, Univ. of California, in cooperation with Publisher's Inc., 1979. xiv, 697pp.
It all started with Ordean Hagen's Who Done It? (A65). Recognizing the deficiencies of that pioneering work, Allen Hubin embarked on a fresh compilation of English-language crime fiction. The results were first presented as supplements to his magazine The Armchair Detective from 1971 to 1976. A further year and a half of additions and corrections produced the bibliography presented in this volume. In the Author Index, something over 50,000 crime fiction titles are listed by author, with each book listed under the byline most commonly associated with it. Pseudonyms are thoroughly cross-referenced. First American and first British editions are listed, with publisher and date; title changes and series characters are indicated. This listing occupies the first 449 triple-columned pages. Pages 453-683 contain a cross-index by title, compiled by Allen Hubin's son, Loren. Pages 687-697 contain an index of series and series characters, as identified in the main Author Index. This is a monumental work, impressive in both its comprehensiveness and its accuracy. As a cornerstone of any reference library on mystery fiction, the book is surpassed only by Hubin's own expansion of this material in his Crime Fiction, 1749-1980 (A83). Breen 18. (REB)

A83. ______. Crime Fiction, 1749-1980: A Comprehensive Bibliography. Garland Reference Library of the Humanities, vol. 371. NY & London: Garland Publishing, Inc., 1984. xix, 711pp.
This enlarged edition of Hubin's Bibliography (A82) does more than just extend the coverage by five years. The listings in the previous edition have been re-examined, some doubtful titles have been removed, and approximately 2600 new titles from the pre-1976 period have been added. Together with the 6000 titles from 1976-1980, this brings the total number of books listed to about 60, 000. Each entry in the Author Index (pages 1-438) lists the titles published under that byline, with cross-references to other bylines used by the same author. First U. S. and first British editions are listed, plus any additional editions involving title changes. Books which are part of series are noted. Many more birth and death dates are given than in the previous edition. There is an attempt to indicate those authors who are included in certain standard reference works such as A Catalogue of Crime (A10) and Encyclopedia of Mystery and Detection (A160), and for many authors not included in such works there are brief biographical or career notes. The Title Index occupies

pages 441-631 and is followed by a new feature: a Settings Index listing some 343 locales and the crime fiction books set in each. There is also an expanded Series Index and a Series Character Chronology, expanded from that in "Patterns in Mystery Fiction" (A84), which lists over 700 series characters, their authors, character type, year of first appearance, and the number of books in which each has appeared (through 1980). This volume, even more than its predecessor, is an indispensable component of any reference library on mystery fiction. (REB)

A84. ______. "Patterns in Mystery Fiction: The Durable Series Character." In Ball, The Mystery Story (B15), pp. 291-318.
A chronological listing of series characters appearing in five or more books by type, country, format, number of books, and author.

A85. Hyatt, Ruth. "Who Done it? A Bibliography of Detectives in Fiction." WLB 14 (June 40): 720. Additions by Maud D.Brooks, WLB 15 (Oct 40):126; and by Arloine Burtich, PW (Jan 41):374.
An alphabetical listing by detective.

A86. J. & S. Graphics. Catalogues of mystery and detective fiction. Chicago, IL. Various dates.
A series of annotated and profusely illustrated catalogues, usually of first editions in fine condition. Among the most famous of these catalogues is 15 (1972, 340 pp., over 4000 entries). (REB)

A87. Jaffery, Sheldon. Horrors and Unpleasantries. A Bibliographical History and Collector's Price Guide to Arkham House. Bowling Green, OH: Bowling Green State University Popular Press, 1982. Hardbound and paperbound editions published simultaneously. Cover design by Gary Dunn. 142pp.
Extensively annotated list of the 162 books published by Arkham House and its associated imprints through the end of 1982. One of the associated imprints is Mycroft & Moran, and books published under this imprint include all of August Derleth's Solar Pons books as well as volumes of detective stories (frequently of the "psychic detective" type) by M. P. Shiel, Seabury Quinn, William Hope Hodgson, and Margery Lawrence. Jaffery's annotations are knowledgeable and enjoyably informal. (REB)

A88. Johnson, Timothy W. and Julia Johnson. Crime Fiction Criticism: An Annotated Bibliography. NY: Garland, 1981. 431pp. Index of critics.
Part One is a listing of general reference books and articles; Part Two is a listing of critical references for authors. Includes material from TAD but not other fanzines. Some foreign entries. 1810 entries. Reviews: Choice 18 (1981):1528; WLB 55 (June 81):774; LJ 106 (1981):1208.

A89. Katatchnik, Amnon, and Aucott, Robert. "A Readers' Supplementary List to the Haycraft/Queen Definitive Library of Detective-Crime-Mystery Fiction." TAD 9 (1976):87-90.
Additions, with a cut-off date of December 31, 1948, as in the original Haycraft-Queen list (A71).

A90. Keio Gijuku Daigaku Suiri Shosetsu Doko-kai. Hoseki Sankuhin Somokuroku |Hoseki index|. Tokyo: Keio Gijuku University Mystery Club, 1973. 368pp.
A list of contents of and index to Hoseki Magazine, Vols. 1-9 (1946-1964) and Bessatsu Hoseki |Extra Hoseki|, nos. 1-129 (1948-1964). Published as number 37 of Suiri Shosetsu Ronso |Mystery Review|, the periodical of

Keio Gijuku University Mystery Club. Limited to 200 copies. (HS/TT)

A90a. Labeau, Dennis, editor. Author Biographies Master Index. 2 vols. Detroit, Michigan: Gale Research Company, 1980. Supplement. Edited by Barbara McNeil and Miranda C. Herbert. Detroit: Gale, 1980.

This useful index gives access to almost 150 standard reference works. It includes information on foreign as well as English and American writers. Writers in Section IV (Authors) of this bibliography who are listed in this index will be so noted in the Reference sources by the abbrevations ABMI, ABMIS, and ABMI(S).

A91. Lachman, Marvin. "Forgotten Men." TAD 2 (1969): 217-223.

Descriptions of 26 series detectives and rogues not listed in Queen's Quorum.

A92. la Cour, Tage. The Short Detective Story 1925-1982. A Personal Checklist. Copenhagen, Denmark: Pinkertons Antikvariat, 1983. Illustrated by Henry Lauritzen. Edition limited to 200 copies.

A listing of la Cour's favorite short detective fiction, based on more than 50 years as a reader and collector. Not seen. Reviewed In DAST 17:1 (1984). (REB)

A93. Landrum, Larry. "Detective and Mystery Novels." In Handbook of American Popular Culture, edited by M. Thomas Inge, pp. 103-120. Westport, CT: Greenwood Press, 1978.

A short history of the genre is followed by information on research collections and criticism, with an annotated bibliography of reference materials.

A94. Lebrun, Michel. L'Almanach du crime 1980 |The crime almanach 1980|. Paris: Guénaud Polar, 1980. 312pp. Also: L'Almanach du crime 1981. Paris: Veyrier Polar, 1981; L'Almanach du crime 1982. Paris: Veyrier Polar, 1982. 318pp.

Making use of a traditional editorial formula, Michel Lebrun annually concocts a monumental compilation on detective fiction, deliberately placed under the sign of humor and the incongruous, but of unfaltering scholarship. For each almanac, Lebrun collects numerous headings distributed throughout the calendar with a diabolical skill in suspense: weapons, collections, criminals, detectives, novelists' humor, famous sayings, secret societies.... In a second section, he examines critically the year's publications. Each year, Lebrun calls on notable collaborators: Jean-Claude Dinguirard, Paul Gayot and Léo Malet in 1980; Michel Renaud and Alex Varoux in 1981; Jean Patrick Manchette and Pierre Siniac in 1982. An inexhaustible mine of information presented in an attractive format. (JB)

A95. _____. "Dictionnaire des auteurs" |Dictionary of authors|. Enigmatika 1:1 (1976):(29-33) - .

In the first issue of this important French specialty journal, Lebrun began publishing an international dictionary of writers of detective fiction with concise biocritical notes and a bibliography of the writers' works. The dictionary was published with some regularity through issue 17 (Jan 1981), and in issues 16 and 17 Lebrun published additions to the roster. In issue 22 (May 1982), Lebrun published an apology for the hiatus, pleading the press of other activities, but promised to devote himself full-time to the enterprise when his hair will have turned sufficiently white to allow him to retire from public life. With this tongue-in-cheek statement, he included the latest installment, an entry for Georges Bernanos. Anyone who is aware of his numerous writing and publishing projects can only hope that he will find some time to complete the letter "B" by the end of the decade.

A96. Lee, Billy C., and Laughlin, Charlotte. "Alfred Hitchock: Dell Paperbacks." PQ 3:1 (1980):23-36. Illus.
A publishing history of this paperback anthology reprint series.

A97. Lewis, Dave. "Rare Books Are Getting Scarce." CP? 2:5 (1980):1923. Illus.
A discussion of hard-boiled fiction with a selective bibliography.

A98. Lewis, K. W. "Checklist of Detectives." PW 140 (9 Aug 41):386-9.
An alphabetic list of detectives with author attributions.

A99. Laughlin, Charlotte. "Dell Mysteries." PQ 3:4(1980):13-18. Illus.
A list of titles in the Scene of the Crime and Murder Ink series.

A100. Lindsay, Ethel. Here Be Mystery and Murder. Reference books in the mystery genre, excluding Sherlockiana. Carnoustie, Scotland: privately published, April 1982. Not paginated (62pp). Wraps. Edition limited to 100 numbered copies.
Checklist of 748 reference books in the mystery genre, listed by title and cross-indexed by author. The compiler cast a wide net, and included some anthologies of mystery fiction and some nonfiction "true-crime" studies in the list. With a number of incomplete or incorrect citations and a lack of categorization by subject, this is useful raw material for further research, rather than finished reference work in itself. (REB)

A101. Lingblom, Hans E. 1257. Förteckning över deckare, thrillers, faktaböcker, memoarer, kolportageromaner |Bibliography of mystery novels, thrillers, nonfiction, memoirs and colportage novels|. Ostersund: Berntssons, 1979.
A bibliography of Swedish mystery novels published from 1833 to the present. The book was later reprinted as JURY 36. (IH)

A102. Locke, George. "The Annotated Addendum." In Ferret Fantasy's Christmas Annual for 1972, pp. 29-76. London: Ferret Fantasy Ltd., 1973. See also (Part 2) in Ferret Fantasy's Christmas Annual for 1973, pp.1-27. London: Ferret Fantasy, Ltd., 1974.
Additions to the Bleiler Checklist of Fantastic Literature (A18). Of interest for its inclusions of material that may be characterized as "weird mystery."

A103. ______. "Fantasy and Mystery Fiction in The Yellow Magazine." Search and Research 1:2 (June 74):23-27.
An annotated list of the fantasy and mystery fiction in the biweekly British Yellow Magazine, its continuation under the title All-Story Magazine, and a sister title, The Green Magazine, 1921-1926. Many stories and serials by thriller writers Edmund Snell, John G. Brandon, and Fred M. White, and single appearances by Earl Derr Biggers, Sax Rohmer, W. Somerset Maugham, and Edgar Wallace. (REB)

A104. ______. "Fantasy in The Red Magazine." Search and Research 1:2 (Nov 73):1-9.

Although mainly devoted to the fantasy fiction in The Red Magazine (Brit.), 1908-1939, this checklist also notes a number of crime and detective short stories by William Hope Hodgson, as well as Edgar Wallace's "Gospel Truth Mortimer" series. (REB)

A105. ______. "Hush Magazine Checklist." Search and Research 1:1 (Nov 73):13-14.

Brief descriptive note and issue-by-issue contents list of rare fiction magazine edited by Edgar Wallace and published by the Detective Story Club Ltd. (an affiliate of the British publishing house of William Collins), 1929-1931. The magazine published several of Agatha Christie's Miss Marple short stories, as well as work by Wallace, G. D. H. and M. Cole, J. S. Fletcher, Arthur B. Reeve, etc. (REB)

A106. Lofts, W(illiam) O(liver) G(uillemont), and Adley, D(erek) J. The Men Behind Boys' Fiction. Introduction by Leslie Charteris. London: Howard Baker, 1970. 361pp.

This book offers an annotated alphabetical listing of all known writers who contributed to the British boys' papers from the 1870s through the early 1950s. At a minimum, each entry lists the papers to which that writer contributed. For many of the writers listed, there are biographical and career notes and information about real names and/or pseudonyms. There is a separate list of the 176 contributors to the Sexton Blake series, arranged chronologically by date of first appearance. The main catalogue includes not only authors who wrote directly for the boys' papers but also authors whose works were reprinted therein. Among the authors included are Margery Allingham and her father, Herbert John Allingham, Delano Ames, Agatha Christie, Leslie Charteris, John Creasey, E. W. Hornung, Barry Perowne, Jack Trevor Story, and Edgar Wallace, plus many lesser lights of British thriller fiction. This is the only compilation of its kind and is filled with interesting tidbits of information. (REB)

A107. Lyles, William H. Dell Paperbacks, 1942 to Mid-1962: A Catalog-Index. Westport, Ct: Greenwood, Press, 1983. xxxv, 471pp. Illus. Indices.

From its first release in March 1943 until the discontinuance of serial numbering in mid-1962, Dell Books published 2168 titles, of which 971 were mysteries, both reprint and original. In the first part of this monumental reference work, "Catalog of Series Listings" (pp. 25-299), the 2168 titles are individually listed and described, with publication date, print run, pagination, back-cover maps, blurbs, and other distinctive features. It is safe to say that any question on the physical appearance or publishing history of any Dell paperback will be answered by this work. The remainder of the book consists of a cross-index by author (pp. 303-441) plus indexes by subject, cover artist, and the locations depicted in the back-cover maps. Among the 971 mysteries are many by Agatha Christie and Brett Halliday, the Dell Great Mystery Library, and several of John D. MacDonald's paperback originals. A companion volume is Lyles: Putting Dell on the Map: A History of the Dell Paperbacks (B234). (REB)

A108. ______. "Keyhole: Confidential." CP? 3:2 (May 81):30-34.

A listing of Dell Books 1-100 with descriptions of characteristic features and printing dates.

A109. Lynn, Richard John. Chinese Literature: A Draft Bibliography in Western

European Languages. Oriental Monograph Series No. 24. Canberra: Australian National University Press, 1979. 102pp.

An attempt at a comprehensive list of books and monographs in Western European languages which treat the subject of Chinese literature. Arranged chronologically by dynasty, it includes sections on reference works, general studies, fiction, and individual literary figures. Lynn attempts to list all relevant Ph.D. dissertations, but for some reason does not include George A. Hayden's 1971 dissertation, "The Judge Pao Plays of the Yuan Dynasty." Because much scholarly work has been done on the novels of Magistrate (Judge) Pao and other ancient Chinese detectives since 1971, this book is a valuable aid. Includes an index of authors and translators. Along with Winston L. Y. Yang's Classical Chinese Fiction (B449), this is one of the best sources for background research into ancient Chinese detective fiction. (GG)

A110. McCormick, Donald. Who's Who in Spy Fiction. London: Elm Tree Books/Hamish Hamilton, Apr 1977; NY: Taplinger, 1977. 216pp. Bibliography.

This is an alphabetically arranged guide to some 90 writers of spy fiction and their work, from Eric Ambler and John le Carré to Edgar Wallace and Dennis Wheatley. Each entry contains biographical information, critical comments, and sometimes a quotation from the writer himself. McCormick also comments on the development of the spy story and the extent to which spy fiction is based on spy fact. Although highly selective and weak on American authors (both Manning Coles and Donald Hamilton are omitted, for example), and marred by typographical and other errors, the book contains a great deal of biographical and critical coverage of British writers, including several who are almost unknown in the U. S., such as Ted Allbeury. Breen 20. (F. M. Nevins, Jr./REB)

A111. Menendez, Albert J. Mistetoe Malice. Silver Springs, MD: Holly Tree Press, 1982. 35pp.

Descriptive guide to the use of Christmas in mystery novels; bibliography of 89 titles. (REB)

A112. Mermet, H. Y., and Naudon, J. F.. Catalogue des nouvelles policières |Catalogue of detective short stories|. 1 (Oct 1980): A/B; 2 (Nov 1980): C.

Published by the French fanzine Les Amis du crime, this was projected as the first in a series of catalogues in which detective short stories published in French magazines would be indexed by author.

A113. Mesplède, Claude, and Schleret, Jean-Jacques. Voyage au bout de la noire |Voyage to the end of the "série noire"|. Paris: Futuropolis, 1982. 478pp. Illus.

This inventory of the 732 authors published in the Gallimard série noire is a virtual bible. There is a biographical and bibliographical note for each author. There is also a filmography with credits for film versions of série noire publications. (JB)

A114. Meyerson, Jeffrey. "The Avon Classic Crime Collection." TMF 1:5 (Sept 77):19.

A short history and a checklist.

A115. ______. "A Bestseller Mystery Checklist." TPP 1:5 (Sept 78):B1-4.

A116. ______. "A Jonathan Press Checklist." TPP 1:3 (May 78):J1-2.

A117. ______. "A Mercury Mystery Checklist." TPP 1:4 (July 78):M1-4.

A118. Miller, Anita. Afrikaanse speurverhale uitgee tot die einde van 1950 |Afrikaan detective fiction published through 1950|. Johannesburg: University of the Witwatersrand, 1967. iv, 23pp.
A list of detective fiction in Afrikaans, by author. Title index.

A119. Morse, Laurence Alan. "The Best Crime Stories of the Last Twenty Years." Bakka Magazine No. 5 (Spring/Summer 77), pp. 98-110.
A proposed updating of July Symons' list of "The Hundred Best Crime Stories (A165). Eighteen titles are offered, with detailed reviews. (REB)

A120. Mundell, E. H., Jr., and Rausch, G. Ray. The Detective Short Story: A Bibliography. Bibliographic Series No. 14. Manhattan, Kansas: Kansas State Univ. Library, 1974. iii, 493pp. Wraps.
The 1439 books listed in this bibliography are divided into several categories, of which the most important are single-author story collections (1-868), and detective story anthologies (901-1213). For each book the compilers give publication data, sometimes including reprint editions, and a list of the detective stories contained in the book. The names of the detectives in the stories are also given. Other categories are Sherlockiana, Secret Service story collections and anthologies, crime puzzle books, true detective experiences, and unexamined titles. The short stories in all categories are cross-indexed by author, and there is a separate index of detective characters. The insistence on "detection" is the key both to the intended purpose of this compilation and to the frustration attendant on using it. Only those short stories which meet the compilers' strict definition (taken from Carolyn Wells) of "detective story" are listed---if a collection or anthology contains stories which do not involve detection, these stories are not listed in this bibliography, and their very existence is not even mentioned. Another awkward feature is that, in the anthology listings, only the last names of story authors (and detectives) are given; for the authors, the omitted first names are almost all included in the cross-index by author. Breen 21. (REB)

A121. Nakajima, Kawataro. Sengo Suiri Shosetsu Somokuroku, Vols. 1-3 |Post-war mystery fiction index|. Tokyo: Nippon Suiri Sakka Kyokai |Mystery Writers of Japan|, 1970-80.
An index of mystery stories published in Japan since 1945 through 1979, by author. It focuses on the stories which first appeared in magazines, and includes only the novels that were originally written in book form. (HS/TT)

A122. ______ Shinseinen Kessaku-sen |Best of "Shinseinen"|. Vol. 5. Tokyo: Rippu Shobo, 1970. 430pp. Illus.
An anthology of the best stories from "Shinseinen" magazine, edited by K. Nakajima. This fifth volume contains non-fiction and a list of contents of the magazine, vols. 1-31 (1920-1950). (HS/TT)

A123. Nehr, Ellen. "Mystery League, Inc." TPP 2:6 (Nov/Dec 79):3-5.
Series history and checklist.

A124. Neuberg, Victor. The Popular Press Companion to Popular Literature. Bowling Green, KY: Popular Press, 1983. 207pp. Illus.
A dictionary of entries on writers, characters, titles, and terms drawn

from popular literature. By its very nature, a highly selective list but of some interest to generalists and larger collections. A guide-book that may serve as an introduction to the field.

A125. Nielsen, Bjarne. Hvem begik hvad. Dansk kriminallitteratur indtil 1979 |Who did what? the Danish bibliography of crime fiction to 1979|. Copenhagen: Pinkerton Antivvariat, 1981. 132pp.
With author index, title index, checklists of anonymous and collective works, series index. (IH)

A126. Nieminski, John. "Closing the Gap: A Critique." TMF 7:3 (May/June 83):6-15, 31.
A detailed review-essay of Michael Cook's Monthly Murders (A34).

A127. _____. "EQA 30: An Index to Issues 1-30 of Ellery Queen's Anthology." TMN 11 (June 77):I1-I28.
An index by author and title, with appendices showing title changes and series characters.

A128. Nieminski, John, compiler. EQMM 350. An Author/Title Index to Ellery Queen's Mystery Magazine, Fall 1941 through January 1973. White Bear Lake, MN: The Armchair Detective, 1974. 116pp. Printed on recto only, stapled in pictorial wrappers.
There is a checklist of issues indexed, giving volume and number, whole number, cover date, and number of pages. The main index (page 5173) is an alphabetical index-by-author of the contents of the first 350 issues of EQMM, giving issue date and pagination for each title. Reprints are noted. The entries are numbered (1 through 4121) for easy reference. The index by title (pages 73-107) uses these reference numbers. Numerous appendices list title changes, series characters, nonfiction pieces, true crime, book reviews, verse, parodies and pastiches, Sherlockiana, and other filler items. An indispensable adjunct to any file of EQMM, and an essential reference work for collectors and students of the mystery short story. Breen 22. (REB)

A129. _____. The Saint Magazine Index: Authors and titles, Spring 1953 - October 1967. Evansville, IN: Cook & McDowell Publications, 1980. 68pp. Stapled in heavy paper covers.
In this index to the U. S. edition of The Saint Detective (or Mystery) Magazine, the scope and overall organization are the same as for this compiler's EQMM 350. Another essential reference work. Breen 23. (REB)

A130. "Office 221." Hikkei Mystery Techo |Indispensable mystery handbook|. Tokyo: Kagyu-sha, 1979. 2 vols.
The first volume deals with the Japanese mystery and the second with the non-Japanese mystery. This handbook not only contains a list of major works by major writers, but also an award-winner list, reference book and magazine lists, a chronological table and other data. The editing is somewhat rough, for lack of space. (HS/TT)

A132. Pronzini, Bill. "Edgar and Special Awards 1945-1978." In The Edgar Winners, edited by Bill Pronzini, pp. 411-420. NY: Random House, 1980.
Listings of Edgar winners in all categories for the years indicated.

A133. Queen, Ellery. The Detective Short Story: A Bibliography. Boston: Little, Brown, 1942; reprint, with new Introduction, NY: Biblo & Tannen, 1969. Biblo & Tannen edition: pp. xii, 146pp. Index.
Annotated bibliography of anthologies and single-author collections of detective short stories. Breen 26. CC 3004. (REB)

A134. ______. "Detective's Dictionary." Good Housekeeping, Feb 44, pp. 27, 154-56.
Twenty-six "tidbits," curious items about detectives, detection and writers. Breezy and informative. Described as from a work-in-progress.

A135. ______. Queen's Quorum: A History of the Detective-Crime Short Story as Revealed in the 106 Most Important Books Published in This Field Since 1845. Boston: Little, Brown, 1951; London: Gollancz, 1953; new edition, with Supplements through 1967, NY: Biblo & Tannen, 1969. Biblo & Tannen edition: ix, 146pp. Indices.
The subtitle says it all: indispensable to anyone interested in short crime fiction. The 1967 supplements bring the total up to 125 books. Breen 27. (REB)

A136. ______. "The Ten Most Important Books of Detective Short Stories." Good Housekeeping, May 44, pp. 25, 124-125. Illus.
From Poe's Tales (1845) to Bailey's Call Mr. Fortune (1920). With five candidates for post-1920 honors.

A137. ______. "The Ten Most Important Detective Novels." Good Housekeeping, June 44, pp. 64, 1160.
Gaboriau's L'Affaire Lerouge to Iles' Before the Fact. With brief, incisive commentaries and a short list of honorable mentions. This list and the preceding were combined and published in Murder Cavalcade (MWA Anthology, 1946). (J. R. Christopher)

A138. Queen, Ellery, editor. Ellery Queen's 1976 Mystery Calendar. NY, NY: Davis Publications, Inc. (distributed by Harper & Row), 1975. (28pp. unnumbered)
A wall calendar featuring 135 photographs (many of them rare) of mystery writers, plus birth and death dates and a few historical events of importance in mystery fiction. One photograph is mis-labeled: on the November page, the photo identified as Maurice Leblanc is actually Sax Rohmer. (See also Eck, Frank: EQ's 1978 Mystery Calendar, A49.) (REB)

A139. ______. Ellery Queen's 1977 Mystery Calendar. NY: Davis Publications Inc., 1976.
Wall calendar featuring photographs and capsule biographies of 24 mystery writers with notes of important dates in their careers. (REB)

A140. Radcliffe, Elsa J. Gothic Novels of the 20th Century. An Annotated Bibliography. Metuchen, N.J.: Scarecrow Press, 1979. xix, 272pp. Index.
Lists 1,973 American English 'Gothic' novels published since 1900 (alphabetically by author, cross-indexed by title), including many examples from the paperback Gothic boom of the 1960's. Marred by errors of fact and of organization and inconsistent in the application of critical standards, it is still the only reference work on its topic. Breen 28. (REB)

A141. Randall, David A. The First Hundred Years of Detective Fiction,

1841-1941. Lilly Publication No. 18. Bloomington, IN: The Lilly Library, Indiana Univ., 1973.

Annotated, illustrated catalogue issued to accompany an exhibit of detective story milestones. (REB)

A142. Redmond, Anne, et al. Enquête sur le roman policier |Investigation of the detective novel|. Paris: Bibliothèques de la ville de Paris, 1978. 143pp.

There is a short history of the genre and a list of critical references but the major part of the volume consists of a dictionary of authors with biographies and selective bibliographies. Particularly useful for information on French writers but international in scope.

A143. Reilly, John M., ed. Twentieth Century Crime and Mystery Writers. NY: St. Martin's Press, 1980; London: MacMillan, 1980. xxiv, 1568pp. (In series: Twentieth Century Writers of the English Language)

This is, and is likely to remain, the primary reference work on English-language crime writers. No other work except Allen Hubin's Crime Fiction bibliography has attempted so much nor come so close to achieving its goals. For each of 614 authors, it offers a thumbnail biographical sketch (Who's Who-style), a bibliography of books and uncollected short fiction in all fields, and a critical/evaluative essay. The list of authors to be included was drawn up with the help of a 21-member advisory board, and the essays were written by more than 130 contributors. In addition to the main entries, separate sections include coverage of nine 19th century writers and sixteen foreign-language writers. The editor's Preface includes an 8-page "Reading List" of important secondary works. The critical essays are not, of course, of uniform quality; some suffer from academic stuffiness, some from superficiality, and one (on Jack Webb, confusing this crime writer with the actor and director of the same name) is just plain wrong. But the average quality is impressively high. Some of the bibliographies need more work, especially in the area of short stories. However, for many of the authors, the lists in this volume are the first attempts to compile bibliographies, and incomplete lists are better than none. A revised edition of this monumental work, with more than a hundred new entries, is due in 1985. Breen 29. (REB)

A144. Rivière, François. "Petit Guide chronologique de la fiction policière |A little chronological guide to detective fiction|." Europe, nos. 571-2 (Nov-Dec 76), pp. 166-71.

Annotated list of authors and works from Poe's Tales (1845) to Hugh Fleetwood's The Order of Death (1976).

A145. Rosenberg, Betty. Genreflecting: A Guide to Reading Interests in Genre Fiction. Littleton, Colorado: Libraries Unlimited, 1982. 254pp.

Since this guide does not claim to be comprehensive in any of the six topic areas it treats (romance, science fiction, thriller, fantasy, horror, Western), it cannot be recommended for any except the most general collections. The book developed from syllabi in a course the author teaches and reflects her enthusiastic appreciation of genre. An amiable hodge-podge that is fun to browse through and that provides some secondary sources for further work. Expensive at $26.95, it would have been more attractive--and recommendable--as a paperback manual. Detective fiction is included in the thriller section. Indices of authors and secondary sources.

A146. ______. The Letter Killeth: Three Bibliographic Essays for Bibliomaniacs. Los Angeles: Kenneth Karmiole, Bookseller, 1982. Index. Wraps. $30.
The author seems unaware of any previous work on this topic and her listings are far from being complete surveys of the field of books, bookdealers, bibliomania and mysteries. Like her Genreflecting, an overpriced and under-researched project.

A147. Sandoe, James. "The Detective Story and Academe." WLB 18 (Apr 44):619-623.
A basic, annotated list of mystery anthologies, fiction and reference. Based on two Haycraft lists (WLB, Feb 38, pp. 371-77, and Ch. XIV in Murder for Pleasure, B143) and submitted, before publication, to a "number of critics, writers, editors, and readers" for comments.

A148. ______. The Hard-Boiled Dick: A Personal Check List. Chicago: Arthur Lovell, 1952. Reprinted in TAD 1 (1967/68):38-42; revised and expanded version published as "The Private Eye" in The Mystery Story (B15), pp.111-123. See also Nevins letter in TAD 1 (1967/68):106, for reservations and additions; and Lachman letter in TAD 1 (1967/68):107, for an annotated supplement. Wraps. 9pp. Edition limited to approximately 300 copies.
An annotated list of 31 writers of "tough" detective stories for "the reader who, having Hammett and Spillane to choose between, prefers the former." In What About Murder? (A22), Jon Breen calls this "the most famous nine-page pamphlet in the annals of the genre, and justly so." Breen 47. CC 3018. (REB)

A149. Schantz, Tom and Enid. Murder: Plain and Fanciful. Catalog 29. Boulder, CO: The Aspen Bookhouse, May 1976. 24pp. Pictorial wraps.
During the 1970s the Aspen Bookhouse issued a lengthy series of illustrated and annotated catalogues of detective fiction. Catalog 29 is notable because it is devoted to 336 items from the library of critic and anthologist James Sandoe. The Schantzes contribute a brief appreciation of Sandoe, and many of the annotations quote his opinions and comments. (REB)

A150. Schleret, Jean-Jacques. "De quelques noirs absents du Voyage au bout de la Noire." Polar 28 (Winter 83):139-47.
Additions to the Mesplède/Schleret Voyage (A113).

A151. Schweitzer, Darrell. "An Index to the Not at Night series." Megavore no. 10 (Aug 1980), pp. 46-7.
A listing by volume of the contents of the ten English anthologies published in the late 20s and early 30s which drew heavily on Weird Tales for selections.

A152. Shibuk, Charles. "A Preliminary Checklist of the Detective Novel and Its Variants." Privately printed, (1967). 6 pp. mimeographed.
A checklist, with 2 supplements, of writers with brief commentaries on their principal contributions and recommended titles.

A153. ______. "Who Done It?: The Mystery Novel on the Screen." TAD 3 (1970):255-69.
Additions to the section on "cinematized mystery fiction" in Hagen's Who Done It? (A65). See Shibuk letter in TAD 4 (1970/71):125, for corrections and additions.

A154. Shibuk, Charles and Marvin Lachman. "What the World Waited For." TAD 9 (1975/76): 203-207.

An updating of the Haycraft/Queen "Definitive Library of Detective-Crime-Mystery Fiction" (A71) through 1975. The contributions of Robert Aucott, Jon L. Breen, Francis M. Nevins, Jr. and John Nieminski are acknowledged.

A155. Shulman, David, editor. An Annotated Bibliography of Cryptography. Garland Reference Library of the Humanities, Vol. 37. NY: Garland Publishing, 1976. Index.

Cites many works of mystery fiction. Not seen. (REB)

A156. Skene Melvin, David and Ann, compilers. Crime, Detective, Espionage, Mystery and Thriller Fiction and Film. A Comprehensive Bibliography of Critical Writing through 1979. Westport, CT: Greenwood Press, 1980. xx, 367pp. Title Index. Subject Index.

The main entries comprise 1,628 numbered items, arranged alphabetically by author (pp. 3-204). These entries are then cross-indexed by title (pp. 205-265) and by subject (pp. 267-355). An Appendix (pp. 357-367) indexes those main entries which are in languages other than English, grouping them by language (two items in Afrikaans, three in Czechoslovakian, etc.). In the Introduction the compilers list categories which have been excluded from this work. Most of these are expected and sensible: Holmesiana, major literary figures who sometimes deal with crime, and supernatural/fantasy/science fiction. Material on pre-Poe writers has largely been excluded as well. The major omission, however, is that of material from the "amateur" or "fan" journals such as TAD, TMF, TPP, etc. A few items from TAD or The Mystery Lover's Newsletter have been included but only when they have been legitimized by being cited in a more "respectable" source. Of course TAD now has its own index(A163),and the fan publications in general are treated in Michael Cook's Mystery Fanfare (A38), but these works did not exist when the Skene Melvin compilation was in progress, and the compilers' reasons for exclusion of this material are unconvincing. Even within the boundaries set by the compilers, there are peculiarities of organization and cross-indexing. Works published without a byline are listed by title in the main alphabetical sequence. Thus the main entry for Bibliography of Dr. R. H. van Gulik is under 'B'. The same treatment is accorded collections of essays by assorted authors, so that the main entry for H. R. F. Keating's Agatha Christie: First Lady of Crime is under 'A'. The same book suffers other mischances. Item 1534, "Music and Mystery" by William Weaver, is said to have appeared in a book titled Agatha Christie. When we look in the title index, we find two books of this title, one by Agatha Christie herself and one by G. C. Ramsey. Both are cited with incomplete titles. Keating's symposium, where the Weaver article actually was published, does not appear in the title index at all. One also finds items that should not have been included, such as 1083, "A Word from Dr. Lyndon Parker" by Lyndon Parker, listed as if it were a critical essay rather than part of the fictional contents of In Re: Sherlock Holmes: The Adventures of Solar Pons. In sum, this bibliography is less than its title and introduction promise and must be used with care. Nevertheless, it collects much useful information not otherwise easily available. (REB)

A157. Smith, Myron J., Jr. Cloak-and-Dagger Bibliography: An Annotated Guide to Spy Fiction, 1937-1935. Metuchen, NJ: The Scarecrow Press, 1976. xi, 225pp. Index of titles.

Annotated author-entry bibliography of 1675 spy novels, selected for adult and young-adult readers. Smith chooses the 1937-75 period in order to concentrate on novels of WW II and Cold War interest. In addition to plot summaries for most of the books listed, annotations are included which give information on printings, suitability for under-10th graders, and sexual content. There are many errors of commission and omission. The British edition is never listed if there is an American edition. Michael Avallone's name is misspelled; it is overlooked that Duncan Kyle, Berkeley Mather, Alan Caillou and George Bartram are pseudonyms. Many important novelizations from TV shows are missing, such as the "I Spy" and "Mission: Impossible" series. The "Man from U.N.C.L.E." and "Get Smart" series are incomplete. Many of these errors were corrected in Smith's expanded Cloak and Dagger Fiction, 2nd edition. Breen 30. (GG)

A158. ______. Cloak and Dagger Fiction: An Annotated Guide to Spy Thrillers. 2nd ed. Santa Barbara, CA: ABC-Clio, Inc., 1982; Oxford, England: Clio Press Ltd., 1982. xxvi, 431pp. Short foreword by Clive Cussler; preface by James C. Stam; three "Introductions" by Smith. Bibliography of secondary sources; indices for pseudonyms, series characters, authors, titles, and intelligence and terrorist organizations.

Much expanded and improved edition of Smith's Cloak-and-Dagger Bibliography. Where the earlier work lists 1675 novels, this lists 3435. Some of the errors have been corrected. Many pseudonyms have been identified. The "I Spy" and "Man from U.N.C.L.E." series are complete, and the "Get Smart" and "Mission: Impossible" series are present. But Michael Avallone's name is still misspelled. Eric Ambler's first book, The Dark Frontier (1936) is overlooked. Smith states that the pseudonym of Trevanian (i.e., Rodney H. Whitaker) is unknown. Sax Rohmer's real name (Arthur Henry Sarsfield Ward) is listed as Arthur S. Wade, and all of Simon Harvester's novels listed which feature Malcolm Kenton are listed as Dorian Silk novels. Despite these and similar errors, the book is very informative, for it gives thousands of plot summaries, including the Nick Carter series. Many books from the pre-1940 period have been added. If used with care in conjunction with Hubin (A83), East (A48), or Reilly (A143), this book, written for junior high and high school library consultation, can be quite useful. (GG)

A159. Steinbrunner, Chris; Shibuk, Charles; Penzler, Otto; Lachman, Marvin; and Nevins, Francis M., Jr. Detectionary: A Biographical Dictionary of the Leading Characters in Detective and Mystery Fiction. Privately published (Lock Haven, PA: Hammermill Paper Co),1971. xiv, 586pp. Illus. Index. Revised edition, Woodstock, NY: The Overlook Press, 1977. xi, 299pp. Illus. Index. The Overlook Press hardcover edition incorporates revisions and corrections to the original edition and has many more illustrations.

An interestingly designed and well-illustrated volume. Entries are arranged in four sections: Detectives, Rogues & Helpers, Cases, and Movies, thoroughly cross-referenced and indexed. A unique compilation. Breen 32. (REB)

A160. Steinbrunner, Chris; Penzler, Otto; Lachman, Marvin; and Shibuk, Charles, editors. Encyclopedia of Mystery and Detection. NY: McGraw-Hill, 1976. 436pp.

A basic reference work on the mystery genre, both in written form and on film. Author biographies, checklists, plot summaries, descriptions of principal detectives and villains, with more than 300 illustrations. Breen 31. (REB)

A161. Stern, Peter L. Detective Fiction and Sherlockiana. Sharon, MA: Peter L. Stern, 1976 - . Illustrated wraps.
A series of booksellers' catalogues, varying from 36 to 64 pages, listing short story collections, novels, and miscellany. Choice items are illustrated--not only covers but title pages and other features. Catalogue 3 (May 1977) contains a section of autograph letters by Wilkie Collins, Maurice Leblanc, and Dorothy L. Sayers; the Sayers letters and part of the Collins are reproduced in facsimile. In addition to his own annotations, Stern frequently quotes apposite comments from standard references on crime fiction. (REB)

A162. Stewart, Enola. Gravesend Books Catalogues. Pocono Pines, PA: Gravesend Books, 1971- . Nos. 1-24 are offset, stapled in decorative or pictorial covers; from no. 25 on the catalogues are printed booklets.
Notable for the detailed bibliographical citations and the concise, knowledgeable annotations, these catalogues retain permanent value for their information on both the standard works and the esoterica of mystery fiction and its associated secondary material. (REB)

A163. Stilwell, Steve. The Armchair Detective Index (Volumes 1-10) 1967-79. NY: Mysterious Press, 1979. 64pp. plus unpaginated front matter. Paper covers.
Indexes not only the titled articles from TAD but also reviews, letters and filler material, by author, title, and subject. An indispensable adjunct to the magazines themselves. (REB)

A164. Swedish Library Service. Vandringar med böcker |A guided tour with books|.
Lists published by the Swedish Library Service that include the following titles: Bo Lundin, Deckare-inte bara pussel |Mysteries-not only puzzles|, no. 2, 1970, 4pp; Lundin, Mord i andra hand |Murder at second hand|, no. 3, 1981, 6pp; Roland Adlerberth, Med pistol i bagaget |With a gun in the luggage|, no. 6, 1969, 4pp. (IH)

A165. Symons, Julian, ed. The 100 Best Crime Stories. London: The Sunday Times, 1959. 21pp. Wraps. Illus.
The results of a survey, compiled, introduced, and annotated by Symons, based on consultations with more than a dozen well-known mystery writers and critics. Some author portraits are included. Breen 35. (REB)

A166. ______. "De 99 bästa kriminalhistorierna |The 99 best criminal stories|." Jury 1:2 (1972):29-32.
Symons' 1959 list with data on Swedish editions of books that have been translated. (MS)

A167. Taylor, Bruce. "Rare Books Are Getting Scarce." CP? 3:2 (May 81):28-29.
A checklist of the Pyramid Green Door Mystery series.

A168. Ting, Nai-Tung. A Type Index of Chinese Folktales in the Oral Tradition and Major Works of Non-Religious Classical Literature. FF Communications No. 223. Helsinki: Academia Scientarum Fennica, 1978. 294pp.
A detailed, well researched, scholarly topic index to Chinese oral folktales. Divided by sections into major topics, such as Animal Tales, Ordinary Folktales, Formula Tales, etc. Of greatest criminous use is the special subject index in an appendix, pp. 280-94, where can be found

page listings of plot outlines of detective stories in the body of the Index. The subject index contains such entries as "Corpse..." or "Judge...," or "Magistrate...." The bibliography consists of primary sources, pp. 252-266, lists over 500 works in Asian and Western languages which contain written versions of the tales, many of them detective stories. This is a good source for the study of the oral origins of the kung-an story. (GG)

A169. Triviallitteratur, Kriminalromaner, Science Fiction |Popular literature, crime novels, science fiction|. Copenhagen: Royal Danish Library, 1980. 62pp.

A catalogue published by the Royal Danish Library of genre titles and their location. (IH)

A170. Trott, Floyd. The Mafia: A Select Annotated Bibliography. Cambridge, England: Institute of Criminology, Univ. of Cambridge Press, 1978. 141pp.

Author and subject indices. Not seen. Review: TLS, 28 Apr 78, p. 481.

A171. Tuck, Donald H., compiler. The Encyclopedia of Science Fiction and Fantasy, Through 1968. A bibliographic survey of the fields of science fiction, fantasy, and weird fiction through 1968. 3 vols. Chicago, IL: Advent: Publishers, Inc. Volume 1: Who's Who, A-L, March 1974, xii, 286pp.; Volume 2: Who's Who, M-Z, January 1978,pp. xviii-xx, 287-530; Volume 3: Miscellaneous, December 1982, pp. xxvi-xxviii, 531-920.

In 474 double-columned pages of small print, the 'Who's Who and Works' section of the encyclopedia covers hundreds of major and minor writers in the sf, fantasy and weird fiction genres. For each writer, the entry gives birth and death dates, a biographical and career sketch, and a list of that writer's fantasy fiction and related nonfiction in book form, with selected magazine pieces. The bibliographies aim at completeness, listing all editions in all languages. The Checklist of Fantastic Literature (A18) of 1948 is taken as a starting point, and information found in that compilation is generally not duplicated in the Encyclopedia. Complete contents of story collections and anthologies are given. Many writers of crime fiction are included in the author entries: Bloch, Borges, Boucher, Chesterton, Christie, Conan Doyle, Fleming, John D. MacDonald, Edith Pargeter ('Ellis Peters'), Dorothy L. Sayers, and dozens more. All book titles cited in the author entries are cross-indexed in the 'Listing by Title' (pp. 479-530). Volume 3 covers the publishing histories of the various sf/fantasy magazines, checklists of paperbacks issued by various publishers, extensive lists of pseudonyms (many from crime fiction) and series characters, Science Fiction Book Club selections, and other miscellany. The amount and diversity of information included in these three volumes almost beggars description. Supplements are planned to extend the coverage up to date. (REB)

A172. ______. A Handbook of Science Fiction and Fantasy. Hobart, Tasmania: (compiler), January 1954. Mimeographed. 2nd edition, Revised and Enlarged. Hobart, Tasmania: (compiler), April 1959. Legal size, mimeographed, bound in card covers. In two volumes: Part 1 (A-L), viii-ix, 1-194pp.; Part 2 (M-Z), pp. 185-396.

Superseded by the same compiler's Encyclopedia. (REB)

A173. Tullberg, Sigurd. O och A. Detektivromaner pa Svenska under 1900-talet |Mystery novels in Swedish during the 19th century|. Stockholm: Bibliotekens Bokformedling, 1954. 95pp. Title and pseudonym indices. (IH)

A174. Tymm, Marshall B., editor. Horror Literature. A Core Collection and Reference Guide. NY & London: R. R. Bowker Co., 1981. xviii, 559pp. Author and Title Index.
The boundaries between supernatural and crime fiction are not very clearly marked, and although many detective fiction specialists think that the supernatural is contrary to the ratiocinative history of the genre, much supernatural fiction contains criminous elements, and some very good detective fiction has supernatural elements. This annotated guide and history is particularly interesting for its survey of the Gothic Romance by Frederick S. Frank and the "Residual Gothic Impulse" by Benjamin F. Fisher IV, but it also has a section on the "Horror Pulps" (Robert Weinberg), a genre that was a horrific blend of mystery and terror. There are also a "Reference Sources" section and a Core Collection Checklist.

A175. Van Tilburg, Barry. "Spy Series Characters in Hardback." TMF 4 (1980), issues 2-6; 5 (1981), issues 1, 3 and 5; 6 (1982), issues 1-3.
Series checklists organized as charts with bibliographies.

A176. Waterhouse, Howard. "The American Detective Series." PQ 2:3 (Fall 79):32-39.
A history and a list of the titles published in the Arthur Westbrooke Company series, 1906-1937.

A177. ______. "The Green Door Mystery." PQ 1:2 (1978):39-43.
A brief publishing history and a checklist of this pb series.

A178. ______. "Mighty, Miraculous, Murder Mystery Monthly." PQ.1:4 (1978):31-36. Illus.
Digest history and checklist.

A179. ______. "The Popular Library Short Story Collections." CP? 2:1 (1980):12-14.
Checklists of collections of stories by William Irish, G. K. Chesteron, Sax Rohmer and Hugh Wiley.

A180. Whitt, J. F. 'The Strand Magazine' 1891-1950. A Selective Checklist: Listing All Material Relating to Arthur Conan Doyle, All Stories by P. G. Wodehouse, and a Selection of Detective, Mystery, or Fantasy Fiction. London: J. F. Whitt, 1979, 48pp. Wraps.
Among the authors included in the 'Selection' are John Dickson Carr and Agatha Christie. (REB)

A181. Wuyek, George. "The Future is Upon Us: A Necrology for the Year 1981." TAD 15 (1982):238-41.

A182. Yamamura, Masao. Meitantei Shinshiroku: Umi no Oya kara Suiri-ho made Tettei-chosa Shita Igai na Yokogao [Great detective who's who: completely investigated, unexpected profiles from their creators to their ways of detecting]. Tokyo: Goma Shobo, 1977. Illus., bibl., index.
A guide to the major works and chief characteristics of 30 non-Japanese series characters and 19 Japanese, in dictionary format. The selection is somewhat inappropriate, and the misquotations are regrettable. (HS/TT)

II. General Reference Works: Historical & Critical

A. Books

B1. Abrahams, Etta Claire. "Vision and Values in the Action Detective Novel: A Study of the Works of Raymond Chandler, Kenneth Millar, and John D. MacDonald." Unpublished Ph. D. Dissertation. Michigan State University, 1973. 209pp. Dissertation Abstracts 34/06-A, pp. 3378-79.

B2. Adams, Donald K., ed. The Mystery and Detection Annual 1972. Beverly Hills, CA: Donald Adams, 1972. xi, 264pp. Illus. Designed and printed by Grant Dahlstrom at The Castle Press.
Anthology of essays, reviews, notes and queries (plus verse and illustrations) on all aspects of mystery fiction. The reviews are detailed and often constitute short essays. Contents: Leon Howard, "Poe's Eureka: The Detective Story That Failed," pp. 1-14; Terrence Hipolito, "On the Two Poes," pp. 16-20 (the grotesque and ratiocinative worlds of EAP); Liahna Klenman Babener, "The Shadow's Shadow: The Motif of the Double in Edgar Allan Poe's 'The Purloined Letter'," pp. 21-32 (E2091); Burton R. Pollin, "Poe's Illustration for 'The Island of the Fay': A Hoax Detected," pp. 33-45; J. E. Harrison, "The Detective," pp. 46-47 (poem); Donald K.Adams, "The Second Mrs. Radcliffe," pp. 48-64 (Mary Ann Radcliffe, Gothic novelist); Arthur J.Cox, "The Haggard Woman," pp. 65-77 (the "opium woman" in Dickens' Drood); Benedict Freedman, "The Thinking Machine," pp. 79-85 (E1222); Norman Donaldson, "A Freeman Postscript," pp. 86-92 (E1181); Penelope Wallace, "A Man and His Books," pp. 93-97 (on her father, Edgar Wallace); Nigel Morland, "Incident in Shanghai," pp. 98-101 (E2008); Lawrence D. Stewart, "Gertrude Stein and the Vital Dead," pp. 102-124 (E2766); Ann Stanford, "The Prologue to the Mystery Poem," pp. 125-135 (poem); Thomas Sturak, "Horace McCoy, Captain Shaw, and the Black Mask," pp. 139-158 (E1805); Donald K. Adams, "The First Thin Man," pp. 160-177 (E1358); Daniel R. Barnes, "'I'm the Eye': Archer as Narrator in the Novels of Ross Macdonald," pp. 178-190 (E1854); "Conversations With a Psychoanalyst: Janet A. Kennedy, M.D.," pp. 191-197 (comments on real-life crime and crime fiction); Paul Bowles, "Etiquette," p. 198 (poem). Reviews (pp. 199-253); Notes and Queries: Daniel R. Barnes, "A Note on The Murder of Roger Ackroyd," pp. 254-55 (E527); Jean Beckner, "Arthur Conan Doyle and Joaquin Miller," pp. 256-58; "The Erle Stanley Gardner Collection at the University of Texas," p. 259 (E1238). Breen 76. (REB)

B3. ______. The Mystery and Detection Annual 1973. Beverly Hills, CA: Donald Adams, 1974. vii-x, 337pp. Illus. Designed and printed by Grant Dahlstrom.
The second, and final volume of this series. Part of this 1973 edition is devoted to California private detective fiction ("the golden age of realistic American detective fiction"), including the first publication of a

novella, "Death in Hollywood," by Horace McCoy. Contents: Leon Howard, "Raymond Chandler's Not-So-Great Gatsby," pp. 1-15 (E413); Thomas Sturak, "A Foreword to 'Death in Hollywood'," pp. 16-19 (E1804); Horace McCoy, "Death in Hollywood," pp. 20-52 (fiction); Ralph Bruno Sipper, "An Interview with Ross Macdonald," pp. 53-58; Steven R. Carter, "Ross Macdonald: the Complexity of the Modern Quest for Justice," pp. 59-84 (E1859); Ann Stanford, "The Mystery Poem," pp. 85-96 (poem); Robert L. Chianese, "James Hogg's Confessions of a Justified Sinner: an Anatomy of Terror," pp. 97-112; Martin Roth, "The Poet's Purloined Letter," pp. 113-28 (E2174); Benjamin Franklin Fisher IV, "Poe in the Seventies: the Poet Among the Critics," pp. 129-41 (critical studies of Poe published in the 1970s); Donald K. Adams, "Recalled and Awakened: the Romantic Fiction of William Godwin, Jr.," pp. 142-66 (E2186); Albert D. Hutter and Mary W. Miller, "The Detective, an Early Journal of Detection," pp. 167-92 (England, 1859-60); Wilbur Jordan Smith, "Mystery Fiction in the Nineteenth Century," pp. 193-205 (D74); Mark McCloskey, "At the Bottom of the Pool," p. 205 (poem); Mark McCloskey, "Clues (for Sukey)," pp. 207-208 (poem); Ngaio Marsh, "Starting with People," pp. 209-210 (E1955); Thomas D. O'Donnell, "Michel Butor's Passing Time and the Detective Hero,"; pp. 211-20 (E307); J. Stuart Whiteley, "Simenon: the Shadow and the Self. An Interview with Georges Simenon," pp. 221-36 (E2702); John Robertson, "Consider, Sir, the Hyacinth Hair," p. 237 (poem); Julian Symons, "Progress of a Crime Writer," pp. 238-44 (E2843); Lawrence D. Stewart, "Paul Bowles: Up above the World So High," pp. 245-70 (Bowles' novel and Gide's Les Caves du Vatican); Henry Binder, "West," p. 271 (poem); Laura Krugman Ray, "The Mysteries of Gaudy Night: Feminism, Faith and the Depths of Character," pp. 272-85 (E2551); J. E. Harrison, "The Passage," p. 286 (poem); Reviews (pp. 287-325); Notes and Queries: Vern L. Bullough, "Deviant Sex and the Detective Story," pp. 326-30 (Ian Fleming, Mark Twain, Mickey Spillane, Joseph Hansen); Lawrence D. Stewart, "The Dust Jackets of The Great Gatsby and The Long Goodbye," pp. 331-334. Breen 77. (REB)

B4. Aisenberg, Nadja. A Common Spring: Crime Novel and Classic. Bowling Green, OH: Popular Press, 1980. 271pp. Index. Selected bibliography of primary and secondary sources; extensive notes with discussion of secondary literature.

After a brief overview of the history of detective fiction (C7), the book consists of chapters on Dickens (E825), Conrad (E703), and Graham Greene (E1310). Breen 236.

B5. Allen, Dick, and Chacko, David, eds. Detective Fiction: Crime and Compromise. NY: Harcourt Brace Jovanovich, 1974. 481pp.

Well thought out textbook/anthology for courses in crime fiction. A general introduction, research and discussion topics, suggestions for further reading. Section IV consists of critical essays on the genre of which the following are relevant to this bibliography: Sayers, "The Omnibus of Crime" (C725); Chesterton, "A Defense of Detective Stories," (C178); Raymond Chandler, "The Simple Art of Murder," (C168); W. H. Auden, "The Guilty Vicarage," (C34); George Grella, "Murder and the Mean Streets: The Hard-Boiled Detective Novel," (C341). Review: TAD 7 (1973/74):218-19. (REB)

B6. Allen, L. David. Detective in Fiction. Lincoln, Nebraska: Cliff Notes Inc., 1978. 128pp.

One in a series of classroom text guides. Although many teachers deplore the use of this by students who use the handy plot resumes as a substitute for the reading of primary texts, Detectives in Fiction, in addition to mini-essays on 11 novels and stories which do include the usual plot summaries but also some judicious critical commentary, also has a short introduction with the Ronald K. Knox and S. S. Van Dine "rules" for writing detective fiction and a discussion of the underlying premises of the classical detective story; a listing of MWA Edgars for best first mystery and best novel through 1975; and selected bibliographies of primary and secondary sources. The texts do not include any hardboiled fiction and only three works published since 1945. The authors and texts discussed are as follows: E. A. Poe, "The Purloined Letter," pp. 17-22; Wilkie Collins, The Moonstone, pp. 22-30; A. Conan Doyle, "The Adventure of the Speckled Band," pp. 30-34; Dorothy (L.) Sayers, Whose Body?, pp. 34-42; S. S. Van Dine, The Benson Murder Case, pp. 42-49; Agatha Christie, The Murder of Roger Ackroyd and What Mrs. McGillicuddy Saw, pp. 49-56, 56-63; Margery Allingham, The Fashion in Shrouds, pp. 63-72; Rex Stout, Black Orchids, pp. 72-80; Philip MacDonald, The List of Adrian Messenger, pp. 80-89; Ellis Peters, Death and the Joyful Woman, pp. 89-97.

B7. Anglo, Michael. Penny Dreadfuls and Other Victorian Horrors. London: Jupiter Press, 1977. 125pp. Illus.

"Penny Dreadfuls" were 19th-century escapist reading for "working-class youth." There is an introductory chapter on the Gothic foundations of the literature and chapters on Dick Turpin and other bandit "heroes," Sweeney Todd, Spring-Heeled Jack, smaller publishers and series fiction, penny dreadful writers, and miscellaneous topics. The period illustrations, many in color, enhance the informal text.

B8. Anker, Jens. Kriminalromaner med en Bibliografi |Detective novels with a bibliography|. Copenhagen: Forlaget Forum, 1948. 126pp. Index by author and title.

Historical first chapter and then a survey of mystery fiction by country: England, America, Austria, Holland, France, Switzerland, Czechoslovakia, Germany and Scandinavia. (IH)

B9. Aoki, Amehiko. Kagai Jugyo: Mystery ni Okeru Otoko to On'na no Kenkyu |Extra-curricular lessons: studies on men and women in mystery fiction|. Tokyo: Hayakawa Shobo, 1977. 266pp.

A collection of essays in which Aoki expresses his views on love relationships, quoting dialogues and descriptions from then newly-published non-Japanese mysteries. The book won the Mystery Writers of Japan award as the best critical book of 1978. He has also written, in the same vein: Yakan Hiko |Night flights|. Tokyo: Hayakawa Shobo, 1976; and Otono no Kaiwa |Adult Dialogues|. Tokyo: Diamond-sha, 1981. Each shows his individualistic way of reading and his almost complete lack of a critical sense, but he should be recognized for his accomplishment in arousing the interest of general readers, and women, in particular, in mystery fiction. The collections were first serialized in a magazine. (HS/TT)

B10. ______. On'na wa Itsumo Mystery |Women are always a mystery|. Tokyo: Bunka Shuppankyoku, 1981. 254pp.

A collection of essays on mystery fiction which originally appeared in periodicals. (HS/TT)

B11. Aramata, Hiroshi; Ishigami, Mitsutoshi; Kozumi, Rei; and Taniguchi, Takao. Taishu Shosetsu no Sekai: Genso Kaiki, Tantei, SF |The world of popular fiction: fantasy, horror, detective, and science fiction|. Tokyo: Kyugei Shuppan, 1978. 238pp.

Each of the four authors writes of the characteristics and a short history of each of the four genres. Ishigami, who writes on detective fiction, is a scholar/critic of films, comics, mysteries and science fiction, and he has written Otoko-Tachi no Tame no Guwa |Fairy tales for men| in which he shows his affection for the heroes of these genres. (HS/TT)

B12. Arnaud, Noel; Lacassin, Francis; and Tortel, Jean. Entretiens sur la Paralittérature |Discussions of paraliterature|. Paris: Plon, 1970. 478pp. Proceedings of the Colloquium of Cérisy-la-Salle, 1-10 September 1967.

Several reports are devoted to the detective novel: Francis Lacassin, "De Georges Sim à Simenon |From Georges Sim to Simenon|," (E2644); Juliette Raabe, "Le Phénomène Série noire |The série noire phenomenon|" (C666); and Charles Grivel, "Observation du roman policier |Observing the detective novel|" (C344). The solidity of the first two presentations contrasts vividly with the mediocrity of Mr. Grivel's analysis of a skeletal body of work. (JB)

B13. Arnold, Armin, and Schmidt, Josef. Reclams Kriminalromanführer |Reclam's crime fiction guidebook|. Stuttgart: Reclam, 1978. 455pp.

Part of German publisher Reclam's well-known guidebook series on the arts and culture, this is an historical, encyclopedic, bibliographical and critical overview of crime fiction around the world. Compiled by two German professors at McGill University, it is divided into three main sections. Section I (pp. 7-44) includes historical material, such as an essay on the development of the genre which includes comments on Biblical crime, ancient Chinese detective stories and dime novels, as well as a timetable of the most important dates in the history of the genre. Section II (pp. 45-362) is encyclopedic in format, similar to Encyclopedia of Mystery and Detection (A160). Biographical and bibliographical data are recorded as well as plot summaries which reveal endings. Section III (pp. 363-455) includes essays by various writers on crime fiction in various countries and areas, along with a list of 100 important crime novels, a character index of over 800 detectives and criminals, a bibliography of secondary sources, and an author index. There is much information throughout on English- and non-English-language novels which is unavailable in any of the standard critical works in English. The errors are mostly those of omission, and some of the subsections are weak. For example, neither the historical essay nor the essays on world crime fiction mention the vast number of crime novels published in India; neither the bibliography of secondary sources nor the essay on Chinese crime fiction even scratches the surface of the mass of critical material extant on the ancient Chinese detective story. Finally, some of the biobibliographical data in the encyclopedic section is sketchier than need be. But all in all, Reclams Kriminalromanführer is one of the single best guides to crime fiction around the world. (GG)

B14. Awasaka, Tsumao. Trick Kokyokyoku |Trick symphony|. Tokyo: JijiTsushinsha, 1981. 253pp. Illus.

The author is a mystery writer, very popular among a certain circle of fans and famous for his tricky writing style. He is also a magician. This book is a collection of essays strongly reflecting his interests, pointing out the similarities of detective fiction and magic and jointly classifying the tricks of detective fiction and those of magic. (HS/TT)

B15. Ball, John, ed. The Mystery Story. Preface by William D. McElroy and introduction by Martin N. Chamberlain. San Diego and Del Mar, CA: University of California and Publisher's Inc., 1976. Second printing, 1977. xiv, 390pp. Illustrated. Bibliography. (Dust jacket and spine identify the book as part of The Mystery Library.)

Collection of 16 essays and an annotated bibliography on mystery fiction, by 13 authors. Chapter Five, "The Private Eye" by James Sandoe, is an expanded version of this author's pamphlet The Hard-Boiled Dick: A Personal Checklist (A148). All of the other contents are original with this volume. Biography sketches and portraits of the contributors are included. In the second printing, the pen-and-ink sketches by Steve Pileggi from the first printing are replaced by new portraits (uncredited), and some typographical errors in the text are corrected. The paperback edition (New York, NY: Penguin Books, 1978) is a facsimile of the second printing. In 1983, distribution of this and other Mystery Library volumes was taken over by Bowling Green University Popular Press. Contents: John Ball, "Murder at Large," pp. 1-25 (C42); Aaron Marc Stein, "The Mystery Story in Cultural Perspective," pp. 29-59 (C781a); Hillary Waugh, "The Mystery Versus the Novel," pp. 61-80 (C845); Otto Penzler, "The Amateur Detectives," pp. 83-109 (C625); James Sandoe, "The Private Eye," pp. 111-23 (A148); Michele Slung, "Women in Detective Fiction," pp. 125-40 (C762); John Ball, "The Ethnic Detective," pp. 143-60 (C41); Hillary Waugh, "The Police Procedural," pp. 163-87 (C846); Donald A. Yates, "Locked Rooms and Puzzles: A Critical Memoir," pp. 189-203 (C881); Michael Gilbert, "The Spy in Fact and Fiction," pp. 205-221 (C320); Phyllis Whitney, "Gothic Mysteries," pp. 223-32 (C858); Robert E. Briney, "Death Rays, Demons, and Worms Unknown to Science," pp. 235-89 (C130); Allen J. Hubin, "Patterns in Mystery Fiction; The Durable Series Character," pp. 291-318 (A84); Otto Penzler, "The Great Crooks," p. 321-41 (C627); Francis M. Nevins, Jr., "Name Games: Mystery Writers and Their Pseudonyms," pp. 343-58 (C582); E. T. Guymon, Jr., "Why Do We Read This Stuff?", pp. 361-63 (C354); Robert E. Briney, "The Literature of the Subject: An Annotated Bibliography," pp. 365-90 (A25). Breen 63. (REB)

B16. Bargainnier, Earl F., editor. 10 Women of Mystery. Bowling Green, OH: Popular Press, 1981. 304pp. Indices: Characters and Titles.

Essays--some of which reveal endings--on major female writers. Each article is accompanied by a chronology of author discussed. In his introduction, Bargainnier states that the essays are intended to present the "achievements" of the ten women writers included and the format of the volume is that of a series of detailed surveys of the writers' work. Contents: Earl F. Bargainnier, "Introduction," pp. 1-5; Kathleen Gregory Klein, "Dorothy Sayers," pp. 8-39 (E2539); Nancy Ellen Talburt, "Josephine Tey," pp. 40-76 (E2862); Earl F. Bargainnier, "Ngaio Marsh," pp. 78-105 (E1947); Nancy C. Joyner, "P. D. James," pp. 106-123 (E1539); Jane S. Bakerman, "Ruth Rendell," pp. 124-29; Barrie Hayne, "Anna Katharine Green," pp. 150-78 (E1304); Jan Cohn, "Mary Roberts Rinehart," pp. 180-220 (E2351); John M. Reilly, "Margaret Millar," pp. 223-46 (E1987); Jeanne F. Bedell, "Emma Lathen," pp. 248-67 (E1627); Steven F. Carter, "Amanda Cross," pp. 269-96. (KLM)

B17. Barzun, Jacques and Wendell Hertig Taylor. A Book of Prefaces to Fifty

Classics of Crime Fiction 1900-1950. New York: Garland Publishing Co., 1976. vii, 112pp. Edition limted to 250 numbered copies.

Contains Barzun and Taylor's introduction to the Prospectus for the Garland reprint series Fifty Classics of Crime Fiction, together with the prefaces to the fifty reprint volumes, arranged alphabetically by author of book. A brief biographical paragraph on each author is also included. In the introduction the authors state: "By noticing the indicated points (in the prefaces), the amateur of the genre can if he wishes turn into an expert, thus ennancing his pleasure and strengthening his judgment against the dull or imitative works." This somewhat overstates the virtues of the prefaces (which are not negligible), if not of the books themselves. The commentary is very much in the spirit and style of A Catalogue of Crime (A10). A few minor errors in biography and bibliography are repeated from the earlier book. (Examples: Rex Stout did not start writing in 1920; he had published fiction as early as 1912, and some verse even earlier. And Follow My Dust is a biography of Arthur Upfield by another author---it is not his autobiography.) The series includes 49 novels and one collection of short stories, Classic Stories of Crime and Detection. The Prefaces will be cited in the Authors section, as follows: Margery Allingham, H. C. Bailey, E. C. Bentley, Nicholas Blake, Ernest Bramah, Gerald Bullett, Miles Burton, Raymond Chandler, G. K. Chesterton, Agatha Christie, G. D. H. and Margaret Cole, Edmund Crispin, Freeman Wills Crofts, Arthur Conan Doyle, Helen Eustis, Kenneth Fearing, R. Austin Freeman, Erle Stanley Gardner, Andrew Garve, Michael Gilbert, C. W. Grafton, Anna Katharine Green, Cyril Hare, Matthew Head, Georgette Heyer, James Hilton, Elspeth Huxley, Michael Innes, Thomas Kindon, Thomas Kyd, Lange Lewis, Ross Macdonald, Pat McGerr, Paul McGuire, Ngaio Marsh, A. A. Milne, Dermot Morrah, Oliver Onions, Marco Page, Virginia Perdue, Eden Phillpotts, Dorothy L. Sayers, C. P. Snow, Rex Stout, Arthur Upfield, Henry Wade, Henry Kitchell Webster, Ellen Wilkinson, and Clifford Witting. Breen 64. (REB)

B18. ______. "Crime Fiction 1950-1975." NY: Garland Publishing, 1983.

A second series of fifty volumes of fifty "classics of American and British mysteries, detective stories, procedurals, and thrillers," published in the period 1950-1975. Each of the volumes contains an introduction consisting of the announcement brochure's general introduction (slightly rewritten) along with a brief biographical statement about the author of that particular volume. There are no analyses of plot, or of the importance of the book or author. The introductions will be cited in the Authors section, as follows: Frank Arthur, Alex Atkinson, John and Emery Bonett, Fredric Brown, Leo Bruce, Joanna Cannan, Philip Clark, K. C. Constantine, A. H. Z. Carr, Glynn Carr, Amanda Cross, Elizabeth Daly, Thomas B. Dewey, Stanley Ellin, Nigel Fitzgerald, Dick Francis, Edward Grierson, Bruce Hamilton, M. V. Heberden, Tony Hillerman, Stanley Hough, P. M. Hubbard, Michael Innes, P. D. James, Carlton Keith, Henry Kuttner, Christopher Landon, Emma Lathen, Norman Longmate, John D. MacDonald, J. J. Marric, John Miles, William Mole, Patricia Moyes, Simon Nash, Ellis Peters, J. B. Priestley, Maurice Procter, Ruth Rendell, Helen Robertson, Jean Scholey, Frank Swinnerton, Julian Symons, Josephine Tey, Simon Troy, Walter Tyrer, Robert Van Gulik, Colin Watson, and Hillary Waugh. (Ralph Carlson)

B19. Becker, Jens-Peter. Der englische Spionageroman. Historische Entwicklung,

Thematik literarische Form |The English spy novel: historical development, themes, literary form|. Munich: Wilhelm Goldmann Verlag, 1973. 202pp. Index.

A revised version of Becker's 1973 doctoral dissertation at Christian-Albrechts University in Kiel, Germany. Includes sections on the secondary literature of the subject, historical development, the realistic spy novel, and the modern (post-W.W. II) spy novel. Pp. 194-200 contain a bibliography of secondary sources. The book is written in an unpretentious style, and shows impressive familiarity with English-language critical material. (GG)

B20. _____. Sherlock Holmes & Co.: Essays zur englischen und amerikanischen Detektivliteratur |Essays on English and American detective literature|. Munich: Wilhelm Goldmann Verlag, 1975. 163pp. Paperbound. Notes. Bibliography. Index.

A collection of ten essays on English-language detective writers and (in one essay) on films. The title was chosen to indicate that all later detective heroes are, in some sense, variations on Holmes. Each essay has an extensive set of notes. The last essay in the book contains extensive annotations on 29 selected secondary works: English, French, German, and Scandinavian. There is in addition a 10-page bibliography of secondary sources in the same languages. Contents: "Statt einer Einleitung: Sherlock Holmes |In place of an introduction: Sherlock Holmes|," pp. 9-14; "Edgar Wallace: Versuch einer Ehrenrettung |EW: attempt at a rehabilitation|," pp. 15-27; "Die Marchenwelt der Margery Allingham |Margery Allingham's fairytale world|," pp. 28-36; "The Man Who Wrote Detective Stories: Michael Innes," pp. 37-46; "Ian Flemings James Bond-Romane und die Kritiker |Ian Fleming's James Bond novels and the critics|," pp. 47-59; "'Locus horridus' und Mayhem Parva: Typische Schauplatze des Detektivromans |'Locus horridus' and Mayhem Parva: typical settings in detective novels|," pp. 60-81; "Die Hartgesottenen:der Held des amerikanischen Detektivromans der 30er Jahre |The hardboiled heroes of American detective novels of the thirties|," pp. 82-93; "Gangsterfilm und 'Serie Noire'," pp. 94-109; "'To Tell It Like It Is': Chester Himes," pp. 110-20; "Die Literatur zu Detektivroman -- Ein polemischer Bericht |The literature on the detective novel -- a polemical report|," pp. 121-49; "Literatur," pp. 150-59 (bibliography); "Namenverzeichnis," pp. 160-63 (Index of Names). (REB)

B21. Bedford-Jones, H. The Graduate Fictioneer. Introduction by Erle Stanley Gardner. Denver, CO: Author & Journalist Publishing Co., 1932. 126pp. Pictorial wraps.

How to write popular fiction. Chapter 9 is "The Detective Story Formula." There is also a chapter on adventure fiction. (REB)

B22. _____. This Fiction Business. NY: Covici, Friede, Publishers, 1929. ix, 179pp. Originally published in 1922; this is an enlarged and updated edition.

A manual on the "rudiments" of fiction writing. Bedford-Jones was one of the most successful and prolific contributors to the pulps in the 1920s and 1930s, and there are some references to his writing and the writing of some of his contemporaries. However, this is principally an encouraging, practical manual for writers.

B23. Bedomda Detektiv- & Kriminalromaner 1975-1978 |Detective and crime novel reviews 1975-1978|. Boras: Bibliotekshogskolan, 1980. 53pp.

A comparison of reviews compiled by librarians from 9 different newspapers/genre magazines/library review services. (IH)

B24. Bennett, Arnold. The Evening Standard Years, edited by Andrew Mylett. London: Chatto & Windus, 1974; Hamden, CT: Archon Press, 1974.
A compilation of Bennett's "Books and Persons" columns appearing in the London Evening Standard from 1926-1931. A number of the columns demonstrate Bennett's interest in detective fiction although it must be said that he finds very little to praise in the books submitted to him for review. There is a running controversy with his readers suggesting that Bennett was probably viewed by them with the same antipathy that readers of Edmund Wilson were to demonstrate for the American critic in the 1940s (C866-C868). The relevant columns are as follows: "The Art of the Crime Story: Conan Doyle, A. E. W. Mason, and Some Others," pp. 80-82 (8 Sept 27; Bennett likes Mason but greatly prefers a non-mystery writer, Katherine Mansfield); "Some Good Detective Stories," pp. 151-53 (3 May 28; reviews of Gaboriau, Shiel and others); "I Read a Thriller--and Startle My Friends," pp. 176-78 (19 July 28; Edgar Wallace); "No Really First-Rate Detective Stories," pp. 225-27 (27 Dec 28; Anna Katherine Green's The Leavenworth Case and some true crime books); "I Take Up the Challenge of Detective Fiction Lovers," pp. 232-34 (17 Jan 29; Gaboriau and J. J. Connington's The Case with Nine Solutions); "Recipe for a Classic Mystery Novel," pp. 278-80 (20 June 29; a call for fresh writing and conception); "Why Not a Novelist's Detective Tale?," pp. 345-47 (6 Feb 30); "Mistakes Detective-Novel Writers Make," pp. 359-61 (27 March 30; books reviewed include John Dickson Carr's It Walks by Night); "Detective-Story Writers Hot on the Trail," pp. 374-76 (15 May 30; on the birth of the Crime Club).

B25. Bennich-Bjorkman, Bo. Forskning om detektivromanen 1907-1977 |Research on the mystery story from 1907-1977|. Uppsala: Avd for litteratursociologi, 1977. Reprinted by Jury, 1977.
A critical look at the most important work in England, USA, France and Germany. (IH)

B26. Benstock, Bernard, editor. Art in Crime Writing. Essays on Detective Fiction. NY: St. Martin's Press, 1983. xi, 218pp. Index.
Essays on eleven modern writers of detective fiction. Short bibliography or notes with critical references for each of the writers and a chronological listing of primary sources. The essays are annotated by author, as follows: Christie (E553), Sayers (E2545), Ngaio Marsh (E1952), Hammett (E1406), Chandler (E384), Ross Macdonald (E1892), P. D. James (E1537), Peter Lovesey (E1780), Nicolas Freeling (E1148), Simenon (E2701), and Sjöwall/Wahlöö (E2709).

B27. Benvenuti, Stefan, and Rizzoni, Gianni. Il romanzo giallo: Storia, autori e personaggi |The giallo novel: history, authors and characters|. Consultant: Alberto Tedeschi. Milan: Mondadori, 1979. English-language edition: The Whodunit. An Informal History of Detective Fiction. English translation by Anthony Eyre. London: Collier Macmillan Publishers, 1980. NY: Macmillan Books, 1980. Trade paperbound edition, NY: Collier, 1981. With a report on the current scene in England and America by Edward D. Hoch. A French translation was published in 1982 (Paris: L'Atalante), with a chapter by Michel Lebrun on the recent French detective novel.
The first illustrated history of the detective novel published in Italy through the efforts of two knowledgeable journalists. The introduction is

signed by Alberto Tedeschi, the best Italian expert in the field, while the vicissitudes of the Italian giallo are summed up separately in a final chapter. The appendix contains a Who's Who which lists the principal protagonists, authors and characters of the detective novel's history. Separate paragraphs are devoted, among other subjects, to the rules of the giallo, to the problem of the locked room crime, to a review of the major writers of a "high" level who have been associated with the genre, to the most recent attempts at structural analysis, to the spy novel and to recent market trends. (RC) Addendum: Not a true history, even an "informal" one, but rather a collection of short essays on the authors' choices of the best and most interesting detective writers from Poe onward. The two chapters on French detective fiction--one on Gaston Leroux, Maurice Leblanc, and Fantomas, the other on Pierre Very, Simenon, and more modern writers--contain materials not readily found in other general books on detective fiction. The authors' account of English-language detective stories concluded with writers whose fame was already well established by the 1950s---Gardner, Stout, Cheyney, Woolrich, Chandler--so Edward D. Hoch was called upon to add a chapter bringing the coverage up to date. A final chapter, "Who's Who in Whodunits," (pp. 187-209) is a biographical dictionary of mystery writers and their fictional characters. (REB)

B28. Berkeley, Anthony, and Dane, Clemence, editors. The Scoop and Behind the Screen. NY: Harper & Row, 1983. 175pp.

An edition of two collaboratively written detective plays broadcast over the BBC. The authors involved were Agatha Christie, Dorothy L. Sayers, Hugh Walpole, E. C. Bentley, Clemence Dane and Freeman Wills Crofts.

B29. Bermúdez, Maria Elvira. Los mejores cuentos policiacos mexicanos |The best Mexican detective stories|. Biblioteca mínima mexicana, vol. 15. Mexico City: Libro-Mexicano editores, 1955. With an introduction, a bibliography of primary material, and an anthology of detective short stories by Mexican writers.

In her introduction (pp. 7-20), Bermúdez discusses the reasons detective fiction has not been as prominent in Latin America as in England and North America which she finds chiefly in the "fact" that detective fiction tends to flourish in countries where respect for the law and its representatives is greatest. She notes the traditional critical attitude of disdain toward the genre and the failure to recognize its merits and comments briefly on the stories in the anthology and on native Mexican writers of detective fiction.

B30. Bilker, Harvey L., and Bilker, Audrey L. Writing Mysteries That Sell. Chicago: Contemporary Books, Inc., 1982. 134pp. Index.

A writers' manual with a list of magazine and book markets. There is an introductory chapter with a brief history and definitions by category (thriller, detectives, etc.).

B31. Bishop, John Lyman. The Colloquial Short Story in China: A Study of the "San-Yen" Collections. Harvard-Yenching Institute Studies XIV. Cambridge: Harvard University Press, 1956. 144pp.

Relatively early study of the Chinese popular short story, including material on detective stories. Chapter II, pp. 29-46, contains titles of and references to several Chinese detective stories, as well as some remarks which seem to be borrowed from Robert Van Gulik's commentaries in Dee Goong An (Toppan Printing Co., 1949; reprinted as

Celebrated Cases of Judge Dee, Dover, 1976). Chapter II, pp. 47-64, contains a translation of a Chinese detective story: "Master Shen's Bird Destroys Seven Lives." Bishop's introduction merely calls it "a clear-cut example" of the detective story. (GG)

B32. Blader, Susan Roberta. "A Critical Study of the San-Hsia Wu-Yi and Relationship to the Lung-t'u Kung-an Songbook." Unpublished Doctoral dissertation. University of Pennsylvania, 1977. 402pp.
A comparison of the famous collection of Magistrate Pao stories, Lung-t'u Kung-an |The criminal cases of the Lord of the Imperial Sketch| and the late 19th century novel which is often described as its sequel, San-Hsia Wu-Yi |Three heroes and five gallants|. Blader concludes that the former is a story-teller's songbook unsuitable as written literature, and that the San-Hsia Wu-Yi is better suited as literature, being smoother and having a greater emphasis on plot. This is one of the few Sinological works to treat in depth the supposed sequel to the famous collection of Pao cases. (GG)

B33. Bleiler, Everett F., editor. A Treasury of Victorian Detective Stories. NY: Scribners, 1979. 406pp.
An anthology of Victorian detective fiction with a general introduction (pp. 1-5), introductions to each of the stories, and a list of sources (pp. 405-406).

B34. Block, Lawrence. Writing the Novel: From Plot to Print. Cincinnati: Writer's Digest Books, 1979. 197pp.

B34A. ______. Telling Lies for Fun and Profit. NY: Arbor House, 1981.
Block is one of the most skillful and entertaining of contemporary mystery writers and these writers' manuals are almost as engaging as his own fiction. He often uses examples drawn from crime fiction (many of them relating to his own work). How-to books whose interest is not limited to the needs of student writers.

B35. Blom, K. Arne. Tankar om mord. En bok om kriminal-genren |Thoughts about murder. A book on the crime genre|. Uddevalla: Zindermans, 1978. 192pp.
32 essays by English, Swedish and Danish writers on detective fiction. (IH)

B35A. Boardman, F. W., Jr., compiler. The Pleasures of Publishing. NY: New York University Press, 14 Apr 41. Condensed version appeared in PW 139 (26 Apr 41):1714.
A report based on a survey of the "preferences and prejudices" of "several hundred detective story addicts."

B36. Boeri, Emilio, and Pini, Donatella, editors. Giallo e nero |Giallo and roman noir|. Milan: Sugar, 1963. 639pp.
This volume provides an ample selection of texts, from François Vidocq to Leslie Charteris, relative to the origins and to the early development of the "tales of investigation and mystery." "The detective novel," the editors observe, "is also and predominantly a narrative having as protagonist an outlaw." According to the perspective of this volume, it was born in the first years of the 19th century and closed its circle with World War I which marked the end of "la belle époque." (LR)

B37. Boileau, Pierre, and Narcejac, Thomas. Le Roman policier |The detective novel|. Collection petite bibliothèque Payot no. 70. Paris: Editions Payot, 1964. 234pp. Japanese edition: Suiri Shosetsu-ron (Tokyo: Kinokuni-ya Shoten, 1967; translated by Yasuhiko Terakado).

More than a history of the detective novel, Boileau-Narcejac's essay is an analysis of the genre and of its development articulated in three great periods: the puzzle novel, the Gothic novel and suspense. The authors situate their work personally in relation to that evolution, by sharing their attempt to institute "a detective novel which, instead of demonstrating the triumph of logic, is dedicated to the failure of reason." A work which shrewdly examines the detective genre but surveys it somewhat hastily. (JB)

B38. ______. Le Roman policier. Collection que sais-je?, no. 1623. Paris: Presses universitaires de France, 1975. 128pp. Japanese edition: Tantei Shosetsu (Tokyo: Hakusui-sha, 1977; translated by Katushide Shinoda).

Boileau-Narcejac return to the theses of their earlier study, modifying some details but devoting a chapter to the "Sharp Shooters," to the marginal writers, which clearly departs from certain of their earlier opinions. (JB)

B39. Bonn, Thomas L. Paperback Primer: A Guide for Collectors. Introduction by Ray Walters. Brownwood, TX: Paperback Quarterly Publications, 1981. 65pp. Hardback and paperback editions.

Long essay on the history of mass market paperbacks, combined with an 18 page bibliography of secondary sources on mass market paperback publishing. Bibliography expanded and updated from an earlier version in PQ 1:4 (Winter 1978). (GG)

B40. Bonn, Thomas L. Undercover: An Illustrated History of American Mass Market Paperbacks. Foreword by John Tebbel. New York: Penguin Books, 1982. 144pp. Illus. Index.

A history with sections on cover art and design, collecting, and suggestions for further reading. The numerous color plates of paperback covers enhance this well-written study and emphasize the importance of design in the marketing of paperbacks.

B41. The Bookman. Special Christmas Number, 1929. London: Hodder & Stoughton, Dec. 1929. pp. (157), 158-227, 1-182 + separately mounted advertising pages (i-xxvi). vol. 76, No. 459.

Pages 157-182 comprise a special section billed on the cover as devoted to "Magic, Ghosts, Detectives & the Mysterious in Literature," with contributions by G. K. Chesterton, Montague Rhodes James, Alfred Noyes, Algernon Blackwood, R. Ellis Roberts, and Edgar Wallace, with shorter notes by J. S. Fletcher, Edgar Jepson, F. Britten Austin, and others. Only Edgar Wallace ("Mystery Stories To-Day and Yesterday") writes on mystery/detective fiction as opposed to fantasy and the supernatural. There are many illustrations for mystery stories, reprinted from Strand Magazine and other sources, plus photographs from stage productions of mystery plays. There are full-page portraits of the major contributors, including the famous Howard Coster portrait of Chesterton. All in all, this is a collection of many small pleasures rather than a substantial contribution to the secondary literature. (The portfolio of color plates by Edmund Dulac illustrating scenes from Poe's poems is generally missing from the copies still in circulation today.) CC 2904. (REB)

B42. Borowitz, Albert. Innocence and Arsenic: Studies in Crime and Literature. NY: Harper & Row, 1977. xiv, 170pp.

Borowitz is mainly concerned with accounts of, and speculations upon, true criminal cases. Crime fiction is dealt with in portions of four essays: "The Snows on the Moors," pp. 1-25 (E2724); "Dr. Jekyll and Mr. Stevenson," pp. 26-32; "The Mystery of Edwin Drood," pp. 53-62 (E889); and "New Gaslight on Jack the Ripper," pp. 87-99 (C111). The latter two pieces appeared originally, in slightly different form, in The Armchair Detective. (REB)

B43. Boucher, Anthony. Multiplying Villainies: Selected Mystery Criticism, 1942-1968. Edited by Robert E. Briney and Francis M. Nevins Jr. Foreword by Helen McCloy. (Boston): A Bouchercon Book, 1973. xii, 136pp. Edition limited to 500 numbered copies. Author and title indices. Published by the organizing committee of the 4th annual Anthony Boucher Memorial Mystery Convention, Boston, MA, 5-7 October 1973. In most copies a portrait of Boucher by Frank Kelly Freas was included as a loose insert.

Boucher was arguably the best and certainly the most influential mystery critic of his time. This book offers an overview of his career through a representative sample of his criticism for the San Francisco Chronicle and The New York Times, plus book introductions and numerous essays. One of the latter, "Opera and Murder," had not previously been published. In all cases this book presents Boucher's original text, free of the editorial changes which had sometimes been made in the published versions. Contents: Foreword, "Tony Boucher as I Knew Him," by Helen McCloy, pp. vii-x; Phyllis White, Note, p. x; Robert E. Briney and Francis M. Nevins, Jr., (Introduction), pp. xi-xii; Reviews and Columns from the San Francisco Chronicle, 1942-1946, pp. 13-32; "Speaking of Crime: The Short Shudder," pp. 33-36 (EQMM, Apr 49; reviews); Selections from "Criminals at Large," 1951-1967, pp. 37-108 (Consists of the annual best-of-the-year summary columns, plus individual reviews and longer selections from more than two dozen other columns); "The Mystery Novels of Henry Kuttner," pp. 109-110 (E1616); "Opera and Murder: Notes on the relation between two of the fine arts," pp. 111-116 (C118); Book Introductions: Brackett (E198), Carr (E346), Innes (E1528), Perutz (E2082), Woolrich (E3112), pp. 117-126 (reprinted from Collier Books editions, 1962-64); "Baker Street Immortal," pp. 127-32 (lengthy review of Baring-Gould's The Annotated Sherlock Holmes, from NYTBR, 21 Jan 68); Index, pp. 133-35; Acknowledgements, p. 136. Breen 66. (REB)

B44. Boucher, Anthony, ed. Best Detective Stories of the Year. NY: E. P. Dutton. 18th Annual Collection (1963) through 22nd Annual Collection (1967).

Each volume has an introduction, notes on the stories included, and a "Yearbook of the Detective Story" (containing a bibliography of relevant fiction and non-fiction from the previous year, a list of the year's awards in mystery fiction, a necrology, and an Honor Roll of additional stories). The 23rd Annual Collection (1968) was published shortly after the editor's death, and includes only the Honor Roll for that year. See also Hoch (B154) and Hubin (B160). (REB)

B45. _____. Four-&-Twenty Bloodhounds. NY: Simon and Schuster, 1950. v-vii, 406pp.

An MWA anthology with Foreword, introduction and biographical notes on the detectives. Boucher pays tribute to Kenneth MacGowan (B238) who "first conceived the idea of detectival Who's Who notes...."

B46. Böving/Eriksson/Roos. Aventyrsromaner och Thrillers |Adventure novels and thrillers|. Boras: Bibliotekshögskolan, 1977. 72pp.
A guide-book consisting of short reviews of 300 different titles.(IH)

B47. Brauchli, Jakob. Der englische Schauerroman um 1880 unter Berücksichtigung der unbekannten Bücher. Weidà, Germany, 1928; reprinted by Garland Publishing in 1979. 260pp.
Brauchli's monograph remains the most thorough description of the Gothic novel, with considerable material that is not generally available elsewhere. After establishing a classification of various subtypes of the Gothic novel, Brauchli discusses its international aspects among Great Britain, France, and Germany; its readership and social significance; chapbook publications; and concepts of the supernatural. Many works are described and a long bibliography of Gothic novels, classified according to type and period, is provided. (EFB)

B48. Brean, Herbert, editor. The Mystery Writer's Handbook. A Handbook on the Writing of Detective, Suspense, Mystery and Crime Stories. By the Mystery Writers of America. New York: Harper & Brothers, 1956. xx, 268pp.
More than fifty members of the Mystery Writers of America contribute everything from handy hints to extended discussions on all aspects of the writing of mystery fiction. There are short biographies of some of the contributors and in the chapter introductions responses to a questionnaire circulated to contributors are excerpted. Some of the discussion is inevitably dated now, such as the treatments of radio writing and paperback originals, but most of it retains its interest, not only for aspiring writers but for enthusiasts of mystery fiction in general. An extensively revised edition of the Handbook was prepared in 1976, edited by Lawrence Treat (B409). Contents: H. Brean, "By Way of Preface," pp. v-xi; "Brief Biographies of Some of the Contributors," pp. xvi-xx; A. Boucher, "What Kind of Mystery Story Appeals to Today's Public?," pp. 1-8;"How to Start a Story," pp. 9-12 (S. Ellin, Sidney Porcelain, David Alexander, John D. MacDonald, Malden Grange Bishop, Dorothy Salisbury Davis, Harold Q. Masur, Anna Mary Wells, Lawrence Treat, Jack Webb, Michael Gilbert, Stuart Palmer); Fredric Brown, "Where Do You Get Your Plot?," pp. 13-18; Frederick C. Davis, "How to Organize a Book," pp. 19-30; Hillary Waugh, "Why I Don't Outline," pp. 31-33; Pauline Bloom, "How to Achieve Story Structure,"pp. 34-41; Dana Lyon, "Plotting from a Situation," pp. 42-44; Lester Dent, "The Master Fiction Plot," pp. 45-56; Michael Gilbert, "'Technicalese'," pp. 57-65; Lawrence Treat, "The Real-Life Policeman," pp. 66-72; Edward D. Radin, "Police Procedure in Homicide Investigation," pp. 73-86 (true crime); Barbara Frost, "How to Make It Authentic," pp. 87-91; Lawrence G. Blochman, "Plot and Background"/Perry D. Westbrook, "The Creation of Atmosphere"/The Gordons, "Problems in the Creation of Background," pp. 92-112; Eleazar Lipsky, "Suspense," pp. 103-112; John D. MacDonald, "How a Character Becomes Believable," pp. 113-122; Dorothy Gardiner, "Proper Names and Proper Introductions," pp. 123-130; Ben Benson, "Character and Action"/Emma Lou Fetta, "Second-Impression Characterization"/Harold Q. Masur, "Criminal Motives," pp. 131-37; Harry Whittington, "Why I Write"/Amber Dean, "Why I Write"/Austin F. Roberts, "Don't Be a Writing Bum"/Samm S. Baker, "Words from a Master," pp. 139-46; "When I Write," pp. 147-151 (Anthony Gilbert, Sidney Porcelain, Frederick C.

Davis, Harold Q. Masur, Dorothy Salisbury Davis, Lawrence Treat, Ben Benson, John D. MacDonald, The Gordons, Ruth Fenisong, Hillary Waugh, Malden Grange Bishop, David Alexander, Stanley Ellin, Stuart Palmer, Anna Mary Wells, Jack Webb, Barbara Frost, Michael Gilbert, Perry Westbrook); Sidney Porcelain, "Credibility and Vividness in Writing," pp. 152-7; "The Biggest Stumbling Block," pp. 158-61 (B. Frost, Austin Roberts, A. M. Wells, S. Porcelain, D. S. Davis, Ruth Wilson, A. Boucher, J. Webb, J. D. MacDonald, D. Lyon, S. Ellin, B. Benson); Rex Stout, "What to Do About a Watson"/Margery Allingham, "Dialogue"/Carl G. Hodges, "Dialogue"/John Dickson Carr, "Story Development"/MWA Membership, "Mystery Story Cliches," pp. 161-72; M. G. Bishop, "Fact Crime Writing," pp. 173-84; Henry Klinger, "The Story That Sells to the Movies," pp. 185-92; Robert Arthur, "Radio Is Not Well"/John Roeburt, "The Outlook for Radio Mysteries," pp. 193-202; Clayre and Michael Lipman, "The Crime Short-Short," pp. 203-12; "Source Books and Notable Examples, Featuring the Haycraft-Queen Library of Detective-Crime-Mystery Fiction," pp. 213-28 (A71); Paul Reynolds, "The Dollars and Cents of Mystery Writing," pp. 229-34 (contributor is a literary agent); Anthony Gilbert, "The British or the American Story"/John Creasey, "Selling Overseas," pp. 235-42; Harry Whittington, "The Paperback Original," pp. 243-47; Bruno Fischer, "Contracts," pp. 248-56; A. Boucher, "You and the Reviews and the Reviewers," pp. 257-65; "The Best Tricks of the Mystery Trade," pp. 266-8 (R. Fenisong, J. Webb, H. S. Keeler, A. M. Wells, S. Porcelain, L. Treat, A. Dean, D. S. Davis, H. Q. Masur, A. Boucher, B. Benson, S. Palmer, D. Alexander, S. Ellin, Morris Hershman). Breen 94. CC 2908. (REB)

B49. Broberg, Jan. Brottsliga sidor |Criminal pages|. Vänersborg: Bokad, 1979.
A collection of essays on various topics. Some of the material is directed at a Scandinavian reader but Broberg's incisive analyses and wide knowledge of the field make it of interest to readers outside Scandinavia. Broberg is known as the "living computer" because of his extensive knowledge. (IH)

B50. ______. Korsforhor |Cross-examination|. Halmstad: Spectra, 1976. 106pp.
12 mystery writers in the witness box; interviews conducted by Broberg with Margery Allingham, Victor Canning, Francis Clifford, Edmund Crispin, Andrew Garve, Michael Innes, Ed McBain, Patricia Moyes, Anthony Price, Ellery Queen, Rex Stout, and Julian Symons. (IH)

B51. ______. Lilla deckarguiden |The little mystery-guide|. Höganäs: Boklubben Bra Deckare, 1975. 42pp.
A booklet with mini-essays on such subjects as "the locked room," "who done it?", "Had I but known," etc. (IH)

B52. ______. Meningar om mord |Meanings of murder|. Stockholm: Cavefors, 1968. 136pp.
15 articles on novels, authors and heroes. (IH)

B53. ______. Mord för ro skull |Murder for leisure|. Uddevalla; Cavefors, 1964. 301pp. Illus.
A history of the detective novel, comparable in scope to Haycraft's Murder for Pleasure (B143). Indices: authors, detectives/heroes, titles. One of the first critical works published in Scandinavia and still one of the best. (IH)

B54. ______. Mord i minne |Murder in memory|. Uddevalla: Zindermans, 1976. 152pp. Illus. Index.

12 essays on mystery novels and authors. (IH)

B55. ______. Mordisk familjebok |The family book of murder|. Uddevalla: Zindermans, 1972.

A collection of articles and essays intended for both new and experienced readers of mystery fiction. (IH)

B56. ______. Ord om mord |Words about murder|. Halmstad: Spektra, 1974. 269pp.

35 essays in which 22 authors and critics discuss a variety of topics. (IH)

B57. ______. Spionen i spegeln |Spies and spying|. Stockholm: Bo Cavefors Bokforlag, 1974. Photographs.

An anthology of essays by a number of Scandinavian and foreign critics (in translation).

B58. Brookes, Canon J(oshua) A(lfred) R(owland). Murder in Fact and Fiction. London: Hurst & Blackett, (1926). 284pp.

Contains two chapters on murders in fiction, mainly mainstream. Material on Mrs. Belloc Lowndes and Edwin Drood. No discussion of the detective genre as such. (REB)

B59. Brunori, Vittorio. La grande impostura: Indagine sul romanzo popolare |The great imposture: inquiries on the popular novel|. Introduction by G. Luti. Venice: Marsilio, 1978.

The third and concluding chapter is devoted to the French detective novel, from Balzac to San Antonio. (RC)

B60. Buchloh, Paul G., and Becker, Jens P., eds. Der Detektivroman. Studien zur Geschichte und Form der englischen und amerikanischen detektivliteratur |The detective novel: studies in the history and form of English and American detective fiction|. Darmstadt: Wissenschaftliche Buchgesellschaft, 1973. 199pp. With contributions by Antje Wulff and Walter T. Rix.

German-language overview, theory and history of the genre. Through the years this has become the standard German-language book-length treatment of the subject. Contents: Buchloh/Becker, "Der Detektivroman: Zur allgemeinen Problematik |The detective novel: on general difficulties|," pp. 1-33 (C138); P. Buchloh, "Edgar Allan Poe und die Detektivgeschichte |E. A. Poe and detective history|," pp. 34-36 (E2102); P. Buchloh, "Der viktorianische Detektivroman |The victorian detective novel: Dickens and Collins|," pp. 47-56 (C136); P. Buchloh, "Arthur Conan Doyle und Gilbert Keith Chesterton," pp. 57-68 (E482); J. P. Becker, "'The Golden Age of the Detective Novel': Formen des englischen Detektivromans zwischen 1914 und 1939 |Forms of the English detective novel between 1914 and 1939|," pp. 69-80 (C73); Antje Wulff, "Die Spielregeln der Detektiverzählung |The rules of the game of the detective story|," pp. 81-95 (C878); J. P. Becker, "Die amerikanische 'Hard-Boiled School' |The American hard-boiled school|," pp. 96-107 (C71); J. P. Becker, "Der englische Spionageroman |The English spy novel|," pp. 108-20 (C72); Walter T. Rix, "Wesen und Wandel des Detektivromans im totalitären Staat |Substance and mutation of the detective novel in the totalitarian state|," pp. 121-33 (C696); J. P. Becker, "Der moderne Englische Detektivroman: Rückkehn zur Tradition und 'Crime Novel' |the modern English detective novel: return to tradition and the 'crime novel'|," pp. 134-44 (C76); Buchloh/Becker, "Der amerikanische Detektivroman nach 1945 |The American detective novel since 1945|," pp. 145-55 (C137); Concluding Observation, pp. 157-58; Bibliography of Secondary Sources, pp. 159-84; Checklist of Authors and Their Works, pp. 185-99. (GG)

B61. _____. Der Detektiverzaehlung auf der Spur. Essays sur Form und Wertung der Englischen Detektivliteratur |On the trail of the detective story: essays on the form and appraisal of English detective fiction|. Darmstadt: Wissenschaftliche Buchgesellschaft, 1977. vii, 395pp. Index.

German-language essay anthology on English-language (primarily British) detective fiction. This is the first such anthology that includes primarily translations of English-language essays, such as those by E. M. Wrong, Dorothy L. Sayers, Ronald A. Knox and other well-known writers. There are also original German language essays. The contents are as follows: Introduction, pp. 1-17; "Das Verbrechen in der Gegenwartsliteratur |Crime in current literature|," pp. 19-33 (C203); G. K. Chesterton, "Verteidigung von Kriminalromanen |A defense of detective stories|," pp. 34-37 (C178); "Die Vergaenglichkeit des Detektivs in der Literatur |The passing of the detective in literature|," pp. 38-40 (C615); Brander Matthews, "Edgar Allan Poe und die Detektivgeschichte |Poe and the detective story|," pp. 41-57 (E2155); Carolyn Wells, "Die Kriminal-literatur |Crime fiction|," pp. 58-66 (C849); Friedrich Depken, "Sherlock Holmes, Raffles und ihre Vorbilder (Auszuege) |Sherlock Holmes, Raffles and their prototypes (excerpts)|," pp. 67-102 (C222); R. Austin Freeman, "Die Kunst der Detektivgeschichte |The art of the detective story|," pp. 103-115 (C291); E. M. Wrong, "Einleitung zu 'Crime and Detection'" |Introduction to....|," pp. 116-33 (C877); T.S. Eliot, "Einleitung zu Wilkie Collins' 'The Moonstone' |Introduction to....|," pp. 134-41 (E657); Dorothy L. Sayers, "Einleitung zu "Great Short Stories of Detection, Mystery and Horror' |Introduction to....|," pp. 142-90 (C725); Ronald A. Knox, "Zehn Regeln fuer einen guten Detektivroman |Ten rules for a good detective story|," pp. 191-92 (C458); Ronald A. Knox, "Mystery Stories," pp. 193-96 (source not located); Anthony Berkeley, "Vorwort zu "The Second Shot' |Preface to....)," p. 196 (excerpt) (C89); C. P. Snow, "Der Autor zu seinem Roman 'Mord unterm Segel' |The author on his novel 'Death Under Sail'|," pp. 198-99 (E2728); Joseph Wood Krutch, "Nur ein Detektivroman |Only a detective story|," pp. 200-207 (C464); George Orwell, "Raffles und Miss Blandish," pp. 208-55 (C606); Edmund Wilson, "Wen interessiert es schon, wer Roger Ackroyd ermordete? |Who cares who killed Roger Ackroyd?|," pp. 226-33 (C867); Nicholas Blake, "Wozu Detektivgeschichten? |The detective story--why?)," pp. 234-42 (C97); Vincent Starrett, "Kriminalgeschichten |Mystery stories|," pp. 243-61 (source not located); Raymond Chandler, "Gelegentliche Notizen ueber den Kriminalroman, niedergeschrieben 1949 |Occasional notes on the crime novel written down in 1949|," pp. 262-71 (C167); Somerset Maugham, "Der Verfall und Untergang des Detektivromans |The decline and fall of the detective story|," pp. 272-98 (C543); John Bingham, "Vorwort zur deutschen Ausgabe von 'Murder Plan Six' |Preface to the German edition of "Murder Plan Six"|," pp. 314-315; Mary Hottinger, "Vorwort zu 'Mord. angelsaechsische Kriminalgeschichten' |Forward to murder: Anglo-Saxon crime stories|," pp. 316-33 (C414); Edmund Crispin, "Vorwort zu 'Best Detective Stories' |Preface to ....|," pp. 334-42 (C205); Norman Shrapnel, "Die Literatur der Gewalttaetigkeit und der Verfolgung |The literature of violence and pursuit|," pp. 342-51 (C754); A. C. Ward, "Literature des 20. Jahrhunderts (Auszug) |"Twentieth century literature 1901-1960 (excerpt)|," pp. 352-55 (C839); Pierre Boileau and Thomas Narcejac, "Der detektivroman (Auszuege))," pp. 356-70 (C107a); Harry Kemelman, "Vorwort zur deutschen Ausgabe von 'The Nine Mile Walk' |Preface to the German edition of ....|," pp. 371-74 (C1583); Julian Symons, "Aux dem Weg zur "Crime Novel' |Towards the crime novel)," pp. 375-79 (B391); Selected bibliography, Index, Bibliography of novels mentioned, pp. 381-389. CC S46. (GG)

B62. Burack, A. S., editor. Writing Detective and Mystery Fiction. Boston: The Writer, 1945. x, 237pp.

26 essays, most of them first published in The Writer but including such classic essays (published elsewhere) as S. S. Van Dine's "Twenty Rules for Writing Detective Stories," Dorothy L. Sayers' introduction to the first volume of her series of anthologies of horror and mystery fiction, and Haycraft's "The Rules of the Game" from Murder for Pleasure. The material is generally restricted to technical issues such as plotting and characterization, but the writers often use their own experience as an example and the essays are, therefore, valuable for research on the individual writers. This is the first of three editions compiled by A.S. Burack. Contents: A. S. Burack, "Foreword," pp. v-vii; Dorothy L. Sayers, "Detective Fictions: Origins and Development," pp. 3-48 (C725); Valentine Williams, "Crime Fiction," pp. 49-58; Zelda Popkin, "A Corpse Can't Leer," pp. 59-64; Q. Patrick, "The 'Naughty Child' of Fiction," pp. 65-72; A. A. Fair, "A Method to Mystery," pp. 73-78; George Harmon Coxe, "Starting that Mystery Book," pp. 79-86; Craig Rice, "It's a Mystery to Me," pp. 87-96; Van Wyck Mason, "The Detective Story," pp. 97-108; Cleve F. Adams, "Motivation in Mystery Fiction," pp. 109-113; Howard Haycraft, "The Rules of the Game," pp. 114-37 (B143); Ogden Nash, "Don't Guess, Let Me Tell You," pp. 138-9 (poem); Guiles Davenport, "Foundations of the Detective-Mystery Story," pp. 140-6; Richard Lockridge, "The Perfect Crime," pp. 147-55; Julius Long, "Guilty as Hell, But--," pp. 156-63; Elliot Paul, "Whodunit," pp. 164-72 (C618); Clyde B. Clason, "Making Crime Pay," pp. 173-9; Todd Downing, "Murder Is a Rather Serious Business," pp. 180-85; Lee Wright, "Dividends for Death," pp. 186-90; Kurt Steel, "So You're Going To Write a Mystery," pp. 191-95; S. S. Van Dine, "Twenty Rules for Writing Detective Stories," pp. 196-201 (C827); Trentwell Mason White, "Detective Story Writing," pp. 202-208; Frederick C. Davis, "Mysteries Plus," pp. 209-13; Dana Lyon, "Mysteries Are Different," pp. 214-9; M. Scott Michel, "The Hard-Boiled Detective Novel," pp. 220-24; Cortland Fitzsimmons, "The Mystery Story Method," pp. 225-31; Dorothy B. Hughes, "It's Fun To Write a Mystery," pp. 232-7. Breen 87.

B63. ______. Writing Detective and Mystery Fiction. Boston: The Writer, 1967. viii, 280pp.

Certain essays (by Sayers, Van Dine, Haycraft, Coxe, Fair, Fitzsimmons, Lockridge, Long, Patrick and Williams) which Burack considers important for their historical interest have been retained from the 1945 edition. Only those essays which are new to this edition will be cited in the contents listing. Contents (partial): Raymond Chandler, "Casual Notes on the Mystery Novel," pp. 81-88 (C167); Charlotte Armstrong, "Razzle-Dazzle," pp. 90-94; Cecilia Bartholomew, "The Man in the Closet," pp. 95-100; Stewart Beach, "How To Write the Mystery and Suspense Story," pp. 101-24; Frances Crane, "Starting That Mystery Book," pp. 133-38; Miriam Allen deFord, "The Psychology of Mystery Story Writing," pp. 146-51; Dorothy Gardiner, "'Casting' Your Mystery Novel," pp. 172-78;

The Gordons, "Eleven Check Points for Writers," pp. 179-85; Jack Iams, "Getting Away with Murder," pp. 186-93; Ed Lacy, "Whodunit?--You?," pp. 194-99; Robert Martin, "The Detective Novel: Tricks and Facts," pp. 217-23; Harold Q. Masur, "That Mystery Novel," pp. 224-30; Q. Patrick, "The Mystery Short Short," pp. 239-41; Richard Powell, "Mysteries with the Light Touch," pp. 242-48; Mary Stewart, "Setting and Background in the Novel," pp. 249-54; Darwin Teilheit, "Blueprint for a Suspense Thriller," pp. 255-60; Phyllis A. Whitney, "Writing the Juvenile Mystery," pp. 261-70. Not recorded in Breen.

B64. ______. Writing Suspense and Mystery Fiction. Boston: The Writer, 1977. ix, 341pp.
Apart from the change in title which reflects the contemporary decline in importance of the classic tale of detection, editor Burack has retained his now classic historical section (Sayers, Van Dine, Chandler, Haycraft and Ogden Nash) but shifted their essays from the opening to the middle section and replaced a number of essays in the 1967 edition by authors not currently fashionable (Stewart Beach, Cortland Fitzsimmons, Ed Lacy, among others) by a more up-to-date roster. The contents listing will cite only the material new to this volume. Contents: Joan Aiken, "Thoughts on Plots," pp. 1-8; Charlotte Armstrong, "The Three Basics of Suspense," pp. 9-13; Jean L. Backus, "Tricks and Traps in Writing Suspense Fiction," pp. 14-20; Rex Burns, "Elements of the Police Procedural Novel," pp. 27-34; Babs H. Deal, "The 'I-Can't-Put-It-Down' Factor," pp. 41-46; Rosemary Gatenby, "How to Devise an Ingenious Plot," pp. 60-67; The Gordons, "Excitement for Sale," pp. 68-75; Joe Gores, "Short Fiction--With a Difference," pp. 76-82; Naomi A. Hintze, "Make Your Reader Wonder," pp. 83-89; Edward D. Hoch, "Plotting the Mystery Short Story," pp. 90-96; Joan Kahn, "The Changing Mystery Novel," pp. 97-108 (an editor's comments); John Lutz, "Setting for Suspense," pp. 109-14; Margaret Maron, "Plotting Short Mysteries," pp. 115-23; Harold Q. Masur, "Notes on the Suspense Novel," pp. 129-39; Patricia Moyes, "Mysteries within Mysteries," pp. 140-45; Albert F. Nussbaum, "Versimilitude in the Crime Story," pp. 146-52; Elisabeth Ogilvie, "Suspense Fiction and a Sense of Place," pp. 153-63; Joyce Porter, "To a Would-Be Detective Story Writer," pp. 164-70; Bill Pronzini, "The Elements of Suspense," pp. 171-79; Willo Davis Roberts, "Creating Heroines for Gothic Novels," pp. 180-84; Richard Martin Stern, "What Will Happen--and When?," pp. 185-89; Michael Underwood, "Plots in Crime Fiction," pp. 197-203; Phyllis A. Whitney, "Springboard to Suspense Fiction," pp. 204-13; Collin Wilcox, "Writing and Selling the Police Procedural Novel," pp. 213-18; American Bar Association, "A Layman's Guide to Law and the Courts," pp. 311-28; American Bar Association, "Glossary of Legal Terms," pp. 329-41. Breen 88.

B65. ______. Techniques of Novel Writing. Boston: The Writer, 1973.
A collection of articles on writing by writers. A number of the articles are by authors of mystery fiction and will be cited in a partial contents listing. Contents: Mary Stewart, "Teller of Tales," pp. 39-47; Evan Hunter, "An Interview with Evan Hunter--Ed McBain," pp. 85-91; Phyllis A. Whitney, "I Couldn't Put It Down," pp. 155-63; Catherine Aird, "The Detective Novel," pp. 164-71; Dorothy Eden, "The Elusive Plot," pp. 181-85; Hillary Waugh, "Plots and People in Mystery Novels," pp. 193-200; Ellis Peters, "The Thriller is a Novel," pp. 213-18; Bruce Cassiday, "Write Me an Adventure Novel," pp. 225-32; Desmond Bagley, "Writing Action Fiction," pp. 248-53; Joan Aiken, "How to Keep the Reader on

the Edge of the Chair," pp. 262-71; Patricia Moyes, "Writing a Mystery," pp. 272-77; Elsie Lee, "When You Write a Gothic," pp. 278-85; Stanley Ellin, "Ideas for Mystery Novels," pp. 286-91.

B66. Carling, Bjørn. Norsk kriminallitteratur gjennom 150 ar |Norwegian crime literature through 150 years|. Oslo: Gyldendal, 1976. 240pp.

A history with a bibliography of all crime fiction published in Norway by Norwegian authors. Includes pseudonyms. (IH)

B67. Carr, John C. The Craft of Crime: Conversations with Crime Writers. Boston: Houghton Mifflin, 1983. ix, 349pp.

The texts of interviews conducted by Carr with 13 writers. An attentive reader will note that there are only 12 interviews, but Carr explains somewhat engagingly in his brief preface that Emma Lathen counts as two, and remarks by Mary Jane Latsis and Martha Henissart are scrupulously attributed during the interview. Contents: "Ed McBain," pp. 1-23; "James McClure," pp. 24-55; "June Thomson," pp. 56-78; "Jane Langton," pp. 79-103; "Gregory McDonald," pp. 104-142; "Robert B. Parker," pp. 143-175; "Emma Lathen," pp. 176-201; "Dick Francis," pp. 202-226; "Ruth Rendell," pp. 227-257; "Peter Lovesey," pp. 258-288; "Mark Smith," pp. 322-349.

B68. Cassiday, Bruce, editor. Roots of Detection: The Art of Detection before Sherlock Holmes. "Recognitions" series. NY: Frederick Ungar Pub. Co., 1983. 195pp.

In his brief introduction (pp. 1-5), Cassiday talks about the meaning of the term "detection" and comments briefly on his choice of selections. There are short introductions for each of the selections (ranging from Herodotus to Gaboriau). No bibliography or notes. For the general reader.

B69. Cawelti, John G. Adventure, Mystery, and Romance. Formula Stories as Art and Popular Culture. Chicago: University of Chicago Press, 1976. 336pp. Index.

One of the most influential books in the field of popular culture, and a point of reference for any study of popular literary formulas. The book is both a general introduction to modern critical theory on popular literature (with the bibliographical notes on pp. 319-329 an invaluable reference guide) and a detailed study of crime and detection fiction (pp. 51-191). The particular forms he studies are the classical detective story and the hard-boiled school, with a substantial chapter (pp. 162-191) on Hammett, Chandler and Spillane. With the proliferation of short author studies of recent years, this wide-ranging theoretical and pragmatic discussion raises the level of critical discourse and extends its range. Cawelti has his supporters and his detractors, but the text must be taken note of by any serious researcher in the field. Reviews: TLS,18 June 1976:732; TAD 9 (1976):304-305; Novel 11 (1977/78):93-96. Breen 38.

B70. Champigny, Robert. What Will Have Happened: A Philosophical and Technical Essay on Mystery Stories. Bloomington, IN: Indiana Univ. Press, 1977. 183pp. Index. Bibliography.

An original discussion by a philosopher and poet. Champigny talks about such elements as point of view, setting, and atmosphere in a dense and challenging text. The study is an extension of his well-known work on literary forms (poetry, novel and theatre). To demonstrate his theories,

Champigny cites examples from a number of writers but his most extensive--and straightforward--analysis is of Joel Townsley Rogers' The Red Right Hand, pp. 122-26. Review: TMF 5:4(1981):28.

B71. Chandler, Frank Wadleigh. The Literature of Roguery. 2 vols. Boston: Houghton Mifflin, 1907. Index in Vol. II and annotatd bibliographies at the end of each chapter. Reprinted in 2 vols. NY: Burt Franklin, 1958; no. IX in the Burt Franklin Bibliographical series.

An entertaining history of the literature in which a rogue of the lower class is an anti-hero. CC 2917.

B72. Charney, Hannah. The Detective Novel of Manners: Hedonism, Morality and the Life of Reason. Rutherford, N.J.: Fairleigh Dickinson Press, 1981. 125pp. Bibliography and index.

Charney's study is meant to show that the detective novel is the literary successor to the 19th century English novel of manners. This is a reasonable theory, at least when applied to soft-boiled mysteries, but Charney's stylistic affectations (expressions like "historical paradigms" and "conventional teleological aims") make the text, at times, practically unreadable. Reviews: TLS, 27 Nov 81, p. 1402; Choice 19 (1981):376. (KLM)

B73. Coma, Javier. La Novela Negra |The hardboiled novel|. (Spain): Ediciones 2001, circa 1983.

A panorama of the American hardboiled novel, including discussions of Hammett, W. R. Burnett, James M. Cain, Horace McCoy, Don Tracy, Jim Thompson, R. Chandler, Ross Macdonald, David Goodis, William McGivern, Chester Himes, and Donald Westlake. With a chronology, filmography, and a bibliography of Spanish translations. (JB)

B74. Conrad, Horst. Die literarische Angst. Das Schreckliche in Schauerromantik und Detektivgeschichte |Literary fear: the dreadful in thrillers and detective fiction|. Literatur in der Gesellschaft 21. Dusseldorf: Bertlsmann Universitaetsverlag, 1974. 230pp. Index; bibliography of primary and secondary sources.

Detailed scholarly examination of the uses and purposes of fear in German and English thrillers. Conrad traces the use of fear to Greek drama and examines its development from The Castle of Otranto (1764) to Agatha Christie. The tales of E. T. A. Hoffmann, such as Das Fraulein von Scuderi (1819), receive special attention. (GG)

B75. Cooper-Clark, Diana. Designs of Darkness: Interviews with Detective Novelists. Bowling Green, OH: Bowling Green University Popular Press, 1983. Photographs by Al Clark. 239pp.

Interviews with 13 novelists: P. D. James, Jean Stubbs, Peter Lovesey, Margaret Millar, Ross Macdonald, Howard Engel, Ruth Rendell, Janwillen van de Wetering, Patricia Highsmith, Julian Symons, Amanda Cross, Anne Perry and Dick Francis. Cooper-Clark's lengthy, leading questions often leave very little for the authors to say except to agree with her. Peter Lovesey seems particularly uncomfortable with the questions and contributes relatively little to the discussion. Review: TMF 7:5 (Sept/Oct 83):35-39.

B76. Corsaut, Aneta; Singer, Muff; and Wagner, Robert. The Mystery Reader's Quiz Book. NY: M. Evans & Co., Inc., 1981. 191pp.

A collection of more than 60 quizzes of all types (multiple choice, short answer, matching, crosswords, etc.) arranged in 10 groups, with scoring methods and answers. The topics range throughout mystery fiction--titles, authors, detectives, plot devices, details of setting and style, mysteries in the movies and on TV. There is "A Master Sleuth's Quiz" at the end for those who think they are experts. The quizzes range from trivial to demanding. There are the inevitable errors (such as referring to Ganesh Ghote and Gordon Craigie as "fictional bad guys"), and one quiz gives away the murderer's identity in each of ten famous crime novels. (REB)

B77. Craig, Patricia and Mary Cadogan. The Lady Investigates. Women Detectives and Spies in Fiction. London: Gollancz, 1982; New York: St. Martin's Press, 1982. 252pp.

An important subject written in a pleasant, accessible style but with numerous errors, omissions and weaknesses. Especially weak on American women sleuths, policewomen and hard-boiled females. Strong on British schoolpaper sleuths. (KLM)

B78. Cremante, Renzo, and Rambelli, Loris, eds. La Trama del Delitto. Teoria e Analisi del racconto poliziesco |The fabric of crime. Theory and analysis of detective fiction|. Parma: Pratriche Editrice, 1980. (294 pp.) Bibliliography of secondary sources.

An anthology of essays on detective fiction. The majority of the contents have been published previously. The Bibliography (pp. 259-291) is particularly useful for its inclusion of entries by a number of non-English language critics. Contents: G. K. Chesterton, "Apologia del racconto poliziesco |A defense of the detective story|," pp. 11-14 (C178); R. A. Freeman, "L'arte del romanzo poliziesco |The art of the detective story, excerpt|," pp. 15-22 (C291); Victor Sklovskij (also as Schklovskij), "La novella dei misteri |The story of mysteries|," pp. 23-41 (C732); Marjorie Nicolson, "Delitto 'cum laude' |Crime cum laude|," pp. 43-51 (C584); Bertolt Brecht, "Sulla popolarità del romanzo poliziesco |On the popularity of the detective novel|," pp. 53-59 (C124); Jorge Luis Borges, "Le due parabole (sopra Chesterton) |Two parables (after Chesterton)|," pp. 61-63 (Poe, Baudelaire, Kafka, Chesterton); Dorothy L. Sayers, "Il racconto polizieco secondo la 'Poetica' di Aristotele, ovvero l'arte di raccontare il falso |Detective fiction according to Aristotle's 'poetics", or the art of telling lies|," pp. 65-76 (C724); Mary McCarthy, "Il delitto e Carlo Marx |Crime and Karl Marx|," p. 77-83 (C503); Alberto Savinio, "Georges Simenon: il romanzo della verità nuda |Georges Simenon: the novel of the naked truth|," pp. 85-93 (E2677); Sergei Eisenstein, "La negazione della negazione |The Negative of the negative|," pp. 95-98 (C251); Roger Caillois, "Il ritorno all'ordine |The return to order|," pp. 99-102 (C145); Edmund Wilson, "Che importanza ha sapere chi ha ucciso Roger Ackroyd? |Who cares who killed Roger Ackroyd?|," pp. 103-109 (C867); W. H. Auden, "La parrocchia delittuosa. Osservazioni su romanzo poliziesco |The guilty vicarage. Observations on detective fiction|," pp. 111-120 (C34); Antonio Santucci, "Per una storia del romanzo giallo |For a history of the giallo|," pp. 121-29 (C718); Eric Hobsbawm, "Il criminale: eroe e mito |The criminal: hero and myth|," pp. 131-37 (C399); Helmut Heissenbuttel, "Le regole del gioco |The rules of the game)," pp. 139-51 (C392); Tzvetan Todorov, "Tipologia del romanzo poliziesco |Typology of the detective novel|," pp. 153-63 (C816); Carlo Emilio Gadda, "Incantagione e paura (Le Trame del 'Pisticciaccio') |Incantation and fear (the plots of the "Pisticciaccio') |," pp. 165-67 (E1235); René Ballet, "Una parodia di rapporti equivoci |A parody of equivocal reports|," pp.

169-81 (C43); Victor Zmegac, "Il paradosso storia-letteraio del romanzo poliziesco |The literary-historical paradox of detective fiction|," pp. 183-93 (C884); Walter T. Rix, "Romanzo poliziesco e dittatura |Detective fiction and dictatorship|," pp. 195-203 (C696); Giorgio Melchiori, "L'arbitrio della ragione |The arbitrary nature of reason|," pp. 205-208 (E583); Maxime Chastaing, "La casa del delitto |The house of crime|," pp. 209-25 (C174); Loris Rambelli, "La demitizzazione italiana del romanzo giallo |The demythologizing of the giallo|," pp. 227-39 (E821); Bibliography, pp. 259-291.

B79. Crider, Allen Billy. "The Private-Eye Hero: A Study of the Novels of Dashiell Hammett, Raymond Chandler, and Ross Macdonald." Unpublished doctoral dissertation. University of Texas at Austin, 1972. 176pp. Dissertation Abstracts 34/02A, pp. 722-723.

B80. Crider, Allen Billy, ed. Mass Market Publishing in America. Boston, MA: G. K. Hall & Co, 1982. v-xii, 294pp. Index. Illus.
A history of the mass-market publishing of paperbacks with chapters on individual publishing imprints by a number of contributors.

B81. "Crime and Criminology." TLS, 26 Sept 75.
Although there are some reviews of fiction in this issue, most of the contributions are on real-life crime and criminals.

B82. "Crime and Detection." TLS, 5 June 81.
Although a considerable portion of this issue is devoted to detective fiction much of the material consists of essay-reviews of particular books rather than essays on various topics. There is an editorial by Russell Davies ("Viewpoint," p. 631) on the subject of crime fiction and short statements by a number of writers ("Not to be overlooked," pp. 632-33) in which they promote unjustly neglected authors or works.

B83. "Crime, Detective and Society." TLS 3095, 23 June 1961, Supplement i-xi. Contents: Norman Shrapnel, "The Literature of Violence and Pursuit," pp. i-ii (C754); Anthony Storr, "A Black-and-White World," p. ii (C786); Lord Berkett, "The Fascination of the Courts," p. iii (public interest in court cases); Julian Symons and Edmund Crispin, "Is the Detective Story Dead?," pp. iv-v (C805); "And Is It Ever True?," p. v (C23); Eric Hobsbawn, "The Criminal as Hero and Myth," p. vi (C399); Anthony Lejeune, "Age of the Great Detective," p. vii (C489); "What Policemen Read," p. viii (C854); Percy Hopkins, "Police Reporting and Its Role," p. ix (improvement in quality of crime reporting); "Detection, Thrillers and Crime," pp. x-xi (reviews); "The Publisher's Share," p. xi (C655); Terrence Morris, "The Suggestible Offender," p. xii; "The Red Hand," p. 387 (editorial).

B84. Crime Writers' Association. The Crime Writer: The Journal of the Crime Writers' Association, circa 1951 - .
An annual newsletter (with some years omitted) published by Britain's Crime Writers' Association; notes and short articles by CWA members such as John Creasey, Christianna Brand, Michael Gilbert, Josephine Bell, etc. The CWA has also published, since 1956, Red Herrings, a news bulletin. Not seen. (REB)

B85. "Croisade pour l'énigme et le roman d'énigme |The puzzle crusade and the puzzle novel|." Subsidia Pataphysica, no. 24-25, pp. 39-171.

The Subsidia is a publishing forum for an organization based on the work and principles of French absurdist playwright Alfred Jarry. Its publications are characterized by a pronounced sense of play and its writings may be difficult for the outsider to follow. In this issue, there is an announcement of the formation of a sub-group within the order, the Oulipopo or Ouvroir de Littérature Potentielle Policière |The bureau of potential detective literature|, one of whose members is Jacques Baudou, editor of the specialist journal Enigmatika which reflects some of the aims of pataphysical writings but is reasonably accessible to the uninitiated. This dossier on the puzzle-novel is an excellent introduction to Oulipopian research and is itself, at times, something of a puzzle, a reflection of the pataphysical belief in form as a function of content, or vice versa. There is an index and a checklist of parody-novels. The dossier demonstrates the group's interest in patterns and structures and there is an attempt to identify underlying patterns in detective fiction. The range of material is not limited to what is usually considered to be genre fiction and that, too, is an expression of the pataphysical belief that the visible universe is an enigma. This is symptomatic of the breakdown in genre boundaries which is characteristic of much contemporary critical theory and contributes to the blurring of distinctions between popular and mainstream fiction.

B86. Dahl, Willy. Bla briller og losskjegg i kristiania |Blue glasses and falcebird in Kristiania|. Oslo: Gyldendal, 1975. 117pp. Illus.

On the Norwegian mystery novel and the thriller from the time of the first World War. A continuation of the treatment in 'Darlig' (B87).(IH)

B87. ______. 'Darlig' lesening under parfinlampen |Bad reading under the oil-lamp|. Oslo: Gylendal, 1974. 102pp. Illus.

A study of popular literature that is largely neglected by literary historians. (IH)

B88. Day, Bradford M., compiler & editor. Bibliography of Adventure: Mundy, Burroughs, Rohmer, Haggard. Denver, NY: Science-Fiction & Fantasy Publications, 1964. 125pp. Wraps. Edition limited to 300 copies.

Of the four authors treated in this book, only Sax Rohmer is a recognized name in mystery fiction. Many of Talbot Mundy's books also qualify for this label, since they deal at least peripherally with espionage in colonial India and the Middle East. (Hubin 2 (A83) also lists three Burroughs titles and one by Haggard.) Day's Mundy bibliography, useful in its time, has now been completely superseded by Donald M. Grant's Talbot Mundy (E202) although J. Lloyd Eaton's "His Sagas: with a story sequence of various characters" is still of interest to anyone who wants to read Mundy's various series in their appropriate order. The Rohmer bibliography, covering both books and magazine stories, is still the most complete gathered in one place, though marred by a few errors (citation of nonexistent editions, mis-quoting of story titles, and a few incorrect dates). All of the Burroughs and Haggard information can be found in other sources. (REB)

B89. Del Monte, Alberto. Breve storia del romanzo poliziesco |A short history of the detective novel|. Bari: Editori paterza. Trans. into Spanish by Florentino Perez and published as: Breve historia de la novela policiaca (Madrid: Taurus, 1962). 233pp. Bibliography of secondary sources and an author index.

This is the first book in Italian devoted to the history of detective fiction, undertaken as a study and provided with an ample bibliography. The author, a student of Romance philology, treats first the concept of a literary genre (or "infraliterary" as in the case of the detective story) and, aware that "the peculiarities of a genre must result from the investigation of its historical development," studies systmatically the basic stages of the detective novel, from the illuministic and romantic antecedents to the neo-romantic phase of Spillane, illustrating at the same time the "continuous process of osmosis" which is established between learned literature and popular literature. (LR)

B90. Del Monte, Alberto, editor. Il racconto poliziesco |The detective story|. Florence: La Nuova Italia, 1967. 113pp.

Anthology of detective stories, chosen among those of particular literary value, directed at young students in the lower secondary schools. The introduction and introductory sketches of the authors (Poe, Doyle, Chesterton, Simenon, Borges) are those treated in large part in Del Monte's Breve storia (B89). (LR)

B91. Depken, Friedrich. Sherlock Holmes, Raffles und ihre Vorbilder. Ein Beitrag zur Entwicklungsgeschichte und Technik der Kriminalerzaehlung |Sherlock Homes, Raffles and their prototypes: a contribution to the historical development and techniques of crime fiction|. Heidelberg: Carl Winter, 1914. Reprint: NY: Garland, 1979. Index; bibliography of primary and secondary sources.

Monograph on the development of crime fiction from Poe and Gaboriau to Doyle and Hornung, in whom Depken sees the genre's final stages. Included are chapters on various narrative techniques, the deductive method, and on various heroes of the genre. (GG)

B91a. The Detection Club. The Floating Admiral. Introduction by Dorothy L. Sayers. London: Hodder, 1931; NY: Doubleday, Doran, 1932. Reprint: NY: Charter House, 1980.

A "round-robin" mystery novel to which the following members of London's Detection Club contributed: G. K. Chesterton, Victor L. Whitechurch, G. D. H. and Margaret Cole, Henry Wade, Agatha Christie, John Rhode, Milward kennedy, Dorothy L. Sayers, Ronald A. Knox, Freeman Wills Crofts, Edgar Jepson, Clemence Dane and Anthony Berkeley. Of interest to this bibliography for Sayers' introduction and the authors' solutions in the appendix which give some information on the various writers' methods.

B92. "Detective & Suspense." Modern Fiction Studies 29 (Autumn 83):387-582.

The entire issue of this literary journal is devoted to detective and suspense fiction. Contents: William T. Stafford, "Editor's Preface," pp. 387-388; Peter Wolfe, "The Critics Did It: An Essay Review," pp. 389-434 (C873); Timothy Steele, "Matter and Mystery: Neglected Works and Background Materials of Detective Fiction," pp. 435-50 (C779); T. R. Steiner, "Stanislaw Lem's Detective Stories: A Genre Extended," pp. 451-62; William Nelson and Nancy Avery, "Art Where You Least Expect It: Myth and Ritual in the Detective Series," pp. 463-74 (C576); Thomas M. Leitch, "From Detective Story to Detective Novel," pp. 475-84 (C488a); Virginia B. Morris, "Arsenic and Blue Lace: Sayers' Criminal Women," pp. 485-96; SueEllen Campbell, "The Detective Heroine and the Death of Her Hero: Dorothy Sayers to P. D. James," pp. 497-510 (C151); Erlene Hubly, "The Formula Challenged: The Novels of P. D. James," pp. 511-22; JoAnn Cannon, "The Detective Fiction of Leonardo Sciascia," pp.

523-534; Larry E. Grimes, "Stepsons of Sam: Re-Visions of the Hard-Boiled Detective Formula in Recent American Fiction," pp. 535-44 (C343); Keith Newlin, "C. W. Sughrue's Whiskey Visions," pp. 545-56 (E753a); Frederic Svoboda, "The Snub-Nosed Mystique: Observations on the American Detective Hero," pp. 557-68 (C798); David Monaghan, "John le Carré and England: A Spy's-Eye View," pp. 569-82.

B93. ("Detective Fiction.") Chimera: A Literary Quarterly 5:4 (Summer 47). The earliest example of a literary review devoting an entire issue to critical studies of detective fiction. Although there is no explicit editorial statement, references in some of the articles suggest that writers were invited to defend to the editor a genre he was not convinced merited serious critical consideration. The quality of the contributions varies, but the essay on Graham Greene, Barzun's predictable but literate homily on the death of the classical English detective story, and, most notably, the excerpt from Caillois' "Le Roman policier" make still valid contributions to the field. Contents: José F. Montesinos, "Imperfect Myths," pp. 2-11 (C562); Q. Patrick/Patrick Quentin/Jonathan Stagge, "Who'd Do It?," pp. 12-17 (C617); Donat O'Donnell, "Graham Greene," pp. 18-30 (E1319); G. Robert Stange, "The Detective Story Mystery," pp. 31-38 (C776); Hector Hoppin, "Notes on Primitive Notes of Detection," pp. 39-48 (C411); Ruthven Todd, "A Trinity of 'Tecs: From There to Where?," pp. 49-58 (C815); Jacques Barzun, "Requiescat," pp. 59-66 (C64); Roger Caillois, "Order and License," pp. 67-68 (C144).

B94. "Detective Fiction." TLS, 25 Feb 55, pp. i-xii.
Contents: "The Secret Attraction," pp. i-ii (C743); "Tram Cars or 'Dodgems': Detection, Thrills and Horror," p. ii (C819); "Images of Horror: The Unknown and Familiar," pp. iii-iv (on the horror story); "Entertaining Inquiry: The Nature of the Detective Story," p. iv (C264); "Cops and Novels: The Sleuth in Fact and Fancy," p. v (C196); "Out of the Ordinary: The Novel of Pursuit and Suspense," pp. vi-vii (C609); "Publishing Detective Novels," p. vii (C656); "In the Best Tradition: Mystification and Art," p. vii (C421); "Love of Heroes: Some Detectives of Character," p. ix (C497); C. H. B. Kitchin, "Five Writers in One: The Versatility of Agatha Christie," p. x (E565); "The Silver Age: Crime Fiction from Its Heyday until Now," pp. xi-xii (C755); Sir Ronald Hare, "A Personal Reaction," p. xii (C368).

B95. Díaz, César E. La novela policiaca |The detective novel|. Barcelona: Ediciones acervo, 1973. 202pp. With a list of the 222 "best" works in the field.
A chronological history of the genre in England and North America with a separate chapter on France and a "brief" survey of "the rest of the world." The short list of secondary sources includes only three articles in Spanish; the other references are to English-language, French or Italian sources.

B96. Dove, George N. The Police Procedural. Bowling Green, OH: Popular Press, 1982. 274pp. Index.
This book--although there is no acknowledgment of it--appears to be a considerably reworked and expanded version of a series of articles published in TAD in volumes 10 and 11 (C241). Dove examines not only works of fiction that may be called "police procedurals" but detective fiction in which the private detective is the protagonist and where the

role of the police is subordinate. This allows Dove to range widely in his discussion and to include writers as far removed from the police procedural as Chandler and Hammett but, at the same time, by defining the procedural as a novel in which policemen investigate a mystery, he excludes the enormously popular and influential writer Joseph Wambaugh. Dove's comments on writers are often perceptive but his study gives the impression of a treatment that has been extended beyond its subject with little consideration for the problems posed. What might have been a substantial study of a significant contemporary trend has become, instead, a disorganized series of chapters with little internal coherence. There are individual chapters on the following writers: John Creasey (pp. 177-83), Maurice Procter (pp. 184-88), Hillary Waugh (pp. 189-95), Ed McBain (pp. 196-205), Bill Knox (pp. 206-210), Nicolas Freeling (pp. 211-16), Maj Sjöwall and Per Wahlöö (pp. 217-25), Collin Wilcox (pp. 225-29), and James McClure (pp. 225-29).

B97. Duhamel, Marcel. Raconte pas ta vie |Don't talk about your life|. Paris: Mercure de France, 1972. 620pp.
Marcel Duhamel devotes part of his autobiography to the birth of the série noire which he initiated and to his memory of encounters with certain of his authors. (JB)

B98. Dupuy, Josée. Le Roman policier. Collection: Textes pour aujourd'hui. Paris: Larousse, 1974. 192pp.
This work directed at a student audience opens with a brief history, continues with an anthology of selections intended to illustrate the elements of the detective narative (the crime, the investigation, the solution, etc.) or those of a popular mythology (the hero, places and things) before concluding with a pedagogical section with some suggested exercises. (JB)

B99. Eames, Hugh. Sleuths, Inc.: Studies of Problem Solvers. Doyle, Simenon, Hammett, Ambler, Chandler. Philadelphia: Lippincott, 1978. 228pp. Bibliography.
Biocritical studies of 5 writers. The chapters are badly organized and the discussions are, in general, reworking of familiar material. Eames' intention was to describe different kinds of detectives but his categories are not well defined while his mistaken belief that "cops as problem solvers are rare in American fiction" leads him to insert a brief chapter on real-life lawman Pat Garrett. Contents: "Sherlock Holmes-Arthur Conan Doyle," pp. 9-47; "Jules Maigret-Georges Simenon," pp. 48-97; "Sam Spade-Dashiell Hammett," pp. 98-140; "A Note on Pat Garrett," pp. 141-47; "Eric Ambler," pp. 148-84; and "Philip Marlowe-Raymond Chandler," pp. 185-221. Breen 67.

B100. Eco, Umberto, and Sebeok, Thomas A., editors. Dupin, Holmes and Pierce: The Sign of Three. Bloomington: Indiana University Press, 1983. v-xi, 236pp. Bibliography.
The methods of Charles Sanders Pierce, considered to be the founder of modern semiotics, are compared with the epistemological methods of Sherlock Homes and with Poe's Dupin. The emphasis is on Holmes rather than on Dupin, with the exception of Chapter 9, an essay by Nancy Harrowitz on "The Body of the Detective Model: Charles S. Pierce and Edgar Allan Poe" (E2133).

B101. Edwards, P. D. Some Mid-Victorian Thrillers: The Sensation Novel, Its

Friends and Its Foes. St. Lucia, Queensland (Australia): University of Queensland Press, 1971. 34pp. Wraps.

Pamphlet reprinting an original lecture at the University of Queensland, delivered in September 1970. Dr. Edwards describes the category of the "sensation novel," introduced in the 1860s, and discusses three important examples (The Woman in White, East Lynne, Lady Audley's Secret) and their authors, with numerous quotations from contemporary reactions, including three satiric jabs from Punch. Sympathetic treatment, scholarly without being stuffy, and carefully annotated. (REB)

B102. Eisinger, Erica M. "The Adaptation of Detective Story Techniques in the French New Novel." Unpublished doctoral dissertation. Yale, 1973. 212pp. Dissertation Abstracts 34 (1973/74), pp. 310A-311A.

On Nathalie Sarraute, Michel Butor, Alain Robbe-Grillet, Claude Simon and Marguerite Duras.

B103. Elgström, Jörgen E.; la Cour, Tage; and Runnquist, Ake R., eds. Mord i biblioteket |Murder in the library|. Stockholm: Bonniers, 1961; Copenhagen, 1965. 223pp. Illus.

A history of the mystery novel comparable to Haycraft's Murder for Pleasure (B143). (IH)

B104. Elgstrom, Jörgen, and Runnquist, Ake R. Svensk mordbok |Swedish murderbook|. Stockholm: Bokvannernas bibliotek nr 36, 1957.

A history of the Swedish mystery novel, 1900-1950. (IH)

B105. "The Eternal World of Mystery and Suspense." Publishers Weekly 213:11 (13 March 78):45-69.

Special section edited by Thomas Chastain. Contents: Dorothy Salisbury Davis, "View from the Middle Window," pp. 46-47 (C217); T. M. McDade, "True or Fact Crime," p. 48 (books on true crimes); Brian Garfield, "The State of the Art," pp. 50-51 (C300); Stefan Kanfer, "Archetype Casting (About)," pp. 54-55 (humor); Edward D. Hoch, "Mystery Writers' Organizations," p. 55 (England, America, Japan, Scandinavia); Thomas Chastain, "Q. 'Who Cares Who Killed Roger Ackroyd?' A. Millions of Readers Do," p. 58 (mystery best-sellers); Julian Symons, "A Personal Pantheon," pp. 60-61 ("best" works); Edward D. Hoch, "Mystery Book Clubs," p. 61; Dilys Winn, "The Case of Mysterious Bookseller," pp. 62-64 (a bookseller's perspective); Daisy Maryles, "Tracking the Mystery Bookstores," p. 64 (speciality book stores, a listing); Jean F. Mercier, "Starting Young," p. 65 (young readers' mysteries); Eugene Franklin Bandy, "Jacques Barzun: A Critic Talks about Mystery Criticism," pp. 68-69 (interview); Edward D. Hoch, "Grand Masters," p. 69 (MWA awards in Grand Master category).

B106. "Etudes de littérature policière potentielle." Organographes du cymbalum pataphysicum, no. 17 (15 July 82), pp. 174. Illus.

A dossier largely devoted to the Golden Age British puzzle mystery. Charts, graphs, and outlines, with some narrative discussion.

B107. (Fanzines, French) See Cook (A37), pp. 649-51, for descriptions of Enigmatika (1976 -); Polar (1979-84), p. 648; and Les Amis du crime (1977 -), pp. 652-54. In addition, the following fanzines are also relevant to this bibliography and should be noted:

Bulletin 813. An irregularly published newsletter, sponsored by a group of writers and fans. The material is often slight but it contains material on the annual convention in Reims to which American writers have been invited as guests-of-honor. Bill Pronzini was the guest at the 1983 convention.

Désiré (1965 -). A quarterly newsletter of studies of pictorial papers, serial papers, and popular books, founded by Jean Leclercq, a self-taught worker. Beginning as a modest newsletter, it gradually increased in size and in importance, acquiring numerous contributors and becoming the first critical journal of popular literature. Two series have been published: Series 1 (Oct 65-June 71); Series 2, Jan 74-1981. Published in very limited printings, items will not be further cited in this bibliography but the writers studied have included Léo Malet, Simenon, Gaboriau, Leroux, Christie, San Antonio, Nick Carter, Jean Ray and Allain/Souvestre. (JB)

Le Fulmar. Editor: François Ducos. Devoted to all forms of popular literature, including the comic strip. Issues are usually devoted to a single writer or theme and the following subjects are of interest for this bibliography: No. 1, Edgar Wallace; No. 2, Doc Savage Dossier; No. 7, Sherlock Holmes Dossier; No. 8, Bob Morane Dossier; No. 10, Nick Jordan Dossier; No. 11, Psychic Detectives.

Hard-Boiled Dicks. 1981 - . Editor: Roger Martin. An attractive digest-sized fanzine devoted to hard-boiled writers. At least seven issues have appeared, each consisting of a dossier on one or two writers. The following issues have been seen: No. 1 (Marvin H. Albert); No. 2 (Michael Collins); No. 4 (Joseph Hansen and Joe L. Hensley); and No. 7 (Richard Deming). Interviews, bibliographies and filmographies, and short articles.

B108. (Fanzines, Japanese) A very large number of professional and amateur magazines devoted to fiction and criticism are published in Japan. Some of these magazines will be cited in the Authors section. Among the general magazines, the following may be noted as examples of the range of publications: Annual Proceedings of the Society of Mystery & Science Fiction, Tokyo, edited by Masao Ushida, in an edition of 35 copies; Eagle (newsletter of the Adventure Fiction Fan Club), Tokyo, quarterly edited by Yoshiaki Hamada; Jusan Kaidan |13 Steps|, Kanagawa (Japan), bimonthly edited by Setsuya Hiroshima; The Maltese Falcon Flyer, monthly, edited by Jiro Kimura, Tokyo; Nazo-Nazo |Puzzle|, published irregularly by the Nazo-Nazo Mystery Club, Miyagi, Japan; Rom Gazzette |Revisiting old mysteries|, published irregularly and edited by Yoshio Kase, Tokyo; and SR Monthly (official publication of the Sealed Room Society), bimonthly, edited alternately by Masatoshi Saito, Tokyo area, and Masato Matsuura, Osaka area. (Listings based on information supplied by Jiro Kimura.)

B109. Ferrini, Franco. Il ghetto letterario. Rome: Armando, 1976.
The second chapter (pp. 87-131) is explicitly devoted to the detective narrative, described in structural and historical terms. (RC)

B110. "La Fiction policière |Detective fiction|." Special issue of Europe, nos. 571-72 (Nov/Dec 76), pp. 3-171.
Contents: Pierre Gamarra, "L'Enquête est ouverte |The investigation is begun|," pp. 3-7 (C296); François Rivière, "La Fiction policière ou le meurtre du roman |Detective fiction or the murder of the novel|," pp. 8-25 (C694); Maxime Chastaing, "Le Roman policier classique |The classic

detective novel|," pp. 26-49 (C174); Bernard Endrèbe, "Pérennité du roman d'énigme |Durability of the puzzle-novel|," pp. 50-54 (C261); Roger Bonniot, "A la recherche d'Emile Gaboriau |In search of Emile Gaboriau|,"-pp. 55-60 (E1226); François Bussière, "Arsène Lupin, homme de lettres |Arsène Lupin, man of letters|," pp. 61-70 (E1646); Christian Robin, "Le 'vrai' mystère de la chambre jaune |The 'real' mystery of the yellow room|," pp. 71-90 (E1758); Francis Albany, "Ellery Queen, le logicien du mystère |Ellery Queen, the logician of mystery|," pp. 91-98 (E2222); Marie-Hélène Huet, "Enquête et représentation dans le roman policier |Investigation and representation in the detective novel|," pp. 99-103 (C416); François Rivière, "Fascination de la réalité travestie |Fascination with travestied reality|," pp. 104-116 (C693); Yves di Manno, "Roman policier et société |Detective novel and society|," pp. 117-124; Véronique Auricoste, "Horace McCoy," pp. 125-131 (E1802); François Guérif, "Raymond Chandler,", pp. 132-36 (E410); F. Guérif, "William Irish," pp. 137-41 (E3118); Michel Lebrun, "Pages d'agenda |Pages from an agenda|," pp. 142-43; Yves Olivier-Martin, "Origines secrètes du roman policier français |Secret origins of the French detective novel|," pp. 144-49 (C599); Jacques Baudou, "Les Petits-Maîtres du roman policier français |Minor masters of the French detective novel|," pp. 150-53 (C67); K. Arne Blom and Jan Broberg, "Panorama du roman policier suédois |Panorama of the Swedish detective novel|, pp. 154-59 (C106); François Rivière, "Notes sur trois romans d'Addington Symonds |Notes on three novels by Addington Symonds|," pp. 160-63 (E4); Paul Gayot, "Sur la littérature policière potentielle |On potential detective literature|," pp. 164-65 (C304); François Rivière, "Petit guide chronologique |A little chronological guide|," pp. 166-71.

B111. Filler, Louis, ed. Seasoned Authors for a New Season: The Search for Standards in Popular Writing: A Question of Quality 2. Bowling Green, OH: Popular Press.
For relevant material see Himes (E1494), John D. MacDonald (E1820), and Ross Macdonald (E1856).

B112. Finckh, Eckhard, ed. Theorie des Kriminalromans |The theory of the crime novel|. Stuttgart: Philipp Reclam, 1974. 88pp.
Anthology containing 23 short exercepts from essays on the genre. Planned for instructional use in German secondary schools, this book contains study questions and a short bibliography of secondary sources. Writers covered include Ernst Bloch, Edgar Marsch, Fritz Woelcken, Viktor Zmegac, Bertolt Brecht and Helmut Heissenbuettel as well as W. H. Auden, Dorothy L. Sayers, and Julian Symons, 11 of whose essays have been collected full length into other anthologies. (GG)

B113. Fleenor, Juliann E., ed. The Female Gothic. Montreal & London: Eden Press, 1983. 311pp.
A collection of essays on 19th and 20th century Gothic novels with an introduction by editor Fleenor and four essays in which there is some treatment of the relationship between Gothic and mystery fiction: Russ (C711), Musell (C569), Bowman (E1507), and Maio (C530).

B114. Forsberg, Thomas E. "The Science-Fiction Detective Story: The Emergence of a Hybrid Genre." M.A. thesis. Bowling Green University, 1976. pp. iii, 57 leaves. Not seen.

B115. Fosca, François. Histoire et technique du roman policier |History and technique of the detective novel|. Paris: Editions de la Nouvelle Revue Critique, 1937. 288pp. Japanese edition, translated by Hachiro Nagasaki. Tantei Shosetsu no Rekishi to Giko. Tokyo: Ikusei-sha, 1938.

After a first chapter in which Fosca--himself author of detective novels--tries to define the detective novel and the different types, there is a series of chapters devoted to its history: the precursors, E. A. Poe, "Between Dupin and Sherlock Homes," Conan Doyle and Sherlock Holmes, French authors from Maurice Leblanc to Georges Simenon. Chapter VII treats the "management of the narrative in the detective novel," Chapter VIII the character of the detective, and Chapter IX that of the criminal. Chapter XI looks into the future of the detective novel. On the whole, a somewhat cursory historical section but one which efficiently traces the major outlines, and a very appropriate and quite interesting first attempt at an analysis of the genre. (JB)

B116. Fossati, Franco, and di Vanni, Roberto. Guida al 'giallo' |Guide to the giallo|. Milano: Gammalibri, 1980.

This guide takes up, in alphabetical order, 99 of the most famous international writers of detective fiction (from Margery Allingham to Israel Zangwill), offering for each one, in addition to a brief critical profile, appendices with bibliographical references (in particular of Italian translations) and overviews of film and television versions of the works. With a short dictionary of Italian authors, compiled by Giorgio Ferrari, of 124 entries--including authors of the stature of Carlo Emilio Gadda, Leonardo Sciascia, and Giovanni Comisso--and a basic bibliography of secondary material. The introduction presents the principal "rules" of the giallo, drawn up by S. S. Van Dine, Chandler, Fox and Fosca. (RC)

B117. Freeman, Lucy, editor. The Murder Mystique. Crime Writers on their Art. New York: Ungar, 1982. Series: Recognitions. v-ix, 140pp.

Historical, critical and technical essays by 11 MWA members. Many of the contributors have both worked in the publishing/editing field and published extensively. Contents: Part One/On the Genre: Bruce Cassiday, "Murder in the Mainstream: A Study in Bloodlines," pp. 2-26 (capsule history of the mystery novel); Thomas Chastain, "The Case for the Private Eye," pp. 27-32 (C173); Hillary Waugh,"The Human Rather Than Superhuman Sleuth," pp. 33-45 (police procedurals); Lucy Freeman, "The Whydunit Emerges, Thanks to Freud," pp. 46-56 (C29); Helen Wells, "Murder in Mother Goose?," pp. 57-72 (mysteries in children's and juvenile fiction); Part Two/On Technique: Ken Follett, "The Spy as Hero and Villain," pp. 74-81 (espionage fiction); D. R. Bensen, "The Education of a Mystery Writer," pp. 82-89 (brief memoir of Bensen's 25 years as an editor; tensions between 'high' literature and genre fiction); Franklin Bandy, "If the Book Is So Good, Why Isn't It in Hardcover?," pp. 90-103 (hardcover versus paperback originals); Edward D. Hoch, "Mystery Movies: Behind the Scenes," pp. 104-17 (movie and TV adaptations from the viewpoint of the author of the original story); Eleanor Sullivan, "Writers on Their Mysterious Calling," pp. 118-25 (quotations from many different writers on their work);; Shannon OCork, "The Truth, More or Less, as Long as It Makes a Good Story," pp. 126-38 (E2035). (REB/WA)

B118. Friedburg, Maurice. A Decade of Euphoria. Western Slavic Literature in Post-Stalin Russia, 1954-64. Bloomington, Indiana: Indiana University Press, 1977. 371pp. Index.

A scholarly study of the reception of and attitudes toward Western authors translated into Russian. There are publishing data, and references to official attitudes toward genre literature. See especially pp. 104-107 for a discussion of thrillers and detective fiction and passim for Poe, Doyle and Wilkie Collins.

B119. Fujisaki, Makoto. Sekai Meitantei Zukan |World great detective pictorial book|. Tokyo: Rippu Shobo, 1975. 189pp. Illus.
An introductory book for juveniles by a mystery reviewer, Takeshi Setogawa (using a pseudonym), with a lot of mystery puzzles in digest form. The book introduces detectives in print and on TV. For a juvenile book of this kind, the description is relatively accurate if desultory. Many illustrations are not appropriate. (HS/TT)

B120. Fukunaga, Takehiko; Nakamaura, Shinchiro; and Maruya, Saiichi. Shinya no Sanpo: Mystery no Tanoshimi |Night walk: the pleasure of mysteries|. Tokyo: Hayakawa Shobo, 1963; revised edition, Tokyo: Kodan-sha, 1978. 261pp. Illus.
These writers are all novelists who love mysteries. A compilation of serialized humorous essays on overseas mysteries. For essays by amateurs, this book reaches the highest standards with original viewpoints and good writing. (HS/TT)

B121. Geherin, David. Sons of Sam Spade: The Private Eye Novel in the 70s. Recognitions series. NY: Frederick Ungar Publishing Co., 1980; second printing 1982. 168pp. Bibliography and index.
Studies of three writers: Robert B. Parker, Roger L. Simon (E2705), and Andrew Bergman (E127). Endings are revealed in the plot summaries that comprise major portions of the chapters.

B122. Gerteis, Walter. Detektive. Ihre Geschichte im Leben und in der Literatur. |Detectives. Their history in life and literature.| Munich: Heimeran Verlag, 1953. (Meitantei was Shinazu. Translated from the German by Michisuke Maekawa. Tokyo: Kobundo, 1962.) 187pp. Index.
Informal popular introduction to real and fictional detectives. Chapters on fictional detectives include Vidocq, Dupin, Inspectors Bucket and Cuff, Sherlock Holmes and Father Brown. Chapters on real-life detectives include the Bow Street Runners, Pinkerton's, Lombroso and the FBI. (GG)

B123. Gilbert, Elliot L. The World of Mystery Fiction. San Diego and Del Mar, CA: University of California, San Diego and Publisher's Inc., 1978. xxi, 441pp. Illus.

B123a. ______. The World of Mystery Fiction: A Guide. Preface by Ellery Queen. San Diego and Del Mar, 1978. 153pp.
The World of Mystery Fiction is an annotated, historical anthology of the detective short story; 24 stories, together with a meaty introduction and excellent head-notes by the editor. The Guide is a textbook for a university-level course in mystery fiction, designed to be used in conjunction with the anthology and selected additional readings. Embedded in the classroom apparatus is an original and penetrating study of detective fiction, well worth any reader's attention. Each of the 12 chapters is accompanied by a bibliography and a set of objectives and review questions. Breen 42. (REB)

B124. Gilbert, Michael, editor. Crime in Good Company. Essays on Criminals and Crime-writing. London: Constable, 1959. x, 242pp.

Compiled by Gilbert on "behalf of the Crime Writers' Association," this collection is a mixture of theoretical and technical essays on various aspects of mystery fiction and its craft. Each of the selections is prefaced by a short introduction to the writer by editor Gilbert. Most of the material has not been published previously. Contents: Josephine Bell, "The Criminal seen by the Doctor. The Psycho-pathology of Crime," pp. 3-26 (C79); Michael Underwood, "The Criminal Seen by the Lawyer," pp. 27-38 (C823); Maurice Procter, "The Criminal Seen by the Policeman," pp. 39-52 (C650); Cyril Hare, "The Classic Form," pp. 55-85 (C367); Raymond Chandler "The Simple Art of Murder," pp. 85-104 (C168); Michael Gilbert, "The Moment of Violence," pp. 105-25 (C319); Julian Symons, "The Face in the Mirror," pp. 126-33 (C802); Jacques Barzun, "Detection in Extremis," pp. 134-45 (C63); L.A.G. Strong, "The Crime Short Story-An English View," pp. 149-62 (C792); Stanley Ellin, "The Crime Short Story-An American View," pp, 163-77 (C258); Roy Vickers, "Crime on the Stage-the Criminological Illusion," pp. 178-91; Eric Ambler, "The Novelist and Films," pp. 192-209; Mary Fitt, "Crime on the Radio," pp. 210-31; David Alexander, "Is Television Necessary?," pp. 232-42. Breen 68. CC 2947.

B125. Glatzer, Richard Mark. "Truth in Detail: Essays on American Detective Fiction." Unpublished doctoral dissertation. University of Virginia, 1978. 269pp. Dissertation Abstracts 40/02A, pp. 850-51.

Poe, Hammett, Chandler and Faulkner.

B126. Goette, Juergen-Wolfgang, and Kircher, Hartmut, eds. Der Kriminalroman. Texte zur Theorie und Kritik |The crime novel: texts on theory and criticism|. Texte und materilien zum Literaturunterricht, Diesterweg 6229. Frankfurt a.M.: Verlag Moritz Diesterweg, 1978. 123pp. Bibliography of secondary sources.

Part of a series of didactic and instruction-oriented books for German secondary schools which includes volumes on comics, science fiction, socialist, political and "high" literature, this volume is a collection of excerpts from essays on the genre as well as on such topics as violence and society, violence in literature and on TV, etc. The excerpts dealing with crime fiction are from writers such as Ulrich Suerbaum (C795), Gerhard Schmidt-Henkel (C734), Hans Christoph Buch (E1089) and Ernst Kaemmel (C439) whose essays are available full-length elsewhere. Also included are study questions for use in the classroom. (GG)

B127. Gonda, Manji, ed. Kyoyo to shite no Satsujin |Murder for culture|. Tokyo: Kagyu-sha, 1979. 336pp. Index.

An anthology of 26 critical essays on mystery fiction by Japanese authors. It contrasts the historical changes in Japanese mystery fiction with those in mystery criticism, with emphasis on the essence. The title is a parody of Howard Haycraft's Murder for Pleasure (B143). (HS/TT)

B128. ______. Nippon Tantei Sakka-ron |Comments on Japanese detective writers|. Tokyo: Gen'eijo, 1975. 262pp.

A collection of comments on 18 Japanese mystery writers who debuted before World War II. Some of the comments overlap with his Shukumei no Bigaku (B129). This book won the Mystery Writers of Japan award as the best critical book in 1976, the first year an award was offered in this category. (HS/TT)

B129. ______. Shukumei no Bigaku: Suiri Shosetsu no Sekai |Esthetics of fate: world of mystery fiction|. Tokyo: Daisan Bunmei-sha, 1973. 302pp.
The author is Japan's leading mystery critic. He debuted with an essay on Raymond Chandler which appears in this book along with comments on Japanese and non-Japanese writers, and on mystery fiction in general. This book illustrates his position that there is artistic value in mystery fiction. (HS/TT)

B130. ______. Shumi to Shite no Satsujin |Murder for a hobby|. Tokyo: Kagyu-sha, 1980. 328pp. Index.
A sequel to Kyoyo to Shite no Satsujin (B127), and as its subtitle "Volume on Practices" suggests, a collection of essays on technical problems in writing, appreciation and criticism. (HS/TT)

B131. Gordon, Mark, and Jack Nachbar, assisted by James Von Shilling; editors and compilers. Currents of Warm Life: Popular Culture in American Higher Education. Bowling Green, OH: Popular Press, 1980. 272pp.
Results of a national survey, conducted in 1979, of popular culture courses at American four-year colleges. Includes course syllabi, and appendices on courses, departments and schools in the survey, with a section on detective fiction. (David H. Doerrer)

B132. Goulart, Ron, editor. The Great British Detectives. A Mentor Book. NY: New American Library, 1980.
An anthology of 15 stories featuring British detectives, with a short introduction, notes on each author, and a list of authors and books for further reading.

B133. ______. The Hardboiled Dick: An Anthology and Study of Pulp Detective Fiction. Los Angeles, CA: Sherbourne Press, 1965.
With an introduction, an informal reading list, and headnotes to individual stories. (REB)

B134. (Gregg Press Mystery Fiction Series) Series editor: Otto Penzler.
The introductions in the Gregg Press reprint volumes are generally of high quality, often containing biographical, bibliographical, or critical material of substance. The Introductions by Christianna Brand (E231), Edward D. Hoch (E196), and Francis M. Nevins, Jr. (E3128, E3131), are especially good. Hoch's introduction for Boston Blackie presents the results of considerable original research on the book's author, Jack Boyle. The introductions were written for the reissue of books by the following writers and will be cited with the critical material in the author section of the bibliography: Anthony Boucher (E189a), Jack Boyle (E196), Christianna Brand (E231), Fredric Brown (E260), James M. Cain (E312), John Dickson Carr/Carter Dickson (E366), Carroll John Daly (E764), Dorothy Salisbury Davis (E779), Stanley Ellin (E1039), Richard Hallas (E1346), Francis Iles (E130), Jonathan Latimer (E1634), Edgar Lustgarten (E1782), Cameron McCabe (E1795), Ross Macdonald (E1862), Frederick Nebel (E2027), Clayton Rawson (E2298, E2302, E2303, E2306, E2307), Seely Regester (E2324), Richard Stark (E3067, E3068, E3071, E3077, E3079, E3080), S. S. Van Dine (E2950), Raoul Whitfield (E3089), Cornell Woolrich (E3128, E3131). (REB/WA)

B135. Grossvogel, David I. Mystery & Its Fictions: From Oedipus to Agatha Christie. Baltimore, Md: Johns Hopkins Press, 1979, ix-xi, 203pp. Bibliography and index.

A heavy-handed study of divine and human mysteries which takes the subject of mystery from such an Olympian perspective that it is often only of peripheral interest for this bibliography. Of the authors he discusses, Christie (E552), Poe (E2129), Borges and Robbe-Grillet (E2371) are most frequently associated with the genre. At the same time that one can complain of a somewhat uneasy mix of popular and "high" culture literature, it should be noted that Grossvogel's comments are sometimes perceptive and a patient reader may be rewarded for the laborious reading. Breen 44

B136. Hackett, Alice Payne. 50 Years ot Best Sellers 1895-1945. Foreword by Frederic G. Melcher. NY: Bowker, 1945. v-viii, 140pp. With a selective bibliography.

There is some information on the period 1880-1895 and the pre-1880 period. There is a descriptive narrative, by subject, with sections on detective stories (pp. 96-97) and dime novels (97-98). An absorbing document on American tastes in popular literature. Allen J. Hubin comments in TAD 1 (1967/68): 99 on the information relating to mystery fiction.

B137a. ______. 60 Years of Best Sellers 1895-1955. NY: Bowker, 1956.

B137b. ______. 70 Years of Best Sellers 1895-1965. NY: Bowker, 1967.

B137c. Hackett, Alice, and Burkes, James H. Eighty Years of Best Sellers 1895-1975. NY: Bowker, 1977.

B138. Haining, Peter. Mystery! An Illustrated History of Crime and Detective Fiction. Designed by Christopher Scott. London: Souvenir Press, 1977; NY: Stein & Day, 1981. 176pp.

Each of the 15 chapters consists of a single page of text followed by numerous illustrations, with captions of varying lengths. Thus, in the book's subtitle, "Illustrated" is more accurate than "History." After a general introduction, the book's arrangement is roughly chronological, from the Newgate period up to the advent of the hard-boiled school. The illustrations, from both original and reprint editions of a wide variety of books and stories, are interesting and well reproduced, but the captions are often confusingly worded. Acknowledgements of sources are completely inadequate, and the lack of an index seriously curtails the use of the book for other than casual browsing. No more than the usual number of factual errors seem to be present. In the U. S. reprint the quality of reproduction of the illustrations is not as good as in the British edition. Breen 100 (REB)

B139. Hanan, Patrick. The Chinese Vernacular Story. Harvard East Asian Series, 94. Cambridge, MA: Harvard Univ. Press, 1981. 276pp.

A critical history of the vernacular short story in China. Includes two sections on "court case" stories, including those of Magistrate Pao. Pp. 39-44 contain information on court case literature from the Sung (1127-1279) and Yuan (1271-1368) dynasties. Hanan states that the themes of crime and punishment are more important in the traditional literature of China than anywhere else up until the advent of Western detective fiction. Pp. 72-74 contain information on Ming court case fiction. (GG)

B140. Harper, Ralph. The World of the Thriller. Cleveland: The Press of Case Western Reserve Univ., 1969; paperback, Baltimore: Johns Hopkins

University Press, 1974. xii, 142pp. Index.

A study of thriller fiction and its readers from the viewpoint of modern philosophy and psychology. Review: JPC 3 (Spring 1970):876-78. Breen 46. (REB)

B141. Hart, James D. The Popular Book; A History of America's Literary Taste. NY: Oxford University Press, 1950. Index.

Of limited interest for some brief comments on dime novels and on detective fiction.

B142. Haycraft, Howard, ed. The Art of the Mystery Story. A Collection of Critical Essays. NY: Simon & Schuster, 1946; paperbound, NY: Grosset & Dunlap, 1961; NY: Carroll & Graf Publishers, 1983. 565pp. Index. (Japanese edition: Suiri Shosetsu no Bigaku. 2 vols. Tokyo: Kenkyu-sha, 1974, 1976. Selections translated by Yukio Suzuki and others.

In itself an entire library of detective story commentary and criticism. An indispensable volume. Contents: Chesterton,"A Defence of Detective Stories," pp. 3-6 (C178); R. Austin Freeman, "The Art of the Detective Story," pp. 7-17 (C291); E. M. Wrong, "Crime and Detection," pp. 18-32 (C877); Willard Huntington Wright, "The Great Detective Stories," pp. 33-70 (C825); Dorothy L. Sayers, "The Omnibus of Crime," pp. 71-109 (C725); Marjorie Nicolson, "The Professor and the Detective," pp. 110-127 (C584); H. Douglas Thomson, "Masters of Mystery," pp. 128-45 (B404); Vincent Starrett, "The Private Life of Sherlock Holmes," pp. 146-57; Howard Haycraft, "Murder for Pleasure," pp. 158-77 (B143); Joseph Wood Krutch, "'Only a Detective Story,'" pp. 178-188(C464);S. S. Van Dine, "Twenty Rules for Writing Detective Stories," pp. 189-93 (C827); Ronald A. Knox, "Detective Story Decalogue," pp. 194-97 (C458); "The Detection Club Oath," pp. 197-202 (C224); E. S. Gardner, "The Case of the Early Beginning," pp. 203-207 (C298); Dorothy L. Sayers, "Gaudy Night," pp. 208-21 (E2560); Raymond Chandler, "The Simple Art of Murder," pp. 222-37 (C168); Craig Rice, "Murder Makes Merry," pp. 238-44 (C690); Anthony Boucher, "Trojan Horse Opera," pp. 245-49 (C120); James Sandoe, "Dagger of the Mind," pp. 250-63 (C715); Marie F. Rodell, "Clues," pp. 264-72 (B344); John Dickson Carr, "The Locked-Room Lecture," pp. 273-86 (C160); Lee Wright, "Command Performance," pp. 287-91 (C876); Isabelle Taylor, "Mystery Midwife: The Crime Editor's Job," pp. 292-97 (C809); Richard Mealand, "Hollywoodunit," pp. 298-303; Ken Crossen, "There's Murder in the Air," pp. 304-310; Rex Stout, "Watson Was a Woman," pp. 311-18 (Sherlockiana); Ogden Nash, "Don't Guess, Let me tell you (poem)," pp. 319-20; Christopher Ward, "The Pink Murder Case (S.S.Van Dine parody)," pp. 321-26; Stephen Leacock, "Murder at $2.50 a Crime (humorous essay)," pp. 327-37; Richard Armour, "Everything under Control (poem)," p. 338; Ben Hecht, "The Whistling Corpse (parody)," pp. 339-43; Robert J. Casey, "Oh, England! Full of Sin (humor)," pp. 343-51; E. V. Lucas, "Murders and Motives (humor)," pp. 352-54; Pierre Véry, "Murder on Parnassus (humor)," pp. 355-62 (C830); Isaac Anderson, "The Life of Riley," pp. 363-66 (C22); 'Judge Lynch', "Battle of the Sexes: The Judge and His Wife Look at Mysteries," pp. 367-72 (C435); Will Cuppy, "How to Read a Whodunit," pp. 373-76 (C208); "Four Mystery Reviews," pp. 377-83 (contemporary reviews of The Moonstone, The Sign of Four, and Trent's Last Case by anonymous reviewers and of Van Dine's The Benson Murder Case by Dashiell Hammett); Anthony Boucher, "The Ethics of the Mystery Novel," pp. 384-89 (C115); Edmund Wilson, "Who Cares Who Killed Roger Ackroyd?," pp. 390-98 (C867); Nicholas Blake, "The Detective Story--

Why?," pp. 398-405 (C97); Ellery Queen, "Leaves from the Editors' Notebook," pp. 406-16 (C661); Dashiell Hammett,"From the Memoirs of a Private Detective," pp. 417-22 (E1378); R. Philmore, "Inquest on Detective Stories," pp. 423-35 (C632); J. B. Waite, "The Lawyer Looks at Detective Fiction," pp. 436-46 (C835); F. Sherwood Taylor, "The Crux of a Murder: Disposal of the Body," pp. 447-52 (C808); John Carter, "Collecting Detective Fiction," pp. 453-75 (C161); Ellery Queen, "The Detective Short Story:The First Hundred Years," pp. 476-91 (C659); James Sandoe, "Readers' Guide to Crime," pp. 492-510 (an annotated list of recommendations, with an introduction by Haycraft); "The Passing of the Detective in Literature," pp. 511-12 (C615); Harrison R. Steeves, "A Sober Word on the Detective Story," pp. 513-26 (problems faced by the modern writer of detective fiction); Philip Van Doren Stern, "The Case of the Corpse in the Blind Alley," pp. 527-35 (advice to writers); Howard Haycraft, "The Whodunit in World War II and After," pp. 536-42 (C376). Breen 69. CC 2955.

B143. Haycraft, Howard. Murder for Pleasure: The Life and Times of the Detective Story. NY: Appleton-Century, 1941; newly enlarged edition, NY: Biblo & Tannen, 1968. xviii, 409pp. Illustrations. Index. (Japanese edition: Tantei Shosetsu: Seicho to Jidai. Translated by Shun'ichiro Hayashi. Tokyo: Togen-sha, 1961.)

A comprehehensive history of the "pure" detective story, covering both British and American practitioners. A treasure-house of information and informed critical opinion. The "Newly Enlarged Edition" contains, in 14 unnumbered pages preceding page 1, a reprint of Haycraft's "Notes on Additions to a Cornerstone Library" and "The Haycraft-Queen Definitive Library of Detective-Crime-Mystery Fiction" reprinted from EQMM Oct 1951. The illustrations contain photographs of fifty famous writers of mystery fiction. Breen 1. CC 2957. (REB)

B144. Hays, Rhys W. Selected Writings of Rhys W. Hays. Edited by Justus F. Paul. Privately printed by the Department of History, the University of Wisconsin-Stevens Point, and the Honorable Judge Paul R. Hays, (1977). 213pp.

This memorial volume collects the major essays of historian and detective story buff Rhys W. Hays (d. 1976). Pages 155-210 contain eleven articles reprinted from The Armchair Detective. A bibliography of Hays' writings is included (pp. 211-213). The reprinted articles are as follows: "Joseph Harrington's First Three Books," pp. 155-60 (E1444); "The Private Life of Father Brown," pp. 161-72 (E487); "Chess in the Detective Story," pp. 173-82 (E380); "A Note on Medieval Detection," pp. 183-85 (C384); "A Note from Francis Parkman," p. 186 (C383); "The Clue of the Dying Message," pp. 187-92 (C381); "A Note about Lewis Carroll," pp. 193-94; "Addenda to 'Chess in the Detective Story'," pp. 195-97 (C380)); "Religion and the Detective Story," pp. 198-203 (C385); "More 'Shades of Dupin!'," pp. 204-207 (C382); "A Lesser Chesterton Detective: Mr. Pond," pp. 208-210 (E486).

B145. Hazama, Yotaro. Mystery Hakubutsukan |Mystery museum|. Tokyo: Misaki Shobo, 1971. Revised edition: Mystery Hyakka Jiten |Mystery encyclopedia|. Tokyo: Shakai Shiso-sha, 1981. Illus. Index.

A collection of miscellaneous essays on various entries such as parts of the human body, animals and plants, snow, ice, timepiece, and telphone, and commentaries with quotations from mystery stories. (HS/TT)

B146. Heggelund, Kjell, and Nordberg, Nils, editors. Kriminallitteraturen |Crime literature|. Oslo: Gylendal, 1978. 218pp.
11 essays on subjects ranging from Julian Symons, G. K. Chesterton and Bertold Brecht to Raymond Chandler. With checklists of the authors discussed. (IH)

B147. Heibon-sha, ed. Meisaku Sashie Zenshu, Vol. 8: Showa Senzen Suiri/Kaiki Shosetsu Hen |Masterpiece illustration collection. Vol. 8: pre-war mystery/horror fiction|. Tokyo: Heibon-sha, 1980. 145pp. Illus.
One of the volumes in a series which deals with illustrations for Japanese popular fiction, compiled chronologically, by genre. This volume contains works by major illustrators of Japanese mystery fiction, 1926-41. (HS/TT)

B148. Hennemann, Horst Siegfried. "Der Japanische Kriminalroman: Eine Literarhistorische Darstellung der Gattung |The Japanese crime novel: a literary-historical description of the genre|." Doctoral dissertation. Ruhr-Universität Bochum (West Germany), 1973. 264pp.
Hennemann's dissertation is intended as a continuation of Nihon Suiri Shosetsu-shi (1964) |History of Japanese detective fiction| by Nakajima Kawataro. Hennemann, who spent two years at the Waseda University in Japan, mentions that critical activity in the field of Japanese crime fiction began with the journal Shin Seinen |New youth| in 1920. Der Japanische Kriminalroman is probably the only book-length study of the subject in a Western language. (GG)

B149. Herman, Linda and Beth Stiel. Corpus Delicti of Mystery Fiction: A Guide to the Body of the Case. Metuchen, N.J.: Scarecrow Press, 1974. viii, 180pp.
Oversimplified and misleading attempt at a guide for librarians and collectors: definitions of categories are not well thought out and are inconsistently applied, and the reliance on secondary sources rather than direct knowledge limits the usefulness of the work. Breen 17. (REB)

B150. Highsmith, Patricia. Plotting and Writing Suspense Fiction. Boston: The Writer, Inc., 1946. 149pp. Reprinted, with new introduction, 1972. viii, 149pp.
The author says, "This is not a how-to-do-it handbook." It is, instead, a volume of straightforward advice that all writers and prospective writers should find interesting and useful. Highsmith discusses the use of personal experience, the problems of plotting, pacing, and revision. A detailed case history of her novel The Glass Cell is used as illustration. (REB)

B151. Hikage, Jokichi. Meitantei Who's Who |Great detective who's who|. Tokyo: Asahi Shinbun-sha, 1977. 254pp. Illus.
A collection of essays introducing 50 overseas (non-Japanese) "print" detectives with a major case for each. In order to make it comprehensive, Hikage includes a long essay on the history of non-Japanese "print" detectives by Kunihiko Sugano, editor of Hayakawa's Mystery Magazine. Mistakes can be found here and there because the author did not check his data, but this is one of the best examples of this kind of writing. (HS/TT)

B152. _____. Mikaku Genso: Mystery Bungaku to Gastronomy |Taste fantasy: mystery literature and gastronomy|. Tokyo: Bokushin-sha, 1974. Revised edition: Mystery Shokujigaku |Mystery gastronomy|. Tokyo: Shakai Shiso-sha, 1981. Illus.
The author is a mystery writer, translator and French cuisine critic. This

is a collection of desultory essays on cuisine and mystery fiction, and it is to be regretted that these two subjects do not mix completely. (HS/TT)

B153. Hirabayashi, Hatsunosuke. Hirabayashi Hatsunosuke Ikoshu |Collected posthumous essays by Hatsunosuke Hirabayashi|. Tokyo: Heibon-sha, 1932. 741pp.
The author is famous in the field of socialist literary criticism. He treats mystery fiction with the same serious attitude, and his incisive arguments led the Japanese mystery field in the early years. Though this book has only a few essays relating to mystery fiction, it should be regarded as valuable. (HS/TT)

B154. Hoch, Edward D. ed. Best Detective Stories of the Year. NY: E. P. Dutton, 1976-81; The Year's Best Mystery and Suspense Stories. NY: Walker & Co, 1982- .
An annual collection. Continues the Boucher and Hubin (B44, B160) tradition of story annotations and "Yearbook of the Detective Story," and adds capsule biographies of authors whose stories are included in the collection. (REB)

B155. Hogarth, Basil. Writing Thrillers for Profit: A Practical Guide. The Writers' and Artists' Library VI. London: A. & C. Black, Ltd., 1936. Pp. v-xii, 13-158.
A manual of interest because of the comments sollicited by Hogarth from a number of writers about their craft and included in the text. After a general survey in which the operative definition is of "detective thrillers," there are chapters on plot, the fair-play element, characterization, structure and other topics. Most of the writers cited are British and should provide insights into the pre-W. W. II mystery field. Breen 90.

B156. Hoveyda, Fereydoun. Histoire du roman policier |History of the detective novel|. Paris: Editions du Pavillon, 1965. 262pp. Japanese edition--Suiri Shosetsu no Rekishi wa Archimedes ni Hajimaru--translated by Hidehiko Miwa. Tokyo: Sogen-sha, 1981. Sp. trans.: Madrid: Alianza Editorial, 1967. Collection: El libro de Bolsillo, 69.
The author has returned to and developed his "little history" of 1956, replacing his third part by a chapter covering authors from Lemmy Caution to James Bond and adding a series of short chapters on the "physiology" of the lover of detective novels. A somewhat unusual work whose liveliness and passion impell approval (in spite of numerous errors!). (JB)

B157. ______. Petite Histoire du roman policier |Little history of the detective novel|. Preface by Jean Cocteau. Paris: Editions du Pavillon, 1956. 92pp. Japanese edition--Suiri Shosetsu no Rekishi--translated by Takehiko Fukunaga. Tokyo: Sogen-sha, 1960.
A brief essay whose author says that it could have been called "A Lover of Detective Novels Broods Over His Past." A rapid overview but one in which the author often demonstrates critical acuity. (JB)

B158. Hsun, Lu. A Brief History of Chinese Fiction. Peking: Foreign Languages Press, 1959.
Contains a short chapter on novels of adventure and detection from the Ching dynasty. Not seen. (REB)

B159. Hubin, Allen J. ed. The Armchair Detective, Volume One. Madison, IN: Brownstone Books, 1981. viii, 158pp. Illus.
Facsimile reprint of the first four issues of TAD, Allen J. Hubin's journal for mystery fiction enthusiasts, with a new introduction by Hubin and a quality cloth binding. Included in these four issues are "The Hardboiled Dick: A Personal Checklist," by James Sandoe (A148), "Dramatizations of the Great Literary Detectives and Criminals" (3 installments) by Charles Shibuk and Marvin Lachman, "Henry Wade" by Charles Shibuk (E3009), articles by William S. Baring-Gould, Norman Donaldson, J. R. Christopher, Francis M. Nevins, Jr., Nigel Morland, and others, plus the always fascinating and informative letter column. Surprisingly little of the material has become dated, and it remains as entertaining as it was in 1967-68. (REB)

B160. ______. Best Detective Stories of the Year. NY: 24th Annual Collection (1970) through 29th Annual Collection (1975).
Each volume contains the editor's Introduction, notes on the individual stories, and a "Yearbook of the Detective Story" (bibliography, awards, necrology, and honor roll). See also B44 and B160. (REB)

B161. Huegel, Hans-Otto. Untersuchungsrichter-Diebesfaneger-Detective. Theorie und Geschichte der Deutschen Detektiverzaehlung im 19. Jahrhundert |Investigating judges-thief takers-detectives: theory and history of the German detective story in the 19th century|. Stuttgart: Metzler, 1978. xi, 359pp. Bibliographies of primary and secondary sources. Index.
Published version of Huegel's 1977 doctoral dissertation at Mainz University. Part I examines the essential aspects of German crime fiction and distinguishes among true crime literature, crime stories, and detective stories proper. Part II examines the history of German crime fiction. Huegel cites German and English-language critical literature throughout which asserts that Germany has no detective fiction tradition because of its "anti-democratic" culture, and that what German detective fiction exists is derivative from that of other cultures. His book is an authoritative argument to the contrary and Huegel is generally recognized as the first to push back the German tradition so far. (GG)

B162. Hughes, Catherine. "The Detective Form: A Study of Its Sources and Meaning in Late Nineteenth-Century Popular Fiction and Works of James and Conrad." Unpublished doctoral dissertation. Brandeis University, 1981. 550pp. Dissertation Abstracts 42/09A, pp. 4006-7. Not seen.

B163. Hughes, Winifred. The Maniac in the Cellar: Sensation Novels of the 1860s. Princeton Univ. Press, 1980. 2llpp.
A detailed discussion of the sensation novelists of the 1860s: Mary Elizabeth Braddon, Wilkie Collins and others. Review-essay: Nineteenth Century Fiction 36 (1981-82):221-25.

B164. Hull, Helen. The Writer's Book. NY: Harper & Brothers, 1950. 355pp.
40 pieces on various aspects of writing, including "The Mystery Novel" by Rex Stout (pp. 62-67), "The Craft of Crime" by Richard Lockridge (pp. 55-61), and "The Pulp Story" by Myron Orr (pp. 156-62). (REB)

B164a. Hull, Helen, and Drury, Michael, eds. Writer's Roundtable. NY: Harper & Brothers, 1959. 201pp.
An anthology of 21 pieces on the craft of writing, including the

following: Daphne duMaurier, "How Will It All End?," pp. 28-34; Rex Stout, "Cinderella Paperback," pp. 112-119.

B165. Ikushima, Jiro. Hardboiled Fu Ni Ikite Minai Ka?: Otoko no Kodo Genri |Don't you live in a hardboiled way?: men's principles of action|. Tokyo: K.K. Bestsellers, 1979. 234pp.

The author is a writer of hardboiled mysteries and former editor of the Japanese edition of EQMM. Introducing dialogues and actions of characters in non-Japanese hardboiled fiction, this book is a philosophy lecture on life for young people and, at the same time, an expression of Ikushima's own views on mystery fiction. The author has also written two collections of dialogues and a chronicle of friendships with other writers, Kon'na No Sunpo, Otoko No Sunpo |Women's measure, men's measure, 1981|. (HS/TT)

B166. Ikushima, Jiro, ed. Nemureru Ishiki O Sogeki Seyo |Snipe at your sleeping senses|. Tokyo: Futaba-sha, 1974. 260pp. Illus.

B166a. ______. Hangyaku no Kokoro O Torimodose |Recover your rebellious spirit|. Tokyo: Futaba-sha, 1974. 293pp. Illus.

These two books are compilations of Ikushima's dialogues with 14 mystery writers and fans, serialized as "Jiro Ikushima's Leading Questions." As his guests are mainly his close friends, the dialogues are pleasantly atmospheric and tend to digress. (HS/TT)

B167. In'naa Torippu-sha, ed. Hoseki Suiri Shosetsu Kessakusen |Best of Hoseki mystery stories|. 3 vols. Tokyo: In'naa Torippu-sha, 1974. 575pp. 574pp. 581pp. Illus.

These collections of best mystery stories are selected from Hoseki, the major Japanese mystery magazine. The three volumes contain not only 74 stories, but also 23 essays, critical articles and panel discussions. The third volume has a list of contents of all the issues of the magazine, compiled by Kawataro Nakajima. (HS/TT)

B168. Ishikawa, Takashi. Gokuraku no Oni: My Mystery Saiten-Yo |Devil in heaven: my mystery judge paper|. Tokyo: Kodan-sha, 1981. 258pp. Illus. Index.

A collection of reviews of overseas mysteries serialized in EQMM (Japanese edition) in 1964-65. Another book with the same title was published in 1966, with part of the sequel volume, Jigoku no Hotoke |Saint in Hell, 1966-69|. This 1981 edition is the first to combine both Gokuraku no Oni and its sequel. (HS/TT)

B169. ______. SF, Mystery Omoro Daihyakka |Great encyclopedia of sf & mystery|. Tokyo: Hayakawa Shobo, 1977. 357pp. Illus. Bibliography. Revised edition: Yume Tantei |Dream detective|. Tokyo: Kodansha, 1982.

The author is a critic of SF, mysteries and horse racing. This book is a collection of SF/mystery reviews serialized in a magazine for young people. The selection of subjects aims chiefly at entertaining readers, but Ishikawa's background knowledge is accurate. (HS/TT)

B170. Ishikawa, Takashi, and Yamaguchi, Masaya, eds. Ellery Queen to sono Rival-tachi |Ellery Queen and his rivals|. 1979. ix, 250pp. Meitantei series (B254).

A discussion of six detectives: Ellery Queen, Drury Lane, Philo Vance, Dr. Gideon Fell, Sir Henry Merrivale and Nero Wolfe. (HS/TT)

B171. Janus 4 (1981)
A special issue of this magazine--published in Kristianstad, Sweden--on Swedish mystery fiction. (IH)

B172. Jensen, Mogens. Laç25/stips I Urval |Tips to the readers|. Lund: Bibliotekstjänst, 1981. 6pp.
A short reader's guide to thriller/adventure books. (IH)

B173. Jinga, Katuso. Kaigai Mystery Nyumon |An introduction to the overseas mystery|. Tokyo: Asahi Sonorama, 1976. 271pp. Illus.
An analysis of the history of mystery fiction, definitions of and comments on sub-genres, gimmicks, relationships with visual media, all presented clearly and plainly. (HS/TT)

B174. Johansson, Hans Olof. Utgivningen av Populärpocketböcker 1965-1974 |The publishing of popular pocketbooks 1965-1974|. Uppsala: Avd for litteratursociologi, 1977. (IH)

B175. Kagami, Saburo. Akai Nishin no Iru Umi: Gendai Suiri Shosetsu Nyumon |Sea with red herrings: an introduction to modern mystery fiction|. Tokyo: Yomiuri Shinbunsha, 1977. 270pp.
While his previous book Mystery Sanpo (B176) is for beginners, this is for fairly advanced readers familiar with the field. Kagami explains how post-war mystery fiction in England and the United States has broken away from the puzzle-novel, discusses several sub-genres and cites titles. (HS/TT)

B176. ______. Mystery Sanpo |Mystery walk|. Tokyo: Bunsen, 1973. 286pp.
The author is a former editor of Hayakawa's Mystery Magazine. This book is an introductory handbook compiled mainly from essays which first appeared in the magazine. There are some original views but, as a whole, it is not penetrating or satisfying. (HS/TT)

B177. ______. Suiri Shosetsu no Seiri-gaku (Gaikokuhen): Zokuzoku Suru Sekai no Meisaku, Kessaku Sagashi |Filing of mystery fiction (overseas): search for thrilling masterpieces of the world|. Tokyo: Kanki Shuppan, 1977. 203pp. Illus.
While his two previous books are desultory collections of previously published essays, this is an introductory book, clearly produced with the intention of recommending books for beginners. (HS/TT)

B178. Kagami, Saburo, ed. Hard-boiled no Tantei-tachi |The hard-boiled detectives|. Meitantei series (B254). 1979. x, 269pp.
This book on private detectives features Sam Spade, Philip Marlowe and Lew Archer. (HS/TT)

B179. Keating, H.R.F., editor. Crime Writers. London: BBC, 1978. 160pp. Index. Illus.
Using the format of a BBC television series in which writers talk about writers and methods of crime fiction, Keating has encouraged contributors to expand on the material of the TV programs, to "lay down more facts" and to treat the writers they discuss in a "wider and more subtle manner." Mike Pavett has supplied an introduction in which he surveys the rise of the detective in 19th century England and linking material between chapters which provides an historical context for the essays. There are also quotes from various writers and specialists who

have been interviewed on the series, and suggestions for further reading. Contents: Reginald Hill, "Holmes: The Hamlet of Crime Fiction," 20-41; Colin Watson, "Mayhem Parva and Wicked Belgravia," 48-63 (sociology of crime fiction); P.D. James, "Dorothy L. Sayers: From Puzzle to Novel," 64-75 (E2535); Julian Symons, "Dashiell Hammett: The Onlie Begetter," 80-93 (E1424); Maurice Richardson, "Simenon and Highsmith: Into the Criminal's Head," 100-117 (E2673); Troy Kennedy Martin, "Four of a Kind?," 122-133 (TV crime series); H.R.F. Keating, "New Patents Pending," 138-155 (speculations on the future of crime fiction). Breen 101.

B180. ______. Murder Must Appetize. London: Lemon Tree Press, 1975; NY and London: The Mysterious Press and Lemon Tree Press, 1981. 63pp. Illus.

Reminiscences and commentary, mostly on "Golden Age" British mystery writers. Breen 48. (REB)

B181. ______ Whodunit? A Guide to Crime, Suspense & Crime Fiction. NY: Van Nostrand Reinhold Co, 1982. 320pp. Illus. Index.

An immensely enjoyable compendium of short articles on crime fiction, statements by ten writers on their own working methods, a 140-page biographical dictionary and consumer's guide to crime fiction, and a portrait gallery of famous characters (mostly detectives, with a few villains mixed in). The only feature that seems not to work as planned is the "consumer's guide," where a small number of works by each author are rated on a scale of 1 to 10 according to characterization, plot, readability, and tension. The rating standards are not consistent or clearly explained, the choice of representative works is sometimes strange, and almost all entries seem to get long strings of stars, so that the system fails to make clear distinctions for the reader. The book concludes with a psychiatrist's attempt to explain why people read crime fiction. The pictorial aspects of the book are superb. The Crime Fiction and Its Categories section is as follows: Reginald Hill, "A Pre-History," pp. 20-25; H. R. F. Keating, "The Godfather and the Father," pp. 26-29; Robert Barnard, "The English Detective Story," pp. 30-36; Julian Symons, "The American Detective Story," pp. 37-42; Hillary Waugh, "the American Police Procedural," pp. 43-46; Michael Gilbert, "The British Police Procedural," pp. 47-50; Eleanor Sullivan, "The Short Story," pp. 51-55; Jessica Mann, "The Suspense Novel," pp. 56-60; Jerry Palmer, "The Thriller," pp. 61-64; Michelle Slung, "The Gothic," pp. 65-69; and John Gardner, "The Espionage Novel," pp. 70-80. The ten writers who supplied statements on "How I Write My Books" are Stanley Ellin (pp. 82-84), P. D. James (pp. 85-86), Desmond Bagley (pp. 87-89), Dorothy Eden (pp. 90-91), Patricia Highsmith (pp. 92-93), Gregory McDonald (pp. 94-96), Lionel Davidson (pp. 97-98), Len Deighton (pp. 99-103), Eric Ambler (pp. 104-106), and H. R. F. Keating (pp. 107-108). (REB)

B181a. Kelly, Alexander, and Wilson, Colin. Jack the Ripper. A Bibliography and Review of the Literature, by Alexander Kelly /with/ An Introduction to the Murders and the Theories, by Colin Wilson. London: Association of Assistant Librarians, S. E. D., 1973. pp. (3), 5-55. Sewn in wraps.

Colin Wilson provides a concise summary of the Ripper murders and a survey of the various theories about the identity of Jack the Ripper. The remainder of this well-organized and interestingly illustrated pamphlet is an annotated bibliography of the written material on the Ripper, including treatments in fiction, drama, music, and films. Minor errors do not detract from its interest or usefulness. (REB)

B182. Kigi, Takataro. Suiri Shosetsu Tokuhon |Mystery fiction reader|. Tokyo: Yomiuri Shinbunsha, 1964. 230pp. Illus.
The author is famous for advocating the argument that mystery fiction is the highest form of art. As this book is a guidebook for general readers, he tries to explain comprehensibly mystery fiction from a universal point of view.' (HS/TT)

B183. Kigi, Takataro, and Arima, Yorichika, eds. Suiri Shosetsu Nyumon |An introduction to mystery fiction|. Tokyo: Kobun-sha, 1960. 212pp.
An anthology of seven critical essay on related subjects such as scientific crime investigation and forensic medicine. A sequel to Rampo and Masumoto's Suiri Shosetsu Saho (B328). (HS/TT)

B184. Kimura, Jiro. Jinmon, Jikyo: 25 Nin no Mystery Writer |Interrogation and confession: 25 mystery writers|. Tokyo: Hayakawa Shobo, 1981. 331pp. Bibliography. Illus.
A collection of interviews with mystery writers and critics, most of whom live in Manhattan. While using the style of private eye fiction, Kimura considerately includes checklists of each writer. (HS/TT)

B185. ______ Kagai Mystery Sakka no Kao |Faces of overseas mystery writers|. Tokyo: Herald Enterprises, 1979. 55pp. Illus. International edition, B187.
The second International Congress of Crime Writers photo book. It includes writers' profiles as an appendix by Nobumitsu Kodaka, with no birth or death dates given. (HS/TT)

B186. ______. New York No Flic(k) o Shitteru kai?: Cinema & Mystery Scrap |Do you know the New York flic(k)?: cinema & mystery scraps|. Tokyo: Kodan-sha, 1981. 266pp. Illus. Index.
The author is a mystery critic and translator who lived for a number of years in New York. "Flic(k)" is a pun: flick as a film and flic as a detective. A collection of serial essays with the then new-on-the-scene information on films and mysteries. (HS/TT)

B187. ______. The Second International Congress of Crime Writers Picture Book, March 14-17, 1978. Osaka, Japan: Kikugoro & Co., April 1979. pp. 3-48. Large 4to, bound in pictorial boards. Edition limited to 800 copies.
A deluxe pictorial record of the events and people of the Congress, including the 33rd annual Edgar Awards dinner of the MWA. There are two articles reprinted from the MWA newsletter The Third Degree: "A Personal Journal" by Robert J. Randisi and "Special Memories of the Congress" by Lucy Freeman. In the pictorial section, pages 8-45, photographs are captioned in both English and Japanese. The complete Program of the Congress is also reproduced. The book concludes with a 3-page article by Kimura in Japanese. (REB)

B188. Kimura, Ki. Taishu Bungaku 16 Ko |16 lectures on popular literature|. Tokyo: Tachibana Shoten, 1933. 415pp.
A collection of essays with a number of references to mystery fiction. The author is a well-known comparatist. (HS/TT)

B189. Knight, Damon. In Search of Wonder: Essays on Modern Science Fiction. Chicago: IL: Advent: Publishers, September 1956. xii, 180pp. Illustrated. Bibliography. Index. Second Edition, Revised and Enlarged: March 1967. xii, 306pp. Illus. Bibliography. Index. Introduction by Anthony Boucher.

In the 1950s, Damon Knight was known for his trenchant, no-holds-barred essays and reviews of current science fiction. This volume, one of the first books of science fiction criticism ever published, collects these pieces from the magazines where they first appeared. Portions of at least three chapters are of interest to students of mystery fiction, since they deal with sf/mystery hybrids: Isaac Asimov's The Caves of Steel in Ch. 8, "Asimov and Empire" (pp. 66-68 in the first edition, pp. 91-93 in the second); Murder in Millenium VI by Curme Gray in Ch. 18, "New Stars" (pp. 121-25; in the second edition, Ch. 20, pp. 182-87); and Frank M. Robinson's The Power in Ch. 22, "What's Next?" (pp. 160-65 in the first edition; Ch. 27, pp. 277-83, in the second). (REB)

B190. Knight, Stephen. Form and Ideology in Crime Fiction. Bloomington, IN: Indiana University Press, 1980. 202pp. Index and bibliographical notes.
The sociology of crime fiction in he work of Poe, Conan Doyle, Christie, Chandler and McBain. Contents: "'...some men come up'--the Detective appears," pp. 8-38 (C454); "'...his rich ideality," pp. 39-66 (E2145); "'a great blue triumphant cloud'--The Adventures of Sherlock Holmes," pp. 67-106; "'...done from within'--Agatha Christie's World," pp. 107-134; "'...a hard-boiled gentleman'--Raymond Chandler's Hero," pp. 135-167; "'...a deceptive coolness'--Ed McBain's Police Novels," pp. 168-193 (E1791). Review: TLS, 9 Jan 81, p. 30.

B191. Kobayashi, Nobuhiko. Jigoku no Dokushoroku |Reading chronicle of Hell| Tokyo: Shuei-sha, 1980. 308pp. Index.
The author is a writer and critic of movies, performing arts and mysteries. His two previous books, Tokyo no Robinson Crusoe |A Robinson Crusoe in Tokyo, 1974| and Tokyo no Don Quixote |A Don Quixote in Tokyo, 1976|, contain numerous references to mystery fiction, while this book is a collection of book reviews, many of them on mystery fiction, appearing in magazines from 1959-63, 1965-69. (HS/TT)

B192. Kodaka, Nobumitsu. My Mystery: Shin Seiyo Suiri Shosetsu Jijo |My mystery: new scenes in western mystery fiction|. Tokyo: Yomiuri Shinbunsha, 1982. xv, 414pp. Illus. Bibliography and index.
A collection of the writer's book reviews and articles which originally appeared in magazines and newspapers, and of essays not previously published in book form. It shows his deep knowledge of the hardboiled school and of American contemporary mystery fiction. (HS/TT)

B193. ______. Papyrus No Fune |Ship of papyrus|. Tokyo: Hayakawa Shobo, 1975. 306pp. Illus.
The author is a mystery critic, reviewer, writer and member of the Mystery Writers of America. A collection of expert studies on overseas mysteries, especially of hardboiled fiction. Though there are insights that one does not normally find in books of this kind, it leans toward the trivial. (HS/TT)

B194. Koontz, Dean R. Writing Popular Fiction. Cincinnati: Writer's Digest Books, 1972. 232pp. Index.
Practical advice for writers, with chapters on suspense fiction, mysteries and the modern gothic-romance. Breen 91.

B195. Kozakai, Fuboku. Hanzai Bungaku Kenkyu |Studies of crime literature|. Tokyo: Shun'yodo, 1926. 333pp.
A unique book which reveals the criminality lurking in Japanese classic

literature. There are comparisons to modern crime literature and some references to Shakespeare and Poe. (HS/TT)

B196. ______. Shumi no Tantei-Dan |Discussion of the detective for pleasure|. Tokyo: Reimei-sha, 1925. 383pp.

A non-technical explanation of scientific criminal investigating and a presentation of mystery stories relating to the two fields. (HS/TT)

B197. Kracauer, Siegfried. Der Detektiv-Roman. Ein philosophischer Traktat |The detective novel: a philosophical treatise|. Frankfurt am Main: Suhrkamp Verlag, 1975. 135pp. First published in Kraucauer's multi-volume Schriften |Writings|, Vol. 1 (Suhrkamp Verlag, 1971), pp. 103-204. Translated into French by Geneviève and Rainer Rochlitz as Le Roman policier (Paris: Petite Bibliothèque Payot, 1981).

The essay bears the date 1925 although the chapter "Die Hotelhalle |The hotel lounge|" bears the date 1922 and was first published in Das Ornament der Masse |The ornamentation of the multitude| (Suhrkamp, 1963), pp. 157 ff. Extremely abstract, fully philosophical treament of the detective novel. Kracauer uses Kantian and Hegelian concepts to argue that the detective novel portrays a process of reality which becomes determinate through Reason. This process is seen in the development of the plot from the lack of clues and facts at the beginning of the story, to the solution of the puzzle at the conclusion. The physical abilities of the detective, such as driving cars, chasing suspects and fighting, are the embodiment of Reason. (GG)

B198. Kuki, Shiro. Suiri Shosetsu Nyumon |An introduction to mystery fiction|. Tokyo: Kin'en-sha, 1979. 293pp. Illus.

For young people who want to write, with the catch phrase "you can produce mystery fiction." However, it is, in fact, a supplement to his previous book Tantei Shosetsu Hayakka (B199)), with a guide to great detectives and to the best non-Japanese works and a lesson on gimmicks, none of which was included in Tantei. (HS/TT)

B199. ______. Tantei Shosetsu Hyakka |The detective story and all that|. Tokyo: Kin'en-sha, 1975. 516pp.

An ambitious book with the claim that "you can understand everything about the detective story with this one book." It serves this purpose to some degree but as the author is a fiction writer rather than a critic the book is filled with quotations, many of them cited incorrectly. (HS/TT)

B200. Kvam, Lorentz N. Om norsk kriminallitteratur |On Norwegian mystery-literature|. Oslo: N. W.Damn & Son, 1942. 19pp.

An essay. (IH)

B201. Lacassin, Francis. Mythologie du roman policier |Mythology of the detective novel|. 2 vols. 10/18 series. Paris: Union générale d'éditions, 1978. Wraps. Vol 1, 320pp. Vol 2, 317pp.

Essays previously published in which a well-known critic of popular culture considers a number of writers of detective fiction from the perspective of their relationship to epic myths and the changes which myths undergo in their historical voyage. There are bibliographies of primary sources for each of the writers Lacassin discusses and filmographies, where appropriate. Contents: Vol. I: "Le Fantastique des villes |The fantastic quality of cities|," pp. 11-18 (domestication of the epic landscape as the urban setting of much crime fiction); "Le Chevalier

Dupin ou les faux mystères de Paris |The knight Dupin or the false mysteries of Paris|," pp. 19-68 (E. A. Poe); "Sherlock Holmes ou le matin des logiciens |Sherlock Holmes or the morning of the logicians|," pp. 69-130; "Arsène Lupin ou du cambriolage comme un service public |Arsène Lupin or burglary as a public service|," pp. 131-60 (E1666); "Father Brown ou à la recherche du ciel perdu |Father Brown or in search of the lost paradise|," pp. 161-270; "Le Loup solitaire ou le 'marché commun' du cambriolage |The Lone Wolf or the "common market" of burglary|," pp. 271-88 (Louis Joseph Vance); "Charlie Chan ou le sage aux sept fleurs |Charlie Chan or the wise man of the seven flowers|," pp. 289-317 (E146). Vol II: "Dashiell Hammett ou la littérature à haute tension |Dashiell Hammett or high tension literature|," pp. 5-40 (E1388); "Pierre Véry ou la police au pays des fées |Pierre Véry or detecting in fairyland|," pp. 41-113 (E2971); "William Irish ou l'oeil qui voit l'intérieur des êtres |William Irish or the eye that sees inside people|," pp. 114-53 (E3121); "Philip Marlowe ou le clair de lune du roman noir |Philip Marlowe or the moonlight of the gothic novel|," pp. 154-215 (E418); "Jean-Louis Bouquet ou l'exploration des âmes en crise |Jean-Louis Bouquet or the exploration of souls in crisis|," pp. 216-42 (E191); "Le Grand Horloger ou le poète, le destin et la mort |The great watchmaker or the poet, destiny and death|," pp. 243-54 (E1067); "Fredric Brown ou Alice de ce côté du miroir |Fredric Brown or Alice on this side of the mirror|," pp. 255-67 (E262); "Boileau-Narcejac ou la province et l'absence (Boileau-Narcejac or the Provinces and Absence)," pp. 268-93 (E170); "Chester Himes ou la fête des fous |Chester Himes or the festival of the madmen|," pp. 294-309 (E1483); General Bibliography, 311-313 (a brief, unannotated bibliography of secondary sources).

B202. ______. Passagers clandestins |Clandestine passengers|. 10/18 series no. 1319. Paris: Union générale d'éditions, 1979. 376pp. Wraps.

A collection of essays in which Lacassin, admitting to a fondness for paradoxes, uncovers hitherto unsuspected aspects of a variety of fictional and real-life characters, personalities and events. The following material is pertinent to the subject of this bibliography: "L'Abbé Faria ou pélérinage au Lourdes de la littérature populaire |The Abbé Faria or the pilgrimage to the Lourdes of popular literature|," pp. 65-97 (E1010); "Robert-Louis Stevenson ou postérité littéraire d'un repas servi pour des fantômes |Robert-Louis Stevenson or literary legacy of a meal served for phantoms|," pp. 163-93 (E2768); "Harry Dickson ou le détective trouvé à Vannes |Harry Dickson or the detective discovered in Vannes|," pp. 336-68 (E2314).

B203. Lacombe, Alain. Le Roman noir americain |The American roman noir|. 10/18 series, no. 918. Paris: Union générale d'éditions, 1975. 188pp.

In spite of numerous errors and rough guesses, a lack of perspective and a failure to take into account the economic and historical conditions of the appearance of the roman noir as well as its evolution, this is a basic treatment of the genre which defines its constituent elements in a series of chapters: "Heros and characters," "The Initiatory Voyage," "The City," "Violence," and "The Woman and Eroticism." (JB)

B204. la Cour, Tage. En gentleman pa Temple Station og andre mystiske herrer |A gentleman in Temple Station and other mysterious gentlemen|. Skjern: Gullanders, 1977. 28pp.

Baroness Orczy, Edgar Wallace, The Viriginian and other authors. (IH)

B205. ______. En merkelig Dame |A curious dame|. Skjern: Gullanders, 1976. 24pp. Illus. Published in an edition of 150 copies.

An essay on Dorothy L. Sayers, Father Brown, Holmes and others. (IH)

B206. ______. Kaleidoskop |Kaleidoscope|. Skjern: Selskabet Bogvennerne, 1975.

A hommage to la Cour on his 60th birthday with articles and essays by la Cour. (IH)

B207. ______. Med hälsningar - fran Ellery Queen och Tage La Cour |With compliments - from Ellery Queen and Tage la Cour|. Stockholm: Bokvännerna, 1968. 60pp. Illus. (IH)

B208. ______. Mord i biblioteket |Murder in the library|. Stockholm: Sällskapet Bokvännerna, 1953. 83pp. Illus.

7 essays on such subjects as Poe and Doyle, Fergus Hume, awards, collecting, representative titles, anthologies and handbooks. (IH)

B209. ______. Studier i rodt |Studies in red|. Copenhagen: Selskabet Bogvennerna, Carit Andersens, 1956. 1500 numbered copies. Revised edition, n.d.

In addition to the 7 essays on mystery fiction in the original edition, the revised edition includes an article on Scandinavian mystery novels and other material. (IH)

B210. la Cour, Tage, and Mogensen, Harald. Kriminallitteratur Kavalkade: kriminal-og detektivhistorien i billeder og tekst. Copenhagen: Lademann Forlagsaktieselskab, 1983. 176pp. Index.

Although the authors, in their introduction, claim that this is not a revised edition of The Murder Book (B211), there is considerable overlap between the two books. The tendency has been to enlarge the emphasis on thrillers and procedurals at the expense of other types of mystery-detection. Stress in the illustrations is now on film stills and frames and many of the author portraits from the earlier volume are missing. Loss of information from The Murder Book is a flaw and this volume cannot be recommended over its earlier incarnation. (EFB)

B211. ______. The Murder Book: An Illustrated History of the Detective Story. Translated from the Danish by Roy Duffell. Foreword by Julian Symons. London: Allen & Unwin, 1971; NY: Herder & Herder, 1971. (Originally published in Danish under the title Mordbogen, Copenhagen: Lademann Forlagsaktieselskab, 1969.) 192pp. Illustrations, bibliography, index.

The text consists of eighty-three brief encyclopedia-style articles on various aspects of mystery fiction. Much information on European material is included, in addition to the major English-language books and authors. Hundreds of drawings and photographs, in both color and black-and-white, form the heart of the book. Breen 102. (REB)

B212. la Cour, Tage; Mogensen, Harald; and Larsen, Else, eds. Dansk og Udenladsk Kriminallitteratur. Hven skrev hvad |Danish and foreign mystery literature. Who wrote what|? Copenhagen, 1975. 350pp. Illus.

A handbook with indexes. (IH)

B213. De Laet, Danny. Les Anarchistes de l'ordre. La Littérature policière en Belgique |Anarchists of order. Detective literature in Belgium|.

Brussels: Editions Recto-verson, 1980.
An excellent panorama of the Belgian detective novel in 4 parts: a study, an anthology of short stories (Duchâteau, Simenon, Steeman, John Flanders, etc....), a dictionary of authors and a list of collections.(JB)

B214. Lafforgue, Jorge; and Jorge B. Rivera, editors. Asesinos de papél |Paper murderers|. Buenos Aires: Calicanto Editorial S. R. L., 1977. 226pp.
An extremely well-edited text on Argentinian and Latin-American detective fiction. The editors have contributed a history of the detective narrative in Argentina (pp. 13-46); include transcriptions of two meetings at which several writers of detective fiction (Borges, Marco Denevi, Augusto Roa Bastos, Jaime Rest, Ricardo Piglia and Ruben Tizziani) respond to questions on a number of topics relating to genre writing (both their own and that of writers in English as well as in Spanish and Portugese); and have compiled an anthology of ten stories originally published from 1903-1975. In an "end-note," the editors give an extensively annotated bibliography of the publishing history of the anthology stories and of the previous publication in journals of the historical narrative and writer discussions. Although there is no general bibliography, there are lengthy notes with detailed references that provide a kind of mini-history of Latin-American criticism of detective fiction. For these discussions, see espcially pp. 14, 16, 17-19, and 26-27.

B215. Lambert, Gavin. The Dangerous Edge. London: Barrie & Jenkins, 1975; NY: Grossman, 1976. xv, 271pp. Bibliography.
Essays on nine "crime-artists." The author emphasizes the psychological underpinnings of the works of these writers, and how their fiction grew out of circumstances in their own lives. Contents: "Prologue," pp. xi-xiii; "Enemy Country: Wilkie Collins," pp. 1-30 (E670); "Final Problems: l. Sir Arthur Conan Doyle/2. G. K. Chesterton (E492)," pp. 31-78; "The Thin Protection: l. John Buchan (E290)/2. Eric Ambler (E47)," pp. 79-131; "The Double Agent: Graham Greene," pp. 132-70 (E1317); "Night Vision: Georges Simenon," pp. 171-209 (E2648); "A Private Eye: Raymond Chandler," pp. 210-35 (E420); "The Benefits of Shock: Alfred Hitchcock," pp. 235-64; "Epilogue," pp. 265-70; "Bibliography," pp. 271-71. Reviews: TLS, 15 Aug 75, p. 912 (Patricia Highsmith); NYTBR, 25 Apr 76, p. 8 (Paul Theroux). Breen 71. (REB)

B216. Landrum, Larry N.; Browne, Pat; and Browne, Ray B., editors. Dimensions of Detective Fiction. Bowling Green, OH:Popular Press, 1976. 290pp.
Contents: Editors, "Introduction," 1-10 (An overview of the genre and a summary introduction to the essays); Jan R. Van Meter, "Sophocles and the Rest of the Boys in the Pulps: Myth and the Detective Novel," pp. 12-21 (C828); Elliot L. Gilbert, "McWatters' Law: The Best Kept Secret of the Secret Service," pp. 22-36 (C318); George Grella, "Murder and Manners: The Formal Detective Novel," pp. 37-57 (C340); Geraldine Pederson-Krag, "Detective Stories and the Primal Scene," pp. 58-63 (C622); Patrick Parrinder, "George Orwell and the Detective Story," pp. 64-67 (C614); William O. Aydelotte, "The Detective Story as a Historical Source," pp. 68-82 (C36); Edward Margolies, "The American Detective Thriller and the Idea of Society," pp. 83-87 (C537); D. F. Rauber, "Sherlock Holmes and Nero Wolfe: The Role of the 'Great Detective' in Intellectual History," pp. 89-96 (E2813); Nancy Y. Hoffman, "Mistresses of Malfeasance," pp. 97-101 (C403); Ronald Ambrosetti, "The World of Eric Ambler: From Detective to Spy," pp. 102-109 (E38); Allen B. Crider, "Race Williams-Private Investigator," pp. 110-113 (E759); Kay Weibel,

"Mickey Spillane as a Fifties Phenomenon," pp. 114-23 (E2749); R. Jeff Banks, "Spillane's Anti-Establishment Heroes," pp. 124-39 (E2732); Darwin T. Turner, "The Rocky Steele Novels of John B. West," pp. 140-48 (E3065); R. Gordon Kelly, "The Precarious World of John D. MacDonald," pp. 149-61 (E1828); Raymond Nelson, "Domestic Harlem: the Detective Fiction of Chester Himes," pp. 162-73 (E1493); Elmer Pry, "Lew Archer's 'Moral Landscape'," pp. 174-81 (E1896); Sam L. Grogg, Jr., "Interview with Ross Macdonald," pp. 182-92; Charles R. Carlisle, "Strangers Within, Enemies without: Alienation in Popular Mafia Fiction," pp. 194-202 (C157); Richard Gid Powers, "J. Edgar Hoover and the Detective Hero," pp. 203-27 (C647); Mick Gidley, "Elements of the Detective Story in William Faulkner's Fiction," pp. 228-46 (E1055); Douglas G.Tallack, "William Faulkner and the Tradition of Tough-Guy Fiction," pp. 247-64 (Hammett, Chandler, Cain and McCoy); Steven R. Carter, "Ishmael Reed's Neo-Hoodoo Detection," pp. 265-74 (E2318); Notes, pp. 275-290. Breen 72.

B217. Larmoth, Jeanine. _Murder on the Menu._ NY: Scribner's, 1972. xv, 268pp. Index.

Entertaining essays on the English mystery novel, with emphasis on the role of food and drink, and enlivened with appropriate essays by Charlotte Turgeon. Breen 49. (REB)

B218. Lasić, Stanko. _Poetika kriminalistic-kog Romana. Pokusaj strukturalne analize._ Zagreg: Liber, 1973. 176pp. With charts, a basic list of 100 novels and a bibliography of secondary sources.

Analytical study of basic structures in detective fiction.

B219. Laura, Ernesto G. _Storia del giallo da Poe a Borges_ |History of detective fiction from Poe to Borges|. Nuova Universale Studium, no. 39. Rome: Edizioni Studium, 1981. 384pp.

A general history with chapters on the detective novel in Italy and in Western Europe, Asia and Latin America. There is no bibliography of secondary sources but the notes include bibliographical references.

B220. Lauritzen, Henry. _Detektivernes Fest_ |The detectives' party|. Aalborg: Scolins, 1966.

9 detectives come to a party on the anniversary of Poe's first Dupin story. A humorous essay. (IH)

B221. ______. _Mesterdetektiver under lup_ |Master-detectives under the magnifying glass|. Silkeborg: Silkeborg, 1970-71. 67pp. Photos and illus.

General essays and then a list of detectives with their authors. (IH)

B222. Lee, Peter Hacksoo. _Korean Literature; Topics and Themes._ The Association for Asian Studies: Monographs and papers, no. 16. Tucson: University of Arizona Press, 1965. x,141pp.

An authoritative guide to Korean literature written by its foremost interpreter in the west. Chapter 8 ("Fiction in Korean," pp. 71-82) gives relatively uncommon information about Korean _kongan_ ("public case") novels and draws comparisons between them and several Magistrate Pao plays and stories. Summarizes the action of the anonymous _Changhwa Hongnyon Chon_ |Tale of Rose Flower and Pink Lotus| with its warrior-detective hero, Chong Tong-u. Mentions other Korean detective novels, such as _Chin Taebang Chon_ |Story of Chin Taebang| and _Pak Munsu Chon_ |Pak Munsu, the royal inspector|. Unfortunately, Lee gives no information about their dates, authors or possible translations. (GG)

B223. Liebman, Arthur, editor. Thirteen Classical Detective Stories, A Critical History of Detective Fiction. NY: R. Rosen Press, 1974. xii, 239pp. Bibl. pp. 226-37.
Anthology with introduction and notes. Liebman has also edited the following anthologies: Classic Crime Stories: The Criminal in Literature (NY: R. Rosen Press, 1975); Ms Mysteries (NY: Washington Square Press, 1976); Quickie Thrillers (NY: Washington Sq. Press, 1975); Tales of Espionage and Intrigue (NY: R. Rosen Press, 1977).

B224. Lindroth, Per. Deckarintriger fran Berlin till Stockholm - S. A. Duse och Paul Rosenhayn |Mystery intrigues from Berlin by S. A. Duse and Paul Rosenhayn|. Uppsala: Avd för litteratursociologi, 1978.
Study of Swedish writer Duse and Danish writer Rosenhayn. (IH)

B225. Lindung, Yngve. Aventyr och kärlek. Om kiosklitteraturen |Adventures and love. On newsstand literature|. Arlöv: Esselte, 1980. 98pp. Index. Illus. Some charts of sales.
The author examines newsstand literature, its producers, its form and contents, its style, readership, etc. (IH)

B226. Lindung, Ynge, et al. Kiosklitteraturen. 6 analyser |Newsstand literature. 6 studies|. Jönköping: Tiden, 1977. 275pp. Bibliography of Secondary Sources.
Lindung is a teacher at a Swedish Library High School. The studies are of such phenomena as Mickey Spillane, hospital novels, Westerns in Swedish, etc. (IH)

B227. Lins, Alvaro. No Mundo do romance policial |The world of the detective novel|. Rio de Janeiro: Ministério da Educaçao e Saûde, Serviço de Documentaçao, 1953. 26pp. Not seen.

B228. Locard, Edmond. Policiers de roman et de laboratoire |Detectives in the novel and in the laboratory|. Paris: Payot, 1924.
The famous criminologist compares fiction and reality. (JB)

B229. Lu, Hsun (Pseud. for Chou, Shu-jen). A Brief History of Chinese Fiction. Translated by Yang Hsien-yi and Gladys Yang. Peking: Foreign Language Press, 1959. 462pp.
Interesting, informative survey of Chinese fiction. Chapter 27 ("Novels of Adventure and Detection in the Ching Dynasty," pp. 355-71) tells about the connection between the Chinese picaresque novel and the detective novel. When the literati tired of reading such "Great Novels" as Dream of the Red Chamber in the 18th and 19th centuries, they turned to the lighter novels. Includes a plot summary of the barely literate and almost ungrammatical Magistrate Pao novel, Three Heroes and Five Gallants, and dates the Pao story "The Ghost in the Black Pot" (which is readily available in English) in the Yuan dynasty (1260-1368). Gives some information on the tangled authorship of several Pao novels and their 19th century imitative "sequels," as well as mentioning novels of other ancient fictional Chinese detectives, such as Lord Liu, Lord Ti (Judge Dee), Lord Shih, and Lord Peng. Interestingly enough, author Lu takes picaresque and detective fiction much more seriously than do other Sinologists writing on the topic. One of the best pieces on the ancient Chinese detective story. (GG)

B230. Lundin, Bo. Salongsbodlarna |The elegant executioners|. Lund: Cavefors, 1971. 203pp.

An excellent study on the values expressed in popular fiction, including mysteries. (IH)

B231. ______. Sparhundarna. Berömda detektiver i närbild |Bloodhounds. famous detectives up close|. Uddevalla: Rabén & Sjögren, 1973. 252pp. Illus. with photos and cartoons.

Portraits of some 50 Swedish, American and English problem solvers. (IH)

B232. ______. The Swedish Crime Story/Svenska deckare. Sundbyberg: Tidscriften Jury. 1981. Both the English and the Swedish versions are published in this volume. Translated from the Swedish by Anna Lena Ringarp, Ralph A. Wilson and Bo Lundin. 127pp. Index of writers and titles.

A concise history of detective fiction in Sweden.

B233. Lundqvist, Ake. Masslitteraturen. Förströelse-Förförelse-fara? |Mass literature. Entertainment-seduction-danger?|. Stockholm: Bonniers, 1977. 174pp.

A pioneering work and the best general study in which popular literature is analyzed. (IH)

B234. Lyles, William H. Putting Dell on the Map. A History of the Dell Paperbacks. Contributions to the Study of Popular Culture, Number 5. Westport, CT & London: Greenwood Press, 1983. xxiv, 178pp. Bibliography. Index. Illustrated.

This is, in the author's words, "a historical treatment of the Dell paperbacks" listed and described in the companion work Dell Paperbacks (A107). It contains a history of the Dell Publishing Company and its association with Western Printing & Lithographing in the production of the Dell paperbacks, together with an analysis of the changing editorial and design aspects of the company's products through the years. Throughout the book there are extensive quotations from letters and interviews with Dell authors on their relations with the company and their reactions to the Dell editions of their books. Contributions from nearly two dozen authors of mysteries are included: Delano Ames, George Harmon Coxe, Frederic Dannay, Mignon G. Eberhart, Leslie Ford, Donald Hamilton, Dorothy B. Hughes, Patricia McGerr, Harold Q. Masur, Lenore Glen Offord, Aaron Marc Stein, Lawrence Treat, and others. The excellent index permits rapid access to all the mystery-related aspects of the book, but the entire book is worth reading for anyone interested in the history of paperbacks. (REB)

B235. Ma, Yau-woon. "The Pao-Kung Tradition in Chinese Popular Literature." Doctoral dissertation. Yale University, 1971. 357pp.

Traces the development of the character of Magistrate Pao and its relation to the historical figure Pao Cheng (999-1062) on which the character is based. Ma states that the literary Pao reaches mythic proportions in the famous collection of stories Lung-T'u Kung-an and is entirely different from the historical Pao. (GG)

B236. MacAndrew, Elizabeth. The Gothic Tradition in Fiction. NY: Columbia Univ. Press, 1980. 289pp.

On p. 171, MacAndre comments that she sees detective fiction as opposed to Gothic fiction in its triumph of reason over brutality. However, in The Gothic Flame (B421) D. Varma makes a substantial argument for the continuity of Gothic and detective fiction based not on an opposition but on parallels and similarities. Review-essay: Nineteenth Century Fiction 36 (1981/82):471-75.

B237. McCleary, G. F. On Detective Fiction and Other Things. London: Hollis & Carter, 1960; Norwood, PA: Norwood Editions, 1974. 161pp.

Mostly other things. Casual, chatty essays of which the following should be noted for their subject, if not their content: "The Popularity of Detective Fiction," pp. 11-18 (C505); "A Victorian Manuscript: The Moonstone," pp. 19-25 (E672); "The Apotheosis of Sherlock Holmes," pp. 26-33; "The Original of Sherlock Holmes," pp. 34-51; "Three Examination Papers: Pickwick, Sherlock Holmes, Jane Austen," pp. 52-65. Breen 73.

B238. MacGowan, Kenneth, ed. Sleuths. Twenty-Three Great Detectives of Fiction and Their Best Stories. NY: Harcourt, Brace & Co., 1931. xv, 595pp.

A classic anthology noteworthy for the "Who's Who" profiles of detectives written, where possible, by the original author. MacGowan, in his introduction, expresses a preference for the short story over the novel of detection. CC 2642.

B239. Madden, David, editor. Tough-Guy Writers of the Thirties. Carbondale, IL: Southern Illinois Univ. Press, 1968. London and Amsterdam: Fefer & Simons, Inc., 1968. v-xxxix, 247pp. Index. Preface by Harry T. Moore.

In his introduction, editor Madden comments on ways the tough-guy novel might be defined and offers a spirited defense of the study of popular fiction on both esthetic and social grounds. He concludes with a short list of further readings in the subject. Contents (partial): Sheldon Norman Grebstein, "The Tough Hemingway and his Hard-Boiled Children," pp. 18-41 (Hammett, Chandler); Philip Durham, "The 'Black Mask' School," pp. 51-79 (D343); Robert I. Edenbaum, "The Poetics of the Private-Eye: The Novels of Dashiell Hammett," pp. 80-103 (E1370); Irving Malin, "Focus on 'The Maltese Falcon': The Metaphysical Falcon," pp. 104-109 (E1397); Joyce Carol Oates, "Man Under Sentence of Death: The Novels of James M. Cain," pp. 110-28 (E327); Thomas Sturak, "Horace McCoy's Objective Lyricism," pp. 137-62 (E1806); E. R. Hagemann, "Focus on 'You Play the Black and the Red Comes Up': 'No Bet'," pp. 163-70 (E1346); Herbert Ruhm, "Raymond Chandler: From Bloomsbury and the Jungle-and Beyond," pp. 171-85 (general biocritical survey); George Grella, "The Gangster Novel: The Urban Pastoral," pp. 186-98 (B340); Carolyn See, "The Hollywood Novel: The American Dream Cheat," p. 199 (C743a); Charles Shapiro, "'Nightmare Alley': Geeks, Cons, Tips, and Marks," pp. 218-24 (William Lindsay Gresham); Charles Alva Hoyt, "The Damned: Good Intentions: The Tough Guy as Hero and Villain," pp. 224-30 (Sherlock Holmes and John D. MacDonald); R. V. Cassill, "'The Killer Inside Me': Fear, Purgation, and the Sophoclean Light," pp. 230-238 (E2869). Breen 74.

B240. Magazine littéraire (Paris). August 1970.

Special issue with supplement on espionage novels, concentrating on James Bond. An article by Francis Lacassin and Juliette Raabe discusses Buchan, Cheyney, Deighton, le Carré, Greene, and others. There is a checklist of "favorite spies." Not seen. (REB)

B241. Mann, Jessica. Deadlier Than the Male. NY: Macmillan, 1981. First publication: London: David & Charles, 1981. Bibliography and index.

The original sub-title of the British edition ("an investigation into feminine crime writing") was a poor one, for Mann's book was woefully incomplete and half-hearted. The American sub-title--"why are respectable English women so good at murder?"--is more appropriate but Mann never satisfactorily answers her own question. Part I is a general essay on the genre. Part II consists of essays on the "big five": Christie, Sayers, Allingham, Tey, and Marsh. Hardly thought-provoking analysis, the essays largely ignore American or less famous English authors. Mann's book is of interest primarily as one mystery-woman tries to come to terms with her field and her most famous predecessors. (KLM)

B242. Margolies, Edward. Which Way Did He Go? The Private Eye in Dashiell Hammett, Raymond Chandler, Chester Himes, and Ross Macdonald. New York & London: Holmes & Meier, 1982. ix-xii, 97pp. Photos. Index. Bibliographies of primary sources and, in his "Sources and Acknowledgements," Margolies discusses relevant secondary material.

In his introduction, Margolies discusses the sources of the private eye tradition and, in his conclusion, its resurgence in the 70s and 80s. The individual essays are serviceable introductions to the writers' lives and works. Margolies has written extensively on black American writers and the essay on Himes will be cited and annotated in the Authors section. Contents: "Introduction," pp. 1-16; "Dashiell Hammett: Success as Failure," pp. 17-31; "Raymond Chandler," pp. 33-52; "Chester Himes's Black Comedy: The Genre is the Message," pp. 53-70 (E1487); "Ross Macdonald: Gentle Tough Guy," pp. 71-84; "Conclusion," pp. 85-87; "Bibliography," pp. 89-90.

B243. Marsch, Edgar. Die Kriminalerzaehlung. Theorie-Geschichte-Analyse |Crime fiction: theory, history and analysis|. Munich: Winkler Verlag, 1972. 295pp. Index, bibliography of primary and secondary sources.

Limits discussion to authors such as Poe, Doyle, Collins and the German E. T. A. Hoffman, who are considered world literary figures as well as crime fiction authors. Marsch sketches a history of the genre, and sees it as composed of three formal narrative elements: the narrative state-of-being before the crime takes place, the crime itself, and the element of detection to which the presence of the detective is not essential. Scholarly and formal. (GG)

B244. Martens, Michel. Underwood:U.S.A. Balade sur les touches du roman noir |Underwood U.S.A. A stroll on the keys of the roman noir|. Paris: Balland, 1980.288pp. With a bibliography and biography of 100 American writers of romans noirs compiled by François Guérif.

The sub-title "Stroll" makes clear the endeavour by Michel Martens, author in collaboration with J. P. Bastid of some admirable detective novels, with respect to the American novel: a subjective and affective approach rather than a scholarly study. Usefully completed by a precise, well-documented dictionary of authors. (JB)

B245. Maruya, Saiichi, ed. Tantei-tachi yo, Spy-tachi yo |Detectives and spies. Tokyo: Shuei-sha, 1981. 259pp.

An anthology of 17 essays (some of them translated from other languages) on mystery and spy fiction, with three tables of masterpieces. (HS/TT)

B246. Maslowski, Igor B. La Douzaine du diable |The devil's dozen|. Collection de la tour pointue. Paris: Editions de la première chance, 1953.

This first anthology--and, as of this date, the only one for the genre--covers the French detective short story, represented by 13 excellent examples (by Simenon, Véry, Steeman, Malet, Jean Bommart, J. Decrest, T. Narcejac, M. B. Endrèbe, Pierre Boileau, and others). There is also an excellent introduction by Maslowsky and a bibliography. (JB)

B247. Matsuda, Michihiro. Trick Monogatari |Trick story|. Tokyo: Chikuma Shobo, 1979. 218pp. Illus.

The author is a critic of card games and magic, and has a deep knowledge of mystery fiction. His other books (Kijutsu no Tanoshimi |Pleasure of magic, 1972|, Trick Senka |Trick lessons, 1982| and Trick Trip, 1982) include many references to mystery fiction. This book is a collection of essays serialized in a mystery magazine, dealing with the relationship of magic, gambling and puzzle gimmicks, and of mystery fiction. There is an attempt at a re-evaluation of John Dickson Carr in Chapter 4. (HS/TT)

B248. Matsumoto, Tai. Gendai Eikoku Taishu Bungaku |Modern English popular literature|. Tokyo: Eigo Eibungaku Kanko-kai, 1934. 35pp. One of the booklets in the "English Language and Literature Lecture" series.

Despite its title, this only deals with mystery fiction and comments on J. S. Fletcher, William Le Queux, E. Phillips Oppenheim, G. K. Chesterton, Edgar Wallace, Baroness Orczy, Agatha Christie and others. (HS/TT)

B249. _____. Robe to Kokage |By the fireside and under the tree|. Tokyo: Okakura Shobo, 1935. 247pp.

Thirty-seven essays, several of which deal with mystery fiction. (HS/TT)

B250. _____. Tantei Shosetsu-Tsu |Detective fiction connoisseur|. Tokyo: Shiroku Shoin, 1930. 165pp. Illus. Bibliography.

A tactful survey book for general readers. In the sections dealing with the history of mystery fiction and its writers, he includes unfamiliar German and Scandinavian writers. (HS/TT)

B251. Medeiros e Albuquerque, Paulo de. O Mundo Emocionante do Romance Policier |The exciting world of the detective novel|. Rio de Janeiro: Livraria Francisco Alves Editora S.A., 1977. xxii, 508pp. Illus.

Excellent survey of detective fiction from Voltaire, Vidocq and Poe to the present day. Concentrates on English- and French-language material but includes a chapter on Brazilian detective fiction and another chapter surveying the genre in other countries. Over half of the book consists of a series of bibliographical and biographical appendices. The author is thoroughly familiar with the critical literature in English and French, and synthesizes this material with his own opinions. The book is illustrated with many (small) film stills and reproductions of book covers. (REB)

B252. _____. Os Maiores Detetives de Todos os Tempos: O herói na evoluçao da estória policial. Ensaio |The best detectives of all time. The hero: evolution of the detective novel. Essay|. Rio de Janeiro: Editora civilizaçao Brasileira S.A., 1973. 191pp. With a selective bibliography of authors and titles.

A descriptive history with short chapters on major fictional detectives. No notes, no index, no sources for critical references. A superficial overview with little critical substance, although the two chapters on Portuguese and Brazilian writers are of some interest for their discussion of writers unfamiliar to English-speaking audiences.

B253. Meet the Detective. Introduction by Cecil Madden. London: Allen and Unwin, 1935. 142pp. New York: The Telegraph Press, 1935. 158pp.

Fictional detectives presented in informal portraits by their creators. Transcribed from an English radio series. N.B.: All page references are to the American edition. Meet: "Bull-Dog Drummond," pp. 13-19 ("Sapper"); "Hanaud," pp. 20-35 (A. E. W. Mason); "Dr. Fu Manchu," pp. 36-41 (Sax Rohmer); "Gun Cotton," pp. 42-50 (Rupert Grayson); "The Saint," pp. 51-60 (Leslie Charteris); "Tiger Standish," pp. 61-70 (Sydney Horler); "Professor Wells," pp. 71-79 (Francis D. Grierson); "Chief-Inspector French," pp. 80-89 (Freeman Wills Crofts); "Mr. Fortune," pp. 90-97 (H. C. Bailey); "Trent," pp. 98-105 (E. C. Bentley); "Phineas Spinnet," pp. 106-115 (Andrew Soutar); "Superintendent Wilson," pp. 116-128 (G.D.H. and M. Cole); "Dr.Thorndyke," pp. 129-138 (R. Austin Freeman); "Dr. Eustace Hailey," pp. 139-147 (Anthony Wynne); "The Scarlet Pimpernel," pp. 148-158 (Baroness Orczy). Breen 75.

B254. Meitantei Tokuhon |The great detective reader|. 8 volumes. Tokyo: Pacifica, 1978-79. Illus.

This critical series focuses on series detectives popular in Japan. Each volume has essays by Japanese and non-Japanese writers, checklists, and much visual material (illustrations, movie stills, and photographs). Characters are introduced and their appeal is analyzed. Volume I is devoted to Sherlock Holmes. The remaining volumes in the series are: 2. Nagashima, Ryozo, editor. Maigret Keishi |Inspector Maigret|; 3. Yano, Kozaburo, and Yasuo Sudo, editors. Poirot to Miss Marple |Poirot and Miss Marple|; 4. Ishikawa, Takashi, and Masaya Yamaguchi, editors. Ellery Queen to Sono Rival-tachi |Ellery Queen and his rivals| (B170); 5. Nakajima, Kawataro and Hiroshi Oshikawa, editors. Sherlock Holmes no Rival-tachi |The rivals of Sherlock Holmes|. 6. Kagami, Saburo, editor. Hard-Boiled no Tantei-tachi |The hard-boiled detectives|; 7. Sakakibara, Kozo, editor. Kaito Lupin |Arsene Lupin, the thief|; 8. Nakajima, Kawataro, editor. Kindaichi Kosuke |Kosuke Kindaichi|. (HS/TT)

B255. Melling, John Kennedy. Murder Done to Death: A Survey of Pastiche and Parody of the Detective Story. 8pp. 1979. Privately published (by the author); place not listed. Edition limited to 500 copies.

Not seen but cited by Richard H. Fawcett in August Derleth Society Newsletter 6:1 (Nov 82):8. (REB)

B256. Merry, Bruce. Anatomy of the Spy Thriller. Dublin: Gill and Macmillan, 1977. 253pp. Index.

The author draws on a broad sample of 20th century espionage narratives in his analysis. He describes the ground rules and the recurring structural patterns of the spy thriller. The subject matter moves from Conrad's The Secret Agent to Goldberg's The Karamazov Equation, from Buchan to Forsyth and Ludlum. Intended as a work of serious scholarship and literary research, the book is in some places forbidding; in others, pretentious. But there is much plain good sense and entertaining commentary within the academic framework. Breen 51. (REB)

B257. Messac, Régis. Le "Detective Novel" et l'influence de la pensée scientifique |The detective novel and the influence of scientific thought|. Paris: Librairie ancienne Honoré Champion, 1929. Reprint: Bibliothèque de la revue de littérature comparée no. 59. Geneve: Slatkine Reprints, 1975. 698pp. Index. Bibliography of Secondary Sources.

In this basic work, the first in France devoted to the detective novel, Régis Messac wrote a study of the "prehistory" of the genre and of its emergence in the second half of the 19th century. In a vast survey which covers the literature of the mystery and the riddle from antiquity to the period of Nick Carter and Sherlock Holmes, the author examines its roots, analyzing all the literary forms from the most scholarly to the most popular, from the litterature of colportage and the serial paper to Dickens, Poe and Balzac, in which the genre is still imperfectly drawn, studying all the metamorphoses it will undergo to reach one day its flowering. A study which is still, for its erudition and the delicacy of its critical approach, unequaled. CC 2981. (JB)

B258. Mira, Juan Jose. Biografia de la novela policiaca (Historia y crítica). Barcelona: Editorial AHR, 1955 (copyright 1956). 254pp. Not seen.

B259. Moebius, Hans. The Gothic Romance. Leipzig, 1902. Reprinted: Garland Press, 1979.

Moebius' monograph was probably the pioneer study of the Gothic novel, and all later examinations have been indebted to his work. Starting with the Gothic episodes in Smollett's Ferdinand Count Fathom, Moebius provides very detailed analyses of the most important books in the form: Walpole's Castle of Otranto, Reeve's Old English Baron, and the novels of Ann Radcliffe. (EFB)

B260. Mooney, Joan M. "Best-Selling American Detective Fiction." TAD 3 (1969/70):98-114, 141-160, 215-239; 4 (1970/71):12-29, 87-103. Bibliography. Publication of a doctoral dissertation presented at the University of Minnesota (1968).

The publication of this dissertation provoked some of the most extensive letter commentary in TAD's history. Some readers objected to TAD's printing this "academic" study but many readers recognized the contribution of Mooney's research and wrote in with constructive comments, correcting details where appropriate. Corrections appeared as follows: 3 (1969/70):204, 207; 4 (1970/71):71-72, 129; 5 (1971/72):44-45. The author responded to the letters, discussing questions raised by readers and justifying some of her comments and choice of authors in TAD 4 (1970/71):246-51.

B261. Mogensen, Harald. Berømte detektiver fra Sherlock Holmes til Kojak |Famous detectives from Sherlock Holmes to Kojak|. Albertslund: Rosenberg, 1980. Illustrated. Index.

By one of Scandinavia's leading critics. (IH)

B262. ______. Blood in Their Ink. Vojens: P. J. Schmidt, 1981. 64pp. Illus. Index of English words in text.

A book used in Danish schools consisting of a historical survey with an author and genre analysis. (IH)

B263. Morland, Nigel. How to Write Detective Novels. Practical Handbook Series no. 32. London: Allen & Unwin, 1936. 74pp. Bibliography. Not seen. Breen 92.

B264. Most, Glenn W., and Stowe, William W., eds. The Poetics of Murder. Detective Fiction & Literary Theory. NY: Harcourt Brace Jovanovich, 1983. xv, 394pp. Index and suggestions for further reading.

A collection of what the editors see as the most "important studies of detective fiction" published in the last 40 years. This does not take into acount the material published in Nevins' The Mystery Writer's Art (B290), none of which is duplicated here. The essays reflect a wide range of critical methodology and include several essays by European critics. This collection is also interesting as a demonstration of some of the directions criticism of detective fiction has taken in the last decades. Most of the selections have been published previously. Contents: Roger Caillois, "The Detective Novel as Game," pp. 2-12 (C145); Geraldine Pederson-Krag, "Detective Stories and the Primal Scene," pp. 14-20 (C622); Jacques Lacan, "Seminar on 'The Purloined Letter'," pp. 21-54 (E2146); Ernst Kaemmel, "Literature under the Table: The Detective Novel and its Social Mission," pp. 55-61 (C439); Richard Alewyn, "The Origin of the Detective Novel," pp. 62-78 (C13); Helmut Heissenbuttel, "Rules of the Game of the Crime Novel," pp. 79-92 (C392); Umberto Eco, "Narrative Structures in Fleming," pp. 93-117 (E1095); Roland Barthes, "Delay and the Hermeneutic Sentence," pp. 118-21 (C54); F. R. Jameson, "On Raymond Chandler," pp. 122-48 (E416); Michael Holquist, "Whodunit and Other Questions: Metaphysical Detective Stories in Postwar Fiction," pp. 149-74 (C407); Frank Kermode, "Novel and Narrative," pp. 175-96 (C447); Steven Marcus, "Dashiell Hammett," pp. 197-209 (E1398); Geoffrey H. Hartman, "Literature High and Low: The Case of the Mystery Story," pp. 210-29 (C369); Albert D. Hutter, "Dreams, Transformations, and Literature: The Implications of Detective Fiction," pp. 230-51 (C419); David I. Grossvogel, "Agatha Christie: Containment of the Unknown," pp. 252-65 (E552); Steven Knight, "'...some men come up'--the Detective Appears," pp. 266-98 (E454); D. A. Miller, "The Novel and the Police," pp. 299-326 (C555); Dennis Porter, "Backward Construction and the Art of Suspense," pp. 327-40 (C640); Glenn W. Most, "The Hippocrates Smile: John le Carré and the Traditions of the Detective Novel," pp. 341-65 (E1708); William W. Stowe, "From Semiotics to Hermeneutics: Modes of Detection in Doyle and Chandler," pp. 366-83 (E449).

B265. Mueller-Fraureth, Carl. Die Ritter- und Räuberromane |The bandit and robber novel|. Halle, 1894. Reprint: Garland, 1979 (with Agnes C. Murphy's Banditry, Chivalry and Terror in German Fiction, 1790-1830; Chicago, 1935).
The theme of banditry reached its height in German literature in Schiller's Die Rauber, where the bandits were seen as Promethean figures in revolt against an oppressive society. Banditry quickly become one of the strongest motives in both English and German Gothic novels, but it soon lost its social significance and became simply a thrill mechanism. Mueller-Fraureuth's work covers banditry, supernaturalism, and the importance of the Italian setting in Gothic romances. (EFB)

B266. Murata, Hiroo. Suiri Shosetsu no Nazo |Mysteries of mystery fiction|. Tokyo: Kobun-sha, 1976. 197pp.
The author, an official in the Japanese Supreme Court, focuses on the relationship between real crimes and real social situations, and mystery fiction. He has also written Hanzai to Tantei |Crime and detective, 1956| where he explains forensic medicine and scientific investigation for general readers. (HS/TT)

B267. Murch, A. E. The Development of the Detective Novel. London: Peter Owen, 1958; NY: Philosophical Library, 1958; Port Washington, NY: The Kennikat Press, 1968. 272pp. General Bibliography and Index.
Much of the book is devoted to pre-WW I fiction and the treatment of

this material is good; the brief comments on more modern material are less satisfactory. (REB)

B268. Murder Manual: A Handbook for Mystery Writers. Introduction by H. F. Wight. East San Diego, CA: Wight House Press, 1936. Not seen. Breen 93.

B269. Mystère Magazine. Jan 48-Oct 76. 343 issues.
French edition of EQMM founded by Maurice Renault, Mystère Magazine was never a simple reprinting of the American magazine but published contributions by French writers and wasted no time in acquiring columns signed by Igor G. Maslowski, Michel Lebrun, Jacqueline Barde, Maurice Bernard Endrèbe, and other notable French detective fiction specialists. Like its American counterpart, Mystère Magazine has published interviews with many writers; these will be cited in the Authors section. It has also published numerous critical articles, among them studies on Vidocq, the "roman noir," Fitz James O'Brien, Herman Melville, Maturin, and Gaboriau, all by André Ferran; theoretical and historical articles by Thomas Narcejac, Roger Caillois, and Fereydoun Hoveyda; and studies of Fantômas, Chandler's Los Angeles, John Dickson Carr, Sherlock Holmes, William Irish, Fu Manchu, Fredric Brown, Kenneth Fearing, G.K. Chesterton, and Agatha Christie, many of these by Francis Lacassin and subsequently published in one or the other of his several collections. In general, these articles will only be cited and annotated where they have been reprinted in essay collections. (Information furnished by Jacques Baudou.)

B270. The Mystery Library. A publication series of the University Extension, University of California, San Diego, CA. in cooperation with Publisher's Inc., Del Mar, CA.
In addition to publishing The Armchair Detective during the middle and late 70s, the extension division of the University of California, San Diego in cooperation with Publisher's Inc., Del Mar, CA also published a generally well-edited series of critical editions of classics of detective fiction. Each of the 12 volumes contained an introduction by a well-known critic, the novel, and an appendix with bibliographies, filmographies, critical notes, contemporary reviews and other useful material. The twelve volumes are as follows: 1. Arthur William Upfield, The New Shoe (E2927); 2. John Dickson Carr, The Crooked Hinge (E352); 3. Mary Roberts Rinehart, The Circular Staircase (E2360); 4. Melville Davisson Post, The Complete Uncle Abner (E2206); 5. E. C. Bentley, Trent's Last Case (E119); 6. Eric Ambler, A Coffin for Dimitrios (E37); 7. Ellery Queen, The Tragedy of X (E2271); 8. John Buchan, The Thirty-Nine Steps (E277); 9. Christianna Brand, Green for Danger (E229); 10. Joel Townsley Rogers, The Red Right Hand (E2377); 11. Hillary Waugh, Last Seen Wearing... (E3058); 12. Anthony Berkeley, The Poisoned Chocolates Case (E128). The series, and other University Extension publications, is now distributed by the the Bowling Green University Popular Press.

B271. Mystery Writers of America. The Third Degree. circa 1945 - .
Newsletter of the Mystery Writers of America, Inc. Includes market reports, news items, letters, obituary notices and tributes to MWA members who have died. At various times the newsletter was edited by Clayton Rawson, Donald R. Bensen, and Bruce Cassiday; since March 1975 it has been edited by Chris Steinbrunner. An important feature in most issues since May 1975 is "MWA in Print," a checklist of new publications

by MWA members, compiled by Ed and Pat Hoch. The Third Degree sometimes prints reports from the organization's regional chapters, most of which have their own newsletters: The Lineup (Northern California), March of Crime (Southern California), The Semi-Private Eye (New England), etc. (REB)

B272. ______. Mystery Writers' Annual. 1946 - . Wraps. Usually 32pp. Illus. This is the "souvenir book" prepared in conjunction with the annual Edgar Allan Poe Awards Banquet of the MWA. Each issue contains messages from the incoming and outgoing presidents of the organization, a list of the year's award nominees, and an assortment of articles and features by MWA members. There are numerous photographs, as well as advertisements for current mysteries. From time to time there have been anagrams, crossword puzzles, clerihews (the best assortment by Aaron Marc Stein in the 1977 edition, p. 14), punning menus (table d'Hoch, carrots Julienne Symons, etc.), and the texts of the humorous sketches (many written by Clayton Rawson) which used to be a feature of the awards dinner. Editors of the Annual have included Clayton Rawson, Donald R. Bensen, Bruce Cassiday, Dorothy Salisbury Davis, and Brian Garfield. Since 1979 the editorial chores have been in the hands of Otto Penzler. Several of the annual issues contain material of permanent archival value. In the 1979 edition there is a comprehensive list of "Previous Award Members" (pp. 25-37), listing all of the Edgar winners from past years in all categories. The 1980 edition contains a brief article, "Thirty-Five Years of MWA Anthologies" by Edward D. Hoch plus a checklist of the contents of all of these anthologies (pp. 31-37). The 1980 edition contains "Thirty-Five Years of Edgar Night Winners," an alphabetical directory of all Edgar and Raven winners, compiled by Otto Penzler, Edward D. Hoch, and Sandra Miller Christie. (REB)

B273. Nagaanuma, Koki. Mysteriani. Tokyo: Kodan-sha, 1965. 272pp. Bibliography.
A collection of desultory essays on various topics in mystery fiction. These topics are "borrowed" from Sutherland Scott's Blood in Their Ink (B364), which the author translated into Japanese, and it is difficult to understand why this talented author did such a thing. (HS/TT)

B274. ______. Suiri Shosetsu Seminar: Mystery Kaidoku-jutsu |Mystery fiction seminar: how to decode mysteries|. Tokyo: Kodan-sha, 19621. 254pp.
The author, a famous Sherlockian in Japan, has written nine Sherlockian books. This book shows how to appreciate mystery fiction, using as examples five mystery stories by E. A. Poe. It also includes a study of Poe's influence on Conan Doyle and other material on mystery fiction in general. (HS/TT)

B275. Nagata, Junko. Suiri Shosetsu to Ango |Mystery and cipher|. Tokyo: Diamond-sha, 1979. 212pp. Illus. Bibliography.
The author is an expert on cryptography. He analyzes the codes and ciphers used in the works of Leblanc, Verne and Mushitaro Oguri (a Japanese writer) as well as those of Poe and Doyle, and suggests future possibilities for cipher mysteries. (HS/TT)

B276. Nakajima, Kawataro. Suiri Shosetsu Note |Notes on mystery fiction|. Tokyo: Shakai Shiso-sha, 1960. 235pp. Illus.
The first half is a general history of mystery fiction. In the second half, there are comments on 40 great detectives, explanatory notes for 117

masterpieces (Japanese and non-Japanese), and 13 lists of masterpieces selected by 13 critics, Japanese and non-Japanese. (HS/TT)

B277. ______. Suiri Shosetsu Tenbo |Views on mystery fiction|. Tokyo: Toto Shobo, 1965. 238pp.
Part one contains 6 critical essays which develop a systematic approach to mystery fiction; part two consists of short biographies of 145 non-Japanese writers. It also includes, as an appendix, a chronological chart. One of the few books which can be recommended as a reference tool. Winner of a Mystery Writers of Japan award in 1966. (HS/TT)

B278. ______. Suiri Shosetsu no Yomikata |How to read mystery fiction|. Tokyo: Popura-sha, 1971. 237pp. Illus.
An introductory book for boys on mystery fiction, with numerous photographs and illustrations. Although it is written for juveniles, this survey maintains a fairly high level of discussion. (HS/TT)

B279. Nakajima, Kawataro, ed. Mystery Handbook. Tokyo: Kodan-sha, 1980. 525pp.
An anthology of 14 critical essays on Japanese mystery fiction, with a history, an encyclopedia and a chronological chart. It is a reference tool which shows the present state of Japanese mystery fiction. (HS/TT)

B280. Nakajima, Kawataro, and Ara, Masahito, eds. Suiri Shosetsu e no Shotai |An invitation to mystery fiction|. Tokyo: Nanboku-sha, 1959. 299pp.
A concise introductory book with a general survey of mystery fiction and its gimmicks, profiles of Japanese and non-Japanese writers, a history of controversies about mystery fiction, profiles of great detectives, and commentaries on masterpieces. (HS/TT)

B281. Nakajima, Kawataro, and Oshikawa, Hiroshi, eds. Sherlock Holmes no Rival-tachi |The rivals of Sherlock Holmes|. Meitantei series (B254). 1979. v, 234pp.
The book deals with four detectives: Freeman's Dr. Thorndyke, Futrelle's The Thinking Machine, Orczy's The Old Man in the Corner, and Morrison's Martin Hewitt. (HS/TT)

B282. Nakamura, Katsuhiko, supervisor. Suiri Shosetsu Zatsugaku Jiten |Informal dictionary of mystery fiction|. Tokyo: Kosaido Shuppan, 1976. 254pp. Illus. Bibliography.
A collection of miscellaneous essays by members of the Keio Gijuku University Mystery Club, which Nakamura once served as an adviser. With many quotations from other sources, it is useful only as a book for general readers. (HS/TT)

B283. Nakata, Koji, ed. Suiri Shosetsu o do Yomuka? |How to read mystery fiction|. Tokyo: San'ichi Shobo, 1971. 238pp.
An anthology of essays of a uniformly high standard by Raymond Chandler, Cyril Hare, Ernst Bloch, Michael Gilbert, Maurice Procter, Josephine Bell and others. (HS/TT).

B284. Nakazono, Eisuke. Yami No Carnival: Spy Mystery e no Shotai |Carnival in the dark: an invitation to the spy mystery|. Tokyo: JijiTsushin-sha, 1980. 274pp.
The author is the only writer in Japan who writes only spy fiction. His two previous books, Genday Spy-ron |Comments on the modern spy, 1965|

and Kau Spy, Jessen Spy |Fictional spies, real spies, 1967|, focus on the analysis of real spy cases. Comprised of selections from his two previous books, this volume--which won the Mystery Writers of Japan award as the best critical book of 1981--communicates the pleasure of writing and reading spy fiction. (HS/TT)

B285. Narcejac, Thomas. Esthétique du roman policier |Esthetic of the detective novel|. Paris: Editions le Portulan, 1947. 208pp.
An analysis of fundamental elements of the genre: plot, characters, dialogue, psychology. Considered by some critics to be a study that still has much of value to offer. (JB)

B286. ______. La Fin d'un bluff |Calling a bluff|. Paris: Editions le Portulan, 1949. 181pp.
This essay which wears the tinsel of a pamphlet is a violent diatribe against the American roman noir, and certain of its excesses. At the time of its publication, it aroused violent reactions and rebuttals. (JB)

B287. ______. Une Machien à lire: le roman policier |A reading-machine: the detective novel|. Preface by Francois Le Lionnais. Collection Méditations no. 124. Paris: Denoël-Gonthier, 1975. 248pp. (Japanese translation by Hiromitsu Arakawak. Tokyo: Sogen-sha, 1981.)
A literary/philosophical (but far from stuffy) study of the detective novel: its origins, some of its important practioners, and its relationships with politics, religion, literature, and even cybernetics. There are individual chapters on R. Austin Freeman (E1211, E1212), Ellery Queen (E2261), John Dickson Carr (E373), G. K. Chesterton (E495), and Agatha Christie (E586). Narcejac is widely read in the secondary literature of crime fiction and makes use of extracts from essays by Raymond Chandler, Nicholas Blake, Anthony Boucher, John Dickson Carr, and many other commentators, in building his own analysis. (REB)

B288. Neuberg, Victor E. Popular Literature: A History and Guide. London: Penguin Books, 1977. 302pp. Index. Critical bibliography. Illus.
A general study of early popular literature from "the beginning of printing to the year 1897." An ambitious project but, in fact, about half of the book is devoted to the 19th century. The critical bibliography will help a neophyte reader to find fuller treatments of the material. Of peripheral interest for this bibliography but the discussion touches on readers and reading in the 19th century and can help to provide a context for genre literature.

B289. Neuhaus, Volker. Typen Multiperspektivischen Erzaehlens |Types of multi-perspective narration|. Literatur und Leben, n.s., Vol. 13. Cologne: Boehlau Verlag, 1971. 179pp. Index, bibliography of primary and secondary sources.
Study of the narrative structures in fiction. Chapter III (pp. 75-109) on the document novel--in which letters and documents help carry the narrative--includes analyses of The Woman in White, Sayers and Eustace's The Documents in the Case and other crime novels. Chapter IV (pp. 110-117) is about multiple perspectives in the detective novel, and discusses Sayers' Clouds of Witnesses, A. Berkeley's The Poisoned Chocolates Case and Ryunosuke Akutagawa's Rashomon. (GG)

B290. Nevins, Francis M., Jr., ed. The Mystery Writer's Art. Bowling Green, OH: Popular Press, 1970. xii, 338pp.
Introduction and twenty-one essays on topics ranging from Poe to science fiction mysteries. The material has all been previously published in a variety of sources, many of them virtually unattainable. A state-of-the-art (as of 1970) of criticism and, as such, an important supplement to Haycraft's Art of the Mystery Story (B142). Contents: Robert A. W. Lowndes, "The Contributions of Edgar Allan Poe," pp. 1-18 (E2150); J. R. Christopher, "Poe and the Tradition of the Detective Story," pp. 19-36 (E2105); Ellery Queen, "Who Shall Ever Forget?," pp. 37-41 (Sherlock Holmes); Robert E. Briney, "Sax Rohmer: An Informal Survey," pp. 42-78 (E2390); Norman Donaldson,"R. Austin Freeman: The Invention of Inversion," pp. 79-87 (E1188); Charles Shibuk, "Henry Wade," pp. 88-97 (E3009); Robert I. Edenbaum, "The Poetics of the Private Eye: The Novels of Dashiell Hammett," pp. 98-121 (E1370); Francis M. Nevins, Jr., "The Drury Lane Quartet," pp. 122-35 (E2262); Frank E. Robbins, "The Firm of Cool and Lam," pp. 136-48 (E1252); Robin Wood, "Hitchcock's Psycho," pp. 149-61; Donald Richie, "High and Low," pp. 162-79 (Akiro Kurosawa; Ed McBain; film); William K. Everson, "Six Mystery Movies and Their Makers," pp. 180-95; Philip Durham, "The Black Mask School," pp. 197-226 (D343); John Dickson Carr, "The Grandest Game in the World," pp. 227-47 (C158); Jacques Barzun, "Detection and the Literary Art," pp. 248-62 (C59); Frank D. McSherry, Jr., "The Janus Resolution," pp. 263-71 (C523); Donald A. Yates, "An Essay on Locked Rooms," pp. 272-84 (C881); Elliot L. Gilbert, "The Detective as Metaphor in the Nineteenth Century," pp. 285-94 (C317); Ross Macdonald, "The Writer as Detective Hero," pp. 295-305 (C512); William O. Aydelotte, "The Detective Story as a Historical Source," pp. 306-25 (C36); Frank D. McSherry, Jr., "The Shape of Crimes to Come," pp. 326-38 (C524). Breen 78.

B291. Nippon Hoso Shuppan Kyokai, ed. Suiri Kyoshitsu |The mystery class|. Tokyo: Nippon Hoso Shuppan Kyokai, 1975. 197pp. Illus.
A book version of selections from the "World of Hobbies" TV series. More than one-third is taken up with three whodunits. An introductory, low-level book. (HS/TT)

B292. Nishikawa, Kiyoyuki. Asobi o Sen to ya Umarekemu: Mystery to Rakugo no Kosaten |Born to be at play: intersection of the mystery and the rakugo|. Tokyo: Hayakawa Shobo, 1982. 274pp.
"Rakugo" is a traditional Japanese art form of humorous narrative storytelling. Although this is a unique attempt to introduce several "rakugo" stories which deal with the same themes as mystery stories, its repetitive subject matter makes it of limited interest. (HS/TT)

B293. Nixon, Joan Lowery. Writing Mysteries for Young People. Boston: The Writer, Inc., 1977. x, 123pp.
A manual of techniques for writing mystery and suspense fiction for young readers; covers books, serials and magazine stories, with examples and marketing information. Breen 96. (REB)

B294. Nogueras, Luis Rogelio. Por la novela policial. Havana: Cuadernos Union, 1982.
This collection of essays contains the following material: three separate reviews of Cuban "detective novels" and a review article dealing with Bulgarian writer Bogomil Rainov's La novela negra (Havana: Editorial Arte y Literatura, 1978); a short note on the reception of Cuban

detective literature abroad; an autobiographical account of how Nogueras and Guillermo Rodriguez Rivera wrote their Cuban detective novel, El curato círculo (Havana: Ed. Letras Cubanas, 1979); and two historical-theoretical pieces on the origins and nature of detective fiction. (Donald A. Yates)

B295. Nusser, Peter. Der Kriminalroman |The crime novel|. Samlung Metzler M 191. Stuttgart: Metzler, 1980. viii, 186pp. Index.
Serious, systematic, academic study of the detective novel. Included are chapters on the "method of investigation," structure and history of the detective novel, and psycho-sociological explanations of the detective novel's effects on its readers. Nusser maintains a sharp distinction between the detective novel and the thriller, which for him includes the hard-boiled novel. In the chapter on the method of investigation (pp. 1-25), Nusser makes further distinctions, with crime literature being the general category which includes criminal literature (Dostoyevsky's Crime and Punishment), criminal adventure stories, spy novels, and detective novels proper. The chapter on the history of the genre (pp. 74-115) is primarily about the history of Anglo-Saxon detective fiction, although Nusser numbers François Gayot de Pitaval's 20 volume Causes célèbres et intéressantes, avec les jugements qui les ont décidées |Interesting famous cases, with the verdicts which decided them| (1734-43) as a literary forerunner. For readers already familiar with English-language book-length treatments of the genre, the most informative parts of the book are the chapters on structure and the effect of detective novels on the reader. Especially informative are the more than 25 bibliographies of secondary sources. Perhaps because of the attempt at comprehensiveness, errors have crept in, such as the statement that Robert L. Fish and Robert L. Pike are pennames of Ed McBain (p. 137). Elsewhere Nusser discusses the well-known "democracy and detective stories" question without mentioning the books of Russian authors such as Marietta Sergejewna Schaginjan or Benjamin Alexandrowitsch Kawerin, whose books have been translated into German. And nowhere is Asian detective literature mentioned. Most of the footnoting and documentation is of secondary sources; relatively few novels are named so that one gets the impression that Nusser is more familiar with the secondary literature than with the genre itself. However, as an overview of the critical literature on the topics discussed, the book is excellent, and, along with Buchloh amd Becker's Der Detektivroman (B66), Schulz-Buschaus' Formen und Ideologien des Kriminalromans (B362) and Vogt's critical anthology Der Kriminalroman (B424), this is one of the most important modern German critical works. (GG)

B296. ______. Romane fuer die Unterschicht. Groschenhefte und ihre Leser |Novels for the lower stratum: dime novels and their readers|. Texte Metzler 27. Stuttgart: Metzler, 1981. 123pp. Bibliography of secondary sources.
Statistical, sociological and linguistic study of contemporary German dime novel-format booklets called Groschenhefte. Of all the genres, from romance to horror, criminous dime novels are one of the most popular, and the majority of readers come from the "blue collar" or working class. The syntax and speech used in the Groschenhefte, especially in the most popular crime series, Jerry Cotton, are found to be similar to that of their readers. (GG)

B297. O'Brien, Geoffrey. Hardboiled America. The Lurid Years of Paperbacks.

NY: Van Nostrand Reinhold, 1981. 144pp. Index. Illus. With a checklist by year (1929-58) listing major hard-boiled novels and mainstream fiction. Selected bibliography.

The first half of the book deals with cover art for paperbacks; the second half is a discussion of some of the major writers. Reviews: PQ 4:2 (1981):49-50; TLS, 25 Dec 81, p.1482.

B298. Oe, Sen'ichi. America Taishu Shosetsu |American popular fiction|. Tokyo: Eigo Eibungaku Kanko-kai, 1934. 52pp.

This study starts with a presentation of bestsellers, touches upon Beadle's Dime Novels, and surveys the styles of Ellery Queen, S. S. Van Dine, Anna Katharine Green, Mary Roberts Rinehart, Arthur Reeve, Hulbert Footner, Herman Landon, Octavus Roy Cohen and others. (HS/TT)

B299. Olivier-Martin, Yves. Histoire du roman populaire en France |History of the popular novel in France|. Paris: Albin Michel, 1980. 301pp. Index and bibliography.

A study of the French popular novel that excludes the detective novel but includes descendents of the Gothic novel. The author is preparing a study of the "magic origins" of the detective novel, 1820-70.

B300. Ousby, Ian. Bloodhounds of Heaven. The Detective in English Fiction from Godwin to Doyle. Cambridge, MA: Harvard University Press, 1976. vii-x, 194pp. Illus. Index.

Ousby takes issue with a commonly held critical theory that the rise of detection in 19th century fiction can be explained by the growth of science and the popularization of scientific methodology. He points out that this is a late 19th century development and does not account for the appearance of the detective much earlier in the century. Ousby proposes to study the figure of the detective with particular reference to social history and the organization and growth of an organized police force in England. After an introductory chapter in which he traces the role of the rogue/thief from 18th to 19th century England and shows the early relationship between the criminal and the detector, he focuses on four writers: William Godwin, Vidocq and his English translations, Dickens, Wilkie Collins and other sensation novelists. Ousby's study--a revised version of his Harvard doctoral thesis--is a major contribution to a largely neglected and misunderstood period of the development of detective fiction. Reviews: Yale Review, Spring 77, pp. 444-47; New Yorker, 25 Apr 77, pp. 141-48.

B301. Ozaki, Hotsuki, and others. Takshu Bungaku Taikei: Bekkan |Survey of popular literature: supplement|. Tokyo: Kodan-sha, 1980. 793pp.

An anthology of reference materials on popular fiction in general, with a history of mystery fiction compiled by Kawataro Nakajima and a list of stories printed in various kinds of popular literary magazines. (HS/TT)

B302. Palmer, Jerry. Thrillers: Genesis and Structure of a Popular Genre. London: Edward Arnold, 1978; NY: St. Martin's, 1979. vi, 234pp. Bibliography and index.

Academic literary criticism at its most formidable, offering little to those who read crime fiction for enjoyment. Palmer subsumes all of crime fiction under the "thriller" heading, including even the classical detective story as written by Doyle and Christie. The absence from their work of the sex and violence found in many modern thrillers is calmly ascribed to "literary propriety in general." Many of the specific examples cited are taken from Ian Fleming or Mickey Spillane; other authors are mentioned less frequently, and so prolific and popular a thriller writer as Edgar Wallace does not appear at all. Review: Choice 16:8 (Oct 79):1010-12. Breen 52. (REB)

B303. Panek, Leroy L. The Special Branch: The British Spy Novel, 1890-1980. Bowling Green, OH: Popular Press, 1981. 288pp.
Some bibliography included as end-of-chapter notes; no index. Essays on 17 British writers of espionage novels. Panek points out in his preface that he has not tried to write a comprehensive study and has not included either Joseph Conrad or W. Somerset Maugham because he feels that there is sufficient criticism available on them and he wished to present some lesser-known authors. Contents: "William Le Queux," pp. 5-16; "E. Phillips Oppenheim," pp. 17-31 (E2043); "Erskine Childers," pp. 32-38 (E515); "John Buchan," pp. 39-67 (E291); "Sapper," pp. 68-83 (E2475); "Francis Beeding," pp. 84-97; "Sidney Horler," pp. 98-111; "Graham Greene," pp. 112-37; "Eric Ambler," pp. 138-54; "Geoffrey Household," pp. 155-70; "Peter Cheyney," pp. 171-84 (E506); "Manning Coles," pp. 185-200 (E632); "Ian Fleming," pp. 201-219 (E1106); "Len Deighton," pp. 220-35 (E788); "John LeCarre (sic)," pp. 236-57 (E1710); "Adam Hall," pp. 258-71 (E1345); "Frederick Forsyth," pp. 272-281 (E1131).

B304. ______. Watteau's Shepherds: The Detective Novel in Britain 1914-1940. Bowling Green, OH: Bowling Green Univ. Popular Press, 1979. 232pp. Index.
In his introduction, Panek expresses his dissatisfaction with the limited perspective of previous critics of detective fiction who have tended to discuss the writers of the period as creators of puzzles and have, claimed Panek, neglected alternate ways of looking at the period and its writers. In the first chapter, he discusses the background of the detective fiction of the period and most particularly the thriller and its relationship to writers like Sayers and Christie. The remainder of the book consists of treatments of individual writers: E. C. Bentley, Christie, A. A. Milne, Sayers, A. B. Cox, Margery Allingham, John Dickson Carr and Ngaio Marsh. There are two appendices. In the first of these, Panek analyses plot structures and there are several charts in which recurrent elements are identified and organized in various ways. The second appendix is a listing of works published by the subject authors during the period between the two wars. Breen 80.

B305. Paris noir. Paris: Le dernier terrain vague, 1980.
This anthology-manifesto was conceived by the editorial team of the short-lived Gang magazine (2 issues, circa 1980) and presents the authors of the "neo-polar" wave. (JB)

B306. Parker, Robert Brown. "The Violent Hero, Wilderness Heritage and Urban Reality: A Study of the Private Eye in the Novels of Dashiell Hammett, Raymond Chandler and Ross Macdonald." Unpublished doctoral dissertation. Boston University, 1971. 188pp. Dissertation Abstracts 32/04-A, pp. 206-66.

B307. Pate, Janet. The Book of Sleuths: from Sherlock Holmes to Kojak. London: New English Library, March 1977; Chicago: Contemporary Books Inc., 1977. (U. S. Edition lacks subtitle; issued in both hardcover and paperback editions.) 124pp.
Each of the 40 brief chapters profiles a fictional detective, starting with

Poe's Dupin and concluding with Kojak. Capsule accounts of the detectives' creators are also included, with checklists of "publications and performances" featuring the detective. Each chapter is illustrated with magazine illustrations and/or movie stills. Some of Pate's choices are bizarre, with Lew Archer and Virgil Tibbs and Martin Beck never mentioned, while whole chapters are devoted to Rin Tin Tin and Batman. With British and continental detectives, Pate is reliable and even innovative both in her choice of subjects and in what she says about them. This "illustrated chronicle" will be a helpful companion for beginners. Advanced students, however, will do better to look elsewhere. Breen 104. (F. M. Nevins, Jr./REB)

B308. _____. The Book of Spies and Secret Agents. London: Galley Press, 1978. 119pp.

Heavily illustrated coffee-table survey of fictional spys and agents, divided into three categories: Traitors and Patriots, The Professionals, and Superstars and Anti-Heroes. Sources range from the Apocrypha (Judith) to historical novels, espionage and detective fiction, TV, and comic strips. Characters range from Kipling's Kim to the Scarlet Pimpernel, Richard Hannay, Ashenden, James Bond, Harry Palmer, Modesty Blaise, Boysie Oakes, Napoleon Solo and Ilya Kuryakin. Oddities include the villains from Michael Innes's The Secret Vanguard and Margery Allingham's Traitor's Purse (unblushingly giving away the denouements of these novels), Nick Fury from Marvel Comics, and Mad magazine's 'Spy vs. Spy.' Pate supplies a thumbnail sketch of each character and his or her creator, with a bibliography, filmography, and notes on stage productions. Pictorial and popular appeal were obviously more important than literary or genre significance in determing the characters to be included. (REB)

B309. Penzler, Otto, editor. The Great Detectives. Boston: Little, Brown, 1978. xii-xvii, 281pp. Illus.

An anthology of portraits of famous fictional detectives written by their creators. Each of the writers is introduced by editor Penzler. This kind of text reflects, as Penzler correctly points out in his preface, the importance of the detective in the history of the genre from its inception. Contents: Ngaio Marsh, "Roderick Alleyn," pp. 2-8; Michael Innes, "John Appleby," pp. 10-15; Ross Macdonald, "Lew Archer," pp. 18-24; Leonard Holton, "Father Bredder," pp. 26-35; George Harmon Coxe, "Flash Casey," pp. 38-46; Hugh Pentecost, "Pierre Chambrun," pp. 48-55; Christianna Brand, "Inspector Cockrill," pp. 58-66; Robert L. Fish, "Captain José da Silva," pp. 68-77; Carolyn Keene, "Nancy Drew," pp. 80-86; Ed McBain, "The 87th Precinct," pp. 88-97; Hillary Waugh, "Fred Fellows," pp. 100-108; H. R. F. Keating, "Inspector Ghote," pp. 110-117; Donald Hamilton, "Matt Helm," pp. 120-26; Baynard H. Kendrick, "Duncan Maclain," pp. 128-40; Vera Caspary, "Mark McPherson," pp. 142-46; Dell Shannon, "Luis Mendoza," pp. 148-53; Richard Lockridge, "Mr. and Mrs. North, " pp. 156-63; Michael Gilbert, "Patrick Petrella," pp. 166-74; Peter Dickinson, "Superintendent Pibble," pp. 176-82; Adam Hall, "Quiller," pp. 184-92; George Bagby, "Inspector Schmidt," pp. 194-204; Maxwell Grant, "The Shadow," pp. 206-16; Brett Halliday, "Michael Shayne," pp. 218-25; John Ball, "Virgil Tibbs," pp. 228-34; Chester Gould, "Dick Tracy," pp. 236-45; Nicolas Freeling, "Inspector Van der Valk," pp. 248-57. Bibliography and Filmography, pp. 281. Breen 81.

B310. ______. The Private Lives of Private Eyes, Spies, Crime Fighters and other Good Guys. New York: Grosset & Dunlap, 1977. Simultaneous hardcover and paperback editions. vii-viii, 214pp. Index. Illus.

More profiles of great detectives, with bibliographies and filmographies, written and compiled by Penzler. The emphasis in the illustrations is on film versions of the detectives' cases. Contents: Lew Archer, pp. 1-8 (Ross Macdonald); Modesty Blaise, pp. 9-16 (Peter O'Donnell); James Bond, pp. 17-23 (Ian Fleming); Nick Carter, pp. 33-42; Charlie Chan, pp. 43-51 (Earl Derr Biggers); Nick and Nora Charles, pp. 52-58 (Hammett); Bulldog Drummond, pp. 59-68 ("Sapper"); C. Auguste Dupin, pp. 69-76 (Poe); Mike Hammer, pp. 77-85 (Mickey Spillane); Sherlock Holmes, pp. 86-105 (Conan Doyle); Jules Maigret, pp. 106-115 (Simenon); Philip Marlowe, pp. 115-22 (Chandler); Miss Jane Marple, pp. 123-28 (Christie); Perry Mason, pp. 129-39 (Erle Stanley Gardner); Mr. Moto, pp. 140-43 (John P. Marquand); Hercule Poirot, pp. 144-52 (Christie); Ellery Queen, pp. 153-60; The Shadow, pp. 161-66 (Maxwell Grant/Walter Gibson); John Shaft, pp. 167-72 (Ernest Tidyman); Sam Spade, pp. 173-78 (Hammett); Dr. Thorndyke, pp. 179-84 (R. A. Freeman); Philo Vance, pp. 185-93 (S. S. Van Dine); Lord Peter Wimsey, pp. 194-200 (Dorothy L. Sayers); Nero Wolfe, pp. 201-212 (Rex Stout). Index, pp. 213-214.

B311. Phillips, Walter C. Dickens, Reade and Collins, Sensation Novelists. New York, 1919; reprinted by Garland, 1979. 238pp.

An important subgenre of the Victorian novel was the so-called sensation novel, which offered lurid, melodramatic subject matter, often in association with domestic or society elements. Charles Reade and Wilkie Collins were considered the leading practitioners, although there were many other well-known authors involved, like Miss Braddon and Mrs. Wood. Professor Phillips covers the psychological aspects of sensation; the historical background, including a survey of the Newgate novel; the importance of the Byronic hero; and the individual authors. Since today we tend to forget that much of Dickens's early work, like Oliver Twist, was based on this aesthetic, Phillips's book is a useful reminder. (EFB)

B312. Pierce, Hazel Beasley. A Literary Symbosis: Science Fiction/Fantasy Mystery. Westport, CT: Greenwood Press, 1983. Pp. ix, 1-255. Index.

After an introduction in which she reviews unsuccessful efforts to provide a "compact" definition of science fiction and the difficulties in combining "idea-oriented" science fiction with "situation-oriented" mystery fiction, Pierce surveys the history of detective fiction through the hard-boiled writers of the 20s and 30s. This survey presents the two major innovations of 20th century detective fiction as the inverted mystery of R. Austin Freeman and the hard-boiled school of Chandler, Hammett and Ross Macdonald. There is no discussion of the classical puzzle story and in spite of the discussion of post-World War II science fiction, Pierce is either not interested in or is unfamiliar with the complex history of contemporary detective fiction. The reader of mystery fiction will be disturbed by the fragmented survey of his field which ignores the historically important puzzle mystery, fails to define precisely or give examples of the the "crime" story, treats the thriller as another designation for the novel of espionage, and concludes with a discussion of the Gothic mystery which presumes to give an historical survey in 3 pages and then discusses a mixed bag filled with lycanthropes, vampires and psychic detectives in which the only criterion seems to be some form of detection or "mystery" (and this term consistently used imprecisely) mixed with the supernatural. She sums up her enterprise by re-stating her hypothesis that the authors she has been discussing have "wedded the idea-oriented mode with the situation-oriented mystery mode." This simplistic formulation is not without its eccentric charm, and if Pierce's historical and theoretical supports are shaky, it should be noted that she has recorded a great deal of raw research data that will be useful to other researchers. This is not, however, a book that can be recommended as an authoritative treatment of its subject.

B313. Ponder, Eleanor Anne. "The American Detective Form in Novels and Film, 1929-1947." Unpublished doctoral dissertation. University of North Carolina at Chapel Hill, 1979. 149pp. Dissertation Abstracts 40/08A, pp. 4599-4600. Not seen.

B314. Populärlitteratur. Sex kritiker om nagra representative genrer [Popular litterature. Six critics on some representative genres]. Bibliotekstjänst-serien no. 42. Lund: Bibliotekstjänst, 1972. 81pp.
Index of authors and names. (IH)

B315. Porter, Dennis. The Pursuit of Crime: Art and Ideology in Detective Fiction. New Haven, CT: Yale Univ. Press, 1981. 267pp. Index.
Bibliographical references included in footnotes. A structuralist study of patterns in detective fiction and the nature of reader response. Porter shows the relationships between genre fiction and "serious" fiction, especially in the anti-detective narratives of the French New Novel and Borges, and covers some of the same areas treated by Cawelti (B69). The style is uneven, alternating between the ponderous and the graceful, and may reflect, in part, his ambivalent feelings about detective fiction. Chapter X is devoted to Simenon's Maigret novels (E2670). Reviews: TLS, 9 Apr 82, p. 403; New Republic, 27 Jan 82, p. 38.

B316. Portuondo, Jose. En torno a la novela policial [On the detective novel]. Cuadernos cubanos. Havana: Páginas, 1947. 70pp. Bibliography. Not seen.

B317. Poupart, Jean-Marie. Les Recréants. Essai portant, entre autres choses, sur le roman policier [The 'recreationists,' essay bearing, among other things, on the detective novel]. Montreal: Les Editions du Jour, 1972. 123pp.
A novelist meditates on the novel, on writing, on reading, and, coincidentally, on detective fiction. Poupart's comments show him to be a well-read and thoughtful partisan of detective fiction. His discussions of individual authors are short but he returns several times to Simenon and Donald Westlake, and the latter most particularly when he is writing as Richard Stark. Neither an original argument or history, but the elements for a substantial study are present in this rambling, intelligent and engaging essay.

B318. Powers, Richard Gid. G-Men: Hoover's FBI in American Popular Culture. Carbondale: Southern Illinois University Press, 1983.
Powers tries to make a case for the G-Man as a continuation of the "action detective" in popular fiction. A section on the dime novel is filled with clichés and based solely on secondary sources. (JRC)

B319. Pronzini, Bill. Gun in Cheek. A Study of "Alternative" Crime Fiction. Introduction by Ed McBain. NY: Coward, McCann & Geoghegan, 1982. 264pp. Bibliography and index.

For "alternative," read "so bad they're funny": that is the sub-category of mystery fiction covered by this hilarious book. From Hanshew to Avallone, from Leroux to Carter Brown, Pronzini offers a guided tour of the overwritten and underthought, the dopey and the just plain inept--all convicted by their own words. In chapter 4, "The Saga of the Risen Phoenix," the entire output of a publishing house, Phoenix Press, is held up before our disbelieving gaze. With only a few exceptions, Pronzini's targets are "safe"--too obscure or too dead to object to their inclusion in this book. (REB)

B320. Prusek, Jaroslav. Chinese History and Literature: Collection of Studies. Dordrecht: Reidel Publishing Co., 1970. 587pp. Part I, Ch. 13, pp. 281-86, previously published as part of "Researches into the Beginnings of the Chinese Popular," Archiv Orientalni 23 (11955):620-52.

Detailed and erudite but informally, nontechnically written collection of essays by the top Czechoslovakian Sinologist. Pp. 281-86 examined kung-an (courtroom) tales. Prusek dates the advent of these stories at the Yuan dynasty, but speculates that cycles of oral stories with officials or magistrates as detective heroes circulated in the Sun (960-1279). States that the kung-an stories generally are well constructed and as logical as European detective stories. Summarizes several stories, including some Magistrate Pao stories from the Ming era Ch'ing-p'ing-shan-t'ang collection. Prusek renders a valuable service by being one of the few writers to relate the kung-an stories to Chinese culture in general. He speculates that their origins were due to the presence of large masses of people in big cities, hungering for stories about serious crimes. Prusek notes that Chinese storytellers (just like their Western counterparts) found that people were much more interested in stories with familiar heroes, hence the birth of the several series detectives, such as Magistrate Pao, Judge P'eng, Judge Shih, etc. Finally Prusek notes how the stories developed from kung-an stories into adventure stories. This is one of the most interesting and important pieces on the ancient Chinese detective story. (GG)

B321. Punter, David. The Literature of Terror: A History of Gothic Fictions from 1765 to the Present Day. London: Longmans, 1980. 449pp. Bibliography and index.

Detective fiction is mentioned only in passing (p. 202) and Punter's observation that there are "detective story elements in the Gothic novel" is not developed. Reviews: TLS, 5 Dec 80, p. 138; British Book News, Jan 81, pp. 52-53.

B322. Quayle, Eric. The Collector's Book of Detective Fiction. London: Studio Vista, 1972. 143pp.

Large, "coffee-table" format, excellent illustrations. Good treatment of selected Victorian and Edwardian mystery writers, but the comments on more recent writers are too often merely paraphrases of Barzun/Taylor or other sources. Plentiful attention to the pleasures and problems of collecting detective fiction, with many mouth-watering color photographs of rare editions. Breen 106. (REB)

B323. Queen, Ellery. In the Queens' Parlor and Other Leaves from the Editors' Notebook. NY: Simon Schuster, 1957; London: Gollancz, 1957; NY: Biblo & Tannen, 1969. 195pp. Index.

Editorial shoptalk (mostly from EQMM) and miscellaneous writings on crime fiction and its bibliography. Breen 82. CC 3005. (REB)

B324. Raabe, Juliette, and Lacassin, Francis. La Bibliothèque idéale des littératures d'évasion |The ideal library of the literatures of escape|. Paris: Editions universitaires, 1969. 216pp.

In this catalogue of the literatures of escape which registers the best works and authors of genres like science fiction, the novel of adventure or the sentimental novel, one chapter is devoted to the detective novel (Ch. IV, pp. 83-136) and another to the spy novel (Ch. VII, pp. 179-204). A very practical guide for neophytes. (JB)

B325. Radine, Serge. Quelques Aspects du roman policier psychologique |Some aspects of the psychological detective novel|. Geneva: Editions du Mont Blanc, 1960. 295pp.

An attempt to show that some detective novels are not inferior to mainstream novels in their style and psychology. (JB)

B326. Rainov, Bogomil. La novela negra |The roman noir|. Havana, Cuba: Editorial Arte y literatura, 1978. Translated from the Bulgarian.

This may well be Bulgaria's principal--perhaps only--authority on detective fiction, a Professor of Aesthetics at Sofia. Reviewed in Nogueras, Por la novela policia (B294). (Donald A. Yates)

B327. Rambelli, Loris. Storia del 'giallo' italiano |History of the Italian giallo|. Milan: Garzanti, 1979. 256pp.

Historical-bibliographical guide to Italian detective literature from the origins to the 70s. The author reports on the works of about 250 writers but he emphasizes those which are representative of taste and custom and in particular those which, within the limits of the genre, present the characteristic--however minimal--of a literary experiment. (LR)

B328. Rampo, Edogawa, and Matsumoto, Seisho, eds. Suiri Shosetsu Saho |How to write mystery fiction|. Tokyo: Kobun-sha, 1959. 248pp.

Compiled as a handbook for writers and readers, this is a collection of eight articles and essays on the history of mystery fiction, gimmicks, motives, conception of ideas, writers' experiences and other subjects. (HS/TT)

B329. Rampo, Edogawa. Akunin Shigan |Desire to be a crook|. Tokyo: Hakubunkan, 1929. 318pp.

The first collection of critical essays by Japan's leading writer of mystery fiction and his sharp critical eye is much in evidence. There can also be glimpsed the talent of an author who left an immortal accomplishment both in mystery fiction and in mystery criticism. (HS/TT)

B330. ______. Gen'eijo |Castle of illusion|. Tokyo: Iwaya Shoten, 1951. xvii,403pp. 14 critical and review essays. With an index and bibliography.

In order to meet the requirements of an introductory handbook, Rampo systematically arranged each chapter, revised when necessary and included as an index a list of mystery magazines and critical books. The volume is carefully produced and is considered as the most authoritative critical reference text. Winner of the Mystery Writrs of Japan Award in 1952. (HS/TT)

B331. ______. Kaigai Tantei Shosetsu: Sakka to Sakuhin |Overseas detective fiction: writers and their works|. Tokyo: Hayakawa Shobo, 1957. cxi, 385pp. Illus. Bibliography.

These essays deal with 80 non-Japanese writers and contain their profiles, short biographies, reviews of their works and checklists. One of the few essential reference books. It is not just a series of biographies but has critical comments on each writer. A fascinating text. (HS/TT)

B332. ______. Oni no Kotoba |Devil's words|. Tokyo: Shunju-sha, 1936. 268pp. Bibliography.
The writer's second collection of critical essays, mainly on the essence of mystery fiction. He defines mystery fiction as a category, clearly describes several sub-genres and mentions borderline genres. (HS/TT)

B333. ______. Tantei Shosetsu no "Nazo" |"Mystery" in detective fiction|. Tokyo: Shiso-stet, 1956. 202pp. Illus.
16 essays analyzing several "tricks" in mystery fiction. The best introductory book for the general reader. This book shows the author's profoundly expert knowledge and will enlighten even experienced aficionados. (HS/TT)

B334. ______. Tantei Shosetsu 40 Nen |40 years of detective fiction|. Tokyo: Togen-sha, 1961. 562pp. Illus. Index.
The chronological memoirs of the author, Japan's leading mystery writer. With numerous quotes from documents and other materials, it is highly regarded as a first-class literary work for researching the history of Japanese mystery fiction. (HS/TT)

B335. ______. Zoku Gen'eijo |Castle of illusion, part two|. Tokyo: Hayakawa Shobo, 1954. xciii, 295pp. Bibliography and index.
16 critical and review essays. Particularly highly regarded are the detailed analysis of classic mystery short stories in the United States and England, and the table classifying mystery gimmicks. One of the leading Japanese research texts, with a detailed index and a bibliography. (HS/TT)

B336. ______. Zuihlitsu Tantei Shosetsu |Essays on detective fiction|. Tokyo: Seiryu-shu, 1947. xx, 242pp. Bibliography and index.
28 essays and reviews which first appeared in numerous magazines. Discussions of John Dickson Carr, Ellery Queen and others. (HS/TT)

B337. Reggiani, Renée. Poliziesco al microscopio: Letteratura popolare e mass-media |Detective story under the microscope: popular literature and mass media|. Turin: E. R. I., 1981.
This volume, which originated in a series of radio broadcasts, offers a coherent historical and critical panorama of the detective genre, related to the area of myth and of fantastic literature and especially the classical tradition of detection. The individual chapters are devoted to Vidocq, Poe, Collins ("a feminist before the fact"), Conan Doyle, Chesterton (Father Brown is treated as a kind of "God's Puck" rather than as an Oberon), S. S. Van Dine, Agatha Christie, Simenon and Stout, with whom the "Present" of the "Super-U.S.A." takes the place of the Ibsenian "Past" of Conan Doyle. (RC)

B338. Reinert, Claus. Das Unheimliche und die Detektivliteratur. Entwurf einer poetologischen Theorie ueber Entstehung, Entfaltung und Problematik der Detektivliterature |The uncanny and detective fiction: sketch of a poetic-aesthetic theory on the origin, development and problematics of detective fiction|. Bonn: Bouvier Verlag Herbert Grundmann, 1973. 158pp.

Abstract, academic treatise on the place of the uncanny in the genre and its relation to aesthetic dimensions such as plot, style and the methods of puzzle solving. Reinert attributes the foundation and development of detective fiction to the literary consciousness of the reality of the uncanny. The discussion is restricted primarily to Poe, Doyle, Chesterton, Samuel Beckett, Wilhelm Raabe and E. T. A. Hoffmann. (GG)

B339. Reynolds, Paul R. The Middle Man: The Adventures of a Literary Agent. NY: William Morrow & Co., Inc., 1972. 223pp. Index.

A lively memoir of Reynold's 44-year career (as of 1971) as a literary agent. Among his clients at various times were H. Bedford Jones, Sax Rohmer, P. G. Wodehouse, Margery Allingham, Stuart Palmer, Elizabeth Sanxay Holding, Howard Fast ('E. V. Cunningham'), and Samuel Shellabarger (who started his career with mysteries under the name 'John Esteven'). All of these writers, and many more, figure in the anecdotes which fill this book. There is little critical or analytical content--this was not the author's intention--but the behind-the-scenes views of writers and their books are fascinating. (REB)

B340. Rhode, John, editor. Detection Medley. London: Hutchinson, 1939. 578pp. Published as Line-Up (New York: Dodd, Mead, 1940). v-ix, 378pp. N.B.:page references will be to the English edition.

An anthology of fiction written by members of the Detection Club of London. In his foreword, editor Rhode details the history of the club and describes the editing of this volume. A. A. Milne contributes a brief introduction in which he speaks of his preference for the amateur detective and on his tendency to identify with him. There are also three essays: G. K. Chesterton, "The Best Detective Story," pp. 60-61; J. J. Connington, "A Criminologist's Book-Shelf," pp. 129-44; and R. Austin Freeman, "The Art of the Detective Story," pp. 214-25 (C291). CC 2765.

B341. Rice-Sayre, Laura Prindle. "Abra-Cadaver: The Anti-Detective Story in Postmodern Fiction." Unpublished Ph. D. dissertation. University of Washington, 1976. 354pp. DAI 37/071-A, p. 4339.

B342. Richardson, Maurice. Crime Ration No. 1. N.p.(England); Library Association branch and Mobile Libraries Group, 1967. Printed wraps.

Reprint of short reviews of detective, suspense and spy novels, originally published in The Observer, April 1966 to March 1967. Not seen. (REB)

B343. Richert, J. Gust. Detektiven i romanen och verkligheten |The detective in fiction and reality|. Stockholm: Ahlén & Akerlunds, 1928. 209pp. Bibliography of secondary sources.

On the villain in reality and fiction, the detective in the novel (Poe, Gaboriau, Doyle, A. E. W. Mason, G. K. Chesterton and Edgar Wallace), real detectives and criminal police in Stockholm and Scotland Yard. (IH)

B344. Rodell, Marie F(ried). Mystery Fiction: Theory and Technique. NY: Duell, Sloan and Pearce, 1943. x, 230pp. Introduction by John W. Vandercook. Bibliography. Revised edition, NY: Hermitage House, Inc., 1952; a volume in the "Professional Writers Library." Pagination not known. London: Hammond, Hammond & Co., 1954. xviii, 171pp. Introduction by Maurice Richardson. Japanese edition: Mystery Nyumon (Tokyo: Shakai Shiso-Stet, 1962). Excerpt published in Haycraft (B142), pp. 264-72.

In 1940-41, Mrs. Rodell published three mystery novels under the byline Marion Randolph, and under her own name she was a long-time editor of crime fiction. In 1942 she taught the "crime fiction" portion of a course at New York University on writing for the pulp magazines. Her book deals with crime fiction as a commercial category, with specific requirements which she analyzes and on which she gives concrete and often useful advice. The 1952 edition is slightly revised, and the Hammond revision is a thorough revision aimed specifically at a British audience: "(A)ll legal procedures, police practices, and publishing standards have been Anglicized." A final brief chapter on "Copyright and Libel under English Law" was added by the publishers. Breen 97. CC 3016. (REB)

B345. Rodriguez Joulia St.-Cyr, Carlos. La novela di intriga. Madrid: Asociación nacional de bibliotecarios archiveros y arqueólogos, 1970. 126pp. Author/title/character index. Bibliography of secondary sources.

The author groups the detective, crime, mystery, and spy novels under the general heading of "novel of intrigue." General considerations of definitions of categories and crossover categories, followed by a historical survey of each of the four types. Interesting section (pp. 67-74) on Spanish authors of detective fiction.

B346. "Roman policier." littérature no. 49 (Feb 83).

A complete issue of this academic French journal is devoted to detective fiction. Contents: Uri Eisenzweig, "Présentation du genre |Presentation of the genre|," pp. 3-15 (C253); Alain Robbe-Grillet, "Entretien |Interview|," pp. 16-22; Shoshana Felman, "De Sophocle à Japrisot (via Freud), ou pourquoi le policier? |From Sophocles to Japrisot (via Freud), or why detective fiction?|," pp. 23-42 (C272); Alain Rey, "Polarités |Polarities|," pp. 43-49 (C685); Marc Angenot, "On est toujours le disciple de quelqu'un, ou le Mystère du pousse-au-crime |You are always somebody's disciple, or the mystery of the 'inciter-to-crime'|," pp. 50-62 (E192); "Poe, Paris 1846: la Lettre pillée |Poe, Paris 1946: the purloined letter|," pp. 63-68 (E2104); Roger Dadoun, "Un 'sublime amour' de Sherlock Holmes et de Sigmund Freud |A 'sublime love" of Sherlock Holmes and Sigmund Freud|," pp. 69-76; Michel Korinman, "Vi(e)sages d'Allemagne, le genre neutre |Life/faces of Germany, the neutral genre|," pp. 77-88 (C461); Fredric Jameson, "L'éclatement du récit et la clôture californienne |The breaking open of the narrative and Californian closure|," pp. 89-101 (E415); Jean-Patrick Manchette, "Réponses |Answers|," pp. 102-107 (interview); "Bibliographie raisonnée de la littérature critique |Annotated bibliography of critical literature|," p. 108-27.

B347. Rosal, Juan del. Crimen y criminal en la novela policial |Crime and criminal in the detective novel|. Madrid: Instituto Editorial Reus, 1947. 411pp. Not seen.

B348. Rosenberg, Bernard and David Manning White, eds. Mass Culture. The Popular Arts in America. New York: The Free Press, 1957.

In a section on detective fiction, the following articles are reprinted: Edmund Wilson, "Who Cares Who Killed Roger Ackroyd?," pp. 149-53 (C867); George Orwell, "Raffles and Miss Blandish," pp. 154-64 (C606); Charles J. Rolo, "Simenon and Spillane: The Metaphysics of Murder for the Millions," pp. 165-75 (E2676); and Christopher La Farge, "Mickey Spillane and His Bloody Hammer," pp. 176-85 (E2743).

B349. Routley, Erik. The Puritan Pleasures of the Detective Story: A Personal Monograph. London: Gollancz, 1972. 253pp. Bibliography and index.
Excellent chapters on Doyle and Chesterton; distinctive approach to modern British writers; totally unreliable on American writers (even including Poe). Breen 55. CC S51. (REB)

B350. Ruehlmann, William. Saint with a Gun: The Unlawful Private Eye. NY: New York University Press, 1974. xvi, 155pp.
One-sided study of the American private eye story, condemning the entire genre as "vigilante literature." Breen 56. (REB)

B351. Sadoul, Jacques, ed. Anthologie de la littérature policière |Anthology of detective literature|. Paris: Editions Ramsay, 1980.
An enormous anthology which goes from Conan Doyle to Jerome Charyn and collects 33 detective short stories supposed to cover the subject. Introduction, introductory notes to stories and a bibliography. (JB)

B352. Sakabe, Goro. Sekai Tantei Hishi |World secret history of the detective|. Nagano: Hoshi Shobo, 1946. 317pp. Bibliography.
This study deals with real and fictional detectives and traces their historical development. Extensive treatment of Lecoq, Conan Doyle and others. (HS/TT)

B353. Sakaguchi, Ango. Watashi no Tantei Shosetsu |My detective fiction|. Tokyo: Kadokawa Shoten, 1978. 196pp.
This famous author advocates his position that detective fiction is a game of wits between writers and readers, a position he supported in his own several masterpieces. This book is a collection of 26 essays on literature which features all five of the essays in which he presented his own views on detective fiction. (HS/TT)

B354. Sakurai, Hajime and others. Mystery Map: Meitantei-Tachi no Ashiato |Mystery maps: footprints of great detectives|. Tokyo: Hayakawa Shobo, (1982). 115pp. Illus.
An enjoyable book in the which the author-illustrator selects 25 great detectives of America, Britain and France, from Sherlock Holmes to Cordelia Gray, and their major cases, presenting the backgrounds and characters of the stories in maps and illustrations. It includes essays by other writers on each detective. (HS/TT)

B355. Sandoe, James, ed. Murder: Plain and Fanciful, with Some Milder Malefactions. Written by Divers Hands & Gathered here by James Sandoe. NY: Sheridan House, 1948. pp. xii, 628pp.
Characterized by Barzun & Taylor as a "virtually perfect anthology." Critical and scholarly contributions by the editor include an excellent Foreword and an annotated checklist, "Criminal Clef: Tales and Plays Based on Real Crimes," pp. 591-628, including a checklist of "Cases and Persons Cited." The "murder plain" is non-fictional accounts of real crimes; the "murder fanciful" is fictional accounts. CC 2774. (REB)

B356. Sano, Yo. Suiri Nikki |Mystery diary|. Tokyo: Ushio Shuppansha, 1976. 384pp.

B356a. ______. Shin Suiri Nikki |New mystery diary|. Tokyo: Kobun-sha, 1980. 262pp.
The author is a popular mystery writer, and is still writing periodical essays with the title of "mystery diary." The books are collections of

these essays, with random thoughts on mystery fiction in general and reviews of the current scene. His comments on mystery fiction are logical, impartial and persuasive. This first book has almost all of his non-periodical mystery essays as well as the periodical essays. (HS/TT)

B357. Sayers, Dorothy L. ed. Great Short Stories of Detection, Mystery and Horror. London; Gollancz, 1928; as The Omnibus of Crime, NY: Payson & Clarke, 1929. CC 2778.

B357a. ______. Great Short Stories of Detection, Mystery and Horror: Second Series. London: Gollancz, 1931; as The Second Omnibus of Crime, NY: Coward-McCann, 1932. CC 2779.

B357b. ______. Great Short Stories of Detection, Mystery and Horror: Third Series. London: Gollancz, 1934; as The Third Omnibus of Crime, NY: Coward-McCann, 1935.

Mammoth compendia of mystery fiction in its widest sense, with superb Introductions by the editor. The Introduction to the first volume has been frequently reprinted (C725). CC 2781. (REB)

B358. Schiller, Friedrich. (Foreword). In Merkwuerdige Rechtsfaelle als ein Bietrag zur Geschichte der Menschheit |Noteworthy legal cases as a contribution to the history of mankind|, Vol. I, edited by Friedrich I. Niethammer, pp. 2-4. Jena: Christian Heinrich Cuno's Erben, 1792. Reprinted in Fricke, Gerhard and Herbert Goepfert, eds. Friedrich Schiller, Saemliche Werke |Friedrich Schiller, complete works|, Vol. 5 (Munich: Hauser Verlag, 1960), pp. 864-66.

Recommendation of the educational as well as entertainment value of the François Gayot de Pitaval collection of true crime cases, Causes célèbres et intéressantes, avec les jugements qui les ont décidées |Interesting and famous cases, with the verdicts which decided them|, 20 vols., 1734-1743. Schiller attributes the popularity of sensational literature of all kinds to the human tendency towards emotional and complicated situations. He states that these law cases fit the needs quite well: they are beneficial for one's moral development and are as excitingly written as novels. (GG)

B359. Schimmelpfennig, Arthur. Beitraege zur Geschichte des Kriminalromans. Ein Wegweiser durch die Kriminal-Literatur der Vergangenheit und Gegenwart |Contributions toward the history of the crime novel: a guide through the crime fiction of the past and present|. Dresden and Leipzeig: Moewig & Hoeffner, 1908. 16pp.

Short but informative monograph tracing the history of German, French, Italian, Russian and English crime fiction from literary ancestors such as Schiller, Dostoyevsky and Dickens. In addition, Schimmelpfennig distinguishes carefully among crime, detective and "cracksman" fiction. One of the first German monographs in the genre.(GG)

B360. Schoenhaar, Rainer F. Novelle und Kriminalschema. Ein Strukturmodell deutscher Erzaehlkunst um 1800 |Novella and criminal schema: a structural model of German narrative art circa 1800|. Bad Homburg and Berlin: Verlag Gehlen, 1969. 223pp. Index. Bibliography of primary and secondary sources.

Often read, cited and discussed study of criminous elements in late German romantic literature. Schoenhaar traces the "detection narrative schema" back to Schiller, Meissner, Brentano, Armin, E. T. A. Hoffmann and other important figures in German literature. However, he has been widely criticized for basing his study on the assumption that the personal figure of a detective is not essential to the detection structure as well as for excluding less than "high" literature. The result is that not much detective fiction is covered. But Schoenhaar's book is important in that it is the most painstaking effort to find the criminous elements in German literature. Reviews: Arcadia 6:3(1971):321-26; MLQ 31 (Sept (1980):388-91. (GG)

B361. Schreuders, Piet. Paperbacks, U.S.A.: A Graphic History, 1939-1959. Translated from the Dutch by Josh Pachter. San Diego, CA: Blue Dolphin Enterprises, 1981. (Original edition published by Loeb (Amsterdam) and Baart, Borbesck (Belgium), 1980; and by Virgin Books (London), 1981, as The Book of Paperbacks.) 259pp. Wraps. Bibliography and index. Illustrated.

A history of the major paperback publishing houses. The focus is on design and artwork and there are short biographies of major artists. Review: PQ 4 (1981), pp. 46-49.

B362. Schulz-Buschhaus, Ulrich. Formen und Ideologien des Kriminalromans. Ein Gattungsgeschichtlicher Essays [Forms and ideologies of the crime novel: a genre-historical essay]. Schwerpunkte Romanistik 14. Frankfurt a. M.: Athenaion, 1975. 244pp. Index.

Serious, scholarly examination of the structural and literary qualities in the crime fiction genre. The author proceeds by selecting authors whose narrative forms and plot structures are exemplary of the form and vary widely from one another. Included are chapters on Poe, Collins, Gaboriau, Doyle, Sayers, Boileau-Narcejac, Hammett and Chandler, the Sicilian author Leonardo Sciascia, as well as on the characters Arsène Lupin, Fantômas and Maigret. This is one of the most quoted critical works in German, and is written from an approach similar to that of the American "Popular Culture" school. (GG)

B363. Schwartz, Saul, ed. The Detective Story: An Introduction to the Whodunit. Skokie, Illinois: National Textbook Co., 1975.

Compendium of representative mystery fiction from Poe through contemporary authors, with commentaries, annotations and class "activity" assignments by the editor. Compiled as a textbook for high school-level courses on the detective story. (REB)

B364. Scott, Sutherland. Blood in Their Ink: The March of the Modern Mystery Novel. Foreword by A. Beverley Baxter. London: Stanley Paul, 1953; Folcroft, Pa: Folcroft Library Editions, 1973. (Japanese edition translated by Koki Naganuma. Gendai Suiri Shosetsu no Ayumi. Tokyo: Sogen-sha.) 200pp. Index.

Descriptive treatment of modern mystery fiction, with much information on plots, characters and settings of individual works. Scott sometimes hits on a telling phrase, such as his reference to R. Austin Freeman's inverted detective stories as the "backside foremost type of story," but more often exhibits a tin ear for language: the "Had-I-but-known" school is referred to as "If-I-had-done-it," for example. Some of the opinions are eccentric, such as the judgment that early Ellery Queen novels such as The Egyptian Cross Mystery are "pleasantly down-to-earth." Scott casually and without warning gives away the murderer's identity in several novels---The Murder of Roger Ackroyd, The Egyptian Cross Mystery, The Siamese Twin Mystery, and others. Names and titles are sometimes slightly skewed: "Phoebe Atwell Taylor," Rex Stout's They Buried Caesar, Elizabeth Daly's The Wrong Way Up (instead of down). And throughout the book there is an overwhelming preference for "the native British product." With all its faults, this is an oddly charming and enjoyable book, but be wary of its "facts." Breen 3. CC 3023. (REB)

B365. Seymour-Smith, Martin. Novels and Novelists. NY: St. Martin's Press, 1980. 288pp. Index of titles. Illus.
The essay on Crime Fiction (pp 51-52) is written by H. R. F. Keating who maintains that crime fiction is still a "thing apart" and is written for entertainment. There are some references to mystery fiction in the section on "Fiction and Illustration" (pp. 241-252) and some genre writers are included in the alphabetical guide of author biographies which occupies about 154pp of the book.

B366. Shenker, Israel. Words and Their Masters. NY: Doubleday & Co., 1974. Photographs by Jill Krementz. pp. 15-368.
Interviews with, and profiles of, several dozen writers, plus miscellaneous essays on words and writing. Subjects include Jorge Luis Borges (pp. 38-42), Graham Greene (pp. 75-81), Georges Simenon (pp. 109-114), Alain Robbe-Grillet (pp. 135-140), Isaac Asimov (pp. 253-55), Rex Stout (pp. 260-64), and Gore Vidal (pp. 271-76). Most of the pieces originally appeared, sometimes in abbreviated form, in The New York Times. (REB)

B367. Shinpyo-sha, editor. Bessatsu Shinpyo |Extra Shinpyo|. Tokyo: Shinpyo-sha, 1975. Illus. Bibliographies.
This is a critical series, mainly focusing on popular literature, published irregularly as special issues of Shinpyo magazine. For the most part, it contains short comments on and subjective views of targeted writers. The majority of the contributions are published for the first time, but there are some reprints. Each issue has scholarly materials such as photographs, a bibliography and a chronology. The writers covered are as follows: Toshiyuki Kajiyana, Haruhiko Oyabu, Tsutomu Minakami, Futaro Yamada, Jiro Nitta, Michio Tsuzuki and Nobuhiko Kobayashi. (HS/TT)

B368. Shin-seinen Henshubu, ed. Sekai Tantei Shosetsu Zenshu: Dai Ikkan |World mystery fiction series: volume I|. Tokyo: Hakubunkan, 1930, 441pp.
This volume contains 26 detective short stories by Voltaire, Schiller and others. Also included is a history of mystery fiction. (HS/TT)

B369. Shiraishi, Kiyoshi. Kodo Bungaku toshiteno Tantei Shosetsu |Detective fiction as action literature|. Tokyo: Jiyu Shupan, 1949. 213pp.
A collection of 14 critical essays, with emphasis on the essence of mystery fiction. (HS/TT)

B370. ______. Tantei Shosetsu no Kyoshu ni tsuite |On nostalgia for detective fiction|. Tokyo: Fuji Shobo, 1949. 163pp.
A collection of 10 critical essays from the viewpoint of social philosophy. Mystery fiction is advocated as an art form and the critical perspective is impressive but, with its numerous lapses in logic, the book has not had much influence. (HS/TT)

B371. Skenazy, Paul. The New Wild West: The Urban Mysteries of Dashiell Hammett and Raymond Chandler. BSU Western Writers Series, Number 54. Boise, Idaho: Boise State University, 1982. 52pp. Wraps. With primary and secondary bibliographies for Hammett and Chandler and a general bibliography of secondary sources for detective fiction.
A good discussion of the tradition of the private eye and the roots of the modern street-wise detective in several traditions, most importantly that

of the Western hero. Skenazy sees Hammett as expanding the range of American literary language as Mark Twain did with the tradition of Southwestern humor. He discusses, in Chandler, the writer's "moralistic impulses," his struggles with the detective form and uses of it for direct commentary. There are also some comments on Ross Macdonald's work (pp. 44-47).

B372. Skvorecký, Josef. Nápady ctemáre detektivek |Reading detective stories|. Prague: československý spisovatel, 1965. 164pp. Illus. No index or notes. Photos and drawings.
Reviewed in Books Abroad 40:4 (1966):474-75 by Josef Rysan (Vanderbilt University) as a history of "the practice and theory of the detective story in Anglo-Saxon countries." Includes biocritical chapters on Poe, Collins, Doyle, Ronald Knox, Hammett and Sayers.

B373. Slung, Michele B., ed. Crime on Her Mind. Fifteen Stories of Female Sleuths from the Victorian Era to the Forties. NY: Pantheon Books, 1975 (hb); 1976 (pb). xxx, 380pp.
In addition to the fiction, there are an editor's Introduction, notes, a "Selective Bibliography" and an annotated list of characters, "The Women Detectives: A Chronological Survey," pp. 357-77. (REB)

B374. Smith, Herbert F. The Popular American Novel, 1865-1920. Boston: Twayne, 1980. 192pp. Bibliography and index.
Detective story writers are only referred to in passing--and not always favorably--but there is one reference to William Dean Howells who wrote some "exquisite detective stories featuring M. Joly, who might be a model for some parts of Simenon's Maigret" (p. 120).

B375. Smyth, Frank, and Ludwig, Myles. The Detectives: Crime and Detection in Fact and Fiction. Philadelphia & NY: J. B. Lippincott, 1978. 191pp. Illus.
Introductory chapter on the "first" professional detectives who inspired Poe, Dickens, and Balzac through the era of Hammett and Chandler. References to fictional detectives in other parts of the text but this is mainly a book on real-life murderers.

B376. Society of Crime Writers in Stockholm. By Us! Translations by Claudia Brannback. Härnösand, Sweden: Harnosands Boktryckeri AB, 1981. 54pp. Wraps.
It might more accurately have been called Buy Us!: a promotional brochure (in English) describing 27 crime novels by nine contemporary Swedish writers (Jan Eric Arvastson, Ulf Durling, Jan Olof Ekholm, Jan Ekström, Kjell E. Genberg, Tage Giron, Olov Svedelid, Sven Sörmark, and Ulla Trenter). The booklet was prepared for distribution at the International Crime Writers Conference in Stockholm, 1981. The writers of the blurbs/plot summaries are not credited, but the translation into English was by Claudia Brannback. The cover has postage-stamp size photos of the writers. A separate 8-page brochure in the same format describes three psychological crime novels by Marianne Jeffmar (giving away the plot and the murderer's identity in all three cases). (REB/WA)

B377. Sormano, Elena. Il romanzo giallo e i suoi meccanismi |The giallo novel and its techniques|. Turin: Paravia, 1979.
Written especially for an interdisciplinary series intended for secondary-school students, the volume illustrates with many examples the basic elements of the detective novel, from mystery/peril plots to the character of the private investigator, the various kinds of policemen, the

motive for the crime, etc. The analysis is enriched with questions for use by teachers, with suggestions for possible discussion topics and with a basic glossary. While proclaiming the positive value of the giallo in the school curriculum, the author considers the giallo for children to be "much less stimulating and positive," because it inculcuates in an infantile way "a false reality, false problems, false situations, a false heroism, an idea of false justice; it is moralistic with the result that it is separated from reality and therefore scarcely believable." (RC)

B378. "Spécial Polar: vingt ans de littérature policière |Polar "special": 20 years of detective literature|." Magazine littéraire no. 194 (April 83), pp. 14-58. Photos, film stills and drawings.
Contents: François Guérif, "Spécial Polar," pp. 14-15 (editor's introduction); Alain Demouzon, Jean Vautrin and Alexandre Lous, "Polar? Vous avez dit, Polar? |Polar? did you say polar?|," pp. 16-18 (three writers talk about detective fiction); Jean-Pierre Deloux, "Le Noir New-Look |The série noire new-look|," pp. 21-23 (new trends in French detective fiction); W. Somerset Maugham and Edmund Wilson, "Pour ou contre le roman policier |For or against the detective novel|," pp. 24-29; Robert Louit, "Le Grand Ami du crime, Harry Whittington |The great friend of crime, H.W.|," pp. 30-31 (interview; photo); Jean-Jacques Brochier, "L'Anarchiste cérébral |The cerebral anarchist|," pp. 32-33 (Simenon, E2600); Léo Malet, "Excellent pour les nerfs |Excellent for your nerves|," pp. 33-35 (fiction excerpt); Alexandre Lous, "Meurtres au féminin," p. 36 (Agatha Christie, Patricia Highsmith, Ruth Rendell); Jacques Baudou, Jean-Pierre Deloux, François Guérif and Alexandre Lous, "54 auteurs fichés |Dossier: 54 authors|," pp. 37-49 (A13); Jacques Baudou and Michel Lebrun, "Polars and antipodes |Polars from the antipodes|," pp. 50-51 (C68); Francois Truffaut, Claude Miller, Jean-Jacques Beineix, "Noires Scènes de tournage |Série noire scenes on film|," pp. 52-53 (film directors' statements); Pierre Lebedel, "Polaroïdes," pp. 54-55 (comic-strip detectives); Jacques Baudou, Jean-Pierre Delous and Francois Guerif, "Polars en series |Polars in séries|," pp. 56-58 (A14); "Bonnes Reférénces," p. 58 (short, annotated bibliography of reference works).

B379. Steele, Timothy Reid. "Lawful Meaning, Sinful Fact: A Study of the Sources and Development of Detective Fiction." Unpublished doctoral dissertation. Brandeis, 1977. 204pp. DAI 38/01A, p. 237. Not seen.

B380. Stewart, R. F. ...and Always a Detective: Chapters on the History of Detective Fiction. London & North Pomfret, VT: David & Charles, Inc., 1980. 351pp. Bibliography and index.
An interesting, if rambling, attempt to bring some order to the "vaguely defined" parameters of the field of detective fiction and to trace its early history. Stewart is particularly concerned with the detective and detection and uses these subjects as his focus. There is a useful appendix in which he corrects numerous errors in the descriptions accompanying the entries in Victorian Detective Fiction (A58). Breen 4. CC S116 (TAD 13:4).

B381. Suiri Shosetsu Kenku-kai, ed. Subarashiki Tatei-tachi |Wonderful detectives|. Tokyo: Seinen Shokan, 1979. 208pp. Illus.
Detection puzzles based on one case for each of 21 non-Japanese and 4 Japanese series detectives. Though profiles of each detective are included, the material is derivative and of no critical value. The editing organization exists in name only, created by Tomoyuki Sato, a journalist,

and others for this book. When the dust-wrapper was changed, the title was changed to Sekai no Meitantei to Suiri o Shinai ka? |Won't you play a detection game with the world's greatest detectives?, 1979| and then to Suiri Shosetsu no Nazo o Toku Hon |The book to solve puzzles in mystery dtories, 1980|. (HS/TT)

B382. Sunano, Kyohei. Meitantei Hyobanki |Essays on the great detectives|. Tokyo: Bun'yu-sha, 1978. 277pp.
A collection of essays on 11 non-Japanese fictional detectives. Filled with irrelevant quotations, superficial discussion and careless errors, the only valuable part is the appendix, "An Introduction to the Ways of Private Eyes." (HS/TT)

B383. Sutherland, John. Bestsellers: Popular Fiction of the 1970s. London & Boston: Routledge and Kegan Paul, 1981. Index and bibliography.
See chapters 18 and 19 for material on mystery/thriller/spy fiction.

B384. Suzuki, Yukio. Eibei no Suiri Sakka-tachi |Mystery writers of America and England|. Tokyo: Hyoron-sha, 1980. 284pp. Bibliography and index. Illus.
The author, a critic of English literature, translates and writes mystery fiction. This book is a survey of the mystery fiction of the United States and England, intended as a reference book for college students. It is loosely compiled from previously published articles, with too much emphasis on Poe and Conan Doyle, and too little unity. (HS/TT)

B385. Suzuki, Yukio, ed. Satsujin Geijutsu |Murder art|. Tokyo: Arechi Shuppansha, 1959. 274pp.
An anthology of 18 critical essays by Japanese and non-Japanese writers. The non-Japanese writers are Dorothy Sayers, G. K. Chesterton, W. H. Auden, Nicholas Blake, George Orwell, Edmund Wilson, Alfred Hitchcock, E. S. Gardner, Raymond Chandler, S. S. Van Dine and Ronald Knox. (HS/TT)

B386. "Swedish Crime-Writers." Dast Magazine Vol. 14 Special Issue (1981). Photographs and illustrations.
An all English-language issue containing a mixture of short critical essays on and interviews with 19 Swedish crime writers, including 8 of those included in the By Us! booklet (B376). The essays consist mostly of plot summaries with some brief critical evaluations. Material other than interviews will be so noted in the contents listing. Contents: Tomas Arvidsson, pp. 3-4; Jenny Berthelius, pp. 5-6; K. Arne Blom, pp. 7-9; Jean Bolinder, pp. 10-12 (includes introductory biographical material, some bibliography, and some "opinions" on his books); Claes Brenman, p. 14; Ulf Durling, pp. 16-17 (short critical essay on his life and work; no interview material); Jan Olof Ekholm, pp. 19-20 (Ekholm is interviewed by his fictional character, Gran Sandahl); Rolf Nilsen, "Jan Ekström - The Intellectual Crime Novelist," pp. 21-22 (essay; no interview material); Kjell E. Genberg, pp. 24-26; Tage Giron, pp. 27, 30-31; Nils Hövenmark, pp. 32-33 (biocritical essay; no interview material); Elisabeth Kagerman, pp. 34-35; Maria Lang, pp. 36-37 (short essay; no interview material); Bertil Martensson, pp. 38-38 ("A Dast International Profile" with some interview material); Jan Martenson, pp. 40-42 (critical study); "Samuel Rosenbaum," pp. 43-44 (character in a series of novels by Leif Silbersky and Olov Svedelid; character profile by Rolf Nilsen); Olov Svedelid, pp. 45-46 (profile of writer's work; no interview material); Sven Sörmark, pp. 48-49 (critical essay by Johan Asplund; no

interview material); Ulla Trenter, pp. 50-51 (short critical essay; no interview material).

B387. Symons, Julian. Bloody Murder. A History from the Detective Story to the Crime Novel. London: Faber & Faber, 1972. U. S. title: Mortal Consequences. NY: Harper & Row, 1972. x, 269pp. Index.
A knowledgeable, entertaining and sometimes controversial account of the development of the detective story to what Symons views as the natural next step in its evolution. Breen 5. (REB)

B388. _____. British Crime Fiction. London: British Council and National Book League, 1974. 52pp. Pictorial wrapper.
Commentary and criticism largely extracted from Symons's book-length study Bloody Murder. Not seen. (REB)

B389. _____. Critical Observations. New Haven and New York: Ticknor and Fields, 1981. 213pp.
A collection of essays. The essays in part III ("Criminal Matters") will be cited by author, as follows: Christie (E602), Symons (C800), Simenon (E2694), Chandler (E452) and Hammett (E1424). All of the material was published previously and original sources--not given in the text--will be cited where possible. Sources for quotations are not given, and footnotes are incomplete. It is unfortunate that basic bibliographical information is not routinely cited for critical material but a prejudice against footnotes has led to a a widespread practice of either eliminating notes and failing to incorporate relevant information in the text or citing irregularly and incompletely.

B390. _____. Critical Occasions. London: Hamish Hamilton Ltd., 1966. 213pp. Anthology of Symons' literary essays, including five on matters pertaining to crime fiction, as follows: "The Face in the Mirror," pp. 149-153 (C902); "The Man Who Lost Himself," pp. 154-160 (true crime); "Reconstructing the Crime," pp. 161-167 (true crime); "Confidential Agents," pp. 168-73 (spy fiction); "Marlowe's Victim," pp. 174-80 (E451). Most of the essays are reprinted from the Times Literary Supplement. (GG)

B391. _____. The Detective Story in Britain. Writers and Their Work: No. 145, published for the British Council and the National Book League. London: Longmans, Green & Co., 1962; reprinted 1969 "with minor amendments to the text and a revised bibliography." 48pp. Wraps. Bibliography.
A thirty-page overview, containing many of the points made at greater length in Bloody Murder, plus a twelve-page "select bibliography" of representative works. The bibliography also contains a brief annotated list of critical and bibliographical studies. Frontispiece portraits of Collins, Doyle, Sayers, and Christie; includes Ronald Searle's drawing of Holmes's consulting rooms at 221b Baker Street. Breen 6. CC3043. (REB)

B392. _____. The Great Detectives. London: Orbis Publishing Ltd, Oct 1981. pp. 144pp. Illus. Bibliography. U. S. Edition: Great Detectives: Seven Original Investigations. NY: Abrams, 1981. 144pp. Illus. Bibliography.
Seven apocryphal episodes in the careers of famous fictional detectives: Sherlock Holmes, Miss Marple, Nero Wolfe, Ellery Queen, Inspector Maigret, Hercule Poirot, and Philip Marlowe. No direct critical commentary is involved, but the "Notes to the Investigations" relate Symons' pastiches to their original models, and there are bibliographies of each detective's exploits. A large part of the interest in this volume is

due to the illustrations: 40 color plates and 30 monochrome illustrations by Tom Adams (with help from Roy Coombes and Ivan Lapper). (REB)

B393. ______. The Modern Crime Story. Edinburgh: Tragara Press, 1980. Wraps. Edition limited to 25 copies with marbled paper covers, 125 copies with card covers. Not seen. (REB)

B394. ______. The Mystique of the Detective Story. Vancouver, BC, 1982. Wraps. Edition limited to 100 numbered copies. Fine press chapbook containing title essay. Not seen. (REB)

B395. Takagi, Akimitsu. Zuihitsu Tantei Shosetsu |Essays on detective fiction|. Tokyo: Masu Shobo, 1956. 245pp. Illus.
A collection of essays the author has written for various magazines, with emphasis on presentation and studies of gimmicks in mystery stories. (HS/TT)

B396. Talburt, Nancy Ellen, and Montgomery, Lyna Lee, eds. A Mystery Reader: Stories of Detection, Adventure, and Horror. NY: Scribners, 1974. 458pp.
A school text, with an introduction, notes and study aids. The critical notes are sketchy and would require considerable additional material to give students any substantive understanding of the field. Some previously published critical articles are included, as follows: W. H. Auden, "The Guilty Vicarage (excerpt)," pp. 208-214 (C34); Raymond Chandler, "The Simple Art of Murder (excerpt)," pp. 274-80 (C168); Ross Macdonald, "The Writer as Detective Hero," pp. 338-48 (C512); and Frank D. McSherry, "The Shape of Things to Come," pp. 433-44 (C524).

B397. Tamburini, Pico, editor. La polizia indaga |The police investigate|. Florence: Vallecchi, 1958. Vol. 15. 521pp.
This volume is part of a collection for children and is an anthology of detective stories preceded by an introduction and by notes on individual writers, from Poe to Faulkner. The author maintains that the relationship between the criminal and the detective is not a banal struggle betwen good and evil but, at its best, "the living emblem of a breach between man and his environment, between the individual and society, until the necessary balance is established." (RC)

B398. Tamura, Ryuichi. Shosai no Shitai |The body in the library|. Tokyo: Kawade Shoboshinsha, 1978. 270pp.
The author, a poet, has translated a lot of mystery stories, especially those by Agatha Christie. One-third of this book is taken up by mystery-related essays, such as afterwords he has written for the Japanese edition of books by Barnaby Ross, F.W. Crofts, Roald Dahl and others. (HS/TT)

B399. Tanaka, Junji. Ango no Hanashi |The cipher story|. Tokyo: Tokuma Shoten, 1967. 229pp. Illus., bibl.
In addition to references to research books on ciphers, there are also many references to codes and ciphers in detective fiction. (HS/TT)

B400. Tanaka, Komimasa. Neko wa Yonaka ni Sanpo Suru |Cats prowl at night|. Tokyo: Tojusha, 1980. 277pp.
A collection of essays by the author, a writer and translator of mystery fiction, especially hard-boiled fiction. Although one-third of the book is taken up with his afterwords for the books he has translated, these essays are mostly miscellaneous notes, and, like his 1981 book, Komi-san

no Futsuka-yoi Note |Mr. Komimasa's hangover notes|, have very little to do with mysteries. (HS/TT)

B401. Tani, Stefano. "The Contribution of the Detective Novel Genre to Postmodern American and Italian Fiction." Unpublished doctoral dissertation. DAI (1981) 42/4, p. 1627A.

The French new novel, Borges, Nabokov; the anti-detective novel. Scheduled for publication by Southern Illinois University Press in 1984 as The Doomed Detective: The Contribution of the Detective Novel to Postmodern American and Italian Fiction.

B402. Temanummer om Popularkulturen |Special issue on popular literature|. Vår lösen (Magazine) 62:8 (1971).

Miscellaneous essays; about half this issue deals with genre material. (IH)

B403. Thomas, Gilbert. How to Enjoy Detective Fiction. London: Rockliff, 1947. 108pp. Bibliography and index.

Contributes little to the enlightenment promised in the title, but contains a brief history of the genre and numerous references to specific authors and books, both important and obscure. Breen 58. (REB)

B404. Thomson, H. Douglas. Masters of Mystery: A Study of the Detective Story. London: Collins, 1931; Folcroft, PA: Folcroft Library Editions, 1973; NY: Dover Publications, 1978, with a new introduction and notes by E. F. Bleiler. Excerpted in Haycraft (B142). (Japanese edition translated by Banshu Hiro. Tantei Sakkaron. Tokyo: Shunju-sha, 1937)

An early attempt at a history and critical survey of mystery fiction, done with wit and verve. Only one chapter is devoted to the American detective story, concentrating on Van Dine and Queen. There are three indexes, containing separate listings of the detective stories, authors, and detectives mentioned in the text. In the Dover edition, Bleiler's introduction and notes contribute to a modern evaluation of Thomson's theoretical position. Breen 7. CC 3047. (REB)

B405. Ti kriminelle minutter (Ten Criminal Minutes). Copenhagen: Spektrum, 1966.

Ten essays. (IH)

B406. Tonoyama, Taiji. Tonoyama Taiji no Mystery & Jazz Nikki |Taiji Tonoyama's mystery & jazz diary|. Tokyo: Kodan-sha, 1981. 215pp.

The author, an actor and enthusiastic mystery lover, writes journal essays, most of which include reviews with grades for mysteries he has read. This book is a collection of these essays. He has written another book, in the same vein, Jam Jam Nikki |Jam jam diary|, 1977. (HS/TT)

B407. Tournier, Marcel. Le Roman policier. Tunis: La rose des sables, 1941. 43pp.

Text of a lecture (April 1, 1941) in which the author celebrates the highly diverting virtues of the detective novel. (JB)

B408. Tourteau, Jean-Jacques. D'Arsène Lupin à San Antonio: Le Roman policier français de 1900 a 1970 |From Arsène Lupin to San Antonio: the French detective novel from 1900-1970|. Tours: Editions Mame, 1971. 372pp. Ill.

A doctoral thesis in which the author studies the genre from a historical and a psycho-sociological viewpoint. There are also studies of individual authors and descriptive analyses of about 20 important works.

B409. Treat, Lawrence, editor. Mystery Writer's Handbook, by the Mystery Writers of America. Cincinnati, OH: Writer's Digest Books, 1976. Hardcover and paperback. 284pp. Index.

The first edition of this handbook was edited by Herbert Brean (B48). This revision is virtually a new book: of its 33 chapters, only 7 (by Brown, Waugh, Bloom, Lyon, John D. MacDonald, Barbara Frost, Rex Stout and Allingham/Hodges) are carried over from the earlier edition. Six of the chapters are compiled from responses sent to MWA members. Most of the differences between editions reflect the changes in the mystery field and in its roster of practitioners over a period of twenty years. The new material will be cited in the partial contents listing. Contents (partial): Lawrence Treat, "Preface," pp. 1-6; (various), "Why Do You Write?," pp. 7-11; Bruce Cassiday, "Into Something Rich and Strange," pp. 13-21; (various), "Where Do You Get Your Ideas?," pp. 22-31; (various), "When and How Do You Write?," pp. 56-66; Hillary Waugh, "The Series vs. the Non-Series Detective," pp. 69-72; Thomas M. McDade, "Homicide and Other Investigations," pp. 75-90 (true crime); Eleanor Sullivan, "How to Please an Editor," pp. 93-100; Michael Avallone, "The Narrative Hook," pp. 109-111; Janet Gregory Vermandel, "Deciding on Viewpoint," pp. 125-28; Richard Martin Stern, "Suspense," pp. 135-39; Dorothy Salisbury Davis, "Background and Atmosphere," pp. 141-47; Aaron Marc Stein, "Style," pp. 155-63; Stanley Ellin, "The Ungentle Art of Revision," pp. 165-69; Lawrence Treat, "Once Over--Not Lightly," pp. 171-75; Helen McCloy, "Cutting: Surgery or Butchery?," pp. 177-81; (various), "Avoiding Cliches Like the Plague," pp. 182-86; (various), "How Do You Handle Those Stumbling Blocks?," pp. 187-94; Phyllis A. Whitney, "What Do You Mean, 'Gothic'?," pp. 197-202; Dan Marlowe, "The Softcover Original," pp. 205-209; Edward D. Hoch, "The Pleasure of the Short Story," pp. 211-15; William T. Brannon, "Writing the True Crime Story," pp. 217-27; William P. McGivern, "Writing for Television and Movies," pp. 229-49; Bill Pronzini, "On Agents," pp. 251-55; Harold Q. Masur, "Legal Aspects," pp. 257-62; (various), "Tricks of the Trade," pp. 263-71; Index by author. (REB & WA)

B410. Tschimmel, Ira. Kriminalroman und Gesellschaftsdarstellung. Eine vergleichende Untersuchung zu Werken von Christie, Simenon, Dürrenmatt und Capote. |The crime novel and the representation of society: a comparative study of the works of Christie, Simenon, Dürrenmatt and Capote). Bonn: Bouvier Verlag Herbert Grundmann, 1979. 277pp.

Dissertation-like comparison of four authors to illustrate the point that social realism and the presence of the puzzle element are inversely proportional in crime fiction. The works of the four authors are seen as lying on a sliding scale from most puzzle-bound and least realistic to least puzzle-bound and most realistic. (GG)

B411. Tsuide, Ikuteru. Tantei Shosetsu-ron |Comments on detective fiction|. Tokyo: Gen'eijo, 1977. 290pp. Bibliography.

This long critical essay comments on the definition, classification and essence of mystery fiction. The attempt is praiseworthy but, unfortunately, the text is not persuasive and is boring. (HS/TT)

B412. Tsuzuki, Michio. Kiiroi Heya wa Ika ni Kaiso Sareta ka? |How is the yellow room remodeled?|. Tokyo: Shobun-sha, 1975. 247pp.

This long critical essay comments on ideal puzzle-stories, with Japanese and non-Japanese mystery stories as examples. The author's position is that the appeal of puzzle-stories is in the puzzle and their logical interpretation, and insists on the resurgence of "great detectives" neglected in Japan. The book includes his essay, "My way of writing mystery fiction." (HS/TT)

B413. ______. Shitai o Buji ni Kesu Made |Until I safely dispose of the body|. Tokyo: Shobun-sha, 1973. 357pp.
The author is a former mystery translator, former editor of the Japanese edition of EQMM and now a mystery writer. This book is a collection of essays on mystery fiction from the writer's viewpoint and on Japanese mystery writers like Juran Hisao and of introductory articles (written during his EQMM editorship) on non-Japanese writers like Ian Fleming. (HS/TT)

B414. Tuska, Jon. The Detective in Hollywood. Garden City, NY: Doubleday & Company, Inc., 1978. xx, 436pp. Illus. Index.
An idiosyncratic, occasionally opaque, but consistently fascinating and information-packed study of the American detective film. The book is based on extensive original research in film studio archives and on interviews with many of the principals involved in the films discussed. There is much commentary on mystery fiction and on writers such as Chandler, Charteris, Hammett, Ross Macdonald, Ellery Queen, and S. S. Van Dine. The book is illustrated with nearly 200 carefully chosen film stills and candid photographs. Breen 59. (REB)

B415. Uekusa, Jun'ichi. Amefuri dakara Mystery demo Benkyo Shiyo |Studying the mystery as it rains|. Tokyo: Shobun-sha, 1972. Reissued in two volumes, Tantei Shosetsu no Tanoshimi |Pleasure of detective fiction|, 1979; and Crime Club e Yokoso |Welcome to the Crime Club|, 1978. 446pp. Index. Illus.
The author is a critic of mystery fiction, modern jazz, movies and overseas culture. The first part consists of essays in which he introduces mystery writers and novels that are not yet known in Japan. The second part is a collection of his articles for the Crime Club series (Japanese edition) which he supervised. (HS/TT)

B416. ______. Edogawa Ranpo to Watashi |Edogawa Rampo and me|. Tokyo: Shobun-sha, 1976. 245pp.
A collection of the writer's essays not included in his first collection (s). (HS/TT)

B417. ______. Mystery no Genko wa Yonaka ni Tetsuya de Kako |Writing mystery essays all through the night|. Tokyo: Hayakawa Shobo, 1978. 366pp. Illus.
Essays written after the publication of his first two books. Though there are some errors in these essays written late in his life, the book won the Mystery Writers of Japanese award as the best critical book in 1979 in consideration of his past accomplishments. (HS/TT)

B418. Ueno, Takashi. Shijo de Yume Miru: Gendai Taishu Shosetsu-ron |Dreaming on paper: comments on modern popular fiction|. Tokyo: Kagyu-sha, 1980. 220pp.
A collection of critical essays in which Ueno deals with 10 widely-read popular fiction writers in Japan from an original viewpoint. Among these writers, there are four mystery writers: Haruhiko Oyabu, Futaro Yamada, Seishi Yokomizo, and Edogawa Rampo. (HS/TT)

B419. Unicorn Mystery Book Club News. August 1948 - October 1952.
Edited by Clayton Rawson, this eight-page, then 16-page newsletter mailed to subscribers to the Unicorn Book Club, described the following month's selections; carried news items of MWA members, with photographs of the annual awards dinners and texts of the dinner "playets," written, among others, by Clayton Rawson, John Dickson Carr, and Harold Q. Masur; and published often lengthy profiles of Unicorn Club authors. These profiles will be cited in the Authors section of the bibliography. They present much valuable contemporary biographical information on the writers, some of whom are not included in any of the standard critical sources. The Unicorn is always readable, often instructive, and has only previously been cited by Edward D. Hoch in a TAD article (C400) where he describes it as "the best history of MWA during the years 1948-1952." His evaluation of its importance is accurate and it is unfortunate that the newsletter is not more widely available to scholars and fans.

B420. Usborne, Richard. Clubland Heroes. London: Constable, 1953; revised edition, London: Barrie & Jenkins, 1974; third edition, Hutchinson, 1983. 186pp.
A "nostalgic" study of the fiction of John Buchan (E296), "Sapper" (E2478) and Dornford Yates (E3147). Breen 60.

B421. Varma, Devendra D. The Gothic Flame. London: Arthur Barker Ltd., 1957. Bibliography and Index.
Unlike many students of the Gothic novel, Varma believes that its influence on modern detective fiction is "by itself a fruitful topic for independent research." There are occasional references to this relationship in the main body of the text, but Appendix III (pp. 237-241) is a concise treatment of the subject. With the disintegration of "pure" Gothic fiction, Varma sees the creation of "building stones" for both detective fiction and thrillers. He refers to sensation novels, Doyle, Christie, James Fenimore Cooper and the frontier tracker/detective in this thoughtful introduction to a topic on which a major study is long overdue.

B422. Veraldi, Gabriel. Roman d'espionnage. Series: Que sais-je, no. 2025. 1983.
The underlying thesis of this study of the espionage novel is that only "a real secret agent can write a good spy novel." A mediocre effort which is absurdly reductive of the topic, and shows a total lack of critical judgement along with ideological short-sightedness. (Annie Matiquat)

B423. Ves Losada, Alfredo. En torno al gênero policial |Concerning the detective genre|. Buenos Aires: Ediciones del Ministerio de Educacion, 1957. Not seen.

B424. Vogt, Jochen, ed. Der Kriminalroman. Zur Theorie und Geschichte einer Gattung |The crime novel: on the theory and history of a genre|. 2 vols. Munich: Wilhelm Fink Verlag, 1971. Vol. I, 307pp; Vol. II, 315-595pp., including index.
German-language anthology of 40 essays on the crime story. Includes translations from English, French, Italian and Russian. The essays in Vol. I are primarily historical and in Vol. II primarily analytic. Vol. I: Klaus Guenther Just, "Edgar Allan Poe und die Folgen |E. A. Poe and the consequences|," pp. 9-32 (C436); Manfred Smuda, "Variation and Innovation," pp. 33-63 (C766); Willy Haas, "Mysteries," pp. 63-71 (C356);

Pierre Boileau/Thomas Narcejac, "Emil Gaboriau," pp. 71-76 (B37); Viktor Schklovsky, "Die Kriminalerzaehlung bei Conan Doyle |Conan Doyle's detective stories|," pp. 79-64 (C732); G. K. Chesterton, "Verteidigung von Detektivgeschichten |Defense of the detective story|," pp. 95-98 (C178); Jean Roudaut, "Gaston Leroux," pp. 98-116 (E1760); Willy Haas, "Die Theologie im Kriminalroman (Theology in the crime novel|," pp. 116-22 (E3020); Dorothy Sayers, "Aristoteles ueber Detektivliteratur," pp. 123-38 (C724); I. I. Revzin, "Zur semiotischen Analyse des Detektivromans am Beispiel der Romane Agatha Christies |Towards a semiotic analysis of the detective novel: example--the novels of Agatha Christie|," pp. 139-42 (E595); S. S. Van Dine, "Zwanzig Regeln fuer das Schreiben von Detektivgeschichten |Twenty rules for writing detective stories|," pp. 143-47 (C827); Walter Blair, "Dashiell Hammett. Motive und Erzaehlstrukturen |D.H. themes and techniques|," pp. 147-64 (E1364); Raymond Chandler, "Mord ist keine Kunst |The simple art of murder|," pp. 164-85 (C168); Peter Fischer, "Neue Haeuser in der Rue Morgue |New houses in the Rue Morgue|," pp. 185-200 (C281); Hans Altenheim, "Ein Traum von Maigret |A dream from Maigret|," pp. 200-206 (E2583); Guenter Waldmann, "Kriminalroman--Anti-Kriminalroman; Duerrenmatts Requiem auf den Kriminalroman und die Anti-Aufklaerung |The crime novel--anti-crime novel; Dürrenmatt's requiem for the crime novel and the anti-crime novel|," pp. 206-27 (E1029); Hans Christoph Buch, "James Bond, oder der Kleinbuerger in Waffen |James Bond; or, the small citizen with weapons|," pp. 227-50 (E1089); Umberto Eco, "Die Erzaehlstrukturen bei ian Fleming |Ian Fleming's narrative structure|," pp. 250-93 (E1095); Pierre Boileau/Thomas Narcejac, "...Den Bankrott des Denkens Zelebrieren |To celebrate the bankruptcy of thought|," pp. 293-97 (C107a); Heinrich Vormweg, "Detektiven auf der Spur. Eine kritische Revue neuer Kriminalromane |Detectives on the trail. A critical review of new crime novels|," pp. 300-307 (C831). Vol. II: Bertolt Brecht, "Ueber die Popularitaet des Kriminalromans |On the popularity of the crime novel|," pp. 315-21 (C124); Ernst Bloch, "Philosophische Ansicht des Detektivromans |Philsophical view of the detective novel|," pp. 322-43 (C104); Siegfried Kracauer, "Detektiv |The detective|," pp. 343-56 (C462); Helmut Heissenbuettel, "Spielregeln des Kriminalromans |The crime novel's rules of the game|," pp. 356-71 (C392); Richard Alewyn, "Anatomie des Detektivromans |Anatomy of the detective novel|," pp. 372-404 (C12); Richard Gerber, "Verbrechungsdichtung und Kriminalroman |Criminal fiction and the crime novel|," pp. 404-20 (C308); Hans Daiber, "Nachahmung der Vorsehung |Imitation of providence|," pp. 421-36 (C213); Ulrich Suerbaum, "Der gefesselte Detekrivroman |The detective novel in shackles|," pp. 437-56 (C795); Guenter Bien, "Abenteuer und verborgene Wahrheit |Adventure and hidden truth|," pp. 457-72 (C95); Dietrich Naumann, "Kriminalroman und Dichtung |The crime novel and fiction|," pp. 473-83 (C570); Erich Thier, "Ueber den Detektivroman |On the detective novel|," pp. 483-99 (C80); Harry Proll, "Die Wirkung der Kriminalromane |The effect of crime novels|," pp. 500-515 (C652); Ernest Kaemmel, "Literatur unterm Tisch |Literature under the table|," pp. 516-32 (C439); Rudolf Roeder, "Zur Frage des Kriminalromans |On the question of the crime novel|," pp. 523-28 (C701); Otto Eckert, "Der Kriminalroman als Gattung |The crime novel as genre|," pp. 528-32 (C248); Karl Anders, "Der Kriminalroman |The crime novel|," pp. 533-45 (C19); Franz Hrastnik, "Das Verbrechen macht sich doch bezahlt |Crime does indeed pay|," pp. 545-59 (C415); Klaus Kunkel, "Ein artiger James Bond. Jerry Cotton under der Bastei-Verlag |A sort of James Bond: Jerry Cotton and the Bastei press|," pp. 559-78 (E714); Erika Dingeldey, "Wer ist der Schuldige? |Who is the guilty one?|," pp. 578-84 (C234); Bibliography of Sources, pp. 585-87; Index, 588-95.(GG)

B425. Watanabe, Kenji. Mystery Cocktail: Suiri Shosetsu Trick no Subete |Mystery cocktail: all the gimmicks of mystery fiction|. Tokyo: Kodan-sha, 1975. 262pp. Illus. Index.

An original introductory book. The author writes it as an entertaining book which is largely based on Edogawa Rampo's expert study, "A Collection of Categorical Gimmicks." Because of the author's accurate, deep knowledge, this is very pleasant reading. (HS/TT)

B426. Watson, Colin. Snobbery with Violence: Crime Stories and Their Audience. London: Eyre & Spottiswoode, 1971; NY: St. Martin's Press, 1972. 256pp (British edition). Index. Illus.

A sharply witty though seriously intended look at thriller fiction (mainly British) as a reflection of, and an influence upon, the social attitudes and prejudices of the reading audience. The 10 illustrations are cartoons reprinted from Punch. Breen 61. (REB)

B427. Wells, Carolyn. The Technique of the Mystery Story. Introduction by J. Berg Eisenwein. Springfield, MA: The Home Correspondence School, 1913. Pp. xiv, 336. Illus. Series: The Writer's Library. Revised Edition, 1929. Pp. xiv, 435. Illus. Index.

Wells' Technique is both a writer's manual, with well illustrated discussions of the various elements of narrative construction and a history of the genre. Wells includes ghost stories in her discussion, a genre that many purists would exclude. The 1929 edition was expanded and the index was revised. Breen 99.

B428. Wells, Walter. Tycoons and Locusts: A Regional Look at Hollywood Fiction of the 1930s. Carbondale: Southern Illinois University Press, 1973. vii-xiii, 139pp. Index, notes and a bibliographical narrative (pp. 132-134) reviewing relevant critical material.

A study of the relationships between literature and setting. The second chapter is a discussion of Horace McCoy's They Shoot Horses, Don't They? and James M. Cain's The Postman Always Rings Twice (E330), while chapter five is devoted to Raymond Chandler's Farewell, My Lovely (E456).

B429. Whitley, John S. Detectives and Friends: Dashiell Hammett's The Glass Key and Raymond Chandler's The Long Goodbye. American Arts Pamphlet No. 6. Exeter, England: University of Exeter, 1981. 38pp. Wraps.

In addition to the title essay, the pamphlet also includes: "Dashiell Hammett & Raymond Chandler: A Chronology," notes and a selective bibliography. A study of the ways in which genre conventions were extended in both these novels which became, in effect, "farewells to the genre." Review: JAmStud 16 (1982):292-93.

B430. Williams, Blanche Colton. The Mystery and the Detective: A Collection of Stories. NY: D. Appleton-Century Co., Inc., 1938. vii-xii, 364pp.

A high-school text consisting of an introduction, and of an anthology of twenty short stories, each of them with a short biography of the writer and questions for class discussion. The selections include stories by Poe, Melville Davisson Post, O. Henry, and E. Phillips Oppenheim. There are also stories by writers like Barry Pain, Algernon Blackwood, John Russell, F. Marion Crawford and Frank R. Stockton, who are not thought of primarily as writers of detective fiction; and by writers like Richard

Washburn Child, Carolyn Darling, Charles Caldwell Dobie, and Frederick Greene who are unfamiliar names to contemporary readers. Interesting as perhaps the earliest school anthology text. The introduction is largely a discussion of the puzzle-story.

B431. Williams, Lisa Wall. "Libraries and Librarians in Murder-Mystery-Suspense Fiction, 1931-1980: A Content Analysis." Unpublished M. A. thesis. School of Library Science, University of North Carolina at Chapel Hill, 1981. iii, 35pp. Not seen.

B432. Williamson, J. N. A Critical History and Analysis of the 'Whodunit.' Privately printed, 1951. 22pp. Mimeographed on one side of paper, spiral bound in stiff card covers. Not seen.

B433. Wilt, Judith. Ghosts of the Gothic: Austen, Eliot and Lawrence. Princeton: Princeton University Press, 1980. xii, 307pp. Illus. Index. Bibliographical references.

There is no attempt to relate the Gothic tradition to detective fiction.

B434. Winks, Robin, ed. Detective Fiction: A Collection of Critical Essays. Series: Twentieth-Century Views. Englewood Cliffs, N. J.: Prentice-Hall, 1980. 246pp. Wraps.

An anthology of critical material with an introduction by the editor, a bibliography of critical and historical literature, a checklist of Wink's "favorites," syllabi for two courses on detective fiction and a list of four book dealers offering current and out-of-print material. Contents: R. Winks, "Introduction," pp. 1-14; W. H. Auden, "The Guilty Vicerage," pp. 15-24 (C34); Dorothy L. Sayers, "Aristotle on Detective Fiction," pp. 25-34 (C724); Edmund Wilson, "Who Cares Who Killed Roger Ackroyd?," pp. 35-40 (C867); Joseph Wood Krutch, "Only a Detective Story," pp. 41-46 (C464); Gavin Lambert, "The Dangerous Edge (excerpt)," pp. 47-52 (B215); Dorothy L. Sayers, "The Omnibus of Crime," pp. 53-83 (C725); George Grella, "The Formal Detective Novel," pp. 84-102 (C340a); George Grella, "The Hard-Boiled Detective Novel," pp. 103-120 (C341); John Cawelti, "The Study of Literary Formulas," pp. 121-43 (C165); Jacques Barzun, "Detection and the Literary Art," pp. 144-53 (C59); Julian Symons, "The Short Story's Mutations," pp. 154-60 (C804); Erik Routley, "The Case against the Detective Story," pp. 161-78 (C707); Ross MacDonald (sic), "The Writer as Detective Hero," pp. 179-87 (C512); John Cawelti, "Artistic Failures and Successes: Christie and Sayers," pp. 188-99 (B69); Ronald A. Knox, "A Detective Story Decalogue," pp. 200-203 (C458); George N. Dove, "The Criticism of Detective Fiction," pp. 203-209 (C239); Robin W. Winks, "The Sordid Truth: Four Cases," pp. 209-228; "Two Sample University Courses on Detective Fiction," pp. 229-232; "Where to Obtain Out-of-Print Detective Stories," pp. 233; "Critical and Historical Literature," pp. 234-238; "A Personal List of 200 Favorites," pp. 239-246. Reviews: TLS, 9 Jan 81, p. 30; Choice, Dec 80, p. 521.

B435. ______. The Historian as Detective: Essays on Evidence. NY: Harper & Row, 1969. 543pp.

The parallels between the professor of history and the detective are lovingly explored in these essays in investigation. In his introductions and footnotes Winks discusses some of the great and not-so-great detective stories relevant to the historical subjects. (REB)

B436. Winks, Robin. Modus Operandi: An Excursion into Detective Fiction.

Boston: David R. Godine, 1982. 131pp. Index.

This is the tale of a respectable academic who became rather publicly engaged in the promotion of popular literature through his mystery fiction review column in The New Republic, to the consternation, it appears, of some of his family and colleagues. It is, to some extent, a contemporary moral tract but there is very little remorse in evidence. As one might expect, he talks both about the art of the mystery story and its pleasures. His writing is often graceful and sometimes affected but always entertaining.

B437. Winn, Dilys, perpetrator. Murder Ink: The Mystery Reader's Companion. NY: Workman Publishing, 1977. (Japanese edition of about one-third of the material translated by Shinpei Tokiwa and others. Mystery Zatsugaku Tokuhon. Tokyo: Shuei-sha, 1982.) 522pp. Index. Illus. Simultaneous hardover and paperback printings. xx, 522pp.

Like no other book in the genre, this compendium of essays, anecdotes, checklists, quizzes, photographs, cartoons, jokes, quotations and what-not is devoted to the sheer fun of mystery fiction. Contains contributions--some reprinted, but most written especially for this book--by dozens of writers and other celebrities. A new delight pops to the surface every time the book is opened. Breen 107. (REB)

B438. ______. Murderess Ink. NY: Workman Publishing, 1979. xv, 304pp. Index.

A potpourri of short pieces on women of mystery fiction and women in mystery fiction.

B439. Wivell, Charles Joseph. "Adaptation and Coherence in Late Ming Short Vernacular Fiction: A Study of the Second West Lake Collection." Doctoral dissertation. University of Washington, 1969. 304pp.

Traces and examines the methods used by storytellers of the Ming dynasty (1369-1644) to make unified stories out of numerous disjointed anecdotes. Ch. 2, esp. pp. 45-48, discusses how the figure of a magistrate-detective, Judge Chou, is used to tie together the various anecdotes. Ch. 4, esp. pp. 118-129, compares Judge Chou stories to several of Van Gulik's Judge Dee stories. Interestingly enough, Wivell notes that the adaptation for which Van Gulik is noted for making in his stories in order to make them more palatable for Western readers had also been made by early Chinese adaptors of the same stories. (GG)

B440. Woecklen, Fritz. Der literarische Mord. Eine Untersuchung ueber die englische & amerikanische Detektivliteratur |Literary murder: an investigation of British and American detective fiction|. Nuremberg, 1953; Garland Press, 1969. 348pp. Index.

Generally acknowledged as the first German book-length study of the English-language genre (although there were earlier German doctoral dissertations). This is sometimes called the "German Haycraft" and Woelcken is quite familiar with English-language critical material. Included are chapters on historical and thematic issues, e.g., the 19th century, Holmesiana, as well as on the typology of crimes and detectives, on literary criticism of detective fiction, "democracy and detectives," the problem of realism, and on various religious and moral issues. (GG)

B441. The Writer. Editor: Sylvia K. Burack. Monthly.

In its earliest years (The Writer was first published in 1887), the magazine reprinted articles from newspapers and magazines on writers and it is, for this reason, an historical document of some importance, and a record of material that is otherwise very difficult to track down. In the 1930s, the magazine began to specialize in the practical advice and market news that characterize its present format. It has consistently published many articles by writers of mystery, suspense and espionage fiction who furnish practical advice on plotting, characterization, and setting. In addition, the authors often use examples from their own work and it is this commentary which makes the material of interest to students of their work. Some biographical information has been provided, with the biographies either written by the subject author or, very often, based on interviews and/or correspondence. Although individual items from this magazine will, in general, not be annotated, they will be cited in the Authors section. The Writer is often dismissed by scholars who are only aware of its advisory aspect. They should be aware that it is also a record of changing tastes in popular literature and a source of primary information on writers and writing.

B442. Writer's Digest. Editor: William Brohaugh. Published monthly.
Writer's Digest, although it does publish "articles of instruction" for the neophyte writer, is more a market newsletter than The Writer. "We like plenty of examples, anecdotes and $$$ in our articles," the editors advise in their annual publication Writer's Market, and Writer's Digest has an attractive format, with lots of photographs that present the profession as a glamorous field. It publishes relatively few articles specifically designed to improve the writing skills of the mystery writer but Lawrence Block, in "Fiction" (his monthly column), includes many examples from his and other writers' mystery fiction. Appropriate material will be cited in the Authors section.

B443. Wu, William F. The Yellow Peril: Chinese Americans in American Fiction 1850-1940. Hamden, CT: Archon Books, 1982. ix, 241pp. Bibliography of primary and secondary sources. Index.
An outgrowth of Wu's doctoral dissertation (University of Michigan, 1979), this book attempts to survey and analyze the depiction of Chinese and Chinese Americans in American fiction from the first immigrants up until the outbreak of WW II. Most of the fiction is genre material. There are chapters on frontier stories, "Chinese invasion" stories, Chinatown stories, Fu Manchu and Charlie Chan (Ch. VI) and on the pulps (Ch. VII). Wu asserts the usual claim that Fu Manchu was the image evoked by future Chinese villains for years to come. Also states that Charlie Chan overcompensates for the Yellow Peril image by exaggerated "good guy" posture. In the chapter on pulps Wu covers villains such as Hammett's Chang Li Ching, Stockbridge's Ssu Hsi Tze, Hogan's Wu Fang, Keyhoe's Yen Sin, and Chang, of Secret Agent X fame. Wu's coverage of stories in the "slicks" and pulps is perfectly adequate, but one wishes that he had treated the dime novel villains and tongs, of which there were many. Review: TLS, 9 Apr 82, p. 403. (GG)

B444. Würtemberger, Thomas. Die deutsche Kriminalerzählung |The German crime tale|. Erlangen, 1941; Garland, 1979.
Wurtemberger's thesis seems to be the only account of the German crime story from the Victorian period through the early twentieth century. The author analyzes the work of Annette von Droste-Hulshoff, Hermann Kurz, Clara Viebig, literary historian and poet Ricards Huch, criminologist Erich Wulffen and lesser authors. (EFB)

B445. Yamamota, Sansei, ed. Nihon Bungaku Koza: Dai Ju-yon kan; Taishu Bungaku-hen |Lectures on Japanese literature: vol. 14; the volume on popular literature|. Tokyo: Kaizo-sha, 1933. 380pp.

Though the main theme is popular literature in general, among the contributors are many mystery writers such as Jun Mizutani (who writes the "Study of Detective Fiction"). Since mystery fiction is included in the this academic publication series, it cannot be ignored. (HS/TT)

B446. Yamamura, Masao. Suiri Bundan Sengoshi: Mystery Boom no Kiseki o Tadoru |Post-war history of the mystery world: tracing the track of the mystery boom|. 3 vols. Tokyo: Futabasha, 1973, 1978, 1980. Illus. Vol I, 293pp; Vol II, 282pp; Vol III, 323pp.
An informal history of the mystery circle from the end of WW II to 1965 when the great pioneer Edogawa Rampo died. This book is based on the direct experiences of the author who was a member of the circle. (HS/TT)

B447. ______. Waga Kaikyuteki Tantei Sakka-ron |My reminiscent comments on mystery fiction|. Tokyo: Gen'eijo, 1976. 300pp. Illus.
While his earlier book is a chronicle reminiscence, this is a personal commentary on 20 individual writers and their works. It won the Mystery Writers of Japan award as the best critical book in 1977, seemingly in consideration of Yamamura's accomplishment in his previous book. (HS/TT)

B448. Yanagida, Tzumi. Zoku Zuihitsu Meiji Bungaku |Essays on the literature of the Meiji epoch, part II|. Tokyo: Shunju-sha, 1938. 540pp.
A collection of critical essays. A study of the literature of the Meiji Epoch (1868-1912) from the viewpoint of comparative literature. "An Essay on the History of Detective Fiction" is a unique study and a good guide for young scholars. (HS/TT)

B449. Yang, Winston L. Y.; Li, Peter; and Mao, Nathan K. Classical Chinese Fiction: A Guide to Its Study and Appreciation: Essays and Bibliographies. Boston: G. K. Hall & Co, 1978. xxvi, 302pp.
A reference guide to Chinese fiction from the Chou dynasty (c1000-221 B.C.) to the Ch'ing dynasty (1644-1911). Emphasizing Western scholarship, especially that done in English, it includes several general essays on fiction of different areas (pp. 3-116) and bibliographies (pp. 117-278). The bibliography section is further divided into sections, including reference works, general studies and anthologies, fictional works by historical period, and individual literary works. The bibliographical entries are all annotated and are divided into two parts, translations of Chinese fictional works and studies of them. The studies include monographs and articles. For example, in the chapter "Other Sung, Yuan, and Ming Works" (pp. 231-38) can be found the heading "The Court Cases of Judge Pao Lung-t'u," under which are listed a translation of the Magistrate Pao novel Lung-t'u kung-an and studies of it. Although several pieces of criminous interest are not to be found in the bibliography, such as Vincent Starrett's essay on Chinese detective stories (C778a) and some of George A. Hayden's pieces (C377, C378v), and although there are some errors or misprints (Leon Comber's name is spelled "Chomber"), this is still a very useful guide. With all the information in its several introductions, appendices, and author index, it is quite informative and well organized. Along with Richard Lynn's Chinese Literature (A109) this is one of the best single sources for background research into ancient Chinese detective fiction. (GG)

B450. Yates, Donald A. "The Argentine Detective Story." Unpublished doctoral dissertation. University of Michigan, 1961. With a bibliography of secondary sources, pp. 272-274.

An important study whose updating and publication are long overdue. Yates corresponded extensively with a number of writers and excerpts from the correspondence are included. DA 22/02, p. 578.

B451. Zmegac, Viktor. Der wohltemperiete Mord. Zur Theorie und Geschichte des Detektivromans |Good-tempered murder: on the theory and history of the detective novel|. Schwerpunkte Germanistik 4. Frankfurt: Athenaeum Verlag, 1971. 278pp.

Along with Jochen Vogt, ed., Der Kriminalroman (B424) also published in 1971, this is one of the first and most important German anthologies of critical essays on the genre. Although 6 of the 12 essays here also appear in Vogt, this work contains the influential, oft quoted essay by Richard Alewyn, as well as two essays from Yugoslavian literary critics. Contents: Viktor Zmegac, "Aspekte des Detektivromans. Statt einer Einleitung |Aspects of the detective novel: instead of an introduction|," pp. 9-34 (C884); Zdenko Skreb, "Die neue Gattung. Zur Geschichte und Poetik des Detektivromans |The new genre: on the history and poetics of the detective novel|," pp. 35-95 (C758); Bertolt Brecht, "Ueber die Popularitaet des Kriminalromans |On the popularity of the crime novel|," pp. 97-103 (C124); E. Wilson, "Warum werden Detektivromane gelesen? |Why do people read detective stories?|," pp. 105-110 (C868); Ernest Bloch, "Philosophische Ansicht des Detektivromans |Philosophical view of the detective novel|," pp. 111-31 (C103); W. H. Auden, "Des verbrecherische Pfarrhaus |The guilty vicarage|," pp. 133-47 (C103); Gerhard Schmidt-Henkel, "Kriminalroman und Trivialliteratur |The crime novel and popular fiction|," pp. 149-76 (C734); Ernst Kaemmel, "Literatur Unterm Tisch. Der Detektivroman un sein gesellschaftlicher Auftrag |Literature under the table: the detective novel and its social mandate|," pp. 177-83 (C439); Richard Alewyn, "Die Anfaenge des Detektivromans |The beginnings of the detective novel|," pp. 185-202 (C13); Helmut Heissenbuettel, "Spielregeln des Kriminalromans |The crime novel's rules of the game|," pp. 203-19 (C392); Ulrich Suerbaum, "Der gefesselte Detektivroman. ein gattungstheoretischer Versuch |The detective novel in shackles: a genre-theoretical attempt|," pp. 221-40 (C795); Dietrich Naumann, "Zur Typologie des Kriminalromans |On the typology of the crime novel|," pp. 241-60 (C571); Peter Fischer, "Neue Haeuser in der Rue Morgue. Entwicklungslinien des modernen Kriminalromans |New houses in the Rue Morgue: lines of development in the modern crime novel|," pp. 261-75 (C281); Bibliography of Sources, pp. 277-78.(GG)

B. Articles

C1. Abartis, Caesarea. "The Ugly-Pretty, Dull-Bright, Weak-Strong Girl in the Gothic Mansion." JPC 13:2 (Fall 79):257-63.
A study of the ambivalent nature of the Gothic heroine.

C2. Adams, Gail. "Double Jeopardy: Husband and Wife Teams in Detective Fiction." TAD 8 (1974/75):251-56.
Series partners in fiction by Agatha Christie, Dashiell Hammett and the Lockridges.

C3. Adey, Robert C. S. "Behind a Victorian Locked Door: A Brief History of the Early Years of the Locked Room Detective Story." Antiquarian Book Monthly Review 2 (April 1975):15-16.
A short piece that finishes with the turn of the century. (RCSA)

C4. ______. "Symbolic Motifs." TMRN 3:4 (1970):27-32. Illus.
60 British publishers' logos reproduced and identified.

C5. Adrian, Jack. "Mystoricals." Books and Bookmen no. 324 (Sept 82), pp. 17-19.
In reviewing four current mysteries by Francis Selwyn, Jeremy Sturrock, Ellis Peters and Julian Symons with historical settings, the reviewer discusses why such settings are used. (RCSA)

C6. Agassi, Joseph. "The Detective Novel and Scientific Method." Poetics Today 3:1 (Winter 1982):99-108.
On the ambiguous nature of the detective's method and the uncertainty about whether it is a comonplace, rational solving of problems or intuitive and romantic. Agassi also attempts to find analogies between the ways scientists and detectives function and speculates on the origins of detective fiction.

C7. Aisenberg, Nadya. "Myth, Fairytale, and the Crime Novel." In A Common Spring (B4), pp. 16-67.
Basing her discussion on the Stith Thompson Motif-Index of Folk Literature, Aisenberg discusses relationships between the hero and villain, the themes of quest, pursuit and identity, and the detective story as allegory and fairy-tale. Her thesis that in the "thriller" characterization is possible while it is not in the ratiocinative detective story is highly questionable and her categories, supported by references to Camus, Dostoyevsky, and Kafka (among others) would have benefitted from more specific references to detective fiction. Most of her genre citations are from Hammett and Chandler.

C8. Albert, Walter. "The Skene Melvin Bibliography of Critical Writing." TMF 5:3 (1981):11-14.
A review-essay of the Greenwood Press bibliography (A156).

C9. Albrecht, Wilma and Richard. "'Krimi'-- und Literaturwissenschaft. Zu einiger literaturwissenschaftlichen Diskussionsschwerpunkten um fiktionale Verbrechensliteratur |Crime fiction -- and literary criticism: on several literary points with respect to fictional crime literature|." Literatur in Wissenschaft und Unterricht 13:124-42.
Article assesses the value of crime fiction for instruction in schools.

After differentiating between crime and detective fiction, and extensively quoting other scholars and critics, the Albrechts conclude that crime novels can be taught in a way that does not "a priori" prevent them from being enjoyed. (GG)

C10. Alderson, Martha. "Deadly Edges of the Gay Blade." TMF 7:3 (May/June 1983):23-28.
A survey of series by Joseph Hansen and Nathan Aldyne with gay detectives. With an annotated checklist.

C11. ______. "Death at the Stage Door: Anne Morice's Theresa Crichton and Simon Brett's Charles Paris." Clues 4:2 (Fall/Winter 83):21-29.
A discussion of the particular effectiveness of actors as detectives.

C12. Alewyn, Richard. "Die Anfaenge des Detektivromans |The beginnings of the detective novel|." In Zmegac (B451), pp. 185-202; and in Most/Stowe (B264), pp. 62-78. Previously published as "Das Raetsel des Detektivromans |The mystery of the detective novel'|." In Definitionen, edited by A. Frise, pp. 117-136. Frankfurt: Vittorio Klostermann Verlag, 1963.
Influential, oft-quoted, oft-discussed article arguing that the detective novel is a product of 18th and 19th century Romanticism and not of Rationalism or Positivism. By comparing Poe to E. T. A. Hoffmann, who wrote some 25 years earlier, Alewyn argues that the essential elements of crime, mystery, misplaced suspicion, and old secrets place the detective novel more firmly in the romantic than the rationalistic tradition. Alewyn is perhaps the first German writer to have recognized Hoffmann's Das Fraulein von Scuderi (1818) as a detective novel. (GG)

C13. ______. "Anatomie des Detektivromans |Anatomy of the detective novel|." Die Zeit, 22 Nov and 29 Nov 1968. Reprinted in Vogt (B424), pp. 372-404.
Influential and oft-discussed essay which distinguishes between detective and crime fiction on the basis of narrative structure. Alewyn also makes several observations for which he has later become well-known: the detective is sociologically an outsider and the detective novel is concerned not only with the secret of a whodunit but with many secondary secrets as well. (GG)

C14. Allbeury, Ted. "Crime & Thrillers." Bookcase. The W. H. Smith Book Review. Undated (August 1983), pp. 14-15. Illus.
Brief, opinionated sketch of the development of the crime/thriller novel, putting down Christie and Sayers in favor of the modern crime and spy novel as written by Greene, Deighton, le Carré, and Trevanian. (REB)

C15. Amis, Kingsley. "Here Comes a Chopper." The Spectator, 8 Apr 72, pp. 547-8.
Essay-review of Symons Bloody Murder (B387).

C16. ______. "My Favorite Sleuths." Playboy, Dec 66, pp. 343-44, 346-49.
Amis notes that detectives are now all the rage and examines, in some detail, Holmes, Father Brown, Gideon Fell and Nero Wolfe. In passing, he fires pot shots at Christie, Innes, Sayers and Queen. He also refers to a number of other fictional detectives.

C17. ______. "Unreal Policemen." In his What Became of Jane Austen? and Other Questions, pp. 108-25. London: Jonathan Cape, 1970.

An overview of a century of detective fiction which establishes Amis' appreciation of the plodding, uneccentric policemen like Van der Valk and Maigret, his lack of enthusiasm for private eyes of the Hammett-Chandler school (although he speaks with great warmth of Spillane as the "best writer" of the group) and his particular admiration for private detectives like Holmes, Father Brown, Nero Wolfe and Gideon Fell. Amis dismisses most of the British "golden age" writers and marks a decline as setting in around 1950. He finds John Dickson Carr to be a "first-rate artist" who will not receive general recognition while genre fiction is undervalued by critics.

C18. Amoruso, Vito. "Visita guidata del mistero |Guided visit to the mystery|. L'Unità, 31 August 1980.
The historical roots of the detective story are to be found in the crisis of middle-class reason, in its complete bankruptcy: "the mystery narrative in all its variants becomes the true expression of those irreversible historical changes," even if it offers a formally consoling resolution. (RC)

C19. Anders, Karl. "Der Kriminalroman." Bucherei und Bildung 4 (1952):509-15. Reprinted in Vogt (B424), pp. 533-45.
Arguments against the widely held prejudices against the crime novel. After dealing with the charges that crime fiction depicts a less than optimal world and that it corrupts young readers, Anders devotes most of the article to the charge that the crime novel is of low literary value. His solution is to distinguish between good and bad crime fiction. (GG)

C20. Andersson, Bernt. "Deckaren i Italien |The detective novel in Italy|." Jury 6:4 (1977):22-32.
Historical overview. (MS)

C21. _____. "Mussolini och detektivromanen |Mussolini and the detective novel|." Jury 7:2 (1978):37-39.
Mussolini's influence and censorship. (MS)

C22. Anderson, Isaac. "The Life of Riley." In Haycraft (B142), pp. 363-66.
A New York Times' reviewer talks about a life of reviewing mystery fiction.

C23. "And Is It Ever True?" TLS, 23 June 61, p. V.
Mysteries may not be true to actual police procedures, but they teach us something about ourselves: love of mystery, our fascination with flight and pursuit, a need to believe in situations for puzzles and to escape into a world of "legality."

C24. Anton, Edoardo (pseudonym of Edoardo Antonelli). "La letteratura poliziesca. Natura e cause del sul successo |Detective fiction. Its nature and the reasons for its success|." Quadrivio, 25 Nov 1934, p. 8.
The author (who in the 30s ventured into the genre both in the narrative and the dramatic fields) defines the detective novel as an enquiry into an event which has already happened. (In the handling of the narrative "nothing must happen after the crime, since the action has already been crystallized in the rigidity of a corpse." The only form of action is represented by the "continuous change of the position of the characters in the confrontations with the suspect.") The detective novel, by its particular nature and structure, proposes to the reader a problem of acquaintance whose analytic method consists in rising from the particular

to the whole (induction) according to the fundamental need of synthesis which, besides being proper to every recognizable process, is also the inevitable outcome of modern times. (LR)

C25. Antonini, Giacomo. "Maesteria del giallo |Mastery of the giallo|." La Fiera Letteraria, 4 December 55, p. 5.
British detective novels have some characteristics in common which distinguish them from the American ones. The diversity in climate and environment (middle and upper bourgeoisie, rural aristocracy and London intelligentsia on the one hand; gangsters and underworld types of the U. S. metropolis on the other) involves a difference in tone and attitude. The norms of good breeding and the strong dose of humor, infallible in a novel belonging to the tradition of Conan Doyle, are replaced in the American novel by a rough and precise realism. At the center of a British giallo there is an enigma to be solved; at the center of an American, there are emotions - violent and unexpected stage effects. The author focuses on the cases of Hammett and Chandler who impose themselves through literary qualities in the same way as the entertainments of Graham Greene, Clifford Kitchin, Cecil Day Lewis and Roy Fuller in the British sector. (LR)

C26. Apostolou, John L. "Japanese Mystery Fiction in English Translation." TAD 13 (1980):310-12.
Descriptive history with a checklist of authors and titles.

C27. ______. "Japanese Mystery Fiction Revisited." TAD 15 (1982):184-85.
Additions to C26.

C28. ______. "Sons of Mr. Moto." TPP 5:3 (May/June 83):26-28.
An introduction to mysteries featuring Japanese detectives; with a checklist.

C29. Arnold, Armin. "Bärlach, Marlowe und Maigret." In Keel, Daniel, ed., Uber Friedrich Dürrenmatt (Zurich: Diogenes Verlag AG, 1980), pp. 237-51. Previously published in Arnold's Friedrich Dürrenmatt (Berlin: Colloquium Verlag, 1974).
German language excerpt from a work written by one of the compilers of Reclams Kriminalromanführer (B13). This piece briefly compares Dürrenmatt's Inspector Hans Bärlach to Philip Marlowe and Jules Maigret. Like Marlowe, Bärlach is an outsider with respect to his society and like Maigret, he is humane and does not operate strictly according to modern police procedure. But primarily this piece is a summary of the four Bärlach novels, A Dangerous Game, The Judge and His Hangman, The Pledge and The Quarry. (GG)

C30. Asfour, J.-C. "Du tirage dans l'édition 'Fleuve noir' |On circulation in the 'Fleuve noir' edition|. Gang 1 (n.d.), pp. 70-72.
Interview with staff member of the 'Fleuve noir' series.

C31. Astaldi, Maria Luisa. "Gli antenati del libro giallo (1958) |The ancestors of the giallo|." In Il poeta e la regina e altre letture inglesi pp. 57-60. Florence: Sansoni, 1963.
Detective literature is one of the most recent forms of the narrative of terror which has ancient origins and tends to be represented under new aspects in each generation. The author advances the hypothesis that this literary phenomenon is to be interpreted with the tools of anthropology, relating it to the instinct of a game and specifically "in the way that

children and primitive people play which consists of inducing in oneself and in others the sense of fear, of apprehension, of terror." (LR)

C32. Auburn, Mark S. "The Pleasures of Espionage Fiction." Clues 4:2 (Fall/Winter 83):30-42.
Auburn discusses four elements which he sees as common to most espionage novels: a "simplistic atonement of sin," our vicarious pleasure in the protagonist's freedom, versimilitude and action. Auburn uses several contemporary writers of espionage thrillers as examples.

C33. Aucott, Robert. "When Was the Golden Age, Anyway?" TAD 5 (1971/72):207-208.
On the critical confusion over the dating of the Golden Age of mystery fiction. With critical boldness and tongue-in-cheek, Aucott appends a list of the best books published in the "Golden Year of 1930."

C34. Auden, W. H. "The Guilty Vicarage." Harper's Magazine 196 (May 1948):406-12. Reprinted in Zmegac (B451), Winks (B434), and Cremante/Rambelli (B78).
A poet's analysis of the classical detective novel with its conventions described as precisely as if they were the stylistic features of a Shakespearean sonnet. Auden does not think that detective fiction is high art but that an anlysis of it may "throw light" on works of art. The fantasy of the reader of detective fiction is that of the innocent who feels guilty and wishes to be restored to his innocence.

C35. Axelson, A. E. "Brött och shack |Crime and chess|." Jury 4:4 (1975):49-50.
A thematic study in which these authors are cited: Poe, Bentley, Chandler, Christie, Van Dine, Stout and Mason. (MS)

C36. Aydelotte, William O. "The Detective Novel as a Historical Source." Yale Review 39 (Sept 49):76-95. Reprinted in Landrum (B216) and in Nevins (B290).
The author-historian argues that while detective fiction is not an accurate reflection of the age in which it is written, its reflections of readers' fantasy-wishes tell something about the frustrations and tensions of the time. Aydelotte refutes the argument that detective fiction can only develop in a democratic society where there is a well-developed judicial system and rather, in its depiction of a perfect, unreal order and in its dependence on an authoritarian detective working outside the official judicial system, tends toward a dependence on a dictator and a system in which the guilt of the criminal is that of a scapegoat justifying paranoid fantasies in which everyone is potentially guilty. Finally, Aydelotte suggests that his thesis may be pedantic and concludes that detective stories deal with "the most essential and urgent problems in the human condition."

C37. Babener, Liahna K. "California Babylon: The World of Detective Fiction." Clues 1:2 (1980):77-89.
Writers who have written about the "traitrous American dream" foundering in Southern California. Chandler, Hammett, Cain and Ross Macdonald.

C38. Bagley, Desmond. "On the Importance of Reading." DAST 11:5 (1978):10.
Reading in general. Despite McLuhan, the book is here to stay. (MS)

C39. Baird, Newton. "Aristotle's Operative, or the Case of the Classic Barzun." TAD 8 (1974/75):15-23.

An argument for an ethics in fiction that "encourages men to be better than they are." Baird maintains that detective story writers like Christie and Fredric Brown, working through apparent disorder to order, are doing precisely that. A somewhat unfocused essay that critizes art in which emotion takes precedence over the intellect.

C40. Bakerman, Jane S. "Advice Unheeded: Shakespeare in Some Modern Mystery Novels." TAD 14:2 (1981):134-39.

Shakespearean puzzles in Josephine Tey's _The Daughter of Time_, Marvin Kaye's _Bullets for Macbeth_, Michael Innes' _Hamlet, Revenge!_ and Charlotte Armstrong's _A Little Less Than Kind_.

C41. Ball, John. "The Ethnic Detective." In Ball (B15), pp. 143-160.

A narrative description of a number of ethnic detectives with the observation that many of them, whatever their status in society, have been popular and accepted by the reader.

C42. ______. "Murder at Large." In Ball (B15), pp. 1-28.

A retrospective look at the genre, with some comments on its conventions.

C43. Ballet, René. "Structures du roman policier; une parodie des rapports équivoques [Structures of the detective novel; a parody of equivocal relationships]." _La Pensée_ no. 135 (1967), pp. 165-74. Reprinted in Cremante/Rambelli (B78), pp. 169-81.

A quasi-sociological study of relationships in society and the uses that detective fiction makes of them.

C44. Ballinger, John. "Bibliomysteries." _American Book Collector_ (new series) 3:2 (March/Apr 82):23-28.

Account of a collector's interest in mysteries with "plots centered around books." Bookselling, book collecting, institutional libraries, book publishing. With a checklist of "Thirty-Six Book-Related Mysteries."

C45. Bander, Elaine. "The English Detective Novel Between the Wars: 1919-1939." TAD 11 (1978):262-73. Illus.

Bander traces the path of the detective novel of this period from the puzzle novel of the 20s to a more flexible form in the 30s closer to the novel of manners. She examines its relation to the society of the period and the nature of its readership and popularity. Extensive notes.

C46. Bandy, Eugene Franklin. "Jacques Barzun: A Critic Talks about Mystery Criticism." PW, 13 March 78, pp. 68-69.

An interview with Jacques Barzun who thinks that good criticism has reduced the number of trashy detective novels. He also comments briefly on several writers, the importance of plotting and his familiar stance that mystery fiction must be thought of as "tales" rather than as as novels.

C47. Barbato, Joseph. "The Mysteries of the Pseudonymous Professors." _Chronicles of Higher Education_, 28 March 77, p. 21.

Academics as pseudonymous writers of mystery stories. Robert Parker and Carolyn Heilbrun ("Amanda Cross") comment on their mystery writing.

C48. Barbolini, Robert. "Giocare col morto |Playing with death|." Terzo occhio 8:23 (1980):48-50.
Referring to Symons' Great Detectives (B392) and to essays by Caillois (C145) and Gramigna (C331), the author recalls the profound structural relationships existing between detective stories and games: "Everything comes back to the same point. There is no bildung; there is no privileged experience. At any mmoment a customer may enter or a bullet may whistle by. And the game begins again. Chance is futile and fatal. But cheating is also part of the game." (RC)

C49. ______. "Le istituzioni del romanzo poliziesco |The institutions of the detective novel|." Il Verri, sixth series, 8 (1977), pp. 127-54.
Raising the detective novel to the level of a literary trope and literary institution, the author formulates the hypothesis that "the narrative, mimicking the behaviour of the detective, like a vampire revives to cannibalize painstakingly the reader's emotional 'charge'." (RC)

C50. Bargainnier, Earl F. "British Murder and British Detective Fiction." TMF 6:4 (1982):19-22.
Bargainnier analyses the British crimes described in J. H. H. Gaute and Robin Odell's encyclopedia of true crimes, Murderers' Who's Who (Montreal: Optimum Publishing Company, Ltd., 1979) and concludes that many of them closely parallel crimes in British detective fiction. He does not maintain that detective fiction is necessarily realistic but that murder does occur in real life with some frequency in the milieux depicted in classical British detective fiction.

C51. ______. "I Disagree." Journal of Communications 25 (Spring 1975):113-119.
A reply to M. J. Jones' article, C434.

C52. Barnes, Bruce. "T.H.R.U.S.H.'s Insidious Weapons or 'What Will They Think of Next?'." PQ 5:4 (1982):13-18. Illus.
An article on the Man from U.N.C.L.E. paperbacks of the 1960s with a checklist of the titles.

C53 Barry, Charles. "Why Do They Read the Stuff?" The Crime-Book Magazine 3:8 (Oct 36):7.
Humorous treatment of the subject in general terms. (RCSA)

C54. Barthes, Roland. "Delay and the Hermeneutic Sentence." In Most/Stowe (B264), pp. 118-21.
An excerpt from an extended analysis (1970) by Barthes of Balzac's tale, Sarrasine (S/Z). Barthe describes narrative and linguistic codes using terms that could be applied to detective fiction: enigma, delay, disclosure, etc.

C55. Bartolini, Luigi. "Apprendono dai gialli il mestiere dei criminali |They learn from the gialli the trade of criminals|." Il giornale d'Italia, 20 Feb 1959.
Violent attack on detective novels as "guides pointing to the ways of delinquency." (LR)

C56. Barzun, Jacques. "The Book, the Bibliographer, and the Absence of Mind." American Scholar 39 (1969-70):138-48.
Review-essay of Hagen's Who Done It? (A65). Barzun sees this bibliography as the failure of a system based on information rather than knowledge. It will be of little comfort to other bibliographers that

Barzun, possibly only half-facetiously, considers such an undertaking "proper work for a rum-soaked reader of detective fiction, preferably one hundred and twenty years old."

C57. _____. "Books about Books of Crime, and the Criticism Thereof." TAD 5 (1971/72):15.
Barzun comments on reviews of the Barzun/Taylor A Catalogue of Crime (A10) in which he admits the incompleteness of references but protests that the Catalogue is not a bibliography but a list with comments on titles "known to the authors."

C58. _____. "A Critical Vocabulary for Crime Fiction." TAD 4 (1970/71):75-78.
An explanation of the basic critical vocabulary developed and employed by Barzun and Wendell Hertig Taylor in the Catalogue of Crime (A10).

C59. _____. "Detection and the Literary Art." New Republic 144, 24 April 61, pp. 17-20. Also appears--in a longer version--as the Introduction to his anthology The Delights of Detection (Criterion Books, 1961), pp. 9-23. Reprinted in Nevins (B290) and in Winks (B434).
Barzun distinguishes the detective "tale" from the "real novel" and describes the sophisticated pleasures it offers its readers. A graceful and persuasive essay.

C60. _____. "From Phèdre to Sherlock Holmes." In The Energies of Art , pp. 303-23. NY: Harper & Bros., 1956.
The classical story of detection is dead, according to Barzun, and he proceeds to trace the rise and fall of this "strictest" of popular genres from Poe to the height of the form in the 1920s and 1930s. He dismisses Maigret and the French roman policier and, while finding some charm in the hard-boiled novel, characterizes its practitioners as petulant and wordy.

C61. _____. "Meditations on the Literature of Spying." American Scholar 34 (1965):167-78.
Barzun reflects on the "trashy literature" of espionage and the reasons it attracts so many readers in the "afternoon of this century." He finds the whole business of spying, as it is now practised, a distasteful one, and extends his distaste to the fiction based on it. Although one may take exception to his fairly general denunication of this literature and think that he has overstated his case, his description of the nature of present-day espionage may not be an inaccurate one.

C62. _____. "Not 'Whodunit?' but 'How?'." SRL 27 (4 Nov 44):9-11.
A reminder by critic Barzun--in a period of the decline of the classical detective story--that "genuine detection" is necessary to detective fiction.

C63. _____. "Party of One." Holiday 24 (July 58): 6, 8-11, 138. Illus. Reprinted as "Detection in Extremis" in Gilbert (B124).
The decline in standards of the contemporary detective novel with detection taking second place to psychology and "case histories." Barzun traces this change from S. S. Van Dine's pseudo-psychology through the Black Mask writers, and the lure of Existentialism. The detective novel, he complains, has ceased to "give entertainment."

C64. ______. "Requiescat." Chimera 5:4 (Summer 47):59-66.
The passing of the "Detective Story" proper, with its emphasis on the "systematic consideration of things" and not on "chancy speculation about human character."

C65. ______. "Suspense Suspended." American Scholar 27 (Fall 58):496-500, 504-508.
Reviews of recent detective fiction to show that with the defiance of respected conventions, detection fiction has fallen on bad days.

B66. Basney, Lionel. "Corpses, Clues, and the Truth." Christianity Today, 30 Aug 74, pp. 16-17.
The reading of detective stories is a civilized pastime and, for the Christian, provides an opportunity to escape into another world where, as in "God's sight," good and bad are clearly defined and distinguished.

C67. Baudou, Jacques. "Les petits maîtres du roman policier français." Europe 571-2 (Nov-Dec 76):150-54.
Minor French detective writers of the period 1945-50.

C68. Baudou, Jacques and Michel Lebrun. "Polars des antipodes." Magazine littéraire 194 (Apr 83), pp. 50-51.
Brief comments on detective fiction in China, Japan and Spain.

C69. Bauer, Wolfgang. "The Tradition of the Criminal Cases of Master Pao, Pao Kung-an (Lung-t'u kung-an)." Oriens 23-23 (1974):433-49.
Scholarly, but interesting and readable, essay on Lung-t'u kung-an and other collections of Judge Pao court cases. Bauer characterises Pao as "a peculiar mixture between King Solomon and Sherlock Holmes." (JLA)

C69a. Beach, Stewart. "How to Write the Mystery and Suspense Story." The Writer 71:3 (March 58):10-14; 71:4 (April 58):16-21.
On characterization, plot, "suspense." By the editor of This Week's Stories of Mystery and Suspense.

C70. Beattie, Anna B. "Whet Your Wits on a Clue." Survey 64 (15 July 30): 350-52. With a "five-foot shelf of thrillers" for suggested reading.
Beattie advocates the reading of detective fiction by social workers to develop techniques that may help them professionally: observation of detail, of people, of the abnormal, and training in the ability to analyze and the development of judgment. Additions to list by Celia Frances Beck in Survey 65 (15 Nov 30):232.

C71. Becker, Jens P. "Die amerikanische 'Hard-Boiled School' |The American hard-boiled school|." In Buchloh/Becker I (B60), pp. 96-107.
Subtitled "The Honest Hero in a Corrupt Society," this chapter discusses the work of Hammett and Chandler as well as "tough guy" literature of the 30s and European reactions to it. (GG)

C72. ______. "Der englische Spionageroman |The English spy novel|." In Buchloh/Becker I (B60), pp. 108-120.
Discusses the novels of Childers, Buchan, Ambler, Maugham, Graham Greene, Deighton, Fleming and John le Carré. (GG)

C73. ______. "'The Golden Age of the Detective Novel': Formen des englischen Detektivromans zwischen 1914 und 1939 |Forms of the English detective novel between 1914 and 1939|." In Buchloh/Becker I (B60), pp. 69-80.

Four major types of Golden Age detective novels are discussed: the puzzle novel, the novel of manners, the psychological crime novel and the thriller. (GG)

C76. ______. "Der moderne Englische Detektivroman: Rückkehr zur Tradition und 'Crime Novel' |The modern English detective novel: return to tradition and the 'crime novel'|." In Buchloh/Becker I (B60), pp. 134-44.
Several characteristics of post WW II crime fiction are discussed, including humor, realism, historical accuracy in setting, and the importance of psychological factors. The novels of Edmund Crispin, Margery Allingham, Josephine Tey, Michael Innes and Nicolas Freeling (through he is Dutch) are examined. (GG)

C77. Becker, May Lamberton. "The Mystery Story." In First Adventures in Reading, pp. 271-86. NY: Frederick A. Stokes Co., 1936.
A discussion of some childrens' mysteries by a noted editor who confesses to a liking for mysteries but does not believe they can ever be considered as "real" novels in which there is character development.

C78. Bedell, Jeanne F. "Melodrama and Manners: Changing Attitudes toward Class Distinctions in English Detective Fiction, 1868-1939." Clues 1:1 (1980): 15-24.
Bedell claims that the virtual exclusion of working class and radical characters from English detective fiction reflects the genre's relationship to the comedy of manners and melodrama and may account for the rigid coventions to which it adheres, with its class bias and idealized setting.

C79. Bell, Josephine. "The Criminal Seen by the Doctor: The Psycho-pathology of Crime." In Gilbert (B124), pp. 3-26.
An examination of the kinds of mental illnesses, congenital and otherwise, that can produce criminal acts. Bell also argues for treatment but for recognition of responsability for one's acts even if they are not controllable.

C80. Bellak, Leopold. "On the Psychology of Detective Stories and Related Problems." Psychoanalytic Review 32 (1945):403-407.
On the reading of detective stories, principles of identification (criminal/victim/sleuth) and release from tension through a problem-solving mechanism. Comparison to other addictions (like gambling), and some discussion of relationship of the writer to his work: plot manipulation, projection by author of his personality into work and style.

C81. Benét, Stephen Vincent. "Bigger and Better Murders." Bookman 63 (1926):291-96.
Benét comments on the present vogue for detective fiction and isolates three reasons for it: Holmes, President Wilson, and the decline of plot and other "sound conventions" in the modern novel. He also includes a list of his favorite writers and pet peeves (mysterious poisons, love interest, implausible murder devices, etc.).

C82. Benét, William Rose. "Here's to Crime!" SRL 4 (1928):605-606, 610, 618.
After paying tribute to W. H. Wright's introduction to The Great Detective Stories (C825) and identifying Wright as S. S. Van Dine, Benét describes his own taste which runs to mysteries "wherein much of the dramatic suspense is produced by hidden forces not revealed until the denouement." He talks with enthusiasm of international thrillers, super-villains, damsels in peril, etc. and appends an annotated list of his

reading over the past few months. A delightful essay and it is refreshing to read a defense of the thriller at a time when it was just becoming fashionable for literary people to confess to a liking for classical detective fiction.

C83. Bengel, Michael. "Detektive tragen heute einen deutschen Pass: Englisches Muster kein Vorbild mehr |Detectives carry German passports these days: English model no longer the pattern|." Koelner Stadt Anzeiger 302 (30 Dec 82):7.

News article about a convention on German detective fiction held at the Loccum Evangelist Academy. Present were authors, publishers, scholars, reviewers and critics. At the convention it was generally agreed that contemporary German detective fiction is relying less and less on Anglo-American examples and is becoming more German. Also notable were the differences in critical opinion among publishers, authors and scholars. (GG)

C84. Bennett, Donna. "The Detective Story: Towards a Definition of Genre." PTL: A Journal for Descriptive Poetics and Theory of Literature (Holland) 4 (1979):233-66.

An interesting attempt to distinguish the detective/mystery genre from horror, Gothic and suspense and to analyze the basic structures. She defines some basic terminology and applies it to a "typical" structure, discusses point of view, author/reader, reader/text and author/text relationships and narrative/narrator reliability. She seems to approach her subject as a professional linguist but claims that the deception(s) in detective stories are of situation not of language, a point many readers would argue. She also tends to make large statements based on an undetermined acquaintance with primary sources.

C85. Benoit, Claude. "Le Retour du détective privé dans le roman policier des années 70 |The return of the private detective in the detective novel of the 70s|." Polar 27 (Spring 83):57-89.

A short history of the private detective and his resurgence in the 1970s is followed by a bibliography of works of the writers discussed.

C86. Berg, Stanton O. "Sherlock Holmes: Father of Scientific Crime Detection." TAD 5 (1971/72):81-88, 98.

Speculations on the influence of Holmes on the development of modern scientific crime detection.

C87. Bergier, Jacques. "Le Roman policier de science fiction." Enigmatika 5, Jan 77, pp. 6-8.

A commentary on Larry Niven's essay (C589) on the relationship between detective fiction and science fiction.

C88. Bergler, Edmund. "Mystery Fans and the Problem of 'Potential Murderers'." American Journal of Orthopsychiatry 15 (1945): 309-17.

On the basis of data collected from his patients, Bergler concludes that readers of mysteries are passive types who excuse their passivity by reading fiction where agressive impulses are generated but exorcised through the medium of a harmless game. Bergler's theory depends on uncontrolled data and a theory of reader identification with criminal or victim. His observations on why people "consciously" read detective stories (a liking for puzzles, fascination with eccentric detectives, etc.) are the same arguments presented by many critics in the field. Haycraft (B143) is cited as support for his observations.

C89. Berkeley, Anthony. "To A. D. Peters." Introduction to The Second Shot, pp. 5-7. Garden City, NY: The Crime Club, 1931; reprinted in Buchloh/Becker 2 (B61), p. 197.

Berkeley thinks that the day of the puzzle novel is over and that it is developing into a novel in which characterization and atmosphere are more important than plot. He also states that "strictly speaking, (The Second Shot) is not a detective story at all."

C90. Bermúdez, María Elvira. "Ensayo sobre la literatura policiaca |Essay on detective literature|." Revista Mexicana de cultura no. 46 (Feb 48), p. 13; no. 49 (7 March 48), p. 2; no. 52 (23 March 48), pp. 2, 10, 12; no. 55 (18 April 48), p. 2.

A substantial essay by a novelist and critic in which she discusses the history and forms of detective fiction and comments on its lesser importance in Latin American countries as opposed to England and North America.

C91. Bertolucci, Attilio. "I gialli alla radio |Gialli on the radio|." Radiocorriere, 20-26 June 1954, p. 10.

The central complex of the detective novel is formed by the hero-detective, "heir of the paladins, of the knights of the Round Table and of the musketeers." However, the industrial revolution and technical progress have given rise to the "civilization of the detective," an expression of the middle class between the end of the 19th century and the the first world war. (LR)

C92. Besana, Renato. "Il 'giallo' come narrativa insolita |The giallo as an unusual narrative|." La Collina I (1980):125-30.

The often somewhat diffuse presence of giallo novels in generically learned series and the contamination of giallo and literature (which is also an avant-garde victory as the values of plot are recovered through the giallo in a neo-conservative world) lead the author to reflect on the apparent paradox in which "the novels of intelligent authors...are neglected," while the giallo, "a consumer's product, a formula for entertaining, remains. And creates a school." (RC)

C93. "Bestiaire du roman policier |A bestiary of the detective novel)." Enigmatika 16, Sept 80, pp. 5-42.

This dossier is devoted to the subject of animals in detective fiction with classification by species. This is not just a listing of novels in which animals figure prominently but a series of articles in which the subject is explored in some depth. The most thorough articles are on cats and dogs. Notes and bibliographies.

C94. Bezzola, Guido. "Preistoria e storia del giallo all'italiana |Pre-history and history of the giallo in the Italian style|." Pubblico (1977), pp. 103-25.

Historical and sociological analysis of the reasons for the delayed fortune of an autonomous Italian detective literature and of the changes in the literary market which justify today the affirmation of a new school of giallistes (giallo writers). (RC)

C95. Bien, Guenter. "Abenteuer und verborgene Wahrheit. Gibt es den literarischen Detektivroman? |Adventure and hidden truth; is there a literary detective novel?|." Hochland 57 (1965): 456-66. Reprinted in Vogt (B424), pp. 457-72.

Academic essay which places detective fiction within the genre of adventure fiction, such as that by James Fenimore Cooper. Bien argues that Friedrich Dürrenmatt and Raymond Chandler come the closest of all authors to writing literary detective novels. (GG)

C96. Biederstadt, Lynn. "To the Very Last: The Dying Message." TAD 12 (1979): 209-10.
General comments on this device of relaying information and Ellery Queen's effective handling of it.

C97. Blake, Nicholas. Introduction. In Murder for Pleasure, edited by H. Haycraft. London: Davies, 1942. Excerpted as "The Detective Story--Why?" in Haycraft (B142), pp. 398-405; and in Buchloh/Becker 2 (B61), pp. 234-42.
Blake notes that the readership of detective fiction seems to be from the middle and upper classes. He proposes a dubious sociological principle that the lower classes kill out of passion and seldom, as is the case with the upper classes, for gain. He concludes with some comments on present-day trends in the genre. A good example of the insularity of British critical perspectives and the tendency--not restricted to British writers--to generalize on the basis of faulty or incomplete data.

C98. ______. "School of Red Herrings." In Diversions, edited by James Sutro, pp. 58-69. London: Max Parrish, 1950. Illus.
The detective novel as fairy tale, fantasy and puzzle but with believable characters in unrealistic situations. Blake tells about his methods of plotting and describes some of the options available to writers.

C99. Bleiler, E.F. "Chinese Detectives in Poland." TAD 11 (1978):343-45.
Translation of an essay on Chinese popular literature "dealing with crime and its punishment" by Polish Sinologist Tadeus Zbikowski, with critical commentary by Bleiler.

C100. ______. "His Own Desert." TMF 3:4 (July/Aug 79):11, 15.
A review of A. Q. Morton's Literary Detection (Scribner's, 1979) in which Bleiler disucsses the importance of stylometry for mystery fiction scholarship.

C101. ______. "Introduction." In Three Victorian Detective Novels, pp. vii-xvi. NY: Dover, 1978.
Biocritical surveys of the work of Andrew Forrester, Wilkie Collins and Israel Zangwill.

C102. ______. "The Policeman: A Victorian Novel." TMF 6:2 (March/April 82):7-10.
The description of an anonymous novel, published in 1841 in Liverpool, England.

C103. Bloch, Ernst. "Die Form der Detektivgeschichte und die Philosophie. Ein Vortrag |The form of the detective story and philosophy: a lecture|." Die Neue Rundschau 71 (1960):665-83. Reprinted as "Philosophische Ansicht des Detektivromans |Philosophical view of the detective novel|," in Vogt (B424), pp. 322-43; in Zmegac (B451), pp. 111-31; and, translated into English by Roswitha Mueller and Stephan Thaman as "A Philosophical View of the Detective Novel," in Discourse 2 (Summer 81):32-51.
Philosophical embellishment of three criteria found in the detective story which Bloch sees as distinguishing it from all other forms of narration:

tension or suspense, detection or disclosure through clues, and an unnarrated prehistory which is later reconstructed in the story. (GG)

C103a. Block, Lawrence. "Fiction." Writer's Digest 57:2 (Feb 77):13, 58, 60- . Bi-Monthly publication until April 1978; monthly to present.
On fiction writing. Block, a well-known writer of mystery fiction, discusses his own work and the work of other genre writers.

C104. Blom, K. Arne. "The Crime Story in Sweden." TMF 7:5 (Sept/Oct 83): 16-25.
An historical survey of Swedish detective fiction.

C105. Blom, K. Arne, and Broberg, Jan. "Detective Fiction in Sweden." TAD 9 (1975/76):272-73.
A short history.

C106. ______. "Panorama du roman policier suédois |Panorama of the Swedish detective novel|." Translated by François Rivière. Europe, no. 571-72 (Nov-Dec 76):154-59.
A descriptive history.

C107. Bogan, Louise. "The Time of the Assassins." Nation 158 (22 April 44): 475-76, 478.
An essay by poet Louise Bogan, based in part on her reading of Roger Caillois' "Le Roman policier" (C145), in which she traces the history of the detective novel and reflects on it as a form "snobbishly" cut off from great literature but perhaps harboring in its admission of every "rejected and denied human impulse" the "secrets of what we are and shall be." See also "Discussion" in the Nation 158 (27 May 44): 635. Here Jacques Barzun takes issue with Miss Bogan's statement that the detective story in the 19th century was a return to form and logic, pointing out that it was often less rigorous in its construction. He also criticizes her for not separating novels of detection from other forms. Miss Bogan replies with citations from Caillois and other writers to establish a wider frame of reference for the genre than Barzun might allow.

C107a. Boileau, Pierre and Thomas Narcejac. "...Den Bankrott des Denkens Zelebrieren |To celebrate the bankruptcy of thought|." Excerpted from their Roman policier (B37). In Vogt (B424), pp. 293-307.

C108. Bonetti, Deborah. "Murder Can Happen Anywhere." TAD 14 (1981): 257-64. Illus.
The importance of place in mystery fiction and some comments on urban and rural settings.

C109. Bongiovanni, Giannetto. "Parliamo del romanzo giallo |Let's talk about the giallo novel|." L'Ora (Palermo), 1 April 1939.
The author, himself a writer of novels and with a background of mystery and detective work, affirms that one cannot, in consideration of the authentic and great novelists who nourish it, a priori deny to the genre the possibility of being appraised as a literary product. In the orbit of the Italian narrative he considers the novels of Augusto De Angelis a confirmation of his thesis. (LR)

C110. Bonn, Thomas L. "American Mass-Market Paperbacks." In Collectible Books: Some New Paths, edited by Jean Peters, pp. 118-50. NY: Bowker, 1979. Illus.

A definition and history of mass-market paperbacks with some information on imprints, authors and artists. There is an annotated bibliography of secondary sources.

C111. Borowitz, Albert. "New Gaslight on Jack the Ripper." In his Innocence and Arsenic (B42), pp. 87-99.
A review of the leading claimants in the "gallery of suspects," with some comments on the fictional treatments.

C112. Boucher, Anthony. "Best Mysteries of the Month." EQMM, Nov 1957 - Feb 1968.

C113. ______. "Criminals at Large." New York Times Book Review, 1951-28 Apr 1968.
More than 850 weekly columns containing reviews of specific books (usually at least six in each column) plus general commentary on mystery fiction and its writers. Mid-year and end-of-the-year summary columns gave Boucher's choices of the best of each year's works. Selections from this column reprinted in Boucher, Multiplying Villainies (B43). (REB)

C114. ______. "Department of Criminal Investigation." San Francisco Chronicle, 1941-47.
A series of monthly essays, supplemented by weekly brief-mention lists, in the This World section of the Sunday Chronicle. Reviews of current mystery novels and commentary on the field of mystery fiction (covering such topics as spy novels, the economic status of the mystery field, arguments with Ellery Queen's lists, as published in Good Housekeeping (A134, A136, A137), of "important" works, etc.). Selections from this column were reprinted in Boucher, Multiplying Villainies (B43). (REB)

C115. ______. "The Ethics of the Mystery Novel." In Haycraft (B142), pp. 384-99. Reprinted from Tricolor, Oct 44.
Boucher describes, and cites examples of, detective fiction's slow evolution from a conservative medium to one that is more responsive to a wider spectrum of social and political attitudes.

C116. ______. "It's Murder, Amigos." PW 151 (19 Apr 47):2105-2106.
A survey of detective fiction in Latin America with the comment that quality is high because writers cannot support themselves by it.

C117. ______. "Murder Up to Date." The Writer 67 (1954):227-29.
On the fusion of the mystery with the mainstream novel and an analysis of trends/changes based on publishers' classifications for 1943 and 1953.

C118. ______. "Opera and Murder: Notes on the Relation between Two of the Fine Arts." In his Multiplying Villainies (B43), pp. 111-116.
Originally written for Opera News but not published there. Discusses, in predictably witty and informed fashion, both operas that involve murder and murder mysteries that involve opera or opera singers. (REB)

C119. ______. "Speaking of Crime." EQMM, 1949-1950. Four columns.

C120. ______. "Trojan Horse Opera." In Haycraft (B142), pp. 245-49.
The spy novel is becoming more popular as readers tire of the routine detective story and are attracted to suspense fiction. Boucher thinks the spy novel will move away from the detective novel and will be subordinated to the suspense story.

C121. Boutell, Clarence V. "England's other Crisis: How Howard Spring...Wrestled with Mystery Fiction." PW 135 (1939):1426-29. Illus. by Clayton Rawson.
A description of the controversy provoked by Howard Spring's unfavorable review of Christie's *Murder for Christmas* in the London *Evening Standard*, 22 Dec 38. Boutell notes the favorable reviews for the book in America and supports the principle that a reviewer should not reveal all of the plot twists.

C122. Brandt, Bruce E. "Reflections of the 'Paranoid Style' in the Current Suspense Novel." CLUES 3:1 (1982):62-69.
A discussion of the conspiracy novel, and its contemporary historical importance as seen in novels by Robert Ludlum, Trevanian, and John D. MacDonald.

C123. Brantlinger, Patrick. "What is 'Sensational' about the 'Sensation Novel'?" *19th Century Fiction* 37 (June 82):1-28.
Characterizing the Sensation novel as a "minor subgenre that flourished in the 1860s...and lives on in several forms of popular culture...modern mystery, detective and suspense," Brantlinger discusses the characteristics of this literary phenomenon in Collins, Le Fanu, Braddon, Charles Reade and Mrs. Henry Wood. Brantlinger also discusses the relationship of the Gothic mystery to the modern mystery story.

C124. Brecht, Bertolt. "Ueber die Popularitaet des Kriminalromans |On the popularity of the crime novel|." In his *Schriften zur Kunst und Literatur*, Vol. 3, pp. 93-102. Frankfurt: Suhrkamp, 1967. Reprinted in Zmegac (B451), pp. 97-103; in Vogt (B424), pp. 315-21; and, translated into Italian by B. Zigari, in Cremante/Rambelli (B78), pp. 53-59. Carries no internal date but was presumably written during the mid-1930s.
Against the accusation that detective novels are all the same, Brecht explains and defends their popularity by arguing that they let the thinking reader into the "inside story" behind crimes and the workings of society. (GG)

C125. Breen, Jon L. "Detective Fiction and the Turf." TAD 5 (1971/72):24.
A note on the popularity of horse-racing as a subject for writers of detective fiction.

C126. ______. "On Science Fiction Detective Stories." *Isaac Asimov's SF Magazine*, June 1979. Not seen.

C127. ______. "Preface." In his *Hair of the Sleuthhound: Parodies of Mystery Fiction*, pp. vii-x. Metuchen, N. J. and London: Scarecrow Press, Inc., 1982.
A short essay on distinctions between pastiche and parody and some discussion of previous anthologies of parodies. There are afterwords to some of the stories in which authors parodied comment on the parody. The authors who supplied material for the afterwords are as follows: Ed McBain, John D. MacDonald, Isaac Asimov, Edward D. Hoch, Michael Avallone, and Donald Hamilton.

C128. Bremner, Marjorie. "Crime Fiction for Intellectuals." *Twentieth Century* 156 (Sept 54):246-52.
After a brief discussion of Edmund Wilson's negative views on detective

fiction (E866-E868) and a report on a June 1954 "Crime Book Exhibition" sponsored in London by the newly formed Crime Writers Association, Bremner looks for the intellectual's interest in detective fiction in the lack of excitement for individuals "at the higher levels of society" and the ways in which detective fiction provides it.

C129. Brin, Irene. "Libri gialli |Giallo books|." In Usi e costumi, pp. 15-16. Rome: De Luigi, 1944.
Detective novels which--in the 20 years from 1920-40 in Italy--were number one on best-seller lists were directed to the mass of readers who "incapable of an adherence to everyday life or to its romantic stylizations (and therefore condemned the best and the worst literature) sought comfort in a fantasy which had become mathematical." In the characters and in the situations of the detective story, Brin, a brilliant journalist, finds "a secret relationship with the horsemen of De Chirico and the giant worms of Dali," demonstrating a vein of surrealism which has entered "innocently" to become a part of the public's taste. (LR)

C130. Briney, Robert E. "Death Rays, Demons and Worms Unknown to Science: The Fantastic Element in Mystery Fiction." In Ball (B15), pp. 235-89.
An informative and entertaining survey of mystery stories and science fiction stories with detective elements in which the supernatural and the occult intrude. There are lengthy discussions of Sax Rohmer and John Dickson Carr, who excelled in this material, and shorter discussions of a score of other authors. The essay begins with a concise look at the supernatural in the 19th century detective novel and short story. Excellent notes.

C131. Broberg, Jan. "Deckarvykort fran Paris |Detective postcard from Paris|." Jury 11:3 (1982): 43-52.
A miscellany of items on the French detective scene, including French authors, novels taking place in Paris, French detectives. (MS)

C132. ______. "Den inverterade deckaren -- ett klarläggande |The inverted detective novel -- a clarification|." Jury 8:1 (1979):63-67.
R. Austin Freeman, Anthony Berkeley and others. (MS)

C133. Bronski, Michael. "Skeletons out of the Closet: Pulp Fiction Goes Gay." Boston Phoenix Section 3, 2 Dec 80, p. 5.
On Gay Gothics and mysteries (especially Nathan Aldyne's Vermillion). (KLM)

C134. Brophy, Brigid. "Detective Fiction: A Modern Myth of Violence?" Hudson Review 18 (Spring 65):11-30. Reprinted in her Don't Never Forget: Collected Views and Reviews, pp. 121-42. NY: Holt, Rinehart and Winston, 1966.
Genre fiction as latterday myths, sharing with ancient myth a faithfulness to types. A subtle and wide-ranging essay on and defense of the detective novel as a modern exemplar of the pattern that, in Greek myth, brought the hero to the city to rid it of a monster and, in so doing, absolved the people of their guilt and restored to them something of their innocence.

C135. Bruers, Antonio. "L'insegnamento dei romanzi polizieschi |The teaching of detective novels|." L'Italia che scrive, 4 Oct 31, pp. 25-26.
The detective novel is the form which is assumed by the narrative of entertainment in the twentieth century, "the century of the airplane and

the radio," like the romance of chivalry in the Middle Ages and in the Renaissance or the social novel in the nineteenth century. The great success of the detective novel represents the reaction of the public to the modern novel weighed down by philosophy and psychology and is an implicit warning to writers to return to a taste for the plot. (LR)

C137. Buchloh, Paul G. and Jens P. Becker. "Der amerikanische Detektivroman nach 1975 |The American detective novel since 1945|." In Buchloh/Becker I (B60), pp. 145-55.
On the work of Ross Macdonald, Robert L. Pike, Ed McBain. Chester Himes and Harry Kemelman. Sees the production of modern short criminous stories as an especially American phenomenon. (GG)

C138. ______. "Der Detektivroman: Zur allgemeinen Problematik |The detective novel: on general difficulties|." in Buchloh/Becker I (B60), pp. 1-33.
Discusses taxonomical distinctions, history, and various aspects of the form such as setting, motive, the Great Detective phenomenon, etc. (GG)

C140. Byerly, Ann. "The Bouchercon Report." MSMM 45:2 (Feb 81):77-83.
Report on the 1980 Anthony Boucher Memorial Mystery Convention in Washington, D.C., with summary of major program items and thumbnail sketches of many participants. (REB)

C141. Buxbaum, Edith. "The Role of Detective Stories in a Child Analysis." Psychoanalytical Quarterly 10 (1941):373-81.
A description of the analytical treatment of a 12-year-old boy whose learning problems in school were aggravated by the detective stories to which he was addicted and whose characters embodied his various fantasy roles (detective, victim and murderer).

C142. Byfield, Barbara Ninde. "A Cast of Characters" ('Off the Record' Column). AHMM 28: 8 (Aug 83):62-73.
A satiric look, in the form of drawings and commentary, at the standard characters and situations in the classic British mystery. (REB)

C143. Byrd, Max. "The Detective Detected: From Sophocles to Ross Macdonald." Yale Review, Autumn 74, pp. 72-83.
An essay on the limitations of the detective story which is not high tragedy because the hero "experiences no fall, no change...."

C145. ______. "Le Roman Policier: évolution, jeu, drame |The detective novel: evolution, game, drama|." In his Puissances du roman, pp. 75-148. Buenos Aires: Editions des lettres françaises, 1941; Marseille: Editions du Sagittaire, 1942. Reprinted in his Approches de l'imaginaire, pp. 177-205. Paris: Gallimard, 1974. Excerpts published as follows: in Chimera 5:4 (Summer 47):67-79; in Cremante/Rambelli (B78), translated by Alfonso Zaccaria, pp. 99-102; in Most/Stowe (B264), translated by Glenn W. Most, pp. 1-12.
In this short but dense essay, Roger Caillois analyses the evolution of the detective novel. He shows that the genre's inevitable origin is located in the beginning of the 19th century and that it was born from the new conditions of life: urban development, creation of politicial police, most notably by Fouché. He shows how one goes from the artisan's novel (Sherlock Holmes) to the puzzle novel by the creation and the observing of a series of rules progressively more arbitrary and restrictive. He studies the different components of the puzzle novel, the various questions the detective must answer, and insists on the limited situations

that constitute the locked-room mystery and the serial murders. He states that apparently the detective novel is at the farthest remove from the novel which freed itself, during that time, from all rules. Finally, in the last third he studies the evolution of the heroes of the detective novel, in particular the prototypes of the hard-boiled private eye (in Hammett and Raoul Whitfield who were the only writers translated into French at that time). He shows that this type of hero reintroduces the most "shameless" novelistic qualities and opposes sensationalism to investigation, anarchy to the police. He concludes by declaring that "the detective novel represents the struggle between order and chaos." (JB) Addendum: The essay was reviewed by Jorge Luis Borges in Sur (Buenos Aires) 91, April 42, pp. 56-57. Borges critized Caillois' history of the origins of the genre, pointing out errors in dates that Borges thought undermined his historical points. Caillois replied on pp. 71-72 of the same issue that Caillois had misunderstood him. Borges closed the public debate in Sur 92, pp. 72-3, by saying that Caillois' version of the origins of the genre is unverifiable.

C146. Calendrillo, Linda T. "Role Playing and 'Atmosphere' in Four Modern British Spy Novels." Clues 3:1 (1982):111-19.
The relationship of role playing and setting in novels by John Buchan, John le Carré, Graham Greene and Joseph Conrad.

C147. Callendar, Newgate. "We Care, Roger." NYTBR, 23 July 78, pp. 3, 33.
A belated, unoriginal reply to Edmund Wilson's often cited essay (C867).

C148. Camerino, Aldo. "I 'gialli': storia di un'anima |The gialli: history of a mind|." La Fiera Letteraria, 25 Nov 51, p. 7.
The author declares his preference as a reader for the ingenuous texts of pre-W. W. I when the awkwardness of the production met with the "candor" of the public and the rules of the detective novel had not yet been rigidly codified. He refers especially to the stories of Arsène Lupin but finds an echo of the old school in the stories of Roy Vickers (The Department of Dead Ends, 1949). (LR)

C149. _____. "Giallo stil nuovo (1953) |Giallo, new style|." In Scrittori di lingua inglese, pp. 331-34. Milan-Naples: Ricciardi, 1968.
The novels of Mickey Spillane (launched in Italy by the publisher Garzanti of Milan, 1953) confront the reader with a new school of detective story which, with the introduction of violent and gratuitous action, destroys the formula of the classic giallo, based on the delineation and clarity of logical design. In addition, with this innovation the detective story confirms that it belongs to "those which Charles Lamb would have defined as 'non-book books'." According to Lamb, these are books that require a passive, lazy reader who skims the pages hastily and forgets everything that he has read. (LR)

C150. Cameron, Mary S. "The UNC Detective Collection." The Bookmark, Friends of the University of North Carolina, no. 38 (Sept 68), pp. 1-6; a shorter version was printed in TAD 1 (1967/68):51-52.
Introductory notes on the collection.

C151. Campbell, SueEllen. "The Detective Heroine and the Death of Her Hero: Dorothy Sayers to P. D. James." MFS 29:3 (Autumn 83):497-510.
Patterns of "gradually redefined and partially resolved problems" in the novels of Sayers and James.

C152. Campos, Jorge. "Crimen y bibliofilia |Crime and the bibliophile|." Bibliofilia VII. Valencia: Editorial Castalia, 1953.

An essay on the role of book-collecting in detective fiction. (Donald A. Yates)

C152. Cannon, Mary. "Booked & Printed." Review column in Alfred Hitchcock's Mystery Magazine from Aug 1982.

This column, which has so far appeared in every issue since its inception except that of Aug 1983, consists of a short essay/review on the career of a single author, followed by a selection of miscellaneous reviews. The subjects of the essay/review (Aug 82-Oct 83) are: Allingham, Bentley, van de Wetering, Crispin, Langton, Moyes, Hare, Sjöwall/Wahlöö, Hilda Lawrence, Rendell, Dunnett, John le Carré, Kallen, Michael Innes, Leo Bruce and Peter Lovesey. Date of appearance and pagination will be cited in the Authors section. (REB)

C154. Capek, Karel. "Holmesiani, or About Detective Stories." In his In Praise of Newspapers, pp. 101-124. London: Allen & Unwin, 1951. Translated by M. and R. Wetherall.

A substantial essay in which Capek, in what amounts to a series of topics treated like entries in an imaginary Universal Encyclopedia, talks about the detective story and fairy tales, the dual attractions of crime and justice, the detective as epic hero/hunter, riddles and puzzles, Great Detectives, the modern detective and science, and the role of chance in the most relentlessly deductive stories. This essay was first published in 1924 but in its good humor and intelligence it is superior to most later work by critics writing on these subjects.

C155. Carboni, Guido. "Introduction." In Polizieschi americani |American detective stories|, edited by F. Moretti, pp. 7-14. Rome: Savelli, 1978.

Correcting a famous judgment by Edmund Wilson (C867), Carboni concludes that people read the giallo because in an indirect, vicarious way they can fix on an expiatory scape-goat the responsibility for their own social and personal anguish, but perhaps the same people pick up another giallo because they know that this expiatory scapegoat is false and sometimes instead of soothing the anguish ends up by releasing it. (RC)

C156. ______. "Un matrimonio ben riuscito? Note sul giallo d'azione negli USA |A very successful marriage? Notes on the American action giallo|." Calibano 2 (1978), pp. 109-37.

Moving from the affirmation of Chandler who characterizes the contemporary age as "not war nor atomic energy but the marriage of an idealist to a gangster and how their home life and children turned out," Carboni retraces the traditional tensions and contradictions "between the Utopian project to which American society traces its own origin and the anti-Utopian violence of the means through which this project has been realized." To the Utopia-violence polarity can also be attributed the various opposing functions which constitute the narrative and writing structure. (RC)

C157. Carlisle, Charles R. "Strangers Within, Enemies Without: Alienation in Popular Mafia Fiction." In Landrum, Dimensions (B216), pp. 194-202.

Carlisle sees Mafia fiction as reflecting one of the principal elements of contemporary life. The mafioso is alienated both from society and from his own kind. The argument is not supported by references to any significant number of texts.

C158. Carr, John Dickson. "The Grandest Game in the World." EQMM, March 63, pp. 53-68. Also published as a privately printed chapbook, The Grandest Game in the World, in an edition limited to 300 copies, (New York, 1963), 22pp., wraps. Reprinted in Nevins (B240)), pp. 227-47; and in The Door to Doom (E354), pp. 308-25.

This essay was written in 1946 as an introduction to an anthology but the project was not realised and the EQMM appearance is its first publication. Carr writes both a spirited, totally committed defense of the well-plotted, fair-to-the-reader detective novel and a scornful denunciation of the hard-boiled mystery which he thinks returns to the outworn devices of the thriller, rejected by the generation of 1920. The essay was apparently intended as a response to Raymond Chandler's 1944 essay, "The Simple Art of Murder." (C168)

C159. ______. "Introduction." In Maiden Murders by the Mystery Writers of America, pp. ix-xiv. NY: Harper & Bros., 1952.

In addition to Carr's introduction, there are writers' introductions to each story, with information on the writing and publishing of the story.

C160. ______. "The Locked-Room Lecture." In Haycraft (B142), pp. 273-86. This "lecture" was delivered by Dr. Gideon Fell in Carr's novel The Hollow Men (1935; American title, The Three Coffins).

The problem of murder in the "hermetically sealed room" is analysed by by a fictional character created by this demanding technique's most inventive practioner.

C161. Carter, John. "Detective Fiction." In his New Paths in Book-Collecting. London: Constable, 1934. Published separately as Collecting Detective Fiction (London: Constable, 1938). Reprinted in Haycraft (B142), pp. 453-75; and in Books and Book-Collectors (London: Rupert Hart-Davis, 1956), pp. 77-93.

A landmark historical essay by a noted bookman, with copiously annotated notes on nineteenth- and twentieth-century detective fiction.

C162. Carter, Steven R. "The Science Fiction Mystery Novels of Asimov, Bester and Lem: Fusions and Foundations." Clues 1:1 (Spring 1980):109-115.

The problems of fairness in sf crime and detective novels. (James R. McCahery)

B163. Cassiday, Bruce. "Write Me an Adventure Novel." The Writer 82:3 (March 69):11-14.

The contemporary adventure story in a discussion of the hero, villain, plot and setting.

C165. Cawelti, John G. "The Study of Literary Formulas." In Winks (B434), pp. 121-43. Originally published in Cawelti (B69), pp. 5-9, 16-18, 20-33, 35-36.

Cawelti defines literary formulas, as he understands them, in relation to society and culture. He also talks about the danger of talking about literature with terms borrowed from other disciplines. Formula fiction is, he maintains, an artistic work and can be described like other literary works.

C166. Chandler, Frank W. "The Literature of Crime Detection." In his Literature of Roguery (B71), Vol 2, pp. 524-49.

This final chapter in the two-volume study of the rogue in literature discusses the "the literature of crime detection" which Chandler sees as having supplanted and partially replaced the older genre. He discusses briefly the development of modern police forces in England and France, an investigative system which he views as the historical event necessary for the creation of this new literature. He distinguishes between the analytic and sensational methods of Poe and Gaboriau and concludes with a lengthy discussion of the Sherlock Holmes stories. The bibliography of the genre is not significant, he claims, although he does credit some sources. He reserves his major praise for an unpublished essay, "The Detective Story," written by one of his former pupils.

C167. Chandler, Raymond. "Casual Notes on the Mystery Novel." The Writer 76:7 (July 63): 13-16, 46. Excerpts from Raymond Chandler Speaking (E397), pp. 63-70. Translated into German and reprinted in Buchloh/Becker 2 (B61), pp. 262-71.

Comments on plotting, appeal to the reader's intelligence, setting, the classical detective story and a number of other topics.

C168. ______. "The Simple Art of Murder." Atlantic Monthly 174 (Dec 44):53-59. Revised version published in Haycraft, (B142), pp. 222-37; in Chandler, The Simple Art of Murder (Houghton Mifflin, 1950), pp. 519-33; in Gilbert (B124), pp. 85-104; and in Vogt (B424), pp. 164-85. (This essay, and the following one, have been frequently reprinted; in this bibliography, only the major hardcover reprintings have been recorded.)

This is the first of two essays that Chandler wrote with this title; it is the longer and the more comprehensive. It is a defense of detective fiction as an art form; an attack on the British classical detective story, with a detailed analysis of the implausible elements in A. A. Milne's novel, The Red House Mystery; a discussion of Dashiell Hammett's contribution to the genre; and, finally, a personal, elegaic evocation of a detective who sounds very much like Chandler's hero, Philip Marlowe. The revisions for the Haycraft anthology are minor and consist largely of a revised first section.

C169. ______. "The Simple Art of Murder." SRL 33 (15 April 50), pp. 13-14. Reprinted as follows: as the Introduction to Chandler, The Simple Art of Murder (Houghton Mifflin, 1950), pp. vii-x; and as "Raymond Chandler Introduces 'The Simple Art of Murder,'" in The Midnight Raymond Chandler (Houghton Mifflin, 1971), pp. vii-xi.

This short essay is Chandler's tribute to the pulp writers of the Black Mask school.

C170. ______. "Twelve Notes on the Mystery Story" and "Addenda." Antaeus 25/26, Spring/Summer 1977, pp. 100-105.

These two selections from The Notebooks of Raymond Chandler (E396) served as the introduction to the Detective Fiction section in this Popular Fiction Issue of Antaeus, edited by Daniel Halpern and published by the Ecco Press. (REB)

C171. Chantland, Gloria. "The Case of the Reluctant Readers." Today's Education, Nov/Dec 76, pp. 32-33.

Case-study of the use of detection to improve reading comprehension, listening skills, and interest in reading in a below-average high school English class. (REB)

C172. Charney, Hanna. "Pourquoi Le 'Nouveau Roman' policier? (Why the Detective 'New Novel'?)." French Review 46 (1972):17-23.

As the formal detective novel seemed to react against the loosening of structures in the serious novel in the early decades of this century, so do the French new novelists revolt against their fictional predecessors. They use techniques of the detective novel but often as parody and the mystery for them has gaps that can never be closed.

C173. Chastain, Thomas. "The Case for the Private Eye." In Freeman (B117), pp. 27-33.
Chastain pays tribute to Hammett and Chandler as the creators of the models for the private-eye novel and tells briefly how he used their technique of mis-directing the reader in his own work.

C174. Chastaing, Maxime. "Le Roman policier classique." Journal de psychologie normale et pathologique 64 (1967):313-42. Reprinted in Europe, Nov/Dec 76, pp. 26-50; and in Cremante/Rambelli (B78), pp. 209-26.
A brief history of the genre (with particular attention to its origins in France) and an analysis of typical structures. There is some discussion of the nature of psychology in the stories and the mental aberrations of the criminal.

C175. Ch'en, Jerome. "Rebels between Rebellions -- Secret Societies in the Novel, P'eng Kung an." The Journal of Asian Studies 29 (1970):807-22.
A study of dissension and upheavals in 19th century Chinese secret socieites using as a literary-historical source the novel P'eng Kung an |The cases of Judge Peng|, published in 1860-70. Includes some historical and bibliographical information on 19th century kung-an ("courtroom" or "crime-case") novels, as well as biographical data on the historical figure P'eng P'eng (1630-1704), on which the stories are loosely based. (GG)

C176. Chesterton, Cecil. "Art and the Detective." Temple Bar (London), Oct 1906; Living Age 251 (24 Nov 1906):505-511.
A defense of detective fiction (and, incidentally, of genre fiction) in which Chesterton maintains that there is good and bad detective fiction and that it is the function of good criticism to distinguish between the two. The mystery should be "mysterious" and the explanation should be well-prepared, even inevitable. He has a splendid paragraph detailing the absurd coincidence as a device and cites approvingly Poe, Gaboriau, Collins, A. K. Green and Florence Warden. He values technical mastery and skillful characterization. Chesterton concludes with a defense of the philosophic detective story, a plea for ideas in the form, and a definition of the genre that is, as he puts it, the essence of all philosophy: "the presence of visible phenomena with a hidden explanation." A little-known essay that deserves to be reprinted.

C177. Chesterton, G(ilbert) K(eith). "About Shockers." In his As I Was Saying, pp. 200-210. London: Methuen, 1930; NY: Dodd, Mead, 1936.
Chesterton protests against a trend in detective fiction toward "savage fatalism," a psychological realism which blurs the moral distinctions that have served the genre so well.

C178. ______. "A Defense of Detective Stories." In his The Defendant. London: R.B. Johnson, 1901; NY: Dodd, Mead, 1902; reprinted by J. M. Dent, Wayfarer Library series, n.d., pp. 157-67. Essay reprinted in: New and Old Essays, edited by R.W. Jepson (London and NY: Longmans, 1937); Essays of To-Day: An Anthology, edited by F. H. Pritchard (Boston: Little, Brown, 1924), pp. 227-31; Haycraft (B142, pp. 3-6; Buchloh/Becker 2 (B62), pp. 34-37; Vogt (B424), pp. 95-98; and in Cremante/Rambelli (B78), pp. 11-14.

A delightful essay on the detective novel as the poetry of the modern world and the detective as the knight errant defending social order against the criminal barbarian who would return society to the primitive forests.

C179. ______. "A Defense of Penny Dreadfuls." In his The Defendant. London: R.B. Johnson, 1901; NY: Dodd, Mead, 1902; Reprinted in the Wayfarer's Library (London: J. M. Dent, n.d.), pp. 19-27.
The lowest popular literature (boys' fiction) may be trash but it is not injurious to one's mental health--as is much modern fiction read by the upper classes--and it maintains the old, hopeful virtues of the popular romance.

C180. ______. "Detective Stories." Preface to The Wrong Letter by W. S. Masterman. London: Methuen, 1926; New York: Dutton, 1926. Reprinted in The Man Who Was Chesterton, edited by Raymond T. Bond (NY: Dodd, Mead, 1921), pp. 79-83.
How to write a detective story: keep it simple, not sensational and short.

C181. ______. "The Domesticity of Detectives." In his The Uses of Diversity, pp. 34-42. London: Methuen, 1920; NY: Dodd, Mead, 1921.
French detective story writers have the French "spirit of definition" which is a way of writing precisely and of constructing plots in which every detail contributes to their development. The English have what Chesterton calls "the spirit of irrelevancy" in which the best moments are often unrelated to the main plot. Chesterton uses the term "the Yellow Peril" to characterize the Oriental threat but also sensational fictions with international conspiracies of other kinds. A nice re-statement of the genius of French classicism.

C182. ______. "On Detective Novels." In his Generally Speaking. NY: Dodd, Mead, 1929. Reprinted in Readings in the Modern Essay, edited by E. S. Noyes (Boston: Houghton Mifflin, 1933), pp. 471-76.
Chesterton wonders why no one has written a book on "how to write a detective story." He proposes two rules: (1) the secret should be simple; and (2) the roman policier is more effective as a short story than a novel. People, he says, wear masks in each story and characters cannot really be discussed or presented until the end when the masks are taken off. He also comments on the low level of reviewing of detective fiction, a situation which some people may think has not changed significantly.

C183. ______. "On Detective Story Writers." In his Come to Think of It, pp. 33-38. London: Methuen, 1930; NY: Dodd, Mead, 1931. (Originally published in Illustrated London Daily News; no date cited.)
Chesterton notes that Edgar Wallace's name figures most prominently on laudatory ads for Bentley's Trent's Last Case and muses on the popularity of writers like Wallace who do not write well and on the greater merit of a less rapturously received work that may also be better written. He also points out that Wallace writes adventures (which Chesterton also enjoys) rather than detective stories.

C184. "Chinese Apathy toward Crime Detection." Literary Digest, 23 Sep 33, p. 14.
Report on an article in The China Critic (Shanghai) by T.K.C. claiming that detective fiction cannot be popular in any country "like China" where there is no love or respect for law and order. The Chinese are a "matter-of-fact people...not interested in mysteries."

C185. Christopher, J. R. "The Case of the Vanishing Locomotives or A Hell of a Way to Run a Railroad." TAD 1 (1967/68):56-58.
Crimes involving the disappearance of a moving train from its tracks.

C186. ______. "Commentary on Joan Mooney's 'Best-Selling American Detective Fiction'." TAD 5 (1977/72):11-14.
A discussion of the Mooney thesis (B260), in which Christopher questions the narrowness of the theoretical premises of chapters 1-3 but attempts to show both the validity of her discussions and ways in which she might have extended them to bring out the wider implications of her subject. On the whole, Christopher's comments are favorable and his comments are the kind of suggestions for strengthening a dissertation that one normally expects from dissertation directors and committees. Corrections by J. Randolph Cox in a letter, TAD 5:109; a reponse by Mooney in TAD 5:118-125; and final comments by JRC in TAD 5:249.

C187. ______. "Murder at the Crossroads; or Oedipus the Detective." TAD 2 (1968/69):225-26.
The making of a case for the dramatic work of Sophocles as the "originating and basic detective form."

C188. ______. "The Rites of a Mystery Cult." TAD 5 (1971/72): 152-153.
Christopher takes issue with Brigid Brophy's argument (C134) that "mystery stories offer society absolution from guilt."

C189. Chung, Sue Fawn. "From Fu Manchu, Evil Genius, to James Lee Wong, Popular Hero: A Study of the Chinese-American in Popular Periodical Fiction from 1920 to 1940." JPC 10 (1976):534-47.
A thoroughly annotated and documented survey of the changing Western treatment of the Chinese in popular fiction, from the Yellow Peril stereotype of the early Sax Rohmer books to the more benign figures of Charlie Chan and James Lee Wong. Another treatment of the same topic is Wu's The Yellow Peril (B443). (REB)

C190. Cohen, Ralph. "Private Eyes and Public Critics." Partisan Review 24 (1957):235-43.
A strained and unconvincing attempt to show similarities between literary criticism and murder mysteries. Cohen never focuses on what other writers have seen as a similar function: the detective and the critic as readers of enigmatic texts.

C191. Colbron, Grace Isabel. "The Detective Story in Germany and Scandinavia." Bookman 30 (1909):407-12.
A survey of the field with particular attention to Augusta Groner of Austria (whom Colbron compares to A. K. Green) and Eric Sorensen and Baron Palle Rosenkrantz of Denmark.

C192. Cole, Don. "High Adventure Fiction." TMRN 4:1 (Oct 70):3-7.
A discussion of some contemporary writers of high adventure fiction and their works. Cole is particularly knowledgeable about Hammond Innes and there are some quotes from correspondence with Innes and a checklist of his works.

C193. Cone, Edward T. "Three Ways of Reading a Detective Story - or a Brahms Intermezzo." Georgia Review 31 (1977):554-74.

Using Doyle's "The Speckled Band" as his basic example, Cone develops a hypothesis of reading in which the third reading (where the reader must again experience the narrative freshly, suppressing what he knows of the "sub-text" as best he can) is the true reading and extends this to a comparison with a listener's experience with music.

C194. Connolly, Cyril. "Deduction from Detectives." New Statesman and Nation (London) 2 (new series), no. 41 (5 Dec 31):vii-viii (Christmas supplement). Reprinted in his Evening Colonnade, pp. 490-95. London: David Bruce & Watson, 1974.
A defense of detective fiction as a social document and "pure" form opposed to the progressively more sprawling novel. The British, Connolly claims, are the masters of the form while in America too much is thought of "horror and psychology."

C195. Consiglio, Alberto. "Cauto elogio del 'giallo' |Cautious praise of the giallo|." L'Italia letteraria, 19 Nov 33, pp. 1-2.
The detective novel as the "document of an era" was born in the industrialized countries (England and the U.S.A.) and bears witness to the interest directed toward the social which is derived in the modern taste from organized industrialism. The genre involves high and low literature: as the "coarse realistic and passionate novel" of the 19th century goes back to Maupassant and Zola so the detective novel has its origins in Poe and Chesterton, who had the "poetic" intuition to lead into the domain of fantasy the logical procedures of pure mathematics. (LR)

C196. "Cops and Novels: The Sleuth in Fact and Fancy." TLS, 25 Sept 55, p. v.
Professional detectives are well-trained; fictional detectives may be more cavalier but professional detectives have admitted to finding useful information in detective novels.

C197. Corbett, James. "The Art of Writing Thrillers." Contemporary Review 182 (1952):240-43.
A somewhat humorous essay on writing thrillers by a writer of thrillers.

C198. Cotton, John. "Editorial." Private Libraries 7 (1974):135-38.
Comments on the reprinting of the Union Jack Christmas numbers from 1925-28 as Crime at Christmas (London: Wyn Evans). Cotton describes the material as "formula detective fiction."

C199. Cox, J. Randolph. "Detection in the Guilt-Age." TAD 8 (1974/75): 111-20.
A survey of detective fiction from Poe to the British Golden Age with comments on the writers, the fiction and the audience. See comment by Elmer R. Pry in letter, TAD 8:239.

C200. ______. "The Detective Story: Its Study and Appreciation. A Syllabus." In 2 parts. TMRN 4:4 (May 71):3-6; 4:5 (Jly/Aug 71):19-22.
A detailed syllabus for a course on detective fiction that Cox taught at St. Olaf's College in Northfield, MN, in 1971. Texts, definitions, supplementary reading, study questions: a complete and fascinating outline for the course.

C201. Creasey, John. "The Social Consequences of Crime-Writing." TAD 4 (1970/71):38-40.
The reader and the effect crime novels may have on him.

C202. "Crime and the Reader." Nation 86 (1908):143-44.
The ambivalence of the reader's liking for detective fiction in which he both exults in the criminal's capture by the astute detective and admires his daring and ingenuity.

C203. "Crime in Current Literature." Westminster Review 147 (1897):429-38; reprinted in Buchloh/Becker 2 (B62), pp. 19-38.
A moralistic tract condemming the flood of crime stories and claiming that such stories may incite the reader to crime and degrade the public morality. A somewhat reluctant admission that there may be literary merit in some of the works can occasionally be detected.

C204. "Crime in Fiction." Blackwood's (Edinburgh), Aug 1890, pp. 172-89.
While recognizing that there is a considerable range from high quality to the dregs in criminal romances, the anonymous author thinks that, in general, crime stories leave a bitter after-taste and are incapable of exalting the reader in the manner of the "highest" art. He finds the French to be the superiors of the English in this genre and after a discussion of Daudet, Balzac, Gaboriau and others, moves to the "sensation" school of English writers with his highest praise reserved for the "English" Gaboriau, Wilkie Collins. He also comments on Mrs. Henry Wood, Miss Braddon, and Mrs. Gaskell.

C205. Crispin, Edmund. "Preface." To Best Detective Stories, edited by Robert Bruce Montgomery ("Edmund Crispin"), pp. 9-15. London: Faber and Faber, 1959; reprinted, in a German translation by Wolfgang Thrun, in Buchloh/Becker 2 (B61)pp. 334-42.

C206. Cumberland, Marten. "Murmurs in the Rue Morgue." Dublin Magazine (new series) 27 (Oct/Dec 52):29-38.
As the thriller and puzzle novel are joined by a "new crime novel of character," new problems of definition and perspective are created for critics and readers.

C207. Cummings, J. C. "Detective Stories." Bookman 30 (1910):499-500.
The Chief of the New York Special Agents of the US Secret Service sees the difference between real and fictional detectives in the fact that where the real detective frequently solves his case from early clues, the important clue in fictional cases may not be revealed until close to the end. He cites Doyle's Holmes as the most realistic of fictional detectives because he's not "muddled in silly romances," works from early clues and generally keeps his mouth closed.

C208. Cuppy, Will. "How to Read a Whodunit." Mystery Book Magazine, Jan 46; reprinted in Haycraft (B142), pp. 373-76.
Some light-hearted advice from a humorist and reviewer which is to open the book and start reading. If you like what you are reading, continue; if not, try another book.

C209. Cushing, Charles Phelps. "Who Writes These Mystery Yarns?" Independent 118 (9 Apr 27):382-84. On pp. 385-88, a photo section of writers. Article subitled "The Great Detective Solves Another Puzzle."
An imaginary dialogue in which the G. D. explains the interest of trained professionals in the mystery story by the "fact" that so many of the writers themselves are trained professionals (doctors, lawyers, engineers

and "high-brow essayists") who have turned the analytical tools of their profession to the writing of detective stories.

C210. Dahl, Tor Edvin. "En eksplosjon av mord! Den utenlanske kriminalroman i Norge |An explosion of murder! the foreign crime novel in Norway|." Jury 5:3 (1976):21-22, 58. (MS)

C211. ______. "Mesterdetektiven Knut Gribb og Norge i 70-arene |Master detective Knut Gribb and Norway in the 70s|." Jury 5:3 (1976):44-46, 59.
Knut Gribbe's adventures, begun in magazines, are now in a book series, by various hands. (MS)

C212 Dahlin, Robert. "PW Interviews Eleanor Sullivan." PW 218 (19 Dec 80):8-9. Photo.
An interview with EQMM editor, Eleanor Sullivan.

C213. Daiber, Hans. "Nachahmung der Vorsehung |Imitation of providence|." Merkur 257 (1969):856-66; reprinted in Vogt (B424), Vol. 2, pp. 421-36.
Essay on various aspects of European and English-language crime fiction. Observations include commentary on the popularity of crime fiction under socialism and Naziism, the difficulty of capturing or defining the genre with rules, and the role of reason in the genre. (GG)

C214. Dane, Clemence. "The Best Detective Story in the World." Bookman 75 (1932):539.
A dialogue with a "young friend" in which Dane proposes Daniel (of Biblical Apocrypha) as the "father of all detectives."

C215. Danesford, Earle. "Famous Fiction Detectives." The Champion Annual 1925, pp. 80-81.
A short study with a natural tendency towards those detectives created for the juvenile market. However, in his survey practically all of the big names receive mention, including at this rather early date Hercule Poirot. (RCSA)

C216. Davenport, Guiles. "Foundations of the Detective-Mystery Story." The Writer 50 (1937):153-55.
The crime writer should widen the "scope of his camera" to respond to social upheaval and change. Criminals may be considered as products of that society.

C217. Davis, Dorothy Salisbury. "View from the Middle Window." PW 213 (13 Mar 78):46-47.
General essay on the current state of mystery fiction and a brief historical survey.

C218. De Angelis, Augusto. "Il romanzo giallo. Confessioni e meditazioni |The giallo novel. Confessions and meditations|." Preface to Le sette picche doppiate, pp. 11-20. "Romanzo Mondiale," 211. Milan: Sonzogno, 1940.
Passionate apology for detection fiction by one of the masters of the Italian detective story in the years 1930-40. The writer maintains that the psychological study of the characters is fundamental in a narrative genre like the detective story in which the plot is presented as "a pitiless struggle of brains." The contrast of psychologies contributes to creating that climate of "tense, vibrant, frantic as well as calculated action," which is the artistic effect of detective literature. (RC)

C219. DeFord, Miriam Allen. "The Psychology of Mystery Story Writing." The Writer 77 (June 64):12-14.
Mystery fiction as an expression of latent interest in violence in all of us and sources for ideas with examples taken from DeFord's writing.

C220. De Laet, Danny. "Le nouveau polar belge |The new Belgian polar|." Enigmatika 20 (Jan 82), pp. 20-24.
After noting the surge in the publication of detective novels by Belgian writers during the German Occupation, De Laet gives a rapid survey of a number of Belgian writers publishing in the 70s and 80s. Brief mentions of Jean Ray and Georges Simenon.

C220a. Dennington, Charlotte. "Crime Really Does Pay." Writer (British), March/April 83, pp. 12-17.
Generalized advice for novices on the writing of crime and suspense novels. (REB)

C221. DePaolo, Rosemary. "From Howtoits to Whodunits: Jane Austen to Agatha Christie." Clues 2:2 (Fall/Winter 1981):8-14.
Realistic detail and the closed society in Austen and Christie.

C222. Depken, Friedrich. "Sherlock Holmes, Raffles und ihre Vorbilder (Auszuege) |Sherlock Holmes, Raffles and their prototypes (excerpts)|." From Depken (B91), pp. 8-24, 29-47, 92-100; reprinted in Buchloh/Becker 2 (B61), pp. 67-102.
Discussion of the techniques of creating suspense and other aesthetic modes as practiced by Gaboriau, Poe, Doyle and Hornung. (GG)

C223. "Detection Club." The Floating Admiral. London: Hodder, 1931; NY: Doubleday, 1932. Reprinted in the Gregg Press Mystery Fiction Series (B134). With introductions by Christianna Brand and Dorothy Sayers.
A collaboration by members of the London Detection Club on a round-robin mystery. The original introduction is by Dorothy S. Sayers; Christianna has written a new introduction for the Gregg Press reprint. CC 2135.

C224. "Detection Club Oath." In Haycraft (B142), pp. 197-202.
The ritual ceremony initiating a member into the London-based mystery writer's club.

C225. "Detectiveness in Fiction." Nation 95 (15 Aug 1912):141-42; also in The Writer 23:10 (October 1912):158-59.
The best detective stories appeal primarily to the intellect and certain formalities (the maintenance of the "chain of causation" and the presence of a "confronting" detective) must be observed.

C226. "The Detective Novel." TLS, 25 Feb 55, Suppl. ix, x-xi; reprinted in Buchloh/Becker 2 (B61), pp. 299-313.
Desultory essay on several aspects of the detective novel. The most interesting comment is that noteworthy characters such as Dupin, Poirot, Dr.Thorndyke and Philo Vance have their authors as prototypes. (GG)

C227. "Detectives." The Saturday Review (London), 5 May 1883, pp. 558-59.
Comments on French police and their special attributes, with some references to fictional treatments of crime and their popularity.

C228. "Detectives in Fiction." The Writer 21:9 (Sept 1909):128-39.

On detectives before Holmes (Cuff, Dupin, Lecoq, Martin Hewitt and Dick Donovan) and their remarkable feats of tracking criminals.

C229. "Detectives in Fiction." TLS, 12 Aug 26; reprinted in Living Age 330 (18 Sept 26): 638-43; and in Men and Books, edited by Malcolm S. MacLean and Elisabeth K. Holmes, pp. 334-35 (London: Long & Smith, 1932).
A concise survey of the current scene in which the detective novel is described as a modern phenomenon, not yet fixed in its conventions and allowing for change and development. The writer discusses the conventions of the Watson-narrator, the prohibition of love interest and, in most detail, H. C. Bailey's Reggie Fortune and R. A. Freeman's Dr. Thorndyke.

C230. De Waal, Ronald Burt. "Literary Parallels and Comparisons." In his World Bibliography of Sherlock Holmes and Dr. Watson, pp. 258-65. Boston: New York Graphic Society, 1974.
An annotated bibliography of articles which are a mixture of discussions of imaginary relationships between Holmes & Watson and other fictional detectives and Doyle's influence on other writers of mysteries. Much of the material originally appeared in journals devoted to the writings of Conan Doyle; appropriate items will be cited in the Authors section.

C231. De Zuani. "Il lettore di 'gialli' |The reader of gialli|." Quadrivio, 11 Feb 40, pp. 1-2.
The writer denounces a phenomenon of decadent taste, and, at the same time, of editorial bad manners. The sensational ingredients which characterize the detective novel (shivers, fear, shudders, horror: all that, in short, which in Italy is expressed in the word giallo) invade and consume a part of every other genre destined for the public of average culture. (LR)

C232. Dickson, Carl Byron. "Edmund Wilson and the Detective Story." TAD 9 (1975/76):189-90.
A defense of the detective story in response to Wilson's attack (C867) on it.

C233. Dickstein, Morris. "Beyond Good and Evil: The Morality of Thrillers." American Film 1:9 (Jly/Aug 81):49-52, 67-69.
Discusses both film and printed versions: le Carré, Greene, Buchan, Ambler, Hitchcock, Welles, etc. (REB)

C234. Dingeldey, Erika. "Wer ist der Schuldige? Aspekte der Frau im amerikanischen Kriminalroman |Who is the guilty one? Aspects of the woman in the American crime novel|." Frankfurter Runschau, SV section, 1 Nov 69. Expanded and reprinted in Vogt (B424), Vol. II, pp. 578-84.
Article taking Chandler, Spillane, Erle Stanley Gardner and other male writers to task for their portrayal of women as unrealistic, nymphomaniacal or dependent upon the male. Only Hammett is spared, because of Hammett's Nora Charles whom Dingeldey found to be charming, high-spirited, intelligent, and a true partner throughout the case. (GG)

C235. Dogana, Fernando. "Il colpevole non sono io: Psicologia del lettore di romanzi polizieschi |I am not the guilty one: psychology of the reader of detective novels|." Psicologia contemporanea 5:27 (1978):42-46.
Panorama of the principal psychological and psychoanalytical interpretations of the "behavior" of readers of detective novels. (RC)

C236. Dömötör, Tekla. "Folktales and the Detective Story." Translated from the German by Elizabeth Tucker and Antony Hellenberg. Folklore Forum 8 (1975):335-43.

A comparison of detective story elements with the numbered classifications in The Types of the Folktale, referred to as "Aarne-Thompson." The discussion excludes the "literary" detective story and concentrates on newsstand thrillers. The author acknowledges that there are several transitional forms leading from the marchen to the modern detective story: the chapbook, dime novel, Western and similar forms.

C237. Donaldson-Evans, Lance K. "Conspiracy, Betrayal, and the Popularity of a Genre: Ludlum, Forsyth, Gérard de Villiers and the Spy Novel Format." Clues 4:2 (Fall/Winter 83):92-114.

After speculating on the reasons spy fiction has received less critical attention than detective fiction, Donaldson-Evans tries to separate the two by isolating the themes of conspiracy and betrayal and then examines the work of three writers.

C238. Donovan, Frank P. "Mystery Rides the Rails." In four parts. TAD 1 (1967/78):124-27; 2 (1968/69):46-48, 103-7, 176-78.

Additions were contributed by readers as follows: letter (Frank D. McSherry, Jr.), TAD 2 (1968/69):1334; letter (Robert E. Briney), 2:201; letter (Robert Garasha), 2:277; letter (Robert J. Gores), 2: 278; letter (Francis M. Nevins, Jr.), 3 (1969/70): 137-8; letter (McSherry), 4 (1970/71):54; and letter (Nevins), 4:192. The installments have the following titles: "Railroad Short Stories of Mystery and Detection in America," "English Railway Novels of Mystery and Detection and Translations," and "English Railway Short Stories of Mystery and Detection." Each section consists of a narrative history with a bibliography of titles.

C239. Dove, George N. "The Criticism of Detective Fiction." PCS 1 (Winter 77): 1-7; reprinted in Winks (B438), pp. 203-8.

Brief summary of five modes of criticism of detective fiction. Also, a prospectus for studies of the relationship between the writer and his reader and the development of "a body of theory of the special sense of reality in detective fiction."

C240. ______. "Intruder in the Rose Garden." TAD 9 (1975/76):278-80.

On the modern private investigator as an intruder in stories in the classic tradition (J. S. Fletcher, Philip MacDonald, Ellery Queen and Agatha Christie). Dove does not see these characters as prototypes of the modern private eye.

C241. ______. "The Police Procedural." Part 1, "Realism, Routine, Stubborness and System," TAD 10 (1977):133-137; Part 2, "The Cops and the Cop-Haters," TAD 10 (1977):241-43; Part 2, "Brother Officers Be Damned," TAD 10 (1977): 320-23; Part 4, "The Police Are Always There," TAD 11 (1978):74-77; Part 5, "The Tangled Emotions," TAD 11 (1978):150-52; Part 6, "The Rookie Type," TAD 11 (1978):249-51.

The material was revised, expanded and published as The Police Procedural (B96).

C242. ______. "'Shades of Dupin!': Fictional Detectives on Detective Fiction." TAD 8 (1974/75):12-14.

References by characters in detective stories to characters in other detective stories.

C243. ______"The Weevil in Beancurd: Or, The Cop Abroad." TMF 2:6 (Nov/Dec 78):17-19, 16.
Foreign procedural series. Sjöwall/Wahlöö are examined in greatest detail but there is some mention of other series.

C244. Drew, Bernard A. "Murder by Mail; or, The Great Postage Stamp Mysteries." Scott's Monthly Stamp Journal 60:4 (April 79):4-9, 59.
Survey of mystery novels and pulp-magazine stories involving postage stamps and philately, illustrated with photos of pulp magazine and paperback covers. Also see three follow-up letters by Drew, Herman Herst, Jr., and Dorothy L. Truhon in 60:6 (June 1979):64. Drew's letter recounts the background of the first Hugh Pentecost novel, Cancelled in Red. (REB)

C245. Dunae, Patrick A. "Penny Dreadfuls: Late Nineteenth-Century Boys' Literature and Crime." Victorian Studies 22 (1978/79):133-50. Illustrated.
On the pernicious effect on juveniles attributed by nineteenth-century critics to popular literature. However, by the end of the century, a grudging acceptance of the literature can be seen as the violence is channeled into more acceptable modes.

C247. Durham, Philip, and Jones, Everett L. "The Books of WWA." The Roundup (official organ of the Western Writers of America) 17:1 (Jan 69) - 17:3 (Mar 70).
A checklist of the book publications of the active members of the Western Writers of America, through 1968. Serialized in 14 parts. Gives title, byline, and year of publication; the overall organization is alphabetical by author's real name. There are many errors and omissions, but for most of the authors, this was the first attempt to list their works. Among the mystery writers included are W. T. Ballard, Leigh Brackett, John Creasey, Davis Dresser, Brian Garfield, Frank Gruber, Donald Hamilton, and Richard Wormser. (REB)

C248. Eckert, Otto. "Der Kriminalroman als Gattung |The crime novel as genre|." Buecherei und Bildung 3 (1951):679-81; reprinted in Vogt (B424), Vol II, pp. 528-32.
Argument that the crime novel has dangerous and harmful effects. Not only do such books spoil readers for works of real literary value, argues Eckert, but they may also ruin the sense and morals of the public. Dorothy L. Sayers' Murder Must Advertise and Graham Greene's Orient Express (Stamboul Train) are so blamed. (GG)

C249. Edgar, George. "The Unromantic Detective." The Outlook, 3 Dec 1910, pp. 788-89.
Readers of detective fiction may expect too much of real-life detectives.

C250. Edmiston, Susan. "The Nine Most Devilish Murders." Esquire, Aug 75, pp. 66-67, 136-37.
Murder methods in nine novels and short stories.

C251. Eisenstein, Sergei. "La negazione della negazione |The negative of the negative|." Voprosy Literatury (Moscow), 1968; reprinted in an Italian translation in Rinascita no. 34, 30 Aug 68, p. 27; and in Cremante/Rambelli (B78), pp. 95-98.
Notes on detective fiction: its appeal to a large popular audience and its development during the period of the rise of the bourgeoisie.

C252. Eisenzweig, Uri. "Chaos et maîtrise: Le discours romanesque de la méthode policière |Chaos and mastery: the novelistic discourse of the detective method|. In Michigan Romance Studies, Vol II: Discours et pouvoirs, Wtr 81. Not seen.

C253. ______. "Présentation du genre |Presentation of the genre|." Littérature no. 49 (Feb 83), pp. 3-15.
This introduction to a series of studies on detective fiction in an issue devoted to the subject provides a critical overview of the genre. The essay also proposes textual strategies and new critical methodologies.

C254. Eisinger, Erica M. "Detective Story Aspects of the Nouveau Roman." TAD 12 (1979):362-65.
A good discussion of the ways the French New Novelists of the 50s and 60s incorporated detective story elements into their novels. This subject has been touched upon frequently in academic criticism; Eisinger's article focuses on the nature of the relationship between the popular novel and the avant-garde novel.

C257. Elizalde, Luis de. "Reflexions sobre la novela |Reflections on the novel|." Sur 195-196 (Jan/Feb 51), pp. 6-24; 197 (March 1951), pp. 23-24.
Renato Ghiotto, in Sur 202 (Aug 51), pp. 78-81, takes Elizalde to task for locating the interest of detective fiction in the feeling of fear which readers find in it. Ghiotto sees it as a game and intellectual exercise most popular in liberal societies where the reader is "well protected" from these primordial feelings. Elizalde replies (pp. 81-86) that detective novels are something more than intellectual games, a point of view he holds in spite of arguments to the contrary by Borges and Roger Caillois.

C258. Ellin, Stanley. "The Crime Short Story -- An American View." In Gilbert (B124), pp. 163-77.
A brief history of the form in the 19th century, comments on the decline in quality in the first three decades of this century, and the role of EQMM in rehabilitating the form.

C259. Elwin, Malcolm. "Psychology of the Thriller." The Spectator, 26 Aug 33, p. 230.
Elwin confuses detective fiction and the thriller, including among the writers he discusses Poe, Wilkie Collins, A. E. W. Mason, and the modern master of the "true thriller," Hugh Walpole. Thrillers must, he says, "grip" the reader.

C260. Endrèbe, Maurice Bernard. "Les Mystères de la chambre |Locked-room mysteries|." Revue de criminologie et de police techniques Vol. 4 (1956); reprinted in Enigmatika 19 (June 81):50-60.
Discussions of locked-room mysteries in, among others, Poe, Chesterton, John Dickson Carr, and Pierre Boileau.

C261. ______. "Pérennité du roman d'énigme |Endurance of the riddle novel|." Europe, no. 571-2, Nov-Dec 76, pp. 50-53.
The riddle novel is not, as some would have it, dead and its continuing popularity reflects our basic interest in riddles.

C262. ______. "Le Prix du quai des orfèvres |The 'Quai des orfèvres' award|." Enigmatika, no. 5 (Jan 77), pp. 9-10.

A list of the prizewinners followed by a discussion of the most recent laureates.

C263. Enna, Franco. "La storia del romanzo giallo |The history of the giallo novel|." La Notte 10, 14, 16, 17 July 1959.
Series of informal articles in which are described in general terms the ramifications of the vast popular literature "born of the cult of justice." The modern developments of this production are represented by detective novels. (The author, whose real name is Franco Cannarozzo, is among the most prolific writers of detective stories, signed, for the most part, with foreign pseudonyms.) (LR)

C264. "Entertaining Inquiry: The Nature of the Detective Story." TLS, 25 Sept 55, p. iv.
On the popularity of detective fiction and its ingredients: plotting, characters, background, story-telling techniques.

C265 Erhardt, Pat. "The Double Life of Gloria Amoury." TMRN 3:5 (June 70):3-6.
An interview with the executive secretary of the Mystery Writers of America. There is some discussion of the MWA newsletter The Third Degree and of Amoury's own short stories.

C266. Erisman, Fred. "Crime Fiction: Some Varieties of Historical Experience." Clues 1:1 (1980):1-8.
A thoughtful study on how detective fiction not only has its sources in its culture but "sheds light" on the myths the culture develops.

C267. Estleman, Loren D. "No Trap So Deadly: Recurring Devices in the Private Eye Story." AHMM 28:13 (Dec 83):69-76. "Off the Record" column.
Estleman enumerates several common elements in private eye stories--overall story structure, the ritualistic beating suffered by the protagonist, the betrayal by a woman, the uneasy relationship with the police--and illustrates them with quotations from Hammett, Chandler, Ross Macdonald, Mickey Spillane, John D. MacDonald, and others. (REB)

C267a. ______. "Plus Expenses: The Private Eye as Great American Hero." AHMM 28:9 (Sept 83):64-72. "Off the Record" column.
Discussion of the essential features of the private eye character, with specific references to (and quotations from) Daly, Hammett, Chandler, Spillane, and Ross Macdonald. Also traces the sources of the private eye to dime novel characters. (REB)

C268. Evans, Verda. "Mystery as Mind-Stretcher." English Journal 61 (72): 495-503.
Text of a speech by the Cleveland Plain Dealer's mystery reviewer in which she discusses the reasons people read mysteries and classifies mysteries as classic detective, police procedural, situational, Gothic, espionage and social comment. Her categories obviously overlap. An elementary treatment for a general audience.

C269. Fabbretti, Nazareno. "Decadenza del 'giallo' |Decadence of the giallo|." Il Popolo, 23 July 58.
The author, a Catholic intellectual, laments the disappearance of the good authors of the traditional detective novel and sees "a blossoming of deformities" inaugurated by Spillane which is evidenced on the level of taste "even before the strictly moral level." (LR)

C270. Fadiman, Clifton. "On Reading Mysteries." Good Housekeeping 116 (Feb 43):30, 79. Illus.
Fadiman reads mysteries for pleasure and as an escape from chaos into orderly conventions where he can "flatter" his intellect.

C271. Farrar, John. "Have You a Detective in Your Home?" Century 118, new series (1929):84-89. Subtitle: "Today's Craze for Crime in Fiction, and Its Causes."
The renewal of interest in the crime novel is attributed to a national interest in cross-word puzzles and other intellectual games and to our snobbishness as exemplified in the popularity of Philo Vance. Farrar classifies the genre into six sub-species as follows: Horror, Puzzle, Mystery, Fantastic Pursuit, Underworld and Murder, with examples of each. He thinks that women are joining what he sees as the largely male readership.

C272. Felman, Shoshana. "De Sophocle à Japrisot (via Freud), ou pourquoi le policier |From Sophocles to Japrisot (via Freud), or why the detective novel|?" Littérature (B346), pp. 24-42.
A reading of Japrisot's Piège pour Cendrillon in tandem with Sophocles' Oedipus cycle, buttressed by references to Freud.

C272. Ferguson, Suzanne. "A Sherlock at Dubliners: Structural and Thematic Analogues in Detective Stories and the Modern Short Story." James Joyce Quarterly 16 (1978/79):111-21.
To support her thesis, Ferguson cites Chesterton on the poetry of detective stories and their relationship to fairy tales, adapts Vladimir Propp's morphology of fairy tales to her purposes and then discusses stories in Joyce's Dubliners, using the referents she has described. An interesting attempt to bridge the gap between elite and popular literature.

C273. Ferri, Enrico. "I delinquenti nell'arte (1896) |Delinquents in art|." In I delinquenti nell'arte ed altre conferenze, esp. pp. 55-68. 2nd edition. Turin: Utet, 1926.
Text of a famous lecture which the psychologist-criminologist gave for the first time in Pisa in 1892. The author, who treats judiciary novels (romans judiciaires) and dramas in the fifth paragraph of his essay, sees in Emile Gaboriau the initiator of the genre and extracts the typical plot of the judiciary novel from L'Affaire Lerouge (1863). The genre is centered on the judiciary vicissitudes and not on the psychology of the delinquent and interests the reader by keeping him suspended between two opposite emotions produced either by the discovery of a guilty person, through "marvelous" logical inductions, or by the persecution of an innocent person as a result of judicial error. (LR)

C274. Field, Louise Maunsell. "Philo Vance & Co., Benefactors." North American Review 235 (1933):254-60.
A humorous piece. Field explains the passion for mysteries by the fact that every "normal" person has, sometime, wanted to murder somebody. With the disappearance of other deterrents to murder, fiction which depicts the capture of the murderer dissuades people from doing it in real life.

C275. Filstrup, Jane Merrill. "Cats in Mysteries." Part I, TAD 11 (1978):58-62; part II, TAD 11 (1978): 134-38. Illus.

Some general remarks on cats in fiction and folklore, but the articles are largely descriptive reports on novels and stories in which cats have important roles.

C276. ______. "A KAHNfidential Interview." Clues 2:2 (Fall/Winter 81):15-22.
An interview with the long-time editor of the prestigious Harper & Row detective fiction series. Other interviews with Kahn: American Bookseller, Dec 80; Mystery 3:1 (July 81):16-17, 61-62.

C277. _____. "The Shattered Calm: Libraries in Detective Fiction." Part I, "The Librarian as Victim," WLB, Dec 78, pp. 320-7; Part II, "The Librarian as Sleuth," and Part III, "Scene of the Crime," WLB, Jan 79, pp. 392-98. Illus.
A descriptive report.

C278. Finch, G.A. "From Spade to Marlowe to Archer." TAD 4 (1970/71): 107-110.
An essay on the development of the private eye from Hammett through Chandler to Ross Macdonald.

C279. Fiscalini, Janet. "Elementary, My Dear Watson." Commonweal 75 (27 Oct 61):116-18.
A perceptive analysis of the dissimilar--but imaginative--fiction of the ratiocinative and hard-boiled schools and some brief comments on the more recent procedurals and novels in which abnormal psychology figures importantly.

C280. Fiscella, Joan B. "A Sense of the Under Toad: Play in Mystery Fiction." Clues 1:2 (1980):1-7.
The "Under Toad" is something threatening that may be covered up by the apparent light-heartedness of games. Fiscella notes the ambivalence of writers toward play and talks about three mystery stories in which there is something "foreboding" in games.

C281. Fischer, Peter. "Neue Haeuser in der Rue Morgue. Entwicklungslinien des modernen Kriminalromans |New houses in the Rue Morgue: lines of development in the modern crime novel|." Merkur 257 (1969):846-56; expanded and reprinted in Vogt (B424), pp. 185-200; and in Zmegac (B451), pp. 261-75.
Essay on trends since Poe and Doyle. Topics include types of detectives, realism, recent espionage fiction and parody. Writers cited include the Simenon, Julian Symons, Hammett and Margery Allingham. (GG)

C282. Fletcher, Connie. "The Case of the Missing Criminal. Crime Fiction's Unpaid Debt to Its Ne'er-Do-Wells." TAD 10 (1977):17-20.
Based on a talk delivered at Bouchercon 6 in Chicago, 1975. How attitudes toward the criminal have changed from the 18th to the 20th centuries; after the "moralistic" eighteenth and the "rational" nineteenth, we are now in a time of "pervasive evil" when anyone can slip into the villain's role.

C283. Flora, Francesco. "Un romanzo poliziesco |A detective novel|." L'Illustrazione italiana, 6 Sept 31, p. 374.
The author, historian and critic of literature of idealistic inspiration, expresses a negative judgment on the spreading of the genre: "the literature of detective novels is the least exquisite and least witty malady of our time." (LR)

C284. Flori, Fausto. "Libri gialli |Giallo books|." Meridiano di Roma, 27 Oct 40, p. xii.
In harmony with the provisions of Fascist censorship, in the recrudescent phase of the war period (abolition of the "black chronicle" by the dailies, embargo on publications considered harmful for children, growing hostility in confrontations with Anglo-Saxon literature), the author proposes to eliminate from the Italian book market detective novels in the name of the moral and literary education of the people and of nationalist sentiment, because "these books are written by Englishmen and by Americans, more or less declared enemies of Italy." (LR)

C285. Follett, Ken. "The Spy as Hero and Villain." In Freeman (B17), pp. 74-81.
Under this general title lurks an article by Follett on how he creates suspense in his spy novels.

C286. Fong, Gilbert Chee Fun. "Time in Nine Murders: Western Influence and Domestic Tradition." In The Chinese Novel at the Turn of the Century, edited by Milena Dolezelova-Velingerova, pp. 116-28. Toronto: Univ. of Toronto Press, 1980.
An analysis of the unconventional temporal (i. e. non-linear) structure of Wu Wayao's Jiuming Giyuan |The strange case of nine murders|, first published serially in 1906. According to Fong, this novel is a variant on the traditional Chinese crime novel, gong-an. Fong points out that in Chinese crime fiction the emphasis is on the punishment of the criminal rather than on the solving of a mystery, as in Western detective fiction. Fong notes the popularity of Western mysteries during this period.

C287. Fredriksson, Karl G. "Frid pa jorden! eller Mordet pa jultomten." |Peace on earth! or the murder of the Christmas elf|." Jury 10:4 (1981):5-13.
Christmas murders in Christie, Hare, Innes, McClure and others including Swedish authors. (MS)

C289. Fredriksson, Karl G. "Wien bleibt Wien |Vienna remains Vienna|." Jury 11:2 (1982):47-53.
The author looks for the Vienna of Dagobert Trostler, the Viennese Sherlock Holmes, and of Graham Greene's Third Man. (MS)

C288. Fredriksson, Karl G. and Lilian. "Hasta Manana." Jury 8:4 (1979): 16-27.
Detective fiction in Spain. (MS)

C290. Freeman, Lucy. "The Whydunit Emerges, Thanks to Freud." In her Murder Mystique (B117), pp. 46-56.
An essay based on the psychological "principle" that if we know the motive of the murderer we will have the added thrill of "identifying" with it--if it is related to a family conflict-- since we have "all" had murderous feelings directed at our parents. Freeman cites several writers and works she feels are appropriate. She does not cite any of the numerous 19th century works to which the subject might have been applied and concludes with a eulogy to Freud for enriching the literature and our lives.

C291. Freeman, R. Austin. "The Art of the Detective Story." Nineteenth Century and After 95 (1924): 713-21. Reprinted in: Haycraft (B142), pp. 7-17; Buchloh/Becker 2 (B61), pp. 103-115; in Cremante/Rambelli (B78), pp. 15-22; and in The Thorndyke File no. 10 (Fall 80), pp. 12-23.
The detective story is too often judged by its failures rather than by its successes and it is an uncommonly difficult form to master. It demands

all the qualities of good fiction and an intellectual satisfaction which is "unique" to it. Such stories most commonly fail in the introduction of logical fallacies and a failure to conclude properly and fairly. Freeman finds the explanation at the end of "Murders in the Rue Morgue" to be an example of an unconvincing explanation.

C292. Friedman, Mickey. "Shades of Sam Spade." The San Francisco Bay Guardian 10:18 (6 Feb-13 Feb 76):9-13.
Photos (pp. 12-13) of Collin Wilcox, Joe Gores and Bill Pronzini, three Bay Area mystery writers. Profiles.

C293. Fritz, Kathlyn Ann, and Hevener, Natalie Kaufman. "An Unsuitable Job for a Woman: Female Protagonists in the Detective Novel." International Journal of Women's Studies 2: 2 (1979): 105-28.
A survey of 28 female detectives. (KLM)

C294. Funghi, Franco. "Il romanzo poliziesco |The detective novel|." Il Calendario del Popolo, July 52, p. 1186.
Following the indications furnished by Gorki (first Congress of Soviet Writers, 1934), the author maintains that the modern detective novel, "founded on the individual search for the culprit," begins with Sherlock Holmes at the time when the cheat, the rogue, and the gentleman thief yield their position as heroes of the novel to the police-spy, "symbol of bourgeois justice triumphing over the forces of evil." (LR)

C295. Gadney, Reginald. "Criminal Tendencies." London Magazine (new series) 12:2 (1972):110-22. Illus.
As the traditional boundaries between good and evil blur and villains are less villanous, Gadney sees the emergence of a more literate crime fiction. In his discussion, he mentions Patricia Highsmith, Ross Macdonald, and Simenon. Since detective fiction has--during much of its history--been characterized by its appeal to the reader's intelligence and by the often high level of its writing, it is difficult see much merit in Gadney's argument.

C296. Gamarra, Pierre. "L'Enquête est ouverte |The investigation is opened|." Europe, no. 571/72 (1976):3-7.
An introduction to this issue of Europe, much of which is devoted to the detective novel. Gamarra takes issue with Narcejac's distinction between a literature of entertainment (popular literature) and a more "serious" literature.

C297. Gardner, F. M. "The Golden Age?" Library Association Record 74:3 (1972): 45-46.
A review of Colin Watson's Snobbery with Violence (B426), in which the reviewer questions Waton's sociological basis and his interpretation of data.

C298. Gardner, Erle Stanley. "The Case of the Early Beginning." In Haycraft (B426), pp. 203-208.
ESG remembers the early days of Black Mask and its writers, and pays tribute to readers who, as detective stories become more "logical in treatment," develop unsuspected powers of deduction from their reading.

C299. ______. "Getting Away with Murder." Atlantic Monthly 215: 1 (Jan 65): 72-75.
On Carroll John Daly, why Della Street will never marry Perry Mason, and

Hammett's use of "gunsel" and "shamus."

C300. Garfield, Brian. "The State of the Art: A Symposium Conducted by Brian Garfield." PW, 13 Mar 78, pp. 50-1. Photos.
Answers by a dozen American and European mystery-suspense writers to queries submitted by Garfield.

C301. ______. "Suspense Fiction: The Problem of Definition." PCS 1:1 (Winter 77):8-11.
Garfield defines suspense fiction as a work in which "a character is malignantly menaced" and in which that threat is the dominating element of the story. With examples.

C302. Gass, Sherlock Bronson. "Disipere in Loco." In his Criers of the Shops, pp. 335-52. Boston: Marshall Jones, 1925.
A casual description of the pleasures afforded by the reading of a mystery novel; the author prefers country-house mysteries. An unoriginal reworking of tired materials.

C303. Gattegno, Jean. "Criminels et dêtectives ou la prêhistoire du roman policier: A propos d'un livre de Ian Ousby |Criminals and detectives or the prehistory of the detective novel: concerning a book by Ian Ousby|." Etudes anglaises 31 (1978):188-97.
A review of Ousby's Bloodhounds of Heaven (B300) in which Gattegno traces the creation of the detective hero at the expense of the criminal who is no longer necessarily the romantic rogue of the pre-Vidocq era. Gattegno fails to note the survival of the rogue-hero in his haste to prove his thesis.

C304. Gayot, Paul. "Sur la littêrature policiêre potentielle |On potential detective literature|." Europe no. 571-2 (Nov/Dec 76):164-66.
Discussion of the history and aims of OULIPOPO (Ouvroir de Littêrature Policiêre Potentielle), a group of writers and critics who formed a subgroup within the Pataphysical Society which is devoted to the promotion of the principles of French absurdist writer Alfred Jarry. OULIPOPO, in addition to supporting the magazine Enigmatika, seeks to widen the discussion of detective fiction beyond the genre classification.

C305. Geherin, David J. "The Hard-Boiled Detective Hero in the 1970s: Some New Candidates." TAD 11 (1978):49-51. Illus.
Robert Parker, Roger Simon and Andrew Bergman.

C306. Genberg, Kjell E. "Deckaren i Holland |The detective novel in Holland|." Jury 9:2 (1980):43-46.
Interview with Martien Carton who discusses her own works and Dutch crime fiction in general. (MS)

C307 ______. "Sa här ser deckarna ut i Sovjet! |So that's how detective novels look in the Soviet Union|." Jury 6:1 (1977): 11-13. (MS)

C308. Gerber, Richard. "Verbrechensdichtung und Kriminalroman |Criminal fiction and the crime novel|." Neue Deutsche Hefte 3:3 (1966): 101-117. Revised and reprinted in Vogt (B424), pp. 404-20.
This article, which contains critical remarks on Alewyn (C12, C13), aims at outlining a clear German terminology. for the detective novel and related works. Both the detective story with its emphasis on ratiocination and the thriller are seen as subgenres of the Kriminalroman (crime novel)

in which a "sleuth" either investigates or prevents a crime. This genre, however, has to be distinguished from literature of crime in general (Verbrechensdichtung), i. e. works like Crime and Punishment dealing with crime, but not according to the conventions of the Kriminalroman. (Barbara Korte)

C309. Gerould, Katherine Fullerton. "Men, Women and Thrillers." Yale Review 19 (1930):689-701.

An attempt to distinguish between the reading tastes of men and women. Detective fiction, Gerould believes, is read by more men than women. Men read objectively, for information; women are seldom involved in fiction with which they can not identify. She does not find this to be a satisfactory state of affairs but she thinks it should be noted. Gerould also speaks for feminism and the newly emancipated woman. Her research seems to have been based on discussions with friends.

C310. ______. "Murder for Pastime." SRL 12:14 (3 Aug 45):3-4, 14. Photos.

They do everything mysterious better in England. American writers feature the detective over the crime and are deficient in the intellectual department.

C310a. Geslin, Luc, and Rieben, Georges. "L'Interview du mois: Marcel Duhamel." Mystère Magazine no. 293, July 72.

Interview with the creator of the serie noire reprint series; interesting glimpse into the world of French reprints of English-language crime fiction. (REB)

C311. "Il giallo in biblioteca |The giallo in the library|." Il Giornale d'Italia, 20-21 January 1966.

A collection of opinions of some Italian writers on the relations between the detective novel and the more committed modern literature. With the participation of Dino Buzzati, Carlo Cassola, Giuseppe Berto, Attilio Bertolucci, Giorgio Caproni, Ignazio Silone, Indro Montanelli, Denti di Pirajno, Manlio Gancogni, Mario Soldati, and Oreste Del Buono. The reply of Carlo Emilio Gadda, because of its interest and with the author's consent, has been published separately under the title "Incantagione e paura" (E1235). (LR)

C312. Giani, Renato. "Il libro giallo (ovvero l'amante degli enigmi) |The giallo (or the lover of enigmas)|." Comunità 12 (1957):xxv-xxxii.

A wide-ranging discussion of genre anthologies, sociological data, genre history and Anglo-Saxon criticism. The author maintains that the novel is not popular reading, but was born and was spread (even in Italy) in the milieu of a middle-class public. (LR)

C313. Giardinelli, Mempo. "Coincidencias y divergencias en la literature 'negra' (apuntes para una explicación de las relaciones de la novela latinoamericana con la norteamericana del género policial |Coincidences and divergencies in roman noir literature (notes for an explanation of the relationship of the Latin American novel to the North American detective genre)|." Revista Mexicana de Ciencas Sociales, no. 100 (July 1980), pp. 125-42.

A wide-ranging essay that suggests principal sources of the influence on contemporary Latin American literature that can be ascribed to American writers--and not exclusively detective fiction authors--of the past sixty years. (Donald A. Yates)

C314. ______. "Acerca de los orígenes de la 'Novela Negra |On the origins of the roman noir|." Revista 'Comunidad Conacyt,' Jan/Feb 82, pp. 9-12; March/April 82, pp. 29-30; May/June 82, pp. 19-20; July/Aug 82, pp. 27-29.
A four-part article that examines the sources of the roman noir in the U. S. The author traces the essences of this literary sensibility back through the "realistic" detective novels of the 30s to the American novel of the West. (Donald A. Yates)

C315. Giardini, Cesare. "Del leggere libri gialli |On reading gialli|." In Il naso di cartone, edited by E. D'Errico, pp. 233-38. Series: "I Libri Gialli," 242. Milan: Mondadori, 1940.
The detective novel denotes a particular quality of reading. While in the serial novel the reader satisfies his taste for horror stories, in the detective novel he admires the constructions of the intelligence similar to "the supreme and unstable balancing of jugglers who, for a few seconds, seem to overcome and upset the laws of the universe." What interests the reader of detective novels is not so much seeing the guilty punished (as happens in the serial novel), as "knowing who the guilty one is and by what paths one succeeds in discovering him." The author traces the archetype of the modern detective back to the Rhetorical Maximus of Plutarch. (LR)

C316. Giglio, Tommaso, editor. "Inchiesta sui gialli |Inquiry into the gialli|." Il Calendario del Popolo. 7 parts: no. 107, Aug 53, pp. 1506-1507; no. 108, Sept 53, p. 1530; no. 109, Oct 53, p. 1555; no. 110, Nov 53, pp. 1578-1579; no. 112, Jan 54, p. 1627; no. 113, Feb 54, p. 1651; no. 114, March 54, p. 1674.
The author, proceeding from the gramscian hypothesis on popular literature (see C332), conducts an inquiry on the detective novel among readers, publishers, and writers (the latter represented by Oreste Del Buono, Domenico Porzio and the woman Polish writer Wanda Melcer). From the debate emerge (1) the need to distinguish the various kinds of detective novels, compressed in Italy into the conventional label (giallo) which mixes various products of different historical periods; (2) the establishment of the fact that "detective literature has a limited character": it is connected, usually, to a definite period in the life of each reader, corresponds to marginal exigencies and in the long run ends up leaving them unsatisfied; (3) the preferences of the public for the so-called classic giallo, à la Conan Doyle, and the open disapproval of the American current of Spillane, bearer of conservative-reactionary tendencies; (4) the desire, expressed also by the most assiduous readers, for a new type of detective novel "more attentive to man and to social and historical phenomena," which, beyond the shudder and the mystery, may help us to know reality better. (LR)

C317. Gilbert, Elliot G. "The Detective as Metaphor in the Nineteenth Century." JPC 1 (1967): 256-62. Reprinted in Nevins (B240), pp. 285-94.
In reponse to the usual view that the detective is a rational being whose development corresponds to that of science in the 19th century, Gilbert shows that the detective is, in fact, often an irrational being symbolic of the century's disillusion with scientific logic.

C318. ______. "McWatter's Law: The Best Kept Secret of the Secret Service." In Landrum (B216), pp. 22-36.
The detective as defeated investigator as the detective novel turns from a structure in which order is resolved to one in which initial order

deteriorates into complex and, for the most part, unresolvable mysteries.

C319. Gilbert, Michael. "The Moment of Violence." In his Crime in Good Company (B124), pp. 106-25.
Thrillers are, Gilbert claims, more difficult to write than detective stories. His examples are largely drawn from Hammett and Chandler. In the thriller, characters are three-dimensional and there are no rules. He sees the attraction of the thriller, as compared to the puzzle novel, in the excitement of its obligatory shocks and violence.

C320. ______. "The Spy in Fact and Fiction." In Ball (B15), pp. 205-221.
Gilbert describes present-day intelligence organizations in various countries and, referring to Buchan, observes that the ideal of the "honorable" spy is dying. He comments on several of his favorite writers of spy novels--with special praise for Len Deighton--and on some of the common errors writers of spy fiction make.

C321. Gillespie, Robert. "The Recent Future: Secret Agents and the Cold World War." Samalgundi, no. 13 (Summer 1970), pp. 45-60.
A thoughtful, detailed essay on recent espionage fiction and the ways its morality differs from the classic models of the pre-Cold War period.

C322. Glover, David. "The Frontiers of Genre." JAmStud 15 (Aug 81):249-52.
Noting that Whitley (B429) has posited a conscious subversion of hard-boiled fiction by Hammett, Glover shifts the discussion to genre definitions to suggest that hard-boiled may only be a sub-text in a wider category that includes spy, gothic, suspense, and classical detective fiction. Until the forms are more clearly defined in their relationships to one another and to a more inclusive category, it will be difficult for any critic to speak of the subversion of a particular sub-species.

C323. Goldstone, Adrian. "The Quacks in the Quorum." TAD 12 (1979): 226-27. Illus.
Goldstone questions the designation of "rare" and "scarce" for some of the books in Queen's Quorum (A135).

C324. Goode, Greg. "German Secondary Literature." TMF 7:5 (Sept/Oct 83):7-15.
A review of the general characteristics of German criticism of detective fiction and comments on significant works.

C325. ______. "The Oriental in Mystery Fiction: The Sinister Oriental." Part I, TAD 15 (1982):196-202. Part II, "The Orient," TAD 15:306-13. Part III, "The Oriental Detective," TAD 16 (1983):62-74. Part IV, "Martial Arts," TAD 16 (1983):257-61. Illus.
In Part I, there is an introduction and a copiously annotated bibliography of secondary sources on the Oriental in fiction and film; part II, in addition to a discussion of the Orient as "character," consists of a comprehensive overview of fiction. For corrections and additions see letters (Goode), TAD 16 (1983):96, 218, 322.

C326.. Gottschalk, Jane. "Criminous Christmases." TAD 13 (1980):281-85. Illustrated.
Novels of Christmas cheer and murder.

C327. ______. "Detective Fiction and Things Shakespearean." TAD 14 (1981):100-107. Illus.

An introductory survey of the subject of Shakespearean references in detective fiction.

C328. ______. "The Games of Detective Fiction." TAD 10 (1977):74-76. Photo of John Dickson Carr and illustrations.
Clues, parodies, allusions in detective novels to other fictional detectives, identification with characters: games for writers and readers. See letter (Nevins), TAD 10:100, for correction.

C329. ______. "Mystery, Murder and Academe." TAD 11 (1978):159-69. Illustrated.
Detectives on college campuses.

C330. Graham, Janis. "So You Want to Write a Medical Thriller." MD, Jan 84, pp. 95-98,103.
Photographs of Robin Cook, Jerry Bauer, William Patrick and David Lindsey. The medical thriller and four practioners.

C331. Gramigna, Giuliano. "Il sogno di Robinson |Robinson's dream|." Il Caffe 17:2 (1971):3-10.
"Danger, pursuit, ambush, struggle are the common property of the detective novel and the novel of adventure: but the two branches diverge at the ending. While the detective novel functions naturally according to a specific and in the final analysis well defined semantics (how the crime was committed, who committed it), in the adventure novel the true and proper meaning is never (or ought not to be) mentioned." (RC)

C332. Gramsci, Antonio. "Sul romanzo poliziesco e Romanzi polizieschi (1934-35) |On the detective novel and detective novels|." In Quaderni del carcere , pp. 2128-30. Turin: Einaudi, 1975.
Gramsci, an author, critic and political figure (founder of the Italian Communist party), attemps to define the bases of popular culture. The feuilleton novel of Dumas and Sue and the detective novel rise "on the margin of literature of celebrated legal suits" and are fed by the interest which the administration of justice always arouses in popular psychology. The ideological content-- which ranges from democratic to conservative reactionary tendencies--can be traced and related to the historical period and the cultural stratum of the public among whom the genre is distributed. Gramsci finally recognizes two traditions in the history of the detective novel: one is mechanical, with an increasingly more prominent schematization of the plot; and another is artistic, represented by Poe and Chesterton. (LR)

C333. Granata, Giorgio. "Decadenza del romanzo poliziesco classico |Decadence of the classic detective novel|." Il Resto del Carlino, 20 Jan 56.
Re-reading the rules dictated by the Detection Club and comparing them with the new course of the detective novel, Granata points out the end of the "detective story" and the arrival of the "thriller," characterized by incidents of violence and of cruelty which seem, moreover, to fulfill "a cathartic function," permitting the reader to "discharge destructive instincts in a figurative, allusive, and symbolic manner." (LR)

C334. Green, Martin. "Our Detective Heroes." In his Transatlantic Patterns: Cultural Comparisons of England with America, pp. 101-30. NY: Basic Books, 1977.
Sayers' Wimsey novels are discussed as descendents of Hornung's Raffles stories and Wimsey's detecting is seen as creating a tension arising from

a conflict between his social rank and his avocation. Both Wimsey and Travis McGee are viewed as conducting investigations because of their "social conscience" and working more as professionals than as amateurs. There is some discussion of John D. MacDonald's "preoccupation" with sex and of the physical "imagination" of Travis McGee.

C335. Greene, Hugh. "Introduction." In his The Rivals of Sherlock Holmes: Early Detective stories, pp. 9-20. London: The Bodley Head, 1970.

C336. ______. "Introduction." In his More Rivals of Sherlock Holmes: Cosmopolitan Crimes. London: The Bodley Head, 1971. U.S. ed. published as Cosmopolitan Crimes: Foreign Rivals of Sherlock Holmes. NY: Pantheon Books, 1971.

C337. ______. "Introduction." In his The Crooked Counties. London: The Bodley Head, 1973. U.S. ed. published as The Further Rivals of Sherlock Holmes. NY: Pantheon, 1973.

C338. ______. "Introduction." In his The American Rivals of Sherlock Holmes. London: The Bodley Head, 1976; NY: Pantheon Books, 1976.
These four anthologies of Victorian detective stories all contain introductions with information on the authors whose stories are reprinted.

C339. Greene, Suzanne Ellery. "The Whounits: Escape and Realism." In her Books for Pleasure: Popular Fiction 1914-45, pp. 94-115. Bowling Green, OH: Popular Press, 1974.
Greene analyzes best-selling detective novels of the period 1926-41 when the following writers turn up on the best seller lists: Christie, E. S. Gardner, Chandler, Queen, S. S. Van Dine, Biggers, Charteris, Hammett, Latimer, Ambler and Marco Page. She concludes that they reflect the "exoticism" of the 20s, escapism of the 30s and the new realistic trend of the late 30s and early 40s.

C340. Grella, George. "The Gangster Novel: The Urban Pastoral." In Madden (B239), pp. 186-98.
The gangster novel and film, like the Western, is an artistically stylized form. It reflects traditions of American culture and as the city has become an important setting for modern literature, the detective becomes an important literary figure.

C340a. ______. "Murder and Manners: The Formal Detective Novel." Novel 4 (1970): 30-48. Reprinted in Winks (B434), pp. 84-102; and in Landrum (B216), pp. 37-57.
A concise and penetrating discussion of the classical British puzzle-novel, perhaps the best treatment of the subject.

C341. ______. "Murder and the Mean Streets:The Hard-Boiled Detective Novel." Contempora 1 (March 70): 6-15; reprinted in TAD 5 1971/(72):1-10; and in Winks (B434), pp. 103-20.
A thoughtful study of the hard-boiled school with its roots in American romance (Cooper and Twain) and in the dime-novel tradition, a distinctively native form opposed to the British formal detective novel. Grella discusses the classic writers (Hammett, Chandler, Ross Macdonald), the private eye and the nightmare vision of the urban landscape. Grella sees Mickey Spillane's Mike Hammer as the fascist, right-wing perversion of the errant knight of the Black Mask writers. He

makes a strong case for the centrality of the hard-boiled novel in modern American fiction. An illuminating, important study.

C342. Grimes, Larry E. "Doing, Knowing and Mystery: A Study of Religious Types in Detective Fiction." PCS 1:1 (Winter 77):24-35.
With a definition of "mystery" based on Rudolf Otto's study of the religious experience of man confronting the unknowable and fearful "Other," Grimes posits three kinds of detectives: the solver of mysteries (Chesteron's Gilbert Symes), the "detective-as-doer" who is not paralyzed by the "nothingness" he confronts (Hammett's Sam Spade), and the secular-priest (Ross Macdonald's Lew Archer).

C343. ______. "Stepsons of Sam: Re-Visions of the Hard-Boiled Detective Formula in Recent American Fiction." MFS 29:3 (Autumn 83):535-44.
"Spill-over" of detective fiction formulas onto serious fiction. A discussion of uses of the formula by three writers: Jules Feiffer in Ackroyd, Richard Brautigan in Dreaming of Babylon, and Thomas Berger in Who is Teddy Villanova?

C344. Grivel, Charles. "Observation du roman policier." In Arnaud (B12), pp. 231-47. General discussion, pp. 248-58.
A transcript of a paper on a literary subject in which there is virtually no reference to any literary work. A study of patterns, models, types, myths. In the general discussion following the paper, there was evidence on the part of several participants of extreme uneasiness about the paper, although there was at least one defender of Grivel's work.

C345. Grochokowski, Mary Ann. "A Beastly Case of Murder." TPP 1:6 (Nov 78):3-10.
Animals in mystery fiction, with a checklist of works in which they appear.

C346. Groff, Mary. "All Too True." TPP 1:1 (Jan 78):3-6; 1:2 (March 78):15-18; 1:3 (May 78):16-19, 12; 1:4 (Jly 78):17-20; 1:5 (Sept 78):13-16; 1:6 (Nov 78):14-17, 10; 2:1 (Jan/Feb 79):23-26, 8; 2:2 (Mar/Apr 79): 20-23, 18; 2:3 (May/June 79):15-18; 2:4 (Jly/Aug 79):21-24; 2:5 (Sept/Oct 79):19-22, 18; 2:6 (Nov/Dec 79):19-22, 24; 3:1(Jan/Feb 80):29-32; 3:2 (Mar/Apr 80):19-23; 3:3 (May/June 80):22-25, 12; 3:4 (Jly/Aug 80):25-28, 22; 3:5 (Oct 80):21-24; 3:6 (Dec 80):21-24, 9; 4:1 (Feb 81):24-27; 4:2 (April 81):15-18; 4:3 (June 81):15-18; 4:4 (Aug 81):21-23; 4:5/6 (Dec 81):59-62.
An annotated listing, by subject, of real-life criminals and crimes and their fictional treatments. The listings concluded in issue 5 of volume 3. A series of additions ran through issue 4, Vol. 4, which also included an annotated list of secondary sources. The listings in issue 5/6, Vol. 4, were of a partial bibliography of film references. The entire series is being revised and expanded for book publication.

C347. ______. "Bloody but Readable." TAD 11 (1978): 234-6.
A survey of English mystery and spy fiction published during WW I.

C348. ______. "Friday, February 25, 1955." TAD 10 (1977):232-34. Illus.
A description of the contents of a special number of the London Times Literary Supplement devoted to detective fiction (B94).

C349. ______. "The Last Year." TAD 11 (1978): 145-49. Illus.
The year is 1939, the last year of the "Golden Age."

C350. Guagnini, Elvio. "L'importazione di un genere: Il "giallo' italiano tra gli anni Trenta e gli inizi degli anni Quaranta. Appunti e problemi |The 'importation' of a genre: the Italian giallo between the thirties and the early forties. Notes and problems|." In Note novecentesche, pp. 221-57. Pordenone: Edizioni Studio Tesi, 1971.

In the course of a more general reflection on the different types and levels of literary consumption, the author, teacher of Italian literature in the University of Trieste, examines the first phase of the true and proper history of the Italian "giallo" (1929-41), whose stages, beginning with the "artificial" birth, are scanned also in relation to the cultural politics of the Fascist regime. The analysis includes writers like Varaldo, Scerbanenco, De Angelis, Lanocita, D'Errico and others, but it is only Carlo Emilio Gadda who perceived, before the others, "the possibility of a use of the plot and technique of the 'giallo' in order to promote the mechanisms of contemporary society dominated by changing customs in a mass society characterized by signs of a diffuse violence." (RC)

C351. Guetti, James. "Aggressive Reading: Detective Fiction and Realistic Narrative." Raritan (Rutgers) 2:1 (Summer 82):133-54.

Hammett, in his minutely detailed descriptions, forces both the reader and the detective to work aggressively to see some order in the investigations. Guetti also sees this technique in Chandler, Ross Macdonald, Theodore Weesner (The Car Thief), and Thomas Pynchon (V.). He concludes with general remarks on the detective novel where the reader's impulse may be to manipulate the literature to see in it more than "pieces." In earlier stories where there is no detective the reader assumes his role.

C352. Gurko, Leo. "Folklore of the American Hero." In his Heroes, Highbrows and the Popular Mind, pp. 187-90. Indianapolis: Bobbs-Merrill, 1953.

The Hammett-Chandler-Spillane tough guy hero "as an expression of Darwinism and the survival of the fittest carried . . . to its ferociously lyrical extreme."

C353. Guymon, Ned. "Why Do We Read This Stuff?" In Ball (B15), pp. 361-63.

A noted collector talks about the pleasures of reading detective fiction.

C354. Gutzen, Dieter. "Jakob Studer, Katherina Ledermacher und Martin Beck. Themen und Tendenzen des modernen Detektivromans am Beispiel der Werke Friedrich Glausers, Richard Heys sowie Maj Sjowalls und Per Wahloos |Jakob Studer, Katherina Ledermacher and Martin Beck: themes and tendencies of the modern detective novel from the examples of the works of Friedrich Glauser, Richard Hey as well as Maj Sjöwall and Per Wahlöö|." Arcadia, Sonderheft fuer Horst Ruediger zum siebzigsten Geburtstag (Berlin and New York: Verlag Walter de Gruyter, 1978), pp. 66-79.

Academic argument that the modern detective novel has become socially conscious and that the novels of Glauser, Hey and Sjöwall/Wahlöö are primarily means to communicate social ideas. (GG)

C355. Gwilt, Peter R. and John R. "The Use of Poison in Detective Fiction." Clues 1:2 (1980):8-17.

A thematic study.

C356. Haas, Willy. "'Mysteries.' Von den Anfaengen des Kriminalromans |Mysteries: from the beginnings of the crime novel|." Imprimatur 2 (1958/9):184-190; reprinted in Vogt (B424), Vol. 1, pp. 63-71.

Interesting, readable essay on the early history of the crime genre, including Collins, Dickens, M. G. ("Monk") Lewis, Ann Radcliffe, Horace Walpole and William Godwin. Interprets the mystery, pursuit, revenge and horror novels of these authors as natural predecessors to the rational-deductive stories of Poe and Doyle. (GG)

C357. "Hablan les implicados |The concerned parties speak|." Crisis (Buenos Aires), no. 33 (Jan 76); reprinted in Lafforgue (B214), pp. 57-67.
Four writers of mystery fiction (Jorge Luis Borges, Jaime Rest, Ricardo Piglia, and Ruben Tizziani) present papers on various topics relating to the genre.

C358. Hackett, A.P. "Hasta la vista, amigos." PW 201 (6 March 72):37.
Drawing on an earlier PW article by Boucher (C116) and Donald Yates' introduction to his Latin Blood (C880), Hackett gives an overview of the growing interest in crime and detective fiction written in Latin America.

C359. Hagen, Ordean. "How I 'Done' It." TAD 1 (1968):45-47.
Hagen discusses the genesis of his Who Done It? (A65) and the problems he encountered in its compilation.

C360. Halte, Jean-Francois; Michel, Raymond; and Petitjean, André. "L'aiguille creuse: l'enjeu idéologique d'un roman policier |The hollow needle: the ideological 'stake' of a detective novel|." Pratiques 11-12 (Nov 76). Not seen.

C361. Hamilton, Cicely. "The Detective in Fiction." In The English Spirit, edited by Anthony Weymouth, pp. 130-35. London: Allen & Unwin, 1942.
Enthusiastic but thin discussion of Sherlock Holmes, Christie, Sayers, E. C. Bentley and Edgar Wallace.

C362 Hamilton, K. M. "Murder and Morality: An Interpretation of Detection Fiction." Dalhousie Review 33:2 (Summer 53):102-108.
A view of the detective story as "an allegory, expressing and justifying fundamental beliefs." Hamilton also makes a distinction between the detective story and the thriller with the writer expressing the hope that detective fiction will not lose its "values" and descend to the level of the shocker.

C363. Hanan, Patrick. "Court Case Story." In his Chinese Vernacular Story, pp. 39-44, 72-74. Cambridge, MA: Harvard Univ. Press, 1981.
After stating that crime and punishment are, perhaps, more important themes in traditional Chinese literature than in any other national literature before the advent of Western detective and crime fiction, Hanan analyses three early court cases.

C364. ______. "Judge Bao's Hundred Cases Reconstructed." Harvard Journal of Asiatic Studies 40 (1980): 301-323.
An essay on a pioneering, 16th century collection of Judge Bao (Pao) court cases, with emphasis on the question of authorship. Noting stylistic differences in the text, Hanan maintains that the collection was the work of three anonymous authors. (JLA)

C365. Hankiss, Jean. "Littérature 'populaire' et roman policier |Popular literature and detective novel|." Revue de littérature comparée 8 (1928): 556-63.

An academic defense of detective fiction which traces summarily from the Middle Ages to the late 19th century the taste for the mysterious and the criminal, culminating in the introduction by Poe of the detective whose investigations orient the genre toward the puzzle and away from the moral and psychological. Detective fiction as a literature of escape from the banal and the routine.

C366. Hardy, Thomas John. "The Romance of Crime." In his Books on the Shelf, pp. 219-35. London: Philip Allan, 1934.
An undemanding study of English writers of mystery from Wilkie Collins to Crofts and Fletcher in which the contribution of Poe is minimized and science and the scientific method are seen as the chief influence on Collins.

C367. Hare, Cyril. "The Classic Form." In Gilbert, Crime in Good Company (B124), pp. 55-84.
Hare largely limits his discussion to modern English puzzle fiction, with its limitations (chiefly in portraying characters), its construction, the choice of detective and the moral aspect (an imaginary world).

C368. Hare, Sir Ronald. "A Personal Reaction." TLS, 25 Sept 55, p. xii.
The Deputy Commissioner at Scotland Yard discusses the art of the professional policeman with some comments on fictional detectives (amateur) and their license to flee restrictions.

C369. Hartman, Geoffrey. "The Mystery of Mysteries." NYRB, 18 May 72, pp. 31-34. Revised and expanded version, "Literature High and Low: The Case of the Mystery Story," published in The Fate of Reading (Chicago and London: Univ. of Chicago Press, 1975), pp. 203-22; and in Most/Stowe (B264), pp. 210-29.
A review of Ross Macdonald's The Underground Man which is also an essay on the limitations of American detective fiction, with particular attention to Chandler and Macdonald. A more sympathetic view of detective fiction than Edmund Wilson's (C867), but nonetheless a statement of what Hartman sees as the principal limitation of the genre, its inability (or refusal) to transcend the mechanical limitations of plot conventions ("the mystery must be solved") and explore rather than solve the problems encompassed.

C370. Harwood, H. C. "Detective Stories." The Outlook, 1 Jan 27, pp. 7-8.
Brief comments on conventions of the detective story, this "noble craft."

C371. Haslinger, Adolf. "Oedoen von Horvaths Jugend ohne Gott als Detektivroman. Ein Beitrag zur oesterreichischen Kriminalliteratur [Odon von Horváth's Youth without God as a detective novel: a contribution to Austrian crime fiction]." In Studien zur Literatur des 19. um 20. Jahrhunderts in Oesterreich: Festschrift fuer Alfred Doppler zur 60. Geburtstag, edited by Johann Holzner, Michael Klein and Wolfgang Weismueller, pp. 197-204. Innsbrucker Beitraeger zur Kulturwissenschaft: Germanistische Reihe, Vol. 12. Innsbruck: Kowatsch, 1981.
Scholarly argument for the conclusion that the novel Youth without God by Austrian poet Horvath has the form and theme of a detective novel. Haslinger sees this murder story as falling into the same literary category as Friedrich Dürrenmatt's crime novels. (GG)

C372. Hawthorne, Julian. "Riddle Stories." Introduction to The Library of the World's Best Mystery and Detective Stories, Vol. 1, pp. 9-19. NY: Review of Reviews, 1908.

A defense of the riddle story (which Hawthorne equates with the detective story). Hawthorne does not exclude the supernatural story from his definition.

C373. Haycraft, Howard. "Corpse with the Raised Eyebrows." PW 140 (9 Aug 41): 382-86. Photos.

Haycraft's comments on publishing practices such as jacket copy and inappropriate titles.

C374. ______. "Decennial detective digest; with Haycraft-Queen list of detective-crime-mystery fiction." WLB 26 (Nov 51):242-46. Also published in EQMM, Oct 51, pp. 66-79; and in Haycraft (B143), as an unpaginated introductory section.

An updating of the list of detective story "cornerstones" published in the United States, Great Britain, and France from 1845-1938 through 1948. Originally published in Murder for Pleasure (1941), pp. 302-6. The update includes an introductory essay by Haycraft and Queen's comments on and additions to Mr. Haycraft's amended list.

C375. ______. "Dictators, Democrats and Detectives." SRL 20 (7 Oct 39): 8. Also published in Spectator (London), 17 Nov 39; and in Murder for Pleasure (B143), pp. 312-318. Editorial.

Noting the banning of novels by Christie and Edgar Wallace in Fascist Italy, Haycraft maintains that the detective story has traditionally flourished in democracies where there is some attempt to safeguard evidence and punish the actual perpetrators of crimes rather than politically acceptable victims.

C376. ______. "The Whodunit in World War II and After." In his Art of the Mystery Story (B142), pp. 536-42.

A general survey. Haycraft discusses the importance of paperback editions, the spy novel and the suspense novel and names several authors (Chandler, Simenon, Raymond Postgate and Dorothy Hughes) he sees as major writers. He also talks briefly about the increasing attention paid to the genre by critics.

C377. Hayden, George. "The Courtroom Plays of the Yuan and early Ming periods." Harvard Journal of Asiatic Studies 34 (1974): 192-220. Revised and expanded version of Hayden's 1971 doctoral dissertation at Stanford, "The Judge Pao Plays of the Yuan Dynasty."

In this scholarly article Hayden examines the applicability of the terms "kung-an" and "courtroom" to plays of the Yuan dynasty (1279-1368). States that one of the defining characteristics of kung-an plays is the courtroom scene and implies that several Magistrate Pao plays are not courtroom plays. Includes a roughly chronological checklist of kung-an plays in Chinese. (GG)

C378. ______. "The Legend of Judge Pao: From the Beginnings through the Yuan Drama." In Laurence G. Thompson, ed., Studia Asiatica, pp. 339-55. San Francisco: Chinese Materials Center, 1975. Revision of Chs. 2 and 4 of Hayden's 1971 doctoral dissertation at Stanford University, "The Judge Pao Plays of the Yuan Dynasty," and appears again, slightly altered, as Ch. 1 of Hayden's Crime and Punishment in Medieval Chinese Drama: Three Judge Pao Plays (Cambridge: Harvard Univ. Press, 1978).

Traces the growth of the legend of the historical Pao Cheng (999-1062), upon whom many of the Magistrate Pao stories were based. Also examines that legend's influence on the Pao plays. (GG)

C379. Hays, H. R. "A Defense of the Thriller." Partisan Review 12 (Winter 45):135-37.

Critics like Mary McCarthy and Edmund Wilson refuse to recognize the new forms of the detective story which have elements of theater/drama and are being modified to reflect the political tensions of the time. Dostoyevsky is proof that the crime story "can be made into a work of art."

C380. Hays, R. W. "Chess in the Detective Story." TAD 5 (1971/72):19-23; reprinted in Selected Writings (B144), pp. 173-82. Also, "Addenda to 'Chess in the Detective Story,'" TAD 5 (1971/72):203-4; reprinted in Selected Writings, pp. 195-97.

A thematic study which--unlike many genre thematic studies--is more than a listing of appropriate titles. In these two articles, Hays analyses the use of chess in a number of writers, pointing out weaknesses in their understanding of the game and the ways chess serves the plot.

C381. ______. "The Clue of the Dying Message." TAD 7 (1973/74):1-3; reprinted in Selected Writings (B144), pp. 187-92.

A systematic study of the uses to which this device is put in detective fiction.

C382. ______. "More 'Shades of Dupin!'" TAD 8 (1974/75):288-89; reprinted in Selected Writings (B144), pp. 204-7.

A note on fictional detectives who refer to other fictional detectives, assume the role of other detectives or express awareness of themselves as fictional characters.

C383. ______. "A Note from Francis Parkman." TAD 5 (1971/72):193; reprinted in Selected Writings (B144), p. 186.

A citation from Parkman which testifies to the skill of American Indians in certain types of detection and, perhaps, supports the claim that Fenimore Cooper's Indians are the first American sleuths.

C384. ______. "A Note on Medieval Detection." TAD 5 (1971/72):88, 90; reprinted in Selected Writings (B144), pp. 183-85.

Translation of a passage from St. Augustine's Confessions (circa 397 A. D.) to help "bridge the gap between Ancient Rome and the twelfth century" in the history of the detective story.

C385. ______. "Religion and the Detective Story." TAD 8 (1974/75):24-26; reprinted in Selected Writings (B144), pp. 203. Addenda as follows: F. N. Nevins, Jr. in TAD 8 (1974/75):159-60; Jay Jeffries, TAD 8 :312. Reply by Hays in a letter, TAD 8:324-25.

A critical survey of detective stories in which religion is a major element.

C386. Hedman, Iwan. "Faktaböcker om Deckare/Thriller-Genre i Skandinavien [Reference books in the dectective/thriller genre in Scandinavia]." DAST Magazine 15:3 (1982):32-35.

A listing of critical material appearing in books, magazines and in pamphlets in Scandinavia.

C387. Hedman, Iwan. "Intervju med Otto Penzler i New York i April 1979." DAST 12:3 (1979):16-18.
An interview with the publisher of TAD and the Mysterious Press.

C388. ______. "Mystery Fiction in Scandinavia." TAD 3 (1970):173-75. Addenda by F. M. Nevins, Jr. in letter, TAD 3 (1969/70): 276.
A brief historical survey of the field.

C389. ______. "Swedish Mystery Writers." TMRN 3:4 (April 70):7-8.
A mini-survey.

390. Heilbrun, Carolyn G. "Female Sleuths and Others." Hecate 2 (July 1976): 74-79.
On Michele Slung's anthology Crime on Her Mind (B373) and the general topic of women in mystery fiction. (KLM)

C391. ______. "A Feminist Looks at Women in Detective Novels." Graduate Woman 74 (Jly/Aug 80):15-24.
The author, who is also "Amanda Cross," sees British detective fiction as a form for autonomous women characters and "tender" male sleuths. (KLM)

C392. Heissembuettel, Helmut. "Spielregeln des Kriminalromans |The crime novel's rules of the game|." Der Monat 15:181 (1963): 51-60; reprinted in Vogt (B424), Vol. 2, pp. 356-71; and in Zmegac (B451), pp. 203-19.
The article contains some remarks on conventions of the detective novel: different types of detectives, the genre's lack of realism, its limited portrayal of character and its stereotyped structural pattern. Heissembuettel sees some new directions of development emerge with Simenon's Maigret, a detective with empathy with the criminals he hunts down. (Barbara Korte)

C393. Hellerstein, Marjorie H. "Murder Mysteries: The Object of Suspicion is Life." College English 32:4 (Jan 71):477-80.
On the act of reading mysteries and their style: "bond of suspicion of life and suppression of emotion" between reader and writer. Rehash of usual genre criticism.

C394. Hellyer, C. David. "TAD: The First Decade." TAD 10 (1977):143-48.
An interview with Allen J. Hubin, editor and publisher of The Armchair Detective through Volume 9, no. 2 (February 1976). For other interviews with Hubin, see the following: DAST 5:6 (1972):8-9; Jury 1:3/4 (1972):38-9; TPP 4:5/6 (Dec 81):24-6.

C395. Hendricks, Denis. "Red Herrings Are Bad Business." PW 140 (5 July 41): 19-20.
A reader rails against the sloppy practice of red herrings in mystery novels. James Sandoe replies in the August 2 issue (pp. 304-305) that the problem is not the convention but the abuse of it.

C396. Higgins, George V. "Private Eye as Illegal Hero." Esquire, Dec 72, pp. 348-51.
A discussion of changes in attitude that permit recourse to violence as a first rather than last resort.

C397. Highet, Gilbert. "The Case of the Disappearing Detectives." In People,

<u>Places, Books</u>, pp. 256-64. NY: Oxford University Press, 1953.

Why detective fiction is not generally high art: sloppy writing, unrealistic detectives, bogus investigative techniques. Only writers with the tragic sense that accompanies crime will qualify. As examples, Highet lists Dostoyevsky, Mable Seely, Simenon, Graham Greene and William Faulkner.

C398. Hilfer, A. C. "Invasion and Excess; Texts of Bliss in Popular Culture." <u>Texas Studies in Literature and Language</u> 22 (Summer 80):125-37.

Elements of reassurance and subversion in popular art with particular reference to Hammett, E. C. Bentley and Christie. An attempt to introduce some flexibility into critical systems that see popular art as a lollypop and avant-garde art as an irritant that undermines popular myths. A good-natured discussion.

C399. Hobsbawn, Eric. "The Criminal as Hero and Myth." TLS, 23 June 61, p. vi; translated into Italian and reprinted in Cremante/Rambelli (B78), pp. 131-37.

The transformation of the criminal as rebel against an unjust society (Robin Hood) into the gangster and (in Chandler) businessman who may be an "authentic force for social order" in a corrupt society.

C400. Hoch, Edward D. "Hans Stefan Santesson and the Unicorn Mystery Book Club." TAD 8 (1974/75):185-92.

A tribute to editor Santesson with a list of his writings; a history of the Book Club; a list of the contents of the club volumes, no.s 1-83; and a brief history of the club's newsletter <u>The Unicorn News</u> (B419), edited by Clayton Rawson. Addendum in letter (Hoch), TAD 8:321.

C401. ______. "Introduction." In <u>All But Impossible!</u>, pp. ix-xi. New Haven, CT & New York, NY: Ticknor & Fields, 1981.

Reports the results of a poll of seventeen mystery writers, critics and fans on their favorite locked room and impossible crime novels. (REB)

C402. ______. "A Mirror to Our Crimes." TAD 12 (1979):280-88. Illus.

Fictionalized true crime.

C403 Hoffman, Nancy Y. "Mistresses of Malfeasance." In Landrum (B216), pp. 97-101.

A highly selective discussion of women mystery writers from Anna K. Green to Jean Dodds Freeman.

C404. Hoftrichter, Paul. "Hammett, Gardner and Chandler." <u>AB Bookman's Weekly</u>, 3 May 82, pp. 3460, 3462-64.

On the hard-boiled mystery with particular reference to the three writers. A number of factual errors which are pointed out by readers and corrected in letters in the issue of 18 Oct 82, pp. 2004-2005.

C405. Holman, C. Hugh. "Detective Fiction as American Realism." In <u>Popular Literature in America: A Symposium in Honor of Lyon N. Richardson</u>, edited by James C. Austin and Donald A. Koch, pp. 30-41. Bowling Green, OH: Popular Press, 1972.

Another look at the birth of detective fiction in the climate of logic and scientific thought of the 19th century, proposed at least as early as 1928 by Régis Messac (B257) and both repeated and refuted by subsequent critics. Some comments on American realism in the 19th century novel and its survival in detective fiction. A superficial and derivative essay.

C406. Holdheim, W. Wolfgang. "Novelle und Kriminalschema: Ein Strukturmodell deutscher Erzaelkunst um 1800 |Novella and criminal schema: a structural model of German narrative art circa 1800|." MLQ 31 (1970): 388-91.
Essay-length review of Rainer Schoenhaar's book Novella and Criminal Schema (B360). Holdheim praises Schoenhaar's conceptual clarity and the skill with which he relates German romanticism to detective narration but criticizes his arguments that the presence of a detective is not necessary and causes otherwise "literary" works to be "trivial".(GG)

C407. Holquist, Michael. "Whodunit and Other Questions: Metaphysical Detective Stories in Postwar Fiction." New Literary History 3 (1971): 134-56; reprinted in Most/Stowe (B264), pp. 149-74.
The bridging of the gap between the high art of the "novel" and the popular art of the detective story in writers like Borges, Robbe-Grillet and Nabokov.

C408. Holmberg, John-Henri. "Mord längs rymdvägarna |Murder along the paths of space|." Jury 10: 4 (1981):57-74.
Science fiction detective novels.(MS)

C409. Holmes, Elizabeth, and Strenski, Ellen. "Hard and Soft Boiled Detectives." PCS 1:1 (Winter 77): 75-79.
Detectives and food and drink.

C410. Honce, Charles. "Detective Stories as Literature." In Mark Twain's Associated Press Speech (NY: privately printed, 1940), pp. 47-57.
Honce writes about the detective short story and his preference for it over the novel, turning into a discussion of Melville Davisson Post and Frederick Irving Anderson. Contains checklists of their first editions and also prints a letter from Anderson to Honce discussing the art of writing. An important source for Anderson. (SAS)

C411. Hoppin, Hector. "Notes on Primitive Modes of Detection." Chimera 5:4 (Summer 47):39-48.
Popularity of detective fiction and reader identification with hero/heroine/criminal seen as a process of sympathetic magic.

C412. Hottinger, Mary. "Eine persoenliche Meinung |A personal opinion|." Forward to her Noch Mehr Morder |Still more murders|, pp. 5-14. Zurich: Diogenes Verlag, 1963.
This is the third of Hottinger's three anthologies of German translations of English and American mystery short stories. She defends the genre against doomsayers, and calls for a truce between those with rigid, classical tastes and the aficionados who read even trashy crime stories for pleasure and relaxation. Hottinger is unique among German-language critics for her cheerful tone and spirit. (GG)

C413. ______. "Elegie fuer den Grossen Detektiv |Elegy for the great detective|." Forward to her Nehr Morder |More murders|, pp. 5-16. Zurich: Diogenes Verlag, 1961.
Enthusiastic introduction to the second of her anthologies. She compares the passing of the Great Detective of the early Golden Age to a transformation found in any form of art, music or drama: when the classic form no longer pleases, there is a rush "back to nature" and in the case of the detective story the result is greater realism. (GG)

C414. _____. "Vorwort |Foreward|." In her Mord: Angelsaechsische Kriminalgeschichten |Murder: Anglo-Saxon crime stories|, pp. 5-25. Zurich: Diogenes Verlag, 1959. Reprinted in Buchloh/Becker 2 (B61), pp. 316-33.
Essay about various aspects of the genre from the viewpoint of a well-read, critical fan. A loose chain of argument throughout suggests that from the 19th century to the post-WW II era, murder has decreased in importance as an element in detective fiction. (GG)

C415. Hrastnik, Franz. "Das Berbrechen macht sich doch bezahlt |Crime does indeed pay|." Der Monat 155: 8 (1961):77-83. Reprinted in Vogt (B424), Vol. II, pp. 545-59.
Subtitled "The Big Business of Crime Fiction," this article argues energetically that the crime novel's opponents should examine its huge success before condemning it. Hrastnik argues from authority, dropping names such as Bertrand Russell, Winston Churchill and Bertolt Brecht as aficionados of the genre. (GG)

C416. Huet, Marie-Hélène. "Enquête et représentation dans le roman police |Investigation and representation in the detective novel|." Europe no. 571/72 (Nov/Dec 76), pp. 98-104.
The detective as reader of a decipherable text with a single explanation and Borges, Nabokov, and Robbe-Grillet as murderers of this reducible text.

C417. Hugo, Grant. "The Political Influence of the Thriller." Contemporary Review 221 (1972):284-89.
A survey of books by contemporary writers of mystery, suspense and spy novels, in which Hugo postulates that since these novels reach a wide audience and can be powerful instruments of propaganda, their political influence may be uncertain but is worth studying by sociologists and students of politics.

C418. Hutchinson, Horace G. "Detective Fiction." Quarterly Review 253 (July 29):148-60.
A rambling discussion of the highlights of the genre's history and a plea for good writing and some attempt at characterization.

C419. Hutter, Albert D. "Dreams, Transformations and Literature: The Implications of Detective Fiction." Victorian Studies 19 (1975-6):181-219; reprinted in Most/Stowe (B264), pp. 230-51.
An essay in two parts: Part I is a discussion of Freud's theory of crimes as fulfillment of infantile experiences and revisions of this theory by contemporary psychoanalysis; Part II is a study of The Moonstone, seen as a prototypical detective fiction in which the reader must take the contradictory information provided in the rational/objective and irrational/subjective narrative to build an integrated account. Hutter proposes a shift in psychoanalytic and literary analysis from a study of latent content to latent structure. Extensive notes incorporating numerous bibliographical references.

C420. Ilyina, Natalia, and Adamov, Arkadi. "Detective Novels: A Game and Life." Translated from the Russian by Peter Mann. Soviet Literature, no. 323 (no. 3, 1975), pp. 142-50.
Adamov is a writer of detective fiction and he objects to Ilyina's use of the word "game" which he feels denigrates the serious purpose of detective fiction to "raise the most important questions of the life of society." There are references to an on-going polemic and to a number of

other writers of detective fiction. Both participants demonstrate wide reading in the field of non-Russian authors.

C421. "In the Best Tradition: Mystification and Art." TLS, 25 Sept 55, p. viii. Christie, Iles, Bardin, Hammett, all represent what the modern crime novelist is capable of as the novel of "problems" blends with the "angel of art."

C422. "Interrogatorio l. Cuatro preguntas a Jorge Luis Borges, Marco Denevi and Augusto Roa Bastos. [Interrogation l. Four Questions for J. L. Borges, M. Denevi and A. R. Bastos]." In Lafforgue (B214, pp. 49-56. First published as "Los detectives de la literatura" in Siete Dias Ilustrados (Buenos Aires), Vol. 9, no. 420 (20-26 June 75):64-67.
A roundtable discussion by three writers of mystery fiction.

C423. "An Interview with Howard Haycraft." TMRN 5:1 (Nov/Dec 71):11-13. Photo.
Haycraft talks about his career as anthologist and editor. With a checklist of his publications.

C424. "And Is It Ever True?" TLS, 23 June 61, p. v.
Mysteries may not be true to actual police procedures but they teach us something about ourselves (need for solutions, escape, fascination with flight and pursuit).

C425. Isaac, Frederick. "The Changing Face of Evil in the Hard-Boiled Novel." TAD 16 (1983):241-47.
A study of evil, the moral "backdrop" in the hard-boiled novel against which the hero acts, from Chandler and Hammett to Robert Parker.

C426. Isola, Apinwumi. "The Detective Novel in Yoruba." Seminar Series (Ile-Ife). 1976-77; 1 (2):490-508. Not seen. Cited in MLA 1981 Bibliography, item no. 14559.

C427. Jacobs, David. "Photo Detection: The Image as Evidence." Clues 1:2 (1980):18-23.
The various uses of photographs in detective fiction. (James R. McCahery)

C428. James, P. D. "In Mystery Fiction, Rooms Furnished One Clue at a Time." NYT "Home Section," 25 Aug 83, pp. C1-C2. Illus.
An essay on the use of setting. James comments that she works in the tradition of Margery Allingham and that it is often a setting, rather than a character or a murder method, that excites her imagination and "gives rise" to a story.

C429. Janvier, Ludovic. "Le Point de vue du policier [Point-of-view in detective fiction]." In his Une Parole exigeante, pp. 39-49. Paris: Editions de Minuit, 1964.
The French New Novel is, claims Janvier, detective fiction taken "seriously." He discusses policier elements (detective, investigation, a world of potential suspects) in Butor and Robbe-Grillet and refers to the "atmosphere of suspicion" in Nathalie Sarraute's novels.

C430. Jeffrey, David K. "The Mythology of Crime and Violence." Clues 1:1 (1980): 75-81.
Detective fiction as romantic myth. (James R. McCahery)

C431. Jennings, Edith. "Mystery Story Solution Wanted." Library Journal 56 (15 Oct 31):865-66.

Mystery fiction does not lead children to reading "higher types of books" and should be gradually barred from juvenile fiction shelves as the books wear out. Jennings does not address the question of whether mystery fiction inhibits children from reading other kinds of books but she clearly knew the answer she wanted when she asked her question. This essay is typical of the attitudes of many librarians toward genre fiction in the 30s and 40s.

C432. Jinka, Katsuo. "Mystery Stories in Japan." TAD 9 (1975/76):112-113.

A cursory survey of the genre's history and its present popularity.

C433. Jones, Archie H. "Cops, Robbers, Heroes and Anti-Heroines: The American Need to Create." JPC 1:2 (Fall 1967):114-27.

The lonely, resourceful American individualist strain in Western myth and urban crime and detective stories from Buffalo Bill and the dime novel through Van Dine and Hammett. In the final section, Jones talks of sex, women and the American hero, concluding with the TV Kildare hero-physician. A wide-ranging discussion that may leave some readers a bit breathless.

C434. Jones, Mary Jane. "The Spinster Detective." Journal of Communications 25 (1975):106-12.

The spinister detective in the British classical detective story. Jones thinks her basic qualities fit the conventions of the genre and its limitations are perfectly suited to hers. See Bargainnier (C51) for a reply to this article.

C435. "Judge Lynch." "Battle of the Sexes: The Judge and His Wife Look at Mysteries." In Haycraft (B142), pp. 367-72.

SRL's male mystery fiction reviewer tells what women like and what they don't like in mysteries. A tongue-in-cheek treatment that is probably to be taken seriously...by men.

C436. Just, Klaus Guenther. "Edgar Allan Poe und die Folgen |Edgar Allan Poe and the consequences|." In his Uebergaenge. Probleme und Gestalten der Literatur, pp. 58-78. Bern and Munich: Francke, 1966. Reprinted in Vogt (B424), Vol. I, pp. 9-32.

Historical article tracing the development of the genre through Poe, Doyle, Chesterton, Christie and Sayers. Just states that Poe's "Murders in the Rue Morgue" was the consciously conceived beginning of a new genre and that the detectives of Christie and Sayers provide insights into the British national character. (GG)

C437. Justice, Keith L. "Publishers' Codes and Collecting Contemporary Editions." Megavore 11 (Oct 80), pp. 23-24.

C438. Kabatchnik, Amnon. "The Suspense Novel - and the Middle East." TMRN 3:1 (Oct 69):3-6.

Some comments on several novels with Middle Eastern settings.

C439. Kaemmel, Ernst. "Literatur unterm Tisch. Der Detektivroman und sein gesellschaftlicher Auftrag |Literature under the table: the detective novel and its social mandate|." Neue Deutsche Literatur 10: 5 (1962):152-6;

reprinted in Vogt (B424), Vol. II, pp. 516-23; in Zmegac (B451), pp. 177-83; and, translated into English by Glenn W. Most, in Most/Stowe (B264), pp. 55-61.

The author tries to show that the detective novel could only emerge and survive in the capitalist world. He sees the criminal actions described in many novels as attacks against private wealth. Apart from this thesis, the article contains some general remarks on genre conventions. (Barbara Korte)

C440. Kahn, Joan. "Editing the Mystery and Suspense Novel." The Writer 79:7 (July 66):18-21.

Editor Kahn talks about the mystery/suspense field and offers some suggestions to authors submitting manuscripts. For other articles by Joan Kahn on the field see the following: TAD 2: (1978/79):169-70; The Writer 82:3 (March 69):19-21; and The Writer 86 (Jan 73):18-21 (with a biographical afterword by Stanley Ellin).

C441. Keating, H. R. F. "How I Write My Books." Writer's Digest, Oct 83, pp. 22-29. Excerpted from Whodunit (B181). Illus.

Seven writers of mystery and suspense fiction (Stanley Ellin, P. D. James, Gregory McDonald, Patricia Highsmith, Len Deighton, Eric Ambler and Desmond Bagley) talk about their writing methods.

C442. Keddie, James, Jr. "Rambling Thoughts on a 'Tec Collection." TAD 1 (1967/68):5-8.

Some favorite authors and their collectibility; suggested reading list.

C443. Kellett, E. E. "Marginal Comments." The Spectator, 26 Feb 37, p. 354.

A humorous request of detective story writers that their detectives "stalk" virtues which are probably more "secret" and harder to identify than villainy.

C444. Kelly, R. Gordon. "Explaining the Detective Story." TAD 5 (1971/72): 214-15.

A follow-up to J. R. Christopher's "Rites of a Mystery Cult" (C118) with reservations and further speculations.

C445. Kennedy, Foster. "From Whodunits to Poetry." SR 24, 18 Oct 41, p. 34.

Compares restrictions of detective fiction to (lesser) ones of poetry. (KLM)

C446. Kennedy, Milward. "Murderers in Fiction." Lovat Dickson's Magazine 3:6 (Dec 34):676-83.

Discussion of the question of premeditated murder, illustrated by reference to famous murders in fiction. (RCSA)

C447. Kermode, Frank. "Novel and Narrative." In Theory of the Novel, edited by John Halperin, pp. 154-74. NY: Oxford Univ. Press, 1974; reprinted in Most/Stowe (B264), pp. 175-96.

A reading of the "old style" detective novel in E. C. Bentley's Trent's Last Case and of the "new" in Michel Butor's Passing Time embedded in a theoretical discussion of fictional forms.

C448. Kimura, Jiro. "34th Annual Edgar Allan Poe Awards Dinner." TAD 13 (1980):205-7.

A photographic record of the event.

C449. King, Daniel P. "Collecting Detective Stories." Antiquarian Book Monthly Review 3 (June/July 76): 162-64.
Patchy essay with little new to offer. (RCSA)

C450. King, Margaret J. "Binocular Eyes: Cross-Cultural Detectives." TAD 13 (1980): 253-60.
Upfield, McClure, Biggers and others, with a selective bibliography.

C451. Kircher, Hartmut. "Schema und Anspruch. Zur Destruktion des Kriminalromans bei Dürrenmatt, Robbe-Grillet und Handke. |Scheme and pretension: on the destruction of the crime novel by Dürrenmatt, Robbe-Grillet and Handke|." Germanischromanische Monatsschrift (new series) 28:2 (1978): 195-215.
Academic argument that the crime novels of Dürrenmatt, Robbe-Grillet and Peter Handke break away from the conventions and style of the crime genre. Kircher argues for the serious study of crime fiction. (GG)

C452. Kittredge, William, and Krautzer, Steven M. "Introduction." In The Great American Detective, pp. x-xxxiv. NY: New American Library, 1978. Reprinted as "The Evolution of the Great American Detective: The Reader as Detective Hero" in TAD 11 (1978): 318-30.
The authors trace the evolution of the private detective from Poe, through the British classical detective, the native American sleuth and the private eye of hard-boiled fiction. They discuss at some length the "vengeance" hero of Mickey Spillane and the outlaw hero of the 60s and 70s. A concise and comprehensive survey.

C453. Klein, Kathleen Gregory. "Feminists as Detectives: Harriet Vane, Kate Fansler, Sarah Chayse." TAD 113 (1980):31-35. Illus.
Klein examines 9 novels by three writers (Dorothy L. Sayers, Amanda Cross and Lynn Meyer) to support her contention that they have created a more positive image of the female detective in contrast to the eccentric, often "unbelievable" portrayals in earlier writers. Klein does not document her blanket denunciation.

C454. Knight, Stephen. "'...some men come up'--the Detective appears." In Most/Stowe (B264), pp. 266-98.
This essay appears as the first chapter in Knight's Form and Ideology in Crime Fiction (B190), pp. 8-37. Knight attempts to show how the patterns of crime control were initiated in the Newgate Calendar without the intervention of a detective whose role--he believes--only began to develop in William Godwin's Caleb Williams (1794) and Vidocq's Memoirs (1828/9).

C455. Knott, Harold. "Some Important Detective Fiction First Editions in Paperback Books." TMRN 3:1 (Oct 69):2-6.
Books Knott has identified as first editions with contents listed. Most of the volumes are collections of short stories.

C456. ______. "Who Really Wrote It?" TMRN 3:6 (Aug 70):2-5.
A disorganized account of pseudonyms and writers who have used them.

C457. Knox, Ronald A. "Detective Fiction." In his Literary Distractions, pp. 180-98. London: Sheed & Ward, 1958.
Repeats his famous "Detective Story Decalogue" (C458) with slightly expanded commentary. (REB)

C458. ______. "Introduction." In The Best (English) Detective Stories of 1928, edited by Father Ronald Knox and H. Harrington, pp. 9-23. London: Faber and Faber, 1929; NY: Liveright, 1929.

This introduction contains his ten "rules" for the classic English detective story frequently published separately as "A Detective Story Decalogue," as in PW 116 (5 Oct 29):1729; in Haycraft (B142), pp. 194-96; in Buchloh/Becker 2 (B61), pp. 191-92; and in Winks (B434), pp. 200-202.

C459. ______. "Introduction." In his The Best (English) Detective Stories of 1929, pp. 9-10. London: Faber and Faber, 1929; NY: Liveright, 1930.

The detective short story is probably harder to write than the novel and its success depends on its selection of details.

C460. Kondo, Thomas M., and Marks, Alfred H. Introduction to Tales of Japanese Justice by Ihara Saikaku, pp. xi-xix. Honolulu: University Press of Hawaii, 1980.

Informative introduction to a classic collection of 44 court cases, originally published in 1689. The book--whose Japanese title is Honcho Oin Hiji--is considered a prototypical work of Japanese crime fiction. Although Kondo and Marks--who also translated the book into English--include some facts about the career of Saikaku, they concentrate on the judicial system in seventeenth-century Japan, in which the local magistrate acted as detective, prosecutor, judge and jury. (JLA)

C461. Korinman, Michel. "Vi(e)sages d'Allemagne: le genre neutre |German lives/faces: the neutral genre|." In Littérature 49 (Feb 83), pp. 77-88.

Detective fiction in the 19th century in Germany.

C462. Kracauer, Siegfried. "Detektiv." In Vogt (B424), Vol. II, pp. 343-56. Originally published as Chapter VI of Der Detektiv-Roman (B197).

The "abstract shadow' of the detective wanders in the "emptiness" among the characters.

C463. Krouse, Agate Nesaule, and Peters, Margot. "Murder in Academe." Southwest Review 62 (1977): 371-78.

The authors contemplate the academic locale in the detective story and conclude that the Vietnam era and a push for realism have tarnished the image of university as Eden. (Parker's The Godwulf Manuscript is their prime example of academia's new, negative reputation.) (KLM)

C464. Krutch, Joseph Wood. "Only a Detective Story." Nation, 25 Nov 44, pp. 647-48. Reprinted in Haycraft (B142), pp. 178-88; Buchloh/Becker 2 (B61), pp. 200-207; and Winks (B434), pp. 41-46.

After rejecting Louise Bogan's theory (C107) that the popularity of the detective novel is related to its sense of dread as not generally characteristic of the field, Krutch suggests that its popularity may more properly be traced to its basic novelistic virtues (a good story well-told) and to its classical form.

C465. Labianca, D. A., and Reeves, W. J. "Coked Criminals, Doped Drinks and the Detective's Dilemma." Clues 3:1 (1982): 80-85.

The use of drugs in fiction by Doyle, Collins, Hammett and Christie. The authors appear to have selected what they consider to be "highpoints" in the history of drugs as a plot device. Their sampling is limited and no general conclusions should be drawn from it.

C466. Lachman, Marvin. "The American Regional Mystery."
A series of articles on mysteries and their settings. Lachman admits that his listings are not encyclopedic but he has clearly researched his subject extensively and his discussions of writers and the ways they have used local settings in their fiction is an important and useful taxonomical project. He had initially divided the subject into ten areas but at the time of the compilation of this bibliography 13 segments have appeared, as follows: I. New England. TMRN 3:3 (Feb 70):13-21; Appendix, with additional listings and comments, in TMRN 3:4 (Apr 70):22-23. II. New York City (Part One). TMRN 3:5 (June 70):23-30; III. New York City (Part Two). TMRN 4:1 (Oct 70):8-17. IV. New York State. TMRN 4:3 (Mar 71):3-11. V. New Jersey and Pennsylvania. TMRN 4:5 (Jly/Aug 71):2-7. VI. Washington,D.C. and Maryland. TMRN 5:1 (Nov/Dec 71):3-9. VII. The South. TMRN 5:3 (Jan/Mar 72):1-11. VIII. Florida. TMRN 5:5 (1972):3-11, 26. IX. Midwest. TMRN 6:1 (1973):1-13. X. The Southwest. TMRN 6:2 (1973):23-31. XI. The Mountain States, Pacific Northwest, and Alaska. TAD 9 (1975/76):11-13. XII. Hawaii and Northern California. TAD 9 (1975/76):260-66. XIII. Southern California. TAD 10 (1977):294-306.

C467. ______. "Department of Unknown Mystery Writers."
A regular feature, appearing in The Poisoned Pen, beginning with volume 1, number 2. A valuable supplement to reference works like TCCMW (A143) and EMD (A160) since Lachman provides biographical and bibliographical information on writers who have published relatively little or have not been considered of sufficient stature for inclusion in major reference sources. Individual entries in this series will be noted in the Authors section with volume, issue and pagination information given.

C468. ______. "Murder at the Opera." Opera News, July 1980, pp. 22-24+.
Detective fiction with operatic settings.

C469. ______. "Mystery Stories and the Presidency." TMRN 2:1 (Oct 68):8-10.
Detective fiction in which a President has played a role. Addenda by ML in letter, TMRN 2:3 (Feb 69):11.

C470. ______. "The President and the Mystery Story." Mystery 2:3 (May 1981):6-9. Illus.
U. S. Presidents as "fans, authors and characters."

C471. ______. "Religion and Detection." TAD 1 (1967/68):20-24.
Brief comments on writers who have have used other writers' characters in their fiction and a pastiched conversation between Rabbi Small and Father Brown.

C472. ______. "Sports and the Mystery Story." I. Tennis. TAD 6 (1972/73):1-6. II. Prizefighting and Bullfighting. TAD 6 (1972/73):83-86. III. Baseball and Basketball. TAD 6 (1972/73):243-45. IV. Football. TAD 7 (1973/74):195-97. V. Golf. TAD 7 (1973/74):261-62, 269. VI. Cricket. TAD 8 (1974/75):108-10. Additions were suggested by correspondents in the letter column as follows: Frank F. McSherry, Jr., TAD 6 (1972/73):127 and TAD 7 (1973/74):302; R. W. Hays, TAD 6 (1972/73):198; F. M. Nevins, Jr., TAD 6 (1972/73):203-204 and TAD 7 (1973/74):67; John Harwood, TAD 6 (1972/73):204; and Bob Adey, TAD 8 (1974/75):238.

C473. ______. "Virgil Tibbs and the American Negro in Mystery Fiction." TAD 1 (1967/68):86-89. Additions by Frank D. McSherry, Jr., TAD 1 (1967/68):155;

F. M. Nevins, Jr., TAD 1 (1967/68):158; and Pat Erhardt, TAD 2 (1968/69):64.

C475. la Cour, Tage. "Viktoriansk kriminallitteratur |Victorian criminal literature|." Jury 1:2 (1972): 24-8. Includes bibliography. (MS)

C476. Lacourbe, Roland. "Espionnage et littérature ou Regard sur le roman d'espionnage |Espionage and literature or a look at the espionage novel|." Polar 28 (Winter 83), pp. 58-103. With a bibliography of authors cited (pp. 90-103).

A survey that includes, in addition to American and English writers, French writers like Jean Bruce, Pierre Nord and Jean Bommart. The bibliography was compiled by Stéphane Bourgoin, Francis Lacassin and Jean-Jacques Schleret.

C477. Lafforgue, Jorge, and Rivera, Jorge B. "La morgue está de fiesta. Literatura policial en la Argentina |Death is on vacation. Detective literature in Argentina|." Crisis (Buenos Aires) 3:3 (Jan 76): 16-26; revised and expanded version published in Lafforgue(B214), pp. 13-46.

A history of detective fiction in Argentina.

C478. Lafforgue, Jorge, and Rivera, Jorge B., editors. "El Prologo." In El Cuento policial. Buenos Aires: Centro editorial de América Latina, 1981.

In this introduction to an anthology of Argentine detective stories, the editors give a brief history of the genre in Argentina and its relationship to English, French and American authors. The earliest story in the anthology dates from 1897.

C479. Laîn Entralgo, Pedro. "La novela policiaca." In his La Aventura de leer |The adventure of reading|, pp. 91-119. Coleccion Austral. Madrid: Espasa-Calpe, S. A., 1956.

After establishing a definition based on comparison and contrast with the novel of adventure, Lain Entralgo discusses the character types, plot structure and history of the detective novel in English. Very few references to writers; Poe, Dostoyevsky, Conan Doyle and Christie are his principal points of reference. He sees the detective novel as being in a period of decline and foresees a more juvenile form of literature replacing it in the affections of readers.

C481. Land, Irene Stokvis, editor. "First Novelists. Gothic, Guns and Games." Library Journal 94 (1 Feb 69):583-84.

John Alexander Graham (Arthur, Harper), and Charles Larson (The Chinese Game, Lippincott) comment on the writing of their first novels and other matters.

C482. Lanham, Cathryn. "A Dream of Reason: The Great Detective as True Believer." Clues 2:2 (1981):22-27.

The deterioration of the belief in a rational universe with cause, effect and order and the increasing recognition of a less comprehensible world.

C483. Lanocita, Arturo. "I segreti del romanzo giallo |The secrets of the giallo Novel|." La Lettura, Sept 34, pp. 832-36.

The author does not regard the detective novel as a literary product, but as having as its only purpose that of entertaining and astonishing. In order to construct it one "needs the ability of a chess player, rather than that of a writer." The author of detective novels has his repertory of techniques and of games, he is a "manipulator" of the novelistic vicissitudes which require certain dosages in order to produce, on the emotional level, the desired effects. The reading becomes, therefore, a "duel of astuteness engaged apparently between the criminal and the detective, but in reality between the writer and the reader." He points out the characteristics of the French, English, and American schools. (The author, a movie critic, has published three detective novels in the period 1932-45.) (LR)

C484. Lauri Conti, Lucio. "Perché piacciono i gialli |Why do gialli please|?" Appendix to Un testamento diabolico, by Pierre Véry. Milan: Pagotto, 1949.
The author admits that detective novels offer the reader a pleasure of an intellectual nature but denies that they can be compared to the puzzle problems. "And that it is thus is proved by the fact that only by chance could the reader find the solution chosen by the novelist. Usually he either finds none or he finds others equally logical." (LR)

C485. Lauterbach, Edward and Karen. "The Crossword Puzzle Metaphor and Some Crossword Puzzle Mysteries." TAD 10 (1977):167-74. Addenda by E. Lauterbach in TAD 10 (1977): 284.
The detective novel as riddle and novels in which crossword puzzles play a crucial role.

C486. Lauterbach, Edward. "Parodies." Yellowback Library, no. 11 (Sept/Oct 82), pp. 14, 20.
A note with references to parodies of dime novel detective series.

C487. Lawrence, Barbara. "Female Detectives: The Feminist--Anti-Feminist Debate." Clues 3:1 (1982):38-48.
Lawrence begins well with some good comments on feminist elements in A. K. Green's novels but she soon abandons her attempt to provide some sort of chronological/historical foundation for the purported topic and the essay deteriorates into a series of anedoctal plot observations.

C488. Lawrence, Tom. "Sisters in Crime." Everywoman 19, no. 221 (July 1958), pp. 252 et seq.
Chatty description of nine lady writers and their methods: Allingham, Anthony Gilbert, Margot Bennett, Christianna Brand, Mary Fitt, Josephine Bell, Stratford Davis, Elizabeth Ferrars and Annette Kerner.(RCSA)

C488a. Leitch, Thomas M. "From Detective Story to Detective Novel." MFS 29:3 (Autumn 83):475-84.
Writers who have turned short stories into novels: Chandler, Sayers, Helen McCloy, and Anthony Berkeley. Leitch concludes with some comments on differences in concept between detective short stories and novels.

C489. Lejeune, Anthony. "Age of the Great Detective." TLS, 23 June 61, p. vii.
As symbol of hope in a rational solution to the mystery of life as well as art.

C490. Leonard, John. "I Care Who Killed Roger Ackroyd." Esquire, Aug 75, pp. 60-61, 120.
A profession of interest in detective fiction because "stories" are interesting. Discusses also how a campaign was mounted to promote the novels of Ross Macdonald and to bring him to the attention of readers and critics.

C491. Lewis, Caleb A. "Iwan Hedman: An Interview." TAD 13 (1980):166-68. Photos.
Hedman is the editor/publisher of the Swedish detective fiction critical journal DAST.

C492. Lewis, Paul. "Beyond Mystery: Emergence from Delusion as a Pattern in Gothic Fiction." Gothic 2 (1980):7-13.
Essay at least in part on Thomas Burke as a writer of horror/gothic literature. (GG)

C493. Lingeman, Richard R. "How to Tell Sam Spade from Philip Marlowe from Lew Archer." Esquire 84 (Aug 75):62, 64.
Chart in which Spade/Marlowe/Archer are compared and contrasted according to categories which include "physical description," "personal habits," "mannerisms," "known associates," and "background."

C494. Ljunglöf, Lennart. "Fran Nordirland til Sinai i terroristernas spar |From Northern Ireland to the Sinai in the terrorists' footsteps|." Jury 6:3 (1977):57-62.
Today's political thrillers as reflections of terrorism. (MS)

C494a. ______. "Storpolitiken i thrillerns spegel |High politics in the mirror of the thriller|." Jury 4:3 (1975):8-14.
Ambler, MacInnes, Maclean, le Carré, Greene. (MS)

C495. LLewellyn, Owen. "Guide to Murder." Victory (The Weekly for India Command, published in New Delhi) 18:5 (31 Dec 45):26-29.
A general study noteworthy because the recommendations--Jonathan Latimer, F. L. Green, J. B. Fearnley, Alice Tilton--include one or two less well-known authors. (RCSA)

C496. Lochte, Richard S., II. "The Private Eye: Enduring as a $1.29 Streak." TAD 3 (1969/70):117-19.
Notes on Hammett, Chandler and Ross Macdonald.

C497. "Love of Heroes: Some Detectives of Character." TLS, 25 Sept 55, p. ix.
Character is as much a part of detective fiction as plot springs. A defense of detectives and their characters. Doyle, Poe, Christie, Bramah, et al.

C498. Lucas, E. V. "The Search." The Outlook, 22 Sept 1906, pp. 379-80.
A plea for the restoration of character to the "quest" novel and a search for people rather than a criminal.

C499. Ludwig, Hans-Werner. "Der Ich-Erzaehler im englisch-amerikanischen Detektiv- und Kriminalroman |The first-person narrator in the English-American detective and crime novel|." Deutsche Vierteljahrsschrift fuer Literaturwissenschaft und Geistgeschichte 45:3 (1971):434-50.
Academic study of the narrative art of Agatha Christie, Raymond Chandler and Peter Cheyney. (GG)

C500. Lundin, Bo. "Det är mest turister some stryker i gränderna--Om deckare i romerska miljöer |It's mainly tourists who roam in the alleys--detective novels in Roman milieus|." Jury 10:4 (1981):43-52.
Includes Marsh, Chapman Pincher, Derek Lambert, Jon Cleary. (MS)

C500a. ______. "Flera mord i Rom |More murders in Rome|." Jury 11:1 (1982): 75.
Additions to C500. (MS)

C501. Ma, Yau-woon. "Themes and Characterization in the Lung-t'un kung-an." T'oung Pao 59 (1973):179-202.
Called by Ma a "companion study" to his 1971 doctoral dissertation at Yale, "The Pao-Kung Tradition in Chinese Popular Literature." Drawing from the 100 stories of the Lung-t'u kung-an, the best known Chinese collection of Magistrate Pao stories, Ma attempts to differentiate several different themes. Although Ma does not go so far as to say that there are sub-genres within the kung-an stories, he does distinguish certain types of stories, such as those featuring lecherous Buddhist monks, roving gangs of criminals or disloyal, murderous wives. Unlike most other scholarly Sinologists who write on ancient Chinese detective stories, Ma shows evidence of awareness of the Western tradition of crime fiction and its criticism. (GG)

C502. McAleer, John. "The Game's Afoot: Detective Fiction in the Present Day." KQ 10:4 (Fall 78):421-38.
The present popularity of detective fiction, various theories as to its popularity, college courses, critical work, some historical notes. A pot-pourri of rambling observations.

C503. McCarthy, Mary. "Murder and Karl Marx: Class-Conscious Detective Stories." Nation 142 (25 March 36): 381-3. Reprinted in Cremante/Rambelli (B78), pp. 77-84.
The exhaustion of the puzzle story has turned some mystery novelists toward political and social problems while native and foreign proletariats are often the most likely murder suspects. McCarthy sees detective writers as, by and large, naive political and social conservatives. In the April 15, 1936 issue, pp. 494-95, William Seagle replies that the ideological detective story is not new and cites as examples Chesterton, A. K. Green and Dashiell Hammett, among others.

C504. Macchiavelli, Loriano. "Il senso giusto del mondo alla rovescia |The true sense of the world in reverse|." Orient Express 2 (1982):67-70.
Transferring the conclusions of Rambelli to the experiments of the contemporary Italian giallo, the author, a confirmed writer of detective novels, characterizes the renunciation of a motive for the crime and of the necessity of a reassuring solution as the most significant structural innovation of the genre. (RC)

C505. McCleary, G. F. "The Popularity of Detective Fiction." Fortnightly Review 167 (n.s. 161, Jan 47): 61-7. Reprinted in his On Detective Fiction and Other Things (B237), pp. 11-18.
A brief history of detective fiction up to and including Sherlock Holmes, with concluding comments on the difficulty of writing a good puzzle story and its contradictory attraction for the "lazy" reader.

C506. McCourt, Edward A. "'Home on the Range': Detective Story vs. the Western." SRL, 2 Nov 46, p. 23. Illus.
The detective story is not an important contribution to literature whatever the current debaters may claim. McCourt prefers the Western for which no such extravagant claims are made and there is no pretense of literature. A humorous piece by a professor of English.

C507. McDiarmid, John F. "The Quality of Play: Agatha among British Mystery Writers." Mid-Hudson Language Studies 5 (1982):91-105. Not seen.

C508 MacDonald, John D. "Strikeouts? Shootouts? Nah! They're Too Busy Kissing and Getting Funny Haircuts!" TV Guide, 9 Oct 82, pp. 14-15. Illus. Disgruntled comments on the current TV police/detective programs and the superiority of TV detectives of the 50s those of the 80s.

C509. Macdonald, Ross. "A Catalogue of Crime." NYTBR, 16 May 71, p. 3; reprinted in A Collection of Reviews (E1879).
A review of the Catalogue of Crime (A10). After pointing out significant omissions in the authors' bibliography, Macdonald takes issue with Barzun's insistence upon fixed conventions and his statement that the "tough" story was born in the thirties and has a "Marxist coloring."

C510. ______. "Down These Streets a Mean Man Must Go." Antaeus 25/25, Spring/Summer 77, pp. 211-216; reprinted in Self-Portrait (E1888).
Macdonald's discovery of, and attitudes towards, detective fiction. "I can think of few more complex critical exercises than disentangling the mind and life of a first-person story writer from the mask of his detective-narrator." (REB)

C511. ______. "Research into the History of Detective Fiction." San Francisco Chronicle--This World, 18 Jan 59, p. 15.; reprinted in A Collection of Reviews (E1879).
A review of Murch, The Development of the Detective novel (B267).

C512. ______. "The Writer as Detective Hero." Show Magazine 1964. Reprinted in Nevins (B290), pp. 295-305; in Ross Macdonald, On Crime Writing (Capra Press, 1973), pp. 9-24; and in Winks (B434), pp. 179-87.
After stating that he believes the detective hero always, to some extent, is based on the writer, Macdonald talks about Poe's contributions, his theory that Baudelaire is the source for much of the modern detective story, and analyzes Hammett's Sam Spade, Chandler's Philip Marlowe and his own Archer.

C513. MacDonell, A. G. "The Present Convention of the Mystery Story." London Mercury 23 (Dec 1930):158-65.
While agreeing with Dorothy Sayers about the limitations of the currently popular puzzle story, MacDonell insists upon the high standard of achievement among the best of the writers of these stories but concludes that the author is not a "free man" at any point.

C514. McElroy, Charles F. "The Clichés of the Mystery Writers." SRL 21 (13 Jan 40):9.
A letter to the editor in which McElroy lists clichés he runs across frequently in his reading of detective novels published in the period 1934-39.

C515. McGill, V. J. "Henry James: Master Detective." Bookman 72 (Nov 30):251-56.
Mystery novels have great appeal for the scientist in their patient sorting out of alternatives but they lack psychological insight. While there are no murders as such in James, there are mysteries of the self and the acute psychological study that clarifies these mysteries makes of James the "master detective." A perceptive essay that predates by two decades the innovations of the French new novelists in this area.

C517. McLuhan, Herbert Marshall. "Footprints in the Sands of Crime." Sewanee Review 54 (1946):617-34.

A disorganized attempt to trace Holmes' antecedents to English philosopher Thomas Hobbes. Simon Templar is, according to McLuhan, a descendent of Charles Stuart, Holmes' stalking-hat links him to Cooper's Indian readers of signs and Robinson Crusoe is apparently included to give some fleeting significance to the title. This "essay" reads like a series of notes jotted down in the heat of passion and not subjected to any revision or objective re-ordering.

C518. McSherry, Frank D., Jr. "The Armchair Criminal." TAD 14 (1981):57-70. Illus. by the author.

Discussions of fiction by Doyle, Frederick Irving Andersson, Melville Davisson Post, Ellery Queen, Rex Stout, Christie and L.Sprague de Camp. Addition by author in letter to TAD 14:4 (1981):382-83.

C519. ______. "The Amateurs' Hour." TAD 3 (1969/70):14-22.

Fictional characters who are forced to turn to detecting. McSherry discusses, among others, Horatio Hornblower, Tom Sawyer and Judge Priest.

C520. ______. "The Golden Road to Samarkand: The Arabian Nights in Detective Fiction." TAD 7 (1973/74):77-94.

Detective fiction "steeped in the atmosphere of the Arabian nights like a rose in perfume...." Among the writers discussed are Theodore Roscoe, A. Merritt, Murray Leinster, Donn Byrne and Clark Ashton Smith. McSherry published a follow-up piece ("Footsteps on the Golden Road. An Addendum to 'The Golden Road....'") in TAD 7:264, 282. Other additions and corrections were made in letters by Charles Shibuk in TAD 7:227, by Marvin Lachman in TAD 7:223, and by McSherry in TAD 7:301-302.

C521. ______. "Judge Crater and His Fellow Travellers." TAD 4 (1970/71):195-218.

Impossible crimes: "vanishers" in fiction and fact. Additions and corrections in letters in Vol. 5, as follows: by McSherry, pp. 48-51, 111-13, 247-48; by John Harwood, pp. 53-54; by John Nieminski, pp. 56-57; by Francis M. Nevins, Jr., p. 126; by W. O. G. Lofts, pp. 126-28; and by G. A. Finch, pp. 187-88.

C522. ______. "Lady in a Straitjacket." TAD 9 (1975/76):201-202.

A discussion of the crossword-puzzle short stories, devised by Margaret Petherbridge, that appeared in Mystery Book Magazine in the 1940s.

C523. ______. "A New Category of the Mystery Story." TAD 2 (1968/69): 23-24.

Some examples of mystery stories that have two possible solutions, one natural and one supernatural. Additions by John Nieminski in TAD 2:128 and by J. P. King in TAD 2:132. "The Janus Resolution," a revised version of this article, was published in Nevins (B290), pp.263-71.

C524. ______. "The Shape of Crimes to Come." In Nevins (B290), pp. 326-38; reprinted in Popular Culture and the Expanding Consciousness, edited by Ray B. Browne, pp. 67-80. NY: Wiley, 1973.

Science fiction stories in which the crime involved is not now a crime. Among the topics McSherry examines are the consequences of the population explosion and attempts to prevent a nuclear war.

C525. ______. "The Smallest Sub-Genre." TAD 10 (1977):267-70. Illustrated.

Fiction in which the reader is the detective. Addenda in volume 10 in letters from McSherry, p. 379 and from Francis M. Nevins, Jr., p. 379.

C526. ______. "A Study in Black." TMRN 5:5 (1972):23-26; 5:6 (March 73):3-8; 6:1 (July 73):29-32; 6:2 (Nov 73):39-43. Illustrations by McSherry.
A study of detective stories in which the detective or his quarry is not "entirely human," and of stories in which the solution may be understood naturally or supernaturally (the "Janus" resolution). This long essay was not completed when TMRN ceased publication and it has not been completed in another publication or the integral version published separately. Illustrations by McSherry.

C527. ______. "Under Two Flags: The Detective Story in Science Fiction." TAD 2 (1968/69):171-73.
Cross-over stories by Poul Anderson, Hal Clement, Alfred Bester, Randall Garrett, Isaac Asimov and others.

C528. ______. "Who-Really-Dun-It? Two Sub-Branches of the Detective Story." TAD 2 (1968/69):88-93.
The fictional writer's attempts to solve a true crime, either with himself or his fictional alter ego as detective. Addenda in letters from J. R. Christopher, TAD 2:200; and from McSherry, TAD 3 (1969/70):276-77.

C529. Mahan, Jeffrey H. "The Hard-Boiled Detective in the Fallen World." Clues (Fall/Winter 80):90-99.
Chandler, Hammett, Ross Macdonald.

C530. Maio, Kathleen L. "Had-I-But-Known: The Marriage of Gothic Terror and Detection." In Fleenor (B113), pp. 82-90.
Stressing the link between the English Gothic and early detective fiction, Maio shows that HIBK is both a Gothic thriller and a form of detective story in which a woman is the chief protagonist. Discussions of Rinehart (as the chief innovator) and Mabel Seely (Rinehart's most important successor). Also a discussion of an HIBK "adjunct," the romantic suspense novel, a celebration of women's submissiveness rather than their strength. Rae Foley, Elaine Wagner, and Mary Linn Roby are briefly discussed in this context.

C531. ______. "Oh! Sweet Mystery." Sojourner, July 1979, pp. 7, 23.
Mystery fiction as a formula largely created and nutured by women. Maio discusses a number of British and American female writers of detective fiction from the nineteenth century to the present.

C532. ______. "(Skeleton in the) Closet Literature: A Look at Women's Mystery Fiction." Second Wave 4 (Summer/Fall 76):8-20.
A detailed study of detective fiction written by women from the English Gothic mystery to the present day. Maio is particularly interesting on the subject of the 19th century writers and in her analysis of the effect the introduction of Harriet Vane had on the character and will-to-detect of Lord Peter Wimsey.

C533. ______. "A Strange and Fierce Delight: The Early Days of Women's Mystery Fiction." Chrysalis 10:93-105.
Biographical and critical studies of 19th century women who wrote

detective fiction. A sympathetic and detailed account which is not at all limited to the comments on Mrs. Braddon and Anna Katharine Green that such pieces often parade as surveys of the subject.

C534. Maloney, Martin. "A Grammar of Assassination." ETC: A Review of General Semantics 11 (53/54):83-95; reprinted in Our Language and Our World: Selections from ETC, edited by S. I. Hayakawa, pp. 256-71. NY: Harper and Row, 1959.

Maloney believes that critics of crime fiction, who berate it for not being "high" art, miss the point: it is a popular art of its time and needs a different critical apparatus for study. Maloney's purpose is to sketch the "bare outlines" of such a grammar/apparatus. Comments on the history of crime fiction, with observations on stylistic/grammatical peculiarities of several writers: Doyle, Horning, hard-boiled American writers. Some speculations on possible further development of crime fiction with reference to Spillane where fiction reflects the violent contemporary world, a society "badly in need of therapy."

C535. Manchester, H. F. "How Philo Vance, Clubfoot and Charlie Chan Were Born." The Writer 43:9 (Sept 31):249-52.

An article on the origins of detectives created by S. S. Van Dine, Valentine Williams and Earl Derr Biggers, including information received in interviews with the writers.

C536. Manno, D. Yves. "Roman policier et société |Detective novel and society|." Europe, 571/2 (Nov/Dec 76):117-25.

Historically-oriented study of the ways in which the detective novel has reflected order in society. Manno maintains that more recent French writers have tended to attack rather than support the prevailing political system.

C537. Margolies, Edward. "The American Detective Thriller and the Idea of Society." In Landrum (B216), pp. 83-87.

To answer Orwell's complaint that the amoral American thriller has caused the British detective novel to deteriorate, Margolies discusses the hard-boiled hero and his relationship to society and the law. Margolies thinks that the development of American society has contributed to the creation of the distinctive hard-boiled hero.

C538. Marshment, Margaret. "Racist Ideology and Popular Fiction." Race & Class 19:4 (Spring 78):331-44.

Ian Fleming, Nicholas Montserrat and Nevil Shute and the "ideology of racisim" in their fiction. Fleming's ideology is presented as that of a capitalist society, so "embedded in the narrative structure and characterization as to appear 'natural'."

C539. Martí, Agenor. Introduction to his Varios Cuentos Policiacos Cubanos, pp. 5-10. Havana: Editorial letras cubanas, 1980.

Unlike detective fiction written in capitalist countries as a defense of the bourgeois and their legal system, the rejuvenated detective novel in Communist countries defends justice and the people as well as the legal system.

C540. Martí-Ibánez, Felix. "The Cosmic Saboteur: A Meditation on Crime." MD Medical Newsmagazine 10:3 (March 66):9-16.

This editorial essay in an issue of MD devoted to 'Criminology and Medicine" ranges over a wide variety of topics on crime in real life and in literature. Under the latter heading, there are extensive comments on Fu Manchu, Bulldog Drummond, John Buchan, John Creasey, with passing mention of many other figures from crime fiction. (REB)

C541. ______. "The Magicians of the Thrill." MD Medical Newsmagazine 7:1 (June 63):11-13. A survey of thriller writers, past and present.
After bows in the direction of Buchan and Edgar Wallace, the author discusses John Creasey, Peter Cheyney, Sax Rohmer, Mark Derby, Eric Ambler, Hammond Innes, Alistair MacLean, and Graham Greene. Dr. Martí-Ibánez, former professor and chairman of the Department of History of Medicine at New York Medical College, and founding editor and publisher of MD, was a knowledgeable enthusiast of mystery fiction and author of some excellent fantasy short stories. (REB)

C542. Matthew, Christopher. "Guilty of Concealing Criminals." The Daily Telegraph Magazine no. 478 (4 Jan 1974):40-46.
Discussion of crime writers as compared with detective story writers. The writers concerned are Roy Fuller, Patricia Highsmith, John Bingham, Michael Innes and Julian Symons. Photos. (RCSA)

C543. Maugham, W. Somerset. "The Decline and Fall of the Detective Story." In his Vagrant Mood, pp. 101-32. Garden City, N.Y.: Doubleday, 1953. An excerpt was published in TMRN 1:5 (June 68):7-8.
After describing the appeal of the classical mystery, Maugham writes with enthusiasm of the hard-boiled writers and of Hammett and Chandler. However, he concludes by saying that he cannot imagine a successor to Chandler or the story of pure deduction although he will continue to read the stories written in those traditions.

C544. ______. "Give Me a Murder." Sat Eve Post, 28 Dec 40, pp. 27, 46-49.
Maugham, describing himself as something of a lowbrow, confesses to a liking for detective stories and offers some rules to be observed in writing them: there must be, at the most, 2 murders; the crime must be motivated; the victim should deserve his fate and so forth. Maugham attributes their success to the "namby-pamby" nature of the modern novel and wonders if future critics might not see the crime novel as more significant than it is now taken to be.

C545. ______. "In Defense of Who-Done-It." Scholastic 46:9 (2 Apr 45):15. Illus.
Reprinted from the New York Post (date not known). Maugham enjoys detective stories because the writers are genuine story tellers at a time when serious novelists are not.

C546. May, Clifford. "'Whatever Happened to Sam Spade?': The Private Eye in Fact and Fiction." Atlantic Monthly, Aug 75, pp. 27-35.
A brief history of the fictional and real-life private eye with a demonstration through anecdote of the fact that the real-life investigator's lot is a much more routine and unglamorous one than the fictional private eye's.

C547. May, H. R. D. "The Immortality of the Modern Burglar Story and Burglar Play." Nineteenth Century and After 77 (Feb 1915):432-44; excerpted under the title "Burglar Stories and Plays" in The Writer 27:6 (June 1915):190-91.
A moralistic tract based on the principle that if vice is made attractive it will win converts. The major part of the essay is a discussion of the

morality of the burglar-hero Raffles with a conclusion in which Arsene Lupin is "cleared" of any charge of immorality.

C550. Melville, James. "The Edogawa Rampo Tradition." TLS, 30 Oct 81, p. 1265.
Despite some minor errors involving dates and the spelling of names, this is an excellent article on Japanese mystery fiction. Included are short reviews of books by Seicho Matsumoto, Seishi Yokomizo, Shizuko Natsuki, Seiichi Morimura, and other Japanese mystery writers. Melville concludes with the interesting comment that, apart from the language in which they are written and the local color involved, Japanese mysteries differ little from those produced in the west. (JLA)

C551. Meyer, Nicholas. "Mystery!" TV Guide, 9 Feb 80, pp. 23-24.
Reflections on the appeal of detective novels.

C552. Mierow, Charles C. "Through Seas of Blood." Sewanee Review 41 (Jan 33):1-22.
An informal and engaging ramble through adventure, detective, mystery and ghost tales. In the category of "I recommend these because I like them." The detective fiction is of the Doyle/Gaboriau/Hornung variety and the adventure and mystery titles will be familiar to readers of fantasy pulps and the Munsey magazines.

C553. Millar, Dr. A. M. "The Detective in Literature." Humberside (England), Oct 38, pp. 74-94.
Deals largely with the period up to Doyle with much about Poe and those biblical and historical stories in which detection can itself be detected. (RCSA)

C554. Miller, D. A. "Language of Detective Fiction: Fiction of Detective Language." In The State of the Language, edited by Leonard Michaels and Christopher Ricks, pp. 478-85. Berkeley: Univ. of California Press, 1980.
Language as a concealer of truths, as a signifier freed from the signified, in detective fiction. Although in British detective fiction the detective through the interrogation of multiple witnesses arrives at the truth of a deceitful language, Miller sees the American violent, hard-boiled novel as a form in which language itself is the conveyer of violence done to the reader's need to know and to understand. A subtle discussion of the uses to which language is put in a genre which has often been seen as largely devoid of literary and linguistic substance.

C555. ______. "The Novel and the Police." Glyph 8 (1981), pp. 127-47; reprinted in Most/Stowe (B264), pp. 299-326.
Miller questions the assumption that the novel is the most "lawless" of all literary forms by pointing out the frequent use of police and the theme of policing in novels--particularly of the 18th and 19th centuries--to suggest that the novel, like other literary forms, is subject to laws and constraints. In his discussion, Miller includes Newgate fiction, sensation fiction and detective fiction.

C556. Miller, P. Schuyler. In a letter in TAD 7 (1974):74, writer Miller reveals himself to be the "J. Hamilton Edwards" discussed in Chapter 7 of Frank Gruber's The Pulp Jungle (D308) and comments briefly on Gruber's narrative, adding some general comments on the importance of detective stories (as contrasted with science fiction stories) as a portrait of their times.

C557. Milne, A. A. "Introducing Crime." In his By Way of Introduction, pp. 47-51. London: Methuen, 1929; NY: Dutton, 1929. Originally published as an introduction to an edition of Milne's The Red House Mystery.
In detective stories, Milne wants literate English, no love interest and a detective who is an amateur and a Watson.

C558. ______. "The Watson Touch." In his If I May, pp. 179-83. London: Methuen, 1920; New York: Dutton, 1921.
Milnes admits he would write another detective story if he had a good idea for one.

C559. Mintz, Phil. "PW Interviews Alberto Tedeschi." PW, 28 May 78, pp. 16-17. Photo.
Interview with the creator and editorial of the paperback mystery series, with a distinctive yellow cover, published by Arnaldo Mondadori. Tedeschi received an MWA Raven on April 27 and, a few days later, a "Red Herring" from the British Crime Writers' Association. Died on May 16, 1978.

C560. Monblatt, Bruce L. "The Detective Story: Pertinent?" TAD 4 (1971): 170-71.
Ways in which the contemporary detective novel mirrors society.

C561. Monsivais, Carlos. "Acerca de la literatura policiada |On detective literature|." Medio Siglo 2a epoca, No. 1 (Oct/Dec 56):108-22.
A study of the birth and development of the detective novel with both a criticism and a defense of its literary value. Monsivais concludes with a short description of detective fiction written in Spanish.

C562. Montesinos, José F. "Imperfect Myths: Being an Observation on Detective Stories by a Continental Reader." Chimera 5:4 (Summer 47):2-11.
Although the detective novel has evolved and attained some literary respectability, it should never "transcend" its own limitations but aspire for perfection within its constraints.

C563. Moretti, Franco. "Indizi |Signs|." In Polizieschi classici, pp. 7-35. Rome: Savelli, 1978.
Using a broad spectrum of sociological, structural and psychoanalytical interpretations, Moretti supports his hypothesis of the intrinsic contradition he sees in the detective genre: the detective story, "which in the detective celebrates the 'man who gives meaning to the world,' in its structure embodies the opposite principle that will be manifested in the mass culture: a process of institutionalizing signifiers which leaves out the active and conscious consensus of its members." (RC)

C564. Morris, Terrence. "The Suggestible Offender." TLS, 23 June 61, p. xii.
People may be influenced by what they read.

C565. Moskowitz, Sam. "The Gaslight Detective Series."
A series of short stories from the Victorian period was published in Mike Shayne's Mystery Magazine from March 1973 to Jan 1974, with biocritical introductions. The following authors are included: Arthur Morrison, R. Austin Freeman and Dr. J. J. Pitcairn, Sax Rohmer, W. H. Hodgson, B. Fletcher Robinson, Albert Payson Terhune, Sir Edmund C. Cox, M. McDonnell Bodkin, L. T. Meade & Clifford Halifax, and Rodriguez

Ottolengui. The stories and introductions will be cited in the Authors section.

C566. ______. "The Sleuth in Science Fiction." Worlds of Tomorrow, January 1966, pp. 66-77. Part II published as "The Super-Sleuths of Science Fiction," in WOT, March 1966, pp. 66-77. Combined, slightly expanded, and published as "From Sherlocks to Space Ships" in his Strange Horizons, pp. 122-59. NY: Charles Scribner's Sons, 1976.

Moskowitz discusses a number of writers who have combined science fiction and detective elements in their fiction. The early section, in which he deals with writers of the late 19th century and the early decades of the 20th, is of particular interest for the breadth of his knowledge of the period.

C567. Moy, Paul R. "Exclusive! The Detective Club's First Collaborations. Unpublished Christies and Others." TPP 4:5/6 (Dec 81):15-18.

The Detection Club's radio script collaborations "Behind the Screen" and "The Scoop" with episodes written by Hugh Walpole, Christie, Sayers, Bentley, Knox, Clemence Dane and Crofts.

C568. Murphy, Michael. "Vincent Starrett on the Hard-Boiled School." Xenophile 21 (Feb 76), pp. 47-48.

Starrett's high opinion of Hammett and Chandler and his lower opinion of Hemingway, based on written evaluations and on conversations Murphy had with Starrett. He concludes by stating there there are references other than those he cited in Starrett's writing to the hard-boiled school and these may be organized for "future" publication.

C569. Mussell, Kay J. "'But Why Do They Read These Things?': The Female Audience and the Gothic Novel." In Fleenor (B113), pp. 37-68.

The modern "feminine romantic mystery novels" in which traditional roles for women are validated. They also show women in unaccustomed, "adventurous" situations from which they extricate themselves and provide reading for women whose lives are lacking in adventure and excitement. Musell sees a reconciliation between roles from which women want to escape and the unaccustomed roles the female protagonists experience in gothics. They are active in the solving of mysteries but passive in their relationship with men.

C570. Naumann, Dietrich. "Kriminalroman und Dichtung |The crime novel and fiction|." Diskus 15:6 (1965):10f. Reprinted in Vogt (B424), Vol. II, pp. 473-83.

The author rejects the view of the detective novel as a genre entirely without esthetic merits. Despite their stereotyped structural patterns, the novels of writers like Boileau/Narcejac, Hammett, Chandler and Simenon display literary qualities. Furthermore, authors like Faulkner, Dürrenmatt and Robbe-Grillet have employed the pattern of the detective novel for purposes outside the normal scope of the genre. (Barbara Korte)

C571. ______. "Zur Typologie des Kriminalromans |On the typology of the crime novel|." Studien zur Trivialliteratur, edited by H. D. Burger, pp. 225-41. Frankfurt: Vittorio Klostermann Verlag, 1968. Reprinted in Zmegac (B451), pp. 241-60.

Discusses two sorts of typologies in crime novels: plot typologies, such as the differences among detective stories, crime stories, private eye stories, etc.; and literary typologies, which have to do with how far authors such as Dürrenmatt or Chandler depart from genre conventions in order to achieve a literary point. (GG)

C572. Nehr, Ellen. "Did It All Start with Ellery?" TPP 3:4 (July/August 80): 3-8.
Mysteries in which a mystery writer solves the crime.

C573. ______. "Little Old Ladies I Have Known and Love." TMF 3:4 (Jly/Aug 79): 3-7.
A preliminary study of mysteries in which the detective is a LOL.

C574. ______. "Little Old Men with Whom I'm Only Slightly Acquainted." TMF 4:4 (Jly/Aug 80):2-6.
Mysteries with LOM detectives.

C575. Nelson, James. "Judge Lynch of the Saturday Review's 'Criminal Record'." PW 136 (5 Aug 39):363.
Photo of masked man. A fictitious portrait of the Saturday Review's detective fiction reviewer.

C576. Nelson, William, and Avery, Nancy. "Art Where You Least Expect It: Myth and Ritual in the Detective Series." MFS 29:3 (Autumn 83):463-74.
The detective is seen in his mythic role in which he seeks to cleanse and purify his world. The authors use Lawrence Sanders' Edward X. Delaney and Martin Beck, from the series by Sjöwall/Wahlöö, as examples of their mythic heroes.

C577. Neuhaus, Volker. "Father Brown und Rabbi Small." In Teilnahme und Spielgelung. Festschrift fuer H. Ruediger, pp. 548-69. Berlin and New York: De Gruyter, 1975.
Serious academic essay relating the Father Brown and Rabbi Small stories to the theologies of their authors. Neuhaus also argues that the Father Brown stories are "orthodox" in their exemplification of certain classical detective story conventions, and that the Rabbi Small stories are "unorthodox" in having departed from these conventions. (GG)

C578. ______. "Rainer F. Schoenhaar: Novelle und Kriminalschema -- Ein Strukturmodell deutscher Erzaehlkunst um 1800." Arcadia 6:3 (1971):321-26.
Essay-length review of Schoenhaar's Novelle (B360).Neuhaus recapitulates Schoenhaar's arguments about the foundation of German detective narration, then takes him to task for having excluded popular literature from his field of study. (GG)

C579. ______. "Vorueberlegungen zu einer Geschichte des detektorischen Erzaehlens |Considerations toward a history of the detective narrative|." Arcadia 12:3 (1977):258-72.
Literary study of the narrative form in the detective story, its history and essential elements. Neuhaus discusses elements such as that of a secret, mystery or puzzle being explained at the conclusion and how these elements affect the narrative form. (GG)

C580. Nevins, Francis M., Jr. "The Criminal Justice System As Seen by Mystery Writers." St. Louis University Law Journal 18:2 (Winter 73):197-213; revised and reprinted as "The Law of the Mystery Writers vs. the Law of the Courts" in PCS 1:1 (1977):12-23.
Nevins cites an earlier article on this subject by John Barker Waite (C835) and parts company with him on Waite's contention that a legally

faulty case ruins many a detective story. Nevins believes that the subject of detective fiction is the triumph of truth over falsehood, rather than of law over crime, and discusses this point with numerous examples.

C581. ______. "Law, Lawyers and Justice in Popular Fiction and Film." Humanities Education 1:2 (May 84):3-12.
Describes a "law and literature" seminar created by the author and taught by him at St. Louis University Law School. Materials from mystery fiction used in the course have included the works of Melville Davisson Post, Arthur Train, Erle Stanley Gardner, Ellery Queen, Joseph Wambaugh, and others. The article includes brief descriptions of these materials and why they are relevant to the course. (REB)

C582. ______. "Name Games: Mystery Writers and Their Pseudonyms." In Ball (B15), pp. 343-58.
Writers and their pseudonyms and the reasons they adopt them.

C583. Nevins, Francis M., Jr.; Yates, Donald A.; Washer, Robert E.; Donaldson, Norman; and Hubin, Allen J. "Social and Political Images in American Crime Fiction." TAD 5 (1971/72):61-78.
Transcript of a panel discussion, chaired by Nevins, held on April 10, 1971,at a Popular Culture Association meeting, Michigan State University. The panel (and members of the audience) responded to this question: is mystery fiction a politically and socially conservative literature? There seemed to be some general agreement that all art is political to some extent but there was very little agreement on the political commitment of particular writers although the British mystery is seen as more establishment-oriented and the American hard-boiled tradition as more resistant to the system. An important topic and an intelligently guided discussion.

C584. Nicolson, Marjorie. "The Professor and the Detective." Atlantic Monthly 143 (April 1929): 483-93. Reprinted in Men and Books (NY: R. R. Smith, 1930), edited by Malcolm S. Smith and Elisabeth K. Holmes, pp. 315-33; in Haycraft (B142), pp. 110-27; and in Cremante/Rambelli (B78), pp. 43-51.
Professor Nicolson attributes academic interest in detective fiction to a surfeit of the contemporary "psychological," subjective, realistic novel and a desire to return to the currently out-of-fashion novel of plot and incident. It appeals to the intellect, is impersonal in tone and manner and, like the puzzle, must be rigorously worked out. Nicolson thinks that it is a male genre in contrast to the "feminized" contemporary novel and women have only two roles, as victim and villainess. A nod is given to the "three or four women who have written surprisingly good detective novels of the purest type." She compares the detective's work to that of the research scholar or scientist.

C585. Niceforo, Alfredo. "Lontani e lontanissimi precursori del romanzo giudiziario moderno |Distant and very distant precursors of the modern judiciary novel|." Il Secolo XX (1917), pp. 767-72.
According to the author, a criminologist of the scientific school, the judiciary novel, whose literary forms end in Poe and in Balzac, has numerous percursors. He cites two examples: Volaire's novel Zadig (1979) and the Declamations of the 1st to 2nd century A. D., attributed erroneously to Quintilian. He points out, in passing, the novels of James Fenimore Cooper, set among the Indians; Le Voyage et les aventures de trois princes de Sarendip, translated (from Italian and not from Persian) by the Chevalier de Mailly (1719); and the 3rd novella (also found in the

Thousand and One Nights) of the Novellina (13th-14th centuries). He observes that whereas in the judiciary novel the solving of the mystery comes about through the merit of an individual of exceptional gifts, in reality the modern instructional judge bases his research on the objective methods furnished by science. The author uses the expression romanzo poliziesco, which should be compared to the French roman policier. (LR)

C586. Nieminski, John. "Pow-Wow on the Potomac. A Report on Bouchercon XI." TMF 4:6 (Nov/Dec 80):12-18.
In addition to the Bouchercon report, there are also a number of candid, sometimes irreverent photographs (pp. 19-30) taken by Nieminski.

C587. Nietzel, Michael T., and Baker, Robert. "Eye to Eye: A Survey of the Private Eye Writers of America." TAD 16 (83):228-34.
Ratings of a number of private eyes (1920-70 and 1970-82) by writers in the field.

C588. Nilsén, Rolf. "Politiska thrillers och vardagsbrott |Political thrillers and everyday crime|." Jury 9:1 (1980):56-59.
Real-life crime and political thrillers from 1914 on. (MS)

C589. Niven, Larry. "The Last Word about SF Detectives." In his The Long Arm of Gil Hamilton, pp. 177-82. NY: Ballantine, 1976. Wraps.
An afterword to his novel in which he talks about cross-over works of science fiction with detective story elements.

C590. "The Noble Art of Mystery." Nation 125 (14 Sep 27):242.
Mystery novels are not inferior to other kinds of fiction and are honorable descendents of the Gothic romance.

C591. Nordberg, Nils. "Ar 151 -- Norske kriminalromaner i aret som gikk |Year 151 -- Norwegian crime novels in the past year|." Jury 6:1 (1977):36-42. (MS)

C592. ______. "Norge 1972 -- en kriminell översikt |Norway 1972 -- a criminal overview|." Jury 2:1 (1973): 24-27, 47-48.
Review of the year's activity. (MS)

C592a. Nussbaum, Albert F. "Versimilitude in the Crime Story." The Writer 84:1 (Jan 71):13-15.
Errors and clichés in crime fiction that destroy versimilitude.

C593. Nusser, Peter. "Neuansaetze des deutschen Kriminalromans der Gegenwart |New beginnings of the contemporary German crime novel|." Wirkendes Wort 31:5 (1981):309-34.
Academic discussion of the new style of crime novel being written in Germany since the 1960s. Nusser notes and argues that the new style of novel has become realistic in the way of Simenon and is used as a vehicle of social criticism, similar to the novels of Sjöwall and Wahlöö. The works of Jacob Wittenbourg, Richard Hey, Irene Rodrian, Michael Molsner and Horst Bosetzky are discussed. (GG)

C594. Nye, Russel. "Murderers and Detectives." In his The Unembarrassed Muse, pp. 244-68. NY: The Dial Press, 1970.
A good capsule history of American detective fiction, marred by careless errors ranging all the way from misspellings (Luther "Trent" and "Saxe" Rohmer) to more serious matters: the claim that Ellery Queen won a

$7500 prize contest for The Roman Hat Mystery (that's not the way it happened), the repeated references to John D. MacDonald's Travis McGee and Donald Hamilton's Matt Helm as "hard-boiled dicks," the claim that there were 40 Fu Manchu books (rather than 14), and the gaffe of crediting The Third Man to Eric Ambler rather than to Graham Greene. Nye also, in true chauvinist fashion, segregates female authors in a category of their own, grouping everyone from Mary Roberts Rinehart to Mabel Seeley to Helen McCloy to Emma Lathen under the same rubric. (REB)

C595. Obstfield, Raymond. "Opus in G Minor Blunt Instrument: The Development of Motive in Detective Fiction." TAD 14 (1981):9-13.

The portrayal of the murderer and his motive and society's attitude toward crime and the criminal.

C596. Ocampo, Victoria. "Detective Story: An English Institution." Books Abroad 16 (Jan 42):38-39.

A short excerpt from the Argentinian journal Sur on the "surprising" predilection of intellectuals for detective fiction. Ocampo is an important Argentinian editor and writer, and Sur has included discussions of detective fiction by Borges and others.

C597. Odell, Ruth. "Mystery Fiction." American Speech 25 (1950): 310-11.

On the origins and meanings of "whodunit," whydunit" and "howdunit."

C598. O'Faoláin, Seán. "Give Us Back Bill Sikes." The Spectator, 15 Feb 35, pp. 242-43.

On the lack of characterization in detective fiction.

C599. Olivier-Martin, Yves. "Origines secrètes du roman policier français |Secret origins of the French detective novel|." Europe, no. 571/2 (Nov/Dec 76): 144-49.

Newspaper serial stories and mainstream detective fiction.

C600. Ollie, James G. "the Literature on the Detective Story." Library World 62 (July 60):11-14.

A narrative survey of critical writings on detective fiction. Includes general historical studies, biographies and reader-guides. No articles included.

C601. Orel, Harold. "The American Detective-Hero." JPC 2:3 (Winter 1968):395-403.

Contributions to the creation of the American detective-hero by Poe, Futrelle, Post, Hammett and Chandler and by Ross Macdonald who has added "compassion to the hard-boiled story." Orel sees this latest contribution as justifying the claim of detective fiction to be a part of the humanistic tradition. The conclusion is a debatable one and the author does not prepare for it or illustrate it sufficiently.

C602. O'Riordan, Conal. "The Vicious Circle." The New Statesman, 28 June 30, pp. 364-65.

Notes on crime fiction. Slight.

C603. Orowan-Cornish, Florella. "A Sense of Unreality: Noir in Fiction." Noir Newsletter (1980). Distributed by Fiction, Literature and the Arts Bookstore, The Arcade, 318 Harvard Street, Cambridge, MA.

Large size--11 X 14--one-page broadside containing a three-column article attempting to characterize noir fiction. Includes a checklist of representative, in-print titles, both mystery and non-mystery. Crumley's The Last Good Kiss and Gores' Hammett are both listed as "noir parodies." (REB)

C604. Orr, Clifford. "Miss Clink and Mr. Crump Talk Mysteries." PW 116 (20 July 29):256-7.
Photo of mystery writer Orr. A comical dialogue on the saleability of mysteries that follow the conventions.

C605. Orwell, George. "Grandeur et décadence du roman policier anglais |Grandeur and decadence of the English detective novel|." Fontaine nos. 37-40 (Algiers, 1944): 69/213-75/219.
The original English essay was translated into French by Fernand Auberjonois and the English version has not been published separately. Orwell sees a deterioration from 1920-40 as violence increases in the English detective novel. In the period 1880-1920, Orwell discusses the qualities of the three masters (Doyle, Ernest Bramah and R. Austin Freeman), speaking of their leisurely plots, abundant detail and digressions. According to Orwell, Chesterton and Edgar Wallace are the only two "moderns" who make us believe in their detectives. After 1920, mysteries have, says Orwell, as little to do with literature as the construction of crossword puzzles.

C606. ______. "Raffles and Miss Blandish." Horizon 10 (Oct 44): 232-44. Reprinted in his Dickens, Dali, and Others: Studies in Popular Culture (NY: Reynal and Hitchcock, 1946), pp. 202-221; in Mass Culture: The Popular Arts in America (Glencoe, IL: Free Press, 1957), edited by Bernard Rosenberg and David Manning White, pp. 154-64; in The Collected Essays, Journalism and Letters of George Orwell (NY: Harcourt, Brace, 1968), edited by Sonia Orwell and Ian Angus, Vol. III, pp. 212-24; in The Art of the Essay (NY: Thomas Crowell, 1958), edited by Leslie Fiedler, pp. 465-76; and in Buchloh/Becker 2 (B61), pp. 208-25.
This essay is clearly related to the essay in Fontaine (C605), published the same year, but instead of writing generally on the deterioration of the detective novel as violence increases, Orwell focuses on the same phenomenon in Hornung's novels about the gentleman crook, Raffles, and James Hadley Chase's No Orchids for Miss Blandish. There is, he believes, a significant change in morality between the two novels (and, by implication, the periods in which they were written). Raffles is a gentleman with standards that are not to be violated; in Chase, there is the assumption that power dictates its own prerogatives, and those include excessive tolerance of violence against the system, others and even oneself. Orwell compares Chase's novel to William Faulkner's Sanctuary and deplores the Americanization of the English crime novel.

C607. Osborne, E. A. "Collecting Detective Fiction." The Bookman, Feb 32, pp. 287-88.
Useful information on some of the earlier writers such as Poe and Gaboriau. Brief mention of some later authors - Mrs. Meade, Doyle, Collins. (RCSA)

C608. O'Toole, L. M. "Analytic and Synthetic Approaches to Narrative Structure. Sherlock Holmes and the 'Sussex Vampire'." In Style and Structure in Literature, edited by Roger Fowler, pp. 142-76. Ithaca, NY: Cornell University Press, 1975.

Using methodological systems developed by Russian formalist critics, O'Toole analyses Conan Doyle's story, "The Adventure of the Sussex Vampire." The article, in addition to its contribution to critical readings of the Holmes canon, is of interest as an example of modern critical methods applied to genre fiction.

C609. "Out of the Ordinary: The Novel of Pursuit and Suspense." TLS, 25 Sept 55, pp. vi-vii.
Novelists of international intrigue: Buchan, Ambler, Greene, Innes and others. A rapid survey.

C610. Overton, Grant. "A Breathless Chapter." In his American Nights Entertainment, pp. 51-63. New York and London: Appleton, 1923.
A casual, chatty ramble through the works of some of Overton's favorite writers, including Emile Gaboriau.

C611. ______. "Where the Plot Thickens." In When Winter Comes to Main Street, pp. 68-77. NY: Doran, 1922.
Reviews of books by, among others, Hulbert Footner, Frank L. Packard, Sapper, Albert Payson Terhune and Mrs. Belloc-Lowndes. There is interview material in the discussions of Terhune and Footner.

C612. Pacheco, Audrey I. "In Search of the Female Protagonist." TMRN 5:4 (1972):23-25. Addenda in a letter by Francis M. Nevins, Jr., in 5:5:17-20.
An informal description (with lists) of some works by several novelists with female protagonists.

C613. Paladini, Vinicio. "Giallo." Quadrivio, 1 Apr 34, p. 7.
Everything is derived from Poe: "The Pleasure of the logical construction of the 'Murders in the Rue Morgue' and of 'The Mystery of Marie Roget' is similar to that of the illogical creation of 'The Fall of the House of Usher'." The essential components of the detective novel, logic and fright, are the product of a modern form of fantasy which has a liking for mental abstractions, whether they are hallucinations or mathematical reasonings, surrealism or functional architecture. From this type of fantasy spring other manifestations of modern life which together with the giallo constitute an important chapter in culture: bridge, puzzle, jazz, Luna Park. (LR)

C614. Parrinder, Patrick. "George Orwell and the Detective Story." JPC 6 (1973):692-97; reprinted in Landrum (B216), pp. 64-67.
Parrinder cites Orwell's two essays (C605, C606) on detective fiction to show that he was an early and astute critic of popular literature.

C615. "The Passing of the Detective." The Academy (London), 30 Dec 1905, pp. 1356-57; reprinted in Haycraft (B142), pp. 511-12; and in Buchloh/Becker 2 (B61), pp. 38-40.
As modern methods of crime detection become more prevalent, the fictional "great detective" will fade from the scene and become, like the dodo, extinct.

C616. Paterson, John. "A Cosmic View of the Private Eye." SR 36 (22 Aug 53):7-8, 31-33. Illus.
Paterson contrasts the transcendant detective of the puzzle novel with the private eye. He sees Sam Spade as a sympathetic figure, lonely, even tragic; Philip Marlowe is a moralist, perhaps a prude. Since Hammett and Chandler the detective has deteriorated into the softboiled, sentimental

hero. In the issue of Oct 31, 1953, Anthony Boucher replies that there are inaccuracies in Paterson's discussion and he fails to deal adequately with the contemporary scene. Paterson's rejoinder is that Boucher is wrong to say that Spillane's Mike Hammer bears no relation to the detectives of Hammett and Chandler and maintains that, like their characters, Hammer is an "executor of private justice," even if in a debased and degenerate form.

C617. Patrick, Q. ; Quentin, Patrick; and Stagge, Jonathan. "Who'd Do It?" Chimera 5:4 (Summer 47):12-17.
Patrick/Quentin/Stagge (Richard Wilson Webb and Hugh Wheeler) talk about the plight of the "poor" detective writer who, in accepting genre limitations, inhibits his growth. A somewhat tongue-in-cheek essav.

C618. Paul, Elliot. "Whodunit." Atlantic Monthly 168 (July 41):36-40; reprinted in Burack (B62), pp. 164-72.
Paul rejects the theory that the best detective stories are intellectual puzzles constructed according to proscriptive rules. He speaks of the salubrious qualities of the detective novel for allowing the reader to experience violence vicariously and thinks the future of the genre is in Simenon's reconciliation of a "profound humanity with the mystery-story form." He also ventures a guess that the majority of detective story readers are women.

C619. Pavolini, Corrado. "Giallo cromo |The yellow giallo|." Scenario, Sept 35, pp. 471-74.
The detective novel, although placing itself at the antipodes of literature, ends by raising "a conspicuous question of esthetics." The rough and elementary writing (common to other non-literary productions like private letters, intimate diaries, chronicles of ugly facts) through its absolute finality produces strongly evocative effects and suggestions which have something "metaphysical." The detective novel is the only modern genre in which a "mythical" dimension of existence is manifested. The sense of the myths of metamorphoses comes again to life in the unstoppable and extraordinary transformations experienced by the characters of the detective novel according to the lights and shadows which the suspect, from time to time, throws upon them. (LR)

C620. ______. "Non vi lascierà dormire |He won't let you sleep|." L'Italia letteraria, 18 Oct 31, p. 7. (The title reproduces the publicity slogan used by publisher Arnold Mondadori to launch his anthology I Libri gialli).
The author objects to a statement by A. Bruers (C135) that writers cannot draw any instruction from the detective narrative because literature and detective fiction are two profoundly different realities and devoid of points of contact. In the detective novel "the characters are brutally presented as in a documentary film, and just as in a piece of discarded film are suddenly, in a broken gesture, abandoned to their fate." Nevertheless the genre, because of its lack of definition, exercises a strong attraction for intellectuals. (LR)

C620a. Pearce, Jack. "Crime Writer's Bookshelf." The Writer 58:2 (Feb 45):53-54.
Books on criminal investigation with which the crime writer should be familiar.

C620b. Peck, Harry Thurston. "The Detective Story." In his Studies in Several Literatures, pp. 257-78. NY: Dodd, Mead, 1909.

Voltaire's Zadig, Poe, Gaboriau and Doyle. Peck sees Poe as the intellectual, Gaboriau as the great constructor of plots, and Doyle as the introducer of the human element, the great fictional character.

C621. Pederin, Ivan. "Na Izvoristima Trivigalne Knjizevnosti: Njemacka Sablasna Pripovedka (Geistergeschichte) i Engleska Gotska Privopedka (Gothic Story) Prema Kriminalistickom Romanu." Izraz 22 (1978):1517-33.
On the derivation of detective novels from Gothic Fiction. Not seen.

C622. Pederson-Krag, Geraldine. "Detective Stories and the Primal Scene." Psychoanalytic Quarterly 18 (1949): 207-14; reprinted in Most/Stowe (B264), pp. 13-20.
An early attempt to apply Freudian concepts to the reader's pleasure in the detective story. Rejecting the usual theories of reader identification, Dr. Pederson-Krag, insisting upon the element of curiosity satisfied by the genre, relates the reader's fascination with the crime and its investigation to a less threatening version of the "primal scene" in which the child witnesses the parents' sexuality and rejects it.

C623. Pellegrini, Giuseppe. "Un filone della letteratura popolare |A vein of popular literature|." La Fiera Letteraria, 5 May 57, p. 4.
The author describes the characteristics of the suspense genre (introduced into Italy especially by the publisher Longanesi of Milan who published an anthology entitled "Suspense"), and briefly traces its history from the economic depression of the thirties to the period after World War II, from the commercial production of the pulp magazines, "destined for the American reader--pessministic and disappointed--of the crisis," to the revolutionary texts of novelists like Hammett, Chandler, Burnett, Latimer, and Cain. (LR)

C624. Pellizzi, Camillo. "Variazioni sul 'giallo' |Variations of the giallo|." Corriere della Sera, 20 Dec 37.
The author, particularly attentive to the sociology of literature, reflects on the fact that historical periods survive in the "picturesque" testimonies of the fables and the legends which in those ages are born through the merit of poets, professional storytellers and "fabricators" of literary genres like the modern detective novel. "Detective novels are the epic novels of the modern Protestant middle-class, more or less Anglo-Saxon, Quaker and democratic. And they contain all that psychological, social, environmental truth which emerges from the great legends and is not found for the most part in histories." Those observations are then grafted onto the much debated question about the lack of popular literarature in Italy. (LR)

C624a. Pember, John E. "Clichés in Mystery Stories." The Writer 56:8 (Aug 43):242-44.
Former newspaperman journalist Pember writes engagingly of his least favorite often used expressions and situations. He suggests a return to a "few accepted standards of good English practice."

C625. Penzler, Otto. "The Amateur Detectives." In Ball, The Mystery Story (B15), pp. 83-109.
Penzler discusses some of the famous amateur detectives and notes that although their time seems to have passed, we are more in need of them than ever in an increasingly mechanistic and dehumanized world.

C626. ______. "Collecting Mystery Fiction." TAD 15 (1982):13-17.

General advice to book collectors, some basic booksellers' terms, and an annotated list of reference materials.

C627. ______. "The Great Crooks." In Ball, The Mystery Story (B15), pp. 321-41.
Affectionate comments on great criminals of detective fiction and a regret that they, like the gifted, charming, amateur detective, are largely no longer to be found.

C628. ______. "Incunabular Detective Fiction." In A Miscellany for Bibliophiles, edited by H. George Fletcher, pp. 221-31. NY: Grastorf and Lang, 1979.
Entertaining and informative discussion of early examples of detective fiction with a bibliography and an appendix liting ten of the most significant works before Poe.

C630. Peters, Margot, and Krouse, Agate Nesaule. "Women and Crime: Sexism in Allingham, Sayers, and Christie." Southwest Review 59 (Spring 74):144-52.
The authors come to the somewhat surprising conclusion that, in terms of sexist stereotypes, "Christie offends the least." Sayers, generally considered a feminist, is criticized for selling Harriet Vane into the reactionary "insignificance" of marriage. (KLM)

C631. Phillips, Louis. "The Oddly Colored Thread: Logic in Detective Fiction." TAD 16 (1983):310-13.
An essay on the "violations of deductive reasoning" in detective fiction. The reasoning in these entertainments, claims Phillips in an amusing discussion, should not be confused with the "reasoning that brings us to truth and justice."

C632. Philmore, R., and Yudkin, John. "Inquest on Detective Stories." Discovery (London), April 1938 and September 1938; reprinted in Haycraft (B142), pp. 423-35.
A two part essay. In Part 1, Philmore, a pseudonymous English writer of detective stories, selects five novels in which murders are carried out by medical means; an English physician, Dr. John Yudkin, discusses their medical validity. In Part 2, Philmore analyzes the plausibility of the psychological motives for committing murder in a number of novels.

C633. Pike, Barry A. "Pen Profiles."
A series of biographical and critical pròfiles of writers and their detective protagonists. The column has appeared regularly in The Poisoned Pen since volume 2, number 2, and most of the writers profiled have been British. Entries in the series will be recorded in the Author section with volume, issue and pagination information.

C634. Pintilie, Petro. "Deckaren i öst |The detective novel in the East|." Jury 9:1 (1980):13-17. Translated by Ioan Gindi and Hans Stertman.
Espionage, puzzle novels and whodunits in the U.S.S.R., Czechoslovakia, Hungary, Bulgaria and East Germany. About thirty writers are discussed. (MS)

C635. ______. "Polisromanen i Rumanien |The police novel in Rumania|." DAST 12: (1979): 53-54. Translated by Ioan Gindi. (MS)

C636. Piovene, Guido. "Libri gialli a Londra |Gialli in London|." Corriere della sera, 27 Apr 35.
The author, at the time of the publication of this article, was the London

correspondent for the Corriere (Milan). He catalogues the principal reasons why, in his opinion, detective fiction flourishes principally in England and America. 1. The English press, following the rule of Sherlock Holmes ("that which is is not"), keeps the detective instinct alive in the public and therefore creates a need for the detective novel. 2. The genre was born in countries, like England, where social differences are marked, because the crime must take place in an aristocratic environment about which people are inclined to fantasize. 3. The rigor of the English law, which foresees the penalty of death, makes the struggle of the murderer to escape the gallows an emotional one. 4. The literary model of detection derives from the model of the Anglo-Saxon policeman who before arresting a suspect must provide real proof to demonstrate his guilt. 5. The London metropolis, considered by the English as something threatening which is never defeated, is reflected in the detective novel ("in the metropolis a murderer gets lost," "the metropolis itself struggles against the police"). 6. The typical idea of the murderer of the detective novels finds its archetype in Dr. Jekyll and is fed by a certain Protestant manicheism, diffused in the popular consciousness, which separates and contrasts good and bad instincts in two distinct categories. (LR)

C637. Plummer, Bonnie C. "Humor and the Detective: Who's Laughing Now." Clues 3:2 (Fall/Winter 82):17-23.

The changing nature of humor in the detective novel as seen in Poe, Hammett, William DeAndrea and Lawrence Block.

C638. Podolsky, Edward. "Writing the Detective Story." The Writer 36:1 (Jan 24): 2-3.

The field is a wide one but the writer should read up on modern methods of criminal investigation. Brief comments on the deductive detective (Holmes), the psychological detective (Balmer and MacHarg's Luther Trant), and the scientific detective (Craig Kennedy and Scientific Sprague).

C639. Poli, Vincenzo. "Treatro giallo della malora |Giallo theater of ruin|." Corriere padano, 24 Dec 35.

A defense of the giallo against the arguments of E. Terracina. The author attributes the birth of the detective novel to the tensions of modern society which are manifested in America earlier than elsewhere and are echoed in Europe: from a criminality, fed by immigration, to the rise of the great cities, in which millions of readers ask the printed page to satisfy the growing thirst for sensations. The novel is followed by the detective drama which has its own tradition because it is connected with the Grand Guignol of which it is the natural and logical continuation on a plane of greater artistic decorum. (LR)

C640. Porter, Dennis. "Backward Construction and the Art of Suspense." In Most/Stowe (B264), pp. 327-40. An abridgment of an essay that originally appeared as chapter 2 of his book The Pursuit of Crime (B315).

The ways in which writers of detective fiction handle the creation of suspense in a narrative in which the effect is revealed before the cause.

C641. Portugal, Eustace. "Death to the Detectives!" The Bookman, Spring special number (April 1933), p. 28.

A discussion of the author's favorite detectives and whether or not he would like to see them bumped off. He is charitable to most and fears Lieutenant Valcour above all the others. (RCSA)

C642. Portuondo, José Antonio. "Holmes y Lupin de América |The Holmes and Lupin of America|." Americas 6:9 (Sept 54):13-16, 26-27.
Well-researched article by the author of En torno de la novela policial (B316) on the history of crime fiction in Latin America, especially that of Argentina and Chile. States that the genre began in Latin America with the appearance of Alberto Edwards' stories in Pacifico Magazine about Roman Calvo, the Chilean Sherlock Holmes, then flowered in the 1930s, inspired by Doyle, Gaboriau, and Leblanc. Later, in the 1950s, the Latin American crime story became more naturalistic and psychological, for example with Ensayo de un crime by Usigli, which Portuondo praises highly. (GG)

C643. ______. "La novela policial revolucionaria |The revolutionary detective novel|." Introduction to, La Justicia por su mano, by José Lamadrid Vega, pp. 7-15. Havana: Editorial de arte y literatura, 1973.
A brief history of the detective novel as a "bourgeois" genre followed by a discussion of a new revolutionary form in which human justice and legality will go hand in hand.

C644. Post, Melville Davisson. "The Blight." Sat Eve Post, 26 Dec 1914, pp. 21-25.
On the need to recognize the ""primacy of storytelling."

C645. ______. "The Mystery Story." Sat Eve Post, 27 February 1915, pp. 21- 23.
Rules are necessary to art and in this, the age of the mystery short story, these rules should be observed: unified plot, agreeable characters, essentialities, incidents taken from life, surprise at the end but not an "outside" explanation.

C647. Powers, Richard Gid. "J. Edgar Hoover and the Detective Hero." JPC 9:2 (1975/76): pp. 257-78; reprinted in Landrum (B216), pp. 203-27.
Hoover in the self-created role of archetypal detective.

C648. Powys, John Cowper. "The Crime Wave in Fiction." The World Today (London), Sept 29, pp. 317-22.
An attempt to explain the popularity of crime fiction. Some discussion of the appeal for a masculine audience and the suspicion that crime fiction may give incentives to real crime.

C649. Prezzolini, Giuseppe. "Il romanzo poliziesco è frutto della civiltà moderna |The detective novel is the fruit of modern civilization|." L'Illustrazione italiana, July 1953, pp. 55-60.
Basing his argument on a famous essay of Chesterton (C178), the author, one of the leaders of 20th century Italian culture, sees in the theme of the city one of the fundamental elements of detective literature. "The taste for the giallo is a taste of city dwellers educated to see the imposing operations of the intelligence as something other than breathing the supernatural air of vices and delights which ripen over the city." A new facet of the modern American city is mirrored by the hard-boiled school which brings to the genre basic stylistic innovations. In connection with the technique of the novel where everything centered on the action, the author traces a parallel between the criminal and the detective and the masks of the ancient commedia dell'arte. (LR)

C650. Procter, Maurice. "The Criminal Seen by the Policeman." In Gilbert (B124), pp. 39-52.

An anecdotal discussion by a detective novelist and former policeman of the British policeman's approach to and understanding of criminals.

C651. "Projet de crime parfait |Project for a perfect crime|." Organographes du cymbalum pataphysicum 1 (n.d.): 41-45.
A schematic presentation of the nature of perfect crimes (legal or esthetic) and two appendices, one on perfect crimes involving God, the other on projects to be undertaken by the pataphysical detective research group OULIPOPO which include committing actual perfect crimes and imaginary ones. The usual pataphysical mix of the serious and the playful.

C652. Proll, Harry. "Die Wirkung der Kriminalromane (|he effect of crime novels|." In Vogt (B424), Vol. II, pp. 500-15. Previously published in Zeitschrift fuer Politische Psychologie und Sexualoekomomie (1938).
Interesting argument by a socialist writer quite well-read in the genre. Proll argues that the popularity in Germany of crime fiction represents needs in the mass of the reading public to be liberated from capitalism. He then calls for a socialist popular literature that would be as exciting and fun to read as is capitalist-influenced crime fiction. (GG)

C653. Pronzini, Bill. "Popular Library." CP? 2:1 (March 80):7-14. Illustrated.
History of the paperback publishing house.

C654. ______. "The Saga of the Phoenix That Probably Should Never Have Arisen." TAD 10 (1977):106-11. Illus.
A survey of Phoenix Press, a 1930s publishing house, and some of their forgettable authors. In an addendum, Pronzini and F. M. Nevins, Jr. exchange letters on several points in the article. See also: Pronzini, letter 10:273; Mary Groff, letter 10:378.

C655. "The Publisher's Share." TLS, 25 June 61, p. xi. From a "correspondent."
The roles of the editor and the publisher in the writing and marketing of crime fiction.

C656. "Publishing Detective Novels." TLS, 25 Sept 51, p. vii.
A response to Edmund Wilson (C867). The "correspondent" claims that the question is not one of quality but of recognition. Cites the Crime Club series as an example of quality.

C657. Pudlowski, Gilles. "De la série noire aux polars marrons |From the série noire to the maroon polar|." NL, 17-24 March 77, p. 6.
Reflections on the present and future of Gallimard's série noire, on the occasion of the death of founder Marcel Duhamel. A recent addition to the French language has been the term "polar" which is now generally used in the popular press and much journal criticism to refer to the roman policier |detective novel|.

C658. ______. "La Marée noire du nouveau polar |The dark tide of the new polar|." NL, no. 2717 (1979), p. 19. Illus.
Série noire and new trends in the field.

C659. Queen, Ellery. "The Detective Short Story: The First Hundred Years." In Haycraft (B142), pp. 476-91. A revised version of the Introduction to Queen's anthology 101 Years' Entertainment: The Great Detective Stories,

1841-1941 (Boston: Little, Brown, 1941), pp. v-xviii; an excerpt appears in SRL 24 (22 Nov 41):5-7.
A history and typology of the detective short story and of short story anthologies. For a more complete bibliographical coverage of the subject, see Queen's The Detective Short Story (A133).

C660. ______. "Introduction." In Ellery Queen's Japanese Golden Dozen, edited by Ellery Queen, pp. 7-12. Rutland, VT: Charles E. Tuttle, 1978.
Ellery Queen was commissioned by the Suedit Corporation of Japan to select twelve Japanese mystery short stories. The introduction gives information on the history of Japanese mysteries and writers, as well as on the Mystery Writers of Japan and Japanese mystery magazines while the chapter heads contain profiles of the writers selected for inclusion. In the inimitable Queen manner, Queen relates how he searched for information on Japanese crime fiction and sifted through 2,500 stories -- the resultant introduction itself is almost as suspenseful as a mystery story.(GG)

C661. ______. "Leaves from the Editors' Notebook." In Haycraft (B142), pp. 406-16.
Short critical commentaries on a variety of subjects taken from the introductory notes to stories published in EQMM.

C662. "Quincunx." "In General." SR (London), 6 Dec 30, p. 746.
On the limitations of detective fiction and the inhibiting effect of a steady diet of such material on the mind.

C663. "Quintus Quiz." "Mental Holidays." Christian Century 51:30 (25 July 34):968.
An editorial, presented as a "letter-to-the-editor," touting the reading of a detective story as a mental holiday taking the reader into an artificial world.

C664. ______. "A Resolution and a Protest." Christian Century 56:6 (8 Feb 39):177-78.
A complaint that detective stories are now too ingenious and writers are not playing fair with readers. Kurt Steel replies, in a letter in the May 17, 1939 issue, p. 646, that some writers do pay attention to maintaining a general reader's interest in a story longer on "human sympathy" than on ingenuity.

C665. ______. "Should Serious Persons Read Thrillers?" Christian Century 62 (12 Sept 45):1033.
A letter to the editor in which "Q.Q." defends serious people's right to read frivolous material like thrillers.

C666. Raabe, Juliette. "Le Phénomène série noire |The série noire phenomenon|." In Arnaud (B12), pp. 290-302. Discussion follows on pp. 302-11.
A first-rate article on the Gallimard series of paper editions of detective novels. Although the series is usually thought as being largely translations of American fiction, Raabe points out that 25% of the books are either British or French. The expression série noire suggests a readily identifiable kind of fiction and Raabe analyzes some of its elements, using Robert Page-Jones' Capot (1966) as a model for an extended analysis. Although detective fiction has aroused a great deal of negative criticism, Raabe presents it as an "intersection" where the serious and

genre novel meet and where the boundaries that separate them dissolve. In the discussion, Raabe talks about editorial policies and the readership and expands on her analysis of structures.

C667. Radius, Emilio. "Autarchia ed etica del romanzo giallo |Autarchy and ethics of the giallo|." Corriere della sera, 29 Apr 39.
The extensive publication in Italy of detective novels, most of them of foreign authorship, poses, according to Radius, "an autarchial problem," and, at the same time, "a moral problem." In order not to import, along with their narrative, social models which are not suitable for Italians, the Italian authors will have to dedicate themselves to the genre and produce a truly national detective novel, much more independent from the canonical rules fixed by Anglo-Saxon authors. He points out a prime example in a novel by A. Lanocita. (LR)

C668. Raffaelli, Raffaella. "Il genere poliziesco in Italia prima del 1928: Le collane a carattere poliziesco |The detective genre in Italy before 1928: detective-type series|." Problemi 65 (1982), pp. 230-41.
Documented, rigorous analysis of the early fortunes of detective literature in Italy. While at its origin, with the first translations of Conan Doyle and Leroux, "there was not yet any awareness of the differences in form and content which separate the detective novel from the feuilleton (serial) literature," a specific initiative begins in 1915 with the series "I Romanzi polizieschi" for the Milanese publisher, Sonzogno, dedicated almost completely to the "Avventure di William Tharps, celebre poliziotto ingelese," of Giorgio Meirs. With this and other collections one witnesses "the first consciousness of the existence of detective fiction as an autonomous genre." With Ventura Almanzi's Le avventure del poliziotto americano Ben Wilson, published by Bietti (Milan) from 1914-1920, finally appears the first example in Italian of the American roman noir, even if the new elements are embedded "in a cornerstone which still preserves elements of the serial and adventure novels of the 19th century." (RC)

C669. Rambelli, Loris. "Il rovescio del mondo alla rovescia |The upsetting of the topsy-turvy world|." Orient Express I (1982), pp. 67-70.
The carnival milieu of many detective novels leads the author to relate the giallo to the carnival, in the sense that the "giallo is the carnival in reverse, or the reverse of the world in reverse," a game of mirrors "that is resolved in plays on words and in errors of logic." (RC)

C670. Ramsey, G. C. "Criticism and the Detective Story." TAD 1 (1967):90-93.
Ramsey notes that mystery fiction has received little serious critical attention, describes the reasons he sees for this and answers reservations expressed by some critics.

C671. Raskin, Richard. "The Pleasures and Politics of Detective Fiction: A Functional Approach." (Pre)publications 52 (1979):3-57. Published by L'Institut d'Etudes romanes, Université d'Aarhus. Bibliography.
An overview of the explanations of the satisfactions of reading detective stories and their politics: how they may "reinforce or...modify certain of the reader's conceptions, values or behavorial patterns." Raskin considers these functions to be equally applicable to film. There is an appendix ("A General Typology of the Psychological and Social Functions of Literary Work") which is the original source of Raskin's article.

C672. Rausch, G. Ray, and Rausch, Diane Kay. "Developments in Espionage Fiction." KQ 10:4 (Fall 78):71-82.
An historical survey of the genre and its various modes ranging from the heroic to the anti-heroic. A somewhat disorganized, cursory treatment.

C673. Ravegnani, Giuseppe. "Agonia del giallo |Agony of the giallo|." Corriere padano, 21 January 40.
The critic distinguishes, within the genre, two types of narrative structure: the novella, created by Poe, and the novel which, in the tradition of the popular French novel, is identified with Emile Gaboriau. Ravegnani upholds the thesis of the progressive decadence of the genre. (LR)

C674. Rawson, Clayton, and Brown, Fredric. "Science Mysteries Again." UN 4:1 (51):2-3.
A discussion of crossover science fiction/mystery fiction and of problems inherent in the genre.

C675. Raynor, Henry. "Decline and Fall of the Detective Story." Fortnightly 179/new series 173 (Feb 53):125-33.
A valedictory for the classical English story of detection; as there is a decay of belief in thought and reason in society, so has "unreason" overtaken the detective story and the detective hero has departed. Along with the valedictory, there is also an intelligent examination of the sources of the strengths of classical mystery fiction.

C676. Recupito, Anna Maria. "Un secolo di gialli |A century of gialli|." Radiocorriere no. 28, 9-15 Jly 61, pp. 15-17; no. 29, 16-22 Jly 61, pp. 15-17; no. 30, 23-29 Jly 61, pp. 17-18; no. 31, 30 Jly-5 Aug 61, pp. 17-18; no. 32, 6-12 Aug 61, pp. 12-13; no. 33, 13-19 Aug 61, pp. 12-14.
The history of the detective genre (from Poe to Hitchcock) is subdivided into three phases: the first is characterized by the terrifying intrigue of related narrative genres (roman noir, feuilleton, paperback); the second by the classic or psychological giallo and has its golden age near the end of the first world war; in the third, which begins in the second postwar period, the genre divides into several branches of which the most important is the action giallo which with its sentimental, humoristic, and psychoanalytical components uses all the forms of mass communication, such as film, radio, and television. (LR)

C677. "The Red Hand." TLS, 23 June 61, p. 387.
Editorial on the international aspects of mysteries with signs of decreasing hostility in Communist countries toward mysteries. The writer interprets this as a break in the traditional antagonism of the Soviets to this Western, anti-socialist literature.

C678. Redman, Ben Ray. "Decline and Fall of the Whodunit." SR 35 (31 May 52): 8-9, 31-32. Portraits.
The Hammett-Chandler-Spillane genealogy as a demonstration of Redman's thesis.

C679. Reeve, Arthur B. "In Defense of the Detective Story." Independent 75 (10 July 1913):91-94.
A brief history of detective fiction (Poe, Gaboriau, Doyle, dime novels) and the current interest in scientific detection. A defense of the genre to establish it as more likely to serve good ends than as a training ground for criminals.

C680. Reilly, John M. "Classic and Hard-Boiled Detective Fiction." TAD 9:4 (1975/76):289-91, 334.

The analysis of a "fundamental similarity" between classic and hard-boiled detective fiction to show a common attempt to restore an order upset by crime.

C681. ______. "On Reading Detective Fiction." TAD 12:1 (1979):64-65.

The reading of detective stories, with their movement toward resolution of crimes, may be reassuring to readers as an esthetic contrast to "free-floating" anxieties for which there is no clear source, no certain resolution.

C682. ______. "The Politics of Tough-Guy Mysteries." University of Dayton Review 10:1 (Summer 73):25-31.

Reilly describes the politics of the fiction of Hammett and Chandler as "disillusioned populism" which probably both reflects and shapes the culture from which it springs. There is also some discussion of the importance of milieu in Hammett and of Chandler's role in refining the innovations of Hammett.

C683. Remar, Frits. "Danske kriminalromaner i 1976 |Danish crime novels in 1976|." Jury 6:1 (1977):21-23. (MS)

C684. ______. "Deckaren i Danmark |The Detective Novel in Denmark|." Jury 5:4 (1976):39-43.

Development of the detective novel in Denmark. (MS)

C685. Rey, Alain. "Polarités." Littérature no. 49 (Feb 83):43-49.

A discussion of terms (roman policier, detective, récit policier) in an attempt to define them and to characterize their relationship to texts. There is also some examination of specific characteristics of the genre.

C686. Reyes, Alfonso. "Sobre la novela policial |On the detective novel|." In Los trabajos y los días. Mexico: Ed. Occidente, 1945. Not seen.

C687. Reynolds, William. "The Detection Club on the Air: 'Behind the Screen' and 'Scoop'." Clues 4:2 (Fall/Winter 83):1-20.

A study of the contributions of Sayers, Christie, Bentley, Hugh Walpole, Ronald Knox and Anthony Berkeley to a BBC dramatic detective series. The essay is badly organized with vital details (like dates) missing from the text and a reader unfamiliar with the series will find it both perplexing and frustrating. There are copious notes, none of which clarifies the muddle.

C688. ______. "Seven 'Crimefiles' of the 1930s: The Purest Puzzles of the Golden Age." Clues 1:2 (Fall/Winter 80):42-53.

The artifact dossiers of Dennis Wheatley, Helen Reilly and Q. Patrick. (James R. McCahery)

C689. Rhodes, Henry T. F. "The Detective in Fiction--and in Fact." Cornhill, Jan 38, pp. 53-67.

Freeman Wills Crofts has brought a new realism to the detective story and given it a greater respect than it has had. Some comments on the departures from realism in R.A. Freeman and Sayers and the distinctions between real and fictional detectives.

C690. Rice. Craig. "Murder Makes Merry." In Haycraft, The Art of the Mystery Story (B142), pp. 238-44.
Examples of "humor-in-homicide."

C691. Richard, Jean-Pierre. "Petites notes sur le roman policier |Little notes on the detective novel|." Le Français dans le monde 50 (Jly/Aug 67):23-28. Not seen.

C692. Rickman, H. P. "Quixote Rides Again: The Popularity of the Thriller." Clues 3:2 (Fall/Winter 82):9-16.
An analysis of the thriller to distinguish it from the detective story and to establish the reasons for its continuing popularity.

C693. Rivière, François. "Fascination de la réalité travestie |Fascination with travestied reality|." Europe no. 571/72 (Nov/Dec 76):104-117.
A theoretical discussion of the author/reader and victim/criminal/detective relationship in detective fiction. The tricks and deceptions that make of the genre novel a subverting of the illusory conventions of the "bourgeois" novel.

C694. ______. "La Fiction policière ou le meurtre du roman |Detective fiction or the murder of the novel|." Europe no. 671/72 (Nov/Dec 76):8-25.
An attempt to raise detective fiction from the status of an unloved stepchild of the Novel to that of an essential Fiction which "explores signs of the ultimate reality, the one perceived in the mirror of the unconscious."

C695. ______. "Du neuf dans le polar français |The new in the French polar|." NL no. 2714 (1979), pp. 21-22. Illus.
New trends in French mystery fiction.

C696. Rix, Walter T. "Wesen und Wandel des Detektivromans im totalitären Staat |Substance and mutation in the totalitarian state|." In Buchloh/Becker 1 (B60), pp. 121-33; reprinted in Cremante/Rambelli (B78), pp. 195-204.
Takes issue with Haycraft's famous pronouncement (C375) about democracy and detectives by discussing detective novels in Nazi Germany and in post-WW II East Germany. Rix mentions that there were half-a-million copies of detective novels published in Germany in 1939. Makes the interesting point that Anglo-Saxon crime fiction was banned and burned at the time not because of its genre, but because it was foreign. Discusses Communist influences on the crime novels of East Germany. (GG)

C697. Roark, Anne C. "Professors Give an 'A' to Mysteries." Los Angeles Times, 18 Feb 83, pp. 1, 24.
On the greater willingness of academics and university departments to accept popular literature in the curriculum and in research. Some comments on writers, the genre history and the belief that "standards of literary excellence" should be applied to the study of detective fiction.

C698. Roberts, Kenneth. "For Authors Only." Sat Eve Post, 24 Sept 32, pp. 14-15, 46, 48, 50. Photos of A. P. Herbert, Warwick Deeping and J. P. Priestly.
In British mysteries, unlike real life, the crimes are always solved. The heroines are ignorant and, in particular, the obligatory American is inaccurately portrayed (particularly in his speech). The rest of the

article is devoted to Roberts' concerns about the murkiness of the criteria for the Pulitzer Prize for Best American Novel.

C699. Robertson, John M. "The Murder Novel." The Living Age 221 (29 April 1899):267-72.
Not so much on mystery fiction as on murder in fiction and on the recent taste for bloodshed in "serious" novels. (KLM)

C700. Rockwell, Joan. "Normative Attitudes of Spies in Fiction." In Mass Culture Revisited, edited by Bernard Rosenberg and David Manning White, pp. 325-40. NY: Van Nostrand Reinhold Co., 1971.
On the demotion of the British spy from his status in Kipling's Kim as gentleman to his present status as a working-class product with conscious and subconscious feelings of agression toward the upper class. Rockwell also points out there is mutual distrust in the modern spy novel between control agents and their subordinates.

C701. Roeder, Rudolf. "Zur Frage des Kriminalromans |On the question of the crime novel|." Buecherie und Bildung 2 (1950):964-66; reprinted in Vogt (B424), Vol. II, pp. 523-28.
Article by a German librarian on the worth of crime novels. Following Friederich Schiller, Roeder argues that well-written, literary crime novels can be of pedagogical value to society. (GG)

C702. Rogers, Cameron. "We Dare You to Read the First Three Pages." World's Work 49:3 (Jan 25):335-39.
A colorful historical survey of major figures (Doyle, Gaboriau, Rohmer et al) and reviews of some recent books in the field. A sturdy defense of the pleasures of detective fiction.

C703. Rosenbach, A. S. W. "The Trail of Scarlet." Sat Eve Post, 1 Oct 32, pp. 8-9, 32, 34, 36. Illus.
A leisurely essay on Rosenbach's fondness for detectives (although not The Moonstone), on the fascination both writers and the general public exhibit for murder and criminals and appreciative comments on Poe, Dickens, R. L. Stevenson, and Thackeray. The author also describes how he came into the possession of Conan Doyle's reference library which largely consisted of records of court trials and the like.

C704. Ross, Helaine. "A Woman's Intuition: Wives and Lovers in British Golden Age Detective Novels." Clues 2:1 (Spring/Summer 1981):17-25.
Female characters in Sayers, Marsh, Blake and Allingham as wives/lovers and professionals with their own careers.

C705. Ross, Mary B. "They Deal in Intrigue: New England's Mystery Writers." Country Journal 3 (Oct 76):66-71.
Includes Helen McCloy and Miriam Lynch. Portraits. (KLM)

C706. Rossi, Alberto. "Il romanzo criminale |The criminal novel|." Gazzetta del Popolo, 25 Feb 31.
The author translates the expression romanzo criminale as "thriller," a genre which, if it cannot always be defined by "detective" and almost never by "adventures," is, however, in almost all cases focused on a crime. The criminal novel is the 20th century successor to the serial novel, but it requires a different narrative structure and a different reading tempo. The purpose of the crime novel is to hold the attention of the reader for a few hours, "transposing into the novel what was the

characteristic of the short story, of the novella." The "aristocratic perfection" of the genre is in fixing from the beginning the reader's curiosity on one or more elements of the mystery and in maintaining the uncertainty of the solution until the end. All detective fiction achieves more or less the intended purpose because it acts upon two fundamental instincts: the pleasure of discovering the truth and the desire to project into an imaginary existence those possiblities which daily existence does not permit. In short, the crime novel exploits the new need for escape created by the modern city. (LR)

C707. Routley, Erik. "The Case against the Detective Story." In Winks (B434), pp. 161-78; excerpts from material originally published in Routley (B349).
A defense of the detective story on moral, ethic and philosophical grounds against charges of immorality, sexual license and lack of compassion for the vitime. A sensible and compassionate argument for the "puritan pleasures of the detective story."

C708. Roy, David T. "The Fifteenth-Century Sho-ch'ang Tz'u-hu as Examples of Written Formulaic Composition." Chinoperl Papers 10:97-128. Ithaca, NY: The Conference on Chinese Oral and Performing Literature, Cornell University, 1981.
Scholarly examination of one Magistrate Pao chantefable from a collection of woodblock-printed specimens recently found in a 15th century Chinese coffin. Roy's paper is part of the continuing Sinological debate as to the extent to which Chinese written stories (including many detective stories) were copies or transcripts of or promptbooks for oral tales. Of greatest benefit to readers of mystery fiction is Roy's eleven page summary of the story. Illustrated with reproductions of the woodblock text and picture carvings. (GG)

C709. Ruhm, Herbert. "Introduction." In The Hard-Boiled Detective: Stories from Black Mask Magazine (1920-1951), edited by H. Ruhm, pp. viii-xviii. NY: Vintage Books, 1977.

C710. "Rules for Detective Stories by One Who Buys Them." The Writer 46:4 (Apr 34):119-22; 46:5 (May 34):154-57.
In Part One, a discussion of the detective and the plot, defining the various kinds of detective stories; in Part Two, the murder, detection, the culprit (s), and the issue of fairness to the reader.

C711. Russ, Joanna. "Somebody's Trying to Kill Me and I Think It's My Husband: The Modern Gothic." JPC 6 (1972/73):666-91; reprinted in Fleenor (B113), pp. 31-56.
A somewhat irreverent study of the modern "crossbreeds" of Jane Eyre and Rebecca. With an appendix devoted to examples of the following categories: Supermales, heroines, shadowmales and the "other woman."

C712. Rycroft, Charles. "A Detective Story: Psychoanalytic Observations." Psychoanalytic Quarterly 26 (1957):229-45; reprinted in Imagination and Reality (London: Hogarth Press, 1975).
Rycroft maintains that Pederson-Krag (C622) should have included the reader/child/detective-as-criminal in her analysis. He finds support for this in The Moonstone and in Collins' earlier novel Basil.

C713. Sánchez Riva, Arturo. "Genealogía filosófica de la novela policial |Philosophical genealogy of the detective novel|." Sur no. 43 (Sept 46), pp. 69-73.

The "scientific detective" novel was born and died with Poe. A variant is introduced in Chesterton that returns this vagrant genre to the "intellect." Also, some brief, appreciative comments on Borges.

C714. Sandoe, James. "The Case of the Respectable Corpse." PW 143 (20 Feb 43):930-32. Photo of a group of writers including Boucher, Leonore Offord, Lee Thayer and Richard Shattuck.

Sandoe objects to the indifferent treatment mystery fiction is given by many reviewers.

C715. ______. "Dagger of the Mind." Poetry 68 (1946):146-63; reprinted in Haycraft (B142).

A rambling essay based on a talk given on the psychological thriller. Sandoe discusses Margaret Millar, Graham Greene and Freeman Wills Crofts.

C716. Sanguinetti, Edoardo. "In principio era il crimine |In the beginning was the crime|." L'Unità, 13 Dec 79.

In this very brief note the author, poet and critic of the Italian neo-avant-garde, declares himself in agreement with Brecht in maintaining that the giallo "while it is reassuring on the power of rationalization (...), demonstrates its literally posthumous character," underlining its "crafty ethical deceit, which is displayed in its supreme neutralization." The reader, "adopting an abstract and impassive inquisitorial perspective, excludes himself from the risk of projecting himself into a complicity with the guilty one as well as the victim." (RC)

C717. Sannino, Laura. "Appendice II: Nota sulla diffusione della paraletteratura in Italia (1908-1976) |Appendix II: note on the spread of paralitterature in Italy (1908-1976)|." In La Paraletteratura, edited by Noel Arnaud, Francis Lacassin and Jean Tortel, pp. 301-12. Rome: Liguori Editore, 1977.

Chapter written for the Italian edition of Arnaud (B12). Sannino traces rapidly the history of paraliterary forms in Italy but devotes only two brief paragraphs to the spy story and the yellowback (giallo) in which mystery fiction began to reach a wider audience in Italy in the 1960s.

C718. Santucci, Antonio. "Per una storia del romanzo giallo |For a history of the giallo novel|." Il Mulino, no. 1 (1951), pp. 78-86; reprinted in Cremante/Rambelli (B78), pp. 121-29.

The first attempt to lay down the lines of a history of the genre with a serious critical method, by a philosopher particularly close to the neo-illuministic current of the period after the war. Having postulated a definition of the detective novel as a development in narrative form of the techniques of mystery and fear and having excluded the genre from every consideration of an esthetic-literary nature, he fixes the origin in Wilkie Collins and the extreme point of the evolutionary parabola in Ellery Queen when the novel becomes a pure and simple formulation of a problem of logic (almost a reflection of the American schools of positive logic). He illustrates briefly the most notable contribution of the authors examined (Collins, Conan Doyle, Leblanc, Wallace, Simenon, Van Dine, Christie and Queen), and researches the sociological counterpart of the most significant historical stages, with notes directed especially to the Italian situation. (LR)

C719. Sarjeant, William A. S. "Detectives and Geology: An Investigation." TAD 11 (1978):294-97.

Sarjeant praises the geological expertise of R. A. Freeman's Dr.

Thorndyke and mentions some other writers who have used geological data in their works.

C720. Sauder, Rae Norden. "They Kill and Tell." Independent Woman 21 (Oct 42):303, 317-18. Photo.

An article on women mystery writers, based on an interview with Doubleday Crime Club editor, Isabelle Taylor. In spite of the great popularity of mysteries, writing is an avocation for most authors and Sander comments briefly on a number of different women writers. Only the opening section attributes direct quotes to Mrs. Taylor but the rest of the article contains sale figures and "behind-the-scenes" information that should probably be attributed to her.

C721. Savi, Tullio. "Dateci il nostro morto quotidiano (appunti sul libro giallo e i suoi lettori) |Give us our daily dead (notes on the giallo and its readers|." La Cultura Popolare, Feb 61, pp. 8-26.

These notes are intended to serve as a guide to the selecting of texts for a library of popular literature. It is the author's conviction that the detective story is justifiable only if it acts as a stimulus to reading and leads to more intellectually provocative experiences. The author analyzes the main elements of the giallo structure in order to show how its narrative mechanisms are infinitely repeated. The reader must realize this if he is to approach the genre with the proper critical attitude. The author concludes with a catalogue of Italian historical- detective anthologies, arranging them in order of quality. (LR)

C722. Savinio, Alberto. "Ripresa e novità |Revival and originality|." Omnibus, 17 July 37, p. 11.

"The Italian giallo is hypothetically absurd." The author, one of the most original Italian Surrealist writers of the 20th century, gives the reasons he thinks an Italian detective mode would be impossible to maintain. The Italian detective story is condemned to the imitation of foreign models. It does not possess the "criminal romanticism" of the Anglo-Saxon novels and the Italian city and the peaceful bourgeoisie are inadequate for the setting the genre requires. (LR)

C723. Savonuzzi, Luca. "La via italiana al delitto |The Italian road to crime|." Il Resto del Carlino, 24 Aug 76.

Favorable verification of the growing increase, quantitative and qualitative, of Italian writers of gialli. Not always, however, do the new experiments succeed in freeing themselves from that growth on the foot of the Italian giallo which is the "literary complex, the inability to create as an artisan a popular story." (RC)

C724. Sayers, Dorothy L. "Aristotle on Detective Fiction." English, 1 Jan 36, pp. 23-35. Reprinted in Unpopular Opinions, pp. 222-36 (American edition). London: Gollancz, 1946; NY: Harcourt, Brace, 1947. Also in Winks (B434), pp. 25-34; in Vogt (B424), Vol. I, pp. 95-98; and in Cremante/Rambelli (B78), pp. 65-76.

Text of a lecture delivered at Oxford, March 5th, 1935. Aristotle's comments on plotting in Tragedy applied to detective fiction.

C725. ______. Introductions to her Great Short Stories of Detection, Mystery and Horror. First series: London: Gollancz, 1928; NY: Payson & Clarke, 1929 as The Omnibus of Crime. Second Series: London: Gollancz, 1931; NY: Coward-McCann, 1932, The Second Omnibus of Crime. Third Series: London: Gollancz, 1934; NY: Coward-McCann, 1935, The Third Omnibus of Crime.

A landmark series of anthologies with important introductions by Sayers. The first of these has been reprinted frequently, as follows: Haycraft (B142), pp. 71-109; Winks (B434), pp. 53-84; Buchloh/Becker 2 (B61), pp. 142-90; as "Alla slags brott," first publication in Swedish, Goteborg, Korpen, 1977. In the first of the three introductions (pp. 9-47, American edition), Sayers provides a superb history of the genre, with remarks on various techniques and the observation that characters must now be believable and "lively," if not "too profoundly studied." In the second introduction (pp. 11-26, English edition), Sayers discusses the subject of the composition of the "average" detective story and the opinion that someone may find a way to combine the older type of detection machine and the new psychological suspense story. She also talks about the short story which she sees as in a precarious position as editors become more demanding about constraints, making it difficult for writers to move in the direction toward which the longer stories seem to be headed. In the third introduction (pp. 1-7, American edition), Sayers discusses briefly the technique of the detective short story and contrasts it with the horror story and supernatural mystery.

C726. ______. "Introduction." In _Tales of Detection_, edited by Dorothy L. Sayers, pp. vii-xiv. Everyman's Library. London: Dent, 1936.
An introduction to an anthology of short stories which "illustrate certain tendencies in the development of the detective story." An overview of the history of the genre, with comments on "fair play," the intellectualization of the detective story, the "sensation" novelists, thrillers, and a move back toward the novel of character.

C727. ______. "The Present Status of the Mystery Story." _London Mercury_ 23 (Nov 30):47-52.
Mystery stories can--like a sonnet--be "great" within genre restrictions and the works that endure will be a combination of fine writing and common feeling.

C728. ______. "The Sport of Noble Minds." SRL 6:2 (3 Aug 29):22-23.
A short excerpt from her introduction to the _Great Stories_, first series (C725).

C729. ______. "Trials and Sorrows of a Mystery Writer." _Listener_ 7 (6 Jan 32), p. 26.
General essay. (KLM)

C730. Schantz, Tom and Enid. "James Sandoe: A Retrospective." TAD 13 (1980): 288-93.
A tribute to the late researcher and reviewer with some notes by Sandoe on books in his collection.

C731. ______. "With Intent to Deceive: The Not-so-guilty Pleasures of Detective Fiction." _Bloomsbury Review_ (Denver) 2:2 (Feb/March 82):15-16.
A general survey of the contemporary scene with a number of writers and works mentioned.

C732. Schklovskij, Viktor. "Die Kriminalerzaehlung bei Conan Doyle |Conan Doyle's detective stories|." A slightly shortened version of a chapter in his _Teorii prozy_, pp. 129-42. 2nd ed., Leningrad, 1929. Reprinted in Vogt (B424), Vol. I, pp. 76-94; and in Cremante/Rambelli (B78), pp. 23-41.
Academic article on the relation between the "flashback" style of

narration and the detective story, using the Holmes stories as examples. Concludes with an outline of the plot mechanisms of the stories as well as the imputation that some of the plot ideas might have been taken from Poe's "The Gold Bug." (GG)

C733. Schlegov, Y. K. "Opisanie structury detektivnoi novelly (A Description of Detective Story Structure)." In Preprints for the International Symposium on Semiotics (Warsaw, 1968). Reprinted in Recherches sur les systemes signifiants, edited by J. Rey-Debove, pp. 343-72. Mouton: The Hague, 1973.
O'Toole (C608) states that Schlegov deals only wih the "outer story" or prelude to the Sherlock Holmes stories, i. e. the coming together of Holmes, Watson and the client, and the initial narration of the problem before the investigation proper begins. In this prelude, the constituent elements of the inner narrative are exposed before their development and elaboration. It might be noted that the elaborate methodological apparatus brings the critic to the same conclusions that more traditional critics have already reached with much simpler analytical tools.

C734. Schmidt-Henkel, Gerhard. "Kriminalroman und Trivialliteratur |The crime novel and popular fiction|." Sprache im technischen Zeitalter 3 (1962): 202-27. Reprinted in an expanded version in Zmegac (B451), pp. 149-76.
Academic essay which discusses whether detective novels should be considered subliterary. Schmidt-Henkel argues cleverly that there is nothing a priori subliterary about them. One of the few German essayists to mention Rex Stout, John Dickson Carr and Carroll John Daly.(GG)

C735. Schonberg, Harold C. "Writers of Mysteries Compare Notes." New York Times, 15 Dec 83, C17. Photos of Donald Westlake, Stanley Ellin, Robin Winks.
Report on a discussion by a panel of writers of detective fiction, including William Buckley (moderator), Ellin, Westlake, Robert Parker. Also, critic Robin Winks.

C736. Schopen, Bernard A. "From Puzzles to People: the Development of the American Detective Novel." Studies in American Fiction 7:2 (Autumn 79):175-90.
Hammett, Chandler and Ross Macdonald have written novels whose protagonists are detectives but in which the detective format is used for "serious esthetic and moral purposes." Ross Macdonald, in particular, has "expanded" the possibilities of the genre.

C737. Sciascia, Leonardo. "Appunti sul 'giallo' |Notes on the giallo|." Nuova corrente no. 1 (June 54), pp. 23-24.
Taking up again a question raised by E. Vittorini (in Il Politecnico, Jan-March 47), the author maintains that the detective story comes from the English Gothic novel of the 18th century. Both traditions are read psychoanalytically as modern manifestions of the feeling for the sacred. Detective literature is "the literature of the human underground" because it awakens in the reader the unconscious and ambivalent processes of the totem and of the taboo. Comments on the "logical schematizations of the traditional or Victorian novel" and on the "violence, atrocity and sensual degeneration" in the innovations of Spillane. (LR)

C738. ______. "Letteratura del 'giallo' |Literature of the giallo|." Letteratura III (1953):65-67.

The future novelist points out the appropriateness of studying detective literature which, even in its limited existence as a sub-product, has followed the path of the contemporary narrative, "often with mutual exchange of elements" and interesting reciprocal effects, either on the level of thematics (the city, the street "nocturnes") or on the technical/structural level. (LR)

C739. Scott-James, R. A. "Detective Novels." London Mercury 39 (Feb 39):377-79.
Editorial comments on a piece by Howard Spring in the Evening Standard in which he writes of the "devitalizing" effect of the mountains of trashy detective novels. Scott-James distinguishes pure detective fiction from the novel but still lists Sayers' Nine Tailors among the best novels produced since the war.

C740. Scowcroft, P. L. "Murder Isn't Cricket: Some Notes on Cricket in Crime Fiction." The Journal of the Cricket Society 8:3 (Autumn 77):38-42.
Reasonably comprehensive study from Doyle and Hornung through to the 1970s. (RCSA)

C741. ______. "Railways and Detective Fiction." Journal of the Railway and Canal Historical Society 23:3 (Nov 77):87-93.
A study from Victorian to modern times relying, in the short story references, on popular or often anthologized stories. (RCSA)

C742. Seaborne, E. A. "Introduction." In his The Detective in Fiction: A Posse of Eight, edited by E. A. Seaborne. London: G. Bell and Sons, 1931. Not seen.

C743. "The Secret Attraction." TLS, 25 Feb 55, pp. i, ii.
As the classical detective story has declined ("the well has run dry"), the thriller has become more popular. A plea for a thoughtful practitioner to combine sensation with "rightness of form"--as did the Brontes, Hardy, Balzac.

C743a. See, Carolyn. "The Hollywood Novel: The American Dream Cheat." In Madden (B239), pp. 199-217.
Hollywood as the fantasy city where dreams are throught to "come true." Among the writers discussed are Paul Cain, Chandler and Horace McCoy.

C744. Seelye, John. "Buckskin and Ballistics: William Leggett and the American Detective Story." JPC 1:1 (Summer 67): 52-57.
Natty Bumpo, J. F. Cooper's western detective, similarities between western and detective fiction and 4 stories by William Leggett published circa 1820-40 which "fit the detective story pattern." In contrast to Poe's cosmopolitan, European version, Seelye establishes a native American current.

C745. Seldes, Gilbert. "Diplomat's Delight." Bookman 66 (Sept 27): 91-93.
Reviews. Seldes believes that detective fiction should be well written and cites T. S. Eliot in support of his thesis. He is not enthusiastic about S. S. Van Dine.

C746. Seesslen, Georg and Kling, Bernt. "Das Kriminalgenre |The crime genre|." In their Romantik & Gewalt., Vol. I, pp. 236-37. Munich: Manz Verlag, 1973.

Long section in a two-volume encyclopedia-format book on film, sport, music, and the various literary genres. This section on the crime genre has entries for well-known authors, as well as for film stars, directors (e.g. Bogart and Roger Corman), and characters in contemporary German TV and dime novel format crime fiction (e.g. Jerry Cotton and The Commissar). Includes a bibliography of secondary sources. Illustrated with photos of book covers and stills from films and TV shows. (GG)

C747. "Seven Who Do the Whodunits." Newsweek 77 (22 March 71):102-103. Photos.

Brief biographies, with some interview material, of John D. MacDonald, Ellery Queen, Rext Stout, Dorothy Uhnak, Donald Westlake and Mickey Spillane.

C748. Shaginyan, Marietta. "A Defense of the Detective Story." East Europe 10:2 (1961): 20-22. Originally published in Literarni Noviny 15 (Prague, 1960).

A sensitive defense of detective fiction on the grounds that it is artistic, realistic, presents believable characters and is unlike much contemporary literature in its reliance on reason to resolve a "maze of circumstances." Interesting for comments on the official party line which is that detective novels are trash and dangerous to the reader's mental health, a point of view promoted by many critics who privately are devoted to the genre. According to the editor's introduction, such fiction was virtually unobtainable in the USSR at the time of the publication of the article. (RCSA and WA)

C749. Shaw, Joseph T. "Introduction." In The Hard-Boiled Omnibus, pp. v-ix. NY: Simon and Schuster, 1946.

Using the editorial "we," editor Shaw talks about the qualities of Black Mask fiction and its contribution to the mystery field.

C750. Sheed, Wilfred. "The Good Word: It All Depends on Your Genre." NYTBR, 5 Sept 71, pp. 2, 22.

Genre writers are usually hacks, although often gifted ones. Ross Macdonald ventures close to the "serious" novel. Some appreciative comments on Graham Greene's entertainments.

C751. Shibuk, Charles. "The Golden Age of the Detective Story: Its Rise and Fall." TQCB 1:4 (Aug 69):14-16.

Argues that the "golden age" of mystery fiction began in 1920 with the appearance of Freeman Wills Crofts' The Cask and Agatha Christie's The Mysterious Affair at Styles and ended with the onset of World War II in 1939. Agrees with Julian Symons that the novel of crime dominates the field today but sees continuing manifestations of the "classic" form in the work of here unnamed newcomers. (JN)

C752. "Shifting the Apology." SRL 3:7 (11 Sept 26):97.

The detective story is no longer to be apologized for and, whatever the reasons for this, it is still a "relief from the actual."

C753. Showalter, Elaine. "Rethinking the Seventies: Women Writers and Violence." Antioch Review 39 (Spring 81):156-170.

Passing references to Judith Rossner's Looking for Mr. Goodbar and Diane Johnson's The Shadow Knows in this thematic study of the changing preoccupations of women writers of the 1970s.

C754. Shrapnel, Norman. "The Literature of Violence and Pursuit." TLS, 23 June 61, pp. i-ii; translated into German and reprinted in Buchloh/Becker 2 (B61), pp. 343-51.

A defense of detective fiction as a serious endeavor, with short appreciations of Poe, Simenon and Conrad's The Secret Agent, concluding that this form may be instructive for other novelists in its "appalling" relevance to current events.

C755. "The Silver Age: Crime Fiction from Its Heyday until Now." TLS, 25 Sept 55, pp. xi-xii.

A rapid survey of the period from Collins to the present.

C756. Sinisgalli, Leonardo. "Romanzi gialli |Giallo Novels|." L'Italia letteraria, 1 Dec 29, p. 8.

The author, future poet of the hermetic school, introduces the first four volumes of the "most prestigious Italian anthology devoted to the police narrative," I Libri Gialli (Milan, Mondadori), characterized by yellow dust jackets. (These dust jackets were first used in 1929, suppressed by the intervention of the Fascist regime in 1944, reappearing in 1946 and now solidly established in the book market.) The author sees detective literature, like the cinema, as an expression of a return to the fable, to a taste for extraordinary stories, to fantasies of an infantile nature, although against the background of the 20th century. (The expression giallo is a typically Italian neologism which, derived from the Mondadori collection, designates approximately what the English and Americans call the "detective novel.") (LR)

C757. Sisk, John P. "Crime and Criticism." Commonweal 54 (20 Apr 56):72-74.

The writer complains about the lack of criticism of mystery fiction and goes on to talk about non-threatening, controlled violence and mystery and the attractions of this stylized genre in which there is an "amazing amount of good writing." Gerry Cashman replies in the issue of May 18, 1956, p. 182, that mystery stories can never be more than crossword puzzles with "continuity." Sisk's rejoinder (May 18, 1956, p. 275) is that he is not discussing the literary worth of mysteries but why people read them.

C758. Skreb, Zdenko. "Die neue Gattung. Zur Geschichte und Poetik des Detektivromans |The new genre: on the history and poetics of the detective novel|." In Zmegac (B451), pp. 35-95. Not previously published.

Using the examples of the works of Doyle, Poe, Gaboriau, Christie, Hammett and Chandler, Skreb, a Yugoslavian literary historian, examines the poetic and formal aspects of the genre. Methods of narration, commonalities among detective, horror and gothic fiction, the function of a Watson, and Cawelti-like comments on genre schemas are among the topics discussed. Although several of Skreb's comments are mistaken, such as the claims that a detective novel cannot be narrated in the first person or that Germany has no detective fiction tradition (cf. Hans Otto Huegel, B161), his insights are interesting. (GG)

C759. Slung, Michele. "Crime Writers' International Congress." American Bookman, 3 May 82, pp. 3473-79.

A report on the Congress which includes interviews with writers, and observations on the popularity of detective fiction in Europe.

C760. ______. "Fan Fare." American Bookseller, Dec 80.

Mystery fans and their organizations.

C761. ______. "70-talets deckare om, med och av kvinnor |Detective novels of the 70s about, including and by women|." Jury 11: (1982): 5-15. Translated by Lena Persson. (MS)

C762. ______. "Women in Detective Fiction." In Ball (B15), pp. 125-40.
A subjective, "lighthearted" survey of women writers of mysteries. Slung concludes with the comment that she has observed that most of the books written since the 1970s which feature intelligent women sleuths have been written by women with the result that she can not only enjoy them but respect them.

C763. ______. "Women in Detective Fiction." Mystery 3:1 (Jly 81): 8-15. Photos and one illustration.
A skimpy study of the "unusual and appealing" in the 70s.

C764. Smith, Susan Harris. "The Case of the Corpse in the Classroom." The CEA Critic 38:4 (May 76):18-22.
On teaching detective fiction.

C765. ______. "The History of British and American Detective Fiction." The Shanghai Foreign Language Institute Journal, Dec 79, pp. 52-69; abridged and in Chinese Translation, in A Forest of Translations, Spring 80, pp. 162-69. Not seen.

C766. Smuda, Manfred. "Variation und Innovation. Modelle literarischer Moeglichkeiten der Prosa in der Nachfolge Edgar Allan Poes |Variation and innovation: models of literary possibilities of prose in the successors of E. A. Poe|." Poetica 3:1/2 (1970):165-87; reprinted in Vogt (B444), Vol. I, pp. 33-63.
Using concepts from cybernetics and communications theory, Smuda states that all crime novels lie on a spectrum between perfect originality and perfect banality. The closer they lie to the former, the better. Poe's three detective stories, Smuda states, lie quite close to perfect originality. Hammett's "crime novels" lie closer to banality; Spillane's are perfectly banal, and Fleming's Bond stories swing back to originality.(GG)

C767. "Snillen spekulerar |Geniuses speculate|?" Jury 10:3 (1981):5-13.
Think tank of Jury staff and Dorothy B. Hughes, Tony Hillerman, H. R. F. Keating, Julian Semjonow (Soviet author), and Nils Nordberg (Norwegian critic). The topics discussed were: the future of the genre, the possibility of the survival of detectives (ethnic, etc.) and "conservative" and "liberal" fiction. (MS)

C768. Snow, C. P. "The Classic Detective Story." In From Parnassus, edited by Dora B. Weiner and Wm. R. Keylor, pp. 16-22. NY: Harper and Row, 1976.
After briefly surveying the classical and hard-boiled mystery, and noting Barzun's objection to the romantic strain in detective fiction, Snow writes approvingly of several English women writers, in particular P. D. James.

C770. Soler Canas, Luis. "La novela policial argentina |The Argentinian detective novel|." Esto es (Buenos Aires) no. 18 (30 March 54) and no. 19 (6 Apr 54). Not seen.

C771. Sorani, Aldo. "Conan Doyle e la fortuna del romanzo poliziesco |Conan Doyle and the fortune of the detective novel|." Pegaso, Aug 30, pp. 212-220.

The author, always attentive to the problems of the sociology of the book and of literary taste, illustrates the variations of the detective novel and of the dilettante detectives modeled on Sherlock Holmes. Among the successors of Conan Doyle, distinguishing between authors of the detective novel and authors of the adventure novel, he focuses on S. S. Van Dine and G. K. Chesterton where the detective novel is "an ingeniously constructed machine, regulated like a clock." The author of detective novels is, therefore, a "manipulator" of criminological gear-meshing. (Sorani cites, in particular, the essay of Marjorie Nicolson on "The Professor and the Detective," C584.) (LR)

C772. ______. "Effetti del romanzo poliziesco |Effects of the detective novel|." La Nazione, 15 Aug 31.

Article written in a semi-serious tone, in dialogue form. Sorani observes that the detective story transmits a pessimistic vision of the world: to the reader, trusting in the confrontations of life, sure of himself and tranquil in his own well-being, opens the hidden and disquieting dimension of mystery, of danger, of plotting, of doubt. (LR)

C773. Spagnoletti, Giacinto. "A proposito del romanzo poliziesco |On the detective novel|." La Fiera Letteraria, 10 Feb 57, pp. 3, 6.

The critic, taking his cue from the famous essay of W. H. Auden, "The Guilty Vicarage" (C34), takes up the problem of the relationship between the detective story and "high" literature. He observes that the detective novel is "produced in series for readers in series" and that the genre would remain completely obscure and unknown on the level of literary history if it were not for great puzzle-creators (Stevenson, Chesterton, Hammett, Simenon, Greene) who, treating the material traditionally devoted to the detective genre, attract the critic's attention with a quality of writing not expected by serial readers. The revolution of these writers "is based solely on style." (LR)

C774. Spanos, William V. "The Detective and the Boundary: Some Notes on the Postmodern Literary Imagination." boundary 2, 1, no. 1 (1972):147-68.

The existentialist crime of existence and the subverting of fictional conventions in modern fiction. Marginal.

C775. Spicer, Christopher H. "A Hard-Boiled Philosophy of Human Nature: Understanding People according to Spade, Marlowe and Archer." Clues 4:1 (Spring/Summer 83):93-104.

A report on statistical analyses of character traits (trustworthiness, altruism, independence, strength of will, complexity, variety) to confirm an evolution in which Archer is the most humane of the three detectives treated.

C776. Stange, G. Robert. "The Detective Story Mystery." Chimera 5:4 (Summer 47):31-38.

On the synthetic values of detective fiction and its addictive and unsatisfying nature.

C777. Starrett, Vincent. "From Poe to Poirot." In Books Alive, pp. 184-210. NY: Random House, 1940.

On reading detection fiction, and the unoriginality of much of the product, followed by a general history of the genre.

C778. ______. "Of Detective Literature." In Fourteen Great Detective Stories, edited by Vincent Starrett, pp. ix-xv. NY: Modern Library, 1928.
A leisurely essay on the pleasures of detective reading and a tribute to the detective story.

C778a. ______. "Some Chinese Detective Stories." In his Bookman's Holiday, pp. 3-26. NY: Random House, 1942. Not seen.

C779. Steele, Timothy. "Matter and Mystery: Neglected Works and Background Materials of Detective Fiction." MFS 29:3 (Autumn 83):435-450.
A re-examination of classical rhetoric and its contribution to understanding the art of the detective story. Steele thinks that it is incorrect to see Aristotle's Poetics in this connection; he looks instead to Aristotle's Rhetoric and to Cicero and Quintilian. Some classical antecedents of the detective are located and there is also a fruitful discussion of 19th century detective fiction, in particular works of Balzac and James Fenimore Cooper. Steele concludes with an artful and eloquent defense of the genre. An important essay that should help to direct critical attention away from the interminable preoccupation with a few modern writers and toward research into the historical sources of the genre.

C780. ______. "The Structure of the Detective Story: Classical or Modern?" MFS 27 (1981/82):555-70.
Modern detective fiction should be understood as deriving from 18th century concepts of aesthetics insofar as it is an end unto itself. Steele suggests that the appeal of the detective story is, in part, its extreme formalist position, which is also its chief limitation.

C781. Stein, Aaron Marc. "The Detective Story - How and Why." The Princeton University Chronicle, Autumn 1974, pp. 19-46. Not seen.

C782. Stein, Aaron Marc. "The Mystery Story in Cultural Perspective." In Ball (C42), pp. 29-59.
Stein traces the history and describes the characteristics of the detective story. He distinguishes it from other categories of mystery fiction and discusses its roots in pre-Poe literature.

C783. Steiner, George. "Sleuths." The New Yorker, 25 Apr 77, pp. 141-46, 148.
Essay-review of Ousby's Bloodhounds of Heaven (B300). Steiner also surveys the history of detection and the detective and concludes with a discussion of the "primal pairing" of Holmes and Watson, in the "realm of squire and knight."

C784. Stern, Peter. "Mystery and Detective Fiction." In Annual Report of the American Rare Book Trade, 1978/79, edited by Dennis Carbonneau. NY: BCAR, 1979.

C785. Stertman, Hans. "Finlandssvenska deckare--finns dom? |The Finno-Swedish detective novel--does it exist?|." Jury 5:3 (1976):23-24, 58. (MS)

C785a. ______. "Mord pa teatern |Murder in the theatre|." Jury 10:4 (1981):32-36. For other thematic studies by Stertman see: Jury 1:3/4 (1972):22-23, 67 (women fictional detectives); and Jury 2:1 (1973):21-23 (beverages in the detective novel).

Commentary on murders in the theatre, including Marsh, Quentin, and Brett and Swedish authors Stieg Trenter and Tage Giron. (MS)

C786. Storr, Anthony. "A Black-and-White World." TLS, 23 June 61, p. ii.
On the limitations of the genre: its adolescent fantasizing, primitive morality, meagre emotional content and unconvincing characterization.

C787. Stout, Rex. "Grim Fairy Tales." SRL 32 (2 Apr 49):7-8, 34. Illus.
"A detective story ends when reason's work is done." Reason must control emotion, the author must know his detective-hero intimately, the story cannot be narrated by the detective, 1st person narrative is preferable to third. The detective story is a fairy tale because the basic premise is that man is "the reasoning animal." Interesting not for Stout's limited concept of fairy tale elements in detective fiction but for his comments on the genre.

C788. ______. "We Mystery-Story Writers Don't Kid Ourselves." PW 138 (28 Dec 40):2312-14. Photo of Stout.
A humorous talk demonstrating the popularity of detective fiction and predicting it will take over the Herald-Tribune Book Review in the future.

C789. Strachey, John. "The Golden Age of English Detection." SRL 19 (7 Jan 39): 12-14. Photos.
In what Strachey sees as the Golden Age, there is a vitality and promise of growth not apparent in other imaginative fiction. Among the new writers Strachey singles out are Michael Innes and Nicholas Blake and he asks himself if the conventions are not responsible for the success of its practitioners.

C790. Strenski, Ellen. "Civilized Recipes of Crime." TAD 16 (1983):443-45.
A comparison of the affinities between a taste for mysteries and a taste for cooking.

C791. Ström, Sven. "Idrott och deckare |Sport and the detective novel|." Jury 6:2 (1977):17-24. (MS)

C792. Strong, L. A. G. "The Crime Short Story--An English View." In Gilbert (B124), pp. 149-62.
A defense of the short story's artistry and potential: it must be perfectly constructed, harmoniously balanced and accurately focused but not delighting in virtuosity for its own sake.

C793. Strunsky, Simeon. "Cold Chills of 1928." In Essays for Discussion, edited by Anita P. Forbes, pp. 185-92. NY: Harper, 1931.
The vicarious pleasure of reading detective stories and an affectionately humorous consideration of some of the conventions.

C794. ______. "On the Floor of the Library." Nation 103 (5 Oct 1916): 317-318; reprinted in his Sinbad and His Friends (NY: Holt, 1921), pp. 191-95; Essays by Present-Day Writers (NY: Macmillan, 1924), edited by R. W. Pence; Introducing Essays (Chicago: Scott, Foresman, 1933), edited by Sterling A. Leonard and Robert C. Pooley, pp. 121-28.
An amusing essay on detective fiction conventions as clichés.

C795. Suerbaum, Ulrich. "Der gefesselte Detektivroman |The detective novel in shackles|." Poetica 1:3 (1967):360-74; reprinted in Vogt (B424), Vol. II, pp. 437-56; and in Zmegac (B451), pp. 221-40.
Recommendable article focusing on aspects of narrative technique connected with the detective novel. Suerbaum points out that the genre is defined by strict conventions concerning theme, structure of plot, functionality of details, action and characters. Because of such restrictions, the detective novel has more affinities with short forms of prose fiction than with the novel proper; it is only a short story stretched to the size of a novel. (Barbara Korte)

C795a. Sullivan, Eleanor. "Questions Mystery Writers Ask." The Writer 87:1 (Jan 74):22-24.
EQMM's editor describes, in question and answer form, EQMM as a market. (REB).

C795b. Sullivan, Hazel. "Suspense--Fake and Genuine." The Writer 64:12 (Dec 51):395-98.
Contrived suspense and "genuine, inherent-in-the-situation" suspense. The article is largely about the latter (as the author describes the various kinds she can identify) but the form is, she admits, hard to recognize. Fuzzy and disorganized.

C796. Sussan, René. "Défense et illustration du roman policier |Defense and illustration of the detective novel|." Mélanges de la Bibliothèque de la Sorbonne 2 (1981):70-81. Illus.
A superficial look at critical attitudes toward detective fiction and its relationship to the novel.

C797. Svedlid, Olov. "Vaclav Erben Tjeckisk Mästare i Brott |Vaclac Erben, Czech master of crime|." DAST 14:6 (1981):21-22.
About Erben's eleven books and the general popularity of crime fiction in Czechoslovakia. (MS)

C798. Svoboda, Frederic. "The Snub-Nosed Mystique: Observations on the American Detective Hero." MFS 29:3 (Autumn 83):557-68.
A comparison of the Western and its hero to hard-boiled detective fiction and the private eye.

C799. Swinnerton, Frank. "An Inter-War Symptom." In The Georgian Scene, pp. 328-35. Revised edition. London: Hutchinson, 1969. Essay originally published as "A Post-War Symptom," in 1935.
A slight piece on Edgar Wallace and Dorothy L. Sayers. Swinnerton speaks more favorably of Wallace than of Sayers who "crafted the story to death."

C800. Symons, Julian. "The Crime Collector's Cabinet of Curiosities." In his Critical Observations, pp. 131-38. Boston: Ticknor and Fields, 1981.
Symons' candidate for the first full-length detective story is "Charles Felix's" The Nottinghill Mystery (1862, 1865). Symons also discusses the first crime story with a transvestite theme and topics like murder dossiers and parodies.

C801. ______. "The Detection Club." NYTBR, 30 Sept 79, pp. 14, 26.
In 1976 Symons succeeded Christie as president of the London-based Detection Club. On the traditions and history of the organization. See

also Symons' introduction to Verdict of 13: A Detection Club Anthology (Harper, 1978), pp. vii-x.

C802. ______. "The Face in the Mirror." In Gilbert (B124), pp. 126-33; and in Symons (B390), pp. 149-53.
Argument for the conclusion that one element in the definition of "crime novel" ought to be that the novel be written seriously and be considered by its author as capable of being a work of art. Symons names The Glass Key, Malice Aforethought, Bardin's Devil Take the Blue Fly and Margaret Millar's Beast in View as examples of the crime novel at its best. (GG)

C803. ______. "The Great Detective." In The Saturday Book 14, pp. 47-53. NY: Macmillan, 1954.
A survey of the great detective who has now "passed away."

C804. ______. "The Short Story's Mutations." In Winks (B434), pp. 154-60. From material originally published in Symons (B387).
The earlier decline in quality and popularity of detective short story and its revival sparked by the editorial policies of EQMM.

C805. Symons, Julian and Edmund Crispin. "Is the Detective Story Dead? A Dialogue." TLS, 23 June 61, pp. iv-v; reprinted in TMRN 4:2(1970/71): 3-7.
On the death of the puzzle novel and Symons' pious hope that a "really serious novelist" may do something exciting with it in 10 years. Crispin talks of his present interest in science fiction rather than mysteries because he thinks science fiction has taken over the detective novel's puzzle function.

C806. Talburt, Nancy Ellen. "Red is the Color of My True Love's Blood: Fetishism in Mystery Fiction." In Objects of Special Devotion: Fetishism in Popular Culture, edited by Ray B. Browne, pp. 69-98. Bowling Green, OH: Popular Press, n.d. With notes and bibliography.
A discussion of the "natural" partnership of crime and the fetish in a number of English and American detective novels.

C807. Taublieb, Paul. "Profile: Alfred Hitchcock's Mystery Magazine." Mystery 2:3 (May 81):34-5 Illus.
Includes an interview with editor Eleanor Sullivan.

C808. Taylor, F. Sherwood. "The Crux of a Murder: Disposal of the Body." The Spectator (London), 9 April 37; reprinted in Haycraft (B142), pp. 447-52.
A humorous piece on disposing in a satisfactory manner of bodies with Taylor's suggestion for a viable solution to the problem.

C809. Taylor, Isabelle. "Just Mysteries--and Proud of It." PW 139 (22 Feb 41):903-4.
Crime Club editor Isabelle Taylor says that until the rental library system (which depresses sales of mysteries) is changed, it will not be possible to increase royalties and encourage writers to write better books. For other articles by Taylor, see also: Haycraft (B142), pp. 292-97; Library Journal 76 (Aug 51):1172-77; PW 163 (25 Apr 53):1734-37 (photo; a history of the Crime Club imprint).

C810. Thier, Erich. "Ueber den Detektivroman |On the detective novel|." Die Bücherei 7 (1940):206-17; reprinted in Vogt (B424), Vol. II, pp. 483-99.
Essay from the viewpoint of German National Socialism arguing that the detective novel is a civic-capitalistic phenomenon whose rationalism is

harmful to the belief in the fuhrer. Thier also hints that the genre is coming to an end but speculates on the possibility of a truly German form to take its place. (GG)

C811. Thompson, Leslie M., and Banks, R. Jeff. "When Is This Stiff Dead? Detective Stories and Definitions of Death." TMF 2:6 (Nov/Dec 78):11-16.
The authors find the same misconceptions in detective fiction as in the general public about the manner of establishing the precise moment of death.

C812. "Throw Out the Detective." SRL 5:19 (1 Dec 28):421-22.
An editorial in which the writer complains that the detective story has become routine and the detective (a hackneyed device) should be eliminated to allow for some novel plotting and writing in the field.

C813. (Titta Rosa, Giovanni) "Poliziesca |Of the police|." Corriere padano, 20 Nov 31. Published under the pseudonym of "Il Doni."
The typical characteristic of the detective novel is that the narrative material is laid down and resolved like a theorem. The last chapter, which is equivalent to the solution of a mathematical demonstration, is the most difficult point to master: here the author's logic and, consequently, the reader's interest, often falter. (LR)

C814. Tiverton, Dana. "An Academy of Detectioneers. The Writer 44:9 (Sept 32): 255-56.
London's Detection Club and its rules for detective fiction.

C815. Todd, Ruthven. "A Trinity of 'Tecs: From There to Where?" Chimera 5:4 (Summer 47):49-58.
The professional police detective, the "great" detective and the hard-boiled detective.

C816. Todorov, Tzvetan. "Typologie du roman policier |Topology of the detective novel|." In his Poétique de la prose |Poètics of prose|, pp. 55-65. Paris: Ed. du Seuil, 1971. The book was published in an English translation by Richard Howard by Cornell University Press, 1977.
An attempt to describe two detective fiction types, the whodunit and the thriller. The whodunit is seen as a duality composed of story (event) and plot (the way the event is presented); in the thriller the event is suppressed and the plot is "vitalized" as "prospection takes the place of retrospection." See also pp. 85-88 and p. 135 for further comments on detective fiction. Todorov is one of the most lucid and least dogmatic of contemporary French critics.

C817. Tonic, Albert. "Interview with John Nanovic." Megavore 9 (June 80):44-45.
Interview with Street & Smith editor.

C818. Tortel, Jean. "Le Roman populaire." In Arnaud (B12), pp. 55-75.
An attempt to discover structural constants that make it possible to arrive at a categorial definition of the "popular novel." Among the authors cited are Eugene Sue, Gaboriau, Marcel Allain, Maurice Leblanc, and Gaston Leroux.

C819. "Tram Cars or 'Dodgems': Detection, Thrills and Horror." TLS, 25 Sept 55, p. ii.
The detective story is constrained by its formal limitations; the thriller

takes chances and is a "more hasardous" form of writing that may have "cousins" higher on the literary scale. Cites Charles Williams, C. S. Lewis, Graham Greene.

C820. Tuska, Jon. "Preface to 'The Popular Detectives'." Views & Reviews 1:1 (Summer 69):32-36.
Preface to a projected series of articles (by various authors) on detective books and films. The Preface establishes guidelines for the series and makes some general comments. The guidelines proved to be elastic, and the series (as an entity) was eventually abandoned. (REB)

C821. Ulanov, Barry. "The Mystery Story." In The Two Worlds of American Art: The Private and the Popular, pp. 284-97. NY: Macmillan, 1965.
On the puzzle novel, and fiction as a game of chess. The best of detective fiction is "orderly." Comments on post-World War II detective fiction, notes the rise in interest in psychiatry and discourses randomly on other topics.

C822. Ullman, Allan Gordon. "Making Crime Pay." PW 126 (7 Jly 34):37-39.
The market for detective fiction is depressed and Ullman attributes it to publishers' willingness to publicize bad books and ignore good ones and to the booksellers' ignorance of the field, compounded by lazy reviewers and no handy, reputable guides to the field.

C823. Underwood, Michael. "The Criminal Seen by the Lawyer." In Gilbert (B124), pp. 27-38.
Underwood, who is both a writer of detective fiction and a lawyer, describes what constitutes a crime in England and Wales and how the system of prosecution and defense works.

C824. Valentié, María Eugenia. "La novela policial |The detective novel|." La Torre 2:5 (Jan/March 54):75-92.
A general introduction to the genre.

C825. Van Dine, S. S. (Willard Huntington Wright). "The Detective Novel." Scribner's Magazine 80 (1926):532-39. Reprinted as the Introduction to his anthology The Great Detective Stories (NY: Scribner's, 1927) and in Haycraft (B142), pp. 33-70.
A history of the detective (or puzzle) novel and an analysis of its chief characteristics: its realism, psychology, style, characterization and mood. Wright's style lacks some of the zest and color of Chesterton's critical writing but, otherwise, his essay can be favorably compared with that of the best English writers on the subject.

C826. ______. "I Used To Be a Highbrow But Look At Me Now." American Magazine 106: 3 (Sept 28):14-15, 118, 122, 124-131. Illustrated by Herbert Morton Stoops.
An autobiobiographical account of how Van Dine (coyly hiding his real name) came to write detective stories.

C827. ______. "Twenty Rules for Detective Stories." American Magazine 106:3 (Sept 28):129-31. Reprinted in his Philo Vance's Murder Cases (Scribner's, 1936), pp. 74-81; in Haycraft (B142), pp. 189-93; in The Writer 52:3 (March 39):71-72; as "How I Got Away with Murder," in Readers' Digest, July 36, pp. 53-55; and in Vogt (B424), vol. I, pp. 143-46.
In this frequently recycled appendix to the preceding entry, Van Dine

lists both caveats and prescriptions for this "intellectual game."

C828. Van Meter, Jan R. "Sophocles and the Rest of the Boys in the Pulps: Myth and the Detective Novel." In Landrum (B216), pp. 12-21.
A comparison of the similarity of formulaic qualities in myth and detective fiction.

C829. Varaldo, Alessandro. "Dramma e romanzo poliziesco |Detective drama and novel|." Comoedia, May/June 32, pp. 9-10.
In the theatrical and narrative works of the detective genre, the author distinguishes an English and an American school; he attributes to the former characteristics of greater refinement and literary maturity and to the latter rougher and more "primordial" traits. In drama, the detective play subverts some rules of dramaturgy considered fundamental to the traditional theater of the 19th century and introduces, also in the area of the novel, a significant novelty: the co-involvement of the spectator or the reader in a kind of competition in rascality with the author. He also notes the birth in Italy--as well as in France with Simenon--of a detective school which advertises abroad national "customs," "characters," and "ideas." To compensate for the lack of an indigenous detective tradition, the author himself published, between 1931-34, detective novels and stories with Italian backgrounds and characters. (LR)

C830. Véry, Pierre. "Murder on Parnassus." Living Age 348 (Apr 35): 163-6. Originally published (in French) in Marianne, a "topical Parisian weekly." Reference not confirmed.
The essay consists of a satirical look at a future in which detective fiction, at present scorned by academics, has taken precedence over all other forms of literature.

C831. Vormweg, Heinrich. "Detektiven auf der Spur. Eine kritische Revue neuer Kriminalromane |Detectives on the trail: a critical review of new crime novels|." In Vogt (B424), Vol. I., pp. 300-307.
Optimistic essay illustrating with examples from Patricia Highsmith, Chester Himes, Westlake/Coe/Stark and several German authors the thesis that the modern crime novel is flourishing. (GG)

C832. Voskresensky, D. M. "The Kung-an Story in China." Narodii Asii i Afriki 1 1966):107-15.
Scholarly introduction to the kung-an (crime or courtcase) or ancient Chinese detective story, which Voskresensky traces from dramatic and oral traditions. Dates the beginnings of criminal prose as far back as the pre-T'ang period (pre-618 A. D.) where fantastic and magical elements were common to prose. Includes morphology and socio-literary analysis. Voskresensky is one of the few to state that the kung-an story was influential in the formation and development of Chinese prose and colloquial language; he seems to favor what he calls the "democratic" world view implicit in the stories, as well as the stories' emphasis on lower and middle class characters. Relatively early study by a Russian Sinologist. (GG)

C833. Wager, Walter. "Making Crime Pay in Stockholm." PW, 11 Sept 81, pp. 40-42. Photo.
A report on the Crime Writers 3rd International Congress. Wager summarizes sessions at which there were presentations on the status of mystery fiction in European countries.

C834. Waite, John Barker. "If Judges Wrote Detective Stories." Scribner's 95 (Apr 34):274-77.

A criticism of investigative procedures in R. Denbie's Death on the Limited leads into a discussion of how laws may inhibit solutions of crimes in ways often violated by fiction writers. Denbie replies (p. 22, Appendix) that, in fact, laws are often flouted by the police and an author should imitate life rather than the law.

C835. Waite, J. B., and Kimball, Miles W. "The Lawyer Looks at Detective Fiction." Bookman 69 (Aug 29): 616-21. Reprinted in Haycraft (B142, pp. 436-46.

A discussion of several novels in which police authorities act in ways that would be legally impossible in real life or in which there is not sufficient evidence to convict the accused. Condensed in Literary Digest, 26 Oct 29, pp. 47-9, with a reply by S. S. Van Dine who states that real detectives, in spite of arguments to the contrary, have the privileges of fictional detectives and asks Professor Waite to consult "the record" to verify his defense.

C836. Wallace, Edgar. "Why Mystery Stories Are So Popular." Everybody's Weekly, 24 Nov 28.

A few well-worded comments from someone who should certainly have known the answer. (RCSA)

C837. Walsh, Rodolfo. "Introduction" to his anthology, Diez cuentos policiales argentinos, pp. 7-8. Buenos Aires: Libreria Hachette, 1953.

A disappointingly cursory survey of the detective novel in Argentina by one of its leading writers.

C838. Walters, Margaret. "English Whodunits: Where Are They Now?" New Republic 170 (20 Apr 74):21-23.

A survey of the classic English detective novel and its survival in the work of Ian Fleming and Julian Symons.

C839. Ward, Alfred C. "Detective Stories." In his Twentieth Century Literature, 1901-1940, pp. 80-82. 7th ed., revised. London: Methuen, 1940. Reprinted in Buchloh/Becker 2 (B61), pp. 352-55.

Generalities and commonplaces.

C840. Warner, Nicholas O. "City of Illusion: The Role of Hollywood in Californian Detective Fiction." TAD 16 (1983):22-25. Illus.

Hollywood settings and motifs in Chandler and Ross Macdonald.

C841. Watson, Colin. "Passport---Tickets---." British Airways High Life, Aug 76.

Len Deighton, Barbara Cartland, Frederick Forsyth and Arthur Hailey talk about travel and its effect on their writing. (RCSA)

C842. Waugh, Charles G. "Introduction. The Fantastic Mystery: A Neglected Genre." In Mysterious Visions: Great Science Fiction by Masters of the Mystery, edited by Charles G. Waugh, Martin Harry Greenberg and Joseph Olander, pp. xix-xxvi. NY: St. Martin's Press, 1979.

Offers a useful classification scheme for fantastic (including science-fictional) mystery stories, dividing the sub-genre into ten categories and giving examples for each category. (REB)

C843. Waugh, Hillary. "Edgars, Anyone?" TAD 2 (1968/69):53-54.

Comments on the Edgar awards-judging process by a member of Edgar committees. Also, a brief biography of Waugh by Allen Hubin and some further comments by Waugh.

C844. ______. "The Human Rather Than Superhuman Sleuth." In Freeman (B117), pp. 33-45.
On the police procedural as a revolt against the hard-boiled writers and as an attempt to make police novels more realistic.

C845. ______. "The Mystery Versus the Novel." In Ball (B15), pp. 61-80.
An attempt to distinguish mystery fiction from the "serious" novel.

C846. ______. "The Police Procedural." In Ball (B15), pp. 163-87.
A defense of the procedural which Waugh sees as providing a "social message" and a new plausibility and realism in contrast to the private-eye and classical detective novels which are often characterized as "light" reading. Waugh's discussion of his conversion to the procedural is interesting for a better understanding of his own work but the polemical aspects of this essay are highly debatable.

C847. Wellershoff, Dieter. "Voruebergehende Entwirklichung. Zur Theorie des Kriminalromans |Passing realization: on the theory of the crime novel|." In his Literatur und Lustprinzip, pp. 77-138. Cologne: Verlag Kiepenheuer & Witsch, 1973.
Criticism from popular psychoanalytical, sociological and information theoretical viewpoints on the crime novel and its effects on readers. Wellershoff argues that people have twin needs for security and stimulation, and that in secure societies the latter need is supplied artificially, e. g., by crime fiction. (GG)

C848. Wells, Carolyn. "Introduction." In Best American Mystery Stories, edited by Carolyn Wells, pp. vii-xviii. NY: Albert and Charles Boni, 1931. Excerpted in part from her Technique of the Mystery Story (B427).
A survey of the genre with comments on its conventions, the role of the detective and the investigative process in fiction.

C849. ______. "Die Kriminalliteratur |Crime fiction|." In Buchloh/Becker 2 (C61), pp. 58-66. Excerpted from her Technique (B427), pp. 10-19.

C850. ______. "The Detective Story's Place in Literature." The World Review, 21 Jan 29, pp. 247, 254. Illus.
A defense of detective fiction and of the short story as its most effective medium.

C852. Weston, Louise E., and Ruggiero, Josephine A. "Male-Female Relationships in Best-Selling 'Modern Gothic' Novels." Sex Roles 4:5 (1978):647-55.
A study based on 38 romantic suspense/modern Gothic novels by 7 writers, published between 1950 and 1974. The heroine is usually non-traditional in her behavior, the "other woman" traditional so that the hero is offered a choice. The hero chooses the non-traditional female but is himself traditional in his behavior. The authors surveyed are Mary Stewart, Victoria Holt, Jane Blackmore, Dorothy Eden, Phyllis Eden, Susan Howatch and Anne Maybury.

C853. Whaley, Bob, and Antonelli, George A. "Healing under the Bare Bulb: The Detective as Therapist." Clues 2:2 (1981):1-7.

Authors relate some fictional detectives and their methods to popular therapeutic schools (Rogerian, Transactional Analysis, Gestalt, etc.).

C854. "What Policemen Read." TLS, 23 June 61, p. viii. From "a correspondent."
Policemen are more likely to read thrillers than detective fiction or works in which there is a sound knowledge of police routine.

C855. Whipple, Leon. "Nirvana for 2 Dollars." Survey 62:3 (1 May 29): 191-92.
Detective fiction as a literature of escape and as a bed-time narcotic. An uneasy blend of defensiveness and defense.

C856. White, Trentwell Mason. "The Detective Story." In his How To Write for a Living, pp. 112-19. NY: Reynal and Hitchcock, 1937.
Advice to the writer based on Ronald Knox's rules (C458).

C857. Whiteside, Thomas. "A Murder a Minute." Collier's 123 (5 Feb 49):28-29, 68-69. Illus.
The popularity of murder novels, the varied backgrounds of writers, the role of the MWA in promoting accuracy in detective fiction, a brief historical survey, the readership and the primal interest in violence as an explanation of the phenomenon's durability.

C858. Whitney, Phyllis A. "Gothic Mysteries." In Ball (B15), pp. 223-32.
An explanation of the "rules" of the modern romantic suspense novel of which Whitney is a leading practitioner.

C859. "Who Done It - As Dickens Did It." Colliers 131 (14 March 53):74. Illus.
Editorial defense of Collier's continuing publication of detective stories and a short history from Poe to Dickens to establish its literary credentials.

C860. Williams, H. L. "The Germ of the Detective Novel." The Book Buyer 21, new series, no. 4 (Nov 1900):268-74. Illus.
A sprawling discussion of the 19th century detective novel. The subjects include the writers, Goboriau and his popularity in the American serial newspapers, detective heroes in French fiction before Gaboriau, the origin of the term "hawkshaw," and the female detective.

C861. Williams, Valentine. "Detective Fiction." Bookman 67 (July 28): 521-24.
The detective story, a recent arrival, should not be confused with the adventure tale. A brief chronology is followed by a reaffirmation of the importance of sound plot construction and Williams' admission that his two professional detectives are based on real-life policemen.

C862. ______. "The Detective in Fiction." Fortnightly Review 134 (Sept 30):381-92.
Williams excludes from his discussion novels in which crime and the criminal figure prominently but in which there is no detective. A survey of the genre in the contributions of Vidocq, Poe and Gaboriau, with a tribute to Conan Doyle and his creation of Sherlock Holmes.

C863. ______. "On Crime Fiction." In What Is a Book?, edited by Dale Warren, pp. 119-33. Boston: Houghton Mifflin, 1936; London: Allen & Unwin, 1936.
Detective fiction must be well constructed even though the

characterizations are wooden and the psychology non-existent. Ingredients of a successful fiction: suspense, surprise, a modicum of characterization, plausibility and, above all, action.

C864. ______. "Putting the Shocks into 'Shockers'." Bookman 66 (Nov 1927): 270-72.

Successful thrillers depend on sound plot construction.

C865. Wilson, Edmund. "The Boys in the Back Room." In Classics and Commercials, pp. 19-56. NY: Farrar, Straus, 1950; London: W. H. Allen, 1951.

Recent writers most of whom have been influenced by Hemingway and live (or have lived) in California and write about it. Wilson begins with James M. Cain and "his school" (Horace McCoy, and Richard Hallas) and characterizes them as "poets of the tabloid murder." He considers Cain the best of the group, which is, at best, faint praise and sees him primarily as a writer for films who writes his novels in his "off-time."

C866. ______. "'Mr. Holmes, They Were the Footprints of a Gigantic Hound!'" New Yorker 21 (17 Feb 45):66-70; reprinted in Classics and Commercials (Farrar, Straus, 1950), pp. 266-74.

An appreciative discussion of Doyle's "imaginative fairy-tales" which, in contrast to his present-day imitations, are a form of literature.

C867. ______. "Who Cares Who Killed Roger Ackroyd? A Second Report on Detective Fiction." New Yorker 20 (20 Jan 45):52-58. Reprinted in Haycraft (B142), pp. 390-97; in Classics and Commercials (Farrar, Straus, 1950), pp. 257-65; in Winks (B434), pp. 35-40; in Buchloh/Becker 2 (B61), pp. 226-33; and in Cremante/Rambelli (B78), pp. 103-110.

Provoked by a flood of letters protesting his put-down of detective fiction (see next entry), Wilson reads books by Allingham, Sayers, Marsh, Chandler and John Dickson Carr. He finds the ladies' books unreadable, likes Chandler's Farewell, My Lovely but calls it a spy/adventure story variation, and enjoys the spookiness and plotting of Carr's The Burning Court. He concludes with a scathing denunciation of the lax mental habits of readers of detective stories and replies to points raised by Jacques Barzun, W. S. Maugham, Joseph Krutch and Bernard de Voto (about whose "messy" style and "total" insensitivity to style he is particularly vehement). An acidly funny piece.

C868. ______. "Why Do People Read Detective Stories?" New Yorker 20 (14 Oct 44):73-4, 76; reprinted in Classics and Commercials (Farrar, Straus, 1950), pp. 231-37; and in Zmegac (B451), pp. 105-10.

Disappointed by the ineffective imitation of Conan Doyle he sees in several Rex Stout novels, Wilson turns to another admired practitioner, Agatha Christie. Her "card tricks" bore him so in desperation he reads Hammett's The Maltese Falcon which he compares to a comic strip. Finally, he concludes that the detective story, as a "department of imaginative writing," is "completely dead."

C869. Wingate, Nancy. "Getting Away with Murder." JPC 12 (1979): 581-603.

Truth rather than justice is often served in the traditional detective novel. Examples from writers like E. C. Bentley, A. B. Cox, A. Christie and others.

C870. Winkauf, Mary S. "Murder Most Poetic." Clues 4:2 (Fall/Winter 83): 115-29.

A discussion of the relationship of poetry and detective fiction. Winkauf gives examples of poems and verse-dramas which serve as sources for titles of mysteries, poems which deal with murder, verse citations used as clues, and detectives who are poets or lovers of poetry.

C871. Winks, Robin W. "American Detective Fiction." In Sources for American Studies, edited by Jefferson B. Kellogg and Robert H. Walker, pp. 48-61. Contributions in American Studies, no. 64. Westport, CT: Greenwood Press, 1983.

A general survey of critical attitudes toward detective fiction which Winks finds generally lack the high seriousness that the genre deserves. There is also an annotated bibliography (pp. 55-61) of secondary sources.

C872. Wodehouse, P. G. "About These Mysteries." Sat Eve Post, 25 May 29, pp. 33, 187. Illus.

A humorous consideration of the popularity of detective fiction and the difficulties it poses for the writer trying to interest the jaded reader.

C873. Wolfe, Peter. "The Critics Did It: An Essay Review." MFS 29:3 (Autumn 83):389-34.

A review of some thirty books of criticism published in the period 1980-82. A survey in which many of the judgments are sound but, as always with general coverage of this kind, the critic has certain areas in which he seems more comfortable than others. The coverage of the hard-boiled writers is generally good; the comments on the material on such areas as the British mystery and police procedural show more good will than critical judgment.

C874. Wood, Neville. "The Golden Age of the Detective Story." TPP 1:1 (Jan 78):11-16.

A general survey of the 1920s and 1930s, mostly devoted to British writers. There is a chart of authors with dates, first book publication, favorite detective(s) and other comments.

C875. Woods, Katharine Pearson. "Renaissance of Wonder." Bookman 10 (Dec 1899):340-43.

A defense of detective fiction as worthy of serious consideration, and an attempt to establish common characteristics to justify the writer's use of the word "school." She cites Gaboriau, Collins and Doyle as writers of quality.

C876. Wright, Lee. "Murder for Profit." PW 131 (10 Apr 37):1591-92.

Wright was the long-time editor of the Simon & Schuster "Inner Sanctum" mystery series and she writes on ways of "servicing" mystery readers (a "pleasant and intelligent lot") to create more fans and sell more mysteries. Wright has also written several other articles in which she touches on a number of topics and writers. See also: Haycraft (B142), pp. 287-91; PW 139 (25 Jan 41):384-85; The Writer 58:9 (Sept 45):266-67; McCall's 96 (Apr 69):97-98, 185; The Writer 92:5 (May 79):14.

C876a. "Writing Mystery Stories." The Writer 27:1 (Jan 1915):10-11. Originally published in the New York Sun (reference not confirmed.)

A formula for successful writing is to keep two stories going at the same time: one is written down, the other occasionally feeds into the written version.

C877. Wrong, E. M. "Introduction." In Crime and Detection, pp. ix-xxx. London: Oxford Press, 1926. Reprinted in Haycraft (B142), pp. 18-32; and in Buchloh/Becker 2 (B61), pp. 116-33.

An historical survey with some critical/theoretical comments on the relationship between detective fiction and "art," and some of the pitfalls of the genre to be avoided. CC 2875.

C878. Wulff, Antje. "Die Spielregeln der Detektiverzahlung |The rules of the game of the detective story|." In Buchloh/Becker 1 (B60), pp. 81-95.

The importance of the detective story as a challenge to the reader during the Golden Age is discussed. Puzzle phenomena such as locked-room mysteries and Dennis Wheatley's crime dossiers are seen as outcomes of the same attitudes which gave rise to the rules of Father Knox and S. S. Van Dine, and the oath of the London Detection Club. (GG)

C879. Yates, Donald A. "The Detective Literature of the Americas." TAD 4:1 (1970/71):5-9.

Changes in detective fiction since World War II and a survey of detective fiction written by Latin American writers since 1929 when, according to Yates, the first "genuine" detective novel written by a Latin American was published.

C880. ______. "Introduction." In his Latin Blood: The Best Crime and Detective Stories of South America, pp. xi-xv. NY: Herder and Herder, 1972.

Useful capsule history of Latin American detective fiction ("most of which is translated from English-language originals"), ending with a tribute to Anthony Boucher as "the first American critic of Spanish American detective literature." (REB)

C881. ______. "The Locked Room." The Michigan Alumnus Quarterly Review, Spring 1957; revised and published as "An Essay on Locked Rooms" in Nevins (B240), pp. 272-84; as "Locked Rooms and Puzzles: A Critical Memoir" in Ball (B15), pp. 189-203; and as "The Locked House: An Essay on Locked Rooms" in TAD 3 (1969/70):81-84. For corrections/additions, see J. R. Christopher, letter, TAD 3:3:205.

A survey of locked-room murders with some speculations on the reasons for the continuing popularity of this phenomenon.

C882. ______. "The Spanish American Detective Story." Modern Language Journal 40 (1956):228-32. A revised and expanded Spanish version was published as "La novela policial en las Americas" in Temas culturales (publication of the U. S. Cultural and Information Service, Buenos Aires) 3:3 (1966); this version also appeared in Letras nuevas (publication of the Asociacion de Escritores Venezolanos, Caracas), no. 7 (Jan/March 71); and as the introduction to El cuento policial latinoamericano (Mexico City: Edicions de Andrea, 1964).

Yates discusses reasons why an indigenous detective fiction developed so late in Latin America and describes the form it has taken in Chile, Mexico, Uraguay and Argentina where genre writers are most active.

C883. Zandel, Diego. "Il 'giallo,' un oggetto misterioso |The giallo, a mysterious object|." Star 2 (June 1983), p. 69.

Brief note on the variegated panorama of the various literary genres relating to the criminal world and all labeled indiscriminately, in the Italian tradition, under the term giallo. (RC)

C884. Zmegac, Viktor. "Aspekte des Detektivromans. Statt einer Einleitung

|Aspects of the detective novel: instead of an introduction|." Umjetnost rijeci (Yugoslavia) 1/2 (1970), pp. 285-92; reprinted in Zmegac (B451), pp. 9-34; and in Cremante/Rambelli (B78), pp. 183-94.

Zmegac, a Yugoslovakian literary critic, examines several facets of the genre such as the heroic, eccentric figure of the detective, the importance of the reader's belief in the power of reason, and the meaning of murder as the principal crime. Also interesting is Zmegac's Marxist criticism and observations on the socially determined nature of crime fiction. (GG)

C885. Zone, Ray. "Mean Streets Revisited." Mystery 2:3 (May 81):18-19. Photo.

Passim for quotes by Timothy Harris, Arthur Lyons, Andrew Fenady, Murray Sinclair, Elliott Lewis and Karl Alexander.

C886. Zurlo, Leopoldo. "Commedia poliziesca (1934) |Detective comedy|." in Memorie inutili. La Censura teatrale nel ventennio, pp. 291-94. Rome: Edizioni dell'Ateneo, 1952.

A study of a part of the report on the censorship of the 1933/34 theatrical season which the author, official censor of the Fascist regime, sent to Benito Mussolini. A caricatural text in dialogue presenting the arguments which the committed moralists used in their confrontations with detective theater. In reality, it is a defense of the genre regarded as innocuous as fiction (riddle, pure mechanism, diversion) or even moral in its unmasking of the ambiguous game between innocence and guilt, between appearance and reality. (LR)

III. Dime Novels, Juvenile Series & Pulps

A. Dime Novel & Juvenile

1. General References

D1. Ade, George. Bang! Bang! Freeport, New York: Books for Libraries, 1971.
Originally published in 1928, this collection of parodies of dime novels includes several about "Eddie Parks, the Newsboy Detective" that clearly display the conventions of the form. Illus. by John T. McCutcheon. (JRC)

D2. Anderson, David. "Thinking about Popular Literature: The Example of the Dime Novel." DNR 50 (1981):13-16.
A reponse to J. Randolph Cox's "The Detective-Hero in the American Dime Novel" (printed in the same issue), arguing that detective dime novels are similar to detective fiction only in that both have detectives as characters: in detective fiction, the characters and crime contribute to a thematic purpose, while in detective dime novels, characters and theme are sacrificed for narrative. Anderson questions whether the two forms can be compared. (DJ)

D3. Anglo, Michael. Penny Dreadfuls and Other Victorian Horrors. London: Jupiter, 1977. 125pp. Illus.
Dick Turpin, Sweeney Todd and others in an informal survey of the Victorian serial periodicals.

D4. (Barbour, Ralph Henry) Chenu, Bob. "Ralph Henry Barbour's Books." TBBC 1:4 (Summer 70):118-24; 3:2 (Spring 72):319 ("addenda"); updated and reprinted in YL 1:6 (Nov/Dec 81):17-22.
Checklists of this prolific writer's series and non-series boys' fiction which includes some mystery titles.

D5. Barry, Beatrice. "Did Mottern Commit Murder from Reading Dime Novels?" DNR 17 (Sept 49):73-75. Reprinted from a feature story syndicated by the Public Ledger in 1917.
An argument against the theory that the reading of dime novels contributes to a desire to murder and steal, based on a case in Pennsylvania. Whatever influence the dime novel may have had has been lessened and supplanted by melodramatic movies. Nick Carter's publishers did not consider the stories to be dime novels in the original sense of the word. (JRC)

D6. Becket, Margaret. "Dime Novels." Sunday Democrat and Chronicle (Rochester, NY) Upstate, 21 March 82, pp. 6-9. Illustrated.

On dime novels and an exhibit from the University of Rochester's Rush Rees Library collection. Includes material from interviews with University of Rochester English faculty members George Grella and Frank Shuffleton on the role of dime novels in American culture and their descendents in pulps, comic strips and comic books.

D7. Bellous, Robert Peabody. "The Degeneration of the Dime Novel." The Writer 12:7 (July 1899):97-98.
The decline in popularity of the dime novel as yellow journalism and the new rage for realism replace the romanticism of the dime novel.

D9. Bleiler, E. F., ed. Eight Dime Novels. NY: Dover Publications, 1974.
Anthology of representative examples, including "The Bradys and the Girl Smuggler" (Secret Service, no. 79, 27 July 1900) and "Scylla the Sea Robber" (Nick Carter Weekly, no. 465, 25 Nov 1905). Informed and informative introduction (pp. vii-xv) sets the stories in the context of literary and social history with comments on authorship. (JRC)

D10. "The Blood-and-Thunder 'Yen'." Literary Digest, 21 June 30, pp. 20-21.
Report on an article by Charles Willis Thompson in the New York Post (no date given) on how the dime novel has been supplanted by magazines featuring detectives and inspectors catering to the human "yen for blood-and-thunder."

D11. Blythe, Robert. "In the Beginning." CDA, 1951, pp. 30-35.
Discussion of the early years of the Nelson Lee Library when the paper was a competitor in the detective field to the Union Jack. (JRC)

D12. The Boys' Book Collector (TBBC). Editor: Alan S. Dikty; Publisher, T. E. Dikty. Eleven issues published between Fall 1969 (1:1) and 1973 (3:3).
A digest-sized periodical, generously illustrated, on juvenile fiction. A well-edited magazine with checklists, book reviews, author and series pieces, historical essays, letters, information for collectors and advertisements. Although few of the contributions focus on detection elements in dime novels and juvenile fiction, it is evident from the titles of many of the series that are described in bibliographic essay that mystery/detection was a wide-spread feature of the series. Material will be included from this journal in both the author and series sections. An excellent source for the study of juvenile series and, to a lesser extent, of dime novels.

D13. Burns, William B. "Old Story Papers: Boys of New York." DNR 26 (1958):17-19; 28-30; 37-38. Illus.
Article in three installments on the contents of the last 285 issues of Boys of New York. Part one gives an overview of a typical issues; the second installment includes a list of the Old King Brady, Young Sleuth, and Jerry Owens detective stories published in the later issues; the third part mentions Handsome Harry tales and some detective fiction that was continued in Happy Days, the successor to Boys of New York. (DJ)

D14. Cobb, Irvin S. "A Plea for Old Cap Collier." Sat Eve Post 193 (5 July 20): 3-4; reprinted as book, New York: George H. Doran, 1921 (Frontis. by Tony Sarg; 56pp).
A humorous and nostalgic look at the joys of dime novel reading and the part dime novels played in the early years of anyone who grew up at the

turn of the century. Indicates the popularity of Nick Carter and Old Cap Collier. (JRC)

D15. Cook, Michael L. Dime Novel Roundup: Annotated Index 1931-1981. Bowling Green, OH: Bowling Green University Popular Press, 1983. 105pp.
With an introduction which includes reminiscences by Ralph F. Cummings, the original editor/publisher of DNR, on his publishing career and a survey by editor Cook of the history of popular literature in the 19th century. The index is organized by title, author and subject; the annotations are short content designations.

D16. Cordier, George H. "The Boys of New York." DNR 11 (Oct 43):1-4.
Nostalgic sketch of the Tousey story paper with lists of some titles reprinted in other Tousey publications. (Boys of New York serialized stories of Old King Brady, Young Sleuth and other detectives.) (JRC)

D17. Cox, J. Randolph. "The Detective-Hero in the American Dime Novel." DNR 50 (1981):2-13.
A history of dime novel detectives, including a discussion of the influence of early detective tales (fiction and non-fiction) on dime novels; an overview of dime novels; and an analysis of the characteristics of dime novel detective-heroes. The analysis is supported by descriptions of dime novel detectives Old Sleuth, Kate Edwards, Old King Brady, and Nick Carter, and by excerpts from stories in which they appeared. (DJ)

D18. ______. "The Heyday of the Dime Novel." WLB, Dec 80, pp. 262-66, Illus.
A concise, informative history of dime novels with references to "Old Sleuth" as perhaps the first detective series (1872) and to several other dime novel detective series.

D19. Cummings, Ralph. "The English Novels of Today." DNR 2 (July-Aug 1933):1-3.
Account of contemporary British papers, Thriller, Detective Weekly, and Bullseye, which publish stories to appeal to dime novel readers. (JRC)

D20. ______. "Newsy News." DNR 18 (July 50):52-54.
A regular column of miscellaneous items about dime novels. This time the subjects are Varick Vanardy as pseudonym for Frederic Van Rensselaer Dey, the possibility that Dey wrote some of the "Jack Wright" science fiction stories for Tousey, and an obituary notice (16 June 50) for Mrs. Haryot Holt Dey, widow of the Nick Carter author. (JRC)

D21. ______. "My First Novel." DNR 4 (April 35):1-3.
Reminiscences of reading an issue of Secret Service as a boy. Collecting dime novels began in 1917, the Happy Hours Brotherhood was founded in 1924, the Happy Hours Magazine in 1925, and the Dime Novel Round-Up in 1931. (JRC)

D22. Cure, Raymond. "Christmas and It's Pantomime Time Again." CDA, 1976, pp. 64-65.
In 1931, the Union Jack offered "The Phantom of the Pantomime," by W. J. Elliott, in place of the traditional Christmas story by Gwyn Evans who was gravely ill. (JRC)

D23. Dizer, John T., Jr. Tom Swift & Company. "Boys Books" by Stratemeyer and Others. Introduction by J. Randolph Cox. Jefferson, North Carolina:

McFarland & Co, Inc., 1982. 192pp. Illus. Bibliography and index.
Entertaining tribute to boys' fiction. Of marginal interest for this bibliography. Reviews: DNR 51:2(April 82):26-28; PBSA 77:1(1983):67-74.

D24. Donelson, Ken. "Nancy, Tom and Assorted Friends in the Stratemeyer Syndicate Then and Now." Children's Literature 7 (1978), pp. 17-44.
An excellent scholarly article, copiously footnoted, analyzing the creations of the Stratemeyer Syndicate and providing much background information. Synopses of various series are given, the Franklin K. Mathiews controversy is described, and the article concludes with a summation of modern day series book criticism. ("Some English teachers and librarians still apparently believe it is their duty to attack Nancy Drew and the Hardy Boys.") (Jack Bales)

D25. Doyle, Brian. The Who's Who of Children's Literature. NY: Schocken Books, 1968.
Biographical sketches of over 400 authors and artists from 1800 to the present. Bibliography, illustrations. Includes some of the "Sexton Blake" writers (Harry Blyth, Edwy Searles Brooks), as well as the dean of Blake illustrators, Eric R. Parker. (JRC)

D27. Ellis, Edward S. Introduction to "Seth Jones of New Hampshire." TBBC 3:3 (1973):336-43. Photo.
Reprinting of an article by author Ellis on the dime novel with a defense against charges that the dime novel is a corruptor of youth. There are also some comments on other writers with whom Ellis was acquainted.

D28. Ferris, Laurana Sheldon. "Letter Sent to George French, Jan. 10th, 1938." DNR 11 (June 43):4-5.
Fragmentary autobiography of the prolific contributor to My Queen and other series. Admits to having written only one Old King Brady story (but doesn't say which) but several Buffalo Bills, Jesse James, Bertha M. Clays, and others. Includes list of periodicals to which she contributed as Laurana Sheldon (her maiden name) and some of her pseudonyms. (JRC)

D29. (Fitzhugh, Percy Keese) O'Gara, Gil. "Tom Slade and Friends." YL 1:4 (Jly/Aug 81):21-22; part 2 (by Bob Chenu) YL 1:5 (Sept/Oct 81):16-18.
O'Gara writes on Fitzhugh's Boy Scout series in part 1 while in part 2, Bob Chenu presents checklists of Fitzhugh's writing for boys, 1912-34. Titles indicate mystery/adventure elements in some of the fiction.

D30. (Fitzhugh, Percy Keese) Sullivan, John F. "The Do Good Boys and the Grave Peril or Percy Keese Hits the Road." TBBC 3:2 (Spring 72):290-301.
A survey of Fitzhugh's boys' fiction. The article contains letters, interviews with Fitzhugh's associates and family, and a list of his books.

D31. Fronval, George. "Dime Novels in France." Translated by Albert J. Dumoulin, Jr. DNR 33 (1964):27-37. Illus.
A detailed history of dime novels in France, including a discussion of French editions of American, German, and English dime novels. Contains some publication information for Nick Carter, Nat Pinkerton, Claude Duval, and Harry Dickson. (DJ)

D32. Gantner, Joe. "Authors of Old Weeklies." DNR 12 (Jan 44):1-2.
Identifies authors behind many dime novels series, including (Samuel) Spalding, John R. Coryell, and Frederic Van Rensselaer Dey. Excerpted from a series, "If You Must Write" by Harry A. Keller, which appeared in

The Editor in the 1930s. Keller, a former editor at Street & Smith, worked on a Nick Carter story (not identified by title) in 1915. (JRC)

D33. Godsave, R. J. "The Supernatural." CDA, 1977, pp. 101-102.
The most memorable of Edwy Searles Brooks' supernatural stories were the Dr. Karnak and Ezra Quirk series in the Nelson Lee Library. (JRC)

D34. Goulart, Ron. Cheap Thrills: An Informal History of the Pulp Magazines. New Rochelle, NY: Arlington House, 1972. See especially pp. 20-29.
Traces the origin of pulp heroes to the story papers and dime novels. Research appears to be based on Mary Noel's article (D61) from American Heritage, Robert Clurman's introduction to Nick Carter, Detective (D133), and E. S. Turner's Boys Will Be Boys (D77). Superficial but lively. (JRC)

D35. Haining, Peter. "The Sensational Sleuths." In Mystery (B138), pp. 46-55.
Brief survey of the dime novel detective in a chapter devoted to "Railway Fiction" and "Yellow Backs." An oversimplified account. (JRC)

D36. Haining, Peter, editor. Blood and Thunder: An Illustrated History of the First Super Heroes. London: New English Library, Feb 1980. Illustrated.
This is primarily a selection of stories and illustrations from various series of story papers published by the Aldine Publishing company, the major British publisher of blood-and-thunder stories. The papers featured such characters as Nick Carter, Deadwood Dick, Ned Kelly, etc. Haining's commentary discusses the publishing history and contents of the various series. Many of the original cover illustrations are reproduced in full color. (REB)

D37. ______. The Penny Dreadful, or, Strange, Horrid & Sensational Tales! London: Gollancz, 1975. 382pp.
An anthology of Victorian sensational fiction, including selections from American dime novels. Mr. Haining includes background material and biography where possible, stressing the social aspects of "fiction for the working man" in Great Britain. An occasional date or title is incorrect, probably because the editor trusted his sources a little too much: in this field one can trust very little of the earlier work. But these small points do not affect the collection's overall value. (EFB)

D38. ______. The Shilling Shockers: Tales of Terror from the Gothic Bluebooks. London: Gollancz, 1978. 183pp.
Selections from the English "Bluebooks," paper-covered pamphlets published in the early nineteeth century during the vogue for Gothic fiction. Includes some supernatural mysteries. In a short introduction, Haining discusses the popularity of this fiction and, although he does not say so, the material and its paperbound, mass market publication seem somewhat comparable to the later phenomenon of the dime novel.

D39. Holmes, Harold C. "New Magnet Library No. 1036." DNR 7 (Feb 39):2.
Stories from Shield Weekly 13, 19, and 21 were used in Magnet Library 280, reprinted as Magnet Library No. 1036. (JRC)

D40. ______. "New York Detective Library No. 171." DNR 10 (Nov 42):1-8.
Plot synopsis of The Broadway Detective; Or, A Midday Robbery, by Francis W. Doughty, from the New York Detective Library 171 (13 March 1886). Not an Old King Brady story. (JRC)

D41. ______. "Shield Weekly." DNR 12 (March 44):1-3.
Bibliographical essay on the short-lived Street & Smith Series, Shield Weekly (22 numbers), which was reprinted in the paper-covered Magnet Library novels as Nick Carter stories. Some misinformation: Adventures of Harrison Keith, Detective (Magnet No. 93) has no textual connection with Shield Weekly and the authorship of the stories in the latter was unknown at the time this was written. Illustration of one cover. (JRC)

D42. Hoppenstand, Gary, ed. The Dime Novel Detective. Bowling Green, OH: Popular Press, 1982.
Anthology of five representative examples reproduced in facsimile, but without the original cover illustrations. Old King Brady, Old Cap. Collier, Old Sleuth, and Bob Brooks are represented here, with checklists of titles in their respective Libraries and Weeklies with the addition of the Young Sleuth Library. The introduction contains a confused and inaccurate description of the dime novel as a publication type. Preface by Edward T. LeBlanc, Editor of the Dime Novel Round-Up. (JRC)

D43. Hudson, Harry K. A Bibliography of Hard-Cover (Series Type) Boys' Books. Revised edition. Tampa, FL: Data Print, 1977. v-xiv, 280pp.
Listed by series with bibliographic information the original publication and reprints including description of bindings and dustjackets. Illustrators, where known, are given. Additions to the bibliography were published in issues of Yellowback Library from number 3 (May/June 81) through 15 (May /June 83).

D44. Jenks, George. "Dime Novel Makers." The Bookman, Oct 1904; reprinted in Age of the Unicorn 2:2 (n.d.):119-34; and in YL 1:3 (May/June 81):20-23 and 1:4 (July/Aug 81):11-13.
A writer of dime novels gives a brief history and discusses writing techniques characteristic of dime novelists with excerpts as examples.

D45. Johanssen, Albert. The House of Beadle and Adams and Its Dime and Nickle Novels: The Story of a Vanished Literature. Norman: University of Oklahoma Press, 1950. 2 vols., illus. v. 3, Supplement, Addenda, Corrigenda, Etc., 1961.
Definitive history and bibliography of the oldest firm of dime novel publishers whose speciality was the frontier tale but did not wholly ignore detective fiction. Vol. 2 is a biographical encyclopedia of dime novel authors who wrote for Beadle as well as for other firms. A model of scholarship. (JRC)

D46. Johnson, Deidre, compiler/editor. Stratemeyer Pseudonyms and Series Books: An Annotated Checklist of Stratemeyer and Stratemeyer Syndicate Publications. Westport, CT and London, England: Greenwood Press, 1982. vii-xl, 343pp.
In her introduction, Johnson provides a detailed history of the Stratemeyer Syndicate with portraits of the leading contributors. The entries are classified by pseudonym and, within that category, as series and non-series. There are several appendices with summary indexes of the information in the main bibliography. Of particular interest to researchers will be the bibliography of secondary material which is a basic guide to published research on juvenile series including the Hardy Boys and Nancy Drew series. Included in the main bibliography are Nick Carter reprint series. Review/essay: Samuel Pickering, Jr. in PBSA 77:1 (1983):67-74.

D47. Kodaka, Nobumitsu. Hardboiled Izen: America ga Aishita Hero tachi, 1840-1920 |Before hard-boiled fiction: heroes America loved|. Tokyo: Soshi-sha, 1980. 252pp. Illus., index.

A study focussing on dime novels, pulp fiction and other material often ignored in studies of detective fiction. The author concludes that Western heroes are the ancestors of hard-boiled private detectives. (HS/TT)

D48. Leblanc, Edward T., and Scollo, Peter A. A Bibliography of Four Tousey Dime-Novel Story Papers. Fall River, MA; 1965, 1966. Reprinted by Garland Press, 1979.

Frank Tousey, one of the major dime-novel publishers, and his successors issued four important story papers, from 1875-1924. These were The Boys of New York (usually considered the greatest of all such periodicals) and its continuation, Happy Days, and Young Men of America and its continuation, The Golden Weekly. In them first appeared many science-fiction stories about Frank Reade, Frank Reade, Jr., and Jack Wright; detective stories about Old King Brady and Young Sleuth; westerns about Kit Carson and Jesse James; circus stories; humor stories; railroad stories; baseball stories; fireman stories; get-rich stories, and all the other dime-novel types. Many of these stories were illustrated much more profusely and better than their later reprints as individual books. In each of the bibliographies (prepared by Leblanc with Peter A. Scollo assisting on Happy Days), after general introductory information about dates and publishing circumstances, Messrs. Leblanc and Scollo offer story listings with precise dates, cross-references to the later reprintings in other Tousey publications, titles changes, pseudonyms, and similar material. Both author and story indexes are also provided. (EFB)

D49. Leckenby, Herbert. "Detectives in Boys' Literature." CDA, 1952, pp. 46-51.

The two most popular genres within the boys' papers were school stories and detective stories. Sexton Blake wasn't alone and there were many reprints from American dime novels. Includes checklist of authors, detectives, and papers in which they appeared. (JRC)

D50. Leithead, J. Edward. "The Anatomy of Dime Novels: The Arthur Westbrook Company." DNR 37 (1968):56-60; Part II 37 (1968):68-73.

A two-part discussion of Arthur Westbrook Company dime novel series. Part I includes the Old Sleuth Weekly; part II contains a long excerpt from a Jeff Clayton detective story and the issue numbers of detective tales in Westbrook's Adventure Series. (DJ)

D51. ______. "The Anatomy of Dime Novels: Bootblack Detectives." DNR 37 (1968):78-83.

A brief history of bootblack detectives, primarily Broadway Billy and Bowery Billy, which includes excerpts, lists of titles, and some information about the authors of the tales. (DJ)

D52. ______. "Boy Detectives." DNR 20 (1952):66-71; part II 20 (1952):74-79. Illus.

Two parts. Part I contains a list of titles featuring boy detectives from early dime novel series: Beadle's Dime Library and Half Dime Library, Munro's Old Cap Collier Library and Old Sleuth Library, Tousey's New York Detective Library and Young Sleuth Library. Includes minor background information on Deadwood Dick, Jr. and Broadway Billy, with excerpts from two of their adventures. Part II continues the list, covering Street & Smith's Brave and Bold series, with some information about Young Broadbrim Weekly and Shield Weekly. Also contains excerpts from the Bowery Boy Library and descriptions of Bowery Billy Barlow and some of the characters in this series. (DJ)

D53. ______. "Tales of Klondike Gold in Dime Novels." DNR 25 (1957):87-92. Illus.
A brief history of the Klondike gold rush and its treatment in dime novel series. Includes a list of titles from Diamond Dick, Jr., Weekly, Nick Carter Weekly, Secret Service, Medal Library, and Old Cap Collier Library on the subject. (DJ)

D54. ______. "This 'Sleuth' Business." DNR 31 (1963):50-54; 62-65; 70-75.
Article in three installments covering detectives in dime novels issued by various publishers. Part one, arranged by detective, provides a detailed list of detective tales in Beadle & Adams publications; part two deals with Arthur Westbrook Company publications, the various Old Sleuth series, and Munro publications, especially the Old Cap Collier Library, and gives bibliographic information for the Old Broadbrim tales reprinted therein; part three continues the reprint information and lists detectives in Tousey's dime novels, with emphasis on Old King Brady. (DJ)

D55. Lofts, W. O. G., and Adley, D. J. The Men Behind Boys' Fiction. London: Howard Baker, 1970.
Data on over 2,000 authors and editors of British juvenile literature, some biographical sketches, a list of all the writers of the Sexton Blake stories with date of publication of first contribution to the series. Pseudonyms and real names noted. Many of the writers also wrote adult books of fiction. (JRC)

D56. Mason, Bobbie Ann. The Girl Sleuth: A Feminist Guide. Old Westbury, NY: Feminist Press, 1975. xi, 145pp. Illus.
A recent Ph. D. turns to the series sleuths of her childhood and writes a study of rediscovery and analysis. Breen 50.

D57. Maurice, Arthur Bartlett. "The Detective in Fiction." Bookman 15 (May 1902):231-36.
The dime novel sleuths were superior to the present-day "shockers." There is also a brief examination of the merits of Doyle's Holmes and Gaboriau's Lecoq.

D58. Morgan, L. "Old New York After Nightfall." DNR 10 (March 42):6-7.
A walk through New York Streets while recalling dime novel novel stories, especially the Chinatown ones from Secret Service. Apparently a reprint from 30 Sept 1941, source not given. (JRC)

D59. Moskowitz,Sam. "A History of 'The Scientific Romance' in the Munsey Magazines, 1912-1920." In Under the Moons of Mars: A History and Anthology, pp. 291-433. NY: Holt, Rinehart and Winston, 1970.
The transition between the dime novel and detective pulp is decribed (p. 386), but the vehicle was Nick Carter Stories (160 issues, 1912-1915) and not Nick Carter Weekly. (JRC)

D60. The Mystery and Adventure Series Review. Edited and published by Fred Woodworth, P. O. Box 3488, Tucson, Arizona 85722.

A digest-sized magazine, published quarterly. 1:1 published Summer, 1980. To date (December 1983), 13 issues have appeared. Review articles on juvenile series, with letters and advertisements. Many interior illustrations and jacket and binding artwork from the original books.

D61. Noel, Mary. "Dime Novels." American Heritage 7 (Feb 56):50-55, 112-13.
Entertaining survey of the style and content of the dime novel which "worshipped success, as it exalted danger and adventure; it instilled many of our subconscious habits of thought" and thus teaches us about our "nationalistic ways and creed of self-reliance." No footnotes or bibliography and few dates of publication cited. The author has obviously read widely and deeply into the genre and does not consider the dime novel detective story any sort of predecessor to the "mystery" since there is little mystery in a dime novel. Well illustrated with covers from publications of Street & Smith and Frank Tousey. (JRC)

D62. Noel, Mary. Villains Galore: The Heyday of the Popular Story Weekly. NY: Macmillan Co., 1954.
The history of the story papers in which serialized adventures of Old Sleuth, Old Cap Collier, and Nick Carter first appeared. Includes an account of the legal battle over the rights to the phrase "Old Sleuth." (JRC)

D63. Nye, Russel. "The Dime Novel Tradition." In The Unembarrassed Muse: The Popular Arts in America, pp. 200-215. NY: Dial Press, 1970.
Research based largely on secondary sources and a necessary compressing of much information into too small a space result in inaccuracies of fact and sweeping generalizations. "Old Sleuth" was the house name used as author of a long series of novels but appeared as the hero of less than a dozen. There were no Nick Carter comic book stories after 1949. Young King Brady was not Old King Brady's son. Old Cap Collier did not appear in 800 novels (more like two dozen). Edward Wheeler wrote about Deadwood Dick, not Diamond Dick. Good selective bibliography. (JRC)

D64. "Old Slob's Detective Library: Strong Armed Sam; or, the Sleuth at 16." DNR 20 (1952):57-60. Illus.
Reprint of a satire of a dime novel detective story; source dated April 24, 1898, and tentatively identified in the article as the New York American. (DJ)

D65. Pachon, Stanley A. "William Wallace Cook." DNR 25 (1957):67-75. Illustrated.
A biography of Cook, including a year-by-year account of Cook's stories for Street & Smith from 1894-1910 (usually by series or pseudonym, not individual titles) and a list of Cook's pseudonyms. Contributed to a number of series, among them the Nick Carter series. (DJ)

D66. Packman, Josie. "The Curious Case of the Once or Twicers." CDA, 1979, pp. 12-13.
A survey of those writers for the Union Jack who only contributed one or two stories. (JRC)

D67. Parratt, C. J. "The Paper of a Thousand Thrills." CDA, 1950, pp. 66-68.
Brief survey of the history of the Thriller with a checklist of all authors whose work appeared there (589 nos, 1929-1940). (JRC)

D68. Pearson, Edmund. Dime Novels; or, Following an Old Trail in Popular Literature. Boston: Little, Brown, 1929; Port Washington, NY: Kennikat Press, 1968.

A somewhat tongue-in-cheek and not entirely accurate historical treatment of the dime novel which nevertheless preserves something of the flavor of the era. Chapters on Old Cap Collier, Old Sleuth, and Nick Carter preserve in synopsis some of the now vanished episodes in their careers. Interviews with individuals on their youthful exposure to dime novels. (JRC)

D69. Pegler, Westbrook. "Fair Enough." Worcester (Mass.) Telegram and Evening Gazette, 15 Oct 43; reprinted in DNR 12 (Dec 43):1-2.

Anecdotal comparisons between dime novel detective adventures and their counterparts in comic strips and radio serials. (JRC)

D70. Reynolds, Quentin. The Fiction Factory; or, From Pulp Row to Quality Street. NY: Random House, 1955.

Anecdotal history of Street & Smith publishing Co., sections of which deal with the dime novels and especially Nick Carter. Inaccurate in many details since it was based in part on interviews with people too far removed from the period. Illustrated and indexed. Illustrations include page one of the first Nick Carter serial in the New York Weekly. (JRC)

D71. Rogers, Denis R. "The Detective Stories of Edward S. Ellis." DNR 51 (1982):94-101; 52 (1983):2-10, 23-24.

In two installments. A brief history of Ellis's detective fiction, followed by a checklist of the Ellis stories that contained a detective as one of the featured characters. The checklist, arranged in chronological order, includes reprint information and plot synopses. (DJ)

D72. Sampson, Robert. "A Time of Lively Fiction." DNR 48 (1979):93-97; Part II 49 (1980):8-13. Illus.

First two parts of a seven part article tracing the history of cheap fiction from dime novels through the pulp era. Part I provides an overview of dime novels and the transition to pulp magazines; part II classifies and discusses different types of dime novel heroes, many of them sleuths. (DJ)

D73. Smeltzer, Robert H. "Sherlock Holmes." DNR 13 (Nov 44):1-2.

Nostalgic recollections of reading dime novels along with Sherlock Holmes. (JRC)

D74. Smith, Wilbur Jordan. "Mystery Fiction in the Nineteenth Century." In MDA 1973 (B3), pp. 193-205.

Speculations on the extent of 19th century mystery publishing based on the holdings of the Department of Special Collections of the Research Library at the University of California, Los Angeles, as well as existing bibliographies. Photos of rare dime novel titles and a complete bibliography (62 titles) of Street & Smith's Secret Service Series (1887-1892). Incorrectly assigns all Nick Carter titles to John R. Coryell. (JRC)

D75. Soderbergh, Peter A. "The Stratemeyer Strain: Educators and the Juveniles Series Book, 1900-1973." JPC 7 (Spring 74):864-72.

A detailed discussion outlining the unending controversy between Stratemeyer and the proponents of "good" literature for children. The Hardy Boys and other favorites are mentioned. Includes footnotes. (Jack Bales)

D77. Stern, Madeleine B., ed. Publishers for Mass Entertainment in Nineteenth Century America. Boston: G. K. Hall & Co., 1980.
An uneven reference book which nevertheless should not be ignored. A lack of adequate source material and the compression of too much data into a short space lead to misleading statements of fact in too many entries in this compilation of short histories of 46 publishers, many of whom issued detective dime novels. Well illustrated with selective bibliographies. Author-Title Index. (JRC)

D78. Turner, E. S. Boys Will Be Boys: The Story of Sweeney Todd, Deadwood Dick, Sexton Blake, Billy Bunter, Dick Barton et al. London: Michael Joseph, 1948, 1957, 1975.
Primarily a survey of British boys' stories, but includes an account of the British editions (reprinted, revised, and newly written) of Nick Carter. Subsequent editions of Turner have been sufficiently revised and expanded to include the later boys' papers. Chapter 8 is called "Five-Five Years of Sexton Blake" in the original edition and "The Odyssey of Sexton Blake" in later editions. (JRC)

D79. Wormull, Len. "A Nugget in Search of Gold." CDA, 1975, pp. 51-55.
The Nugget Weekly was a merger of three other publications and as such included stories as diverse as those about Buffalo Bill, Nelson Lee, and Sexton Blake, as well as Robin Hood. (JRC)

D80. Wright, Charles. "Speaking of Aldines." CDA, 1953, pp. 39-45.
A survey of many series of paper-covered books published in England by the Aldine Publishing Co. Many of these were reprinted from American dime novels. Included was a series called Detective Tales. (JRC)

D81. Yellowback Library. Edited and published by Gil O'Gara, 811 Boulder Ave., Des Moines, IA 50315. Bi-monthly.
First issue published in January/February 1981. To date (December 1983), 18 issues have appeared. Primarily devoted to hardback juvenile series but information on dime novels is also occasionally included. Articles, checklists, columns of miscellaneous information and advertisements. Illustrated. A large amount of material on Leo Edwards, Nancy Drew and the Hardy Boys is published here, along with some fiction reprints. Index to the first 18 issues in no. 19 (Jan/Feb 84):12-13.

2. Series

"Agent Nine"

D82. "Agent Nine. A 'G' Man Series." YL 1:3 (May/June 81):3-5.
An overview of Graham M. Dean's "Agent Nine" series with an addendum listing books in two other "G" men series: "The G-Man's Son" by Warren F. Robinson and "G-Men" by William Engle and Laurence Dwight Smith.

"The Boy Spies"

D83. Chenu, Bob. "The Boy Spies and Navy Boys Series." YL 13 (Jan/Feb 83):3-5.
An early juvenile espionage series.

"Dave Fearless"

D84. Brahce, Jack. "Fearless Dave Fearless." YL 10 (July/Aug 82):14-15, 17; 11 (Sept/Oct 82):1-6, 24; 12 (Nov/Dec 82):4-6.
A checklist and overview of a mystery/adventure series. See also "Dave Fearless and the Development of Apathy," by Cecil K. Bilgewater, in YL 11, pp. 7-13.

"Deadwood Dick, Junior"

D85. Johanssen, Albert. "The Deadwood Dick, Junior, Stories Not Written by Wheeler." DNR 25 (1957):54-57.
Shows George Cowdrick to be the author of the sixty-first through the eighty-fifth Deadwood Dick, Jr., stories and suggests he may have written the last twelve stories as well. (DJ)

"Dick Dobbs"

D86. French, George. "Dick Dobbs Detective Weekly." DNR 4 (June 35):1.
Bibliographic essay on the short-run series which may have been the last dime novel series of all, a publication of the George Marsh Company in 1909. (JRC)

"Dixon Hawke"

D87. McMahon, J. "Dixon Hawke Library." CDA, 1970, pp. 77-78.
Nostalgic recollections of a series which rivaled that of Sexton Blake, the _Dixon Hawke Library_ ran 576 numbers (1919-1941). "Anything Sexton Blake could do, Hawke could do--much better." (JRC)

"George Marsden Plummer"

D88. Rowe, Cyril. "Plummer in _Pluck_." CDA, 1979, pp. 46-47.
An account of the early career of George Marsden Plummer, the renegade Detective Sergeant of Scotland Yard which appeared in the pages of _Pluck_. (JRC)

"G-Man's Son"

See "Agent Nine" (D82).

"G-Men"

See "Agent Nine" (D82).

"Hal Keen"

D89. Erickson, Byron. "A Glimpse of the Hal Keen Series." M&ASR 8 (Spring 82):(9)-(11).
With a checklist of the series by Hugh LLoyd (Percy Keese Fitzhugh). A boys' mystery series in which the main character seems to be modeled on Dorothy L. Sayers' Lord Peter Wimsey and the writing is generally superior to that of other boys' series.

"The Hardy Boys"

D90. Bales, Jack. "Those Indomitable Hardy Boys." YL 14 (March/April 83):6-8, 10; 15 (May/June 83):9-12; 16 (July/August 83):7-8; 17 (Sept/Oct 83):12-13; 18 (Nov/Dec 83):5-6.
A five-part series on miscellaneous subjects relating to the Hardy Boys series, including textual revisions in recent editions of the early titles, non-story collectibles, librarians' attitudes toward juvenile series and, in number 19, an annotated bibliography of secondary literature.

D91. "The Hardy Boys." M&ASR 4 (Spring 81).
An issue devoted to the series. Numerous illustrations from the books. The issue is not paginated. Contents: "Bayport's Famous Sleuths," pp. (1)-(2) (general essay); John M. Enright, "Mr. McFarlane's Magic," pp. (3)-(6) (characterization, plotting and artwork); John M. Enright, "Hardy Boys Tie-Ins," pp. (7)-(8) (TV series and comic books); "Dates of Origins and Rewrites," pp. (9) (this chronological chart also indicates the extent of revisions from "slightly altered" to "wholly different"; see also p. (10) for a chronological list of revisions); John M. Enright, "The Dust-Jacket Era, 1927-1961," pp. (10)-(13) (a "graded" listing with plot summaries; some comments on dust-jackets and bindings); Kent Winslow, "A Laughing Ghost," pp. (13)-(16) (a review of Leslie MacFarlane's Ghost of the Hardy Boys (D92)); Fred Woodworth, "Capwell Wyckoff--A Hardy Author?," pp. (16)-(19) (speculates that Wyckoff may have written some of the later books; theory demolished in issue 5, p. 9).

D92. McFarlane, Leslie. Ghost of the Hardy Boys. Toronto & New York: Methuen, 1976. 211pp.
The humorous, funny, irreverent and iconoclastic autobiography of the man who began the Hardy Boys' books in 1927 and who contributed over two million words in this series during the years he was "Franklin W. Dixon." McFarlane details much about Edward Stratemeyer and his literary syndicate, and also weaves into the narrative with remarkable skill his experiences as a journalist on small mining town newspapers in Canada. Highly recommended. (Jack Bales)

D93. O'Connor, Gerard. "The Hardy Boys Revisited: A Study in Prejudice." In Challenges in American Culture, edited by Ray B. Browne, pp. 234-41. Bowling Green, OH: Popular Press, 1970.
A rather bitter article aimed at confronting the "racism" in the Hardy Boys series. The author maintains that the Hardy Boys' world is "a world of gross prejudice, of insulting stereotypes, of crude caricature." See also Paul C. Deane, "The Persistence of Uncle Tom: An Examination of the Negro in Children's Fiction Series." The Journal of Negro Education 37 (Spring 68):140-45. (Jack Bales; YL 18, p. 6)

D94. Phillips, Louis. "Me and the Hardy Boys." TAD 15:2 (82):174-77. Illus.
A reader recounts his early addiction to the Hardy Boys series and discusses the characters and plots.

D95. Prager, Arthur. "Rascals at Large." In his Rascals at Large (Doubleday, 1971), pp. 97-123.
This is perhaps one of the first modern pieces written on the Hardys that is devoid of all the miserable claptrap that haunts series book criticism. Background material on Stratemeyer is given, and Prager presents a very readable, entertaining overview of the Hardy Boys books, complete with quotations from the texts. (Jack Bales)

D96. Riordan, Robert V. "A Half Century of The Hardy Boys, or Clues to an Obscure Chronology." DNR 47 (April 78):34-47.
In spite of some errors, this is still noteworthy as the first serious attempt to create order out of dozens of complexities facing the Hardy Boys bibliographer. Riordan discusses bindings, endpapers, frontispieces, book notes, length, dust jackets, and first editions. (Jack Bales)

D97. Wasylyshyn, John. "A Neo-Freudian Analysis of The Hardy Boys Mystery Series." In Researching American Culture, edited by Phillip Kottak, pp. 111-115. Ann Arbor: University of Michigan Press, 1982.
The author sees the popularity of the Hardy Boys books as deriving from their relevancy to the psychosexual development of their readers. The readers are usually in the "latent" developmental stage while the Hardy Boys, in their late teens, have successfully integrated several stages. Some discussion of Oedipal and id/superego relationship in the series.

D98. ______. "An Analysis of American Culture as Presented in Two Hardy Boys Books That Differ in Time." In Researching American Culture (D97), pp. 116-27.
A discussion of ways the two versions (1935 and 1961) of The Hidden Harbour Mystery differ and how these differences relate to changes in regionalism, kinship and family ties, women in society and race portrayals. Wasylyshyn maintains that their readers were not "lower" class because the books were not in libraries and had to be purchased and it is his experience that no one can read just one. His hypothesis is that even if a lower-class youth read one, he could not get "hooked" because he would not have the money to buy other titles. Wasylyshyn lists some of the differences in the second version: the boys are two years older and more independent, anti-Southern references have been deleted and a stereotypical black character has been removed.

D99. Zuckerman, Ed. "The Great Hardy Boys' Whodunit." Rolling Stone, issue no. 221 (9 Sept 76), pp. 36-40.
Perhaps the best article yet written on the dynamic duo. Zuckerman compares the original volumes with the insipidly rewritten books, and although he does not mention Leslie McFarlane, he offers considerable background information on Stratemeyer and the Syndicate. Beautifully illustrated. (Jack Bales)

"Harrison Keith"

D100. Leithead, J. Edward. "The Harrison Keith Stories." DNR 5 (Nov 36):2-3.
Brief bibliographic essay concernfing the 51 volumes about Harrison Keith in the Magnet Library with some speculations on the use of material from Shield Weekly and Old Broadbrim Weekly there. (JRC)

"Jerry Todd"

D101. Chenu, Bob. "Edition Variations of Leo Edwards Books Published by Grosset & Dunlap." TBBC 3:1 (Fall 71/Wtr 71):282-84.
Bibliographical data.

D102. ______. "Leo Edwards and His Books." YL 1:2 (March/April 81):15-18.
Biography with checklists of Edwards several boys' series.

D103. ______. "The Leo Edwards Saga: The Jerry Todd Series. YL 17 (Sept/Oct 83), pp. 3-6.
Characters and settings.

D105. Lee, Eugene. "Leo Edwards." TBBC 1:3 (Spring 70):92-95. Photos and illustrations.
Personal memories of Edwards and his readers by his son.

D106. O'Gara, Gil. "Leo Edwards: In Appreciation of." YL 1:1 (Jan/Feb 81):13-18. Illus.
On Edwards' series books. The Jerry Todd and Nicholas Carter Sherlock Holmes "Poppy" Ott series are most closely related to detective fiction.

D107. The Tutter Bugle. Editors: Robert L. Johnson and Julius R. Chenu. Two series of this fanzine, published by the Leo Edwards Juvenile Jupiter Detective Association, appeared for a total of 26 issues between December 1967 through February 1975. Not seen. Cook, pp. 583-84.

"Jocko Kelly"

D108. LeBlanc, Edward T. "Rare Dime Novels: 4, the Hub 10 Cent Novels." DNR 20 (Jan 52):1-4.
Bibliographic description of a rare dime novel series and a plot synopsis of one of the Jocko Kelly stories which were based on the exploits of a real crook of the 1890s in Boston. Includes a checklist of titles and an illustration of the cover of No. 1. (JRC)

"Judy Bolton"

D109. Russell, Luana. "A Judy Bolton Mystery - 'Blacklisted Classics'." Clues 2:1 (Spring/Summer 81):35-44.
A defense of a juvenile series for girls disparaged by librarians. Russell considers the series as being related to the "larger historical perspective of detective fiction" and discusses it in the context of adult mysteries with female heroines. One of the few attempts to bring juvenile mystery fiction out of the critical ghetto to which it is customarily relegated.

"Ken Holt"

D110. Woodworth, Fred. "The Ken Holt Mystery Stories by Bruce Campbell." M&ASR 2 (Fall 80):7-20. Illustrated.
An in-depth look at this boys' mystery series. Woodworth provides considerable information on the author of the series, Samuel Epstein, as well as a detailed examination of the 18 titles and some information on British, Dutch and German editions. In a prefatory editorial, editor Woodworth makes a case for examining juvenile fiction as literature.

"Martin Dale"

D111. Hockley, Geoff. "That Other Detective, or Maxwell Scott's Second String." CDA, 1957, pp. 37-45.
Maxwell Scott had another detective series besides that about Nelson Lee, the Martin Dale stories of 1911-1916. (JRC)

"Melody Lane"

D112. Abreu, John E. "Down Melody Lane with Lilian Garis." YL 9 (May/June 82):2-8.
A short biography of the author and a survey of this girls' mystery series.

"The Mystery Hunters"

D113. Holbrook, Don. "Wyckoff's Stories of Adventure." M&ASR 5 (Summer 81):6-20. Illus. Includes a biography of Capwell Wyckoff (p. 21).
There were four titles published in this series (1934-26) but other series and non-series titles (as listed) also appear to have mystery elements.

"Nancy Drew"

D114. Conger, Lesley. "Nancy Drew and the Secret Fort." The Writer, Feb 76, pp. 9-10.
On the reading habits of the author's daughters. Oblique references to Nancy Drew.

D115. Farah, Dave. "Basic Nancy Drew." YL 6 (Nov/Dec 81):6-7.
The first in a series of articles appearing in each issue, with thirteen installments published through issue 18 (Nov/Dec 83). The first 9 installments dealt with the format of the volumes and variants. In installments 10-13, the focus shifted to collectibles; in installment 13 (issue 17), Farah comments on some magazine and newspaper articles on the series, without claiming to present a complete checklist of secondary material. In the 14th installment (issue 18), he returns to a consideration of format with a close study of the early editions of Password to Larkspur Lane and the comment that he has yet to see a 1932 edition of the novel. A valuable, if somewhat disorganized, contribution to the critical history of the series.

D116. ______. "Cameo Edition Nancy Drews." YL 5 (Sept/Oct 81):3.
A bibliographic study. See also installment 10 of the "Basic Nancy Drew" for additional information on the cameo editions.

D117. Jones, James P. "Nancy Drew, WASP Super Girl of the 1930's." JPC 6 (73):707-717.
Racial stereotypes, class snobbery and period references in the series.

D118. ______. "Negro Stereotypes in Children's Literature: The Case of Nancy Drew." The Journal of Negro Education, Spring 71, pp. 121-25. Not seen.

D119. Keene, Carolyn (Harriet Adams). "Nancy Drew." In Penzler, The Great Detectives (B309), pp. 79-86.
A portrait of Nancy Drew with comments on the rewriting of earlier titles "which are no longer in line with customs and language of today."

D120. Lapin, Geoffrey S. "Carolyn Keene, Pseud." YL 16 (July/August 83): 3-5.
The authorship of series titles by Mildred A. Wirt based on research and interviews with Miss Wirt.

D121. ______. "Carolyn Keene, pseud." YL 18 (Nov/Dec 83):13-17. Photo.
An essay on the Nancy Drew titles written by Walter Karig with biographical and Stratemeyer Syndicate data.

D122. Miller, Margo. "Nancy Drew Follows Wellesley Motto." Boston Globe, 4 March 78, p. 8.
Article on Harriet Stratemeyer Adams (Carolyn Keene) on the occasion of her receiving an "alumnae achievement award" from Wellesley College. (REB)

D123. "Nancy Drew." M&ASR 7 (Winter 81). Illustrated. Not paginated.
Contents: John M. Enright, "Nancy Drew in Review," pp. (6)-(12) (overview, artwork, dust-jackets); Don Holbrook, "Nancy Drew in Japanese," p. (13) (format of Japanese editions); John M. Enright, "TV's Nancy Drew," pp. (14)-(15) (1977 series starring Pamela Sue Martin); Kent Winslow, "The Critic's Clew...to Miss Drew," pp. (16)-(21) (authorship and narrative weaknesses).

D124. Praeger, Arthur. "The Secret of Nancy Drew: Pushing Forty and Going Strong." In Rascals at Large (Doubleday, 1971), pp. 71-95.
A funny but affectionate survey of the series and the reasons for its popularity (fantasy adventures for pre-pubescent girls) with an epilogue in which Praeger visits Harriet S. Adams, is taken gently to task by her for some of his statements, and surveys, briefly, some other juvenile girls' series.

D125. Williams, Donna Kay. "That Drew Girl Gumshoes in Bobbysox." Boston Phoenix, 2 Dec 80, sect. 3, pp. 3, 12-13.
A general article on girl sleuths with principal emphasis on Nancy Drew. (KLM)

"Nelson Lee"

D126. Churchill, C. E. "You May Not Remember." CDA, 1965, pp. 112-16.
Synopsis of A Christmas of Peril which appeared in the Nelson Lee Library No. 78 (2 Dec 16), the first Christmas number of the paper. Nelson Lee vs. Prof. Zingrave. Story by Edwy Searles Brooks. (JRC)

D127. Godsave, Reuben. "The Black Wolf." In Collectors' Digest Annual, 1961, pp. 26-35.
Entertaining synopsis of the third series of stories featuring Mademoiselle Miton, the Black Wolf, in the Nelson Lee detective stories (Nelson Lee Library, 1915), by G. H. Teed. (JRC)

D128. Lister, William. "There's a Fortune Coming Someone's Way." CDA, 1978, pp. 67-68.
Nelson Lee may not have been the world's greatest detective as the editor claimed in 1931, but "The Final Round" in which Professor Mark Rymer tries to gain a fortune delivers the appropriate thrills. (JRC)

D129. Wood, Jack. "A Dead Man's Secret, or, Nelson Lee in Fact and Faction." CDA, 1954, pp. 29-45.
The early years of the career of Nelson Lee in the stories by Maxwell Scott (John Staniworth), 1894-1912, with an account of the actor and dramatist whose name was used for the hero of the series. Includes checklist of titles and publications. (JRC)

D130. ______. "The Nelson Lee Story." CDA, 1955, pp. 133-143.
Further discussion of the detective stories about Nelson Lee, the major rival in popularity to Sexton Blake in the British papers. (JRC)

"Nick Carter"

D131. Burgess, Gelett. "The Confessions of a Dime Novelist." Bookman (NY) 15 (Aug 1902):528-33. (Rptd. with an introduction as "Blood and Thunder Novels of the Nineties." Welcome News 14 (March 1941):8-10; same in DNR 9 (May 41):2-5).
Tongue-in-cheek interview with Eugene T. Sawyer who appears to indicate that he created Nick Carter if one doesn't read closely, was paid $50 each for the stories, but found it difficult to find plausible ways to bring Nick back to life when other writers would kill him off. Identifies specifically only one of the stories which Sawyer wrote (The Dead Man's Hand; or, Nick Carter's Matchless Method). (JRC)

D132. Burns, William M. "Our Old Story Papers, No. 3, 'New York Weekly.'" DNR 17 (May 49):37-45.
Historical survey of the story paper which published the first Nick Carter serial with a brief list of some of the other detective stories which appeared there. Suggests that the success of the publication was largely due to its detective fiction. (JRC)

D133. Clurman, Robert O., ed. Nick Carter Detective: Fiction's Most Celebrated Detective. Six Astonishing Adventures. NY: Macmillan, 1963.
Anthology of 6 novelettes, 4 taken from Nick Carter Library, 2 from Nick Carter Weekly. Stories 1-2 by Frederic Van Rensselaer Dey; story 3 by George Waldo Browne; story 4 by O. P. Caylor; stories 5-6 by Frederick R. Burton. Eight page introduction by a writer for the New York Times, researched using only secondary sources, is a virtual compendium of all the misinformation about the character and series which has ever appeared in print. Correctly attributes Nick's success to that "willing suspension of disbelief" brought to the stories by readers in a less complex age. (JRC)

D134. Coryell, John Russell. "Reminiscences of Nick Carter by His Creator." Street & Smith's Detective Story Magazine 13 (5 March 1918):46-52.
An account of the correspondence received by Coryell from Nick Carter readers and his attempts to be an armchair consultant and problem-solver for those who believed in the reality of the great detective. Compares his creation to d'Artagnan as a hero of romance. (No specific information on the creation or the writing of the stories.) (JRC)

D135. Coryell, Russell M. "The Birth of Nick Carter." Bookman (NY) 69 (July 1929):495-502.
Reminiscences of John R. Coryell, creator of Nick Carter, written by his son. Charming account of how the three Coryell brothers discovered their father was the famous Nick Carter, but were forbidden to tell anyone because the older Coryell did not want to be known as the author of dime novels. On re-reading his youthful indiscretions he found them surprisingly good. (JRC)

D136. Couch, Frisco Bert. "Blood & Thunder Novels of the Gay Nineties Period." DNR 9 (May 41):1.
Takes issue with the statement that John R. Coryell created Nick Carter and offers as proof the text of Gelett Burgess's interview with Eugene T. Sawyer from the New York Bookman (D131). For a rebuttal, see Woodson's article from Welcome News (D198). (JRC)

D137. Cox, J. Randolph. "Bibliographic Listing: New Nick Carter Weekly." Supplement to DNR 44 (1975). Illus.

A bibliographic listing, in chronological order, of the Nick Carter Weekly, with author and reprint information. A detailed introduction discusses the series' contents, format, and cover illustrations, and offers comments on and analysis of Frederick Van Rensselaer Dey's contributions. A second section covers reprints and includes a list of Old Cap Collier Library issues reprinted in Nick Carter Weekly. A list of significant Nick Carter Weekly issues notes important events in the series: format changes, first and final appearances of key characters, etc. A separate section has errata for Cox's "Bibliographic Listing: The Nick Carter Library" (supplement to DNR 43 (1974)). Errata for this listing is in J. Randolph Cox, "Bibliographic Listing" (D139). (DJ)

D138. ______. "Bibliographic Listings: The Nick Carter Library." Supplement to DNR 43 (1974). Illus.

A bibliographic listing, chronologically arranged, of the Nick Carter Library, with author and reprint information. An introduction gives a detailed look at the Nick Carter Library, including format, authors, publication history, and cover illustrations, as well as some summary and analysis of content. A separate list highlights significant Nick Carter Library issues (format changes, first appearance of recurring characters, etc.); short sections discuss reprints, both by Street & Smith and by other publishers. Errata published in J. Randolph Cox, "Bibliographic Listing: New Nick Carter Weekly" (supplement to DNR 44 (1975)). (DJ)

D139. ______. "Bibliographic Listing: Nick Carter Stories and Other Series Containing Stories About Nick Carter." Supplement to DNR 46 (1977); Part II Supplement to DNR 49 (1980). Illus.

Two parts. Part I has an introduction discussing the format of Nick Carter Stories, with information about contents; a list of key issues in the series (i. e. format changes, introduction of important characters, etc.); and a bibliographic listing, in chronological order, for Nick Carter Stories, with author and reprint information. Part II contains a list of Nick Carter tales published in Detective Story Magazine, Nick Carter Magazine, Clues--Detective, Crime Busters, The Shadow, New York Weekly, Ainslee's, Rough Rider Weekly, New Medal Library, and Western Story Library. Also included are bibliographic listings for Shield Weekly and Old Broadbrim Weekly; a list of Old Cap Collier Library issues reprinted in Old Broadbrim Weekly; lists of Old Cap Collier and Union Jack Library issues rewritten as Nick Carter tales; an introduction discussing Nick Carter's publishing history; and errata for Part I and for Cox's "Bibliographic Listing: New Nick Carter Weekly" (supplement to DNR 44 (1975)). (DJ)

D140. ______. "Chapters from the Chronicles of Nick Carter." DNR 43 (1974):50-55; 62-67.

Two installments. Part one provides an historical perspective on Nick Carter's place among both dime novels and detective fiction, gives an overview of Nick Carter's publishing history, and begins plot summaries of Nick Carter Weekly stories from 1905. Part two continues the plot synopses for the Nick Carter Weekly through late 1905. (DJ)

D141. ______. "The Many Lives of Nick Carter." The Pulp Era, no. 71 (March/April 69), pp. 8-11.

Survey of the many incarnations of Nick Carter, from dime novels to modern paperbacks. (REB)

D142. ______. "Nick Carter in the Movies." DNR 47 (1978);:114-19.
History of French and American Nick Carter Movies, with references to their dime novel origins, and a synopsis of A Cry at Midnight (1920). (DJ)

D143. ______. "Nick Carter: The Man and the Myth." TMRN 2:3 (Feb 69):15-18.
Dispells the myths that Nick Carter did not drink or smoke and corrects information about his marriage.

D144. ______. "Nick Carter Studies: Nick Carter's Capitol Case; or, The Daring Detective's Defiance." DNR 45 (1976):22-25.
A satire of a Nick Carter tale, but one which incorporates a great deal of information about the recurring characters in the Nick Carter dime novels. (DJ)

D145. ______. "The Pulp Career of Nicholas Carter." Xenophile 22 (March/April 76):15-19.
The continuation of the Nick Carter saga in Detective Story Magazine, a Street & Smith pulp, with a checklist of stories in the magazine.

D146. ______. "Some Notes Toward a Study of Nick Carter." DNR 38 (1969):44-46.
A discussion of approaches to and problems with compiling information (primarily bibliographic) on the various Nick Carter series. (DJ)

D147. ______. "Strange Encounter." DNR 34 (1965):70-71.
A fanciful account of an encounter with Nick Carter which incorporates information about the history of Nick Carter from the early dime novels through the Killmaster series. (DJ)

D148. "The Creator of 'Nick Carter'." Literary Digest 73 (20 May 1922): 40, 42.
Account of the life and work of Frederic Van Rensselaer Dey as reported by several newspapers after his death. Photo of Dey, three New Magnet Library covers and a facsimile of a page from chapter 8 of The Hunter of Men (ironically, a chapter written by Charles W. Hooke, a protege of Dey's). (JRC)

D149. "Creator of 'Nick Carter' Kills Himself; Penniless after Writing 40,000,000 Words." New York Times, 27 Apr 22, p. 1.
Obituary of Frederick Van Rensselaer Dey. Similar articles in other newspapers provoked a number of editorial exercises in nostalgia. (JRC)

D150. "Davis, Nick Carter's Ghost Writer, Dies in New Bedford." DNR 3 (Nov 34):1.
Obituary notice for Frederick W. Davis, a major writer for the Nick Carter series, reprinted from the Boston Transcript, 5 Jan 33. (JRC)

D151. Dey, Frederic Van Rensselaer. "How I Wrote a Thousand 'Nick Carter' Novels." American Magazine 89 (Feb 1920):18-19, 159-61, 163.
Autobiographical sketch of the prolific writer of most of the Nick Carter series. Some of the basic errors (mis-naming Nick's father "Seth Carter" instead of "Sim Carter" among others) found in later articles can be traced to this source. Publisher's records attribute less than 600 to Dey instead of his own round-figure of 1,000. (JRC)

D152. ______. "Who Created Nick Carter?" New York Tribune, 5 Jan 1917, n. p.
Letter to the editor in response to obituary notice of Alfred B. Tozer, reprinted in the Tribune from the Philadelphia Inquirer, setting straight some of the facts regarding the authorship of the Nick Carter stories. See also: "An Authentic Solution to the Mystery of the Celebrated Nick Carter." Current Opinion 62 (March 1917):206 (review of Dey's Tribune letter). (JRC)

D153. "'Diamond Dick' Author Dies in Rustic." DNR 2 (May/June 33):2-3.
Obituary notice of George C. Jenks who contributed much to the later years of the Nick Carter series. (JRC)

D154. "Dime Novel Days." DNR 10 (Jan 42):2-3.
Anecdotes of the creation of Nick Carter, the continuing of the series by Frederic Van Rensselaer Dey, his methods of writing, and the authorship of 10 Bertha Clay novels laid at the feet of Philadelphian William J. Benners. (JRC)

D155. Dobbin, William James. "'Nick Carter's' Father and His Last Fight." New York Tribune, 7 May 22, pp. 4-5.
Lengthy tribute to the memory of Frederic Van Rensselaer Dey whose "stories have thrilled two generations of boys." Photos of Dey's home and the author at work at the typewriter. Text of a prayer written by Dey. The author's masterpiece is considered to be the short story "The Magic Story," the theme of which is success by being oneself and being true to oneself. Dey's favorite Nick Carter novel was Tracked Across the Atlantic, an early serial for the New York Weekly. (JRC)

D156. "First 'Nick Carter' Story Was Accepted." DNR 7 (April 38):4-5.
Biographical sketch of Eugene T. Sawyer (1846-1924) who is credited here with 300 Nick Carter stories (an exaggeration). Reprinted from unspecified newspaper. (JRC)

D157. "F. W. Davis, 74, of 'Nick Carter' Authors, Dead." DNR 39 (1970):19-20.
Reprint of an obituary. Source unidentified; dateline New Bedford, Mass., January 4 (1933). (DJ)

D158. Gantner, Joe. ("Letter to Ralph Cummings.") DNR 13 (June 45):4.
Ideas for a new series of detective stories about the son of Nick Carter, Nick Carter, Jr. (DJ)

D159. ______. "My Search for Old Nick Carter." DNR 10 (Nov/Dec 41):1-2.
Nostalgia about reading Nick Carter and the Liberty Boys as a youth and the joys of finding some old stories as an adult. (JRC)

D160. ______. "Old Nick Carters." DNR 11 (June 43):1-4.
The desire to read again the novels of his boyhood is satisfied after the discovery of 19 numbers of the Nick Carter Weekly. Theories about the reasons for their appeal: the colored cover and the best period of the stories being those published between 1900 and 1904. Illus. of 3 covers. (Error in dating John Coryell's three serial stories in the 1870s.) (JRC)

D161. "Goods of Noted Writer Bring $1000." DNR 8 (Nov 39):2.
Newspaper account of the disposition of the estate of Thomas C. Harbaugh whom tradition has linked with the authorship of some of the Nick Carter stories, but which has never been substantiated. (JRC)

D162. Goodyear, R. A. H. "Fifteen Years Non-Stop Carter." Story Paper Collector 2 (Oct 48):85-87.
An accidental receipt of a shipment of Nick Carter stories amid bundles of The Smart Set and Redbook introduced the writer to American dime novels. Nick Carter's appeal was in "plot and swift incident rather than in the leisurely unravelling of a mystery." (JRC)

D163. Holmes, Harold C. "A 'Bit' on Nick Carter Library." DNR 8 (Sept 39):1-2.
Critique and excerpts from two early Nick Carter stories. Notes ways in which dime novel writers made their stories seem real. (JRC)

D164. ______. "The First Nick Carter." DNR 7 (Oct 38):1-5.
Detailed plot synopsis of The Old Detective's Pupil, by John R. Coryell. (JRC)

D165. ______. "Information on the Shield Weekly and New Maget (sic) Library." DNR 6 (May 37):5-6.
Patterns of reprinting stories from one weekly into another, in this case from the Shield Weekly into the Magnet Library and then again into Nick Carter Stories, are discussed. (JRC)

D166. ______. "New Magnet Library No. 1088." DNR 7 (April 39):1.
Shield Weekly nos. 20, 14, and 10 were reused in Magnet Library 236 (reprinted as New Magnet Library 1091) with Nick Carter substituted for Sheridan Keene. Other changes noted as well. (JRC)

D167. ______. "Nick Carter Weekly Nos. 91 and 92." DNR 5 (Oct 36):1-5.
Plot synopses of two issues of the Nick Carter Weekly: "Nick Carter in Harness; or, The Stolen Safe Combination" and "An Attempt to Bunco Nick Carter; or, Barking Up the Wrong Tree." Includes detailed bibliographic description of format which was not uniform with the remainder of the series. (JRC)

D168. Jackson, C. A. G. "Meet Col. Dey Who Adopted Nick Carter, Brought Him Up." Sunday Herald, 30 Jan 21, pp. 12-13.
Interview with Frederick Van Rensselaer Dey who admits to having Nick Carter do those things he himself would have liked to do. Dey patterned Nick after strong man and physical culturist, Eugene Sandow. Illustrated with photo of Dey and two covers from the New Magnet Library. (JRC)

D169. Lahmon, L. H. "Nick Carter." DNR 5 (Feb 37):1.
Reminiscences of reading Nick Carter as a boy in response to the article by Harold C. Holmes (D163) on Nick Carter Weekly nos. 91 and 92. (JRC)

D170. Leithead, J. Edward. "The Anatomy of Dime Novels: No. 1-Nick Carter." DNR 33 (15 Sept 64):76-79; (15 Oct 64):84-89.
Several factors went into the popularity of the dime novels, perhaps the chief one being the covers. Synopsis and discussion of the Morris Carruthers eries (Nick Carter Weekly Nos. 407-412 (1904)). (JRC)

D171. ______. "Author and Artist of the Street & Smith Staff." DNR 30 (1962):92-96; Part II 30 (1962):99-105, 110. Illus.
Two part article in three installments on W. Bert Foster and Charles L. Wrenn. Part I (spanning two issues) gives a summary of Foster's writings and some biographical information. Although the emphasis is on Foster's Western tales, his contributions to the Nick Carter and Bowery Billy series are also discussed. Part II contains a biography of Wrenn and identifies many of the illustrators for the Buffalo Bill Stories. (DJ)

D172. ______. "Dr. Quartz and Other Nine-Lived Villains." DNR 33 (15 May 64):40-44; (15 June 64):48-49.
A detailed, two-part survey of the Dr. Quartz, Dazaar, and Sacred Valley of the Himalayas series which first appeared in the Nick Carter Library and Nick Carter Weekly, and subsequently in the Magnet and New Magnet Library (with the exception of the third series). Some errors of fact (Richard Wormser did not write all of the Nick Carter stories which appeared in Nick Carter Magazine) but otherwise informed and informative. (JRC)

D173. ______. "Frederick (sic) Van Rensselaer Dey." DNR 35 (1966):14-18. Supplement in DNR 35 (1966):51.
A summary, with many excerpts, of The Night Wind's Promise, a Dey novel published under the pseudonym Varick Vanardy. Also included are long excerpts from a 1933 biographical article from the Philadelphia Evening Bulletin, mostly on Dey's writing habits, his connection with the Nick Carter series, and his death. The supplement has a summary of some of the biographical information in National Encyclopedia (sic) of American Biography, followed by several excerpts on Dey's travel experiences and Nick Carter stories, quoted from an autobiographical article from February, 1920, American Magazine. (DJ)

D174. ______. "The Greatest Sleuth That Ever Lived." DNR 23 (15 May 55):38-43.
Further information regarding authorship and reprinting of the Nick Carter stories, based on responses to the article in the Dime Novel Round-Up (Feb 53). Includes a checklist of volumes of short stories in the Magnet and New Magnet Libraries. Doubts that Frederick W. Davis was the author of more than the first 16 numbers of the Shield Weekly or that he wrote the stories expressly for that publication. (JRC)

D175. ______."More About the Nick Carter Libraries." DNR 21(Feb 53):10-13.
A follow-up to his earlier article, "Nick Carter in Print," (DNR, Oct 47) with further information on stories from the weeklies which were reprinted in the Magnet Library, on volumes of the Magnet Library which were re-issued in the New Magnet Library, authorship, the agreement that Street & Smith be allowed to use Sexton Blake stories in their publications by changing the names of the characters, etc. Some of this is based on correspondence with others and personal knowledge; other information is conjecture. Not entirely accurate, as later research has revealed different conclusions. (JRC)

D176. ______. "New News of Nick Carter." Happy Hours Magazine 11 (Sept/Oct 35):2.
Miscellaneous information about the publishing history of Nick Carter with references to the pulp magazine. Speculations on the source of the short stories collected as The Detective's Pretty Neighbor. (JRC)

D177. ______. "Nick Carter and Buffalo Bill Items." DNR 6 (April 37):1-2.
Discrepancies between cover titles and page one titles noted for several Nick Carter stories along with a notice of the passing of the pulp Nick Carter Magazine with the issue of March 1936. (JRC)

D178. ______. "Nick Carter Detective Tales in Magnet and New Magnet Library." DNR 18 (May 50):33-38.
A checklist by series number of all the stories with Nick Carter as main character which appeared in Street & Smith's paper-covered novel series, the Magnet Library and New Magnet Library with the corresponding number of the reprint in the later numbers of the New Magnet Library. Any volumes not reprinted are so designated. An invaluable reference source. (JRC)

D179. ______. "Nick Carter in Another Man's Shoes." DNR 29 (15 Nov 61):112-16; (15 Dec 61):120-25.
Two-part discussion of the stories which Samuel Spalding rewrote from Sexton Blake adventures for the Nick Carter series. List of stories in the New Magnet Library (1910-1916) which may have been Spalding's work. (JRC)

D180. ______. "Nick Carter in Print." DNR 15 (Oct 47):75-83.
Anecdotal and somewhat rambling, but informed and informative, this attempts to cover the Nick Carter series from 1886 to 1936 by discussing the recurring characters, favorite themes of individual writers, and the pattern of reprinting stories from one bibliographical fonnat to another. Identifies authors, cover artists for the Nick Carter Weekly and comments on specific titles. Variants on this article under different titles appeared every few years. (JRC)

D181. ______. "Nick Carter Reprints." DNR 28 (15 Oct 60):82-85; (15 Nov 60):92-95.
A free-form, two-part discussion of the patterns of reprinting the Nick Carter stories from nickel weekly to paperback library with a checklist of those titles in the Magnet Library which were never re-issued in the New Magnet Library. Quotes letters from several correspondents on these questions. Cites Ralph Adimari as source for suggestion that the name "Nick Carter" was chosen for the hero of a regular weekly series to serve as competition for a character named Cool Carter in the Old Cap. Collier Library. (JRC)

D182. ______. "On Stage, Mr. Carter." (3 parts) DNR 26 (15 Nov 58):140-42; (15 Dec 58):151, 154-56; 27 (15 Jan 59):9-10.
Reprints and changes in the Nick Carter stories over the years. Sources of information are varied, secondary as well as personal knowledge. A free-form discussion of the stories and their authors which leans a bit too heavily in some places on Quentin Reynolds' The Fiction Factory (D70) without being critical enough of that source. Mentions some of the other series of detective stories and the striking similarity between the covers of the Nick Carter Weekly and the Dick Dobbs Detective Weekly. Considers that the Dobbs series might have developed into real competition for Nick Carter. (JRC)

D183. ______. "That Matchless Detective, Nick Carter." Happy Hours Magazine 9 (May/June, July/Aug, Sept/Oct, Nov/Dec 33); 10 (Jan/Feb 34). (Pages vary, 2-3 for the most part.)

Anecdotal, rambling, yet delightfully informative survey of the publishing history of the Nick Carter stories. See also the variants and revisions of this essay in the DNR under other titles. (JRC)

D184. ______. "W. Bert Foster, Master Fictioneer." Happy Hours Magazine 12 (May/June 36):1-2.
Biographical sketch of the prolific writer who made major contributions to the Nick Carter and Harrison Keith series. Revised and expanded as "Pulp King - W.Bert Foster." Relics 2 (Summer 68):10-12. (JRC)

D185. McCafferty, William Burton. "Odds and Ends." DNR 17 (April 49):33-34.
Comparisons between modern Nick Carter novels (presumably the Vital Books editions of the 1930s pulp novels), the radio show, and the original dime novel hero. Brief reference to a detective named Zed in the nickel weekly, Young Klondike. (JRC)

D186. Morgan, L. "Collection of Horror and thrills." DNR 10 (July 42):1-2.
Description of covers of several dime novels which depict "weird and thrilling" scenes. Included are Nick Carter Weekly no. 484 ("A Battle among the Clouds"), Secret Service no. 450 ("The Brady's Church Vault Mystery"), and Secret Service no. 254 ("The Bradys' Graveyard Clew"). (JRC)

D187. "Nick Carter's Father." Literary Digest 46 (10 May 1913):1095-98.
The story of Frederic Van Rensselaer Dey's authorship of 1,076 Nick Carter stories with some sidelights on his favorite authors (Dumas and Charles Lever) and methods of working. References to some of the famous men of the day who read Nick Carter. (Based on an article by Frank O'Brien in the New York Press, date unspecified.) Breezy and exaggerated but not uninformative. (JRC)

D188. Pate, Janet. "Nick Carter/J. R. Coryell" and "Sexton Blake/Hal Meredith." In Pate (B307), pp. 23-26, 13-15.
Breezy and concise to the point of confusion. Illustrated accounts of fictional detectives, including Sexton Blake and Nick Carter. Incorrectly states that Frederick W. Davis did not write stories about Nick Carter and that there was no theatrical production featuring the detective when, in fact, there was a French play. Nick Carter Weekly cover reproduced is of the British edition, but not so identified. Other errors. Bibliographies and filmographies inadequate, but preserve some useful details. (JRC)

D189. Penzler, Otto. "Nick Carter." In Penzler (B310), pp. 32-41.
One of the better surveys of the history of Nick Carter from dime novel to paperbacks. The captions to the illustrations leave something to be desired and two of them (pp. 34, 40) have been reversed. Filmography includes only the 3 Walter Pidgeon films. (JRC)

D190. "Rev. S. C. Spalding, Author, Was 83." New York Times, 10 Feb 62, p. 23.
Obituary of Samuel C. Spalding, author of Nick Carter stories between 1910 and 1916. (JRC)

D191. Roff, William R. "The Mystery of the First Malay Novel (and Who Was

Rokumbul?)." Bijdragen Tot de Taal-, Land- En Volkenkunde 130 (1974):450-64.

A translation of a Nick Carter story was the first novel published in Malaya. Includes an informed discussion of the Nick Carter series as well as other early detective fiction. (JRC)

D192. "Rome Bans Nick Carter, Buffalo Bill and Lincoln." DNR 8 (August 39):1.

News item reprinted from Associated Press that Nick Carter appeared on a list of stories found to be "unsuited to the Fascist spirit." (JRC)

D193. Smelzer, Robert H. "Nick Carter Again." DNR 2 (Sept 33):1-2.

Synopsis of Nick Carter's Double Catch; or, Dazaar the Vindictive (Magnet Library No. 409). (JRC)

D194. Smith, Derek. "Nick Carter--America's Sexton Blake." CDA, 1967, pp. 133-36.

Brief survey of the career of Nick Carter from dime novel to paperback in the 1960s. Not without the usual errors. (JRC)

D195. Spalding, Samuel Charles. I've Had Me A Time! Great Barrington, Mass.: The Friends of Gould Farm, 1961. 72pp. Frontis.

Autobiography of the minister who turned to full-time writing after suffering a crippling disability in 1907. Spalding rewrote Sexton Blake stories from the Union Jack for the requirements of the Nick Carter series from 1910 to 1915 (the latter date may be only an estimate) and also appeared briefly in a silent film as "the author of Nick Carter." Includes selected poems and three sermons from 1960. (JRC)

D196. ______. "A Letter from the Last of the Nick Carter Authors." DNR 28 (1960):11-12.

A letter from Spalding verifying his authorship of some Nick Carter stories, both originals and rewrites. (DJ)

D197. Van Raalte, Joseph. "Nick Carter, The Picturesque Career of the Man Who Made Him." Century Magazine 115 (Nov 27):91-97.

A character sketch of Frederic Van Rensselaer Dey who has become identified with the persona of Nick Carter. According to Van Raalte, Dey "never achieved the wealth or distinction he merited. His career was a picturesque extreme of wrongheadedness and his death, like his life, was an absurd moral disaster." (JRC)

D198. Woodson, Weldon D. "The Nick Carter Question Again." Welcome News 14 (Sept 41):5.

Proof offered that John R. Coryell and not Eugene T. Sawyer created Nick Carter. Reproduces letter from H. W. Ralston, vice-pres. of Street & Smith, to substantiate assertions which are based on a comparison between Gelett Burgess's interview with Sawyer and Russell Coryell's memoir of his father. (JRC)

D199. ______. "Who Wrote Nick Carter?" Welcome News (Nov 40):10-11.

Considers John R. Coryell to be the creator of Nick Carter in spite of claims made for Thomas Chalmers Harbaugh (whom he erroneously calls Charles Harbaugh), Frederic Van Rensselaer Dey, and Eugene T. Sawyer. (JRC)

"Old Cap Collier"

D200. Craufurd, Ross. "Old Cap Collier: A Dossier." DNR 51 (1981):42-50. Illus.
A publishing history of Old Cap Collier and the Old Cap Collier Library that includes some discussion of different settings for Old Cap Collier tales. Approximately half of the article describes detectives who appeared in single issues of Old Cap Collier Library and gives excerpts from or plot synopses of the appropriate stories. (DJ)

D201. Lahmon, L.H. "Old Cap Collier and Norman L. Munro." DNR 6 (July 37):3.
Recollections of reading Old Cap Collier in Munro's Family Story Paper with some comments on specific stories. Prefers the old stories to anything being published in 1937. (JRC)

"Old King Brady"

D202. Bragin, Charles. "Francis Worcester Doughty, Uncrowned King of the Dime Novel Writers." DNR 4 (Aug/Sept 35):1-4.
Biographical sketch of the creator of Old King Brady with succinct and informative comments on his work. (JRC)

D203. ______. "Items of Interest." DNR 3 (May 34):2.
Note on the authorship of Old King Brady and the James Boys stories (a combined series) in the New York Detective Library. F. W. Doughty was the highest paid author who wrote for Tousey publications. (JRC)

D204. Cordier, George H. "Old King Brady." DNR 4 (June 53):3; (Jan 36):3; (May 36):2-3.
The publishing history of Old King Brady ("beside him the Nick Carters, Old Sleuth, Young Sleuth, and Old Cap Collier pale into insignificance") from Boys of New York and the New York Detective Library through Secret Service. Nostalgic and anecdotal with excerpts frosm the stories. (Uncompleted series of articles, revised and reprinted, DNR Special Birthday Number, 1938; largely superseded by Leithead (D212).) (JRC)

D205. Craufurd, Ross. "The Early Doughty--Master of Mysteries and Wonders." DNR 45 (1976):106-15. Illus.
A brief analysis, with excerpts, of some of Doughty's dime novels, including an Old King Brady detective story, followed by a chronological list of Doughty's works from 1884 through 1890. (DJ)

D206. "From Movie Picture Stories of Sept 3, 1915." DNR 25 (1957):16-17.

Reprint of a short biography of Doughty. (DJ)

D207. Holmes, Harold C. "Old King Brady, the Sleuth-Hound." DNR 8 (Sept 40):1-4.
Plot synopsis of the first story about Old King Brady, Old King Brady, the Sleuth-Hound, by a New York Detective (F. W. Doughty), New York Detective Library, no. 154 (14 Nov 1885). (JRC)

D208. ______. "Pluck and Luck 118." DNR 16 (May 48):37-47.
Plot synopsis of Howard Austin's The Scarlet Shroud; or, The Fate of the Five which appeared in Pluck and Luck, no. 118 (5 Sept 1900). Austin was pen name for Doughty. In this story he rings the changes on an old

plot: villain who is second in line for a fortune plots death of hero who is first in line for same. (JRC)

D209. ______. "Secret Service 258." DNR 13 (July 45):1-4; (Aug 45):1-4. Plot synopsis of "The Brady's and 'Joe Jinger'; or, The Clew in the Convict Camp," by F. W. Doughty (as "A New York Detective") from Secret Service no. 258 (1 Jan 1904) with illus. of cover. (JRC)

D210. Leithead, J. Edward. "The Great Detective Team: Old and Young King Brady." American Book Collector 20 (Nov/Dec 69):25-31.
Anecdotal and informative survey of the Old King Brady stories with references to many specific titles. Stories not authored by Doughty suggested to be the work of Lu Senarens and Walter Fenton Mott. Identifies cover artist on Secret Service as A. Berghaus. Illus. with covers of Secret Service. (JRC)

D211. ______. "The Nickel Novel Almost Everybody Liked: Pluck and Luck." DNR 30 (1962):60-65.
An overview of Pluck and Luck, with emphasis on enumerating Francis W. Doughty's pseudonymous contributions to this dime novel series. (DJ)

D212. ______. "The Two King Bradys and Their Girl Detective." DNR 31 (1963):80-85; 90-95.
Two installments. Part one has a history of Old King Brady, including early publication information and background on the different authors of the stories, as well as an analysis of some types of Brady tales; part two continues the analysis, comments on the cover illustrations, and includes a long excerpt from and summary of a Brady tale. (DJ)

D213. O'Gara, Gil. "Old King Brady: His Rise and Decline." Age of the Unicorn 2 (April 80):19-22; reprinted YL 1 (Jan/Feb 81):5-7.
Brief but accurate survey of the publishing history of the Old King Brady stories considered in the context of the genre of dime novel detective fiction. (JRC)

D214. Smeltzer, Robert H. "Retrospect--Francis Worcester Doughty." DNR 29 (1961):54-55.
Short biography of Doughty. (DJ)

D215. White, Percy W. "King Bradys Not Related." DNR 9 (March 41):4.
News clipping referring to a question in a quiz in Liberty for March 9 which asked for the identity of two detectives, father and son, who "solved more crimes than J. Edgar Hoover." The answer, Old and Young King Brady, is false since they were not blood relatives. (JRC)

"Old Sleuth"

D216. Godfrey, Lydia. "Old Sleuth, Nineteenth Century 'Nipper' America's First Serialized Detective and His World." Clues 1:1 (Spring 80):53-56.
The importance of the Old Sleuth stories was in their effect on readers for they shifted the focus of popular fiction to detective stories and created a demand for the genre which lasted into the 20th century. Lengthy description of the persona of Old Sleuth. Notes the publication by George Munro of 6 stories about Old Sleuth and the difficulties of reading all of them due to gaps in the files at the Library of Congress.

(Since this article was written the author has improved her acquaintance with Old Sleuth by a visit to the Hess Collection at the University of Minnesota Library where a more complete set may be found.) (JRC)

D217. Smelzer, Robert H. "Old Sleuth Library." DNR 14 (Aug 46):2-3. Reminiscences of the enjoyment of dime novel reading with a selected checklist of the Old Sleuth Library. (JRC)

"Perry Pierce"

D218. Abreu, John E. "Perry Pierce and the Who Series." M&ASR 11 (Spring 83):(22)-(25).
A short-lived series (four titles published from 1921-34) by Clinton W. Locke about an amateur boy detective and his friends who "encounter ghosts and weird happenings while looking for treasure and mysteries to solve." Abreu points out the weak plots in which circumstances are manufactured to fit the mysteries.

"Peter Flint"

D219. Hockley, Geoffrey. "The Cases of Peter Flint--Detective Extraordinary." CDA, 1954, pp. 19-28.
An account of the brief, but memorable series of stories by Stephen H. Agney in the Nugget Library (James Henderson, pub.) in 1913. Includes checklist of 10 titles. (JRC)

"Roger Baxter"

D220. Ybarra, Bob. "Ken Holt's Predecessor: The Roger Baxter Series." M&ASR 3 (Winter 80):23-25.
Three books in this series, written by Samuel Epstein, were published by Julian Messner in the late 1940s. Roger Baxter is a Ken Holt prototype and scenes and characters from this series turn up again in the later series.

"Roy Stover"

D221. Abreu, John E. "The Roy Stover Mysteries." M&ASR 8 (Spring 82):(14)-(18). Illus.
A four-volume series published by Grosset & Dunlap in the early 30s about a cub reporter who "becomes involved in mystery and adventure while tracking down leads to big news stories."

"Rupert Waldo"

D222. Packman, Josie. "Waldo the Wonderman." CDA, 1977, pp. 21-24.
A survey of the 37 stories (beginning with 1918) about Rupert Waldo by Edwy Searles Brooks which appeared in the Union Jack. (JRC)

D223. Smith, Derek. "Waldo's Wonder Stunt." CDA, 1969, pp. 115-118.
Discussion of two of the stories featuring "Rupert Waldo, the Wonder Man," and some thoughts about their basis in fact. (Union Jack 1054, and 1077, from 1923-24.) (JRC)

"Sexton Blake"

See also: D188.

D224. Adrian, Jack. "The Sexton Blake Story." Radio Times 220, no. 2861, 9-15 Sept 78, pp. 4-5.
A brief account of Britain's most enduring detective and a few words about some of the many authors who wrote about him. Illustrated with covers from some of the early Blake stories and a scene from the television serial the article served to introduce. (RCSA)

D225. Bond, H. M. "Characters in Sexton Blake Stories." CDA, 1947, pp. 36-43.
A review of the major recurring characters in the Sexton Blake stories. (JRC)

D226. ______. "Sexton Blake and Myself." CDA, 1950, pp. 71-72.
Attempts to survey the basic humane qualities of the Sexton Blake saga. (JRC)

D227. ______. "Topicality was the Keynote." CDA, 1950, pp. 71-72.
Examines 10 years of the Union Jack (1923-1933) with comments on the topical nature of the Sexton Blake stories, from the illicit diamond racket to South American revolutions. (JRC)

D228. Bridgwater, John. "A Corner in Union Jacks." CDA, 1979, pp. 24-25.
A poetic tribute to the Criminals Confederation series in the Sexton Blake saga. (JRC)

D229. ______. "Mrs. Bardell--Authoress." CDA, 1977, pp. 29-31.
Sexton Blake's landlady plans writing a novel (adapted from Union Jack no. 432 (Jan. 1912), "The Publisher's Secret" by W. M. Graydon). (JRC)

D230. ______. "A Sexton Blake Scrapbook." CDA, 1975, pp. 24-32.
A sampler of some 30 quotations from the Sexton Blake stories to illustrate the varied styles of the writers. Sources for the quotations are given at the end. (JRC)

D231. ______. "A Unique Case of Interblakenisation." CDA, 1978, pp. 57-60.
A tongue-in-cheek look at the changes made on a Sexton Blake story by George Dilnot which had originally appeared as a non-Blake serial in the Thriller. (JRC)

______

D232. Burns, William M. "Exit Union Jack." DNR 2 (July/Aug 33):5-6; (Oct 33):2-3.
Nostalgic account of some of the highlights of the career of Sexton Blake whose adventures appeared in the Union Jack. (JRC)

D233. Colby, Victor. "Pensive Ramblings." CDA, 1964, pp. 137-39.
Comments on the lengthy saga of Sexton Blake on hearing that the Sexton Blake Library is to be revived. (JRC)

D234. ______. "Sexton Blake in The Champion." CDA , 1965, pp. 102-105.
Comments on the Sexton Blake stories which appeared in The Champion in 1922, with further information on the work of those regulars among Blake authors and artists who contributed other stories to this paper. (JRC)

authors and artists who contributed other stories to this paper. (JRC)

D235. ______. "Sexton Blake in The Penny Popular." CDA, 1964, pp. 100-107. A checklist with comments on the stories reprinted from the Union Jack in The Penny Popular (1912-1916). Article reprinted from Golden Hours Magazine (Australia). (JRC)

D236. Colcombe, William. "Reprinted Stories in the Sexton Blake Library." CDA, 1948, pp. 28-29.
A list of stories in the Sexton Blake Library (2nd series) which were reprinted from earlier numbers of the 1st or 2nd series. (JRC)

D237. ______. "With Blake on Their Spot." CDA, 1948, pp. 53-56.
Discusses the various locales in which the Sexton Blake stories were set, with specific references. (JRC)

D238. Cox, J. Randolph. "My Friend, Sexton Blake." CDA, 1973, pp. 30-32.
Nostalgic recollections of the first time this writer read a Sexton Blake story. The appeal seems to have been in the believability of the character. (JRC)

D239. Cure, Raymond. "Villains Come in All Shapes and Sizes." CDA, 1974, pp. 81-82.
The villains in the Sexton Blake series were a varied lot. Six are examined to support that claim. (JRC)

D240. Dolphin, Rex. "Friends at the Yard." CDA, 1947, pp. 44-51.
Commentary and quotations about the major Scotland Yard officers who figure in the Sexton Blake stories: Detective Inspector Coutts, Det. Inspector Harker, Supt. Venner, Det.-Sgt. Belford, and the Commissioner of Police, Sir Henry Fairfax. (JRC)

D241. ______. "Dr. Ferraro and His Creator." CDA, 1948, pp. 79-81.
Discusses the stories by Coutts Brisbane in which Sexton Blake battled the master criminal, Dr. Ferraro. (JRC)

D242. Homer, Harry. "Monograph on the Criminals Confederation." CDA, 1950, pp. 73-87.
A discussion of the longest running series within the Sexton Blake saga, the battle with Mr. Reece and the Criminals Confederation, which lasted for 50 stories. (JRC)

D243. ______. "Monograph on Sexton Blake." CDA, 1949, pp. 118-21.
An attempt to explain the continuing appeal of Sexton Blake with examples from the series which demonstrate his realistic characterization. (JRC)

D244. ______. "Monograph on Yvonne Cartier." CDA, 1951, pp. 49-62.
Discussion of the stories featuring Yvonne Cartier, from the Sexton Blake series (1912-26) with a checklist of titles. (JRC)

D245. Homer, Harry, ed. "More of the Man from Baker Street." CDA, 1954, pp. 85-99.
The third compilation of information by the members of the Sexton Blake circle of the Old Boys' Book Club. Checklists of the Sexton Blake stories by Lewis Jackson and Andrew Murray with further comments on Sexton

Blake and sport, the Captain Dack stories of John Hunger and other recurring figures in the series. Corrigenda to previous volumes of the Annual. (JRC)

D246. ______. "They Wrote of Sexton Blake." CDA, 1953, pp. 84-107.
Discussions, checklist, letters, all dealing with the Sexton Blake stories of Gwyn Evans, Pierre Quiroule (W. W. Sayers), Anthony Skene, Cecil Hayter, Allan Blair (William J. Bayfield), John G. Brandon, and Coutts Brisbane. Additional essay on the women in the Blake series. (JRC)

D247. Homer, Harry and Members of the Sexton Blake Circle. "Kings of Crime." CDA, 1952, pp. 61-89.
"A complete and authentic record of (Sexton Blake's) campaigns against the major master criminals" in the Union Jack, and Sexton Blake Library. Extensive checklists and copies of letters from Blake author, Anthony Skene. (JRC)

D248. Hudson, Gordon. "...By Any Other Name?..." CDA, 1972, pp. 131-32.
The practice of republishing Sexton Blake stories with the hero changed continues with those by Howard Baker which reappeared as stories about Richard Quintain. Checklist included. (JRC)

D249. Leckenby, Herbert. "They Wrote of Sexton Blake." CDA, 1950, pp. 88-91.
A list, with introduction, of the 74 authors who had contributed stories to the Sexton Blake Library from 1915 to Oct 1950, with the number of stories credited to each. (JRC)

D250. Leithead, J. Edward. "Jeff Clayton--Sexton Blake; or, Another Mystery Solved." DNR 39 (1970):21.
A short article linking the Jeff Clayton detective tales to Sexton Blake stories and suggesting the former were actually reprints of the latter. (JRC)

D251. Lister, William. "Once to Everyman--Comes the Moment to Decide." CDA, 1977, pp. 124-25.
In choosing among Sexton Blake stories to read, one begins with the cover illustration, but the final decision is based on a combination of author and co-star. (JRC)

D252. ______. "Sexton Blake and the Man with a Thousand Names." CDA, 1972, p. 132.
Brief tribute to the work of Edwy Searles Brooks in the Sexton Blake series. (JRC)

D253. Lofts, W. O. G. "Sexton Blake." DNR 38 (15 Apr 69):40-43.
The origin of the name and the publication of the early stories of the longest running detective series in literature was solely the work of Harry Blyth, who died before he had written more than a handful of the stories. (JRC)

D254. ______. "Sexton Blake." DNR 23 (June 55):48-50.
Overview of the creation, authorship, character and publications in which Sexton Blake appeared from 1892 to date. Notes that the editor of the Sexton Blake Library has remained the same since it began in 1915. Brief

reference to film versions, the comic strip in Knockout, and the practice of individual authors being allowed to republish their Blake stories in hardcover with the characters changed. (JRC)

D255. ______. "Sexton Blake." The Saint Magazine 24 (Dec 66):150-59.
A detailed, yet concise survey of 73 years of Sexton Blake and the many changes over the years in the series. (Article reprinted from The Record, Fleetway Publications house organ, Nov/Dec 62.) (JRC)

D256. Lofts, W. O. G., and Adley, D. J. "Favorite Boyhood Characters on the British Screen." DNR 46 (June 77):66-70.
Few fictional heroes have been transferred to the screen. None of the 26 films based on the Sexton Blake stories has been up to the standard set by the original character. (Part II of this article appeared in Dec. 77, pp. 122-26, but dealt with other than detective figures.) (JRC)

D257. Lowder, Christopher A.J. "The Base of the Pyramid." CDA, 1968, pp. 33-40.
A look at the first 14 thrillers in the 4th Series of the Sexton Blake Library (the early "New Look," 1956) attributes the success and revitalization of the series to the greater characterization and attention to detail introduced by the author-editor, W. Howard Baker. (JRC)

D258. ______. "On First Reading The Yellow Tiger." CDA, 1971, pp. 63-71.
The first novel in the Sexton Blake Library (1915) is still considered to be a good story and a reflection of days of thrillers past. (JRC)

D259. ______. "The Progressive Phase of G. H. Teed." CDA, 1972, pp. 78-88.
A discussion of the Sexton Blake stories by G. H. Teed which were published after 1915, with suggestions on the influence of the occult on the Prince Menes series. (JRC)

D260. M., J. E. "Mrs. Walker's Academy and the Teaching of Sexton Blake." CDA, 1978, pp. 64-66.
A second-hand story-paper shop served as a surrogate school to those who purchased the Union Jack and had a wider world opened to them in its pages. (JRC)

D261. McLean, Arthur. "In Reply to Cries of Anger." CDA, 1956, pp.135-8.
A reply to complaints about changes in the style of the Sexton Blake stories in the 1950s, written by one of the new Blake authors. (JRC)

D262. Norton, Ray. "Blake's Blunders." CDA, 1966, pp. 109-11.
The occasions when the great detective made mistakes. (All quotations are from the stories of John Hunter. (JRC)

D263. Packman, Josie. "Around the World in 80 Years." CDA,1975, pp.47-50.
The journeys made and countries visited by Sexton Blake in the many stories published since 1893. (JRC)

D264. ______."The Birth of the Sexton Blake Library." CDA,1964, pp.124-5.
The beginning of the first Sexton Blake Library (1915) is recalled with the news that yet a new series is to begin shortly. Includes copy of the advertisement for that first story, "The Yellow Tiger," from the Union Jack of August 14, 1915. (JRC)

D265. ______. "The Dr. Huxton Rymer Story." CDA, 1973, pp. 3-11.

An account of the stories in which Sexton Blake meets his recurring adversary, Dr. Huxton Rymer, as related by the prolific G. H. Teed. The last recorded story is considered to be out of character and possibly not the work of Teed. (JRC)

D266. ______. "A New Look at the 'New Look' SBL's." CDA, 1978, pp. 32-33. A re-reading of the 5th series of Sexton Blake Library (the paperbacks published by Mayflower Books) suggests that while not as pleasurable as the older stories they are on a par with other modern detective stories with those by Martin Thomas being more interesting on the second time around. (JRC)

D267. _____."The Third Murray and the Hon. John Lawless." CDA,1976, pp.52-4 Among the more memorable stories in the Sexton Blake series, Andrew Murray was responsible for those featuring that English gentleman, the Hon. John Lawless (20 stories in the Union Jack, beginning in 1914, and 33 in the Sexton Blake Library, 1917-1923). (Title of this article is a sort of "in" joke: the other two "Murrays" were William Murray Graydon and Robert Murray, also contributors to the saga.) (JRC)

D268. Packman, Josephine,ed. "Blakiana." Collectors' Digest v 1- (1946-). Monthly column. Earliest issue examined, February 1957. Presumably included in all issues. Reviews of individual Sexton Blake stories, discussions of the merits of individual authors, checklists of stories by specific authors, and debate over the qualities of the New Look introduced in the late 1950s. A rich source of information about the Man from Baker Street, but too voluminous for individual abstracts, each column contains from one to four separate items in the form of brief 300-500 word articles. (JRC)

D269. Packman, Len, ed. "The Man from Baker Street." CDA, 1955, pp.96-119. The fourth collection of articles by members of the Sexton Blake Circle: Marie Galante, Voodoo Queen, a brief survey of the stories through the years, the story of Tinker, data on criminals who figured in the stories, the artists who illustrated the stories, and other topics. (JRC)

D270. ______. "The Man from Baker Street." CDA, 1956, pp. 94-120. The fifth collection of articles by members of the Sexton Blake Circle covers the Prince Menes stories, the works of Gilbert Chester, miscellaneous matters dealing with authorship of the early stories, popular recurring characters, and the floorplan of Blake's Berkeley Square offices. (JRC)

D271. ______. "The Man from Baker Street." CDA, 1957, pp. 89-113. The sixth collection includes a discussion of the stories about Rupert Waldo, the many feminine characters, and the stories by Robert Murray. (JRC)

D272. ______. "The Man from Baker Street." CDA, 1958, pp. 113-133. The seventh compilation: a checklist and statistical paper on the many authors of the stories, an account of the Blake stories by John C. Brandon which were reprinted in hardcovers with slight revisions, the "New Look" Sexton Blake of the 1950s and how it came about, and a discussion of the "Black Eagle" stories of the 1920s. (JRC)

D273. ______. "The Man from Baker Street." CDA, 1959, pp. 98-128. The earlier Sexton Blake stories, a revision of the who's who of Sexton

Blake authors (from the previous Annual), a collection of the opening lines from a selection of stories, and an attempt to account for the continuing appeal of the saga: all included in this eighth symposium of materials by members of the Blake Circle. (JRC)

D274. ______. "The Man from Baker Street (9)." CDA, 1960, pp. 112-143. Discussions of favorite stories, a checklist of the major characters in the Sexton Blake stories, a checklist of Sexton Blake stories in Detective Weekly and Nugget Weekly, comments on the new stories by Martin Thomas (one of the authors) and Michael Moorcock. (JRC)

D275. ______. "The Man from Baker Street (10)." CDA, 1961, pp. 125-46. Reprints a tribute to Sexton Blake by Gwyn Evans, discussions of the early editors of the stories, an obituary for Francis H. Warren (a Blake artist), statistical evidence that George F. Teed wrote more stories about Blake while William Murray Graydon wrote more words, the probable identity of "Michael Storm," and a checklist of Blake writers and their work in other fields. (JRC)

D276. ______. "The Man from Baker Street (11)." CDA, 1962, pp. 115-32. Sexton Blake on the stage and a checklist of the stories that appeared in the Boys' Friend Library form the bulk of this entry. Included is a pastiche by Eric Fayne, editor of Collectors' Digest and the successor to Herbert Leckenby. (JRC)

277. ______. "The Man from Baker Street (12)." CDA, 1963, pp. 121-28. Some comments on the work of Alfred Edgar in the Blake series, and the Sexton Blake stories with China settings. This is the last of the symposium series of material by members of the Sexton Blake circle. (JRC)

D278. Packman, Leonard and Josie (and members of the Sexton Blake Circle). Sexton Blake Catalogue. London: Sexton Blake Circle, n. d. Supplement to the Sexton Blake Catalogue. London: Sexton Blake Circle, n. d. Complete listing by publications series of all Sexton Blake stories with authors identified, character index, and information concerning stories reprinted in later issues of the Blake publications. Includes Annuals, the 5th Series SBL and hardover edition issued in the 1960s. Dates given are for 1st numbers of each year, not for individual stories. (JRC)

D279. Rowe, Cecil. "Stormy?" CDA, 1976, pp. 104-110. A bibliography and discussion of the work of the mysterious "Michael Storm," one of the Sexton Blake writers. According to The Men Behind Boys' Fiction (D55), a pseudonym for Ernest Sempill. (JRC)

D279a. Swan, S. Gordon. "A Clergyman in Disgrace." CDA, 1975, pp.121-4. Recurring appearances in the Sexton Blake stories of the Rev. Lionel Stainer began with Union Jack 300 ("Unfrocked" by W. Murray Graydon) and ended with Union Jack 314 ("Sexton Blake, Playwright"), also by Graydon. (JRC)

D279b. ______. "A Dangerous Partnership." CDA, 1974, pp. 60-62. Dr. Huxton Rymer served not only as an adversary for Sexton Blake, but was featured in three Nelson Lee serials in the Prairie Library in 1920. (JRC)

D280. ______. "A Sexton Blake Anthology." CDA, 1972, pp. 48-50.

A choice, with annotations, of the 20 best Sexton Blake stories which would make up an ideal anthology of his adventures. (JRC)

D281. ______. "Sexton Blake's Past." CDA, 1976, pp. 61-63; also in CDA, 1977, pp. 94-96.
There were two separate versions of the boyhood of Sexton Blake, one which appeared as serials and then in the Boys' Friend Library (First Series), the other in The Pilot in 1937. (JRC)

D282. ______. "They Were Already Famous." CDA, 1970, pp. 75-76.
A number of fictional characters stepped out of their own series to appear briefly in the Sexton Blake saga: Ferrers Lord, the schoolboys of Calcroft School, Cora Twyford, Captain John Christman, Mr. Preed, and Captain Dack. (JRC)

D283. ______. "Tinker's Romance." CDA, 1971, pp. 75-77.
A penchant for the opposite sex has been a traditional theme as far as Sexton Blake's young assistant is concerned. (JRC)

D284. Twyman, H. W. "Men at Work." CDA, 1958, pp. 78-81.
The working habits of several of the Sexton Blake writers as described by the editor of the Union Jack and Detective Weekly, 1921-1937. (JRC)

D285. Unwin, Frank. "Sexton Blake, 1958." CDA, 1958, pp. 46, 55, 64, 74.
A survey of the "new look" in Sexton Blake stories published in 1958, its strengths and weaknesses, but primarily the way it revived the series. (JRC)

D286. Wearing, F. N. "Sexton Blake: How Did the Name Originate?" CDA, 1966, pp. 133, 1381.
Some basic information on the origin of the name Sexton Blake who may have been based on an American dime novel hero, Jackson Blakė, whose adventures were running in Beadle's Dime Library authored by Albert W. Aiken. (Reprinted from an early number of the Collector's Digest.) (JRC)

D287. Webb, Walter. "The Strange Case of the Author Who Died Twice." CDA, 1967, pp. 105-110.
Investigation into the real person behind the pen name "Michael Storm" reveals a husband and wife who each wrote stories for the Sexton Blake series. (JRC)

D288. Wilde, Geoffrey. "The Sexton Blake Work of Anthony Parsons." CDA, 1979, pp. 71-83.
A detailed analysis of the stories contributed to the Sexton Blake Library (1937-1956) by Anthony Parsons who ranks second only to G. H. Teed "in terms of sustained quality." Includes checklist. (JRC)

D289. Wood, J. F. "The Dead Man Laughs." CDA, 1951, pp. 88-89.
A brief look at the work of Edwy Searles Brooks, author of many Sexton Blake stories as well as the Norman Conquest and Inspector Ironsides Cromwell detective novels. (JRC)

D290. Wright, Norman. "Sherlock Holmes--Detective, Par Excellence." CDA, 1965, pp. 11-14.
Bibliographical and historical survey of the stories which were the prototype for the Sexton Blake saga. (JRC)

D291. York, James. "Goodness, Sexton Blake." CDA, 1976, pp. 131-33.
While the stories maintained their topicality, Sexton Blake was always the old-fashioned untarnished hero. (JRC)

"Troy Nesbit"

D292. Holbrook, Don. "An Overlooked Series - The Troy Nesbit Books." M&ASR 10 (Fall 82):(4)-(15).
Six books were published between 1962 in this series set in the southwest and characterized by a strong sense of natural phenomena and an archaelogical sense of the past. With a photo of Franklin Folsom and some biographical information.

B. Pulps

1. General References

D293. Anderson, Virginia Combs ("Nanek") and William Papilia. "A Remembrance of Early Pulp Collecting and Fandom 1938-1943." Xenophile 40 (July 78) pp. 3-38, 87-119. Illus.
Includes a number of letters from Norvell W. Page ("Richard Wentworth," author of Spider novels) and from Rogers Terrill of Popular Publications. Interspersed with facsimiles of text from The Spider pulp.

D294. Attic Revivals. Ed./pub. Bernard A. Drew. 53 Gilmore Ave., Great Barrington, MA 01230.
Each issue is usually devoted to one pulp magazine writer, providing brief biographical sketches, checklists, and a short story reprint. Published irregularly. (RS)

D295. Blackbeard, Bill. "The Pulps." In Handbook of American Popular Culture, edited by Thomas Inge, pp. 195-24.
An "historic outline" of the pulp era, an overview of history and criticism devoted to the pulps and an annotated bibliography of secondary sources.

D296. Bonnett, Hal Murray. "It Was Never That Much Fun!" Xenophile 36 (Nov 77), 141. Illus.
A pulp writer's reminiscences.

D297. Carr, Wooda Nicholas. "The Pulp Hero." DNR 51:1 (Feb 82):2-8. Illus. by Frank Hamilton.
A survey of pulp heroes. Short profiles of Doc Savage, The Shadow, The Spider, G-8, The Phantom Detective and The Avenger.

D299. Drew, Bernard A. "The Domino Lady: Introduction." Attic Revivals 5, 1982, p. l.
Three-paragraph note mentioning the rarity of female protagonists in pulp fiction, especially "costumed heroines." (REB)

D300. ______. "In the Days of the Shadow." Yesteryear, Feb 80, pp. 6-7.
Reminiscences of pulp writers: Walter Gibson, Bill Severin, Judson Philips and William R. Cox. Photo of Gibson and reproductions of pulp covers.

D301. _____. "The Vanishing Resource - Old Pulp Writers." Age of the Unicorn 1:2 (June 79):2-6.
General remarks on Drew's encounters with pulp writers and bibliography of articles on the pulps and their writers that appeared in a variety of newspapers and regional and local magazines.

D302. _____. "Secretaries in the Pulps." Age of the Unicorn 1:2 (June 79):7-8. Originally published in Modern Secretary April 79.
This discussion of secretary roles in pulp fiction includes appearances in stories by Frederick Nebel and Erle Stanley Gardner.

D303. Echoes. Publisher: Tom Johnson; editor: Ginger Johnson. 504 E. Morris St. Seymour, TX. 76380. Bi-monthly.
Fanzine devoted to material on the pulps. First published: June 1982. With contributions from some of the best known pulp scholars (Robert Sampson, Will Murray, and Wooda Nicholas Carr) and illustrations by Frank Hamilton, Echoes fills some of the void left by the demise of Xenophile (Cook, 617-19). In addition to the essays, editorial comment, columns and letters, there are lists of items for sale and trade and the magazine is an important resource for the reader, researcher and collector of pulps. Not listed in Cook.

D303. Fisher, Steve. "Pulp Literature. Subculture Revolution in the Late 1930s." TAD 5 (1971/72):91-2, 95.
Personal notes on writing for the pulps.

D304. Goodstone, Tony, compiler and editor. The Pulps. Fifty Years of American Pop Culture. NY: Chelsea House, 1970. v-xvi, 239pp. Illustrated.
An anthology of facsimile stories from the pulps with a portfolio of color illustrations (covers). In his introduction, Goodstone provides a general survey of the pulp era.

D305. Goulart, Ron. Cheap Thrills. An Informal History of the Pulp Magazines. New Rochelle, NY: Arlington House, 1972; NY: Ace Books, 1973. The texts of the two editions are identical. 192pp.
The accent is on "informal" and there are individual chapters on the Shadow, Doc Savage, Special Agents and Dime Detectives. An entertaining, informative look at the magazines and their writers. In the final chapter, Goulart includes short statements by a number of writers about pulp writing. Breen 43

D306. Goulart, Ron, editor. The Hardboiled Dicks. An Anthology and Study of Pulp Fiction. Los Angeles: Sherbourne Press, 1965; NY: Pocket Books, 1967. xviii, 268pp.
The introduction consists of a survey of the history of the pulps and each of the stories has a brief preface. There is a useful "Informal Reading List" (pp. 265-68) in which Goulart suggests additional titles and comments on his recommendations. The Pronzini Arbor House (D323) anthology has the more substantial critical notes but this is a good selection of stories with sensible, if cursory, notes.

D307. Gruber, Frank. "The Life and Times of the Pulp Story." Foreword (pp. 7-46) to Brass Knuckles: The Oliver Quade, Human Encyclopedia Stories. Los Angeles: Sherbourne Press Inc., 1966.
Anecdotal account of Gruber's early career: how he became a successful writer for the pulp magazines, and the origins of his first hardcover mystery, The French Key. All the material here presented was

incorporated into the author's The Pulp Jungle (D308). (REB)

D308. ______. The Pulp Jungle. Los Angeles: Sherbourne Press Inc., 1967. 189pp.
Anecdotal memoir of Gruber's years as a pulp fiction writer, with commentary on the mystery pulps, their editors and writers. Also gives the background of Gruber's first hardcover mystery novel. The book is greatly expanded from Gruber's introduction to Brass Knuckles (D307). Breen 45. (REB)

D309. Hagemann, E. R., editor. "Focus on Pulp Detective Fiction." Clues 2:2 (Fall/Winter 81):38-153.
The articles cover a number of writers with an emphasis on Black Mask and its contributors. Contents: William F. Nolan, "A Walk in the Pulpwoods: Random Recollections," pp. 38-41 (D32); Bill Pronzini, "Ante-Bellum Days; Or, 'My Roscoe Sneezed Ka-chee!'," pp. 41-51 (E111); J. Randolph Cox, "More Mystery for a Dime: Street & Smith and the First Pulp Detective Magazine," pp. 52-59 (D362); Robert Sampson, "Life as a Series of Abstract Analyses," pp. 61-76 (E2832); Herman Petersen, "The Barbless Arrow," pp. 77-87 (western pulp story; first published in Action Stories, 5 (Oct 25), pp. 88-96); Bernard A. Drew, "Hoh-Hoh to Satan:, Detective Fiction Weekly's Nutty Series Heroes of the 1930s," pp. 88-102 (D361); Michael S. Barson, "'There's No Sex in Crime': The Two-Fisted Homilies of Race Williams," pp. 103-12 (E758); Carroll John Daly, "The Ambulating Lady," pp. 113-16 (E760); Dave Lewis, "The Backbone of Black Mask," pp. 117-27 (E2026); Will Murray, "Lester Dent: The Last of the Joe Shaw's Black Mask Boys," pp. 128-34 (E800); Robert S. Powell, "Including Murder: An Unpublished Hammett Collection," pp. 135-42 (E1417); E. R. Hagemann, "Cap Shaw and His 'Great and Regular Fellows': The Making of The Hard-Boiled Omnibus," pp. 143-52 (D345).

D310. Haining, Peter. The Fantastic Pulps. London: Gollancz Ltd., 1975. 420pp. Anthology with introduction and prefatory notes. Mostly SF and fantasy but Ray Cummings' "Madman's Murder Melody," reprinted from Horror Stories, is of interest to the field.

D311. Hersey, Harold B. Pulpwood Editor. NY: Frederick A. Stokes, 1937; reprinted by Greenwood Press, 1974. vii-viii; 301pp. With an index and a list of publications with which Hersey was associated.
Hersey was an editor and sometimes publisher for a number of pulp magazines including Underworld Magazine, Spy Stories, Murder Stories, Gangster Stories, Racketeer Stories and others. There is little specific information on the day-to-day editorial work but this is still a valuable document on the pulp publishing world.

D312. Hickman, Lynn. "The Pulp Collector." The Pulp Era, no. 75 (Spring 71), pp. 6-11.
Checklist of issues published (by volume, number and date) for pulps including Captain Satan, Dr. Yen Sin, The Mysterious Wu Fang, The Octopus, Secret Six, and The Scorpion. (REB)

D313. Hogan, Robert J. "Inside an Author's Brain." Writer's Digest, Oct 35, pp. 13-
Hogan wrote the entire contents of the G-8 and His Battle Aces pulp, as well as the featured novels in The Mysterious Wu Fang. When asked to tell "how I get my ideas and how I build my plots," he revealed that he

used "mechanical help" in the form of a set of books called "The Plot Genie." Article also includes comments on pulp villains. (REB; information paraphrased from Nick Carr's The Flying Spy, p. 13)

D313a. Hullar, Link. "The Pulps and American History: An Informal History." DSCR 6 (1979).
General discussion of the pulps as a reflection of their time. (WM)

D313b. Hutchinson, Don. "Those Mad, Mad, Mad Pulp Villains." Collector's Magazine 1:2 (not dated, probably 1977), pp. 10-21. Illus. Published by G & T Enterprises, Toronto.
A sprightly and entertaining survey of the single character pulp magazines which featured super-villains rather than super-heroes as their main characters (Dr. Death, Dr. Yen Sin, The Mysterious Wu Fang, and others) as well as related stories from other magazines, such as the Doctor Satan series in Weird Tales. Profusely illustrated with pulps and paperback cover reproductions. (REB)

D314. Johnson, Tom. "Fading Shadows: Corinth/Regency Paperbacks." Megavore 10 (1 Aug 80):36-39. Illus.
In the early 1960s, novels and stories featuring several pulp characters were reprinted in paperback by a West Coast publishing house. Johnson has written a short introduction on the series and on the individual pulp characters and compiled a list of the titles. The series included the Phantom Detective, Operator "5", Dusty Ayres and Doctor Death.

D315. ______. "Fighting Men Extraordinary." Xenophile 22 (March/Apr 76), pp. 26-28, 33, 35; reprinted in a revised and expanded version as "Fantastic Fighting Men of Fiction," in Age of the Unicorn 2:2:66-72, 74, 136. Illus.
The awesome fighting skills of a number of pulp characters.

D316. Jones, Robert Kenneth. The Shudder Pulps. A History of the Weird Menace Magazines of the 1930's. West Linn, Oregon: FAX Collector's Editions, 1975. v-xv, 238pp. Index. Illus.
Detailed survey of a mystery-related subgenre of pulp figures. Among the writers who wrote in this backwater are Paul Ernst, Bruno Fischer, Steve Fisher, Frank Gruber, and Richard Sale. In an epilogue, Jones reports on interviews with Baynard Kendrick, Paul Ernst and Wyatt Blassingame. Chapter 11 is a treatment of "defective detectives" (detectives with physical handicaps). A shorter version of this material was originally published in The Pulp Era, no. 68 (Nov/Dec 67), pp. 21-23, 8. Earlier versions of other chapters were published in Bronze Shadows, nos. 10-15 (1967/68). (REB, RS)

D317. Lowndes, Robert A. W. In a letter in TAD 5 (1971/72): 106-9, Lowndes describes his job as editor for the digest series of pulp reprints (Startling Mystery Stories, Magazine of Horror, and others) published by Health Knowledge, Inc. in the 1960s.

D318. "The Men Who Make the Argosy." Series of author profiles in Argosy magazine, published irregularly from 1929-1937.
There are no critical comments but some biographical information is provided for writers on whom little information is presently available. Approximately 130 profiles were published in the series. An attempt has been made to identify those writers whose work included detective/mystery elements and references to this source for authors will be to Argosy, with date of profile and pagination (where available). Since genre

categories were often flexible in the pulp magazines, further research may establish the use of mystery fiction formulas by writers not included in this bibliography.

D319. Murray, Will. "The Ancestors of Batman." TBG, 7 Oct 83, pp. 50, 52, 54.
Pulp characters, ancestors of the comic book masked hero, Batman. Includes characters created by Norman Daniels, Murray Leinster and "C. K. M. Scanlon."

D321. Nolan, William F. "A Walk in the Pulpwoods: Random Recollections." Clues 2:2 (Fall/Winter 81):38-40.
A tribute to the pulp writers and Nolan's debt to them.

D322. Odyssey Publications, Inc. P. O. Box G-148, Greenwood, MA 01880.
A small publishing house, directed by pulp researcher Will Murray, which has built up a well-edited list of publications that include Duende magazine, pamphlets, and facsimile reprints of pulp stories and magazines.

D323. Pronzini, Bill, editor. The Arbor House Treasury of Detective & Mystery Stories from the Great Pulps. NY: Arbor House, 1983. 342pp.
In his five-page introduction, Pronzini provides a concise history of the pulp era. Each of the stories is prefaced by editor Pronzini with a biocritical introduction.

D324. Pulp and Pulp Press. Published by Robert Weinberg, 15145 Oxford Drive, Oak Forest, Ill. 60452. 13 issues of Pulp magazine published as of December 1983.
Weinberg is a specialty book dealer who is also one of the most knowledgeable writers on pulp subjects and, in addition to reprints of fiction from the pulp magazines, he has published a number of collections of essays on pulp characters and contributed articles to a number of other publications. Articles in Pulp cover a variety of genre topics and will be included in this bibliography as appropriate. Cook, pp. 432-34.

D325. Sampson, Robert. "Faces from the Shadow." TMRN 6:2 (Nov 73):7-14.
Series characters in the pulps with brief references to a number of detective characters.

D326. ______. "A Time of Lively Fiction." In 7 parts. DNR 48:6 (Dec 79):93-97; Pt 2 (Chapter 2) DNR 49:1 (Feb 80):8-13; Pt 3 (Ch. 3) DNR 49:2 (34-40); Pt 4 (Ch. 4-5) DNR 49:3 (June 80):52-55; Pt 5 (Ch. 5, concl.) DNR 49:4 (Aug 80):71-74; Pt 6 (Ch. 5-7) DNR 49:5 (Oct 80):87-91; Pt 7 (Ch. 7-8) DNR 49:6 (Dec 80):104-109.
A seven-part article tracing the history of cheap fiction from dime novels through the pulp era. Part I provides an overview of dime novels and the transition to pulp magazines. Part 2: A classification and discussion of different types of dime novel heroes, many of them sleuths. Part 3: The development (1920-1930) of the detective story, the crook story, the interplanetary romance, historical and war fiction, with emphasis on series characters and the magazines in which they appeared. Part 4: The influences leading to the creation of the single-character pulp magazines of the 1930s; begins a discussion of the more influential of these magazines, including The Shadow and The Whisperer. Part 5: Continues the discussion of influential single-character magazines, including The Spider, Phantom Detective, Doc Savage, and G-8. Part 6:

Concludes discussion of the single-character magazines, including Operator 5. The development of major mystery magazines is followed, citing typical characters illustrative of the changing fictional patterns. Early science-fiction magazines are then examined. Part 7: The rise of fantasy, love, and spicy magazines is examined and the second wave of single-character magazines described. Effects on the pulps of the Second World War are noted and their final decline traced into the 1950s. (DJ and RS)

D327. ______. Yesterday's Faces. A Study of Series Characters in the Early Pulp Magazines. Vol. 1: Glory Figures. Bowling Green, OH: Bowling Green Univ. Popular Press, 1983. Issued in both paperbound and hardbound editions. 270pp. Illustrated. Index.

Antecedents of pulp fiction (the dime novelists), and some prototypes (by Hanshew, Edgar Wallace, Frank Packard) of pulp characters.

D328. ______. Yesterday's Faces. Vol. 2: Strange Days. 1984. vii, 290pp. Issued in both hardcover and paperbound editions. Illustrated. Notes, bibliographies. Index.

An introduction and four long essays, continuing the author's study of series characters in the American pulp magazines. Chapter I, "Willemite Flourescing," discusses scientific detectives: The Thinking Machine, Luther Trant, Dr. Thorndyke, Craig Kennedy. Chapter II, "Strange Days," covers occult or psychic detectives: John Silence, Carnacki, Semi-Dual, Morris Klaw, Godfrey Usher, Jules de Grandin, and--somewhat unexpectedly--Robert E. Howard's Solomon Kane and King Kull. The other two chapters deal with Tarzan and other jungle heroes, and with the "scientific romance." The various series are analyzed, compared, and related to their authors' other work and to the larger pulp-magazine and popular fiction milieus of their time. There are extensive notes, a bibliography of primary and secondary sources, and checklists of the magazine appearances of all the series under discussion. Two dozen black-and-white reproductions of pulp magazine covers are included. Some of the material has appeared in a different form in magazines. (REB)

D329. Shaner, Carl. "Pulp Heroes You Never Knew Existed." Echoes 1:6 (June 83):32-35.

Little known pulp heroes published in the Boy's Friend Library (England).

D330. Smalley, Jack. "I Wrote for the Pulps." Modern Maturity (Dec/Jan 74/75):59-60. A condensation of a Westway Magazine article.

Smalley was a reader, editor and writer for pulps from 1922-1933 and he discusses the writers he knew, the style of the pulp writings and--surprisingly--what he sees as their decline during the depression, a time when most students of the field consider the pulps to be most popular. (RS & WA)

D331. Tonik,Al. "Immobile Faces." DSQ 10 (1982), pp. 4-5, 9.

On pulp characters whose faces lend themselves to disguise. (WM)

D332. Turner, Robert. "The Not-So-Literary Digests." Xenophile 38 (March/April 78), p. 19.

Reminiscences by a pulp writer, with a list of Turner's stories published in Manhunt under his own name and under the pseudonym of Roy Carroll. Checklist compiled by Bill Clark.

D333. ______. Some of My Best Friends Are Writers, But I Wouldn't Want My Daughter to Marry One! Los Angeles: Sherbourne Press, 1970. 253pp.

Turner describes the process of breaking into the pulps of the late Thirties, the editors and agents and fellow pulp-writers he dealt with, what happened to him when the pulps folded in the early Fifties, the rise and fall of Manhunt, teleplay-writing and the Mike Hammer TV series. Among the writers encountered are John D. MacDonald, Steve Fisher, Harold Q. Masur, Frank Kane and Day Keene. He is uncompromisingly honest about himself and his trade, he has some excellent anecdotes to tell, and his sidelights on the business of pulp writing deserve the attention of all devotees of the genre. (F. M. Nevins, Jr.)

D334. Weinberg, Robert, and McKinstry, Lohr. The Hero Pulp Index. (Hillside, NJ); no publisher given, 1970. v, 54pp. Stapled in heavy covers. "This edition is a limited one, of 250 numbered copies." Second edition (revised and enlarged): Evergreen, CO: Opar Press, June 1971. iv, 48pp. Wraps. Illustrated. (In spite of the limitation statement in the first edition, copies with numbers higher than 250 have been seen.)

The "hero pulps" were those pulp magazines which featured stories, usually of novel length, built around continuing larger-than-life characters: The Shadow, Doc Savage, Operator 5, etc.This Index lists the known appearances of 56 such characters. The listing is alphabetical by character name and gives, for each appearance, the magazine title, author's name, whole number, volume and number, cover date, and title of the featured novel. There is a separate alphabetical list of authors, with many pseudonyms identified. "A Guide to the Hero Pulps," a collection of capsule descriptions of the major pulp heroes, and a set of notes describing the reprints (mostly in paperback) of the pulp novels are also included. Nearly two-thirds of the characters listed fall into the crime/mystery category: detectives, "caped crusaders," G-men, spies, or super-criminals. Among the authors are many known for crime fiction outside of the pulp magazine field: Edward S. Aarons, Kendell Foster Crossen, Norman A. Daniels, Frederick C. Davis, Clayton Rawson, Stewart Sterling, Richard Wormser, and others. Initial work on the Index was done by Lohn McKinstry, who brought in Robert Weinberg as a collaborator on the first edition. The revised and expanded second edition was prepared by Weinberg. This second edition is illustrated with 16 full-page reproductions (black and white) of pulp magazine covers. (REB)

2. Single-character Series, Magazines & Publishers

Alfred Hitchcock's Mystery Magazine

D335. Suzuki, Seiichi, compiler. Hitchcock Magazine Somokuroku (Hitchcock Magazine Index). Private publication, 1981. 208pp.

The compiler is a librarian and the index contains a list of and an index to all 50 issues of the Japanese edition of AHMM. (HS/TT)

"Alias Mr. Death"

D336. "The Self-Appointed Avenger of Crime." Pulp 1:5 (Winter 73):17-19.

Annotated list of the "Alias Mr. Death" short stories by G. Wayman Jones from Thrilling Detective. (REB)

"The Avenger"

D337. Banks, R. Jeff. "Goulart's Version of the Avenger: New Wine, Old Bottles and Something Extra." TAD 9 (1975/76):122-24.
New episodes in the Avenger pulp series in which writer Ron Goulart varies the formula by original series writer Paul Ernst.

D338. Carr, Wooda Nicholas (Nick). "The Avenger." TMRN 3:6 (Aug 70):13-16.
A survey of the series with a list of novels by year and month.

D339. ______. "The Avenger's Aides." Pulp 1:5 (Winter 73):6-15.
"Biographies" of the associates of The Avenger. (REB)

D340. Hullar, Link, and Carr, Nick (Wooda Nicholas). "Vengeance is Mine: The Life and Times of Richard Henry Benson and Justice, Inc." Echoes 1:6 (June 83):16-22.
An overview of the series.

"The Black Bat"

D341. Lewandowski, Joseph. "Smashing the Buckle." Nemesis 15 (Spring 83), pp. 28-37.
Long article on the German version of the American pulp hero, the Black Bat, and how the characters for this new series were changed. (WM)

D341a. Ward, Rex E. "The Black Bat Remembered." Echoes 1:1 (Aug 82):29-36.
An outside-the-law crime fighter appearing in Black Book Detective 1939-53. With a series checklist.

Black Mask

D342. Boys in the 'Black Mask.': An Exhibit in the UCLA Library, Jan 6-Feb 10, 1961. Los Angeles, CA: University of California Library, 1961. 12pp. Pictorial wrappers.
Catalogue with a short preface by Philip Durham and a list of the items in an exhibit of material related to Joseph T. Shaw and the Black Mask writers. Items include books, magazines (mostly pulps), manuscripts, photographs, letters, etc. Excerpts from the catalogue were published in TMRN 3:2 (1969):23-26, with an introduction by Wilbur J. Smith. (JLA)

D343. Durham, Philip. "The 'Black Mask' School." In Madden (B239), pp. 51-79. Reprinted in Nevins (B290), pp. 197-26.
Durham discusses the history of the Black Mask magazine, its contribution to the creation of the hard-boiled mystery under the editorship of Joseph Shaw, and the writers whom Shaw encouraged and published: Hammett, Caroll John Daly, Frederick Nebel, Raoul Whitfield, Raymond Chandler and others. An essential source for anyone interested in these writers and the magazine.

D344. Hagemann, E. R. "The Black Mask." Mystery 2:1 (Jan 81):51-53, 59. Photo of a display of Black Mask covers.
A short survey of the early years (those preceding the appointment of Captain Joseph Shaw as editor) and the magazine's editorial policies which, according to Hagemann, remained virtually unchanged during the ten years (1926-36) of Shaw's reign.

D345. ______. "Capt. Shaw and His 'Great and Regular Fellows': The Making of The Hard-Boiled Omnibus, 1945-46." Clues 2:2 (Fall/Winter 81):143-52.
An essay on the assembling of The Hard-Boiled Anthology (C749). With the first publication of a tentative list of writers and stories Shaw drew up at the beginning of the project.

D346. ______. "Captain Joseph T. Shaw's Black Mask Scrapbook." TMF 7:1 (Jan/Feb 83):2-6.
Discussion of a scrapbook kept by editor Shaw, roughly covering the years 1929-36 of Black Mask. The material falls into four categories: Hammett, Raoul Whitfield, Black Mask and Shaw. Hagemann examines some of the material relating to the latter two subjects.

D347. Hagemann, E. R., compiler and editor. A Comprehensive Index to Black Mask, 1920-1951, With Brief Annotations, Preface, and Editorial Apparatus. Bowling Green, OH: Bowling Green University Popular Press, 1982. 236pp. Simultaneous clothbound and paperbound editions. Selected bibliography.
The main portion of the Index, comprising 2509 numbered items, lists all fiction and "most non-fiction deemed of interest" alphabetically by author. Pen-names and series characters are noted, and brief notations of plot devices or settings are included for many entries. Editorials, departments, letters, and filler material are generally not listed, with the exception of letters by selected Black Mask writers (such as Hammett) and published biographical notes on these writers, which are mentioned in the annotations. There is a checklist of issues indexed and a register of BM editors and writers, arranged in order of first appearance in the magazine, and including notes on frequency of appearance and on series figures. As the compiler takes pains to point out, the Index is "comprehensive, not complete." It still remains for someone to produce a complete issue-by-issue list of contents and a cross-index by title. Most, if not all, of the necessary data have been collected and transcribed, but the task of preparing the material for publication (and finding a publisher) is a formidable one. (REB)

D348. Mertz, Stephen. "Captain Shaw's Hard-Boiled Boys." TAD 12 (1979):264-65.
Editor Shaw's notes on several hard-boiled writers, part of his working file for The Hard-Boiled Omnibus (C749).

D349. Ruhm, Herbert, editor. The Hard-Boiled Detective: Stories from Black Mask Magazine 1920-1951. NY: Vintage Books, 1977. xviii, 396pp. Wraps.
In his introduction Ruhm discusses the importance of the Black Mask pulp to the development of hard-boiled writing, Shaw and his editorship and some of the writers who contributed to the magazine.

"Blue Jean Billy"

D351. Sampson, Robert. "Pirates in Candyland." TMF 6:3 (May/June 82):7-13.
On Blue Jean Billy, a pulp villainess, pirate and "Highway Woman of the Sea." With a checklist of her appearances in Detective Story Magazine and Best Detective.

"Captain Satan"

See also: D312.

D352. Grennell, Dean. "Captain Satan." The Pulp Era, 72 (Sept 69), pp. 15-17. Reminiscences on Captain Satan pulp; reprinted from Grue 28, May 1956.

D353. Jones, Robert Gibson (Bob). "The World's Weirdest Criminal." The Pulp Era, no. 72 (Sept 69), pp. 12-13.
Survey of the Weird Tales series.

"Captain Zero"

D354. Johnson, Ginger. "Zero at Midnight." Echoes 1:4 (Feb 83):29-32.
G. T. Fleming-Roberts' Captain Zero series. A less-than-charismatic crime fighter of the 1949-50 period.

Columbia Pulp Chain

D355. Lowndes, Robert A. W. "The Columbia Pulps." The Pulp Era, no. 67 (May/June 67), pp. 5-20.
Anecdotal history of the Columbia Pulp chain, by one of its long-time editors. Mentions a few detective pulp titles. Invaluable eye-witness account of a portion of pulp-magazine history. (REB)

Crime Busters/Mystery Magazine

D356. Murray, Will. "Street & Smith's Crime Busters." Xenophile 38 (March/April 78), pp. 132-37.
A critical history of the Crime Busters pulp whose name was changed to Mystery Magazine with the first issue of volume 5 (Nov 39). With a contents index by issue.

"The Crimson Mask"

D357. Carr, Nick. "The Crimson Mask." Echoes 2:3 (Dec 83):10-19.
An overview of the masked detective appearing in Detective Novels Magazine 1940-44.

"Dan Fowler"

D358. "The 'Dan Fowler' Novels in G-Men Magazine." Pulp 1:1 (Fall 70):1921.
Checklist giving magazine date & title of featured novel. (REB)

"Dan Turner"

D359. Carr, Nick. "Dan Turner." Xenophile 21 (Feb 76), pp. 51, 53, 54.
A brief portrait of "Hollywood's number one private-eye."

D360. Wooley, John. "Introduction." In Dan Turner, Hollywood Detective, edited by John Wooley, pp. 1-4. Bowling Green, OH: Popular Press, 1983.
A light, amusing introduction that touches on the pulps, Dan Turner, the hard-boiled tradition, parody in Bellem's work, the use of language, narrative speed, and why trashy fiction is good for you. (RS)

Detective Fiction Weekly

D361. Drew, Bernard A. "Hoh-Hoh to Satan. Detective Fiction Weekly's Nutty Series Heroes of the 1930s." Clues 2:2 (Fall/Winter 81):88-202. Illustrated.
A history and bibliography of selected DFW series characters from 1933-1937.

Detective Story Magazine

D362. Cox, J. Randolph. "More Mystery for a Dime: Street & Smith and the First Pulp Detective Magazine." Clues 2:2 (Fall/Winter 81):52-59.
An important study of Street & Smith's Detective Story Magazine, the successor, in 1915, to Nick Carter Weekly and, according to Cox, the "primary source of the transition between the dime novel of the 1890s and the 'hero pulp' of the 1930s."

D363. Sampson, Robert. "The Other Spider." Echoes, "special issue" (June 82):(27)-(32).
Johnston McCulley's Spider, a "superior master criminal." Published in DSM, 1918-1919.

Dime Mystery

See: D437.

"Doc Savage"

See also: E3028; Cook (A37), pp. 177-85.

D364. Clark, William J. An Author Index to the Doc Savage Magazine. Los Angeles, CA: M & B Publishers, Dec 71. 4to, stapled in pictorial wrappers. pp. 2-21.
The fiction contents of the 181 issues of Doc Savage magazine are indexed alphabetically by author, with publication date, title, and number of pages for each story. House names and pseudonyms are indicated where known. Probably the most famous contributor is John D. MacDonald, with 19 stories under his own name and four pen-names. Steve Fisher, William Campbell Gault, and Q. Patrick are also among the authors listed. (REB)

D366. Farmer, Philip Jose. Doc Savage: His Apocalyptic Life. Garden City, NY: Doubleday, 1973; paperback, NY: Bantam Books, 1975.
A "biography" of Doc Savage based on the one hundred and eighty-one pulp magazine novels, plus Farmer's elaborations. This book is part of Farmer's intricate exercise in "creative mythology" which ties together most of the famous characters in popular fiction (including detective fiction) into a single incredible network. (REB)

D367. Herrick, Daryl S. "The Doc Savage Lawsuit That Wasn't." DSF 1 (1978), pp. 6-15.
Presents correspondence exchanged between Frank A. Munsey Company and Street & Smith, Will Jenkins, and Lester Dent, concerning apparent similarities between a "Murray Leinster" (Jenkins) Argosy serial and a Dent Doc Savage novel. A plagiarism suit was averted. (RS)

D368. ______. "The Doc Savage Story That Wasn't." Age of the Unicorn 1:6 (Feb 80):19-21.
A Wm. Bogart/Robeson novel published in Mammoth Action Adventure, Nov 46.

D368a. Hullar, Link. "Doc Savage and the Great Depression." DSCR 7 (1979).
Examination of Doc Savage as a hero responding to the needs of Depression America. (WM)

D368b. Lai, Rick. "Fantastic Islands in the Stream." SSB 4 (Summer 83):25-26.
Comparisons between a Doc Savage novel, Fantastic Island, and Fleming's Dr. No. (WM)

D369. Laidlaw, Bill. "A Recurring Little Villain." DSQ 5 (Apr 81), pp. 9-13. On Doc Savage and The Avenger's dwarf villains. (WM)

D370. McGregor, Herman S. "A Critical Analysis of the Doc Savage Novels." Bronze Shadows 2 (Dec 65) - 15 (Nov 68).
An issue-by-issue analysis of the Doc Savage novels beginning with Doc Savage Vol. 1, no. 1 and concluding with Vol. 7, no. 5 in the last issue of Bronze Shadows. In the last two installments, the title was changed to "A Comprehensive Survey of the Doc Savage Novels."

D371. Murray, Will. "The Doc Savage Influence." SSB 1 (Sept 82), pp. 12-13. Doc Savage's influence on the mystery/SF field. (WM)

D372. ______. Doc Savage:Reflections in Bronze. Melrose, MA: Odyssey Publications, Inc. 24pp. Wraps. Illus.
Reprinting of two articles--"Reflections in a Flake-Gold Eye" (D381) and "The Girl Who Loved Doc Savage" (D377)--which originally appeared in DSR, nos. 2-3 and 4. (WM)

D373. ______. "The Duende Doc Savage Index." Duende 2 (Winter 76/77), pp. 27-31.
Compiled in order of composition with author names--where known--attributed. Also includes original titles to the novels. Data based on Street & Smith files and on internal evidence as analyzed by Murray.

D374. ______. "The Feathered Serpent Motif in Doc Savage and The Shadow." Fantasy Mongers 5 (Jan 83), pp. 10-12.
On Mayan/Aztec villains. (WM)

D375. ______. "The Forgotten Doc Savage." In Secrets of Doc Savage. Odyssey Publications, 1981. Wraps.
Article on Col. Richard Henry Savage, the soldier of fortune whose life inspired Doc Savage and the Avenger. (WM)

D376. ______. "The Fortress of Solitude." In Secrets of Doc Savage, pp. 24-29. Article on Doc Savage's fortress retreat. (WM)

D377. ______. "The Girl Who Loved Doc Savage." DSR 4 (1973), pp. 6-10 (as by Bill Murray); reprinted in Doc Savage: Reflections in Bronze (Odyssey Publications, 1978), pp. 14-22.
On Doc Savage's relationship with the Mayan Princess Monja. (WM)

D378. ______. "The Great Monk." Attic Revivals No. 2 (1980), pp.2-3. Examines an early Lester Dent character which served as prototype for Monk Mayfair of the Doc Savage series. (RS)

D379. ______. "Indestructible Doc Savage." TCBG, 22 Jly 83, pp. 56, 58. Illus. The publishing history of the Bantam reprint series with an author guide giving authors of titles not by Lester Dent.

D380. ______. "Pulpularity: Doc Savage vs. The Shadow." SSB 3 (March 83), pp. 4-6.
A critical comparison of the two characters. (WM)

D381. ______. "Reflection in a Flake-Gold Eye." DSR 2-3 (Spring 1973), pp. 16-22 (as by Bill Murray); reprinted in Doc Savage: Reflections in Bronze (Odyssey, 1978), pp. 2-13.
Speculative article on Doc Savage's career from a psychological point of view.

B381a. ______. "The Resurrection of In Hell, Madonna." DSCR 5 (1979).
Background on the newly discovered "lost" Doc Savage novel, published by Bantam as The Red Spider. (WM)

D382. ______. "The Secret Kenneth Robesons." Duende 2 (Winter 76/77), pp. 3-26.
On the ghost writers used by Lester Dent to help him write Doc Savage.

D383. ______. "The Top Ten Doc Savage Novels--and One Stinker." Age of the Unicorn 2:2 (June 80):22-29.
Personal lists by Will Murray and seven other readers.

D384. ______. "The Untold Adventures of Doc Savage." In Secrets of Doc Savage (Odyssey, 1981), pp. 3-19.
On the aborted Doc Savage novels and outlines by Lester Dent and his ghost writers. (WM)

D385. ______. "The War Sower." In Secrets of Doc Savage (Odyssey, 1981), pp. 20-23.
Article on Jonas Sown, a Doc Savage foe. (WM)

D386. Sampson, Robert. "Cover Story." SSB 3 (March 83), pp. 6-10.
Doc Savage cover artists. (WM)

D387. ______. "The Digest Docs." Pulp 1:2 (Spring 71):3-14.
Critical examination of changes in narrative style, and characterization, and format of the digest-sized issues of Doc Savage, 1944-48.

D388. ______. "That Terrible Sunlight." Pulp 1:4 (Spring 72):26-31.
Descriptive article on John Sunlight, Doc Savage's principal antagonist. (REB)

D389. Smith, Bill. "A Visit with 'Mrs. Doc Savage'." Bronze Shadows 6 (Sept 66):3-5.
An interview with Mrs. Lester Dent.

D390. Tonik, Al. "Documents on Doc." SSB 1 (1982), pp. 14-16.
Article/bibliography on Doc Savage articles in print. (WM)

Double Detective

D391. Birch, Victor. (Double Detective: A Checklist.) Echoes 3:1 (Feb 84):7.
By volume, number and date.

"Dr. Death"

D392. Dewitt, Jack. "The Return of Dr. Death." Bronze Shadows No. 5 (July 66), pp. 4-5.
Discusses the three-issue Doctor Death pulp magazine. With checklist of contents. (RS)

D393. Myers, Dick. "the Birth of (Dr.) Death." Bronze Shadows No. 6 (Sept 66), p. 5.
Cites initial appearance of Dr. Death novelettes in All Detective Magazine (1934-35). (RS)

"Dr. Nancy Dayland"

D393a. Sampson, Robert. "Doctor Wonderful." TMF 5:6 (Nov/Dec 81):13-18.
An overview of the series featuring Florence Mae Pettee's pulp detective heroine, Dr. Nancy Dayland. Includes a partial bibliography.

"Dr. Yen Sin"

See also: D312.

D394. Carr, Nick. "Introducing the Yellow Peril." Megavore 12 (Dec 80), pp. 39-46. Illus.
Dr. Yen Sin, pulp super villain, his villainous plots and his principal antagonists.

D395. Lewandowski, Joseph. "An Index to Dr. Yen Sen, a Popular Publication." Age of the Unicorn 1:5 (Dec 79):32-33. Illus.

"Dusty Ayres"

D396. Carr, Nick. "The Emperor of the World." Megavore 10 (Aug 80), pp. 42-45. Illus.
Examination of "Fire-Eyes," villain in the Dusty Ayres pulp series.

D397. Carr, Nick and Tom Johnson. "They Called Him Agent 10." Echoes 1:3 (Dec 82):13-17; 1:4 (Feb 83):23-27.
A descriptive, two-part narrative study of Secret Agent 10, a recurrent character in the Dusty Ayres saga.

D398. "Dusty Ayres." Pulp 1:1 (Fall 70):22-23.
Brief survey and checklist of the 12 issues of Dusty Ayres and His Battle Birds. (REB)

Ellery Queen's Mystery Magazine (EQMM)

See also: E2255.

D399. Boucher, Anthony. "There Was No Mystery in What the Crime Editor Was After." NYTBR, 26 Feb 61, pp. 4-5, 50.
A tribute to EQMM on its 20th anniversary. Boucher traces the history of American detective fiction magazines and describes EQMM's contribution.

D400. Hosei Daigaku Suiri Shosetsu Kenkyu-kai, Mystery Magazine Index. Tokyo: Hosei University Mystery Study Group, 1976. 232pp.
An index to the Japanese edition of EQMM, nos. 1-115 (1956-65), and

Hayakawa's Mystery Magazine (formerly EQMM, Japanese edition), nos. 116-200 (1966-1972). Limited to 300 copies. (HS/TT)

D401. Nieminski, John, compiler. EQMM 350. Author/Title Index to Ellery Queen's Mystery Magazine, Fall 1941 Through January 1973. White Bear Lake, MN: The Armchair Detective Press, 1974. 116pp. Wraps.

A comprehensive index that includes non-fiction material. With appendices as follows: A. Title Changes (for reprint material); B. Series Characters; C-K: indices identifying articles/essays/features, true crime, book reviews, poems and verse, quizzes and puzzles, cartoons, translators, Sherlockiana, and non-Sherlockian parodies/pastiches/satires/take-offs and other genre-related narrative fiction.

"Felix Boyd"

D402. Sampson, Robert. "Half Nick Carter and Half Sherlock Holmes." DNR 50 (1981):118-22.

A well-written history and analysis of the Felix Boyd detective stories in The Popular Magazine; many excerpts and plot synopses are included. (DJ)

"G-8"

See also: D313 (qv).

D403. Carr, Nick. The Flying Spy: A History of G-8. Pulp Classic 18. Chicago, IL: (Robert Weinberg, Publisher), 1978. 160pp. Illus. With an introduction by Jack Devenny and a biography of author Robert Jasper Hogan by Sid Bradd.

What Eisgruber's Gangland's Doom (D455) did for The Shadow, this book does for the featured character of the air-war pulp G-8 and His Battle Aces (110 issues, Oct 1933 - June 1944). There are two short chapters (8 pages) dealing with G-8's author and the genesis of the magazine. The rest is an exhausting treatment of the minutiae of plot and characters in the 110 novels, of interest only to the most dedicated pulp fiction addict. The illustrations include pulp cover reproductions and some fine drawings by the estimable Frank Hamilton. (REB) Addendum: for the publication of miscellaneous comments which where deleted from this book see Carr's article "The Flying Spy," DSCR 6 (1979). (WM)

D404. ______. "G-8 versus Chu Lung." Pulp 1:4 (Spring 72):3-14.

Summary of G-8's battles against Oriental villain Chu Lung. Partly incorporated into Carr, The Flying Spy, (D403). (REB)

"The Ghost"

D405. Sampson, Robert. "Ghost Story." Pulp 1:5 (Winter 73):20-33.

Survey of the single-character novels from The Ghost (and title variations) and Thrilling Mystery. (REB)

"Health Knowledge Magazines"

See also: D317.

D406. Marshall, Gene, and Waedt, Carl F. "An Index to the Health Knowledge Magazines." SFC 3 (1977):3-42. Illus.

A listing of the contents--by issue--with an author index--of the group of digest pulp magazines edited in the 1960s by Robert A. W. Lowndes. Most of the material was reprinted from the pulps of the 30s and 40s and included many stories from Weird Tales. Among the magazines was Startling Mystery Stories and editor Lowndes' knowledgeable introductions contain information on pulp writers and magazines that make them a valuable source of information.

"The Honeymoon Detectives"

D407. Sampson, Robert. "Amazing Grace." TMF 6:4 (July/Aug 82):23-29.
A survey of the six serial novels featuring Robert and Grace Duvall, published in The Cavalier (and title variants) from 1912-1917. An early husband-and-wife detective team.

Horror Stories

See: D437.

"Jerry Wade, the Candid Camera Kid"

D408. Grossman, Al. "A Snappy Hero--Jerry Wade." Pulp 1:2 (Spring 71):20-21.
Brief discussion of amateur detective appearing in Detective Novels magazine, 1939-44. With checklist. (RS)

"Jim Hatfield"

D409. Tonik, Albert. "Jim Hatfield: Texas Ranger." Echoes 1:3 (Dec 82):23-32.
A publishing history of the adventures of this pulp western detective. With a series checklist, including information on pb reprints, and an addendum (pp. 33-36), a biography of writer "Jackson Cole" (A. Leslie Scott) based on information supplied by Mrs. Scott.

"The Masked Detective"

D410. Carr, Wooda Nicholas. "The Masked Detective." Pulp 8 (Spring 76), pp. 3-7.
On the detective hero in a Popular Publications pulp magazine. With a checklist.

"Mr. Chang"

D411. Sampson, Robert. "The Chang Monster." SFC 14 (May 81), pp.41-46.
An examination of A. E. Apple's pulp series featuring Mr. Chang. Sampson suggests that the Chang stories may be a parody of sinister Oriental fiction. Includes a partial checklist of Mr. Chang's pulp appearances between 1919 and 1936. (GG)

"Mr. Death"

D412. "Death in the Skies." Pulp 1:4 (Spring 72):20-21.
Survey of the air-war villain Mr. Death, created by Steve Fisher in Daredevil Aces. (REB)

The Munsey Magazines

D413. Moskowitz, Sam. "A History of 'The Scientific Romance' in The Munsey Magazines, 1912-1920." In his Under the Moons of Mars, pp. 289-433.

A brilliant tour de force covering not only the development of science fiction in the Munsey magazines, but the early years of pulp magazine fiction, both mystery and adventure, through 1920. (RS)

Mystery Book Magazine

D414. Briney, Robert E. "Mystery Book Magazine: An Appreciation and Index." TAD 8 (1974/75):245-50.

A publication history and an index of fiction by author, with separate listings of Samuel Mines' true-crime series, Will Cuppy's review columns and Margaret Petherbridge's crossword puzzle-stories.

Mystery League

D415. Hardin, Nils. "Mystery League: A Summary." Xenophile 14 (June 75), pp. 8-13.

A review of the contents of this four-issue magazine, with a contents checklist.

D416. Hubin, Allen J. (Mystery League Magazine: a history and complete description.) TAD letter, 3 (1969/70):64-65.

A publishing history and contents description of the Queen-edited magazine, interpolated into the letter column in response to a comment by a reader.

Mystery Magazine. See Crimebusters

New Mystery Adventures

D418. Cook, Fred and Gordon Huber. "Index to New Mystery Adventures/Mystery Adventure Magazine/Mystery Adventures Magazine." Xenophile 22 (March/Apr 76), p. 47.

A listing of the contents of Volume I, issues 1-6, and Volume 2, issues 1 and 2. Although this installment was listed as "part 1," the publication of the index was not completed.

"Nick Kennedy and His River Police"

D419. Wormull, Len. "Bullseye, Spellbinder Extraordinary." CDA, 1974, pp. 126-30.

Stories of the bizarre were a feature of the Bullseye in the 1930s. Included were the stories of Nick Kennedy and his River Police against the Red Shadow Tong, headed by Fang Wu. (JRC)

"Norgil"

D420. Gibson, Walter B. "Introduction." In Grant, Norgil the Magician, pp. ix-xv. NY: Mysterious Press, 1977.

An anthology of 8 stories with an introduction in which Gibson talks about magic and mystery, his professional association with magicians Harry Thurston and Houdini, and his use of magic in The Shadow Magazine and in the creation of magician-detective Norgil.

D421. ______. "Introduction: In Retrospect." In Grant, Norgil, More Tales of Prestigitection, pp. ix-xi. NY: Mysterious Press, 1979.

In his introduction to this collection of eight crime-detecting adventures of Norgil the Magician from the 1938-39 Crime Busters Magazine, author

Gibson ("Maxwell Grant") explains the dedication ("to Jay Marshall") of his first Norgil collection. (RS)

"The Octopus"

See: D312.

"Operator 5"

D422. Carr, Wooda Nicholas ("Nick"). *America's Secret Service Ace*. Oak Lawn, IL: Robert Weinberg, 1974. 63pp. Illus. Wraps.
Detailed analysis of the *Operator 5* pulp magazine novels (most of them written by Frederick C. Davis): heroes, villains, plot summaries, chronology. Illustrated with numberous pulp magazine cover reproductions. Breen 147. (REB)

D423. ______. "Beware of the Leopard." *Echoes*, special issue (June 82), pp. 33-36.
Operator 5 "pulp evildoer," the Leopard, who appeared in *War-Masters from the Orient* (*Operator 5*, March 36).

D424. ______. "Emperor Rudolph." *Pulp* 1:4 (Spring 72):22-25.
Description of one of Operator 5's antagonists. (REB)

D425. ______. "Let's Face It! A Look at the Disguises of Operator 5 during the Purple Invasion." *Age of the Unicorn* 1:3 (Aug 79):3-8, 21. Illus.

D426. ______. "Operator 5." *Pulp* 1:1 (Fall 70):3-18.
"Biographical" sketch and personality analysis of Jimmy Christopher (Operator 5), detailed review of the May 1935 (4:2) issue of the pulp--the summary and analysis of the lead novel, *Blood Reign of the Dictator*, occupies more than 4 pages--and a summary of the Purple Invasion series of 13 novels. Some of this material was incorporated, in rewritten form, into Carr, *America's Secret Service Ace* (D422). (REB)

D427. Grennell, Dean A. "Jumping Jimmy Christopher." *Xenophile* 30 (March 77):17-19. Illus.
The principal characters in the *Operator 5* series.

D428. Murray, Will. "The Three Worlds of Jimmy Christopher." *Echoes* 1:5 (Apr 83):6-30.
A lengthy survey of the *Operator 5* series with up-dated information on the writers behind the "Curtis Steele" house name. A checklist and an afterword by Nick Carr commenting further on the series and its author.

D429. Weinberg, Robert. "Who Wrote *Operator 5*?" *Pulp* 13 (Fall 81), pp. 14-20. Illus.
A checklist of issues of *Operator 5* showing the author's real name and the amount of money he was paid for the story. The list was compiled, with the assistance of Joel Frieman, from the files of Popular Publications.

"The Phantom Detective"

D430. Carr, Wooda Nicholas. "Ryerson Johnson and the Phantom Detective." *Age of the Unicorn* 1:6 (Feb 80):9-12.
Interview with author of Phantom Detective no. 46, *The Silent Death*.

D431. Hutchison, Don. "Twenty Years of Murder." Echoes 2:2 (Oct 83):5-12.
A profile of the Phantom Detective series and its lead character.

D432. Murray, Will. "Foe of the Phantom." Echoes 1:1 (Aug 82):20-24.
Clifford Boniface, super spy opponent of the Phantom Detective, who appeared in two 1939 novels.

D433. Sampson, Robert. "Blood Chronicle." TMRN 3:3 (Feb 70):3-10.
On the twenty-year career of the Phantom Detective with a checklist of novels by year of publication and a list of the Corinth paperback reprints.

D434. Tonik, Albert. "D'Arcy Lyndon Champion." Echoes 2:1 (Aug 83):7-9.
A profile of the author of the Phantom Detective.

D435. Wermers, Bernie. "A Checklist for the Phantom Detective." Bronze Shadows 11 (Aug 67):4-6.
A list of the Phantom Detective lead novels by year and month (1933-53). No information available to compiler on December 1935 issue.

Popular Publications

D436. Hardin, Nils. "An Interview with Henry Steeger." Xenophile 33 (July 77), pp. 3-18.
Steeger, the publisher of Popular Publications, talks about the company's pulp magazines, the series and their authors. With a checklist of Popular Publications titles (1930-55), compiled by Hardin and George Hocutt. Followed, on pp. 25-36, by a portfolio of pulp magazine covers.

D437. Jones, Robert Gibson. "Popular's Weird Menace Pulps" and "Index to Weird Menace Pulps," in The Weird Menace, edited by C. E. Cazedessus, Jr. Evergreen, CO: Opar Press, June 1972. Wraps.
The Weird Menace is a paperbound booklet reprinting two stories by John H. Knox, "Man Out of Hell" and "Frozen Energy!", from Dime Mystery Magazine. Bound in as a 20-page center section of the booklet are Jones's brief essay on the "weird menace" pulps issued by Popular Publications in the period from 1934 to 1941, and an index by author to the contents of these magazines: Dime Mystery, Horror Stories, Sinister Stories, Startling Mystery, Terror Tales, and Thrilling Mysteries. Among the stories listed are three by Cornell Woolrich, two by John Dickson (here spelled "Dixon") Carr, and two by Edgar Wallace. Bruno Fischer was a prolific contributor under his "Russell Gray" and "Harrison Storm" pseudonyms, and other familiar names include Hugh B. Cave, Paul Ernst, David Goodis, Frank Gruber, Henry Kuttner, and "Archie" Oboler. Seven full-page reproductions of pulp covers are included. (REB)

D438. Steeger, Henry. "The Popular Publications." The Pulp Era, no. 67 (May/June 67), pp. 31-34.
Checklist of Popular Publications pulp titles, with year of first issue plus brief commentary by Steeger, mostly on Argosy. Includes about 20 different detective pulps. (REB)

"Ranger Calhoun"

D439. Sampson, Robert. "Bring Them in Dead." Echoes 1:1 (Aug 82):25-28.
The Ranger Calhoun series in Flynn's Weekly and Flynn's Detective Fiction Weekly, from the mid-twenties to the mid-thirties.

Red Star Mystery

D440. Briney, Robert E. "Red Star Mystery." The Pulp Era, no. 64 (July/Aug 66), pp. 14-16.
Brief descriptive article and index to RSM, whose lead novels featuring "Don Diavolo, The Scarlet Wizard" were written by Clayton Rawson as Stuart Towne. (REB)

The Saint/Detective/Mystery Magazine

D441. Nieminski, John, compiler. The Saint Magazine Index. Authors and Titles, Spring 1953-October 1967. Evansville, In: Cook & McDowell Publications, 1980. 68pp. Wraps.
In addition to author and title, there is also indexing of title changes, series characters, non-fiction and Sherlockiana.

Scientific Detective Monthly

D442. Lowndes, Robert A. W. "The Unique Mystery Magazine: Hugo Gernsback's Scientific Detective Monthly." Parts 1 through VII. TAD 14 (1982):24-30, 157-62, 243-46, 367-71; 15 (1982):18-22; 16 (1983):153-63, 269-74. Correction by John L. Apostolou in letter, TAD 14 (1981):383.
An issue-by-issue description of the contents of the 10 issues--all published in 1930--of the Gernsback pulp magazine which featured Arthur Reeve's Craig Kenney. The most recently published installment examines the July 1930 issue; the last issue was published in October 1930. In 16 (1983):163, there is an index, by author, of all stories published in the magazine. The series is continuing in volume 17 (1984).

"The Scorpion"

See D312

Scotland Yard

D443. Sampson, Robert. "Fourteen Issues." Xenophile 22 (March/Apr 76), pp. 4-11. Illus.
An analysis of the fiction in the Scotland Yard pulp (1930/31), with a table of contents listing for each issue.

"Secret Agent X"

D444. Johnson, Tom. "City of Madness." Echoes 3:1 (Feb 84):2-13.
A review of the plots of what Johnson considers to be the best stories in the Secret Agent X series.

D445. Johnson, Tom, and Murray, Will. Secret Agent-X--A History. Pulp Classics 22. Chicago: Robert Weinberg, 1980. pp. 6-96. 8vo, wraps. Illus.
A history and analysis of the Secret Agent X pulp magazine. More than half of the book is devoted to plot summaries of the featured novels and reconstructed 'biographies' of the main characters, and is of interest only to the diehard pulp enthusiast. But there is also solid information about the publishing history of the magazine, biographical sketches of the authors of the Agent X novels (Paul Chadwick and G. T. Fleming-Roberts, both using the 'Brant House' pseudonym), and checklists of related pulp series. The book is awkwardly organized, with

bibliographical information scattered throughout the various chapters and with no index to help locate it. Small photographs of 41 of the Secret Agent X covers are included. (REB)

D446. Murray, Will. "The Unknown Brant Houses." In Secret Agent X, pp. 120-127. Melrose Highlands, MA: Odyssey Publications, 1977. Illus.
Some general comments on the history of the "wedding" of the horror tale to the detective story in the late 20s pulps and biographies of the authors who wrote the Secret Agent X series under the house name of "Brant House."

"Semi-Dual"

D447. Clark, William J. "The Occult Detector by J. U. Giesy and Junius B. Smith." Xenophile 17 (Sept 75), p. 55.
A checklist of the "Semi-Dual" stories with a short introduction.

D448. Sampson, Robert. "Detection by Other Means." TMF 7:1 (Jan/Feb 83):7-17. With a checklist of stories.
Description of a series featuring Prince Abdull Omar, an occult detective known as "Semi-Dual," whose cases appeared in several pulps from 1912-35. Written by J. U. Giesy and J. B. Smith.

"The Secret Six"

See: D312.

D449. "The Not-So-Secret Six." Pulp 1:4 (Spring 72):18-19.
Supposed interview with the leader of The Secret Six. (REB)

"The Shadow"

See also: EMD (A160), pp. 58-59; Wallace/Lai (E3028); D380; Penzler (B310).

D450. Avallone, Michael. "Golden Age Pulp Heroes: The Shadow." MSMM, March 81, pp. 86-87.
Nostaglic reminiscence. (REB)

D451. Blackbeard, Bill. "ForeSHADOWings." 2 pts. Xenophile 17 (Sept 75), pp. 6-7, 59-60; 22 (March/Apr 76), pp. 30-33.
Masked crime-fighters, antecedents of the Street & Smith popular 1930s series characters. Among other subjects, Blackbeard discusses the contributions of Guy Boothby and Frank L. Packard. First two installments of a projected series. No additional parts published to date.

D452. Cox, J. Randolph. "That Mysterious Aide to the Forces of Law and Order." TAD 3 (1970/71):221-29.
The Shadow and the tradition of the masked avenger in literature.

D453. Edwards, John. "From Shadow to Superman." Age of the Unicorn 2:1 (Apr 80):10-18.
On the Belmont paperback Shadow series revival.

D454. Eisgruber, Frank, Jr. "Crime Undercover." Pulp 1:4 (Spring 72):15-17.
Spy rings and other secret groups against which The Shadow fought.

D455. ______. Gangland's Doom: The Shadow of the Pulps. Oak Lawn, IL: Robert Weinberg, 1974.
Exhaustive analysis of the pulp magazine novels about the Shadow. Illustrated.

D456. ______. "Only the Shadow Knows." Pulp 1:4 (Summer 71):28-37.
Survey of those Shadow novels in which the title character supposedly unmasks or reveals facts about his origins. Incorporated in rewritten form into Eisgruber's Gangland's Doom. (REB)

D457. Gibson, Walter B. "Introduction." In The Shadow: Crime Over Casco & The Mother Goose Murders, pp. xi-xiii. NY: Crime Club, 1979.
Gibson discusses the three general phases into which The Shadow novels fell during the years of their publication (1931-1949). Also discusses events influencing the writing of these reprinted novels. (RS)

D458. ______. "Introduction." In The Shadow: Jade Dragon & House of Ghosts, p. ix. NY: Crime Club, 1981.
Gibson explains his choice of novels for this volume. (RS)

D459. ______. "Introduction." In The Shadow: The Mask of Mephisto & Murder by Magic, pp. ix-xi. NY: Crime Club, 1975.
Gibson briefly reminisces about his years of writing The Shadow. (RS)

D460. ______. "Introduction." In The Shadow: A Quarter of Eight & The Freak Show Murders, pp. xi-xv. NY: Crime Club, 1978.
Gibson gives a condensed account of pulp magazine history and describes the initiation of The Shadow magazine. (RS)

D461. ______. The Shadow Scrapbook. NY: Harcourt Brace Jovanovich, 1979. vi, 162pp. Pictorial wraps. "An Original Harvest/HBJ Book." Preface by Chris Steinbrunner. Contributing Editor: Anthony Tollin. Illus.
Covers The Shadow in all his incarnations, from the original pulp magazine through the paperback and hardcover revivals of the 1960s and 1970s, as well as the long-running radio show, the movies, and the comic strips. "Introducing the Shadow" by Walter Gibson (pp. 1-25) is an account of the genesis and development of The Shadow, accompanied by a checklist of the 325 magazine novels with publication date and author. "Writing The Shadow" offers a sample of the story outlines which Gibson used in planning the novels. "The Invisible Shadow" (pp. 75-92) by Anthony Tollin surveys the Shadow radio program, and includes a complete episode log. (Among the familar names which appear as scriptwriters are Alfred Bester, Max Ehrlich, and Frank Kane.) The very first Shadow radio script (by Edward Hale Bierstadt) is reproduced. There is a 16-page Shadow comic strip story. The illustrations include a portfolio of 25 Shadow pulp covers in color and another 17 in black and white, plus many interior drawings from the magazine, and a wealth of photographs. If this book doesn't tell you everything you want to know about The Shadow, you can always go on to The Duende History of The Shadow (D467). (REB)

D462. ______. "My Years with The Shadow." In his Two Adventures of the Shadow, pp. vii-xix. NY: Dover, 1975.
Reminiscences by The Shadow's creator.

D463. Goulart, Ron. "A.K.A. The Shadow." In Cheap Thrills (D305), pp. 43-58.

Informal comments on The Shadow and other masked avengers of the 1930s.

D464. Grennell, Dean. "The Fallen Mighty: The Shadow." Xenophile 22 (March/April 76), pp. 20-23, 54.
The Shadow and his associates.

D465. ______. "The Shadow." The Pulp Era no. 61 (July 64), pp. 13-24.
Disenchanted retrospective look at The Shadow--the magazine, the character, the stories; reprinted from Grennell's fanzine Grue, Nov. 1955 (25), with a one-page addendum dated 26 Aug 62. (REB)

D466. McSherry, Frank D., Jr. "The Shadow of Ying Ko." TRR 16 (July 77):1-24. Illus. by Frank Hamilton.
The Shadow and his oriental foe, the Golden Master, with references to Nero Wolfe and Zeck, and Sherlock Holmes and Moriarty.

D467. Murray, Will. The Duende History of The Shadow Magazine. Greenwood, MA: Odyssey Publications, 1980. 128pp. Illustrated with pulp covers and interior drawings, photographs and original art by Frank Hamilton.
An exhaustively-researched and entertainingly written history of The Shadow pulp magazine, using not only the texts of the magazine novels themselves but also interviews with the writers and editors involved and material from the publisher's files. The discussions clearly distinguish the attitudes and contributions of the four Shadow writers and relate these to the circumstances in which they wrote. There is less obsessive concern with the fictional minutiae of the stories than in Eisgruber's Gangland's Doom (D455). Contents: Will Murray, "The Men Who Cast The Shadow," pp. 5-59 (a detailed survey of the series, its publishing history and the fiction); Will Murray, "The Duende Shadow Index," pp. 60-66 (a chronological list of stories, with the working title and the author); Bob Sampson & Will Murray, "The Golden Shadow," pp. 67-76 (Lester Dent's original Shadow novel and Walter Gibson's revision); Bob Sampson, "The Vulnerable Shadow," pp. 77-84 (Theodore Tinsley's contributions to the series); "Theodore Tinsley--Maxwell Grant's Shadow," pp. 85-92 (interview); Bob Sampson, "The Third Cranston," pp. 93-99 (the Bruce Elliott Shadow novels); Walter B. Gibson, "The Purple Girasol," pp. 100-102 (fiction); Walter B. Gibson, "Blackmail Bay," pp. 103-114 (fiction); "Walter B. Gibson Revisited," pp. 115-24 (interview); Will Murray, "The Sinister Sanctum," pp. 124-25 (The Shadow's inner sanctum). Breen 173. (REB)

D468. ______. "The Top 25 Shadow Novels." Unicorn 1:4 (Oct 79):3-17.

D469. Nanovic, John L. "I Never Called Him Bill." In Two Adventures with the Shadow, pp. xxi-xxv. NY: Dover, 1975.
Street & Smith editor Nanovic recalls his assocation with Walter Gibson.

D470. Ostermann, Robert. "Where are the Pulp Fictioneers?" Bronze Shadows, no. 2 (Dec 65), pp. 15-21.
Includes anecdotes from Gibson's years writing The Shadow. (RS)

D471. Sampson, Robert. "A Footnote for Shadow Collectors." TMRN 4:2 (Jan 71):9-13.
4 Shadow novels with duplicate titles and Shadow novel reprints.

D472. ______. The Night Master. Chicago: Pulp Press, 1982. pp. 7-216. Large

8vo. Bibliography. Illus.

This book-length study of The Shadow (the pulp character and the magazine in which he appeared) fits in with the same author's Yesterday's Faces series (D327, D328) on series characters from the pulp magazines. The Appendices contain useful checklists of The Shadow in both magazine and book form, and a 12-page gallery of illustrations and covers from the original pulp. There are also three new drawings and a dust-jacket illustration by Frank Hamilton. The author's discursive style sometimes gets out of hand, and the lack of an index, as well as some typesetting peculiarities, make it harder than it should be to locate specific information. (REB)

D473. ______. "The Vulnerable Shadow." Pulp 1:1 (Fall 70):24-33; reprinted in the Will Murray Duende History (D467).
Analysis and checklist of the Theodore Tinsley Shadow novels. (REB)

D474. "The Shadow Speaks." Pulp 1:5 (Winter 73):3-4.
Question-and-answer session between Nick Carr and Walter Gibson. (REB)

D475. Ven, These. "An Interview with Harry Vincent." Echoes from the Pulps, No. 1 (Summer 78), pp. 1-7.
Speculative article concerning the unwritten history of The Shadow, couched as an interview with his chief agent. (RS)

Sinister Stories

See: D437.

"The Skipper"

D476. Hullar, Link, and Murray, Will. "The Fighting Fury." Megavore 12 (Dec 80), pp. 3-12. Illus.
A Doc Savage imitation adventure series with some detection and espionnage.

Spicy Mystery Stories

D477. Miller, Steve. (Spicy Mystery Stories: A Checklist.) Echoes 3:1 (Feb 84):5-6.
A contents listing of story and author by date, volume and number.

"The Spider"

See also: D293.

D478. Avallone, Michael. "Golden Age Pulp Stories: The Spider." MSMM, June 81, pp. 75-77.
One of a series. Brief nostalgic reminiscence, illustrated by Frank Hamilton. (REB)

D479. Carr, Wooda Nicholas. "Alias Blinky McQuade and Other Characters." Echoes 1:6 (June 83):23-25.
Recurrent characters in The Spider series.

D480. ______. "The Spider...A Personal View." Unicorn 2:2 (June 80):62-65.
Notes on the pulp series.

D481. ______. "Spider Notes." Echoes 1:1 (Aug 82):37-39; 2:2 (October 83): 31-32.
From Carr's Spider notebook. Miscellaneous comments.

D482. MacGregor, Herman S. "A Comprehensive Survey of The Spider Novels." The Pulp Era, no. 66 (March/Apr 67); pp. 40-52; no. 67 (May/June 67), pp. 76-82; no. 68 (Nov/Dec 67), pp. 27-31; no. 70 (Jan/Feb 69), pp. 13-24; no. 71 (March/Apr 69), pp. 15-17. In 5 installments.
Covers Oct 1933-Aug 1934 issues of the pulp magazine. Complete cast of characters, plot summary, critical comments, and supplementary remarks for each novel. (REB)

D483. Murray, Will. "The Top Ten Spiders." Megavore 13 (March 81), pp. 5-13. Illus.

D484. Sampson, Robert. "Sex and the Spider." Echoes 1:2 (Sept/Oct 82):21-34.
A thematic study in which RS shows that sexual activity is a "deadly danger" to a pulp hero in whose wake comes death.

D485. Sampson, Robert; Weinberg, Robert; and Freiman, Joel. "Who Wrote The Spider?" Pulp 13 (Fall 81), pp. 4-12. Illus.
A checklist with authors and prices paid them for writing series novels. Research based on Popular Publications files.

D486. "The Spider Checklist." The Pulp Era 67 (May/June 67), pp.73-75.
A chronological checklist of issues with lead novel identified. (REB)

D487. "The Spider vs. Munro." Pulp 1:4 (Spring 72):25.
Brief note on Munro, The Faceless One, a continuing villain in the Spider novels. (REB)

D488. Thorpe, Dickson. "The Wounds and Injuries of Richard Wentworth." Echoes 1:2 (Sept/Oct 82):35-39.

D489. Ven, These. "An Interview with Jackson." Echoes from the Pulps, No. 2 (Winter 78), pp. 1-9.
Speculative article concerning the unwritten history of the Spider in the form of an interview conducted with his assistant, Ronald Jackson. (RS)

D490. Weinberg, Robert. "The Man from the East." Pulp 1:2 (Spring 72):32-35.
Descriptive article on The Living Pharoah, one of the Spider's antagonists. (REB)

Startling Mystery

See: D437.

Startling Mystery Stories

See: D406.

Strange Detective Stories

D491. Lord, Glenn. "Strange Detective Stories." The Pulp Era, no. 65 (Sept/Oct 66), pp. 12-14.
Descriptive article and index to SDS. (REB)

Street & Smith

See also: C817, B362, and D70.

D492. Ostermann, Robert. "Where Are the Pulp Fictioneers?" Bronze Shadows, No. 2 (Dec 65), pp. 15-21.
A general discussion of the Street & Smith single-character magazines, with anecdotes concerning writers and editors. (RS)

Terror Tales

See: D437.

The Thrill Book

D493. Jones, Robert Kenneth. "The Thrill Book." Xenophile 30 (March 77), pp. 4-9. Illus. Originally published in WSFA Journal, March-Nov 1970.
Detective elements in some of the fiction but this early, elusive pulp seems to have emphasized adventure/fantasy stories. With a contents list.

Thrilling Mysteries

See: D437.

Thrilling Detective

D494. Tipton, Gene. "Remembrances of Thrilling Detective." Echoes 3:1 (Feb 84):14-17.
A survey of TD and some of the writers and stories.

"Thunderbolt"

D495. Sampson, Robert. "Thunderbolt!" Echoes 2:3 (Dec 83):7-10.
A series of six novelettes that appeared in Detective Story Monthly, 1920-21, and one of the earliest examples of a costumed mystery figure in pulp fiction.

Underworld Romances

D496. (Lachman, Marvin.) "Underworld Romances." Echoes 2:3 (Dec 83):19-22.
A review of the contents of the first three issues of UR, Popular Publications, 1931-32. Not listed in Cook (A37).

"Vivian Legrand"

D497. Jennings, Robert. "The Lady from Hell." Mystic Agent Double X, no. 1 (1980), unpaginated.
Long article on the Detective Fiction Weekly series concerning Vivian Legrand, The Lady from Hell, perhaps the most successful feminine series criminal of the pulps. Checklist and story abstracts. (RS)

Weird Tales

D498. Weinberg, Robert. "The Index - Weird Tales." In 5 parts. Weird Tales Collector 1 (1977), pp. 16-32; 2 (1977), pp. 17-31; 3 (1978), pp. 18-32; 4 (1978), pp. 18-32; 5 (1979), pp. 24-30.

A chronological listing of the contents page of WT. Many of the stories in WT were mystery with supernatural elements and readers with the patience to work through the listings will find many items of interest. A more useful listing is the index by author, compiled by T. G. L. Cockcroft, of the Weird Fiction Magazines, including WT. This was published privately by the compiler in 1964 and a second edition was issued in 1967. A dealer at the 1983 Pulpcon (Dayton, Ohio) had several copies and other copies may possibly still be obtained from speciality dealers. Weird Tales featured many stories with mystery/detection elements but secondary material dealing with Weird Tales usually focuses on the fantasy and supernatural elements and, for this reason, the substantial WT critical bibliography is not included in this bibliography.

D499. Weinberg, Robert. The Weird Tales Story. West Linn, Oregon: Fax Collector's Editions, 1977. 134pp. Illustrated.
A handsome tribute to the magazine. There are chapters on the editor, Farnsworth Wright, the stories, the cover and interior art and other topics. Of particular interest are the recollections by contributors to the magazine. Among these writers are Frank Belknap Long, Edmond Hamilton, Manly Wade Wellman and Robert E. Howard.

D500. Weinberg, Robert, ed. WT 50: A Tribute to Weird Tales. Chicago: Robert Weinberg, 1974. Wraps. Illustrated. 135pp.
An anthology of tributes to WT, along with some fiction. Among the contributors are writers Robert Bloch, Manly Wade Wellman, Frank Belknap Long, and Edmond Hamilton. This volume and The Weird Tales Story are not scholarly histories but they convey some of the flavor of the magazine and demonstrate the range of material it published.

"The Whisperer"

D501. Murray, Will. "The Many Faces of The Whisperer." Pulp 7 (Spring 75):3-18.
Detailed discussion of the pulp magazine justice figure, The Whisperer, who appeared from 1939 to 1942 in 24 novels and 25 short stories. The article places the character in the mainstream of pulp fiction, identifies main themes, continuing characters within the series, provides numerous story summaries, and reviews changes to the character as he evolved in the context of changing magazine fiction requirements. (RS)

"The Wizard"

D502. Herrick, Daryl S. "A Look at The Wizard Magazine." Echoes 1:6 (June 83):28-29.
A Street & Smith publication featuring a "maverick financier" on the lookout for shady operations in the business world. With a contents listing of the six issues (1940/41).

"Wu Fang"

See also: D312, D313.

D503. Carr, Wooda Nicholas. "The Mysterious Wu Fang." DSCR 7 (1979).
A lengthy discussion of the pulp villain, Wu Fang, his background, methods and origin in Fu Manchu. (WM)

IV. Authors

AARONS, EDWARD A.

Ref: Hubin 2, TCCMW, EMD, CC, SN, AMBI; UN 1:5 (1948):4-5 (photo; as "Edward Ronns."

See also: D334.

ABBOT, ANTHONY

Ref: Hubin 2, TCCMW, EMD, CC, ABMI; The Writer 58:12 (Dec 45):371-76.

E1. Breen, Jon L. "About the Murders of Anthony Abbot." TAD 3 (1969/70):1-5.
A study of Abbot's Thatcher Colt novels. Breen points out Abbot's debt to the S. S. Van Dine Philo Vance novels and the ways in which the series differs from the Van Dine model. With a list of the novels and short stories in the Colt canon.

E2. Nevins, Francis M, Jr. "About the Output of Anthony Abbot." TM(R)N 2:1 (Oct 68):12-15.
A survey of Abbot's mystery fiction.

ADAMS, CLEVE F.

Ref: Hubin 2, TCCMW, EMD, CC, ABMI, SN; The Writer 55:5 (May 42):141-43 (characterization).

E3. Nevins, Francis, M., Jr. "The World of Cleve F. Adams." TAD 8 (1974/755):195-201.
A study of Adam's fiction with a checklist of novels and magazine appearances, established by Nevins and William J. Clark.

ADAMS, EUSTACE L.

Ref: Hubin 2, ABMI; Argosy, 26 Oct 35; 27 Sept 30.

ADDINGTON-SYMONS, FRANCIS

E4. Rivière, François. "Notes sur trois romans d'Addington-Symons |Notes on three novels of Addington-Symons|." Europe, no. 571/2 (Nov/Dec 76), pp. 160-64.
An analysis of structural elements in Murder of Me, Smile and Murder and Stone Dead.

A. D. G. (pseud. for Alain Fournier)

Ref: SN.

Int: MM no. 279, Jan 73.

AIKEN, JOAN

Ref: Hubin2, TCCMW, CC, ABMI; The Writer 81:5 (May 68):9-12, 54 (plotting).

AINSWORTH, WILLIAM HARRISON

E5. Ellis, S(tewart) M. William Harrison Ainsworth and His Friends. London and New York, 1911; reprinted by Garland Press, 1979. 2 vols. 910pp.
Ainsworth, author of Jack Sheppard, Rookwood, and many other novels, was the most important writer of Newgate novels--early nineteenth-century sensational crime fiction. He was also a central figure in the British literary world. Editor of Bentley's Magazine, founder of Ainsworth's Magazine, he was closely associated with Dickens, Thackeray, Bulwer, the Cruickshanks, and most of the other literary and publishing personalities of the day. Ellis's rich study of the period is definitive and has not been superseded. (EFB)

AIRD, CATHERINE

Ref: Hubin 2, TCCMW, EMD, CC, ABMI, The Writer 82:8 (Aug 69):11-14 (plotting); The Writer 84:10 (Oct 71):14-16; The Writer 92:3 (March 79):14-16.

Int: TMRN 4:2 (Jan 71):29-31.

ALBERT, MARVIN H.

Ref: Hubin 2, ABMI (S), SN.

E6. Martin, Roger, compiler. "Marvin H. Albert." Hard-Boiled Dicks, no. 1 (Nov 81). 44pp. Pamphlet. Photos and illustrations.
First in a series of pamphlets on American writers of hard-boiled detective fiction. The material is in French. There is a long interview conducted by Martin (pp. 6-22), a bibliography, a filmography, and biographical and critical notes extracted from a variety of sources.

ALBRAND, MARTHA

Ref: Hubin 2, TCCMW, EMD, CC, ABMI; The Writer 58:9 (Sept 45):270-71; UN 5:2 (1952):4-5 (photo).

ALCOTT, LOUISA MAY

Ref: Hubin 2; ABMI.

E7. MacDonald, Ruth K. Louisa May Alcott. Twayne's United States author series 457. Boston, Twayne Publishers, 1883. 111pp. Index. Bibliography of primary and secondary sources.
A general introduction to Alcott's life and works; discussion of her "gothic potboilers and their relationship to her other writing," pp. 81-84.

E8. Payne, Alma J. Louisa May Alcott: A Reference Guide. Boston: G. K. Hall, 1980.
An annotated bibliography of secondary sources.

E9. Rostenberg, Leona. "Some Pseudonymous Thrillers of Louisa M. Alcott." PBSA 37:2 (1943):131-40.
A description of Rostenberg's pioneering attempt to uncover the extent of Alcott's thriller writing.

E10. Stern, Madeleine B. "Behind the Mask of Louisa May Alcott." In Books and Book People in 19th Century America, pp. 165-73. NY: Bowker, 1978.
Some preliminary remarks on the economic and psychological reasons which impelled Alcott to the "gory inkstand" to write her pseudonymous thrillers, followed by an account of Stern's introduction to the subject and a short survey of the material.

E11. ______. "Introduction." In Behind a Mask: The Unknown Thrillers of Louisa May Alcott, edited by Madeleine Stern, pp. vii-xxviii. NY: Wm. Morrow, 1975. The introduction was published prior to book publication, as follows: School Library Journal 21 (Jan 75):13-17.
A detailed essay by editor Stern on Alcott's career as a writer of Gothic thrillers. There are numerous notes and the first modern publication of these "buried" thrillers, with their critical context, is an important contribution to 19th century popular literature. Reviews: NYTBR, 1 June 75, 4-5, 30-31; TAD 9 (1975/76):149.

E12. ______. "Introduction." To Plots and Counterplots: More Unknown Thrillers of Louisa May Alcott, edited by M. Stern, pp. 7-29. NY: Wm. Morrow and Co., 1976.
This edition also includes, as an appendix (pp. 315-318), a thematic chart and checklist of Alcott's thrillers. In the introduction, Stern continues the history of these thrillers begun in Behind a Mask. Reviews: NYTBR, 26 Jly 76, p. 74; TLS, 14 May 76, p. 569.

E13. ______. Louisa May Alcott. Norman: University of Oklahoma Press, 1950; revised edition, 1971.
Considered the definitive Alcott biography, the second edition contains a comprehensive bibliography of her writings.

ALDRIDGE, HOWARD F.

Ref: Hubin 2; Lachman, TPP 1:4 (July 78):16.

ALEXANDER, DAVID

Ref: EMD, CC, SN; UN 3:10 (1951):4-6 (photo).

ALLAIN, MARCEL, and SOUVESTRE, PIERRE

Ref: Hubin 2.

E14. Alfu. L'Encyclopédie de Fantômas. Paris: Autoéditions, 1981. 330pp.
This comprehensive study of the 32 Fantômas adventures by Allain and Souvestre is presented in the form of an encyclopedia from an article on "props" to one devoted to the novel Voleur de feu. The 32 volumes are summarized and analyzed, while different aspects of the saga are the subject of articles, sometimes accompanied by graphics or by charts: the geography of Fantômas (articles on Germany, England, Paris, etc.), the principal characters (Juve, Fandor, Vladimir, Lady Beltham), the secondary characters (tramps, tough guys, etc.), publishing details, themes (money, spectacle, plot, the erotic, murder). On pp. 261-64, there is a list of the leading characters. This volume constitutes an interesting study of the series, although the fragmentation is bothersome: the encyclopedia format was probably not the most coherent one to use. (JB)

E15. Allain, Marcel. "Confessions." In Arnaud, Paralittératures (B12), pp. 79-103.
After some modest comments on his biography, Allain talks about the Fantômas series and, after his presentation, answers questions from the platform and the audience.

E16. "Fantômas." Europe, no. 590/91 (June/July 78), pp. 1-161.
This excellent issue of the magazine Europe contains numerous texts of Marcel Allain on the popular novel, on Fantômas, on Tigris, and selections from his correspondence. There is an extensive bibliography compiled by Francis Lacassin. Contents: F. Lacassin, "Fantômas ou

l'opéra de treize sous |Fantômas or the thirteen-penny opera|," pp. 3-6 (introductory tribute); Hubert Juin, "Pour éveiller nos joies un beau crime est bien fort |A fine crime is strong enough to make us joyful)," pp. 7-11 (poetic implications of the Fantômas series); Michel Carrouges, "Le Noyau noir du mythe |The dark core of the myth|," pp. 18-20 (Fantômas as a modern tragic hero); Marcel Allain, "Du Roman populaire et de ses possibilités commerciales |On the popular novel and its commercial possibilities)," pp. 21-33 (A 1938 theoretical essay on the popular novel); M. Allain, "Fantômas et les autres vus du premier rang de l'orchestre |Fantômas and the others seen from the first row of the orchestra|," pp. 34-39 (1958; physical and psychological portraits of the principal characters); M. Allain, "Fantômas voleur d'amour |Fantômas, the thief of love|," pp. 40-41, (1935; plot summary of Fantômas contre l'amour); M. Allain, "Pour une couverture attirante de 'Si c'était Tigris?' |For a striking cover for 'if it were Tigris?')," pp. 42-43 (1949; suggestions for a cover illustration); M. Allain, "Lettres à Jean Duperray |Letters to Jean Duperray|," pp. 43-44; M. Allain, "'Je suis donc un homme de gauche |I am, therefore, a leftist|," pp. 45-48 (1967; a quasi-serious political statement); Correspondence, pp. 49-55; Madeleine Cacaret-Allain, "Mon frère, Marcel Allain |My brother, Marcel Allain|," pp. 55-57; Yves Olivier-Martin, "Souvenirs sur Marcel Allain |Memories of Marcel Allain|," pp. 57-58; Jean Duperray, "Marcel Allain démasque Fantômas |Marcel Allain unmasks Fantômas|," pp. 59-63 (report on an "outing" with Allain); Louis Chavance, "La Morale de Fantômas |Fantômas' ethics|," pp. 64-7; Jean-Pierre Bouyxou, "Dégénérescence d'un mythe |Degeneration of a myth|," pp. 68-71 (faulty readings of the Fantômas myth); Roland Stragliati, "'Fantômas'? Oui, mais.... |'Fantômas'? yes, but....|," pp. 72-78 (the poetry of the myth; other writers and the myth); Maurice Dubourg, "Fantômas voyage |Fantômas travels|," pp. 79-95 (geography in the Fantômas cycle); Jean-Paul Colin, "Les verbes de la mort dans Fantômas |The verbs of death in Fantômas|," pp. 96-104 (a statistical analysis); Yves Olivier-Martin, "Héroïnes et cruauté |Heroines and cruelty|," pp. 104-107 (female roles); Geo Vadieu, "Fantomin et Lupinas," pp. 108-111 (Fantômas and Arsène Lupin); Claude Dauphine, "La société dans 'le policier apache' |Society in the 'hooligan detective novel'|," pp. 112-119 (the nature of the portrait of pre-W. W. I society); Yves Olivier-Martin, "Géographie de Fantômas: Paris," pp. 119-140 (Paris in the Fantômas novels); Francis Lacassin, "Bibliographie de Fantômas," pp. 141-61. (JB)

E17. "Fantômas, ... c'est Marcel Allain |Fantômas is Marcel Allain|." La Tour de feu, no. 88, Dec 1965.
This poetry journal edited by Pierre Bojut devoted one of its issues to the Fantômas myth. The contents include a long essay by Jean Duperray , "Le cinéma imprimé de Fantômas |The printed theater of Fantômas|," pp. 17-77, a text by Marcel Allain on "La Grande Colère de Fantômas |Fantômas' great anger|," some reproductions of splendid covers by Starce, an article by Jean Paul Colin, and a very fine text by Pierre Boujut, "Pour en finir avec Fantômas |To put an end to Fantômas|." A bibliography compiled by Jean Duperray and some poems complete the contents. This poetic approach to the Fantômas myth is decorated with a cover which cheerfully avoids the Fayard style. (JB)

E18. Peske, Antoinette, and Marty, Pierre. Les Terribles. Series: Visage No. 2. Paris: Frédéric Chambrian, 1951.
The third part (pp. 133-90) of this work is devoted to Marcel Allain and Fantômas. After a brief biography of Allain, the authors tell about the

meeting of Allain with Souvestre, and the birth of Fantômas. Then they attempt an analysis of the character: "Avec Fantômas, le diable devient cartésien |With Fantômas, the devil becomes a cartesian philosopher|." They touch on the rest of Allain's work (Fatala, Miss Teria, Drames ignorés) and especially his social work, "Les cris de la misère humaine |The cries of human misery|." Finally, in the chapter titled "Le Roi des surréalistes |The king of the surrealists|," they take note of the interest shown by numerous writers and poets (Apollinaire, Blaise Cendrars, Robert Desnos, Raymond Queneau, Jean Cocteau, and others) in Fantômas. (JB)

E19. Queneau, Raymond. "Fantômas." In his Bâtons, chiffres et lettres, pp. 259-60. Gallimard: Collection Idées, 1965 (original publication, 1950).
A statistical chart showing the kinds and number of crimes committed by Fantômas. Queneau confesses that he had, at one time, intended to write a biography of this fictional character.

E20. Tortel, Jean. "Fantômas et le phénomène de la destruction |Fantômas and the phenomenon of destruction|." Critique, Oct 63.
Review of the publication of the Laffont (1960-63) seven volume edition of the series and an analytic study.

E21. Torteau, Jean-Jacques. "Fantômas, le roman feuilleton du pauvre |The poor person's serial novel|." In Tourteau (B408), pp. 97-103.
A survey of the series. See also pp. 276-79 for an analysis of the novel Fantômas (1911).

ALLARDYCE, PAULA. See BLACKSTOCK, CHARITY

ALLBEURY TED

Ref: Hubin 2, TCCMW, ABMI.

ALLEN, GRANT

Ref: Hubin 2, CC, ABMI.

E22. Donaldson, Norman. "Introduction." In An African Millionaire, pp. v-xiv. NY: Dover, 1980.
Frederic Dannay has described Colonel Clay as the "first great thief of short mystery fiction." After a biocritical survey of Allen's career, Donaldson describes the publishing history of the Dover collection and the character of the thief protagonist, Colonel Clay.

E23. Dueren, Fred. "Rogues for the New Century." TMF 5:3 (May/June 81):11-14.
A comparison of Allen's An African Millionaire (1897) with George Randolph Chester's Get-Rich-Quick Wallingford (1908). Dueren points out similarities and differences between these two novels with "a common interest in swindlers and businessmen."

E24. Schantz, Tom and Enid. "Editor's Note." In The Reluctant Hangman and Other Stories of Crime, by Grant Allen, pp. vii-viii. Boulder, CO: the Aspen Press, 1973.
Informative introduction to a reprint of three Grant Allen crime stories.

ALLINGHAM, MARGERY

Ref: Hubin, TCCMW, EMD, CC, ABMI.

See also: B6, B20, B241, B301, B349, E2535.

E25. Allingham, Margery. "Party of One." Holiday 34 (Sept 63):11-15.
Allingham talks about her coming-of-age as a writer and about the contemporary English climate for fiction and the evolution of detective fiction during her lifetime. An attractive, apparently honest, lightly serious self-examination.

E26. Barzun, Jacques and Wendell Hertig Taylor. Preface to Dancers in Mourning, by Margery Allingham (New York, 1937). In A Book of Prefaces (B17), pp. 15-16.

E27. Cox, J. Randolph. "Miss Allingham's Knight: The Saga of Albert Campion." TAD 15 (1982):86-91. Illus.
A survey of the Campion saga: characters and characterization, and the distinctive qualities of the series.

E28. Huey, Talbott W. "Mr. Campion and the Survival of the Great Detective." Clues 3:1 (Spring/Summer 82):90-104.
Campion's ability to adapt to changing social conditions, as the novels reflect Allingham's portrait of the society of her time.

E29. Keddie, James. Letter, TAD 1 (1967/68):65.
In his letter, Keddie quotes comments to him (in a letter) from Joyce Allingham (Margery's sister) on the publishing history of The White Cottage Mystery and on Margery Allingham's dislike of the novel.

E30. Lachman, Marvin. "The Detective Who Would Be King." TPP 5:2 (1982): 17-20.
An analysis of "clues" in Allingham's Campion saga to the model for Albert Campion, King Edward VIII. Lachman believes that Allingham had misgivings about basing the character so recognizably on Edward and also drew on Lord Mountbatten for some aspects of the character.

E32. Pike, B. A. "Margery Allingham's Albert Campion: A Chronological Examination of the Novels in Which He Appears." A lengthy survey of the novels of the Campion saga, appearing in TAD, as follows: 9 (1975/76):1-6, 95-101; 10 (1977):25-29, 84-87, 117-25, 244-48, 324-55; 11 (1978):34-44, 177-85, 274-84, 372-78; 12 (1979):34-39, 168-73, 348-50.

E33. Queen, Ellery. "Introduction." In The Case Book of Mr. Campion, by Margery Allingham, pp. 3-4. Mercury Book No. 112. NY: The American Mercury, 1947.

ALLISON, HUGHES

Ref: Hubin 2, ABMI; Lachman, TPP 1:4 (July 78):16; with addendum in TPP 4:1 (Feb 81):18.

ALMANZI, VENTURA

E34. Raffaelli, Raffaella. "La donna che 'smette di essere angelica può solo diventare perversa |The woman who stops being angelic may only become perverse|." Orient Express 3 (1982), pp. 17-18.
Phenomenology of the female characters in the detective novels of Ventura Almanzi, which illustrates how much the writer remains "linked to the end to the culture, the taste and the social models" of pre-20th century Italy. (RC)

E35. ______. "Il giallo di Ventura Almanzi: Un caso particolare |The giallo of Ventura Almanzi: a particular case|." Orient Express 2 (1982), pp. 67-68. Brief note on the series of Le avventure del poliziotto americano Ben Wilson published in Milan between 1914 and 1920. While she underlines, among the novel elements of the gialli of Almanzi, the themes and the violence of the American novel of action, Raffaelli notes also how such ingredients lose "their excessive, often brutal character, to be freshly composed in a more moderate form suitable to the tastes of an Italian public." (RC)

ALMQUIST, C. J. L.

E36. Borowitz, Albert I. "Innocence and Arsenic: The Literary and Criminal Careers of C. J. L. Almquist." TAD 9 (1975/76):17-22.
Swedish novelist Almquist (1793-1866) as a theorist of crime in his novels and as a real-life practitioner.

AMBLER, ERIC

Ref: Hubin 2, TCCMW, EMD, CC, AMBI.

See also: B99, B303, C541.

Interviews: PW, 9 Sept 74, pp. 6-7; Sunday Times Magazine (London), 5 Jan 75, pp. 30-32; JPC 9:2 (Fall 75):285-93; EQMM, May 77, pp. 76-77; Jury 6:2 (1977): 74-80; NYTBR, 13 Sept 81, pp. 3, 22, 24; Mystère Magazine 1 (Dec 81), pp. 4-5 (photo).

E37. Ambler, Eric. A Coffin for Demetrios. The Mystery Library (B270), no. 6. 1977. v-xii, 289pp.
Contents: John Ball, "Editor's Note: Concerning Two Authors," pp. v-vi (Ambler and Elleston Trevor/Adam Hall); Elleston Trevor, "Introduction," pp. vii-xii; A Coffin for Demetrios, pp. 1-264; James Sandoe, "The Workings of Eric Ambler: A Checklist," pp. 266-70 (an annotated bibliography with some information on his writing for films, a filmography, and selected secondary material); "MWA Tribute to Eric Ambler," p. 271; "Dust Jackets (photos)," pp. 272-73; Ronald Ambrosetti, "The World of Eric Ambler: From Detective to Spy," pp. 274-79 (E38); "Film Photos," pp. 280-1; Gavin Lambert, "The Thin Protection: Part 2--Eric Ambler," pp. 282-89 (E47).

E38. Ambrosetti, Ronald. "The World of Eric Ambler: From Detective to Spy." In Landrum (B216), pp. 102-109; excerpt printed in Ambler (E37), pp. 282-89.
Ambrosetti sees Ambler's contribution to the spy novel in his linking of the detective story with the novel of espionnage.

E39. Blumenberg, Hans C. "Ein britischer Romancier |A British novelist|." In Diogenes (E42), pp. 70-75. First published as "Der Palastinenser im Haus. Eric Amblers roman Der Levantiner." Die Zeit (Hamburg), 26 Oct 73.
Essay-length review of Ambler's The Levanter. Blumenberg speculates on the reasons Hitchcock has not filmed any of Ambler's books and calls Ambler one of the greatest romantic novelists of the 20th century. (GG)

E40. Busche, Jurgen. "Anatomie einer modernen Form des spannenden Romans |Anatomy of a modern form of the spy novel|." Frankfurter Allgemeinen Zeitung, 23 July 75; reprinted in Diogenes (E42), pp. 86-94.
Academic-style article arguing for the conclusion that because of the realism, tone, narrative style and sheer readability of Ambler's novels,

they can be considered as literature. This is one of the more serious and involved treatments of Ambler's work. (GG)

E41. Davis, Paxton. "The Worlds We Live in: The Novels of Eric Ambler." The Hollins Critic (Virginia) 8:1 (Feb 71): 1-11; reprinted, in a German translation, in Diogenes (E42), pp. 45-49.
Davis argues that Ambler has done for the spy novel what Chandler said Hammett did for the murder mystery--gave it back to the people who in real life "do it." Similar to many other American academic style analyses. (GG)

E42. Diogenes Verlag. Uber Eric Ambler. Diogenes Verlag 187. Zurich: Diogenes Verlag AG, 1979. 192pp.
Well-edited German collection of essays on the work of Eric Ambler. Contains a German translation of the Ambler short story, "The Blood Bargain" (1972), as well as the following essays: Alfred Hitchcock, "Empfiehlt Eric Ambler," pp. 39-40 (E45); Gabriel Veraldi, "Vom Nutzen und Nachteil der Literatur," pp. 41-44 (E50); Paxton Davis, "Die Welt in der wir leben oder die Romane Eric Amblers," pp. 45-49 (E41); Francis Lacassin, "Eric Ambler und der nouveau roman," pp. 50-69 (E46); Helmut Heissenbuttel, "Eric Ambler," pp. 76-85 (E44); Jurgen Busche, "Anatomie einer modernen Form des spannenen Romans," pp. 86-94 (E40); and Aurel Schmidt, "Wie es zugeht auf der Welt," pp. 99-113 (E48). In addition, this volume contains an Eric Ambler interview, an essay by Ambler entitled "Der Romanautor und die Filmleute |The novelist and the film-makers|," a short Ambler biography, and bibliographies of primary and secondary sources. Generously illustrated with photos which are accompanied by personal remarks which Ambler prepared especially for this volume. Of the essays and commentary, what was not written originally in German has been translated into German. Several of the critical essays first appeared in German periodicals or in forwards to French translations of Ambler's books, and the distinctly European critical slant is intriguing and edifying for English-speaking readers. Undoubtedly an important collection (GG)

E44. Heissenbuttel, Helmut. "Eric Ambler." Die Weltwoche (Zurich), 2 Apr 75; and in Das Tintenfass (Zurich) 11:25 (1975). Reprinted in Diogenes (E42), pp. 76-85.
Academic analysis of Ambler primarily as political critic and diagnostician. Heissenbuttel praises Ambler's political acuity as seen in the pre-WW II books and distinguishes his realism from the distinct political prejudices he sees in the spy novels of Fleming, Oppenheim, Buchan and Donald Hamilton. Interesting European social-political critical approach. (GG)

E45. Hitchcock, Alfred. "Empfiehlt Eric Ambler |Recommending Eric Ambler|." First published in Hitchcock's foreword to the Ambler omnibus Intrigue (Knopf, 1943); reprinted in Diogenes (E42), pp. 39-40.
Hitchcock praises Ambler's realistic plots and heroes whom Hitchcock calls "normal, nice people." (GG)

E46. Lacassin, Francis. "Eric Ambler ou la forêt hantée par les mensonges |Eric Ambler or the forest haunted by lies|." Foreword to French edition of A Kind of Anger (Paris: Plon, 1973). Fr. title: Le Rendez-vous de Nice. Reprinted in Diogenes (E42), pp. 50-69.
Argues cleverly that Orson Welles' film work was influenced by Ambler's books. Lacassin claims to be the first to see that Ambler's books are

similar to those of the French new novel (but see Gabriel Veraldi, E50) and argues that most of what new novelist Alain Robbe-Grillet became known for had been anticipated some 15-20 years previously by Ambler. Interesting and well argued. (GG)

E47. Lambert, Gavin. "The Thin Protection: 2. Eric Ambler." In his Dangerous Edge (B215), pp. 104-31; reprinted in Ambler (E37), pp. 282-89.
A skillful blend of biographical and critical information that provides an overview of Ambler's life and work.

E48. Schmidt, Aurel. "Wie es zugeht auf der Welt |How it is in the world|." In Diogenes (E42), pp. 95-113.
Leisurely tour through the world of Ambler's writings. Schmidt examines the style of Ambler's books, as well as their plots, characters, political settings and realism. Ambler the man and his cynicism, skepticism and moral outlook are discussed. Schmidt seems to have had the opportunity to speak with Ambler about his work and there are several quotations from Ambler. This article is a bit too desultory but it does give a well fleshed-out view of the man and his work. (GG)

E49. Symons, Julian. "Confidential Agents." TLS (1966); reprinted in Critical Occasions (B390), pp. 168-73.
Ostensibly a review of Ambler's The Night-Comers, this essay gives at least as much commentary on other Ambler books, such as The Mask of Demetrios and Journey into Fear. Symons calls The Night-Comers Ambler's best post-war book and says that it might be a step in the direction of the "straight" novel. (GG)

E50. Veraldi, Gabriel. "Vom Nutzen und Nachteil der Literatur |On the use and disadvantage of literature|." German-translated excerpt from Veraldi's foreward to the French edition of The Mask of Demetrios (Paris, 1965) in Diogenes (E42), pp. 41-44.
Veraldi argues that under a new definition of literature--one in which literature is used for personal development and the formation of world-views--Ambler's work qualifies as literature. Veraldi also hints that Ambler's success is partly due to his books falling into the category of nouveau roman. This is a relatively early serious look at a modern espionnage author. (GG)

AMILA, JEAN

Ref: SN.

Int: MM 300, Feb 73.

AMIS, KINGSLEY

Ref: Hubin 2, TCCMW, ABMI.

E51. Salwak, Dale. Kingsley Amis: A Reference Guide. Boston: G. K. Hall, 1978.
An annotated listing of secondary material on Amis, with reviews of his fiction including his thrillers and detective fiction.

ANDERSON, FREDERICK IRVING

Ref: Hubin 2, TCCMW, EMD, CC, ABMI.

See also: B142, B143.

E52. Bleiler, Everett F. "Anderson, Frederick Irving." In Reilly (A143), pp. 35-36.
Anderson's career and publications are outlined. A partial list of uncollected stories appears. The Notorious Sophie Lang (1925) is erroneously listed as a novel instead of a group of stories collected from magazines. Anderson is bracketed with Robert Louis Stevenson for imparting a "fairy tale quality" to detective fiction. Bleiler remarks that Anderson continues to be undervalued. (BFF)

E53. Honce, Charles. Mark Twain's Associated Press Speech and other News Stories on Murder, Modes, Mysteries, and Makers of Books. NY: privately printed, 1940. See esp. pp. 50-57.
Honce admired and met Anderson. Praise for superb literary style and a checklist of book-length publications are included. Anderson is not better known because he wrote only short stories and many remain uncollected. (BFF)

E54. Fisher, Ben. "The Book of Murder by Frederick Irving Anderson." TPP 2:2 (March/Apr 79):25-26.
Anderson's creativeness in circumstances of characterization and sense of place are evident in these stories--originally pieces in the Saturday Evening Post. Derivation from Poe in the opening story, "Beyond All Conjecture," is clear. (BFF)

E55. _____. "Frederick Irving Anderson. The Notorious Sophie Lang." TPP 4:3 (June 81):20-21.
The genesis of Anderson's book, in the form of stories first published in McClure's and The Saturday Evening Post, is outlined. Sophie and Deputy Parr respectively evince intuition and logic--which trait defeats Parr at every turn. Sophie derives from Gothic tradition, and she is altogether a heroine who would align with those of Hawthorne, Faulkner, and O'Neill. Anderson's richly textured language, his ironies, and his handling of the appearance-vs.-reality theme are complimented. (BFF)

E56. _____. "Fugitive Poe References: A Bibliography." Poe Studies 12 (1979):31.
The link between Poe's "Murders" and Anderson's "Beyond All Conjecture" is noticed. (BF)

ANDERSON, JAMES

Ref: Hubin 2, TCCMW.

ANONYMOUS

Ref: TCCMW (Richmond, p. 1531).

E57. Bleiler, E. F. "Female Detectives, Ghost Books and the Relative Importance of It All." TAD 8 (1974/75):202.
A bibliographical description of Experiences of a Lady Detective establishing it as a later publication of Revelations of a Lady Detective (1864).

E58. _____. "Introduction." In Richmond: Scenes in the Life of a Bow Street Runner, pp. v-xviii. NY: Dover, 1976.
An accurate, modern statement about Bow Street, based on research in parliamentary reports and records and a survey of fiction dealing with Bow Street. Bleiler also makes the first serious attempt to identify the

author, rejecting traditional ascription.

ANTHONY, EVELYN

Ref: Hubin 2, TCCMW, ABMI.

ANTONY, PETER

Ref: Hubin 2, TCCMW, EMD, CC, ABMI.

APPLE, A. E.

Ref: Hubin 2.

See also: D411.

E59. Hubbard, D. C. "Popular Detective Story Writers: A. E. Apple." Detective Story Magazine 101:2 (12 May 28):122-23.
Discussion of Apple and his work for DSM, with scanty biographical material. Portrait. Series characters: Mr. Chang (D411), Rafferty. (RS)

ARD, WILLIAM

Ref: Hubin 2, CC, SN, ABMI.

E60. Nevins, Francis M., Jr. "Other Names, Same World: The Pseudonymous Crime Novels of William Ard." TAD 16 (1983):386-90.
In this sequel to his 1982 TAD article, Nevins proves to his satisfaction that the nine pseudonymous novels are consistent with the portrait he drew from the 16 books published under Ard's own name.

E61. ______. "The World of William Ard." TAD 15 (1982):158-66.
A survey of the life and works of an American writer of private-eye novels.

ARDEN, WILLIAM. See COLLINS, MICHAEL

ARDIES, TOM

Ref: Hubin 2, TCCMW, ABMI.

ARLEY, CATHERINE

Int: MM 296, Oct 72.

ARMSTRONG, ANTHONY

Ref: Hubin 2, TCCMW, CC, ABMI.

ARMSTRONG, CHARLOTTE

Ref: Hubin 2, TCCMW, EMD, CC, ABMI; The Writer 61 (Jan 55):3-5 (Characterization); The Writer 80:10 (Oct 67):17-19 (plotting).

ARNAUD, G.-J.

Ref: Hubin 2, ABMI.

E62. Deloux, Jean-Pierre. "La Maison-Dieu |God's house|." Polar 26 (Winter 83):5-18.
A survey of Arnaud's work to show both its eclectic nature and its evolution. His mystery novels are detailed studies of contemporary France.

E63. "Dossier G.-J. Arnaud." Polar 26 (Winter 83):5-58. Illustrated.
Contents: Jean-Pierre Deloux, "La Maison-Dieu," pp. 5-18 (E62);

François Guérif, "Entretien avec Georges-J. Arnaud," pp. 21-24 (interview); G.-J. Arnaud, "Puzzle," pp. 25-34 (short story); Jean-Pierre Deloux, "La statue du Commandeur |The statue of the Commander|," pp. 35-42 (on Arnaud's spy novels); Alfu, in collaboration with Pierre Turpin, "Bibliographie de Georges-J. Arnaud," pp. 43-54; J.-J. Schleret and G.-J. Arnaud, "Filmographie de G.-J. Arnaud," pp. 55-58.

ARTHUR, FRANK

Ref: Hubin 2, TCCMW, CC, ABMI.

E64. Barzun, Jacques and Wendell Hertig Taylor. "Introduction." In Another Mystery in Suva (London, 1956), by Frank Arthur. "Crime Fiction 1950-1975" (B18).

ASIMOV, ISAAC

Ref: Hubin 2, TCCMW, CC, ABMI (S); UN 2:5 (1950):10-11, 16 (photo).

See also: B189.

Int: EQMM, May 76, pp. 101-102; B366.

E65. Asimov, Isaac. In Memory Yet Green: The Autobiography of Isaac Asimov, 1920-54. NY: Doubleday, 1979. In Joy Still Felt: The Autobiography of Isaac Asimov, 1944-1978. NY: Doubleday, 1980. 732pp., Illus., Index; 828pp., Illus., Index.

Although known primarily as a writer of science fiction, Asimov has published about forty stories about the Black Widowers, two cross-over novels (The Caves of Steel and The Naked Sun), and two straight mysteries, Whiff of Death and Death at the ABA. He and Edward D. Hoch are, almost by themselves, keeping alive the detective story in which the author presents clues and plays fair with the reader and, thus, his autobiography is of interest to the mystery genre. There are some interesting sidelights regarding mystery writers Ben Benson and Cornell Woolrich, as well as details on the purchase of AHMM. A fascinating and relevant autobiography. (Marvin Lachman)

E66. Miller, Marjorie M. Isaac Asimov: A Checklist of Works Published in the United States, March 1939--May 1972. The Serif Series: Bibliographies and Checklists, No. 25 Kent, OH: the Kent State University Press, 1972. xii, 98pp. Index. .

All of Asimov's books, articles, stories, and verse through mid-1972 are listed chronologically by publication date, with reprint appearances noted. There is also a "Selected Criticism and Works about Asimov," listing 28 items, and an index of titles. No annotations. (REB)

E67. Patrouch, Joseph F., Jr. The Science Fiction of Isaac Asimov. Garden City, NY: Doubleday, 1974. xxvii, 283pp. Bibliography. Index.

This is an exercise in what the author calls "practical criticism": an analysis of Isaac Asimov's literary craftsmanship "aimed at a popular rather than an academic audience." The emphasis is on story construction and narrative techniques; critical evaluation is subordinate. Asimov's science-fictional mysteries are discussed in Chapter Six (pp. 151-180) for the novels and a portion of Chapter Eight (pp. 221-233) for the short story collection Asimov's Mysteries. The bibliography lists books and stories (by Asimov and other sf writers) mentioned in the text, plus a selection of secondary materials. (REB)

ATKINSON, ALEX

Ref: Hubin 2, CC.

E68. Barzun, Jacques and Wendell Hertig Taylor. "Introduction." In Exit Charlie (NY, 1956), by Alex Atkinson. "Crime Fiction 1950-1975" (B18).

ATLEE, PHILIP

Ref: Hubin 2, TCCMW; UN 4:5 (1951):6-7, 14 (photo).

E69. Kelley, George, and Banks, R. Jeff. "The Joe Gall Series." TMF 3:2 (March/April 79):26-35.
Introductory remarks by George Kelley on the spy series with a chart by Banks highlighting such elements as setting, characterization and plot.

ATODA, TAKASHI

E70. Atoda, Takashi. Kyofu Collection |Horror collection|. Tokyo: Shincho-sha, 1982. 222pp. Bibliography.
The author is popular for his short stories in the manner of Roald Dahl. In this book, he tells of his experiences, introduces several works--Japanese and non-Japanese, in addition to his own stories--, and comments on the horrors lurking in everyday life. His first collection of essays, Nomiso Tsushin |Brain newsletter, 1981| has very few mystery references. (HS/TT)

AUDEMARS, PIERRE

Ref: Hubin 2, TCCMW, CC, ABMI.

AUSTWICK, JOHN

Ref: Hubin 2, TCCMW, ABMI.

AVALLONE, MICHAEL

Ref: Hubin 2, TCCMW, EMD, SN, ABMI; Writer's Digest 43:1 (Jan 63):24-25, 26; The Writer 82:2 (Feb 69):21-22, 30.

Int: PQ 3:1 (Spring 80):10-18 (photo; illustrations); Writers Digest 56:10 (Oct 76):38-39 (photos)

See also: C127.

E71. Adrian, Kelly. "Mike Avallone: One of the Un-Angry Young Men." TMRN 1:5 (June 68):3-5.
A biographical sketch that includes interview material. With a checklist of his work.

E72. Avallone, Michael. "For Mystery Critics Only: Hard-Boiled Detective Division." Xenophile 21 (Feb 76), p. 10.
Some personal comments on other mystery writers followed by an apparently autobiographical note (as by "Ed Noon") on the "D'Artagnan of the Typewriter: Michael Avallone."

E73. _____. "The Greatest Mystery Ever Told." TMF 1:1 (Jan 77):3-5.
On the compilation of the collection ostensibly edited by Boris Karloff, Tales of the Frightened (Belmont, 1963).

E74. _____. "How I Sold a series of Paperback Mystery Novels." Writers Digest 51 (Jan 71):24-25, 54.

On the writing and marketing of the Ed Noon series. Included is the original four-page prospectus sent to New American Library.

E75. ______. "Kiss My Deadly Typewriter No. 539." TQCB 2:2 (July 70):9-12.
A polemical indictment of the acumen and perspicacity of unnamed "Scholars and Young Critics" in the mystery fiction field which challenges the presumed standing of various genre authors and works. In TQCB 3:1 (April 71):14-17, appeared letters of reaction, some unfavorable and some mixed, from Marvin Lachman, Francis M. Nevins, Jr., Charles MacDonald, Stanley A. Carlin, Jon L. Breen, and Joe Gores, along with a brief rejoinder thereto by Avallone. (JN)

E76. ______. "Kiss My Deadly Typewriter No. 7654." TMF 1:2 (March 77): 11-14.
On the writer and his friends and former friends. The former friends are discreetly replaced by dashes.

E77. ______. "This Little Paperback Went to Market or Kiss My Deadly Typewriter." TMRN 3:2 (Dec 69):27-28.
Avallone rails against unprincipled publishers.

E78. Cook, Michael. "Michael Avallone-Writer Extraordinaire." _Age of the Unicorn_ no. 8 (June 80), pp. 75-103. Illus.
Newspaper reports, letters, tributes, and a bibliography.

E79. Johnson, Tom. "Fading Shadows: Avallone." _Megavore_ 9 (June 80), pp. 21-24. Illus.
A list of Avallone's contributions to the _Mike Shayne Mystery Magazine_ and brief comments on his work.

E80. Mertz, Stephen. "Rapping with Mike. A Michael Avallone Appreciation, Interview and Checklist." TNSPE 8 (1980), pp. 2-9.

E81. ______. "Michael Avallone: A Checklist." TAD 9 (1975/76): 132-34. See also letter (Avallone), TAD 9:239, for corrections.
A checklist of fiction by Avallone writing under his own name and pseudonyms.

E82. "Michael Avallone." _Amis du crime_ 8 (Feb 81). 39pp. Wraps.
A bibliography of American and French editions of Avallone's books, a listing of his short stories and critical material which includes an interview first published in _The Not So Private Eye_ (E80), Francis M. Nevins' "Ed Noon et le ciel t'aidera" (originally published as "Murder at Noon," E84), and an article by Avallone from _Writer's Yearbook 1977_. Jean-Pierre Deloux, in "Flash sur Michael Avallone," discusses his career.

E83. Nevins, Francis M., Jr. "The Crime Column." _Views & Reviews_ 4:2 (Winter 72):77-79.
On the Avallone Ed Noon series. A general survey and comments on several specific novels.

E84. ______. "Murder at Noon." _The New Republic_, 22 July 78, pp. 26-28; reprinted in _Amis du crime_ 8 (E84), in French.
A sympathetic view of Avallone's work with particular emphasis on the film references in his fiction. Nevins quotes some characteristic examples of Avallone's style from his "Nooniverse."

AVELINE, CLAUDE

Ref: Hubin 2, ABMI.

Int: MM 275, Jan 71.

E85. Endrèbe, Maurice Bernard. "Postface à L'abonné de la ligne U." Enigmatika 19 (June 81), pp. 37-41.
Afterword written by Endrèbe for a 1947 reprinting of Aveline's first detective novel. Endrèbe describes the reception of the novel at the time of its publication and characterizes Aveline as a writer who, although Russian by heritage, has done much for the French detective novel. The essay includes material from an interview with Aveline.

E86. Tourteau, Jean-Jacques. "La Double Mort de Frederic Belot (1932)." In Tourteau (B408), pp. 280-83.
An analysis of Aveline's novel.

BACKUS, J(EAN) L(OUISE)

Ref: Hubin 2, ABMI (S); The Writer 90:3 (March 77):11-14 (on suspense fiction).

BACON, PEGGY

Ref: Hubin, ABMI.

E87. Boucher, Anthony. "Introduction." In Lady Marked for Murder (orig. title: The Inward Eye, Scribner, 1952), by Peggy Bacon. NY: A Mercury Mystery, 1953.

BAGBY, GEORGE. See STEIN, AARON MARK

BAGLEY, DESMOND

Ref: Hubin 2, TCCMW, ABMI; The Writer 92:10 (Oct 79):18-21 (on settings).

Int: TAD 7 (1973/74):258-60; DAST 11:4 (1978):30-33; DAST 12:2 (1979): 14-16; TMF 7:2 (March/Apr 83):13-18, 26.

E88. Bagley, Desmond. "Notes on Running Blind." DAST 13:1 (1980): 38-39. (MS)

BAILEY, H. C.

Ref: Hubin 2, TCCMW, EMD, CC, ABMI.

See also: B253, E349.

E89. Barzun, Jacques and Wendell Hertig Taylor. Preface to Mr. Fortune: Eight of His Adventures, by H. C. Bailey (London, various dates). In A Book of Prefaces (B17), pp. 17-18.

E91. Poster, Constance Hammett. "H. C. Bailey: The Case of the Culinary Dr. Jekyll and Mr. Hyde." Clues 4:1 (Spring/Summer 83):67-78.
On Reggie Fortune and Joshua Clunk, hero and anti-hero counterpart, and food as social and psychological codes in Bailey's detective fiction. With a bibliography of Bailey's work and relevant references on food, cooking and eating.

E92. Purcell, Mark. "The Reggie Fortune Short Stories: An Appreciation and Partial Bibliography." TMRN 5:4 (circa 1972):1-3.
Some very brief comments on the stories followed by a bibliography of the collections with contents for each volume listed. Purcell credits

Francis M. Nevins, Jr. for contributing to the bibliography.

E93. Sarjeant, William Antony S. "In Defense of Mr. Fortune." TAD 14 (1981):302-12. Illus.
Sarjeant regrets the contemporary neglect of Bailey's fiction and, after quoting some adverse criticisms, he presents a detailed portrait of Mr. Fortune to support his contention that the stories are still entertaining and not deserving of their present neglect.

E94. Waugh, Thomas D. "The Parables of H. C. Bailey." TAD 6 (1972/73):75-77.
A brief assessment of Bailey's short stories followed by a bibliography of collections with contents listed.

BAKER, RICHARD M.

Ref: Hubin 2, CC.

E95. Van Dine, S. S. "Introduction." in Death Stops the Manuscript: Franklin Russell's First Case." NY: Scribner's, 1936. Not seen.

BAKER, SAMM SINCLAIR

Ref: Hubin 2, ABMI; Lachman, TPP 4:1 (Feb 81):17-18.

BALL, JOHN

Ref: Hubin 2, TCCMW, EMD, CC, ABMI; The Writer 94:8 (Aug 81):12-14 (on flashbacks).

Int: TMRN 5:5 (1971/72):9-14; EQMM, Feb 76, pp. 119-20; Mystery 1:3 (1980):31-34.

See also: B309.

E96. Lachman, Marvin. "Virgil Tibbs and the American Negro in Mystery Fiction." TAD 1 (1967/68):86-89.
An overview of blacks in detective fiction with extended comments on Ball's Virgil Tibbs.

BALLARD, K. G. See ROTH, HOLLY

BALLARD, W. T.

Ref: Hubin 2, TCCMW, ABMI, SN.

E97. Mertz, Stephen. "W. T. Ballard: An Interview." TAD 12 (1979):14-20.
A substantial interview in which Ballard talks about the pulp years and the writers he knew, and about his more recent career as a writer of pb originals. With a checklist of his crime and detective fiction.

BALLINGER, BILL S.

Ref: Hubin 2, TCCMW, EMD, ABMI, SN.

E99. Erhardt, Pat. "Bill Ballinger: His Work, His Women and His World." TMRN 4:6 (Sept/Oct 71):3-10. Photo. With a checklist of his publications.
Erhardt discusses his life and writings and includes comments made by Ballinger in a recent interview with her.

BALMER, EDWIN

Ref: Hubin 2, TCCMW, EMD, ABMI.

BALZAC, HONORE DE

Ref: Hubin 2, EMD, CC, ABMI.

E100. Weinstein, Arnold. "Solvable Mysteries: Balzac and Dickens." In *Vision and Response in Modern Fiction*, pp. 25-29. Ithaca, NY: Cornell University Press, 1974.
Not concerned so much with the mysteries of detective fiction as with the world as an enigmatic text to be read.

BANKIER, WILLIAM

Int: EQMM, 7 Oct 81, pp. 92-93; 4 Nov 81, pp. 99-100.

BARBETTE, JAY. See SPICER, BART

BARDIN, JOHN FRANKLIN

Ref: Hubin 2, TCCMW.

E101. Marcus, Greil. "The Mechanics of Fear." *The New Yorker*, 30 Aug 76, pp. 88-89. A review of the Bardin *Omnibus* (Penguin, 1976).
Marcus sees paranoia as the subject of Bardin's fiction and as related to *film noir* where horror invades the "order of everyday life."

E102. Symons, Julian. "Introduction." In *The John Franklin Bardin Omnibus*, pp. 7-11. Harmondsworth (England) and Baltimore: Penguin Books, 1976.
Biographical detail on a writer whose works, Symons believes, clearly draw on his autobiography.

BARNES, DALLAS

Ref: Hubin 2.

E103. Bishop, Paul. "The Enigma of the Policeman/Writer. A Look at the Police 'Insider Novels'." *Mystery* 2:1 (Jan 81):34-40.
Novels written by policemen; includes an interview with Barnes.

BARRY, JEROME

Ref: Hubin 2, ABMI; *Writer's Digest* 45:7 (July 65):34-37 (plotting, etc.).

BARTON, BILLY

E104. Barton, Billy. "Interview with Myself." TMF 5:4 (Jly/Aug 81):113-17.
Barton, in dual role of interviewer and interviewee, discusses his recently published mystery novel *Past Murder Imperfect* (Bilbar Books), mystery fiction and writers and his work-in-progress.

BARTON, GEORGE

Ref: Hubin 2, ABMI; *The Writer* 32:4 (April 1920):50-51 (on plotting his *Mystery of the Red Flame*).

BAR-ZOHAR, MICHAEL

Int: DAST 11:3 (1978):30-2.

E105. Blom, K. Arne. "Interationellt känd thriller-författare kommer pa besök till Sverige |Internationally known thriller author visits Sweden|." DAST 12:4 (1979):54-56.
Bar-Zohar's visit and works. (MS)

BASTIANI, ANGE

Ref: SN.

E106. Bastiani, Ange. Le Bréviaire du crime |The crime breviary|. Paris: Editions Raoul Solar, 1968. 346pp.
Ange Bastiani, one of the most interesting French writers of the period 1950-70, engages in a butterfly-like Quinceyian examination of the detective novel. (JB)

BAWDEN, NINA

Ref: Hubin 2, TCCMW, CC, ABMI.

BAXT, GEORGE

Ref: Hubin 2, TCCMW, ABMI, SN.

Int: EQMM, 27 Jan 82, 82-83; 24 Feb 82, pp. 92-94.

BEDFORD-JONES, H.

Ref: Hubin 2, ABMI; Argosy, 16 Nov 29; 18 Feb 33 (as Gordon MacCreagh).

E107. Clark, William J. "H. Bedford-Jones in Bluebook." Xenophile 22 (March/Apr 76), pp. 42-45.
A list of publications by year and issue with name of principal character and page count for each story.

BEEDING, FRANCIS

Ref: Hubin 2, TCCMW, EMD, CC, ABMI.

E108. Panek, LeRoy. "Francis Beeding." In The Special Branch (B303), pp. 84-94.
Beeding's spy novels represent the "best of conventional spy writing between the wars."

BEHN, NOEL

Ref: Hubin 2, TCCMW.

BELL, JOSEPHINE

Ref: Hubin 2, TCCMW, EMD, CC.

BELLAIRS, GEORGE

Ref: Hubin 2, TCCMW, EMD, CC, ABMI.

BELLEM, ROBERT LESLIE

Ref: Hubin 2, TCCMW; Writer's Digest 24:8 (July 44):17-19 (dialogue and style; excerpted in Clues 2:2 (Fall/Winter 81):50-51).

See also: D36, D359.

E109. Mertz, Stephen. "Robert Leslie Bellem: The Great Unknown." Xenophile 21 (Feb 76):49-51.
A profile of Bellem's life and work.

E110. ______. "The Further Adventures of Robert Leslie Bellem or the Bellem-Adams Connection." Xenophile 38 (Mar/April 78), p. 13. Photo.
Detective work in the Bellem file in the UCLA library which established the titles and authorship of three missing Bellem items.

E111. Pronzini, Bill. "Ante-Bellem Days; or, 'My Roscoe Sneezed Ka-chee!'" Clues 2:2 (Fall/Winter 81):41-48.
A survey of the outrageous shenanigans of Bellem's Hollywood private-eye, Dan Turner. With a partial checklist of stories in which Turner appeared.

BENET, JAMES

Ref: Hubin 2, ABMI; UN 2:9 (1950):12-13 (photo).

BENNETT, ARNOLD

Ref: Hubin 2, EMD, CC, ABMI.

E112. Ravenscroft, N. C. "Arnold Bennett--as a Writer of Crime Fiction." TAD 10 (1977):182. Photo.
A description of Bennett's juvenile crime-fiction novel, Sydney Yorke's Friend (1893).

BENNETT, JAY

Ref: Hubin 2, SN.

E113. Janeczko, Paul B. "An Interview with Jay Bennett." English Journal, May 76, pp. 86-88; an expanded version was published in TAD 10 (1977):342-46. Photo.

BENNETT, MARGOT

Ref: Hubin 2, TCCMW, CC, ABMI.

E114. Amelin, Michel. "Margot Bennett." Enigmatika 24 (July 83):10.
Biocritical essay with a bibliography.

BENSEN, D. R.

Ref: Hubin 2, ABMI; The Writer 85:2 (Feb 72):22-23.

See also: B117.

BENSON, BEN

Ref: Hubin 2, TCCMW, EMD, CC; UN 3:6 (1951):6-7; UN 4:2 (1951):8-9, 16 (photos); The Writer 66:8 (Aug 53):265-67.

BENSON, E. F.

Ref: Hubin 2, TCCMW, CC, ABMI.

BENTLEY, E(DMUND) C(LERIHEW)

Ref: Hubin 2, TCCMW, EMD, CC, ABMI; Cannon, AHMM 27:9 (Sept 82):70-72.

See also: B253, B304, B349.

E115. Barzun, Jacques and Wendell Hertig Taylor. Preface to Trent's Last Case (London, 1912), by E. C. Bentley. In A Book of Prefaces (B17), pp. 19-20.

E116. Baker, Isadore Lewis. E. C. Bentley: Trent's Last Case. Notes on Chosen English Texts series. London: James Brodie, 1956. 54pp. Not seen.

E118. Bentley, E. C. These Days: An Autobiography. London: Constable, 1940.
A chapter is devoted to Trent's Last Case. There is also material on Chesterton and the pre-golden-age of detective fiction. This

autobiography is essential for an understanding of Bentley and his work, and has received high praise from Barzun and Taylor. CC 2899. Breen 110. (Charles Shibuk)

E119. ______. Trent's Last Case. The Mystery Library 5 (B270). 1977.
Contents: Aaron Marc Stein, Introduction (pp. ix-xxv) and annotations; Trent's Last Case, pp. 1-250; Charles Shibuk, "Edmund Clerihew Bentley," pp. 253-57 (E123); Bentley, "Meet Trent," pp. 258-61 (B253); Howard Haycraft, "'Trent's Last Case' Reopened," pp. 266-68 (E120); "E. C. Bentley's 'The Woman in Black'," p. 269 (review from The Bookman, May 1913).

E120. Haycraft, Howard. "'Trent's Last Case' Reopened." NYTBR, 15 Dec 63; reprinted in Bentley, Trent's Last Case (E119), pp. 266-68.
A retrospective review in which Haycraft discusses the origin and publication of the novel, and surveys the novel's enduring qualities and Bentley's subsequent career.

E121. Menon, K. R. A Guide to E. C. Bentley's Trent's Last Case. Singapore: India Publishing House, 1957. 104pp. Not seen.

E123. Shibuk, Charles. "Edmund Clerihew Bentley." TAD 4 (1970/71):30-31; a revised version appeared in Bentley (E119), pp. 253-57.
An annotated bibliography.

BENTLEY, NICOLAS (CLERIHEW)

Ref: Hubin 2, TCCMW, CC, ABMI; UN 2:2 (1949):8-10 (photo).

BENTLEY, PHYLLIS

Ref: Hubin 2, TCCMW, EMD, ABMI.

E124. Bentley, Phyllis. O Dreams, O Destinations. London: Gollancz, 1962; NY: Macmillan, 1962. 272pp. Photos.
An autobiography in which her detective short stories are largely ignored. (REB)

BENTON, KENNETH

Ref: Hubin 2, TCCMW, ABMI.

Int: DAST 10:5 (1977):24-28.

BERCKMAN, EVELYN

Ref: Hubin 2, TCCMW, EMD, CC, ABMI.

BERESFORD, J. D.

Ref: Hubin 2, CC, ABMI.

E125. Johnson, Reginald Brimley. "J. D. Beresford." In Some Contemporary Novelists (Men). Leonard Parsons, 1922; reprint, Freeport, NY: Books for Libraries Press, 1970. Not seen.

BERGER, THOMAS

Ref: Hubin 2, ABMI.

E126. Madden, David. "Thomas Berger's Comic-Absurd Vision in Who Is Teddy Villanova?" TAD 14 (1981):37-43. Illus.

Ways in which Berger uses conventions of the hard-boiled mystery in his 1977 parody novel.

BERGMAN, ANDREW

Ref: Hubin 2, TCCMW, SN.

E127. Geherin, David. "Andrew Bergman." In his Sons of Sam Spade (B121), pp. 129-53.
Geherin finds the 40s skillfully evoked in Bergman's two private eye novels (The Big Kiss-Off of 1944 and Hollywood and LeVine), but sees them as more than nostalgic exercises. They are also, claims Geherin, serious novels of character and situation, a successful blend of politics, history and the detective novel.

BERKELEY, ANTHONY

Ref: Hubin 2, TCCMW, EMD, CC, ABMI; Pike, TPP 5:4 (Oct 83):3-10.

E128. Berkeley, Anthony. The Poisoned Chocolates Case. The Mystery Library 12 (B270). 1979.
Contents: James Sandoe, "Foreword," pp. vii-ix; A. Berkeley, "The Avenging Chance," pp. 1-23 (ss; genesis of The Poisoned Chocolates Case); The Poisoned Chocolates Case, pp. 1-270; Christianna Brand, "A New Denouement," pp. 272-76 (an alternate version of the ending, written for this edition); A. Berkeley, "Concerning Roger Sheringham," pp. 277-78 (fictional biography); "The Detection Club Oath," pp. 279-82 (C224); Mary Smith, "Notes on the Parallel Poisonings," pp. 283-87 (E137); John Dickson Carr, "A Tribute to Cox," pp. 288-90 (E129); James Sandoe, "A Checklist with Some Notes," pp. 291-303 (annotated bibliography for Cox/Berkeley/Iles).

E129. Carr, John Dickson. "A Tribute to Cox." EQMM, July 172; reprinted in Berkeley, Poisoned Chocolates (E128), pp. 288-90.
A survey of A. B. Cox's work in which Carr confesses to a preference for the "Berkeley" titles.

E130. Keating, H. R. F. "Introduction." In Before the Fact, published as by Francis Iles, pp. v-xi. Gregg Press Mystery Fiction Series (B134).

E131. Moy, Paul R. "Anthony Berkeley's Unknown Pseudonymn: A 'Lost' Detective Story Discovered." TPP 5:3 (May/June 83):12.
A bibliographic note on Cicely Disappears, published as by A. Monmouth Platts in 1927.

E132. ______. "A Bibliography of the Works of Anthony Berkeley Cox (Francis Iles)," TAD 14 (1981):236-38.
A list of Cox's writings under his own name and his two pseudonyms of Anthony Berkeley and Francis Iles. Corrections by Moy in 2 letters, TAD 14:381 and 15 (1982):181.

E133. ______. "A Bibliography of the Works of Anthony Berkeley Cox (Francis Iles)." TPP 5:4 (Oct 83):11-18.
A revised version of the TAD bibliography (E132).

E134. Panek, LeRoy. "Anthony Berkeley Cox." In his Watteau's Shepherds (B304), pp. 111-25.
A study of Cox's work as Berkeley and as Iles. Panek sees Cox as, perhaps, the "most important" of the Golden Age writers both for his

role as founder of the Detection Club and for his understanding of the detective novel, the "most sophisticated" of any writer of his generation. Panek devotes a substantial portion of his essay to the three novels by "Frances Iles," which he characterizes as crime novels with a special interest in psychology.

E136. Shibuk, Charles. "The Literary Career of Mr. Anthony Berkeley Cox." TAD 2 (1968/69):164-68, 170.
An annotated bibliography with information on publication, a brief plot summary and critical summaries.

E137. Smith, Mary. "Notes on the Parallel Poisonings." In Berkeley, Poisoned Chocolates (E128), pp. 283-87.
Smith clarifies the textual references to real-life poisonings which parallel the events in Berkeley's novel.

BERNA, PAUL

E138. Baudou, Jacques. "Le mystère Berna |The Berna mystery|." Enigmatika 24 (July 83), pp. 29-35.
A study of Berna's detective fiction for young people. Baudou invites readers to assist him in finding other titles by Berna for a "global" study of his work.

BERNANOS, GEORGES

Ref: Hubin 2, ABMI.

E139. Astier, Colette. "La tentation du roman policier dans deux romans: Un Crime de Georges Bernanos, Le Rocher de Brighton, de Graham Greene |The temptation of the detective novel in two novels|." Revue de littérature comparée 44 (1970):224-43.
Both Bernanos and Greene use the detective novel not to create diversions but to adapt it to their notion of evil. Both novelists "rise above" the banalities of the genre.

E140. Dubourg, Maurice. "Un Crime de Georges Bernanos." Enigmatika 24 (July 83):21-28.
A report on the composition of Bernanos' novel and its critical reception. Dubourg also discusses a complementary text, Un Mauvais Rêve.

BERTHELIUS, JENNY

Ref: Hubin 2.

Int: Jury 2:2 (1973): 26-29.

BEYNON, JANE. See LEWIS, LANGE

BIERCE, AMBROSE

Ref: EMD, ABMI.

E141. Stein, William Bysshe. "Bierce's 'The Death of Halpin Frayser': The Poetics of Gothic Consciousness." Emerson Society Newsletter 18 (1972):115-22; reprinted in Critical Essays on Ambrose Bierce, edited by Cathy N. Davidson, pp. 217. Boston: G. K. Hall, 1982.
A detective is identified and a murder committed but this is a tale of horror and not a tale of detection.

BIGGERS, EARL DERR

Ref: Hubin 2, TCCMW, EMD, CC, ABMI.

Int: NYT, 22 March 31, p. 12.

See also: C535.

E142. Breen, Jon L. "Charlie Chan: The Man Behind the Curtain." Views & Reviews 6:1 (Fall 74):29-35. Illus.
Sections I-III of what was intended to be a chronological survey of the Charlie Chan novels--this portion is a discussion of the first two novels in the series. Views & Reviews ceased publication with this issue, and the rest of the article remains unpublished. (REB)

E143. ______. "Murder Number One: Earl Derr Biggers." New Republic, 30 July 77, pp. 38-39.
An overview of Biggers' ethnic detective series in which Breen insists on Biggers' "exceptional" racial sympathy and sees the interest of the series in the conflict of Western and Eastern cultural values.

E144. Ellman, Neil. "Charlie Chan Carries On." TAD 10 (1977):183-84.
A study of the character of Chan and the way Biggers modified it to make of him the first "domestic" detective in fiction. Ellman also discusses the film portrayals of Chan. Corrections by William K. Everson in a letter, TAD 10:274.

E145. Hill, M. C. "The Illustrious Charlie Chan." CP? 4:3 (1982):4-23. Illus.
Some introductory remarks on the fiction and film series with a publishing history of paperback editions of the novels and a filmography.

E146. Lacassin, Francis. "Charlie Chan ou le sage aux sept fleurs." In Lacassin (B201), Vol. I, pp. 289-317.
A discussion of the character of Charlie Chan, of the ethnic and professional ties and tensions, and the slow, methodical rhythms of the narrative.

E147. Penzler, Otto. "Charlie Chan." In Penzler (B310), pp. 42-51.
Biography and personality profile of the Chan of Biggers' six novels. In keeping with the theme of the book, the profile emphasizes the personal life of Chan, including his family and personality traits. Included are bibliography, filmography and sketch of author Biggers' life. Illustrated with reproductions from the Saturday Evening Post serializations and stills from the films. This is the longest and perhaps best biography of Chan, and includes more epigrams from the books than any other piece, as well as some information not easily to be found on Chan's elusive prototype, Chang Apana. (GG)

E148. Penzler, Otto. "Collecting Mystery Fiction." TAD 15 (1982):119-25. Illus.
Incarnations and re-incarnations of the Chan series and its appearance in forms other than the novels and films. With an annotated bibliography of the first editions of the novels.

E149. Rivière, François. "Charlie Chan: ombres chinoises sur ciel californien |Charlie Chan: Chinese shadows against a California sky|." Preface to Alfred Andriola's Charlie Chan: 1938-1939, Vol I, pp. 5-14. Paris: Futuropolis, 1980.
This introduction to a book-length reprinting of artist Andriola's Chan

comic strip for the McNaught Syndicate in 1938-39 includes a summary of the Chan literary and film sagas. Substantial amounts of material are taken from Detectionary (A159), Encyclopedia of Mystery and Detection (A160), and other sources. Lavishly illustrated with reproductions of Chan film material and book covers from French Chan editions. (GG)

BINGHAM, JOHN

Ref: Hubin 2, TCCMW, CC, SN, ABMIS.

See also: B61, B349.

BLACK, GAVIN

Ref: Hubin 2, TCCMW, ABMI(S).

BLACK, LIONEL

Ref: Hubin 2, TCCMW, CC, ABMI.

BLACK, THOMAS B.

Ref: Hubin 2, SN, ABMI(S).

E150. Boucher, Anthony. "Introduction." In The Pinball Murders (Reynal, 1947), by Thomas B. Black. NY: Mercury, n.d.

BLACKBURN JOHN

Ref: Hubin 2, TCCMW, CC, ABMI.

BLACKMORE, RICHARD

Ref: ABMI.

E151. Jiggens, Clifford. "Inspector Bucket's Rival." TAD 12 (1979):270-72. Photo.

On Inspector Cutting in Richard Blackmore's Clara Vaughan (1864).

BLACKSTOCK, CHARITY

Ref: Hubin 2, TCCMW, CC, ABMI.

E152. Boucher, Anthony. "Introduction." In The Foggy, Foggy Dew by Charity Blackstock. London House & Maxwell, 1958.

BLACKSTOCK, LEE. See BLACKSTOCK, CHARITY

BLACKWOOD, ALGERNON

Ref: Hubin 2, TCCMW, EMD, CC, ABMI.

E153. Colombo, John Robert. Blackwood's Books: A Bibliography Devoted to Algernon Blackwood. Toronto: Hounslow Press, 1981. Frontis. (pen-and-ink portrait of Blackwood by Isaac Bickerstaff). Wraps. Bibliography.

The bulk of this work is devoted to a descriptive bibliographical listing of Blackwood's 58 books published between 1906 and 1977. Appendices contain a chronological list of book titles, an alphabetical list of the stories contained in Blackwood's 13 short story collections, brief biographical articles and appreciations. Appendix V deals with Blackwood's works for the theatre, radio and television. Blackwood created one of the best known of "occult detectives" in the book John Silence, Physician Extraordinary (1917), and a number of his short stories deal with crime, mystery and the macabre as opposed to the overtly supernatural. (REB)

BLAKE, NICHOLAS

Ref: Hubin 2, TCCMW, EMD, CC, ABMI.

E154. Barzun, Jacques and Wendell Hertig Taylor. Preface to Minute for Murder (London 1974), by Nicholas Blake. In A Book of Prefaces (B17), pp. 21-22.

E155. Broberg, Jan. "Conversation with Nicholas Blake." TMRN 2:3 (Feb 69):3-4. Translated from the Swedish by Rev. Thompson, Portland, Maine.
Text of a 1964 interview in which Blake comments on his work and that of other writers, and on readers of mysteries. With a checklist compiled by Charles Shibuk.

E156. Lewis, C. Day. The Buried Day. London: Chatto & Windus, 1960; NY: Harper & Bros., 1960. Translated into Japanese by Satoru Tsuchiya and published as Uzumoreta Jidai (Tokyo: Nan'undo, 1962).
Autobiography of the British poet-laureate who writes detective novels as Nicholas Blake; passing references to his detective fiction (esp. Chapter III). CC 157. (REB)

E157. Day-Lewis, Sean. C. Day-Lewis: An English Literary Life. London: Weidenfeld & Nicolson, March 1979, 360pp. Illus.
Sean Day-Lewis is the son of Cecil Day-Lewis. This biography of the elder Day-Lewis, written with a mixture of affection and detachment, makes use of the autobiographical content of Day-Lewis's poetry (he was Poet Laureate of England from 1968 until his death in 1972) and of his Nicholas Blake novels, as well as many previously unpublished letters. The emphasis is on Day-Lewis's personal life and his participation in British intellectual and literary circles in the 1930s; his detective ficion is relegated to a subsidiary role. (REB)

E158. Lundin, Bo. "Poeten och deckaren |Poet and detective|." Jury 1:1 (1972):21-23.
Analysis of Blake's detective, Nigel Strangeways. (MS)

BLANC, SUZANNE

Ref: Hubin 2, TCCMW, ABMI.

BLANKFORT, MICHAEL

Ref: Hubin 2, ABMI.

E159. Boucher, Anthony. "Introduction." In The Widow-Makers (Simon & Schuster, 1946), by Michael Blankfort. NY: Mercury Press, n. d.

BLOCH, ROBERT

Ref: Hubin 2, TCCMW, EMD, SN, ABMI.

Int: Black Oracle 2 (1969), 4 (1970); Castle of Frankenstein 16 (1971), pp. 4-11 & 17, pp. 21-26; Fandom Unlimited 1 (1971) (n.b. the preceding three interviews were combined in "Robert Bloch: A Collaborative Interview," The Robert Bloch Fanzine (E165), pp. 36-43); EQMM, March 76, pp. 118-119.

E160. Bloch, Robert. "Author, Author" department in The Fanscient No. 8, 3:2 (Summer 49), pp. 19-23. Reprinted (without photo or checklist) in Graeme Flanagan (E163), pp. 6-9.

Autobiographical article; much information on Bloch's writing, focusing on his weird fiction and science fiction. The checklist covers only these areas. Only one Bloch novel, The Scarf, had been published at the time of this essay, and most of the author's crime fiction was yet to be written. (REB)

E161. ______. "Introduction." In his Out of the Mouths of Graves, pp. ix-xiii. NY: Mysterious Press, 1979.

E162. "Dossier Robert Bloch." Polar 3 (June 79):3-35.
Although the focus is on his films and science fiction, the bibliography is particularly interesting for the inclusion of comments by Bloch on his fiction. Profusely illustrated, mostly with film stills. Contents: "Entretien avec Robert Bloch," pp. 4-12 (interview); "Filmographie," pp. 13-17; R. Bloch, "La Nouvelle Belzébuth," pp. 18-23 (ss, translated by Gérard de Chergé); "Robert Bloch et Psychose," pp. 24-28 (on the film Psycho); "Bibliographie," pp. 30-35.

E163. Flanagan, Graeme, editor. Robert Bloch: A Bio-Bibliography. Canberra City, Australia: Graeme Flanagan, July 1979, 64pp. Wraps. Includes 12pp. of photographs.
The treatment is similar to that in Randall Larson's Robert Bloch Fanzine (E165), but more extensive. The interviews, biographical material, and appreciations by colleagues are new. "The Robert Bloch Collection" describes the collection of Bloch material---including published work, manuscripts, correspondence, and memorabilia---in the Division of Rare Books and Special Collections at the University of Wyoming library. Part 1 of the "Biography" is a reprint of "Author, Author" department in The Fanscient (E160). The bibliography is based on Larson's, brought up to date and rearranged into more useful form by Flanagan. There are separate listings for magazine fiction (first printings only), non-fiction, novels, story collections, miscellanea (book introductions, interviews, speeches, biographical sketches), and work for radio, TV and films. Wordage for individual stories is not given. Reprints are listed only for those stories which have not been included in Bloch's own story collections. In spite of these omissions, this is the most useful existing bibliography of Bloch's work. Contents: G. Flanagan, "Introduction," pp. 3-4; Harlan Ellison, "Robert Bloch: A Few Words of Friendship," p. 5; "Biography," pp. 6-12 (Part 1, by Robert Bloch; part 2 by G. Flanagan); G. Flanagan, "The Robert Bloch Collection," pp. 12-13; Robert Weinberg, "Mr. Weird Tales," pp. 15-16; G. Flanagan, "Interview One," pp. 17-23; G. Flanagan, "A Few Notes on three Important Cthulhu Mythos Tales," p. 24; Fritz Leiber, "When Screwballs Meet...," pp. 25-26; G. Flanagan, "Interview Two," pp. 27-36; "Bibliography," pp. 38-59, 62; Mary Elizabeth Counselman, "My Weird Little Brother, Bob," pp. 60-61; Ramsay Campbell, "From a British Point of View...," p. 61; plus one- or two-paragraph comments on Bloch by Richard Matheson, Sam Moskowitz, and Ray Bradbury. (REB)

E164. Hall, Graham M. (compiler). Robert Bloch Bibliography. Tewkesbury, England: Graham M. Hall, January 1965. Pages (34) not numbered. Mimeographed, stapled at left edge. Artwork by Brian McCabe.
The bibliography is in three parts. "Listing - Chronological" lists all of Bloch's work, both original and reprint, chronologically by publication date, through Fall 1964. Wordage is given for each item. In "Listing - By Magazine," Bloch's magazine fiction and some non-fiction are listed according to the magazine in which they appeared; the arrangement is

alphabetically by magazine title and chronologically within each magazine, with prior appearances cross-indexed. An "Addendum" lists Bloch's novels, the anthologies in which his stories have been reprinted (the stories themselves are not identified), miscellaneous book appearances, the contents of the short story collections, the "Lefty Feep" series, radio plays, and TV and movie adaptations. The latter listings are very condensed, with no dates given. In addition, the booklet contains a brief appreciation, "Building Bloch" by Samuel A. Peeples (E167) and a 14-line "Author's Note" by Bloch. (REB)

E165. Larson, Randall D. (editor). The Robert Bloch Fanzine. Los Altos, CA: Fandom Unlimited Enterprises, Sept 1972. Mimeographed. Second edition, Sept 1973. pp. 1-50 (including covers). Offset, stapled in heavy covers. Illustrated.

Contents: R. Bloch, "By the Author of Psycho?," p. 4 (introduction); Sam Moskowitz, "Psycho-Logical Bloch," pp. 5-7 (reprint of Moskowitz (E166), with added note by Bloch); Joe Pumilia, "I Met the Author of Psycho!!," p. 8; *R. Bloch, "Fan Mags," p. 9 (Items marked * are reprints of material from various science fiction fanzines); "1935-1973 Chronological Bibliography," pp. 10-28; *R. Bloch, "Lefty Feep and I," pp. 30-31; Loay Hall, "Blochitis," pp. 32-33; *R. Bloch, "Unsolved Mysteries of Fandom," p. 33; Judith Lichtenberger, "A Poem for Robert Bloch," p. 34; Terry Dale, "Vampire Killer Extraordinaire," p. 35; John Stanley, "On Visiting Robert Bloch," p. 36; "Robert Bloch: A Collaborative Interview," pp. 36-43; *R. Bloch, "How To Be an SF Critic," pp. 43-44; Samuel Peeples, "Building Bloch," pp. 46-47 (E167). The main items of interest are the bibliography, the "collaborative interview," and the illustrations. The bibliography is an expansion of Graham Hall's chronological list (E164), without credit to the source. It gathers magazine fiction, non-fiction, books, columns, and interviews, including pseudonymous works, reprints, and foreign translations, into a single list arranged chronologically by publication date. Wordage is given for each item. There are supplementary lists of TV and movie adaptations, radio plays, the contents of Bloch's short story collections, the stories in the "Lefty Feep" series, and awards received. There is no cross-index by story title, so that locating individual items becomes a tedious business. The illustrations include movie stills, movie ads, snapshots of Bloch with family members and friends, and pen-and-ink drawings. (REB)

E166. Moskowitz, Sam. "'Psycho'-Logical Bloch." Amazing Stories, Dec 62, pp. 109-119; reprinted as chapter 19, "Robert Bloch," in Seekers of Tomorrow: Modern Masters of Science Fiction, by Sam Moskowitz (World Publ. Co., 1966), pp. 335-351; reprinted in Bogey Men, by Robert Bloch (NY: Pyramid Books F-839, 1963), pp. 146-59; and in Larson (E165).

An overview of Bloch's career, with emphasis on his science fiction and weird fiction. Coverage of the period after 1945 is sketchy. Bloch's psychological and crime novels are mentioned, with his own comments on his favorite, The Kidnaper. (REB)

E167. Peeples, Samuel A. "Building Bloch." In Hall (E164) and in Larson (E165). Brief appreciation, pointing out the quality and importance of Bloch's psychological novels and paperback-original crime fiction. (REB)

BLOCHMAN, LAWRENCE G.

Ref: Hubin 2, TCCMW, EMD, CC, SN, ABMI; Argosy, 14 May 32.

E168. Boucher, Anthony. "Introduction." In <u>See You at the Morgue</u> (Duell, 1941), by Lawrence G. Blochman. NY: <u>Collier Books, 1962.</u>

BLOCK, LAWRENCE

Ref: Hubin 2, TCCMW, SN, ABMI; <u>Writer's Digest</u>, Sept 76, pp. 15-17; Writer's Digest, Oct 81, pp. 24-29.

Int: EQMM, March 79, pp. 96-97.

See also: C103a, C637.

BLOOMFIELD, ROBERT

Ref: Hubin 2; UN 4:8 (1952):10-11, 15; UN 5:1 (1952):6-7 (photos).

BODKIN, M. MCDONNELL

Ref: Hubin 2, TCCMW, EMD, ABMI.

E169. Moskowitz, Sam. "M. McDonnell Bodkin, 'The Vanishing Diamonds'." "Gaslight Detectives" series (C565). MSMM, Oct 73, pp. 60-63.

BOILEAU, PIERRE, AND NARCEJAC, THOMAS

Ref: HUBIN 2, CC, ABMI.

Int: MM 20, Sept 49 (Pierre Boileau); MM 274, Dec 70.

E170. Lacassin, Francis. "Boileau-Narcejac ou la province et l'absence |Boileau-Narcejac or the province and absence|." In Lacassin (B201), pp. 268-293. Bibliography and filmography.

Lacassin uses the elements of his first meeting with Boileau and Narcejac (dramatic use of an ordinary setting, suspense moderated by humour, skill in manipulating the unexpected, a mystification based on the absurd) as the basis of his discussion of their work.

E170a. Tourteau, Jean-Jacques. "<u>Les Louves.</u>" In Tourteau (B408), pp. 298-301. An analysis of a 1955 novel.

BOLAND, JOHN

Ref: Hubin, TCCMW, ABMI.

BOMMART, JEAN

Ref: SN.

Int: MM 24, Jan 50; MM, Apr 76.

BONETT, JOHN and EMERY

Ref: Hubin 2, TCCMW, EMD, CC, ABMI.

E171. Barzun, Jacques and Wendell Hertig Taylor. "Introduction." In <u>Not in the Script</u> (NY, 1951), by John and Emery Bonett. "Crime Fiction 1950-1975" (B18).

BONNER, MARGERIE

Ref: Hubin 2.

E172. Grace, Sherrill. "Margerie Bonner's Three Forgotten Novels." <u>Journal of Modern Literature</u> 6 (1977):321-24.

Among the fiction of writer Malcolm Lowery's wife Margerie Bonner are two detective novels which Grace calls comparable to Agatha Christie's work: The Last Twist of the Knife and The Shapes That Creep, both published by Scribner's in 1946.

BOOTH, CHRISTOPHER B.

Ref: Hubin 2, ABMI.

E173. Hubbard, D. C. "Popular Detective Story Writers: Christopher B. Booth." Detective Story Magazine 103:4 (18 Aug 28):113-114. Portrait.
Biographical sketch. Series character: Mr. Clackworthy, Con Man. (RS)

BOOTHBY, GUY

Ref: Hubin 2, EMD, ABMI.

See also: D451.

E174. Davidson, M. "Doctor Nikola." CDA, 1969, pp. 19-20.
Brief synopsis of the first story in the series by Boothby and the appeal it had for one youthful reader. (JRC)

BORGENICHT, MIRIAM

Ref: Hubin, TCCMW; UN 1:9 (1949):10-11 (photo).

BORGES, JORGE LUIS

Ref: Hubin 2, TCCMW, ABMI.

Int: EQMM, Apr 78, 103-104; May 78, 103-104.

See also: B135, B366.

E175. Gayton, Gillian. "Jorge Luis Borges y G. K. Chesterton." In Actas del Sexto Congreso Internacional de Hispanistas celebrado en Toronto del 21 al 26 agosto de 1977, edited by Alan M. Gordon, et al., pp. 312-15. Toronto: Dept. of Spanish and Portuguese, University of Toronto, 1980.
Stylistic devices used by Borges in three stories that Gordon believes are indebted to Chesterton. The author spends too much time arguing that Borges might borrow from a writer of lesser rank and seems unaware of earlier work on Borges and Chesterton by Anglo-Saxon writers.

E176. Gillespie, Robert. "Detections: Borges and Father Brown." Novel (Spring 1974):220-30.
Ways in which both Borges and Chesterton experiment with genre conventions to "examine the supernatural and the nature of evil."

E177. Hayes, Aden W. and Khachib Toloyan. "The Cross and the Compass: Patterns of Order in Chesterton and Borges." Hispanic Review 49 (Autumn 81):395-405.
An analysis of the materials Borges adapts from Chesterton's "The Blue Cross" for use in his story "La muerte y la brújula."

E178. Holzapfel, Tamara. "Crime and Detection in a Defective World: The Detective Fictions of Borges and Dürrenmatt." Studies in 20th Century Literature 3:1 (Fall 79). Not seen.

E179. Imbert, Enrique Anderson. "Chesterton en Borges." Anales de Literatura hispanoamericana (Madrid), nos. 2-3 (1973-74), pp. 469-94. Cited by Hayes and Toloyan (E177); not seen.

E180. Irby, James E. "The Structures of the Stories of Jorge Luis Borges." Unpublished Ph.D. dissertation. University of Michigan, 1962.
Includes interview material with Borges who speaks (on p. 309) of his debt to Chesterton's "The Three Horsemen of the Apocalypse" for "La muerte y la brújula." As cited by Hayes and Toloyan (E177); not seen.

E181. Merivale, Patricia. "The Flaunting of Artifice in Vladimir Nabokov and Jorge Borges." Wisconsin Studies in Contemporary Literature 8 (1967):294-309.
Passim for comments on the hero-detective in search of his identify and on the conventions of the detective story converted to a metaphysics of form.

BOSSE, MALCOLM

Ref: Hubin 2, SN.

Int: PW, 20 May 83, pp. 238-39 (photo; 1979 MWA nominee).

BOUCHER, ANTHONY

Ref: Hubin 2, TCCMW, EMD, CC, ABMI.

E182. A Boucher Portrait: Anthony Boucher as Seen by His Friends and Colleagues. Compiled by Lenore Glen Offord (with) A. Boucher Bibliography, compiled by J. R. Christopher, with D. W. Dickensheet and R. E. Briney. White Bear Lake, Minn.: (Allen J. Hubin), 1969. Offprint from TAD, vol. 2, nos. 2,3,4. pp. 69-85, 143-55, 263-73.
Collection of brief but cogent memorial statements by a dozen of Boucher's friends and fellow writers, together with an exhaustively annotated bibliography of Boucher's writings in all fields. (REB)

E183. Boucher, Anthony. "Author, Author" department in The Fanscient 4:2 (Summer 50):21-24. Photo, p. 20. Checklist, pp. 24-25.
Autobiographical article; the commentary on his writing emphasizes his fantasy and science fiction. The mystery fiction gets only a brief paragraph. "I'll sum up the Mystery business hastily by saying that I have worked in just about every branch of non-punishable murder...." Checklist includes only sf/fantasy works. (REB)

E184. Christopher, J. R., R. E. Briney and D. W. Dickensheet, compilers. "A. Boucher Bibliography." TAD 2 (1968/69):77-85, 143-56, 263-73.
Reprinted with Offord (E189) as (E182). Additions and corrections to the bibliography in letters to TAD, as follows: Edward D. Hoch, 2:202; Steve Lewis, 2:202; R. E. Briney, 2:275; Steve Lewis, 3 (1969/70):60; R. E. Briney, 3:66, 137; Don Yates, 5 (1971/72):51.

E185. Hahn, Robert W., editor. Sincerely, Tony/Faithfully, Vincent. The Correspondence of Anthony Boucher and Vincent Starrett. Chicago, IL: The Catullus Press, 1975. 55pp. Illus. Wraps.
About 35 postcards, telegrams and letters comprise this collection. The correspondence was conducted intermittently from 1941 to 1958 and while much of the material is slight, it is an engaging perspective on two notable mystery critics and writers of the period. There are extensive explanatory notes which include excerpts from the text of Starrett's essay on detective fiction that appeared in the 14th edition of the Encyclopedia Britannica (1944) and was reprinted in Buchloh/Becker 2 (B61).

E186. Nevins, Francis M., Jr. "Anthony Boucher." Mystery 3:2 (Sept 81):18-19, 63. Photo.
A survey of Boucher's career with a bibliography of his novels and short stories.

E187. ______. "A Checklist of the Fiction of Anthony Boucher." In Exeunt Murderers (E187), pp. (299), 300-307.
The checklist consists of an annotated list of Boucher's novels and story collections, giving first U. S. and first British hardcover and first U. S. paperback editions; a list of Boucher's magazine fiction, both mystery and science fiction, arranged by magazine, with reprint appearances noted; and a list of stories which first appeared in anthologies. Several instances are noted where the date of composition differed markedly from date of first publication. (REB)

E188. ______. "Introduction: The World of Anthony Boucher." In Exeunt Murderers: The Best Mystery Stories of Anthony Boucher, edited by Francis M. Nevins, Jr. and Martin H. Greenberg, pp. viii-xvi. "Mystery Makers" Series: Volume 1. Carbondale and Edwardsville, IL: Southern Illinois University Press, 1983.
Nevins's knowledgeable and perceptive introduction is the best account yet written of Anthony Boucher's multiple careers as author, editor, and critic. An earlier version, somewhat the worse for editorial and typesetting interference, appeared as "Anthony Boucher" (E186). (REB)

E189. Offord, Lenore Glen, compiler. "A Boucher Portrait. Anthony Boucher as Seen by His Friends and Colleagues." TAD 2 (1968/69):69-76, 119. Reprinted in A Boucher Portrait (E182).
By subject: "As Editor," "As Mystery Writer," "As Sherlockian," etc.

E189. Penzler, Otto. "Introduction." In The Case of the Baker Street Irregulars (Simon & Schuster, 1940), by Anthony Boucher. Gregg Press Mystery Fiction Series (B134).

E190. Spencer, David G. "The Case of the Man Who Could Do Everything." Rhodomagnetic Digest 2:2 (Sept 1950):7-10.
Biographical and career sketch (up to 1950) of Anthony Boucher, by a fellow member of the Elves', Gnomes', and Little Men's Science-Fiction, Chowder and Marching Society. (REB).

BOULLE, PIERRE

Ref: Hubin 2, TCCMW, ABMI.

BOUQUET, JEAN-LOUIS

E191. Lacassin, Francis. "Jean-Louis Bouquet ou l'exploration des âmes en crise |Jean-Louis Bouquet or the exploration of souls in crisis|." In Lacassin (B201), Vol. 2, pp. 216-42.
Bouquet has worked extensively in films (from the early 1920s) as writer and production assistant but has also written numerous works of science fiction, the fantastic and detective fiction. His chief characteristic, according to Lacassin, is the study of tortured souls in a shadowy, chiaroscuro world. His work can be compared to the Fantômas adventures (Allain and Souvestre) and appears to be colored by the chapter films of his early silent film work.

BOURGET, PAUL

E192. Angenot, Marc. "On est toujours le disciple de quelqu'un, ou le mystère du pousse-au-crime |You are always somebody's disciple, or the mystery of the 'pousse-au-crime'|." Littérature 49 (Feb 83), pp. 50-62.
The "pousse-au-crime" (literally, "incites to crime") is a beverage with a very strong alcoholic content but the "crime" element makes it a very apt pun for this article on a character who is not himself a murderer but incites others to commit murder. The discussion includes Bourget's novel Le Disciple and Agatha Christie.

BOX, EDGAR

Ref: Hubin 2, TCCMW, EMD, CC, ABMI.

Int: B366.

E193. Bargainnier, Earl F. "The Mysteries of Edgar Box (aka Gore Vidal)." Clues 2:1 (Spring/Summer 1981):45-52.
Vidal's three mysteries, written under the pseudonym of Edgar Box, considered as mysteries and as part of Vidal's total work. Bargainnier studies most closely elements of social satire in the novels.

E194. Broberg, Jan. "Brobergs brottstycke 19 |Broberg's crime piece no. 19|." Jury 4:4 (1975):31.
On Edgar Box/Gore Vidal. (MS)

E195. Nevins, Francis M., Jr. "Gore Vidal, Mystery Writer." TMRN 4:2 (Jan 71):25-28.
Nevins describes what he sees as Vidal's partial success at writing mystery novels without, apparently, knowing much about the form.

BOYLE, JACK

Ref: Hubin 2, TCCMW, EMD, ABMI.

E196. Hoch, Edward D. "Introduction." In Boston Blackie (Fly, 1919), by Jack Boyle. Gregg Press Mystery Fiction Series (B134).

BRACKETT, LEIGH

Ref: Hubin 2, SN, ABMI.

E197. Arbur, Rosemarie. Leigh Brackett, Marion Zimmer Bradley, Anne McCaffrey: A Primary and Secondary Bibliography. Boston, MA: G. K. Hall, 1982. xlviii, 277pp. Indexed.
Although primarily known as authors of science fiction and fantasy, all three of the writers covered in this book wrote some mystery or suspense fiction. The hardcover mystery novels of Leigh Brackett are noted, as are the Gothic ("romantic suspense") paperback novels by Bradley and McCaffrey. Brackett's detective fiction for the pulp magazines (1943-45) is not mentioned. Even more surprising is the omission of the published edition of the script for The Big Sleep by Brackett, William Faulkner, and Jules Furthman (in Film Scripts One, edited by Garrett et al., Appleton-Century Crofts, 1971). The extensive listings of critical studies (including reviews) are almost exclusively restricted to the authors' science fiction and fantasy works. (REB)

E198. Boucher, Anthony. "Introduction." In No Good from a Corpse (Coward, 1944), by Leigh Brackett. NY: Collier Books, 1964. Reprinted in Multiplying Villainies (B43), pp. 117-18.

E199. Briney, Robert E. "In Memoriam: Leigh Brackett." TAD 11 (1978): 258-59.
A thoughtful and detailed survey of Brackett's life and works with comments on her detective fiction and on the hard-boiled elements which she had "consciously" incorporated into her science fiction.

E200. Truesdale, David, and McGuire, Paul. "Tangent Interviews: Leigh Brackett and Edmond Hamilton." Tangent 5, Summer 76, pp. 7-25. Photos. Reprinted as "An interview with Leigh Brackett and Edmond Hamilton." Science Fiction Review 6:2 (whole no. 21, May 77):6-15. Photos.
A wide-ranging joint interview with Leigh Brackett and her husband Edmond Hamilton, covering the careers of both writers. Contains comments on Brackett's first novel, No Good from a Corpse, anecdotes about writing colleagues such as Henry Kuttner (including his mystery writing) and Ray Bradbury, and a lengthy discussion of her work on the screenplay for The Big Sleep. (REB)

BRADBURY, RAY

Ref: Hubin 2, TCCMW, ABMI.

E201. Albright, Donn. "Ray Bradbury." Xenophile 13 (May 75), pp. 10-20, 61-66; no. 26 (Sept 76), pp. 4-10; no. 36 (Nov 77), pp. R2-R7.
A bibliography of Ray Bradbury's writings described as a "supplementary index to all those that preceded it." The listings include fanzine appearances and stories in pulp magazines. An invaluable guide to material that--at the time of the compilation--seldom made its way into subject bibliographies.

E202. Bradbury, Ray. "Author, Author" department in The Fanscient 2:3 (whole no. 6, Winter 49):19-22. Photo, p. 18. Checklist, pp. 22-24.
Autobiographical article, with comments on his stories and on his attitude towards his work. Feels that the way to grow as a writer is not to read other works in the same field but to devote his reading time to general literature. The checklist contains a list of Bradbury stories in the detective pulp magazines. (REB)

E203. ______. "Introduction: Hammett? Chandler? Not to Worry!" In A Memory of Murder, by Ray Bradbury, pp. 7-9. NY: Dell, 1984.
Introduction to an anthology of short stories from pulps, among them Dime Mystery Magazine and Flynn's Detective Fiction. The book is dedicated to Leigh Brackett who read Bradbury's stories and advised him on revisions.

E204. Nolan, William F. "Bradbury in the Pulps." Xenophile 36 (Nov 77), pp. R21-R24, R31.
This includes a section on Bradbury's appearances in detective pulp magazines.

E205. ______. "The Crime/Suspense Fiction of Ray Bradbury: A Listing." TAD 4 (1970/71):155.
The 30 stories Nolan considers to be Bradbury's contributions to the genre.

E206. ______. The Ray Bradbury Companion: A Life and Career History, Photolog, and Comprehensive Checklist of Writings, with Facsimiles from Ray Bradbury's Unpublished and Uncollected Work in All Media.

Introduction by Ray Bradbury. Detroit Gale Research, 1975. 339pp. Illus.
A well-researched and presented bibliography. The Albright supplements (E201) in Xenophile build on Nolan's work and include material by Nolan originally intended for inclusion in the bibliography.

E207. ______. "The Ray Bradbury Index." In Ray Bradbury Review (San Diego, CA: William F. Nolan, 1952), pp. 46-63; and "An Index to the Works of Ray Bradbury," in The Magazine of Fantasy and Science Fiction 24:5 (May 63):40-51.
In the period 1944-48 Bradbury had seventeen stories published in the detective pulp magazines, and in later years several crime-related stories appeared in Manhunt and EQMM. These stories are listed, along with Bradbury's other short fiction and books, in the two checklists cited above. The Review index is arranged by magazine, the other is chronological. (REB)

BRADDON, MARY ELIZABETH

Ref: Hubin 2, TCCMW, EMD, CC, ABMI.

E208. Bedell, Jeanne F. "Amateur and Professional Detectives in the Fiction of Mary Elizabeth Braddon." Clues 4:1 (Spring/Summer 83):19-34.
Crime, detection, and detectives in Braddon's sensation fiction and her contribution to the novel of "domesticity."

E209. Donaldson, Norman. "Introduction." In Lady Audley's Secret, by Mary Elizabeth Braddon, pp. v-xiv. NY: Dover, 1974.
A good, basic biocritical study, although Donaldson refers to interviews and other material for which no references are given.

E210. Elliott, Jeanne B. "A Lady to the End: The Case of Isabel Vane." Victorian Studies 19 (March 1976):(329)-344.
On sensation fiction, primarily Braddon's Lady Audley's Secret. (KLM)

E211. Heywood, Christopher. "Lady Audley's Secret: A T. S. Eliot Source?" Review of English Studies 27:106 (May 76):182-88.
Of interest to Braddon and genre scholars for the ways in which more "serious" writers may use popular sources.

E212. "Mary E. Braddon." The Writer 10:11 (Nov 97):167-68.
A portrait of the writer and her writing habits, with acknowledgement of a "recent" number of Windsor Magazine as the source for the information. The source has not been confirmed but in the early years of its publication, The Writer reprinted a great deal of material on writers that had appeared in magazines and newspapers and is an invaluable--if often unverifiable--source for ephemeral material on popular authors of the day.

E213. "Mary E. Braddon." The Writer 14:8 (Aug 1901):122.
An excerpt from the Philadelphia Times (no date given) with details on Braddon's domestic life and the way she wrote Lady Audley's Secret in two months.

E214. Wolff, Robert Lee. Sensational Victorian: The Life and Times of Mary Elizabeth Braddon. NY: Garland Press, 1979. pp. xiv, 519. Index and bibliography.
A massive biographical study. Review: Victorian Studies 23: 402-3; Choice 16:1027.

BRADLEY, MARY HASTINGS

Ref: Hubin 2, ABMI; UN 4:5 (1951):8-11, 14; UN 5:2 (1942):6-7, 9 (photos).

BRAHMS, CARYL

Ref: Hubin 2, TCCMW, ABMI.

BRAMAH, ERNEST

Ref: Hubin 2, TCCMW, EMD, CC, ABMI.

See also: B349.

E215. Barzun, Jacques and Wendell Hertig Taylor. Preface to _Max Carrados_ (London, 1914), by Ernest Bramah. In _A Book of Prefaces_ (B17), pp. 23-24.

E216. Goldberg, Joshua. "What's in a Name? or Playfully on a Tangent?" TAD 7 (1973/74):122-24.
Etymological speculations on the origin of the name of Bramah's blind detective, Max Carrados, in the word "mask" (and its etymons).

E217. Penzler, Otto. "Collecting Mystery Fiction: Max Carrados." TAD 16 (1983):199-201. Illus.
One of a series on mystery writers. A bibliographical article on editions.

E218. White, William. "Ernest Bramah: A First Checklist." BoB 22:6 (1958):127-31.
A checklist of works by and about Bramah. White states that this is a preliminary effort done in preparation for his paper, "Kai Lung in America: The Critical Reception of Ernest Bramah" (E226). Furthermore, White states that he knows that he has missed many of Bramah's stories in English journals. Nevertheless, his checklist is impressive, giving the contents of the short story collections in the Kai Lung and Max Carrados books, as well as some reprint information. Also included are Bramah's appearances in periodicals and anthologies, and reviews of his books. The section on biography and criticism is a checklist of secondary sources, including books, prefaces, articles and obituary notices, and is knowledgeably and amusingly annotated. There are citations from Haycraft (B142, B143). This is a very good "first effort" on a writer who is generally said to be obscure. (GG)

E219. ______. "Ernest Bramah in Anthologies, 1914-1972." TAD 10 (1977):30-32. Photo and illustrations.
An updating of White (E218). Additions by Frank D. McSherry, Jr. in a letter, TAD 10 (1977):100.

E220. ______. "Ernest Bramah in China: An Important Letter." PMLA 87 (May 72):511-13.
Biographical data. See also comments by White in a letter, TAD 8 (1975): 237-8 and a reply by E. F. Bleiler in TAD 8:317.

E221. ______. "Ernest Bramah in Periodicals, 1890-1972." BoB 32:1 (Jan/March 75):33-34, 44.
A checklist of Bramah writings, primarily short stories, including reprints. This is a handy place to find the citations of the first appearances of many of the stories which later appeared in the Kai Lung collections. Some entries are briefly annotated. (GG)

E222. ______. "Ernest Bramah on Max Carrados: An Unpublished BBC Talk." TAD 15 (1982): 80-83.

A typescript of a talk aired on 7 May 1935. The typescript was found among the Bramah papers in the Humanities Research Center, University of Texas at Austin. A rambling but interesting talk in which Bramah describes the origin of his blind detective and defends his use of an infirmity for which some critics have taken him to task. Without presuming to be a scholar on the subject of blind detectives, Bramah reminds his listeners of the cyclops Polyphemus who, blinded by Ulysses, had to depend on his other senses and his native wit to locate his persecutors. Bramah also seizes on a description of his detective as a fairy-tale character to say that all fictional detectives are fairies who can accomplish things no ordinary human can.

E223. ______. "Ernest Bramah's Max Carrados." TMRN 2:2 (Dec 68):7-10.

Comments on editions and popularity of the Bramah mysteries. White also includes comments by Bramah on his books taken from an unpublished manuscript in the University of Texas (Austin) Bramah collection. White published two addenda, as follows: a letter from Bramah, dated 4 June 40, with annotations by White, in TMRN 2:3 (Feb 69):8-9; and a footnote about Bramah's story "The Bunch of Violets" in TMRN 2:4 (April 69):19-20.

E224. ______. "Ernest Bramah's Published Letters: A Survey." BoB 31:1 (1975): 5.

An annotated list of 8 letters from Bramah to others, including Howard Haycraft. As White states, this is an introductory effort. He mentions, but does not include, the 200 letters from Bramah to the Ralph Pinker agency. See also: "An Unpublished Ernest Bramah Letter," American Notes & Queries 5 (Nov 66):35-36. (GG)

E225. ______. "Is There an Ernest Bramah?" American Book Collector 16:10 (Summer 66):12. Photo.

A report on some biographic sleuthing by White in which he gathered data on Bramah. White examined the University of Texas manuscript collection which included some unpublished biographical material by Bramah.

E226. ______. "Kai Lung in America: The Critical Reception of Ernest Bramah in America." American Book Collector 9 (June 59): 15-19.

A history of Bramah's writing career and a discussion of Kai Lung and Max Carrados.

E227. ______. "An Unpublished Ernest Bramah Letter on Max Carrados." TAD 3 (1969/70): 92-3.

White discusses the lack of critical notice of Bramah and quotes some favorable comments by several critics. The body of the article consists of a letter from Bramah to his publisher suggesting six titles for the book finally published as The Eyes of Max Carrados (1923) with some comments by White. See TAD 3:203 for a letter from Francis M. Nevins, Jr., clarifying a point in White's article.

BRAMHALL, MARION

Ref: Hubin 2; UN 1:10 (1949):8-9, 15 (photo).

BRAND, CHRISTIANNA

Ref: Hubin 2, TCCMW, EMD, CC, ABMI.

Int: EQMM, Aug 78, pp. 108-109; DAST 14:4 (1981):34-5 (photo).

See also: B309.

E228. Brand, Christianna."The Author Comments." In Brand, Green for Danger (E229), pp. xiii-xiv.
The author describes the conditions under which she wrote this now classic novel (during the war as an amateur at fiction) and sees in it an expression of the universal themes of man as the hunter and the hunted.

E229. _____. Green for Danger. The Mystery Library (B270) 9. 1978.
Contents: Otto Penzler, "Introduction," pp. vii-xii (E234); Christianna Brand, "The Author Comments," pp. xiii-xiv (E228); Green for Danger, pp. 1-254; Otto Penzler, "The Works of Christianna Brand," p. 256-60 (E235); Christianna Brand, "Inspector Cockrill," pp. 261-66 (B309); Anthony Boucher, "Introduction," pp. 268-69 (Originally published as the Introduction to the Bantam Books edition of Green for Danger, Jan 1965); "Reviews of Green for Danger," pp. 270-71.

E231. _____. "Introduction." In Fog of Doubt (Scribner, 1953; as London Particular, Joseph (London), 1952), by Christianna Brand, pp. v-x. Gregg Press Mystery Fiction Series (B134).

E232. Briney, Robert E. "Introduction: The World of Christiana Brand." In Buffet for Unwelcome Guests: The Best Mystery Stories of Christianna Brand, edited by Francis M. Nevins, Jr., and Martin H. Greenberg, pp. vii-xv. The "Mystery Makers" Series, Vol 2. Carbondale and Edwardsville, IL: Southern Illinois University Press, 1983.
Briney's introduction catches the flavor of Brand's personality with his account of her appearances at various mystery gatherings and conventions. In addition, he presents a detailed biography that includes information on the writing and publication of her novels and short stories. He concludes by pointing out that there were often substantial differences between the American and English editions of the stories chosen for this collection; in every case, the version chosen is the one preferred by the author.

E233. _____. "Christianna Brand: A Checklist." In Brand, Buffet (as described in E232), pp. 291-300.
A bibliography of her writing. Both American and English editions are given, with both titles (where different) and original serial publication, as appropriate. Also included are short stories, short story collections (with contents listed), and non-fiction.

E234. Penzler, Otto. "Introduction." In Brand (E229), pp. vii-xii.
A biographical and critical study of Brand in which Penzler discusses the circumstances of the writing of this novel, her life and other writings, and the film based on Green for Danger.

E235. _____. "The Works of Christianna Brand." In Brand (E229), pp. 256-60.
An annotated bibliography of her novels and short story collections. Superseded by Briney (E233).

BRAND, MAX

Ref: Hubin 2, TCCMW, EMD, ABMI; Argosy, 10 Dec 32.

E236. Clark, Bill. "Max Brand and the Mystery Story." TAD 2 (1968/69):255. Bibliographic notes on Brand's mystery fiction.

E237. Easton, Robert. Max Brand: The Big "Westerner". Norman: The Univ. of Oklahoma Press, 1970. xii, 330pp. Illus. Bibliog. Index.
This is a biography of Frederick Faust, the incredibly prolific writer of Westerns, historical romances, crime and spy fiction, the Dr. Kildare stories, plays, and poetry, who published more than 30 million words during his career. His crime fiction is mentioned in a number of places in the biography, with occasional quotations from contemporary reviews. "A Faust Bibliography" (pp. 273-301) lists all of Faust's published work through 1969, magazine stories and books under all bylines, in a single chronological listing. (This bibliography was based on a Faust index compiled by William J. Clark from original sources, supplemented by material from papers of the Faust family and of Faust's agent.) There is also a filmography and an excellent index. (REB)

E238. Herzog, Evelyn. "Young Doctor Kildare." TMF 7:2 (March/April 83):2-10. On detective story elements in the Kildare medical series.

E239. Nolan, William F. "Max Brand--Pulp King." With "Postscript: Max Brand's Pulp Fiction Characters." Xenophile 32 (May/June 77): pp. 2-12.
Biography with brief critical postscript. This list includes series for detective pulp magazines.

E240. Richardson, Darrell C., editor & compiler. Max Brand, The Man and His Work: Critical Appreciations and Bibliography. Los Angeles, CA: Fantasy Publishing Company, Inc, 1952. 198pp. Illus.
The first part of this book consists of nine biographical essays, memoirs and appreciations of Frederick Faust (Max Brand and some 18 other pseudonyms) by the compiler, John L. Schoolcraft, Steve Fisher, William F. Nolan, and others. Faust/Brand was and is best known as a writer of Westerns and as the creator of Dr. Kildare, but contributed a considerable amount of spy and crime fiction to both pulp and slick magazines. At least ten crime novels have been published in book form. This crime fiction is mentioned in Nolan's brief article, "Interesting Facts about Faust's Prolific Production" (pp. 93-103), and is listed in the "Bibliography of the Works of Frederick Faust" which constitutes the second part of the book (pp. 129-98). Published books are arranged alphabetically by pseudonym and cross-indexed by title. Magazine works are arranged according to the magazine in which each work first appeared. Series characters, book publications, and changes of byline are noted. (REB)

BRANDON, JOHN G.

Ref: Hubin 2, TCCMW, ABMI.

See also: D246, D272.

BRANSON, H. C.

Ref: Hubin 2, TCCMW, EMD, CC, ABMI.

BRAUN, LILLIAN JACKSON

Ref: Hubin 2, TCCMW.

BREAN, HERBERT

Ref: Hubin 2, TCCMW, EMD, CC, ABMI.

BREEN, JON L.

Ref: EMD, ABMI.

Int: EQMM, June 79, pp. 57-58.

See also: C127.

E241. Greene, Doug(las). "Jon L. Breen and the Tradition of Parody." TPP 5:3 (May/June 83):15-18, 22.
On Breen's Hair of the Sleuthhound (1982) as one of only three volumes of successful mystery parodies known to Greene. The others are John Riddell's John Riddell Murder Case (1930) and I*n Fl*m*ng's Alligator (1962).

BRETT, SIMON

Ref: Hubin 2, TCCMW.

Int: EQMM, Aug 79, pp. 107-108.

BREWER, GIL

Ref: Hubin 2, TCCMW, SN, ABMI.

Int: PQ 3:4 (Wtr 80):6-11.

E242. Barson, Michael. "Gil Brewer's Fables of Evil Women, Driven Men and Doom." PQ 3:4 (Wtr 80):3-5.
Short essay on Brewer's fiction. Barson cites Cain and Spillane as influences but thinks that the fiction really reminds "of nothing so much as Gil Brewer." With an interview (pp. 6-11) and a checklist of Brewer's paperback originals. Photo and reproductions of paperback covers.

BRIDGE, ANN

Ref: Hubin 2, TCCMW, ABMI.

E243. Bridge, Ann. "Writing Thrillers." In Facts and Fictions: Some Literary Recollections. NY: McGraw-Hill, 1968.
Discussion of the mystery thriller part of her output, by a prolific writer who is the wife of a British diplomat. Not seen. (REB)

BRIDGES, VICTOR

Ref: Hubin 2, TCCMW, CC, ABMI.

BRITTAIN, WILLIAM

Ref: TCCMW, ABMI.

BROCK, LYNN

Ref: Hubin 2, TCCMW, EMD, CC, ABMI.

BRONSON, F. W.

Ref: Hubin 2, ABMI; UN 2:3 (1949):6-7 (photo).

BROOKS, EDWY SEARLES

Ref: Hubin 2, TCCMW, EMD, AMBI(S).

See also: D25, D222, D252, D289.

E244. Blythe, Robert C. A Bibliography of the Writings of Edwy Searles Brooks. Privately printed, 1971. 72pp.

Edy Searles Brooks was a very prolific writer of English school stories as well as the creator of Ironsides Cromwell of the Yard and the Saint-like adventurer, Norman Conquest. The exploits of these last two gentlemen were published under his pen names "Victor Gunn" and "Berkeley Gray." This extensive bibliography of his periodical and book appearances centers, and rightly so, on his school stories, but his mysteries are not slighted. The miscellaneous information in Part Three relates entirely to the world of the St. Franks school and includes illustrations taken from the magazines in which the stories appeared. His earliest story was published in 1907, his last in 1966, although his wife and son continued the Norman Conquest series and wrote two novels (Conquest Calls the Tune and Conquest in Ireland) using the "Berkeley Gray" signature. A remarkable piece of research, this bibliography should be of interest to anyone who is a student of the British thriller between the wars. (JRC; TAD 5 (1971-72):162)

BROWN, CARTER

Ref: Hubin 2, TCCMW, SN, ABMI.

BROWN, CHARLES BROCKDEN

Ref: Hubin 2, EMD, CC, ABMI.

E245. Bernard, Kenneth. "Edgar Huntley: Charles Brocken Brown's Unsolved Murder." Library Chronicle (University of Pennsylvania) 33 (1967):30-53.

An attempt to integrate what many critics of Brown's novel Edgar Huntley have seen as two irreconcilable plots, the Huntley-Clithero and Huntley-Indian sections. Bernard does not discuss the novel as a prototype of the detective novel but the subjects of theft, murder and pursuit are discussed..

E246. Christensen, Peter J. "The First Locked-Room Mystery? Charles Brockden Brown's Wieland." TAD 10 (1977):368-69.

Christensen believes this novel, published in 1798, may have influenced Poe. It has been established that Poe had read Brown and Christensen sees the general influence in the writers' common interest in Gothic terror, morbidity and the psychology of characters placed in extreme situations. Christensen discusses the locked-room device in Brown's novel and while he does not claim a specific influence of Poe on Brown does build a convincing case to demonstrate the use of the locked room convention prior to Poe.

E247. Hemenway, Robert E. and Dean H. Keller. "Charles Brockden Brown, America's First Important Novelist: A Checklist of Biography and Criticism." PBSA 60 (July/Sept 66):349-63.

According to Parker (E249), the most extensive bibliography of biography and criticism to date.

E248. Hobson, Robert W. "Voices of Corwin and Other Mysteries in Charles Brockden Brown's Wieland." Early American Fiction 10 (1975):307-309.

Of marginal interest. The "mysteries" are not specifically detective fiction elements.

E249. Parker, Patricia L. Charles Brockden Brown: A Reference Guide. Boston: G. K. Hall, 1980. ix-xxv, 132pp. Author index and a subject and title index.

An annotated bibliography of critical writings on Brown and his work, arranged chronologically. Some general references to "mystery" and "mysteries" but no publication describing Brown as a precursor of modern/mystery detective fiction is cited. Passim for references to Brown as a writer of American Gothic fiction. The following items may be of some relevance to genre fiction: Prescott, 1834.4; Beers, 1887.5; Newcomber, 1901.4; Nye, 1970.11; Lewis, 1977.7.

E250. Witherington, Paul. "Charles Brockden Brown: A Bibliographical Essay." Early American Literature 9 (Fall 1974): 164-87.
Annotated bibliography of primary sources, and of biography and criticism.

BROWN, FREDRIC

Ref: Hubin 2, TCCMW, EMD, CC, ABMI; UN 1:3 (1948):6-7; UN 1:7 (1948):6-7; UN 2:9 (1950):6-7; UN 3:6 (1951):10-11; UN 3:8 (1951):4-5; UN 4:1 (1951):8-9; UN 4:4 (1951):6-7, 14 (includes profile by Beth Brown); UN 4:10 91952):4-15, 16 (numerous photos with articles).

E251. Altshuler, Harry. "The Early Career of Fredric Brown." In Baird (E252), pp. 23-24. An earlier version was published, in French, in Les Amis du crime no. 3 (Spring 1979).
Brief article about Brown's early career in the pulps, introduction to science fiction, and first few hardcover novels. Altshuler was Brown's first literary agent. The version of the article in Baird is rewritten by Alshuler from the original correspondance with French editor Jean-Jacques Schleret, and contains an additional lengthy footnote.(REB)

E252. Baird, Newton. A Key to Fredric Brown's Wonderland. A Study and an Annotated Bibliographical Checklist by Newton Baird. With Reminiscences by Elizabeth Brown and Harry Altshuler and "It's Only Everything" by Fredric Brown. Georgetown, CA: Talisman Literary Research, Inc., (Nov) 1981. 63pp. Edition limited to 360 copies. Index, pp. 54-63.
Brief analytical study of Brown's work, chronology of his life and career, reminiscences by his widow and first literary agent, and an extensive annotated bibliography of all of Brown's work, including reprint editions and foreign-language translations. Although the title essay is separate from Baird's long study "Paradox and Plot" (E253) and states some opinions and conclusions different from those in this earlier study, the checklist is a revision and expansion of the one published in TAD. The book is illustrated with 20 photographs, including reproductions of book and magazine covers featuring Brown's work. Contents: title essay by Newton Baird, pp. 9-15; Chronology of Fredric Brown, pp. 16-19; Elizabeth C. Brown, "Fredric Brown, My Husband," pp. 20-22 (E257); Harry Altshuler, "The Early Career of Fredric Brown," pp. 23-24 (E251); Fredric Brown, "It's Only Everything," pp. 25-26 (E255); Newton Baird, "An Annotated Bibliographical Checklist of Fredric Brown's Writing," pp. 27-53; Index, pp. 54-63. (REB)

E253. ______. "Paradox and Plot: The Fiction of Fredric Brown." A six-part essay and bibliography appearing in TAD, as follows: 9 (1975/76):282-88; 10 (1977):33-38, 85-87, 151-59, 249-60, 370-75; 11 (1978):86-91, 102.
As Robert Briney points out in his annotation for Baird (E252), this essay is a different one from the 1981 Talisman Press publication although the later checklist is a revision and expansion of the TAD series material.

E254. Barzun, Jacques, and Taylor, Wendell Hertig. "Introduction." In The Deep End (NY, 1952), by Fredric Brown. "Crime Fiction 1950-1975" (B18).

E255. Brown, Fredric. "It's Only Everything." In Baird (E252), pp. 25-26. Originally published in Goliard (fanzine published for Spectator Amateur Press Society by Karen Anderson), April 1965.
Brief autobiographical article on the foundations of Brown's atheism. (REB)

E256. ______. "Où trouvez-vous vos intrigues |Where do you get your plots|?" Translated by Gérard de Chergé. In Polar 23, pp. 22-26. The source for this article is not given.
A business-like account of plot construction in which Brown takes his initial idea and adds to it to arrive eventually at a completed story.

E257. Brown, Elizabeth C. "Fredric Brown, My Husband." In Baird (E252), pp. 20-22. Version, in French, published in Les Amis du crime, no. 3 (Spring 1979).
Brief interview conducted via letter by editor Jean-Jacques Schleret, focusing on Brown's life, his and his wife's opinions of his work, favorite stories, work habits, personal qualities. (REB)

E258. Deloux, Jean-Pierre. "Mouvement Brownien |Brownian Movement|." Polar 23, pp. 5-14.
A dense thematic study of Brown's work, in particular the element of time which Deloux examines closely in the seven novels of the Ed and Am Hunter series. Deloux also discusses the search for the self and the interior spiritual voyage which Deloux compares to the medieval epic romances.

E259. "Dossier Fredric Brown." Polar 23 (15 April 82).
Contents: Jean-Pierre Deloux, "Mouvement Brownien," pp. 5-14 (E258); Elizabeth C. Brown, "Fredric Brown, mon mari," pp. 15-21 (E257); Fredric Brown, "Où trouvez-vous vos intrigues?," pp. 22-26 (E256); Jean-François Naudon, "Bibliographie de Fredric Brown," pp. 41-63 (E264); Jean-Jacques Schleret and Newton Baird, "Filmographie de Fredric Brown," pp. 64-68 (E266a); "Elements bio-bibliographiques," pp. 69-70.

E260. Goulart, Ron. "Introduction." In The Fabulous Clipjoint (Dutton, 1947), by Fredric Brown, pp. v-vii. Gregg Press Mystery Fiction Series (B134).

E261. Keating, H. R. F. "Introduction." In 4 Novels, by Fredric Brown, pp. v-ix. London: Zomba Books, 1983.
Excellent brief appreciation of Brown's writing. (REB)

E262. Lacassin, Fredric. "Fredric Brown ou Alice de ce côté du miroir |Fredric Brown or Alice on this side of the mirror|." In Lacassin (B201), Vol. II, pp. 255-67.
Lacassin sees Brown as a writer who emmeshes the reader in a dense action rather than in analysis and reflection. He also discusses the role of dreams and the fantastic and of the absurd in Brown's fictional universe.

E263. McMillan, Dennis. "The Uncollected fiction of Fredric Brown." CP? 3:1 (March 1981):15-19.
A list of stories not anthologized or expanded into novels. In CP? 3:2 (May 1981): 25-27, there is a list of republished and/or expanded material.

E264. Naudon, Jean-François. "Bibliographie de Fredric Brown." Polar 23, pp. 41-63. Ilus.
A list of the novels and short story collections followed by an alphabetical list of stories. Naudon acknowledges the earlier work of Newton Baird (E252, E253) and Jean-Jacques Schleret (E265).

E265. Nolan, William F. "Thoughts on Fredric Brown." TAD 5 (1971/72):191-93.
A checklist of Brown's books with some biographical comments by Nolan.

E266. Schleret, Jean-Jacques. "Fredric Brown." Les Amis du crime 3 (circa 1979).
Not seen, but one in a series of excellent bibliographies of American and English writers published by this French fanzine.

E266a. Schleret, Jean-Jacques and Newton Baird. "Filmographie de Fredric Brown." Polar 23, pp. 64-68.
A filmography that includes adaptations of Brown's work for both the movies and television.

BROWNE, HOWARD

Ref: Hubin 2, EMD, SN, ABMI.

E267. Browne, Howard. "A Profit without Honor." Amazing Science Fiction Stories 58:1 (May 84):71-81.
Although much of this entertaining essay by Browne is devoted to his association with Raymond A. Palmer, editor of Amazing Stories during the heady years of the Richard S. Shaver controversy, Browne also describes how he was hired as editor of Mammoth Detective and how he wrote and published under Mickey Spillane's byline the story "The Veiled Lady." An informative behind-the-scenes evocation of the pulp years.

E268. Lewis, Caleb. "Interview with Howard Browne." TAD 11 (1978):172-76. Photo and illustration.
Browne talks about the series of private eye novels featuring investigator Paul Pine which he published in the 1950s under the pseudonym of John Evans. Since 1957, Browne has been living in Los Angeles and working as a screenwriter but he tells interviewer Lewis that he is writing a fifth Paul Pine novel (The Paper Gun) and discusses the book in general terms.

E269. ______. "The Return of Paul Pine." TAD 11 (1978):79-85.
Lewis announces the imminent publication of a fifth Paul Pine novel, by Howard Browne and uses it as the occasion to review the earlier novels in the series. However, the book had not been published as of 1983.

E270. Sandoe, James. "The Reviewer at Work." TAD 11 (1978):84-85.
Sandoe offers an appreciative evaluation of the Paul Pine series and includes his working notes for reviews of three of the series novels.

BRUCE, GEORGE

Ref: Hubin 2; Argosy, 22 June 35.

BRUCE, JEAN

Ref: Hubin 2, CC.

E271. Dukeshire, Theodore P. "Jean Bruce." DAST 6:1 (1973):7-9.
Brief description with checklist of the works of Jean Bruce (Jean-Alexandre Brochet). (IH)

E272. Tourteau, Jean-Jacques. "Valse viennoise pour OSS 117." In Tourteau (B408), pp. 318-322.
Analysis of a Bruce novel.

BRUCE, JOSETTE

Int: MM 303, May 73.

BRUCE, LEO

Ref: Hubin 2, TCCMW, CC, ABMI; Cannon, AHMM 28-10 (Mid-Sep 83):70-72.

E273a. Adey, R. C. S. "My Favourite Detectives. 3. Sergeant Beef by Leo Bruce." TMRN 5:3 (1971/72):20-22, 30. Illus.
A profile of Sergeant Beef and a list of the novels in which he has appeared, with short annotations.

E273b. Barzun, Jacques, and Taylor, Wendell Hertig. "Introduction." In _Furious Old Women_ (London, 1950) by Leo Bruce. "Crime Fiction 1950-1975" (B18).

BRUTON, ERIC

Ref: Hubin 2, TCCMW, CC, ABMI.

BUCHAN, JOHN

Ref: Hubin 2, TCCMW, EMD, CC, ABMI.

See also: C540, C541.

E274. Binyon, T. J. "Introduction." In _The Courts of Morning_ (Hodder, 1929), by John Buchan. "Classic Thrillers Series." London: John Dent, 1983. Paperback.

E275. Blanchard, Robert G. _The First Editions of John Buchan: A Collector's Bibliography_. Hamden, CT: Archon Books, 1981. xi, 284pp.
Supersedes Hanna (E287). _Review_: PBSA 77:1 (1983):97-98.

E276. Buchan, John. _Pilgrim's Way: An Essay in Recollection_. Boston: Houghton, Mifflin, 1940. 336pp. Index.
Autobiography, completed only a week before the author's death. (REB)

E277. ______. _The Thirty-Nine Steps_. Mystery Library series (B270) no. 8. 1978. _Contents_: Michael Gilbert, "Introduction," pp. vii-xiv (life and writings); _The Thirty-Nine Steps_, pp. 1-158; Janet Adam Smith, "List of Books by John Buchan," pp. 161-65 (a chronological bibliography); "Reviews of _The Thirty-Nine Steps_," pp. 166-68; "In Memoriam," p. 169 (cartoon from _Punch_, 1940); J. Randolph Cox, "John Buchan: A Philosophy of High Adventure," pp. 170-84 (E280); Robert A. Harris & Michael S. Lasky, "The Films of Alfred Hitchcock," pp. 186-89 (excerpt from _The Films of Alfred Hitchcock_, Lyle Stuart, 1976); François Truffaut, "An Interview with Alfred Hitchcock," pp. 190-95; Contemporary reviews of Hitchcock's version of _The Thirty-Nine Steps_, pp. 196-200; "Film Photos from _The Thirty-Nine Steps_," pp. 201-55; Review of 1960 film version of the novel, pp. 206-207.

E278. Cox, J. Randolph, compiler. "An Annotated Bibliography of Writings about John Buchan, Lord Tweedsmuir." _English Literature in Transition_ 9:5 (1966):241-91; 9:6 (1966):292-325.
A list of secondary material arranged alphabetically, by author.

E279. ______. "The Genie and His Pen: The Fiction of John Buchan." ELT 9:5 (1966):236-40.
A biography with a survey of his thrillers.

E280. ______. "John Buchan: A Philosophy of High Adventure." TAD 2 (1968/69):207-214; reprinted in Buchan (E277), pp. 170-84.
A biography with comments on Buchan's writing, especially on the writers who influenced him.

E281. Daniell, David. "Introduction." In Castle Gay (Hodder, 1930), by John Buchan. "Classic Thrillers Series." London: Dent, 1983. Paperback.

E282. ______. "The War and Richard Hannay." In The Interpreter's House, pp. 118-43. London: Thomas Nelson and Sons, 1975.
An essay on the Hannay spy-adventure series..

E283. ______. "The Modern Romances 1921-1936." In The Interpreter's House, pp. 144-70. London: Thomas Nelson and Sons, 1975.
Critical assessments of Buchan's fiction.

E285. "Dossier John Buchan." Polar 18 (April 81), pp. 3-29.
Contents: François Guérif, "Editorial," p. 3; Jean-Pierre Deloux, "Salut à un coureur d'aventures |Tribute to an adventurer|," pp. 4-12; J. F. Naudon and J. P. Deloux, "Bibliographie," pp. 12-16 (includes French editions); J. J. Schleret, "Filmographie de John Buchan," pp. 17-20; John Buchan, "Dr. Lartius," pp. 22-29 (short story, translated by Danièle Bondil).

E286. Dukeshire, Theodore F. "John Buchan." TAD 7 (1973/74):198-202.
A biography and a checklist of his writings.

E287. Hanna, Archibald. John Buchan, 1875-1940: A Bibliography. Hamden, CT: Shoe String Press, 1953. pp. xi, 135. Index. Introduction by Robert Metzdorf.
The bibliography is arranged in four sections: Books and Pamphlets, Contributions to Books, Contributions to Periodicals, and Writings about John Buchan. Not seen. (REB)

E288. John Buchan by His Wife and Friends. London: Hodder & Stoughton, 1977. 304pp. Index.
A collection of miscellaneous essays on Buchan's life.

E289. Johnson, Reginald Brimley. "John Buchan." In Some Contemporary Novelists (Men). Leonard Parsons, 1922; reprint, Freeport, NY: Books for Libraries Press, 1970. Not seen.

E290. Lambert, Gavin. "The Thin Protection. 1. John Buchan." In The Dangerous Edge (B215), pp. 79-104.
A psychological study of the writer with reference to his life and works.

E291. Panek, LeRoy L. "John Buchan." In The Special Branch (B303), pp. 39-67.
The influence of schoolboy fiction and detective fiction on Buchan's spy novels, with discussions of his protagonists and suspense and adventure elements.

E292. Runnquist, Ake. "Generalagenten. Generalmajor, Sir Richard Hannay en av de klassika förebilderna till dagens agenter |Major general sir Richard Hannay, one of the classic models for today's agents|." Jury 4:3 (1975):18-21. (MS)

E293. Smith, Janet Adam. John Buchan. London: Rupert Hart-Davis, 1965; NY: Little, Brown, 1965.
See esp. pp. 251-98 where Smith discusses Buchan's stories of adventure and suspense. Review: J. R. Cox in English Literature in Transition 9:1 (1966):49-50.

E294. ______. John Buchan and His World. London: Thames and Hudson, 1979. Illus.
A biographical study of Buchan and his times in the format of a family/portrait album.

E295. Turnbaugh, Roy. "Images of Empire: George Alfred Henty and John Buchan." JPC 9 (1975/76):734-40.
Includes some comments on the Hannay novels.

E296. Usborne, Richard. "John Buchan." In Usborne (B420), pp. 81-130.
Essays on Buchan's "shockers," with studies of Hannay, Sandy Arbuthnot and Edward Leithen.

E297. Voorhees, Richard J. "Flashman and Richard Hannay." Dalhousie Review 53 (Spring 73):113-20.
A study of George MacDonald Fraser's Flashman and Buchan's Richard Hannay. According to Voorhees, these series novels have some international intrigue elements but are more properly identified as anti-romantic thrillers.

E298. ______. "John Buchan Today: The Richard Hannay Novels." University of Windsor Review, Spring 74, pp. 30-39.
Buchan's Hannay novels may be seen in part as exercises in nostalgia, with the character of Hannay, in spite of its English schoolboy characteristics, embodying noble qualities in contrast to the contemporary anti-hero's loss of these qualities.

BUCKLEY, WILLIAM F., JR.

Ref: Hubin 2, ABMI.

Int: NYTBR, 30 March 80, p. 32 (photo).

See also: C735.

BUDE, JOHN

Ref: Hubin 2, TCCMW, CC.

BULLETT, GERALD

Ref: Hubin 2, CC.

E299. Barzun, Jacques, and Taylor, Wendell Hertig. "Preface" to The Jury (London, 1935), by Gerald Bullett. In A Book of Prefaces (B17), pp. 25-26.

BURGESS, GELETT

Ref: Hubin 2, TCCMW, EMD, CC, ABMI.

BURKE, JOHN F.

Ref: Hubin 2, TCCMW, ABMI.

BURKE, THOMAS

Ref: Hubin 2, TCCMW, EMD, CC, ABMI.

See also: C492.

E300. Bronner, Milton. "Burke of Limehouse." Bookman 46 (Sept 1917):15-17. Literary profile in praise of Burke's style as demonstrated in a thin volume of poetry and especially Limehouse Nights. Included are plot summaries to several of the stories. Bronner treats Burke seriously, calling his subjects brutal, his prose poetic, and his style as powerful and forceful as Kipling's. This is a refreshing view of a writer often accused of writing Yellow Peril fiction. (GG)

E301. Ferguson, Malcolm M. "Thomas Burke of Limehouse." Romantist 2 (1978):41-42; reprint of 1950 article (source not located). Not seen.

E302. "A New Master of the Mystery and Romance of London's Underworld." Current Opinion 63:5 (Nov 1917):337.
Review-essay of Burke's Limehouse Nights by a critic who defends his own opinion by citing excerpts from British and American newspaper reviews. States that Burke's book gives the best evocation of London's slums since Arthur Morrison's Tales of Mean Streets but adds that Burke relied too heavily on exotic atmosphere and at times descended into "moth-eaten melodrama." Illus. (GG)

E303. Seldes, Gilbert Vivian. "Rediscovery and Romance." The Dial 63 (July 1917):65-67.
Review-essay of Burke's Limehouse Nights and his London autobiography Nights in Town. States that Burke "never quite succeeds" with his tales of Chinatown in the former book, adding that he exaggerates the strangeness of people in the tales. Calls Burke's books "at once vigorous and wanton" but concludes that they are wonderful to read. This piece serves to point up the difference between criticism of a writer from without the genre of crime fiction, and criticism within the genre. Many genre critics approve of Burke's evocation of the mood of Chinatown, though they may admit that Burke exaggerates. (GG)

BURLEY, W. J.

Ref: Hubin 2, TCCMW, EMD, CC, ABMI.

BURNETT, W. R.

Ref: Hubin 2, TCCMW, EMD, SN, ABMI; UN 1:12 (1949):6-7; UN 5:2 (1952):8-9 (photos).

Int: Mystery 3:2 (Sept 81):26-26 (photos); Polar 15 (Nov 80):10-18; Film Comment 19:1 (1983):59-68, 70.

E304. "Dossier W. R. Burnett." Polar 15 (Nov 80):4-38.
Contents: Jean-Pierre Deloux, "Dossier W. R. Burnett," pp. 4-9 (general survey of his fiction); "Entretien avec William Riley Burnett," pp. 10-18 (interview); Claude Benoit, "Filmographie de William R. Burnett," pp. 19-24 (illustrated with numerous stills); W. R. Burnett, "Voyageurs sans bagages," pp. 26-35 (short story, translated by Jean-Paul Gratias); J. J.

Schleret, "Bibliographie de William Riley Burnett," pp. 36-38.

E305. Mate, Ken, and McGilligan, Pat. "Burnett." Film Comment 19:1 (1983):59-68, 70. Photos.
Filmography compiled by Dennis L. White. Biographical introduction and lengthy comments by Burnett on his writing for books and films in the course of an interview conducted in January 1981.

BURNS, REX

Ref: Hubin 2, TCCMW, SN, ABMIS; The Writer 90:7 (July 77):14-17 (on police procedurals); The Writer 94:3 (March 81):11-14 (procedurals).

Int: The Bloomsbury Review (Denver) 2:2 (Feb/March 82):21, 23-24.

BURTIS, THOMSON

Ref: Hubin 2, ABMI; Argosy, 15 Aug 31.

BURTON, MILES. See RHODE, JOHN

BUSBY, ROGER

Ref: Hubin 2, TCCMW.

BUSH, CHRISTOPHER

Ref: Hubin 2, TCCMW, EMD, CC, ABMI(S).

See also: E701.

BUTLER, GWENDOLINE

Ref: Hubin 2, TCCMW, CC, ABMI(S).

BUTOR, MICHEL

Ref: Hubin 2, TCCMW, ABMI.

E306. Delcourt, Xavier. "Pour Michel Butor, les frontières entre science-fiction et littérature tendent à s'effacer |For Michel Butor, the frontiers between science fiction and literature tendent to disappear|." Quinzaine littéraire no. 225, 16-31 Jan 76, pp. 5-7.
In the course of an interview in which Butor discusses contemporary science fiction, he talks about classic and hard-boiled detective fiction, the importance of série noire and the detective/investigator as a scientist of sorts.

E307. O'Donnell, Thomas D. "Michel Butor's Passing Time and the Detective Hero." In MDA 1973 (B3), pp. 211-20.
Crime, the detective and detection in Butor's novel.

CAILLOU, ALAN

Ref: Hubin 2, TCCMW, SN.

CAIN, JAMES M.

Ref: Hubin 2, TCCMW, EMD, CC, ABMI.

See also: E1879.

Int: Akron Beacon Journal, 21 July 74 (rpt. in Authors in the News, I, p. 84); Film Comment, May/June 76, pp. 50-57; NYTBR, 13 May 62, p. 8; TAD 16 (1983):4-21 (includes biographical notes on individuals mentioned by Cain and a bibliography; conducted by John Carr).

E308. Cain, James M. "Preface (1942)." In Three of a Kind, by James M. Cain, pp. vii-xv. NY: Knopf, 1944.
Cain writes about his early failure at writing, his meeting and association with screenwriter Harry Vincent, and his opinion of the three works (Double Indemnity, Career in C-Major and Serenade) reprinted in this anthology.

E309. Deloux, Jean-Pierre. "Qu'as-tu fait de ton frère |What have you done with your brother|?" Polar 21 (Oct 81), pp. 4-9.
A study of Cain's work, with frequent references to statements by Cain and by other critics.

E310. "Dossier James M. Cain." Polar 21 (Oct 81):3-36. Illustrated.
Contents: François Guérif, "Editorial," p. 3; Jean-Pierre Deloux, "Qu'as-tu fait de ton frère," pp. 4-9 (E309); Jean-François Naudon, "Bibliographie: James Mallahan Cain (1/7/1892-27/10/1977)," pp. 10-16 (illustrated with paperback cover reproductions; French, English and American editions); François Guérif, "James Cain et le cinéma," pp. 17-23; François Guérif, "Filmographie," pp. 24-26; François Forestier and François Guérif, "Entretien avec Bob Rafelson," pp. 27-29 (interview with American director of 1980 film version of The Postman Always Rings Twice); James M. Cain, "Une fille dans la tempête," pp. 30-36 (French translation, by Frédérique Brengues, of Cain's "The Girl in the Storm").

E311. Durham, Philip. "James M. Cain's Struggle with Style." Neuphilologische Mitteilungen 57:9 (1956):133-48.
The importance of Cain's assertion that he found his writing style in the "West" and the extent of his work's relationship to the American frontier.

E312. Ellison, Harlan. "Introduction." In Hard Cain, stories by James M. Cain. "Gregg Press Mystery Fiction Series" (B134).

E313. Fine, David M. "James M. Cain and the Los Angeles Novel." American Studies 20 (Spring 79):25-34.
A discussion of the pessimistic vision of Cain in the three Los Angeles Novels (The Postman Always Rings Twice, Mildred Pierce and Double Indemnity) and of the death of the American dream in Southern California. Fine also talks about the tradition of the American "bitch" in the fiction of the 20s, the symbolic use of automobiles and architecture and the gangster "tough guy" in films and fiction.

E314. Frohock, William M. "The Tabloid Tragedy of James M. Cain." In The Novel of Violence in America 1920-1950. Dallas, TX: Southern Methodist University Press, 1950. In the revised edition of this book (1957), the material in this chapter was incoporated into the introduction, pp. 13-22.
Frohock sees Cain's work as a "bourgeois tragedy," exploiting the reader and the "climate of sensibility" which produced the best novels of Faulkner and Hemingway.

E315. Hagemann, E. R., and Durham, Philip C. "James M. Cain, 1922-1958: A Selected Checklist." BoB 23:3 (Sept/Dec 60):57-61.
Covers primary material: articles, plays, short stories, novels, and foreign translations of his works.

E316. Hoopes, Roy. "An Appreciation of James M. Cain." New Republic, 22 July 78, pp. 23-6. Photo.
A survey of Cain's fiction.

E317. ______, ed. The Baby in the Icebox...and other short fiction by James M. Cain. NY: Holt, Rinehart and Winston, 1981. 312pp.
An introduction and notes on Cain's life and works. The anthology collects the "best" of his short fiction and includes one novella, "Money and the Woman" ("The Embezzler").

E318. ______. Cain. NY: Holt, Rinehart and Winston, 1982. xvi, 684pp. Index. Extensive notes and bibliography of primary sources.
Hoopes interviewed Cain in the final years of his life and this massive biography is based on the interviews and research. Reviews: NYTBR, 28 Nov 82, pp. 13, 26; NYRB, 3 Feb 83, pp. 21-25.

E319. ______. "Hack Slays Movie Colony." American Film 7:1 (Oct 81):53-56, 84. 4 photos.
An account of Cain's screenwriting career and the novels he wrote while in California. (REB)

E320. ______. "Raising Cain." West Coast Review of Books, Oct 81. Not seen.

E321. Madden, David. "James M. Cain's The Postman Always Rings Twice and Albert Camus' L'Etranger." Papers on Language and Literature 6 (Fall 70): 407-19.
Madden cites a number of French writers (including Sartre) who believe Cain's Postman may have influenced Camus and then proceeds to compare the two novels to identify the influence. His conclusion is that if Camus did use Cain's novel as a model, he transformed it into "something finer."

E322. ______. James M. Cain. Twayne's U. S. Author Series 171. NY: Twayne, 1970. 200pp. Selective bibliography of primary and secondary sources, with annotations, and an index.
A fine bio-critical assessment of Cain's writing in the context of other American and European work of the period. Also provides a perspective on changing critical attitudes toward Cain and other writers of popular literature. One of the earliest--and still one of the best--studies on a writer associated with the hard-boiled school of the 20s and 30s.

E323. ______. "James M. Cain and the Pure Novel." The University Review 30:2 (Winter 1963):143-8. Followed by: "The 'Pure' Novel and James M. Cain." The University Review 30:3 (Spring 64): 235-9.
Madden tries to extend the concept of "pure" poetry associated with writers like Mallarmé and Valéry to Cain's novels with generally unsatisfying results. The concept of a pure literature is not clearly defined by Madden but is usually understood as related to the ideal of a "harmonious" beauty in the plastic arts. Madden is trying to shift critical focus from Cain's sensationalism to an appreciation of his fiction as carefully crafted, self-contained works of art. He sees the novels not as works that engage us emotionally but as objects which we admire with some detachment. An esthetician's view of Cain.

E324. ______. "James M. Cain and the Tough Guy Novelists of the 30s." In The Thirties: Fiction, Poetry and Drama, edited by Warren French, pp. 63-71. Deland,FL: Everett Edwards, Inc., 1967.

A study of Cain's fiction (in particular, The Postman Always Rings Twice), the role of violence in his novels and in that of the hard-boiled school with its influence on European fiction, and the theme of the American dream gone sour. Passing references to Hammett, Chandler, Horace McCoy and the gangster cycle in 30s films.

E325. ______. "James M.Cain: Twenty-Minute Eggs of the Hard-Boiled School." JPC 1 (Winter 1967):178-92.
Madden describes the tough guy protagonist of the Black Mask writers of the thirties, placing him in the context of the historical development of the detective novel, and focuses on Cain for a succinct overview of his novels. He sees Cain as more interested in action associated with the crime "as it is being perpetrated" than with the classical technique of investigation and discovery.

E326. ______. "Morris' Cannibals, Cain's Serenade: The Dynamics of Style and Technique." JPC 8:1 (1974-75):59-70.
A classroom exercise in "understanding and a receptivity to the aesthetics of both serious and popular fiction." Also includes a discussion of point-of-view in Cain's fiction.

E327. Oates, Joyce Carol. "Man under Sentence of Death: The Novels of James M. Cain." In Madden (B239), pp. 110-28.
A superb examination of Cain and his "catering" to his audience by giving them versions of American mythologies in which uncontrolled desires provoke the antagonists into acts which threaten society and for which they must be punished. Oates does not see Cain as an "artist" writing literature but examines in detail Postman and Serenade which she thinks is Cain's best novel. Although some readers may be disturbed by her refusal to read Cain's fiction as literature, she is no less severe with Dostoesvsky (in a passing comment) and her analyses give more critical "weight" to Cain's fictions than many studies of more academically acceptable writers.

E328. Reck, Tom S. "James M. Cain's Los Angeles Novels." Colorado Quarterly 22 (Winter 74):375-87.
A study of Cain's sense of the "pure" novel, this time taken to be a fiction in which nothing extraneous intrudes. Reck discusses Cain's refusal of middle-class morality along with the role of seduction and amorality in the novels and the reader's uneasy relationship to them.

E329. Starr, Kevin. "It's Chinatown: James M. Cain." New Republic, 26 July 75, 31-32.
A terse but substantial introduction to Cain. Starr outlines his work and his relative importance in exposing the sordid reality behind the Southern California showfront.

E330. Wells, Walter. "The Postman and the Marathon." In Wells (B428), pp. 14-35.
A study of the "ties" between place (the "Southland") and fiction in Horace McCoy's They Shoot Horses, Don't They? and Cain's Postman. Wells finds that McCoy draws more richly from the region than Cain does and that that his novel is the better of the two. Essentially, however, the essay is a comparative study of thematic material, in particular that of dissolution and collapse as old values break down and relationships repeatedly fall apart and briefly reform until a final destruction.

E331. Wilson, Edmund. "The Boys in the Back Room: 1. James M. Cain." In his Classics and Commercials, pp. 19-22. NY: Farrar, Straus, 1950; London: W. H. Allen, 1951.

Wilson characterizes Cain as a "poet of the tabloids" and speaks of his "imagination" but Wilson's discussion of Cain's work is simplistic (weak men are dominated by strong women and led astray) and nothing in this short article--as Joyce Carol Oates has rightly pointed out (E327)--justifies Wilson's designation of Cain as a poet.

CAIN, PAUL

Ref: Hubin 2, SN.

E332. Faust, Irvin. "Afterword." To Paul Cain's Fast One, pp. 305-13. Carbondale: Southern Illinois Univ. Press, 1979.

Faust is particularly interested in Cain's career as a screenwriter and compares the novel to a good, tight script for a B movie. Faust sees in the unrelenting, "one-note" action the chief limitation of Fast One. Faust refers to the publication (in 1933) as coinciding with the rise of the Black Mask school. He does not seem aware--or does not mention--that the novel was first published in the Black Mask.

E333. Hagemann, E. R. "Introducing Paul Cain and His Fast One: A Forgotten Hard-Boiled Writer--A Forgotten Gangster Novel." TAD 12 (1979):72-76.

A biographical study of George Sims, who wrote for Black Mask as Paul Cain and for the movies as Peter Ruric. The first substantial look at this writer about whom very little is known and on whom the documentation is meager. Hagemann quotes from the Joseph T. Shaw correspondence file, from interviews and from newspaper and magazine reviews of Cain's novel and films.

CAIRD, JANET

Ref: Hubin 2, TCCMW, CC, ABMI.

CAMERON, OWEN

Ref: Hubin 2, SN; UN 2:5 (1950):6-7 (photo).

CAMPBELL, JOHN FRANKLIN

Ref: Lachman, TPP 2:3 (May/June 79):22.

CANDY, EDWARD

Ref: Hubin 2, TCCMW, CC, ABMI.

CANNAN, JOANNA

Ref: Hubin 2, TCCMW, CC, ABMI; UN 3:1 (1950):8-9.

See also: B349.

E334. Barzun, Jacques, and Taylor, Wendell Hertig. "Introduction." In The Body in the Beck (London, 1952), by Joanna Cannan. "Crime Fiction 1950-1975" (B18).

CANNING, VICTOR

Ref: Hubin 2, TCCMW, EMD, CC, ABMI.

CAPEK, KAREL

Ref: Hubin 2, CC, ABMI.

See also: E480.

E335. Harkins, William E. Karel Čapek. NY: Columbia Univ. Press, 1962. 193pp. Index. Some bibliography in end-of-chapter notes.
In Chapter 6, Harkins discusses a collection of stories (Wayside Crosses) which Čapek thought of as detective stories and which Harkins compares to Chesterton's use of the form as an allegory of the search for God. These are metaphysical and appear to be only marginally related to the genre. Tales from Two Pockets (Faber & Faber, 1932) consists of a selection of stories from two volumes originally published in Czech and some of the stories involve a crime and an investigation. Harkins discusses these in Chapter 3 (pp. 119-28) and calls them "police tales" more often concerned with "aspects of crime other than detection." Čapek is candid about police brutality in his native Czechoslovakia and the stories were criticized by "leftish" critics. It is Harkins' opinion that Čapek "humanized' the traditional tale and there are further references to Chesterton.

E336. Skvorecký, Josef. "A Discovery in Čapek." TAD 8 (1975):180-84.
An interpretation (with extensive, useful notes) of Čapek's story "The Footprint" as a tribute to E. A. Poe.

E337. Vey, Marc. "Une Source de Karel Čapek?" Revue des études slaves 36 (1959):59-63.
Vey believes that Čapek used O'Henry's cryptological story "Calloway's Code" as a basis for his story, "Professor Rouss' Experiment." Čapek may or may not have had access to the O'Henry story in its original form or in a Czech translation. Speculative and largely unsupported.

CAREY, BERNICE

Ref: Hubin 2; UN 3:12 (1951):4-5, 11; UN 4:6 (1952):6-7, 16 (photos).

E338. Amelin, Michel. "Bernice Carey." Enigmatika 24 (July 83), p. 10.
A short essay on Carey's The Reluctant Murderer (Doubleday, 1949).

E339. Boucher, Anthony. "Introduction." In The Missing Heiress (Doubleday, 1952), by Bernice Carey. NY: Mercury, n.d.

E340. ______. "Introduction." In The Frightened Widow (originally published as Their Nearest and Dearest, Doubleday, 1953), by Bernice Carey. NY: Mercury, 1954.

CARLE, C. E. See MORGAN, MICHAEL

CARLETON, MARJORIE

Ref: Hubin 2, CC; UN 2:10 (1950):6-7 (photo).

CARMICHAEL, HARRY

Ref: Hubin 2, TCCMW, CC, ABMI.

CARNAC, CAROL

Ref: Hubin 2, TCCMW, EMD, CC, ABMI; UN 1:12 (1949):4-5, 7; 4:3 (1951): 8-9 (photos).

CARR, A. H. Z.

Ref: Hubin 2, TCCMW, EMD, CC, ABMI.

E341. Barzun, Jacques, and Taylor, Wendell Hertig. "Introduction." In Finding Maubee (NY, 1971), by A. H. Z. Carr. "Crime Fiction 1950-1975" (B18).

CARR, GLYNN

Ref: Hubin 2, TCCMW, CC.

E342. Barzun, Jacques, and Taylor, Wendell Hertig. "Introduction." In Death Finds a Foothold (London 1961), by Glynn Carr. "Crime Fiction 1950-1975" (B18).

E343. Sarjeant, William A. S. "Detection among the Mountains: The Writings of Glyn Carr." TPP 4:5 (Sept/Oct 81):3-14.
An essay on the life and works of British writer Frank Showell Styles, author of 15 mysteries published from 1951 to 1969.

CARR, JOHN DICKSON (aka CARTER DICKSON)

Ref: Hubin 2, TCCMW, EMD, CC, ABMI(S).

See also: D437.

E344. Adey, R. C. S. "My Favorite Detectives: Sir Henry Merrivale." TMRN 3:2 (Dec 69):11-14.
A profile of Carter Dickson's detective with an annotated list of novels and collections of short stories in which he appeared.

E345. Bleiler, E. F. "Some Thoughts on Peacock Feet." TMF 6:3 (May/June 82):14-21.
A thoughtful essay on flaws in the plotting and characterization of Carr's The Peacock Feather Murders.

E346. Boucher, Anthony. "Introduction." In The Blind Barber (Harper, 1934), by John Dickson Carr. NY: Collier Books, 1962. Reprinted in Multiplying Villanies (B43), pp. 118-20.

E347. ______. "Introduction." In Hag's Nook (Harper, 1933), by John Dickson Carr. NY: Collier, 1963.

E348. Briney, Robert E. "The Books of John Dickson Carr/Carter Dickson: A Checklist." In Carr (E352), pp. 277-83.
Titles of British editions are given in brackets and the contents of short story collections are listed. Briney, in a letter, TAD 10 (1977):160, corrects errors in the checklist.

E349. ______. "Introduction: The Art of the Magician." In Carr (E352), pp. vi-xv.
Briney compares Carr's basic technique to that of the illusionist misdirecting the audience's attention. He then recounts Carr's biography and writing career to the time of the publication of The Crooked Hinge in 1938, including a profile of Gideon Fell who is based on the model of G. K. Chesterton.

E350. ______. "Notes for the Curious." In Carr (E352), pp. 274-76.
Notes on The Crooked Hinge.

E351. Busch, Lloyd. "A Checklist of the Paperback Editions of John Dickson Carr." CP? 2:2 (May 80):9-18. Illus.

E352. Carr, John Dickson. The Crooked Hinge. The Mystery Library (B270) 2. 1976.

Contents: Robert E.Briney: "Introduction: The Art of the Magician," pp. vi-xv (E349); The Crooked Hinge, pp. 1-273; "Notes for the Curious," pp. 274-76 (E350); "The Books of John Dickson Carr/Carter Dickson--A Checklist," pp. 277-83 (E348).

E353. Carr, John Dickson. (Address.) The Bookmark, Friends of the University of North Carolina, no. 38 (Sept 68), pp. 9-17. Introd. by Hugh Holman, pp. 7-8.

A survey of the detective fiction in which Carr discusses Poe, Conan Doyle, and the Detection Club (London).

E354. ______. The Door to Doom and Other Detections. Edited and with an introduction by Douglas G. Greene. NY: Harper & Row, 1980. 352pp.

An anthology of short stories, radio plays, Sherlockian parodies and essays (C158) by Carr, with a critical introduction (E362) and a bibliography (E360) of Carr's work by editor Greene.

E355. Endrèbe, Maurice Bernard. "Préface de La Chambre Ardente |Preface to The Burning Court|." Enigmatika 19 (June 81), p. 46. Originally published in Mystère Magazine, no. 271.

A history of the publishing and film fortunes of the French translation of Carr's novel, and a biocritical introduction of Carr for a non-specialist French audience.

E356. French, Larry L. "The Baker Street-Carrian Conection: The Influence of Sherlock Holmes on John Dickson Carr." Baker Street Journal 29:1 (March 79):6-10. Not seen.

E358. French, Larry L., ed. Notes for the Curious. A John Dickson Carr Memorial Journal. Carrian Press, 1978. Wraps. iv, 32pp. Limited to 500 numbered copies.

In spite of the editor's admiration for his subject and his knowledge of Carr's works, this chapbook is something of a slapdash affair, sloppily organized and often just as sloppily written. Its main virtue is that it collects, in one place, in addition to the editorial text, comments on Carr from a number of editors and critics, as well as some brief material by Carr himself. The checklist of Carr's works is rudimentary, dropping initial articles from most titles, omitting publishers, failing to distinguish between novels and shorter works, and ignoring British editions. The short alternate titles attached to most of the novels are, however, useful as reminders of "which case is which." Contents: R. E. Briney, "John Dickson Carr, 30 November 1906 - 27 February 1977," pp. 1-2 (from TAD 10:2); Larry L. French, "The Man Who Was John Dickson Carr," pp. 3-7 (biographical sketch; comments on Carr by other authors are quoted, and sometimes mis-quoted); J. D. Carr, "The Man Who Read (and Published) John Dickson Carr/Carter Dickson," pp. 8-11 (a patchwork of quoted comments by Carr and Ellery Queen; includes Carr's short essay from the dust-jacket of Night at the Mocking Widow); "Commentaries for the Curious," pp. 11-19 (Comments on Carr, some of them written especially for this chapbook, by Otto Penzler, Chris Steinbrunner, Marvin Lachman, Jon L. Breen, Robert Lewis Taylor, Michael Harrison, and others); "Carrian Canon for the Curious," pp. 20-26 (checklist of Carr's work, with capsule biographies of his 3 most famous detectives: Dr. Fell, H. M., and Bencolin); John Dickson Carr, "Epilogue: Culprit Confesses," pp. 27-28 (miscellanea); "The Carr Chronology," pp. 29-30 (chronological list of the high points of Carr's life and career). There is also a list of contributors and an Afterword by the editor. (REB)

E359. Greene, Douglas G. "Adolf Hitler and John Dickson Carr's Least-Known Locked Room." TAD 14 (1981):295-96.
JDC as a writer of war-time scripts for BBC.

E360. ______. "A Bibliography of the Works of John Dickson Carr." In Carr, The Door to Doom (E354), 327-52.
In addition to the novels, published under Carr's own name and pseudonyms, the bibliography includes short fiction, nonfiction articles and reviews, introductions to books by other authors, radio scripts, stage plays and adaptations. An indispensable critical tool.

E361. ______. "John Dickson Carr, Alias Roger Fairbairn, and the Historical Novel." TAD 11 (1978):339-41.
An essay on one of Carr's innovations, the detective novel with a historical setting.

E362. ______. "Introduction--John Dickson Carr: The Man Who Created Miracles." In Carr, The Door to Doom (E354), pp. 9-26.
A concise and wide-ranging essay on Carr's life and writing in which Greene discusses his innovations, his relationship to the traditional mystery novel, and his interest in the past and in historical subjects. An excellent introduction to the subject.

E363. ______. "Introduction: John Dickson Carr and the Radio Mystery." In Carr, The Dead Sleep Lightly, edited by Douglas Greene, pp. 1-11. Garden City, NY: Crime Club (Doubleday), 1983.
Survey of Carr's career as radio script writer for Suspense, Appointment with Fear and other series. Greene also provided short individual Prefaces to the nine radio scripts in this collection. (REB)

E364. ______. "John Dickson Carr on British Radio." TAD 12 (1979):69-71.
A chronological checklist of Carr's British radio plays.

E365. Herzel, Roger. "John Dickson Carr." In Minor American Novelists, edited by Charles Alva Hoyt, pp. 67-80. Carbondale, IL: Southern Illinois Univ. Press, 1970.
The first major discussion in print on Carr and still one of the best sources of informed commentary on this locked-room specialist. (REB)

E366. Kahn, Joan. "Introduction." In The Three Coffins (Harper, 1935), by John Dickson Carr, pp. v-vii. "Gregg Press Mystery Fiction Series" (B134).

E367. Kingman, James. "John Dickson Carr and the Aura of Genius." TAD 14 (1981):166-67.
A discussion of the "impossible gimmick" in Carr's The Crooked Hinge.

E368. Lachman, Marvin. "The Life and Times of Gideon Fell." TMF 2:3 (May 78):3-18.
A checklist of works in which the detective is Gideon Fell, with an addendum containing information on the elusive Mrs. Fell.

E369. Levinson, Richard and William Link. "Introduction." In The Department of Queer Complaints (Morrow, 1940), by "Carter Dickson." "Gregg Press Crime Fiction Series" (B134).

E370. Lithner, Klas. "Bravo, John Dickson Carr." DAST 14:2 (1981): 53-54. The historical background of the Bravo case, on which Carr based Below Suspicion. (MS)

E371. Lundin, Bo. "Den gamle mästaren |The old master|." Jury 1:3-4 (1972):16-18.
Carr's Sir Henry Merrivale. With checklist. (MS)

E372. Miller, Edmund. "Stanislaw Lem and John Dickson Carr: Critics of the Scientific World-View." TAD 14 (1981):341-3.
A brief, tenuous discussion linking two dissimilar writers on the basis of their common dissatisfaction with scientific rationalism.

E373. Narcejac, Thomas. "John Dickson Carr." In Narcejac (B287), pp. 127-42. An analysis of The Burning Court. Narcejac discusses Doyle and spiritualism as it affects Carr's work, and sees the obsessive use of the "locked-room" problem as a metaphore for the human body and the intrusion of the supernatural as a threat to the body.

E374. Nevins, Francis M., Jr. "The Sound of Suspense. John Dickson Carr as a Radio Writer." TAD 11 (1978):334-38. Illus.
A discussion with a checklist of the scripts Carr wrote for Suspense.

E375. Panek, LeRoy L. "John Dickson Carr." In Panek (B304), pp. 145-84. Carr's attempts to write the "perfect entertainment." Panek discusses the various detective series and analyzes recurrent plot structures in Carr's work.

E376. Sneary, Rick. "A John Dickson Carr Checklist." TMRN 3:4 (April 71):13-15.
An updating of a bibliography which Sneary originally compiled and published privately in 1966. Additions/corrections in letter, TMRN 4:1 (Oct 70):13-15.

E377. Taylor, Robert Lewis. "Profiles: Two Authors in an Attic." New Yorker, 8 Sept 51, pp. 39-44, 47-48; 15 Sept 51, pp. 36-40, 43-44, 46, 48.
An extensive profile of Carr based on interviews and research. There are comments on other writers and a mini-history of the genre. Informative and entertaining.

CARR, MARGARET

Ref: Hubin 2, TCCMW, ABMI.

CARROLL, JAMES

Ref: Hubin, ABMI.

Int: PW 221:23 (4 June 82):10-11 (photo).

CARSE, ROBERT

Ref: ABMI; Argosy, 1 March 30; 4 Jan 36.

CARTER, JOHN FRANKLIN. See "DIPLOMAT"

CARTER, NICK

Ref: Hubin 2, EMD, CC, ABMI.

See also: D131-D199.

CARTON, MARTIEN

E378. Genberg, Kjell E. "Deckaren i Holland |The detective novel in Holland|." Jury 9:2 (1980):43-46.
Woman author talks about her own works and Dutch crime fiction in general. (MS)

CARVIC, HERON

Ref: Hubin 2, TCCMW, CC, ABMI(S).

CASPARY, VERA

Ref: Hubin 2, TCCMW, EMD, ABMI(S).

See also: B309.

E379. Bakerman, Jane S. "Vera Caspary's Fascinating Females: Laura, Evvie and Bedelia." Clues 1:1 (Spring 80):46-52.
Character studies.

E381. Caspary, Vera. The Secrets of Grown-Ups. NY: McGraw-Hill, 1979. 287pp. Illus. Index.
Autobiography focusing mainly on personal matters; some mention of her writing and of other writers whom she knew. Breen 115. (REB)

CECIL, HENRY

Ref: Hubin 2, TCCMW, EMD, CC, ABMI(S).

CHAMBERLAIN, ANNE

Ref: Hubin 2, ABMIS; The Writer 90:8 (Aug 77):20-22, 29; The Writer 92:10 (Oct 79):12-14; The Writer 94:4 (Apr 81):13-16, 45.

CHANCE, JOHN NEWTON

Ref: Hubin 2, TCCMW, CC, ABMI(S).

CHANDLER, RAYMOND

Ref: Hubin 2, TCCMW, EMD, CC, SN, ABMI(S); The Writer 76:7 (July 63):13-16, 46 (excerpt from E397).

See also: B1, B79, B99, B190, B239, B310, B371, B429, C278, C404, E1873, E2110.

E382. Aldrich, Pearl G. "The Glimmer of Magic." PCS 1:1 (Winter 77):52-56.
Material from Chandler's letters arranged chronologically to "illuminate (his) philosophy of writing."

E383. Anderson, Stig. "Herr Marlowe och hans värld |Mr. Marlowe and his world|." DAST 6:3 (1973):19-22.
Chandler's realism. (MS)

E384. Arden, Leon. "A Knock at the Backdoor of Art: The Entrance of Raymond Chandler." In Benstock (B26), pp. 73-96.
A routine chronological survey of Chandler's novels.

E385. Barzun, Jacques. "The Illusion of the Real." In Gross (E409), pp. 159-63.
A critique of Chandler's "The Simple Art of Murder" (C168) to demonstrate that the hard-boiled mystery is no more realistic than the "tender" school Chandler chastized in his essay. Barzun also remarks on what he sees as the Marxist "flavoring" of the hard-boiled school.

E386. Barzun, Jacques, and Taylor, Wendell Hertig. Preface to The Lady in the Lake (NY, 1943), by Raymond Chandler. In A Book of Prefaces (B17), pp. 29-30.

E387. Becker, Jens P. "Murder Considered as One of the Fine Arts." Literatur in Wissenschaft und Unterricht 6 (March 73):31-42.
An analysis of Chandler's short story "I'll Be Waiting" in which Becker attempts to "work out some of the essential characteristics of Chandler and of the Black Mask school." Francis M. Nevins, Jr. is right to point out that "I'll Be Waiting" was first published, not in Black Mask, but in the Saturday Evening Post, 14 Dec 39, pp. 10-11, 72, 74-75, 78.

E388. Beekman, E. M. "Raymond Chandler and an American Genre." Massachusetts Review 14 (Winter 73):149-73.
Beekman sees Hammett as the first crime writer to revolt against the classic mystery but claims that Chandler is the better writer. A crowded study of Chandler's style, Philip Marlowe as a hero in the Romantic tradition, the metaphoric treatment of the American landscape and society, the melancholy tone of Chandler's work, and his successors. In an appendix, Beekman presents an annotated list of leading mystery writers and critics in several European countries. Beekman also claims --against the evidence of style, content and chronology--that Chandler and Hammett "fathered" modern procedural fiction and such diverse writers as Simenon, Freeling and Wahlöö.

E389. Binyon, T. J. "A Lasting Influence?" In Gross (E409), pp. 171-83.
The influence, direct and indirect, of Chandler on private eye fiction. Binyon thinks that as the influence has turned more recently to parody and pastiche it may be coming to an end in detective fiction; it may still, however, continue to exert some influence on the spy novel and the adventure story.

E390. Bishop, Paul. "The Longest Goodbye or the Search for Chandler's Los Angeles." Mystery 1:2 (March/April 80):33-36. Photos.
The search for Chandler landmarks in contemporary Los Angeles.

E391. Bruccoli, Matthew J. "Afterword: Raymond Chandler and Hollywood." In Chandler, The Blue Dahlia, pp. 129-37. Carbondale: Southern Illinois Univ. Press, 1976.
Chandler's career as a screenwriter.

E392. ______. Raymond Chandler: A Checklist. The Serif Series: no. 2. Kent, OH: Kent State Univ. Press, 1968. ix, 35pp.
Lists Chandler's books (including reprint editions) and the first appearances of his fiction, articles, reviews, verse, and miscellaneous prose. Now superseded by Bruccoli (E392). Breen 116. (REB)

E393. ______. Raymond Chandler: A Descriptive Bibliography. Pittsburgh Series in Bibliography, No. 11. Pittsburgh, PA: Univ. of Pittsburgh Press, 1979. xv, 146pp. Appendices. Index.
The first 106 pages are devoted to meticulously detailed descriptions of all books by Chandler, in all editions, with reproductions of the dustjackets and paperback covers, title pages, and copyright pages. The remainder of the bibliography lists first appearance contributions to books, and first periodical appearances of Chandler's fiction, nonfiction,

and verse. A separate section lists his screenplays. Breen 117. Review: PBSA 74:3 (1980):194-95. (REB)

E394. Bruccoli, Matthew, ed. Chandler Before Marlowe. Raymond Chandler's Early Prose and Poetry, 1908-12. Columbia: University of South Carolina Press, 1973. Foreword by Jacques Barzun. Also printed in a limited, boxed edition of 499 copies. The trade edition has a "Chandler Checklist" by Bruccoli not present in the limited edition.

A useful text for its view of Chandler as a writer a quarter of a century before he achieved fame with his detective fiction. Barzun finds some characteristics of the mature Chandler in these early works in his concern for style and his obsessive concentration on one or two ideas. Bruccoli also comments briefly on the problems involved in the editing of the texts in this anthology.

E395. Cawelti, John G. "Hammett, Chandler, and Spillane." In Cawelti (B69), pp. 162-91.

A discussion of the three writers to "examine some of (their) central differences...and to define more fully their individual characteristics and artistic significance."

E396. Chandler, Raymond. The Notebooks of Raymond Chandler and English Summer: A Gothic Romance. Edited and with a Foreword by Frank MacShane. NY: The Ecco Press, 1976; London: Weidenfeld & Nicolson, 1977. 113pp.

The longer portion of this book presents the contents of two notebooks of literary observations, clippings, story ideas, and miscellany which Chandler began compiling in the 1930s. Highlights include a Hemingway parody, some witty verses to a proofreader, "Twelve Notes on the Mystery Story," Chandler's farewell to film writing, and a review of a Fleming James Bond novel. Collectively these items provide invaluable insight into Chandler's attitudes and techniques. The book also includes five pages of photographs and the text of an early Chandler short story, illustrated by Edward Gorey. (REB)

E397. (Chandler, Raymond.) Raymond Chandler Speaking. Edited by Dorothy Gardiner and Kathrine Sorley Walker. Boston: Houghton Mifflin, 1962. London: Allison & Busby, 1983 (paperbound). 271pp. Index. Japanese edition, translated by Shunji Shimizu as Raymond Chandler Kataru. Tokyo: Hayakawa Shobo, 1967.)

A skillfully arranged volume of Chandler's correspondence, providing fresh evidence on every page that he was one of the last great letter-writers. Also included are a previously unpublished Chandler short story and a fragment of an unfinished Philip Marlowe novel. Breen 118. CC 2918. (REB)

E398. (Chandler, Raymond.) Selected Letters of Raymond Chandler. Edited by Frank MacShane. NY: Columbia Univ. Press, 1981. London: Jonathan Cape, 1981. Both editions: xx, 501pp. Index.

In spite of MacShane's statement, in his introduction, that "wherever possible, I have reproduced the entire letter," only about one-third of the letters are printed without significant cuts. Selections in Raymond Chandler Speaking (E397) included passages from 28 letters cut by MacShane and these cuts are damaging both to the context of certain letters and in the distorted view they give of Chandler's comments on mystery fiction and writers. When Chandler says something favorable about mysteries or mystery writers, MacShane usually cuts it; when

Chandler says something unfavorable, the comment is not edited. Annotations which might have been helpful are not supplied, while many of those which are prove to be irrelevant or obvious. What survives MacShane's cutting is entertaining and enlightening but it is unfortunate that editorial decisions were made which seriously compromise Chandler's opinions and his complex views. CC S139. Reviews: New Yorker, 8 March 82, pp. 138, 140-41; NYTBR, 15 Nov 81, pp. 7, 45-46. (Brian KenKnight)

E399. Chandler, Raymond and James M. Fox. Raymond Chandler and James M. Fox: A Correspondence. Santa Barbara, CA: Neville-Yellin, 1978. 66pp. Edition limited to 350 numbered copies.
Letters exchanged by Chandler and Fox, none previously published. (REB)

E400. Clark, Al Raymond Chandler in Hollywood. London & New York: Proteus, 1983. 160pp. Index. Filmography.
Clark went to Los Angeles and interviewed people involved in the production of Chandler's films and people who knew Chandler, and his narrative is a mixture of production information and film analysis. In his preface, Clark describes the sources he will be citing but there are no notes or bibliography. The illustrations include stills, lobbycards and other advertising material for the films.

E401. Conrad, Peter. "The Private Dick as Dandy." TLS, 10 Jan 78, p. 60.
Review-essay of Miriam Gross (E409) and Chandler (E396).

E402. Davies, Russell. "Omnes Me Impune Lacessunt." In Gross (E409), pp. 31-51.
Davies links the first person narrator (Marlowe) to Chandler and analyses the contradictory movements in the character's speech and actions and the writer's personality. The Chandler knight, as Davies reminds us, is often passive and Davies discusses the way he is treated by other people and his complex, often mocking, psychologically oblique reactions to them.

E403. "Dossier Philip Marlowe." Polar 13 (Aug 80), pp. 3-14.
On the character of Philip Marlowe and the screen versions of the Chandler novels. Illustrated with film stills. Contents: François Guérif, "Editorial," p. 3; Jean-Pierre Deloux, "'Trouble Is My Business'," pp. 4-10 (on the Marlowe character and persona); "Filmographie," pp. 11-13; "Bibliographie de Philip Marlowe," pp. 14-15 (bibliography of the fiction).

E404. Dove, George. "The Complex Art of Raymond Chandler." TAD 8 (1974/75):271-74.
Chandler's complex plot structures with innovations like the "residue of mystery" where a plot thread, introduced after the main plot, is unresolved and carried forward after its resolution.

E405. Durham, Philip. Down These Mean Streets A Man Must Go. Raymond Chandler's Knight. Chapel Hill: Univ. of North Carolina Press, 1963. viii, 173pp. Index, bibliography of secondary sources consulted and a chronological checklist of Chandler's work.
The first biographical/critical book on Chandler: knowledgeable, enthusiastic, and charming. (REB)

E406. ______. "Introduction." In Killer in the Rain, by Raymond Chandler, pp. vii-xii. Boston: Houghton Mifflin, 1964.

E408. Gilbert, Michael. "Autumn in London." In Gross (E409), pp. 103-14. Gilbert chronicles his friendship with Chandler and includes some excerpts from Chandler's letters to him.

E409. Gross, Miriam, ed. The World of Raymond Chandler. Introduction by Patricia Highsmith. London: Weidenfeld and Nicolson, 1977; NY: A & W Publishers, Inc., 1978. ix, 190 + 24pp. of photographs.
A useful compilation of thirteen essays and one interview covering the major aspects of Chandler's life and writing. Of the 24 pages of photographs, 8 deal with Chandler himself and the other 16 with the films made from his work. Contents: Eric Homberger, "The Man of Letters (1908-12)," pp. 7-18 (E411a); Julian Symons, "An Esthete Discovers the Pulps," pp. 19-29 (E452); Russell Davies, "Omnes Me Impune Lacessunt," pp. 31-51 (E402); Ivan Moffatt, "On the Fourth Floor of Paramount: Interview with Billy Wilder," pp. 43-51 (E431); John Houseman, "Lost Fortnight," pp. 53-55 (E412); Philip French, "Media Marlowes," pp. 67-79 (film versions of Chandler's novels); Dilys Powell, "Ray and Cissy," pp. 81-87 (E439); Michael Mason, "Marlowe, Men and Women," pp. 89-101 (E427); Michael Gilbert, "Autumn in London," pp. 103-14 (E408); Clive James, "The Country Behind the Hill," pp. 115-26 (E414); Natasha Spender, "His Own Long Goodbye," pp. 127-58 (E 448); Jacques Barzun, "The Illusion of the Real," pp. 159-63 (E 385); Frank Norman, "Friend and Mentor," pp. 165-70 (E436); T. J. Binyon, "A Lasting Influence?," pp. 171-83 (E389); Bibliography, pp. 185-86. Breen 121. (REB & WA)

E410. Guérif, François. "Raymond Chandler." Europe no. 571/2 (Nov/Dec 76), pp. 132-37.
Film adaptations of Chandler's novels.

E411. Holden, Jonathan. "The Case for Raymond Chandler's Fiction as Romance." KQ 10:4 (Fall 78):41-47.
An attempt to develop remarks by other commentators on Chandler's fiction as a modern version of chivalric romance with specific examples from the novels.

E411a. Homberger, Eric. "The Man of Letters (1908-1912)." In Gross (E409), pp. 7-18.
An oblique attempt to study the Chandler of the London years and the poetry and essays he wrote for little reviews.

E412. Houseman, John. "Lost Fortnight." Harper's Magazine 231 (August 1965); reprinted in Chandler, The Blue Dahlia (Southern Illinois Univ. Press, 1976), pp. ix-xxi; and in Gross (E409), pp. 53-66.
Houseman writes about Chandler during the period he was working on the film The Blue Dahlia which Houseman produced for Paramount in 1945.

E413. Howard, Leon. "Raymond Chandler's Not-So-Great Gatsby." In Adams, MDA 1973 (B3), pp. 1-15.
A comparison of Chandler's The Long Goodbye with F. Scott Fitzgerald's The Great Gatsby.

E414. James, Clive. "The Country behind the Hill." In Gross (E409), pp. 115-26. On style in Chandler. James examines Chandler's wit, his metaphors (even some of the overextended ones), and his skill at description from The Big Sleep to the unfinished novel, The Poodle Springs Mystery.

E415. Jameson, Fredric. "L'éclatement du récit et la clôture californienne |The rupturing of the narrative and Californian closure|." Littérature 49 (Feb 83), pp. 89-101. Translated by Marcelle Mékiés.

In Chandler, the portrayal of a social "totality" is accomplished by the use of a closed space (material or geographic). In The High Window, this enclosure cannot take place because the natural space has not been adequately charted and the novel breaks into fragments.

E416. ______. "On Raymond Chandler." Southern Review (new series) 6:3 (July 70):624-50; reprinted in Most/Stowe (B264), pp. 122-48.

An extended discussion of Chandler's prophetic depiction of the fragmented, anonymous American landscape through the medium of the detective/observer. Chandler thought of himself as a stylist and Jameson analyses the way he creates style through dialogue. In the final section, Jameson deals with nostalgia, views of the past, attitudes toward objects and manufactured products and with the novels' structure and distinctive rhythms.

E417. Kaye, Howard. "Raymond Chandler's Sentimental Novel." Western American Literature 10 (Aug 75):135-45.

Chandler's affiliation with Western fiction in terms of setting and characteristics of the hero. The connection is tenuous and Kaye is more interested in the "sentimentalization" of Marlowe in the last novels.

E418. Lacassin, Francis. "Philip Marlowe ou le clair de lune du roman noir |Philip Marlowe or the moonlight of the tough guy novel|." In Lacassin (B201), Vol. 2, pp. 154-215.

Lacassin thinks the principal interest of Chandler's work comes from his distinctive treatment of his private eye hero and he analyzes--with numerous quotations from the novels--Marlowe and the art of portraiture in Chandler. There are also comments on the role of setting, and short sections on Chandler's biography and "The Simple Art of Murder" (C168). With a bibliography and a filmography.

E419. Lachtman, Howard. "The Legendary Sleuths of Pre-WW II Los Angeles." San Francisco Chronicle Review, 1 Feb 81, pp. 10-11.

On Chandler and Erle Stanley Gardner. (KLM)

E420. Lambert, Gavin. "A Private Eye: Raymond Chandler." In Lambert (B215), pp. 210-34.

An intelligent mixture of biographical datal and comments on Chandler's fiction. Lambert is particularly good at selecting a telling detail that illuminates a passage or a work and this essay is an excellent introduction to Chandler.

E421. Lid, R. W. "Philip Marlowe Speaking." Kenyon Review 31 (1977):153-78.

A major essay on Chandler as a social critic, on his control of American vernacular, on the role of landscape in his ficton, on the souring of the American dream and, most persuasively, on Marlowe as a vehicle for the release of some of the deepest facets of Chandler's peronality. There is also (pp. 165-66) a discussion of a "nameless detective" who may remind some readers of Bill Pronzini's more recent private eye. Finally, Lid discusses Chandler's sentimentality and how he sees it as a betrayal of the "moral vision" of the fiction. Lid analyzes The Long Goodbye as thinly disguised autobiography but in this instance Lid's hypotheses are supported by very little concrete information. In spite of the disappointing conclusion, the first half of the essay is one of the best general discussions of Chandler's fiction.

E422. Luhr, William. Raymond Chandler and Film. NY: Frederick Ungar, 1982. xv, 208pp.
A fine study of the films based on Chandler's novels. Luhr first presents an overview of Chandler's Hollywood years, his relationship to people in the industry, and his influential role in the establishment of "film noir." He notes that the film versions show an unusual concern with the stylistic elements of the novels and often incorporate large portions of the text into the screenplays. Luhr's analysis of the films also includes perceptive discussions of the fiction.

E423. MacDermott, K. A. "Ideology and Narrative Stereotyping: The Case of Raymond Chandler." Clues 2:1 (Spring/Summer 81):77-90.
Stylistic stereotyping of characters in Chandler's work and the gradual replacement of the ideological concerns characteristic of the Depression years by those characteristic of the Cold War. MacDermott examines most closely The Little Sister to support his thesis.

E424. Maclaren-Ross, J. "Chandler and Hammett." London Magazine (new series) 3:12 (March 64):70-79.
An introductory survey of the life and works of Chandler and Hammett with the acknowledgement of Hammett as the pioneer and, perhaps, the greater of the two writers.

E425. MacShane, Frank. The Life of Raymond Chandler. NY: Dutton, 1976. 306pp. Index. Japanese edition translated by Shunji Shimizu as Raymond Chandler no Shogai. Tokyo: Hayakawa Shobo, 1981.
The authorized biography of Chandler, but quite limited as a literary study. MacShane's distaste for pulp detective magazines and his unfamiliarity with 1940s crime movies prevents him from seeing Chandler in his proper context as a writer. Breen 122. CC S24 (TAD 9:4). (REB)

E427. Mason, Michael. "Marlowe, Men and Women." In Gross (E409), pp. 89-101.
An essay on Marlowe's ambivalent sexual feelings. Mason cites a number of passages to demonstrate Marlowe's feminine qualities and is particularly concerned about Marlowe's "excessive" interest in domestic activites. Mason admits that there is little agreement on what constitutes feminine qualities and that the sexual ambiguities are apparent in the novels and not in the short stories. An inconclusive study.

E428. Mawer, Randall R. "Raymond Chandler's Self-Parody." TAD 14 (1981):355-59. Photo.
Mawrer treats Chandler's skillful use of language for comic effect although he takes issue with MacShane's analysis of burlesque elements in the fiction.

E429. Meador, Ray. "Chandler in the Thirties: Apprenticeship of an Angry Man." Book Forum 6:2 (1982):143-53.
A biographical essay on Chandler and his apprenticeship writing for the pulps as a prelude to his major work in the 1940s.

E430. Milner, Jay G. "Morality and the Detective Hero: Raymond Chandler's Philip Marlowe." Clues 1:1 (Spring 80):116-18.
Chandler gave, according to Milner, the hard-boiled detective hero a "viable code of ethics" and a new dimension to the genre. A short, cliché-ridden piece filled with unsupported general statements about detective fiction.

E431. Moffat, Ivan. "On the Fourth Floor of Paramount: Interview with Billy Wilder." In Gross (E409), pp. 43-51.
Wilder talks about his relationship with Chandler when they collaborated on the film scenario for Double Indemnity. The relationship was not a warm one but Wilder respected Chandler and his comments about him are consistent with other biographical information on Chandler.

E432. Moran, Carlos Alberto. "A Latin American Reading of Raymond Chandler." Imagen nos. 103/104 (1975); reprinted in Review 76 (Spring 1976), pp. 47-53.
A thematic (solitude, decadence, violence) and political/social reading: Marlowe's acts call society into question although they do not produce social change.

E433. Morgan, Neil. "The Long Goodbye." California (formerly New West), June 82, pp. 81, 159, 161-62, 164.
A memoir-essay on Chandler and Philip Marlowe based on Morgan's reading of the novels and his friendship with Chandler. He includes descriptions of conversations with the writer and excerpts from their correspondance in a sympathetic, moving account. The essay is preceded (pp. 84-90) by a photo-essay with photographs by Dan Weaks "illustrating" scenes and characters from Chandler's novels. (JLA/WA)

E434. Nolan, William F. "Chandler on Screen, TV and Radio--with a Look at the Many Mr. Marlowes." TAD 3 (1969/70):23-26.
A checklist of the adaptations with a short introduction.

E435. ______. "Portrait of a Tough Guy." Xenophile 38 (Feb 76), pp. 13-17. Illus. Originally published in Rogue (1962); reprinted in a collection of essays, Sinners and Supermen (1965).
A sympathetic portrait of Raymond Chandler, the man and the writer, in a version revised for this publication.

E436. Norman, Frank. "Friend and Mentor." In Gross (E409), pp. 165-70.
Norman, recently out of prison and trying to establish himself as a writer, was befriended by Chandler in London in the 1950s and met and corresponded with him until Chandler's death. His portrait is of the alcoholic last years but tempered by his affection for Chandler and his gratitude for his support of his work.

E437. Parker, Robert B. "Marlowe's Moral Code." PCS 1:1 (Winter 77):36-51.
Extensive quotes from Chandler's fiction give some substance to Parker's meager comments on Marlowe's strong ethical sense and his fictional world.

E438. Pendo, Stephen. Raymond Chandler on Screen: His Novels into Film. Metuchen, NJ: Scarecrow Press, 1976. Folkestone: Scarecrow Press, 1977. xv,240pp. Illus. Bibliography. Index.
Detailed discussion of the book-into-film translations of six Chandler novels. Breen 123. (REB)

E439. Powell, Dilys. "Ray and Cissy." In Gross (E409), pp. 81-87.
A moving view of Chandler's relationship with his wife by an Englishwoman who knew him from the 40s to the time of his death. This may not add a great deal of new information to what we know of Chandler but Powell's analysis of Chandler's relationship with his wife

seems a very perceptive and most probably an accurate one.

E440. Rabinowitz, Peter J. "Rats behind the Wainscoting: Politics, Convention and Chandler's The Big Sleep." Texas Studies in Literature and Language 22 (Summer 80):224-45.
A close reading of The Big Sleep to show how Chandler undercuts what Rabinowitz sees as the three basic rules of detective fiction: there must be one indentifiable culprit; the detective must restore order; and an individual rather than a social fault must motivate the crime. Rabinowitz also discusses the observance of these conventions in the classic detective novel (using Christie as his example). The analysis of Chandler's novel shows the use he made of two short stories, the relationship of Hawks' film to the novel, and the importance of names. Rabinowitz concludes with the statement that detective fiction cannot be profitably studied internally, but "in a social and political context." Thus, Chandler is a political writer because he challenges unstated assumptions in other contemporary novels.

E441. Sissman, L. E. "Raymond Chandler." The New Yorker 48, 11 March 72, pp. 123-25. A review of The Midnight Raymond Chandler (Houghton Mifflin, 1971).
Sissman reviews briefly the hard-boiled tradition, reports on a disenchanted rereading of some Hammett, and praises Chandler's gifts as a storyteller and his prophetic portrait of California.

E442. Skenazy, Paul. The New Wild West: The Urban Mysteries of Dashiell Hammett and Raymond Chandler. Western Writers Series, No. 54. Boise, Idaho: Boise State University, 1982. 52pp. Wraps. Selected bibliography of primary and secondary sources.
After establishing connections between detective fiction and the western novel, Skenazy discusses the work of Hammett and Chandler. The section on Chandler (pp. 28-44) pays tribute to Chandler's two "innovations": the "subservience of realism to a romantic quest" and the emphasis on and development of the setting and verbal irony. Skenazy discusses the role money and power play in Marlowe's world and the chronicle of a changing society. A useful, rapid survey of Chandler's work with a good, selective bibliography.

E443. Smith, David. "The Public Eye of Raymond Chandler." JAmStud 14 (Dec 80):423-41.
A subtle, detailed examination of Chandler's fictional Los Angeles, with references to historical figures and events, and Marlowe's realistic/romantic relationship to the time and plalce. Some comments on Hammett and Ross Macdonald and a reply to what he sees as Barzun's misleading essay (E385) on Chandler.

E445. Soriano, Oswaldo. "Chandler el duro |Chandler the tough guy|." La Opinion cultural, 3 Sept 72. Cited by Moran (E432). Not seen.

E446. ______. "Raymond Chandler, dolor y dignidad |R. C., sorrow and dignity|." La Opinion Literaria, 15 Aug 71. Cited by Moran (E432). Not seen.

E447. Speir, Jerry. Raymond Chandler. NY: Frederick Ungar, 1981. 166pp. Bibliography and index.
A survey of Chandler's fiction. Reviews: TLS, 5 June 81, pp. 619-20; Choice, Sept 81, p. 83; Journal of Modern Studies 16 (1982):141-42.

E448. Spender, Natasha. "His Own Long Goodbye." In Gross (E409), pp. 127-58. Spender, an English concert pianist, met Chandler in England just after the death of his wife, and her essay provides what appears to be a very detailed, full report of his psychological state in the last years of his life. Spender put together a support group to try to retrieve Chandler from his suicidal destructiveness. They saw him "through" several doctors and stays in sanatoriums, in what was a long-term, hopeless struggle against his drinking and depression. There is some discussion of the three portraits of Chandler in The Long Goodbye (three aspects of his personality dispersed among as many characters) but this is essentially a portrait of the private Chandler.

E449. Stowe, William W. "From Semiotics to Hermeutics: Modes of Detection in Doyle and Chandler." In Most/Stowe (B264), pp. 366-83.
A study of the ways Chandler succeeded in moving detective fiction away from the study of signs (semiotics) and the solution of mysteries and toward the conceptual and philosophical understanding of "mystery." Stowe's study is a reflection of the continuing contemporary critical interest in "process" and his comments on Chandler's fiction, while they are neither original or unconventional, avoid the abstract, ill-defined methods of Grossvogel (B135).

E450. Symons, Julian. "The Case of Raymond Chandler." NYT Magazine, 23 Dec 73, pp. 13, 22, 25, 27.
A bio-critical protrait of Chandler, an "introverted Romantic." Symons knew the writer personally and finds his work still fresh, 14 years after his death.

E451. ______. "Marlowe's Victim." In Symons (B390), pp. 174-80. Previously published in TLS, 1962.
Review-essay on Raymond Chandler Speaking (E397) and The Second Chandler Omnibus. Symons gives biographical information on Chandler, praises his descriptive style and ability to create atmosphere and turn a phrase, and laments that the Gardiner and Sorley collection did not give a fuller picture of Chandler the human being. Symons also argues briefly that Marlowe's victim is Chandler himself.

E452. ______. "Raymond Chandler: An Esthete Discovers the Pulps." In Gross (E409), pp. 19-30; reprinted in Symons (E389), pp. 156-65.
Chandler's writing and these characteristics: romantic estheticism, loneliness and its Anglo-American character. Symons also discusses the pulp stories and how Chandler worked them into his novels.

E453. Thomson, James (W.). "Murder with Honor: Raymond Chandler." New Republic, 22 July 78, pp. 28-31. Illus.
Marlowe as Chandler's alter ego in a rapid overview of Chandler's life and work.

E454. ______. "Raymond Chandler: Novelist." Xenophile 21 (Feb 76), pp. 52-53.
A survey of Chandler's writing career.

E455. ______. "The Slumming Angel: The Voice and Vision of Raymond Chandler." Unpublished Ph. D. dissertation. University of Pennsylvania, 1977. 256pp. DAI 38/08A (1977/78), p. 4833.

E456. Wells, Walter. "Grey Knight in the Great Wrong Place." In Wells (B428), pp. 71-86.
On regional involvement in Farewell, My Lovely.

E457. Zinsser, David Lowe. "Watching the Detective (A Literary Analysis of the Works of Raymond Chandler)." Unpublished Dissertation. DAI 43/02, pp. 443A-444A.

CHARTERIS, LESLIE

Ref: Hubin 2, TCCMW, EMD, CC, ABMI(S); The Writer 79:2 (Feb 66):19-21, 46 (the Saint on TV; originally published in The Saint Magazine, Aug 65).

See also: B253.

E458. Alexandersson, Jan, and Hedman, Iwan, editors. Leslie Charteris och Helgonet under 5 Decannier en Bio-Bibliografi |Leslie Charteris and the Saint over 5 decades: a bio-bibliography|. DAST Dossier No. 2. Strängnäs, Sweden: Dast-Förlag AB, 1973. 125pp. Illus. Index.
A biographical introduction and a comprehensive bibliography of the Saint in books, films and on TV.

E459. ______. "Leslie Charteris and the Saint. Five Decades of Partnership." TMF 4:4 (July/Aug 80):21-27.
A biography first published in DAST Dossier No. 2 (E458). Translated and edited by Carl Larsen.

E461. Cox, J. Randolph. "Prologemena to a Bibliography of the Immortal Works of Leslie Charteris." TMRN 5:2 (Jan/Feb/March 72):9-15.
A chronological bibliography of Charteris' work and a filmography.

E462. Dinan, John A. "The Saint's Boston Caper." Xenophile 11 (March 75), pp. 17-19. Photo.
Charteris is interviewed by Boston University's Mugar Memorial Library which will serve as a repository for his papers.

E463. Lofts, W. O. G., and Adley, Derek. The Saint and Leslie Charteris. London: Hutchinson Library Services, 1971; Bowling Green, OH: Popular Press, 1972. 135pp.
An amateurish but enthusiastic little book on one of the great rogues of crime fiction, Simon Templar (the Saint), and his creator. Contains a Charteris bibliography covering only British appearances. (The British edition contains a note saying "First published in Great Britain by Howard Baker Ltd. in 1970;" the Howard Baker edition was, in fact, never published.) Breen 125. (REB)

E464. Lundin, Bo. "Helgonet 50 år! Outsidern som blev inne |The Saint is 50! the outsider who became an insider|." Jury 7:4 (1978):14-20. Includes bibliography. (MS)

E465. Shibuk, Charles. "Notes on Very Early Leslie Charteris." TAD 4 (1970/71):230-31.
Stories published by Charteris in The Thriller in 1929 and 1930. Additions as follows: Frank D. McSherry, Jr., letter TAD 5 (1971/72):110-11; J. Randolph Cox, letter TAD 5:185-86.

E466. Trewin, Ion. "Introduction." In Enter the Saint (Hodder, 1930), by Leslie Charteris. "Classic Thrillers" series. London: Dent, 1983. Paperback.

CHARYN, JEROME

Ref: Hubin 2, SN, ABMI(S).

E467. Deloux, Jean-Pierre. "Jogging with the Geek." Polar 16 (Jan 81):4-7. A short discussion of Charyn's use of New York as a "monstrous Babel" on his series of novels featuring super-detective Isaac Sidel. It might be noted that Charyn's brother is a policeman and that he inadvertently wrote a detective series when he began to record his brother's story.

E468. "Dossier Jerome Charyn." Polar 16 (Jan 81):3-31. In his lead editorial (p. 3), editor François Guérif describes American writer Charyn as the last discovery of série noire editor Marcel Duhamel before his death. In an interview in this issue, Charyn says that he hates detective fiction and cannot read them. Then, paradoxically, he states that he prefers detective novels to literary novels (i. e., Thomas Mann or Virginia Woolf.) Contents: Jean-Pierre Deloux, "Jogging with the Geek," pp. 4-7 (E467); "Entretien avec Jerome Charyn," pp. 8-9 (photo; interview); J. Charyn, "Le nez de Pinocchio," pp. 10-21 (trans. by Leah Berns-Sobol; first chapter of a novel previously unpublished in France); Jean-Pierre Deloux, "Le Bestiaire d'Isaac Sidel," pp. 22-27 (dictionary of names of "fauna who haunt the streets of New York" in the imagination of J. Charyn); J. Charyn, "Marilyn la dingue," pp. 28-30 (chapter XI of Marilyn the Wild, suppressed in the série noire version); "Bibliographie de Jerome Charyn," p. 31.

E469. Martens, Michel. "L'auteur du mois: Jerome Charyn |Author of the Month: Jerome Charyn|." Gang 1 (n. d.; circa 1980), pp. 38-40. A profile-interview. Includes a chapter from a novel-in-progress described as autobiographical.

CHASE, BORDEN

Ref: Hubin 2; Argosy, 17 Aug 35.

CHASE, JAMES HADLEY

Ref: Hubin 2, TCCMW, EMD, CC, SN, ABMI; UN 3:7 (1951):10-11.

See also: C606.

E470. Dukeshire, Theodore P. "James Hadley Chase." TAD 5 (1971/72):32-34. A short biography and a checklist which includes titles by Chase's alter ego "Raymond Marshall." See comments in letters from Francis M. Nevins, Jr., in TAD 5:126; and from J. Randolph Cox in TAD 6 (1972/73):128.

E471. ______. "The Caper Novels of James Hadley Chase." TAD 10 (1977):128-29. Illus. An overview.

E472. Smith, Susan Harris. "No Orchids for George Orwell." TAD 9 (1975/76):114-15. A defense of Chase's novel No Orchids for Miss Blandish which was described by Orwell as glamorizing crime.

CHASTAIN, THOMAS

Ref: Hubin 2, SN, ABMI.

Int: EQMM, Oct 79, pp. 103-4.

See also: B117, C173.

CHESTER, GEORGE RANDOLPH

Ref: Hubin 2, EMD, ABMI(S).

See also: E23.

E473. Borowitz, Albert. "The Many Rises and Falls of J. Rufus Wallingford." TAD 12 (1979):28-19. Illus.

A portrait of Chester's fictional "company promoter and swindler."

CHESTERTON, GILBERT KEITH

Ref: Hubin 2, TCCMW, EMD, CC, ABMI(S).

See also: B201, B310, B349, C177-C188, C471, E175-E177, E179.

E474. Balka, Peggy. "G. K. Chesterton's Father Brown." Antioch Review No. 26 (Summer 76):25-29.

Balka suggests a biographical source for the fictional priest-detective.

E475. Barker, Dudley. G. K. Chesterton. NY: Stein and Day, 1973.

The comments on the Father Brown stories are limited to pp. 194-97. Barker describes Father Brown's biographical source, Father John J. O'Connor, and speaks briefly of Chesterton's tiring of the subject and of the series' gradual deterioration. Superficial.

E476. Barzun, Jacques, and Taylor, Wendell Hertig. Preface to The Innocence of Father Brown (Cassell, 1911), by G. K. Chesterton. In A Book of Prefaces (B17), pp. 31-32.

E477. Borges, Jorge Luis. "Los Laberintos Policiales y Chesterton |Detective labyrinths and Chesterton|." Sur (Buenos Aires) no. 10 (July 35), pp. 92-94.

An essay-review of Chesterton's The Scandal of Father Brown. Borges talks about the dilemma of detective fiction which satisfies two needs: an appetite for adventure and an appetite for legality. He proposes six principles which Chesterton's stories suggest to him: no more than six characters; a statement of all the elements of the problems; economy of means; primacy of the "how" over the "who;" the fear of death; necessity and surprise in the solution.

E478. ______. "Modos de G. K. Chesterton |G.K.C.'s methods|." Sur 22 (July 36):47-53.

An obituary tribute to Chesterton as "church father," detective story teller and writer.

E479. Boucher, Anthony. "Introduction." In Ten Adventures of Father Brown, by G. K. Chesterton. NY: Dell, 1961. Paperback.

On Chesterton and the general subject of religious detectives.

E480. Bradbrook, B. R. "The Literary Relationship between G. K. Chesterton and Karel Čapek." Slavonic and East European Review 39:93 (June 61):327-38.

Although he recognizes that Chesterton and Čapek are temperamentally quite different, Bradbrook compares the two as writers and as essayists ("wit and penetrating detail") and traces Čapek's acknowledged debt to the Father Brown stories. Bradbrook maintains that Čapek's stories transcend the genre and are more "lively" than Chesterton's tales which, he claims, become "tedious." Close comparison of stories where the debt is most obvious.

E481. Breen, Jon L. "The Invisible Man Revisited." TAD 4 (1970/71):154. On the "implausibility" of Chesterton's story, "The Invisible Man."

E482. Buchloh, Paul. "Arthur Conan Doyle and Gilbert Keith Chesterton." In Buchloh/Becker 1 (B160), pp. 57-68.
Doyle and Chesterton are discussed as having founded the tradition of the "Great Detective" with odd, eccentric, perhaps almost contradictory aspects to his character. (GG)

E483. Camerino, Aldo. "Padre Brown (1960)." In _Scrittori di lingua inglese_, pp. 259-62. Milano-Napoli: Ricciardi, 1968.
The perfect detective stories of G. K. Chesterton are the only ones which can approach that unsurpassed masterpiece which remains "The Purloined Letter" of Poe. Father Brown, "born under the sign of poetry," lives in a slightly absurd poetic atmosphere which is totally lacking in Dupin, conceived as a purely logical entity. (LR)

E484. Chesterton, G. K. _Autobiography_. NY: Sheed & Ward, 1936. 360pp. Index of names. Japanese edition, translated by Ken'ichi Yoshida as _Jijoden_. Tokyo: Shunju-sha, 1973.
No discussion of the Father Brown stories. CC 1921.

E485. Dale, Alzina Stone. _The Outline of Sanity: A Biography of G. K. Chesterton_. Grand Rapids, Michigan: Wm. B. Eerdmans, 1982. xvi, 354pp. Illus. Bibliography and index.
A full-scale biography. A well-balanced presentation of Chesterton as a man of letters and a man of flesh and blood. Chesterton's role as a writer of mysteries is not neglected and Dale is especially good on his association with London's Detection Club. (Marvin Lachman)

E486. Hays, R. W. "A Lesser Chesterton Detective: Mr. Pond." TAD 9 (1975/76):125; reprinted in Hays (B144), pp. 208-10.
Observations on Chesterton's _The Paradoxes of Mr. Pond_ (London: Cassell, 1937).

E487. ______. "The Private Life of Father Brown." TAd 4 (1970/71):135-39; reprinted in Hays (B144), pp. 161-72.
A profile of Father Brown with determination of dates, chronology and locale of the stories. For corrections, see letters from James D. Clark, TAD 4:259; and from R. W. Hays, TAD 5 (1971/72):47-48.

E488. Hollis, Christopher. _G. K. Chesterton_. "Writers and Their Work" Series. London: British Council National Book League, 1950. (Translated into Japanese by Teizo Oda. Tokyo: privately published, 1969.) Wraps. Frontispiece; bibliography.
A short biography; some information on Father Brown stories.

E489. Hunter, Lynette. _G. K. Chesterton: Explorations in Allegory_. NY: St. Martin's Press, 1979.
A study of Chesterton's work. See pp. 135-38 (in "Inner Landscapes: 1900-1935") for material on the Father Brown stories.

E490. Jago, David M. "The Metaphysician as Fiction-Writer: G. K. Chesterton's Narrative Techniques." Antigonish Review no. 22 (Summer 76), pp. 85-99.
Not seen but described (in Abstract of English Studies 21: 7 (1977/78), item 2548) as including discussion of the Father Brown stories.

E491. Knox, Ronald. "Father Brown." In his Literary Distractions, pp. 170-79. London: Sheed & Ward, 1958.
We should read the Father Brown stories because they are good Chesterton but not because they are good detective stories. See also the essay on Chesterton (pp. 159-69) for a good general study with some comments on Father Brown.

E492. Lambert, Gavin. "Final Problems. 1. G. K. Chesterton." In Lambert (B215), pp. 63-78.
A bio-critical study of the Father Brown stories. Lambert evokes vividly the figures of both the writer and his detective and summarizes concisely the virtues and shortcomings of the stories.

E493. Lowndes, R. A. W. "G. K. Chesterton's Father Brown." SMS 3:5 (Fall 70):4-9, 118, 120, 122, 124, 128; reprinted in TAD 9 (1975/76):184-88, 235.
A general essay on Father Brown.

E494. Nakano, Kii and Peter Milward. G. K. Chesterton no Sekai |The world of G. K. Chesterton|. Tokyo: Kenkyu-sha, 1970. xiii, 219pp. Illus. Bibliography and index.
A collection of twelve articles on Chesterton. There are a few references to Chesterton as a mystery writer. (HS/TT)

E495. Narcejac, Thomas. "G. K. Chesterton." In Narcejac (B287, pp. 143-54.
Narcejac thinks that Chesterton is not, properly speaking, a detective story writer and discusses his philosophy and his politics in the Father Brown series.

E496. O'Connor, John. Father Brown on Chesterton. London: Frederick Muller, 1937. 173pp. Index. Not seen.

E497. Penzler, Otto. "Collecting Mystery Fiction: Father Brown." TAD 16 (83):248-50. Illus.
On editions and bibliographic points of interest.

E498. Robson, W. W. "G. K. Chesterton's Father Brown Stories." The Southern Review 5:3 (Summer 69):611-29; revised and reprinted in Chesterton: A Century Appraisal, edited by John Sullivan, pp. 58-72. NY: Barnes and Noble, 1974.
Maintaining that Chesterton is a serious, currently unjustly negelected writer, Robson analyzes the "manifest" meaning of the Father Brown stories. He finds the precedent for the stories in Poe's "The Purloined Letter" and in Dickens' The Mystery of Edwin Drood and discusses the character of Father Brown and the stylistic qualities of the fiction. A sympathetic and intelligent essay.

E499. Scheick, William J. "The Twilight Harlequinade of Chesterton's Father Brown Stories." The Chesterton Review 4:1 (Fall/Winter 77/78):104-14.
The art of the "sketch" as practised by GKC in the Father Brown stories which Scheick thinks he found "most suitable for conveying an impression of life as a dreamlike experience." The twilight setting of many of the stories is also appropriate for a view in which man is seen as a twilight

creature, half asleep, half awake. See also a letter from John J. Mulloy in TCR 4:2 (Spring/Summer 78):316:21. Mulloy takes issue with the discussion of the twilight elements in the settings and with other points.

E500. Skvorecký, Josef. "A Sort of Tribute to G. K. Chesterton." The Chesterton Review 3:2 (Spring/Summer 77):240-45. Text of an address delivered at the National Meeting of the Chesterton Society at York University in Toronto on January 28, 1977.

Skvorecký talks about his introduction to Father Brown and the village priest of his childhood. There are also some comments on Skvorecký's own detective fiction.

E501. White, William. "G. K. Chesterton's Father Brown: A Bibliography." TAD 16 (1983):251-56.

A bibliography of primary works, including translations and foreign editions; also, a bibliography of secondary sources listing articles and books in English, French, German, Czech and Swedish.

CHEYNEY, PETER

Ref: Hubin 2, TCCMW, EMD, CC, SN, ABMI(S).

See also: C541.

E502. Boucher, Anthony. "Introduction." In The Dark Omnibus, by Peter Cheyney. NY: Dodd Mead, 1952.

E503. Dukeshire, Theodore P. "Peter Cheyney." TMRN 4:4 (May 71):8-10.

A short appreciation and a checklist of his work. No dates or publishers given.

E504. Harrison, Michael. Peter Cheyney, Prince of Hokum. London: Neville Spearman, 1954.

The life and times of a prolific British thriller-writer who set many of his novels in the United States (although his American is purely a figment of his imagination) and won most of his popularity in France. (REB)

E505. Hedman, Iwan. "Peter Cheyney." TAD 4 (1970/71):111-13.

A Peter Cheyney checklist by series, with date of publication and pagination. Correction by Theodore P. Dukeshire in letter, TAD 4:183.

E506. Panek, LeRoy. "Peter Cheyney." In Panek (B303), pp. 171-84.

Cheyney's contribution to the spy story is seen as his use of conventions from the American hard-boiled detective novel.

E507. "Peter Cheyney." Amis du crime 9 (March 1981). 38pp. Illus.

A bibliography, filmography and a TV-filmography. The bibliography lists American, English and French editions. Critical material by François Guérif on the films, a tribute by J. P. Schweig, and a comparison of French translations showing differences in handling of stylistic elements.

CHICHESTER, JOHN JAY

Ref: Hubin.

E508. Hubbard, D. C. "Popular Detective Story Writers: John Jay Chichester." Detective Story Magazine 100:1 (24 March 28):133-34.

Biographical sketch. Series character: Sanderson, a Raffles-type thief. (RS)

CHIDSEY, DONALD BARR

Ref: Hubin 2; Argosy, 19 Nov 32.

Int: Age of the Unicorn 1:3(Dec 79):17-20.

CHILDERS, ERNEST

Ref: Hubin 2, TCCMW, EMD, CC, ABMI.

E509. Boyle, Andrew. The Riddle of Erskine Childers. London: Hutchinson, 1977. 351pp. Illus. Index.
A list of "sources & references." Not seen.

E510. Childers, Ernest. "Preface." In The Riddle of the Sands, pp. 17-19. Originally published in 1903. Harmondsworth, Middlesex, England: Penguin, 1978.
The author writes about himself and the publication of this novel.

E511. Cox, Tom. Damned Englishman: A Study of Erskine Childers. Hicksville, NY: Exposition Press, 1975. 374pp. Notes. Bibliography. Index.
A vanity press publication, but containing much solid biographical and bibliographical information. (REB)

E512. Donaldson, Norman. "Introduction." In Childer's The Riddle of the Sands, pp. 2-11. NY: Dover, 1976.
Biography and brief comments on the writings.

E513. Household, Geoffrey. "Foreword." In The Riddle of the Sands (E510), pp. 7-15.
A biography of Childers and some brief critical comments on the novel.

E514. Malosse, Jean. "Une curiosité littéraire: L'Enigme des sables |A literary curiosity: The Riddle of the Sands|." Enigmatika 25 (Nov 83):39-41.
Short, introductory essay on the novel.

E515. Panek, LeRoy L. "Erskine Childers." In Panek (B303), pp. 32-38.
According to Panek, in spite of some elements in his one spy novel that may be tedious for present-day readers, Childers is important as the first espionage writer to give precedence to fact over romance, to shape the war prophecy novel into a spy story, and to ally the schoolboy story to espionage fiction in order to "unify" it.

E516. Wilkinson, Burke. The Zeal of the Convert: The Life of Erskine Childers. Washington, DC: R. B. Luce Co., 1976. viii,256pp. Not seen. (REB)

CHIN, SHUNSHIN

E517. Chin, Shunshin. Yosomono no Me |Eyes of the outsider|. Tokyo: Kodansha, 1972. 294pp.
A collection of 54 short essays by a writer of detective fiction although very few of them deal directly with the mystery novel. However, one can see his attitude toward writing and his deep cultural knowledge. (HS/TT)

CHRISTIE, AGATHA

Ref: Hubin 2, TCCMW, EMD, CC, ABMI(S).

See also: B6, B190, B179, B241, B310, B349, E192.

E518. Adams, Tom. Agatha Christie: The Art of Her Crimes. The Paintings of Tom Adams. Commentary by Julian Symons. Introduction by John Fowles. NY: Everest House, 1981; London: Dragon's Dream/Paper Tiger, 1981. British title: Agatha Christie Cover Story. 144pp.
90 paintings in color by Tom Adams, done for British and U. S. paperback editions of Agatha Christie books. Commentary by the artist on the sources and symbolism in the paintings, showing that they were based on a careful and appreciative reading of the books, and opinion by Symons on how well they succeed. The collection, although it is presented as being complete, omits at least 6 covers painted for Pocket Book editions of Christie novels. (REB and Brian KenKnight)

E519. Alonso-Cortés, Carolina-Dafne. Anatomía de Agatha Christie |Anatomy of Agatha Christie|. Madrid: Knossos, Colección de Misterio, 1981. 127pp.
A study of Christie's fiction. The writer sees Christie's work as a reflection of her times and, in the person of Ariadne Oliver, of her own character. Brief studies of places, detectives, motives, point-of-view, her dramatic works and films and adaptations. There is a chronological list of her fiction with plot summaries and alphabetical listings of novels and short stories giving date of first publication. A straightforwrd, sympathetic introduction to Christie's work. Alsonso-Cortés speaks, in her introduction, of the lack of attention detective fiction writers receive, even in their own country, and she seems unaware of the substantial body of critical literature on Christie in English, French, German, Swedish and Japanese.

E520. "Agatha Christie." New Yorker, 16 Jan 76, p. 24.
A tribute to Christie, at the time of her death, including a 1971 letter from Christie in which she explains why she does not usually give interviews.

E521. Bargainnier, Earl F. "Agatha Christie's Other Detectives: Parker Pyne and Harley Quin." TAD 11 (1978):110-115. Illus.

E522. ______. "Another Watson: Captain Hastings." TAD 13 (1980):354-60. Illus.
The recurrent Christie character.

E523. ______. The Gentle Art of Murder: The Detective Fiction of Agatha Christie. Bowling Green, OH: Popular Press, 1981. 232pp. Bibliography and index.
A study of the writer's techniques. Review: Choice, 18 June 81, 1411-12.

E524. ______. "I Disagree." Journal of Communications 25 (Spring 75):113-119.
Bargainnier claims that, rather than being an example of a "generally sexist attitude toward women of the detective fiction genre," Miss Marple is a "liberated woman" because of her independent spirit, toughness of mind and "essential ruthlessness."

E525. Barnard, Robert. "Agatha Christie." London Magazine, Oct 79, pp. 36-54.
After playing devil's advocate and outlining weaknesses in Christie's work, Barnard looks for her continuing popularity in her "dazzling" plotting, her engagment of the reader's sympathy, her detachment, and her drabness of style which gives "relief" from "fine writing."

E526. ______. A Talent to Deceive. An Appreciation of Agatha Christie. London: Collins, 1980; NY: Dodd, Mead & Company, 1980. x, 213pp. With a bibliography and short story index compiled by Louise Barnard and an annotated list of all the novels with "detective interest." Japanese edition translated by Shigeru Koike and Yasushi Nakano as Damashi no Tensai. Tokyo: Shubunsha International, 1982.

Published during the 50th anniversary celebration of the Collins Crime Club, Christie's major British publisher, this is the first book-length analysis of Christie's writing. Barnard analyzes Christie's appeal, the phenomenon of her fantastic sales, and the qualities of the individual works. The book's thoroughness requires that it also be honest. The author passes on the adverse criticism which Christie's books have received, guts her plots, recognizes that in the early years she was somewhat racist and contemptuous of the working class. (He also recalls that in 1940 the Russians called her books "a deliberate attempt by the Cripps-Bevin-Atlee-Churchill hyenas to distract the attention of the masses from the machinations of the warmongers.") It is a measure of the strength of Christie's work that, ultimately, all the negative comments turn out to be beside the point. Breen 127. (REB)

E527. Barnes, Daniel R. "A Note on The Murder of Roger Ackroyd." In Adams, MDA 1972 (B2), pp. 254-55.

Christie's novel as an "effective answer" to an implied challenge in Percy Lubbock's The Craft of Fiction (1921).

E528. Barzun, Jacques, and Taylor, Wendell Hertig. Preface to The Murder of Roger Ackroyd (NY, 1926), by Agatha Christie. In A Book of Prefaces (B17), pp. 33-34.

E529. Behre, Frank. Studies in Agatha Christie's Writings: The Behaviour of A Good (Great) Deal, A Lot, Lots, Much, Plenty, Many, A Good (Great) Many. Gothenberg Studies in English, No. 19. Goteberg, Sweden: Almqvist & Wiksell, 1967. 203pp. Bibliography.

A highly technical study of "quantifiers and modifiers" in Christie's work. Professor Behre is a linguist of some reputation. Breen 128.

E530. Beniamino, Michel, and Roche, Daniel-Rolland. "Du lieu clos à la 'murder party' |From the locked room to the 'murder party'|." Enigmatika 24 (July 83), pp. 51-60.

The "murder party," a form of the traditional "locked room mystery," in Christie's work. With introductory comments surveying the theme in other works of detective fiction.

E531. Birns, Margaret B. "Agatha Christie's Portrait of the Artist." Clues 1:2 (Fall/Winter 80):31-34.

Birns refers to the well-known fact of Christie's dislike of revealing details of her personal life and then shows how her fiction is sometimes a "therapeutic working-through" of private issues. She uses the 1946 novel The Hollow to prove her point.

E532. Boutell, Clarence B. "England's Other Crisis." PW 135 (15 Apr 39):1426-29.

An unfavorable review of Christie's Murder for Christmas by Howard Spring appeared in the London Evening Standard, December 22, 1938. John Dickson Carr replied in a letter on January 4, 1939, defending Christie and Spring stuck to his guns in a letter in the same issue. There was further correspondence (JDC, 5 Jan 39, p. 2; JDC, 6 Jan 39, p. 3; HS, 6 Jan 39, p. 3). On January 7, Dorothy L. Sayers entered the fray to state that an unfavorable review need not spoil a reader's pleasure by revealing vital plot elements, and there were letters in the issue of January 9 from Helen Simpson, Dennis Wheatley and others. Boutell's article (with witty drawings by Clayton Rawson) is a summary of the skirmishes with an appropriate sensitivity to the comic aspects of the controversy.

E533. Brand, Christianna. "Miss Marple - A Portrait." In Keating (E562), pp. 193-204.
A charming character study of Miss Marple. There are introductory comments on a revealing conversation Brand may or may not have had with Christie.

E534. Calder, Ritchie. "Agatha Christie and I." New Statesman 91 (30 Jan 76):128-29.
In 1926, Calder was a junior reporter for the London Daily News and--in conjunction with a senior colleague--he covered Christie's celebrated disappearance. He recounts, unemotionally and precisely, the events of the period from her flight to her discovery and, since he was at the scene of the discovery, his short narrative is of uncommon interest. There is an ironic postscript of his second encounter with Christie in which, as he puts it tellingly, the recognition was "mutual." At least, he felt it to be so.

E535. Cawelti, John. "Artistic Failures and Successes: Christie and Sayers." In Winks (B434), pp. 188-99. Originally published in Cawelti (B69), pp. 111-16, 119-25.
Cawelti analyzes Christie's An Overdose of Death and Third Girl to show how the same basic structure is used very successfully in the first and disastrously in the second.

E536. Christie, Agatha. An Autobiography. London: Collins, 1977. 542pp. NY: Dodd, Mead, 1977. xii, 529pp. Index. Photographs. Japanese edition translated by Shin'ihiro Inui as Agatha Christie Jiden. 2 vols. Tokyo: Hayakawa Shobo, 1978.
This a leisurely and selective account--"I have remembered, I suppose, what I wanted to remember"--of Dame Agatha's childhood up to the end of World War II, with occasional references to later events. The famous disappearance of 1927 is not here but there is much information on the author's writing habits, the genesis of plots and characters, and her attitude toward her own work and toward writing in general. Dame Agatha had an active and adventurous life quite apart from her writing, and she looked back on it with keen perception and great good humour. Breen 129. Reviews: TLS, 11 Nov 77, p. 132; NYTBR, 13 Nov 77, pp. 7, 78, 80. (REB)

E537. Crispin, Edmund. "The Mistress of Simplicity." In Keating (E562), pp. 39-48.
H. R. F. Keating interviews Crispin on Christie. Crispin distinguishes between the simplicity of Christie and the "simple-mindedness" of E. S. Gardner. A low-keyed discussion of her appeal for readers.

E538. Debyser, Francis. "Mais comment est mort le dernier nègre |But how did the last little negro die|?." Enigmatika 24 (July 83), pp. 3-7.
Comments on the problem with coherence in Christie's novels and on structures of detective fiction in general.

E539. Dennis, Nigel. "Genteel Queen of Crime." Life 40 (14 May 56):87-88, 91-92, 97-98, 101-2. Illus.

A portrait of Christie apparently based on reports and speculations. There are numerous quotes by Christie and her characters and the sources for Christie's statements are not given. There is no statement that Dennis was or was not able to interview her. He also discusses her work and the reasons for its popularity.

E540. Dueren, Fred. "Hercule Poirot: The Profile of a Private Eye." TAD 7 (1973/74):115.

E541. East, Andy. Andy East's Agatha Christie Quiz Book. NY: Drake Publishers, 1975; paperback reprint, under the title The Agatha Christie Quizbook (NY: Pocket Books, Feb 76, pp. 11-157). 169pp.

Approximately 300 questions and answers about Christie's works. Not seen. Breen 130.

E542. Feinman, Jeffrey. The Mysterious World of Agatha Christie. NY: Award Books, 1975. Wraps. Distributed in England by Tandem Publishing Company. 190pp. Illus. Bibliography.

Brief biography sketch; facile survey of Christie's literary career, including capsule comments on specific books and quotations from reviews and critical commentary by other writers. Breen 131. (REB)

E543. The First 30 Years of Agatha Christie's "The Mousetrap," 1952-1982. London, 1982. 54pp. Wraps. Not seen. Listed in bookseller's catalogue. (REB)

E544. Fitzgibbon, Russell H. The Agatha Christie Companion. Bowling Green, OH: Popular Press, 1980. ix, 178pp. Simultaneous clothbound and paperbound editions. Bibliography.

Books about Agatha Christie and her works could form an industry by themselves, and many of them seem to recycle the same information: potted biography, survey of critical/analytical commentary, descriptions of her detectives, and bibliographical material. One has to ask what is new or different in a fresh volume of this type. Fitzgibbon's book offers several features that make it a useful addition to the Christie shelf. The biographical sketches of Christie's detectives include three one-book sleuths not normally covered. The bibliography attempts to list some reprint editions (only the first edition from each publisher of a title is listed; reissues and reprints by the same publisher are omitted). Though one could wish for more complete citations, the information on paperback reprints, omnibus volumes, and large print editions is not conveniently available in any other source. There is a checklist of alternate titles, and a "story finder" in chart form, allowing easy identification of those collections which contain any given Christie short story. The last 63 pages are devoted to an index of characters from Christie's fiction. There are a few hundred more names than are included in Randall Toye's Agatha Christie's Who's Who (E605), but Fitzgibbon offers only a one- or two-line entry for each: an identifying phrase and citation of the stories in which the character appears. (REB)

E545. Fredriksson, Karl G. "De bada glömda -- Parker Pyne och Mr. Quin |The two forgotten men -- Parker Pyne and Mr. Quin|." In two parts. Jury 7:3 (1978):76-79; 7:4 (1978):79-83. (MS)

E546. ______. "Vem katten bryr sig om vem som mördade Roger Ackroyd |Who

cares who killed Roger Ackroyd|?." Jury 6:2 (1977):41-48.
An analysis of Who Murdered Roger Ackroyd? (MS)

E547. Fremlin, Celia. "The Christie Everybody Knew." In Keating (E562), pp. 111-20.
Christie's reception by reviewers and the public.

E548. Furness, Adrian. "Mystery of the Dutchess of Death." TV Times Magazine 108:36 (4-10 Sept 82):8-10.
Review of Christie's early years and her famous disappearing trick. (RCSA)

E549. Gilbert, Michael. "A Very English Lady." In Keating (E562), pp. 49-78.
A narrative of Christie's life.

E550. Grant, E. "Tribute to Agatha Christie." Horizon, Autumn 76, pp. 106-9. Photos.
This essay is at once a tribute to Christie and to the genre. A list of 10 essential works of detective fiction, including Christie's Mysterious Affair at Styles, is provided.

E551. Gregg, Hubert. Agatha Christie and All That Mousetrap. London: William Kimber, 1980. 170pp.
A personal portrait of Christie by the man who directed the London productions of five of her plays. Review: TLS, 27 Feb 81, p. 218. (REB)

E552. Grossvogel, David. "Agatha Christie: Containment of the Unknown." In Grossvogel (B135), pp. 39-52; reprinted in Most/Stowe (B264), pp. 252-65.
Some unoriginal remarks on the conventions of fiction of the Golden Age as exemplified by Agatha Christie's novel A Mysterious Affair at Styles and as personified by Hercule Poirot.

E553. ______. "Death Deferred: The Long Life, Splendid Afterlife and Mysterious Workings of Agatha Christie." In Benstock (B26), pp. 1-17.
The continuing attraction of Agatha Christie's books lies in her fictional world, protected from social disturbances of recent years, to which the reader can briefly return. Her books remind us that we "once had faith in the possibility of control, of knowledge and of the power of reason against the irrational."

E554. Hall, Richard Paul. "Dame Agatha Christie." CP? 3:1 (March 81):26-28.
A checklist of pb editions of Christie's novels.

E555. Hamblen, Abigail Ann. "The Inheritance of the Meek: Two Novels by Agatha Christie and Henry James." Discourse 12:3 (Summer 69):409-13.
A comparative study of Christie's Endless Night and James' Wings of the Dove. Not seen and listed as described in Abstract of English Studies 19:9, item no. 2766.

E556. Hardesty, Susan M. "A Literary Approach to Agatha Christie: An Analysis of And Then There Were None." Clues 3:1 (Spring/Summer 82):17-30.
A defense of And Then There Were None in which it is seen as "something more" than a detective novel for its intricate plotting, harmonious balance of stylistic elements and psychological interest.

E557. ______. "Using the 'Little Grey Cells'." English Journal, Sept 83, pp. 37-40.

On the usefulness of Christie's fiction in the classroom and some exercises Hardesty has assigned her students.

E558. Heald, Tim. "Bundle--The Glamorous Sleuth Who Wasn't Bright Enough for Agatha Christie." TV Times 102:11 (7-13 March 81):2-5.
A comparison of the various Christie sleuths and the actors and actresses who have portrayed them. (RCSA)

E559. Holquist, Michael. "Murder She Says: Agatha Christie." New Republic, 26 July 75, pp. 26-28.
"Agatha Christie is an industry that once was an art." A survey of her work with a list of 10 texts that define her "very real contribution." Holquist also maintains that detective stories are best when they are not "hybrids" with novelistic elements but "pure" entertainments.

E560. Hughes, Dorothy B. "The Christie Nobody Knew." In Keating (E562), pp. 121-30.
The fiction written by Christie under her pseudonym, Mary Westmacott.

E561. Jochmans, Betty. "A Note Written on the Day That Agatha Christie's Death Was Announced." Prairie Schooner 50 (Summer 76):183-85.

E562. Keating, H. R. F., ed. Agatha Christie: First Lady of Crime. London: Weidenfeld & Nicolson, 1977. 224pp. Illus. Bibliography and index. U.S. edition - NY: Holt, Rinehart & Winston, 1977. Checklist of titles and index. Photos. Japanese edition: Agatha Christie Tokuhon. With additional essays by Japanese writers, panel discussions and a general re-editing of the original edition. Tokyo: Hayakawa Shobo, 1978.
Contents: Keating, "Introduction," pp. 7-9; Elizabeth Walter, "The Case of the Escalating Sales," pp. 11-24 (E608); Julian Symons, "The Mistress of Complication," pp. 25-38 (E603); Edmund Crispin, "The Mistress of Simplicity," pp. 39-48 (E537); Michael Gilbert, "A Very English Lady," pp. 49-78 (E549); Emma Lathen, "Cornwallis's Revenge," pp. 79-94 (E570); Colin Watson, "The Message of Mayhem Parva," pp. 95-110 (E609); Celia Fremlin, "The Christie Everybody Knew," pp. 111-21 (E547); Dorothy B. Hughes, "The Christie Nobody Knew," pp. 121-30 (E560); J. C. Trewin, "A Midas Gift to the Theatre," pp. 131-54 (E606); Philip Jenkinson, "The Agatha Christie Films," pp. 155-82 (a survey); William Weaver, "Music and Mystery," pp. 183-92 (E610); Christianna Brand, "Miss Marple - A Portrait," pp. 193-204 (E533); H. R. F. Keating, "Hercule Poirot - A Companion Portrait," pp. 205-16 (E563). Breen·132.

E563. ______. "Hercule Poirot - A Companion Portrait." In Keating (E562), pp. 205-16. A revised version was published as "A Sleuth for All Seasons," Saturday Evening Post 250 (March 78).

E564. ______. "Mrs. Christie's Secret." Books 1 (Autumn 70):33-34. Not seen.

E565. Kitchin, C. H. B. "Five Writers in One: The Versatility of Agatha Christie." TLS, 25 Feb 55, p. x.
On Christie as a thriller writer, philosopher, social observer, archaeologist and cosmopolite.

E566. Knepper, Marty S. "Agatha Christie: Feminist?" TAD 16 (1983):398-406. Although there are anti-feminist elements in her novels, Knepper finds sufficient evidence to demonstrate that Christie respects women and has definite feminist tendencies.

E567. Krouse, Agate Nesaule, and Peters, Margot. "Why Women Kill." Journal of Communications 25 (Spring 75):98-104. Illus.
Women as victims and murderers in Christie's world of formulaic conventions.

E568. la Cour, Tage. Detektivfortellingens dronning |The queen of the mystery story|. Skjern: Gullander, 1979. 25pp. Illus.
2 essays on Christie and 2 on Ellery Queen. (IH)

E569. Lane, Thomas D. "Dignity in the Detective Novel." Clues 1:1 (Spring 80):119-22.
Another attempt to see the popularity of Christie and Sayers in the optimistic, orderly alternative their works offer to the pessimistic tone of much of 20th century literature.

E570. Lathen, Emma. "Cornwallis's Revenge." In Keating (E562), pp. 79-94.
A strange piece about the "conquering" of America by the British crime novels of Agatha Christie. The essay is a mixture of favorable and unfavorable comments which imply that her success in this country--which greatly surpasses that of most American detective writers, including Lathen--is not to be explained by the overwhelming superiority of her work to the work of other writers. The tone is humorous but there is a somewhat bitter edge to it.

E571. Legars, Brigitte. "Agatha Christie: la mise en scène de la mort de l'auteur |Agatha Christie: the directing of the author's death|." Critique 33, no. 365 (Oct 77):955-60.
A review of Sleeping Murder that includes an overview of her work.

E572. Legars, Brigitte, and Thibaudeau, Jean. "Agatha Christie." La Nouvelle Critique 96 (Nov 76):46-52.
A Marxist/struturalist reading of Christie's work and an analysis of the reasons for its enormous popularity. A disconnected but provocative essay.

E573. _____. "'La Femme aveugle' ou les peintures d'Agatha Christie |'The blind woman' or the paintings of Agatha Christie|." Cahiers critiques de la littérature 1 (Sept 76). Not seen but cited in E572.

E574. Lithner, Klas. "Agatha Christie och historiens wingslag |Agatha Christie and the wingbeat of history|." DAST 10:4 (1977):10, 9.
The historical background of Murder on the Links. (MS)

E575. Lowndes, R. A. W. "The Editor's Page: On Hercule Poirot." SMS 3:3 (Spring 70):4-7, 121-27.
Lowndes comments on Poirot, Ariadne Oliver, Christie's misdirections to the reader, and other topics.

E576. _____. "The Editor's Page: On Miss Marple." SMS 3:4 (Summer 70):4-10, 126-27.

E577. Lyles, Bill. "Agatha Christie in the Dell Mapbacks." PQ 3:3 (Fall 80):26-38. Illus.
A history of paperback publications of Christie's works.

E578. McCarthy, Paul. "The Short Mystery Stories of Agatha Christie: A

Checklist." TAD 6 (1972/73):16-19; for corrections/additions, see letter from Tom Balow in TAD 6:131.
A listing of the short stories showing the collections in which they appeared and any reprintings in EQMM.

E579. Maida, Patricia, and Spornick, Nicholas B. Murder She Wrote. A Study of Agatha Christie's Detective Fiction. Bowling Green, OH: Popular Press, 1982. 199pp. Portrait.
A study of Christie's life and works with chapters on Poirot, Marple, some of Christie's lesser-known detectives, her settings and her legacy. Notes but no index or bibliography.

E580. Mallowan, Max. Mallowan's Memoirs. London: Collins, 1977; NY: Dodd, Mead, 1977. 322pp.
Memoirs of Christie's second husband. There are four chapters in Part III which are devoted to his wife and her writing career.

E581. Martin, Patrick; Oostvotels, Joe; and Peeters, Frank. "De sociale implikaties van Agatha christies detektiveverhalen." Restant 10:1 (Spring 1982):19-32.
Cited in 1982 MLA bibliography and described as including a semiotic approach in its discussion of Christie's fiction. Not seen.

E582. May, Keith. "The Craft of Agatha Christie." Woman's Journal, March 75, pp. 68-69.
A very general study of the author's techniques, not helped by repeated references to that sharp-eyed village spinster called Miss "Marples." (RCSA)

E583. Melchiore, Giorgio. "L'arbitrio della ragione |The arbiter of reason|." Rinascità, 23 January 76, p. 32; reprinted in Cremante/Rambelli (B78), pp. 205-208.
An attempt to sum up concisely the nature of Christie's contribution to genre fiction and the reasons for her great popularity. Melchiore sees in the novels written after 1930 an increasing awareness of flaws in the "perfect" system she appeared to be writing about.

E584. Moy, Paul R. "The Unpublished Agatha Christie and Other Notes." TPP 5:1 (July 82):19-22.
Appended to his uncoordinated notes on Christie's works is a useful listing of WW II "raid" pamphlets with Poirot short stories and 13 stories which have never been reprinted in book form in England.

E585. Murdoch, Derrick. The Agatha Christie Mystery. Toronto: Pagurian Press, 1976. 192pp. Photos. Bibliography.
The first half deals with biographical material and Part II with the literary work, placing it against a broad spectrum of the history of the genre. There are a number of typographical and factual errors but, on the whole, this is a highly readable, entertaining study. Breen 133 (Charles Shibuk)

E586. Narcejac, Thomas. "Agatha Christie." In Narcejac (B287), pp. 171-84.
Unlike others of her colleagues, Christie understood that readers are interested in characterization. However, her interest is not so much in the psychology of the individual as in the psychology of the community. Some comments on why the detective novel is not a "real" novel.

E587. Osborne, Charles. The Life and Times of Agatha Christie. London: William Collins Sons and Co., Ltd., 1982. NY: Holt, Rinehart and Winston, 1983. 256pp. 32pp. of photographs.

Of all the books about Agatha Christie's life and writings, this is one of the most interesting and useful to the student of mystery fiction. The overall framework is the chronological publishing history of her books, non-mystery as well as mystery. For each book we are given authoritative information on the circumstances in which the book was conceived, written and published, a description of the book itself, and an account of its contemporary critical reception. All of this information is set against the backgroundof the major events in Christie's life. Osborne draws freely on previous critical and biographical writings (always carefully cited), but also offers judgments and opinions of his own. Because of the small print, the text is longer than the page-count might indicate. The photographs are well chosen, with very little duplication of those in Gwen Robyns' biography (E600). (REB)

E588. Panek, LeRoy L. "Agatha Christie." In Panek (B304), pp. 38-63.

Panek discusses Christie's detectives, characterization and her "undistinguished" style and describes recurrent narrative devices. He also comments on what he sees as her departure from the conventions of the puzzle-novel and her use of thriller techniques in her plotting.

E589. Patterson, Sylvia. "Agatha Christie's Alter Ego: Ariadne Oliver." TAD 14 (1981):222-27.

A study of Christie's fictional detective-story writer whom Patterson sees as a "self-parody, self-portrait."

E590. Peeters, Benoît. "Tombeau d'Agatha Christie |Tomb of Agatha Christie|." In his Bibliothèque de Villiers. Paris: Laffont, 1980.

Not seen but described by Paul Emile Meheust, in Enigmatika 20 (1982):53-57, as an appendix in which Peeters discusses the likelihood of using the narrator as the murderer as Christie does in Murder of Roger Ackroyd. This appendix appears to be a text functioning as clues to invite a re-reading of the enigmatic main narrative of Bibliothèque.

E591. Petschek, Willa. "The World's Most Mysterious Woman." McCall's 96 (Feb 69):80, 129-30.

Interviewed at her country home, Christie talks about her writing, how she outlines her plots, her favorite writers, and her archaelogical outings with her husband.

E592. Petscher, May-Brittig; Sjogren, Agneta; Turesson, Yngve; and Westerberg, Nils-Gunnar. Agatha Christie - en lasarlots |Agatha Christie - a reader's guide|. Boras: Bibliotekshogskolan, 1966. 24pp.

Biography, checklists of work, bibliography, reviews. (IH)

E593. Ramsey, Gordon K. Agatha Christie: Mistress of Mystery. NY: Dodd, Mead, 1967; revised, London: Collins, 1968. xi, 124pp. Photographs. Apollo editions (Dodd, Mead) A-231, nd (paperbound version).

A slight, diffuse, poorly organized study that does not come close to doing justice to its subject, but does at least provide sixteen pages of photographs and a useful annotated checklist of Christie's fiction and plays. Breen 134. CC 3009. (REB)

E594. ______. "A Teacher Meets Agatha Christie." TAD 1 (1968):13-18.

How Ramsey became interested in Christie, got a contract for a book on her and travelled to London for an interview. The interview is briefly described.

E595. Revzin, I. I. "Zur semiotischen Analyse des Detektivromans am Beispiel der Romane Agatha Christies |Towards a semiotic analysis of the detective novel: example - the novels of Agatha Christie|." First published in Russian in Programma i terisy dokladov v letnej skole po vtoricnym modelirujuscim sistemam, pp. 38-40. Tartu, 1964. Reprinted in German in Vogt (B424), Vol I, pp. 139-42; translated into English by Julian Graffy and reprinted in New Literary History 9 (Winter 78):385-88.
Semiotic analysis of Christie's The Murder in the Clouds, The Murder on the Links and The Murder of Roger Ackroyd. Discusses the frequently found Christie character types, and states cryptically that "on the level of the aesthetic symbol-system of detective fiction...a construction is presented in which no sort of reality lies behind the symbols."(GG)

E596. Riley, Dick and Pam McAllister, eds. The Bedside Bathtub and Armchair Companion to Agatha Christie. Introduction by Julian Symons. NY: Ungar, 1979. xix, 330pp. Illus. Simultaneous hardcover and paperbound editions. Bibliography. Title index.
Most of the features in this compendium can also be found, in one form or another, in one of the other numerous books on Christie and her works. Here the material gives the Murder Ink treatment: popular-magazine style layout, with numerous illustrations---movie stills and posters (the latter in color), posed photographs, paperback covers, and a map ("The Christie Mystery Map of Southern England"). The text offers one- or two-page plot summaries of 88 Christie books--the mystery novles, some short story collections and plays--interspersed with 30-some articles on all aspects of the Christie books and the films based on them. There are also crossword puzzles, a double-crostic, verse, recipes, and numerous short quotations from Christie's novels and autobiography. (One is tempted to add "kitchen sink" to the book's title....) Forty-nine writers in addition to the book's editors contributed to this assemblage of material. Of most lasting value are several articles and an annotated checklist by Michael Tennenbaum on Christie movies. All of the book's contents will not be listed but the following items are of particular interest: Symons, "Introduction," pp. xv-xix; Sue Ellen York and Pam McAllister, "Crime, Class and Country in Christie's Mysteries," pp. 73-77; Patricia Maida and Nick Spornick, "The Romantic Englishwoman: Agatha Christie as Mary Westmacott," pp. 141-43; Richard Regis, "The Poison Pen: A Guide to Agatha's Toxic Agents," pp. 162-65; Pam McAllister, "Dartmoor--The Deadly Heath," pp. 182-85 (legends of the Devonshire moor where Christie wrote her first story); Jerry Keucher, "Hercule Poirot, the Man and the Myth," pp. 214-218; Norma Siebenheller, "The Marvellous Miss Marple: A Profile," pp. 245-48; Jan Oxenberg, "The Womanly Arts: Gossip and Intuition as Detective Tools," pp. 261-63; and Beth Simon, "Ariadne Oliver: Dame Agatha's Alter Ego." (REB)

E597. Rivière, François. Agatha Christie, Duchesse de la Mort |Agatha Christie, the duchess of death|. Paris: Editions du Seuil, 1981. 187pp. Photos. With a bibliography, filmography and a note on the translation of Christie's novels into French.
A devoted reader of Agatha Christie, François Rivière analyses her work and tries to reveal its mechanisms by basing his opinion on the creator of Hercule Poirot. A perspicacious and intelligent approach. Reviews: NL, 2-9 April 81, p. 3; TLS, 5 June 81, p. 620.(JB)

E598. _____. "James Sheppard, Romancier |James Sheppard, novelist|." Enigmatika 9 (Feb 78):3-7.
A critical study of The Murder of Roger Ackroyd.

E599. Robertson, Sandra D. "Domesticated Murder: Or The Butler Usually Doesn't Do It: Characterization in Agatha Christie." Clues 3:1 (Spring/Summer 82):86-89.
Although Christie's characterizations are two-dimensional, they are "true to life and to type." There may be some truth to Robertson's cliché, but this 3 page article does not document it.

E600. Robyns, Gwen. The Mystery of Agatha Christie. NY: Doubleday, 1978. xiii, 247pp. Illus. Bibliography and index. Japanese edition, translated by Mieko Yoshino as Agatha Christie no Himitsu. Tokyo: Sogen-sha, 1980.
An excellent biography, with more detail on Christie's life than any earlier book except the Autobiography, and containing thorough coverage of the famous disappearance of 1926. In addition to using contemporary newspaper accounts, Robyns was able to interview the only four surviving people who played a significant role in the case, and her account is probably the most thorough we shall get of this important incident in Christie's life. There is almost no attempt at critical assessment or even plain description of Christie's books, though there are comments on Christie's sales figures and general popularity. Read this one for the rounded portrait of the persona who was Agatha Christie. The book won the Edgar Allan Poe Award from the Mystery Writers of America as best biographical/critical work of 1978. Breen 136. (REB)

E601. Sampson, Robert. "The Solving Sixth." TMF 5:5 (Sept/Oct 81):3-6.
A discussion of the birth of Miss Marple in a short story series The Thirteen Problems (Am. title: The Tuesday Club Murders).

E602. Symons, Julian. "Agatha and Agatha." NYRB, 21 Dec 78, p. 39; reprinted in Symons (B389), pp. 139-47.
A short biography of Christie and an analysis of her fictional world as a "fairy tale." Ostensibly a review of four books: Kathleen Tynan, Agatha; and Ten Little Indians, Destination and The Mousetrap and Other Plays, all by Christie.

E603. _____. "The Mistress of Complication." In Keating (E562), pp. 25-38.
A general introduction to Christie whose chief importance is, says Symons, in constructing puzzles. He discusses several of the novels and tries to assess their relative success in relation to one another.

E604. Talbot, David. "Agatha Christie Gives an Interview." Birmingham Post and Gazette, 24 Feb 58.
An interview given on the occasion of the premiere of her play Verdict. (RCSA)

E605. Toye, Randall. The Agatha Christie Who's Who. NY: Holt, Rinehart and Winston, 1980. 264pp. Illus. Bibliography.
A "biographical dictionary" listing more than 2000 characters drawn from Christie's novels and 147 short stories: detectives, victims, suspects, witnesses, heirs, police, murderers. Each entry contains a capsule biography of the character, based on material in the story or stories in which the character appears. For close students of Christie's works, Toye has uncovered a number of anomalies, which he describes in his Introduction to the book. (My favorite is the mention of Tuppence and

Tommy's three children, aged 15, 11, and 7, two of whom were twins.) The bibliography lists all of Christie's novels and story collections chronologically, with the contents of each collection; U. K. editions are given priority in each case, but title changes and other differences in U. S. editions are noted. There are appendices listing the titles in the Poirot, Marple, and Oliver series, and Christie's plays and non-mystery books. Great for browsing, and it doesn't give away any plot secrets. The drawings by Ron Berg are, as the writer of the jacket blurb says, elegant. (REB)

E606. Trewin, J. C. "A Midas Gift to the Theatre." In Keating (E562), pp. 131-54.
An informative survey of Christie's work for the theatre.

E607. Ulam, Adam. "Agatha Christie, Murder and Class." New Republic, 31 July 76, pp. 21-23.
A Harvard professor of government defends the relevance of detective fiction to our times and lists a number of ways in which Christie's work is both a reflection of the contemporary world and a moral lesson for it.

E608. Walter, Elizabeth. "The Case of the Escalating Sales." In Keating (E562), pp. 11-24.
A writer of crime fiction and an editor at Collins, Walter discusses Christie's publication from the editor's viewpoint.

E609. Watson, Colin. "The Message of Mayhem Parva." In Keating (E562), pp. 95-110.
The appeal of Christie's fiction for her reading public and why Poirot was a success and other detectives, contemporary with his appearance, were not.

E610. Weaver, William. "Music and Mystery." In Keating (E562), pp. 183-92.
Some references to music in Christie's work.

E611. Weinkauf, Mary S. "Miss Jane Marple and Aging in Literature." Clues 1:1 (Spring 80):32-40.
A study of the ways in which Marple is an attractive version of the various stereotypes of old people often found in popular fiction.

E612. White, William. "Agatha Christie: A First Checklist of Secondary Sources." BoB 36:1 (1979):14-17.

E613. Williams, Richard. "Agatha Christie in paperback." Antiquarian Book Monthly Review 10:1 (issue 105, Jan 83):16-17, 19-21. Photos.
Assorted bibliographic notes and an alphabetical checklist of British paperback editions of Agatha Christie's books. The checklist cites the original hardback editions and what are apparently the first paperback editions known to the compiler. Only one paperback edition is given for each title, in spite of the existence of numerous reissues and reprints. The covers of six assorted Christie paperbacks are illustrated. (REB)

E614. Winterbrook House Tsushin (The Newsletter of the Agatha Christie Fan Club). Editor: Yasuo Sudo. Editorial Address: 1-11-1-402 Iwato-kita, Komae, Tokyo, Japan. Semi-annual. Subscriptions limited to 200. (JK)

E615. Wyndham, Francis. "Agatha Christie on Mystery Fiction." The Writer 79:8 (Aug 66):27-8.

Excerpted from an interview with Christie in the London Sunday Times (source not verified). Christie talks about her early work and her working methods.

E616. Wynne, Nancy Blue. An Agatha Christie Chronology. NY: Ace Books, 1976. Wraps. 266pp. Bibliography.
A catalogue of all of Christie's books, with plot summaries, annotations, and a detailed bibliography of hardcover editions. Little attempt at critical commentary. Breen 137 (REB)

E617. ______. "The Baker Street-Devon Connection: The Influence of the Sherlock Holmes Stories on Agatha Christie's Early World." Baker Street Journal 27:1 (Mar 77):6-10. Not seen.

E618. Wuyek, George. "End of the Golden Age." TAD 10 (1977):263-64. Photo.
An obituary of Agatha Christie. Appendix (pp. 264-67): a 1975/76 Necrology of Mystery-Crime Writers, containing brief biographies.

CIABATTINI, GIUSEPPE

E620. Rambelli, Loris. "L'avventura di un giallista |Adventure of a writer of gialli|." Orient Express 8 (1982), pp. 18-20.
Brief profile of the Italian writer of detective novels Giuseppe Ciabattini (1882-1962), creator of a hobo character, "I Tre Soldi," who is surely "the most original investigator of the Italian giallo." (RC)

CLARK, DOROTHY PARK

Ref: Hubin 2, ABMI; UN 2:5 (1950):12-13 (photo).

CLARK, DOUGLAS

Ref: Hubin 2, CC.

E621. "Douglas Clark." BMJ, 2 Aug 80, p. 378.
Writer Clark works for a pharmaceutical company, and although he claims to do very little research, prides himself on the accuracy of his medical facts.

CLARK, MARY HIGGINS

Ref: Hubin 2, ABMIS; The Writer 93:9 (Sept 80):9-12.

Int: EQMM, Dec 79, pp. 100-101; Jan 80, pp. 88-89.

E622. Bernard, Bina. "With Five Kids to Support, Could Widow Clark Find Romance? Life, Like Novels, Does End Happily." People 9 (6 March 78):79-80.
Profile.

CLARK, PHILIP

Ref: Hubin 2.

E623. Barzun, Jacques, and Taylor, Wendell Hertig. "Introduction." In The Dark River (London, 1950), by Philip Clark. "Crime Fiction 1950-1975" (B18).

CLARKE, ANNA

Ref: Hubin, TCCMW, ABMIS.

CLARKE, DONALD HENDERSON

Ref: Hubin 2, SN, ABMI.

E624. Clarke, Donald Henderson. Man of the World: Recollections of an Irreverent Reporter. NY: Vanguard Press, 1950. 304pp.
Autobiographical account of Clarke's newspaper career in the 1920's, including his crime reporting. The first of his crime novels, Louis Beretti, appeared in 1929. (REB)

CLASON, CLYDE B.

Ref: Hubin 2, ABMIS; The Writer 52:1 (Jan 39):6-8.

CLAYTON, RICHARD. See HAGGARD, WILLIAM

CLEARY, JON

Ref: Hubin 2, TCCMW, ABMI(S).

CLEEVE, BRIAN

Ref: Hubin 2, TCCMW, SN, ABMI(S).

CLIFFORD, FRANCIS

Ref: Hubin 2, TCCMW, SN, ABMI(S); The Writer 80:11 (Nov 67):17-18 (on characterization and style).

Int: Dast 8:5 (1975):14-16 (with bibliography).

E625. Blom, K. Arne. "Francis Clifford är död |Francis Clifford is dead|." DAST 8:5 (1975):43.
Tribute to Clifford. (MS)

CLINTON-BADDELEY, V. C.

Ref: Hubin 2, TCCMW, CC, ABMI(S).

COATMEUR, JEAN FRANCOIS

Int: MM 305, July 73.

COBB, G. BELTON

Ref: Hubin 2, TCCMW, CC, ABMIS.

COE, CHARLES FRANCIS

Ref: Hubin 2, EMD, ABMI(S).

E626. Coe, Charles Francis. Never a Dull Moment. NY: Hastings House, 1944. 326pp.
Coe was a criminologist and lawyer who also wrote sports and gangland stories, including more than a dozen novels from 1927 onwards. This autobiography is filled with capsule portraits of the famous people whom Coe knew during his first fifty years. (REB)

COE, TUCKER. See WESTLAKE, DONALD

COHEN, OCTAVUS ROY

Ref: Hubin 2, TCCMW, ABMI(S).

COHEN, STANLEY

Ref: Hubin 2, ABMI(S); The Writer 93:11 (Nov 80):20-21 (on dialogue).

COLE, G. D. H. and MARGARET

Ref: Hubin 2, TCCMW, EMD, CC, ABMI(S).

E627. Barzun, Jacques, and Taylor, Wendell Hertig. Preface to The Murder at Crome House (London, 1927). In A Book of Prefaces (B17), pp. 35-36.

E628. Cole, G. D. H. and Margaret. "Crime in Life and Fiction." New Statesman (new series) 2:41 (21 Nov 31):645.
A review of two books on crime and detection in which the reviewers claim that true crime offers little that is useful to the crime novelist.

E629. ______. "Superintendent Wilson." In Meet the Detective (B253), pp. 116-28.
A reader of detective fiction and Superintendent Wilson interview the Coles in a railway carriage. The Coles discuss their collaborative habits (one them writes a first draft and then both revise), the birth of Superintendent Wilson ("he just came to me") and Wilson's lack of distinctive characteristics.

E630. Cole, Dame Margaret. The Life of G. D. H. Cole. London: Macmillan, 1971; NY: St. Martin's Press, 1971. 304pp. Photographs. Index.
Biography of the distinguished teacher, scholar, biographer, and Socialist historian, by his widow. The thirty-odd volumes of detective fiction by G. D. H. and Margaret Cole are dismissed with barely disguised disdain in less than two pages. Although Dame Margaret's brother, Raymond Postgate, plays a prominent role in the book, the fact that he too wrote detective fiction is not even mentioned. (REB)

COLES, MANNING

Ref: Hubin 2, TCCMW, EMD, CC, ABMI(S).

E631. Coldwell, Marion. "Manning Coles: A Checklist and Comments." Aardvarks Booksellers Advance List 4 (July 74):5-7.
Annotated checklist of the books of Manning Coles, with a brief biographical sketch. The annotations include publication date, plot summary, and brief evaluative comment. Published as part of bookseller's catalogue; 3 legal-sized photo-offset pages. (REB)

E632. Panek, LeRoy. "Manning Coles." In Panek (B303), pp. 185-200.
Panek discusses the promise of Coles' first books in which realism seems to triumph over some of the "sillier conventions" of the spy genre and the way the books deteriorate into "repetition and clichés."

E633. Sarjeant, William A. S. "A Toast to the Secret Service: In Tribute to Manning Coles and Tommy Hambledon." TAD 15 (1982):100-114.
A biography of the writers, a chronological summary of the Hambledon spy novels, and some comments on secondary characters. With a checklist of the novels referred to in the article.

COLLIER, JOHN

Ref: Hubin 2, TCCMW, EMD, ABMI(S).

COLLINS, MARY

Ref: Hubin 2; UN 2:2 (1949):6-7, 10 (photo).

COLLINS, MAX

Ref: Hubin 2, SN.

Interviews: TAD (1978):300-304 (photo and illustrations); Spiderweb 1 (Winter 82), pp. 38-45.

E634. Collins, Max. "Confessions of a Crime Writer." Mediascene, Nov/Dec 73, pp. 4-5.

COLLINS, MICHAEL

Ref: Hubin 2, TCCMW, EMD, SN, ABMI(S).

Int: Jury 8:3 (1979):54-57.

E635. Edwards, John. "Dan Fortune--Private Eye." Megavore 9 (June 80), pp. 38-39. Illus.
List of Lynds' Slot Machine Kelly stories for Mike Shayne and Manhunt. Kelly is seen as the prototype of Dan Fortune.

E636. ______. "The Story of Dennis Lynds." Age of the Unicorn 1:4 (Oct 79):21-26; 1:5 (Dec 79):20; 1:6 (Feb 80):36, 71. Illus.
The first segment of this article consists of a short biography and a checklist of the writings of Dennis Lynds. In 1:5, Edwards attributes correctly to Michael Avallone two stories listed as by Lynds and in 1:6, he makes further corrections and additions.

E637. Martin, Roger, ed. "Michael Collins." Hard-Boiled Dicks No. 2 (March 82). 52pp. Wraps. Portrait and illustrations.
Along with biographical and bibliographical material, there is also some critical material on Collins/Lynds. Contents: "Eléments biographiques," pp. 5-7; "Entretien avec Michael Collins |Interview with Michael Collins|," pp. 20-3; Roger Martin, "Michael Collins, le trouble-fête du roman noir," pp. 20-23 (E639); "Bibliographie chronologique," pp. 24-31; Francis M. Nevins, Jr., "Sale temps pour les privés |A bad time for private eyes|," pp. 32-36 (E640); M. Maertens and François Guérif, "Article Collins dans Underwood U.S.A. (B244)," pp. 37-39; Jean-Jacques Schleret, "Michael Collins," pp. 38-39 (E641); Roger Martin, "The Shadow...Les Pulps...Maxwell Grant...et...Michael Collins," pp. 40-41 (E638); Michael Collins, "Meurtre par nuit chaude |Murder on a hot night|," pp. 42-49 (short story).

E638. Martin, Roger. "The Shadow...Les Pulps...Maxwell Grant...et...Michael Collins |The Shadow...the Pulps...Maxwell Grant...and...Michael Collins|." In Hard-Boiled Dicks 2, pp. 40-41. Illus.
Notes on the Shadow pulp series and Michael Collins. Enthusiastic and slight.

E639. ______. "Michael Collins, (le) trouble-fête du roman noir |Michael Collins, the party-pooper of the roman noir|." In Hard-Boiled Dicks 2, pp. 20-23.
A defense of Collins who has been criticized for introducing political concerns into his novels.

E640. Nevins, Francis M., Jr. "Private Eye in an Evil Time: Mark Sadler's Paul Shaw." Xenophile 38 (March/April 78), p. 11; translated into French by Roger Martin and published in Hard-Boiled Dicks 2, pp. 32-36.
An appreciative description of Paul Shaw whom Nevins characterizes as a "soft-boiled, unwisecracking, concerned, compassionate post-Chandler incarnation of the classic private detective."

E641. Schleret, Jean-Jacques. "Michael Collins." Enigmatika 12-13 (June 79), pp. 57-59; an abridged version was published in Hard-Boiled Dicks 2, pp. 38-39.

A discussion of Dan Fortune and the thematic consistency of the novels featuring this one-armed private investigator with some discussion of other novels by Collins/Lynds.

COLLINS, WILKIE

Ref: Hubin 2, TCCMW, EMD, CC, ABMI(S).

See also: A161, B6, C101, C419, C712, E2516.

E642. Andrew, R(ay) V(ernon). "A Wilkie Collins Checklist." English Studies in Africa 3 (1960):79-98.

First publication and alternative titles under which items later appeared are cited. This compilation will assist study of Collins's periodical ventures most notably. (BFF)

E643. ______. Wilkie Collins: A Critical Survey of His Prose Fiction, with a Bibliography. NY: Garland, 1979.

This publication of a 1959 Doctor Litterarum Thesis makes available a sound reading of Collins's writings. Pp. 331-336 in particular discuss the detective tale from ancient China through Collins's time, with special attention to his debts to Poe and to his incorporation of themes, motifs, and types common to the literature of detection into his fiction. (BFF)

E644. Ashley, Robert P. Wilkie Collins. NY: Roy Publishers; London: Arthur Barker, 1952; rpr. Folcroft, PA: Folcroft Library Editions, 1974; NY: Haskell House, 1975.

Ashley sets out to correct misapprehensions about Collins the man and writer. He observes how Cuff (because of his relatively minor role and his inability to solve the mystery of the moonstone) does not attain status as a genuine modern detective. Plot is paramount in The Moonstone. (BFF)

E645. ______. "Wilkie Collins." In Victorian Fiction: A Guide to Research, edited by Lionel Stevenson, pp. 277-84. Cambridge, MA: Harvard University Press, 1964.

Ashley surveys available editions, biography, and critical writing about Collins. This essay is a model guide to its subject. (BFF)

E646. ______. "Wilkie Collins and the Detective Story." Nineteenth-Century Fiction 6 (1951):47-60.

Collins invented and developed many of the most interesting motifs and plot devices in detective fiction, although he apparently did not recognize his pioneer labors as such. (BFF)

E647. ______. "Wilkie Collins Reconsidered." Nineteenth-Century Fiction 4 (1950):265-73.

This major reassessment of all of Collins's fiction assisted in demolishing the walls of obscurity that had long clouded his accomplishments. The Moonstone numbers among his greatest novels, his later work did not betray so much decline as many other critics believe, and Collins's impact upon Dickens was--contrary to detractors--positive. (BFF)

E648. Barton, George. "A Great Novel Dissected." The Writer 21:9 (Sept 1909):129-33.

The Moonstone and how Collins "secures his effects by patient endeavor."

Barton also comments on plot and character construction.

E649. Beetz, Kirk H. Wilkie Collins: An Annotated Bibliography, 1889-1996. Metuchen, N. J. and London: Scarecrow Press, 1978.
Although this book does not list many contemporaneous notices of Collins's fiction, it does chart currents of critical viewpoints since his death--with frequent mention of his works of detection or of his relationships with detective writing in general. (BFF)

E650. Blair, David. "Wilkie Collins and the Crisis of Suspense." In Reading the Victorian Novel, edited by Ian Gregor, pp. 32-50. NY: Barnes & Noble, 1980.
Blair theorizes that although in the detective puzzle-novel and the Gothic novel, detail may be subordinate to form as all ambivalencies suggested appear to be settled by the novel's conclusion, these "intermediate experiences" may, in fact, have a life of their own. Thus the inflexible form of the Gothic novel in which a natural solution is finally proposed for apparently supernatural happenings and the closed system of the classic detective novel may be undermined by the "resonance" of the detail. This can be seen as a "double structure" working at cross-purposes. Blair uses for his analysis Collins's Armadale and Charlotte Bronte's Villette.

E652. Booth, Bradford A. "Wilkie Collins and the Art of Fiction." Nineteenth-Century Fiction 6 (1951):131-43.
Collins's hallmarks are examined. He is often notably theatrical, he reveals a Gothic heritage, and suspense is his chief trait. His plots are good, and often intricate. (BFF)

E653. Buchloh, Paul. "Der viktorianische Detektivroman: Dickens und Collins." In Buchloh/Becker 1 (B60), pp. 47-56.
Dickens and Collins are here discussed as having been the first to develop the detective novel as opposed to detective (short) story. (GG)

E654. Cordasco, Francesco, and Scott, Kenneth W. Wilkie Collins and Charles Reade: A Bibliography of Critical Notices and Studies. Brooklyn, NY: Long Island University Press, 1949. 8pp. Wraps.
104 items listed. (REB)

E655. Davis, Nuel Pharr. The Life of Wilkie Collins. Urbana: Univ. of Illinois Press, 1956. See especially pp. 168-69, 250-58, 285.
History of detectives, Collins's working notes for The Moonstone, and his interest in French detection are noted. Davis attempts altogether too emphatically to link Collins's life with his writings, in psychoanalytic trappings. (BFF)

E656. de la Mare, Walter. "The Early Novels of Wilkie Collins." In The Eighteen-Sixties: Essays by Fellows of the Royal Society of Literature, edited by John Drinkwater, pp. 51-101. London: Cambridge University Press; NY: Macmillan; Tokyo: Maruzen, 1932.
The Moonstone receives praise for plotting and ingenuity. Collins's rather weak male characters, as opposed to unusally strong young women, are also discussed. (BFF)

E657. Eliot, T. S. "Wilkie Collins and Dickens." TLS, 4 Aug 27, pp. 525-26.
Revised, this essay appeared in various printings of Eliot's Selected Essays, and forms the basis for his introduction to The Moonstone

(London: Oxford University Press, 1928), and often reprinted. Collins's greatest influence upon Dickens is evident in Bleak House. Both writers create "melodramas." The Moonstone is lauded as the first and greatest English detective novel. (BFF)

E658. Ellis, S(tuart). Wilkie Collins, Le Fanu and Others. London: Constable, 1931; NY; Richard R. Smith, 1931; rpr. Bombay, Calcutta, and Madras: Orient Longmans, 1951. See pp. 1-53.
Amidst the appreciations come significant bits of information concerning Collins's interest in and use of criminal psychology in fiction, particuarly in The Moonstone and The Woman in White. There is a bibliography that has been superseded more recently by Kirk H. Beetz (E649). (BFF)

E659. Elwin, Malcoln. "Wilkie Collins: The Pioneer of the Thriller." London Mercury 33 (1931):574-84. Revised and reprinted as "Wallflower the Sixth: Wilkie Collins." In Victorian Wallflowers, pp. 203-227. London: Jonathan Cape, 1934; Port Washington: Kennikat Press, 1966.
This general assessment of Collins's art provides many insights along the way that are pertinent to detective fiction. The novels after 1870 do not match the quality of earlier books. Collins's story-telling abilities, his economies of style, and his adaptation of the weird manner of Poe give him the paternity ascribed by Elwin. (BFF)

E660. Fisher, Benjamin Franklin IV. "The Residual Gothic Impulse, 1824-1873." In Horror Literature: A Core Collection and Reference Guide, edited by Marshall B. Tymn, pp. 176-220. NY: R. R. Bowker, 1981.
Collins is placed with other later-nineteenth-century writers in the thriller vein. The Moonstone receives special praise.

E661. ______. "Wilkie Collins and the Critics." Wilkie Collins Society Journal 1 (1981), pp. 5-12.
This survey of scholarship on Collins since the mid-1970s gives information about his reputation as a writer of detective fiction. Some of this secondary material might not initially seem to treat detective fiction, although Collins's affinities with the sensation school in fiction during the 1860s and 1870s makes this vagueness no great wonder. (BFF)

E662. Gasson, Andrew. "Wilkie Collins: A Collector's and a Bibliographer's Challenge." The Private Library, 3rd series, 3 (1980):49-77.
Valuable information in textual matters appears here, since Collins's texts offer interesting revisions. The Moonstone in particular holds out tantalizing variants for collectors. (BFF)

E663. Gregory, E. R. "Murder in Fact." New Republic, 22 July 78, pp. 33-34.
In what is probably the best brief evaluation of Collins's career overall, The Moonstone is praised for atmosphere, plotting, and realism. (BFF)

E664. Haycraft, Howard. Murder for Pleasure (B143).
Collins's name recurs throughout. He is ranked with Dickens for creating compelling characters and for plotting. The Moonstone had an impact upon later detective novels, and it is paraphrased in Michael Innes's Lament for a Maker and Dorothy L. Sayers's The Documents in the Case. There are comparisons with Poe. Some of Haycraft's opinions have been superseded, but his commentary remains nevertheless of "classic" status. (BFF)

E665. Hennelly, Mark M., Jr. "Reading Detection in The Woman in White." Texas Studies in Literature and Language 22 (Winter 80):449-67.
Varieties of detection in Collins' novel and the relationship of the reader to the text.

E666. Hughes, Winifred. "The Triumph of the Detective." In The Maniac in the Cellar (B163), pp. 137-65.
Collins tries to make sense from the sensational, to provide "meaning and esthetic structure." The Moonstone is his greatest accomplishment in this method. (BFF)

E668. Kendrick, William A. "The Sensationalism of The Woman in White." Nineteenth-Century Fiction 32 (1977/78):18-35. Not seen.

E669. Keshokova, Elena S. "'The Father' of the English Detective Novel." Soviet Literature no. 12 (1980), pp. 149-53.
Wilkie Collins, lacking the "genius" of Dickens, saw himself as much an educator and moralist as a writer of entertainments. The writer comments on the "sensation novel" and its depiction of man's complex psychology. Also discussed are the double, man's dual nature, and the examination of the realities of the Victorian age. An enthusiastic, disjointed discussion.

E670. Lambert, Gavin. "Enemy Country: Wilkie Collins." In The Dangerous Edge (B215), pp. 1-30.
Biographical information and analyses of several of Collins's novels, with emphasis on their detective-fiction elements (notably The Dead Secret (1857), The Woman in White (1860) and The Moonstone (1868)) make this important reading for Collinsians. Lambert is excellent on the "explanation scene, that usually fatal curse of the detective story." (BFF)

E671. Lawson, Lewis A. "Wilkie Collins and The Moonstone." American Imago 20 (1963), pp. 61-79.
Sexual symbolism in the novel is studied. (BFF)

E672. McCleary, G. F. "A Victorian Classic." The Fortnightly Review 166 (1946):137-41; rpt. in On Detective Fiction and Other Things (B237), pp. 19-25.
This general discussion of The Moonstone contains fine material. Cuff "is probably the most life-like and convincing sleuth in the whole of mystery fiction." Cuff's original was Jonathan Whicher, of Scotland Yard. Collins's limitations--dull attempts at humor and a faulty style--are also analyzed (although subsequent critics no longer ascribe to these theories). (BFF)

E673. Marshall, William H. Wilkie Collins. NY: Twayne Publishers, 1970.
Tailored to the requirements of the Twayne volumes, this one offers interesting information about and assessments of Collins's detective ventures over many pages. The Moonstone "may well be Collins's most skillfully constructed work...and it fully deserves its place as the first English detective novel" (p. 85). The chapters on the short stories and plays (pp. 47-52) give keen insights into detection literature. (BFF)

E674. Messac, Régis (B257).
Collins's name crops up in many spots. Strangely, Messac minimizes the detective-novel element in The Moonstone, arguing that Collins wished to

avoid a reputation as a writer of mystery fiction. (BFF)

E675. Miller, David A. "From roman policier to roman-police: Wilkie Collins' The Moonstone." Novel 13:2 (Wtr 80):153-70; reprinted, in an Italian translation, in Calibano 3 (1979):100-20.
The Moonstone seen as variations on a "discourse of power."

E676. Murch, A. E. (B267), pp. 92-114, 258-59.
Collins derived much from Poe and from French sources for his novels of crime and detection--those for which he is acclaimed today. This account is informed and useful. (BFF)

E677. Nelson, Bill. "Evil as Illusion in the Detective Story." Clues 1:1 (Spring 80):9-14.
Thematic study with particular attention to The Moonstone and Graham Greene's Brighton Rock. (James R. McCahery)

E678. Ousby, Ian. "Wilkie Collins' The Moonstone and the Constance Kent Case." Notes & Queries, January 74, p. 25.
Sgt. Cuff's penchant for roses and rose-growing may have been suggested by the character of Sgt. Adolphus Williamson who assisted Inspector Whicher in the original investigation of the Kent case and was later appointed the first Chief Constable of the C. I. D.

E679. ______. "Wilkie Collins and Other Sensation Novelists." In Bloodhounds of Heaven (B300), pp. 111-36.
The Moonstone receives lengthy analysis, notably in terms of the creation of Cuff. The Collins-Dickens relationship is also assessed. (BFF)

E680. Page, Norman, ed. Wilkie Collins: The Critical Heritage. London and Boston: Routledge and Kegan Paul, 1974.
There are generous selections from contemporaneous reviews of The Moonstone, pp. 169-81, and Collins's methods and successes in producing detective fiction are treated repeatedly in the contents of this volume. (BFF)

E681. Quayle, Eric. The Collector's Book of Detective Fiction (B322), pp. 42-50.
In addition to bibliophilic information, there is excellent criticism of character and plot in The Moonstone. (BFF)

E682. Quilter, Harry. Preferences in Art, Life and Literature. London: Swan Sonnenschein, 1892. See pp. 247-80.
This is the best early critique of Collins's fiction, condensing two early, hard-to-locate periodical essays by Quilter. He thinks that many critics deliberately denigrated Collins and his writing. There are fine analyses of Collins's pictorial methods, techniques he doubtless learned because of his family's associations with painting and graphic artists. (BFF)

E683. Robinson, Kenneth. Wilkie Collins: A Biography. London: John Lane, 1952; NY: Macmillan, 1952; rpr. Westport, CT: Greenwood Press, 1972; London: Davis-Poynter Ltd., 1974.
This "standard" life of Collins offers little literary criticism, although matters of composition, reception, and serialization of novels like The Moonstone are detailed. Breen 144 (BFF)

E685. Sayers, Dorothy L. "Introduction." In The Moonstone, by Wilkie Collins,

pp. v-xvi. London: J. M. Dent; NY: E. P. Dutton, 1944.
An essay that is packed with critical gems, this one should attract all readers of The Moonstone. Sayers credits Collins as the first to employ scientific machinery in solving the mystery. Treatment of women places Collins far beyond his contemporaries; his women are "strong, resolute, and intellectual." Plot is a strong point in The Moonstone; his style is "on the whole sober and pedestrian." (BFF)

E686. ______. Wilkie Collins: A Critical and Biographical Study. Edited by E. R. Gregory. Toledo, OH: The Friends of the Univ. of Toledo Library, 1977. 120pp. Wraps. Edition limited to 1000 numbered copies.
First publication of this unfinished study, from the ms. at the Manuscript Humanities Research Center in Austin, Texas. Gregory notes Sayers's own debt to Collins. The later pages review the problems inherent in "sensation" fiction, with comment about Collins's detective ventures. This book, a project long mentioned but never completed by Sayers, reveals affinities of the twentieth-century writer with her nineteenth-century subject. Reviews: TLS, 2 Dec 77, 1398; TSR 2;3 (Aug 78):18-21. (BFF & REB)

E687. Sehlbach, Hans. Untersuchungen uber Romankunst von Wilkie Collins |Investigations of the art of the novel in Wilkie Collins|. Jena, 1931; rpt Garland, 1979. 198pp.
While Wilkie Collins is usually considered the most skilled "plotter" in nineteenth-century English literature, very little work has been done in analyzing the means that he used. The present work is the only thorough analysis of his story plans, tension devices, misdirections, and resolutions, as well as of such basic topics as characterization and even sentence structure. As T. S. Eliot has said, almost every modern novelist could learn matters of technique from Collins. (EFB)

E688. Starrett, Vincent. "Introduction." In The Moonstone, by Wilkie Collins, pp. vii-xviii. NY: Heritage Press, 1959.
This introduction was written by a practitioner of detective fiction himself. Collins's sources are set forth; his "firsts"--aligning him with Poe--particularly that of creating "fair play," give him distinction. Betteredge and Cuff stand out above the other characters. (BFF)

E689. Stewart, J. I. M. "Introduction." In The Moonstone, pp. 7-24. Harmondsworth and Baltimore: Penguin Books, 1966 (many reprintings).
Stewart, detective writer Michael Innes, provides a sensible overview to Collins's career and to The Moonstone. Remarks on plot are particularly useful. (BFF)

E690. Stewart, R. F. ...And Always a Detective (B380).
The Moonstone is placed historically with other nineteenth-century detective novels. Collins's derivations from Poe are noted. Stewart corrects many earlier misimpressions and bits of misinformation about Collins's famous detective novel. Collins's name appears throughout this book. (BFF)

E691. Swinburne, Algernon Charles. "Wilkie Collins." Fortnightly Review, 1 Nov 1889, pp. 589-99. Reprinted in Studies in Prose and Poetry, pp. 110-28 (London: Chatto and Windus, 1894); in The Complete Works of Algernon Charles Swinburne, edited by Edmund Gosse and Thomas James Wise, vol 15, pp. 289-306 (London: William Heinemann, 1926); and in Wilkie Collins: The Critical Heritage, edited by Norman Page, pp. 253-64 (London and Boston:

Routledge and Kegan Paul, 1974).
This classic essay is an early assessment of Collins's art by a contemporary and a great admirer. The Moonstone is Collins's greatest accomplishment. (BFF)

E692. Symons, Julian. Bloody Murder (B387), pp. 42-57.
The Moonstone is excellent detective fiction. It is compared with The Notting Hill Mystery (1862) in terms of detection and technique (multiple narration). (BFF)

E693. ______. "Introduction." In The Woman in White, by Wilkie Collins, pp. 7-21. Harmondsworth and Baltimore: Penguin, 1974.

E694. Tillotson, Geoffrey. "Wilkie Collins's No Name." In Criticism and the Nineteenth-Century, pp. 231-43. London: Univ. of London, The Athalone Press, 1951; NY: Barnes & Noble, 1951.
Some references are made to detective fiction, to thrillers and the Gothic novel, but this is basically a study of the novel and of Collins's lack of "a sound sense of morality."

E695. Tillotson, Kathleen. "Dickens, Wilkie Collins, and the Suicidal Curates." Dickensian 69:3 (Sept 75):173. Not seen.

E696. Waugh, Arthur. "Wilkie Collins and His Mantle: A Personal Prediction." The Academy and Literature 62 (1902):364-65.
Waugh compares The Hound of the Baskervilles, a new novel in 1902, with The Moonstone, as regards atmosphere and creation of plausible characters. (BFF)

E697. Wolfe, Peter. "Point of View and Characterization in Wilkie Collins's The Moonstone." Forum (University of Houston) 4 (1965):27-29.
Technically, The Moonstone is Collins's most interesting novel. The narrators reveal interesting characters, although had Rachel Verinder related a section the book overall might be better. (BFF)

COLLINSON, PETER. See HAMMETT, DASHIELL

CONANT, PAUL

Ref: Hubin 2; UN 4:9 (1952):6-7, 15 (photo).

CONDON, RICHARD

Ref: Hubin 2, TCCMW, ABMI(S).

Int: PW, 24 June 83, pp. 66-67 (photo).

E698. Buckley, Tom. "The Literary Conspiracies of Richard Condon." NYT Magazine, 2 Sept 79, pp. 16-17, 30, 35, 44-45. Photograph.
Profile.

E699. Condon, Richard. "Party of One." Holiday 31 (Jan 62):10, 16-20. Illus.
A baroque diversion on how Condon came to write his novels.

E699a. Gonzalez, Arturo F., Jr. "Richard Condon: Booksellers Are His Business." Writer's Digest 56:11 (Nov 76):22-25. Photos.
Profile.

CONNINGTON, J. J.

Ref: Hubin 2, TCCMW, EMD, CC, ABMI(S).

E700. Beams, David. "The Quality of Ingenuity: The Work of J. J. Connington." TAD 15 (1982):4-12. Illus.
A detailed survey of the novels of Connington, creator of a scientific sleuth in the manner of Freeman and Crofts.

E701. Malosse, Jean. "Romanciers anglais 'classiques' oubliés: J. J. Connington et Christopher Bush |Forgotten 'classic' English novelists|." Enigmatika 24 (July 83), pp. 36-41.
Biographies and short critical appreciations.

E702. Stewart, A. W. Alias J. J. Connington. London: Hollis and Carter, 1947. xi, 279pp.
Posthumously published volume of essays on various topics, including a few short comments on Sherlock Holmes, true crime, plotting, the Loch Ness monster, etc. Very little genre material, except for the Preface, pp. vii-xi, in which crime writing and the choice of the "Connington" pseudonym are discussed. (REB & GG)

CONRAD, JOSEPH

Ref: Hubin 2, EMD, CC, ABMI(S).

E703. Aisenberg, Nadya. "Joseph Conrad and the Thriller." In Aisenberg (B4), pp. 111-67.
A complex investigation of thriller (sensation/adventure) and detective fiction elements in Conrad's work. In addition to drawing attention to underlying structural elements (myth and fairy tale), Aisenberg discusses the evolution of the political thriller and the use of devices from melodrama and sensation fiction to "convey the modern sense of crisis, of urgency, of doubt."

E704. Baird, Newton. "Conrad's Probe to Absolute Zero." TAD 9 (1976):43-49.
A study of the characters and plot structure in Conrad's novel The Secret Agent with some discussion of its detective fiction elements.

E705. Walton, James. "Conrad, Dickens and the Detective Novel." Nineteenth-Century Fiction 23 (March 69):446-62.
On Dickens' influence on Conrad with discussion of the "important connection" between the detectives in Bleak House and The Secret Agent.

CONSTANTINE, K. C.

Ref: Hubin 2.

Int: PW, 17 June 83, pp. 76-77.

E706. Barzun, Jacques, and Taylor, Wendell Hertig. "Introduction." In The Man Who Liked to Look at Himself (NY, 1973), by K. C. Constantine. "Crime Fiction 1950-1975" (B18).

E707. Constantine, K. C. "Afterword." In The Man Who Liked to Look at Himself and A Fix Like This, by K. C. Constantine. A Godine Double Detective. Boston: David Godine, 1983.
Constantine, showing a wry sense of humor about himself, discusses his pseudonym and his desire to preserve a "normal" life for himself and his

family, the genesis of Mario Balzic, and his deep seriousness about writing.

E708. Retchko, Bob. "Beer-Drinking Chief Wins Literary Toast." Pittsburgh Press, 11 Dec 77, C1. Interview.
Constantine is a pseudonym and although the writer apparently lives near Pittsburgh his anonymity is preserved.

E709. Winks, Robin. "Afterword." In The Rocksburg Railroad Murders (1972) and The Blank Page (1974), by K. C. Constantine, pp. 151-158. A Godine Double Detective. Boston: David R. Godine, Publisher, 1982.
Winks, who discovered Constantine's fiction almost a decade after its first publication, describes that discovery, a telephone coversation with Constantine (who jealously guards his pseudonymity), and a trip to Southwestern Pennsylvania where he saw the "authentic Americana" that is captured in Constantine's novels.

COOK, ROBIN

Ref: Hubin 2, SN, ABMI(S).

See also: C330.

E710. Jennes, Gail. "Dr. Robin Cook has an Rx for Success: A 'Brain' in the Bookstores and a Beauty at Home." 'Couples' dept. People, 6 Apr 81, pp. 62, 65-66. 4 photos.
Profile of Robin Cook and second wife Barbara. Some biographical information on Cook and comments on his writing methods. (REB)

E711. McFadden, Steve. "Robin Cook and Coma." Boston Today, Apr 78, pp. 12-14.
Profile of author Cook, with cover photo. (REB)

COOPER, BRIAN

Ref: Hubin 2, TCCMW, ABMI(S).

COOPER, COURTNEY RYLEY

Ref: Hubin 2, ABMI(S); Argosy, 15 March 30.

COPPARD, A. E.

Ref: TCCMW, CC.

COPPEL, ALEC

Ref: Hubin 2, TCCMW, SN, ABMI(S).

COPPEL, ALFRED

Ref: Hubin 2, ABMI(S).

Int: DAST 11:5 (1978):14-17 (photo).

COPPER, BASIL

Ref: Hubin 2, TCCMW, ABMI(S).

CORCORAN, WILLIAM

Ref: Hubin 2; Argosy, 7 Feb 31.

CORKHILL, LOUIS

Ref: Hubin 2; UN 3:12 (1951):14-15 (photo).

CORRIGAN, MARK

Ref: Hubin 2, TCCMW, CC.

CORY, DESMOND

Ref: Hubin 2, TCCMW, CC, ABMI(S).

Cotton, Jerry

Ref: Hubin 2.

E712. Duedder, Rolf. "Jerry Cotton vor Gericht |Jerry Cotton before the tribunal|." Die Zeit 9 (26 Feb 71):10.
News article about Heinz Werner Hoeber. Includes information about his efforts to raise his royalty percentage, as well as data on the Cotton series. Illus. with a photo of Hoeber standing in front of a silhouette target. (GG)

E713. Goode, Greg. "Introducing...Jerry Cotton." TPP 5:3 (May/June 83):3-11.
One of the most popular German "Helfroman (series novel)." Jerry Cotton is both the series character and attributed author although the writer who has contributed most to the series is probably Heinz Werner Hoeber. With a partial chronological checklist through 1958. Dime-novel and paperback formats are listed, as are films and movie tie-in editions.

E714. Kunkel, Klaus. "Ein artiger James Bond. Jerry Cotton und der Bastei-Verlag |A sort of James Bond: Jerry Cotton and the Bastei press|." Der Monat 209:1 (1966):61-70; also published in Vogt (B424), Vol. II, pp. 559-78.
The first, longest and most informative article on Germany's most popular dime novel (Heftroman) character, FBI agent Jerry Cotton. Kunkel describes the character, the history and astounding success of the series, which began in the middle 50s, as well as giving lots of information on its "house" operation-style production. (GG)

COULTER, STEPHEN

Ref: Hubin 2, TCCMW, ABMIS.

COURTIER, S(IDNEY) H(OBSON)

Ref: Hubin 2, TCCMW, EMD, CC, ABMI(S).

COWEN, FRANCES

Ref: Hubin 2, TCCMW, ABMI(S).

COX, ANTHONY BERKELEY. See BERKELEY, ANTHONY

COX, (Sir) EDMUND C.

Ref: Hubin, ABMI.

E715. Moskowitz, Sam. "Introduction." To "The Last Story," by Sir Edmund C. Cox. "Gaslight Detectives" series (C565). MSMM, Sept 73, pp. 87-89.

COX, WILLIAM R.

Ref: Hubin 2, SN, ABMI.

See also: D300.

E716. Drew, Bernard. "Pulp Profile: William R. Cox." Attic Revivals 5 (1982):7.

Commentary by Cox on his pulp writing with framing comments by Drew. Only passing mention of crime fiction (series characters used by the author). (REB)

E717. Traylor, Jim. "William R. Cox: An Interview and an Appreciation." TAD 15 (1982):253-66. Photographs and illustrations.
Cox has written for the pulps, the slicks, and television and since 1954 has published some 75 books, of which many are westerns written under pseudonyms. Cox talks about his years as a pulp writer and Traylor comments generally on Cox's work. With a selected bibliography.

COXE, GEORGE HARMON

Ref: Hubin 2, TCCMW, EMD, CC, SN, ABMI; The Writer 50:12 (Dec 37):380-82 (characterization and plotting); The Writer 53:12 (Dec 40):362-65; The Writer 79:9 (Sept 59):15-17 (characterization).

E718. Cox, J. Randolph. "Mystery Master: A Survey and Appreciation of the Fiction of George Harmon Coxe." TAD 6 (1972/73):63-74, 160-62, 232-41; TAD 7 (1973/74):11-23.
A thorough study of the career of writer Coxe. The final installment includes a "chronological list of his writings." The biographical material is based, in part, on interviews with Coxe. Additions to the bibliography as follows: Frank D. McSherry, Jr., letter TAD 7 (1973/74):144; J. R. Cox, letter TAD 9 (1975/76):168.

E719. Coxe, George Harmon. "Flash Casey." In Penzler, Great Detectives (B309), pp. 37-46.
Along with a portrait of his fictional character, Coxe talks about his relationships with editors and publishers.

CRAIG, JONATHAN

Ref: Hubin 2, CC, SN, ABMI.

E720. Schleret, J.-J. "Entretien avec Jonathan Craig (Frank E. Smith)." Enigmatika 24 (July 83), pp. 61-66.
Interview and a bibliography of his work, listing both English-language and French publications, novels and short stories.

CRANE, FRANCES

Ref: Hubin 2, TCCMW, EMD, ABMI; The Writer 59:4 (April 46):111-13 (characterization); The Writer 73:7 (July 60):13-15 (setting); The Writer 78:2 (Feb 65):15-17 (researching a story).

CREASEY, JOHN

Ref: Hubin 2, TCCMW, EMD, CC; UN 1:6 (1948):10-11 (photo); UN 3:9 (1951):10-11, 15 (photo); The Writer 73:1 (Jan 60):18-20.

See also: C540, C541.

E721. Barzun, Jacques, and Taylor, Wendell Hertig. "Introduction." In Gideon's River (NY, 1968), by J. J. Marric. "Crime Fiction 1970-1975" (B18).

E722. Bird, Tom. "John Creasey Remembered." Short Stories Magazine 1:8 (July 81):9-12.
A brief review of Creasey's writing career. (RCSA)

E723. Boyles, John. "A Word for John Creasey: J. J. Marric's Gideon's Risk." TAD

11 (1978):282-83. Illus.
A discussion of an early Gideon series novel that Boyles considers to be representative.

E724. Briney, R. E. and John Creasey. "A John Creasey Bibliography." TAD 2 (1968/69):5-22.
A bibliographic summary of his writings as of September 1968. Corrections and addenda in letters in volume 2, as follows: R. E. Briney, pp. 123-26, 276; John Creasey, p. 127; Joseph J. Coffey, p. 199; Andy Zerbe, p. 201.

E725. Creasey, John. "John Creasey - Faction or Fiction? A Candid Commentary in Third Person." TAD 2 (1968/69):1-3.
An autobiographical memoir by Creasey written in the third person. With a personal note by Allen Jubin on a visit with Creasey and his wife (pp. 3-5).

E726.. (Creasey, John) _John Creasey--Fact or Fiction? A Candid Commentary in Third Person_, by John Creasey (with) _A John Creasey Bibliography_ by R.E. Briney and John Creasey. White Bear Lake, Minn.: (Allen J. Hubin), 1968; revised edition, 1969. Offprint from _The Armchair Detective_, Vol. 2, No. 1, pp. 1-22.
In addition to Creasey's own (auto)biographical commentary, the pamphlet contains a memoir of Creasey by Allen J. Hubin. The bibliography, complete as of January 1969, lists 534 books by Creasey, under twenty-six by-lines. The revised edition includes projected titles through 1971. These offprints were prepared mainly for Creasey's use in responding to letters from his readers. CC 2931. (REB)

E727. Creasey, John. "Mystery the World Over." _Rotarian_ 91 (Dec 57):14-16.
Creasey on the thriller and its popularity. Includes a biographical sketch of the writer.

E728. ______. "What Is a Thriller?" _The Crime-Book Magazine_ 3:3 (March 36):8, 12.
Tongue-in-cheek discussion in dialogue of thrillers as opposed to detective novels. (RCSA)

E730. Harvey, Deryk. "The Best of John Creasey." TAD 7 (1973/74):42-43.
One reader's guide to Creasey's fiction.

E731. ______. "John Creasey." DAST 6:4 (1973):3-6.
Memorial essay. (MS)

E732. Hedman, Iwan. "John Creasey -- Master of Mystery." DAST 6:3 (1973):23-27.
Creasey's extraordinary productivity. (MS)

E733. "How To Be the Most." _Newsweek_ 53 (2 Feb 59):85-6. Portrait.
A fact piece on Creasey's career with some interview comments by the writer.

E734. Nevins, Francis M., Jr. "Remembering John Creasey." _Xenophile_ 4 (June 73/74), pp. 37-38.
A tribute to the man and the writer with information that appears to have been based on meetings with Creasey.

E735. Wood, Jack. "The John Creasey Story." CDA, 1957, pp. 123-25. Brief survey of Creasey's career to date.

CRICHTON, MICHAEL

Ref: Hubin 2, TCCMW, ABMI(S).

CRICHTON, ROBERT

Int: Newark Star-Ledger, 12 Feb 74 (rpt. in Authors in the News, p. 120; photo).

CRISPIN, EDMUND

Ref: Hubin 2, TCCMW, EMD, CC, ABMI(S); Cannon, AHMM 27:11 (Oct 82):77-80.

See also: B349.

E736. Barzun, Jacques, and Taylor, Wendell Hertig. Preface to Buried for Pleasure (New York, 1949), by Edmund Crispin. In A Book of Prefaces (B17), pp. 37-38.

E737. Montgomery, Robert Bruce. "Edmund Crispin." TAD 12 (1979):183-85. Semi-autobiographical sketch by Montgomery/Crispin, written for Walker publicity department. First publication.

E738. Pettersson, Sven-Ingmar. "Deckarportratt Nr 12." DAST 9 (1975/76): 40-41.
Article on Edmund Crispin in DAST writers' portrait series. (MS)

E739. Sarjeant, William A. S. "Edmund Crispin: A Memorial and Appreciation." TPP 3:3 (May/June 80):3-10.
A review of Crispin's life and writing career; with a checklist of his writings and a list of biographical sources.

E740. ______. "Obsequies about Oxford: The Investigations and Eccentricities of Gervase Fen." TAD 14 (1981):196-209. Photo and illustrations.
A profile of Crispin's Oxford don detective.

CROFTS, FREEMAN WILLS

Ref: Hubin 2, TCCMW, EMD, CC, ABMI(S).

See also: B253, B349.

E741. Barzun, Jacques, and Taylor, Wendell Hertig. Preface to The Box Office Murders (London, 1929), by Freeman Wills Crofts. In A Book of Prefaces (B17), pp. 39-40.

E743. Keddie, James, Jr. "Freeman Wills Crofts." TAD 2 (1968/69):137-42. Photo.
A checklist of Crofts' novels and short stories with a brief biographical introduction in which Keddie cites from correspondence and other material by Crofts. Correction by Joy Sanderson in letter, TAD 3 (1969/70):62.

E744. Malosse, Jean. "Mon Ami F. W. Crofts." Enigmatika 20 (1982):64-70.
Malosse re-reads Crofts, finds that he holds up well because of the two elements he finds indispensable to good detective novels: variety and believability. With a short biography and a bibliography of works translated into French.

E745. Thomson, H. Douglas. "The Realistic Detective Story. 2. Freeman Wills Crofts." In Thomson (B404), pp. 176-92.
A discussion of Crofts' matter-of-fact style, his mastery in plotting and his able characterization of Chief-Inspector French, concluding with comments on the novels.

CROSS, AMANDA

Ref: Hubin 2, TCCMW, CC, ABMI(S).

Int: Graduate Woman, July/Aug 80, pp. 14-21; In Cooper-Clark (B18), pp. 187-204.

See also: B16, C453.

E746. Barzun, Jacques, and Taylor, Wendell Hertig. "Introduction." In In the Last Analysis (NY, 1964), by Amanda Cross. "Crime Fiction 1950-1975" (B18).

E747. Cross, Amanda. "The Manners of the Mystery." Washington Post Book World, 19 July 81, p. 5.
Cross on her personal tastes in mystery reading. Essay and reading list of Cross favorites. (KLM)

E748. Persson, Lena. "Pretensiös och pratsam, snobbig och radikal -- den svårätkomliga Amanda Cross lika irriterende som fascinerande |Pretentious and chatty, snobby and radical --- Amanda Cross, difficult to approach, both irritating and fascinating|." Jury 11:1 (1982):31-39.
Somewhat negative view of Cross' work, but expressing the hope that she will continue to write detective fiction. (MS)

E749. Purcell, J. M. "The 'Amanda Cross' Case: Socializing the U. S. Academic Mystery." TAD 13 (1980):36-40. Illus.
An interesting attempt to analyze Cross' style and define the attitudes that are embedded in her work. The polemical and the analytical are not the happiest of companions in this essay but Purcell ranges widely over Cross' work with references to Heilbrun's biography to try to support his arguments and the results are provocative if not always completely convincing.

E750. Wilt, Judith. "Feminism Meets the Detective Novel." Clues 3:2 (Fall/Winter 82):47-51.
Feminist themes in Cross' Death in a Tenured Position compared with Sayers' Gaudy Night and Robert Parker's Looking for Rachel Wallace.

CROSS, JAMES

Ref: Hubin 2, SN, ABMI(S); Lachman, TPP 2:6 (Nov/Dec 79):17-18, 16.

CROSSEN, KENDALL FOSTER

Ref: Hubin 2, TCCMW, CC, ABMI(S).

See also: D334.

E751. "Kendell Foster Crossen." TMN 12 (June 1979):A1-A18, B1-B24.
Much of the issue is devoted to this pulp/comic book/detective fiction writer. Contents: Steve Lewis, "Interview of Kendell Foster Crossen," pp. A1-A4; "A (Partial) Index to Reviews of Crossen Books (w/Extracts)," pp. A5-A10; Myrtis Broset, Art Scott and Don Miller, "A

Selection of Reviews of Crossen Books," pp. A11-A16; "Odds and Ends," pp. A17-A18 (excerpts from Crossen letters, bibliographic note by Francis M. Nevins, Jr.); Don Miller, "Kendell Foster Crossen Bibliography," pp. B1-B24 (by title, by pseudonym/author's name variation, by principal character (s), by magazine or publisher, Secondary Sources, Addenda/Corrigenda).

E752. Thorpe, Dickson. "Will the Real Ken Crossen Please Stand Up?" TMF 1:2 (March 77):5-10.
Biography with a checklist of Crossen's writings under each of his several pseudonyms. See TMN 12 (June 79):B23 for a critical note on information in Thorpe's checklist.

CRUMLEY, JAMES

Ref: Hubin 2, ABMI.

E753. Cahill, Tim. "Screenwriter's Syndrome: Crumley's Missouri Breaks." Rolling Stone, 12 July 79, p. 26, 29. Photo.
Profile incorporating some interview material. (Bill Crider)

E753a. Newlin, Keith. "C. W. Sughrue's Whiskey Visions." MFS 29:3 (Autumn 83):545-55.
Crumley, in The Last Good Kiss, portrays the American landscape as a decaying wasteland. However, he offers a solution in the use of whiskey as a means toward redemption in a transcendental vision of America. Newlin refers to Crumley's irony but his very serious treatment does not take into account the comedy in Crumley's view of the wasteland. The failure to understand the tone undermines Newlin's study.

CULLINGFORD, GUY

Ref: Hubin 2, TCCMW, CC, ABMIS.

CUMBERLAND, MARTEN

Ref: Hubin 2, TCCMW, CC, ABMI(S); UN 2:6 (1950):8-9 (photo).

CUMMINGS, RAY

Ref: Hubin 2, ABMIS; Argosy, 8 Feb 30.

CUNNINGHAM, A. B.

Ref: Hubin 2, CC, ABMI; UN 1:2 (1949):8-9; UN 3:5 (1951):6-7, 14 (photo).

E754. Boucher, Anthony. "Introduction." In Blood Runs Cold (orig. title: The Hunter is the Hunted, Dutton, 1950), by A. B. Cunningham. NY: Mercury, 1954. Wraps.

E755. "Jess Roden." UN 2:6 (1950):10-11. Photo of A. B. Cunningham.
Mock statement by fictional character Roden.

CUNNINGHAM, E. V.

Ref: Hubin 2, TCCMW, SN, ABMI(S).

Int: PW, 1 Apr 83, pp. 64-5 (photo; interview of Howard Fast with no reference to his detective fiction).

E756. Deloux, Jean-Pierre, ed. "Howard Fast." Polar 25 (15 Oct 82):163-85.
An abbreviated Polar dossier with an essay by Deloux, and an interview and a bibliography/filmography prepared by Jean-Jacques Schleret. In the

essay, Deloux examines chronologically Fast's work as E. V. Cunningham. He discusses Fast's political views and their repercussions in his early detective fiction and, while he speaks warmly of the Cunningham series, regrets that Cunningham has finally "silenced" Howard Fast, the political activist. Schleret's short interview was conducted in 1974 with some additional material gathered in 1979, The bibliography records only the detective fiction.

CUNNINGHAM, EUGENE

Ref: Hubin 2, ABMI; Argosy, 7 June 30.

CURTISS, URSULA

Ref: Hubin 2, TCCMW, EMD, CC, ABMI.

Int: TAD 4 (1970/71):140-44; see also Letter, R. W. Hays, TAD 5 (1971/72):51-52.

DAHL, ROALD

Ref: Hubin 2, TCCMW, ABMI(S).

E757. Merrick, Stephen. "Roald Dahl: The Writer Who Gets Paid for What He Throws Away." Argosy 27:8 (Aug 66):20-34.
Long interview report covering many aspects of the writers's life and work. (RCSA)

DALY, CARROLL JOHN

Ref: Hubin 2, TCCMW, EMD, SN, ABMI(S).

See also: D343.

E758. Barson, Michael S. "There's No Sex in Crime: The Two-Fisted Homilies of Race Williams." Clues 2:2 (Fall/Winter 81):103-12.
The major shortcomings and modest successes of Daly as a writer of pulp/hard-boiled fiction.

E759. Crider, Allen B. "Race Williams--Private Investigator." In Landrum (B216), pp. 110-13.
A discussion of Daly's Snarl of the Beast, a novel Crider sees as his masterpiece.

E760. Daly, Carroll John. "The Ambulating Lady." Writer's Digest 27:5 (April 47):19-24; reprinted--with a short letter from Daly published in Black Mask 7:9 (Nov 1924):128--in Clues 2:2 (Fall/Winter 81):113-15.
Daly describes his early verbose, unsaleable manuscripts and argues for simplicity and against vulgarity. He discusses briefly story openings and the need to maintain suspense but with breathing spaces for the reader.

E761. Finch, G.A. "A Fatal Attraction." TAD 13:2 (1980):112-24.
An attempt to analyse the appeal the mediocre, "grotesquely literate" writings of Daly had for the editors of Black Mask and the magazine's readers. Finch argues, in his introduction, for the use of diverse critical techniques for discussing detective fiction and his approach is sociological, literary/historical, and textual.

E762. Nolan, William F. "Pulp Pioneer of the Private Eye." MSMM 44:10 (Oct 80):56-68.
Biographical sketch and survey of Daly's career, pointing out his

influence on later writers such as Spillane. Includes comments by other pulp writers who knew Daly. (REB)

E763. ______. "Carroll John Daly: The Forgotten Pioneer of the Private Eye." TAD 4:1 (1970/71):1-4.
A survey of Daly's life and writing career. Includes an excellent bibliography of material on Daly in books and magazines, much of it short discussions of Daly in multi-subject articles, but an essential, basic list of sources for anyone interested in his work.

E764. Shibuk, Charles. "Introduction." In Snarl of the Beast, by C. J. Daly, pp. v-viii. Gregg Press Mystery Fiction Series (B134).

DALY, ELIZABETH

Ref: Hubin 2, TCCMW, EMD, CC, ABMI(S); The Writer 61:6 (June 48):186-87.

E765. Barzun, Jacques, and Taylor, Wendell Hertig. "Introduction." In Death and Letters (NY, 1950), by Elizabeth Daly. "Crime Fiction 1950-1975" (B18).

E766. Fox, Estelle. "A Profile of Henry Gamadge and an Elizabeth Daly Checklist." TMRN 4:4 (May 71):27.

E767. Waldron, Ann. "The Golden Years of Elizabeth Daly." TAD 7 (1973/74):25-28.
A useful overview of Daly's life and work which includes comments by the writer and some critical evaluations of her fiction.

DANE, CLEMENCE

Ref: Hubin 2, TCCMW, CC, ABMI(S).

DANIEL, GLYN

Ref: Hubin 2, TCCMW, EMD, CC, ABMI(S).

DANIEL, ROLAND

Ref: Hubin 2, TCCMW, ABMI(S).

E768. Lofts, W. O. G. "Roland Daniel--Prolific Mystery Writer." TAD 6 (1972/73):242, 245.
Profile.

DANIELS, NORMAN A.

Ref: Hubin 2, SN, ABMIS.

See also: D334.

E769. Barson, Michael S. "An Interview with Norman Daniels." PQ 4:3 (Fall 81):5-14. Illus.
With a preface on "Norman Daniels--The Writer as Assemblyline" and a chronological list of pb originals. A pulp writer who made the transition to paperbacks.

E770. Murray, Will. "The Amazing Norman A. Daniels." Echoes 1:4 (Feb 83): 7-15.
A profile of writer Daniels with detailed information on series to which he contributed (The Black Bat, The Crimson Mask, and others). Also includes a checklist of publications based on Daniels' records.

DANNAY, FREDERIC. See QUEEN, ELLERY

DARD, FREDERIC (aka "San Antonio")

Ref: Hubin 2.

Int: MM 304, June 73 (as Frédéric Dard); MM 308, Oct 73 (as San Antonio); NL, 13-17 Nov 81, p. 8 (photo).

E771. Dard, Frédéric. Les Mots en épingle de San Antonio |Catchy expressions from San Antonio|. Paris: Fleuve Noir, 1980.
Collection of aphorisms and puns taken from San Antonio's early novels. (JB)

E772. San Antonio. Je le jure |I swear it|. Paris: Editions Stock et Fleuve noir, 1975. Reprinted in the series "J'ai lu," no. 93 (Paris, 1977).
In this very interesting autobiographical confession, the Janus author San Antonio/Frédéric Dard talks about this dichotomy, about the way he practises his art, and his love of language. (JB)

E773. Tourteau, Jean-Jacques. "Méthodes et procédés récents (San Antonio) |Recent methods and techniques|." In Tourteau (B408), pp. 217-36.
After a brief discussion of the ways in which the French crime novelists of the sixties moved away from genre classifications, Tourteau analyzes the popular San Antonio series. With their focus on language and, in particular, argot, Tourteau acknowledges that they are virtually impossible to translate and are thus largely, and perhaps undeservedly, unknown outside France. See also pp. 311-17 for an analysis of a series novel (as by San Antonio), Fleur de nave vinaigrette; and pp. 302-305 for an analysis of Toi le venin (as by F. Dard).

DARK, ELEANOR

Ref: ABMI(S).

E774. Day, A. Grove. Eleanor Dark. Boston, MA: Twayne, 1976. 168pp. Index.
Critical study of Australian novelist whose works included occasional mysteries. (This author is not listed in Hubin 2.) (REB)

DAVEY, JOCELYN

Ref: Hubin 2, TCCMW, CC, ABMI(S).

DAVID-NEEL, ALEXANDRA

E775. van de Wetering, Janwillem. "Introduction." In The Power of Nothingness, by Alexandra David-Neel and Lama Youngden, translated by van de Wetering, pp. vii-xv. Boston: Houghton Mifflin, 1982.
In this introduction to a most unusual mystery thriller, van de Wetering gives us a biographical sketch of world-traveler and Buddhist scholar Madame David-Neel (1868-1969). The book is a translation of a French novel (La Puissance du néant) by David-Neel and her adopted son Yongden, a Tibetan lama. Van de Wetering relates how his interest in this extraordinary woman led to the desire to translate her books into English. (JLA)

DAVIDSON, LIONEL

Ref: Hubin 2, TCCMW, ABMI(S).

Int: DAST 13:3 (1980):24-27.

E776. Duprez, Leif. "Outsidern som ofta vinner |The outsider who often wins|." Jury 11:4 (1982):19-26. Photo.
On the writings of Lionel Davidson. (MS)

DAVIDSON, T. L. (pseudonym for DAVID LANDSBOROUGH THOMSON)
Ref: Hubin 2, CC, ABMI(S).

E777. Barzun, Jacques. "Disposition of a Pair of Ghosts." TAD 6 (1972/73):248.
A note in which T. L. Davidson, author of The Murder in the Laboratory, is identified as scientist D. L. Thomson and item no. 2680 of the Catalogue of Crime (A10) is corrected.

DAVIES, L. P.
Ref: Hubin 2, TCCMW, CC, ABMI(S).

DAVIOT, GORDON. See TEY, JOSEPHINE

DAVIS, DOROTHY SALISBURY
Ref: Hubin 2, TCCMW, EMD, CC, ABMI(S); UN 4:10 (1952):10-11 (photo); The Writer 92:8 (Aug 79):23-25 (on plotting).

Int: PW, 13 March 78, pp. 46-47 (Photo); PW, 13 June 80, pp. 6-7 (photo); Mystery 1:2 (March/April 80):8-9, 25 (photos).

E778. Boucher, Anthony. "Introduction." In The Clay Hand (Scribner, 1950), by Dorothy Salisbury Davis. NY: Collier Books, 1963.

E779. Davis, Dorothy Salisbury. "Introduction." In A Gentle Murderer, by D. S. Davis. Gregg Press Mystery Fiction Series (D422).

DAVIS, FREDERICK C.
Ref: Hubin 2, TCCMW, ABMI; The Writer 53:10 (Oct 40):292-94.

See also: D334, D422.

E780. Whittington, Harry. "Hommage a Frederick C. Davis." Les Amis du crime 5 (March 80), pp. 34-35.
A short tribute to Davis, followed by a bibliography which includes French editions.

DAVIS, MILDRED
Ref: Hubin 2, SN, ABMIS; Lachman, TPP 2:5 (Sept/Oct 79):16-18.

E781. Boucher, Anthony. "Introduction." In They Buried a Man (Simon, 1953), by Mildred Davis. NY: Mercury, n.d.

DAVIS, NORBERT
Ref: Hubin 2, SN, ABMI.

E782. Apostolou, John L. "Norbert Davis: Profile of a Pulp Writer." TAD 15 (1982):30-35. Photo.
A biocritical profile with critical notes and a checklist of Davis' mystery and detective fiction in Black Mask, Detective Fiction Weekly, and Dime Detective.

DEAL, BABS

Ref: Hubin 2, ABMI; The Writer 89:5 (May 76):9-11.

DEAN, AMBER

Ref: Hubin 2, TCCMW, ABMI(S); UN 2:4 (1949):10-11 (photo).

DEAN, SPENCER. See STERLING, STEWART

DeANDREA, WILLIAM L.

Ref: Hubin 2, ABMIS.

Int: EQMM, Nov 79, p. 108.

See also: C637.

DE ANGELIS, AUGUSTO

See also: C218.

E784. Rambelli, Loris. "Acculturazione di un genere letterario: il detective, l'analista italiano |Acculturation of a literary genre: the detective, the Italian analyst|." Lingua e Stile 10 (April 75):97-124.
Monographic study of the detective novels of Augusto De Angelis, in the context of the climate of Italian literary taste of the 1930s and 1940s. (LR)

DEBRETT, HAL

Ref: Hubin 2, ABMI; Int: UN 1:10 (1949):6-7 ("puzzle" interview with clues to Debrett's real identity).

DECREST, JACQUES

Int: MM 22, Nov 49.

DE FORD, MIRIAM ALLEN

Ref: Hubin 2, TCCMW, EMD, ABMI(S); Writer's Digest 45:10 (Oct 65):34-36 (on titling and titles).

DEIGHTON, LEN

Ref: Hubin 2, TCCMW, EMD, CC, ABMI(S).

Int: MM 334, March 76 (in French); NYTBR, 21 June 81, p. 34 (photo).

E785. Banks, Jeff, and Dawson, Harry. "The Len Deighton Series." TMF 3:1 (Jan/Feb 79):10-13.
Schematic checklist of Deighton's spy novel series.

E786. Erisman, Fred. "Romantic Reality in the Spy Stories of Len Deighton." TAD 10 (1977):101-105.
An essay on Deighton's first six spy novels with references to Romantic theorists to support Erisman's belief that Deighton's spy is an individualist firmly grounded in an urban society but with the Romantic's ability to create his own self-contained world.

E787. Grosvenor, Rita. "Up in the Ops Room Len Deighton Talks by Telex and Plans Another Blockbuster." Argosy 30:7 (July 69):18-25.
Rather more about the author's lifestyle than his books but contains nonetheless some interesting information about his methods. (RCSA)

E788. Panek, LeRoy L. "Len Deighton." In Panek (B303), pp. 220-35.
In addition to describing Deighton as a writer of spy novels in the new realistic manner and in showing his roots in the classic spy novel, Panek establishes what he sees as Panek's debt to the writers of hard-boiled detective fiction, especially Raymond Chandler.

DE LA TORRE, LILLIAN

Ref: Hubin 2, TCCMW, EMD, CC, ABMI(S).

Int: EQMM, Feb 83, pp. 65-67; March 83, pp. 83-85.

E789. de la Torre, Lillian. "The Pleasures of Histo-Detection." TAD 7 (1973/74):155-62.
Partial text of a lecture delivered by de la Torre at the University of Colorado on October 19, 1983, and in which she relates anecdotes of her researches into famous crimes of history, both invented and actual.

E790. Purcell, Mark. "Lillian de la Torre, Preliminary Bibliography: Blood on the Periwigs." TMRN 4:5 (July/Aug 71):25-27.
The introductory biography includes information on her writing projects.

E790a. Wallace, Frances J. "Lillian de la Torre." WLB 23 (Jan 49):350. Photo.
Profile.

DELVING, MICHAEL

Ref: Hubin 2, TCCMW, CC,ABMI(S).

DEMARIS, OVID

Ref: Hubin 2, TCCMW, SN, ABMI(S).

DEMING, RICHARD

Ref: Hubin 2, TCCMW, ABMI(S); Writer's Digest 36:4 (March 76):13-16 (on researching for writing fiction).

E791. "Richard Deming." Hard-Boiled Dicks 7 (n.d.). 54pp. Wraps.
Issue devoted to an American writer of some 85 books under three pseudonyms (Max Franklin, Emily Moor, and Jessica Fen) and 7 house names (Nick Morino, Jack Lancer, Franklin W. Dixon, David Wilson, Richard Hale Curtis, Lee Davis Willoughby, and Hasley Clark), as well as his own name and that of Ellery Queen. Illustrated with book, paperback, and pulp covers. Contents: Roger Martin, "Editorial," pp. 7-8; "Eléments biographiques," pp. 9-10; "Entretien avec Richard Deming," pp. 11-22 (interview based on correspondence); Art Scott, "Richard Deming," pp. 23-24 (critical essay from Reilly, A143); "Bibliographie," pp. 25-40; "Filmographie," pp. 41-43; R. Deming, "Le serment de sang," pp. 45-54 (fiction; translated by Roger Martin).

DENNIS, RALPH

Ref: Hubin 2, SN, ABMI.

E792. Finch, G. A. "Have You Met Hardman?" TAD 8 (1974/75):275, 270.
A survey of the Popular Library Atlanta-based private eye series.

E793. Garner, Phil. "Mind If I Kill You Off in Chapter Three?" Atlanta Journal and Constitution, 30 June 74, n.p.; reprinted in Authors in the News, Vol. I, pp. 130-31.
Profile.

E794. Graham, Keith. "Novelist Lives on the Margin." Atlanta Constitution (date unknown), 3-A, 3-B.
Some comments on the Hardman series in this interview.

DENT, LESTER

Ref: Hubin 2, TCCMW, SN, ABMIS; Writer's 1940 Yearbook, pp. 17-21 (on characterization.

See also: D367, D389.

E795. Blosser, Fred. "The Man from Miami - Lester Dent's Oscar Sail." TAD 5 (1971/72):93.
A note on the two Oscar Sail private eye stories, first published in Black Mask.

E796. Dent, Lester. "Pulp Paper Master Plot." Bronze Shadows 11 (Aug 67), pp. 15-19; rpt. in Weinberg, E806. Originally published in Writer's Market, 1939.
Detailed notes for writing a pulp story. (RS)

E796a. Gruber, Frank. "Lester Dent." TAD 2 (1968/69):215-16.
Personal reminiscences by a fellow pulp writer.

E797. Murray, Will. "Dent's Detectives." Duende 1, April 74, pp. 8-19. Illus.
Murray analyzes Dent's pulp series detectives to see what common characteristics they share. He concludes that the archetypal model for all of them is Dent himself and, in the last part of the article, profiles Dent to support his thesis.

E798. _____. "The Great Monk." In Attic Revivals, no. 2 (1980), pp. 2-3. Photo.
Introduction to Dent's story "Bat Trap" in which Murray discusses Dent's early career and his use of stock character-types. (REB)

E799. _____. "InciDENTals." CP? 2:4 (Sept 80):21-2.
Dent's paperback writing career.

E800. _____. "Lester Dent: The Last of the Joe Shaw's Black Mask Boys." Clues 2:2 (Fall/Winter 81):128-35.
A discussion of the publication of two Dent stories in Black Mask and of Dent's relationship with editor Joseph T. Shaw.

E801. Potts, Samuel W. "The Man of Bronze--And His Creator." Bronze Shadows 2, Dec 65, pp. 8-9.
Contains some biographical material. (RS)

E802. Sampson, Robert. "After the Bronze Man." In Weinberg (E806), pp. 68-87. Illus.
Sampson first analyses the later Doc Savage novels, which he sees as transitional works as Dent will successfully move from the pulps to the slicks, and then examines in detail his post-Doc fiction which he characterizes as as a "mass of material, still insufficiently known."

E803. _____. "The Argosy Novels." In Weinberg (E806), pp. 37-55. Illus.
Dent published three serial novels (Hades, Hocus Pocus and Genius Jones) in Argosy (1936-8) and Sampson gives detailed analyses of this "forceful,

vigorous, wonderful, wild formula work." He also relates these novels to Dent's other work (especially the Doc Savage novels).

E804. ______. "The Tall Man." In Weinberg (E806), pp. 15-23.
An essay on Dent's two Black Mask stories. Sampson places the stories in the context of Dent's other fiction and also demolishes the commonly-held belief that complex characterization was not to be found in pulp fiction. He makes the basic--and often overlooked--point that character and situation "interacted" in the best pulp fiction. With a checklist of the reprintings of the two stories.

E805. Smith, Billy G. "Doc Savage's Creator--Lester Dent." Bronze Shadows, 2 (Dec 65), pp. 6-7.
Reminiscences of Lester Dent in La Plata, Missouri. (RS)

E806. Weinberg, Robert, ed. The Man Behind Doc Savage. A Tribute to Lester Dent. Oak Lawn, IL: Robert Weinberg, 1974. Wraps. 127pp. Illus. by Frank Hamilton.
Eight essays on Lester Dent, covering not only his Doc Savage pulp novels (written under the house pseudonym of Kenneth Robeson) but also his stories for Argosy and Black Mask, and his "straight" mystery novels. The booklet also contains reprints of two Dent pulp stories, and is illustrated with reproductions of 39 Doc Savage pulp covers plus other drawings and photographs. Contents: R. Weinberg, "The Man Behind Doc Savage," pp. 5-8 (E807); Will Murray, "The Bronze Genius," pp. 9-14 (on the scientific genius of Doc Savage); Robert Sampson, "The Tall Man," pp. 15-23 (E804); Philip José Farmer, "Writing Doc's Biography," pp. 24-30 (on writing Doc Savage: His Apocalyptic Life, D366); Will Murray, "The Lure of the Lost," pp. 31-36 (lost races and forgotten cities in the Doc Savage novels); Robert Sampson, "The Argosy Novels", pp. 37-55 (E803); Will Murray, "Doc at War," pp. 56-63; Lester Dent, "The Pulp Paper Master Fiction Plot," pp. 64-67 (E795); Robert Sampson, "After the Bronze Man," pp. 68-87 (E802); L. Dent, "Funny Faces," pp. 88-100 (story); L. Dent, "The Death Blast," pp. 101-118 (story). (REB/WA)

E807. Weinberg, Robert. "The Man Behind Doc Savage." In Weinberg (E806), pp. 5-8.
A profile of Dent and his contributions to the pulps.

DE POLO, HAROLD

Ref: Hubin 2; Argosy, 13 Sept 30.

DERLETH, AUGUST

Ref: Hubin 2, TCCMW, EMD, CC, ABMI(S); UN 3:12 (1951):6-7, 16 (photo).

See also: E2424.

E808. Derleth, August, compiler (uncredited). August Derleth: Twenty-Five Years of Writing, 1926-1951. Sauk City, WI: Arkham House, 1951. Wraps. Frontis.
A 2-page biographical sketch, a list of the magazines to which Derleth had contributed, a checklist of published books, lists of book introductions by Derleth, textbook and anthology appearances, and selected critical "appraisals." The booklet was distributed free to patrons of Derleth's Arkham House Publishers. An updated and more elaborate version was issued in 1962 (E808). (REB)

E809. Derleth, August, compiler. 100 Books by August Derleth. Foreword by Donald Wandrei. Sauk City, WI: Arkham House Publishers, 1962. 121pp. Wraps. Illus. Edition limited to 1225 copies.

Detailed bibliography of Derleth's books in all fields through 1962, together with checklists of anthology and textbook appearances, work in progress, magazines that had published his work, and extracts from biographical sketches and critical appraisals. Complete contents list for all of Derleth's short story and poetry collections and edited anthologies are included. (REB)

E810. Derleth, August. A Praed Street Dossier. Sauk City, WI: Mycroft & Moran, 1968. 108pp. Illus.

Contains extensive notes on the creation of Derleth's Holmes surrogate, Solar Pons, and on the origins of the stories, together with three sample tales. (REB)

E811. Dutch, Bill. Publications of August W. Derleth, 1907-1971. No date or place of publication; 'Addendum' dated October 1981. 14pp.

Compiled for the August Derleth Society and distributed free to members. Alphabetical list of August Derleth's books, with an attempt to list all English-language editions. A few foreign language translations are included. There are 2 pages of notes on distinguishing first editions, and a 2-page Addendum lists additions and corrections to the original compilation. (The brochure's title erroneously gives Derleth's birth year as 1907; as noted in the Addendum, the correct year is 1909.) (REB)

E812. Hubin, Allen. "Introduction." In The Chronicles of Solar Pons, by August Derleth, pp. vii-ix. Sauk City, WI: Mycroft & Moran, 1958.

E813. Lowndes, R. A. W. "The Editor's Page: Solar Pons." SMS 2:5 (Winter 68/9):4-5, 124, 126-27.

A profile of Derleth's detective.

E814. Moskowitz, Sam. "I Remember Derleth." Starship (formerly published as Algol) 18:1 (Spring 81):7-14.

Account of a visit by Moskowitz and Dr. David Keller and his wife to Derleth's home in 1948. Moscowitz describes the house, Derleth's collection, and their discussions. Moskowitz saw Derleth only one more time, in 1952, but he talks about Arkham House publishing ventures and his correspondence with Derleth.

E815. Norris, Luther. "Pons and Parker: The Durable Duo." Bakka 5 (Spring/Summer 77), pp. 95-96. Photo of Derleth & Norris, p. 94.

An account of the founding of the Praed Street Irregulars, plus comments on the Solar Pons stories and current (as of 1977) progress in preparing the collected edition of that series. (REB)

E816. Patrick, Robert. "A Chronology of Solar Pons." In The Reminiscences of Solar Pons, by August Derleth, pp. 194-99. Sauk City, WI: Mycroft & Moran, 1961.

E817. Smith, Edgar W. "Introduction." In The Return of Solar Pons, by August Derleth, pp. vii-xiii. Sauk City, WI: Mycroft & Moran, 1958.

E818. Starrett, Vincent. "Introduction." In The Casebook of Solar Pons, by August Derleth, pp. ix-xi. Sauk City, WI: Mycroft & Moran, 1965.

E819. ______. "Introduction." In 'In Re:Sherlock Holmes.' The Adventures of Solar Pons, by August Derleth, pp. ix-xii. Sauk City, WI: Mycroft & Moran, 1945.

E820. Wilson, Alison M. August Derleth: A Bibliography. The Scarecrow Author Bibliographies, No. 59. Metuchen, NJ, & London: Scarecrow Press, 1983. xxvi, 229pp. Frontispiece.

This bibliography is divided into two main sections, "The Fantasy World: Mystery, Science Fiction, and Horror" and "Sac Prairie and the Real World." The boundary is not clear-cut since, on the one hand, the Judge Peck detective novels are set in and around Sac Prairie and, on the other hand, some of the Sac Prairie stories have mystery and supernatural elements. All of Derleth's crime, supernatural, and science fiction short stories are grouped into a single list of 258 annotated works. The collaborations with Mark Schorer are listed separately, as are the "posthumous collaborations" with H. P. Lovecraft. Other subsections list the Solar Pons books, the Judge Peck novels, and the non-series mystery and true-crime writings. The "Steve and Sim" juvenile mysteries are listed in the Sac Prairie section. An alphabetical index of annotated works makes it easy to locate specific titles in the bibliography. An introduction by the compiler discusses Derleth's literary reputation and surveys the many newspaper articles about Derleth. There is also a brief chronology of his life. (REB)

D'ERRICO, EZIO

E821. Rambelli, Loris. "La demitizzazione italiana del romanzo giallo |The Italian demythologizing of the giallo novel|." In Cremante/Rambelli (B78), pp. 227-39.

Essay on the detective novels of Ezio D'Errico, Italian imitator, in the 30s and 40s, of the first series of the Maigrets. The resumption of the classical theme of the couple formed by the detective and the friend of the detective constitutes the demythologizing element in the comparisons of the detective genre and permits the writer to detach himself either from the Simenon model or from the closed structure of the puzzle novel. (LR)

DESMOND, HUGH

Ref: Hubin 2, TCCMW, CC, ABMIS.

DEVI, SHAKUNTALA

Ref: Hubin 2.

E822. Falk, Bertil. "Minns du räknefenomenet Shakuntala Devi? Indiens mänskliga dator skriver numera deckare |Do you remember Shakuntala Devi, the calculating wonder? India's human computer is now writing detective novels|." DAST 13:3 (1980):8-13.

Interview with photo. (MS)

DE VILLIERS, GERARD. See VILLIERS, GERARD DE

DEVINE, D. M.

Ref: Hubin 2, TCCMW, EMD, CC, ABMI(S).

DEWEY, THOMAS B.

Ref: Hubin 2, TCCMW, EMD, CC, ABMI(S); UN 3:1 (1950):10-12; UN 3:8 (1951):12-13 (photos).

E823. Barzun, Jacques, and Taylor, Wendell Hertig. "Introduction." In A Sad Song Singing (NY 1963), by Thomas B. Dewey. "Crime Fiction 1950-1975" (B18).

DEXTER, COLIN

Ref: Hubin 2.

Int: DAST 10:3 (1976):12-13 (photo and bibliography).

DEY, FREDERIC VAN RENSSELAER

Ref: Hubin 2, TCCMW, ABMI(S).

See also: D137, D148, D149, D151, D154, D155, D168, D173, D197, D199.

DICKENS, CHARLES

Ref: Hubin 2, TCCMW, EMD, CC, ABMI(S).

See also: E100, E652, E657, E695, E705

Part I: Non-Drood References

E825. Aisenberg, Nadya. "Dickens and the Crime Novel." In Aisenberg (B4), pp. 68-110.
In his "crime novels", Dickens, like Kafka and Dostoevsky, "subsumes the crime novel." Aisenberg discusses Dicken's attraction to crime and criminals, folklore motifs he shares in common with fairy tales, and also ways he can be distinguished from the sensation novelists and Gothic writers on whose work he draws.

E826. Brice, Alec W., and Fielding, K. J. "On Murder and Detection - New Articles by Dickens." Dickens Studies 5 (May 69):45-61.
Tentative attribution of articles on the Rush murders to Dickens.

E828. Friedman, Stanley. "Notes & Queries: A Loose Thread in Our Mutual Friend." DSN 1:2 (Sept 70):18-20.
A review of the identity of possible assaillants of George Radfoot, concluding with the observation that the identity is "a loose thread" and one that "has not troubled most of the novel's readers."

E829. Gibson, Frank A. "Mysteries in Dickens." The Dickensian 56 (1960):176-78.
A slight piece--little more than an enumeration--of major and minor mysteries in Dickens' fiction.

E830. Kelly, Patrick Joseph. "The Way of the Labyrinth: Mystery and Detection in the Novels of Charles Dickens." Unpublished Ph. D. dissertation. University of Toronto, 1980. DAI 41/06A (1980/81), pp. 2613-14.

E831. Koike, Shigeru. Dickens: 19 seiki Shingoshu |Dickens: the 19th century signalman|. Tokyo: Toju-sha, 1979. 194pp. Illustrated. Index.
The author is an authority on 19th century British literature, and an aficionado of the railroad and of mystery fiction. His book Eikoku Tetsudo Monogatari |The British railway story; 1979| has a number of references to mystery fiction. This volume, one of a series on British and American writers, devotes a great deal of attention to Dickens' crime novels. (HS/TT)

E832. Levy, Diane Wolfe. "Dickens' Bleak House." Explicator 38:3 (Spring 80):40-82.
Detectives and detection in Bleak House.

E833. Lewis, Sinclair. "Detective Stories and Mr. Dickens." Yale University Library Gazette 45:3 (Jan 71):88-92.
Lewis comments on the validity of his abridgement of Bleak House and on the importance of Inspector Bucket as the "real Founding Father" of detective fiction in which the detective is "more important than the ingenuity of the crime." His essay was originally intended to be the introduction to his version of Bleak House, a project he abandoned in 1942.

E834. Melling, John Kennedy. "Dickens and the Detectives." TPP 5:4 (Oct 83):35-36, 38.
Abridged summary of a lecture delivered at the Fifth Dickens Festival, 5 June 1983, at Rochester, Kent, England. A sketchy account of the growth of Dickens' interest in fictional and real-life police and detectives.

E835. Miller, H. Hillis. Charles Dickens: The World of His Novels. Cambridge, MA: Harvard University press, 1958.
In the chapter on Bleak House, Miller discusses (on pp. 169-77) Dickens' use of the techniques of the detective story with the definition of the "mystery" in this novel as the "strange sense that something is hidden."

E836. Ousby, Ian. "Charles Dickens." In Ousby (B300), pp. 79-110.
After noting the increasing interest of the reading public in detectives and in the exploitation by the sensation novelists of this interest, Ousby discusses Dickens' contribution to the phenomenon and analyses the role of Inspector Bucket in Bleak House.

E837. Petrullo, Helen B. "Sinclair Lewis's Condensation of Dickens's Bleak House." The Yale University Gazette 45:3 (Jan 71):85-87.
A discussion of Lewis' aborted edited version of Bleak House in which Lewis intended (E833) to give more importance to Inspector Bucket and the detective's role.

E838. Schklovski, Viktor. "The Mystery Novel: Dickens's Little Dorrit." In Readings in Russian Poetics, edited by Ladislav Matejka and Krystyna Pomorska, pp. 220-226. Cambridge, MA: M. I. T. Press, 1971; rpt. in 1978 by the University of Michigan Press. An abridged version, in English translation, of a Russian text.
A muddled essay, in its present form, on the Gothic mystery (Radcliffe, Maturin and Monk Lewis) and its heritage in Dickens' Little Dorrit. Schklovski comments that the detective novel is the "direct heir" of the mystery novel. He does not define his terms. No mention of Poe. Subjects discussed are plot inversion, simultaneous plot lines (with comparisons made to Russian fiction), the folktale (the "riddle") and others.

E839. Stewart, R. F. ...And Always a Detective (B380).
Passim. Consult index for numerous page references to Dickens' work.

E840. Symons, Julian. "Dickens, Collins, Gaboriau: The Pattern Forms." In Symons (B387), pp. 36-53.
A cursory but wide-ranging discussion of trends in mid-nineteenth century fiction, the reading public, and the contributions of the three writers to the new cult of the detective.

E841. Thomas, Deborah. "Murder and Self-Effacement." In her Dickens and the Short Story, pp. 110-20. Philadelphia: University of Pennsylvania Press, 1982.

The first part of this chapter is a discussion of Dickens' short story "The Bride's Chamber" whose technique of having the events of a murder told by the murderer after the fact is related to Dickens' proposed ending to The Mystery of Edwin Drood.

Part II: The Mystery of Edwin Drood (compiled by E. F. Bleiler)

Introduction

In the earliest period of Drood studies, from the 1870s until World War II, critics and writers were concerned mostly with what Dickens did not write--or a solution to the mystery elements of Drood. This was to some extent justifiable, since Drood is a mystery story.

Two questions were overwhelmingly prominent during this period: was Drood really murdered? Who was Datchery? These questions were variously answered. Until well into the 20th century, Drood's survival was generally favored, but as more information became available (and more Droodists read Drood, instead of talking about it), this position became difficult to sustain and was gradually abandoned. The identification of Datchery, too, varied over the years. A rough chronological sequence of Datchery's identification would be: publication time, mostly a new character; 1880s into the 20th century, Edwin Drood; first quarter of the century, Helena Landless, and, secondarily, Tartar; second quarter of the century, Bazzard, and, secondarily, Grewgious; modern period, Bazzard, and, secondarily, a new character.

In the second quarter of the century, until World War II, other speculations became important, elements in Drood that were perhaps hinted at, but not made explicit. These included the role and identity of the Opium Woman, the disposition of Drood's body, and enlargement of Jasper, as a Thug or a mesmerist.

Since World War II, however, the emphasis in Drood studies has been more on what Dickens did write, which is also justifiable. Dickens the man came to be studied in conjunction with Drood. With Edmund Wilson's essay "Dickens: The Two Scrooges" (1941) the modern study of Drood began. Wilson saw Drood as a projection of elements from Dicken's psyche and set Drood into Dickens' conflicts. Wilson's mode of analysis has dominated Drood studies until recently, and Dickens is still often interpreted in terms of Jasper.

In most recent times Drood and Dickens have been approached in terms of various psychological or aesthetic theories, which have been applied with mixed results. Such studies have been concerned with such matters as character levels in terms of psychological systems, symbolism and analysis of metaphor, and structural analysis of various sorts.

It should be noted that even today, more than one hundred years after the writing of Drood, there is no really definitive study of all aspects of Drood, the closest to this being the introductory material in the Cardwell (1972) Drood, which, however, is historical and avoids controversial or interpretative material.

The literature on Drood is enormous in quantity, running to well over a thousand items. Unfortunately, much of it, particularly in the earlier period, is of limited value, since it is polemic within a narrow range, highly repetitious, and sometimes unscholarly.

The present selective bibliography has been based primarily on scholarly usefulness, and I hope that I have not missed anything of significance. But a certain amount of the earlier material has been included for typological completeness. The old questions, no matter how answered, are still being asked.

Bibliographies

E842. Churchill, Reginald. A Bibliography of Dickensian Criticism 1836-1975. NY: Garland, 1975. Drood material pp. 117-22.
Less useful than Gold or Fenstermaker; skimpy, and without precise locations. 62 items.

E843. Collins, Philip. "Charles Dickens." In Victorian Fiction. A Second Guide to Research, edited by George H. Ford, pp. 30-113. NY: Modern Language Association, 1978.

E844. Dickens Studies Newsletter. Louisville, Ky. Quarterly publication.
Very thorough listings of primary and secondary material, unfortunately not categorized or described.

E845. Fenstermaker, John J. Charles Dickens, 1940-1975. An Analytical Subject Index to Periodical Criticism of his Novels and Christmas Books. Boston: G. K. Hall, 1979. Drood material pp. 235-41.
Analytical index of topics followed by general listing. 47 items.

E846. Gold, Joseph. The Stature of Dickens. A Centenary Bibliography. Toronto: Published for University of Manitoba Press by the University of Toronto Press, 1971.
Drood material items 3081 through 3194. The most useful of the general indexes.

E847. Green, Roger L. "Andrew Lang, Critic and Dickensian." Dickensian 41 (1944/1945):10-14.
The noted folklorist and critic was greatly interested in Drood, but made no outstanding contribution. His interpretation of Drood varied from time to time, but on the whole he accepted the theory that Drood survived and rejected more fanciful identifications of Datchery. Bibliography of 19 items.

E848. Matz, B. W. "The Mystery of Edwin Drood. A Bibliography Compiled by B. W. Matz." Dickensian 7 (1911):130-33.
Lists 83 items up through March 1911. See also Nicoll (1912) which reprinted Matz, extending it to 1912, but omitting a few items.

E849. Matz, Winifred. "A Bibliography of Edwin Drood." Dickensian 24 (1928):236, 301-02; 25 (1928/1929):42-44; 25 (1929):185-87.
Ranges from 1911 through 1928. A continuation of B. W. Matz (1911), and Nicoll (1912). About 450 items, including several letter chains that are difficult to tally.

E850. Nisbet, Ada. "Charles Dickens." In Victorian Fiction. A Guide to Research, edited by Lionel Stevenson, pp. 44-153. Cambridge: Harvard University Press, 1964.

Texts and Documents

E851. Dickens, Charles. (MS. of The Mystery of Edwin Drood) Preserved in John Forster Collection, Victoria and Albert Museum.

Never reproduced, but occasional readings cited in polemic literature. First adequate description in Cardwell (1972) edition of Drood, with divergencies from 1870 text noted as footnotes to printed text. Most of these differences are not substantive. (not seen)

E852. ______. (Notes and Number Plans for The Mystery of Edwin Drood) Mss. in John Forster Collection, Victoria and Albert Museum.

One sheet with alternate titles for Drood and alternate character names. Five sheets with working notes for part divisions. Published in illegible photographic facsimile in Carden (1931). First published in transcription in Nicoll (1912), with some inaccuracies. Mss. are very difficult to read, but transcription in Cardwell (1972) edition of Drood is probably the most accurate. Important for interpretation of Drood. (originals not seen)

E853. ______ (Corrected printer's proofs to The Mystery of Edwin Drood) John Forster's set preserved in the John Forster Collection, Victoria and Albert Museum. Luke Fildes' partial set preserved in the Gimbel Collection, Beinecke Library, Yale University.

Dickens' last corrections and alterations, not always followed in numbers of Drood published after Dickens's death. Forster set transcribed by Nicoll (1912) and often cited elsewhere. Forster set incorporated, Fildes set utilized in Cardwell (1972) edition of Drood. Probably less important for the interpretation of Drood than they used to be considered. (originals not seen)

E854. ______. The Mystery of Edwin Drood, edited by Margaret Cardwell. Oxford: Oxford University Press, the "Clarendon Dickens," 1972. 6 illustrations. Uses 1870 text (with some emendations) as basis, indicating in footnotes variations in ms. and proofs.

A full, scholarly introduction, with much the best general summation of Drood origins. Additional material: descriptive list of editions, 1870-75; the Number Plans and Notes in transcription; the "Sapsea Fragment;" the descriptive headings added in 1875; the illustrations; the Every Saturday and Fields, Osgood one-volume edition of 1870; the after-history of Drood, 1870-78. Appendix covers Fields proofs, which were available too late for inclusion and incorporation. The definitive edition of Drood, indispensable for serious study, but available only at a ridiculously exorbitant price.

E855. ______. The Mystery of Edwin Drood, edited by Margaret Cardwell. Oxford: Oxford University Press, the World's Classics, 1982. 10 illustrations. Uses text of Cardwell (1972) edition, with some emendations. Additional material includes short introduction, note on text, chronology of Charles Dickens, the Number Plans and Notes in transcription, the "Sapsea Fragment," four pages of explanatory notes, and a brief bibliography. The best text available at a reasonable price, but without the footnotes or scholarly wealth of the Cardwell (1972) edition. If this edition is not available, the Penguin (1974) edition of Drood edited by Arthur J. Cox is acceptable. It pays some heed to ms. variations, but by no means as authoritatively as the Cardwell editions.

General Works

(Histories of the detective story and histories of the English novel that mention Drood in passing have not been listed, nor have biographies of Dickens, unless they discuss Drood at length or offer significant material not generally available elsewhere.)

E856. Allen, D. G. MacDonald. The Janus Sex. The Androgynous Challenge. Hicksville, NY: Exposition Press, 1975.
Section on Drood (pp. 164-85) discusses transvestism in Dickens's works and asserts that Dickens was a poor judge of women, both in fiction and in life.

E857. Barnard, Robert. Imagery and Theme in the Novels of Dickens. Bergen, Norway: Universitetsforlaget; NY: Humanities Press, 1974.
Drood coverage (pp. 134-44), despite title of book, has nothing to do with imagery and theme, but is plot reconstruction on a somewhat uncritical level. Argues that Jasper is a ritual murderer, with earlier murder on previous Christmas Eve; that Drood escaped; and that Datchery was Bazzard.

E858. Camerer, Rudi. Die Schuldproblematik im Spaetwerk von Charles Dickens |The problem of guilt in the later work of Charles Dickens|. Frankfurt a. M.: Peter Lang, 1978.
Does not cover Drood directly, but content is applicable to Drood. Guilt can be societal or personal.

E859. Collins, Philip. Dickens and Crime. London: Macmillan, 1964.
Thorough, scholarly account of Dickens's involvement in criminology and reform movements. Frequent references to his fiction, especially Chapters XI ("Murder, from Bill Sikes to Bradley Headstone") and XII ("The Mysteries in Edwin Drood"). Very fine Drood chapter covers composition, interpretation, relation of Drood to Dickens's life, and offers good rebuttal to Wilson (1941).

E860. Hobsbaum, Philip. A Reader's Guide to Charles Dickens. London: Thames and Hudson, 1972; NY: Farrar, Straus, and Giroux, 1973.
Includes workmanlike elementary account of Drood and related questions.

E861. Johnson, Edgar. Charles Dickens: His Tragedy and Triumph. 2 vols. NY: Simon and Schuster, 1952.
General biographical study. Drood material pp. 1113-1126. Still the best of the modern biographies.

E862. Kaplan, Fred. Dickens and Mesmerism. The Hidden Springs of Fiction. Princeton: Princeton University Press, 1975.
Discussion passim of Drood, but Drood material not as developed as might be expected. Extension of Boyd's point of view: Jasper works mesmerically and has dual consciousness. Drood is dead.

E863. Lane, Lauriat, Jr. "Dickens and the Double." Dickensian 55 (1959):47-55.
Sees Jasper as an internalized double, torn by conflict, gradually dissociating himself from criminal second personality.

E864. Leacock, Stephen. Charles Dickens. His Life and Work. Garden City, NY: Doubleday, Doran, 1934.
Drood chapter (pp. 278-301) covers Drood, some continuations, some

studies. Considers Drood alive, and hovers between Drood and Bazzard as Datchery. On the whole, a weak book.

E865. Lindsay, Jack. Charles Dickens. A Biography and Critical Study. London: Andrew Dakers, 1950.
Drood section (pp. 390-409) follows Wilson (1941) in interpreting Drood as a projection of Dickens.

E866. Monod, Sylvere. Dickens the Novelist. Norman, Okla: University of Oklahoma Press, 1968. Introduction by Edward Wagenknecht.
A very fine study of Dickens's working methods, with full, penetrating analysis of several typical novels, notably Copperfield. Section on Drood (pp. 488-502) contrasts high degree of technical mastery with occasional inappropriate grotesquerie, occasionally slovenly style. Is surprisingly timid on most Drood problems.

E867. Pritchett, V. S. The Living Novel. NY: Random House, 1944; London: Chatto and Windus, 1946. Enlarged edition, New York: Random House, 1964.
Essay "Edwin Drood," reprinted from New Statesman (February 1944), terms Drood watershed work between past, where fictional murder was treated as horrible, and moderns, where murder is an intellectual puzzle. Criticizes characterizations, arguing that Dickens can write only monologues. Finds isolation basic aspect of Drood and late Dickens.

E868. Wilson, Angus. The World of Charles Dickens. London: Secker and Warburg, 1970. Penguin reprint, 1972.
Stronger on cultural-historical background than most studies of Dickens. Good, perceptive text. Moderate psychological interpretation of Drood, pp. 286-92. Excellent illustration: 34 color plates, 144 black and white illustrations.

E869. Wilson, Edmund. "Dickens: The Two Scrooges." In The Wound and the Bow. Cambridge: Houghton, Mifflin, 1941, with many later reprintings.
Sees much of Dickens's life as projection of rebel and criminal personality components. Drood section argues that Drood (against background of Dickens's affair with Ellen Ternan) shows criminal aspect. Accepts Duffield on thuggee; Boyd on mesmerism and dual personality; Walters and Nicoll on Helena Landless as Datchery. An extremely influential essay, particularly beyond Droodist circles, on Dickens in general, but very erratic and weak on Drood.

E870. Winters, Warrington. "Dickens and the Psychology of Dreams." PMLA 63 (1948):984-1006.
Describes concept of dreams in several works, including Drood. Argues that Jasper's dreams in Drood show evolution of Dickens's understanding of phenomena.

Critical and Historical.

E871. Aylmer, Felix. "The Drood Case Re-Opened." Dickensian 20 (1924):192-93; 21 (1925):205-09.
Rejects theory that Jasper has secondary personality and argues that he was completely innocent of crime. Also argues that Jasper was son of Opium Woman, who had been seduced and abandoned by Drood, Sr. Far-fetched.

E872. ______. "First Aid for the 'Drood' Audience." Dickensian 47 (1951):133-39.
Advance indications of Aylmer (1964), where argument is developed.

E873. ______. The Drood Case. London: Rupert Hart-Davies, 1964.
Argues for very complex background plot: Drood, Sr., now dead, became object of blood feud in Egypt, and Opium Woman carries on feud against Edwin and Jasper (who is illegitimate son of Drood, Sr., by Arab woman). Opium Woman's grandson tries to kill both Drood and Jasper. Drood mistakenly believes that Jasper has attacked him and flees to Egypt. Datchery is identified as Bazzard. All fantasy, of course, with little relevance to Drood. Book also occasionally reproduces useful source material and cites earlier work. Appendices cover pagination table of various editions, transcription of title sheet and number plans, brief bibliography. Index and 17 illustrations.

E874. Baker, Richard M. "Who Was Dick Datchery? A Study for Droodians." Nineteenth Century Fiction 2 (1948a):201-22; 3 (1948a):35-53.
Reviews earlier theories and argues that Datchery was Grewgious. Reprinted in Baker (1951).

E875. ______. "John Jasper--Murderer." Trollopian 3 (1948b):99-118, 177-88. Describes and analyzes Jasper's actions and words. Accepts theory that Jasper was mesmerist, but rejects thuggee as explanation for murder. Reprinted in Baker (1951).

E876. ______. "The Datchery Assumption: Reply." Nineteenth Century Fiction 4 (1949a):77-81. Reply to MacVicar (1949).
A weak, casuistic response.

E877. ______. "Was Edwin Drood Murdered?" Nineteenth Century Fiction 4 (1949b):111-28, 221-36.
Excellent coverage of information from Dickens's family, Forster, illustrators, plus texual evidence. Concludes that Drood was really murdered by Jasper. Reprinted in Baker (1951).

E878. ______. "The Genesis of Edwin Drood." Nineteenth Century Fiction 3 (1949c):281-95; 4 (1949c):37-50.
Examines three works that have been suggested as either influencing or offering possible competition to Drood: Dickens's early "A Confession Found in a Prison in the Time of Charles the Second;" Emily Jolly's 'An Experience' (sometimes misattributed to Percy Fitzgerald), printed in All the Year Round; Robert Lytton's "The Disappearance of Roger Ackland," which Dickens accepted for All the Year Round, then curtailed in publication, on grounds of possible plagiarism. Reprinted in Baker (1951).

E879. ______. "What Might Have Been: A Study for Droodians." Nineteenth Century Fiction 4 (1950):275-97; 5 (1950):47-65.
Attempts, diffidently, to follow story threads out to end. The Opium Woman was only a blackmailer. Jasper is trapped where Drood's corpse is concealed, chased up tower, and captured. Neville Landless is killed by Jasper. Helena Landless mesmerizes Jasper into confessing. Jasper is hanged. Reprinted in Baker (1951).

E880. ______. The Drood Murder Case. Five Studies in Dickens's Edwin Drood. Berkeley and Los Angeles: University of California Press, 1951. Reprints five essays above: 1948a, 1948b, 1949b, 1949c, 1950.

Very entertaining reading, and all in all the best book about Drood and Droodism, although I do not agree with the identification of Datchery.

E881. Bart, Barry D. "George Silverman's Explanation." Dickensian 60 (1964):48-51.
Relates GSE (minor work written just before Drood) to Drood. Common factors are consequences of ethic renunciation and a self-immolating hero (Jasper).

E882. Bengis, Nathan L. "John Jasper's Devotion." TAD 8 (1974/75):165-78, 257-70; 9 (1975/76):25-40.
Argues that Drood survived (although Jasper believed he had killed him) and returns as Datchery. The last is the idea which Dickens called "incommunicable" in letter to Forster--though Bengis communicates it quite easily. Covers early theories of Drood and provides good selected bibliography.

E883. Bilham, D. M. "Edwin Drood--to Resolve a Mystery." Dickensian 62 (1966):181-83.
Impressionistic argument that Opium Woman is the mother of Drood and sister of Jasper.

E884. Blakeney, T. S. "Problems of Edwin Drood." Dickensian 51 (1955):182-85.
Early attempt to link Drood to Dickens's life situation. Argues that characterization of Helena Landless is based on Dickens's mistress Ellen Lawless Ternan. Also argues that Drood has been murdered by Jasper and that Datchery is a new character, of no consequence. Bazzard is a red herring.

E885. Bleifull, William W. "A Re-examination of Edwin Drood." Dickensian 50 (1954):110-15, 176-86; 51 (1955):24-29.
Argues that Drood should be read and studied not as a a modern detective story, but as a novel of character. Decides that Drood is alive and that Datchery is Bazzard.

E886. Bleiler, Everett F. "The Dilemma of Datchery." TMF 4:4 (1980):7-15.
Early (1955) paper argues that Datchery is a new character, in some way connected with past history of Drood or the Landlesses. Bases argument on internal evidence, names, and Dickens's patterns of age levels in characterization.

E887. ______. "The Names in Drood." Dickens Quarterly (formerly Dickens Studies Newsletter) 14 (1983).
A close analysis of personal names in Drood attempts to isolate plot elements, character identities, and projection of the author's life situation into the work. Main conclusion is that names carry hints of unwritten developments.

E888. ______. "To Be and Not To Be." TMF 6:6 (Nov/Dec 82):3-4, 18.
Comments on Charles Forsyte's The Decoding of Edwin Drood (Scribner's, 1980).

E889. Borowitz, Albert I. "The Mystery of Edwin Drood." TAD 10 (1977):14-16, 82; reprinted in Innocence and Arsenic (NY: Harper, 1977), pp. 53-62.
Pleasant, noncommittal survey of problems.

E890. Boyd, (Peter) Aubrey. "A New Angle on the Drood Mystery." Washington

University Studies: Humanistic Series 9 (1921):35-85.
Also a separate pamphlet. The first extended study of Japser as a mesmerist and split personality. A very important work historically.

E891. Brend, Gavin. "Edwin Drood and the Four Witnesses." Dickensian 52 (1955):20-24.
Argues that four contemporaries (John Forster; Luke Fildes; Charles Dickens, Jr.; Charles Allston Collins) who stated that Dickens told them that Drood was murdered by Jasper are all unreliable and not to be believed in this instance. Unconvincing.

E892. Carden, Percy T. "Datchery. The Case for Tartar Re-stated." Dickensian 15 (1919):189-94.
Argues that Datchery was Tartar, a theory not well received. While Carden was not the originator of this theory, he was its principal exponent.

E893. ______. "Dickens's 'Number Plans' for The Mystery of Edwin Drood." Dickensian 27 (1931):183-85, 200-01, 266-69, 284-85, 300-01.
Photographs of working notes for Drood. Reproductions are very bad, almost illegible, but they seem to be the only reproductions of the whole set. See Dickens (Number Plans).

E894. ______. "Secrets of the Dickens House." Dickensian 34 (1938):232-34.
Comments on acquisition of the Howard Duffield collection of Drood material, with occasional interesting side points.

E895. Cardwell, Margaret. "Dickens's Correspondence with the Illustrator of 'Edwin Drood.'" Dickensian 69 (1973):42-43.
Letters to Luke Fildes, preserved in the Gimbel Collection, Yale University. One letter is somewhat pertinent to Drood.

E896. ______. "A Newly Discovered Version of a Collins Sketch for 'Edwin Drood.'" Dickensian 70 (1974):31-34.
An unsigned version of one of Collins's rejected sketches (Number Three) has turned up. Cardwell considers it genuine. Reproduced here, it does not differ significantly from the two previously known versions.

E897. ______. "Collins's Sketches for 'Edwin Drood.' A Postscript." Dickensian 71 (1975):45-46.
The present location of the sketches, which had been believed lost.

Carr, John Dickson. (See de la Torre, Lillian.)

E898. Clark, William Clark. "Edwin Drood Again." Dickensian 33 (1937):191-95.
Item in controversy about dispensation of Drood's body, with tacit assumption that Cloisterham cathedral corresponds exactly to Rochester cathedral. Argues that Jasper disposed of Drood's body in space over vaulting. Argument is moot, but there are three interesting photographs of architectural features.

E899. Collins, Charles Allston. "The Mystery of Edwin Drood." Dickensian 15 (1919):196.
Reprint of letter of May 1871. Collins, who drew first sketch of the green parts cover and six inside illustrations that were rejected, states that he received from Dickens a "general outline" of the story. Drood was murdered by Jasper, who misleads the investigation of the crime. Tartar

was to marry Rosa. "Young Landless was to die, perhaps, and Jasper certainly would," though does not remember details. An important document.

E900. ______. (Unused art work for Drood). For reproductions, see Lehmann-Haupt (1929) and Cardwell (1974).

E901. Collins, Philip. "Dickens on the Education of Girls." Dickensian 57 (1961):86-96.
Comments on Twinkleton's school.

E902. ______. "Inspector Bucket Visits the Princess Puffer." Dickensian 60 (1946b):89-90.
Reprints contemporary account (Frederick Wellesley, Recollections of a Soldier-Diplomat) of visit by Wellesley and Inspector Field (prototype of Bucket) to opium establishment of Lascar Sal. Reveals that Lascar Sal, despite aged appearance, was a young woman, and suggests that Opium Woman (who was based on Lascar Sal) was also young, perhaps previously seduced by Jasper. Suggestion seems unlikely.

E903. Conway, Eustace. "The Mystery of Edwin Drood." In Anthony Munday and Other Essays, pp. 69-99. NY: Privately printed, 1927. (250 copy edition)
Argues that Jasper killed Drood, but as dual personality, and that final confession will describe crime as if committed by Neville Landless. Datchery is Bazzard. Jasper kills Neville.

E904. Cordery, Garth. "The Cathedral as Setting and Symbol in The Mystery of Edwin Drood." DSN 10 (1979):7 97-103.
As title indicates.

E905. Cox, Arthur J. "The Haggard Woman." In Adams, MDA 1972 (B2), pp. 65-77.
Assuming that the "opium woman" in Edwin Drood is not, as has commonly been supposed old but, rather, young, Cox examines the implications of his hypothesis.

E905a. Cox, Arthur J. "The Morals of Edwin Drood." Dickensian 38 (1962): 32-42.
Argues that Jasper is motivated not so much by love for Rosa Bud as by hatred of Drood for his life style. Jasper, as powerful mesmerist, forced Neville Landless to kill Drood.

E906. ______. "The Drood Remains." Dickens Studies 2 (1966):33-44.
Discusses Dickens's shifting of text within number parts to fulfill length requirements; also cuts made in proofs. Suggests that "Sapsea Fragment" is earlier than generally believed, and accuses Forster of destroying the first part of it. The accusation is backed by no evidence.

E907. ______. "Charles Dickens. The Mystery of Edwin Drood." In Adams, MDA 1973 (B3), pp. 307-312.
Review of Cardwell (1972) Drood. Questions some readings of Number Notes and criticizes treatment of Ackland incident. (See Baker, 1949c; Rosenberg, 1974.)

E908. ______. "Dickens's Last Book: More Mysteries Than One." TAD 14 (1981):31-37.
Argues that Dickens took more from work of Wilkie Collins than is

generally recognized, particularly from Armadale: characters, motifs, situations. (Argument is overstated.) Also argues that Neville murdered Drood under Jasper's mesmeric influence, and that the theme of the book is the guiltlessness of an unwitting instrument of crime.

E909. Cross, J. F.; W. Laurence Gadd; and Sara D. Chinnock. "New Light on the Drood Mystery. Varied Views." Dickensian 24 (1928):144-45.
Reaction to Reuter (1927/28) and other publicity. Comments on Spiritualist claim to have received communications from the spirit of Dickens about Drood. Incredulous rejection.

E910. de la Torre, Lillian. "John Dickson Carr's Solution to The Mystery of Edwin Drood." TAD 14 (1981):291-94.
Undated letter from Carr to de la Torre quoted. Argues that Helena Landless, disguised as a man and mistaken for Neville Landless, bludgeoned Drood to death in a quarrel. Jasper, who had fallen unconscious in opium fit, on awaking and finding Drood's corpse, assumes that he did it and hides body. Perverse overingenuity matching Aylmer's.

E911. (Dexter, Walter) "'Cloisterham,' the City of Drood." Dickensian 25 (1929):263, 304, 319; 26 (1930):17, 21.
Excellent photographs of Rochester cathedral, a street, John Jasper's gatehouse, Sapsea's house, and the Nuns' House.

E912. (Dickens Fellowship) "A New Dickens Bibliography. The Mystery of Edwin Drood." Dickensian 41 (1945):206-07.
First edition information, reproduction of green parts cover, vignette title page, title page. Of value for exceptionally clear reproduction of parts cover, which elsewhere is usually filled in and fuzzy.

E913. Duffield, Howard. "John Jasper-- Strangler." Bookman (New York) 70 (1930):381-88.
Argues that Jasper had early connection with India and was a practitioner of thuggee, and that the murder of Drood was primarily a ritual matter. Covers 19th century literature on Thugs briefly. A very influential paper historically, widely accepted in critical work, although at present, fortunately, it seems to be obsolescent. See Jacobson (1977).

E914. ______. "The Macbeth Motif in 'Edwin Drood.'" Dickensian 30 (1934):263-71.
Considers Macbeth central to Drood: Jasper equals Macbeth; the Opium Woman, the Three Witches; Drood, Duncan, etc. (Perhaps, but others have pointed out that Macbeth memories are common throughout Dickens's work.) Also hints that Drood will return in disguise.

E915. Dyson, A. E. "Edwin Drood: A Horrible Wonder Apart." Critical Quarterly 11 (1969):138-57.
Hidden themes of Drood: mixture of idyll and nightmare; darker side of love; spying and domination; devious plots uniting. Perhaps the finest modern essay on Drood. Reprinted in The Inimitable Dickens, A Reading of the Novels. London: Macmillan; NY: St. Martin, 1970.

E916. Ellis, M. A. "'The Chinaman' in 'The Mystery of Edwin Drood.'" Dickensian 17 (1921):139.
Argues that the Chinaman depicted in the lower right hand corner of the parts cover is Helena Landless, in disguise in an opium den, spying on Jasper. Rejects Helena as Datchery.

E917. Everett, Edward S. "The Cloisterham Murder Case." In The Fred Newton Scott Anniversary Papers, pp. 157-74. Chicago: University of Chicago Press, 1929.
Attempts to tie Drood in with pattern common in Dickens's work: the wrong man is murdered. Argues that Jasper killed Bazzard by error, instead of Drood; that Drood fled to Europe; that Datchery is Bazzard's father. Perhaps first clear recognition of implications of fact that Datchery is a stranger in Cloisterham.

E918. Fildes, Sir Luke. "The Mysteries of Edwin Drood." Dickensian 1 (1905):319. Reprinted from The Times of 3 November 1905.
Fildes, who illustrated Drood, declares categorically that Dickens told him that Jasper was to strangle Drood with a neckerchief. An important document.

E919. Fisher, Benjamin F., IV. "Paperback Editions of The Mystery of Edwin Drood." DSN 8 (1977):19-22.
Compares New American Library, Airmont, and Penguin (Cox) editions, rating Penguin highest. Also interesting side points.

E920. Fleissner, Robert F. "Drood the Obscure: The Evidence of the Names." TAD 13 (1980):12-16.
Argues that Drood is Christ-figure, destined to be sacrificed; basis is element "rood" in "Drood."

E921. Ford, George H. "Dickens's Notebook and 'Edwin Drood.'" Nineteenth Century Fiction 6 (1952):275-80.
Makes points that notebook of ideas that Dickens kept was used more for Drood than is generally recognized, but for textual embellishment, rather than for central ideas.

E922. Fraser, W. A. "Sir Luke Fildes's Illustrations to 'Edwin Drood.'" Dickensian 4 (1908):41-43.
Aesthetic comments on the illustrations to Drood.

E923. Gadd, George F. "Datchery the Enigma: The Case for Tartar." Dickensian 2 (1906):13-16.
Early statement of theory that Datchery was Tartar in disguise.

E924. ______. "A Veteran Droodist Returns." Dickensian 29 (1933):238.
Disputes Rust (1933).

E925. Gadd, W. Laurence. "Modern Writers of Mystery Stories and Edwin Drood." Dickensian 24 (1928):223-24.
Report on Drood Night, Westminster, 11 April 1928, when R. Austin Freeman and Sutton Vane discussed Drood. Both writers agreed that Drood is a simple mystery story, Freeman stating that "mystification (had been created) by numerous writers who had invented stories of their own and grafted them on (Drood)." True.

E926. Gratz, Jeffrey Michael."Notes on the Identity of Dick Datchery." DSN 8 (1977):72-78.
Good clear survey of theories and evidence, but takes no stand. Thinks Datchery is perhaps a new character, but if a known character, Bazzard is the best choice.

E927. Hark, Ina Rae. "Marriage in the Symbolic Framework of The Mystery of

Edwin Drood." Studies in the Novel 9 (1977):154-68.
Feminist position. Is annoyed that Rosa Bud is cavalierly married off to Tartar in most reconstructions. Attempts character analysis on semi-Jungian basis (invoking Mitchell, 1966) to find suitable mate for her. Selects Drood, who survived. Jargon aside, maturation is the topic. More valuable for incidental discussion of symbolism of the Orient in Drood; good insights here.

E928. Harris, Edwin. "The Mystery of Edwin Drood. Some Facts about Rochester Cathedral." Dickensian 30 (1934):305-6.
Refutation of Canon Pythian-Adams (1934), with excellent discussion of internal features of Rochester cathedral, including parts not open to the public.

E929. Hill T(homas) W. "Drood Time in Cloisterham.' Dickensian 40 (1944a):113-17.
Attempts to date action of Drood. Finds that information is not consistent, but considers the early 1850s most reasonable.

E929a. ______. "Notes on The Mystery of Edwin Drood." Dickensian 40 (1944b):198-204; 41 (1944/1945):30-37.
Explanation of topical references, identification of places, other material such as might be found in an annotated Drood. Considers Cloisterham to be somewhat transmogrified Rochester. Probably the most authoritative opinion on linkages between Cloisterham and Rochester.

E930. (Jackson, Henry) About Edwin Drood. Cambridge: Cambridge University Press, 1911.
Published anonymously, but dedication signed H. J. Has consulted manuscript for better readings in several cases, notably in the first paragraph of Drood. Argues that Drood is dead, and that Datchery is Helena Landless. Historically important for theory that Dickens, if he had lived, would have transferred Chapter XIII (introduction of Datchery) to between Chapters XXII and XXIII. The theory was influential for a time, but there never was any reason to accept it, and it now seems abandoned.

E931. Jacobson, Wendy. "John Jasper and Thuggee." Modern Language Review 72 (1977):526-37.
Examines Duffield's theory that Jasper was a thug in much greater detail and with more documentation than did Duffield, and concludes that it is an "interesting and imaginative red herring." Correct.

E932. Jamieson, H. W. and F. M. B. Rosenthal. "The Mystery of Edwin Drood. Some New Keys That Fit." Dickensian 25 (1928/1929):28-36; 25 (1929):100-03.
Argues that Datchery is Grewgious; that Jasper buried Drood under floor of passage at the side of the chancel; that Dickens intended the quicklime to preserve Drood. Also argues, from green parts cover, that woman reading "Lost" poster is Opium Woman's daughter, whom Jasper seduced using Drood's name and wearing a false mustache! Seriously!

E933. Kavanagh, Mary (pseud. of Spain, M. M.) A New Solution of The Mystery of Edwin Drood. London: John Long, 1919.
Argues that Drood escaped death and returns in disguise as Tartar. Jasper is an impostor, and Datchery is the uncle of Drood, the brother of the real Jasper, and father or stepfather of the Landlesses. Reprinted

with Chapman and Hall (1922) edition of Drood (not seen).

E934. ______. "The Drood Mystery. A Reply to Mr. J. Cuming Walters." Dickensian 16 (1920):18-21.
General defense of position taken in A New Solution.

E935. Kustelnick, Charles. "Dickens's Quarrel with the Gothic: Ruskin, Durdles, and Edwin Drood." Dickens Studies Newsletter 8 (1977):104-08.
Argues that Durdles symbolizes Ruskin's Gothic workman. Cathedral itself is both oppressive and redemptive.

E936. Lang, Andrew. The Puzzle of Dickens's Last Plot. London: Chapman and Hall, 1905a.
Holds pretty much to Proctor's theory that Drood survived and returned as Datchery.

E937. ______. "A Mystery of Dickens." Blackwood's Magazine 189 (1911): 670-681.
Is now more inclined to think Drood dead, but notes that by chance or design Dickens has completely clear options either to declare Drood dead or to bring him back into the story. Also estimates copy length for remainder of book.

E938. Lehmann-Haupt, C. F. "New Facts Concerning "Edwin Drood.'" Dickensian 25 (1929):165-75.
Establishes clearly that Fildes reworked Collins's rejected draft of parts cover. Also reproduces six recently discovered drawings by Collins intended as illustrations for Drood, and attempts an analysis of them--which is sometimes questionable. Important for the illustrations, which are clearer than in later reproductions.

E939. ______. "Studies on 'Edwin Drood.'" Dickensian 31 (1935):299-305; 32 (1936):29-34, 135-37, 219-20, 301-06; 33 (1936):57-62.
Describes circumstances of composition of green cover and analyzes motifs. Argues that Sapsea fragment is discarded early draft, Poker being first concept of Datchery. Considers Datchery hitherto unknown relative of Rosa. Places Drood's corpse in Sapsea monument, preserved, not destroyed, by lime. Cites ms. to argue that Dickens first brought Opium Woman to Cloisterham at earlier point, but changed plans. Compares Drood with Our Mutual Friend. An important article.

E940. MacVicar, H. M. "The Datchery Assumption: Expostulation." Nineteenth Century Fiction 4 (1949):75-77.
Argues against Baker's conclusions in Baker (1948a) that Datchery was Grewgious. Baker's reply, same issue, is weak.

E941. Matchett, Willoughby. "A Talk round Drood." Dickensian 10 (1914):11-14.
Among general topics, suggests that Dick Datchery represents Dickens, and that the name is "a sort of inversion of the name Charles Dickens."

E942. Matchett, Willoughby; W. A. Fraser; Francis Studley; G. Forest; J. C. L. Clark; George F. Gadd; and J. W. Wilson. "Last Words on the Drood Mystery." Dickensian 7 (1911):98-104.
The Dickensian declared its columns closed to further Droodism (a closing that did not last long), and offered the present piece as a parting salute. Most of the contributions are of no interest, but Wilson's is a very early statement of the theory that Jasper was a mesmerist.

E943. Matz, B. W. "The Murder of Edwin Drood." Dickensian 20 (1924):41-42. Calls attention to introduction by Charles Dickens, Jr., to new Macmillan edition of Drood. Dickens, Jr., reveals that father stated clearly that Drood was dead.

E944. Mitchell, Charles. "The Mystery of Edwin Drood: The Interior and Exterior of Self." English Literary History 33 (1966):228-46.
Jungian interpretation of characters, on basis of relation of internal self to external self and reality. Stresses symbolism of water. Regards Drood highly as psychological novel. An influential paper, although, stripped of jargon, sometimes rather obvious.

E945. Nicoll, W. Robertson. The Problem of 'Edwin Drood.' A Study in the Methods of Dickens. London: Hodder and Stoughton, 1912.
Still unique source book for Drood studies. Covers text, with some reference to manuscript; transcribes Number Plans and Notes; cites testimony of Dickens's family and associates; analyzes wrapper illustrations; indicates material Dickens cut from Forster proofs; comments on previous work; reprints Matz (1911) with slight extension. In second section, argues that Drood is dead and that Datchery is Helena Landless. Cites history of transvestism on stage and in fiction, and compares Drood with Wilkie Collins's No Name. Some of source material is now a little dated and a little inaccurate, but still a very useful book, even if the Helena assumption now seems very silly.

E946. Pakenham, Pansy. "The Memorandum Book, Forster and Edwin Drood." Dickensian 51 (1955):117-21.
Forster had been caught faking a communication from Dickens (or was an unfortunate victim of circumstances), and anti-Forsterians have made the most of this in Drood studies. Pakenham defends Forster, Collins, and other early sources.

E947. Pearson, Edmund. Murder at Smutty Nose and Other Murders. Garden City, NY: Doubleday, Page, 1926; London: Heinemann, 1927.
In essay on Constance Kent calls attention to parallels between Constance Kent and Helena Landless. The resemblance is trivial, but the article is often cited.

E948. Perugini, Kate Dickens. "'Edwin Drood' and the Last Days of Charles Dickens." Pall Mall Magazine 37 (1906):643-54. 7 illustrations.
Dickens's younger daughter reminisces on CD's last days, Drood, similar matters. Claims father still in excellent mental condition, despite physical disabilities.

E949. Proctor, Richard A. Watched by the Dead: A Loving Study of Dickens' Half-Told Tale. London: W. H. Allen, 1887.
Analysis of Drood, arguing that Drood is not dead, but returns to Cloisterham as Datchery, and confronts Jasper in the crypt. Historically very important as the first of the detailed, extensive solutions to Drood, offering the model for an endless amount of later speculation.

E950. Pythian-Adams, W. J. "A Suggested Solution of The Mystery of Edwin Drood." Dickensian 30 (1934):181-82.
Items in controversy about disposition of Drood's body, with tacit assumption that Cloisterham cathedral corresponds exactly to Rochester cathedral. Argues that crime was committed in clerestory gallery and

body concealed in Indulgence Chamber. See Harris (1934).

E951. Reuter, Florizel von. "New Light. Sir Arthur Conan Doyle's Seance." Dickensian 24 (1927/1928):64-66. Reprints extracts from article in Light (1 October 1927), with brief editorial note.
Reuter describes Spiritualist seances at Doyle's home, during which Doyle and Dickens conversed. Dickens disavowed the James continuation; dodged a question about Datchery; stated had "always hoped you would set Sherlock on his track," and declared Drood alive, sheltered by Cris(parkle). The incident received world-wide publicity, and Doyle occasionally referred to it in his lectures. (Light not seen)

E952. Rines, Edward F. "The Technique of 'Edwin Drood.'" Dickensian 28 (1932):105-08, 287-89.
Attempts to analyze aspects of Drood in terms of a formal detective story. See also Sanders (1932).

E953. Robbins, Sir Alfred. "Datchery's Disguise Dissipated." Dickensian 26 (1930):97-103.
Argues that Datchery is Grewgious, basing identification on community of personality.

E954. Robison, Roselee. "Time, Death and the River in Dickens' Novels." English Studies 53 (1972):436-54.
Symbolism of the river and of water; both as destructive and healing forces.

E955. Rosenberg, Edgar. "Restoration in Cloisterham: The 'Clarendon Drood.'" DSN 5 (1974):70-84.
Long, considered review of Cardwell (1972) Drood, basically very favorable, but criticizes treatment of Ackland incident (see Baker, 1949c) and a few minor matters.

E956. Roussel, Roy. "The Completed Story in The Mystery of Edwin Drood." Criticism 20 (1978):383-402.
Author does not mean solution of mystery, but dialectic or tension between history (real life) and story (fairy tale treatment). Sees both Jasper and Rosa as trapped by life, with different attempts to escape, neither being successful. Drood typifies Dickens's own life situation. Turgid, but with insights.

E957. Rust, S. J. "The Mystery of Edwin Drood. A Plea for a Solution Which Would Make Dickens Something More than a Writer of Inferior Melodrama." Dickensian 29 (1933):96-99.
Argues that Datchery is manager of firm in Egypt and real guardian of Drood; that the Opium Woman had habituated Jasper to opium when he was a child in the Orient.

E958. Sanders, E. L. "The Technique of 'Edwin Drood.'" Dickensian 28 (1932):190-92.
Disputes Rines (1932).

E959. Sanders, E. L.; Katharine Kelly; C. G. Matthews; Deorad. "The Drood Case Re-opened." Dickensian 21 (1925):18-24.
Comments on Aylmer (1924). Sanders disagrees; Kelly agrees; Matthews considers overingenious; Deorad comments that Dickens sometimes changed his mind during composition.

E960. Saunders, Montagu. The Mystery in the Drood Family. Cambridge: Cambridge University Press, 1914.
Argues that Drood is dead, murdered by Jasper. Considers Datchery to be a new character, a member of a legal firm used by Grewgious for miscellaneous work. Turgid, but one of the better older books.

E961. ______. "The Mystery in the Drood Family." Dickensian 11 (1915):65-67.
Reply to critical review of Saunders (1914) by J. Cuming Walters.

E962. ______. "Dickens, Drood and Datchery." Dickensian 15 (1919):182-88.
Argues that Datchery is Datchery, a new character.

E963. ______. "The Murder of Edwin Drood." Dickensian 17 (1921):24-29.
Unfavorable review of Carden's theory that Tartar is Datchery.

E964. Squire, J. C. "The Drood Mystery Insoluble." Dickensian 15 (1919):195-96. Reprinted from Land and Water 22 May 1919.
Against Droodism, which JCS characterizes as having "hypnotic power over the simple-minded." Also questions value of close analysis of text, since Dickens was not a rigorous writer, and in any case, had the right to take liberties.

E965. Suddaby, John. "A Night Amongst the Drood Opium Dens." Dickensian 12 (1916):210-14.
Reprints contemporary accounts of Lascar Sal, the prototype of the Opium Woman.

E966. Thompson, Charles William. "The Track of Edwin Drood." Catholic World 140 (1934):51-58.
Argues that there is no real mystery in the parts of Drood written; the real mystery would have dealt with events anterior to story-present. Jasper is still an unknown character, whose past would have been developed.

E967. Thomson, G. M. Hollingsworth. "When Shall These Three Meet Again?" Dickensian 27 (1931):97-99.
Argues that only Drood himself could have planted the evidences of his "death."

E968. Tuckett, J. E. Shum. "Who Was Jasper?" Dickensian 27 (1931):25-32.
A development of Kavanagh's theory. Argues that Jasper is an impostor, a Eurasian half-brother of the true Jasper, who is present disguised as Datchery.

E969. (Vanes, Alexander R.) "Mr. Sapsea the Murderer of Edwin Drood." Dickensian 29 (1933):217-19.
Argues that Sapsea was in love with Rosa Bud and murdered Drood, and that old Mrs. Crisparkle was Datchery. A joke, of course, but worth reading as a parodic criticism of much analysis of Drood. Published anonymously.

E970. Walters, J. Cuming. Clues to Dickens's Mystery of Edwin Drood. London: Chapman and Hall, 1905.
The first extended argument (and classical statement of theory) that Datchery was Helena Landless in disguise. Also argues that Drood is dead. Walters was an indefatigable polemist with many articles, letters,

lectures expounding these points.

E971. Watt, John V. "Local Events in the Days of Drood." Dickensian 29 (1933):40-42.

Attempts to date Drood as 1842-43.

E972. Werner, Craig. "Fugal Structure in The Mystery of Edwin Drood." DSN 9 (1978):77-80.

Argues that Dickens uses two Jasper motifs--veneer of respectability and self-destructive criminality-- contrapuntally. Bases argument on passage in Monod (1968).

E973. Wing, George. "Edwin Drood and Desperate Remedies. Prototypes of Detective Fiction in 1870." Studies in English Literature 13 (1973):677-78.

General discussion, as early detective fiction.

Continuations, pastiches, parodies: texts

E974. Carden, Percy T. The Murder of Edwin Drood Recounted by John Jasper (etc). London: Cecil Palmer; NY: Putnam, 1920.

A brief restatement (somewhat slanted) of Drood, followed by a continuation in summary. Jasper killed Drood; Jasper kills Neville Landless; Jasper stabs Helena Landless, who recovers; Jasper confesses. Datchery is Tartar. No fictional merit. Appendices cover date of action (argued as 1842); identify Datchery as Tartar; locate Durdles's house in Rochester; discuss green cover.

E975. Forsyte, Charles (pseud.). The Decoding of Edwin Drood. NY: Scribner, 1980.

Extended treatment of Jasper as a true multiple personality (Jasper proper and the Murderer, who do not communicate with one another). Argues that Dickens used techniques of stage magic to plant hints; that Jasper's nature and fate are conveyed by subliminal hints in descriptive passages. Also offers fictional completion of Drood. Drood is dead and Jasper is captured after killing Neville. In prison the Jasper component first learns of his crimes through the Opium Woman, and commits suicide in remorse. Datchery is Bazzard. Argument: sometimes far-fetched; fiction: routine. CC S122.

E976. Freeman, R. Austin. The Mystery of Angelina Frood. London: Hodder and Stoughton, 1924; NY: Dodd, Mead, 1925.

A Dr. Thorndyke mystery based loosely on Drood. Freeman makes point that quicklime would not dissolve a corpse, and establishes conditions for successful male impersonation by young woman. An excellent mystery.

E977. Garfield, Leon. The Mystery of Edwin Drood by Charles Dickens. Concluded by Leon Garfield. London: Andre Deutsch; NY: Pantheon, 1980.

1870 text with Garfield's continuation. Drood is dead. Jasper kills Neville Landless near opium den. Jasper is hanged. Datchery, a friend of Bazzard's, is broken-down actor turned professional detective, hired by Grewgious. Continuation attempts manner of Dickens, but unsuccessfully. Weak characterizations, and dull. Introduction by Edward Blishen and 20 illustrations by Antony Maitland. CC S123.

E978. Harris, Edwin. John Jasper's Gatehouse. A Sequel to the Unfinished Novel "The Mystery of Edwin Drood" by Charles Dickens. Rochester (England): Mackays, Ltd., 1931.

Fictional continuation. Drood was murdered by Jasper. Jasper throws Neville off the tower and is committed for trial. Datchery is Bazzard, acting with knowledge of Grewgious. No fictional merit.

E979. Graeme, Bruce (pseud. of Jeffries, Graham M.). Epilogue. London: Hutchinson, 1933; Philadelphia: Lippincott, 1934.
Supt. Stevens, modern C. I. D. series sleuth, and associate go back in time to Cloisterham to work on Drood case. Jasper murders Datchery (who is Bazzard). In extended trial scene, the detectives create much confusion by references to future. Drood's corpse found. All a dream. Routine work.

E980. Indictment of John Jasper Lay Precentor of Cloisterham Cathedral in the County of Kent for the Murder of Edwin Drood, Engineer. Trial Holden at the Assizes at Westminster, on the 7th of January, 1914. (Short title on cover, The Trial of John Jasper for The Murder of Edwin Drood.) London: Dickens Fellowship, 1914. Prepared from shorthand notes by J. W. T. Ley.
Record of famous London trial of Jasper, with G. K. Chesterton as judge, G. B. Shaw as foreman of jury, and Arthur Morrison, Max Pemberton, Justin McCarthy, William de Morgan, and other literary men as jurors. Droodists Walters and Ley apparently intended the trial as a serious matter which would support their own theories, but others were more frivolous, and at the end, what with Shaw and Chesterton, things got out of hand. This trial received enormous international publicity. See Ley (1914a), Walters (1914a).

E981. (James, Thomas F.) The Mystery of Edwin Drood Complete. Brattleboro, Vt.: T. F. James, 1873. Second title page: Part Second of the Mystery of Edwin Drood by the Spirit-Pen of Charles Dickens through a Medium.
Dickens's text followed by long, sentimental confusion. Durdles rescues Drood; Datchery is a sea captain, son of the Opium Woman. Jasper had seduced Datchery's sister. Jasper goes mad and dies. Drood weds Rosa; Crisparkle weds Helena. Author adds many new characters and subplots. A curiosity only. It is not clear whether Spiritualist claim was meant seriously or for sales. See Reuter (1927/1928) for disavowal by Dickens's spirit!

E982. Jones-Evans, Eric. John Jasper's Secret. A Play in Four Acts. London: Samuel French, 1957.
Helena, disguised as sailor, worms confession out of Jasper in opium den and implants suggestion that he must retrieve the ring. At tomb, Jasper sees Drood-figure (Neville), whom he stabs. A chase up the tower, Jasper leaps, is accidentally caught by scarf on ironwork, and strangles. Datchery is Bazzard, but does not appear in play. Lurid, sensational, with cliched dialogue.

E983. Kerr, Orpheus C. (pseud. of Newell, Robert H.). The Cloven Foot. Being an Adaptation of the English Novel "The Mystery of Edwin Drood" (by Charles Dickens) to American Scenes, Characters, Customs, and Nomenclature. NY: Carleton, 1870.
Very close parody-pastiche that parallels Drood incident by incident. Bladams (Jasper) is an alcoholic, rather than an opium fiend, and sees everything double. On one of his benders he misplaces his nephew, Drood, and his umbrella. Tracey Clews (Datchery), an amateur detective, is gathering information for the great American novel. I found this much more amusing than it is generally considered.

E984. Lang, Andrew. "At the Sign of the Ship." Longman's Magazine 45 (1905b):(473-80).
Holmes and Watson discuss the Drood mystery. Holmes slashes theories of J. Cuming Walters and supports that of Proctor. Mildly amusing at times.

E985. (Morford, Henry) John Jasper's Secret. A Sequel to Charles Dickens' Unfinished Novel "The Mystery of Edwin Drood." Philadelphia: Peterson, 1872. First published in Frank Leslie's Illustrated Newspaper, irregularly, 29 April through 2 September 1871.
Long fictional continuation by American author who traveled to Rochester to obtain background. Jasper tried to strangle Drood, and dropped his body between the double walls of the cathedral, whence Durdles rescued him. Drood fled to London and consulted his friend Bazzard, who (unknown to Grewgious) assumed role of Datchery, while Drood went on to Egypt. Jasper dies in opium den. Jasper had seduced daughter of Opium Woman. Drood returns and marries Helena. A period piece. Often fraudulently attributed to Wilkie Collins and Charles Dickens, Jr. Many cheap reprints in America and Great Britain.

E986. Pearson, Edmund. "Dickens's Secret Book." In The Secret Book, pp. 44-70. NY: Macmillan, 1914. Reprinted from Boston Evening Transcript, 2 April 1913.
Holmes and Watson visit Rochester, and call on Sapsea and Jasper. Watson converses with Datchery and draws all the wrong conclusions. Holmes reveals that Drood is alive, masquerading as Datchery, looking for proof against Jasper. "The improbable is probably true." Mildly amusing. Reprinted as Sherlock Holmes and the Drood Mystery. Freeville, NY: Aspen Press, 1973, with introduction and afterword by Tom Schantz (not seen).

E987. Smith, Harry B. How Sherlock Holmes Solved "The Mystery of Edwin Drood." Glen Rock, PA: W. Klinefelter, 1934. 33 copy edition. Reprinted from Munsey's Magazine, December 1924 (not seen).
The narrator, who is a friend of Watson's, introduces Holmes to Drood. Holmes is fascinated, and concludes that Drood escaped to Egypt. The reason for his silence is that he does not know that he is believed dead. Negligible as fiction.

E988. Vase, Gillan (pseud. of Newton, Mrs. Richard (Elizabeth)). A Great Mystery Solved Being a Continuation of and Conclusion to "The Mystery of Edwin Drood." 3 vols. London: Remington, 1978. Second (badly abridged) edition, edited by Jevons, Shirley Byron. London: Sampson Low, 1913; NY: McBride, Nast, 1914.
Long sentimental continuation. Drood escaped from Jasper, adopted disguise (dark glasses!) and went to work for Grewgious, who did not know him. Datchery is a professional detective, but soon drops out of the story. Drood and Rosa marry. Sometimes praised, but I find it of no fictional merit.

Continuations, pastiches, parodies: critical and historical

E989. Becker, May L. "The Reader's Guide." SRL 1 (1925):653.
Brief discussion of continuaions to Drood and speculations about plot.

E990. Bengis, Nathan L. "Sherlock Holmes and the Edwin Drood Mystery." BSJ 5 (1955):5-12.

Describes and comments on three pastiches in which Holmes considered the Drood case: Lang (1905b), Pearson (1914), Smith (1934). Notes that all three believe that Drood survived. Useful, since stories are hard to find.

E991. Gadd, George F. "The History of a Mystery. A Review of the Solutions to 'Edwin Drood.'" Dickensian 1 (1905): 240-43, 270-73, 293-96, 320-23.
A judicious survey of the early continuations and reconstructions, useful for describing material not generally available.

E992. Ley, J. W. T. "The Trial of John Jasper Alleged Murderer of Edwin Drood in the Dock. A Unique Literary Treat." Dickensian 10 (1914):33-41.
Summarizes London trial, declaring conclusion an outrage. Blames egotism of Shaw and actor who played Bazzard for collapse of trial. (Not wholly supported by the trial record.) See also Indictment of John Jasper (1914).

E993. Morley, Malcolm. "Stage Solutions to the Mystery." Dickensian 53 (1957):46-48, 93-97, 180-84.
Good survey of solutions and presentations, printed and unprinted, 1870 to 1951.

E994. Read, Newbury Frost. "Edwin Drood." Dickensian 25 (1929):144-45.
Discussion, summary of The Cloven Foot by Orpheus C. Kerr.

E995. Sayers, Dorothy. "Angelina Frood." Dickensian 26 (1930):70-71.
Interesting letter calling attention to R. Austin Freeman's The Mystery of Angelina Frood and parallels to Drood.

E996. T., J. K. "American Trial of John Jasper." Dickensian 10 (1914):148-50.
A favorable summary of events at the trial held in Philadelphia, 29 April 1914. Matters did not get out of hand, as happened in the British trial. Jaspers was found not guilty, apparently on the ground that there was no corpus delicti. See also Walters (1917).

E997. Walters, J. Cuming. "The Drood Trial Reviewed." Dickensian 10 (1914a):42-44.
Walters declares himself "utterly disappointed" at the London trial, and blames Shaw and the actor who played Bazzard. Criticism is somewhat disingenuous, since Walters himself violated trial conditions by insinuating the Helena-Datchery theory into the evidence. See also Indictment of John Jasper (1914).

E998. ______. "'Edwin Drood' Continued." Dickensian 10 (1914b):238-41.
Extended review of continuation The Mystery of Edwin. . . Completed in 1914 by W. E. C., edited and revised by Mary L. C. Grant. Drood is dead. Datchery is a new character, an amateur detective. Helena Landless hypnotizes Jasper in the opium den and obtains a confession from him. Walters declares this the best of the continuations from a literary point of view. (W. E. C.'s work not seen)

E999. ______. "A Warning against Drood Trials." Dickensian 13 (1917):149-51.
Reviews the trial book of the Philadelphia 1914 trial, and considers the trial to have been a fiasco. He warns against future similar trials. See also T., J. K. (1914).

DICKENSON, FRED

Ref: Hubin 2; UN 2:11 (1950):12-13 (photo).

DICKINSON, PETER

Ref: Hubin 2, TCCMW, EMD, CC, ABMI(S); Cannon, AHMM 29:1 (Jan 84):56-58.

See also: B309.

DICKENSON, FRED

Ref: Hubin 2; UN 2:11 (1950):12-13 (photo).

DICKINSON, PETER

Ref: Hubin 2, TCCMW, EMD, CC, ABMI(S); Cannon, AHMM 29:1 (Jan 84):56-58.

See also: B309.

E1000. Bargainnier, Earl F. "The Playful Mysteries of Peter Dickinson." TAD 13 (1980):185-93. Illus. See TAD 14 (1981):73 for a letter from Bargainnier correcting printing errors in the article.

After discussing the five mysteries featuring Superintendent James Pibble and creating a profile of the detective, Dickinson discusses the five books that do not feature Pibble. He concludes that Dickinson "extended the range" of British mystery fiction. There is no attempt to compare Dickinson with other writers or to support his claims for Dickinson's "innovations," and, although Bargainnier mentions Dickinson's tenure on the staff of the British humor magazine _Punch_, he does not make any critical use of this important fact.

E1002. "Peter Dickinson." BMJ, 26 July 80, pp. 293-94.

Dickinson's medical data are "sometimes" verified in the local library but, according to this article, based on an interview with the writer, Dickinson's medical inventions are largely based on his own imagination.

DICKSON, CARTER. See CARR, JOHN DICKSON

DIDELOT, FRANCIS

Ref: Hubin 2, CC.

Int: MM 293, July 72, pp. 119-224.

DIEHL, WILLIAM

Ref: Hubin 2.

Int: PW 221:2 (8 Jan 82):12-14 (photo).

DIMENT, ADAM

Ref: Hubin 2, TCCMW, ABMIS.

"DIPLOMAT" (pseud. of JOHN FRANKLIN CARTER)

Ref: Hubin 2, EMD, CC, ABMI(S).

E1003. Panek, Leroy. "Diplomat's New Deal Mysteries." _Clues_ 4:2 (Fall/Winter 83):76-91.

A discussion of the seven mystery novels John Franklin Carter wrote under the pseudonym of "Diplomat." Carter did not think that the mystery novel could say "important things" but his fiction is still entertaining reading.

DISNEY, DORIS MILES

Ref: Hubin 2, TCCMW, EMD, CC, ABMI; UN 3:8 (1951):6-7, 15 (photo); UN 4:9 (1952):8-9 (photo).

E1004. DeMarr, Mary Jean. "Three Gentle Men: Doris Miles Disney's Continuing Detectives." TMF 3:3 (May/June 79):5-14.
A discussion of Disney's Postal Inspector David Madden, Claim Adjuster Jefferson DiMarco and detective Jim O'Neill.

E1005. Mercier, Jean F. "PW Interviews: Doris Miles Disney and Isabelle Taylor." PW 204 (13 Aug 73):24-5.
Some brief comments by Crime Club editor Taylor but largely an interview with Disney who talks about her career and her books.

DISNEY, DOROTHY CAMERON

Ref: Hubin 2, TCCMW, EMD, CC, ABMI.

DODGE, DAVID

Ref: Hubin 2, TCCMW, SN, ABMI(S); UN 1:2 (1948):2-3 (photo).

DOLPH, JACK

Ref: Hubin 2, ABMI; UN 1:4 (1948):6-7 (photo); UN 2:11 (1950):10-11 (photos); UN 3:7 (1951):6-7, 15 (photo).

DOLSON, HILDEGARDE

Ref: Hubin 2, TCCMW, ABMI.

DONOVAN, DICK

Ref: Hubin 2, TCCMW, EMD, ABMIS.

E1006. "Donovan, Dick" (J. E. Preston Muddock). Pages from an Adventurous Life. London: T. Werner Laurie, n. d. (1907). 352pp. Illus. Index.
Autobiography of prolific early British writer of detective thrillers (1890s through the 1920s), which he disparages. (He only did it for the money....) (REB)

DORN, DEAN M. See MORGAN, MICHAEL

DOSTOEVSKY, FYODOR

Ref: Hubin 2, EMD, ABMI(S).

See also: E1062.

E1007. Holquist, Michael. "Puzzle and Mystery, the Narrative Poles of Knowing: Crime and Punishment." In his Dostoevsky and the Novel, pp. 75-101. Princeton, N. J.: Princeton University Press, 1977.
A discussion of the first six books of Crime and Punishment as a complicated variant of the detective novel. Holquist analyses plot in terms of the genre and Russian formalist perspectives. Holquist is not defensive about genre references and this chapter could serve as a model for discussions of literary works in which genre elements can be identified.

DOUGLASS, DONALD MCNUTT

Ref: Hubin 2, CC, ABMI; Lachman, TPP 3:6 (Dec 80):11-12.

DOWNING, TODD

Ref: Hubin 2, ABMI; The Writer 56:12 (Dec 43):357-59 (market advice).

DRAX, PETER

Ref: Hubin 2; The Writer (England) 18:4 (Jan 37):85.

DRESSER, DAVIS. See HALLIDAY, BRETT

DRISCOLL, PETER

Ref: Hubin 2, TCCMW, ABMI(S).

DRUMMOND, IVOR

Ref: Hubin 2, TCCMW, ABMI(S).

DRUMMOND, JUNE

Ref: Hubin 2, TCCMW, CC, ABMI(S).

DUBOIS, THEODORA

Ref: Hubin 2, ABMI(S); UN 1:10 (1949):4-5 (photo).

DUBOISGOBEY, FORTUNE

Ref: Hubin 2, EMD, CC, ABMI.

E1008. Malosse, Jean. "Les Emules de Gaboriau: Fortuné Duboisgobey (1821-1891) |The imitators of Gaboriau|." Enigmatika 24 (July 83):16-20.
A report on a disenchanted reading of La Vieillesse de Monsieur Lecoq (Duboisgobey) and Maman Rocambole (Zaccone).

DUKE, WINIFRED

Ref: Hubin 2, EMD, ABMI(S).

E1009. Donaldson, Norman. "Winifred Duke: A Preliminary Survey." TAD 2 (1968/69):94-96.
Survey of work of British writer who died in 1962.

DUMAS, ALEXANDRE

Ref: CC.

E1010. Lacassin, Francis. "L'Abbé Faria ou inventaire successoral pour une légende défunte |The Abbé Faria or an estate inventory for a deceased legend|." In Lacassin (B202), pp. 65-97.
Lacassin establishes the historical reality of the Abbé Faria who figures in The Man in the Iron Mask as a priest-detective and whom Lacassin sees as an early armchair detective.

DU MAURIER, DAPHNE

Ref: Hubin 2, TCCMW, EMD, ABMI(S).

See also: B164a.

E1011. Bakerman, Jane S. "Tension and Duality: Daphne du Maurier's 'Don't Look Now.'" TMF 3:4 (July/August 79):8-10.
As Bakerman points out, du Maurier--winner of the MWA's Lifetime Achievement Award--does not consider herself to be a writer of detective fiction but she does often write about crimes. This article is a study of the story of psychic phenomena on which Nicolas Roeg's 1973 film was based.

E1012. du Maurier, Daphne. Growing Pains. London: Gollancz, 1973. 173pp. Illus. Autobiographical account of du Maurier's early life, up to the writing of her first novel and her subsequent marriage. Very little foreshadowing of her later career, and little commentary specifically about writing. (REB)

E1013. du Maurier, Daphne. The Rebecca Notebook and Other Memories. Garden City: Doubleday, 1981. 305pp.
Personal recollections of the circumstances surrounding the writing of Rebecca, probably the most famous modern romantic suspense novel. The book also contains new short stories and journalistic pieces. (REB)

DUNCAN, ROBERT L.

Ref: Hubin 2, TCCMW, ABMIS.

E1014. Winks, Robin W. "Murder by Holocaust: Robert L. Duncan/James Hall Roberts." New Republic, 22 July 78, pp. 31-33; reprinted in Winks (B434), pp. 224-28.
Duncan's books have puzzle elements (Duncan "confesses" to having read Ellery Queen at age 12) but Winks relates these well-researched thrillers to writers as diverse as Paul Erdman, Jack Higgins and Robert Ludlum, Harry Patterson, Laurence Sanders, Joseph Wambaugh and Emma Lathen. The comparisons to these other writers are largely name-dropping with some capsule judgements such as that neither Higgins nor Ludlum can write and that Wambaugh "purports" to write of the police.

DUNCAN, W. MURDOCH

Ref: Hubin 2, TCCMW, ABMI(S).

E1015. Ireland, Donald. "W. Murdoch Duncan--Master of Mystery. An Appreciation." TAD 9 (1975/76):116-118.
Under his various pseudonyms, Duncan wrote novels of detection, private detective novels and thrillers. Ireland points out that Duncan spent as much time on characterization as on plotting and considers the novels written under the Malloch byline as the most interesting.

DUNN, J. ALLAN

Ref: Hubin 2, ABMI(S); Argosy, 8 March 30.

DUNNE, JOHN GREGORY

Ref: Hubin 2, TCCMW, ABMI(S).

DUNNETT, DOROTHY (HALLIDAY)

Ref: Hubin 2, TCCMW, CC, ABMI(S); Cannon, AHMM 28:5 (May 83):84-87.

E1016. Haber, Ruth. "'Tant que je vive' -- 'Placetne': Some Parallels between the Lymond Chronicle and the Lord Peter Mysteries." TSR 3:2 (Dec 78):21-28.
Posits the literary influence of Sayers' Wimsey mysteries on Dunnett's Lymond Chronicle.

DURAS, MARGUERITE

Ref: Hubin 2, ABMI(S).

E1017. Eisinger, Erica M. "Crime and Detection in the Novels of Marguerite Duras." Contemporary Literature 15 (Autumn 74):503-20.
Duras' interest in stories of crime is in the "human drama of moral

involvement in the mystery of another's criminal act" where for the French new novelists (like Butor and Robbe-Grillet) it is in the puzzle element. Some comparisons with Simenon are made. The observer as detective; the detective as novelist, creating fiction; investigations result in "communion." A rambling, badly focused discussion.

DURBRIDGE, FRANCIS

Ref: Hubin 2, TCCMW, EMD, CC, ABMI(S).

E1018. Adley, Derek. "The Paul Temple Saga." TAD 9 (1975/76):267-68.
Paul Temple, novelist-private investigator, in radio, TV, fiction and illustrated paperbacks.

E1019. Jones, Michael Wynn. "Investigating the Mastermind behind 30 Years of Violent Crime." Radio Times, 21 Oct 71, pp. 63-71.
Report of a visit to and interview with author Durbridge, and a review of his radio and television work. Lots of photos. (RCSA)

DURRENMATT, FRIEDRICH

Ref: Hubin 2, TCCMW, CC, ABMI.

See also: E178.

E1020. Arnold, Armin. "Friedrich Dürrenmatt and Edgar Wallace." International Fiction Review 3:2 (1976):142-44.
On the influence of Edgar Wallace's "Four Just Men" series on Dürrenmatt's short novel Die Panne (1956) that Dürrenmatt's novel in some ways parodies.

E1021. Beckmeir, Ralph William. "Dürrenmatt and the Detective Novel: Commitment and Responsability." Unpublished dissertation. New York University, 1973. 162pp.
Not seen but described in Dissertation Abstracts 34/08-A, p. 5156, as an analysis of the "political and social social implications of detective novels."

E1022. Gillis, William. "Dürrenmatt and the Detectives." The German Quarterly 35 (Jan 62):71-74.
Dürrenmatt "exalts" the detective story form in his use of it to demonstrate his "basic concept of the absolute certainty of justice."

E1023. Herr, Kay. "The Failure of Two Swiss Sleuths." TAD 13 (1980):163-65.
A discussion of Dürrenmatt's three crime novels in which man's ability to reason is imperfect and thus cannot always provide the solutions that characterize detective fiction novelists like Conan Doyle and Rex Stout.

E1024. Holtan, Orley I. "Freidrich Dürrenmatt: The Detective Story as Moral Fable." TAD 5 (1972):133-6, 144.
Dürrenmatt's The Judge and His Hangman, The Suspicion, The Pledge and Traps as procedurals and as metaphysical fables.

E1025. Leah, Gordon N. "Dürrenmatt's Detective Stories." Modern Languages 48 (June 67):65-69. Not seen.

E1026. Peppard, Murray B. Friedrich Dürrenmatt. NY: Twayne, 1965.
There is some minor discussion of detective fiction elements in Dürrenmatt's work in Chapter 5.

E1027. Ramsey, Roger. "Parody and Mystery in Dürrenmatt's The Pledge." MFS 17 (Winter 71/2):525-32.
Dürrenmatt's novella The Pledge is both a Kriminalroman in which the faith in mystery--Truth inviolate--is not parodied and the conventional "commitment to problem-solving" is.

E1028. Wagner, Geoffrey. "Dürrenmatt and the Kriminalroman." Commonweal 76 (22 June 62):324-6.
Six violations of formal mystery "codes" which Wagner sees as intentional paroy.

E1029. Waldmann, Guenter. "Kriminalroman -- Anti-Kriminalroman: Dürrenmatts Requiem auf den Kriminalroman und die Anti-Aufklaerung |Crime novel -- anti-crime novel: Dürrenmatt's requiem for the crime novel and the anti-enlightment|." In Vogt (B424), Vol. I, pp. 206-27. Previously published as "Requiem auf die Vernunft: Dürrenmatts christlichen Kriminalroman |Requiem for reason: Dürrenmatt's Christian crime novel)" in Paedagogische Provinz 15 (1961):376-84.
Scholarly examination of the The Pledge and The Quarry. Waldmann strives to show that the first represents a religious anti-enlightenment and that the second is a Christian crime novel. (GG)

E1030. Wieckenberg, Ernst-Peter. "Dürrenmatts Detektivromane |Dürrenmatts detective novels|." Text + Kritik 56 (October 77):8-19. Not seen.

DUSE, S. A.

E1031. Saxlund, Tyrgils. "S. A. Duse -- deckarförfattaren |S. A. Duse -- the detective author)." Jury 7:4 (1978):40-43.
Duse was Sweden's most popular detective author in the teens and twenties. (MS)

EASTMAN, ELIZABETH

Ref: Hubin 2, ABMI; UN 1:2 (1948):5 (photo).

EBERHART, MIGNON

Ref: Hubin 2. TCCMW, EMD, CC, ABMI(S); The Writer 51:3 (March 38):67-68.

Int: PW, 16 Sept 74, pp. 10-11.

EBERSOHN, WESSEL

Ref: Hubin 2.

E1032. Isaac, Fred. "Black and White and Dead: James McClure's South Africa." TMF 6:4 (July/Aug 82):12-18.
See the conclusion of this article (pp. 17-18) for some comments on Ebersohn's two crime novels featuring psychologist Yudel Gordon.

ECHOLS, ALLAN K.

Ref: Argosy, 6 Sept 30.

EDEN, DOROTHY

Ref: Hubin 2, TCCMW, ABMI(S).

EDOGAWA, RAMPO. See RAMPO, EDOGAWA

EGAN, LESLEY. See LININGTON, ELIZABETH

EGLETON, CLIVE

Ref: Hubin 2, TCCMW, SN, ABMIS.

Int: DAST 9:1 (1976):38-39 (photo); DAST 14:6 (1981):52-54 (photo and checklist).

EKMAN, KIRSTIN

E1033. Westin, Barbro; Holmblad, Karin; and Berg, Lillemor. "Kerstin Ekmans deckare |Kerstin Ekman's detective novels|." Jury 8:1 (1979): 27-34. (MS)

E1034. Wright, Rochelle. "Kerstin Ekman: Voice of the Vulnerable." World Literature Today 55:2 (Spring 1981):204-209. Photo.

Known as the Swedish "Queen of the Detective Novel," a reputation established by her early works in the genre (circa 1959-67), her novels increasingly moved away from their genre associations. Her three most recent works are historical novels set in the region where she grew up. Ekman was elected to the Swedish Academy in 1978. Wright is uncomfortable with the early novels and does not attempt to relate them to her subsequent work or to say much more than that they are in a genre "generally considered devoid of artistic pretensions."

ELLIN, STANLEY

Ref: Hubin 2, TCCMW, EMD, CC, ABMI(S); UN 4:7 (1952):8-9, 14-15 (photo); The Writer 70:11 (Nov 57):7-10 (irony); The Writer 73:11 (Nov 60):7-10 (literary history; author biography); The Writer 76:5 (May 63):7-9 (point of view); The Writer 79:12 (Dec 66):11-13, 44 (climax; pulp formulas); The Writer 80:12 (Dec 67):11-13 (novel sources); The Writer 86:1 (Jan 73):22-24; The Writer 92:12 (Dec 79):9-11, 43 (plotting and characterization); The Writer 95:8 (Aug 82):9-11 (suspense in fiction).

Int: DAST 9:5 (1976):26-27 (photo and checklist); EQMM, Sept 76, pp. 79-80.

See also: C735.

E1035. Barzun, Jacques, and Taylor, Wendell Hertig. "Introduction." In The Key to Nicholas Street (NY, 1952), by Stanley Ellin. "Crime Fiction 1950-1975" (B18).

E1036. Camerino, Aldo. "Stanley Ellin: 'Strane Storie' (1961) |Stanley Ellin: 'strange stories'|." In Scrittori di lingua inglese, pp. 335-38. Milan-Naples: Ricciardi, 1968.

The author notes the extraordinary fortune of the genre, in Italy and abroad, and its capacity to renew itself, with one of the "variations" of the detective genre bearing the name of Stanley Ellin. This, in spite of the pessimistic predictions of the critics who very early (in Blackwood's Magazine, 1890) and periodically in the course of its history warn of its extinction. (LR)

E1037. Ellin, Stanley. "The Destiny of the House." TAD 12 (1979): 195. Photo.

A tribute to Ellery Queen and EQMM and the genesis of Ellin's first story for EQMM, "The Specialty of the House."

E1038. ______. "Stanley Ellin Talks about Himself and His Writing." TMRN 2:3 (Feb 69):13-14.

An interview in which Ellin also expresses his reservations about the claims to excellence of most "straight" novels which he thinks are often inferior to the best detective novels.

E1039. Penzler, Otto. "Introduction." In The Eighth Circle, by Stanley Ellin (Random, 1958), pp. v-x. Gregg Press Mystery Fiction Series (B134.)

E1040. Queen, Ellery. "Introduction." In Kindly Dig Your Grave and Other Wicked Stories, by Stanley Ellin, pp. 7-9. NY: Davis Publications, Inc., Dec. 1975.

ELLISON, HARLAN

Ref: Hubin 2, ABMI(S).

E1041. Swigart, Leslie Kay. Harlan Ellison: A Bibliographical Checklist.. Dallas, TX: Williams Publishing Co., 1973. v, 118pp. Illus. Index. Edition limited to 1000 numbered copies.

Harlan Ellison's work in all fields is listed in ten categories: books, scripts, fiction, articles and essays, introductions and afterwords, reviews, published letters, interviews, fanzines, and 'titles announced but not yet produced.' (Of 14 books listed in the last section, 12 have yet to appear.) Contents are listed for all short story collections. Original appearances and both English-language and foreign-language reprints are listed for all magazine fiction. In addition to the bibliographic material, there are appreciations or tributes by Isaac Asimov, Ben Bova, Edward Bryant, Joanna Russ, Robert Silverberg, and James Sutherland, as well as an Afterword by Ellison. The illustrations include 90 book and magazine cover reproductions and 22 snapshots or portraits from all periods of Ellison's career. The bibliographic citations are as complete and meticulous as you could want, and the high quality of the design and presentation make this a collector's item as well as a valuable reference tool. (REB)

ELSTON, ALLAN VAUGHAN

Ref: ABMI(S); Argosy, 6 May 33.

ENDREBE, MAURICE BERNARD

Int: MM 284, Oct 71; Enigmatika 19 (June 81), pp. 3-14.

E1042. "Dossier Maurice Bernard Endrèbe." Enigmatika 19 (June 81), pp. 1-72. A dossier on the Belgian writer of detective fiction. Contents: J. Baudou, "Entretien avec M. B. Endrèbe |Interview with M. B. E|," pp. 3-14; "Bibliographie," pp. 15-21; "M. B. E. Critique |M. B. E. critic|," pp. 22-34 (reviews of fiction by Endrèbe); M. B. Endrèbe, "Mes Traductions préférées," pp. 35-36 (E1043); M. B. Endrèbe, "Claude Aveline. Postface à L'Abonne de la ligne U," pp. 37-41 (E85); M. B. Endrèbe, "Postface de La Chambre Ardente, pp. 42-46 (E355); M. B. Endrèbe, "Patrick Quentin. Postface à Assassin pour Dames seules," pp. 47-49 (E2281); M. B. Endrèbe, "Les Mystères de la chambre close, pp. 50-60 (C260); M. B. Endrèbe, "D'après nature |According to nature|," pp. 61-66 (true crime); M. B. Endrèbe, "La Derniere Goutte d'huile |The last drop of oil|," pp. 67-70 (ss); Jean Malosse, "Les Auteurs anglais 'classiques' : 'Sir Morris B. Endrebb', pp. 71-72 (E1044).

E1043. Endrèbe, Maurice Bernard. "Mes Traductions préférées |My favorite translations|." Enigmatika 19 (June 81), pp. 35-36.

Endrèbe has some some notable translations into French of English and American detective fiction and he comments briefly on a number of those novels and others that are not detective novels.

E1044. Malosse, Jean. "Les Auteurs anglais 'classiques': 'Sir Morris B. Endrebb' |The 'classic' English authors: 'Sir Morris B. Endrebb'|." Enigmatika 19, pp. 71-72.

Light-hearted comments on 3 "classical" English detective novels published in French and written by Endrèbe under the pseudonym of Sir Morris B. Endrebb.

ENGEL, HOWARD

E1045. Cooper-Clark, Diana. "Howard Engel." In Cooper-Clark (B75), pp. 103-24. Photo.

A sympathetic and wide-ranging discussion with Canadian novelist Engel, author of three private-eye novels, on the lack of a Canadian detective fiction tradition, the role of criticism, the relationship of mainstream fiction (Faulkner) to the best detective fiction (Hammett, Chandler), and Engel's novels. Probably the best-conducted interview in this collection.

ERDMAN, PAUL E.

Ref: Hubin 2, TCCMW, ABMI(S).

ERICSON, WALTER. See CUNNINGHAM, E. V.

ERNST, PAUL

Ref: Hubin 2, ABMI(S); UN 3:12 (1951):12-13, 16 (photo);

See also: D316, D317.

ERSKINE, MARGARET

Ref: Hubin 2, TCCMW, ABMI(S); UN 1:8 (1948):13, 16 (photo).

ESHLEMAN, JOHN M.

Ref: Hubin.

E1046. Boucher, Anthony. "Introduction." In The Deadly Chase (orig. title: The Long Chase, Washburn, 1954), by John M. Eshleman. NY: Mercury, 1955.

EUSTACE, ROBERT

Ref: Hubin 2, TCCMW, ABMI.

See also: Barton, Dr. Robert Eustace.

EUSTIS, HELEN

Ref: Hubin 2, TCCMW, EMD, CC, SN, ABMI.

E1047. Barzun, Jacques, and Taylor, Wendell Hertig. Preface to The Horizontal Man (NY, 1946), by Helen Eustis. In A Book of Prefaces (B17), pp. 43-44.

EVANS, JOHN. See BROWNE, HOWARD

EXBRAYAT

Ref: Hubin 2.

Int:MM 294, Aug 72.

E1048. Evernden, Margery. "America, ou est-vous (sic): Speculations on Exbrayat." TAD 11 (1978):254-256. Illus.

Everndern sees the failure of Exbrayat's novels to find an English-speaking audience in attitudes that are too "foreign" to us. However, she obviously enjoys his sense of humor, his delight in favoring the "proletariat" and his Southern France settings and does not believe that her tastes are so untypical that other Anglo-Saxon readers would not also enjoy this prolific and very popular novelist.

FABRE, DOMINIQUE

Int: MM 295, Sept 72.

FAIR, A. A. See GARDNER, ERLE STANLEY

FAIRBAIRN, ROGER. See CARR, JOHN DICKSON

FAIRLIE, GERARD

Ref: Hubin 2, TCCMW, ABMI(S).

FALLON, MARTIN. See HIGGINS, JACK

FARLEY, RALPH MILNE

Ref: Argosy, 22 Feb 30.

FARRER, KATHERINE

Ref: Hubin 2, TCCMW, CC, ABMI.

FAST, HOWARD. See CUNNINGHAM, E. V.

FAULKNER, WILLIAM

Ref: Hubin 2, TCCMW, EMD, CC, ABMI(S).

See also: B216 (Tallack), C606.

E1049. Bassett, John (Earl). William Faulkner: An Annotated Checklist of Criticism. NY: David Lewis, 1972. xiii, 551pp. Index of critics.
Some brief annotations, many of them citations from sources rather than critical evaluations. The contents are arranged as follows: studies of individual novels; studies of short stories, poetry and miscellaneous writings; topical studies (including thematic and structural analyses, interviews, and miscellaneous); and "other materials."

E1050. ______. William Faulkner: An Annotated Checklist of Recent Criticism. Serif Series, No. 42. Kent, OH: Kent State University Press, 1983. xi, 272pp. Index.
An update of Bassett (1972), including items from 1971-82.

E1051. Brooks, Cleanth. "History, Tragedy and the Imagination in Absalom, Absalom!" Yale Review 52 (March 63):34-51; reprinted in William Faulkner: The Yoknapatawpha Country, by Cleanth Brooks, pp. 295-325. New Haven, CT: Yale University Press.
A close reading of Faulkner's novel, with some appreciative references to it as a "wonderful detective story," but no major discussion of use of genre material.

E1052. Brown, May Cameron, and Seaton, Esta. "William Faulkner's Unlikely Detective: Quentin Compson in Absalom, Absalom!" Arts and Sciences 8 (May 79):27-33.
Proceeding from the conviction that detective story writers have not

produced any work of the first rank, the authors discuss Faulkner's novel as an example of the way in which a "first-rate" writer makes use of detective story elements. They see the most significant use of such material by Faulkner in the novel's structure rather than in the characters although there is some discussion of the traditional detective contrasted with Faulkner's "unlikely detective," Quentin Compson.

E1053. Fiedler, Leslie. "William Faulkner: An American Dickens." Commentary 10 (Oct 50): 384-87. Reprinted in Love and Death in the American Novel, by Leslie Fiedler, pp. 309-15. NY: Criterion Books, 1960. Revised edition, NY: Stein and Day, 1966, pp. 320-25.

Unlike many academic critics, Fielder sees Faulkner's detective fiction as a high point in his work.

E1054. French, Warren. "William Faulkner and the Detective Story." In The Thirties: Fiction, Poetry, Drama, pp. 55-62. Deland, FL: Everett Edwards, Inc., 1967.

After making the point that detective fiction is decried because so many hack writers are attracted to it, French discusses the merits of Poe and proposes Absalom, Absalom! as "perhaps the greatest detective story in American literature," comparing its double narrative to Poe's "Murders in the Rue Morgue." A rambling essay that, apart from the discussion of Poe and references to Edmund Wilson and Conan Doyle, shows little knowledge of detective fiction and makes no reference to Faulkner's Knight's Gambit.

E1055. Gidley, Mark. "Elements of the Detective Story in William Faulkner's Fiction." JPC 7 (1973):97-123; reprinted in Landrum (B216), pp. 228-46.

Gidley discusses several of Faulkner's works in which there are detective story elements and comments that it is to Faulkner's credit that none of them is a "totally pure detective story" since it is Gidley's belief that works in which detective fiction elements dominate are weaker than those in which they play a subservient role. Although Gidley does not make this connection, his contention that things should not fall neatly into place and that some of the "ultimate mystery" should be preserved is similar to the French new novelists' use of detective fiction elements.

E1056. Holman, C. Hugh. "Absalom, Absalom!: The Historian as Detective." Sewanee Review 79 (Autumn 1971):542-53. Reprinted in The Roots of Southern Writing, by C. Hugh Holman, pp. 168-76. Athens, Georgia: University of Georgia Press, 1972.

The detective story form "puts a high premium on the interpretation of the past." Holman examines this premise in relation to Faulkner's Absalom, Absalom!

E1057. Jordan, Peter Wilson. "Faulkner's Crime Fiction: His Use of the Detective Story and the Thriller." Unpublished dissertation. University of Chicago, 1974. 220pp. Abstract published in DAI 34/05-A (1973/74), pp. 2630-31.

E1058. McHaney, Thomas. William Faulkner: A Reference Guide. Reference Guides in Literature, no. 7. Boston: G. K. Hall, 1976. xx, 568pp. Author/title/subject index.

A well-annotated bibliography of secondary material with a number of references incorporating discussion of genre elements in Faulkner's fiction. Superior to Bassett (E1049, E1050) and Ricks (E1063) and it is to be hoped that an updated version will be issued.

E1059. Malraux, Andre. "Préface à Sanctuaire de William Faulkner." Nouvelle Revue française 41 (Nov 33):744-47; reprinted, in an English translation, in Yale French Studies 10 (Fall 52):92-94.

Malraux discusses Sanctuary as a detective novel that has no detective but elements of Greek tragedy. Briefly compares Faulkner to Poe and E. T. A. Hoffmann.

E1060. O'Brien, Frances Blazer. "Faulkner and Wright: Alias S. S. Van Dine." Mississippi Quarterly 14 (Spring 61):101-107. Not seen.

E1061. O'Connor, William Van. "Sectionalism, and the Detective Story." In The Tangled Fire of William Faulkner, by Wm. Van O'Connor, pp. 136-45.

In the final pages of this chapter (pp. 142-45), O'Connor discusses briefly Knight's Gambit which he uses for his argument that the detective story is "ill-adapted" to Faulkner's language, themes and subject matter.

E1062. Rabinowitz, Peter J. "The Click of the Spring: The Detective Story as Parallel Structure in Dostoevsky and Faulkner." Modern Philology 76:4 (May 79):355-69.

An analysis of the ways in which the detective story is "harnassed" to serve the formal demands of Dostoevsky and Faulkner.

E1063. Ricks, Beatrice, compiler. William Faulkner: A Bibliography of Secondary Works. Metuchen, N. J. & London: The Scarecrow Press, 1981.

Ricks makes little attempt to annotate the material she includes and since this duplicates much of the material in both Bassett and McHaney (E1049, E1050, E1058v), and manages to omit items both of them include, this volume cannot be recommended.

E1064. Speir, Hans. "Faulkner's Knight's Gambit: Detection and Ingenuity." Notes on Mississippi Writers 13:2 (1981):79-83. Not seen.

E1065. Volpe, Edmond L. "'Monk': The Detective Story and the Human Heart." In Faulkner Studies I, edited by Barnett Guttenberg, pp. 86-90. Miami: University of Miami, 1980. Not seen.

FAUST, FREDERICK. See BRAND, MAX

FEARING, KENNETH

Ref: Hubin 2, TCCMW, EMD, CC, ABMI(S).

E1066. Barzun, Jacques, and Taylor, Wendell Hertig. Preface to The Big Clock (NY, 1946), by Kenneth Fearing. In A Book of Prefaces (B17), pp. 45-6.

E1067. Lacassin, Francis. "Le Grand Horloger ou le Poēte, le Destin et la Mort |The big clock or the poet, destiny and death|." In Lacassin (B201), Vol. 2, pp. 243-54.

Poet/novelist Kenneth Fearing's The Big Clock was translated into French by the poet/novelist Boris Vian (author of several detective pastiches under the pseudonym of Vernon Walker) and Lacassin analyzes the attraction of this novel for Vian which he finds in its poetry of death and fate. With a bibliography of Fearing's fiction and poetry.

E1068. Ryley, Robert M. "More than a Thriller: The Big Clock." TAD 16 (1983):354-59.

A discussion of The Big Clock as a "serious, artfully crafted novel," rather than as the potboiler it has often been labeled by critics of Fearing's poetry.

FEARN, JOHN RUSSELL

Ref: Hubin 2, ABMIS.

E1069. Harbottle, Philip. The Multi-Man: A biographic and bibliographic study of John Russell Fearn (1908-60). Wallsend, Northumberland, England: Philip Harbottle, 1968. 69pp. Spiral bound in pictorial covers. Illus. Bibliography.
Although best known as a prolific producer of science fiction for the lower echelon markets, British writer John Russell Fearn also wrote detective fiction, both under his own name and as "Hugo Blayn" and "John Slate." In his "Black Maria" series under the latter name, he used the "webwork" method of plotting made famous (or infamous) by Harry Stephen Keeler, though without the latter's inspired nuttiness. Fearn's crime fiction work is discussed along with his science fiction in "the Ultimate Analysis" by Philip Harbottle, which occupies the first 34 pages of The Multi-Man. His detective and mystery fiction in both magazine and book form is listed on pages 64-66 of the bibliography. The annotations include complete plot summaries. (REB)

FELIX, CHARLES

Ref: Hubin 2.

See also: C800.

FENISONG, RUTH

Ref: Hubin 2, TCCMW, CC; UN 2:1 (1949):6-7 (photo); UN 2:7 (1950):6-7 (photo).

FENWICK, ELIZABETH

Ref: Hubin 2, TCCMW, ABMI.

FERNALD, CHESTER BAILEY

Ref: Hubin 2, ABMI(S).

E1071. Bleiler, E. F. "A Chinese Detective in San Francisco." TMF 5:3 (May/June 81):2-4.
Bleiler analyzes "Chan Tow the Highrob," a dialect story by Fernald appearing in The Cat and the Cherub and Other Stories (Century, 1896), and finds in it a traditional Chinese detective story.

FERNEZ, ANDRE

E1072. "Dossier Nick Jordan." Fulmar no. 10 (July 82), pp. 4-46.
Published in the Marabout-Junior series (see bibliography, p. 46), these juvenile adventure novels feature counter-espionage agent Nick Jordan. . This dossier is a detailed study of the main character, his team of helpers, scientism in the novels, and the writing style. Illustrated with drawings from the books.

FERRARS, E. X.

Ref: Hubin 2, TCCMW, EMD, CC, ABMI(S).

FERRIERE, JEAN-PIERRE

Int: MM 280, June 71.

FIELDING, A.

Ref: Hubin 2, TCCMW, CC, ABMI.

FINDLEY, FERGUSON

Ref: Hubin 2; UN 2:7 (1950):10-11 (photo).

FINNEGAN, ROBERT

Ref: Hubin 2, TCCMW.

FINNEY, JACK

Ref: Hubin 2, TCCMW, ABMI(S).

FISCHER, BRUNO

Ref: Hubin 2, TCCMW, SN, ABMIS; UN 4:1 (1951):4-5 (photo).

See also: B309.

E1073. Crider, Bill. "Paperback Writers." PQ 1:4 (Winter 78):22. Cover photo. Crider comments briefly on Fischer's work. Crider's critical note is followed (pp. 23-24) by an annotated checklist of Fischer's Gold Medal originals and by an interview in which Fischer talks about his writing career.

FISH, ROBERT L.

Ref: Hubin 2, TCCMW, EMD, CC, ABMI(S); The Writer 80:6 (June 67):22-24; The Writer 82:4 (April 69):22-23, 44 (characterization); The Writer 92:9 (Sept 79):14-15 (on creating suspense).

Int: DAST 9:3 (1975):44-46 (photo); TMRN 2:5 (June 69):8-11 (checklist); DAST 9:6 (1976):24-25 (portrait and bibliography); EQMM, July 77, pp. 81-82; Jury 9:4 (1980):51-54.

See also: B309.

E1074. Blom, K. Arne. "Robert L. Fish 1912-1981." DAST 14:2 (1981):20. Memorial tribute with photo. (MS)

E1075. Boucher, Anthony. "Introduction." In The Incredible Schlock Holmes, by Robert L. Fish. NY: Simon & Schuster, 1966.

E1077. _____. "Introduction." In Kek Huuygens, Smuggler, by Robert L. Fish, pp. 9-11. NY: Mysterious Press, 1976.

E1078. "Robert Fish. In Memoriam 1912-1981." TAD 14 (1981):118-21. Photo. Tributes to Fish by a number of writers. The tributes first appeared in The Mystery Writers Annual, 1981 and in the MWA journal, The Third Degree. There is also a tribute in the form of diary entries written by Michael Seidman.

FISHER, STEVE

Ref: Hubin 2, TCCMW, EMD, SN, ABMI(S).

See also: D303, D316, D412.

FITT, MARY

Ref: Hubin 2, TCCMW, CC, ABMI.

E1079. Amelin, Michel. "Mary Fitt." Enigmatika 24 (July 83), pp. 8-10. Biography, critical essay and bibliography.

E1080. Boucher, Anthony. "Introduction." In Pity for Pamela (Macdonald, 1950; Harper, 1951), by Mary Fitt. NY: Collier Books, 1962.

FITZGERALD, NIGEL

Ref: Hubin 2, TCCMW, CC, ABMI(S).

E1081. Barzun, Jacques, and Taylor, Wendell Hertig. "Introduction." In Suffer A Witch (London 1958), by Nigel Fitzgerald. "Crime Fiction 1950-1975" (B18).

FITZSIMMONS, CORTLAND

Ref: Hubin 2, CC, ABMI; The Writer 57:1 (Jan 44):6-8.

E1082. Breen, Jon L. "Cortland Fitzsimmons and the Sports Mystery." TAD 14:2 (1981):129-32.

A survey of Fitzsimmons' sports and non-sports mystery fiction.

FLEMING, IAN

Ref: Hubin 2, TCCMW, EMD, CC, SN, ABMI(S).

See also: B20, C538, D368a.

Int: Show 4 (Nov 64):62-63, 91; Playboy 11 (Dec 69):97-106; Writer's Digest 45:5 (May 65):22-25, 77, 80 (photo).

E1083. Amis, Kingsley. The James Bond Dossier. London: Jonathan Cape, 1965. 159pp. Bibl. NY: New American Library, 1965. xi, 147pp. Bibl. Japanese edition translated by Jun Nagai. James Bond Hakusho (Tokyo: Hayakawa Shobo, 1966).

A witty, enthusiastic look at the reasons behind the popularity of Ian Fleming's secret agent. Includes a chart summarizing the villains, locales, etc., in the Bond books. Breen 152. CC 2883. (REB)

E1084. ______. "M for Murder." New Statesman 69 (new series) (2 Apr 65): 540-41.

Review-essay of Man with the Golden Gun.

E1085. ______. "A New James Bond." In his What Became of Jane Austen? and Other Questions, pp. 65-77. London: Jonathan Cape, 1970.

Amis was asked to continue Fleming's Bond saga and talks about how he constructed his Bond novel. The essay is also a defense of Fleming's Bond in the face of critics who see him as a spokesman for American Vietnamese policies and of popular novels which Amis thinks are better written than "serious" fiction. "John D. MacDonald is by any standards a better writer than Saul Bellow." Amis is against academic hierarchies for writers although he's not above establishing some of his own. In two brief notes appended to the essay, Amis thinks that Bond's Scaramanga in an earlier draft of The Man with the Golden Gun may have been shown to be attracted sexually to Bond and comments on the view in le Carré that spying is a dirty business and "we" are no better than "they" are. This, thinks Amis, is as much a fantasy as Bond's character.

E1086. Antony, Paul, and Friedman, Jacqueline. Ian Fleming's Incredible Creation. Chicago, IL: Novel Books, 1965. 128pp. Pictorial wrappers. (A Three Star Book.)

"My Friend Ian Fleming" and an examination of James Bond by Jacqueline Friedman. (REB)

E1087. Bergonzi, Bernard. "The Case of Mr (.) Fleming." Twentieth Century 163, no. 973 (March 1958):220-28.

On elements not necessary to the plot, "affective superstructures," in Fleming. Distinguishes between Buchan's merits as a high entertainer and Fleming's faults. A patronizing and moralizing essay.

E1088. Boyd, Ann S. The Devil with James Bond! Richmond, VA: John Knox Press, 1967.

A totally straight-faced attempt to establish that Ian Fleming was a theologian manqué and 007 a modern St. George. (REB)

E1089. Buch, Hans Christoph. "James Bond, oder der Kleinbuerger in Waffen |James Bond: or, the small citizen with weapons|." Der Monat 203:8 (1961):39-49; reprinted in Vogt (B424), Vol. I, pp. 227-50.

Essay similar to George Grella's essay "James Bond: Culture Hero" (E1097) explaining Bond's popularity. Buch discusses sex, sadism, ideology and "the good life" as portrayed in the novels, and argues that the Bond figure represents the ancient classical conception of the ideally perfect, fulfilled human being. This essay is notable for having been published two years before the first Bond film was made, and so comments on just the books, without influence from the film-inspired Bond craze. (GG)

E1090. Campbell, Ian. Ian Fleming: A Catalogue of a Collection. Privately published by Ian Campbell, 22 Gambier Terrace, Liverpool l, England. 72pp. Wraps.

"A preliminary to a bibliography." Not seen.

E1091. Carpenter, Edward C. "007 and the Myth of the Hero." JPC 1:2 (Fall 1967):79-89.

Classic myths as sources for the Bond stories. The hero in the labyrinth and on perilous quests. Carpenter sees them as "relatively undiluted myths" in an "age of disillusionment and skepticism."

E1092. Del Buono, Oreste, and Eco, Umberto, editors. The Bond Affair. Translated from the Italian by R. A. Downie. London: Macdonald, 1966. Orginally published as Il Caso Bond (Milan: Casa Ed. Valentino Bompiani, 1965). Italian edition not seen and all references will be to the English edition. 173pp.

A collection of essays on the Bond "phenomenon," with contributions from, among others, an ethnologist, a nuclear physicist, and a student of psychoanalysis. Still the best introduction to this popular phenomenon and it is regrettable that an American edition has not been published. Contents: Lietta Tornabuoni, "A Popular Phenomenon," pp. 13-34 (critical reaction and an overview of the books); Umberto Eco, "The Narrative Structure in Fleming," pp. 35-75 (E1095); Romano Calisi, "Myths and History in the Epic of James Bond," pp. 76-85 (the Bond series as a modern epic related to myth and fairy-tales); Furio Colombo, "Bond's Women," pp. 86-102 (a thematic study); Fausto Antonini, "The Psychoanalysis of 007," pp. 103-121 (Bond on the analyst's couch); G. B. Zorzoli, "Technology in the World of James Bond," pp. 122-31 (on

Fleming's solid scientific documentation); Andrea Barbato, "The Credible and the Incredible in the Films of 007," pp. 133-45 (fantasy and reality in the films); Laura Lilli, "James Bond and Criticism," pp. 146-70 (critical attitudes toward the novels; with a list of sources and references appended, pp. 171-73).

E1093. "Dossier James Bond." Polar 6 (Oct 79), pp. 4-21. Illustrated with film stills and book/paperback cover illustrations.
Contents: François Guérif, "Le Créateur d'un mythe |Creator of a Myth|," p. 4 (editorial); F. Guérif, "Ian Fleming & James Bond," pp. 5-9 (rapid survey of Bond novels); Raymond Lefèvre, "Filmographie," pp. 10-16 (film credits with short critical notes); Jean-François Naudon, "Bibliographie de Ian Fleming," pp. 17-21.

E1094. Durgnat, Raymond. "James Fleming contre Ian Bond ou 'The Man with the Golden Eye'." midi-minuit fantastique no. 12 (May 65), pp. 17-28.
Comments on both the books and the films based on them. (REB)

E1095. Eco, Umberto. "Le strutture narrative in Fleming |Narrative structures in Fleming|." In Il caso Bond, edited by O. Del Buono and U. Eco. Milan: Bompiani, 1965. (Italian original not seen.) Reprinted as follows: (in English translation) in The Bond Case (E1092); (in French translation) Communications 8 (1966):77-93; (in German translation) in Vogt (B424), Vol. I, pp. 250-293; (in English translation) in The Role of the Reader: Explorations in the Semiotics of Texts (Bloomington: Indiana University Press, 1979), pp. 144-63; and in Most/Stowe (B264), pp. 93-117.
Serious, detailed essay examining Fleming's narrative structures in the following modes: the oppositions of characters and values, intrigue as game, and literary technique. (GG)

E1096. Gant, Richard. Ian Fleming: The Fantastic 007 Man. NY: Lancer Books, 1966 (paperback). As Ian Fleming: The Man with the Golden Pen. London: Mayflower books, 1966 (paperback). 172pp.
Quickie biography of Fleming, obviously written and published to cash in on the James Bond boom of the mid-1960s. Breen 157. (REB)

E1097. Grella, George. "James Bond: Culture Hero." The New Republic 150: 22 (30 May 1964):17-18, 20. Reprinted in The Critic as Artist: Essays on Books, 1920-1970, edited by Gilbert A. Harrison, pp. 138-44. NY: Liveright, 1972.
A discussion of the Bond novels not as thrillers but as "historic epic and romance." Grella examines the mythical sources of several of the novels and sees Fleming's success in his creation of a hero of myth for our "mythless age."

E1098. Hedman, Iwan. "Ian Fleming." TAD 5 (1971/72):216-219, 222.
A biography with a bibliography of primary and secondary sources.

E1099. Holbrook, David. "The Problem of Hate in Culture. Ian Fleming's Goldfinger." The Masks of Hate: The Problem of False solutions in the Culture of an Acquisitive Society, pp. 67-144. Oxford: Pergamon Press, 1972.
Detailed analysis of a "popular work of symbolism representative of our time." The symbolism is manifestly that of primitive schizoid hate. The effect of Fleming's work is to "make us act as if we did not have a conscience." Also discussion of fantasies, the primal scene, contempt for women and for being human.

E1100. Hydak, Michael G. "Don Juan Bond." Language Quarterly 14 (Spring/Summer 1976):29-30, 33. Not seen.

E1101. Lane, Sheldon, ed. For Bond Lovers Only. London: Panther Books, 1965. 173pp. Paperback. Illus. NY: Dell Books, 1965. Paperbound, large-sized. 156pp. Illus. Japanese translation: Tokyo: Hayakawa Shobo, 1966.
Interviews (including one with Raymond Chandler) and brief memoirs/appreciations of Ian Fleming and James Bond, illustrated with pin-up photos of the women from the Bond movies. Breen 158. Not seen. (REB)

E1102. Lee, Billy C. "Ian Fleming: Alias James Bond." PQ 4:1 (Spring 81):41-47. Illus.
Background on Fleming and his series and information on the pb publishing history of the Bond novels.

E1103. Martin, Bernard. "James Bond: A Phenomenon of Some Importance." In Cunning Exiles: Studies of Modern Prose Writers, edited by Don Anderson and Stephen Knight, pp. 218-38. London: Angus and Robertson, 1974. Not seen.

E1104. Moore, Tim. "Appendix: Notes towards the Analysis of the Bond Stories." In his Claude Lévi-Strauss and the Cultural Sciences, pp. 35-50. Birmingham, England: Centre for Contemporary Cultural Studies, Birmingham University, n.d. Occasional Papers, no. 4.
A philosopher, with an interest in "structural anthropology, the analysis of myth and story-forms," examines the nature of authority ("the licensing operator") and how it is communicated to Bond in "licensing" episodes. Also a study of the individual (Bond) in action and the relation of this kind of myth to society.

E1104a. Newquist, Roy. "Ian Fleming." In Counterpoint, pp. 209-216. NY: Rand McNally & Co, 1964.
An interview with Fleming. Other writers interviewed include the Gordons (pp. 289-96), Helen MacInnes (pp. 457-64), Mary Stewart (pp. 561-72) and C. P. Snow (pp. 553-60).

E1105. Omerod, David, and Ward, David. "The Bond Game." London Magazine 5 (May 65):41-55. Not seen.

E1106. Panek, LeRoy L. "Ian Fleming." In The Special Branch (B303), pp. 201-19.
According to Panek, James Bond is a "muddled hero created by a third-rate hack." Panek writes, as he states, from the perspective of a study of 4 decades of spy novels and his most generous comment is that Fleming "was a minor writer who...did little to advance the form." In the context of Panek's discussion, this faint praise must be seen as an overstatement.

E1107. Pearson, John. 007 James Bond, The Authorized Biography. London: Sidgwick & Jackson, 1973. American edition published as James Bond: The Authorized Biography of 007, a fictional biography. NY: Wm. Morrow & Co., 1973. Not seen. (REB)

E1108. ______. The Life of Ian Fleming. London: Jonathan Cape, 1966. 352pp. Illus. Index. NY: McGraw-Hill, 1966. vii,338pp. Illus. Index. Breen 159. Not seen. (REB)

E1109. Randall, David A. The Ian Fleming Collection of 19th-20th Century Source Material Concerning Western Civilization, Together with the Originals of the James Bond-007 Tales. Bloomington, IN: Lilly Library, Indiana University, 1971. Lilly Library Publication XII. 55pp.
Descriptive illustrated catalog of the Fleming collection, including typescripts and author's copies of the James Bond stories. (REB)

E1110. Richler, Mordecai. "James Bond Unmasked." Commentary 46 (July 68):74-81. Reprinted in Mass Culture Revisited, edited by Bernard Rosenberg and David Manning White (NY: Van Nostrand, 1971), pp. 341-55; and in Notes on an Endangered Species and Others (NY: Knopf, 1974), pp. 3-35.
After enumerating Fleming's weaknesses in style, concept and characterization, Richler relates Bond to England's diminished international status and its paranoid fear of disruptive forces outside and within the "Empire."

E1111. Sims, George. "Ian Fleming: A Consideration of the Myth." American Bookman Monthly Review 9:3, issue 95 (March 1982):88-89, 91, 93-95 (3 photos); 9:4, issue 96 (April 1982):146-137, 139-141 (4 photos).
Part I: Discussion of Fleming's early life and career in journalism and military intelligence up to the end of WW II, pointing out the origins of settings, people, and events that later appeared in the James Bond novels. Part II: The writing of the Bond novels, their public success and Fleming's reactions to it, his depression and death. Overall thesis is that Fleming was, in Philip Larkin's words, "much more complex, much more intelligent, much more imaginative" than his creation, James Bond. Reproduction of sample ms. page, inscription in Fleming's own copy of Casino Royale giving background of the book; page from Fleming's rare 1st book (nonfiction). (REB)

E1112. Snelling, O. F. 007 James Bond: A Report. London: Neville Spearman, 1964. 160pp. NY: Signet Books, 1965 (paperback). 127pp.
A neat yet loving dissection of Ian Fleming's super-spy in the manner of Richard Usborne's Clubland Heroes. Breen 161. (REB)

E1113. Starkey, Lycurgus M., James Bond's World of Values. Nashville, TN: Abingdon Press, nd (1966). 96pp. Wraps.
A clergyman takes a critical (and unfriendly) look at James Bond's behavior in the light of the Christian faith and ethic. Breen 162. Not seen. (REB)

E1114. White, William. "Ian Fleming: Book Collector." TAD 6 (1973):181-82.
On Fleming as bibliophile and as member of the editorial board of the English journal The Book Collector.

E1115. Zeiger, Henry A. Ian Fleming: The Spy Who Came In with the Gold. NY: Duell, Sloan & Pearce, 1966. 150pp. Pb: Popular Library 60-2131, (n.d. but copyright 1965, before publication of hardcover edition). 125pp. Japanese translation, Tokyo: Arechi Shuppansha, 1966.
Biography of Fleming, with two chapters (more than a third of the book) devoted to Fleming as a writer. Lengthy critique of the James Bond novels and speculations on the causes of their popularity. (REB)

FLEMING, JOAN

Ref: Hubin 2, TCCMW, CC, ABMIS.

FLETCHER, J. S.

Ref: Hubin 2, TCCMW, EMD, CC, ABMI(S).

FLETCHER, LUCILLE

Ref: Hubin 2, TCCMW, CC, ABMI.

FLETCHER, MARY

Ref: Hubin 2.

Int: Fort Lauderdale News, 12 Jan 74; rpt. Authors in the News, p. 157 (photo).

FLORA, FLETCHER

Ref: Hubin 2, TCCMW, CC, ABMI.

FLOWER, PAT

Ref: Hubin 2, TCCMW, ABMI.

FOLEY, RAE

Ref: Hubin 2, TCCMW, CC, ABMIS.

FOLLETT, KEN

Ref: Hubin 2, ABMIS.

Int: EQMM, Dec 78, pp. 95-96; DAST 12:4 (1979):32-34 (photo); DAST 14:6 (1981):23 (photo); Pittsburgh Press Sunday Roto, 8 Jan 81 , pp. 14-15 (photo); New York Post, 29 Oct 83 (not seen; pagination not known).

E1116. Hauptfuhrer, Fred. "When It Comes to Cliff-Hanging, Ken Follett Has, at 29, Clawed into Competition with Le Carre." People, 25 Sept 78 (not paginated).

Profile, with 3 photos. (REB)

FOOTNER, HULBERT

Ref: Hubin 2, TCCMW, EMD, CC, ABMI.

E1117. "The Fiction of Hulbert Footner." Argosy All-Story Weekly 150:3 (31 March 23):321-23.

Brief story resumes of 16 Footner novels and series published between 1911 and 1922 in the Munsey magazines and Outing. (RS)

E1118. Morley, Christopher. "Granules from an Hour-Glass." SRL 4:13 (10 March 28):667.

Included in a column ("The Bowling Green") with general remarks on the detective fiction is an account of an afternoon Morley spent with Footner whose Mme Storey he "greatly" admires.

E1119. ______. "In Memoriam: Hulbert Footner (1879-1944)." In The Ironing Board, by Christopher Morley, pp. 167-72. NY: Doubleday, 1949.

A personal tribute by an old friend. Morley mentions Footner's "30 or so detective novels."

E1120. McCardell, Roy L. "The Men Who Make The Argosy." Argosy 223:5 (5 Sept 31):716. Originally published in the Daily Telegraph (no other data available). Portrait.

Some biographical material concerning Footner's youthful years before he began selling to the magazines. (RS)

E1121. Sampson, Robert. "A Practical Psychologist Specializing in the Feminine." TAD 16 (1983):363-66, 368-74.
A brief study of some female detectives precedes a comprehensive study of Madame Rosika Storey, "celebrated psychologist and consulting detective." Mme Storey, on whom "Holmes' shadow fell heavily," appeared in cases collected into ten volumes. With a checklist of pulp and book appearances.

E1122. Waterhouse, Howard. "Super Detective Person: Rosika Storey." TPP 2:4 (July/August 79):3-6.
Comments on the Footner heroine and series with a bibliography.

FORBES, COLIN

Ref: Hubin 2, ABMI(S).

E1123. Hedman-Morelius, Iwan. "Mitt möte med thrillerförfattaren Colin Forbes |My meeting with thriller author Colin Forbes|." DAST 11:6 (1978):15-19.
Hedman reports on his travels with Forbes as the writer gathers background material for a projected thriller. (MS)

FORBES, STANTON

Ref: Hubin 2, TCCMW, EMD, CC, SN, ABMI(S).

Int: TMRN 2:2 (December 68):19-21 (with a checklist of titles; no dates given).

FORD, LESLIE

Ref: Hubin 2, TCCMW, EMD, CC, ABMI.

Int: TPP 2:4 (July/Aug 79):15, 10.

E1124. Dueren, Fred. "Evan Pinkerton." TAD 7 (1973/74):193-194.
A profile of David Frome's "unobtrusive and timid detective."

E1125. Ford, Leslie. "Why Murder Fascinates Me." <u>Good Housekeeping</u> 110 (May 1940):37.
Ford is interested in the psychological state of the murderer and what leads up to the murder and follows it.

E1126. "Mystery." <u>American Magazine</u> 119 (May 1935):58. Portrait.
Profile of Leslie Ford. (KLM)

E1127. Waldron, Ann. "An Interview with Leslie Ford." TAD 4 (1971):33-36.
Interview material organized as comments on a chronological survey of Ford's life and work.

FORREST, RICHARD

Ref: Hubin 2, ABMI.

Int: <u>Jury</u> 9:3 (1980):58-59.

FORSYTH, FREDERICK

Ref: Hubin 2, TCCMW, ABMI(S).

See also: C237.

E1128. Bear, Andrew. "The Faction-Packed Thriller: The Novels of Frederick Forsyth." <u>Clues</u> 4:2 (Fall/Winter 83):130-48.

"Faction" is borrowed from Alex Haley who used it to mean the "freedom of the writer to extrapolate imaginatively from a base in fact." A study of "factions" in Forsyth's novels and narrative devices.

E1129. Hedman, Iwan. "Frederick Forsyth." DAST 12:6 (1979):30-31.
Short biography with checklist and photo. (MS)

E1130. Merry, Bruce. "The Spy Thriller." London Magazine 16:1 (April/May 1976):8-27.
A detailed analysis of Forsyth's The Day of the Jackal with numerous references to other spy thrillers. Merry shows how Forsyth overcomes what he sees as the basic implausibility of the genre and creates a believable, gripping fiction.

E1131. Panek, LeRoy L. "Frederick Forsyth." In Panek (B303), pp. 272-81.
Forsyth successfully combines the thriller and the historical novel and creates a "perfect entertainment for the seventies" whose readers like the plausibility of historical backgrounds.

E1132. Wolfe, Peter. "Stalking Forsyth's Jackal." TAD 7 (1974):165-74.
A critical discussion of Forsyth's political thriller. See also further comments in a letter from R. W. Hays, TAD 7 (1973/74):298.

FOSTER, JAN

Ref: Hubin 2; UN 1:3 (1948):12-13 (photo).

FOWLER, KENNETH A.

Ref: ABMI(S).

E1133. Drew, Bernard A. "Pulp Profile: Kenneth A. Fowler." Attic Revivals 5 (1982), p. 4.
Commentary by Fowler on his pulp career, with framing comments by Drew. Only passing mention of crime fiction (Fowler's first sale was to Black Mask). (REB)

FOWLER, SYDNEY

Ref: Hubin 2, TCCMW, ABMI(S).

FOWLES, JOHN

Ref: Hubin 2, ABMI(S).

E1134. Brownell, David. "John Fowles' Experiments with the Form of the Mystery Story." TAD 10 (1977):184-86. Illus.
A discussion of Fowles' short story "The Enigma" which appears in the collection, The Ivory Tower.

E1135. Carter, Steven R. "Freedom and Mystery in John Fowles' 'The Enigma'." TMF 3:5 (Sept/Oct 79):14-16.
Fowles' story as an "anti-detective-story detective story" in which the mystery is allowed to flourish and there is an implicit criticism of the detective's role as clarifier of enigmas.

E1136. Ochiogrosso, Frank. "Threats to Rationalism: John Fowles, Stanislaw Lem and the Detective Story." TAD 13 (1980):4-7. Illus.
Ochiogrosso sees the detective novel as the last refuge of rationalism and cites Fowles' "The Enigma" and Lem's The Investigation as examples of an attack on genre conventions. Ochiogrosso does refer to some

earlier examples (Borges, Cortazar and Boll) but there is no mention of the most important subverting of genre conventions in contemporary fiction, the French new novelists Michel Butor and Alain Robbe-Grillet whose important work in this area dates from the fifties.

FOX, JAMES M.

Ref: Hubin 2, SN; UN 4:10 (1952):6-7, 16 (photo).

See also: E399.

FOXX, JACK See PRONZINI, BILL

FRANCIS, DICK

Ref: Hubin 2, TCCMW, EMD,CC, SN, ABMI.

Int: Life 66 (6 June 69):81-2; TAD 6 (1973):151-52; EQMM, Jan 77, pp. 82-83; Jury 9:2 (1980):5-8; NYTBR, 1 June 80, p. 42; NYTBR, 12 Apr 81, p. 47; Boston Globe, 7 Apr 81 (photo); Practical Horseman 44:22 (1981):47-48; Washington Post Book World, 27 March 83 (photo); Carr (B67), pp. 202-26; Cooper-Clark (B75), pp. 225-39.

E1137. Axthelm, Pete. "Writer with a Whip Hand." Newsweek, 6 Apr 81, pp. 98, 100. 'Books' Dept. 2 photos.
Review of Reflex and brief author proile; some interesting biographical information and comments on Francis's work as a whole. (REB)

E1138. Barzun, Jacques, and Taylor, Wendell Hertig. "Introduction." In The Dead Cert (NY, 1962), by Dick Francis. "Crime Fiction 1950-1975" (B18).

E1139. Bauska, Barry. "Endure and Prevail: The Novels of Dick Francis." TAD 11 (1978):238-44. Photo and illustrations.
A biographical and critical survey of Francis' work. The comments on the novels concern characterization and the careful craftsmanship of Francis.

E1140. Francis, Dick. The Sport of Queens. London: Michael Joseph, 1957. 238pp. Illus. NY: Harper & Row, 1969. 247pp. Illus. Index. 2nd edition, revised, London: Michael Joseph, 1974. 248pp. Illus., index. Japanese edition, Tokyo: Shobunsha, 1981.
To today's readers Dick Francis is known as one of the best of contemporary crime novelists, but prior to the 1960s his fame rested on his career as a steeplechase jockey. It is this career that is the subject of the first edition of his autobiography, with an account of the still-mysterious fall of the Queen Mother's horse Devon Loch in the home stretch of the 1956 Grand National. Both Francis and Devon Loch went on to further races. After his retirement from racing in 1957 Francis spent four years as a sports journalist and then, with the publication of Dead Cert in 1962, began his career as a crime novelist. These developments are covered cursorily in a 2-page Afterword in the 1969 Harper & Row edition of the autobiography and in more detail in a new chapter added for the 1974 second edition (pp. 232-42 in the Michael Joseph edition). Breen 165. (REB)

E1141. Hauptfuhrer, Fred. "The Sport of Kings? It's the Knaves that Ex-Jockey Dick Francis Writes Thrillers About." People, 7 June 76, p. 66-68.
Profile with 3 photos. (REB)

E1142. Stanton, Michael N. "Dick Francis: The Worth of Human Love." TAD 15 (1982):137-143.
An overview of Francis' novels with an attempt to show how they have developed since his first novel was published in 1962.

FRASER, ANTONIA

Ref: Hubin 2, TCCMW, ABMI(S).

FREELING, NICOLAS

Ref: Hubin 2, TCCMW, EMD, CC, ABMI(S).

See also: B96, B309.

E1143. Bakerman, Jane S. "Arlette: Nicolas Freeling's Candle against the Dark." TAD 16 (1983):348-52.
A profile of Arlette Van der Valk whom Bakerman sees as a "paradigm for proper, contemporary human behavior."

E1145. Freeling, Nicolas. "Biographical/Critical Note." DAST 8:4 (1975):20-22.
Freeling describes his life and works. (MS)

E1147. Ruble, William. "Van der Valk." TMRN 5:2 (Jan/Feb/March 72):1-5.
A character sketch of Van der Valk, plot summaries of the novels and a checklist.

E1148. Schloss, Carol. "The Van der Valk Novels of Nicolas Freeling: Going by the Book." In Benstock (B26), pp. 159-73.
Van der Valk is a "bad" policeman because he understands that police authority is an obstacle to solving crimes and he is notable for his ability to enter the world of the victim and the crime in a game of search and concealment. Although he habits both the bureaucratic and the social worlds, it is his widow, Arlette, who will abandon completely the world of bureaucratic authority.

FREEMAN, R. AUSTIN

Ref: Hubin 2, TCCMW, EMD, CC, ABMI(S).

See also: B310, B349.

E1149. Adams, John. "Mr. R. Austin Freeman." TTF, no. 6 (Fall 78), pp. 34-39. Originally published in The Bookman (London), April 1913.
An essay-review of Freeman's early fiction. N. B. This article was also reprinted in TTF 15 (pp. 6-12) with no acknowledgement of the earlier TTF reprinting.

E1150. Arnott, Ian. "La Filza di Thorndyke." TTF, no. 3 (Spring 77), pp. 28-36.
On translations of Thorndyke series novels into foreign languages.

E1151. Asdell, Philip T. "John Evelyn Who?" TTF, no. 7 (Spring 79), pp. 35-40.
The historical John Evelyn and possible "clues" to Freeman's choice of J.E. for Dr. J. E. Thorndyke.

E1152. Barzun, Jacques and Taylor, Wendell, Hertig. Preface to The Singing Bone (London, 1912), by R. Austin Freeman. In A Book of Prefaces (B17), pp. 47-48.

E1153. Bleiler, E. F. "Introduction" to The Best Dr. Thorndyke Detective Stories, pp. v-ix. NY: Dover, 1973.
A succinct and perceptive survey of Freeman's writing career, with comments on the historical importance of the stories selected for this volume.

E1154. ______. "Introduction" to The Stoneware Monkey and The Penrose Mystery, pp. iv-viii. NY: Dover, 1973.
Freeman and the art of the scientific detective story.

E1155. Boucher, Anthony. "Introduction." In Mr. Pottermack's Oversight (London, 1930), by R. A. Freeman. NY: Collier Books, 1962.

E1156. Brody, Howard. "The Crime File: One Problem and Three Solutions." TTF 16 (Fall 83), pp. 25-36.
Norman Donaldson has criticized the choice of novels for Dr. Thorndyke's Crime File (1941). Brody attempts to show that the three novels are a "unified" choice and that the volume might have been subtitled "Every Conceivable Way to Use an Egyptian Mummy to Create False Clues in a Murder Case."

E1157. ______. "Drood and Frood: A Commentary or a Solution?" TTF, no. 13 (Spring 82), pp. 5-12.
Brody discusses Angelina Frood and characterizes it not as a solution to Dickens' The Mystery of Edwin Drood but as a tribute to Dickens using the earlier novelist's work as a source.

E1158. ______. "A Guide to Thorndykean Pilopathology." TTF, no. 11 (Spring 81), pp. 3-11.
A coined term for a discussion on the pathology of hair (and skin) in Freeman's work.

E1159. ______. "An Inquiry into Circular Heels." TTF, no. 12 (Fall 81), pp. 8-12.
On the nature and use of circular heels by Freeman in his fiction.

E1160. ______. "Thorndyke on the Art of Disguise." TTF, no. 15 (Spring 83), pp. 28-36.
The use of disguises in the Thornyke novels.

E1161. B. W. S. "R. Austin Freeman." The Writer 42:1 (January 1930):14-15.
A literary portrait of Freeman whose fiction is recommended as a "model to every student of mystery writing."

E1162. Chapman, David Ian. "'The Fairest Inne of Chancerie'." TTF, no. 16 (Fall 83), pp. 3-5.
A description of No. 7 Staple's Inn, Holborn, and the construction of an argument to support Chapman's theory that Freeman may have chosen the name of "John Evelyn Thorndyke" in the "quiet of Staple's Inn."

E1163. Chavdarian, C. G. "A Freeman Bibliographical Supplement." TTF, no. 13 (Spring 82), pp. 42-43.
A supplement to Norman Donaldson's bibliography of primary sources. See TTF 15 (Spring 83), p. 44, for a correction of Chavdarian's supplement by Douglas G. Greene; and TTF 16 (Fall 83), pp. 43-44, for further bibliographic comments by Howard Brody and Ruth McAleer.

E1164. Dembling, Merwin. "Freeman and Anti-Semitism." TTF, no. 15 (Spring 83), pp. 38-42.
Evidence of Freeman's "decent attitude toward the Jews."

E1165. Dirckx, John H. (M. D.) "The Compleat Poisoner." TTF, no. 7 (Spring 79), pp. 3-17.
Poisons and poisoning in Freeman.

E1166. ______. "Cordite: Any Poison Will Do in a Pinch." TTF, no. 13 (Spring 82), pp. 16-18.
Notes on cordite.

E1167. ______. "Dr. Thorndyke's Library." TTF, no. 2 (Fall 76), pp. 35-44.

E1168. ______. "Dr. Thorndyke's Pockets." TTF, no. 4 (Fall 77), pp. 25-30.
"A Catalogue of Thorndyke's customary stock of paraphernalia."

E1169. ______. "The Eye of What's-His-Name." TTF, no. 15 (Spring 83), pp. 13-22.
On Osiris. See TFF 16 (p. 41) for a further note on The Eye of Osiris.

E1170. ______. "The House That Freeman Built." TTF, no. 16 (Fall 83), pp. 6-18.
A tour of Dr. Thorndyke's "establishment."

E1171. ______. "The Inquest: An Inquiry." TTF, no. 9 (Spring 80), pp. 22-27.
The inquest motif in Freeman's fiction.

E1172. ______. "Literary Quotations and Allusions in the Dr. Thorndyke Novels and Short Stories." TTF, no. 1 (Spring 76), pp. 3-25.
A survey and not an "exhaustive catalogue."

E1173. ______. "A Museum of Thorndykean Pathology." TTF, no. 5 (Spring 78), pp. 2-15.
"Medical oddities in the Thorndyke saga."

E1174. ______. "An Open-and-Shut Case." TTF, no. 14 (Fall 82), pp. 3-13.
The research case as Dr. Thorndyke's emblem.

E1175. ______. "Thorndyke the Linguist." TTF, no. 10 (Fall 80), pp. 24-32.
His competency in classical and modern languages.

E1176. Dirckx, John H. and Philip T. Asdell. "Nathaniel Polton, Artificer Extraordinary." TTF, no. 6 (Fall 78), pp. 25-30.
A portrait.

E1177. Donaldson, Norman. "Clifford Ashdown: A Retrospect." In The Further Adventures of Romney Pringle, by "Clifford Ashdown," pp. 13-20. Philadelphia: Oswald Train, Publisher, 1969.
A full account of the collaboration of Freeman and Pitcairn.

E1178. ______. "The Dead Hand and How It Grew." TTF, no. 7 (Spring 79), pp. 18-29.
The publishing history of "The Dead Hand" and its incorporation into the novel The Shadow of the Wolf.

E1179. ______. "Edwin and Angelina." TTF, no. 2 (Fall 76), pp. 2-17.

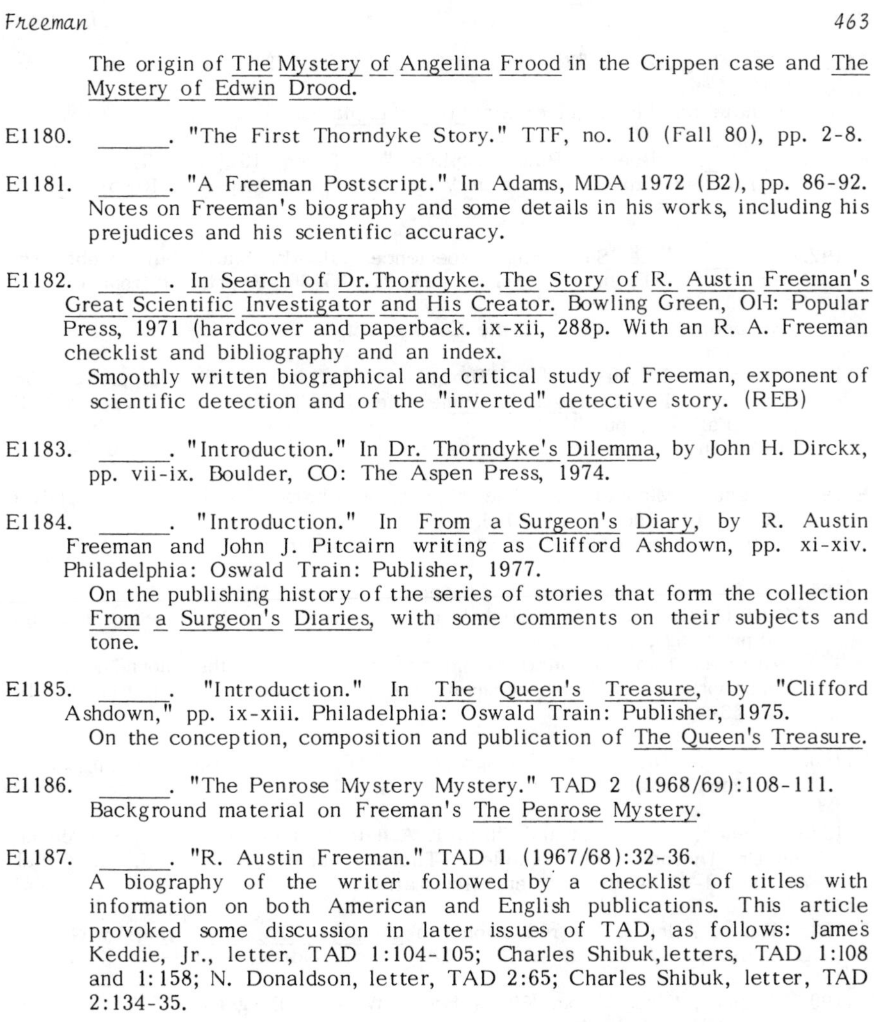

The origin of The Mystery of Angelina Frood in the Crippen case and The Mystery of Edwin Drood.

E1180. ______. "The First Thorndyke Story." TTF, no. 10 (Fall 80), pp. 2-8.

E1181. ______. "A Freeman Postscript." In Adams, MDA 1972 (B2), pp. 86-92.
Notes on Freeman's biography and some details in his works, including his prejudices and his scientific accuracy.

E1182. ______. In Search of Dr. Thorndyke. The Story of R. Austin Freeman's Great Scientific Investigator and His Creator. Bowling Green, OH: Popular Press, 1971 (hardcover and paperback. ix-xii, 288p. With an R. A. Freeman checklist and bibliography and an index.
Smoothly written biographical and critical study of Freeman, exponent of scientific detection and of the "inverted" detective story. (REB)

E1183. ______. "Introduction." In Dr. Thorndyke's Dilemma, by John H. Dirckx, pp. vii-ix. Boulder, CO: The Aspen Press, 1974.

E1184. ______. "Introduction." In From a Surgeon's Diary, by R. Austin Freeman and John J. Pitcairn writing as Clifford Ashdown, pp. xi-xiv. Philadelphia: Oswald Train: Publisher, 1977.
On the publishing history of the series of stories that form the collection From a Surgeon's Diaries, with some comments on their subjects and tone.

E1185. ______. "Introduction." In The Queen's Treasure, by "Clifford Ashdown," pp. ix-xiii. Philadelphia: Oswald Train: Publisher, 1975.
On the conception, composition and publication of The Queen's Treasure.

E1186. ______. "The Penrose Mystery Mystery." TAD 2 (1968/69):108-111.
Background material on Freeman's The Penrose Mystery.

E1187. ______. "R. Austin Freeman." TAD 1 (1967/68):32-36.
A biography of the writer followed by a checklist of titles with information on both American and English publications. This article provoked some discussion in later issues of TAD, as follows: James Keddie, Jr., letter, TAD 1:104-105; Charles Shibuk, letters, TAD 1:108 and 1:158; N. Donaldson, letter, TAD 2:65; Charles Shibuk, letter, TAD 2:134-35.

E1188. ______. "R. Austin Freeman: The Invention of Inversion." In Nevins (B290), pp. 79-87.
An excerpt from Donaldson's In Search of Dr. Thorndyke in which the technique of the inverted mystery story is traced from its inception through its development in Freeman's work.

E1189. ______. "Thorndyke and the Plumber's Oddments." TTF, no. 4 (Fall 77), pp. 8-24.
The use of the Druce-Portland case in Dr. Thorndyke Intervenes. Donaldson observes that Freeman did not realize all the possibilities of the scientific raw materials of the case, a charge he also levels against Freeman in For the Defense: Dr. Thorndyke. For the former novel, Donaldson supplies pastiche material to provide a crucial laboratory sequence lacking in the novel.

E1190. Finzel, James N. "Freeman during the Blitz." TTF, no. 16 (Fall 83), pp. 40-41.
A note on the origin of Mr. Polton Explains.

E1191. _____. "Inspector Rusby Explains." TTF, no. 16 (Fall 83), p. 41.
A reference to Thorndyke in Virgil Markham's Inspector Rusby's Finale (NY, 1933).

E1192. _____. "The Surprising Experiences of Mr. Shuttlebury Cobb Re-Examined." TTF, no. 13 (Spring 82), pp. 35-36. Reprinted from TPP 3:6 (Dec 80):25.
An appreciative view of the Cobb novel.

E1193. Freeman, R. Austin. "Dr. Thorndyke." In Madden (B253), pp. 129-138; reprinted in Dr. Thorndyke's Crime File (Dodd, Mead, 1941); and in TTF, no. 4 (Fall 77), pp. 31-36.
Freeman talks about Thorndyke and, briefly, about Polton and Jervis.

E1194. Heenan, Michael G. "The Names of Characters in The Thorndyke Stories." TTF, no. 4 (Fall 77), pp. 2-7.
General comments and an attempt at categorization.

E1195. _____. "A Note on the Chronology of the 'Dr. Thorndyke' Novels." TAD 9 (1975/76):52-54; a slightly revised version was reprinted in TTF, no. 13 (Spring 82), pp. 26-34.
An attempt to determine the internal chronology of the Thorndyke novels and short stories. For a comment, see J. M. Kinabrew, Jr. in TTF, no. 14, pp. 43-44.

E1196. _____. "Thorndyke's Topography." TTF, no. 5 (Spring 78), pp. 23-27.
Freeman's realism in his use of topography.

E1197. Heenan, Michael G. and Philip T. Asdell. "On the Trails of Dr. Freeman and Dr. Thorndyke or A Guide to Thorndykean England." TTF, no. 8 (Fall 79), pp. 4-40. With maps and illustrations.

E1198. Hubin, Allen J. "Introduction" to Goodbye, Dr. Thorndyke, by Norman Donaldson, p. (iii). Culver City, CA: Luther Norris, Dec 1972. (REB)

E1199. Lithner, Klas. "From King's Bench Walk to Bergsgaten." TTF, no. 13 (Spring 82), pp. 38-40.
On Modern Criminal Investigation (NY, 1935), by Harry Soderman and John J. O'Connell, as the source of an allusion in The Stoneware Monkey.

E1200. Lofts, W. O. G. and D. J. Adley. "Was 'Jack Wylde' Really R. Austin Freeman?" TAD 7 (1974):247-50.
An enquiry into the possibility that Freeman wrote juvenile fiction as "Jack Wylde." See comment by E. F. Bleiler, letter, TAD 8:1:72.

E1201. McAleer, John. "The Eye of Osiris and the Webster-Parkman Case." TTF, no. 12 (Fall 81), pp. 2-7.
Freeman's interest in Dickens and true crime cases.

E1202. _____. "The Freemans of Thorndyke House." TTF, no. 13 (Spring 82), pp. 23-24.
Interview with a former employee of the Freemans.

E1203. ______. "R. Austin Freeman: Toward a Definitive Biography." TTF, no. 11 (Spring 81), pp. 19-32.
An essay-review of Mayo's Freeman biography (E1206) with suggestions for future areas of research on Freeman's life.

E1204. ______. "The Springer Collection." TTF, no. 16 (Fall 83), pp. 19-23.
An examination of the P. M. Stone/R. A. Freeman correspondence from the Lloyd Springer (Chicago) collection.

E1205. McAleer, Ruth D. "Notes for a Freeman Bibliography." TTF, no. 11 (Spring 81), p. 12.

E1206. Mayo, Oliver. R. Austin Freeman: The Anthropologist at Large. Hawthorndene, So. Australia: Investigator Press, 1980. Wraps.
A biography which presents the results of Mayo's extensive research in the records of the British Colonial Service. The book also reflects the cooperation of Freeman's niece, and includes many previously unpublished and revealing letters. The implied thesis of the book is that Freeman's detective, Dr. Thorndyke, was a thinly disguised version of Freeman himself. (REB)

E1207. ______. "Golden Beetles or Blue Bugs?" TTF, no. 11 (Spring 81), pp. 13-18.
Speculation that Freeman's short story "The Blue Scarab" is a commentary on Poe's "The Gold-Bug."

E1208. ______. "Was Doctor Norbury an Imposter." TTF, no. 15 (Spring 83), pp. 23-26.
On Doctor Norbury in The Eye of Osiris.

E1209. Moskowitz, Sam. "R. Austin Freeman and Dr. J. J. Pitcairn, 'The Adventure at Heath Crest'." "Gaslight Detectives" series (C565). MSMM, April 73, pp. 128-29.

E1210. Narasimhan, R. "Notes on a Freeman Bibliography." TTF, no. 8 (Fall 79), pp. 41-44.
Additions to the bibliography in Donaldson (E1183).

E1211. Narcejac, Thomas. "Austin Freeman. La Théorie." In Narcejac (B287), pp. 47-56.
An analysis of Freeman's "Art of the Mystery Story" (C291).

E1212. ______. "Austin Freeman. Le Romancier scientifique |The scientific novelist|." In Narcejac (B287), pp. 57-94.
A lengthy study of Freeman's work. Although he "imposed the idea that the detective novel was a scientific novel," he succeeded only in writing parascientific works.

E1213. Roberts, Daniel G. "The Paperback Dr. John Thorndyke." PQ 5:1 (Spring 82):25-40. Illus.
An introduction to Freeman's work, and an annotated list of his novels that have been published in paperback editions. Roberts also discusses pastiches of Freeman's work and some of the secondary material.

E1214. Spivak, Peter B. "One More Thorndyke Mystery." TTF, no. 14 (Fall 82), p. 32.
On the authorship of the unsigned introduction to the Dr. Thorndyke

Omnibus (Dodd, Mead, 1932). Reponses as follows: J. M. Kinabrew, Jr., TTF, no. 16 (Fall 83), pp. 37-39; R. Narasimhan, no. 16, pp. 39-40. A number of possibilities are presented.

E1215. Stone, P. M. "5A King's Bench Walk." In Dr. Thorndyke's Crime File (Dodd, Mead, 1941), edited by P. M. Stone; reprinted in TTF, no. 3 (Spring 77), pp. 37-51.
Thorndyke's lodgings, its contents, including the laboratory, and his associates.

E1216. Thomson, H. Douglas. "The Realistic Detective Story. l. R. Austin Freeman." In Thomson (B404), pp. 168-76.
A mildly appreciative essay on Freeman's work. Thomson prefers the short stories to the novels where Freeman takes excessive pains and sometimes writes over the "reader's head."

E1217. The Thorndyke File.
The first 10 issues (Spring 1976-Fall 1980) were published under the editorship of Philip T. Asdell; with issue 11, the editorship passed to John McAleer. The magazine is published twice a year for "admirers of Dr. John Thorndyke and R. Austin Freeman." The magazine is rich in bibliographical, biographical and critical information and is an essential research tool for students of Freeman's work.

FREEMANTLE, BRIAN

Ref: Hubin 2, TCCMW, SN, ABMIS.

FREMLIN, CELIA

Ref: Hubin 2, TCCMW, CC, ABMI(S).

Int: DAST 11:1/2 (1978):70-1 (photo); EQMM, Nov 83, pp. 76-79; Dec 83, pp. 96-98.

FROME, DAVID. See FORD, LESLIE

FRUTTERO, CARLO, and LUCENTINI, FRANCO

Ref: Hubin 2.

E1218. Canova, Gian Battista. "La domenica di Fruttero e Lucentini |The "Sunday" of Fruttero and Lucentini|." Pubblico, 1983, pp. 51-67.
The adoption of a detective structure in the "lucky" novels written with four hands by Carlo Fruttero and Franco Lucentini is determined especially by "the opportuneness of playing the appeal to the reader in captivating tones with a strong emotive pull to force him to continue reading even when the narrative course abandons the giallo itinerary in favor of excursions in other and different realms of fable." (RC)

E1219. Citati, Pietro. "Il fascino del capolavoro |The fascination of the masterpiece|." Corriere della Sera, 3 Nov 79.
According to Citati, A che punto e la notte of Fruttero and Lucentini is not only "the grandest cathedral, the most incredible ziggurat that a writer of gialli has ever imagined," but also the "most ambitious novel written in Italy since Gadda's Pasticciaccio." (RC)

FULLER, DEAN

Ref: ABMI.

Int: PW, 15 July 83, pp. 54-55.

FULLER, ROY

Ref: Hubin 2, TCCMW, CC, ABMI(S).

FULLER, SAMUEL

Ref: Hubin 2, TCCMW, SN.

FUTRELLE, JACQUES

Ref: Hubin 2, TCCMW, EMD, Cc, ABMI(S).

E1220. Bleiler, E. F. "Introduction" to Best "Thinking Machine" Detective Stories, pp. v-ix. NY: Dover, 1973.
A survey of Futrelle's work, including novels that are not part of the "thinking machine" series. The introduction also is the first statement of the publishing circumstances of "The Problem of cell 13."

E1221. _____. "Introduction" to Great Cases of the Thinking Machine. NY: Dover, 1976.

E1222. Freedman, Benedict. "The Thinking Machine." In Adams, MDA 1972, pp. 79-85.
An overwritten essay on the "thinking machine" as both a coldly reasoning logician and a "courageous, trusting human being."

E1223. Gilbert, Elliot L. "Murder Without Air. Jacques Futrelle." New Republic, 30 July 77, pp. 33-34.
Gilbert sees the appeal of Futrelle's story "The Problem of Cell 13" in its use of the Easter Myth, recast for the "modern sensibility." Gilbert's analysis of the story seems to justify this interpretation. There is also some commentary on the relationship of Futrelle's work to Poe's.

GABORIAU, EMILE

Ref: Hubin 2, TCCMW, EMD, CC, ABMI.

See also: B179, D57.

E1224. Bleiler, E. F. "Introduction." In Monsieur Lecoq, pp. v-xxviii. NY: Dover, 1975.
A survey of Gaboriau's fiction that places it in the context of the development of detective fiction both within France and abroad. There is much new material in this introduction including the role of Paul Féval in Gaboriau's crime fiction and the first thorough statement of Gaboriau's influence on Conan Doyle. With a bibliography.

E1225. Boileau, Pierre, and Narcejac, Thomas. "Emile Gaboriau." In Vogt (B424), Vol. I, pp. 71-76. Originally published in Boileau/Narcejac (B37).

E1226. Bonniot, Roger. "A la recherche d'Emile Gaboriau |In search of Emile Gaboriau|." Europe 571/2 (Nov/Dec 1976):55-60.
The author describes his attempt to track down materials for a biography of Gaboriau and appeals for a collaborator who is "reasonably knowledgeable about the French mystery novel" to work with Ms. Nancy Loudenslager Curry (E1229) on a study of Goboriau's romans judiciaires, a project Bonniot does not feel qualified to undertake.

E1227. Cambiaire, Célestin Pierre. "Poe and Emile Gaboriau." In The Influence

of Edgar Allan Poe in France, pp. 257-63, 264-80. NY: G. E. Steckert, 1927.
Gaboriau is a disciple of Poe but not an unoriginal one. Gaboriau has added "literary" quality to Poe's "scientific" tales of ratiocination. A comparison of Dupin with Gaboriau's detectives and Gaboriau's method of plotting compared to Poe's to show that the method used is that of "The Murders in the Rue Morgue."

E1228. Colin, Jean-Paul. "Gaboriau: tombeau d'un oublié |Tomb of a forgotten man|." NL, no. 2405, 29 October-4 November 1973, pp. 10-11.
On the centenary of his death, Gaboriau is unjustly forgotten. Characterizing him as the "father of the French detective novel," Colin reviews Gaboriau's career and the sparse interest shown in him by modern readers and critics.

E1229. Curry, Nancy Ellen Loudenslager. The Life and Works of Emile Gaboriau. NY: Garland, 1979. 273pp.
First publication of a an important study on Gaboriau originally presented as a Ph. D. thesis at the University of Kentucky in 1970. Although Gaboriau is second only to Poe in the historical development of the detective story, he has been greatly neglected in literary studies. This thesis, based on extensive research in France, is the only thorough study of Gaboriau in any language, with much unique information about Gaboriau's life, his books, and hitherto-unknown periodical contributions. Dr. Curry also covers the social milieu both around and within Gaboriau's novels. (EFB)

E1230. Fredriksson, Karl G. "Gaboriau och Leroux -- tva glomda |Gaboriau and Leroux -- two forgotten men|?" Jury 11:3 (1982):53-58.
Reevaluation of the two authors. (MS)

E1231. Hardy, Alfred E. Gathorne. "The Examination of Prisoners.--Emile Gaboriau." National Review, July 1884, pp. 591-604.
The focus of the article is legal rather than literary, but there is some discussion of several of Gaboriau's works which the author apparently read because he was told they would help him understand the court system in French.

E1232. Picchi, Mario. "Il signor Lecoq bravo poliziotto |Mr. Lecoq, an able policeman|." La Fiera Letteraria, 28 July 57.
The author considers the character of Lecoq as the protype of the detective because Lecoq introduces a novelty that consists of applying "positivism to police methods." (LR)

E1233. Thomson, H. Douglas. "The French Detective Story. 2. Emile Gaboriau." In Thomson (B404), pp. 93-108.
A sympathetic study of Gaboriau whom Thomson sees as the father of the detective novel. He analyzes Gaboriau's plot devices, points out that Gaboriau is the first detective writer to include adrawing of the scene of the crime, and briefly comments on L'Affaire Lerouge and Le Crime d'Orcival which Thomson considers to be the best of Gaboriau's novels.

E1234. Williams, Valentine. "Gaboriau: Father of the Detective Novel." National Review 82 (December 1923):611-622.
Detailed study of the author and his work. Tribute is paid to Féval, Gaboriau's mentor. The detective novels are distinguished from the romances and the origin of the name Lecoq is revealed. (RCSA)

GADDA, CARLO EMILIO

Ref: Hubin 2, CC, ABMI(S).

E1235. Gadda, Carlo Emilio. "Incantagione e paura |Enchantments and fear|." Il giorno d'Italia, 21-22 Jan 66; reprinted in Nuovi Argumenti, April/June 76, pp. 3-5; and in Cremante/Rambelli (B78), pp. 165-67.
One of the best Italian writers of the 20th century develops a meditation on the themes and motives of his novel Quer pasticciaccio brutto de via Merulana (1946-57), which remains, in Italy, one of the most significant examples of a meeting between high literature and the detective novel. (LR)

GAINHAM, SARAH

Ref: Hubin 2, TCCMW, ABMI(S).

GALWAY, ROBERT CONNINGTON. See MCCUTCHAN, PHILIP.

GARDINER, DOROTHY

Ref: Hubin 2, TCCMW, ABMI(S); The Writer 77:1 (Jan 64):16-19 (characterization).

GARDNER, ERLE STANLEY

Ref: Hubin 2, TCCMW, EMD, CC, ABMI(S); CC; Argosy, 7 Dec 29; The Writer 52:2 (Feb 39):35-36 (general writing comments).

See also: B310, C404.

E1236. Barzun, Jacques, and Taylor, Wendell Hertig. Preface to The Case of the Crooked Candle (NY, 1944), by Erle Stanley Gardner. In A Book of Prefaces (B17), pp. 49-50.

E1237. "Erle Stanley Gardner. An Exhibit - September 1972." Austin, Texas: Humanities Research Center, 1972.
An exhibition catalogue with a cover photograph of Gardner and photographs of exhibited items. The descriptive narrative has information on the collection, Perry Mason, Gardner's non-fiction and his writing methods and manuscripts.

E1238. "The Erle Stanley Gardner Study at the University of Texas." In Adams, MDA 1972 (B2), p. 259.
A note on the collection of important papers, books and memorabilia willed by Gardner to the University of Texas.

E1239. Fugate, Francis L. and Roberta B. Fugate. Secrets of the World's Best-Selling Writer: The Storytelling Techniques of Erle Stanley Gardner. NY: Wm. Morrow, 1980. 286pp.
Based primarily on Gardner's papers in the collection at the University of Texas, this book provides details on Gardner at work, on his characters and on his philosophy of writing (begin with a mystery and tell a story that people want to read). (Steve Lewis)

E1240. Gardner, Erle Stanley. "Getting Away with Murder." Atlantic 215 (January 65):72-75.
Reminiscences on the early days of Black Mask and on fellow pulp writers Carroll John Daly and Dashiell Hammett.

E1241. Hughes, Dorothy B. Erle Stanley Gardner: The Case of the Real Perry Mason. NY: Wm. Morrow, 1978. 350pp. Photos. Bibliography by Ruth Moore; index.

Hughes' book is smoothly readable as a summary of Gardner's life and character and beliefs, but it's not quite a biography since most of the text consists of letters to and from Gardner interspersed with his dictated autobiographical statements. Hughes has filled out these materials with letters and reminiscences from surviving members of Gardner's personal and professional "family," but she has let Gardner speak for himself almost without interruption, so that we learn next to nothing of her own view on Gardner as a mystery writer. It remains for some tireless researcher of the future to provide a judicious assessment of Erle Stanley Gardner. But that person will owe much to Dorothy B. Hughes for this hard-to-pigeonhole book: neither a biography nor an autobiography nor a collection of letters, but a combination of all three. (F. M. Nevins, Jr.)

E1242. Johnston, Alva. The Case of Erle Stanley Gardner. NY: William Morrow, 1947. 87pp. Illus. Bibliography. Originally published in the Saturday Evening Post, as follows: 5 Oct 46, pp. 9-11, 88-89, 91-92, 95 (color photos); 12 Oct 46, pp. 26-27, 102, 105, 108, 110, 112 (2 black-and-white photos); 19 Oct 46, pp. 24, 76, 78, 81, 84, 87, 89 (black-and-white photo of Gardner).

A superficial but entertaining little book, based on Saturday Evening Post articles, relating many of Gardner's courtroom battles which eventually became the basis for the forensic maneuvers of Perry Mason. Breen 169. (REB)

E1243. Kane, Patricia. "Perry Mason: Western Culture Hero." In Heroes of Popular Culture, edited by Ray B. Browne, Marshall Fishwick and Michael T. Marsden, pp. 125-33. Bowling Green, OH: Bowling Green University Popular Press, 1972.

A discussion of Perry Mason as a hero championing right.

E1244. Lachman, Marvin. "The Case of the Unbeaten Attorney or The Secret Life of Perry Mason." TAD 4 (1970/71):147-53. See also R. Gordon Kelly, letter TAD 5 (1972):43-4.

A profile of Gardner's series character.

E1245. Moore, Ruth. "A Bibliography of Erle Stanley Gardner." In Hughes (E1241), pp. 312-41.

Chronological checklist of Gardner's magazine fiction, books, and articles. Magazine and newspaper serializations of the novels are indicated, as are the stories belonging to Gardner's various series. TV and movie scripts edited by Gardner are included. (REB)

E1246. Morton, Charles W. "The World of Erle Stanley Gardner." Atlantic 219 (January 1967):79-86, 91.

Profile of Gardner based on interviews and research into his life and writings.

E1247. Mundell, E. H. Erle Stanley Gardner: A Checklist. Kent, OH: Kent State University Press, 1970. 91pp. See also a letter from Bernard Beauchesne in TMRN 3:5 (June 1970):35-36, for corrections and additions.

A chronological listing of over 400 short stories and of 100 hardcover books. A useful volume but the following reservations should be noted: a number of stories are listed twice, under alternate titles, as if they were different stories; paperback editions are not included; and although lists of stories for many of Gardner's series characters are provided, these lists are incomplete. The bibliography by Ruth Moore (E1245) covers the same material. (Marvin Lachman)

E1248. Nevins, Francis M., Jr. "Aspects of the Unknown Gardner." In two parts. TMRN 5:4 (n.d.; 1972), 13-15, 22; 5:5 (n.d., 1972):27-30.
Discussion of a number of Gardner's little-known pulp stories. In Part 2, Nevins reviews several collections of the short stories, published in paperback and hardcover editions.

E1249. ______. "Notes on Some Uncollected Gardners." JPC 2:3 (Winter 1968):488-92.
Preliminary attempt at classifying Gardner's extensive short story writings, with a discussion of the Depression era Saint variant, Paul Pry.

E1250. Queen, Ellery. "Introduction." In The Amazing Adventures of Lester Leith, by Erle Stanley Gardner, pp. 9-10. NY: Davis Publications Inc., 1980.

E1251. ______. "Introduction.' In The Case of the Murderer's Bride and Other Stories, by Erle Stanley Gardner, pp. 4-7. NY: Davis Publications, Inc., 1969.

E1252. Robbins, Frank E. "The Firm of Cool and Lam." In Nevins (B290), pp. 136-48. Originally published in The Michigan Alumnus Quarterly Review (now The Michigan Quarterly Review) 59 (Spring 1953):222-28.
Profile of the detective team of Bertha Cool and Donald Lam.

E1253. Shapiro, Debbie. "Perry Mason's N.Y. Adviser." Northwestern Alumni News, March 1977, p. 10.
Erle Stanley Gardner and Northwestern University lawyer Paul Klopsteg. (REB)

E1254. Stewart-Gordon, James. "Unforgettable Perry Mason." Reader's Digest, May 1980, pp. 108-112.
ESG and his fictional character.

GARDNER, JOHN

Ref: Hubin 2, TCCMW, CC, ABMI(S).

Int: The Dossier 1:1 (1981):11-13; Boston Globe, 21 May 81, pp. 49-50 (photo); NYTBR, 7 June 81, p. 30.

E1255. Larkin, Philip. "The Batman from Blades." TLS, 5 June 81, p. 625.
Review-essay of License Renewed, Gardner's continuation of the Fleming Bond series.

GARFIELD, BRIAN

Ref: Hubin 2, TCCMW, ABMI(S); The Writer 89:12 (Dec 76):27-31.

Int: DAST 8:2 (1975):16; DAST 8:3 (1975):18-21; EQMM, Sept 77, pp. 82-83; DAST 11:1/2 (1978):70-71 (photo); Films in Review, Nov 80, pp. 549-50; Jury 10:1 (1981); DAST 14:4 (1981):34-35 (photo);

E1256. Garfield, Brian. "Garfield for the Defense. Purcell vs. Bogart." TAD 11 (1978):186-88.
A reply to an article on Humphrey Bogart in TAD 11 (1978):6-16 ("The

De-Canonization of Bogart").

E1257. ______. "Introduction." In Checkpoint Charlie, by Brian Garfield, pp. ix-xiv. NY: Mysterious Press.

E1258. ______. "Introduction." In I, Witness, edited by Brian Garfield, pp. vii-xii. New York, NY: Times Books, 1978.
Includes an account of the real-life event which led to the writing of Death Wish. (REB)

E1259. Tarbell, Marta. "An Amazing New Book on WW I Creates a Stir." 'Author-ized' department. US, 24 June 80, pp. 62, 64. (REB)

GARNET, A. H.

E1260. Paul, Angus. "A Scholarly Team of Mystery Writers and the Case of the Cooked Professor." Chronicle of Higher Education, 27 April 83, pp. 21, 24. On mystery writer "A. H. Garnet." (Ed Lauterbach)

GARRETT, RANDALL

Ref: Hubin 2, ABMI(S).

E1261. Silverberg, Robert, editor. The Best of Randall Garrett. NY: Timescape (Pocket Books), 1982.
Although Garrett is usually classified as a writer of science fiction, his work draws heavily on conventions of detective fiction, particularly in the Lord Darcy series. This anthology of stories contains biographical comments by a number of writers, many of whom comment on detective/mystery elements in the fiction. In the absence of any specific study, this book is essential for a study of Garrett as a writer of "cross-over" genre fiction.

GARVE, ANDREW

Ref: Hubin 2, TCCMW, EMD, CC, ABMI(S).

Int: DAST 13:1 (1980):13-15 (photo)).

E1262. Barzun, Jacques, and Taylor, Wendell Hertig. Preface to No Tears for Hilda (NY, 1950), by Andrew Garve. In A Book of Prefaces (B17), pp. 52-53.

GASKIN, CATHERINE

Ref: Hubin 2, TCCMW, ABMI(S).

GAULT, WILLIAM CAMPBELL

Ref: Hubin 2, TCCMW, EMD, CC, SN, ABMI; The Writer 66:10 (Oct 53):339-40, 357; Writer's Digest 36:6 (May 56):13-15.

Int: PQ 2:2 (Summer 79):8-13; Enigmatika 20 (1982):(34-39); EQMM, Nov 82, pp. 87-88.

E1263. Boucher, Anthony. "Introduction." In Vein of Violence (Simon & Schuster, 1961), by William Campbell Gault. NY: Award, 1965.

E1264. Martin, Roger, ed. "William Campbell Gault." Hard-Boiled Dicks No. 3 (June 82). Wraps. 48pp. Photo and illustrations.
Contents: "Editorial," p. 3-4; "Eléments biographiques," p. 5-6; "Entretien avec William Campbell Gault," p. 8-17 (interview); "William

Campbell Gault, le dernier paladin du roman noir |W. C. G., the last paladin of the hard-boiled novel|," pp. 18-20 (sketchy overview of his work); "Bibliographie chronologique," p. 21-33 (includes short stories); "Un pseudonyme ignoré de W. C. G.: Tommy Lister! |An unknown pseudonymn of W. C. G.: Tommy Lister," p. 34; Art Scott, p. 35 (Gault article from Reilly, A143); Francçois Guérif, p. 36 (Gault article from Martens, B2443); W. C. Gault, "Joue le jeu, franc jeu |Be smart, be really smart|," pp. 38-46 (short story, first published in The Saint Magazine, March 1958).

GERY, R. V.

Ref: Argosy, 14 Sept 35.

GIBSON, WALTER (pseud.: MAXWELL GRANT)

Ref: Hubin 2, TCCMW, EMD, ABMI(S).

Int: EQMM, June 76, 101-102; Duende 2 (Winter 76-77), pp. 33-46; Age of the Unicorn 7 (April 80), pp. 23-25.

See also: D300, D420, D421, D457-D462, D467, D469, D470, D474.

E1265. Drew, Bernard. "Walter Gibson's Magicians: Introduction." Attic Revivals 4 (1982), pp. 1, 8.
Summary of Walter Gibson's career, focusing as much on his crime fiction and true-crime articles as on his Shadow novels. (REB)

E1266. Gruber, Frank. "Walter Gibson." TAD 3 (1969-70):94-95.
Note on the pulp writer and magician by a long-time friend.

E1267. Lauterbach, Edward. "Gibson's Non-Shadow Detective." TAD 6 (1972-73):33-34.
On Gibson's A Blonde for Murder (Vital Books, 1948).

E1268. Murray, Will. "Alias Maxwell Grant." PQ 5:1 (Spring 82):41-48. Illus.
A history of the Shadow paperback reprints with a checklist of titles.

GIDE, ANDRE

Ref: Hubin 2, ABMI(S).

E1269. Horn, Pierre. "Gide's Isabelle, A Detective Novel." Romance Notes 18 (Fall 1977):54-61.
Horn attempts to identify a researcher-investigator as a detective and by showing that a mystery is patiently unraveled that Gide's recit is a detective novel. Although some of the traditional elements of mystery fiction are used, there appears to be no substantial basis for calling this fiction a detective novel. Mr. Horn has himself used a traditional gimmick: the fausse piste (false lead) that goes nowhere.

E1270. ______. "Gide's Vatican Cellars: The Popular Detective Novel Parodied." TMF 6:2 (March/April 1982):11-15.
Horn shows that Gide uses devices from the French popular novel of crime to comic effect. His most interesting point is a comparison of the novel's young anti-hero, Lafcadio, with Arsene Lupin.

GIELGUD, VAL

Ref: Hubin 2, TCCMW, EMD, CC, ABMI(S).

E1271. Gielgud, Val. "Crime or Adventure - Which?" Constable's Quarterly No. 2, Summer 1931, pp. 23-27.
The author puts the case for the adventure novel but admits to liking detective fiction. (RCSA)

GIESY, J. U.

Ref: Hubin 2, ABMI(S).

See also: D447, D448.

E1272. "The Men Who Make The Argosy: J. U. Giesy." Argosy 218:6 (14 Feb 31):860. Portrait.
Useful précis of Giesy's life and career, with considerable specific information. (RS)

GIFFORD, THOMAS

Ref: Hubin 2, TCCMW, ABMIS.

Int: Minneapolis Tribune, 8 Aug 80, p. 20 (photo).

GILBERT, ANTHONY

Ref: Hubin 2, TCCMW, EMD, CC, ABMI.

E1273. Bakerman, Jane S. "Bowlers, Beer, Bravado and Brains: Anthony Gilbert's Arthur Crook." TMF 2:4 (July 78):5-13.
A portrait (with numerous quotes from the novels in which he appears) of Gilbert's eccentric lawyer-detective, "defender of the meek and scourge of the British police."

E1274. Boucher, Anthony. "Introduction." In The Wrong Body (first published as A Nice Cup of Tea, London, 1950), by Anthony Gilbert. NY: Mercury, n. d.

GILBERT, MICHAEL

Ref: Hubin 2, TCCMW, EMD, CC, ABMI(S).

Int: EQMM, 12 Aug 81, pp. 109-110; 9 Sept 81, pp. 108-109.

See also: B309.

E1275. Barzun, Jacques, and Taylor, Wendell Hertig. "Preface" to Smallbone Deceased (New York, 1950), by Michael Gilbert. In A Book of Prefaces (B17), pp. 53-54.

E1277. Heilbrun, Carolyn. "Who Did It? Michael Gilbert and P. D. James." NYTBR, 12 Sept 82, pp. 9, 24.
Overviews of the work of the two writers.

E1278. Queen, Ellery. "Introduction." In Amateur in Violence, by Michael Gilbert. NY: Davis Publications, Inc., 1973.

GILMAN, DOROTHY

Ref: Hubin 2, TCCMW, ABMI; The Writer 91:7 (July 78):13-15 (on humor).

GIOVANNI, JOSE

Ref: Hubin 2, SN.

Int: MM 283, Sept 71.

E1279. "Dossier José Giovanni." Polar 17 (Feb 81), pp. 3-34.
In his lead editorial (p. 3), François Guérif describes Giovanni as responsible for giving , at the end of the 1950s, a "second wind" to the French detective novel with two films based on his work and the publication of his novel Le deuxième souffle in the série noire. In these works, the setting took on a tragic dimension. This issue of Polar examines the fictional and film work of the writer who was responsible for that "new wave." Illustrated with stills. Contents: Jean-Pierre Deloux, "Le milieu et la marge |The setting and living on the fringes of society|," pp. 4-8 (a survey of Giovanni's work); F. Guérif and Jean-Pierre Deloux, "Entretien avec Jose Giovanni," pp. 9-23 (a lengthy interview which focuses on his film work); "Bibliographie," p. 23; J. Giovanni, "Un banque," pp. 24-27 (fiction); Jean-Jacques Schleret, "Filmographie," pp. 29-34 (his work as filmwriter and director).

E1280. Nolan, Jack Edmund. "A Great Contemporary: José Giovanni." TMRN 4:4 (May 71):19-22.
Career biography of French novelist and screenwriter Giovanni.

GODEY, JOHN

Ref: Hubin 2, TCCMW, EMD, SN, ABMI.

Int: Star-Ledger (Newark, N.J.), 5 Nov 74 (photo; reprinted in Authors in the News, p. 159).

E1281. Greenfield, Josh. "A Conversation with John Godey." DAST 6:6 (1973):38-39. (MS)

GODFREY, PETER

Ref: Hubin 2, ABMI(S).

E1282. Adey, Robert C. S. "Peter Godfrey - A Reprise." TPP 3:5 (October 1980):9-11.
Three letters to Mr. Adey from writer Godfrey, in which he discusses his work under various pseudonyms, talks at some length about his Death Under the Table, and reminisces about his career.

E1283. Lachman, Marvin. "Department of Unknown Mystery Writers. Peter Godfrey." TPP 3:2 (March/April 1980):13-14, 12.
See Adey (above) for comments by Godfrey on Lachman's "imaginative research" and further comments on the stories Lachman discusses.

GODWIN, WILLIAM

Ref: Hubin 2, TCCMW, EMD, CC, ABMI(S).

See also: E2182.

E1284. Ousby, Ian. "Caleb Williams." In Ousby (B300), pp. 19-42.
Ousby describes Godwin's novel as the "first work of English fiction to display a sustained interest in the theme of detection." An extensive analysis of the novel which is a revised and expanded version of the article by Ousby described below.

E1285. ______. "My Servant Caleb: Godwin's Caleb Williams and the Political Trials of the 1790s." University of Toronto Quarterly 44 (1974/75):47-55.

The prototypical detective in 18th century England, the spy, and his role as threat to the orderly institution whose trust he violates: the family.

GODWIN, WILLIAM, JR.

Ref: ABMI.

E1286. Adams, Donald K. "Recalled and Awakened: the Romantic Fiction of William Godwin, Jr." In Adams, MDA 1973 (B3), p. 142-66.
A detailed study of the younger Godwin's novel Transfusion which appears to be a variant on the Frankenstein motif. There is extensive biographical data and, although Godwin's work appears to be more Gothic supernatural than detective fiction, Adams makes a number of comparisons of Godwin, Jr.'s work with his father's.

GOINES, DONALD

Ref: Hubin 2, ABMI; Detroit News, 15 Nov 74 (profile; rpt. in Authors in the News, p. 188; photo).

E1287. Stone, Eddie. Donald Writes No More: A Biography of Donald Goines. Los Angeles: Holloway House, 1974. 223p.
Popular biography of black ex-con-turned-writer Donald Goines, one of the first novelists of the "Black Experience" genre. Recounts the flight of Goines' grandparents north from Missippi, and Goines' own experiences as a heroine addict, thief, pimp, pusher, numbers runner and bootlegger before he turned to writing. Covers his literary career until his murder in 1974. Although there are errors relating to dates, chronological inconsistencies and events narrated for which there were most likely no witnesses alive at the time of writing, the book gives interesting summaries and analyses of Goines' 16 novels. (GG)

GOLDSTEIN, ARTHUR

Ref: Hubin 2, TCCMW, ABMIS.

GOODIS, DAVID

Ref: Hubin 2, CC, SN, ABMI.

See also: D316.

E1288. "A la recherche de David Goodis |In search of David Goodis|." Polar 23 (15 April 82):97-106.
Some miscellaneous material on--and by--Goodis which includes reproductions of two letters from Goodis to French director François Truffaut, a transcript of a letter from Truffaut's friend Helen Scott in which she describes vividly a meeting with Goodis in 1960, some stills from Shoot the Piano Player and a review of the 1960 film based on a 1982 viewing.

E1289. "David Goodis." Polar 10.
Not seen but this series usually includes an overview of the work, an interview with the writer or with associates, and a bibliography and filmography (where appropriate).

E1290. O'Brien, Geoffrey. "The Career of David Goodis." PQ 5:4 (Winter 1982):3-12.
Discussion of Goodis' novels and a checklist of his hardcover and paperback publications.

GOODRUM, CHARLES A.

Ref: Hubin 2, ABMI(S).

E1291. Goodrum, Charles A. "Writing the Library Whodunit." American Libraries 8 (April 77):194-96.
A librarian, author of two library mysteries, tells why he wrote a library mystery and how he went about composing his "entertainment."

"THE GORDONS" (MILDRED and GORDON GORDON)

Ref: Hubin 2, TCCMW, EMD, CC, SN, ABMI(S); The Writer 60:2 (Feb 47):40-43 (by Mildred Gordon; on the writing and editing of The Little Man Who Wasn't There); The Writer 75:1 (Jan 62):14-17 (by the Gordons on collaborating; biographical note by Mildred Gordon); The Writer 80:9 (Sept 67):16-17, 43 (on writing dialogue); The Writer 82:11 (Nov 69):9-12 (includes biographical note by the Gordons); The Writer 79:11 (Nov 66):11-14 (biographical note; on plotting); UN 2:10 (1950):8-9, 11; UN 4:12 (1952):6-7, 16 (photo).

GORES, JOE

Ref: Hubin 2, TCCMW, SN, ABMI(S); The Writer 84:8 (Aug 71):13-16, 46.

Int: TPP 3:1 (Jan/Feb 80):19-22; Mystery 3:2 (Sept 81):42-44 (photo); Polar 24 (July 82):28-35.

E1292. Gores, Joe. "Author's Note." Epilogue to his Hammett, A Novel, pp. 243-51. NY: Putnam, 1975.
Notes and comments on the research for and writing of his novel based on Dashiell Hammett's life.

E1293. ______. Letter. TAD 7 (1974):223-24.
Gores discusses his use of dialogue in his novel Interface.

E1294. ______. Letter. TAD 9 (1976):83-4.
A discussion of the "cross-over" scene in his Dead Skip and Donald Westlake's Plunder Squad.

GOULART, RON

Ref: Hubin 2, TCCMW, SN, ABMI(S).

See also: D337.

E1295. Dunn, Bill. "Ron Goulart Pens Names and Novels with a Juggler's Dexterity." US, 28 Oct 80, pp. 50-51. Photo.
Brief profile with some information on Goulart pen-names. (REB)

E1296. Meech, Shirley. "Ron Goulart Checklist." The Comic Buyer's Guide, 16 May 82, pp. 39-42.
Publishers and publishing dates are not given for the novels; extensive list of short stories by magazine, with month and year.

GRADY, JAMES

Ref: Hubin 2, ABMIS.

Int: EQMM, Sept 78, 88-99; DAST 11:3 (1978):22-23.

GRAEME, BRUCE

Ref: Hubin 2, TCCMW, EMD, CC, ABMI(S).

GRAFTON, C. W.

Ref: Hubin 2, CC.

E1297. Barzun, Jacques, and Taylor, Wendell Hertig. Preface to Beyond a Reasonable Doubt (New York, 1940), by C. W. Grafton. In A Book of Prefaces (B17), pp. 55-56.

E1298. Lyles, Bill. "C. W. Grafton." TPP 3:6 (December 80):7-9.
Informative letter from Grafton on his and other writers' fiction.

GRAHAM, JACK. See HIGGINS, JACK

GRAHAM, WINSTON

Ref: Hubin 2, TCCMW, ABMI(S).

GRANBECK, MARILYN

Ref: Hubin 2; Writer's Digest 46:4 (April 66):53-56, 93.

GRAY, BERKELEY. See BROOKS, EDWY SEARLES

GRAY, CURME

Ref: Hubin 2, ABMIS; UN 4:4 (1951):10-11, 15 (photo).

See also: B189.

GRAY, DULCIE

Ref: Hubin 2, TCCMW, CC, ABMI(S).

GREEN, ANNA KATHERINE

Ref: Hubin 2, TCCMW, EMD, CC, ABMI(S).

E1299. (Anna Katharine Green). The Writer 26:10 (Oct 1914):154-55. Originally published in the Strand, Aug 1914 (reference not verified).
On the source of The Leavenworth Case and early writing and revising experiences.

E1300. (Anna Katharine Green). The Writer 30:10 (Oct 1918):154-55.
On plot construction in Green's fiction. Originally published in New York Sun (reference not verified).

E1301. Barzun, Jacques, and Taylor, Wendell Hertig. Preface to The Circular Study (New York, 1900), by Anna Katharine Green. In A Book of Prefaces (B17), pp. 57-58.

E1302. Cornillon, John. "A Case for Violet Strange." In Images of Women in Fiction: Feminist Perspectives, edited by Susan K. Cornillon, pp. 206-215. Bowling Green, OH: Popular Press, 1973.
The Golden Slipper and Other Problems for Violet Strange (1915) consists of short stories about a young woman, apparently the stereotypical Southern belle, who has a gift for detecting and uses it to help, privately, other women oppressed by society's relegation of women to an inferior status. It is Cornillon's opinion that Green uses these stories to "expose many of the ways women are oppressed by society's laws, conventions, attitudes and institutions." A thoughtful and informative article.

E1303. Harkins, Edwin F. "Anna Katharine Green." In Famous Authors, pp. 91-106. Boston: L. C. Page, 1901. Photo.
A portrait of the writer and a survey of her work.

E1304. Hayne, Barrie. "Anna Katharine Green." In Bargainnier (B16), pp. 153-82.
After some preliminary remarks on Green's long career and on her contributions in establishing the detective novel as a realistic art form, the essay is largely a series of plot resumes of her major novels.

E1305. Hatch, Mary R. P. "The Author of The Leavenworth Case." The Writer 2 (1888):159-62.
Biographical profile (with quotes from letters) written by Green's friend and fellow mystery author. (KLM)

E1306. Overton, Grant. "Anna Katharine Green." In The Women Who Make Our Novels, pp. 167-73. NY: Dodd, Mead, 1928.
To demonstrate Green's skill at constructing a story on a single idea and a "sufficient" motive, Overton analyzes Dark Hollow (1914). With a graded checklist of her work.

E1307. Welch, Deshler. "The Home-Life of a Popular 'Story Teller.'" Book News 25 (Sept 1906):27-30.
Profile of and interview with Anna Katharine Green. With portraits of subject and her husband. (KLM)

E1308. Woodward, Kathleen. "Anna Katharine Green." Bookman 70 (October 1929):168-70.
Interview with Green at age 83. Constrasted with Edgar Wallace whom Woodward had also met.

GREENE, GRAHAM

Ref: Hubin 2, TCCMW, EMD, CC, ABMI(S).

See also: B303, B306, C541, E139.

Int: Figaro littéraire, 20 Dec 47, p. 6; E1330.

E1309. Adamson, Judy and Philip Stratford. "Looking for the Third Man: On the Trail in Texas, New York, Hollywood." Encounter 50 (June 78):39-46.
A study of six drafts of the film scenario for The Third Man, and of the conception, writing and publishing history.

E1310. Aisenberg, Nadja. "Graham Greene and the Modern Thriller." In Aisenberg (B4), pp. 168-222.
Of the 3 major figures (Dickens, Conrad, Greene) about whom Aisenberg writes, Graham Greene is probably the writer whose "entertainments" have been most often discussed in relation to the crime/thriller heritage on which he draws. She does note his debt to Conrad, and his divergence from that model, and also, as in the other essays, points out the relation of the narratives to the fairy tale. She comments that Greene rejects the closed, safe world of the puzzle novel where justice restores order in favor of a treatment of the guilt we all share and cannot commit to a scapegoat. A somewhat disjointed discussion but one that does give more insight into the writer's adaptation of popular material than do her essays on Conrad and Dickens.

E1311. Auden, W. H. "The Heresy of Our Time." Renascence 1 (Spring 49):23-4; reprinted in Graham Greene: A Collection of Critical Essays, ed. by Samuel Hynes (Englewood Cliffs, N.J.: Prentice-Hall, 1973, pp. 93-94.
The Ministry of Fear is both a thriller like Buchan's Thirty-Nine Steps and an allegory of a "creature at war with itself."

E1312. Cassis, A. F. Graham Greene: An Annotated Bibliography of Criticism. Author Bibliographies: No. 55. Metuchen, N.J.: Scarecrow Press, 1981. Index.

E1313. Christopher, J. R. "A Detective Searches for a Clue to The Heart of the Matter." TAD 4 (1970/71):32.
Detective fiction motifs in Greene's novel.

E1314. DeVitis, A. A. Graham Greene. NY: Twayne, 1964.
In "The Entertaining Mr. Greene," pp. 51-72, DeVitis discusses the genre-related pre-Brighton Rock novels, characterizing the later work as "religious."

E1315. Greene, Graham. A Sort of Life. NY: Simon & Schuster, 1971. 220pp. Japanese edition translated by Nishijiro Tanaka as Graham Greene Jiden. Tokyo: Hayakawa Shobo, 1974.
Autobiographical account of Greene's early years. (REB)

E1316. Harwood, Ronald. "Time and the Novelist." Listener 94, no. 2425 (4 Dec 75):747-
Greene talks about his play The Return of A. J. Raffles and earlier writings. Not seen.

E1317. Lambert, Gavin. "The Double Agent: Graham Greene." In Lambert (B215), pp. 132-70.
After identifying some of Greene's childhood fears of death and fantasies of self-destruction, Lambert discusses his novels in some detail.

E1318. McCall, Dan. "Brighton Rock: The Price of Order." English Language Notes 3 (June 1966):290-94.
Analysis of the novel as both a detective story and a contrast between "two ways of ordering experience."

E1319. O'Donnell, Donat. "Graham Greene." Chimera 5:4 (Summer 47):18-30.
Although Greene has been "pulled down" by his thriller writing, he is still one of the most "characteristic" English writers of his time.

E1321. Pritchett, V. S. "The Human Factor in Graham Greene." NY Times Magazine, 26 Feb 78, pp. 33-46.
Profile with photos.

E1322. Salter, James. "Like a Retired Confidential Agent, Author Graham Greene Hides Quietly in Paris." People, 19 Jan 76, pp. 64-67.
Profile with 6 illustrations.

E1323. Scott, Carolyn D. "The Urban Romance: A Study of Graham Greene's Thrillers." In Graham Greene, edited by Harry J. Cargas, pp. 1-28. St. Louis: B. Herder Book Co., 1969.
Greene's entertainments have their sources in popular literature (adventure novels, detective fiction, thrillers) as they "catch the essence of our age." Scott cites Chesterton's statement about the mystery story

as the poetry of modern life and devotes some attention to the romance of the city in Greene.

E1324. Smith, A. J. M. "Graham Greene's Theological Thrillers." Queen's Quarterly 68:1 (Spring 61):15-33.
Sees Greene as a religious writer with affinities with Mauriac, Bernanos, Kafka, James and, especially, Conrad's Secret Agent.

E1325. Spier, Ursula. "Melodrama in Graham Greene's The End of the Affair." MFS 3 (1957): 235-40.
Although Greene is reported to have said that he was excluding melodrama, Spiers finds that Greene has, in fact, used some stock melodramatic devices to good artistic effect.

E1326. Steiner, George. "God's Spies." New Yorker, 8 May 78, pp. 149-54.
Essay/review on spy novels in general and Greene's The Human Factor in particular.

E1327. Stratford, Philip. "Graham Greene: Master of Melodrama." Tamarack Review 19 (Spring 1961):67-86.
Characterization in Greene's fiction with some discussion of narratives written from the criminal's point-of-view in his post-1936 "detective fiction."

E1328. Symons, Julian. Essay/review of Greene's Monsignor Quixote. TLS, 8 Oct 82, pp. 1089-90.
An overview of his work.

E1329. Wansbrough, John. "Graham Greene: The Detective in the Wasteland." Harvard Advocate 136 (Dec 52):11-13, 29-31. Not seen.

E1330. Wobbe, R. A. Graham Greene: A Bibliography and Guide to Research. NY: Garland, 1979, vii-xvi, 439pp.
The critical material is not annotated but includes books, dissertations, articles, and essays in books. Also includes a section on published and broadcast interviews. With an index of works by Greene and works reviewed by him.

E1331. Wolfe, Peter. "Graham Greene and the Art of Entertainment." Studies in Twentieth Century Literature no. 6 (Fall 70), pp. 35-61. Not seen.

E1332. ______. Graham Greene. The Entertainer. Carbonale, IL: Southern Illinois University Press, 1972. vi-viii, 181pp. Bibliography and index. Preface by Harry T. Moore.
A thoughtful study of an important element of the work of a writer Wolfe describes as "one of the century's great writers in English." Wolfe distinguishes the thriller from the detective (or puzzle) novel and analyzes its characteristics, noting Greene's debt to Edgar Wallace. Then, in succeeding chapters, Wolfe discusses in detail each of the "entertainments." In the first chapter, Wolfe reviews the critical literature on Greene and comments on its relevance to his topic.

E1333. Zabel, Morton Dauwen. "Graham Greene." The Nation 157 (3 July 43):18-20. Revised and expanded and published as follows: In Craft and Character, pp. 76-96. NY: Viking Press, 1957. In Graham Greene: A Collection of Essays, edited by Samuel Hynes, p. 30-48. Englewood Cliffs, N.J.: Prentice-Hall, 1973.

Greene draws from current materials (newspapers, current events, etc.) but his world is not that of Oppenheim and Edgar Wallace. His fiction is not melodrama but an expression of the guilt and fear that is a part of our lives.

GREENLEAF, STEPHEN

Ref: Hubin 2; Cannon, AHMM 28:12 (Nov 83):64-67.

Int: TAD 15 (1982):346-49 (photo).

GRIBB, KNUT

See also: C211.

E1334. Nordberg, Nils, ed. Mesterdetektiven Knut Gribb. Oslo: Bladkompaniet, 1968. 256pp. Illus.
A bibliography and 2 facsimile stories. (IH)

GRIBBLE, LEONARD

Ref: Hubin 2, TCCMW, EMD, CC, ABMI(S).

GRIEG, MAYSIE

Ref: Hubin 2, ABMI; UN 4:8 (1952):8-9, 13-14 (photo).

GRIERSON, EDWARD

Ref: Hubin 2, TCCMW, CC, ABMI(S).

GRIERSON, FRANCIS D.

Ref: Hubin 2, CC, ABMI(S).

See also: B253.

E1335. Barzun, Jacques, and Taylor, Wendell Hertig. "Introduction." In The Second Man (New York, 1956), by Francis D. Grierson. "Crime Fiction 1950-1975" (B18).

GRUBER, FRANK

Ref: Hubin 2, TCCMW, EMD, CC, SN, ABMI(S); The Writer 61:7 (July 1948):222-25; PW 139 (5 April 41):1450-54 (on writers' earnings; includes details on his own income).

See also: D307, D308, D316.

E1336. Boucher, Anthony. "Introduction." In Kiss the Boss Goodbye (orig. title: The Last Doorbell, as by John K. Vedder, Holt, 1951), by Frank Gruber. NY: Mercury Mystery, 1954.

E1337. Clark, William J. "Frank Gruber." The Pulp Era no. 67 (May/June 67):31-34.
Brief article on Gruber, with checklist of his books arranged in various series, and mentions of the pulp origins of many titles. (REB)

E1338. ______. The Frank Gruber Index. Los Angeles, CA: William J. Clark, 1969. 18pp. Stapled; no covers. Lists Gruber's book and magazine fiction and non-fiction through mid-1969.
Official publication date is given for each book, and magazine cover date for each contribution to a periodical. The magazine listing is arranged

alphabetically by magazine title. Lengths (in pages), series characters, and pseudonyms are listed. Gruber supplied much information from his own files for this compilation. (REB)

E1339. Fisher, Steve. "Frank Gruber -- I Loved You, too, Buddy." TAD 3 (1969/70):170.
A tribute by fellow writer Fisher.

GUILD, NICHOLAS

Ref: Hubin 2.

Int: Columbus Dispatch Magazine, 13 May 1979.

GUNN, VICTOR. See BROOKS, EDWY SEARLES

GURR, DAVID

Ref: Hubin 2.

Int: PW, 20 Aug 79, pp. 10-11 (photo).

GUTHRIE, A. B., JR.

Ref: Hubin 2, SN, ABMI(S).

E1340. Erisman, Fred. "The Education of Jason Beard: A. B. Guthrie's Western Suspense Stories." Clues 1:2 (Fall/Winter 1980):126-31.
The process of learning and maturing in the character of young Jason Beard in Guthrie's 3 western detective/suspense novels.

HAGBERG, DAVID

Ref: Hubin 2.

E1341. Hagberg, David. "'Croc' Revisited." TNSPE 10 (1982):9-13.
Hagberg talks about his "crocodile" thriller and is interviewed. Hagberg has also written 6 Nick Carter novels.

HAGER, JEAN

Ref: Hubin; Writer's Digest, Oct 80, pp. 44-47.

HAGGARD, WILLIAM

Ref: Hubin 2, TCCMW, EMD, CC, ABMI(S).

E1342. Winks, Robin W. "Murder without Blood: William Haggard." New Republic, 30 July 77, pp. 30-33; reprinted in Winks (B434), pp. 218-24.
Winks writes with great admiration of English writer Haggard's professionalism which makes of him the creator of the "thinking man's spy." Winks notes the uneven reception of Haggard's novels by critics, and the complaints that he is too much for the Establishment but defends his accurate, realistic portrayal of characters and milieus and compares his narrative voice to that of Jane Austen, Dickens, Mrs. Gaskell and Anthony Powell.

HALE, CHRISTOPHER

Ref: Hubin 2; UN 1:9 (1948):12.

HALL, ADAM

Ref: Hubin 2, TCCMW, EMD, ABMIS.

Int: EQMM, Jan 78, p. 88.

See also: B309.

E1343. Banks, R. Jeff, and Dawson, Harvey D. "The Quiller Report." TMF 4:1 (Jan/Feb 80):8-11.
An analytical chart of narrative elements in Hall's spy novels.

E1345. Panek, LeRoy L. "Adam Hall." In Panek (B303), pp. 258-71.
Although Hall, writing under several under pseudonyms, has been publishing on the average of one novel a year since 1943, Panek limits his discussion to the eight Quiller novels written by "Adam Hall." Panek thinks that Hall's extensive use of "humanistic psychology" and the adventure story do not fuse successfully in his spy novels. He sees Quiller as a demonstration of Hall's interest in cybernetics, a cybernetic man.

HALL, O. M.

Ref: Hubin 2, ABMI; UN 1:7 (1948):4-5 (photo).

HALLAHAN, WILLIAM H.

Ref: Hubin 2, ABMIS; The Writer 95:3 (March 82):12-14.

HALLAS, RICHARD

Ref: Hubin 2, ABMIS.

E1345a. Feinberg, David. "Introduction." In You Play the Black and the Red Comes Up (McBride, 1939), by Richard Hallas. Gregg Press Mystery Fiction Series (B134).

E1346. Hagemann, E. R. "Focus on 'You Play the Black and the Red Comes Up': 'No Bet'." In Madden (B239), pp. 163-70.
A close reading of Hallas' novel.

HALLIDAY, BRETT

Ref: Hubin 2, TCCMW, EMD, CC, ABMI(S); The Writer 68:10 (Oct 55):325-25 (letter); UN 4:4 (1951):4-5 (photo); UN 4:12 (1952):4-5 (photographed with Helen McCloy).

See also: "Hal Debrett."

E1348. Halliday, Brett. "Mike Shayne." In Penzler (B309), pp. 217-26.
Much of this essay is a striking description of the two encounters Dresser had with the man on whom he later based the character of Mike Shayne. Dresser also reveals, for the first time, the reason why he killed off Phyllis Shayne.

E1349. Johnson, Tom. "Mike Shayne Author Former Area Resident." Age of the Unicorn 1:5 (December 79):30. Reprinted from the Baylor County Banner (Seymour, TX), 27 Sept 79.
Biographical notes on Davis Dresser.

E1350. McCloy, Helen. "The Return of Michael Shayne." TAD 14 (1981):344-45. Illus.
On Brett Halliday/Davis Dresser and the importance of reader identification with fictional characters.

HAMAO, SHIRO

E1351. Hamao, Shiro. Hamao Shiro Zuihitsushu |Shiro Hamao's essay collection|. Tokyo: Shunju-sha, 1936. 503pp. Illus.
The author, an ex-lawyer, established his fame by writing mystery novels à la S. S. Van Dine but died before he was 40. This is a collection of 13 essays, published as a tribute, and including comments on mystery fiction and criminology. (HS/TT)

HAMILL, PETE

Ref: Hubin 2, SN, ABMI(S).

Int: EQMM, Dec 77, pp. 99-100.

HAMILTON, BRUCE

Ref: Hubin 2, EMD, CC, ABMI.

E1352. Barzun, Jacques, and Taylor, Wendell Hertig. "Introduction." In Too Much of Water (London, 1958), by Bruce Hamilton. "Crime Fiction 1950-1975" (B18).

HAMILTON, DONALD

Ref: Hubin 2, TCCMW, EMD, CC, SN, ABMI(S); The Writer 81:6 (June 68):19-20, 54.

See also: B309, C127.

E1353. Banks, R. Jeff, and Townsend, Guy M. "The Matt Helm Series." TMF 2:2 (March 78):3-11.
A short essay by Townsend on Matt Helm, followed by a chronological chart of titles, prepared by Banks, with information on characters, plot and setting. The article is introduced by excerpts from letters of Banks and Townsend on their collaboration.

E1354. Erisman, Fred. "Western Motifs in the Thrillers of Donald Hamilton." Western American Literature 10 (Feb 1976):283-92.
Kinship with Western fiction in plots, setting, themes and characterization.

E1356. Winks, Robin W. "The Sordid Truth: Donald Hamilton." New Republic, 26 July 75, pp. 21-24; reprinted in Winks (B434), pp. 209-15.
Compulsive reading, written on the model of John Buchan. Winks believes that Hamilton has, perhaps more successfully than any other writer, overcome the problems presented by series characters.

HAMILTON, EDMOND

Ref: Hubin 2, ABMI(S).

E1357. Kankowski, Joseph. "Fiction by Edmond Hamilton." Xenophile 30 (March 77), pp. 14-15.
A preliminary checklist including stories from detective pulps.

HAMILTON, PATRICK

Ref: Hubin 2, TCCMW, EMD, CC, ABMI(S).

HAMMETT, DASHIELL

Ref: Hubin 2, TCCMW, EMD, CC, SN, ABMI(S).

See also: B79, B99, B242, B306, B309, B371, C322, C404, C637, D343, D429, E424, E1240, E2110.

E1358. Adams, Donald K. "The First Thin Man." In Adams, MDA 1972 (B2), pp. 160-77.
An earlier, unfinished version of the novel The Thin Man is described by Adams with extensive citations from the typescript copy. This first "Thin Man" was published, in its entirety, in City of San Francisco 9:17 (4 Nov 75):1-12 (center insert). Adams discusses the "modest but significant" influence this version had on Hammett's later work.

E1359. Amoruso, Vito. "Le sorprese dell'intrigo: Dashiell Hammett et la letteratura |Plot surprises: Dashiell Hammett and literature|." Star, 2 June 83, pp. 17-18.
The attention of the author, a teacher of American literature at the University of Bari, is directed especially to defining, from a new perspective, the "singular documentary quality" of the Hammett narrative, traversed by a kind of ambivalence (or even of ambiguity) in the "observation of the fascination of the 'negative' that, particularly in The Dain Curse, is something very different from negative realism, from that lucid capacity for objectization which is often characterized as the most innovative quality of Hammett in the giallo tradition." (RC)

E1360. Anselmi, Luciano. "I romanzi dell'ex-detective |The novels of the ex-detective|." Il Resto del Carlino, 24 Jan 73.
The "pernicious and fabulous fascination" of Hammett (in whose work the author recognizes limits and lacks...of a specific nature) would consist of the contamination of realistic representation and of unrealistic and adventurous themes: contamination which succeeds in striking chords the reader would prefer to keep hidden. (RC)

E1361. Bazelon, David T. "Dashiell Hammett's 'Private Eye'." Commentary 7:5 (May 49):467-72; reprinted in The Scene Before You, edited by Chandler Brossard (NY: Rinehart, 1945), pp. 180-90.
As Hammett the man is a failed human being who has followed the "easy, illusionary pleasures of Hollywood and Communism," the work shows how Hammett has stifled his talent. His private eyes personify the American work ethic in its purest form in which the worker does the job competently without making any moral choices. Barzelon sees The Glass Key as the work closest to a "real" novel and the character of Nick Beaumont "almost" a human being. A moral tract which nonetheless shows that Barzelon is familiar with Hammett's fiction and is capable of some intelligent discussion of character and method in the Continental Op stories, Red Harvest and The Glass Key.

E1362. Bentley, Christopher. "Murder by Client: A Reworked Theme in Dashiell Hammett." TAD 14 (1981):78-79.
Bentley discusses Hammett's use of material from earlier stories in The Maltese Falcon.

E1363. Berkley, Miriam. "PW Interviews Diane Johnson." PW, 9 Sept 83, pp. 66-67. Photo.
Johnson talks about the research for and writing of her biography of Hammett.

E1364. Blair, Walter. "Dashiell Hammett: Themes and Techniques." In Essays on

American Literature in Honor of Jay B. Hubbell, edited by Clarence Gohdes, pp. 295-306. Durham, N. C.: Duke University Press, 1967. Reprinted in Vogt (B424), Vol. I, pp. 147-64.

After gingerly suggesting that Hammett's writings may be closer to literature than to pulp fiction, and giving a brief biography, Blair compares Hammett and Hemingway for style and attitude, and discusses Hammett's use of first-person narration which he reminds us is something that "looms large in the concerns of critics," thus presumably, by implication, confirming his thesis that Hammett is a writer one ought to take seriously. There follows a ponderous, superficial discussion concluding with the statement that Hammett is a "technician of unusual skill." Sources are not given for most of the references.

E1365. Cawelti, John G. "Hammett, Chandler and Spillane." In Cawelti (B69), pp. 162-73.

A discussion of the literariness of Hammett (his use of earlier literary models) and--for a mystery writer--his unusual philosophical power and seriousness.

E1366. "Dashiell Hammett's San Francisco." City of San Francisco Magazine, 4 Nov 75, p. 16-49.

A survey of aspects of Hammett's life and works, profusely illustrated with period photographs and modern drawings, focusing on his years in San Francisco. Contents: Warren Hinckle, "Introduction," pp. 16, 18; Steven Marcus, "Dashing after Hammett," p. 18; Dashiell Hammett/Alex Raymond, "Secret Agent X-9," pp. 19-21 (comic strip reprints with explanatory text); Larry Levinger, "My Father Liked Precision. The Samuels Story," pp. 23-24 (E1393); "Sam Spade's Frisco," pp. 26-28 (alphabetical list of SF places figuring in Hammett's fiction); Joe Gores, "A Foggy Night," pp. 29-32 (E1375); Dashiell Hammett, "The Thin Man," pp. 1-12 center insert (1930 unpublished manuscript; for discussion see E1358); "Phil Haultain Looks Back," pp. 34-35 (E1416); David Feccheimer, "Old Detective Interview II: Jack Knight Looks Back," pp. 35-36 (E1372); David Feccheimer, "Mrs. Hammett Is Alive and Well in San Francisco," pp. 36-39 (E1371); James Martin MacInnis, "The Old Hall," pp. 41-42 (E1396); William F. Nolan, "Dashiell Hammett: Notes from a Casebook," pp. 43-45 (E1408); Fred Gardner,"An Unfinished Man," p. 46 (notes on Hammett's life and work)

E1367. Deloux, Jean-Pierre. "Hard-boiled Dash." Polar 24 (July 82):3-18. Photos.

An essay on Hammett's vision of a world seen "literally" with no metaphysical trappings. Deloux also sees Hammett as endowing the female with an intensity and ambiguity unlike the conventional heroine of detective fiction and analyzes Hammett's detectives, the Op and Sam Spade in some detail.

E1368. "Dossier Hammett." Polar 24 (July 82):3-60. Illus.

Contents: Jean-Pierre Deloux, "Hard-boiled Dash," pp. 3-18 (E1367); Pascal Merigeau/Jean-Pierre Devillers, "Entretien avec Wim Wenders," pp. 19-27 (interview with director of film, Hammett); F. J. D., "Entretien avec Joe Gores," pp. 28-36 (interview with Joe Gores, author of Hammett, the novel and the screenplay); François Guérif, "Bibliographie française," pp. 37-42 (French editions of Hammett's work); Jean-Jacques Schleret, "Filmographie commentée de Dashiell Hammett," pp. 43-57 (annotated filmography); Pascal Merigeau, "Hammett, note sur le film,"pp. 58-60 (film review).

E1370. Edenbaum, Robert I. "The Poetics of the Private-Eye: The Novels of Dashiell Hammett." In Madden (B239), pp. 80-103; reprinted in Nevins (B290), pp. 98-121.
A fine discussion of the "daemonic" nature of Hammett's detectives, "free of sentiment, of the fear of death, of a past, of the temptations of sex and money."

E1371. Feichheimer, David. "Mrs. Hammett Is Alive and Well in L. A." In City (E1366), pp. 36-39. Portrait.
An interview with Josephine Dolan Hammett.

E1372. ______. "Old Detective Interview II: Jack Knight Looks Back." In City (E1366), pp. 35-36. Photo.
A Pinkerton agent and contemporary of Hammett whom Knight never met.

E1373. Finch, G. A. "From Spade to Marlowe to Archer: An Essay." TAD 4 (1970/71):107-10.
Hammett's Sam Spade is discussed as a "new kind of hero" and as the exemplary model for fictional private eyes.

E1375. Gores, Joe. "A Foggy Night." In City (E1366), pp. 29-32.
A tour of Hammett's--and the real--San Francisco.

E1376. ______. "Hammett the Writer." Xenophile 38 (March/April 78), pp. 5-10.
A "slightly edited" transcript of a paper originally delivered in July 1976, as part of a University of California Extension Program in San Francisco. Illus. Portraits of Hammett's Sam Spade and Continental Op.

E1377. Grella, George. "The Wings of the Falcon and the Maltese Dove." In A Question of Quality: Popularity and Value in Modern Creative Writing, edited by Louis Filler, pp. 109-14. Bowling Green, OH: Popular Press, 1976.
A comparison of Henry James' Wings of the Dove and Hammett's Maltese Falcon.

E1378. Hammett, Dashiell. "From the Memoirs of a Private Detective." Smart Set, March 1923; reprinted in Haycraft (B142), pp. 417-22.
Aphoristic reminiscences by Hammett of his years as a Pinkerton detective.

E1379. ______. "Introduction." In The Maltese Falcon, pp. vii-ix. NY: Modern Library, 1934. With a short biography.
On the genesis of the character and the earlier use by Hammett of the novel's "situation" in "The Whosis Kid" and "The Gutting of Couffignal."

E1380. Hammett, Richard T. (Dashiell Hammett.) News-American (Baltimore), 19 Aug 73; reprinted in Authors in the News, Vol. I, p, 209.
A profile by Hammett's nephew. There does not seem to be any fresh information in this article.

E1381. Hellman, Lillian, ed. The Big Knockover: Selected Stories and Short Novels by Dashiell Hammett. NY: Random House, 1966.
This collection offers a generous helping of Hammett's pulp mystery tales and the opening chapter of an unfinished novel. The introduction is an intimate memoir of Hammett by playwright Hellman, with whom he lived for most of the last thirty years of his life. Much material on Hammett (some of it duplicating the contents of the present Introduction) appears

also in Miss Hellman's An Unfinished Woman (Boston: Little, Brown, 1969), Pentimento (Little, Brown, 1973) and Scoundrel Time (Little, Brown, 1976). These memoirs were collected into one volume and published as Three (Little, Brown, 1979) with an introduction by Richard Poirier in which he comments on the memoirs and, among other topics, on the relationship with Hammett. (REB)

E1382. Herron, Don. Dashiell Hammett Tour. Herron's Literary Walks in San Francisco, 1. San Francisco: Dawn Heron Press, 1982. Illus. 95pp. Wraps.
The itinerary of a walk through parts of San Francisco associated with Hammett's fiction. The entertaining narrative provides a great deal of information about Hammett's life and there is an introduction which surveys his career.

E1383. Hill, M. C. "The Short Stories and Novels of Hammett. Dell Mapbacks and Ellery Queen Magazine." CP? 3:2 (May 81):9-17. Illus.
A checklist by title of Hammett stories in EQMM and Dell Mapback collections.

E1384. Hulley, Kathleen. "From the Crystal Sphere to Edge City: Ideology in the Novels of Dashiell Hammett." In Myth and Ideology in American Culture, edited by Regis Durand, pp. 111-27. Lille: University of Lille, 1976.
A closely reasoned essay on Hammett's detectives as story-tellers who "disrupt" their own fictions and as revolutionaries whose "desire is to preserve a mythical state of revolution." Hulley points out that most critics of Hammett have confused his protagonists with those of his followers and that there is no attempt in Hammett's fiction to uphold the "fundamental idealism" of law and democracy. Includes good discussions of Red Harvest and The Glass Key.

E1385. Johnson, Diane. Dashiell Hammett: A Life. NY: Random House, 1983. 344pp. Illus. As: The Life of Dashiell Hammett, London: Chatto/Hogarth, 1983.
This is the first biography of Hammett written with the cooperation of Lillian Hellman, who provided (among other aids) access to Hammett's papers. The result is a detailed examination of Hammett's personal life, with full attention paid to his bouts with the clap, his alcoholism, his tuberculosis and numerous other illnesses, and his involvement with left-wing organizations. It is a dreary picture. Johnson is less successful (and in fact makes less of an attempt) to come to grips with Hammett's writing. William F. Nolan, himself the author of two books on Hammett and therefore not entirely a disinterested observer, has claimed that there are numerous errors of fact and interpretation in Johnson's book ("Setting the Record Straight," TAD 17 (1984):35-38). (REB)

E1386. Kenney, William. "The Dashiell Hammett Tradition and the Modern American Novel." Unpublished dissertation. University of Michigan, 1964. Dissertation Abstracts 25/12 (1964/5):7272.

E1387. Kolb, Bernard. "Remembering the Dashiell Hammett of Julia." NY Times Leisure Section, 25 Sept 77, pp. 15-16.
Kolb's personal memories of Hammett.

E1388. Lacassin, Francis. "Dashiell Hammett ou la littérature à haute tension |Dashiell Hammett or high-tension literature|." In Lacassin (B201), Vol. 2, pp. 5-40. Bibliography and filmography.

A biographical and thematic study of Hammett's work. Lacassin also discusses Hammett's conception of the private operator as an "anarchist" whose role is at odds with that of the detective in the formal British and American puzzle mystery.

E1389. Lamb, Margaret. "Expressionism and American Popular Literature: Hammett as a Continental Op-Eye." Clues 2:1 (Spring/Summer 81):26-34.
A study of similarities between what Hammett saw in American cities and what others saw in a disintegrating Europe.

E1390. Layman, Richard. Dashiell Hammett: A Descriptive Bibliography. Pittsburgh, PA: University of Pittsburgh Press, 1979. vi, 185pp. Illus. Index.
A bibliography of primary sources including books, paperbacks, periodicals, newspapers and movies. There are 6 appendices on advertising copy; radio, TV, movie and stage plays based on Hammett's work; newspaper syndication of the Alex Raymond/Hammett comic strip and several fictional works; compiler's notes on unverified publications; and a very short list of secondary sources. The covers and title pages of all hardcover and paperback first editions are reproduced (in black & white), as well as the contents pages of the short story collections. Reviews: TAD 13 (1980):23-24 (by William F. Nolan); PBSA 76:2 (1982):232-33.

E1391. ______. Shadow Man: The Life of Dashiell Hammett. NY and London: Bruccoli Clark/Harcourt Brace Jovanovich, 1981. xviii, 285pp. Illus. Bibliography. Notes. Index. An appendix contains a bibliography of his writings and the transcript of Hammett's U. S. District Court testimony on July 9, 1951.
In addition to the biography, Layman summarizes Hammett's fiction and makes some critical comments. The account of Hammett's pulp career is cursory and the contributions of Black Mask editor Joseph T. Shaw that many earlier writers have seen as significant editorial contributions to the new hard-boiled literature are described as those of a promoter with little or no involvement in the editorial duties one would normally expect of him. CC S148. Reviews: NYTBR, 23 Aug 81, pp. 9, 20; TLS, 5 June 81, pp. 619-20; TMF 6:1 (Jan/Feb 81):32-34.

E1392. Leverence, John. "The Continental Op." JPC 9 (Winter 1975):741-43.
Leverence cites 15 elements common to Hammett's short stories that, he thinks, contributed to the development of the hard-boiled narrative. Some of the items appear to be arbitrary and a more extended discussion would have been useful. The article is, essentially, a review of the Marcus-edited collection (E1398).

E1393. Levinger, Larry. "The Samuels Story." In City (E1366), pp. 23-24.
Between 1922 and 1927, Hammett worked in the advertising deparment of Albert Samuels' jewelry company. Levinger interviews Albert J. Samuels, Jr. who has almost nothing to say about Hammett's association with the company.

E1394. Lyles, William L. "Dashiell Hammett in the Dell Mapbacks." PQ 4:2 (Summer 1981):15-23. Illus.
A discussion of the Hammett stories published in Dell Mapbacks with print runs, identification of artists and discussion of art work.

E1395. Macdonald, Ross. "Hommage to Dashiell Hammett." Mystery Writers' Annual 1964; reprinted in Macdonald (E1888), pp. 109-12.

A concise essay on Hammett and the tradition of the two-fisted American adventurer, Hemingway, and the character of Sam Spade. A fair number of subsequent critics have used Macdonald's insights and, in effect, added nothing of any consequence to his pared-to-the-bone analysis.

E1396. MacInnis, James Martin. "The Old Hall of Justice." In City (E1366), pp. 41-42.
Martin met Hammett once, briefly. The article is a history of San Francisco's Old Hall of Justice.

E1397. Malin, Irving. "Focus on 'The Maltese Falcon': The Metaphysical Falcon." In Madden (B239), pp. 104-109.
Malin thinks the novel transcends the hard-boiled school in its irony and metaphysical dimension. There are some brief, but useful, comments on Hammett's use of dialogue and the "nonbelief of conversation."

E1398. Marcus, Stephen. "Introduction" to The Continental Op (NY: Random House, 1974), pp. ix-xix. Also published as "Dashiell Hammett and the Continental Op," in Partisan Review 41 (1974):362-77; reprinted in Representations: Essays on Literature and Society (NY: Random House, 1975), pp. 311-21; Part II (pp. xv-xxix) reprinted in Most/Stowe (B264), pp. 197-209.
A substantial essay on ambiguity and deception in art, life and society as they are expressed in Hammett's fiction. Marcus sees Hammett's political views as essential to his writing and it is Marcus' view that when Hammett separated his politics from his writing, he became, first, a hack writer and, then, "no writer at all."

E1400. Marling, William. "The Hammett Succubus." Clues 3:2 (Fall/Winter 82):66-75.
Marling sees the woman-demon as a continuing theme in Hammett's work, a constant threat of "death-through-sexuality." He shifts the discussion of The Maltese Falcon away from Sam Spade's artful duplicity to the "fictional functions of the female types" and points up the use of the Succubus female in his other novels. Marling's language is not always equal to his perceptions and he makes almost no effort to identify this type in Hammett's short stories, but his argument--based on historical and literary precedents--is well-supported and is an important contribution to literary typology in Hammett.

E1401. Michaels, Leonard. "The Continental Op." NYTBR, 8 Dec 74, pp. 1, 10, 12, 14.
Review-essay of Marcus (E1398) in which Michaels discusses the 7 reprinted stories as the products of the "mind and will," perfectly constructed but with "no gift from the muse." Typical product of the Hammett-as-uninspired-genre-craftsman school of criticism.

E1402. Morris, Homer H. "Dashiell Hammett in the Wasteland." Midwest Quarterly 19 (Winter 1978):196-202.
Hammett's use of setting and landscape in his creation of an urban wasteland. Hammett's work is compared to John Gay's Beggar's Opera for characterization and style.

E1403. Moss, Leonard. "Hammett's Heroic Operative." New Republic 154 (8 Jan 66):32-34.
Review-essay of The Novels of Dashiell Hammett (Knopf, 1965). Moss

focuses on Red Harvest and the Continental Op stories. Moss also comments that The Maltese Falcon is "probably" Hammett's worst novel.

E1404. Mundell, E. H. A List of the Original Appearances of Dashiell Hammett's Magazine Work. Serif Series No. 13. Kent, OH: Kent State University Press, 1968: 52pp.
Entries are listed chronologically, with the first few lines of each story quoted. The latter feature is not present in any of the other Hammett bibliographies. Breen 178. (REB)

E1405. Nakjavani, Erik. "Red Harvest: An Archipelago of Micro-Powers." Clues 4:1 (Spring/Summer 83):105-113.
On the role of the Continental Op as he establishes a temporary balance and gives some coherence to a society threatened by competing "micro-powers" within its boundaries.

E1406. Naremore, James. "Dashiell Hammett and the Poetics of Hard-Boiled Detection." In Benstock (B26), pp. 49-72.
Naremore's essay and the essay of Kathleen Hulley (E1384) are probably the two best essays in English to date on the nature and significance of Hammett's work. Naremore discusses Hammett's pulp fiction, his style, the novels, his superiority as a theoretician of fictional language over Chandler, and his role as the potential "Flaubert of detective fiction."

E1407. Nolan, William F. Dashiell Hammett: A Casebook. Santa Barbara, CA: McNally & Loftin, 1969. Introduction by Philip Durham. 189pp. Index.
An all-too-brief account of the life and work of the hard-boiled genre's leading performer. Emphasis is on the biographical and bibliographical facts rather than in-depth analysis. The 50- page annotated checklist of writings by and about Hammett was the first extensive listing of this material. The bibliography of primary material has been superseded by the Layman bibliography (E1390) but the listing of secondary sources is still useful, particularly so since Layman's biography of Hammett (E1391) does not provide a separate bibliography of secondary sources but incorporates them into the notes. Nolan's bibliography includes newspaper reviews and articles. Nolan's Hammett: A Life at the Edge (see below) has a short bibliography of secondary sources but the majority of the sources are cited in the notes. Review/essay by Francis M. Nevins, Jr. in JPC 3 (Spring 1970):878-879. (REB and WA)

E1408. ______. "Dashiell Hammett: Notes from A Casebook." In City (E1366), pp. 43-45.
Excerpts from Nolan's Casebook.

E1409. ______. Hammett: A Life at the Edge. NY: Congdon and Weed, Inc., 1983. xi-xiv, 276pp. Photos. London: Arthur Barker, 1983.
A biography of Hammett with some discussion of his writings. Nolan's style is a more informal one than Layman's (E1391) and there is more detail on Hammett's post-30s career (except for Hammett's congressional testimony). This is also, like Layman's book, an "unofficial" biography, researched without the cooperation of Lillian Hellman. Review: TLS, 16 Dec 83, p. 1394.

E1410. ______. "The Hammett Checklist Revisited." TAD 6 (1973):249-54.
An updating of his Casebook bibliography (E1407). In addition to the TAD items listed in this bibliography, Nolan has written a number of letters with the earliest appearing in TAD 1 (1967/68):105. The letters

contain material on both Nolan's writing and on his Hammett research. See Stilwell's TAD Index (A163) for a listing of the letters through 10:3.

E1411. ______. "Revisiting the Hammett Checklist." TAD 9 (1976):292-295; 324-329.
A second updating of bibliographical material in Nolan's Casebook.

E1412. ______. "Shadowing the Continental Op." TAD 8 (1975):121-123.
A list of first publication of 36 Op stories with a history of their subsequent publication in anthologies.

E1413. Ochiogrosso, Frank. "Murder in the Dark: Dashiell Hammett." New Republic, 30 July 77, pp. 28-30.
The Op is, according to Ochiogrosso, Hammett's essential creation and his subsequent detectives are recognizable variations on this character. Ochiogross refers to the "two dozen stories and two novels" the Op appears in. Nolan (E1412) identifies 36 Op stories.

E1414. O'Neill, James P. "Dashiell Hammett Haunts San Francisco." Second Spring 5:2 (April/May 78):15-19. Illus.
A survey of Hammett's career with emphasis on the San Francisco period.

E1415. Pattow, Donald J. "Order and Disorder in The Maltese Falcon." TAD 11 (1978):171.
A short study of character "pairings" to show patterns of disorder and distrust in Hammett's novel.

E1416. "Phil Haultain Looks Back." In City (E1366), pp. 34-35.
An interview with a Pinkerton operative who occasionally worked with Hammett.

E1417. Powell, Robert S. "Including Murder: An Unpublished Hammett Collection." Clues 2:2 (Fall/Winter 81):135-42.
A report on papers in the Hammett Manuscript Collection at the University of Texas which appear to be a draft for a collection of Continental Op stories.

E1418. Queen, Ellery. "Introduction." In A Man Named Thin and Other Stories, by Dashiell Hammett, pp. 6-12. NY: Mercury Publications (Mercury Mystery 233), 1962.
The introduction contains complete contents lists for all of the earlier Mercury collections of Hammett stories. Queen also supplied copious headnotes and afterwords for all the stories in this collection. (REB)

E1419. Reilly, John M. "Sam Spade Talking." Clues 1:2 (Fall/Winter 80):119-25.
A study of language in The Maltese Falcon. Reilly sees Sam Spade's rhetorical style as that of the vernacular style fashioned by Mark Twain.

E1420. Sales, Roger. "The Hammett Case." NYRB 22 (6 Feb 75):20-22; reprinted in On Not Being Good Enough: Writings of a Working Critic, pp. 73-80. NY: Oxford University Press, 1979.
Review-essay of the Marcus (E1398). According to Sales, the Continental Op stories are mediocre and Hammett overrated. The Glass Key is Hammett's best book.

E1421. Sandoe, James. Notes for reviews of Hammett's The Thin Man and Dead Yellow Women. TAD 14 (1981):74-75.

E1422. Sinda, Gregory J. "The Mystery of Mystery: The Novels of Dashiell Hammett." Unpublished dissertation. University of Illinois at Urbana, 1980. 217pp. DAI 41/09A (1981/82), p. 4044.

E1423. Starrett, Vincent. "In Praise of Dashiell Hammett." In Books and Bipeds, pp. 16-19. NY: Argus Books, Inc., 1947.
An appreciation of Hammett and of his innovations in style and method. (SAS)

E1424. Symons, Julian. "Dashiell Hammett: The Onlie Begetter." In Keating (B179), pp. 80-93; reprinted in Symons (B389), p. 166-77.
Hammett as the originator of the American crime story. Remarks on his style, his short stories and his novels with The Glass Key seen as his masterpiece.

E1425. Thompson, George J., III. "The Problem of Moral Vision in Dashiell Hammett's Novels." Dissertation. University of Connecticut, 1972. 222pp. Dissertation Abstracts 33/06-A (1972/73), pp. 2955-2956. Reprinted in TAD 6 (1972/73):153-156, 213-225; 7 (1973/74):32-40, 178-92, 270-80; 8 (1974/75):27-35, 124-30. Correction by Thompson in letter, TAD 8:2:159.
A detailed chronological thematic study.

E1426. Tuck, Jay Nelson. "Hammett Not Chandler." New Statesman, 18 April 75, p. 513.
Letter in which Tuck states that Hammett rather than Chandler, as it has usually been suggested, popularized the word "gunsel," in The Maltese Falcon.

E1427. Westerberg, Kerstin. "The Going Is Tough." Jury 11:1 (1982):53-61.
Women in Hammett's novels. (MS)

E1428. Whitley, John S. "Stirring Things Up: Dashiell Hammett's Continental Op." JAmStud 14 (December 80):443-55.
A provocative essay on the violent "Jacobean" world of the Continental Op where he is a "shape-changer" who cannot be hurt "because there is nothing inside to be hurt." Whitley's touchstones for comparison are, other than Jacobean drama, the Gothic novel, Highsmith, Bardin and Himes. He sees Hammett's extravagant tales in which the narrator mirrors the violence he investigates as quite distinct from Chandler and Ross Macdonald in their texture, plotting and characterization. See Glover (C322) for a response.

E1429. Wolfe, Peter. Beams Falling: The Art of Dashiell Hammett. Bowling Green, OH: Popular Press, 1980. 168pp. No index; some bibliography in notes.
A study of Hammett's fiction. Chapters on Hammett's use of conventions and his art, his short stories and on each of his novels. Breen 180.

E1430. ______. "Sam Spade: Lover." TAD 11 (1978):366-71.
A detailed study of character in The Maltese Falcon, concluding that Falcon is "a psychological novel with almost no psychology."

E1431. Worpole, Ken. "The American Connection: The Masculine Style in American Fiction." New Left Review 139 (May/June 83):79-94. Reprinted in Dockers & Detectives, by Ken Warpole, pp. 2-48. London: Verson Editions, 1983.

On the democratization of American literature by Hammett and Hemingway. Hammett as social critic; exclusion of women except as "forces of evil," and the reflection of working-class ideals in the fiction. An argument in which polemic takes precedence over common sense. See comment by George V. Higgins, in Boston Globe, 17 Sept 83.

HANDLEY, ALAN

Ref: Hubin 2; UN 1:1 (1948):6 (photo).

HANSEN, JOSEPH

Ref: Hubin 2, TCCMW, SN, ABMI(S).

Int: Books & Bookmen 18:2 (Aug 73):6; PW 222:24 (17 Dec 82):14-15; Hard Boiled Dicks 4 (Oct 82):9-12 (in French); EQMM, Sept 83, pp. 69-71 and Oct 83, pp. 89-91.

E1432. Martin, Roger. "Joseph Hansen." Hard Boiled Dicks 4 (Oct 82):7-17.
A biographical and critical dossier on the American writer. Contents: "Joseph Hansen: éléments biographiques," pp. 7-9 (biography); "Entretien avec Joseph Hansen," pp. 9-12 (interview, in French); "Bibliographie de Joseph Hansen," pp. 13-16; "Critiques," p. 17 (3 book reviews, in French).

HANSHEW, THOMAS W.

Ref: Hubin 2, TCCMW, EMD, CC, ABMI(S).

See also: D327.

E1433. Cox, J. Randolph. "Cleek and His Forty Faces: Or, T. W. Hanshew, a Dime Novelist Who Made Good." DNR 42 (15 March 73):30-34; 42 (15 April 73):41-43.
Survey of Cleek stories and the "unraveling" of some of the bibliographic tangles.

E1434. Greene, Douglas. "The Incredible Hamilton Cleek; or, Sherlock Holmes from Graustark." TPP 5:2 (Nov/Dec 82):11-14.
An introduction to the Hanshew Cleek series, with a bibliography, including uncollected short stories.

E1435. "Master T. W. Hanshew." DNR 8 (Sept 1939):3.
Biographical sketch of the early career of the dime novelist who created Cleek of the Forty Faces. Reprinted here from Boys of the World, 12 April 1877. (JRC)

E1436. "Oh, Girls! Bertha M. Clay is Dead and 'She' was a Man!" Detroit Tribune, 22 March 1914, n.p.
Obituary of Thomas W. Hanshew who is credited (erroneously) with being Bertha M. Clay. (File copy of article in Street & Smith archives, Syracuse University Library, has the word "Liar" scrawled across the bottom.) (JRC)

HARDY, THOMAS

Ref: ABMI(S).

E1437. Moore, R. L. "The Poet within the Architect's Ring: Desperate Remedies, Hardy's Hybrid Detective-Gothic Narrative." Studies in the Novel 14 (Spring 82):31-42.

An exploration of the integration of Gothic and detective traditions in Hardy's first published novel. Moore indicates that the detective element is also present in Hardy's later novels and the subject seems worth pursuing in a more comprehensive essay.

HARE, CYRIL

Ref: Hubin 2, TCCMW, EMD, CC, ABMI(S); Cannon, AHMM 28:1 (Jan 83):69-71.

E1438. Barzun, Jacques, and Taylor, Wendell Hertig. "Preface" to When the Wind Blows (London, 1949), by Cyril Hare. In A Book of Prefaces (B17), pp. 59-60.

E1439. Bennett, Reynold. "Cyril Hare: the Male Agatha Christie." TPP 5:3 (May/June 83):23-25, 28. With a bibliography of primary works.
An introduction to his life and writing.

E1440. Boucher, Anthony. "Introduction." In The Christmas Murder (orig. title: An English Murder, Faber, 1951), by Cyril Hare. NY: Mercury Publications, 1953.

E1441. Gilbert, Michael. "Introduction: Cyril Hare." In Best Detective Stories of Cyril Hare. London: Faber, 1959; NY: Walker & Co, 1961. Reprinted as Death among Friends and other Detective Stories, by Cyril Hare, pp. 7-15. NY: Perennial Library (Harper & Row), 1984.
Biographical sketch of Hare (Alfred Gordon Clark), account of Gilbert's first encounter with Hare's fiction, and concise but acute commentlary on Hare's style and technique. (REB)

E1442. Shibuk, Charles. "Cyril Hare." TAD 3 (1970):28-30.
A concise bio-bibliographical survey of Hare's fiction.

E1443. Strout, Cushing. "Murder with Manners: Cyril Hare." New Republic, 30 July 77, pp. 34-36.
A tribute to this underrated craftsman of the British mystery story.

HARLING, ROBERT

Ref: Hubin 2, TCCMW, CC, ABMIS.

HARRINGTON, JOSEPH

Ref: Hubin 2, TCCMW, EMD, CC, SN, ABMI.

E1444. Hays, R. W. "Joseph Harrington's First Three Books." TAD 4 (1971):104-6; reprinted in Hays (B177), pp. 155-60.
Harrington's three police procedurals, featuring New York City detective Frank Kerrigan are neatly summarized by Hays.

HARRINGTON, JOYCE

Ref: Hubin 2, TCCMW.

Int: EQMM, 22 April 81, pp. 94-96 and 20 May 81, pp. 82-84.

HARRIS, HERBERT

Ref: Hubin 2, TCCMW, EMD, ABMI.

HARRIS, ROSEMARY

Ref: Hubin 2, TCCMW, ABMI(S).

HARRIS, TIMOTHY

Ref: Hubin 2, SN.

Int: Los Angeles Times, 27 February 80, Sect. V, p. 8; Polar 26 (Winter 83):169-71 (in French).

E1445. Deloux, Jean-Pierre. "Des Polars plein la tête |His head full of mysteries|." Polar 26 (Winter 82): 164-68. Photo. Bibliography.
Deloux reviews the novels of the "most promising" writer of his generation whose work he compares to Raymond Chandler's.

HARRISON, MICHAEL

Ref: Hubin 2, TCCMW, CC, ABMI(S).

Int: TMRN 3:6 (Aug 70):17-20 (with a partial checklist of his work).

E1446. Queen, Ellery. "Introduction." In The Exploits of the Chevalier Dupin, by Michael Harrison, pp. ix-xi. Sauk City, WI: Mycroft & Moran, 1968. The same introduction also appears in Murder in the Rue Royale, by Michael Harrison. Lond: Tom Stacey, Ltd., 1972.

HART, FRANCES NOYES

Ref: Hubin 2, TCCMW, EMD, CC, ABMI(S).

HARVESTER, SIMON

Ref: Hubin 2, TCCMW, CC.

HASTINGS, MACDONALD

Ref: Hubin 2, TCCMW, EMD, CC, ABMI(S).

HATCH, Mary R. P.

Ref: Hubin 2, ABMI(S).

E1447. Twitchell, V. B. "Mrs. Mary R. P. Hatch." Granite Monthly 12 (1889):173-175.
Biographical sketch, with portrait, of a little-known mystery author. (KLM)

HAUFF, WILHELM

E1448. Arnold, Armin. "Zadig as a Jew: An Early German Tale of Detection." TAD 13 (1980):173-74. Illustrated.
On Hauff's "Abner der Juder, der nichts gesehen hat," published in 1827.

HAYES, JOSEPH

Ref: Hubin 2, TCCMW, ABMI(S).

HAYS, LEE

Ref: Hubin 2; Lachman, TPP 5:1 (1982):43.

HEAD, MATTHEW

Ref: Hubin 2, TCCMW, EMD, CC, ABMI; UN 3:3 (1950):6-7 (photo).

E1449. Bargainnier, Earl F. "Matthew Head's Dr. Mary Finney and Hopper Taliaferro Novels." Clues 4:1 (Spring/Summer 83):53-66.
Studies of detective Finney and narrator Taliaferro, and of the comic, classic novels of detection in which they appear.

E1450. Barzun, Jacques, and Taylor, Wendell Hertig. "Preface" to The Congo Venus. In A Book of Prefaces (B17), pp. 61-62.

HEALD, TIM

Ref: Hubin 2, TCCMW, ABMI(S).

HEARD, H. F.

Ref: Hubin 2, TCCMW, EMD, CC, ABMI(S).

HEBERDEN, M. V.

Ref: Hubin 2, CC; UN 4:1 (1951):6-7 (photo); UN 4:7 (1952):4-5, 16 (photo).

E1450a. Barzun, Jacques, and Taylor, Wendell Hertig. "Introduction." In Engaged to Murder (NY, 1948), by M. V. Heberden. "Crime Fiction 1950-1975" (B18).

HEILBRUN, CAROLYN. See CROSS, AMANDA

HELLER, FRANK

E1451. Hedman, Dag. Frank Heller födelse. En undersökning av Gunnar Serners debut som underhållningsförfattare 1913-1914 |The birth of Frank Heller. an investigation of Gunnar Serner's debut as a popular writer|. Uppsala, Sweden: Avd för litteratrsociologi, 1980. 110pp.

A biography. (IH)

HENDRYX, JAMES B.

Ref: Hubin 2, ABMI.

E1452. Harwood, John. "The Saint of the North: Black John Smith of Halfaday Creek." TMF 3:6 (1979):3-7.

James B. Hendryx's outlaw hero-villain in a series of novels set in the Northwest at the time of the Yukon gold strike (1896). Includes a list of the novels in which Black John appears.

HENISSART, PAUL

Ref: Hubin 2, ABMI(S); The Writer 91:5 (May 78):15-18 (on spy fiction).

HENSLEY, JOE L.

Ref: Hubin 2, SN, ABMI(S).

Int: TPP 2:3 (May/June 79):19-21; Hard Boiled Dicks 4 (October 82):19-25 (in French).

E1453. Frauenglas, Robert. "Law, Lawyers and Justice in the Novels of Joe L. Hensley."TMF 4:1 (Jan/Feb 80):3-7; published in French translation in Hard Boiled Dicks 4 (Oct 82):32-40.

A survey of his novels followed by short discussions of the law and corruption in his fiction.

E1454. Martin, Roger, ed. "Joe Louis Hensley." Hard Boiled Dicks 4 (Oct 82):19-49.

Contents: "Entretien avec Joe L. Hensley," pp. 19-25 (interview, in French); "Bibliographie de Joe L. Hensley," pp. 26-30; "Filmographie de Joe L. Hensley," p. 31; Robert Frauenglas,"Loi, hommes de loi et justice," pp. 32-40 (E1453); Joe L. Hensley, "Plan de bataille pour un procès," pp. 41-48 (short story).

E1455. Hensley, Joe L. Letter, TAD 7 (1974):74.
Hensley talks about his reading of Detective Fiction Weekly as a youngster.

HERRINGTON, LEE

Ref: Hubin 2, SN; UN 4:2 (1951):10-11, 13 (photo).

HERRON, SHAUN

Ref: Hubin 2, TCCMW, ABMI(S).

HEYER, GEORGETTE

Ref: Hubin 2, TCCMW, EMD, CC, ABMI(S).

E1456. Bargainnier, Earl K. "The Dozen Mysteries of Georgette Heyer." Clues 3:2 (Fall/Winter 82):30-39.
Bargainnier sees Heyer's distinctiveness in her adroit blending of melodrama, romance and mystery.

E1457. Barzun, Jacques, and Taylor, Wendell Hertig. "Preface" to A Blunt Instrument (NY, 1938), by Georgette Heyer. In A Book of Prefaces (B17), pp. 63-64.

E1458. Boucher, Anthony. "Introduction." In A Blunt Instrument, by Georgette Heyer. NY: Bantam, 1966.

HEYES, DOUGLAS

Ref: Hubin 2; UN 3:11 (1951):8-9, 14 (photo).

HIGGINS, GEORGE V.

Ref: Hubin 2, TCCMW, ABMI(S).

E1459. Gadney, Reg. "Boston Bums: The Novels of George V. Higgins." London Magazine (new series) 16:2 (June/July 76):67-70. Photo.
Some impressionistic, disorganized comments on Higgins' The Friends of Eddie Coyle, Boston, the human animals who infest it, and his success in capturing the "intimate voice of the American criminal." There are also some poorly integrated comments on pre- and post-Watergate America.

E1460. McCabe, Bruce. "Higgin's Trade." Boston Globe, 17 May 1974, p. 35. Photo.
Interview; mentions Higgins' law practice ("I don't have to practice law. I want to. It doesn't do the writing any harm, either...."), his business enterprises, the affluence resulting from the success of his 1st three books (a $40,000 office complex in Boston's financial district, 2 sports cars, a boat). "I always worked my butt off. I'd been writing 15, 16 years before (The Friends of Eddie) Coyle, and I taught nights at Northeastern (Univ.)." (REB)

E1461. O'Brian, Don. "The Sage of George V. Higgins: Hardly the Lit'ry Life." Boston Phoenix, 11 Nov 80 (Sect. 1), pp. 1, 6-8, 12-14, 16.
Interview/profile. (KLM)

HIGGINS, JACK

Ref: Hubin 2, TCCMW, ABMI(S).

Int: NYTBR, 24 April 77, p. 46; NYTBR, 20 July 80, p. 22.

E1462. Hauptfuhrer, Fred. "The Eagle Has Landed Jack Higgins in a High Tax Bracket and Given Him Ulcers." People, 17 Jan 77, pp. 68-70. Photos. Profile. (REB)

E1463. Higgins, Jack. "Thriller Writing." Bookcase. The W. H. Smith Book Review. Undated (August 1983), p. 5.
Brief article discussing the writing profession. Higgins's own "formula for success," and the importance of background research, leading up to a plug for his Falklands war novel, Exocet. (REB)

HIGHSMITH, PATRICIA

Ref: Hubin 2, TCCMW, EMD, CC, ABMI(S); The Writer 67:12 (Dec 54):403-406 (on suspense in fiction); The Writer 79:3 (March 66):9-22 (the suspense short story); The Writer 80:10 (Oct 67):23-26 (writer's block).

Int: New Review 4:41 (Aug 77):31-36; in Cooper-Clark (B75), pp. 159-71 (photo); EQMM, Aug 83, 89-92; Mystere no. 279, May 71.

See also: E2673.

E1464. Brophy, Brigid. "Bartleby the Scriptwriter." New Statesman 70 (29 Oct 65):664-65; reprinted in Don't Never Forget (NY: Holt, Rinehart and Winston, 1967), pp. 149-155.
A review of Highsmith's A Suspension of Mercy which Brophy uses as an occasion to pillory detective fiction from Poe to Hammett, Chandler and Macdonald. She excepts Highsmith and Simenon because they have turned this low-class entertainment into an art which does not seek to soothe the reader's "ego."

E1465. Highsmith, Patricia. "Je préfère le Noël français |I prefer the French Christmas|." NL, 23-30 March 78, p. 19. Translated from the English by Philippe Mikriamnos.
The American novelist describes her reactions to life in French.

E1466. Rivière, François. "L'inquiétante Madame Highsmith |The disturbing Mme Highsmith|." Nouvelles litteraires, 19 Sept-6 Oct 77. Portrait.
Highsmith and her work seen as complementing one another in the isolation of the writer and the novels, "an island of cold and desperate hatred in the midst of an American school usually centered on the complacent painting of characters."

E1467. Symons, Julian. "Patricia Highsmith." London Magazine 9:3 (June 69):37-43.
A study of characterization in Highsmith in a review of The Tremor of Forgery that expands to include her earlier work.

E1468. Uber Patricia Highsmith. Zurich: Diogenes, 1980. 222pp. Wraps. Bibliography. Illus.
Essays (in German) on various aspects of Highsmith's work, by Graham Greene, Julian Symons, and others. Not seen. (REB)

E1469. Volpatti, Lia. "C'è delitto e delitto |There is crime and there is crime|." Star I, July 82, pp. 75-76.
Brief profile of Patricia Highsmith, whose artistic cipher is characterized by a suspense transferred from the dynamics of the story to the "lucid

neurotic and pathological rationality" of the characters. (RC)

HILDICK, WALLACE

Ref: Hubin 2, TCCMW, ABMI(S).

HILL, HEADON

Ref: Hubin 2, EMD, ABMI(S).

E1470. Bengis, Nathan L. "Plots for Sale--Cheap; Apply: 221B." TAD 1 (1968):116-117.
Bengis lists the stories in Hill's Zambra the Detective (1894) and shows how they are influenced by Conan Doyle stories.

HILL, REGINALD

Ref: Hubin 2, TCCMW, ABMI(S).

HILLERMAN, TONY

Ref: Hubin 2, TCCMW, CC, SN, ABMI(S).

Int: PW, 24 Oct 80, pp. 6-7 (photo); TAD 14 (1981):93-95 (photo and illustrations).

E1471. Bakerman, Jane S. "Hunter and Hunted. Comparison and Contrast in Tony Hillerman's People of Darkness." TMF 5:1 (Jan/Feb 81):3-10.
Bakerman compares Navajo tribal policeman Jim Chee with Hillerman's series character Joe Leaphorn, and contrasts him with his killer-for-hire antagonist, Colton Wolf.

E1472. ______. "Joe Leaphorn and the Navajo Way: Tony Hillerman's Detective Fiction." Clues 2:1 (Spring/Summer 81):9-16.
An analysis of Hillerman's four mystery novels (as of 1978) with their "authorial command" of the Navajo world and Hillerman's "skillful development of his protagonist."

E1473. Barzun, Jacques, and Taylor, Wendell Hertig. "Introduction." In The Fly on the Wall (New York, 1971), by Tony Hillerman. "Crime Fiction 1950-1975" (B18).

E1474. Broberg, Jan. "Brobergs brottstycke 2 |Broberg's crime piece 1|." Jury 1:2 (1972):23. Photo.
On Tony Hillerman. (MS)

E1475. Schneider, Jack W. "Crime and Navajo Punishment: Tony Hillerman's Novels of Detection." Southwest Review 67 (Spring 82):151-60.
An admiring survey of the Leaphorn and Chee novels in which, claims Schneider, detective fiction has a "richness of content and a substantiality of form it has rarely enjoyed before."

E1476. Strenski, Ellen, and Evans, Robley. "Ritual and Murder in Tony Hillerman's Indian Detective Novels." Western American Literature 16 (Fall 81):105-16.
"Ceremonial and visionary Indian identity" in Hillerman's fiction as the authors see the Joe Leaphorn novels as an important contribution to literature using native American material. Includes information from correspondence with Hillerman.

HILTON, JAMES

Ref: Hubin 2, TCCMW, EMD, CC, ABMI(S): Pike, TPP 3:1 (Jan/Feb 80):28, 24.

E1477. Barzun, Jacques, and Taylor, Wendell Hertig. "Preface" to Was It Murder? (New York, 1935), as by Glen Trevor. In A Book of Prefaces (B17), pp. 65-66.

HILTON, JOHN BUXTON

Ref: Hubin 2, TCCMW, CC, ABMI(S).

HIMES, CHESTER

Ref: Hubin 2, TCCMW, SN, ABMI(S).

See also: B20.

Int: Adam (Nov 64); Sunday Times Magazine (London), 9 Nov 69, pp. 69-70; Life 69:9 (28 Aug 70):60-61; Armistad I, edited by John Williams and Charles H. Harris (NY: Random House/Vintage Books, 1970), pp. 25-93 (includes a Bibliography of Himes' works); PW 201 (3 April 72):20-21 (photo); Les Nouvelles litteraires, 7-14 Dec 78, p. 8 (photos).

E1478. Berry, Jay R., Jr. "Chester Himes and the Hard-Boiled Tradition." TAD 15 (1982):38-43. Photo.

Himes brings to the conventions of Hammett, Chandler and Ross Macdonald, an evocative sense of place, the Black militancy movement and Afro-American detective heroes.

E1479. Campenni, Frank J. "Black Cops and/or Robbers: The Detective Fiction of Chester Himes." TAD 8 (75):206-209.

Text of a paper presented at the Popular Culture Association meeting in Milwaukee, Spring, 1974. Black characters and anarchic plots.

E1480. Feuser, Willifried. "Prophet of Violence: Chester Himes." African Literature Today 9 (1978):58-76.

A survey of Himes' fiction with an emphasis on a theory of violence which makes him one of the first advocates of the Negro revolution. Some discussion of violence in the detective series (pp. 68-72).

E1481. Himes, Chester A. Autobiography. Vol. I. The Quality of Hurt. NY: Doubleday, 1972. 351pp. Vol. II. My Life of Absurdity. NY: Doubleday, 1976. 391pp. Photographs. With an appendix, "The Works of Chester Himes," Vol. II, pp. 395-398, listing domestic and foreign editions.

An anecdotal narrative which concentrates most fully on his long stay in Europe. The violence of his early years in the United States contrasts vividly with his life in Europe as an expatriate writer. Although it is usually stated that his detective fiction was written to make money and should be distinguished from his non-genre writing, it is clear from his autobiography that the anarchistic Harlem scene draws on his earlier experiences in the mid-west.

E1482. Kane, Patricia and Doris Y. Wilkinson. "Survival Strategies: Black Women in Ollie Miss and Cotton Comes to Harlem." Critique 16:1 (1974): 101-109.

Comparative study of a black woman in rural society (in George Wylie Henderson's Ollie Miss) and in an urban society (in Himes' Cotton.)

E1483. Lacassin, Francis. "Chester Himes ou la fête des fous |Chester Himes or holiday for madmen|." In Lacassin (B201), pp. 294-309.

Lacassin compares Himes' Harlem to the lowest circle in a Dantesque inferno. His essay lingers on the most grotesque, most violent elements in Himes' detective cycle in a survey of the 9 novels in the series.

E1484. Lee, A. Robert. "Hurts, Absurdities and Violence: The Contrary Dimensions of Chester Himes." JAmStud 12 (April 78):99-114.

After presenting an overview of critical attitudes toward Himes, Lee discusses his fiction and autobiographical novels with, on pp. 101-103, a brief consideration of his thrillers. Excellent critical notes that include, on pp. 101-102, a listing of American, French and British editions of his 9 detective novels. A very useful introduction to Himes.

E1485. _____. "Violence Real and Imagined: The World of Chester Himes' Novels." Negro American Literature Forum 10 (1976):13-22.

A cross-over discussion linking his genre and non-genre fiction.

E1486. Lundquist, James. "Search Warrants for the Inner City." In Chester Himes, pp. 106-33. NY: Frederick Ungar, 1976.

A discussion of Himes's detective novels. Lundquist thinks that Himes has extended the genre to the core of social "purpose" and shows what it is to be black in America. Also compares Himes' detectives to Chandler's Marlowe.

E1487. Margolies, Edward. "Chester Himes's Black Comedy: The Genre is the Message." In Margolies (B242), pp. 53-70.

On Himes' biography and its relationship to his writing. His detectives, initially somewhat at odds with the society they are hired to protect, find themselves increasingly at odds with it and, finally, unable to perform.

E1488. _____. "Race and Sex: The Novels of Chester Himes." In his Native Sons: A Critical Study of Twentieth Century Negro American Authors, pp. 87-101. Philadelphia: Lippincott, 1968. Not seen.

E1489. _____. "The Thrillers of Chester Himes." Studies in Black Literature 1 (Summer 1970):1-11. Not seen.

E1490. Margolies, Edward, and David Bakish. "Chester Himes." In Afro-American Fiction, 1853-1976: A Guide to Information Sources, pp. 68-70. Detroit: Gale, 1979.

A listing of secondary material.

E1491. Micha, René. "Les Paroissiens de Chester Himes |Chester Himes' parishioners|." Les Temps modernes 20 (Feb 65):1507-23.

Micha finds that Himes, in his Harlem series, has left the 19th century Dickensian white model, to work with a material that is new and that affects the reader in a way his other fiction does not. Micha sees in the thrillers all the conventions of the hard-boiled série noire but distinguished by Himes' affection for the setting, his characters and their lives.

E1492. Milliken, Stephen F. "The Continental Entertainer, The Detective Novellas, Pinktoes." In his Chester Himes: A Critical Appraisal, pp. 207-69. Columbia: Univ. of Missouri Press, 1976.

An excellent study of Himes' detective fiction and his contributions to the French série noire. Milliken comments on the quality of translations of Himes' novels in French and Spanish, analyzes structural elements, characters, the use of violence, humor and satire, and some stylistic elements. The bibliography of secondary sources does not contain all of the sources cited in the book and other useful secondary material, in both English and French, will be found in the running page notes.

E1493. Nelson, Raymond. "Domestic Fiction: The Detective Fiction of Chester Himes." Virginia Quarterly Review 48:2 (Spring 72):260-76; reprinted in Landrum (B216), pp. 162-73.
Nelson sees Himes' detective novels as something other than potboilers as they recapture the spirit of the Harlem Renaissance of the 1920s and draw on the "folk traditions of Black American culture." They are also classic detective stories which Himes saw as a native American genre significant to blacks for the way it highlights the "most pertinent depravity of American life."

E1494. Reilly, John M. "Chester Himes' Harlem Tough Guys." JPC 9:4 (1976):935-47; reprinted in Filler (B111), pp. 58-69.
A discussion of Himes' "tough-guy novels" as a cycle which is a comment on contemporary Harlem and the "entire American culture."

E1495. Smith, Robert P., Jr. "Chester Himes in the France and the Legacy of the roman policier." CLA Journal 25:1 (Sept 81):18-27.
Examination of Qu'on lui jette la première pierre, the French translation of Himes' prison novel, Cast the First Stone (1953). Smith praises Himes' insight and calls his powers of character delineation "limitless." (GG)

HINTZE, NAOMI

Ref: Hubin 2, ABMI; The Writer 85:11 (Nov 72):18-20 (plotting).

HIRSCHBERG, CORNELIUS

Ref: Hubin 2, TCCMW, CC, ABMI(S).

HITCHENS, DOLORES, and HITCHENS, BERT. See OLSEN, D. B.

HOCH, EDWARD D.

Ref: Hubin 2, TCCMW, EMD, CC, ABMI(S); The Writer 93:5 (May 80):13-15 (plotting short stories).

See also: C127, E2239.

Int: EQMM, Aug 76, p. 130.

E1496. Clark, William J.; Hoch, Edward D.; and Nevins, Francis M., Jr. "Edward D. Hoch: A Checklist." TAD 9 (1976):102-11.
Novels, short fiction and non-fiction by Edward D. Hoch/R. L. Stevens/ Mr. X./Pat MacMahon/Irwin Booth. Also includes film adaptations by Hoch.

E1497. Falk, Bertil. "Mordad i Kristi efterföljd |Murdered in imitation of Christ|." DAST 10:6 (1977):4-13.
Religious murders in the work of the Catholic author, Edward D. Hoch. (MS)

E1498. Hoch, Edward D. "Growing Up with Ellery Queen." TAD 12 (1979):200.
Hoch recounts his discovery and reading of Ellery Queen.

E1499. "Introduction." In The Thefts of Nick Velvet, by Edward D. Hoch, pp. ix-xiii. NY: Mysterious Press, 1978.

E1500. ______. "A Simon Ark Bibliography." TAD 3 (1969/70):248-249.
Some comments by Hoch on his series and the lead character preface a list of the short stories with first publication and reprints (if any).

E1501. Queen, Ellery. "Introduction." In The Spy and the Thief, by Edward D. Hoch, pp. 5-7, 9-10, 101-102. NY: Davis Publications, 1971.

HOCKING, ANNE

Ref: Hubin 2, TCCMW, CC, ABMIS.

HODGSON, WILLIAM HOPE

Ref: Hubin 2, TCCMW, EMD, ABMI(S).

E1502. Christensen, Peter. "William Hope Hodgson's Carnacki the Ghost-Finder." TAD 12 (1979):122-24.
The 9 short stories featuring psychic detective Carnacki are among the few genre stories that allow the possibility of a supernatural explantion for the mysterious events in what is usually thought of as a "rational" genre.

E1503. Koenig, H. C. "William Hope Hodgson, Master of the Weird and Fantastic." Introduction to The House on the Borderland and Other Novels, pp. vii-xi. Sauk City, WI: Arkham House, 1946.
A short biographical and critical introduction to the first American publication of Hodgson's major fiction.

E1504. Moskowitz, Sam. "William Hope Hodgson." Introduction to Out of the Storm, pp. 9-117. West Kingston, R. I.: Donald M. Grant, 1975.
An extensive study of Hodgson's life and writing career, drawing on contemporary reviews, biographical notes in period magazines and other material. Bibliographic references are not given.

E1505. ______. "William Hope Hodgson, 'The Thing Invisible'." MSMM, June 73.
"Gaslight Detective" series (C565).

E1506. Searles, A. Langley. "Bibliography of the Published Books of William Hope Hodgson." In House on the Borderland (Arkham House, 1946), pp. 638-39.

HOLDING, ELIZABETH SANXAY

Ref: Hubin 2, TCCMW, CC, SN, ABMI(S).

See also: UN 4:4 (1951):8-9, 14-15.

HOLDING, JAMES

Ref: TCCMC, CC.

HOLMAN, C. HUGH

Ref: Hubin 2, TCCMW, ABMI(S).

HOLMES, H. H. See BOUCHER, ANTHONY

HOLT, VICTORIA

Ref: Hubin 2, ABMI(S).

E1507. Bowman, Barbara. "Victoria Holt's Gothic Romances: A Structuralist Inquiry." In Fleenor (B113), pp. 69-81.
A study of character types (femme fatale, male friend, ideal father, vague mother, and hero) to relate underlying psychological relationships to formulaic plot conventions. Also describes a plot structure corresponding to three "initiatory" changes in the heroine's character culminating in a break with the parental family that "promises" her maturity and ability to influence actively other characters.

HOLTON, LEONARD

Ref: Hubin 2, TCCMW, EMD, ABMI(S).

E1508. Holton, Leonard. "Father Bredder." In Penzler (B309), pp. 26-35.
Holton distinguishes his priest/detective from Chesterton's Father Brown by emphasizing the spiritual dimension he has tried to give his character. His priest is first a practicing religious and then a detective.

HOMES, GEOFFREY

Ref: Hubin 2, TCCMW, EMD, CC, SN, ABMI.

E1509. Dukeshire, Theodore P. "The Books of Geoffrey Homes." TMF 3:3 (May/June 79):19-21.
A selective survey of Homes' mystery fiction, with a checklist.

HORLER, SYDNEY

Ref: Hubin 2, TCCMW, EMD, CC, ABMI(S).

See also: B253.

E1510. Horler, Sydney. _More Strictly Personal_: Six Months in My Life. London: Rich & Cowan, 1935.

E1511. ______. _Strictly Personal_: An Indiscreet Diary. London: Hutchinson, 1934.
The author's informal and highly opinionated memoirs. After reading these two volumes, it becomes clear why Horler was singled out for special attention in Colin Watson's _Snobbery with Violence_ (B426). (REB)

E1513. Panek, LeRoy L. "Sydney Horler." In Panek (B303), pp. 98-111.
Horler was a prolific writer whom Panek finds so dreadful that he includes him only to fulfill the function of criticism which tells readers "what to avoid." He does, however, fulfill another function of criticism which is to provide some information about relevant subjects and his obvious distaste for Horler does not prevent him from describing his espionnage fiction's principal features.

HORNUNG, ERNEST WILLIAM

Ref: Hubin 2, TCCMW, EMD, CC, ABMI(S).

See also: C334, C606.

HOUGH, STANLEY

Ref: Hubin 2, TCCMW, CC, ABMI(S).

E1514. Barzun, Jacques, and Taylor, Wendell Hertig. "Introduction." In _The Tender Killer_ (U.S. title _The Bronze Perseus_; NY 1959), by Stanley

Hough. "Crime Fiction 1950-1975" (B18).

HOUSEHOLD, GEOFFREY

Ref: Hubin 2, TCCMW, EMD, CC, ABMI(S).

Int: Books and Bookmen 19:4 (January 74):40-42 (photo); PW, 4 Apr 77, pp. 6-7; Jury 11:2 (1982):27-34.

See also: B303.

E1515. Household, Geoffrey. Against the Wind. London: Michael Joseph, 1958; Boston: Atlantic Monthly Press/Little, Brown, 1959. 238pp.

Household's autobiography, covering the years 1922 to roughly 1955. Part III, "Craftsman," is Household's analysis of his writing, describing his literary forebears and discussing in detail the creation of Arabesque, A Rough Shoot, A Time to Kill, The High Place, and Fellow Passenger. Breen 184. (REB/Martin Morse Wooster)

HOWARD, CLARK

Ref: Hubin 2, SN.

Int: EQMM, 2 Dec 81, pp. 102-103; 1 Jan 82, p. 99.

HOWARD, ROBERT E.

Ref: ABMI(S)

See also: E2394.

E1516. Briney, Robert E. "Introduction: From Limehouse to River Street." In Lord of the Dead, by Robert E. Howard, pp. 9-17. West Kingston, R.I.: Donald M. Grant, Publisher, 1981.

Surveys Howard's career, with emphasis on his contributions to the subgenre of the exotic mystery story; gives the publishing history of the stories in this collection, and discusses the strong influence of Sax Rohmer on this part of Howard's work. (REB)

HOWATCH, SUSAN

Ref: Hubin 2, ABMI(S); The Writer 84:12 (Dec 71):11-12 (on the writing of Penmarric).

HOWLAND, SIDNEY

Ref: Lachman, TPP 1:4 (July 78):15-16.

HUBBARD, P. M.

Ref: Hubin 2, TCCMW, CC, ABMI(S).

E1517. Barzun, Jacques, and Taylor, Wendell Hertig. "Introduction." In High Tide (NY, 1970), by P. M. Hubbard. "Crime Fiction 1950-1975" (B18).

HUGGINS, ROY

Ref: Hubin 2; Lachman, TPP 3:4 (July/August 80):20-22.

HUGHES, DOROTHY B(ELLE)

Ref: Hubin 2, TCCMW, EMD, CC, SN, ABMI(S); The Writer 56:9 (Sept 43):259-61; The Writer 60:5 (May 47):177-79.

Int: PW, 13 March 78, pp. 6-7 (photo); New York Times, 31 March 78, C24;

EQMM, July 78, pp. 122-23; Polar 27 (Spring 83), pp. 10-12 (photos).

E1518. "Dossier Dorothy Belle Hughes." Polar 27 (Spring 83):5-19. Photos and cover illustrations.
A mini-dossier on the American writer. Contents: Jean-Pierre Deloux, "Missouri Belle," pp. 4-9 (overview of her fiction); François Guérif and Evelyne Dielbolt, "Entretien avec Dorothy B. Hughes," pp. 10-12 (interview); J.-J. Schleret, "Bibliographie de Dorothy B. Hughes," pp. 13-16; J.-J. Schleret, "Filmographie de Dorothy B. Hughes," pp. 17-19.

E1519. Tuska, Jon. "It's Murder, My Sweet: Dorothy B. Hughes and the Mystery Genre." West Coast Review of Books 5:4 (July 79):70-79. Illus.
Interspersed among reviews of some recent mystery fiction critical books is an appreciation of Hughes' fiction.

HULL, HELEN

Ref: Hubin 2, CC, ABMI(S); The Writer 52:5 (June 39) (on writing novelettes).

See also: B164, B164a.

E1520. Hull, Helen. "How to Write a Mystery Story." In Creative Writing: The Story Form. NY: American Book Co., 1932. Not seen.

HULL, RICHARD

Ref: Hubin 2, TCCMW, EMD, CC, ABMI.

HUME, FERGUS

Ref: Hubin 2, TCCMW, EMD, CC, ABMI(S).

See also: A58, B179.

E1521. Hume, Fergus. "Preface." In The Mystery of a Hansom Cab, pp. 7-9. NY: Dover, 1982. Originally published for the revised edition, 1935; the novel was first published in 1882.
Hume describes the genesis of the novel and its publishing history.

HUNT, E. HOWARD

Ref: Hubin 2, EMD, ABMI(S).

Int: PQ 2:1 (Spring 79):11-13; Philadelphia Bulletin 14 Nov 74 (reprinted in Authors in the News, Vol. I, p. 235; photo).

E1522. Davis, Earle. "Howard Hunt and the Peter Ward-CIA Novels." KQ 10:4 (Fall 78):85-95.
A study of the espionage novels of the prolific Hunt, writer and Watergate conspirator.

E1523. Szulc, Tad. Compulsive Spy: The Strange Career of E. Howard Hunt. NY: Viking Press, 1974. 180pp.
Focuses on Hunt's activities in real life rather than fictional crime. (REB)

E1524. Vidal, Gore. "The Art and Arts of Howard Hunt." NYRB, 13 Dec 73, pp. 6, 8, 10-19; reprinted in Matters of Fact and of Fiction: Essays, 1973-1976, pp. 207-35. NY: Random House, 1977.
Hunt's life and works and matters political, private and public. Some comments on his fiction.

HUNTER, ALAN

Ref: Hubin 2, TCCMW, EMD, CC, ABMI(S).

HUNTER, EVAN. See MCBAIN, ED

HUXLEY, ELSPETH

Ref: Hubin 2, TCCMW, EMD, CC, ABMI(S).

E1525. Barzun, Jacques, and Taylor, Wendell Hertig. "Preface" to The African Poison Murders (New York, 1939), by Elspeth Huxley. In A Book of Prefaces (B17), pp. 67-68.

HYLAND, STANLEY

Ref: Hubin 2, TCCMW, CC, ABMI(S).

IAMS, JACK

Ref: Hubin 2, TCCMW, EMD, CC, ABMI; The Writer 63:5 (May 50):152-55.

IANNUZZI, JOHN N.

Ref: Hubin 2, TCCMW.

ILES, FRANCIS. See BERKELEY, ANTHONY

INNES, HAMMOND

Ref: Hubin 2, TCCMW, ABMI(S).

See also: C541.

INNES, MICHAEL

Ref: Hubin 2, TCCMW, EMD, CC, ABMI(S); Cannon, AHMM 28:9 (Sept 83):74-76.

Int: Jury 4: (1975):44-45 (with photo and checklist); Jury 7:2 (1978):4-12.

See also: B20, B349.

E1526. Barzun, Jacques, and Taylor, Wendell Hertig. "Introduction." In One Man Show (NY, 1952), by Michael Innes. "Crime Fiction 1950-1975" (B18).

E1527. ______. Preface to The Daffodil Affair (New York, 1942), by Michael Innes. In A Book of Prefaces (B17), pp. 69-70.

E1528. Boucher, Anthony. "Introduction." In Hamlet, Revenge! (Gollancz, 197), by Michael Innes. NY: Collier Books, 1962. Reprinted in Boucher (B43), pp. 120-22.

E1529. Innes, Michael. "Death as a Game." Esquire 63 (Jan 65):55-56.
A low-keyed defense of detective stories with the recognition that they may be a bit thin in characterization and carried on plot alone.

E1530. ______. "John Appleby." In Penzler (B309), pp. 9-16.
A superior essay on a detective working within a "society remembered rather than observed." Innes himself is an expatriate Scot who has keenly observed a world into which he was not born. Reflections on the English country-house mysteries as well as a portrait of Appleby.

E1531. Neuhaus, Volker. "Michael Innes: From London Far; Spiel und

Glasperlenspiel im Detektivroman |Michael Innes: from London far; play and 'glass bead game' in the detective novel|." Euphorion 71 (1977):195-206.

Literary essay on the themes in Innes' From London Far (1946). By elucidating the quotes and literary references and their place in the plot of the novel, Neuhaus argues that Innes intended his book to be Literature. The quotes are argued to yield the interpretation that Western civilization has not declined (in the novel the chief criminal reads Spengler's The Decline of the West). Neuhaus' title is itself a literary reference, to the Glasperlenspiel by Herman Hesse. (GG)

E1532. Panek, Leroy. "The Novels of Michael Innes." TAD 16 (1983):116-30. Photo and illustrations.

Panek classifies Innes' novels as detective novels and thrillers and discusses each category with respect to the tradition it draws on and Innes' development. Panek sums up Innes' accomplishments as those of a writer of "literate thrillers" deriving from popular fiction in England between the two world wars.

E1533. Unger, Gunnar. "Inte bara lärd men ocksa bildad |Not merely learned but also cultivated|." Jury 4:3 (1975):44-45.

An essay on J. I. M. Stewart. Photo and checklist. (MS)

IRISH, WILLIAM. See WOOLRICH, CORNELL

JACKMAN, STUART

Ref: Hubin 2, TCCMW, ABMI.

JACKSON, SHIRLEY

Ref: Hubin 2, TCCMW, ABMI(S).

JACOBS, T. C. H.

Ref: Hubin 2, TCCMW, CC, ABMI(S).

JAKES, JOHN

Ref: Hubin 2, ABMI(S).

Int: PQ 3:3 (Fall 80):9-21 (photo; bibliography).

JAMES, P. D.

Ref: Hubin 2, TCCMW, EMD, CC, ABMI(S).

Int: EQMM, Dec 76, pp. 98-99; PW, 5 Jan 76, pp. 8-9; TAD 10 (1977):55-57, 92; NYTRB, 11 Dec 77, p. 55; New York Times, 11 Dec 77, p. 86 (photo); Family Weekly, 24 Sept 78, p. 9; NYTBR, 27 Apr 80, p. 28 (photo); TPP 3:3 (May/June 80):11-12; TLS, 5 June 81, pp. 641-42; San Francisco Chronicle, 16 Aug 81, pp. 10-11; Boston Phoenix, 9 Nov 82, pp. 3, 12; in Cooper-Clark (B75), pp. 14-32 (photo).

See also: C151, E1277.

E1534. Bakerman, Jane S. "Piercing the Closed Circle: The Technique of Point of View in Works by P. D. James." TMF 1:5 (Sept 77):3-15.

An analysis of psychological intensity in James achieved through her exploitation of the closed society/group, with multiple points of view, as it is breached by an outsider.

E1535. Barzun, Jacques, and Taylor, Wendell Hertig. "Introduction." In Cover Her Face (NY, 1962), by P. D. James. "Crime Fiction 1950-1975" (B18).

E1536. Clark, S. L. "Gaudy Night's Legacy: P. D. James An Unsuitable Job for a Woman." TSR 4:1 (Sept 80):1-12.
A careful analysis of James' novel to show that it is a conscious reworking of the themes and plot elements and devices of Sayers' Gaudy Night.

E1537. Harkness, Bruce. "P. D. James." In Benstock (B26), pp. 119-41.
P. D. James keeps alive the tradition of the classic British mystery. She should more properly be compared to Dorothy S. Sayers than to Agatha Christie.

E1537a. Hubly, Erlene. "The Formula Challenged: P. D. James." MFS 29:3 (Autumn 83): 511-21.
James has created a hybrid blend out of romantic, realistic, classical and hard-boiled elements.

E1538. James, P. D. "Introduction." In Crime Times Three, pp. v-viii. NY: Charles Scribner's Sons, 1979.
On detective heros--in particular, Adam Dagliesh--and the conventions of detective fiction.

E1539. Joyner, Nancy J. "P. D. James." In Bargainnier (B16), pp. 109-26. Photo.
Quotes James to refute attribution of the writer as the "successor" to Agatha Christie and cites Sayers and Allingham as James' principal influences. The essay includes a discussion of James' settings, plots and characterization.

E1540. Matz, Kerstin. "När barnen börja skolan fick de tid att skriva |When the children started school they got time to write|." Jury 11:1 (1982):16-23.
The works and lives of P. D. James and Margaret Yorke. (MS)

E1541. Siebenheller, Norma. P. D. James. "Recognition" Series. NY: Ungar, 1981. 154pp. Bibliography and index.
A comprehensive study of James' work with individual chapters on major themes, major characters and style. Reviews: Choice, March 82, p. 921; Library Journal, 1 Dec 81, p. 2317.

E1542. Smyer, Richard I. "P. D. James: Crime and the Human Condition." Clues 3:1 (Spring/Summer 82):49-61.
A survey of James' crime novels to show that detective fiction can deal with some of the concerns of more "serious" fiction. Smyer cites a number of critical studies of detective fiction and provides something of a history of changing fashions in the field.

E1543. White, Diane. "She Attacks Life with Fervor." Boston Globe, 4 June 80, p. 29.
Brief profile of P. D. James. (KLM)

E1544. Winks, Robin. "P. D. James: Murder and Dying." New Republic 175 (1 July 76):31-32; reprinted in Winks (B434), pp. 215-218.
A study of a writer whose books are "realistic portrayals of life and death, among the ill and dying." Winks comments on her work to date and gives biographical detail to show the specialist's knowledge she brings to her writing.

E1545. "With Crime in Mind: P. D. James." BMJ, 9 Aug 80, pp. 442-43.
James' hospital experience and her use of it in her novels.

JAPRISOT, SEBASTIEN

Ref: Hubin 2, TCCMW, CC.

Int: MM 287, Jan 72; Jury 11:3 (1982):20-25 (photo).

See also: C272.

JARRETT, CORA

Ref: Hubin 2, TCCMW, EMD, ABMI(S).

JAY, CHARLOTTE

Ref: Hubin 2, TCCMW, CC.

E1546. Boucher, Anthony. "Introduction." In Arms for Adonis (Collins, 1960), by Charlotte Jay. NY: Collier Books, 1964.

JEFFRIES, RODERIC

Ref: Hubin 2, TCCMW, EMD, CC, SN (as Jeffrey Ashford), ABMI.

JENKINS, GEOFFREY

Ref: Hubin 2, ABMI(S).

E1547. Jenkins, Geoffrey. "The Sea Is My Theme." DAST 11:5 (1978):45-47.
Autobiographical article with photo. (MS)

JENKINS, WILL F. See LEINSTER, MURRAY

JEPSON, SELWYN

Ref: Hubin 2, TCCMW, EMD, CC, ABMI(S); UN 2:1 (1949):4-5, 7 (photo); UN 3:1 (1950):4-5 (photo).

JESSE, F. TENNYSON

Ref: Hubin 2, TCCMW, EMD, CC, ABMI(S).

E1548. Jesse, F. Tennyson. "Foreward" to The Solange Stories, pp. ix-xvi. NY: Macmillan, 1931.
Jesse comments on the pleasure of writing detective stories where "the old rules obtain" and on the pertinency of several of Ronald Knox's rules (C458). She also comments on some of her writing techniques in the Solange short stories.

JOBSON, HAMILTON

Ref: Hubin 2, TCCMW, ABMI(S).

JOENSUU, MATTI

E1549. Kukkola, Timo. "Polisen som blev författare --- Matti Joensuu |The policeman who became an author|." Jury 11:4 (1982):50-56. Translated by Tomas M. Bäck.
Interview with Finnish policeman Matti Joensuu, who is compared with Ed McBain and Joseph Wambaugh. (MS)

JOHNS, VERONICA PARKER

Ref: Hubin 2, EMD, ABMI.

E1550. Boucher, Anthony. "Introduction." In Murder by the Day (Doubleday, 1953), by Veronica Parker Johns. NY: Mercury, n.d.

JOHNSON, E. RICHARD

Ref: Hubin 2, TCCMW, CC, SN, ABMIS.

Int: TMRN 2:6 (Aug 69):12-13.

JOHNSON, RYERSON

Ref: Hubin 2.

Int: Echoes 1:2 (Sept/Oct 82):11-12 (photo).

See also: D430.

JONES, JAMES

Ref: Hubin 2, ABMI(S).

Int: Courier-Journal & Times (Louisville), 15 Sept 74 (rpt. in Authors in the News, p. 255); Miami Herald, 5 Jan 75 (Reprinted in Authors in the News, pp. 251-54; photo).

E1551. Carter, Steven. "Karma and Spiritual Responsibility in James Jones' A Touch of Danger." TAD 13 (1980):230-36. Illustrated.
An analysis of Jones' one detective novel which, in spite of technical achievements, cannot "compete" with his other fiction.

JONES, RAYMOND F.

Ref: ABMIS; UN 5:3 (1952):6-7 (photo).

JURDANT, LOUIS-THOMAS

E1552. Schleret, Jean-Jacques. "Louis-Thomas Jurdant." Enigmatika 9 (Feb 78), pp. 26-29.
Biography, bibliography and short interview with the Belgian novelist (b. 1909).

KAJIYAMA, TOSHIYUKI

E1553. Kajiyama Toshiyuki no Sekai |The world of Toshiyuki Kajiyama|. In Shinpyo-sha series (B367). July 1975. 262pp. (HS/TT)

KALLEN, LUCILLE

Ref: Hubin 2; Cannon, AHMM 28:7 (July 83):63-65.

E1554. Bakerman, Jane S. "C. B. Greenfield: The Metaphor is the Man." TMF 7:6 (Nov/Dec 83):24-29.
Contemporary stories on the intrusion of murder into communities at some distance from "urban rot" and on the restorations of order. Bakerman studies the central character, C. B. Greenfield.

KAMINSKY, STUART

Ref: Hubin 2, SN, ABMIS.

Int: TAD 13 (1980):338-41.

KANE, FRANK

Ref: Hubin 2, TCCMW, CC, SN, ABMIS; UN 2:6 (1950):6-7 (photo); UN 4:11 (1952):6-7, 9 (photo).

KANE, HENRY

Ref: Hubin 2, TCCMW, EMD, CC, SN, ABMI.

KANTOR, MACKINLAY

Ref: Hubin 2, EMD, CC, ABMI(S); UN 1:8 (1948):4-5 (photo).

KASSAK, FRED

Ref: Hubin 2.

Int: MM 281, July 71.

KATZENBACH, JOHN

Int: PW 221:17 (23 Apr 82):8-9 (photo).

KEATING, H. R. F.

Ref: Hubin 2, TCCMW, EMD, CC, ABMI(S).

Int: EQMM, Apr 76, pp. 128-29; Clues 4:2 (Fall/Winter 83):43-65.

See also: B309.

E1555. Clark, Meera T. "Detective Fiction and Social Realism: H. R. F. Keating's India." Clues 2:1 (Spring/Summer 81):1-8.
Indian society seen through the eyes of an insider (Inspector Ghote) in Inspector Ghote Breaks an Egg (Doubleday, 1971).

E1556. Hamilton, Alex. "The Pidgin English Fancier." Manchester Guardian, 24 May 74, p. 12. Interview with Keating whose straight novel The Underside had just been published.
Some detail on India and Inspector Ghote. Photo. (RCSA)

E1557. "H. R. F. Keating." BMJ, 5 July 80, p. 48.
Medical details for his novels are given to Keating by a friendly general practitioner.

E1558. "H. R. F. Keating." DAST 6:6 (1973):32-33.
Brief biography and bibliography. (MS)

E1560. Pettersson, Sven-Ingmar. "H. R. F. Keating." TAD 8 (1975):277-9, 270.
An introduction to Keating's fiction with a checklist of the novels.

E1561. Randall, Rona. "Inspector Ghote Takes a Bow." TMRN 5:4 (n.d. circa 1972):17-20. Photo.
Biographical data on Keating which incorporates interview material.

KEELER, HARRY STEPHEN

Ref: Hubin 2, TCCMW, EMD, CC, ABMI(S).

E1562. Bates, David. "Harry Stephen Keeler." TPP 4:2 (April 81):3-6.
A biography and an admittedly partial listing of the novels.

E1563. Beauchesne, Bernard. "Harry Stephen Keeler: Mystery Writer

Extraordinary." TAD 1 (1967/68):143-49.
Biography and a checklist of his writings. For corrections and additions, see Beauchesne, letters TAD 2 (1968/69):9; 127.

E1564. Cuthbert, Jack. "Another Side of Harry Stephen Keeler." TAD 7 (1973/74):101-108.
Commentary based on letters from Keeler in which he discusses his books and writing.

E1565. Gruber, Frank. "Reminiscences: 1. of Harry Stephen Keeler; 2. on Script-writing Holmes and Bulldog Drummond." TAD 2 (1968/69):55-56.
Brief comments on Gruber's acquaintanceship with Keeler and their correspondence.

E1566. Nevins, Francis M., Jr. "Harry Stephen Keeler's Screwball Circus." TAD 5 (1971/72):209-13.
Keeler's circus series with plot summaries and maps of McWhorter country. For correction, see Nevins, letter TAD 6 (1971/72):121-22.

E1567. ______. "Hick Dick from the Sticks: Harry Stephen Keeler's Quiribus Brown." TAD 7 (1973/74):251-52.
Originally conceived for Esquire, the story featuring Quiribus Brown was rejected by the magazine. The article traces the subsequent fortune and, largely, misfortunes of Keeler in his attempt to write a saleable manuscript.

E1568. ______. "Murder Like Crazy: Harry Stephen Keeler." New Republic, 30 July 77, pp. 25-28.
A survey of Keeler's life and fiction, and of his erratic publishing career. Nevins characterizes vividly both Keeler's methods and eccentric plots.

E1569. ______. "The Wild and Wooly World of Harry Stephen Keeler: Scenes from the Last Act." TAD 3 (1969/70):71-76; reprinted in Challenges in American Culture, edited by Ray B. Browne, Larry Landrum and William K. Bottoroff (Bowling Green, OH: Popular Press, 1970), pp. 251-57. Portrait. Text of a paper presented on November 1, 1969, at the second national meeting of the American Studies Association.
A description of the work of Keeler's last period with a bibliography compiled by Nevins with the assistance of the author's widow. The bibliography is not included in the Popular Press reprint.

E1570. ______. "The Wild and Wooly World of Harry Stephen Keeler." JPC 3 (1970):635-43; 4 (1970/71):410-18; 5 (1971):521-29; and 7 (1973):159-71.
The life and work of the "great wack" of American letters. In his plot summaries of HSK's novels, Nevins discusses both the Arabian Nights and "webwork" structuring of the novels, along with his "random selection" methods of composition.

E1571. ______. "The Worst Legal Mystery in the World." TAD 1 (1967/68): 82-85.
A plot resume of Keeler's The Amazing Web.

E1572. Scott, Art(hur C.). "Dumbfounded in Keelerland." TMF 1:1 (Jan 77): 12-17.
Scott finds the major emphasis in Keeler to be on plot mechanisms and discusses the plots of several of the novels.

E1573. ______. "Further Excursions into the Wacky World of Harry Stephen Keeler." TMF 1:4 (July 77):13-24.
Burning with the passion of the true convert, Scott sent out some Keeler novels to several of his friends for review and he prints their responses interspersed with his commentary. An interesting experiment in literary proselytizing.

E1574. Starrett, Vincent. "The Methods of Mr. Keeler." In Books and Bipeds, pp. 72-73. NY: Argus Books, Inc., 1947.
A very short note on Keeler giving the now oft-repeated story of how HSK picked newspaper clippings at random out of a hat to form his plots. (SAS)

KEENE, CAROLYN

Ref: TCCMW, ABMI(S).

See also: D122, D124.

KEENE, DAY

Ref: Hubin 2, TCCMW, CC, SN, ABMIS.

E1575. Naudon, Jean-François, ed. "Day Keene." Amis du crime 10 (Oct 81). 50pp. Wraps.
Contents: Jean Paul Schweig, "Entretien avec Al James (Day Keene, Jr.)," pp. 3-9 (E1578); "Témoignages |Testimony|," pp. 10-12 (comments by other writers on Keene and his work); J.-P. Schweig, "Day Keene et la politique des auteurs," pp. 13-19 (E1577); J.-P. Schweig, "Seeds of Doubt ou le Day Keene inconnu," pp. 20-22 (E1580); J.-P. Schweig, "Petite Note sur Les Houris de Miami," pp. 23-24 (E1579); "Florilège |Anthology|," pp. 25-30 (quotes from Keene's fiction arranged by category); J.-J. Schleret, J.-F. Naudon and J.-P. Schweig, "Day Keene: Bibliographie," pp. 31-48 (E1576); "Filmographie de Day Keene," pp. 49-50.

E1576. Schleret, Jean-Jacques; Naudon, Jean-François; and Schweig, Jean-Paul. "Day Keene: Bibliographie." Amis du crime 10, pp. 31-48. Illus.
A chronological bibliography of Keene's works listing American, English and French editions and a list of his short stories, a reprinting of the listing in Reilly (A143), pp. 885-86. The novels are annotated with plot summaries. There is also a bibliography of secondary sources, most of which are mentions or short entries in general biographies or studies.

E1577. Schweig, Jean-Paul. "Day Keene et la politique des auteurs |Day Keene and writers' politics|." Amis du crime 10, pp. 12-19.
Discussions of several of Keene's novels with some attempts to provide an overview of the work.

E1578. ______. "Entretien avec Al James." Amis du crime 10, pp. 3-9.
This interview with Keene's son, Al James, contains details on Keene's life, writing, his favorite authors, his relationships with other authors, his MWA association and miscellaneous matters. The interview was transcribed in 1980.

E1579. ______. "Petite note sur Les Houris de Miami |A little note on Murder over Miami|." Amis du crime 10, pp. 23-24.
Schweig discusses Murder over Miami as a pastiche of Keene's earlier work.

E1580. ______. "Seeds of Doubt ou le Day Keene inconnu |Seeds of doubt or the unknown Day Keene|." Amis du crime 10, pp. 20-22.
A discussion of a non-genre novel whose subject is artificial insemination.

KEITH, CARLTON

Ref: Hubin 2, ABMI(S).

E1581. Barzun, Jacques, and Taylor, Wendell Hertig. "Introduction." In The Crayfish Dinner (NY, 1966), by Carlton Keith. "Crime Fiction 1950-1975" (B18).

KELLAND, CLARENCE BUDINGTON

Ref: Hubin 2, TCCMW, CC, ABMI(S).

KELLY, MARY

Ref: Hubin 2, TCCMW, CC, ABMI.

KEMELMAN, HARRY

Ref: Hubin 2, TCCMW, EMD, CC, ABMI(S).

Interviews: PW, 28 Apr 75, pp. 8-9; Pittsburgh Press Roto, 14 Sept 75, p. 30. Fort Lauderdale Sun-Sentinel, 20 Jan 75 (reprinted in Authors in the News, Vol I, p. 265; photo).

E1582. Jennes, Gail. "The Rabbi Small Mysteries Are Harry Kemelman's Sneaky Way of Teaching Judaism." People, 30 Sept-76, pp. 45-46.
Brief personality sketch; 3 photos. (REB)

E1583. Kemelman, Harry. "Introduction" to Nine Mile Walk (NY: G. P. Putnam's Sons, 1967), pp. 9-12; reprinted in Buchloh/Becker 2 (B61), pp. 371-74.
Kemelman describes the origin of the Nicky Welt short stories and the way they led to the writing of the Rabbi Small mysteries.

E1584. Lachman, Marvin. "Religion and Detection: Sunday the Rabbi Met Father Brown." TAD 1 (1967):19-24.
Brief notes on the Chesterton and Kemelman novels featuring Father Brown and Rabbi Small preface a pastiche bringing together the two fictional detectives.

E1585. Schlagel, Libby. "Today the Rabbi Gets Looked At." TAD 16 (1983):101-109.
An assessment of the Rabbi Small series now that it is, according to Mrs. Schlagel, completed.

KENDRICK, BAYNARD H.

Ref: Hubin 2, TCCMW, EMD, CC, ABMI(S); UN 5:3 (1952):4-5 (photo).

E1586. Kendrick, Baynard H. "Duncan Maclain." In Penzler (B309), pp. 127-40.
An autobiography by writer Kendrick describing how he was blinded and his career until he began writing the Duncan Maclain series.

KENNEDY, MILWARD

Ref: Hubin 2, TCCMW, EMD, CC, ABMI.

KENYON, MICHAEL

Ref: Hubin 2, TCCMW, CC, SN, ABMI(S).

E1587. Mesplède, Claude. "Un Auteur anglais retiré en France: Michael Kenyon |An English author In retirement in France: Michael Kenyon|." Enigmatika 20 (Jan 82), pp. 46-48.
Includes a brief survey of his life and work, an interview and a bibliography.

KERSH, GERALD

Ref: Hubin 2, TCCMW, EMD, CC, SN, ABMI(S).

E1588. Lauterbach, Edward S. "Smorgasbord Thriller." TAD 4 (1970/71):165-67. Detective story elements in Kersh's The Secret Masters (Ballantine, 1953; English title The Great Wash, Heinemann, 1953).

KEVERNE, RICHARD

Ref: Hubin 2, TCCMW, CC, ABMI(S)

E1589. Keverne, Richard. "Need It Always Be Murder?" Constable's Quarterly No. 1 (Spring 1931), pp. 23-26.
A well-known author poses this interesting question. (RCSA)

KEYES, EDWARD

Ref: Hubin 2, ABMI.

Int: PW, 5 June 81, p. 6.

KIENZLE, WILLIAM X.

Ref: Hubin 2.

Int: PW, 18 April 80, pp. 6-7 (photo); EQMM, 1 Dec 80, pp. 74-75; DAST 14:1 (1981):56-59.

KIGI, TAKATARO

E1590. Kigi, Takataro. Kigi Takataro Zenshu |The complete works of Takataro Kigi|. Vol. 6. Tokyo: Yomiuri Shinbunsha, 1971. 440pp. Bibliography.
A collection of poems and essays, including 13 important essays and comments on mystery fiction. (HS/TT)

E1591. Tsukada, Yuzo, ed. Hayashi Takashi/Kigi Takataro Sensei Tsuitoshu |Takashi Hayashi/Takataro Kigi: memorial book|. Tokyo: Nippon Kagaku Kyokai, Private Publication, 1970. 350pp. Illustrated. Bibliography.
A volume containing the writer's posthumous works, a report on his funeral and the memorial service, 97 memorial tributes, comments from his family and relatives, and his chronology. (HS/TT)

KINDON, THOMAS

Ref: Hubin 2, CC.

E1592. Barzun, Jacques, and Taylor, Wendell Hertig. "Preface" to Murder in the Moor (New York, 1929), by Thomas Kindon. In A Book of Prefaces (B17), p. 71-72.

KING, C. DALY

Ref: Hubin 2, TCCMW, EMD, CC, ABMI(S).

KING, RUFUS

Ref: Hubin 2, TCCMW, EMD, CC, ABMI(S); UN 3:6 (1951):4-5 (photo).

E1593. Purcell, J. M. "A Note on Rufus King's Series Short Stories." TAD 12 (1979):380.
Comments on and checklists of Rufus King's collected stories from Redbook and both collected and uncollected stories from EQMM. No dates are given for the original publication of the Redbook stories and King refers to but does not list a series of uncollected stories in that magazine.

KIRST, HANS HELLMUT

Ref: Hubin 2, TCCMW, ABMI(S).

E1594. Granholm, Arne. "De ona, de goda och de passiva |The evil, the good and the passive|." Jury 7:2 (1978):48-52.
Analysis of Kirst's novels. (MS)

KITCHIN, C. H. B.

Ref: Hubin 2, TCCMW, EMD, CC, ABMI.

KLINGER, HENRY

Ref: Hubin 2, TCCMW, CC.

KNEBEL, FLETCHER

Hubin 2, ABMI(S).

Int: PW, 14 Aug 81, pp. 6-7; Beacon Journal (Akron), 27 Oct 74 (rpt in Authors in the News, pp. 284-86; photo); Philadelphia Enquirer, 26 Aug 74 (rpt. in Authors in the News, p. 287; photo).

KNIGHT, CLIFFORD

Ref: Hubin 2, ABMI(S); UN 2:1 (1949):10-11 (photo; face not identifiable).

KNOWLAND, HELEN

Ref: Hubin 2.

E1595. Boucher, Anthony. "Introduction." In Baltimore Madame (orig. title: Madame Baltimore; Dodd, Mead, 1939), by Helen Knowland. NY: Mercury, 1954.

KNOX, BILL

Ref: Hubin 2, TCCMW, CC, SN, ABMI(S).

See also: B96.

KNOX, RONALD

Ref: Hubin 2, TCCMW, EMD, CC, ABMI(S)

E1597. Donaldson, Norman. "Ronald Arbuthnott Knox." TAD 7 (1973/74): 235-46.
A biography followed by a survey of the detective fiction. Donaldson shows that Knox was a serious student of the "form" and comments on each of the novels with references to the work's critical reception.

E1598. Kingman, James. "In Defense of Ronald Knox." TAD 11 (1978):299. Illus.

Kingman thinks that Knox's novels have suffered from the high expectations for the fiction written by a man who was exceptional in other pursuits but that they are, nonetheless, "good" if not great detective novels.

E1599. Reynolds, William. "The Detective Novels of Ronald A. Knox." TAD 14 (1981):275-83.
Detailed examinations of Knox's fiction. Reynolds finds Knox's fiction of interest for its plotting and for its reflection of the period in which he wrote. Reynold's notes are useful for their survey of and commentary on the critical literature on Knox's detective fiction.

E1600. Speaight, Robert. "Who Dunits." In his Ronald Knox, the Writer, pp. 32-42. London: Sheed and Ward, 1966. Not seen.

E1601. Waugh, Evelyn. The Life of the Right Reverend Ronald Knox. London: Chapman &B Hall, 1959. As Monsignor Ronald Knox: Fellow of Trinity College, Oxford, and Pronotary Apostolic to His Holiness Pope Pius XII. Boston: Little, Brown, 1959. 358pp.
Biography of the distinguished theologian, pioneer of Sherlockian scholarship, and mystery novelist. (REB)

KOBAYASHI, NOBUHIKO

E1602. Kobayashi Nobuhiko no Sekai |The world of Nobuhiko Kobayashi|. In Shinpyo-sha (B367) series. December 1981. 206pp.

KOGA, SABURO

E1603. Koga, Saburo. Hanzai, Tantei, Jinsei |Crime, detective, life|. Tokyo: Shinshosetsu-sha, 1934. 272p.
The author was one of the earliest important Japanese mystery writers and wrote in the popular "puzzle" mode. A collection of his essays, some of which deal with mystery fiction. (HS/TT)

KOIZUMI, KIMIKO

E1604. Koizumi, Kimiko. Mystery wa Watashi no Kosui |Mystery is my fragrance|. Tokyo: Bunka Shuppan-kyoku, 1980. 285pp.
The author is a female mystery writer and translator of several books by writers who include Craig Rice and P. D. James. This book contains her friendship notes, comments on mystery fiction and tributes to Raymond Chandler, Boileau/Narcejac and other non-Japanese mystery writers. (HS/TT)

KOZAKAI, FUBOKU

E1605. Kozakai Fuboku Zenshu |Complete works of Fuboku Kozakai|. Vols. 8 and 12. Tokyo: Kaizo-sha, 1929-30.
Vol. 8 has essays by Kozakai as well as a short autobiography and excerpts from his diary, while Vol. 12 contains personal notes, letters, chronology and a checklist. (HS/TT)

KRASNER, WILLIAM

Ref: Hubin 2, CC, ABMI(S); Lachman, TPP 1:2 (March 78):11-12.

KREBS, ROLAND

E1606. Hubbard, D. C. "Popular Story Writers: Roland Krebs." Detective Story Magazine 119: 5 (28 June 30):111-112.
Biographical sketch. Series character: Sheik. (RS)

KUROIWA, JUGO

E1607. Ozaki, Hotsuki. Kuroiwa Jugo no Sekai |The world of Jugo Kuroiwa|. Tokyo: Tairyu-sha, 1980. 292pp. Illus. Bibliography.
Jugo Kuroiwa (1924-) is a popular writer of genre fiction with an Osaka setting. Ozaki has written afterwords for Kuroiwa's Complete Works, and for many popular editions. He has revised these afterwords and compiled them into a long essay, emphasizing individual works. With a chronology and a checklist.

KUROIWA, RUIKO

E1608. Ito, Hideo. Kuroiwa Ruiko-den |Biography of Ruiko Kuroiwa|. Tokyo: Kokubun-sha, 1975. Illustrated. Bibliography and index.
The first critical biography based on the author's extensive study of Kuroiwa. With a chronology and a detailed bibliography. (HS/TT)

E1609. ______. Kuroiwa Ruiko Kenkyu |Study on Ruiko Kuroiwa|. Tokyo: Gen'eijo, 1978. 318pp. Bibliography.
An anthology of 21 essays which have appeared separately in magazines. With a chronology and bibliography. (HS/TT)

E1610. ______. Kuroiwa Ruiko: Sono Shosetsu no Subete |Ruiko Kuroiwa: all about his novels|. Tokyo: Togensha, 1971. Revised edition, 1979. 430pp. Illustrated. Bibliography and index.
An annotated bibliography of Kuroiwa's novels. The author summarizes each story, and reprints facsimile pages and illustrations from original editions, as appropriate. (HS/TT)

E1611. Miyoshi, Toru. Mamushi no Shuroku |Shuroku the viper|. Tokyo: Chuo-koronsha, 1977. 418pp.
A critical biography of Kuroiwa, focusing on his career as a journalist. Miyoshi is a mystery writer and includes much material on Kuroiwa's detective fiction. "The Viper" is Kuroiwa's nickname. (HS/TT)

E1612. Oka, Naoki. Ijin Ruiko |The great Ruiko|. Kochi: Tosa Bunka Shiryo Chosa Kenkyu-Kai, 1970. 266pp.
Kuroiwa was born in Kochi Prefecture and there is interesting material on his ancestors and his acquaintances. (HS/TT)

E1613. Ruiko-kai, ed. Kuroiwa Ruiko. Tokyo: Fuso-sha, 1922. 930pp. A memorial publication.
A collection of 41 essays by Kuroiwa, and 77 interviews and tributes by other writers. With a chronology. Although there are few references to Kuroiwa as a mystery writer, the book is essential to an understanding of his biography. (HS/TT)

KUTAK, ROSEMARY

Ref: Hubin 2.

E1614. Boucher, Anthony. "Introduction." In I Am the Cat (Farrar, Rinehart, 1948), by Rosemary Kutak, pp. 5-6. NY: Collier Books, 1965.

KUTTNER, HENRY

Ref: Hubin 2, EMD, CC, SN, ABMI(S).

See also: D316.

E1615. Barzun, Jacques, and Taylor, Wendell Hertig. "Introduction." In Murder of a Wife (New York, 1956), by Henry Kuttner. "Crime Fiction 1950-1975" (B18).

E1616. Boucher, Anthony. "The Mystery Novels of Henry Kuttner." In Henry Kuttner: A Memorial Symposium, edited by Karen Anderson, pp. 12-13. Berkeley, CA: Sevagram Entreprises, 1958. Reprinted in Boucher (B43), pp. 109-10.

Survey and appreciation of Kuttner's mystery novels. Includes the observation that many of Kuttner's science fiction stories had the structure of detective and murder-suspense stories. (REB)

KYD, THOMAS

Ref: Hubin 2, TCCMW, EMD, CC, ABMI; UN 2:3 (1949):10-11, 16.

E1617. Barzun, Jacques, and Taylor, Wendell Hertig. "Preface" to Blood on the Bosom Devine. In A Book of Prefaces (B17), pp. 73-74.

KYLE, DUNCAN

Ref: Hubin 2, SN, ABMI(S).

E1618. Hedman, Iwan. "Blixtvisit av Duncan Kyle |Quick visit by Duncan Kyle|. DAST 11:6 (1978):36-37.

English thriller author Duncan Kyle (John Broxholme) visits Sweden. Photo. (MS)

LA BERN, ARTHUR

Ref: Hubin 2, TCCMW.

LACY, ED

Ref: Hubin 2, TCCMW, EMD, CC, SN, ABMI; The Writer 72:2 (Feb 59):14-16 (plotting and characterization; biography); The Writer 77:4 (April 64):16-17, 46.

LAING, ALEXANDER

Ref: Hubin 2, CC, ABMI(S).

E1619. Lauterbach, Edward. "Horror, Detection and Footnotes." TAD 3 (1969/70):12-13.

A bibliographical description of the two "main" editions of Laing's The Cadaver of Gideon Wyck (1934), and a discussion of the horror and detection motifs and the function of the numerous footnotes in the novel. Lauterbach's own use of footnotes is as profuse as Laing's and in them he compares Laing's novel with H. P. Lovecraft's Weird Shadow over Insmouth (1936).

Landon, Christopher

Ref: Hubin 2, CC, SN.

E1620. Barzun, Jacques, and Taylor, Wendell Hertig. "Introduction." In Stone-Cold Dead in the Market (London, 1955), by Christopher Landon. "Crime Fiction 1950-1975" (B18).

LANDON, HERMAN

Ref: Hubin 2, ABMI.

E1621. Hubbard, D. C. "Popular Story Writers: Herman Landon." Detective Story Magazine 99: 2 (18 Feb 28):11.
Sketchy comments on Landon's life and DSM work. (RS)

LANG, MARIA

Ref: Hubin 2.

E1622. Fredriksson, Karl G. "Potzdonnerwetter, hab' ich das alles getan? eller Pa spaning efter den Lang som flytt |Good heavens, did I do all that? or on the track of the Lang who fled|." Jury 8:1 (79):7-20.
Critical essay on the works of the Swedish author Maria Lang. (MS)

E1623. Gylder, Ragnvi. Hej Maria |Hallo, Maria|! Stockholm: Norstetds, 1976.
A portrait of Maria Lang, a female mystery writer of juveniles in Sweden, and mostly written for her younger fans. (IH)

LANGTON, JANE

Ref: Hubin 2, ABMI(S); Cannon, AHMM 27:12 (Nov 82):60-63.

LATHAM, AARON

Ref: Hubin 2, ABMI(S).

Int: PW, 27 June 77, pp. 12, 14.

LATHEN, EMMA

Ref: Hubin 2, TCCMW, EMD, CC, ABMI(S).

Int: Business Week, 9 May 70, p. 48 ("masked" photograph); DAST 8:3 (75):32-34 (photos); Forbes 120 (1 Dec 77):89 (photo); Wall Street Journal, 6 March 81, pp. 1, 9; Carr (B67), pp. 176-201.

E1624. Bakerman, Jane S. "A View from Wall Street: Social Criticism in the Mystery Novels of Emma Lathen." TAD 9 (1975/76):213-17.
An analysis of the adroit blend of formula writing and social criticism in Lathen's fiction.

E1625. ______. "Women and Wall Street: Portraits of Women in Novels by Emma Lathen." TAD 8 (74/75):36-41.
An examination of female characters whom Bakerman finds to be more "fully drawn" than they usually are in detective novels.

E1626. Barzun, Jacques, and Taylor, Wendell Hertig. "Introduction." In Murder Makes the World Go 'Round (NY, 1966), by Emma Lathen. "Crime Fiction 1950-1976" (B18).

E1627. Bedell, Jeanne F. "Emma Lathen." In Bargainnier (B16), pp. 250-70.
A discussion of the novels written under the Lathen and Dominic pseudonyms, with the majority of the essay devoted to the Lathen novels of intrigue and murder in the business world. Bedell discusses their classical form, the comic and farcical elements and concludes with a

tribute to the reasuring social stability reflected in the dominant "business as usual" motif.

E1628. Brownell, David. "Comic Construction in the Novels of Emma Lathen and R. B. Dominic." TAD 9 (75/76):91-92.
An analysis of the Lathen formula plotting. Brief comments on comic elements, in particular authorial detachment which Brownell sees as essential in comedy but not in tragedy. He thinks the Dominic Washington novels are less successful because of the authors' lack of familiarity with the political scene.

E1629. Cawelti, John. "Emma Lathen: Murder and Sophistication." New Republic 175 (31 July 76):25-27.
An exuberant examination of the "fantasies of sophisticated superiority" by the "best" contemporary American writer of classical detective fiction. Cawelti analyses the structure of the classical mystery and shows how Lathen uses it in her Thatcher series.

E1630. Hall, Max. "The Case of the Wall Street Mysteries." Harvard Magazine 77 (July/August 75):57-59; reprinted in Mount Holyoke Alumnae Quarterly, Winter 77, pp. 15-17.
Although this profile was written while Latsis and Henissart were still shielding their names, both women reveal something of their background and a good deal about how they write their Thatcher series. (KLM)

E1631. Lawrence, Barbara. "Emma Lathen: The Art of Escapist Crime Fiction." Clues 3:2 (Fall/Winter 82):76-82.
Lawrence classifies Lathen's novels as procedurals because they present a "wealth" of information about the business world. Lawrence seems not to understand that in the police procedural, on which she bases her inaccurate classification, it is the detailed accounting of police procedures leading to the solution of the crime which is characteristic of this important contemporary form. The novel has traditionally presented detailed information about social and professional milieus and and this does not ally Lathen's classically structured detective novels with the police procedural as Lawrence mistakenly claims.

E1632. Miller, Margo. "White Collar Life and a Bit of Murder." Boston Globe, 20 Aug 78, pp. Bl, B5. Photos.
Profile of Latsis and Henissart, based on an interview. Research, how the two women work together, their projects.

LATIMER, JONATHAN

Ref: Hubin 2, TCCMW, EMD, CC, SN, ABMI.

Int: Schleret (E1635); McCahery (E1636); The Writer 54:12 (Dec 41):370-72.

E1633. Boucher, Anthony. "Introduction." In The Dead Don't Care (Doubleday, 1938), by Jonathan Latimer. New York: Mercury, n.d.

E1634. DeAndrea, William L. "Introduction." In Headed for a Hearse, by Jonathan Latimer. Gregg Press Mystery Fiction Series (B134).

E1635. "Dossier Jonathan Latimer." Polar 7 (Dec 79), pp. 4-19. Photo and film stills.
Contents: Jean-Pierre Deloux, "Un vieux de la veille |An old fellow from 'yesteryear'|," pp. 4-7 (overview of Latimer's work); Jean-Jacques

Schleret, "Entretien avec Jonathan Latimer," pp. 8-11 (interview); François Guérif, "Jonathan Latimer et le cinéma," pp. 12-19 (filmography and TV-filmography).

E1636. McCahery, Jim (James R.). "Jonathan W. Latimer: An Interview." Megavore 11 (1 Oct 80):16-22. Illustrated. With a bibliography and a filmography.

E1637. ______. "Jonathan Latimer's William Crane." TNSPE 1 (Aug/Sept 78):5-10; 2 (Oct/Nov 78):5-13, 48.
A profile of private eye William Crane in a chronological evaluation of the novels in which he appears.

LAW, JANICE

Ref: Hubin 2, ABMIS: The Writer 93:3 (March 80):17-19.

LAWRENCE, HILDA

Ref: Hubin 2, TCCMW, EMD, SN, ABMI; Cannon, AHMM 28:3 (March 83):66-69; SRL 28 (17 Feb 45):16-18 (on characterization; rpt. in The Writer, July 45, pp. 198-200.)

LAWRENCE, JOHN

E1638. Nevins, Francis M., Jr. "The Marquis of Unremembered Manhunters." Xenophile 21 (Feb 76):3-4.
A description of the pulp stories featuring Lieutenant Martin Marquis and his Broadway Squad, "a parade of thieves, blackmailers, sadists and killers." With a partial checklist of Lawrence's pulp fiction.

LAWRENCE, JOSEPH IVERS

Ref: Argosy, 3 May 30.

LEASOR, JAMES

Ref: Hubin 2, TCCMW, CC.

LEBLANC, MAURICE

Ref: Hubin 2, TCCMW, EMD, CC, ABMI(S).

Int: NL, 27 June 31.

See also: B254.

E1639. Albérès, Francis Marill. Le Dernier des dandies, Arsène Lupin. Etude de mythes |The last of the dandies, Arsène Lupin. a study of myths|. Paris: Nizet, 1979. 148pp.
Written by an academic specialist on Stendhal, this volume bears a seductive title which gives a false idea of what it tries to cover: the thesis of Mme Albérès is as difficult to get hold of as the hero she is dealing with and her book is essentially only a series of analyses, too often psychological, of the greater part of the Lupinian cycle. However, there are 9 pages in Chapter XVI where Leblanc and Lupin are justly compared to the dandies of the 19th century. (Henri Bordillon)

E1640. "Arsène Lupin." Europe, nos. 604-605 (Aug/Sept 79), pp. 3-147.
Much of this issue of Europe is devoted to critical material on Leblanc and Arsène Lupin. The issue contains the following bibliographical material: Jean-Pierre Bouyxou, "Éléments pour une filmographie

lupinienne |Material for a Lupinian filmography|," pp. 131-34; Hervé Dumont, "Théâtro-filmographie d'Arsène Lupin," pp. 135-43; Yves Olivier-Martin, "Bibliographie," pp. 143-47 (secondary material). The articles and essays will be listed separately by author and annotated. The material on Lupin is comparable to the literature on Sherlock Holmes in its interest in the biography of the fictional character.

E1641. "Arsène Lupin jugé par nos contemporains |Arsène Lupin judged by our contemporaries|." Europe, nos. 604-605, pp. 104-109.
Comments by a number of contemporary French writers. A comment by Chesterton from his essay "The Domesticity of Detectives" is also included.

E1642. Baudou, Jacques. "Le Secret de Dan Yack |The secret of Dan Yack|." Europe, nos. 604-605, pp. 110-16.
Speculations on Lupin's activities during World War I.

E1643. Bens, Jacques. "Les Trois Crimes d'Arsène Lupin |The three crimes of Arsène Lupin|." Enigmatika 8, pp. 50-61.
A census of the acquired skills Lupin demonstrates in the cycle with an epilogue in which Bens comments on some problems of identity.

E1644. Bordillon, Henri. "Arsène Lupin, Balthazar et Dorothée." Europe nos. 604-605, pp. 78-83.
A discussion of two characters who do not appear in the Lupinian cycle but who shed light on alternative aspects of Lupin: Dorothée, a feminine alter ego, and Professor Balthazar, a "cruelly lucid anti-hero."

E1645. ______. "Arsène Lupin trahi par le professeur Balthazar |A. L. betrayed by professor Balthazar|." Enigmatika 8, pp. 5-8.
Further discussion of Leblanc's "anti-Lupin." With a note in which Bordillon comments on the betrayal of literary characters in Stark/Westlake by references to their literariness.

E1646. Buissière, François. "Arsène Lupin, homme de lettres |A. L., man of letters|." Europe nos. 571/572 (Nov/Dec 76), pp. 61-71.
A close reading of Leblanc's novel L'Ile aux 30 cercueils |The island of the 30 coffins| in which Buissière situates the novel in the context of three writers: Raymond Roussel, Borges and Gaston Leroux.

E1647. Catogan, Valère. Le Secret des rois de France ou la véritable identité d'Arsène Lupin |The secret of the kings of France or the true identity of Arsène Lupin|. Paris: Editions de Minuit, 1955. 68pp.
This is not a literary study of Lupin but a true essay on Lupinian mythology which explains irrefutably the knowledge that Lupin had of the secret of the hollow needle. This pamphlet which devolves upon pure Lupinian speculation had, in France, a sort of legacy in the famous journal of Lupinian studies (E1679). (JB)

E1648. Colin, Jean-Paul. "Modernisme ou modernité du language lupinien |Modernism or modernity of Lupinian language|?" Europe nos. 604-605, pp. 56-60.
In spite of the classical syntax of Leblanc's style, Colin sees the incursion of the modern world in Lupin's linguistic adaptability to every situation, the absence of long, Balzian descriptions, and the constant identification of contemporary technology in the text. Colin admits that "modern" elements date immediately but finds many examples that

establish Lupin's awareness of his contemporary world.

E1649. Compère, Daniel. "La Méthode du discours |Method of discourse|." Enigmatika 8, pp. 30-35.
Linguistic features of Lupin's language.

E1650. Couegnas, Daniel. "La Vitrine mystérieuse ou l'agence Leblanc et cie |The mysterious showcase or the Leblanc agency ltd.|." Enigmatika 8, pp. 14-24.
A stylistic and thematic study of Leblanc's titles.

E1651. Delbègue, Jean-Paul. "La Baguette lente de la fée Maurice Leblanc |The slow wand of the fairy Maurice Leblanc|." Enigmatika 2, pp. 25-28.
In a materialistic age, Lupin performed feats that appeared to be miraculous but were, in fact, carefully engineered tricks.

E1652. Dinguirard, Jean-Claude. "Fifty Years of Lupinian Studies." Baker Street Miscellanea no. 20 (Dec 79), pp. 3-11. Originally published in Annals (New Series) 18:2 (1972); reprinted in Enigmatika 2, pp. 5-11. Translated from the French by Ann Byerly.
This copiously annotated translation is a history of the Revue des études lupiniennes and of the Société des études lupiniennes written by the journal's editor/publisher. The article includes an annotated listing of the magazine's contents, by issue. An invaluable article since only 20 complete collections are known to exist. An excellent translation of an original that presents great difficulties with its specialized information and vocabulary.

E1653. _____. "Le lecteur en peau de Lupin |The reader in Lupin's skin|." Europe nos. 604-605, pp. 67-77.
A subtle and detailed essay on the nature of reader identification with popular heroes in general, and Lupin in particular.

E1654. _____. "Méfiez-vous des contrefaçons |Beware of counterfeits|." Enigmatika 8, pp. 26-29.
Contradictory and inaccurate details in the cycle which reveal Leblanc's lack of contact with Lupin between approximately 1914 and 1925.

E1655. _____. "La première arrestation d'Arsène Lupin |Arsène Lupin's first arrest|." Enigmatika 2, pp. 21-24.
A hypothetical examination of Lupin's first arrest.

E1656. "Dossier Arsène Lupin (1)." Enigmatika 2 (1976), pp. 1-40.
This issue is devoted to biographical, bibliographical and critical material on Leblanc and Arsène Lupin. Much of this material will be listed separately and annotated. The dossier also includes the following articles which will not be listed separately: Jean-Claude Dinguirard, "Lettre à un conservateur de musée," p. 29 (request for a plaque in the Louvre in memory of Lupin and his contributions to the museum); Jacqueline Bestiault, ed., "Petite Bibliographie Lupinienne," p. 31-38 (secondary material, including articles in Revue des études lupiniennes); Jacques Baudou, "Filmographie Lupinienne," pp. 39-40.

E1657. "Dossier Arsene Lupin (2)." Enigmatika 8 (circa 1978), pp. 1-70.
The contents will be listed separately and annotated with the exception of: "Lupiniana," pp. 69-70 (miscellaneous commentary).

E1658. Dubourg, Maurice. "Arsène Lupin, témoin de son temps et de l'histoire |A. L., witness of his time and of history|." Europe no. 605/605, pp. 12-19.
Events in the Lupin cycle related to historical events.

E1659. Faivre, Jean-Paul. "De Jules Verne en Arsène Lupin, ou le vray mistère de l'Aiguille creuse |From J. Verne to A. L., or the true mystery of 'L'Aiguille Creuse')." In Jules Verne, edited by Pierre-André Touttain, pp. 317-23. Paris: Editions de l'Herne, 1974.
Faivre believes Leblanc's "L'Aiguille creuse" is based on Verne's Face au drapeau (1896). With a bibliography and notes.

E1660. Gayot, Paul. "Arsène Dupin gentleman-cambrioleur |Arsène Dupin gentleman-thief|." Enigmatika 8, pp. 62-67.
Poe's influence on Leblanc.

E1661. ______. "Lupin premier |Lupin (was) first|." Europe no. 604/605, pp. 20-23.
Conventions of detective fiction used first by Leblanc.

E1662. George, François. "Arsène Lupin contre Jacques Lacan." Europe no. 604/605, pp. 117-119.
Lupin's influence on the theory of the "division of the subject" put forth by contemporary French philosopher Jacques Lacan.

E1663. ______. La Loi et le phénomène |Law and Its phenomenon|. Paris: Christian Bourgois, 1978. 216pp. Followed by two stories by Maurice Leblanc: "L'homme à la peau de bique" and "Le cabochon d'émeraude."
Francois George has read and thought about all those who, consciously (J. C. Dinguirard, V. Catogan, F. Lacassin) or not (S. Freud, K. Marx), have traced the gentleman thief. If no scientific approach manages to encompass him, it's because the sciences of "fullness" (emplissement) can't deal with Lupin's "Absence." George proposes a philsophy of the "elusive;" Lupin lends himself naturally to a philosophy of the ALMOST like V. Jankelevitch's, or to a philosophy of the contradictory like negative theology: Arsène Lupin is he who is not. It's a book which tells us what is fascinating and arresting in Lupin, written in a dense and sometimes austere style, but always, like its hero, "elegant, ironic, light." (J. Baudou and Patrick Besnier)

E1664. Guasch, Gérard-Philippe. "Psychanalyse d'un caractère |Psychoanalysis of a personality|." Europe no. 604/605, pp. 119-130.
An attempt to do an in-depth analysis of Arsène Lupin.

E1665. Halte, Jean François; Michel, Raymond; and Petitjean, André. "L'aiguille creuse: l'enjeu idéologique d'un roman policier |the ideological commitment of a detective novel|." Pratiques 11-12 (Nov 76). Not seen.

E1666. Lacassin, Francis. "Arsène Lupin ou du cambriolage comme un service public |A. L. or thieving as a public service|." In Lacassin (B201), Vol. 1, pp. 131-60.
A portrait of Lupin followed by a bibliography of the cycle.

E1667. ______. "L'art de cambrioler l'histoire de France (The art of robbing French history|." Europe no. 604-605, pp. 24-34.
Lupin and French history.

E1668. Laucou, Christian. "Un amour inconnu d'Arsène Lupin |An unknown love

affair of A. L.|." Enigmatika 8, pp. 9-13.
Lupin and Elisabeth d'Andréville.

E1669. "Leblanc on Lupin." Translated by Henry H. Babcock. Introduction by Peter L. Stern. Francestown: privately printed, 1978. Wraps. 9pp. French and English on facing pages.
Letter, dated 30 June 1908 from Leblanc to Edgar Jepson, translator into English of the play Arsène Lupin. Leblanc characterizes Lupin for Jepson and discusses some of the devices he uses in his fiction.

E1670. Lebrun, Michel. Éléments pour une étude comparative des imitateurs, émules et épigones d'Arsène Lupin |Elements for a comparative study of the imitators, rivals and descendents of A. L.|. 2 vols. Société des études lupiniennes, 1971. The Introduction and several entries were excerpted in Europe no 604/605, pp. 93-104.
A masterful work, which is never without the characteristic good humor of its author, on the different characters of gentlemen thieves in detective fiction, seen from the perspective of a Lupinian scholar. In the form of a dictionary which goes from Raffles to the Lone Wolf. (JB)

E1671. Limat, Maurice. "Monsieur Maurice Leblanc, écrivain français |M. Maurice Leblanc, French writer|." Europe no. 604-605, pp. 61-67.
A defense of Leblanc whom Limit sees as a popular writer of genius.

E1672. "Maurice Leblanc - Arsène Leblanc." Catalogue of the Exhibition of the Bibliothèque nationale, April 1947.

E1673. Mirku, Q. "De quelques événements récents analysés à la lumière du secret de l'aiguille creuse |Concerning a few recent events analyzed in light of the secret of the hollow needle|." Enigmatika 2, pp. 13-17.
The fall of General de Gaulle explained in light of the imaginary history of the legendary "hollow needle."

E1674. Olivier-Martin, Yves. "Le bal des voleurs |The thieves' ball|." Europe no. 604-605, pp. 5-9.
An essay on the literary reading public at the time of the publication of the first Lupin novel and some speculations on the reasons for its success. There is an interesting note which describes an 1844 novel (Philibert Audebrand's Les Trois Nuits de Sir Richard Cockerill) that, published a year before Poe's Tales, contains all the conventions to be exploited in the puzzle novel.

E1675. ______. "Esthétique du gentleman cambrioleur |The esthetique of the gentleman thief|." Europe no. 604-605, pp. 35-41.
The tradition of the gentleman thief in France from about 1824-1951.

E1676. Peske, Antoinette, and Marty, Pierre. Les Terribles (E18).
This study, the first important one on the "primitives of the French detective novel," devotes the first section to Maurice Leblanc (pp. 7-63). "The fine literary life" treats the debut of Leblanc in the world of letters, "Lupin the Magnificent" celebrates the gentleman thief, "The Demon of Adventure" recalls that Leblanc also wrote other texts dependent on a mystery or on science fiction and analyses the writer in relationship to his hero. A first stage biography, a first exploration of the Lupinian myth, a completely absorbing work. (JB)

E1677. Raymond, François. "Arsène Lupin et le démon de la répétition |Arsène

Lupin and the demon of repetition|." Europe no. 604/605, pp. 42-50.
An essay on the role of the past inscribed in the text of the present and the chief actor "Lupin" as narrator of his own investigations. Raymond sees Ellery Queen as the literary heir of the Lupin tradition.

E1678. ______. "Suivez le guide |Follow the guide|." Enigmatika 8, pp. 36-49.
Raymond compares Lupin's role to that of Legrand in Poe's "The Gold Bug" and develops the idea of Lupin as an intercessor, a mystifier and a decipherer.

E1679. Revue des études lupiniennes. Organ of the Société des études lupiniennes, founded in 1965 by F. Anquéti-Turet and brought to life by Jean-Claude Dinguirard.
The R.E.L. was published in a very limited printing of five issues in reverse numbering. No. 5 (1967, 24pp.) includes the Lupinian chronology of Perry Hammer, and articles of J. Aboucaya, J. C. Dinguirard, M. Costume, Geo Vadieu. This issue was reprinted for Oulipopians in 1979, then by Jacky Goupil who included it in the first issue of his journal Flagrant Délit No. 1, editions Ponte Mirone, 1980. No. 4 (1968, 26pp.) contains the catalogue of Lupinian pseudonyms and identities of F. Anquéti-Turet and J. K. Karlsberg, "Le butin de Lupin" of M. Hovenot and the essay of Q. Mirku "Quelques remarques sur la structure de l'Aiguille creuse." No. 3 (1969, 32pp.) contains the study (E1643) of Jacques Bens "Les 3 crimes d'Arsène Lupin," and "L'essai d'analyse spectrale du discours lupinien" de J. Aboucaya. No. 2 (1970, 37pp.) includes the study of J. K. Karlsberg "Les amours de Lupin," the bibliography of Leblanc by F. Lacassin, and the article of A. Lebois on the play "Arsène Lupin." No. 1-0 (1970, 61pp.): the two issues were grouped together in a single binding as No. 10. Texts of Geo Vadieu, René Alleau, Q. Mirku, J. Roland de Renéville, Jacques Bens, Maurice Dubourg, Ingmar d'Ainjust, J. J. Couderc, Geoffroy de Beaufort, André Lebois, J. C. Dinguirard, etc. (JB)

E1681. Stéphane, Nelly. "Mais où sont les lupins d'antan |But where are the Lupins of yesteryear|?" Europe No. 604/605, pp. 84-89.
Rambling remarks on detective fiction with some focus on the changing fashion in which the hero-criminal is no longer popular and the subversive aspect of the genre which allows the death of the innocent in the pursuit of the guilty.

E1682. Thomson, H. Douglas. "Maurice Leblanc." In Thomson (B404), pp. 118-21.
A sketchy overview of Leblanc's work. Thomson prefers him in his lighter vein and has particular praise for the Sherlock Holmes pastiches.

E1683. Tourteau, Jean-Jacques. "Les Apports de Maurice Leblanc à la littérature policière |The contributions of M. Leblanc to detective literature|." In Tourteau (B408), pp. 83-96.
Technical contributions of Leblanc including the victim/reader relationships, "locked room" devices and suspense techniques.

E1684. ______. "Maurice Leblanc et Arsène Lupin." In Tourteau (B408), pp. 66-82.
The innovations of Leblanc are in his conception of the "hero-thief" and in his various technical devices that support the character. For analyses of three novels (L'Aiguille creuse, le Bouchon de cristal and l'Echarpe de soie rouge), see pp. 262-75.

E1685. Vadieu, Geo. "Fantomin et Lupinas." Europe No. 590/591 (June/July 1978).
Fantomas and Arsène Lupin.

E1686. Vareille, Jean Claude. Filatures: Itinéraire à travers les cycles de Lupin et Rouletabille |Shadowings: guide to the Lupin-Rouletabille cycles|. Grenoble: Presses Universitaires de Grenoble, 1980. 239pp. Extensive notes with detailed bibliographical references and comments; no index.
The cycles of Lupin and Rouletabille have many other aspects than the sociological. One of the merits of Filatures is to reveal them. Lupin and his junior Rouletabille appear as the heroes of a "labyrinthian pursuit," enter into combat with a monster, conjure up with a single stroke the presence of a feminine ambiguity oscillating between the "woman with the two smiles' and the "lady in black." Therefore one subscribes willingly to one of the essay's conclusions: "The detective novel of the Belle Epoque, which is usually seen as naive, is shown through analysis to be strangely crafty." Written by an academician preoccupied for several years with paraliterature, this is a subtle analysis which very often appeals to the essential; that is to say, to the texts themselves. Note should be taken on a very interesting appendix: "Holmes and Fantomas." (JB and François Raymond)

E1687. ______. "Modernité et tradition." Europe No. 604/605, p. 50-55.
Although Leblanc placed his hero under the "double sign of modernity and actuality," the work incites the reader to dream and a tradition of legend and magic underlies the modern exterior.

E1688. "La Vérité sur Arsène Lupin." Magazine littéraire no. 52 (May 1971).
The following texts are included in this issue: Francis Lacassin, "La vraie vie d'Arsène Lupin |The real life of Arsène Lupin|;" Maurice Leblanc, "Un Début littéraire;" Interview with Claude Leblanc; Bibliography. Also includes a short story of Maurice Leblanc, "L'homme à la peau de bique."(JB)

LE BRETON, AUGUSTE

Ref: Hubin 2, SN.

Int: MM 291, May 72.

LEBRUN, MICHEL

Int: MM 286, Dec 71; Polar 19 (May 81), pp. 9-19 (photos).

E1689. Camara, Caroline. "Michel Lebrun vu par ... Caroline Camara |Michel Lebrun seen by...Caroline Camara|." Polar 19, pp. 20-21.
A personal, affectionate tribute to Lebrun by a friend.

E1690. Deloux, Jean-Paul. "De l'assassinat considéré comme l'un des Beaux-Arts |On murder considered as one of the fine arts|." Polar 19, pp. 4-8.
Lebrun has published 80 books and Deloux discusses his successful exploitation of a 50s suburban milieu, reminiscent of a film made just after or just before W. W. II. He also praises his humor, his skilful plotting and his creation of a vast "fresco" of contemporary France.

E1691. "Dossier Michel Lebrun." Polar 19 (May 1981):3-43. Includes a bibliography and a filmography.

Material appropriate to this bibliography indexed by author and annotated. Contents: Jean-Pierre Deloux, "De l'assassinat considéré comme l'un des Beaux-Arts," pp. 4-8 (E1690); François Guérif and J.-P. Deloux, "Entretien avec Michel Lebrun |Interview|," pp. 9-19 (photos); Caroline Camara, "Michel Lebrun vu par Caroline Camara," pp. 20-21 (E1689); Jacques Baudou, Michel Lebrun and Gilles Marchal, "Bibliographie de Michel Lebrun," pp. 22-25; J. J. Schleret, "Filmographie de Michel Lebrun," pp. 25-31; Michel Lebrun, "Mon Oeil," pp. 33-43 (unpublished short story).

E1692. Lebrun, Michel. Le Crime parfait. Collection Idée fixe. Paris: Julliard, 1973. 114ppp.

"It's stronger than me, I have to kill. But not just anything, not just anybody, not just anyway, not just anytime." In this Oulipopian essay, Michel Lebrun explains his novelist's obsession to realize literarily a perfect crime which would, at the same time, be a true work of art. He drafts an actual theory--and an ethic--of the perfect crime. Let us add that demonstrates in it his sense of humor, black or not! (JB)

E1693. _____. "Pages d'agenda |Pages from a diary|." Europe, no. 571/572 (Nov/Dec 1976):142-44.

Notes on writing and writers.

LE CARRE, JOHN

Ref: Hubin 2, TCCMW, EMD, CC, SN, ABMI(S); Cannon, AHMM 28:6 (June 83):72-73.

Int: NYT Magazine, 8 Sept 74, pp. 55-68; Listener 95 (29 Jan 76):90 (television discussion); NYTBR, 25 Sept 77, pp. 9, 44-45 (photo); PW, 19 Sept 77, pp. 56-8 (photo); NYTBR, 13 March 83, pp. 1, 22.

E1694. Banks, R. Jeff and Harry Dawson. "Le Carré's Spy Novels." TMF 2:5 (Sept/Oct 78):22-25.

A survey of le Carré's spy fiction with a chart identifying such features as the setting, characters and plot highlights and with some brief critical comments.

E1695. Dawson, Harry D. "The Fathers and Sons of John le Carré." TMF 5:3 (May/June 81):15-17.

Dawson points out the "commonplace motif in spy fiction of the parallel between spy/spy-master and father/son relationships" and analyzes it in le Carré's Smiley novels.

E1696. Ericson, Carol. "Judas and Other Spies." Christian Century 98 (25 March 81):318-319.

A comparison of the narrative of betrayal in le Carré's Tinker, Tailor, Soldier, Spy with the Maundy Thursday meeting of Jesus and his twelve apostles.

E1697. Garson, Helen S. "Enter George Smiley: le Carré's Call for the Dead." Clues 3:2 (Fall/Winter 82):93-99.

A portrait of Smiley, who has elements of both the hero and the anti-hero, in his first appearance in Call for the Dead.

E1698. Greenway, H. S. D. "Travels with John le Carré." Newsweek, 10 Oct 77, p. 102.

Report by the newsman who helped le Carré with research on The

Honourable Schoolboy.

E1699. Grella, George. "John le Carré: Murder and Loyalty." New Republic, 31 July 76, pp. 23-25.
The moral dimensions of le Carré's fictional world and the role of George Smiley as a character who provides some sense of a moral center.

E1700. Halperin, John. "Between Two Worlds: The Novels of John le Carré." South Atlantic Quarterly 79:1:17-37.
A Victorian scholar discusses le Carré's work which he compares to Victorian fiction in its creation of a world that is "atmospherically familiar from book to book." He also discusses le Carré's two worlds (past and present, East and West), the deglamorization of espionage and the historical basis of le Carre's stories.

E1701. Johnson, Douglas. "Three Cards of Identity." New Society, 3 Nov 77, pp. 247-48. Not seen.

E1702. Kanfer, Stefan. "The Spy Who Came In for the Gold." Time, 3 Oct 77, pp. 58-60, 67-68, 72. Photos and illustrations.
An overview of le Carré's life and writing career. Some interview material is incorporated into the profile.

E1703. King, Holly Beth. "Child's Play in John le Carré's Tinker, Tailor, Soldier, Spy. Clues 3:2 (Fall/Winter 82):87-92.
Adults' relationships and "secret fears" from the perspective of children or contrasted with children.

E1704. ______. "George Smiley-The Reluctant Hero." Clues 2:1 (Spring/Summer 81):70-76.
Le Carré's "survivor hero," a paradoxical character in a morally ambivalent world.

E1705. le Carré, John. "In England Now." NY Times Magazine, 23 Oct 77, pp. 34-35, 86-87. Photos.
Le Carré remembers his private school days and their effect on him and on other Englishmen.

E1706. ______. "Introduction" to The Spy Who Came in from the Cold (50th Anniversary Edition). NY: Coward, McCann and Geogehan. Not seen.

E1707. McIlvanney, Hugh. "The Secret Life of John le Carré." The Observer Magazine, 6 March 83, pp. 18-22.
Discussion of the author's family background, on the eve of publication of The Little Drummer Girl. (RCSA)

E1707a. Monaghan, David. "John Le (sic) Carré and England: A Spy's-Eye View." In MFS 29:3 (Autumn 83):569-82.
Monaghan discusses le Carré's place in the tradition of British spy fiction. He is, according to Monaghan, both a romantic in the patriotic tradition and a realist who keeps an ironic distance from his narratives to comment on present-day British society.

E1708. Most, Glenn W. "The Hippocratic Smile: John le Carré and the Traditions of the Detective Novel." In Most/Stowe (B264), pp. 341-65.
An apocalyptic view of le Carré's place in the tradition of detective fiction as Most conceives of it: two traditions, the English (in which the

detective is not involved in the crime and effects a "joyous" solution) and the American hard-boiled, in which the distinction between detective and criminal may disappear and whose final enigma-mystery is the detective. Most traces le Carré's debts to these two traditions and concludes with a discussion of A Small Town in Germany where the novel ends with the condemnation of the detective to death. Most sees this as an allegory about the death of the detective novel.

E1709. Nolan, Richard. "The Spy Fiction of John le Carré." Clues 1:2 (Fall/Winter 80): 54-70.
After situating le Carré in the tradition of the "radical" writers of spy fiction, Nolan shows, in a survey of the novels, how le Carré has used them as vehicles for "significant social and political statements." Nolan sees le Carré's two major themes as the "bankruptcy of the Cold War and the illusory status of the spy as hero."

E1710. Panek, LeRoy L. "John LeCarre (sic)." In Panek (B303), pp. 236-57.
Le Carré, according to Panek, uses the spy novel for "wider human purposes" than are usually present in the suspense story. He begins his discussion with a comparison of Cornwall's choice of pseudonym with that of William Le Queux. Panek's analysis is based on a dubious reading of "Le Queux" as a form of the French word "la queue |the tail|."

E1711. Pritchett, V. S. "A Spy Romance." NYRB, 7 Feb 80, pp. 22-24.
Essay/review of Smiley's People.

E1712. Rutherford, Andrew. "The Spy as Hero: le Carré and the Cold War." In The Literature of War: Five Studies in Heroic Virtue, p. 135-56. NY: Barnes and Noble, 1978.
A defense of popular literature and its fantasy day-dreaming a response to needs in all of us. The spy thriller in this category of novels provides us with "forepleasures" as we enter a world we acknowledge as fiction so that it is not likely to "carry implications for real life." Some historical survey of spy fiction (Kipling, Buchan, Maugham) and, finally, a discussion of le Carré who combines "psychological release with radical moral concerns." Character studies of some le Carré protagonists conclude the article.

LEE, MANFRED. See QUEEN, ELLERY

LE FANU, JOSEPH SHERIDAN

Ref: Hubin 2, TCCMW, EMD, CC, ABMI(S).

See also: E2111.

E1713. Bleiler, E. F. "Introduction" to Best Ghost Stories of J. S. Le Fanu, pp. v-xi. NY: Dover Publications, 1964.
A biographical and critical study in which Bleiler discusses Le Fanu's esthetics of the supernatural story and the qualities which set him apart from his contemporaries.

E1714. ______. "Introduction." In Ghost Stories and Mysteries, by J. S. Le Fanu, pp. iv-ix. NY: Dover Publications, 1975.
A general introduction to Le Fanu's short mystery and supernatural fiction between which, as Bleiler points out, there is often very little distinction. Bleiler characterizes Le Fanu's Uncle Silas as the best Victorian mystery although, in general, he finds Le Fanu's mystery novels

to be of lesser quality than his short fiction.

E1715. Bowen, Elizabeth. "Introduction" to Uncle Silas, by J. S. Le Fanu, pp. 7-23. London: The Cresset Press, 1947; reprinted in Collected Impressions (London: Longmans, Green, 1950), pp. 3-17.
Bowen calls Uncle Silas a "romance of terror" and in her laudatory introduction writes with particular insight of the "inner" plot, the psychological mainspring of the novel which is not at all, she feels, damaged by certain inconsistences of the "mechanical" plot line. Bowen points out that this is a striking example of the "country house" novel, and although she does not speak of detection elements, refers several times to elements of mystery which might be seen as characteristic of detective fiction. A fine essay in which there are references to "gothic" traditions and "sensational" literature.

E1716. Browne, Nelson. Sheridan Le Fanu. London: Arthur Barker, 1951. NY: Roy, 1951. 135pp. Bibliography. Index. Breen 185. Not seen. (REB)

E1717. Brownell, David. "Wicked Dreams: The World of Sheridan Le Fanu." TAD 9 (1975/76):191-97.
A biography and a survey of the work with a bibliography crediting as source the New Cambridge Bibliography of English Literature 3. After some comments on the selections in the two anthologies edited by E. F. Bleiler and published by Dover (1964, 1975), Brownell discusses the plots of Le Fanu's novels. He considers Wylder's Hand to be Le Fanu's best novel and there is some discussion of mystery/detection elements in the work.

E1718. Donaldson, Norman. "Introduction." In The Rose and the Key, by J. S. Le Fanu, pp. v-xiii. NY: Dover, 1982.

E1719. ______. "Introduction." In Wylder's Hand, by J. S. Le Fanu. NY: Dover.

E1720. Ellis, Stewart Marsh. "Joseph Sheridan Le Fanu." In Wilkie Collins, Le Fanu and Others, pp. 140-91. London: Constable, 1931.
Biographical and critical study with some comments on his "sensation" novels of death.

E1721. McCormack, W. J. Sheridan Le Fanu and Victorian Ireland. NY: Oxford Univ. Press. 310pp. Bibliography and index.
A biography with critical readings of the fiction. Reviews: TLS, 2 May 80, p. 481; Choice, Oct 80, p. 249.

E1722. Shroyer, Frederick B. "A Critical Survey of Representative Works by Joseph Sheridan LeFanu and of Comments upon His Work." Ph.D. Dissertation. University of Southern California, 1955.
Of particular interest is the chapter on "Representative Suspense Novels of Le Fanu" in which there is some discussion of detection elements.

E1723. ______. "Introduction." In Uncle Silas, by J. S. Le Fanu, pp. v-xiii. NY: Dover, 1966.
Considered to be one of the most knowledgeable specialists on Le Fanu's writings but Shroyer unfortunately published very little in his field.

E1724. Varma, Devendra P. "Musings on the Life and Works of Joseph Sheridan Le Fanu, A Forgotten Creator of Ghosts." Published in a brochure announcing the publication of The Collected Works of J. S. Le Fanu, under

the advisory editorship of Varma, pp. 10-29. Illustrated.
Detection elements are frequently referred to and this is an excellent, albeit hard-to-come-by, introduction to Le Fanu's work.

E1725. Wright, A. B. "Sheridan Le Fanu: Harbinger of the Detective Story." Sherlock Holmes Journal 6:3 (Winter 63):88-89.
On Doyle's possible borrowings from Le Fanu's A Lost Name. DeWaal 4092. Not seen.

LEINSTER, MURRAY

Ref: Hubin 2, ABMI(S).

See also: D367.

E1726. McSherry, Frank D., Jr. "Sidewise in Crime: The Mysteries of Murray Leinster." TAD 16 (1983):375-80, 382-85.
With a partial bibliography of his mystery fiction which was only a small part of his total output. Leinster's most significant contribution, according to McSherry, occurs when he combines the plots of science fiction (for which he is principally known) with the themes of mystery fiction.

E1727. Payne, Ronald. The Last Murray Leinster Interview. Richmond, VA: Waves Press, 1982.
A brief interview, published as a finely printed chapbook, in which Leinster (Will F. Jenkins) discussed his mystery and science fiction writing. (REB)

LEJEUNE, ANTHONY

Ref: Hubin 2, TCCMW, ABMI.

LEM, STANISLAW

Ref: Hubin 2, ABMIS.

See also: E372, E1136.

E1727a. Steiner, T. R. "Stanislaw Lem's Detective Stories: A Genre Extended." MFS 29:3 (Autmn 83):451-62.
Steiner first discusses Lem's essay "On the Criminal Novel" (1960; not seen and apparently not translated into English) to establish Lem's relationship to the genre and his attitudes toward the British classic mystery and the American hard-boiled school. Steiner groups Lem with the postmodernist writers (Robbe-Grillet, Borges) and describes him as "raising" the detective novel by its "inner logic." He also discusses Lem's two detective novels in this informative and informed essay.

LEMARCHAND, ELIZABETH

Ref: Hubin 2, TCCMW, CC, ABMI(S).

LEONARD, CHARLES L. See HEBERDEN, M. V.

LEONARD, ELMORE

Ref: Hubin 2, SN, ABMI(S).

Int: The Detroiter, June 74 (reprinted in Authors in the News, Vol. I, pp. 303-304; photo); PW, 25 Feb 83, pp. 32-33 (photo); TAD 16 (1983):235-40 (photo and bibliography).

E1728. Mitgang, Herbert. "Novelist Discovered after 23 Books." NYT, 29 Oct 83. Photo.
Profile; some interview material.

LE QUEUX, WILLIAM

Ref: Hubin 2, TCCMW, EMD, CC, ABMI(S).

See also: B303.

E1729. Le Queux, William. Things I Know about Kings, Celebrities and Crooks. London: Eveleigh Nash and Grayson, 1923. 320pp. Index. Illus. Not seen. Breen 186. (REB)

E1730. Sladen, N. St. Barbe. The Real Le Queux. London: Nicholson & Watson, 1938. pp. xx,239. Illus.
The life of that flamboyant and today almost forgotten writer of lurid thrillers, William Le Queux. Breen 187. Not seen. (REB)

LEROUX, GASTON

Ref: Hubin 2, TCCMW, EMD, CC, ABMI(S).

See also: E1230, E1686, E2103.

E1731. Baudou, Jacques. "Catacombes-Cristo et le marionnettiste |Catacombs-Cristo and the puppeteer|." Europe no. 626/627 (June/July 81):127-31.
Leroux's Le Roi Mystère is in the lineage of novels that use the thematic material of Dumas' Count of Monte Cristo. Baudou also cites novels by other writers in his essay.

E1732. Bizarre No 1, first series, n.d.
The first issue of this remarkable magazine which included on its editorial committee Jean Ferry, Michel Laclos, Ado Kyrou, Jacques Sternberg, Michael Seldow and Romi gave a stirring tribute to Gaston Leroux. The tribute began with a notice by the editors and continued with a "Proposition pour le petit Larousse |Proposal for the shorter Larousse dictionary|," the reprinting of an interview by Frédéric Lefèvre with Gaston Leroux (E1750), a selection from Leroux's work, an article by Ado Kyrou on "Gaston Leroux et le cinéma," a "prospectus pour la poupée sanglante |prospectus for the bloody doll|--signed by Jean Ferry--a text by A.G. Leroux on Gaston Leroux as the father of his heroes, an evocation of "La Reine de Sabbat" by Jean Rougeul, and especially the famous poèmes en italiques ("poems in italics") by Jean Rougeul composed on famous italicized expressions used by G. Leroux in his novels. Also, a text of G. Leroux's "La mansarde en or" and a comic strip by A.P. Sault and G. Leroux, "Un histoire épouvantable."

E1733. Blin, Frédéric. "'L'épouse du soleil' en marionnettes |'The sun's bride' for puppets|." Europe nos. 626/27, pp. 132-35.
A description of a marionette production of Leroux's novel L'épouse du soleil.

E1734. Les Cahiers sémestriels du cercle Gaston Leroux |The quarterly Cahiers of the Gaston Leroux group|.
The cahiers were initiated in 1977 and published 8 reports until the second quarter of 1981. Their publication was suspended on the death of the son-in-law of Gaston Leroux, Pierre Lépine, who sponsored this publication. The cahiers published numerous rare texts, and some

unpublished material by Leroux, in particular articles on Leroux on Russia, on the Russian-Japanese war, the conquest of Morocco and other subjects. Attention should be drawn to an article on Rouletabille in the 5th issue. (JB)

E1735. Colin, Jean-Paul. "Les moyens linguistiques de l'emphase |Linguistic techniques of exageration|." Europe no. 626/27, pp. 75-81.
Colin cites definitions of emphase to show how imprecisely the term is used and then analyzes a number of stylistic devices in Leroux's work.

E1736. Compère, Daniel. "Dossier Gaston Leroux." Compère Guilléri no. 11.
Compère has devoted the 11th issue of his curious little magazine to Gaston Leroux. He reproduces a fascimile text by Leroux on the novel of adventures and adds to it a relevant study on "Gastox Leroux ou l'art du mystère |G.L. or the art of mystery|." (JB)

E1737. ______. "Une écriture romanesque: le reportage |a novelistic style: reportage|." Europe no. 626/27, pp.38-44.
A study of the various techniques that Compère characterizes as reportage and which he believes give stylistic unity to Leroux's work.

E1738. Costaz, Gilles. "Gaston Leroux reporter." Europe no. 626/27, pp. 45-49.
A biographical study of Leroux's reporting career.

E1739. Couegnas, Daniel. "Structures et thèmes de l'énigme dans Les Aventures de Rouletabille |Puzzle structures and themes in the adventures of Rouletabille|." Europe no. 625/26, pp. 113-26.
A structural, thematic and linguistic study of puzzle elements in Leroux's work.

E1740. Diébolt, Evelyne. "Gaston Leroux et la Russie: du journaliste au romancier |G. L. and Russia: from journalist to novelist|" Europe no. 626/27, pp. 65-69.
How Leroux used the documentation he accumulated in Russia in his novels.

E1741. Dubourg, Maurice. "Gaston Leroux, journaliste parisien, journaliste et parisien |G. L., Parisian journalist, journalist and Parisian|." Europe no. 626/27, pp. 56-65.
How Leroux used autobiographical material in his works.

E1742. Ducos, François. "Leroux et la nouvelle insolite |Leroux and the fantasy short story|." Europe no. 625/26, pp. 70-75.
Ducos describes several stories of Leroux which have a mixture of mysterious, fantastic and frightening elements.

E1743. Furth, Pierre-Pascal. "'Alsace' ou le théâtre de l'Oedipe |'Alsace' or the theater of Oedipus|." Europe no. 625/26, pp. 136-45.
A close reading of Leroux's play Alsace.

E1744. "Gaston Leroux." Europe no. 625/26 (June/July 81):1-165.
A dossier on Leroux's life and works. Individual items will be indexed by author and annotated except for items whose content is described in brackets in the listing of the table of contents. Translations of titles will be given with the individual listings. Contents: Yves Olivier-Martin, "Le phenomène Gaston Leroux," pp. 3-14 (E1756); Madeleine Lépine-Leroux, "Comment une petite fille a vu son père," pp. 15-17 (E1751); Gaston

Leroux, fils, "Mon père, Gaston Leroux," pp. 18-20 (E1752); Gaston Leroux, "La course à l'échafaud," pp. 21-27 (unpublished scenario); Daniel Compère, "Une écriture romanesque: le reportage," pp. 38-45 (E1737); Gilles Costaz, "Gaston Leroux reporter," pp. 45-49 (E1738); Maurice Limat, "Un journaliste de l'irréel," pp. 50-55 (E1753); Maurice Dubourg, "Gaston Leroux, journaliste parisien, journaliste et parisien," pp. 56-65 (E1741); Evelyne Diébolt, "Gaston Leroux et la Russie: du journaliste au romancier," pp. 65-69 (E1740); François Ducos, "Leroux et la nouvelle insolite," pp. 70-75 (E1742); Jean-Paul Colin, "Les moyens linguistiques de l'emphase chez Gaston Leroux," pp. 75-81 (E1735); Francis Lacassin, "A l'ombre des italiques en fleur," pp. 81-87 (E1746); Jacques Goimard, "L'Esthetique du mirobolant: sur un chapitre de 'La Reine du Sabbat,'" pp. 87-96 (E1745); Jean Leclerq, "La reine du Sabbat des mystères," pp. 96-101 (E1749); Jean-Claude Vareille, "Chéri-Bibi, intertextualité, baroque et degré zéro de l'écriture," pp. 102-107 (E1764); Jean-Claude Lamy, "Le fauteuil hanté," pp. 107-12 (E1747); Daniel Couëgnas, "Structures et thèmes de l'énigme dans les Aventures de Rouletabille," pp. 113-27 (E1739); Jacques Baudou, "Catacombes-Cristo et le marionnettiste," pp. 127-31 (E1731); Frédéric Blin, "'L'épouse du soleil' en marionnettes," pp. 132-35 (E1733); Pierre-Pascal Furth, "'Alsace' ou le théâtre de l'Oedipe," pp. 136-45 (E1743); Yves Olivier-Martin, "Gaston Leroux et ses contemporains," pp. 146-50 (E1785); Hervé Dumont, "Téléfilmographie de Gaston Leroux," pp. 150-53 (TV-filmography); Francis Lacassin, "Filmographie de Gaston Leroux," pp. 153-58 (filmography); Yves Olivier-Martin, "Chronologie de Gaston Leroux," pp. 158-65 (chronology of the life and works of G.L.).

E1745. Goimard, Jacques. "L'Esthétique du mirobolant: sur un chapitre de 'La reine du Sabbat' |The esthetics of the astonishing: concerning a chapter of 'La reine du Sabbat'|." Europe no. 625/26, pp. 87-96.
A linguistic/stylistic study of the romantic concept of the "astonishing" in a chapter of a Leroux novel.

E1746. Lacassin, Francis. "A l'ombre des italiques en fleur |In the shade of the flowering italics|." Europe no. 625/26, pp. 81-87.
A stylistic study of Leroux's use of italicized expressions in his fiction.

E1747. Lamy, Jean-Claude. "Le fauteuil hanté |The haunted armchair|." Europe no. 625/26, pp. 107-112.
On Leroux's Le Fauteuil hanté and the French Academy to which Leroux was never elected.

E1748. ______. "Gaston Leroux, le vrai Rouletabille |G. L., the real Rouletabille|." In Leroux, Histoires épouvantables, pp. 11-70. Paris: Nouvelles Editions Baudinière, 1977.
A study of Leroux and his fictional character. Includes a bibliography. (JB)

E1749. Leclercq, Jean. "La reine du Sabbat des mystères |The queen of the Sabbath of mysteries|." Europe no. 625/26, pp. 96-101.
An examination of the two of the many "mysteries" introduced by Leroux in his work.

E1750. Lefèvre, Frédéric. "Une heure avec Gaston Leroux." NL, 2 May 1925; reprinted in Bizarre 1 (E1732).
Interview.

E1751. Lépine-Leroux, Madeleine. "Comment une petite fille a vu son père |How a little girl saw her father|." Europe no. 625/26, pp. 15-17.
Leroux's daughter talks about her memories of her father.

E1752. Leroux, Jean-Gaston. "Mon père, Gaston Leroux." Europe no. 625/26, pp. 18-20.
Leroux's son recounts an anecdote concerning his father.

E1753. Limat, Maurice. "Un journaliste de l'irréel |A journalist of the unreal|." Europe no. 626/627, pp. 50-55.
Leroux as reporter and poet.

E1754. Martina, Daniel. Lectoguide: le mystère de la chambre jaune |Reader's guide: "le mystère de la chambre jaune"|. Paris: Pédagogie moderne, 1977.
This series of reader's guides is designed to introduce adolescents to complete works. Martina analyses the novel, proposes various assignments for the students including interesting comparisons between the book and the play, and a study of Henri Aisner's film version, before devoting a chapter to the theme of the locked room. A scholarly work of good quality. (JB)

E1755. Olivier-Martin, Yves. "Gaston Leroux et ses contemporains |G. L. and his contemporaries|." Europe no. 626-627, pp. 146-50.
Excerpts from critical writings (1909-1927) on Leroux. Interesting for its panoramic view of Leroux by some early critics.

E1756. _____. "Le phénomène Gaston Leroux |The Gaston Leroux phenomenon|." Europe no. 626/627, pp. 3-14.
A discussion of early studies of popular litterature, the audience for popular fiction and attitudes toward genre fiction. There are also some comments on examples of detective fiction that pre-date Poe.

E1757. Peske, Antoinette, and Marty, Pierre. Les Terribles (E18), pp. 65-131.
First important study on Leroux who is presented as a journalist, dramatist, and the creator of Rouletabille and Chéri Bibi. The three chapters are as follows: "Le mystère et le parfum |Mystery and perfume|, "Chéri Bibi" and "L'homme et ses visages |The man and His faces|," a discussion of the other aspects of his work. (JB)

E1758. Robin, Christian. "Le 'vrai' mystère de la chambre jaune |The 'true' mystery of the yellow room|." Europe no. 626/627, pp. 71-91.
Robin sees Leroux's Mystère de la chambre jaune as a pastiche of the detective novel used as a pretext for reflexions on the mystery of writing (écriture).

E1759. Rollin, Jean. "Aujourd'hui Gaston Leroux |Gaston Leroux today|." midi-minuit fantastique 23 (Autumn 70); 24 (Winter 70/71).
This long study, appearing in two issues of a magazine devoted to fantastic films, deals especially with Leroux's great serial stories, hailed as grand tragedies, "hymns to 'mad' love (l'amour fou)." A bibliography and a filmography prepared by Francis Lacassin are included in issue 24. (JB)

E1760. Roudaut, Jean. "Gaston Leroux en relief |Highlighting Gaston Leroux|." Critique 164 (Jan 61):19-36; reprinted in a revised and shortened form in Vogt (B424), Vol. I, pp. 98-116.
Intelligent, serious, but informally written article on the technique, style

and atmosphere in Leroux's novels. Much space is devoted to comparing The Mystery of the Yellow Room to "The Purloined Letter" and Leroux to Poe. (GG)

E1761. Thomson, H. Douglas. "Gaston Leroux." In Thomson (B404), pp. 114-18. Thomson cites other critics who support his belief that The Mystery of the Yellow Room is "by general consent, the greatest masterpiece of French detective fiction." He discusses the technique of this novel but speaks briefly and much less enthusiastically of Leroux's other work.

E1762. Tourteau, Jean-Jacques. "La Méthode de Gaston Leroux |G. Leroux's method|." In Tourteau (B408), pp. 53-65.
The structure and narrative devices in Leroux's "problem-novels."

E1763. ______. "Les Personnages de Gaston Leroux |The characters of G. L.|." in Tourteau (B408), pp. 46-52.
Identification and some discussion of character types (narrator, victim, suspects, detective) in the first two volumes of the Rouletabille series. See also pp. 257-61, for an analysis of Le Parfum de la dame en noir.

E1764. Vareille, Jean-Claude. "Chéri-Bibi, intertextualité, baroque et degré zéro de l'écriture |Chéri-Bibi, intertextuality, the baroque and 0 degrees of writing|." Europe no. 626/627, pp. 102-107.
A densely argued analysis of the function of signs and symbols in Chéri-Bibi, the role of pastiche and irony, and references to a number of modern French experimental writers whose work Vareille tries to relate to Leroux's.

LESLIE, JEAN

Ref: Hubin 2; UN 1:6 (1948):4-5 (photo); UN 2:4 (1949):4-5, 16 (photo).

LEVIN, IRA

Ref: Hubin 2, TCCMW, EMD, CC, ABMI(S).

Int: TMRN 3:1 (Oct 69):9-11 (with checklist); DAST 9:4 (1976):24-26 (photo).

E1765. Ornkloo, Ulf. "Ira Levin." Jury 9:3 (80):41-45.
Brief analysis of Levin's works. (MS)

LEVINSON, RICHARD, and LINK, WILLIAM

Ref: Hubin 2, ABMIS.

Int: EQMM, 11 Feb 80, pp. 93-94.

LEWIN, MICHAEL Z.

Ref: Hubin 2, TCCMW, ABMI(S).

Int: TPP 3:3 (May/June 80):13-14, 16.

LEWIS, CECIL DAY. See BLAKE, NICHOLAS

LEWIS, LANGE

Ref: Hubin 2, CC.

E1766. Barzun, Jacques, and Taylor, Wendell Hertig. Preface to The Birthday Murder (Indianapolis, 1945), by Lange Lewis. In A Book of Prefaces (B17), pp. 75-76.

LEWIS, ROY

Ref: Hubin 2, TCCMW, ABMI.

E1767. Pettersson, Sven-Ingmar. "Deckarporträtt Nr 8." DAST 8:2 (75):16-17.
Life and works of Roy Lewis. (MS)

LIEBERMAN, HERBERT

Ref: Hubin 2, ABMI(S).

Int: PW 221:11 (12 March 82):6-7 (photo).

LINEBARGER, PAUL. See SMITH, CARMICHAEL.

LININGTON, ELIZABETH

Ref: Hubin 2, TCCMW, EMD, CC, ABMI; The Writer 80:3 (March 67):11-13, 46 (on "police-routine" novels).

Int: TAD 13 (80):299-307 (photo; see also John Apostolou letter, TAD 14 (81):383).

E1768. Buhrer, Barbara. "A Look at: Dell Shannon." The Mystery Nook 1:3/4 (5 Sept 75):3-5.
A brief survey of the writer's work, a bibliography listed by by-line (Linington, Egan, Shannon, Blaisell and O'Neill), and some book reviews.

E1769. Lachman, Marvin. "People, Philosophy, Politics and the Policeman: Elizabeth Linington's Luis Mendoza." TPP 5:3 (May/June 83):19-22.
Lachman examines the Mendoza series, whose success he finds difficult to understand given weaknesses in plotting and characterization, and Linington's political and social attitudes as they appear in the novels.

E1770. Shannon, Dell. "Writing the Police-Routine Novel." The Writer 80:3 (March 67):11-13, 46.
On the importance of presenting the police as "good guys," the detectives' private lives, gimmicks and cliches, and plotting. Shannon discusses her own writing methods.

E1771. Waldron, Ann. "Past-Mistress of the Police Procedural." Book World, 1 March 70; reprinted in TMRN 3:5 (June 70):32-34.
Introduction to Linington/Shannon/Egan with comments drawn from an interview with the writer.

LINK, WILLIAM. See LEVINSON, RICHARD

LINKLATER, ERIC

Ref: Hubin 2, ABMI(S); UN 3:10 (1951):12-13 (portrait).

LIPSKY, ELEAZAR

Ref: Hubin 2, ABMI; The Writer 72:5 (May 59):10-13).

LISH, GORDON

Int: PW, 13 May 83, pp. 58-59 (photo).

LITTLE, CONSTANCE and GWYNETH

Ref: Hubin 2, TCCMW, CC; UN 1:5 (1948):10, 15; UN 4:12 (1952):10-11, 16.

LITVINOV, IVY

Ref: Hubin 2, TCCMW, ABMIS.

LOCKRIDGE, FRANCES and RICHARD

Ref: Hubin 2, TCCMW, EMD, CC, SN, ABMI(S); The Writer 74:10 (Oct 61):10-11, 37 (defense of mystery fiction by Richard Lockridge).

Int: TAD 11 (1978):382-93 (Richard Lockridge; photo).

E1772. Banks, R. Jeff. "Mr. & Mrs. North." TAD 9 (75/76):182-83.
A survey of the popular series written by Richard and Frances Lockridge. See R. E. Briney letter, TAD 9:247 for corrections.

E1773. Boucher, Anthony. "Introduction." In Trial by Terror (originally published as Death by Association, Lippincott, 1952), by Richard and Frances Lockridge. NY: Mercury, 1954.

E1774. Filstrup, Jane. "Murder for Two: Richard Lockridge." New Republic, 22 July 78, pp. 35-38.
Frances Lockridge provided plot outlines and Richard Lockridge wrote the novels they published during their career. Filstrup discusses series written in collaboration and titles published after Frances Lockridge's death and but she refers most often to Richard as the "writer." An informative survey of the Lockridge publications.

E1775. Hobel, Kathy. "Checklist: Frances and Richard Lockridge." TMRN 2:5 (June 69):6-7. See also, for corrections and additions: R. E. Briney letter, TMRN 2:6 (Aug 69):14-15; and Adrian Goldstone letter, TMRN 2:6:14.

E1776. Lockridge, Richard. "Mr. & Mrs. North." In Pages: The World of Books, Writers, and Writing, edited by Matthew J. Bruccoli and C. E. Frazer Clark, Jr., Vol I, pp. 254-57. Detroit: Gale, 1976. Not seen.

E1777. ______. "Mr. and Mrs. North." In Penzler (B309), pp. 155-64.
Lockridge describes the genesis of the North series and how he and wife Frances worked together.

LOFTS, NORAH

Ref: Hubin 2, TCCMW, CC, ABMI(S).

LONDON, JACK

Ref: Hubin 2, CC, ABMI(S).

E1778. Walker, Dale L. "Jack London, Sherlock Holmes, and the Agent." Baker Street Journal 20:2 (June 70):79-85. DeWaal 4021. Not seen.

LONG, JULIUS

Ref: Hubin 2, ABMI(S); The Writer 54:3 (March 51):81=84.

LONGMATE, NORMAN

Ref: Hubin 2, CC, ABMI(S).

E1779. Barzun, Jacques, and Taylor, Wendell Hertig. "Introduction." In Strip Death Naked (London, 1959), by Norman Longmate. "Crime Fiction 1950-1975" (B18).

LORAINE, PHILIP

Ref: Hubin 2, TCCMW, CC, ABMIS.

LOVESEY, PETER

Ref: Hubin 2, TCCMW, EMD, CC, ABMI(S); The Writer 88:8 (Aug 75):21-23; Cannon, AHMM 28:11 (Oct 83):61-63.

Int: DAST 11:3 (78):3-5 (photo); EQMM, 2 June 80, pp. 103-4; TAD 14 (81):210-17 (photo; reprinted in Cooper-Clark (B75), pp. 53-65); and in Carr (B67), pp. 258-88.

E1780. Hurt, James. "How Unlike the Home Life of Our Own Dear Queen: The Detective Fiction of Peter Lovesey." In Benstock (B26), pp. 142-58.
A discussion of the novels in Lovesey's Victorian era detective series. Hurt points out that the detail is unlike the foggy atmospherics of the Doyle stories and the background is carefully researched by history buff Lovesey.

LOWNDES, MARIE BELLOC

Ref: Hubin 2, TCCMW, EMD, CC, ABMI(S).

LUCKLESS, JOHN

Int: PW, 21 Aug 78, pp. 6-7 (photo).

LUDLUM, ROBERT

Ref: Hubin 2, TCCMW, ABMI(S).

See also: C237.

Int: Writer's Digest 57 (Sept 77):25-6 (photo; conducted by Lawrence Block); DAST 10:4 (77):22-24 (photo); Mystery 1:3 (June/July 80):8-12 (photos).

E1781. Scura, John. "Spies, spies, everywhere! and cloak-and-dagger man Robert Ludlum believes he made them all up." US, 10 June 80, p. 36-37. Photo.
Brief, superficial article. (REB)

LUSTGARTEN, EDGAR

Ref: Hubin 2, TCCMW, EMD, CC, ABMI(S).

E1782. Schantz, Tom and Enid. "Introduction." In One More Unfortunate (Scribner, 1947), by Edgar Lustgarten. Gregg Press Mystery Fiction Series (B134).

LUTZ, JOHN

Ref: Hubin 2, TCCMW, ABMIS; The Writer 91:8 (Aug 78):16-18 (on the use of technology in mysteries); The Writer 93:7 (July 80):17-18 (Lutz comments on his own work).

Int: TAD 12 (1979):276-79 (photo; with a checklist of Lutz's short stories, compiled by F. M. Nevins, Jr.).

E1783. Nevins, Francis M., Jr. "A Checklist of the Short Stories of John Lutz." TPP 1:3 (May 78):13-15.

LYALL, GAVIN

Ref: Hubin 2, TCCNW, EMD, SN, ABMI(S).

Int: DAST 8:6 (1975):14-17.

E1784. Alexandersson. "Gavin Lyall -- forfattaren som kom bort |Gavin Lyall— the author who got away|." DAST 5:6 (1972):17-19.
Biography and bibliography. (MS)

LYNDS, DENNIS. See COLLINS, MICHAEL

LYON, DANA

Ref: Hubin 2, SN, ABMI; The Writer 58:4 (April 45):106-108; Writer's Digest, 47:10 (Oct 67):45-47, 89-91, 93.

LYONS, ARTHUR

Ref: Hubin 2, SN, ABMI(S).

Int: TPP 3:2 (March/April 80):10-12.

MCBAIN, ED

Ref: Hubin 2, TCCMW, EMD, CC, SN, ABMI(S); Writer's Digest 38:4 (March 58):18-19 (photo).

Int: The Writer 82:4 (April 69): 11-14; Jury 7:4 (1978):25-27; Polar 9 (Feb 80), pp. 8-10; PW, 3 April 81, pp. 6-7 (photo); Mystery 2:1 (Jan 81):14-17, 59; Carr (B67), pp. 1-23; The Sunday Times Magazine (London), 12 June 83, pp. 23-25.

See also: C127.

E1785. Boucher, Anthony. "Introduction." The 87th Precinct (omnibus), by Ed McBain, pp. vi-viii. NY: Simon & Schuster, 1959.

E1786. "Dossier Ed McBain." Polar 9 (Feb 80):3-23.
Interview, bibliography and filmography, a previously unpublished short story, and an essay. Contents: François Guérif, "Editorial," p. 3; Jonathan Farren, "Trop McBain pour être Hunter," pp. 5-7 (E1189)); Jean-François Naudon, "Bibliographie de Evan Hunter et compagnie," pp. 11-17 (chronological bibliography of English and American editions and French translations); Evan Hunter, "Les Aveux (The Confession)," translated by J. P. Gratias, pp. 18-23 (short story); Jean-Jacques Schleret, "Filmographie," pp. 24-29 (filmography with stills).

E1787. Dove, George N. "Ed McBain." In Dove (B96), pp. 196-205.
Dove's treatment of McBain's 87th precinct series is more than the routine, almost perfunctory handling of much of the other material in the book. His concise summary of characters and characterization, and of recurrent and innovative plot devices gives a good sense of McBain's achievement in this long-running series. There is evidence of both intellectual and emotional involvement by Dove in this material and his essay is an excellent introduction to the series.

E1788. The 87th Precinct Report. Ed. by Russell William Hultgren. Vol I, no. 1 (Summer 1983). Quarterly.
Enthusiastically edited fanzine for devotees of Ed McBain and his 87th Precinct novels, though all of McBain's (i.e., Evan Hunter's) criminous writing is given attention. Features articles on McBain and his 87th Precinct characters, interviews, and a "Legwork" column partially

written by Hunter about his upcoming projects. Handsomely printed on gray paper which simulates a real precinct report. (GG)

E1789. Farren, Jonathan. "Trop McBain pour être Hunter |Too much McBain to be Hunter|." Polar 9 (Feb 80), pp. 5-7.
Some biographical material on an author too little known in France and a short discussion of the importance of the City in the 87th precinct novels.

E1790. Holmberg, Bo. "En häpnadsväckande produktivitet |Astounding productivity|." Jury 6:3 (1977):62-65.
The career of Evan Hunter/Ed McBain. (MS)

E1791. Knight, Stephen. "'...a deceptive coolness'--Ed McBain's Police Novels." In Knight (B190), pp. 168-93.
Knight sees the 87th precinct series as "pragmatic liberal humanist fables about crime, the police and the city." Knight analyzes the documentary form of the novels, and the illusion of objective reality, but sees McBain as essentially catering to the reader and reasuring him of the ability of the police to maintain some semblance of security and protection in the urban jungle.

E1792. McBain, Ed. "The 87th Precinct." In Penzler (B309), pp. 87-97.
McBain describes how he was persuaded to change the original ending of The Pusher in which Steve Carella was killed and talks about the 87th precinct family and the City. McBain develops the statement by Mel Brooks that any successful series has two elements: a family and a house.

E1793. Pronzini, Bill. "The 'Mystery' Career of Evan Hunter." TAD 5 (71/72):129-32.
A rapid survey of the work of Hunter/Mcbain with a bibliography of mystery fiction written under several pseudonyms.

E1794. Wallin, Lena, and Wennerlund, Staffan. Ed McBain och polisromnerna om 87:e distriktet |Ed McBain and the novels about the 87th precinct|. Boras: Bibliotekshogskolan, 1976. 42pp.
Biography and study of plots and characters. Checklist of all his fiction. (IH)

MCCABE, CAMERON

Ref: Hubin 2 (as McCabe and as Ernest Borneman).

E1795. McCabe, Cameron. The Face on the Cutting Room Floor (London, 1937). Reprinted in "Gregg Press Mystery Fiction series" (B134).
This reprinting of McCabe's novel is described as "including a dossier on a Vanished Author and a Vanished Book by the Editors of Gregg Press and the author." Not seen.

MCCARRY, CHARLES

Ref: Hubin 2, TCCMW, ABMIS.

MCCLOY, HELEN

Ref: Hubin 2, TCCMW, EMD, CC, SN, ABMI(S); The Writer 60:4 (April 47:136-38.

Int: Sojourner, June 80, pp. 6-7 (photo).

E1796. Boucher, Anthony. "Introduction." In Cue for Murder (Morrow, 1942), by Helen McCloy. NY: Collier Books (F3027), 1965.

E1797. McCloy, Helen. "Whodunits--Still a Step Child." New Republic 133 (31 Oct 55):29.
Reviews but with some comments on the blurring of distinctions between the serious and popular novel and on the increasing internationalism in mystery fiction.

MCCLURE, JAMES

Ref: Hubin 2, TCCMW, EMD, CC, ABMI(S).

Int: DAST 12:4 (1979):26-27 (photo); Jury 8:2 (1979):75-78; Carr (B67), pp. 24-55.

E1798. Dove, George N. "James McClure." In Dove (B96), pp. 230-34.
On the political/social context of McClure's South African procedurals with brief comments on his style which "makes heavier demands upon the reader than do the narratives of most mystery writers." In short, his books are better written.

E1799. Isaac, Fred. "Black and White and Dead:James McClure's South Africa." TMF 6:4 (July/Aug 82):12-18.
A brief survey of ethnic detectives and a study of social and political elements in McClure's South African procedurals.

E1800. Wall, Donald. "Apartheid in the Novels of James McClure." TAD 10 (1977):348-51.
Discussions of the "complicated" plots of McClure's first three procedurals. With a short bibliography of books on South Africa and apartheid.

E1801. White, Jean M. "Wahlöö/Sjöwall and James McClure: Murder and Politics." New Republic, 31 July 76, pp. 27-29.
A superficial treatment of two important procedural series.

MCCOY, HORACE

Ref: Hubin 2, TCCMW,SN, ABMI.

See also: E330.

E1802. Auricoste, Véronique. "Horace Mac Coy (sic)." Europe 571/572 (Nov/Dec 76), pp. 125-31.
An analysis of the principal characters in McCoy's fiction, their historical context and the different ways they deal with conflict and crisis. Auricoste finds McCoy's treatment of women to be of particular interest: they are seen as real participants in the action and not relegated, as they often are in detective fiction, to secondary roles.

E1803. Richmond, Lee J. "A Time to Mourn and a Time to Dance: Horace McCoy's They Shoot Horses, Don't They?" Twentieth Century Literature 17:2 (April 71):91-100.
A study of McCoy's novel as "indisputably the best example of absurdist existentialism in American fiction."

E1804. Sturak, Thomas. "A Foreword to 'Death in Hollywood.'" In Adams, MDA 1973 (B3), pp. 16-19.

These prefatory remarks to the first publication of McCoy's story "Death in Hollywood" focus on McCoy's style and his use of descriptive elements ressembling Chandler's before Chandler's first publications. Sturak also provides biographical material on McCoy's early, unsuccessful Hollywood years.

E1805. ______. "Horace McCoy, Captain Shaw and the Black Mask." In Adams, MDA 1972 (B2), pp. 139-58. Photos.
A detailed discussion of McCoy's Black Mask fiction that includes a careful depiction of Shaw's editorial contributions to McCoy's extensive revisions. Perhaps the most thorough examination in print of Shaw's editorship and a substantial rebuttal of the position held by some critics that Shaw made no significant contribution to the fiction he selected and published.

E1806. ______. "Horace McCoy's Objective Lyricism." In Madden (B137-62), pp. 137-62.
Much of this fine essay on McCoy's fiction is devoted to They Shoot Horses, Don't They? but the first third is a survey of his other novels including comments on the original version of No Pockets in a Shroud which was only published, in this country, in expurgated form.

E1807. ______. "The Life and Writings of Horace McCoy, 1897-1955." Unpublished dissertation. University of California, 1966. 609pp. DAI 27/12-A, p. 4266.
Sturak had access to letters, drafts and unpublished manuscripts. Extensive bibliography.

E1808. Winchell, Mark Royden. Horace McCoy. Western Writers Series: Number 51. Boise, Idaho: Boise State University, 1982. 50pp. Wraps. Selective, annotated bibliography.
A short biography and biocritical analyses of McCoy's novels. Winchell does not discuss McCoy's short fiction and his career in the pulps and is mainly interested in plot and character in the longer fiction. The amputation of McCoy's fiction from its pulp roots seems to vitiate much of its strength and the reader misses the rich detail to be found in Sturak's work on McCoy.

MCCULLEY, JOHNSTON

Ref: Hubin 2, ABMI(S).

See also: D363.

E1809. "The Men Who Make the Argosy." Argosy 224:3 (3 Oct 31):427.
Sketchy biographical material, citing hobbies and work habits. Portrait. (RS)

MCCURTIN, PETER

Ref: Hubin 2, SN.

E1810. Banks, R. Jeff. "Carmody: Sagebrush Detective." TAD 8 (1974/75): 42-43.
Detective fiction elements in two paperback western originals.

MCCUTCHAN, PHILIP

Ref: Hubin 2, TCCMW, CC, ABMI(S).

MCDONALD, GREGORY

Ref: Hubin 2, SN, ABMI.

Int: American Way (Aug 78):48-51 (photos); TAD 12 (79):134-135 (photo); Washington Post, 11 Oct 80, FI- (photo); PW, 18 DDec 81, pp. 14-16 (photo); in Carr (B67), pp. 104-42; Polar 27 (Spring 83):163-71 (photo).

E1811. Deloux, Jean-Pierre. "Super MC: Star du polar." Polar 27 (Spring 83):158-62. Two photos.
Brief comments on the Fletch series with some brief excerpts (translated into French) to demonstrate the McDonald "touch."

MACDONALD, JOHN D.

Ref: Hubin 2, TCCMW, EMD, CC, SN, ABMI(S); Writer's Digest 42:12 (Dec 62):15-18 (writer/editor relationships); Writer's Digest 49:6 (June 69):58-61, 96 (on creativity and writing); The Writer 77:9 (Sept 64):14-16, 45 (on Travis McGee; JDM biography); The Writer 87:1 (Jan 74):13-15, 44 (use of description).

Int: NYTBR, 10 March 74, p. 37; Esquire 84 (Aug 75):68, 136-137; NYTBR, 15 May 77, p. 42; PQ 4:1 (Spring 81):5-9 (with a checklist of his paperback originals, pp. 10, 12).

See also: B1, B239, C127, C334, C7747.

E1812. Abrahams, Etta C. "Cops and Detectives." Clues 1:1 (Spring 80):96-98.
JDM's "fully developed" police characters as seen in Sheriff Hyzer of The Long Lavender Look. Comment by JDM in JDM Bibliophile 24, pp. 8-9. (James R. McCahery)

E1813. ______. "Travis McGee: The Thinking Man's Robin Hood." In Dimensions in Popular Culture, edited by Russel B. Nye, pp. 236-46. Bowling Green, OH: Popular Press, 1972.
McGee as an observer of and commenter on society and a righter of wrongs.

E1814. Barzun, Jacques, and Taylor, Wendell Hertig. "Introduction." In Dead Low Tide (NY, 1953), by John D. MacDonald. "Crime Fiction 1950-1975" (B18).

E1815. Benjamin, David A. "John D. MacDonald and the Life and Death of the Mythic Hero." Ph. D. Dissertation. Harvard, 1977. No other information available.

E1816. ______. "Key Witness: John D. MacDonald." New Republic 173 (26 July 75):28-31.
Primarily on the Travis McGee series in which the previously "unknown" MacDonald found a public identity with a best-selling hero. Benjamin sees a certain ennui creeping into recent McGee novels.

E1817. Campbell, Frank D., Jr. John D. Campbell and the Colorful World of Travis McGee. The Milford Series: Popular Writers of Today, Volume 5. San Bernardino, CA: R. Reginald/The Borgo Press, 1977. 63pp. Wraps.
Plot summaries of the first sixteen Travis McGee novels, presented in a jocular and sometimes smart-alecky style, with a minimal amount of generalized criticism and value judgments that read like one-liners. Not to be taken seriously. Breen 188. (REB)

E1818. Cleveland, Carol. "Travis McGee, the Feminists' Friend." TAD 16 (1983):407-413.
A counter-argument to the view of McGee as a writer who "wallows in masochism."

E1819. Cook, Wister. "John D. MacDonald: A Little Ecology Goes a Long Way." Clues 1:1 (Spring 80):57-62.
The humanity of Travis McGee and his ecological concerns. (James R. McCahery)

E1820. Doulis, Thomas. "John D. MacDonald: The Liabilities of Professionalism." JPC 10 (1976):38-53; reprinted in Filler (B111), Vol. 2, pp. 170-86.
Discussions of novels by JDM which Doulis thinks reflect intensely personal concerns and yet contain major structural flaws.There is, in his introduction, the statement that the Travis McGee stories represent JDM's "foremost achievement as a craftsman" and that McGee rescued JDM from the "bumbling heroes that populated his earlier fiction." A rambling and disjointed essay that reads like two separate articles combined into one unwieldy discussion.

E1821. Geherin, David. John D. MacDonald. NY: Frederick Ungar, 1982. 202pp. Bibliography and index. Simultaneous hardback and paperback publication.
Not seen but described in Choice (Oct 82, p. 265) as putting an "emphasis on pre-Travis McGee but (with) a four-chapter summary of McGee's adventures." Review: WLB, Sept 82, p. 62.

E1822. Grimes, Larry. "The Reluctant Hero: Reflections on Vocations and Heroism in the Travis McGee Novels of John D. MacDonald." Clues 1:1 (Spring 80):103-108.
In the early novels, McGee is an archaic hero seeking order in a "vocational formula;" in the later novels, this order is threatened and McGee moves toward a world of "profane adventure" where he is less at home and uncertain of his role. Comment by JDM in JDM Bibliophile 24 (July 79):9-11.

E1823. Hirschberg, Edgar W. "John D. MacDonald as Social Critic." Clues 1:1 (Spring 80):129-34.
On MacDonald's penchant for speculative observations in his fiction.

E1824. Holtsmark, Erling B. "Travis McGee as Traditional Hero." Clues 1:1 (Spring 80:99-102.
McGee as a modern descendent of the classical dragon-slayer, rescuer of maidens and finder of treasure. Comment by JDM in JDM Bibliophile 24 (July 79):11-12.

E1825. Hoyt, Charles Alva. "The Damned: Good Intentions: The Tough Guy as Hero and Villain." In Madden (B239), pp. 224-30.
A "mechanistic" Hemingway imitation, but useful as an illustration of a confrontation of the tough guy as villain and hero.

E1826. The JDM Bibliophile.
An amateur journal devoted to the life and works of John D. MacDonald. The oldest continually published such magazine devoted to a living American author. First published in March 1965 in mimeograph form by Len & June Moffatt of Downey, California in an attempt to compile a checklist of the author's writings, reader interest forced its expansion to

a widespread, on-going fan magazine with as many as 34 pages to an issue. Included excellent critical essays, book reviews, and lengthy letters to the editor. After 22 issues, 4 Bulletins and a 46 page Master Checklist (E1838), the Moffatts, after May 1978, turned the publication of the journal over to the University of South Florida, Tampa, FL 33620, where it continues to be published on a semi-annual basis, Ed Hirschberg, editor. $5 annually. Includes frequent contributions from JDM as well as reprints of his early writing previously published only in newspapers or other difficult-to-find sources. See also Shine (E1848, E1849). (Jean & Walter Shine)

E1827. "John D. MacDonald and the Critics." JDM Bibliophile 24 (July 79):4-12. MacDonald comments on papers on his work read at a conference at the University of South Florida on Nov. 18, 1978. The papers were subsequently published in Clues 1:1 (Spring 1980) and the comments will be cited in this bibliography with the articles that prompted them.

E1828. Kelly, R. Gordon. "The Precarious World of John D. MacDonald." In Landrum (B216), pp. 149-61.
A discussion of The Executioners (1957) with the Flitcraft episode in The Maltese Falcon as point of reference.

E1829. Kennedy, Veronica S. M. "The Prophet Before the Fact: A Note on John D. MacDonald's The End of the Night." TAD 7 (1973/74):41.
The End of the Night (Simon & Schuster, 1960) as prophetic of the Manson murders, or life imitating art.

E1830. MacDonald, John D. "Author's Foreword." In The Good Old Stuff, pp. xv-xviii. NY: Harper and Row, 1982.
How stories were selected for this collection, with recollections of his pulp magazine work. (RS)

E1831. ______. "Introduction." To The Arbor House Treasury of Mystery and Suspense. NY: Arbor House, circa 1980. Not seen.

E1832. ______. "John D. Macdonald vs. Doc Savage." Bronze Shadows No. 3 (Feb 66):3-4.
Short discussion of MacDonald's apprenticeship in pulp writing and how he declined to write a Doc Savage novel. (RS)

E1833. ______. "Pulp Perspective Plus." Bronze Shadows No. 7 (Nov 66):3-6. Writer's view of working in the pulps. Includes checklist of his fiction appearing in Doc Savage and The Shadow, plus list of pseudonyms. (RS)

E1834. Mallory, Margaret I. "John D. MacDonald's Criminal Heroes." JPC 1:1 (Winter 77):57-74.
A detailed discussion of illegal acts performed by the protagonists in five of MacDonald's novels: The Soft Touch, Cancel All Our Vows, The Deceivers, Clemmie and A Key to the Suite.

E1835. Marotta, Joseph. "The Disorderly World of John D. MacDonald: or Travis McGee Meets Thomas Pynchon." Clues 3:1 (Spring/Summer 82):105-110.
An analysis of The Green Ripper and the contemporary themes of apocalypse and dissolution as they are reflected in a popular novel.

E1836. "Master of Suspense." MD Medical News-Magazine 23:11 (Nov 78):117-22. Photographs.

Biography and career profile of the "Dean of Crime Fiction" with interview material.

E1837. Moffatt, Len J. "John D. MacDonald: The Writer's Writer." TMRN 1:6 (Aug 68):11-14.
A tribute to the writer followed by a checklist of hardcover and paperback works.

E1838. Moffatt, Len & June; and William J. Clark. The JDM Master Checklist. A Bibliography of the Published Writings of John D. MacDonald. Downey, CA: Moffatt House, Feb 1969. xvii, 42pp.
This was the first comprehensive bibliography of MacDonald's writings, including both book and magazine work. It has extensive data on pseudonyms, wordage, foreign editions, etc. Until the appearance of the Shine bibliography (E1848) more than 10 years later, this was the primary source of information about McDonald's published work. (REB)

E1839. Moran, Peggy. "McGee's Girls." Clues 1:1 (Spring 80):82-88.
An analysis of the 130 women in the first 17 McGee novels. (James R. McCahery)

E1840. Nelson, John Wiley. "Travis McGee, Tarnished Knight in Modern Armor." In Your God is Alive and Well and Appearing in Popular Culture, pp. 170-92. Philadephia: Westminster Press, 1976. Not seen.

E1841. Nevins, Francis M., Jr. "Introduction." To The Good Old Stuff, pp. ix-xiii. NY: Harper and Row, 1982.
Brief biographical sketch of MacDonald's life and work in pulps and paperbacks. (RS)

E1842. ______. "The Making of a Tale-Spinner: JDM's Early Pulp Mystery Stories." Clues 1:1 (Spring 80):89-95.
The years 1946-52. JDM's apprenticeship at one and two cents a word. Comment by JDM in JDM Bibliophile 24, pp. 7-8. (James R. McCahery)

E1843. Peek, George S. "Beast Imagery and Stereotypes in the Novels of John D. MacDonald." Clues 2:1 (Spring/Summer 81):91-97.
JDM's stereotyped characters, "the very stuff of modern America," and his use of animal imagery in the creation of his stereotypes.

E1844. ______. "Conquering the Stereotypes: On Reading the Novels of John D. MacDonald." TAD 13 (80):90-93. Illus.
Female characters and stereotypes in A Purple Place for Dying, Bright Orange for the Shroud and The Dreadful Lemon Sky.

E1845. Pratt, Allan. "The Chronology of the Travis McGee Novels." TAD 13 (80):83-89.
Dating the McGee novels on the basis of internal evidence and the assumption that no action occurs later than the copyright date.

E1846. Raban, Jonathan. "Suicide of an Eden." Sunday Times (London), 20 Feb 83, pp. 33-34.
Description of a visit to Florida, its new developments, its waterside life. It includes a visit to and discussion of local peculiarities with author John D. MacDonald. (RCSA)

E1847. Sanders, Joe. "Science Fiction and Detection Fiction: The Case of John D. MacDonald." Science-Fiction Studies 2:157-65. Not seen.

E1848. Shine, Walter and Jean. A Bibliography of the Published Works of John D. MacDonald with Selected Biographical Materials and Critical Essays. Gainesville, FL: Patrons of the Libraries, University of Florida, 1980. ix, 109pp. Photographs. Indices. Spiral bound. Edition limited to 500 copies.

In this thorough and carefully organized compilation, all of MacDonald's published work through the end of 1980 is listed both chronologically and alphabetically. Approximate word counts or page counts are given, and the non-fiction, science fiction and sports stories are so indicated. Magazine and book reprints and some reissues are listed as well as translations into 18 languages. Secondary materials--biographical and critical articles and book reviews--are also listed. The covers of all U. S. first editions are illustrated, as well as selected British editions, translations, and covers of magazines and anthologies featuring MacDonald's work. There is also a brief biographical article reprinted from MD magazine. Review: PBSA 77:1 (1983):105-107. (REB)

E1849. ______. An Index to the JDM Bibliophile. An Amateur Publication Devoted to the Life & Work of John D. MacDonald. Issues No. 1 through 30, March 1965---July 1982. Privately published, 1982. 33pp. Mimeographed and stapled.

An index by title, subject and author. Letters to the editor are indexed separately by name. Given the scarcity of and difficulty of access to complete runs of the fanzine, this is an invaluable index. The index demonstrates the nature and range of the published material and is an indication of the Bibliophile's value as a resource for research on MacDonald and his work.

E1850. Tolley, Michael J. "Color Him Quixote: MacDonald's Strategy in the Early McGee Novels." TAD 10 (77):6-13.

Travis McGee as a modern-day Quixote. A portrait of McGee with comments on his attitudes toward women, JDM's debt to Raymond Chandler and comic elements in the novels.

MACDONALD, PHILIP

Ref: Hubin 2, TCCMW, EMD, CC, ABMI(S).

See also: B6, B404.

E1851. Boucher, Anthony. "Introduction." In Murder Gone Mad (Collins, 1931), by Philip MacDonald. NY: Mercury, n.d.

E1852. Donaldson, Norman. "Philip MacDonald: Gethryn and Others." TAD 3 (1969/70):6-11.

Comments on MacDonald's detective fiction with particular emphasis on the Colonel Gethryn saga. The checklist of the fiction includes both American and English publication data. Additions: Donaldson letter, TAD 3:95; Francis M. Nevins, Jr. letter, TAD 3:137.

MACDONALD, ROSS

Ref: Hubin 2, TCCMW, EMD, CC, SN (as Kenneth Millar), ABMI(S).

Int: NYTBR, 1 June 69, pp. 2, 19 (photo); Esquire, June 72, pp. 148-49, 188 (photo); in Adams, MDA 1973 (B3), pp. 53-58 (reprinted in Macdonald (E1888), pp. 87-93); JPC 7 (1973):213-22 (reprinted in Landrum (B216), pp.

182-92); Tamarack Review no. 62 (1974):66-85; South Dakota Review 13:3 (1975):83-84 (reprinted in Macdonald (E1888), pp. 61-62); EQMM, Jan 76, pp. 137-38; Gallery, Jan 76, pp. 84-90; The National Observer, 31 July 76, p. 17; Jury 8:2 (79):9-18; and in Cooper-Clark (B75), pp. 83-100 (photo).

See also: B1, B79, B216, B242, B306, B310, B371, C278, C369.

E1854. Barnes, Daniel R. "'I'm the Eye': Archer as Narrator in the Novels of Ross Macdonald." In Adams, MDA 1972 (B2), pp. 178-90.
A study of first-person narration in Macdonald's fiction. Barnes recognizes that Archer is not an objective narrator but both the observer and the observed. Much of the essay focuses on obsessive eye imagery and the fear of blindness.

E1855. Barzun, Jacques, and Taylor, Wendell Hertig. Preface to The Drowning Pool (New York, 1950), by Ross Macdonald. In A Book of Prefaces (B17), pp. 77-78.

E1856. Brown, Russell. "Ross Macdonald as Canadian Mystery Writer." In Filler (B111), Vol. II, pp. 164-69.
Brown sees the following qualities in Macdonald as a Canadian: use of a mythic landscape, a present explained by a reconstructed past, a concern with individual responsibility and a preoccupation with fathers and father-figures.

E1857. Bruccoli, Matthew J. Kenneth Millar/Ross Macdonald: A Checklist. Introduction by Kenneth Millar. Detroit: Gale Research Co., 1971. xvii, 86pp. Illus. Introduction by Kenneth Millar.
All of Millar/Macdonald's works--books, short stories, articles, reviews, interviews, miscellaneous prose (including college term papers), and verse--are listed and described. The overall organization is chronological. Breen 190. (REB)

E1858. ______. Ross Macdonald. HBJ Album Biographies. NY: Harvest/Harcourt Brace Jovanovich, 1984. xxi, 147pp. Index and Bibliography. Published simultaneously in hardback and trade paperback editions. The abstract for Macdonald's Ph. D. Dissertation (University of Michigan) is published on pp. 123-24.
A mixture of biography and criticism but the biography dominates and the work is seen through the optic of the life. There is very little information on Macdonald's last years and the text seems often little more than expanded captions for the photographs and other illustrative material.

E1859. Carter, Steven R. "Ross Macdonald: the Complexity of the Modern Quest for Justice." In Adams, MDA 1973 (B3), pp. 59-82.
A wide-ranging thematic study (authority figures, money, divine and human justice) with discussions of the influence of Freud and Macdonald's relationship to the fiction of Chandler and Hammett. Carter incorporates materials from his correspondence with Macdonald.

E1860. Champlin, Charles. "A Loss for Detective Fiction." Los Angeles Times Calendar, 31 July 83, p. 23. Photo.
A memorial tribute to Millar/Macdonald in which the autobiographical nature of his writing is stressed.

E1861. Chandler, Raymond. Letter to James Sandoe, April 14, 1959. In Raymond

Chandler Speaking (E397), pp. 54-55.
An often-cited letter in which Chandler talks about Macdonald's "repellent" style.

E1862. Chastain, Thomas. "Introduction." In The Moving Target (as by John Macdonald; Knopf, 1949), by Ross Macdonald, pp. v-vii. Gregg Press Mysytery Fiction Series (B134).

E1863. Combs, William W. "The Detective as Both Tortoise and Achilles: Archer Gets the Feel of the Case in The Chill." Clues 2:1 (Spring/Summer 81):98-105.
Archer's discovery, in The Chill, that his contradictory feelings about his cases (everything is connected/nothing is related, he's solving the case but getting nowhere) were subjects of discourse in Greek philosophy.

E1864. Cook, Bruce. "Ross Macdonald: The Prince in the Poorhouse." Catholic World 214 (Oct 71):27-30.
An essay-review of The Underground Man which Cook sees as Macdonald's weakest novel to date, the one in which his discomfort with detective fiction conventions is most evident, the language most pretentious and strained, and the story most unbelievable in its use of coincidences.

E1865. Darrach, Brad. "Ross Macdonald: The Man Behind the Mysteries." People, 8 July 74, pp. 26-31.
"Personality" article, with 7 photos. (REB)

E1866. Dorinson, Zahava K. "Ross Macdonald: The Personal Paradigm and Popular Fiction." TAD 10 (77):43-45, 87. Photo.
Popular literature is distinguished from "serious" literature in kind, not in quality, as an "artful variation of the familiar." Macdonald's originality is in his invention resulting in an "individuated formula."

E1867. Finch, G. A. "The Case of the Underground Man: Evolution or Devolution." TAD 6 (72/73):210-12.
A review of The Underground Man based on the premise that this novel is inferior to Macdonald's earlier work.

E1868. Fishman, Charles. "Another Heraldic Cry: Heraldic Birds in Five Lew Archer Novels." Clues 2:1 (Spring/Summer 81):106-115.
Macdonald's bird imagery categorized and discussed as sentinels, predators, scavengers and dead birds.

E1869. Geherin, David J. "Archer in Hollywood: The 'Barbarous Coast' of Ross Macdonald." TAD 9 (75/76):55-58. Text of a paper presented at the Popular Culture Association Conference, Spring, 1974.
Hollywood, the dream capital, and its metaphorical role in Macdonald's fiction.

E1870. Goldman, William. "The Goodbye Look." NYTBR, 1 June 69, pp. 1-2.
A review-essay of The Goodbye Look in which Goldman claims that Macdonald is not writing hard-boiled detective fiction but "novels of character about people with ghosts." An important review that signaled the beginning of major critical acceptance of Macdonald's work.

E1871. Grella, George. "Evil Plots: Ross Macdonald." New Republic 173 (26 July 75):24-26.

Grella sees Macdonald as the most distinguished contemporary practitioner of the hard-boiled detective novel. He discusses the obssessive themes of the quest and the search for the past and describes a metamorphic pattern in Archer's process of heightening perception.

E1872. Grogg, Samuel L., Jr. "Between the Mountains and the Sea: Ross Macdonald's Lew Archer Novels." Unpublished Ph. D. dissertation. Bowling Green State University, 1974. DAI 35/02A, pp. 1044-45.

E1873. Hartman, Geoffrey. "The Mystery of Mysteries," NYRB, 18 May 72, pp. 31-34.

Essay-review of Macdonald's The Underground Man. On the liberation of the detective story, its "arrested" development, and Archer and Marlowe.

E1874. Hazard, Johnnine Brown. "The Detective Fiction of Kenneth Millar/Ross Macdonald." Unpublished dissertation. University of Chicago, 1974. No other information available.

E1875. Holtan, Judith and Orley L. Holtan. "The Time-Space Dimension in the Lew Archer Detective Novels." North Dakota Quarterly 40:4 (Autumn 1972):30-41.

A look at the reflection of the mobile California society in Macdonald's novels and the comment it makes on American culture today. The Holtans take Macdonald's California landscape to be used as a microcosmic view of American society. Macdonald is consistently referred to as MacDonald.

E1876. Kiell, N. "Very Private Eye of Ross Macdonald." Literature and Psychology 27 (1977):21-34; 67-73.

The metastasized eye and hypotheses of "an unresolved oedipal conflict, anxieties incurred by fantasies of the primal scene, and the inevitable search for identity in the search for the father." Kiell has determined that Macdonald uses on the average of one eye reference a page in his novels. His discussion of the blind eye is detailed and informative. An intelligent blend of psychoanalytic, thematic and metaphoric criticism.

E1877. Leonard, John. "I Care Who Killed Roger Ackroyd." Esquire 84 (Aug 75):60-61, 120.

A vigorous and entertaining essay in which Leonard traces the behind-the-scenes maneuvering which placed Goldman's NYTBR essay on Macdonald's The Underground Man on page 1 (E1870) and the novel on the best-seller lists, and initiated an extensive correspondence between Macdonald and Eudora Welty. Leonard also gives a brief history of the genre and ends with the statement that detective novels are, "after all," good stories.

E1878. Lynds, Dennis. "In Memoriam: Ross Macdonald." TAD 16 (83):227.

E1879. Macdonald, Ross. A Collection of Reviews. Introduction by Ross Macdonald. Northridge, CA: Lord John Press, 1979. 350 copies. 67pp.

A collection of 14 reviews by Macdonald. Three are directly relevant to this bibliography but all of them are valuable as examples of Macdonald's non-fiction writing and an indication of his critical opinions on a variety of authors and subjects. It should be pointed out that these are only a small fraction of the reviews Macdonald wrote and a more comprehensive selection, at a more reasonable price, would be a welcome addition to the Macdonald bibliography. All reviews, unless otherwise noted, were published in the San Francisco Chronicle--This World section. Contents:

"Foreword," pp. ix-xii; "The Detective in Fiction," pp. 1-4 (C511); "A Catalog of Crime," pp. 5-10 (C509); "The Durable Art of James M. Cain," pp. 11-19 (review of James M. Cain's Cain X 3; published in NYTBR, 2 March 69, pp. 1, 49-51); "Van Wyck Brook's Life of W. D. Howells," pp. 20-25 (8 Nov 59, p. 28); "Strindberg's Love Letters, and Some Other Experiments," pp. 26-30 (not located); "A New Look at the Tradition of the Novel," pp. 31-33 (19 April 59, p. 25); "England and the Continent," pp. 34-48 (not located); "Studies of Cultural Revolution in This and Previous Generations," pp. 39-44 (10 Jan 50, p. 24); "Correspondence of Conrad and His Publishers," pp. 45-47 (19 Apr 59, p. 24); "T. S. Eliot," pp. 48-51 (4 Oct 59, p. 25); "The Stature of Colin Wilson," pp. 52-55 (29 Nov 59, p. 19); "Waugh and Peace," pp. 56-58 (15 Feb 59, p. 26); "Stephen Leacock, Stranger in Paradox," pp. 59-65 (3 Jan 60, p. 21); "Thomas Mann's Last Words," pp. 66-67 (2 Apr 59, p. 35). (David Grothe)

E1880. ______. "Death of the Detective." Paper delivered at World Crime Writers Conference, 1978. Published in Macdonald (E1888), pp. 105-107.
A lyrical tribute to the detective novel as a modern descendent of the Gothic romance.

E1882. ______. "In the First Person." From a Davidson Films shooting script. Published in Macdonald (E1888), pp. 39-46.
Autobiography and the writing of detective fiction.

E1883. ______. "Introduction." In Lew Archer, Private Investigator, by Ross Macdonald, pp. ix-xiii. NY: Mysterious Press, 1977.

E1884. ______. "Introduction." In Ross Macdonald Selects Great Stories of Suspense. NY: Knopf, 1974.

E1885. ______. "Lew Archer." In Penzler (B309), pp. 17-24.
Macdonald comments, not on Lew Archer, but on the private detective and his role.

E1886. ______. On Crime Writing. Yes! Capra Chapbook Series 11. Santa Barbara, CA: Capra Press, 1973. 45pp. Wraps.
Contents: "The Writer as Detective Hero," pp. 9-24 (C512); "Writing the Galton Case," pp. 25-45 (E1887). Translated into Swedish and published as Att skriva romaner om brott. Goteborg: Korpen, 1977.

E1887. ______. "A Preface to The Galton Case." In Afterwords: Novelists on Their Novels, edited by Thomas McCormack. NY: Harper and Row, 1969. Reprinted in Macdonald (E1887), pp. 25-45; and in Macdonald, Self-Portrait (E1888), pp. 47-59.
A detailed analysis by Macdonald of the writing of his novel.

E1888. ______. Self-Portrait: Ceaselessly into the Past. Foreword by Eudora Welty. Santa Barbara, CA: Capra Press, 1981. iv, 131pp.
A collection of essays, reviews, and interviews, most of them previously published. The contents will be listed with some items indexed separately and annotated; the several introductions and articles on ecological concerns will not be annotated. Contents: Eudora Welty, "Foreword," pp. i-iv; "Down These Streets a Mean Man Must Go," pp. 3-9 (C510); "A Collection of Reviews," pp. 11-14 (introduction); "Archer in Jeopardy," pp. 15-16 (introduction); "Lew Archer, Private Investigator," pp. 17-21 (E1883); "Kenneth Millar/Ross Macdonald--A Checklist," pp. 23-28

(introduction); "Archer at Large," pp. 29-32 (introduction); "Find the Woman," pp. 33-34 (introduction); "Archer in Hollywood," pp. 35-37 (introduction); "In the First Person," pp. 39-46 (E1883); "Writing the Galton Case," pp. 47-59 (E1887); "From South Dakota Review," pp. 61-62 (interview); "A Death Road for the Condor," pp. 63-67 (ecology); "Life with the Blob," pp. 69-79 (ecology); "Black Tide," pp. 81-85 (ecology); Ralph B. Sipper, "An Interview with Ross Macdonald," pp. 87-93 (B3); "Great Stories of Suspense," pp. 95-104 (introduction); "The Death of the Detective," pp. 105-107 (E1880); "Homage to Dashiell Hammett," pp. 109-112 (E1395); "The Writer as Detective Hero," pp. 113-133 (C510); "F. Scott Fitzgerald," pp. 123-124; "Eudora Welty," pp. 125-126; Ralph B. Sipper, "Afterword: A Personal Appreciation," pp. 127-129; Acknowledgments, p. (130); Books by Ross Macdonald, p. (131).

E1889. ______. "The Writer as Detective Hero." In Essays: Classic and Contemporary, edited by Richard W. Lid. NY: J. B. Lippincott. Reprinted in Nevins (B290), pp. 295-305; in Macdonald (E1887), pp. 9-24; in Winks (B434), pp. 179-87 (this version also contains material from C510); and in Macdonald (E1888), pp. 113-22.

Macdonald believes that very often the detective hero is modelled, at least in part, on the writer. He discusses this relationship in Poe, Doyle, Hammett, Chandler and in his own work.

E1890. MacShane, Frank. "Meeting Ross Macdonald." NYTBR, 11 Sept 83, pp. pp. 14, 36.

A tribute based on meetings and correspondence.

E1892. Mottram, Eric. "Ross Macdonald and the Past of a Formula." In Benstock (B26), pp. 97-118.

Mottram thinks that Lew Archer--and Macdonald--move the private eye novel into "fictions of self-deception and self-expenditure" and away from the stereotypical models of detection at the "pure disposal of law."

E1893. Mulqueen, James E. "Three Heroes in American Fiction." Illinois Quarterly 36:3 (Feb 74):44-50.

Natty Bumpo, the Virginian and Lew Archer: American heroes living up to their code.

E1894. "Novelist Ross Macdonald Dies." San Francisco Chronicle, 13 July 83, p. 32. Photo.

E1895. Pronzini, Bill. "Introduction." In The Dark Tunnel (as by Kenneth Millar; Dodd, Mead, 1944), by Ross Macdonald. Gregg Press Mystery Fiction Series (B134).

E1896. Pry, Elmer. "Lew Archer's 'Moral Landscape.'" TAD 8 (1974/75):104-106; reprinted in Landrum (B216), pp. 174-81.

People and landscapes in the Macdonald Archer novels.

E1897. Sacks, Sheldon. "The Pursuit of Lew Archer." Critical Inquiry 6 (Winter 79):231-38.

Ross Macdonald has raised the "potentiality" of the detective story form.

E1898. Schickel, Richard. "Detective Story." Commentary 52 (Sept 71):96, 98-99.

A review-essay of Macdonald's The Underground Man. Schickel thinks that Macdonald's reputation is grossly inflated and that, far from being the "social realist" he imagines himself to be, Macdonald is a creator of fantasy which Schickel does not think is art. Schickel's discussion is undermined by his questionable distinction between art and fantasy and by his eccentric comparison of Macdonald to the "stylized whodunits" of Christie, Rex Stout and Ellery Queen.

E1899. Sokolov, Raymond A. "The Art of Murder." Newsweek 77 (22 March 71):101-102, 104, 106, 108. Photos.
A profile of Macdonald and his work. Cover portrait of Macdonald.

E1900. Speir, Jerry. Ross Macdonald. Recognitions series. NY: Frederick Ungar, 1978. vii-ix, 182pp. Index. Bibliography of primary and secondary sources.
A chronological study of Macdonald's work that includes chapters on Archer, Macdonald's style and on critical attitudes toward his work.

E1901. Welty, Eudora. "The Stuff That Nightmares Are Made of." NYTBR, 14 Feb 71, pp. 1, 28, 30.
A review of The Underground Man which Welty finds to be his finest work to date. She discusses the use of fairy tale material, Macdonald's imagery and sees it all as possible only because of the detective novel form "with all its difficult demands and its corresponding charms...."

E1902. Wolfe, Peter. Dreamers Who Live Their Dreams: The World of Ross Macdonald's Novels. Bowling Green, OH: Popular Press, 1976 (1977). 346pp. Notes. Index.
This is not an introductory treatment of Macdonald's writing, but a work of academic literary analysis aimed at synthesizing and illuminating the novels for readers already familiar with them. Few mystery writers' worlds are meaty enough to justify a long book of criticism, and few literary academics know enough about the genre to write such a book on any mystery writer. This book brings together an author and a critic who were made for each other. Breen 193. (F. M. Nevins, Jr.)

MCDOUGALD, ROMAN

Ref: Hubin 2, ABMI; UN 2:12 (1950):4-5, 15 (photo).

McDowell, Michael

Ref: Hubin 2; The Writer 95:4 (April 82):21-23, 46 (on plotting).

MCGERR, PAT(RICIA)

Ref: Hubin 2, TCCMW, CC, SN, ABMI(S); The Writer 78:4 (April 65):9-11; UN 2:11 (1950):6-7 (photo).

Int: Washington Star-News, 26 March 73 (rpt. in Authors in the News 1, p. 331); EQMM, May 82, pp. 95-96.

E1903. Barzun, Jacques, and Taylor, Wendell Hertig. Preface to Pick Your Victim (New York, 1946), by Pat McGerr. In A Book of Prefaces (B17), pp. 79-80.

MCGIRR, EDMUND

Ref: Hubin 2, TCCMW, CC.

MCGIVERN, WILLIAM

Ref: Hubin 2, TCCMW, EMD, CC, ABMI(S); UN 3:5 (1951):4-5 16 (photo); UN 4:8 (1952):6-7 (photo).

Int: PW, 12 March, pp. 8-9 (photo); DAST 11:4 (78):43-45 (photo; includes a bibliography prepared by Iwan Hedman).

E1905. Obituary. New York Times, 21 Nov 82, p. 24.

E1906. "William P. McGivern." Hard-Boiled Dicks 5.
Interview, bibliography and filmography, articles. In French. Not seen.

MCGUIRE, PAUL

Ref: Hubin 2, TCCMW, EMD, CC, ABMI(S).

E1907. Barzun, Jacques, and Taylor, Wendell Hertig. Preface to A Funeral in Eden (New York, 1938), by Paul McGuire. In A Book of Prefaces (B17), pp. 81-82.

MCILVANNEY, WILLIAM

Ref: Hubin 2, ABMI(S).

Int: Jury 8:4 (1979):5-9.

MCINERNY, RALPH

Ref: Hubin 2, SN, ABMI(S).

E1908. McCahery, Jim (James R.). "Father Roger of Fox River." TPP 2:5 (Sept/Oct 79):8-12.
A survey of McInerny's priest detective with some introductory remarks on religious sleuths.

MACINNES, HELEN

Ref: Hubin 2, TCCMW, EMD, CC, ABMI(S).

Int: PW, 17 June 74, pp. 10-11; DAST 9:4 (76):8-10 (photo); NYTBR, 17 Dec 78, p. 42 (photo); DAST 13:4 (80):7-12 (photo; checklist).

See also: 1104a.

E1909. Boyd, Mary K. "The Enduring Appeal of the Spy Thrillers of Helen MacInnes." Clues 4:2 (Fall/Winter 83):66-75.
MacInnes excells at plotting and readers tend to overlook her "extreme" political conservatism.

E1910. Pettersson, Sven-Ingmar. "Helen MacInnes och världens frihet |Helen MacInnes and the world's freedom|." Jury 4:3 (75):5-7. (MS)

MCINTYRE, JOHN THOMAS

Ref: Hubin 2, CC.

E1911. Sampson, Robert. "A Few Kind Words for Ashton-Kirk." TMF 7:6 (Nov/Dec 83):3-12.
A biography of writer McIntyre and some charitable comments on the Ashton-Kirk (criminologist) series.

MACISAAC, FRED

Ref: Hubin 2, ABMI(S); Argosy, 23 Nov 29.

MACKENZIE, DONALD

Ref: Hubin 2, TCCMW, SN, ABMI(S); The Writer 74:8 (Aug 61):20, 38; The

Writer 81:1 (Jan 68):18-19 (characterization of rogues and criminals).

E1912. MacKenzie, Donald. Occupation: Thief. Indianapolis: Bobbs Merrill, 1955; published as Thieves: London: Elek, 1955.

E1912a. ______. Gentlemen at Crime: An Autobiography. London: Elek Books, 1956. pp. 7-200. 8vo. Frontispiece photo.
These two books recount MacKenzie's criminal career ("For twenty-six years I lived by looting the property of others") before he turned to fictional crime. (REB)

MCKIMMEY, JAMES
Ref: Hubin 2, CC, ABMIS; The Writer 83:9 (Sept 70):15-17.

MACKINTOSH, ELIZABETH. See TEY, JOSEPHINE

MACLEAN, ALISTAIR
Ref: Hubin 2, TCCMW, ABMI(S).

See also: C541.

E1913. Gadney, Reg. "Middle-Class Heroics: the Novels of Alistair MacLean." The London Magazine (new series) 12: 5 (Dec 72/Jan 73):94-105.
The professionalism of MacLean's heroes is compared to Chandler's Marlowe. Gadney discusses the shared sympathies ("reciprocal relationship") between MacLean and his readers in an attempt to explain his popularity. A superficial and unconvincing article.

E1914. Hedman, Iwan. "Alistair MacLean: A Bibliography & Biography of the Author." TMRN 4:5 (July/Aug 71):29-31.
The information is based on correspondence with MacLean.

E1915. Lee, Robert A. Alistair MacLean: The Key is Fear. The Milford Series: Popular Writers of Today, Volume Two. San Bernardino, CA: R. Reginald/The Borgo Press, Oct 76. pp. 3-60. Wraps. Bibliography.
An analysis of MacLean's novels (including those published under his Ian Stuart pseudonym) from H. M. S. Ulysses to The Golden Gate, with an attempt--only partially successful--to highlight the themes and techniques which have made this author's books popular. Lee's own prose is unexciting, and he fails to communicate any sense of enthusiasm for his subject. The endings to several books are revealed unnecessarily. Breen 194. (REB)

MACLEOD, CHARLOTTE
Ref: Hubin 2, ABMI(S).

E1916. Bakerman, Jane S. "Bloody Balaclava: Charlotte MacLeod's Campus Comedy Mysteries." TMF 7:1 (Jan/Feb 83):23-29. Includes a short biography and a bibliography in note 1, p. 29.
A discussion of MacLeod's Rest You Merry (1978) and The Luck Runs Out (1979).

MACLEOD, ROBERT
Ref: Hubin 2.

E1917. Hedman, Iwan. "Robert MacLeod - produktiv skotsk forfattare |Robert MacLeod - productive Scottish author|." DAST 11:1/2 (78):64-66.

Interview, with checklists of Bill Knox, Robert MacLeod, Michael Kirk and Noah Webster titles. (MS)

MCMULLEN, MARY

Ref: Hubin 2, TCCMW, EMD, CC, ABMI.

MCNEILE, H. C. See "SAPPER"

MCSHANE, MARK

Ref: Hubin 2, TCCMW, SN, ABMI(S).

Magnan, Pierre

E1918. Baudou, Jacques, and Renaud, Michel. "Entretien avec Pierre Magnan." Enigmatika 20 (Jan 82):5-13. 2 photos.
An interview with the writer preceded by Baudou's review of Magnan's novel Le tombeau d'Hélios.

MAHANNA, FLOYD

Ref: Hubin 2, SN; UN 3:2 (1950):10-11, 13 (photo); UN 3:10 (1951):10-11, 13 (photo).

MAINWARING, DANIEL. See HOMES, GEOFFREY

MAJOR, CLARENCE

Ref: ABMI(S).

E1919. McCaffery, Larry, and Gregory, Linda. "Major's Reflex and Bone Structure and the Anti-Detective Tradition." Black American Literature Forum 13:2 (Summer 79): 39-45.
A discussion of a "postmodern" novel in which detective fiction conventions are subverted; in the tradition of novels about the writing of novels.

MAKIN, WILLIAM J.

Ref: Hubin 2, ABMI(S).

E1920. Lofts, W. O. G. "It's All in the Face." TAD 7 (1973/74):109-110.
On the tradition of the detection of criminals by their facial features with William Makin's Jonathan Jow cited as an example. Lofts traces this only back to 1864 but the tradition--even if not specifically related to the criminals--is, of course, much older.

MALET, LEO

Int: MM 21 (Oct 49); MM 276 (Feb 71); Indépendante no. 147 (Aug 78) (reprinted in Enigmatika 18 Spéciale 81 (E1923), pp. 135-40, 159-63, 187-89; Magazine littéraire no. 155 (Dec 79); Enigmatika 18 (May 80):3-9, 10-18; Nuits Noires 1 (1981):9; Polar 8 (Jan 80):13-21.

E1921. Bens, Jacques. "Ai-je croisé Nestor Burma |Have i run into Nestor Burma|? Enigmatika 18 (May 80):19-22.
A study that identifies the fictional city in Malet's 1942 novel Le cinquième procédé as Marseilles, where Bens lived as a child.

E1922. "Dossier Léo Malet." Polar 8 (Jan 80), pp. 4-43. Photographs, film stills, illustrations.

Contents: François Guérif, "Introduction," p. 4; A. Demouzon, "La Déconnade prodigieuse," pp. 5-6 (reminiscence); F. Guérif, "Frank Harding, Omer Refreger, Leo Latimer, sans oublier Jean de Selneuves," pp. 7-9 (Malet's pseudonymous works); Maurice Bernard Endrèbe, "L'Age du Christ |The time of Christ|," pp. 10-12 (reminiscences); F. Guérif and Richard Bocci, "Entretien avec Léo Malet," pp. 13-21 (interview); Jacques Baudou, "3 Rencontres de premier type |3 encounters of the first kind)," pp. 22-23 (3 meetings with Malet); Jean-Pierre Deloux, "Trilogie noire |Dark trilogy|," pp. 24-25 (discussion of three novels); L. Malet, "Derrière l'Usine à Gaz," pp. 26-40 (fiction); "Bibliographie de Léo Malet," pp. 41-43.

E1923. Enigmatika 18 Spéciale 81. Paris: Edition de la Butte aux Cailles, 1982. 223pp. Illus.

An updated and expanded version of the Enigmatika 18 (E1929) devoted to the life and works of Léo Malet, creator of Nestor Burma. The additional material consists of 2 supplements. The supplements contain mostly interviews and texts of Malet and the contents listing will include brief subject notations. "Supplément I." Claude Rameil, "Léo Malet à La Rue |Léo Malet in La Rue|," pp. 131-32 (list of stories published by Malet in the magazine La Rue, 1946-47); Pierre-Henri Liardon, "France Culture," pp. 132-34 (a tribute to Malet broadcast on August 25, 1978); "Rencontres," pp. 135-40 (interview originally published in L'Indépendante no. 147, Aug 78); Léo Malet, "A l'assassin!", pp. 141-42 (article on detective fiction, originally published in Combat, 30 Jan 48); L. Malet, "Rauch Verboten!," pp. 143-44 (a colorful polemic, originally published in 1945, on an anti-smoking edict for movie theaters); L. Malet, "Le Mystère du 57,3," pp. 145-57 (fiction); Michel Lebrun, "'C.Q.F.D." et "La vache enragee'," pp. 159-63 (interview); "Témoignages," pp. 165-74 (Tributes from Matulu, E1934); Leo Malet, "L'Assassinat de Rudolf Klément |The murder of R. F.|," pp. 175-79 (true crime). "Supplément II." "Extrait des entretiens Lebrun-Malet," pp. 187-89 (interview); L. Malet, "Le deuil en rouge," pp. 191-223 (fiction).

E1924. Gaillard, Noé. "Nestor Burma et cié. |Nestor Burma, ltd.|." Enigmatika 18 (May 80):23-27.

Associates of Nestor Burma in his investigations.

E1925. ______. "Note liminaire à une étude plus approfondie: des femmes dans l'oeuvre de Léo Malet |Introductory note to a more detailed study: women in Léo Malet's work)." Enigmatika 18 (May 80):29-31.

General remarks on women's roles in Malet's fiction.

E1926. ______. "Reflexions sur vif à propos de "Bonne et heureuse" en Ursurpation d'identité de Boileau et Narcejac |First thoughts on "bonne et heureuse" in Boileau-Narcejac's ursurpation d'identité|." Enigmatika 18 (May 80):28.

Objections to the clumsy parody of Malet's style in the short story "Bonne et heureuse."

E1927. Gauteur, Claude. "Léo Malet et le cinéma: un rendez-vous manqué |Léo Malet and film: a missed rendez-vous|." La Revue du cinéma no. 38 (April 79):49-66. Illus.

A discussion of Malet's 56 books of fiction and the missed opportunity: only 3 films have been made from his novels which are "rich in visual qualities."

E1928. Hoog, Armand. "Mythologie du pistolet. Romans policiers de Léo Malet |Mythology of the gun. detective novels by Léo Malet|." Enigmatika 18 (May 80):98-101. First published in Carrefour, 1949.

Hoog finds interest in Malet not in his style (he thinks that Nestor Burma speaks "badly") but in an "energy" which he traces from Stendhal and Maurice Barrès through Arsène Lupin to Malet. He distinguishes Malet from both the English puzzle novel and the American hard-boiled writers and attempts to locate Malet in a French tradition.

E1929. "Léo Malet." Enigmatika 18 (May 80). pp. 1-105.

An extensive dossier on Malet subsequently reprinted, with supplements, as Enigmatika 18 Spéciale 81 (E1923). With book and magazine illustrations and photos. Contents: Jacques Baudou, "13 Questions à Léo Malet |13 questions for Léo Malet|," pp. 3-9 (interview); Paul Parisot, "Qui double qui? |Who is doubling whom?|," pp. 9-11 (interview); Jacques Bens, "Ai-je croisé Nestor Burma?," pp. 19-22 (E1921); Noé Gaillard, "Nestor Burma et cie," p. 23-27 (E1924); N. Gaillard, "Réflexions sur le vif....," p. 28 (E1926); N. Gaillard, "Note liminaire....," p. 29-31 (E1925); Pierre-Henri Liardon, "Un dialogue d'écorché," pp. 32-34 (E1930); "Lettres de René Magritte," pp. 35-36 (two letters from Magritte to Malet); "Titres," p. 37-38 (titles of books contracted for and not written); L. Malet, "Léo Malet et le poisson chinois |L. M. and the Chinese fish|," pp. 39-40 (2 letters, various subjects); "A propos de Leo Malet: Bibliographie," pp. 41-43 (bibliography of secondary sources); Jacques Natanson, "120 rue de la gare," pp. 45-46 (film review); L. Malet, letters and fiction, pp. 49-77; L. Malet, "Cherchez la femme," pp. 78-90 (genre criticism); "Léo Malet critique de romans policiers |Léo Malet, Critic of Detective Novels|," pp. 81-89 (book reviews); "Dossier critique," pp. 89-97 (reviews of Malet fiction and critical tributes); Armand Hoog, "Mythologie du pistolet," pp. 98-101 (E1928); Michel Lebrun, "A la recherche du temps perdu," pp. 102-105 (journal notes on Malet).

E1930. Liardon, Pierre-Henri. "Un dialogue d'écorché |The dialogue of a flayed man|." Enigmatika 18 (May 80):32-34.

Malet's Surrealist poetry and the fictional trilogy, Trilogie noire: a comparison and an analysis.

E1931. Malet, Léo. "L'ouvrier déformé doit retrouver sa forme |The deformed worker must recover his shape|." La Rue no. 11 (20 Sept. 46); reprinted in La rue du cinéma no. 338, pp. 64-5.

Notes on the film medium, updated by a critical note written by Claude Gauteur.

E1932. Mallerin, Daniel, ed. Les cahiers du silence. Paris: Editions Kesselring, 1974.

The first compilation devoted to Léo Malet, this issue directed by Daniel Mallerin focuses on a lengthy interview between Malet and two specialists, Julien Moret and Luc Geslin. It contains numberous rare texts by Malet, poems, dream narratives, tributes by François Caradec and Albert Simonin, with a very rich iconography and a good bibliography. (JB)

E1933. "Préfaces."

Editions Néo (Paris) has reprinted a number of texts written by Malet under various pseudonyms. The editions have critical introductions by Michel Lebrun, Jean-Pierre Deloux, Jacques Baudou, François Guérif,

Michel Marmin, and Léo Malet. (JB)

E1934. "Spécial Léo Malet." Matulu no. 30 (1974).
Texts by Robert Beauvais, M. B. Endrébe, Gilbert Sigaux, Jean Bourdier, Albert Simonin, Jean Rousselot, Michel Lebrun. Interview. Not seen.

MALING, ARTHUR

Ref: Hubin 2, TCCMW, SN, ABMI; The Writer 94:4 (April 81):9-12.

Int: TPP 2:1 (Jan/Feb 79):11-13.

MALLEY, LOUIS

Ref: Hubin 2, SN; UN 4:1 (1951):10-11, 16 (photo).

MALLORY, ARTHUR

Ref. Hubin 2.

E1935. Hubbard, D. C. "Popular Detective Story Writers: Arthur Mallory." Detective Story Magazine 101:5 (2 June 28):102-104.
Brief biographical sketch. Series character: Dr. Krook. (RS)

MANCHETTE, JEAN-PATRICK

Ref: SN.

Int: MM 306, Aug 73; NL, 28 Jan-4 Feb 82, pp. 44-45; Polar 12 (June 80):18-25; Littérature 49 (Feb 83):102-107.

E1936. Deloux, Jean-Pierre. "Noir et rouge." Polar 12 (June 80):4-7.
Deloux uses a comment by Manchette that society makes us all mad to show how his novels draw on and are a criticism of contemporary society.

E1937. "Dossier Jean-Patrick Manchette." Polar 12 (June 80):4-26. Photos and stills.
Contents: Jean-Pierre Deloux, "Noir et rouge," pp. 4-7 (E1936); "Filmographie de J.-P. Manchette," pp. 8-10; J.-P. Manchette, "Le discours de la méthode," pp. 11-17 (short story); François Guérif and J.-P. Deloux, "Entretien avec J.-P. Manchette," pp. 18-25 (interview); Jean-François Naudon, "Bibliographie," pp. 25-26.

E1938. Manchette, Jean-Pierre. "Cinq remarques sur mon gagne-pain |5 comments on my job|." NL, 30 Dec 76-6 Jan 77, p. 4.
Notes on writing.

MANN, JACK

Ref: Hubin 2, ABMI(S).

E1939. Lofts, W. O. G., and Briney, Robert E. "On the Trail of the Mysterious 'Jack Mann'." TMRN 6:2 (Nov 73):19-22.
A biography of the elusive English writer, with a checklist of the novels written by E. Charles Vivian under the Mann pseudonym, compiled by R. E. Briney.

MANN, JESSICA

Ref: Hubin 2, TCCMW, ABMI(S).

MANVEY, CHRISTIAN

Int: Gang 1 (circa 1980), pp. 72-73 (photo; bibliography).

MARKSTEIN, GEORGE

Ref: Hubin 2, SN.

Int: DAST 13:4 (1980):5-6.

MARLOWE, DAN J.

Ref: Hubin 2, TCCMW, EMD, SN, ABMI(S); The Writer 79:12 (Dec 66):17-19.

E1940. Adrian, Kelly. "Dan J. Marlowe: Who Said He Would and He Did." TMRN 3:3 (Feb 70):25-28.

A biography, apparently based on an interview, with a checklist of mystery-suspense book-length publications.

MARLOWE, DEREK

Ref: Hubin 2, TCCMW, ABMI(S).

MARLOWE, HUGH. See HIGGINS, JACK

MARLOWE, STEPHEN

Ref: Hubin 2, TCCMW, SN, ABMI(S).

MARON, MARGARET

Ref: The Writer 89:6 (June 76):26-28, 46 (plotting the short mystery story).

MARQUAND, JOHN P.

Ref: Hubin 2, TCCMW, EMD, CC, ABMI(S).

Int: Christian Science Monitor Weekly Magazine Section, 24 June 39, p. 5 (photo; passing reference to Moto series).

E1941. Birmingham, Stephen. The Late John Marquand: A Biography. Philadelphia, PA and NY: J. B. Lippincott, 1972. 322pp. Index.

Biography of the creator of Mr. Moto by a writer who knew Marquand and had the same literary agent. (REB)

E1942. Penzler, Otto. "Mr. Moto." In Penzler (B310), pp. 140-43. Illus. Bibliography, filmography and a sketch of author Marquand's life.

This is a well-written, balanced profile, managing to capture the now-you-see-him, now-you-don't impression that Mr. Moto makes upon most readers, as well as the lasting impression he makes upon the American characters in the stories. (GG)

E1943. Rausch, George J. "John P. Marquand and Espionage Fiction." TAD 5 (1971/72):194-98.

Espionage and the Moto series.

E1944. White, William. "John P. Marquand: A Preliminary Checklist." BoB 19:10 (1949):268-71.

A first attempt at an annotated checklist of works by Marquand, with a short introductory essay. White includes the Moto books along with citations of their previous serial appearances in Saturday Evening Post. (GG)

E1945. ______. "John P. Marquand Since 1950." BoB 21:10 (1956):230-34.

An updated bibliography of material by and about Marquand, supplementing White's "Preliminary Checklist" and "Marquandia."

Includes citations of reprints of the Moto books, but is a year too early to include Stopover:Tokyo, which was published in 1957. (GG)

E1946. ______. "Marquandiana." BoB 20:1 (1950):8-12. A supplement to White's "Preliminary Checklist" (E1944).
This checklist is of secondary sources, covering books, periodicals, newspaper material and book reviews dealing with Marquand. Includes sections of reviews of the Moto books, even though White states that he has probably not "captured" everything about Moto. (GG)

MARRIC, J. J. See CREASEY, JOHN

MARSH, HOWARD R.

See: Argosy, 8 June 35.

MARSH, NGAIO

Ref: Hubin 2, TCCMW, EMD, CC, ABMI(S); The Writer 90:4 (April 77):23-25.

See also: B16, B241, B309, B349, E2535.

Int: Argosy 30:5 (May 69):40-51; Mystery 3:1 (July 81):23-25 (photo); The New Zealander 1980 Annual, Vol. I, p. 92.

E1948. Bargainnier, Earl F. "Ngaio Marsh's 'Theatrical' Murders." TAD 10 (1977):175-81. Photo and illus.
Dame Marsh's career in the theater and theatricalism in her detective fiction.

E1949. ______. "Roderick Alleyn: Ngaio Marsh's Oxonian Superintendent." TAD 11 (1978):63-71. With a chronology. Illus.
A portrait of the detective.

E1950. Barzun, Jacques, and Taylor, Wendell Hertig. Preface to A Wreath for Rivera (Boston, 1949), by Ngaio Marsh. In A Book of Prefaces (B17), pp. 83-84.

E1951. Boucher, Anthony. "Introduction." In The Bride of Death (originally published as Spinsters in Jeopardy, Collins, 1954), by Ngaio Marsh. NY: Mercury, 1955.

E1952. Dooley, Allan J., and Dooley, Linda J. "Rereading Ngaio Marsh." In Benstock (B26), pp. 33-48.
A review of Marsh's fiction with emphasis on the accuracy of her settings and characterization, and the continuing freshness of her plotting.

E1953. Marsh, Ngaio. Black Beech and Honeydew: An Autobiography. Boston: Little, Brown, 1965. 343pp. Illus. London: Collins, 1966. 287pp. Illus. Revised and enlarged edition, London: Collins, 1981. 310pp. Illus.
This work leaves no doubt that Ngaio Marsh's chief love in life was the stage and that her work in this area--particularly the critically-acclaimed stagings of Shakespeare's plays--was her chief source of satisfaction. In the first edition, her mystery writing received only incidental mentions scattered throughout the text. In the revised edition, Marsh's comments on her mystery fiction are both more extensive and more precise, not only in the two new chapters, "Second Wind" and "A Last Look Back," but in the revised earlier chapters as well. Marsh's friends who were the models for the Lamprey family in her fiction are

described in detail, though not identified by name. The revised edition includes many more photographs than the original (including two of Marsh in company with Agatha Christie and with H. R. F. Keating). Breen 195.

E1955. ______. "Starting with People." In Adams, MDA 1973 (B3), pp. 208-210. Photo.
Marsh classifies herself with the detective story writers who create rounded characters and struggle with the genre's limitations as opposed to the writers of puzzle stores (Christie et al) for whom characterization is secondary.

E1956. Panek, LeRoy. "Ngaio Marsh." In Panek (B304), pp. 185-97.
The last of the Big Four women authors to enter the field, Marsh adapted better than the others to the post-World War II world and combined the best of two currents: the comfortable arcadia and disturbing new country without a name.

E1957. White, Jean M. "Murder Most Tidy: Ngaio Marsh." New Republic 177 (30 July 77):36-38.
Marsh as a 30s writer with more interest in characterization and setting than most with the result that she she sometimes "forgets" that she is not writing a novel of manners and "neglects" to "get on with" the detection.

MARSTEN, RICHARD. See MCBAIN, ED

MARTIN, A. E.

Ref: Hubin 2; Lachman, TPP 1:3 (May 78):11-12.

MARTIN, IAN KENNEDY

Ref: Hubin 2.

Int: DAST 14:2 (81):45-46 (mail interview, photo).

MARTIN, ROBERT (LEE)

Ref: Hubin 2, ABMI; The Writer 71:7 (July 58):5-8, 37; The Writer 75:3 (March 62):7-9, 25.

MASON, A. E. W.

Ref: Hubin 2, TCCMW, EMD, CC, ABMI(S).

See also: B253.

E1958. Green, Roger Lancelyn. A. E. W. Mason. London: Max Parrish, 1952. 272pp. Index and bibliography.
Green knew Mason, saved his notebooks and letters, interviewed people who knew him, is familiar with his books, and has written a fascinating study of the life of a fascinating man. Mason did not write an autobiography but Green has pieced together some of the episodes of Mason's secret service career from conversations with the writer and from his notebooks and published short stories. This is a writer's biography that is certainly deserving of republication. (J. R. Cox)

E1959. Mason, A. E. W. "Detective Novels." The Nation and The Atheneum, 7 Feb 25, pp. 645-46.
Mainly of interest for its author's description of where he got the ideas

for two of his most famous books, At the Villa Rose and The House of the Arrow. (RCSA)

E1961. Thomson, H. Douglas. "Mr. A. E. W. Mason." In Thomson (B404), pp. 229-33.
A discussion of Mason's Hanaud novels.

E1962. Overton, Grant. A. E. W. Mason: Appreciations - with Biographical Particulars and Notes on His Books (A. E. W. Mason's Mystery of the Art of Fiction). NY: George H. Doran, n. d. 222pp. Pictorial wraps. Not seen. (REB)

MASON, F(RANCIS) VAN WYCK

Ref: Hubin 2, TCCMW, EMD, CC, ABMI(S); The Writer 46:6 (June 34):193-94 (on the deductive-mystery story; rpt in The Writer |England|, May 37, p. 203); The Writer 46:7 (July 34):241-42 (on the character-detective story; rpt. in The Writer |England|, June 37, p. 226); The Writer 46:9 (Sept 34):315 (on the horror-mystery story; rpt. in The Writer |England|, Sept 37, p. 310); The Writer 52:9 (Sept 39) (on the story of international intrigue).

E1963. "Antecedents, Past Performances and Future Plans of Hugh North." PW 140 (23 Aug 41):530-31. Photo.
General background information and sales figures on Hugh North series with a biography of the character written by author Van Wyck Mason.

E1964. Mason, Van Wyck. "The Camera as a Literary Element." The Writer 51:1 (Nov 38):325-26.
On the planning and writing of a photo-crime novel, The Castle Island Case.

E1965. ______. "How I Wrote The Seven Seas Murders." The Writer 46:4 (Apr 34):115-118.
How he researched, constructed and wrote the novel.

E1966. ______. "My Budapest Murder." The Writer 47:3 (March 35):89-91.
On The Budapest Parade Murders.

E1967. ______. "Remarks on Adventure-Mystery." The Writer 46:10 (Oct 34):366.
Mason Uses his The Shanghai Bund Murders as an example.

E1968. "The Men Who Make the Argosy." Argosy 212:3 (17 May 30):430. See also biographical sketch in Argosy, 15 June 35.
Concise biographic sketch of life, travel experiences, and professional work to 1930. With portrait. (RS)

MASUR, HAROLD Q.

Ref: Hubin 2, TCCMW, EMD, CC, SN, ABMI(S); UN 5:3 (1952):2-3 (photo); The Writer 63:1 (Jan 50):7-10; Writer's Digest 39:1 (Jan 59):24-31 (marketing advice and information).

Int: EQMM, June 77, pp. 88-89.

MATHER, BERKELY

Ref: Hubin 2, TCCMW, CC, ABMI(S).

MATSUMOTO, SEICHO

Ref: Hubin 2, ABMIS.

E1969. Fukuoka, Takashi. Ningen Matsumoto Seicho |Seicho Matsumoto: human being|. Tokyo: Daiko-sha, 1968. 257pp. Revised edition, 1977.
A memoir by the author who spent nine years as a stenographer/assistant of Seicho Matsumoto, a bestsller writer. Valuable for its insider's view of his writing activities. (HS/TT)

E1970. Matsumoto, Seicho. Hansei no Ki |Half of my life|. Tokyo: Kawade Shobo Shinsha, 1966. Revised edition: Tokyo, 1977.
The autobiography focuses on his life before he began to write. The 1977 edition is an expanded version.(HS/TT)

E1971. ______. Kuroi Techo |Black pocketbook|. Tokyo: Chuo-Koron-sha, 1961. 237pp.
A collection of essays, half of which deal with mystery and his own writing, and the rest with real crimes. In the essays on mystery fiction, he insists on the necessity of social problems as motive. See also his Sakko no Techo |Writer's pocketbook, 1981| for more of the writer's notes. (HS/TT)

E1972. Saito, Doichi. Meitantei Matsumoto Seicho-shi |Mr. Seicho Matsumoto the great detective|. Tokyo: Shirakawa Shoin, 1981. 286pp.
This study deals with many facets of the work of Matsumoto who was not only a successful mystery but also an outstanding journalist. The works are analyzed in detail. The insights into Matsumoto's work as a mystery writer are especially valuable. (HS/TT)

E1973. Tamura, Sakae. Matsumoto Seicho:Sono Jinsei to Bungaku |Seicho Matsumoto: his life and literature|. 2 vols. Tokyo: Seizan-sha, 1976-1977.
A critical biography which deals with a great many works of Seichko. The second volume includes a panel discussion with, as participants, Tamura, Matsumoto and a historian, Eiichi Matsushima. (HS/TT)

MAUGHAM, ROBIN

Ref: Hubin 2, TCCMW, CC, ABMI(S).

MAUGHAM, W. SOMERSET

Ref: Hubin 2, TCCMW, EMD, CC, ABMI(S).

E1974. Cody, Richard. "Secret Service Fiction." Graduate Student of English 3 (Summer 1960):6-12. Not seen.

E1975. Shropshire, F. "W. Somerset Maugham as a Mystery Writer." TAD 14 (81):190-91.
A discussion of the merits of Ashenden (1928).

E1976. Whitehead, John. "'Whodunit' and Somerset Maugham." Notes & Queries 21, new series, 21 (Oct 74):370.
A suggestion that the expression "whodunit" may have been adapted from the phrase "who done it" in Maugham's short story "The Creative Impulse" (Harper's Bazaar, 1926).

MAXWELL, VICTOR

E1977. Sampson, Robert. "The Professionals." TMF 6:1 (Jan/Feb 82):16-20.

A series of police stories featuring Sergeant Riordan and Captain of Detectives Brady that appeared in Flynn's 1925-39. With a series checklist.

MAYSE, ARTHUR

Ref: Hubin 2; UN 2:2 (1949):4-5 (photo).

MAZARIN, JEAN

E1978. Mesplède, Claude, ed. "Jean Mazarin." Les Amis du crime 14 (n.d., circa 1982). Wraps.
Issue devoted to René-Charles Rey who wrote under the name of Jean Mazarin and who also used the pseudonym of Emmanuel Errer. Contents: "Entretien avec Jean Mazarin," pp. 7-19 (interview); "Bibliographie," pp. 22-37; "Personnages," pp. 40-44 (short character portraits); Jean Mazarin, "La conférence pédagogique," pp. 45-56 (short story); "Florilège," pp. 47-51 (quotations from Mazarin's fiction); "Revue de presse," pp. 56-61 (excerpts from reviews of Mazarin's books).

MEADE, MRS. L. T.

Ref: Hubin 2, TCCMW, EMD, ABMI(S).

E1979. Moskowitz, Sam. "L. T. Meade and Clifford Halifax, 'The Horror of Studley Grange'."" Gaslight Detective" series (C565). MSMM, Dec 73, pp. 71-72.

E1980. "Mrs. L. T. Meade." The Writer 14:2 (Feb 1901):28-30.
Excerpt from an autobiographical article in the November 1900 Girl's Realm (not seen), in which Mrs. Meade talks about her writing career.

MEGGS, BROWN

Ref: Hubin 2, TCCMW, ABMI.

MELVILLE, HERMAN

E1981. Fulcher, James. "Melville's 'Benito Cereno'--An American Mystery." Clues 2:1 (Spring/Summer 81):116-122.
Melville's novella as a "story of crime and detection."

MELVILLE, JAMES

Ref: Hubin 2.

Int: TAD 16 (1983):340-47.

E1982. Lundin, Bo. "Det är klart at han borde översättas : James Melville |It's clear that his works should be translated: James Melville|." Jury 11:4 (1982):71-74.
Introduction to his novels, with photo. (MS)

MERRITT, ABRAHAM

Ref: Hubin 2, ABMI(S); Argosy, 25 Oct 30.

E1983. Wentz, Walter J. "A. Merritt's Mysteries." TAD 5 (71/72):204-206.
Discussions of Merritt's Burn, Witch, Burn; Seven Footprints to Satan; and Creep, Shadow!

MERTZ, BARBARA G. See PETERS, ELIZABETH

MEYER, NICHOLAS

Ref: Hubin 2, TCCMW, ABMI(S).

MEYNELL, LAURENCE

Ref: Hubin 2, TCCMW, CC, ABMI(S).

MICHAELS, BARBARA. See PETERS, ELIZABETH

MICHEL, M. SCOTT

Ref: Hubin 2, ABMI(S); The Writer 57:4 (April 44):105-107 (characterization in the hard-boiled novel).

Interview: TPP 4:4 (Aug 81):3-8 (with a bibliography).

MILES, JOHN

Ref: Hubin 2.

E1984. Barzun, Jacques, and Taylor, Wendell Hertig. "Introduction." In The Night Hunters (Indianapolis, 1983), by John Miles. "Crime Fiction 1950-1975" (B18).

MILLAR, KENNETH. See MACDONALD, ROSS

MILLAR, MARGARET

Ref: Hubin 2, TCCMW, EMD, CC, SN, ABMI(S); UN 3:3 (1950):4-5 (photo).

Int: Cooper-Clark (B75), pp. 67-81 (photo).

E1985. Gondi, Ioan. "Margaret Millar - en bibliografisk notis |a bibliographical note|." DAST 10:3 (76):40, 16. (MS)

E1986. Lachman, Marvin. "Margaret Millar: The Checklist of an 'Unknown' Mystery Writer." TAD 3 (69/70):85-88.
Annotated checklist of her fiction.

E1987. Reilly, John M. "Margaret Millar." In Bargainnier (B16), pp. 225-49.
Millar's novels do not fit neatly into any one popular genre and Reilly finds in her fiction a tension between the "institutionalized" forms and her art. Reilly sees her as a revisionist of the detective novel and discusses her novels from this perspective.

MILLER, WADE

Ref: Hubin 2, TCCMW, EMD, SN, ABMI; UN 1:3 (1948):10-11 (photo); UN 2:11 (1950):4-5 (photo); UN 4:5 (1951):12-14 (photo).

E1988. "About the Detective: Max Thursday." UN 3:4 (1950):4-5, 11.
Profile of Thursday.

E1989. Lachman, Marvin. "The Man Who Was Thursday." TAD 8 (74/75):179, 184.
A note on Miller's Max Thursday series.

MILNE, A. A.

Ref: Hubin 2, TCCMW, EMD, CC, ABMI(S).

E1990. Barzun, Jacques, and Taylor, Wendell Hertig. Preface to The Red House

Mystery (London, 1922), by A. A. Milne. In A Book of Prefaces (B17), pp. 85-86.

E1991. Chandler, Raymond. "The Simple Art of Murder (C168)."
Chandler uses Milne's The Red House Mystery as a "classic" example of the weakness of the puzzle mystery.

E1992. Cox, J. Randolph. "Some Notes Toward a Checklist of A. A. Milne's Short Tales of Crime and Detection." TAD 9 (1975/76):270.

E1993. Milne, A. A. Autobiography. NY: Dutton, 1939. Japanese edition translated by Sho Hara and Tokiko Umebayashi. Bokutachi wa Kofuku Ratta. Tokyo: Kenkyu-sha, 1975.)
In the last section ("Author", pp. 271-315), Milne discusses his post-W. W. I career, mostly with reference to his his plays and their writing although there is some general advice to authors.

E1994. Panek, LeRoy. "A. A. Milne." In Panek (B304), pp. 64-71.
In spite of Chandler's criticism of The Red House , Panek sees it as "setting the pattern" for post-war detective fiction.

E1995. Thomson, H. Douglas. "A. A. Milne." In Thomson (B404), pp. 164-66.
A brief discussion of the adroitness of Milne's The Red House Mystery.

MINAKAMI, TSUTOMU

E1996. Minakami Tsutomu no Sekai |The world of Tsutomu Minakami|. Shinpyo-sha series (B367). 226pp. July 1978.

E1997. Minakami, Tsutomu. Minakami Tsutomu ni Yoru Minakami Tsutomu |Tsutomu Minakami by T. Minakami|. Tokyo: Seido-shaa, 1982. Illus. 237pp.
This is a volume in a series on writers which organizes articles by the writer into an autobiography. We learn that Minakami wrote mystery fiction unwillingly. (HS/TT)

E1998. "Omoshiro Hanbun," ed. Kakute Minakami Tsutomu |Therefore, Tsutomu Minakmi|. Tokyo: Omoshiro Hanbun, 1980. 274p. Illus. Bibliography.
Tsutomu Minakami (1919-) established a position as a writer of mystery fiction and a successor to Seicho Matsumoto. Now he has turned from mystery to mainstream fiction. This book, published as an extra issue of Omoshiro Hanbun magazine, has studies on the writer by numerous contributors. There are only a couple of comments on his mystery fiction. (HS/TT)

MITCHELL, GLADYS

Ref: Hubin 2, TCCMW, EMD, CC, ABMI(S).

E1999. Craig, Patricia. "The Corpse in the Copse." TLS, 8 Aug 80, p. 892.
A review of Mitchell's The Whispering Knights (Michael Joseph, 1980) in which the reviewer provides an overview of her work to date.

E2000. Pike, B. A. "In Praise of Gladys Mitchell." TAD 9 (1975/76):250-60.
On the writer and her work, with a bibliography and an interview.

E2001. "With Crime in Mind: Gladys Mitchell." BMJ, 12 July 80, pp. 137-38.
How Mitchell kills her victims.

MITCHELL, JAMES

Ref: Hubin 2, SN, ABMIS.

E2002. Hart, Denis. "The Lonely Man Who Made Callan." The Daily Telegraph Magazine, no. 320 (4 Dec 70), pp. 29-36.
Report of an interview with writer James Mitchell, creator both for television and in books of popular anti-hero spy David Callan. (RCSA)

MIYOSHI, TORU

E2003. Miyoshi, Toru. Toi Tabi, Mezurashii Kajitsu |Long trips, rare fruits|. Tokyo: Kodan-sha, 1980. 331pp.
The author, a mystery writer and ex-journalist, likes to write works with international viewpoints. Most of the essays here are travelogues and social commentary; only a small proportion deal with mystery fiction. (HS/TT)

MOFFAT, GWEN

Ref: Hubin 2, TCCMW, ABMI.

MOFFETT, CLEVELAND

Ref: Hubin 2, EMD, CC, ABMI(S).

E2004. Lauterbach, Edward S. "The Mysterious Card Unsealed." TAD 4 (1970/71):41-43.
Lauterbach describes the publishing history of Moffett's book and analyzes the plot. He also characterizes it as one of the earliest fictional treatments of Jack the Ripper.

MOLE, WILLIAM

Ref: Hubin 2, CC, SN, ABMIS.

E2005. Barzun, Jacques, and Taylor, Wendell Hertig. "Introduction." In Small Venom (New York, 1956), by William Mole. "Crime Fiction 1950-1975" (B18).

MONIG, CHRISTOPHER. See CROSSEN, KEN

MONTAYNE, HAROLD

Ref: Argosy, 18 April 31.

MONTHEILHET, HUBERT

Ref: Hubin 2, TCCMW, CC, ABMI(S).

Int: MM 298, Dec 72.

E2006. Tourteau, Jean-Jacques. "Les Mantes religieuses." In Tourteau (B408), pp. 306-310.
An Analysis of Montheilhet's novel.

MONTGOMERY, BRUCE. See CRISPIN, EDMUND

Moore, Robin

Ref: Hubin 2, ABMI.

Int: Hartford Courant, 15 Sept 74 (rpt. in Authors in the News 1, pp. 354-55; photo); Connecticut (Stratford, CT), July/Aug 73 (rpt. in Authors in the

News 1, pp. 356-57; photo).

MORGAN, MICHAEL

Ref: Hubin 2.

E2007. Morgan, Michael. "Let's Call It Gun in Girdle." TAD 16 (83):275-77. Reminiscences by Dean M. Dorn and C. E. "Teet" Carle, the pseudonymous authors of Decoy called by Bill Pronzini "the worst mystery of all time." See Pronzini's reply in TAD 16 (1983):419-21 in "An Open Letter to Dean and Teet or, 'Look Out, Pronzini's got a Rebuttal in His Girdle'."

MORICE, ANNE

Ref: Hubin 2, TCCMW, ABMIS.

Int: TMF 6:6 (Nov/Dec 82):5-8 (with a checklist of her work).

MORLAND, NIGEL

Ref: Hubin 2, TCCMW, EMD,CC, ABMI(S).

Int: TAD 13 (1980):194-98.

E2008. Morland, Nigel. "Incident in Shanghai." In Adams, MDA 1972 (B2), pp. 98-101.
An autobiographical note on Morland's early career.

MORIMURA, SEIICHI

E2009. Akiba, Toshitaka. Morimura Seiichi-shi Suiri Shosetsu no Machigai Sagashi |Search for mistakes in Mr. Seiichi Morimura's mystery fiction|. 2 vols. Tokyo: Arrow Shuppan-sha, 1978. Illus.
A study of Morimura's mystery fiction in which errors are pointed out in a logical way. (HS/TT)

E2010. Morimura, Seiichi. Roman no Yosegi-zaiku |Mosaic work of Roman|. Tokyo: Kodan-sha, 1975. 282pp.

E2011. ______. Roman no Kiriko-zaiku |Cutting-glass work of Roman)| Tokyo: Kadokawa Shoten, 1980. 295pp.

E2012. ______. Roman no Zoge-zaiku |Ivory work of Roman|. Tokyo: Kodan-sha, 1981. 239pp.
All three books are collections of essays in which Morimura mostly discusses his own works. (HS/TT)

MORRAH, DERMOT

Ref: Hubin 2, CC, ABMI(S).

E2013. Barzun, Jacques, and Taylor, Wendell Hertig. Preface to The Mummy Case (New York, 1933), by Dermot Morrah. In A Book of Prefaces (B17), pp. 87-88.

MORRISON, ARTHUR

Ref: Hubin 2, TCCMW, EMD, CC, ABMI(S).

E2014. Bell, Jocelyn. "A Study of Arthur Morrison." In Essays and Studies 1952, edited by Arundell Esdaile, pp. 77-89. Essays and Studies, new series, Vol.

5. London: John Murray, 1952.
See especially pp. 83-85 where Bell comments on Martin Hewitt stories, relating them to Conan Doyle's Holmes stories. She praises the craftsmanship of the stories but considers detective stories to be just a diversion. The essay is mainly a study of Morrison's other fiction.

E2015. Bleiler, E. F. "Introduction" to Best Martin Hewitt Detective Stories, pp. vi-xiv. NY: Dover, 1976.
A biography and a survey of Morrison's Martin Hewitt stories, with some consideration of his work as a potential not fulfilled.

E2016. Moskowitz, Sam. "Arthur Morrison, 'The Lenton Croft Robberies'." "Gaslight Detective" series (C565). MSMM, March 73.

E2017. Pritchett, V. S. "An East End Novelist." In The Living Novel, pp. 155-60. NY: Reynal & Hitchcock, 1947. Reprinted in The Living Novel and Later Appreciations, pp. 206-22. NY: Random House, 1964.
A good discussion of some of Morrison's qualities as a writer of fiction although there is no mention of the Martin Hewitt stories.

MORTON, ANTHONY. See CREASEY, JOHN

MOYES, PATRICIA

Ref: Hubin 2, TCCMW, EMD, CC, ABMI(S); Cannon, AHMM 27:13 (Dec 82):80-82; The Writer 83:4 (April 70):11-14; The Writer 89:10 (Oct 76):20-22; The Writer 83:4 (April 70):11-14 (includes biography written by Moyes).

Int: EQMM, June 82, pp. 92-93; EQMM, July 82, pp. 105-7.

E2018. Barzun, Jacques, and Taylor, Wendell Hertig. "Introduction." In Johnny Underground (NY, 1966), by Patricia Moyes. "Crime Fiction 1950-1975" (B18).

E2019. Boucher, Anthony. "Introduction." In Murder by 3's (omnibus). NY: Holt, Rinehart and Winston, 1965.

MULLER, MARCIA

Ref: Hubin 2, ABMIS; The Writer 91:10 (Oct 78):20-22, 45.

MUNDY, TALBOT

Ref: Hubin 2, ABMI(S); Argosy, 25 Oct 30.

See also: B88.

E2020. Day, Bradford M. Talbot Mundy Biblio. Materials toward a Bibliography of the Works of Talbot Mundy. South Ozone Park, NY: Science Fiction and Fantasy Publications, 1955. 28pp. Mimeographed, stapled in card covers. Edition limited to 200 copies.
A slightly revised version of this booklet was later incorporated into Day's Bibliography of Adventure (B88). (REB)

E2021. Grant, Donald M., compiler. Talbot Mundy: Messenger of Destiny. West Kingston, RI: Donald M. Grant, Publisher, Inc., 1983. 253pp. Bibliographies. Illustrations.
The first half of this book offers various biographical material on Talbot Mundy (real name: William Lancaster Gribbon), known primarily for his many books of high adventure in colonial India and the Middle East.

There is an autobiographical sketch which Mundy prepared for Adventure magazine (3 Apr 1919), a lengthy biographical article, "Willie--Rogue and Rebel" by Peter Berresford Ellis, and a memoir by Mundy's widow, Dawn Mundy Provost. There are also appreciations of Mundy's writing by Darrel Crombie and Fritz Leiber. The other half of the book consists of a detailed study of Mundy's contributions to Adventure magazine, where all of his best fiction first appeared, and bibliographies of Mundy's books and magazine fiction and non-fiction. Contents: Donald M. Grant, "Introduction," pp. 9-12; Talbot Mundy, "Autobiography," pp. 15-26; Peter Berresford Ellis, "Willie--Rogue and Rebel/Talbot Mundy: The Early Years 1879-1909," pp. 27-72; Dawn Mundy Provost, "Talbot Mundy," pp. 75-113; Darrel Crombie, "Ghosts Walk...," pp. 115-118; Donald M. Grant, "Talbot Mundy in Adventure," pp. 121-70; Fritz Leiber, "The Glory of Tros," pp. 171-73; Donald M. Grant, "Books," pp. 175-216 (bibliography); Donald M. Grant, "Magazine Appearances," pp. 217-40 (bibliography); Peter Berresford Ellis, "The Jerusalem News," pp. 245-48 (periodical contributions); Donald M. Grant, "The Theosophical Path," pp. 249-51 (periodical contributions); Donald M. Grant, "The New York Times," p. 253 (periodical contributions).

MURPHY, WARREN B.

Ref: Hubin 2, SN, ABMI(S).

Int: TAD 11 (1978):284-86 (photos)

See also: E2473.

MURRAY, MAX

Ref: Hubin 2, TCCMW, CC; UN 3:8 (1951):10-11 (photo).

E2022. Nehr, Ellen. "The Max Murray Saga." TPP 5:1 (July 82):27-29.
A checklist of the novels with plot descriptions which support Nehr's statement that the summary in TCCMW (A143) was written by someone who was not well acquainted with Murray's work.

NABOKOV, VLADIMIR

Ref: Hubin 2, ABMI(S).

See also: B366, E181.

E2023. Christopher, J. R. "On Lolita as a Mystery Story." TAD 7 (73/74):29.
On a novel in which there are mystery story elements but where the "rhythm is all wrong."

NARCEJAC, THOMAS. See BOILEAU, PIERRE

NASH, SIMON

Ref: Hubin 2, CC, ABMI(S).

E2024. Barzun, Jacques, and Taylor, Wendell Hertig. "Introduction." In Killed by Scandal (London, 1962), by Simon Nash. "Crime Fiction 1950-1975" (B18).

NATSUKI, SHIZUKO

E2025. Natsuki, Shizuko. Alibi no Nai Onna |Woman without alibi|. Tokyo: Shuei-sha, 1977. 212pp.

The author is one of the leading Japanese female mystery writers. Only about one-seventh of the book contains essays on fiction writing and mystery fiction; the rest deals with the writer's life as a housewife and her friendships. (HS/TT)

NEBEL, FREDERICL

Ref: Hubin 2, TCCMW, SN, ABMI.

See also: D343.

E2026. Lewis, Dave. "The Backbone of Black Mask." Clues 2:2 (Fall/Winter 81):118-127.

A survey of Nebel's series characters for Black Mask and a bibliography of the stories by issue and series.

E2027. Randisi, Robert J. "Introduction." In Six Deadly Dames, by Frederick Nebel. Gregg Press Mystery Fiction Series (B134).

NELSON, HUGH LAURENCE

Ref: Hubin 2, CC; UN 1:3 91948):4-5 (photo); UN 2:3 (1949):12-13, 16 (photo); UN 2:9 (1950):10-11 (photo).

NEMOURS, PIERRE

Int: MM 285, Nov 71.

NEVILLE, BARBARA ALISON. See CANDY, EDWARD

NEVILLE, MARGOT

Ref: Hubin 2, TCCMW, CC; UN 1:10 (1949):10-11 (photos).

NEVINS, FRANCIS M., JR.

Ref: Hubin 2, TCCMW, EMD, ABMI(S).

NEWMAN, BERNARD

Ref: Hubin 2, TCCMW, ABMI(S).

NEWTON, WILLIAM

Ref: Hubin 2, ABMI.

Int: DAST 12:4 (1979):11-12 (photo; in Swedish).

NICHOLS, BEVERLEY

Ref: Hubin 2, TCCMW, ABMI(S).

NICOLE, CHRISTOPHER. See YORK, ANDREW

NIELSEN, HELEN

Ref: Hubin 2, TCCMW, ABMI(S); UN 4:9 (1952):4-5, 15 (photo).

NISHIMURA, JUKO

E2029. Oda, Mitsuo. Shohi Sareru Shomotsu: Nishimura Juko to Taishu Shosetsu no Sekai |Consumed books: Juko Nishimura and the world of popular fiction|. Tokyo: Sorin-sha, 1982. 182pp.

Nishimura (1930-) is at present one of the most widely read authors in Japan. He started in mystery fiction, and turned to adventure fiction. He now specializes in books with excessive sex and violence although he still occasionally produces more serious books. (HS/TT)

NITTA, JIRO

E2030. Nitta Jiro no Sekai |The world of Jiro Nitta|. Tokyo: Shinpyo-sha, 1981. 208pp. "Extra" Shinpyo series (B367).

NOLAN, WILLIAM F.

Ref: Hubin 2, TCCMW, EMD, ABMI(S); The Writer 81:3 (Feb 68):9-11, 53; The Writer 83:6 (June 70):18-20.

See also: D321.

E2031. Nolan, William F. "Nolan Mystery Checklist." TAD 3 (1969/70):26-7.
A bibliography of Nolan's fiction and non-fiction mystery writing, compiled by the author.

E2032. ______. "On Chandler, Hammett, Brand and Bradbury--And an Eye Named Challis." TAD 2 (1968/69):86-87.
A short history of novelist and critic Nolan's favorite writers.

E2033. ______. "Sam Space, An Eye on Mars." Mystery 1:3 (June/July 80): 28-30.
The novelist discusses his space-age private eye.

NOMURA, KODO

E2034. Nomura, Kodo. Zuihitsu Zenigata Heiji |Essays on Heiji Zenigata|. Tokyo: Obun-Sha, 1979. 290pp. Illustrated. Bibliography.
"Torimono-sho" is a sub-genre of Japanese mystery fiction, set in the Tokugawa Period (17th-19th centuries). The author is the best writer in the sub-genre. Heiji Zenigata is the name of his famous serious character who is also seen on TV and in films. This book is a collection of essays about fiction writing, essays with his perspective on mystery fiction, and autobiographical sketches. (HS/TT)

NORMAN, JAMES

Ref: Hubin 2, TCCMW, ABMI(S).

NORTH, GIL

Ref: Hubin 2, TCCMW, CC, ABMI(S).

OCORK, SHANNON

Ref: Hubin 2, SN.

E2035. OCork, Shannon. "The Truth, More or Less, as Long as It Makes a Good Story." In Freeman (B117), pp. 126-38.
On reporting and inventing. Some autobiographical comments and some discussion of her writing.

O'DONNELL, LILLIAN

Ref: Hubin 2, TCCMW, SN, ABMI; The Writer 91:2 (Feb 78):7-19, 46 (on the police procedural); The Writer 95:12 (Dec 82):11-13 (plot versus characterization).

Int: TAD 14 (1981):164-66 (with a list of her novels).

O'DONNELL, PETER

Ref: Hubin 2, TCCMW, EMD, ABMI(S).

Int: DAST 6:1 (1973):20-24 (photo); DAST 11:6 (1978):41-42.

See also: B310.

E2036. Banks, R. Jeff. "Immoderate Homage to Modesty." TMF 4:2 (March/April 80):8-10.

A series summary and a chart with data on characters and plots.

O'FARRELL, WILLIAM

Ref: Hubin 2, CC,SN, ABMIS; UN 2:1 (1949):12-13, 15 (photo); UN 2:8 (1950):8-9 (photo); UN 3:5 (1951):8-9, 11 (photo); UN 4:3 (1951):6-7 (photo).

OFFORD, LENORE GLEN

Ref: Hubin 2, TCCMW,EMD, CC, ABMI(S); UN 2:4 (1949):12-13 (photo).

Int: TPP 5:2 (Nov/Dec 82):3-8, 10.

E2037. Boucher, Anthony. "Introduction." In Clues to Burn (Duell, 1942), by Lenore Offord, pp. 3-4. NY: Mercury Mystery, n.d.

OGDEN, GEORGE WASHINGTON

Ref: Argosy, 1 Feb 30.

OGILVIE, ELISABETH

Ref: Hubin 2, ABMI; The Writer 89:9 (Sept 76):14-16.

O'HANLON, JAMES

Ref: Hubin 2; Lachman, TPP 3:3 (May/June 80):15-16.

OLDEN, MARC

Ref: Hubin 2.

Int: TAD 12 (1979):324-27.

OLLIER, CLAUDE

E2038. Alter, Jean. "L'Enquête policière dans le nouveau roman: La Mise en scène de Claude Ollier |The police investigation in the new novel: Claude Ollier's La Mise en scène|." Revue des lettres modernes 94-99 (1964):83-104.

An analysis of Ollier's novel La Mise en scène which Alter compares to the classic detective novel in its crime, investigation and "anti-hero" detective. Alter also comments briefly on detective fiction elements in Butor's L'Emploi du temps and Robbe-Grillet's Les Gommes.

OLSEN, D. B.

Ref: Hubin 2, TCCMW, CC, ABMI; UN 1:8 (1949):6-7 (photo); UN 4:11 (1952):8-9 (photo).

OLSEN, JACK

Ref: Hubin 2.

Int: PW, 18 Nov 83, 78-79 (photo).

ONIONS, OLIVER

Ref: Hubin 2, CC, ABMI(S).

E2039. Barzun, Jacques, and Taylor, Wendell Hertig. Preface to In Accordance with the Evidence (London, 1915), by Oliver Onions. In A Book of Prefaces (B17), pp. 89-90.

OPPENHEIM, E. PHILLIPS

Ref: Hubin 2, TCCMW, EMD, CC, ABMI(S); The Writer 26:12 (Dec 1914): 183-84.

E2040. Gadney, Reg. "Switch Off the Wireless--It's on Oppenheim." London Magazine, new series, 10:3 (June 70):19-27. Photo.
An attempt to account for Oppenheim's great popularity, now "all lost."

E2041. Oppenheim, E. Phillips. The Pool of Memory. London: Hodder and Stoughton, 1941. ix, 300pp. Illus. Index. Boston, MA: Little, Brown, 1942. vii, 341pp + 5 page bibliography. Illus.
Memoirs, with only occasional references to his own work or to a few mystery writers such as Doyle, Orczy, and Rohmer. Not seen. Breen 197. (REB)

E2042. Overton, Grant. "A Great Impersonation by E. Phillips Oppenheim." In Cargoes for Crusoes, pp. 126-42. NY: D. Appleton, Geo. H. Doran and Little, Brown, 1924.
Biography, Oppenheim's method of dictating his stories and his pre-eminent role as an entertainer. With a checklist of his work, an excerpt from an interview and footnotes with a number of references to interviews and newspaper and magazine pieces on Oppenheim.

E2043. Panek, LeRoy L. "E. Phillips Oppenheim." In Panek (B303), pp. 17-31.
Panek considers Oppenheim's novels to be bad by any standards if not as bad as Le Queux's. He discusses three spy novels he considers to be representative: The Mysterious Mr. Sabin, The Pawns Count and Up the Ladder of Gold. Panek does not discuss Oppenheim's detective fiction.

E2044. Standish, Robert. The Prince of Story-Tellers. London: Peter Davies, 1957. 253pp. Bibliography.
The life of the tireless chronicler of polite international intrigue. Breen 198. (REB)

E2045. Wellman, Ellen, and Brown, Wray D. "Collecting E. Phillips Oppenheim (1866-1946)." The Private Library, Quarterly journal of the Private Libraries Association, U.,. Third series, 6:2 (Summer 83):83-89. Photo on p. 82. Illus.
Discusses Oppenheim's continuing popularity, his style (with quotations) and typical plots, and various points for collectors of his work in book and magazine form. (REB)

ORCZY, BARONESS

Ref: Hubin 2, TCCMW, EMD, CC, ABMI(S).

See also: B253.

E2046. Bargainnier, Earl F. "Lady Molly of Scotland Yard." TMF 7:4 (July/August 83):15-19.
A discussion of the stories E. F. Bleiler claims present the first female

detective at Scotland yard, as well as a female "Watson," in English (British) detective fiction.

E2047. ______. "The Old Man in the Corner." TMF 7:6 (Nov/Dec 83):21-23.
A discussion of the bibliographical problems posed by the "Old Man" stories and some comments on the series.

E2048. Bleiler, E. F. "Introduction" to The Old Man in the Corner, by Baroness Orczy, pp. v-ix. NY: Dover, 1980.
Biography and a discussion of Orczy's "typological" importance in the history of detective fiction as the creator of the first important stories about an armchair detective and the first writer to jettison the story and to concentrate on the denouement.

E2049. Dueren, Fred. "Was the Old Man in the Corner an Armchair Detective?" TAD 14 (1981):232-33.
Mr. Dueren, on the basis of a close reading of the Orczy stories, doubts that he was.

E2050. Orczy, Baroness. The Autobiography of Baroness Orczy: Links in the Chain of Life. London: Hutchinson, n.d. (1945?). Illus. Index.
Contains only scattered and superficial comments about the author's detective fiction. Not seen. Breen 199. (REB)

ORDWAY, PETER

Ref: Hubin 2; UN 5:1 (1952):4-5 (photo).

ORIOL, LAURENCE

Ref: Hubin 2.

Int: MM 289, March 72.

ORMEROD, ROGER

Ref: Hubin 2, TCCMW, ABMIS.

Int: DAST 15:5 (1982):22-25.

ORR, CLIFFORD

Ref: Hubin 2.

E2052. Orr, Clifford. "Miss Clink and Mr. Crump Talk Mysteries." PW 116 (20 July 29):256-7. Photo of Orr.
A comical dialogue on the saleability of mysteries that follow the conventions.

ORUM, POUL

Ref: Hubin 2, TCCMW.

OSBORN, DAVID

Ref: Hubin 2, ABMI.

E2053. Hedman, Iwan. "Biografi David Osborn." DAST 8:3 (1975):14-15. (MS)

OSHITA, UDARA

E2054. Oshita, Udara. Tsuri, Hana, Aji |Fishing, flowers, tastes|. Tokyo: Yojin Shoin, 1967. 246pp. Illustrated. Bibliography. Limited to 700 copies.

A memorial collection of essays. As the title suggests, most of the essays deal with fishing and gastronomy while only eight deal with mystery fiction. A sympathetic portrait of the writer and the only published collection of his essays. (HS/TT)

OTTOLENGUI, RODRIGUES

Ref: Hubin 2, CC, ABMIS.

E2055. Coles, Stephen L. "Dr. Rodrigues Ottolengui." The Writer 7:7 (July 1894):97-98.
A portrait of the writer and his writing methods.

E2056. Moskowitz, Sam. "Rodrigues Ottolengui, 'The Montezuma Emerald'." "Gaslight Detective" series (C565). MSMM, Jan 74, pp. 131-32.

E2057. Taylor, Wendell Hertig. "Rodrigues Ottolengui (1861-1937): A Forgotten American Mystery Writer." TAD 9 (1975/76):181.
An early writer of mysteries of scientific detection.

E2058. Wright, Richardson."Forgotten Dentures." SR 27 (1 Jan 44):8, 21.
A career profile and report on his fiction.

OURSLER, CHARLES FULTON. See ABBOT, ANTHONY

OYABU, HARUHIKO

E2059. Oyabu, Haruhiko. Koya kara no Juka: Oyabu Haruhiko Mind |Rifle fire from the wilderness: the mind of Haruhiko Oyabu|. Tokyo: Kadokawa Shoten, 1979; essays included in Oyabu Haruhiko no Sekai |The world of Haruhiko Oyabu| (B367). 242pp.
A very popular author greatly influenced by Mickey Spillane. Although many critics maintain that his works are not hard-boiled, this book includes several essays on mystery fiction and one of Oyabu's comments is that he does not care whether his works are hard-boiled or not. With a chronology. (HS/TT)

E2060. Oyabu Haruhiko no Sekai |The world of Haruhiko Oyabu|. Tokyo: Shinpyo-sha, 1976; revised edition, 1979. Part of Shinpyo-sha "Extra" series (B367). (HS/TT)

PACKARD, FRANK L.

Ref: Hubin 2, TCCMW, EMD, CC, ABMI(S); Argosy, 26 Sept 31.

See also: D328, D451.

E2061. Davis, Robert H. "The Literati under the Lens." Bookman 69 (Aug 29):635.
Portrait of Packard, with caption telling of character Jimmy Dale, as well as a bit of Packardian philosophy: he thinks counterfeit money is legal tender. (GG)

E2062. Guiterman, Arthur. "Frank L. Packard and His Miracle Man." Bookman 51:4 (June 20):466-70.
Appreciative essay on Packard, occasioned by the recent release of the film adaptation of The Miracle Man. Gives biographical information, including his trips to Samoa, Fiji, and Hawaii. Although Guiterman does not mention Packard's Eastern tales, he says of Packard's detective

fiction that giving readers the "indispensable thrill" was his main concern. (GG)

E2063. Hutchison, Don. "Jimmie Dale, Pulp Archetype." Xenophile 22 (March/April 76), pp. 12-14. Illus.
Frank L. Packard's "Gray Seal," a masked avenger series of novels published at the end of World War I.

E2064. McCafferty, William Burton. "Old King Brady in Disguise." DNR 6 (May 1937):3-4.
Changing tastes in detective fiction are noted along with the names of famous men who were fans and the suggestion that Craig Kennedy is only Old King Brady in disguise. (JRC)

E2065. Overton, Grant. "Frank L. Packard Unlocks a Book." In Cargoes for Crusoes, pp. 330-347. NY: Appleton/Doran/Little, Brown, 1924.
Biography and some critical comments although much of the discussion of the fiction consists of plot summaries.

PAGE, EMMA

Ref: Hubin 2, TCCMW.

PAGE, MARCO

Ref: Hubin 2, TCCMW, EMD, CC, ABMI.

E2066. Barzun, Jacques, and Taylor, Wendell Hertig. Preface to The Shadowy Third (New York, 1946), by Marco Page. In A Book of Prefaces (B17), pp. 91-92.

PAINE, LAURAN BOSWORTH

Ref: Hubin 2, ABMI(S).

Int: TAD 15 (1982):92-94.

PALMER, STUART

Ref: Hubin 2, TCCMW, EMD, CC, ABMI; Writer's Digest 35:12 (Dec 55):14-23, 73-78, 80; Writer's Digest 38:11 (Nov 58):18-21, 80.

PARKER, MAUDE

Ref: Hubin 2; UN 4:6 (1952):10-11, 16 (photo).

PARKER, ROBERT B.

Ref: Hubin 2, TCCMW, SN, ABMI(S).

Int: Boston Phoenix, 12 Apr 77, p. 2 (photo); Carr, Craft of Crime (B67), pp. 143-175; EQMM, May 83, pp. 59-61 and June 83, pp. 83-84.

See also: B121, C735.

E2067. Carter, Steven R. "Spenser Ethics: The Unconventional Morality of Robert B. Parker's Traditional American Hero." Clues 1:2 (Fall/Winter 80):109-18.
Spenser fits into the tradition of the hard-boiled detective, the sports superstar, the Western hero and the movie tough guy yet deviates, in surprising ways, from all these models.

E2068. Drew, Bernard. "Spenser: Hardboiled Roots." Xenophile 21 (Feb 76), pp. 7, 48.
Notes taken by Drew on Parker's view of the American detective hero as explained in a course on "The Novel of Violence," taught by Parker at Northeastern University. Comments on Chandler, Hammett, Stout, Ross Macdonald, the western hero and Spenser's resemblance to Parker.

E2069. Evans, T. Jeff. "Robert B. Parker and the Hardboiled Tradition of American Detective Fiction." Clues 1:2 (Fall/Winter 80):100-108.
Ways in which Parker works both inside and outside the hard-boiled private eye tradition.

E2070. Fridhammer, Christer. "En man fran Boston |A man from Boston|." Jury 7:3 (1978):73-75.
Essay on Parker. (MS)

E2071. Hoffman, Carl. "Spenser: The Illusion of Knighthood." TAD 16 (1983):131-38, 140-43. With a bibliography of primary and secondary sources. Photo and illustrations.
A study of the first six Spenser novels to show the "ups and downs" of the sleuth and the three phases Hoffman sees in the novels. He also speculates on the future direction the series might take and maintains that Spenser is a long way from "being a true knight" like Chandler's Marlowe.

E2072. Parker, Joan H. and Robert B. Parker. Three Weeks in Spring. Boston, MA: Houghton, Mifflin, 1978. pp. v, 1-183. 8vo.
Autobiographical account of Joan Parker's masectomy and its effect on her family. Little or no mention of Parker's mystery writing. (REB)

E2073. Parker, Robert B. "Creating a Series Character." The Writer 94:1 (Jan 81):15-17.
Parker describes how he proceeds from a two-page treatment to a chapter outline to the writing of a book.

E2074. ______. "Spenser's Boston." Boston (Magazine), Feb 81, pp. 82-85.
Photo-essay (with photos by Jerry Berndt) on Parker's use of Boston as a locale in his mysteries. Of little use to the scholar. (KLM)

PARRY, HUGH JONES. See CROSS, JAMES

PARSONS, ELIZA

Ref: Hubin 2, ABMI.

E2075. Roberts, Bette B. "Marital Fears and Polygamous Fantasies in Eliza Parsons' Mysterious Warning." JPC 12 (1978/79):42-51.
Parsons, a late 18th century, early 19th century English novelist, is discussed for her adaptation of Walpole's "gothicism" and for her "assumptions, values and interests" shared with her women readers.

PATRICK, Q. See QUENTIN, PATRICK

PATTERSON, HARRY. See HIGGINS, JACK

PAUL, ELLIOT

Ref: Hubin 2, TCCMW, EMD, CC, ABMI(S); UN 3:9 (1951):6-7 (photo).

PELMAN, BRICE

Int: MM 282, Aug 71.

E2076. "Brice Pelman." MM 292, June 72, pp. 105-107.
One of a series of articles consisting of profiles, biographical sketches or interviews with writers. Pelman is a Moroccan-born French crime writer. He also writes as Pierre Darcis. (REB)

PEMBERTON, MAX

Ref: Hubin 2, TCCMW, EMD, CC, ABMI.

PENDLETON, DON

Ref: Hubin 2, TCCMW, ABMI(S).

Int: Mediascene 7 (Nov/Dec 73):8-10; Writer's Digest 61:3 (March 81):18-19 (photo).

E2077. Pendleton, Don. The Executioner's War Book. NY: Pinnacle Books, 1977. Wraps. 201pp.
Pendleton's series hero Mack Bolan gets the "fan" treatment: Stephen Mertz, "Behind the Executioner: An Introduction to the War Book;" "The Bolan Saga: As Reconstructed in Brief," by Mike Newton, a summary of the first 28 books in the series; an annotated index of characters appearing in these 28 books; 42 pages of diagrams of The Executioner's "war wagon" and weaponry; and 40 pages of letters from Executioners, with Pendleton's replies. For diehard Executioner fans only. (REB)

PENTECOST, HUGH

Ref: Hubin 2, TCCMW, EMD, CC, ABMI(S); Argosy, 5 Oct 35 (as Judson P. Philips).

Int: Hartford Courant, 30 June 74 (rpt. in Authors in the News 1, p. 379; photo); TAD 13 (1980):425-30 (photo); EQMM, 25 Jan 81, pp. 89-90 and 25 Mar 81, pp. 102-103; Writer's Digest, May 81, pp. 14-15 (photo).

See also: D300, C127.

E2078. Clark, William J. "The Park Avenue Hunt Club by Judson P(entecost) Philips." Xenophile 21 (Feb 76), p. 9.
Brief overview of the series and a checklist of stories. In "Pulp Information Center" department.

E2079. Drew, Bernard A. "Meet Judson P. Philips." Attic Revivals no. 1, 1973, pp. (2-3; pages not numbered). Photo of Philips, p. 2.
Descriptive article on Philips' career, particularly his writing for Detective Fiction Weekly and other pulps. Several anecdotes and observations quoted from Philips. (The same issue of Attic Revivals reprints "The Hawk," the first of Philips' Park Avenue Hunt Club Stories, pp. 3-16.) (REB)

E2080. Pentecost, Hugh. "Pierre Chambrun." In Penzler, The Great Detectives (B309), pp. 47-55.
Some comments on Pentecost's transition from the pulps to the slicks but much of the essay consists of a history of the creation of Pentecost's chef-detective.

PERDUE, VIRGINIA

Ref: Hubin 2, CC, ABMI.

E2081. Barzun, Jacques, and Taylor, Wendell Hertig. Preface to Alarum and Excursion (New York, 1944), by Virginia Perdue. In A Book of Prefaces (B17), pp. 93-94.

PEROWNE, BARRY

Ref: Hubin 2, TCCMW, EMD, CC, ABMI.

Int: EQMM, Apr 83, pp. 86-87.

PERRY, ANNE

Ref: Hubin 2.

Int: Clues 3:2 (Fall/Winter 82):52-65 (reprinted in Cooper-Clark B75, pp. 205-23; with photo).

PERRY, RITCHIE

Ref: Hubin 2, TCCMW, ABMI(S).

PERUTZ, LEO

Ref: Hubin 2, CC, ABMIS.

E2082. Boucher, Anthony. "Introduction" and "Afterword." In The Master of the Day of Judgment (Munich, 1923; Boni, 1930), by Leo Perutz. New York: Collier Books, 1963. Reprinted in Boucher (B43), pp. 122-24.

PETERS, ELIZABETH

Ref: Hubin 2, TCCMW, ABMI(S); The Writer 87:2 (Feb 74):15-17.

PETERS, ELLIS

Ref: Hubin 2, TCCMW, CC, ABMI(S); The Writer 85:3 (March 72):9-11.

See also: B6.

E2083. Barzun, Jacques, and Taylor, Wendell Hertig. "Introduction." In Never Pick Up Hitchhikers (NY, 1976), by Ellis Peters. "Crime Fiction 1950-1975" (B18).

PETERS, LUDOVIC

Ref: Hubin 2, TCCMW, ABMI(S).

PETERSEN, HERMAN

Ref: Hubin 2.

E2084. Drew, Bernard A. "Herman Petersen, The Poolville Pulpster." Attic Revivals no. 2 (1980), pp. 17-19.
Biographical article. (RS)

E2085. ______. "A Pulp Chronicle." Attic Revivals no. 2 (1980), pp. 19-23.
Discussion of Petersen's pulp magazine work from the 1922 Black Mask to 1939, based upon his writing records. (RS)

PETIEVICH, GERALD

Ref: The Writer 94:9 (Sept 81):13-14, 45 (characterization).

PETRIE, RHONA

Ref: Hubin 2, TCCMW, CC, ABMI(S).

PHILIPS, JUDSON. See PENTECOST, HUGH

PHILLIPS, JAMES ATLEE. See ATLEE, PHILIP

PHILLPOTTS, EDEN

Ref: Hubin 2, TCCMW, EMD, CC, ABMI(S).

E2086. Barzun, Jacques, and Taylor, Wendell Hertig. Preface to Found Drowned (New York, 1931), by Eden Phillpotts. In A Book of Prefaces (B17), pp. 95-96.

E2087. Rowland, John. "Phillpotts's Detective Fiction." In Eden Phillpotts: An Assessment and a Tribute, edited by Waveney Girvan, pp. 135-59. London: Hutchinson, 1953.

A craftsman whose detective novels have a "flavour of high tragedy." Rowland finds some of the elements of the detective fiction in his other novels. With a selective list of English first editions.

PIKE, ROBERT L. See FISH, ROBERT L.

PIPER, EVELYN

Ref: Hubin 2, TCCMW, ABMI(S); UN 1:8 (1948):10-11, 16; UN 2:8 (1950):4-5, 14.

PLAYER, ROBERT

Ref: Hubin 2, TCCMW.

POATE, ERNEST M.

Ref: Hubin 2, CC.

E2088. Hubbard, D. C. "Popular Detective Story Writers: Ernest M. Poate." Detective Story Magazine 98:5 (28 Jan 28). Not seen.

POE, EDGAR ALLAN

Ref: Hubin 2, TCCMW, EMD, CC, ABMI(S).

See also: B179, B201, B310, C637.

E2089. Allen, L. David. "'The Purloined Letter,' Edgar Allan Poe." In Allen (B6), pp. 17-22.

Dupin is designated "forerunner of a long line of fictional detectives who are eccentric and brilliant." His anonymous comrade also establishes a line of chroniclers of detectives' adventures. Tersely assessing the five ratiocinative tales ("The Murders in the Rue Morgue," "The Mystery of Marie Roget," "The Gold-Bug," "Thou Art the Man," and "The Purloined Letter"), Allen gives palms to the last as Poe's best integration of adventure and reasoning. (BFF)

E2090. Asarch, Joel Kenneth. "A Telling Tale: Poe's Revisions in 'The Murders in the Rue Morgue'." In Poe at Work: Seven Textual Studies, edited by Benjamin Franklin Fisher IV, pp. 83-90. Baltimore: The Edgar Allan Poe Society, 1978.

Poe's changes much improved this tale, transforming it from a "theoretical study of analysis to a practical demonstration of the imagination." (BFF)

E2091. Babener, Liahna Klenman. "The Shadow's Shadow: The Motif of the Double in Edgar Allan Poe's 'The Purloined Letter'." In Adams, MDA 1972 (B2), pp. 21-32.
Dupin and the Minister D_____ are brothers. (BFF)

E2092. Bandy, W. T. "Poe's Solution of the 'Frailey Land Office Cipher'." PMLA 68 (1953):1240-41.
Bandy supplements information assembled by W. K. Wimsatt (E2195) concerning Poe's knowledge of and abilities--and lack thereof--in decoding cryptograms and ciphers. (BFF)

E2093. _____. "Who was Monsieur Dupin?" PMLA 27 (1964):509-510.
"Murders" is "very probably the most widely read and imitated work of fiction that has come out of this hemisphere for almost a century and a quarter." Dupin's origins perhaps combine the name of one S. Maupin, who on 30 September 1940 wrote to Poe mentioning a teacher of French named C. Auguste Dubouchet. (BFF)

E2094. Barnes, Melvin. Best Detective Fiction (A9), passim.
Vidocq's memoirs influenced Poe. Bibliographical information on the detective tales and an outline of their special features are given. (BFF)

E2095. Barzun, Jacques, and Taylor, Wendell Hertig. A Catalogue of Crime (A10).
Passim. Poe's name is repeatedly cited. Valuable references to printings of his detective fiction in anthologies appear. (BFF)

E2096. Baudou, Jacques. "Jules Verne et la cryptographie." In Jules Verne, edited by Pierre-André Touttain, pp. 324-29. Paris: Editions de l'Herne, 1974.
Poe's passion for cryptography and his influence on Jules Verne.

E2097. Belden, Henry M. "The Vulgar Ballad." Sewanee Review 19 (1911): 213-27.
Poe's "Murders" influenced Eugene Sue's Gringulet et Coupe-en-deux, not vice versa. Poe may have learned about a shaving ape from an eighteenth- or nineteenth-century ballad, "The Monkey Turn'd Barber." He may also have known Sir Oran Haut-Ton in T. L. Peacock's Melincourt (1817). (BFF)

E2098. Benton, Richard P. "'The Mystery of Marie Roget'--a Defense." Studies in Short Fiction 6 (1969):144-52.
There are far better demonstrations of mental processes here than in the other Dupin tales. This tale anticipates modernf methods of model construction. (BFF)

E2099. Blanch, Robert J. "The Background of Poe's 'The Gold Bug'." English Record 16 (1966):44-48.
Washington Irving's Tales of a Traveller and Poe's personal experience merged in this tale. (BFF)

E2100. Boll, Ernest. "The Manuscript of Poe's 'The Murders in the Rue Morgue,' and Poe's Revisions." Modern Philology 40 (1943):302-15.
A description of the manuscript, with comments about the nature of Poe's revisions into a printed text, is offered. (BFF)

E2101. Bonaparte, Marie. Edgar Poe: Etude psychanalytique. Foreword by Sigmund Freud. 2 vols. Paris: Denoel & Steele, 1933. Published in English translation as The Life and Works of Edgar Allan Poe: A Psychoanalytic Interpretation. Trans. by John Rodker. London: Hogarth Press, 1949; NY: Humanities Press, 1971.
An influencial study on Poe. See especially Chapter 23, "A Tale of Earth: The Gold-Bug," (pp. 353-69); and sections on "The Man of the Crowd," (pp. 413-26) and "The Murders in the Rue Morgue" (pp. 427-57).

E2102. Buchloh, Paul. "Edgar Allan Poe und die Detektivgeschichte |Edgar Allan Poe and detective history|." In Buchloh/Becker 1 (B60), pp. 34-46.
Discusses the Dupin stories and Poe's historical importance in the genre. (GG)

E2103. Cambiaire, Célestin Pierre. The Influence of Edgar Allan Poe in France. NY: G. E. Stechert, 1927. Part V, "Poe and the Detective Novel in France:" Ch. 1, "Poe, the Father of the Detective Novel," pp. 257-63; Ch. 2, "Poe and Emile Gaboriau," pp. 264-80; Ch. 3, "Poe and Gaston Leroux and Eugêne Sue," pp. 281-82.
The misinformation, furthered by Poe himself, that the Paris Charivari published "Murders," is corrected; an adaptation appeared in La Quotidienne in June 1846. Poe creates the "intellectual sleuth," drawing perhaps upon Vidocq and influencing Gaboriau--whose sleuth is "less analytical, less purely ratiocinative." (BFF)

E2104. Cawelti, John G. Adventure, Mystery and Romance (B69). Pp. 8-111.
Poe created the formula for detective stories, although it was probably only after Doyle wrote that the nature of detective fiction began to be understood. In "Murders" and "The Purloined Letter" Poe defines four common elements of detective fiction: situation, pattern of action, characters and relationships, and setting. (BFF)

E2105. Christopher, J. R. "Poe and the Tradition of the Detective Story." TAD 2 (1968/69):49-51; revised and reprinted in Nevins (B290), pp. 19-36.
An annotated bibliography of secondary material on Poe's detective tales and his contributions to detective fiction is preceded by an essay in which Christopher analyzes the five "canonical" stories and "A Tale of the Ragged Mountains" and "The Man of the Crowd." For comments on Christopher's TAD article, see the following letters: Christopher, TAD 2:132; and Clayton Rawson, TAD 2:129-31.

E2106. Dameron, J. Lasley. "Poe's C. Auguste Dupin." Tennessee Philological Bulletin 17 (1980):5-16.
The popularity of detective stories in English from Poe's day is noted. Dupin is compared with Socrates in terms of "the hero as thinker." Dupin as an American cultural hero is assessed, with comment about heroic types in westerns and in broader areas of American literature. (BFF)

E2107. Dameron, J. Lasley, and Irby B. Cauthen, Jr., editors. Edgar Allan Poe: A Bibliography of Criticism, 1827-1967. Charlottesville: University Press of Virginia, 1974. Also, "Addenda to the Bibliography of Edgar Allan Poe." PBSA 74:1 (1980):70-71.

E2108. Daniel, Robert. "Poe's Detective God." Furioso 6 (1951):45-54; reprinted in Twentieth Century Interpretations of Poe's Tales, edited by William L. Howarth, pp. 103-110 (Englewood Cliffs: Prentice-Hall, 1971).

Dupin fills the role of a secular God in tales that border upon supernaturalism. A remark by Dupin in "The Purloined Letter" suggests Poe's attitudes toward his detective and, implicitly, himself--that he is simultaneously far from society (psychically) and at its service. (BFF)

E2109. Davidson, Edward H. Poe: A Critical Study. Cambridge, MA: Harvard University Press, 1957. pp. 213-222.
The ratiocinative tales are placed within a philosophic framework. Dupin is the lonely hero of American letters, but he makes the commercial world ethic work for his benefit. (BFF)

E2110. Del Buono, Oreste. "La fabbrica delle emozioni |The factory of emotions|." Colloqui, March 58.
The author specifies in the history of the genre two great masters, Edgar Allan Poe, the creator of "ratiocinative stories," and Dashiell Hammett, "the first revolutionary of the genre." Their best pupils are, on the one hand, Conan Doyle and, on the other, Raymond Chandler. (LR)

E2111. Diskin, Patrick. "Poe, Le Fanu, and the Sealed Room Mystery." Notes & Queries, n.s. 13 (1966):337-39.
Poe's borrowings for "Murders." (BFF)

E2112. Durkin, Mary Brian, O. P. Dorothy L. Sayers (E2508), pp. 20, 98-100.
In working up her anthologies of detection and horror stories, Sayers studied those "masters," Poe, Collins, and Le Fanu. Poe is credited with development of the eccentric detective and the "red herring" technique of misleading readers. (BFF)

E2113. Eames, Hugh. Sleuths, Inc. (B99), pp. 10-11, 13, 15, 34, 39, 48.
Holmes owes much to Poe's Dupin, "a man of thought and genius." "Poe placed originality in opposition to social control." Contrary to the information on p. 15, Poe's first Dupin story was written in 1841, not 1842. Vidocq looms behind Poe's ratiocinative fiction. (BFF)

E2114. Eisenzweig, Uri. "Poe, Paris, 1846: La Lettre Pillée |Poe, Paris, 1846: the purloined letter|." Littérature 49 (Feb 83), pp. 63-68.
First publication (in the 20th century) of first 2 versions in French of "Murders in the Rue Morgue," both of them revised/rewritten versions of Poe's originals. Eisenzweig uses these texts to support his theory that here began the divorce between American concision and coherence in the detective story and the sensationalism of Gaboriau, Leblanc, Leroux.

E2115. Engel, Leonard W. "Truth and Detection: Poe's Tales of Ratiocination and His Use of the Enclosure." Clues 3:2 (Fall/Winter 82):83-86.
Le Fanu's "Passage in the Secret History of an Irish Countess" (1838) and the use of the "sealed room" in Poe's detective tales.

E2116. Fiedler, Leslie A. Love and Death in the American Novel. Cleveland and NY: Criterion Books, 1960; Meridian Books, 1962. pp. 474-78.
Dupin, the "half-artist, half-scientist," indicates that grotesquerie can be explained in terms of seeming normalcy. Poe's detective stories and others like them extend the Gothic explained supernatural. Poe's and other American detective stories demonstrate a "recalcitrant" artist's giving way to the "bourgeois community." After Dupin, American detectives are not worthy companions to Holmes, Father Brown, Wimsey, and their fellows. (BFF)

E2117. Fisher, Benjamin Franklin IV. "Ancilla to the Gothic Tradition--A Supplementary Bibliography." American Transcendental Quarterly 30 (1976):14-36.
Many items relevant to detective fiction by Poe or influenced by him are listed. (BFF)

E2118. ______. "Blackwood Articles a la Poe: How to Make a False Start Pay." Revue des langues vivantes/Tijdschrift voor Levende Talen 39 (1973):418-32.
The detective tales, particularly "Murders" and "The Gold-Bug," reveal Poe the hoaxer at work. Specifically, in tales like these, he begins with what appears to be nothing more than a typical Gothic thriller, and then he cleverly leads readers to different regions of literary concern. (BFF)

E2119. ______. "Fugitive Poe References: A Bibliography." Poe Studies 11 (1978):13-14; 12 (1979):31-34; 13 (1980):34-36; 14 (1981):25-30; 15 (1982):18-22.
Many items relevant to Poe's role in detective fiction, or to his appearance as a character or point of reference within such fiction itself, are cited. (BFF)

E2120. ______. "Poe, Blackwood's, and 'The Murders in the Rue Morgue'." American Notes & Queries 11 (1974):109-11.
A source for the great ape who terrified ladies (and in Poe's tale murdered them) appears in "A Chapter on Goblins," in Blackwood's. Poe makes a potentially comic encounter brutal and death-dealing. (BFF)

E2121. ______. "Poe's 'Tarr and Fether': Hoaxing in the Blackwood Mode." Topic 31 (1977):29-40.
In "The System of Dr. Tarr and Professor Fether," a late (1845) and often neglected tale, Poe burlesques themes and motifs from "Murders." (BFF)

E2122. Fusco, Richard. "Poe's Revisions of 'The Mystery of Marie Roget'--A Hoax?" In Poe at Work: Seven Textual Studies, edited by B. F. Fisher IV, pp. 91-99. Baltimore: The E. A. Poe Society, 1978.
Fusco surveys much previous criticism of this tale in his study of Poe's revisions. He concludes that a two-dimensional Poe as person is implicit here: first an egotistical and then an artistic being. (BFF)

E2123. Gavrell, Kenneth. "The Problem of Poe's Purloined Letter." TAD 15 (1982):381-82.
Flaws in the plotting of "The Purloined Letter."

E2124. Goldhurst, William. "Edgar Allan Poe and the Conquest of Death." New Orleans Review 2 (1969):316-319.
A subtle allegory of Legrand's progression from heaven to hell, through death, and to resurrection, underlies the story of "The Gold-Bug." (BFF)

E2125. ______. "Misled by a Box: Variations on a Theme from Poe." Clues 3:1 (Spring/Summer 82):31-37.
Poe's story "The Oblong Box" with its "innocent" narrator who misreads all the clues. Goldhurst then traces the use of the basic situation of the story to Doyle's "The Little Square Box" and Eugene O'Neill's "In the Zone."

E2126. Gravely, W. H., Jr. "An Incipient Libel Suit Involving Poe." Modern

Language Notes 60 (1945):308-311.
The charges of plagiarism leveled at Poe by the New York Herald and the Philadelphia Spirit of the Times are examined. (BFF)

E2127. Griswold, Rufus Wilmot. The Prose Writers of America. Philadelphia: Carey and Hart, 1847. pp. 523-24.
"The analytic subtlety and the singular skill shown in the management of revolting and terrible circumstances in The Murders of (sic) the Rue Morgue produced a deep impression, and made this story perhaps the most popular that Mr. Poe has written. An equal degree of intellectual acuteness marks The Gold Bug and the Purloined Letter, which are more pleasing and scarcely less interesting." (BFF)

E2128. Gross, Seymour. "Native Son and 'The Murders in the Rue Morgue': An Addendum." Poe Studies 8 (1975):23.
Wright felt the impact of Poe's murderous ape when he created Bigger. (BFF)

E2129. Grossvogel, David. "'The Purloined Letter': The Mystery of the Text." In Grossvogel (B135), pp. 93-107.
Poe's name recurs throughout this book of essays but this chapter contains an analysis of "The Purloined Letter." It is not, claims Grossvogel, wholly satisfactory as a detective story, but it lends itself well to psychoanalytic theories devolving from Marie Bonaparte and to critical views of texts, deriving from Jacques Lacan. (BFF)

E2130. Haining, Peter. Mystery! (B138), pp. 7-8, 17-31, 59, 103.
A terse account of Poe's origination of detective fiction--with comment that he never once used "detective" in regard to these tales--is accompanied by illustrations from early editions of his works. Poe's influence upon Doyle and Melville Davisson Post is mentioned. (BFF)

E2131. Halliburton, David. Edgar Allan Poe: A Phenomenological View. Princeton: Princeton University Press, 1973.
Although this book does not center upon the detective fiction, it offers provocative comments about the nature of those tales in a broad perspective. Halliburton is signally keen on matters of characterization. (BFF)

E2132. Harrowitz, Nancy. "The Body of the Detective Model: Charles S. Pierce and Edgar Allan Poe." In Eco/Sebeok (B100), pp. 179-97.
An examination of ways in which the scientist and the poet deal with the phenomena of the empirical world. Pierce used the term "abduction" to describe a process based on observation, intuition, hypothesis. Poe's method is called ratiocination and seems very close to the scientist's.

E2133. Hassell, J. Woodrow, Jr. "The Problem of Realism in 'The Gold Bug'." American Literature 25 (1953):179-92.
Realism and fantasy intermittently conflict. Poe's art is such that he manages to subsume this conflict and make fantasy appear plausible. The "Poet and Reasoner" are evident. (BFF)

E2134. Hawkins, John. "Poe's 'The Murders in the Rue Morgue'." Explicator 23 (Feb 65):item 49.
Checkers and chess motifs are analyzed. (BFF)

E2135. Haycraft, Howard. The Art of the Mystery Story (B142).

Poe's name appears in many of the essays gathered here--generally in praiseworthy terms. Haycraft's own classic first chapter from Murder for Pleasure is reprinted, with its fine analysis of Poe's place among writers of detective fiction. (BFF)

E2136. ______. Murder for Pleasure (B143), pp. ix, 1-27, 222, 251, 253, 302, 334, 387-91. Chapter I reprinted, in an abridged form, as "Father of the Detective Story," in SRL 24 (23 Aug 41):12-15.

The first chapter is a classic exposition of components of good detective fiction, as it derives from Poe's initial efforts in this form. "Murders" is termed "physical" detective fiction because we remember the descriptions instead of the reasoning. "Marie Roget" fails because it errs too much in the opposite direction. "The Purloined Letter," not flawless, is nonetheless the best of the three Dupin tales. Poe's career is sketched, his writings in veins of puzzle-solving, cryptography, and mystery are assessed. (BFF)

E2137. Hoffman, Daniel. PoePoePoePoePoePoe Poe. Garden City: Doubleday, 1972.

Ch. IV centers on the ratiocinative tales. Dupin thinks "by association." There are interesting comments on the theme of doubles in these tales and about their comic substance. (BFF)

E2138. Holman, Harriet R. "Longfellow in the Rue Morgue." In New Approaches to Poe, edited by Richard P. Benton, pp. 58-60. Hartford: Transcendental Books, 1970.

Consequent upon the critic Poe's "Longfellow War," that is, the leveling of "plagiarism" against the famous American poet, Poe punned in satiric hoaxing fashion upon his name in citing a "little fellow" in "Murders." Thus, we comprehend more humor in this tale than might be readily apparent at its surface. (BFF)

E2139. Hubbell, Jay B., ed. Tales and The Raven and other Poems. Columbus, OH: Charles E. Merrill, 1969. pp. v-xxvi.

Doyen to all Americanists, Hubbell places Poe within American literary tradition. He observed Poe's founding of the detective story (the three Dupin stories plus "The Gold-Bug" were selected for the first book publication of the Tales in 1845), the formulaic continuance of the type, and Poe's influence upon Doyle. (BFF)

E2140. Irwin, John T. American Hieroglyphics: The Symbol of the Egyptian Hieroglyphic in the American Renaissance. New Haven and London: Yale University Press, 1980. pp. 44, 118-119, 125-26.

There are interesting comments about Dupin's character, that of a masterful portrait of "scientific intuition" at work. The ape in "Murders" symbolizes the irrational animal lurking in all humankind. (BFF)

E2141. Jones, Buford. "Monsieur Dupin: Further Details on the Reality behind the Legend." Southern Literary Journal 9:1 (Fall 76):70-77.

A review of the hypotheses on Dupin's real-life source and a new proposal of André Marie-Jean-Jacques Duplin (1783-1865), a magistrate involved in two "scandals of international renown.".

E2142. Keller, Mark. "Dupin in the 'Rue Morgue': Another Form of Madness?" Arizona Quarterly 33 (1977):249-55.

Dupin's character is set forth at greater length in "Murders" than in the other two stories featuring him. His interest in analysis becomes monomaniacal, and he is far less sympathetic in "The Purloined Letter" than he was when he first appeared. There is good analysis of Poe's wordplay here. (BFF)

E2143. Kennedy, J. Gerald. "The Limits of Reason: Poe's Deluded Detectives." American Literature 47 (1975):184-96.

"The Man of the Crowd" stands as a transition between Poe's earlier terror tales and the detective fiction of the early 1840s. "The Oblong Box" is a tale filled with ironic stance toward ratiocination, which, Poe fairly soon concluded, was not great art and consequently returned to producing non-ratiocinative fiction of terror. (BFF)

E2144. Ketterer, David. "Tales of Ratiocination." In his The Rationale of Deception in Poe, pp. 238-54. Baton Rouge and London: Louisiana State University Press, 1979.

Ketterer examines the detective tales, all of which he thinks treat the creative process. Dupin is "detective, victim, and criminal in one." His name perhaps is chosen to call up associations of duplicity. (BFF)

E2145. Knight, Stephen. "'...his rich ideality'--Edgar Allan Poe's Detective." In Knight (B190), pp. 39-66.

An analysis of the three Dupin stories to show that, gradually, Poe created a pattern, to be repeated by other writers, in which "disorder could be contained by activating values that leisured readers could all share."

E2146. Lacan, Jacques. "Le séminaire sur 'la Lettre volée' |Seminar on 'the purloined letter'|." In Lacan, Ecrits, pp. 11-61. Paris: Editions du Seuil, 1966; reprinted in Yale French Studies 48 (1973):39-72; and in Most/Stowe (B264), pp. 21-54. English translation by Jeffrey Mehlman.

A psychoanalytic reading of Poe's tale, delivered at a conference in 1955-56, is followed by a more recent discussion of a neo-Freudian principle of repetition. Lacan is one of the seminal figures of modern philosophic and critical thought and this "seminar" is one of his more accessible and most influential writings.

E2147. Lemay, J. A. Leo. "The Psychology of 'The Murders in the Rue Morgue'." American Literature 54 (1982):165-88.

A "head-body dichotomy" pervades the tale, and in it Poe attacked Enlightenment theories of human emotions. The women represent a suppressed emotionalism, the ape and sailor the animal, murderously destructive elements in psychological makeup. As Dupin ultimately frees Le Bon (one of Poe's punning names), after revealing that murder originated with what amounts to repressed libido, readers can discern the necessity of integrating all elements in personality. (BFF)

E2148. Lippit, Noriko Mizuta. "Tanizaki and Poe: The Grotesque and the Quest for Supernal Beauty." Comparative Literature 29 (Summer 77):221-40. Reprinted in slightly revised form in Reality and Fiction in Modern Japanese Literature, by N. M. Lippit, pp. 82-103. White Plains, NY: Sharpe, 1980.

Examines Poe's influence on Junichiro Tanizaki (1886-1965), one of Japan's major literary figures. (JLS)

E2149. London, Rose. Cinema of Mystery. NY: Bounty Books, 1975.

On film versions of Poe's writings, this book furnishes throughout information and illustrations relevant to Poe's detective tales. Naturally, sensational aspects of "Murders" are prominent (just as they are in minds of film makers, apparently, as they went to work on this story and incidentally created an image of Poe the artist). (BFF)

E2150. Lowndes, R. A. W. "The Editor's Page: On Poe, Dupin, etc." SMS 2:6 (Spring 69):4-7, 121-24; 3:1 (Summer 69):4-7, 120-24, 126, 128; revised and reprinted as "The Contributions of Edgar Allan Poe," in Nevins (B290), pp. 1-18.

In the course of analyzing the three Dupin stories, Lowndes lists 32 elements that he feels later authors derived "directly or indirectly" from the stories.

E2151. Mabbott, Maureen Cobb. Mabbott as Poe Scholar: The Early Years. Baltimore: Enoch Pratt Free Library and the Edgar Allan Poe Society, 1980. pp. 30, 36.

This outline of the early career of the world's most renowned Poe scholar, by his widow, affords much valuable information concerning Poe the writer. The designated pages give particular data on "Murders," notably that the so-called "facsimile" printings are actually not duplicates of the manuscript, now in the Gimbel Collection of Poe, in the Free Library of Philadelphia. (BFF)

E2152. Mabbott, Thomas Ollive. "A Poe Manuscript." Bulletin of the New York Public Library 28 (1924):103-105.

Particulars for "'Thou Art the Man'" are provided. (BFF)

E2153. Mabbott, Thomas Ollive, ed., assisted by Eleanor D. Kewer and Maureen Cobb Mabbott. Collected Works of Edgar Allan Poe, vols. 2 & 3. Cambridge, MA: Belknap Press of Harvard Univ. Press, 1978.

Both volumes contain numerous references to the detective tales. The combination of texts with Mabbott's extensive headnotes and annotations makes these books "bibles" for readers of detective fiction. (BFF)

E2154. Marder, Daniel. "Poe's Perverse Imp and M. Dupin." College Literature 8 (1981):175-85.

Dupin projects Poe's self--in part as an intellectual scorned by society, in part as a surrogate for the author's alternation between despair and hope as regards his career and his personal life. (BFF)

E2155. Matthews, J. Brander. "Poe and the Detective Story." Scribner's Magazine 42 (1907):287093; reprinted in The Recognition of Edgar Allan Poe: Selected Criticism since 1829, edited by Eric W. Carlson, pp. 82-94 (Ann Arbor: University of Michigan Press, 1966); and in Buchloh/Becker 2 (B61), pp. 41-57.

Poe's modifications of the earlier Gothic mystery story are set forth, and his move from emphasis upon plot character is noted. Work by predecessors of Poe, mainly Voltaire's Zadig and his successors, is surveyed. (BFF)

E2156. Messac, Regis. Le "Detective Novel" (B257), passim.

Poe figures significantly in this vast survey of detective fiction through the 1890s, although Messac is quick to point out flaws in Poe's knowledge of France. (BFF)

E2157. Moldenhauer, Joseph, Jr. "Murder as a Fine Art: Basic Connections between Poe's Aesthetics, Psychology, and Moral Vision." PMLA 83 (May 68):284-97.

Dupin possesses the "artistic ability of Poe's poet-critic." That is, his powers are intuitional rather than analytical. The detective is principally concerned with "difficult, faulty, or incomplete verbal materials," as demonstrated in the Dupin tales and "The Gold-Bug." Dupin can resolve mysteries because he identifies with the criminal perpetrator of them; he is the criminal's double. (BFF)

E2158. Moore, John Robert. "Poe, Scott, and 'The Murders in the Rue Morgue'." American Literature 8 (1936):52-58.
The ape derives from Walter Scott's novel, Count Robert of Paris, and such a source will overturn arguments for Poe's psychosis showing within the tale. (BFF)

E2159. Mowkowitz, Sam. "Poe on 'Trial'." TAD 4 (1970/71):10-11.
A note commenting on a statement by Harvey H. Hewett-Thayer in Hoffmann: Author of the Tales (Princeton University Press, 1948, p. 319) that E. T. A. Hoffmann, and not Poe, is the father of modern mystery and detective fiction.

E2160. Murch, Alma Elizabeth. "The Short Detective Story. Edgar Allan Poe." In Murch (B267), pp. 67-83.
Poe created the detective short story. Critical comment on the ratiocinative tales is sound. (BFF)

E2161. Orel, Harold. "The American Detective-Hero." JPC 2 (1968):395-403.
Dupin is the first detective, he resembles his creator, he proceeds with the Rue Morgue case for amusement, and he is an urbane, worldly figure. A defense of the narrator in the Dupin tales is tersely offered. (BFF)

E2162. Osborne, Eric. Victorian Detective Fiction (A58), pp. 99-100.
Bibliographical particulars are given for English printings of Poe's Tales (containing "Murders," "Marie Roget," and "The Purloined Letter") as well as for Tales of Mystery, Imagination & Humor (Vizetelly, 1852), the edition read by so wide a British audience. (BFF)

E2163. Ousby, Ian. Bloodhounds of Heaven (B300), passim.
Poe is mentioned throughout. There are particularly interesting links drawn between Godwin's novel Caleb Williams and Poe and between Poe and Doyle. (BFF)

E2164. ______. "'The Murders in the Rue Morgue' and 'Doctor D'Arsac': A Poe Source." Poe Studies 5 (1972):52.
Poe transformed the greed motive in his source--a tale in Burton's Gentleman's Magazine--into something more complicated and rich. (BFF)

E2165. Panek, LeRoy L. "Play and Games: An Approach to Poe's Detective Tales." Poe Studies 10 (1977):39-41.
Modern psychological theories are brought to bear on these tales. (BFF)

E2166. Paul, Raymond. Who Murdered Mary Rogers? Englewood Cliffs, N.J.: Prentice-Hall, 1971.
This fictional treatment of Poe's tale holds out Daniel Payne, Mary Rogers's fiance, as the guilty one. (BFF)

E2167. Poe, Edgar Allan. The Gold-Bug. Foreward by Hervey Allen. Edited by Thomas Ollive Mabbott. NY: Remington & Hooper, 1928; Garden City: Doubleday, Doran, 1929.

The introductory essay gives publication history, the place of the tale among those of "ratiocination," as Poe termed them (instead of "detective stories"), variants, and information concerning Poe's accuracy. (BFF)

E2168. ______. The Letters of Edgar Allan Poe. Edited by John Ward Ostrom. 2 vols. NY: Gordian Press, 1966.

This revision of Ostrom's earlier volumes, published by Harvard University Press in 1948, gives Poe's own thoughts concerning his detective, or "ratiocinative," tales, particularly on pp. 201, 175-76, 328, 336. (BFF)

E2169. ______. Prose Romances. Edited by George E. Hatvary and Thomas O. Mabbott. Jamaica, NY: St. John's Univ. press, 1968.

This facsimile reprint of a projected series of Poe's tales contains "Murders." Variants from Graham's text of April 1841 are mentioned, though not listed (they are in Mabbott's Collected Works, E2153). Other relevant publication history is provided, as are terse comments on Poe's place in the literature of detection. (BFF)

E2170. Pollin, Burton R. "Poe's 'Murders in the Rue Morgue': The Ingenious Web Unravelled." In Studies in the American Renaissance: 1977, pp. 235-60. Boston: G. K. Hall, 1978.

Poe the hoaxer is at work throughout this tale. Many readers have overlooked the numerous improbabilities in this tale. Pollin attempts to correct the record, and his researches include maps of Paris in Poe's era as well as other documentary evidence that others have overlooked. (BFF)

E2171. Prior, Linda T. "A Further Word on Richard Wright's Use of Poe in Native Son." Poe Studies 5 (1972):52-53.

Poe's ape-thought-man killer is transformed by Wright into man-thought-ape, an ironic reversal. (BFF)

E2172. Quayle, Eric. "The Father of the Detective Story." In Quayle (B322), pp. 22-28.

On Poe's contributions and information on editions. With a photograph of Poe and other illustraions.

E2173. Richard, Claude. "Destin, Design, Dasen: Lacan, Derrida and 'The Purloined Letter'." Iowa Review 12:4 (Fall 81):1-11.

Transcript of a lecture in which Richard talks about Lacan's famous reading (E2146) of "The Purloined Letter" and concludes with an inventive and persuasive analysis of the implications of the letter "D" in the narrative. There is a richly annotated "Purloined Letter" dossier of references relating to Lacan's article and the controversy it has generated. There is also an interview with Richard (pp. 12-22) in which he describes Poe's French influence and the difficulty Americans have in understanding the French admiration for Poe. There are also further observations on "The Purloined Letter," in particular on the didactic and symbolic levels of the story. A good introduction to the state of current French critical thinking about and work on Poe.

E2174. Roth, Martin. "The Poet's Purloined Letter." In Adams, MDA 1973 (B3), pp. 113-28.

This tale demonstrated Poe's knowledge of biblical lore and his bent toward satiric hoaxing. (BFF)

E2175. St. Armand, Barton Levi. "Poe's 'Sober Mystification': The Uses of Alchemy in 'The Gold-Bug '." Poe Studies 4 (1971):1-7.
Alchemical lore imparts a consistency to this tale that is not admitted by J. Woodrow Hassell, Jr. (E2133). (BFF)

E2176. Sayers, Dorothy L. Great Short Stories (C725).
Poe is given high honors in Sayers's excellent introduction, and "Marie Roget" is warmly praised for its analytical methods. (BFF)

E2177. ______. Tales of Detection (C726).
Sayers deplores tendencies among modern detection writers to depart from the models set up by Poe. She includes, in the collection, Poe's "The Purloined Letter." (BFF)

E2178. (Smith, Mrs. E. V.) "The Works of the Late Edgar Allan Poe." North American Review 83 (1856):427-55.
The tales of ratiocination have a "philosophical substratum." Pilfering of "Murders" by French journals, Le Commerce and La Quotidienne, is mentioned. Poe's interest in cryptography, autography, and ciphers is noted. (BFF)

E2179. Stauffer, Donald Barlow. "Poe as Phrenologist: The Example of Monsieur Dupin." In Papers on Poe: Essays in Honor of John Ward Ostrom, edited by Richard P. Veler, pp. 113-25. Springfield, OH: Chantry Music Press.
Poe's revisions indicate his knowledge of Phrenology. Dupin is a "poet-artist." (BFF)

E2180. Stein, Aaron Marc. In Ball (B15), pp. 29-60 (passim).
Poe's invention of detective fiction is credited, although the low esteem in which his contemporaries held his detective tales is also pointed out. (BFF)

E2181. Stewart, R. F. ...And Always a Detective (B380), passim.
Despite claims for others, Poe fathered the detective story, although he remained ignorant of his importance in this area, as Wilkie Collins, who wrote shortly afterward, also remained. Too often, twentieth-century evaluators want to see these early works in more recent terms. (BFF)

E2182. Symons, Julian. "Tales of Detection." In his The Tell-Tale Heart: The Life and Works of Edgar Allan Poe, pp. 221-225. NY: Harper & Row, 1978. Translated into Japanese by Toshio Yagi. Tokyo: Sogen-sha, 1981.
A short section on Poe's detective tales and their influence on subsequent literature.

E2183. ______. "The Two Strands: Godwin, Vidocq, Poe." In Symons (B387), pp. 17-35.
All of Poe's detective stories receive attention, much of it historical, although some good critical comment is incorporated. Poe's Gothic heritage is tersely mentioned. (BFF)

E2184. Thomson, H. Douglas. "Edgar Allan Poe." In Thomson (B404), pp. 75-91.
Thomson seems generally unsympathetic to Poe's art in the Dupin tales, and he questions whether "The Gold-Bug" is a genuine detective story. (BFF)

E2185. Varnado, S. L. "The Case of the Sublime Purloin: or Burke's Inquiry as the Source of an Anecdote in 'The Purloined Letter'." Poe Newsletter 1:2:27.

Anecdote of the boy who "gauged opponents' moods by imitating their facial expressions."

E2186. Vines, Lois. "Dupin-Teste: Poe's Direct Influence on Valéry." French Forum 2 (1977):147-59.

Vines presents convincing parallels between Poe's and Valéry's writer-characters, Dupin and Teste. (BFF)

E2187. Walsh, John Evangelist. Poe the Detective: The Curious Circumstances behind 'The Mystery of Marie Roget', New Brunswick, NJ: Rutgers University Press, 1968. Translated into Japanese by Masao Kaiho and published as Meitantei Poe-shi (Tokyo: Soshi-shal, 1980).

With a foreword by Thomas Ollive Mabbott, this book is the most ample survey of primary documents in the case of Mary Rogers and Poe's treatment of it in his tale. Poe's abilities as a hoaxer (evident, Walsh thinks, in the second version of "Marie Roget") are assessed, and much attention goes to the confession of Mrs. Loss, involved in the original Rogers case. (BFF)

E2188. Wertz, S. K., and Linda L. "On Poe's use of 'Mystery'." Poe Studies 4 (1971):7-10.

The term for Poe may best be defined as what "involves the subject and the reader in preternatural or abnormal speculations--in astute analyses of the bizarre." They analzye the term with reference to the detective tales. (BFF)

E2189. Whitty, James H. "The Poe Mystery." Bookman 36 (1913):604.

"Marie Roget" is the topic. (BFF)

E2190. Wigmore, John H. "Did Poe Plagiarize 'The Murders in the Rue Morgue'?" Cornell Law Quarterly 13 (1928):219-36.

Similarities exist between Poe's tale and a case cited by Dr. Karl Loeffler, one-time editor of Judicial News, in Berlin. Poe did not plagiarize from Loeffler, who could have known Poe's work from sources in French. T. O. Mabbott is quoted as a supplier of information. (BFF)

E2191. Wilbur, Richard. "The Poe Mystery Case." NYRB, 13 July 67, pp. 16, 25-28; reprinted in Responses, by Richard Wilbur, pp. 127-38 (Harcourt Brace Jovanovich, 1976).

"Murders" is an allegory of the soul's coming to an understanding of itself. Dupin is representative of all the characters coalescing into a single personality. The ape symbolizes evil or irrationality that desires the destruction of a redemptive force, represented by the two women he kills. (BFF). Addendum: See also Wilbur's introduction to the Poe section of the college text Major Writers of America (1962) for a general introduction to Poe's life and works, with brief comments on the detection tales. Reprinted in Responses (as above), pp. 39-66.

E2192. Williams, Valentine. "The Detective in Fiction." The Fortnightly 134 (1 Sept 30):381-92.

"Doyle did for detective fiction what...Poe was not able to achieve: he made it respectable." Although he invented something original, Poe drew considerable inspiration from Vidocq. Poe's love for unravelling mysteries turned him to creation of detective stories, as did Gothic backgrounds. Holmes owes his popularity to Dupin. Poe's popularity in French, and particuarly his popularity as author of "Murders" is outlined, as is his impact upon Gaboriau. (BFF)

E2193. Wimsatt, W. K., Jr. "Mary Rogers, John Anderson, and Others." American Literature 21 (1950):48k2-84.
Responding to Worthen's 1948 essay (see below), Wimsatt suggests that Mary died from an abortion. John Anderson may have been implicated. These bits of information bear upon "Marie Roget." (BFF)

E2194. ______. "Poe and 'The Mystery of Marie Roget'." PMLA 56 (1941): 230-48.
Poe's signal idea was that the naval officer was connected with Marie's death. A history of Poe's methods and materials is given, with special attention to newspaper accounts. (BFF)

E2195. ______. "What Poe Knew about Cryptography." (PMLA 58 (1943):754-79.
This valuable study reveals that Poe's mastery of this topic, one relevant to his detective stories, was not nearly so accomplished as he claimed. (BFF)

E2196. Worthen, Samuel C. "Poe and the Beautiful Cigar Girl." American Literature 20 (1948):305-312.
Poe's logic is flawed, he does not "solve" the mystery of Mary Rogers, and he overlooks certain facts in the case. (BFF)

E2197. ______. "A Strange Aftermath of 'The Mystery of Marie Roget'." Proceedings of the New Jersey Historical Society 60 (1942):116-23.
A lively court case and Poe's bungling in treating factual background for his tale are discussed. (BFF)

POPKIN, ZELDA

Ref: Hubin 2, TCCMW, ABMI(S); The Writer 55:10 (Oct 42):291-94.

E2198. DeMarr, Mary Jean. "The Mysteries of Zelda Popkin." Clues 3:1 (Spring/Summer 82):1-8.
A biocritical essay with citations from Popkin's autobiography and discussions of her mystery fiction and the "hybrid" serious novel, A Death of Innocence.

E2199. Popkin, Zelda. Open Every Door. NY: E. P. Dutton, 1956.
Autobiography. See especially pages 182-188 for comments on the writing of her mystery fiction.

PORTER, JOYCE

Ref: Hubin 2, TCCMW, EMD, CC, SN, ABMI(S); The Writer 81:8 (Aug 68):16-18 (autobiography and working methods); The Writer 84:12 (Dec 71):9-10, 41.

Int: TMRN 3:2 (1969/70):19-22; EQMM, 24 March 82, pp. 118-20.

POST, MELVILLE DAVISSON

Ref: Hubin 2, TCCMW, EMD, CC, ABMI(S).

E2200. Boucher, Anthony. "Boucher on Post." In Post (E2206), pp. 417-18.
An appreciative tribute to Post; originally published as Boucher (E2201).

E2201. ______. "Introduction." In Uncle Abner, Master of Mystery, by Melville Davisson Post. NY: Collier Books, 1962.

E2202. Hubin, Allen J. "Introduction" to The Complete Uncle Abner (E2206), pp. vi-xvi.
Hubin speculates on the form of the Uncle Abner stories, their particularly American and "fully born rather than evolving" qualities, gives a brief biography and discusses the character of Uncle Abner and the chief characteristics of the stories.

E2203. Norton, Charles A. Melville Davisson Post: Man of Many Mysteries. Bowling Green, OH: Popular Press, 1973 (hardcover and paperback). 261pp.Notes. Post Bibliography. Index of story titles (no general index).
A diligently researched but awkwardly written study of the man whose Uncle Abner tales made him the foremost American writer of detective short stories between Poe and Hammett. The bibliography lists Post's contributions to magazines and newspapers as well as his books. (Warning: Norton reveals the endings of several stories in the course of his discussion.) Breen 200. (REB)

E2204. ______. "The Randolph Mason Stories." TAD 6 (1972/73):86-96.
Excerpted from Norton (E2203).

E2205. Overton, Grant. "Melville Davisson Post and the Use of Plot." Bookman 59 (June 1924):423-30; reprinted--with some minor revisions and additions--as "The Art of Melville Davisson Post" in Cargoes for Crusoes (NY: Appleton/George H. Doran/Little, Brown, 1924), pp. 41-59; and (in abridged form) in Post (E2206), pp. 419-23.
An analysis of "The Doomsdorf Mystery" and a discussion of Post's primary use of plot--rather than character--as his means to his fictional end. He has, claims Overton, lifted the detective story to the dignity of Greek tragedy by reinstating the deus ex machina and creating "the purge of pity and the cleansing of a reverent terror." With a biography and a bibliography. Breen 79.

E2206. Post, Melville Davisson. The Complete Uncle Abner. Edited by Allen J. Hubin. Mystery Library (B270): No. 4. 1977. xvi, 423pp. Illustrations by Darrel Millsap.
Contents: Allen J. Hubin, "Introduction," pp. vi-xvii (E2202); The Complete Uncle Abner, pp. 1-397; Allen J. Hubin, "Annotated Bibliography," pp. 399-410; Charles A. Norton, "Chronology of Melville Davisson Post," pp. 414-416; M. D. Post, "The Detective Short Story," pp. 414-416 (E2207); Anthony Boucher, "Boucher on Post," pp. 417-418 (E2200); Grant Overton, "The Art of Melville Davisson Post," pp. 419-423 (E2205).

E2207. Post, Melville Davisson. "The Mystery Short Story." A summary, apparently dictated by Post, of material in two articles originally published in The Saturday Evening Post 26 Dec 1914 and 27 Feb 1915; summary published in Overton, Cargoes for Crusoes (E2205), pp. 57-59; and in The Complete Uncle Abner (E2206), pp. 414-16.
A theoretical consideration of Post's concept of his contribution to the short story and a defense of the detective story as not inferior, in any way, to any other kind of literary structure. "The mystery story may be structurally so excellent and its workmanship so good that it is the equal of any form of literature."

E2208. Schantz, Tom and Enid. "Introduction: The Book of Abner." In The Methods of Uncle Abner, pp. vi-x. Boulder: The Aspen Press, July 1974.

E2209. Williams, Blanche Colton."Melville Davisson Post." In Our Short Story Writers, pp. 293-308. Originally published 1920. Reprint, NY: Dodd, Mead, 1940.

A discussion of Post's various collections of short stories with an analysis of their distinctive characteristics.

POSTGATE, RAYMOND

Ref: Hubin 2, TCCMW, EMD, CC, ABMI(S).

POTTS, JEAN

Ref: Hubin 2, TCCMW, EMD, CC, ABMI; Writer's Digest 37:9 (Sept 57):21-23, 78.

POWELL, JAMES

Ref: Hubin 2, TCCMW, ABMI.

Int: EQMM, Dec 82, pp. 92-94 and Jan 83, pp. 72-75.

POWELL, RICHARD

Ref: Hubin 2, CC, ABMI; The Writer 61:12 (Dec 48):395-99 (characterization, setting and plotting); The Writer 83:2 (Feb 70):11-14, 45 (sources for stories; illustrated with examples from Powell's writing).

POWELL, TALMAGE

Ref: Hubin 2, SN, ABMI(S).

E2210. Roberts, Ralph. "Talmadge Powell: Southern Mystery Man." TPP 5:4 (Oct 83):37-38.

Brief career profile of prolific short story writer.

PRATHER, RICHARD S.

Ref: Hubin 2, TCCMW, CC, SN, ABMI(S).

PRICE, ANTHONY

Ref: Hubin 2, TCCMW, ABMI(S).

Int: DAST 12:2 (1979):6-8; DAST 13:1 (1980):24-25 (photos); Jury 10:4 (1981):14-19.

E2211. Bedell, Jeanne F. "A Sense of History: The Espionage Fiction of Anthony Price." TAD 15 (1982):114-18.

Plot discussions, with some mention of Price's debt to Rudyard Kipling in their "shared emphasis upon the fusion of past and present."

E2212. Broberg, Jan. "Brobergs brottstycke 3 |Broberg's crime piece 3|." Jury 1: 3/4 (1972):14, 67.

Article on Price's fiction. (MS)

PRIESTLY, J. B.

Ref: Hubin 2, TCCMW, EMD,CC, ABMI(S).

E2213. Barzun, Jacques, and Taylor, Wendell Hertig. "Introduction." In Salt Is Leaving (NY, 1975), by J. B. Priestly. "Crime Fiction 1950-1975" (B18).

E2214. Cooper, Susan. J. B. Priestly: Portrait of an Author. NY: Harper & Row, 1970. 240pp.
Some discussion of his thrillers and Salt is Leaving in Chapter 7.

PRINCE, JEROME and HAROLD

E2215. McSherry, Frank D., Jr. "Avant-Garde Writing in the Detective Story." TAD 3 (1969/70):96.
Movie techniques used in stories published in EQMM in May 1944 and January 1945. In a letter to TAD (3:277), McSherry reports on a letter from Frederick Dannay commenting on the article.

PRIOR, ALLAN

Ref: Hubin 2, TCCMW, SN, ABMI(S).

PROCTER, MAURICE

Ref: Hubin 2, TCCMW, EMD, CC, ABMI(S).

See also: B96.

E2216. Barzun, Jacques, and Taylor, Wendell Hertig. "Introduction." In The Pub Crawler (NY, 1957), by Maurice Proctor. "Crime Fiction 1950-1975" (B18).

PRONZINI, BILL

Ref: Hubin 2, TCCMW, SN, ABMI; The Writer 84:5 (May 71):12-14, 46 (dialogue); The Writer 89:2 (Feb 76):14-17; The Writer 94:11 (Nov 81):11-15 (research tools; comments on Pronzini stories); The Writer 90:12 (Dec 77):19-23 (mystery short-short).

Int: TAD 11 (1978):46-48; TPP 1:6 (Nov 78):11-13; Polar 20 (July 81):11-16 (photos).

E2217. Deloux, Jean-Pierre. "Le Grand jeu |The big game|." Polar 20 (July 81):4-10.
According to Deloux, Pronzini's novels are built on a structure in which there is a gradual shift from an initial physical situation (a hold-up, a crime), toward the psychic and the spiritual. Much of the article focuses on a study of Pronzini's "Nameless" detective.

E2218. "Dossier Bill Pronzini." Polar 20 (July 81):4-31.
Contents: Jean-Pierre Deloux, "Le Grand jeu," pp. 4-10 (E2217); "Entretien avec Bill Pronzini," pp. 11-16 (interview; photos); Jacques Baudou, "Bibliographie de Bill Pronzini," pp. 17-19; and Bill Pronzini, "Un boulot de tout repos |A nice easy job|," pp. 20-32 (short story, translated by Michèle Valencia).

E2219. Isaac, Frederick. "Nameless and Friend: An Afternoon with Bill Pronzini." Clues 4:1 (Spring/Summer 83):35-52.
An interview/essay. A study of the "Nameless" series and Pronzini's sensitive private eye, with a description of Pronzini's opinions on John Dickson Carr, classic British mysteries, John D. MacDonald and his favorite mystery writer, Ed McBain.

E2220. Nevins, Francis M., Jr. and Bill Pronzini. "Bill Pronzini: A Checklist." TAD 13 (1980):345-350. Illustrated.
Includes both the novels and the short fiction, written alone, in collaboration and under pseudonyms.

PROPPER, MILTON

Ref: Hubin 2, TCCMW, EMD, CC, ABMI(S).

E2221. Nevins, Francis M., Jr. "The World of Milton Propper." TAD 10 (1977):196-203.
A biography and discussion of Propper's detective fiction. See comment by Propper's sister in a letter, TAD 10:291; and a correction by J. R. Cox in TAD 10:381.

QUEEN, ELLERY

Ref: Hubin 2, TCCMW, EMD, CC, SN, ABMI(S); UN 4:6 (1952):4-5, 12-15 (Photos; full profile of EQ as writer, editor, and contributor to the field).

Int: Jury 11:4 (1982):14-18; Playboy 26:6 (1979):48 (w/F, Dannay); EQMM, Jan 79, pp. 84-85, and Feb 79, pp. 97-98 (w/F. Dannay); People, 5 March 79, pp. 47-51 (w/F. Dannay; photos; includes career sketch); Pittsburgh Press, 30 Apr 79, B-1 (w/F. Dannay; photos); Polar 25 (15 Oct 82):39-41 (w/Frederic Dannay).

See also: B170, B310, C747, D399-401, D415.

E2222. Albany, Francis. "Ellery Queen, le logicien du mystère |E. Q., the logician of the mystery|." Europe no. 571/572, Nov/Dec 76, pp. 91-98. Trans. into French by François Rivière and the author.
Profiles of the two Queens and an examination of the investigative methods of E. Q.

E2223. Andrews, Angela. "Remembering Ellery Queen." PQ 5:3 (Fall 82):3-9. Illus.
A survey of the Queen career and a list of the first 20 Queen titles published by Pocket Books.

E2224. Bainbridge, John. "Ellery Queen: Crime Made Him Famous and His Authors Rich." Life 15:21 (22 Nov 43):70-76. Photo and 1 illustration.
An informal survey of the Queen publishing phenomenon, ending with a somewhat mystified description of the authors' collaborative methods and their cross-country lecture tours as a masked Barnaby Ross and Ellery Queen. The essay seems to capture some of the quality of the writers' public personae.

E2225. Biederstadt, Lynn. "To The Very Last: The Dying Message." TAD 12 (1979):209-210.
Queen's use of the "dying message" ploy.

E2226. Boucher, Anthony. Ellery Queen: A Double Profile. Boston: Little, Brown Co., 1951.
A 12-page pamphlet published on the occasion of Queen's 25th novel, The Origin of Evil. (F. M. Nevins, Jr.)

E2227. ______. "Introduction." In Cat of Many Tails (Little, Brown, 1949), by Ellery Queen. NY: Bantam, 1965.

E2228. ______. "Introduction." In The Quintessence of Queen, edited by Anthony Boucher. NY: Random House, 1962.

E2229. ______. There Was No Mystery in What the Crime Editor Was After. N.p., n.d. (New York, 1961) 4pp, printed wraps. Edition limited to 500 copies. A privately printed chapbook version of Boucher's essay from the New York Times, 26 Feb 61, reprinted in EQMM, June 1961.

A tribute to Ellery Queen the editor on the 20th anniversary of EQMM. (REB)

E2230. Breen, Jon L. "The Fantastic World-Wide Ellery Queen Poll." TQCB 3:1 (April 1971):7-9.

A report of the results of a poll of readers of the Queen Canon Bibliophile asking them to name their five favorite Ellery Queen novels. Twelve respondents selected, in order, Calamity Town, The Tragedy of Y, The Tragedy of X, Cat of Many Tails, and The Egyptian Cross Mystery. (JN)

E2231. "A Case of Double Identity." MD (Magazine), December 1967. Reprinted in EQR (unnumbered) (October 1971):11-17; and in Queen (E2271), pp. 310-20.

A lengthy personal and professional profile of Frederic Dannay and Manfred B. Lee. Soundly researched and enlivened by some amusing anecdotage found nowhere else, it was, according to Francis M. Nevins, Jr., Dannay's favorite article of its type. (JN)

E2232. "A Century of Thrills and Chills: Ellery Queen Meets the Critics." WLB 16:8 (April 42):638-44, 661.

Transcript of a radio broadcast in which Lee, Howard Haycraft, Granville Hicks and Basil Davenport participated. 101 Years' Entertainment is used as the springboard for a discussion which is historical, taxonomical and rambling.

E2233. Christopher, Joe R. "The Bigamy of Ellery Queen, with a Challenge to the Reader." TQCB 1:2 (Jan 69):11-12 (published as "Challenge to the (TQCB) Reader"); reprinted in Christopher (E2238), pp. 10-11.

Commentary on a footnote in Queen's Quorum, pp. 82-83. (REB)

E2234. ______. "The Case of the Missing Article." TQCB 2:1 (Feb 1970):14; reprinted in Christopher (E2238), pp. 21-22.

Recounts briefly the author's unsuccessful attempt to locate in the pages of Good Housekeeping an article by Ellery Queen on Poe's "Thou Art the Man," stated by Anthony Boucher, in The Great American Detective Stories, to have appeared therein sometime prior to 1945. (JN)

E2235. ______. "Cross-Trumps: A Conjectural Note on Rex Stout and Ellery Queen." TAD 1 (1967/68):9. Revised and enlarged version published as "Cross-Trumps" in TQCB 2:2 (July 70):6-7; and a further revised version as "Cross-Trumps: Rex Stout and Ellery Queen" in Christopher (E2238), pp. 24-26.

A comparison of the poker, travel, chess, and holiday motifs used in the titles of various works, long and short, by Rex Stout and Ellery Queen. (JN)

E2235a. ______. "Ellery's Adventure in Wonderland." Originally published as an untitled review in Jabberwocky: The Journal of the Lewis Carroll Society 6:2 (Spring 77):53-57; reprinted in Christopher (E2238), pp. 13-18.

The use of Lewis Carroll motifs in the Queen short story "The Adventure of the Mad Tea-Party" (1934) and in the TV script (1975) based on it.

E2236. ______. "Last but Not Least." TAD 4:1 (1970):11; reprinted in Christopher (E2238), p. 12.

Note on the EQ stories in which the last words of the text are the murderer's name. (REB)

E2237. ______. "The Mystery of Social Reaction: Two Novels by Ellery Queen." TAD 6 (1972/73):28-32.
The Glass Village and Cop Out as novels of social comment in which the social order is defended.

E2238. ______. Queen's Books Investigated, or Queen is in the Accounting House. Stephenville, TX: The Carolingian Press, 1983. 35pp. Wraps. Edition limited to 30 numbered copies.
Chapbook of short notes and verse on Ellery Queen, typical of the playful but genuine scholarship to be found in the mystery fan journals. Contents: "A Queenly Paeon," p. 5 (limerick); "Murder in the Roman Theatre," pp. 6-7 (outline of Ellery's solution to the dying message puzzle in the first EQ novel; gives away the solution); "The Persian Hat Mystery; or, The Tragedy of Q," pp. 8-9 (parody); "The Bigamy of Ellery Queen, with a Challenge to the Reader," pp. 10-11 (E2233); "Last but Not Least," p. 12 (E2236); "Ellery's Adventure in Wonderland," pp. 13-18 (E2235a); "Joe Meets Ellery," pp. 19-20 (first encounter with an EQ novel); "The Case of the Missing Article," pp. 21-22 (E2234); "Sing a Song of Suspects," p. 23 (verse); "Cross-Trumps: Rex Stout and Ellery Queen," pp. 24-26 (E2235); "The Semi-Precious 'Diamonds in Paradise,'" pp. 27-28 (E2241); "The Retirement of Richard Queen," pp. 29-33 (E2240); "The Re-Shattered Raven: Perhaps an Anti-Climax to this Chapbook but a Suggestion That the Tradition Continues," p. 34 (E2239). (REB)

E2239. ______. "The Re-Shattered Raven: Perhaps an Anti-Climax to This Chapbook but a Suggestion That the Tradition Continues." TAD 3 (1969/70):133; reprinted in Christopher (E2238), p. 34.
Originally published as an untitled review, this note is a clever linking of EQ with Edward D. Hoch's novel The Shattered Raven. (REB)

E2240. ______. "The Retirement of Richard Queen." TQCB 1:1 (1968):(2)-(5); revised version published in Christopher (E2238), pp. 29-33.
A brief examination of thematic and symbolic elements in Queen's Inspector Queen's Own Case and The House of Brass, associating the former with Shakespeare's Seven Ages of Man and the latter with the Gothic tradition in mystery fiction. (JN)

E2241. ______. "The Semi-Precious 'Diamonds in Paradise'." In Christopher (E2238), pp. 27-28.
Comparison of the texts of two versions (magazine and book) of the EQ short story. (REB)

E2242. Del Buono, Oreste. "La spettabile ditta Ellery Queen lascia ancora misteri [The respectable firm of Ellery Queen still leaves mysteries]." Tuttolibri 2, Sept. 82.
Brief profile of Ellery Queen, on the occasion of the death of Frederic Dannay. "The figure of Ellery Queen so elegant, brilliant and fortunate...is really the American dream, rather North American, the dream conceived and hatched by two who do not feel themselves sufficiently North American. It was Ellery Queen who led them by the hand into complete installation, into integration in depth." (RC)

E2243. Deloux, Jean-Pierre. "American Queen." Polar 25 (15 Oct 82):9-26. After a brief preface in which Deloux links Queen to the Western tradition of reason and logic, he proceeds to a straightforward survey of the fiction published as by Ellery Queen and Barnaby Ross.

E2244. "Dossier Ellery Queen." Polar 25 (15 Oct 82). Illus. Includes, on pp. 7-8, a reproduction of a holograph letter from Dannay to François Guérif. Contents: François Guérif, "Editorial," p. 3 (tribute to Dannay); Jacques Baudou, "Il était une fois, Ellery Queen |Once upon a time there was Ellery Queen)," pp. 5-6 (introductory tribute); Jean-Pierre Deloux, "American Queen," p. 9-26 (E2243); François and Catherine Guérif, "Bibliographie d'Ellery Queen," pp. 27-37 (American, English and French first publication, and a list of short stories published in French translation); F. Guérif, "Entretien avec 'Ellery Queen'," pp. 39-41 (interview with F. Dannay, Stockholm, 1981); Paul Gayot, "Le chant du signe: Ellery Queen, poète," pp. 42-48 (E2250); E. Queen, "Du bon usage des pseudonymes |On the proper use of pseudonyms|," pp. 49-55 (comments on pseudonyms used by mystery writers; originally published as the preface to Woman in the Dark; French translation by J. P. Gratias); J.-J. Schleret, "Ellery Queen au cinéma et à la télévision," pp. 56-66 (film and TV adaptations; includes an interview with French director Claude Chabrol who directed a film version of Ten Days' Wonder).

E2245. "Ellery Queen." Xenophile 14 (June 75). Cover portrait of Dannay, Lee and Queen by Frank Hamilton. Contents: Michael Murphy, "A Queen Quandry Quickly Quavered in Quondam Quixotic Quotation: A note on notations re:Queen," pp. 2-3 (note by Vincent Starrett on Queen with explanatory material by Murphy); Francis M. Nevins, Jr., "Editor at Work: Ellery Queen and EQMM," pp. 4-5 (anecdotal account of Dannay as EQMM editor); Nils Hardin, "Mystery League: A Summary," pp. 9-13 (D415); "From TQCB," pp. 55-59 (excerpts from TQCB).

E2246. "Ellery Queen Builds Collection of Rare Detective Short Stories." PW 144 (20 Nov 43):1946-49. Photos. High-lights of Queen's short story collection.

E2247. The Ellery Queen Review. See The Queen Canon Bibliophile.

E2248. Fistell, Ira J. "Ellery Queen: The First Fifty Years." West Coast Review of Books 5:4 (July 79):82-86. Good survey of EQ's career, with the clearest statement in print about the non-EQ EQ paperbacks. Text marred by jumbled paragraphs, transposed lines, no proofreading. (REB)

E2249. Gaiter, Dorothy J. "Frederic Dannay: Obituary." NY Times, 5 Sept 82, p. 24. Photo.

E2250. Gayot, Paul. "Le chant du signe: Ellery Queen poète |The song of the sign: E. Q. poet|." Polar 25 (15 Oct 82):42-48. A study of the uses of language in Queen's fiction.

E2251. Godfrey, Thomas. "The Lamp of God." TAD 12 (1979):212-13. Publishing history of the Queen novelette, with an analysis of fictional techniques.

E2252. Honce, Charles. "The First Lady Flatfoot." In For Loving a Book, pp. 67-70. Mount Vernon, NY: Privately printed, 1945.
A short discussion of the history of women detectives in crime fiction, turning into a history and appreciation of "Ellery Queen". (SS)

E2253. Hubin, Allen J. "Frederic Dannay: Doctor of Humane Letters." TAD 12 (1979):236-37. Photos.
Report on the awarding to Dannay of an honorary degree by Carroll College in Waukesha, Wisconsin.

E2254. Lachman, Marvin. "Ellery Queen and His New York." TQCB 1:3 (March 69):8-12.
A survey of some of the many New York City sites and locales, real and fancied, featured in the Queen canon, offered in support of the argument that Queen "is the New York detective in the same way that Sherlock Holmes, Inspector Maigret, and Philip Marlowe represent London, Paris, and Los Angeles respectively." (JN)

E2255. ______. "The Magazine." TQCB 2:1 (Feb 70):6-12.
A brief history and critique of EQMM 1941-1969, citing both its major contributions to the genre and certain post-1960 trends considered "cause for concern." Appended tables provide "A Chronology" which lists by date major changes in format and the appearance of significant features and stories; a listing of "Outstanding Writers Whose First Stories Were Published in EQMM;" and paid circulation figures for the years 1960-69. (JN)

E2256. ______. "The Misadventures of Ellery Queen." TQCB 1:4 (Aug 69):7-10.
A brief survey, with descriptions, of the numerous parodies and pastiches in print as of 1969 which feature Ellery Queen, both the fictional character and the author. (JN)

E2257. ______. "The Roman Hat Mystery." TQCB 2:1 (Feb 70):13.
A facetious review of the first Ellery Queen novel, written as of "August 1929," in which the work's numerous virtues are viewed as faults, leading the reviewer to the "inescapable conclusion that in 1930, on the first anniversary of this book, no one will even remember the name 'Ellery Queen'." (JN)

E2258. la Cour, Tage. Detektivfortellingens dronning |The queen of the mystery Story|. Skjern: Gullander, 1979. 25pp.
Includes two chapters on Ellery Queen. (IH)

E2259. Lee, Rand. "Dad and Cousin Fred Entered a Writing Contest...That's When Ellery Queen Was Born." TV Guide, 11 Oct 75, pp. 20-24.
Article on the Queen novels by Manfred Lee's son.

E2260. "Mysterious Masked Author." PW 130 (10 Oct 36):1512.
A short news item identifying Dannay and Lee as "Ellery Queen."

E2261. Narcejac, Thomas. "Ellery Queen." In Narcejac (B287), pp. 111-26.
Narcejac sees Queen as moving from the novel as puzzle to the novel as game where the detective novel "ceases to be scientific."

E2262. Nevins, Francis M., Jr. "The Drury Lane Quartet." Originally published as part of Section Two of Nevins QCB series (E2265); revised and reprinted in Nevins (B290), pp. 122-35.

Survey of the four novels written by Dannay and Lee under the pseudonym of Barnaby Ross.

E2263. ______. "Ellery Queen in Wrightsville." TAD 7 (1973/74):4-10.
An excerpt from Royal Bloodline (E2266), in which Nevins discusses the fiction of Queen's third period (1942-48).

E2264. ______. "Introduction" to The Tragedy of Y (E2271), pp. ix-xvii.
A study of the Drury Lane series and of the writing/publishing Queen phenomenon of the 1930s.

E2265. ______. "Royal Bloodline: the Biography of the Queen Canon." TQCB. part One: 1: 1 (1968), (5)-(10); reprinted 3:1 (April 1971):2-7; part Two: 1:1 (January 1969):2-10; part Three: 1:3 (March 1969):2-7; Part Four: 1:4 (August 1969):2-6; Part Five: 2:1 (February 1970):2-6; Part Six: 2:2 (July 1970):1-5; Parts Seven and Eight: The Ellery Queen Review, (unnumbered) (October 1971):2-10.
A serialization of portions of an early version of Nevins' Royal Bloodline (E2266). (REB)

E2266. ______. Royal Bloodline: Ellery Queen, Author and Detective. Bowling Green, OH: Popular Press, 1974; Japanese translation by Tomoko Akizu published as Ellery Queen no Sekai (Tokyo: Hayakawa Shobo, 1980), and includes--in compliance with the wishes of the author--the translation of an article "Ellery Queen on the Small Screen," published in TAD 12 (1979):216-23. 288pp. Illus. Index and a checklist.
After an introduction which consists of biographies of Manfred and Lee and a history of the team's activities, Nevins undertakes a meticulous analysis of the works of Ellery Queen. The checklist of the writings includes titles of works edited by Queen and a short list of secondary material.

E2267. Nevins, Francis M., Jr., and Ray Stanich. The Sound of Detection. Ellery Queen's Adventures in Radio. Madison, IN: Brownstone Books, 1983. viii, 109pp. Photos. Cover drawing by Brad W. Foster.
The first part of this book is a biographical and critical memoir of Ellery Queen by Francis M. Nevins, Jr., which complements and extends the same author's Royal Bloodline (E2266). Although centered around the involvement of Frederic Dannay and Manfred Lee with the Ellery Queen radio program (1939-48), the memoir provides additional biographical details and an invaluable discussion of Dannay's and Lee's working methods. Nevins's impressive knowledge of, and infectious enthusiasm for, his subject are evident throughout. The second part of the book, "The Adventures of Ellery Queen: Chronology and Episode Log" by Nevins and Stanich, lists all of the radio episodes by broadcast date and title, with notes on the cast, guest stars, sponsors, sources of the plots, printed or recorded versions of the episodes, and other details. Overall, the book chronicles an important but previously neglected area of the Dannay/Lee collaboration. (REB)

E2268. Newton, John J. "Ellery Queen: A Checklist." TQCB 1:3 (March 69): 13-18.
A bibliography, essentially complete as of 1969, of the first editions of books written and edited by Ellery Queen, covering all categories both hardcover and paperback. Subsequently superseded by the listing, current as of 1974, in Nevins' Royal Bloodline (E2266), which includes periodical appearances as well. (JN)

E2269. The Queen Canon Bibliophile.
A fan magazine devoted to the life and works of Ellery Queen. Eight mimeographed issues totaling 151 pages, published irregularly from 1968 to October 1971. With eight and final issue, title changed to The Ellery Queen Review. Edited and published by Rev. Robert E. Washer. Contributing Editor: Francis M. Nevins, Jr., beginning with Vol. I, No. 2. Contents included Queen-oriented articles, commentary, letters, and reviews, along with reviews of books by other mystery writers. Some material reprinted from other sources. (JN)

E2270. Queen, Ellery. An Exhibition on the Occasion of the Opening of the Ellery Queen Collection. Austin, TX: The Research Center, The University of Texas, January 16, 1959. 27pp. Illus. Wraps. Foreword: "The Ellery Queen Collection" by F. W. Roberts.
A catalogue of the exhibition marking the opening of the Ellery Queen collection of detective fiction at the University of Texas. Selected books, periodicals, and manuscripts from the Queen collection are listed and annotated by Queen (Frederic Dannay): Poe, Doyle, Twain, Dickens, Collins, Gaboriau, and a selection of over a hundred novels and short story collections from Voltaire's Zadig onward. Inscriptions of holograph letters are noted, and three of the rarest books--Clifford Ashdown's The Adventures of Romney Pringle, Victor L. Whitechurch's Thrilling Stories of the Railway, and C. Daly King's The Curious Mr. Tarrant--receive longer annotations. (REB)

E2271. ______. The Tragedy of X (originally published as by Barnaby Ross). Edited by Francis M. Nevins, Jr. Mystery Library Series (B270): No. 7. 1978. xviii, 320pp. Illustrations by Joyce Kitchell.
Text of the 1932 novel with critical material as follows: Francis M. Nevins, Jr., "Introduction," pp. ix-xvii (E2264); Ellery Queen, "Another Open Letter," pp. xviii-xx; Ellery Queen, "An Open Letter to the Reader," pp. xxi-xxiii; The Tragedy of X, pp. xxiv-xxviii, 1-297; Francis M. Nevins, Jr., "Ellery Queen: A Checklist," pp. 300-303; "Reviews of The Tragedy of X," pp. 304-305; David Hellyer, "The Accolades of Ellery Queen," p. 307 (list of awards); "A Case of Double Identity," pp. 310-320 (E2231).

E2272. Queen, Ellery (Frederic Dannay). "Introduction." In The Roman Hat Mystery, by Ellery Queen, pp. (v-x). "Golden Anniversary Edition." NY: The Mysterious Press, 1979. (REB)

E2273. ______. "Who Shall Ever Forget?" In Nevin (B290), pp. 37-40. First published in Queen, In the Queen's Parlor (B323), pp. 125-29.
Dannay recounts his childhood discovery of Sherlock Holmes.

E2274. Queendom. Editor: Masatoshi Saito. Published by the Ellery Queen Fan Club. Editorial address: 85-1-102 Kanda, Urawa, Saitama, Japan. Quarterly. (JK)

E2275. Ruble, William. "Explaining Ellery Queen." TQCB 2:2 (July 70):8-9.
How the writer introduced his two young teenage children to the Queen Canon, and the problems he encountered in attempting to differentiate Queen the character, the author, the editor, the collector, and the anthologist. (JN)

E2276. A Silver Anniversary Tribute to Ellery Queen from Authors, Critics,

Editors and Famous Fans. Boston: Little, Brown, 1954. 31pp. 8vo, printed wrappers.

A collection of short comments and tributes to Ellery Queen by some 90 contributors, including Boucher, Haycraft, Starrett, and Upfield. Issued to commemorate EQ's 25th anniversary and the publication of his 28th novel, The Glass Village. (REB)

E2277. Sullivan, Eleanor. "Fred Dannay and EQMM." TAD 12 (1979):201-202. Illus.

Personal memories of Dannay by the EQMM editor who was hired by Dannay.

E2278. Touchant, Jean-Louis. "Les Aventures de Ellery Queen en France." Les Amis du crime 7 (Sept 80). Wraps. Illus. 55pp.

A catalogue of works of Queen published in France with a running commentary by Touchant. The narrative describes the history of an addiction and offers what Touchant characterizes as impressions of the fictional world of Ellery Queen. Touchant cites abundantly from the French translations.

E2279. Washer, Rev. Robert E. "An Editor's Outline." TQCB 1:3 (March 69):23-25.

Commentary on the character of the fictional Ellery Queen and the crisis of self doubt he experienced in the novels Ten Days' Wonder and Cat of Many Tails. Washer promised more in a similar vein, but no subsequent installments of the "Outline" appeared. (JN)

E2280. Yates, Donald A. "Van Dine and Queen." TQCB 1:4 (Aug 69):12-14.

"Random jottings," focusing mainly on the more prominent trappings of the S. S. Van Dine mystery novels incorporated into the early works of Ellery Queen. (JN)

QUENTIN, PATRICK

Ref: Hubin 2, TCCMW, EMD, CC, ABMIS; The Writer 55:1 (Jan 42):35-38; The Writer 64:1 (Jan 51):6-7 (on plotting).

See also: Stagge, Jonathan; C617.

E2281. Endrèbe, Maurice-Bernard. "Patrick Quentin." In Enigmatika 19 (June 81), pp. 47-49.

Originally published as a "postface" to a French edition of Assassin pour dames seules. Endrèbe describes his experience with the works of Q. Patrick and Patrick Quentin, and includes some information based on his acquaintanceship with Hugh Wheeler.

E2282. "Patrick Quentin." Les Amis du crime 2 (n.d.). Not paginated.

In addition to a bibliography of the fiction published under the pseudonyms of Q. Patrick, Patrick Quentin and Jonathan Stagge, there is also the following material: an interview with Belgian Writer M.-B. Endrèbe, reviews by French critics of some of the books, a filmography and a grouping of the books by pseudonym.

Quinn, Seabury

Ref: Hubin 2, ABMIS.

E2283. Carter, Lin. "Introduction" to The Adventures of Jules de Grandin, pp. 9-15. NY: Popular Library, 1976. Wraps.

A survey of Quinn's life and writing. In an "Afterword" Robert Weinberg talks about several of the de Grandin stories.

E2284. Lowndes, R. A. W. "The Cases of Jules de Grandin: A chronological listing." SMS 3:1 (Summer 69):76-85.
With an appendix of notes on the illustrations for the stories as they were published in Weird Tales.

E2285. ______. "Introduction" to The Casebook of Jules de Grandin, pp. 9-13. NY: Popular Library, 1976. Wraps.
Lowndes reprinted a number of Quinn stories in Magazine of Horror and Startling Mystery Stories and he describes the correspondance with Quinn as he was preparing them for publication. With an "afterword" by Robert Weinberg on the New Jersey setting of the de Grandin series.

E2286. Quinn, Seabury. "By Way of Explanation." In The Adventures of Jules de Grandin, pp. 16-17. NY: Popular Library, 1976. Wraps.
Quinn comments briefly on the series and on his psychic detective, de Grandin.

E2287. Sampson, Robert. "The Very Much So Clever Fellow." Weird Tales Collector 5 (1979), pp. 3-18. With two illustrations and a photograph of Quinn and his son.
A profile of the series with an evaluation of its effectiveness for today's reader.

E2288. Wellman, Manley Wade. "Introduction" to The Skeleton Closet of Jules de Grandin, pp. 9-13. NY: Popular Library, 1976.
A biographical memoir on Quinn drawing on Wellman's friendship with his fellow Weird Tales author. With incidental remarks on the series by Robert Weinberg in an "Afterword."

RADFORD, E. and M. A.

Ref: Hubin 2, TCCMW, ABMI(S).

RAE, HUGH C.

Ref: Hubin 2, TCCMW, ABMI(S).

RAFFERTY, S. S.

Ref: Hubin 2, TCCMW, ABMI.

RAMPO, EDOGAWA

Ref: Hubin 2, CC.

E2289. Gen'eisha, ed. Edogawa Ranpo no Sekai |The world of Edogawa Rampo|. Tokyo: Gen'eisha, 1975. 312pp. A special issue of Gen'eijo magazine.
A collection of 61 critical articles and essays on Rampo, including both original and reprinted material. With a bibliography and chronology. (HS/TT)

E2290. Harris, James B. Translator's Preface to Japanese Tales of Mystery and Imagination, by Edogawa Rampo, pp. vii-xii. Translated by James B. Harris. Tokyo and Rutland, VT: Charles E. Tuttle Co., 1956.
Biographical sketch of Edogawa Rampo (pseudonym of Taro Hirai), known as "the father of the Japanese detective story," who wrote the first modern Japanese detective story, "Nisen Doka," in 1923. Includes some brief remarks on the history of Japanese mystery fiction and on the

difficulty of translating Japanese into English. (JLA)

E2291. Nakajima, Kawataro, ed. Edogawa Ranpo: Hyoron to Kenkyu |Edogawa Rampo: criticism and study|. Tokyo: Kodan-sha, 1980. 240pp. Bibliography.
An anthology of 28 critical studies on Rampo, from a literary historical perspective. With an appendix, "An Edogawa Rampo Bibliography," compiled by the editor. (HS/TT)

E2292. Rampo, Edogawa. Akunin Shigan |Desire to be a crook|. Tokyo: Hakubunkan, 1929. 318pp.
The first collection of critical essays by Japan's leading writer. Most of them are short essays on subjects other than mystery fiction and Rampo's sharp critical eye can be found everywhere. Also seen is a glimpse of the talent of the author who left behind an immortal accomplishment both in mystery writing and in mystery criticism. (HS/TT)

E2293. ______. Edogawa Ranpo Zenshu, 22: Waga Yume to Shinjitsu |The complete works of Edogawa Rampo, Vol. 22: my dream and truth|. Tokyo: Kodan-sha, 1979. 261pp.
In addition to the autobiographical Waga Yume, there are stories for boys, transcripts of dialogues and of panel discussions, letters and other material. (HS/TT))

E2294. ______. Waga Yume to Shinjitsu |My dream and truth|. Tokyo: Sogen-sha, 1957; Reprinted in Edogawa Ranpo, 22 (E2297). xi, 321pp. Illus.
Bibliography and index. A collection of 80 autobiographical sketches. (HS/TT)

E2295. Ushijima, Hidehiko. Yume no Horosha: Edogawa Ranpo |Dream wanderer: Edogawa Rampo|. Tokyo: Mainichi Shinbunsha, 1980. 274pp. Illustrated. Bibliography.
A biography of Rampo in the context of modern Japanese history. There is an especially moving description of the World War II situation when many writers were forbidden to write and were conscripted into military service. (HS/TT)

RANDOLPH, MARION

Ref: Hubin 2, TCCMW, ABMI.

RANDOLPH, VANCE

E2296. Clements, William M. "The Red Herring as Folklore." TAD 12 (1979):256-59.
An analysis of the use of the convention of the "red herring" and folklore motifs and psychology in The Camp-Meeting Murders (NY: Vanguard, 1936) by Vance Randolph and Nancy Clemens.

RANK, CLAUDE

Int: MM 288, Feb 72.

RATHBONE, JULIAN

Ref: Hubin 2, TCCMW, ABMIS.

RAVEN, SIMON

Ref: Hubin 2, CC, ABMI(S).

E2297. Durrant, Digby. "Devil on Horsback: The Raven Sequence." London

Magazine (new series) 16:2 (June/July 76):71-76. Photo.
A discussion of several of Raven's non-mystery novels. (RCSA)

RAWSON, CLAYTON

Ref: Hubin 2, TCCMW, EMD, CC, ABMI(S).

See also: D334, D440.

E2298. Biederstadt, Lynn. "Introduction." In No Coffin for the Corpse, by Clayton Rawson. Gregg Press Mystery Fiction Series (B134).

E2299. Boucher, Anthony. "Introduction." In The Footprints on the Ceiling (Putnam, 1939), by Clayton Rawson. NY: Collier Books, 1962.

E2300. Dueren, Fred. "The Great Merlini." TMF 4:4 (July/Aug 80):28-32.
Profiles of Merlini, narrator Ross Harte, Inspector Homer Gavigan, and, making two appearances in the Merlini series, mystery author Stuart Towne.

E2301. Erisman, Fred. "Clayton Rawson and the Flexible Formula." TAD 14 (1981):173-75.
Erisman sees the Merlini novels and stories as a conscious manipulation by Rawson of the conventions of the formula puzzle mystery and a "textbook" exploration of its illusory nature.

E2302. Fish, Robert L. "Introduction." In The Footprints on the Ceiling, by Clayton Rawson. Gregg Press Mystery Fiction Series (B134).

E2303. Gibson, Walter. "Introduction." In Death for a Top Hat, by Clayton Rawson. Gregg Press Mystery Fiction Series (B134).

E2304. Nevins, Francis M., Jr. "The Diavolo Quartet." TAD 3 (1969/70):243; reprinted in Xenophile 3 (May 74):(2)-(3). The Xenophile reprint includes additional information published as a letter in TAD 4 (1970/71):193.
The short article is a description of the cases of Rawson's "hocus-pocus hawkshaw" Don Diavolo, originally appearing as four novellas in Red Star Mystery Magazine in 1940.

E2305. Penzler, Otto. "Collecting Mystery Fiction." TAD 15 (1982):249-52. Illus.
A short biography of Rawson, a discussion of the problems posed for collectors attemting to assemble a complete set of his publications and an annotated bibliography of the publications.

E2306. ______. "Introduction." In The Headless Lady (Putnam, 1940), by Clayton Rawson. Gregg Press Mystery Fiction Series (B134).

E2307. Sullivan, Eleanor. "Introduction." In The Great Merlini, by Clayton Rawson, pp. vii-xi. Gregg Press Mystery Fiction Series (B134).
In her introduction to this first book publication of the Merlini short stories, Sullivan talks about her professional relationship with Rawson, the circumstances of the stories' publication in EQMM, and comments briefly on the stories.

RAY, JEAN

Ref: Hubin 2, ABMI(S).

E2308. Baronian, Jean-Baptiste, and Levie, Françoise. Jean Ray l'archange fantastique |Jean Ray the fantastic archangel|. Paris: Librairie des Champs-Elysées, 1981. Not seen.

E2309. Baronian, Jean-Baptiste. "Jean Ray Epistolier |Jean Ray letter-writer|." Bulletin Jean Ray 1 (1982):25-46.
Selections from Ray's correspondence. Baronian does not consider Ray to be a "great" letter writer but the selections are interesting for the glimpses they afford of Ray's personal life and feelings.

E2310. Briot, Murielle, and Michaux, Ginette. "A la jointure du récit fantastique et du roman policier: les Harry Dickson de Jean Ray |Where the fantastic tale and the detective novel meet: the Harry Dickson series by Jean Ray|. Quelle-littérature (74 rue Jacques Ballings, 1140 Brussels) no. 111/12 (Dec 81):25 et seq. Not seen.

E2311. Cahiers Jean Ray. Lobergen-bos 27, 3200 Leuven. Published by Jozef Peeters and the Fondation Jean Ray. Issues 4, 5, 6, 7 and 8 carry articles on Harry Dickson. (JB)

E2312. Craufurd, Ross. "Jean Ray, Last and Greatest of the Dime Novelists." DNR 48 (1979):40-46. Illus.
Brief biography of Jean Ray, Belgian dime novelist, with emphasis on his French dime novels about detective Harry Dickson ("Le Sherlock Holmes américain") and plot synopses of three tales. (DJ)

E2313. Ducos, François. "Les Contes du whiskey de Jean Ray." Le Fulmar 1 (1981), pp. 63-67. Illus.
Essay on stories by Ray which owe a great deal to Dickens, Hodgson and Conan Doyle. The stories were first published in 1925.

E2314. Lacassin, Francis. "Harry Dickson ou le detective trouvé à Vannes (Harry Dickson or the detective found in Vannes|." In Lacassin (B202), pp. 337-68.
A discussion of the Ray novels featuring detective Harry Dickson is linked to film maker Alain Resnais' unsuccessful attempt to bring the detective's adventures to the screen.

E2315. Truchaud, François, and Van Herp, Jacques, eds. Jean Ray. Paris: Editions de l'Herne, 1980.
An elaborate dossier on the Belgian writer who continued in French the adventures--originally published in German--of the "American Sherlock Holmes," Harry Dickson, in over 100 stories. The Harry Dickson saga is only a part of his enormous output and the articles on his life and work and the extensive bibliography chronicle the labyrinthian career of this intriguing mythologist.

E2316. Van Herp, Jacques. Harry Dickson et Jean Ray. Collection "Ides et autres" no. 32-33. Brussels: Editions recto-verso, 1981.
An interesting study on Jean Ray's Harry Dickson series which begins with a study of the serial publications (Eichler) and the fake Sherlock Holmes. (JB)

E2317. Vuijlsteke, Marc. "Jean Ray ou l'expérience d'une écriture protéiforme |Jean Ray or the experience of a protean style|." Bulletin Jean Ray 1 (1982):5-25.
In spite of the range of Ray's writing, Vuijlsteke sees in it a great

uniformity of style and vision. See pp. 18-20 for comments on Harry Dickson. The article is particularly valuable for its documentation which consists of numerous footnotes with references to critical material on Ray's work.

REACH, JAMES

Ref: Hubin 2, ABMI(S); UN 1:7 (1948):10-11, 14 (photo).

REED, ISHMAEL

Ref: Hubin 2, TCCMW, ABMI(S).

E2318. Carter, Steven R. "Ishmael Reed's Neo-Hoodoo Detection." In Landrum B216), pp. 265-74.
A study of two novels by Reed which might be seen as variations on traditional detective forms and as evidence that Reed is "one of the foremost practitioners of experimental mystery fiction."

REEVE, ARTHUR B.

Ref: Hubin 2, TCCMW, EMD, CC, ABMI(S).

See also: D328, D442.

E2319. Cox, J. Randolph. "A Reading of Reeve: Some Thoughts on the Creator of Craig Kennedy." TAD 11 (1978):28-33. Illus.
A short, general introduction to Reeve's detective fiction and two bibliographies: an annotated, chronological listing of Reeve's books; and a list of periodical appearances, by magazine.

E2320. Harwood, John. "Arthur B. Reeve and the American Sherlock Holmes." TAD 10 (1977):354-57.
A survey of Reeve's life and works. See letter, TAD 11 (1978):108 for a correction.

E2321. Olsson, Hans-Olov. "En glömd detektiv: Craig Kennedy |A forgotten detective: Craig Kennedy|." DAST 13:5/6 (1980):8-10.
Study of Reeve's detective, with a checklist. (MS)

E2322. "The Scientific Detective." Dime Detective 8:2 (1 Oct 33):126.
Primarily a superficial rehash of clichés concerning police use of scientific equipment. A short biographical sketch of Reeve is included. (RS)

REEVES, ROBERT

Ref: Hubin 2, SN.

E2323. Boucher, Anthony. "Introduction." In Come Out Killing (orig. published as No Love Lost, Holt, Rinehart, 1941), by Robert Reeves. NY: Mercury, 1953.

REGESTER, SEELEY

Ref: Hubin 2, EMD, ABMI.

E2324. Slung, Michele. "Introduction." In The Dead Letter (Beadle, 1867), by Seeley Regester. Gregg Press Mystery Fiction Series (B134).

REGIS, JUL

Ref: Hubin 2.

E2325. Persson, Gun-Britt, and Halkjaer, Niels. Jul Regis detektiv-thrillers. Uppsala: Avd för litteratursociologi, 1978. 66pp. Illus.
A survey of Regis' mysteries and thrillers. (IH)

REILLY, HELEN

Ref: Hubin 2, TCCMW, EMD,CC, ABMI.

REMAR, FRITS

E2326. Strom, Sven. "Frits Remar -- deckarlitteraturens tusenkonstnär (Frits Remar -- detective fiction's jack-of-all-trades|." Jury 8:4 (1979):46-52.
Critical essay on the works of the Danish author Frits Remar. (MS)

RENDELL, RUTH

Ref: Hubin 2, TCCMW, CC, ABMIS; Cannon, AHMM 28:4 (Apr 83):55-57.

Int: TMN 10 (May 77):A1-A6; EQMM, 6 Oct 80, pp. 80-81 and 3 Nov 80, pp. 99-100; DAST 12:1 (1979):38-40; TAD 14 (1981):108-17 (reprinted in Cooper-Clark B75, pp. 125-42; photo); Carr (B67), pp. 227-57; Polar 28 (Winter 83):17-23.

See also: B16.

E2327. Bakerman, Jane S. "Explorations of Love: An Examination of Some Novels by Ruth Rendell." TAD 11 (1978):139-44. Illus.
Friendship, familial love and sexual passion in six of Rendell's novels.

E2328. ______. "Humor, Horror and Intellect: Giles Mont of Ruth Rendell's A Judgement in Stone." TMF 5:4 (July/Aug 81):5-10.
A character study in which the relationship between characterization and plot is analyzed.

E2329. ______. "One in Two: Some Personality Studies by Ruth Rendell." TMF 5:6 (Nov/Dec 81):21-28.
A discussion of pairs of similar and contrasting characters in two non-series novels, In Sickness and in Health and A Demon in My View.

E2330. ______. "The Writer's Probe: Ruth Rendell as Social Critic." TMF 3:5 (Sept/Oct 79):3-6.
An analysis of A Judgement in Stone in which Rendell makes a "serious social comment" without sacrificing any of the suspense.

E2331. Barnard, Robert. "A Talent to Disturb: An Appreciation of Ruth Rendell." TAD 16 (1983):146-52. Photo and illustrations.
Barnard finds Rendell's Wexford novels to be entertaining but unoriginal and too given to excess in quotations. Barnard is more enthusiastic about four non-Wexford novels which he discusses in some detail.

E2332. Barzun, Jacques and Wendell Hertig Taylor. "Introduction." In A New Lease of Death (NY, 1967), by Ruth Rendell. "Crime Fiction 1950-1975" (B18).

E2333. "Dossier Ruth Rendell." Polar 28 (Winter 83), pp. 5-23.
Contents: Marie-Thérèse Naudon, "Ruth Rendell," pp. 5-13 (photo; survey of her fiction); Jacques Baudou and François Guérif, "Entretien avec Ruth Rendell," pp. 14-16 (interview); J.-F. Naudon, "Bibliographie

de Ruth Rendell," pp. 17-23.

E2334. Fredriksson, Lilian. "'La belle Dame sans merci' och Ruth Rendell --- variationer pa ett kvinnotema |'La belle dame sans merci" and Ruth Rendell --- variations on a woman's theme|." Jury 11:1 (1982):24-30.
Women in Rendell's novels. (MS)

E2335. Larsson, Nils. "En ny deckaardrottning |A new detective novel queen|?" Jury 6:3 (1977):7-12. Includes photo and checklist. (MS)

E2336. Miller, Don. "A Look at the Novels of Ruth Rendell." TMN 10 (May 77):A7-A17.
A survey of Rendell's novels based on a "crash" reading program.

E2337. ______. "A Look at the Short Stories of Ruth Rendell." TMN 10 (May 77):A19-A22.
Brief reports on the stories.

E2338. Pettersson, Sven-Ingmar. "Deckarporträtt Nr 7." DAST 8:2 (1975):24-25.
Life and works of Ruth Rendell. (MS)

E2339. "Ruth Rendell." TMN 10 (May 77):A1-A30.
Contents: Jane S. Bakerman, "Rendell Territory," pp. A1-A6 (interview); "A Selection of Review Extracts," p. A6; Don Miller,"A Look at the Novels of Ruth Rendell," pp. A7-A17 (E2336); Guy Townsend, "Rendell's Latest," p. A18 (review of A Demon in My View); "Selected Review Extracts (Revisited)," p. A18; Don Miller, "A Look at the Short Stories of Ruth Rendell," pp. A19-A22 (E2337); "Another Selection of Review Extracts," p. A22; "A Partial Checklist of Reviews of Books by Ruth Rendell," pp. A23-A25; "Still More Review Extracts," p. A25; "Odds and Ends," p. A26 (editorial miscellany); Don Miller, compiler, "Ruth Rendell: A Bibliography," pp. A27-A29; "Yet Still More Review Extracts," pp. A29-A30; "Tidbits," p. A30.

E2340. Vicarel, Jo Ann Genaro. "A Rendell Dozen Plus One." TAD 9 (1975/76):198-200, 235.
An annotated checklist of the novels published through 1974, citing only first U. S. publication; with brief remarks on each of the novels.

RENO, MARIE

Ref: Hubin 2, ABMIS; The Writer 89:7 (July 76):18-20.

RETCLIFFE, JOHN

E2341. Plass, Paul. "Concerning Nena Sahib." TAD 6 (1972/73):157-59.
Cursory remarks on a locked-room episode in Retcliffe's 1858/1859 novel with the relevant material included in the text of the article.

REVELL, LAURA

Ref: Hubin 2, CC; UN 2:12 (1950):6-7, 16.

REVESZ, ETTA

Int: EQMM, Aug 77, pp. 108-9.

REYNOLDS, G. W. M.

Ref: Hubin 2, ABMI(S).

E2342. Bleiler, E. F. "Introduction" to Wagner, the Wehr-Wolf, pp. vii-xviii. Bibliography, pp. 153-60. NY: Dover, 1975.
In his comprehensive introduction, Bleiler examines Reynolds' life and writings sympathetically but not uncritically. Although Wagner is not primarily a mystery, many of Reynolds' other works are based on crime and the introduction provides a detailed and succinct survey. The important bibliography is the first attempt to disentangle one of the most confused and most complex publishing records in popular literature.

RHODE, JOHN

Ref: Hubin 2, TCCMW, EMD, CC, ABMI(S).

See also: B349.

RICE, CRAIG

Ref: Hubin 2, TCCMW, EMD, CC, SN, ABMI; UN 1:9 (1949):4-5, 12 (photo); The Writer 57:11 (Nov 44):323-27.

E2343. Dueren, Fred. "John J. Malone (and Cohorts)." TAD 8 (1974/75):44-47.
Profiles of Craig Rice's lawyer-detective John J. Malone and of his associates Jake and Helene Justus.

E2344. Grochowski, Mary Ann. "Craig Rice: Merry Mistress of Mystery and Mayhem." TAD 13 (1980):265-67.
An entertaining, informal survey of Rice's life and work.

E2345. Jasen, David A. "The Mysterious Craig Rice." TAD 5 (1971/72):25-27, 34.
A bibliography of novels and short stories by Craig Rice, prefaced by a bio-critical introduction. For additions see the following letters: Francis M. Nevins, Jr., TAD 5:125-126; Tom Balow, TAD 5:173; Robert B. Green, TAD 5:174.

E2346. "Mulled Murder, with Spice." Time 47 (28 Jan 46):84, 86, 88, 90. Photos. Color cover portrait of Craig Rice by Artzybasheff.
A profile of Craig Rice, and some general remarks on American detective fiction, fans, and sales figures. A good profile of Rice but the general remarks suggest that the editors were a bit uncomfortable with their choice of subject and were trying to legitimize it.

RIDDELL, MRS. J. H.

Ref: Hubin 2, ABMI(S).

E2347. Bleiler, E. F. "Introduction" to The Collected Ghost Stories of Mrs. J. H. Riddell, pp. v-xxvi. NY: Dover, 1977. Bibliography, pp. 341-45.
As is usual with Victorian ghost stories, crime situations lie behind much of her work. Bleiler's essay is the fullest treatment of her life and her work in general. The bibliography identifies a hitherto lost work.

RIGSBY, HOWARD

Ref: Hubin 2, ABMI; UN 3:7 (1951):4-5, 15 (photo).

RINEHART, MARY ROBERTS

Ref: Hubin 2, TCCMW, EMD, CC, ABMI(S); The Writer 26:9 (Sept 1914):139-40.

Int: In Writers and Writing, by Robert Van Gelder, NY: Scribner's, 1946, pp. 145-48.

E2348. Breit, Harvey. "Mary Roberts Rinehart." NYTBR, 3 Feb 52; rpt. in The Writer Observed, by Harvey Breit, pp. 227-29. Cleveland and NY: World, 1956.

E2349. Broberg, Jan. "Reverens för Rinehart |Reverence to Rinehart|." Jury 1:1 (1972):16-19.
Rinehart's influence on the genre. (MS)

E2350. Cohn, Jan. Improbable Fiction: The Life of Mary Roberts Rinehart. Pittsburgh: University of Pittsburgh Press, 1980. xv, 293pp. Bibliography and index. Photographs.
The Rinehart papers and files are deposited in the Special Collections of Hillman Library at the University of Pittsburgh and Cohn, who was teaching at Carnegie-Mellon University in Pittsburgh at the time she was researching and writing this book, worked extensively with them. This is primarily a biography but there is information on her writing and Improbable Fiction appears to be a balanced and accurate portrait of Rinehart. There is a chronological list of her works which shows the fees she was paid for magazine publication. The secondary sources are cited in the notes; however, there has been little critical attention paid to Rinehart's work and the sources consist mainly of magazine articles and material in newspapers. An important contribution to the history of popular literature and publishing in the first half of the 20th century. Breen 202. Reviews: Choice, Oct 80, p. 242; Studies in American Fiction 9:1 (1981):132-33.

E2351. ______. "Mary Roberts Rinehart." In Bargainnier (B16), pp. 183-224.
Cohn discusses the mystery fiction chronologically, and in some detail, concluding that Rinehart does not fit into either the hard-boiled or British puzzle traditions, and making a modest attempt to relate her work to the Gothic tradition. There is a bibliography listing only the mystery fiction and a list of sources.

E2352. Disney, Dorothy Cameron, and Mackaye, Milton. Mary Roberts Rinehart. NY: Rinehart, 1948. Wraps.
Annotated checklist of Rinehart's books. Not seen. (REB)

E2353. Doran, George H. Chronicles of Barrabas, 1884-1934. NY: Harcourt, Brace & Co., 1935.
On pp. 187-94, the well-known publisher of Rinehart's books and father of her daughter-in-law, talks about Rinehart and her family.

E2354. Hellman, Geoffrey T. "Mary Roberts Rinehart: For 35 Years She Has Been America's Best-Selling Lady Author." Life 20 (25 Feb 46):55-56, 58, 61-62.
General biographical profile with photographs and plates from her books. (KLM)

E2355. Hoffman, Arnold R. "Social History and the Crime Fiction of Mary Roberts Rinehart." In New Dimensions in Popular Culture, edited by Russel B. Nye, pp. 153-71. Bowling Green, OH: Popular Press, 1972.
Essay on a variety of subjects, including Rinehart's elitism and racism. Includes a list of her works.(KLM)

E2356. Mary Roberts Rinehart: A Sketch of the Woman and Her Work. NY: Geo. H. Doran, 1922. Booklet.
Contents: "My Creed" (1917) and a "short description of the detective story." Not seen and cited as described in Overton, Women Who Make Our Novels (Geo. H. Doran, 1928), p. 285. N.B. The Rinehart article "Writing the Detective Story" (E2363) is cited as appearing in this pamphlet but the title and date differ slightly from the Overton attribution.

E2357. Miller, Donald. "Rinehart 'Treasure Trove' Becomes Improbable Fiction." Pittsburgh Post-Gazette, 3 March 80, Sect. C, p. 25.
An interview with Jan Cohn, author of Improbable Fiction (E2350), in which she discusses her research for the Rinehart biography.

E2358. Overton, Grant. "Mary Roberts Rinehart." In The Women Who Make the Novels, pp. 272-84. Rev. edition. NY: Dodd, Mead, 1928.
Biocritical survey with a graded checklist of her work. (KLM)

E2359. ______. "The Vitality of Mary Roberts Rinehart." In When Winter Comes to Main Street, pp. 102-117. NY: Doran, 1922. Reprinted in Overton, Authors of the Day: Studies in Contemporary Literature, pp. 262-76. NY: George H. Doran, 1924. Photo.
A survey of her life and work with a list of books and sources; Overton quotes generously from his sources in the essay.

E2360. Rinehart, Mary Roberts. The Circular Staircase. Edited by Phyllis Whitney. The Mystery Library Series (B270): No. 3. 1977.
Contents: Phyllis Whitney, "Introduction," pp. vii-xv (a thin survey of Rinehart's life and work); The Circular Staircase, pp. 1-249; Jan Cohn, "A Rinehart Crime Bibliography," pp. 251-55; Robert E. Briney, compiler, "Film Versions of The Circular Staircase and The Bat," p. 256; M. R. Rinehart, "The Early Years," pp. 257-67 (from My Story (E2362), on the writing of The Bat); Jan Cohn, "A Note on the Serial Version of The Circular Staircase," pp. 268-69; J. Cohn, "A Note on "The Housekeeper's Story'," pp. 270-77 (early fiction; note followed by reprinting of story); Harvey Breit, excerpt from "Mary Roberts Rinehart" chapter in A Writer Observed (E2348), pp. 278-79; 2 pp. from Rinehart's logbook of fees; review of The Circular Staircase (NY Times, Aug 22, 1908); Obituary, PW, Oct 12, 1958.

E2361. ______. "My Public." The Bookman 52:4 (Dec 1920):289-91.
On the importance of readers and the rewards of meeting with them.

E2362. ______. My Story. NY: Farrar and Rinehart, 1931; revised and expanded edition, Rinehart, 1948. Illus.
Although Rinehart does not go into great detail about the writing of much of her fiction, this is a fascinating account of her life, told with apparent candor. The early sections in which she talks about her work as a nurse are graphic in their detail and are not only a striking portrait of a medical professional of the time but provide some insight into her preoccupation with crime and death. Breen 203.

E2363. ______. "The Repute of the Crime Story." PW 117 (1 Feb 30):563-66.
Rinehart defends her genre. Included is a portrait page of famous and distinguished mystery fans. (KLM)

E2364. ______. "Writing the Detective Story." In The Free-Lance Writer's Handbook, edited by William Dorsey Kennedy and Margaret Gordon, pp. 67-69. Cambridge, MA: The Writer Publishing Company, 1926. Reprinted from the booklet, "Mary Roberts Rinehart, The Woman and Her Work," (Doran, 1923).

The detective story, according to Mrs. Rinehart, consists of the explicit narrative (which the reader follows) and an implicit one (a "submerged" plot which surfaces as clues and enigmas). Mrs. Rinehart finds the chief weakness of the form in its beginning with a climax (the crime) and ending with an anticlimax (the solution).

E2365. Tebbel, John. George Horace Lorimer and The Saturday Evening Post. Garden City: Doubleday, 1948.

See pp. 55-63 for a description of Lorimer's professional relationship with Rinehart.

E2366. Tiverton, Dana. "The 'Buried Stories' of Mrs. Rinehart." The Writer 44:11 (Nov 32):323-24.

An analysis of Rinehart's technique with discussion of her plotting, first-person narrative, the importance of revision and of sound technique, and the weakness of the anticlimactic explanation chapter.

E2367. Van Gelder, Robert. "An Interview with Mary Roberts Rinehart." Writers and Writing, pp. 145-48. NY: Scribner's, 1946.

An interview dated December 15, 1940 and touching on her entire career. (KLM)

RIPPON, MARION

Ref: Hubin 2; The Writer 83:3 (March 70):12-16 (on writing The Hand of Solange); The Writer 88:5 (May 75):12-14.

RITCHIE, JACK

Ref: Hubin 2, TCCMW.

Int: TAD 6 (1972/73):12-14; EQMM, 17 June 81, pp. 87-89 and 15 July 81, pp. 97-98.

ROBBE-GRILLET, ALAIN

Ref: Hubin 2, TCCMW, ABMI(S).

Int: Littérature 49 (Feb 83):16-22.

See also: B366.

E2369. Besses, Ona D. "A Bibliographic Essay on Alain Robbe-Grillet." BoB 26:2 (1969):52-59. Continued in 26:3 (1969):87-88.

Bibliography of works by and about the author of such crime novels as La Jalousie, Les Gommes, and Le Voyeur, all of which have been translated into English. The part of the bibliography dealing with primary sources gives original and reprint publication data on the novels and on short stories in periodicals. The part dealing with secondary sources is largely in detailed essay form, and is divided into sections on bibliographic coverage, biographical material, theses and monographs on Robbe-Grillet in particular and on the French new novel in general, as well as articles on several of his novels and films. Besses' emphasis is on Robbe-Grillet as a literary figure and not as a writer of crime novels. (GG)

E2370. Boyer, Alain-Michel. "L'Enigme, l'enquête et la quête du récit: la fiction policière dans Les Gommes et Le Voyeur d'Alain Robbe-Grillet |The puzzle, the investigation and the quest for the narrative: detective fiction in Robbe-Grillet's Les Gommes and Le Voyeur|." French Forum 6:1 (Jan 81):74-83.

The substitution, in Robbe-Grillet's two novels, of the investigation of novelistic forms for the crime/investigation/solution model of the classical detective novel.

E2371. Grossvogel, David. "Structure as Mystery (II)." In Grossvogel (B135), pp. 165-79.

Oedipal themes and myth in two of Robbe-Grillet's novels. Of little interest for genre studies.

ROBERTS, JAMES HALL. See DUNCAN, ROBERT L.

ROBERTSON, HELEN

Ref: Hubin 2, CC, ABMI(S).

E2372. Barzun, Jacques, and Taylor, Wendell Hertig. "Introduction." In Swan Song (NY, 1960), by Helen Robertson. "Crime Fiction 1950-1975" (B18).

ROBINSON, B. FLETCHER

Ref: Hubin 2.

E2373. Moskowitz, Sam. "B. Fletcher Robinson, 'The Vanishing Billionaire'." "Gaslight Detectives" series (C565). MSMM, July 73, pp. 67-68.

ROEBURT, JOHN

Ref: Hubin 2, SN, ABMI(S); UN 1:11 (1949):4-5, 15 (photo).

ROGERS, JOEL TOWNSLEY

Ref: Hubin 2, TCCMW, EMD, ABMI(S); Writer's Digest 24:6 (Aug 44):11-21.

E2374. Champigny, Robert. "Story." In Rogers (E2377), pp. 221-224; originally published in Champigny (B70).

A study of stylistic elements that "turn the text into a comprehensive parody."

E2375. Gilbert, Elliot L. "A Bad Dream." In Rogers (E2377), pp. 225-30.

An analysis of The Red Right Hand in which Gilbert discusses the mythic dimensions of the novel and the effect of its haunting images on the reader.

E2376. ______. "Introduction" to The Right Red Hand (E2377), pp. vii-xv.

A report on an interview with Rogers in which the two men browse in Rogers' library and the writer talks on a number of topics related to his life and writing.

E2377. Rogers, Joel Townsley. The Red Right Hand. Edited by Elliot L. Gilbert. Mystery Library Series (B270): No. 10. 1978.

Contents: Elliot Gilbert, "Introduction," pp. vii-xv (E2376); The Red Right Hand, pp. 1-213; Elliot Gilbert, "Checklist: The Novels of Joel Townsley Rogers," pp. 217-20; Robert Champigny, "Story," pp. 221-24 (E2374); Elliot Gilbert, "A Bad Dream," pp. 225-30 (E2375); "Illustrations from New Detective," pp. 231-34; Joel Townsley Rogers, "The Marauders," pp. 235-37 (poem).

ROHMER, SAX

Ref: Hubin 2, TCCMW, EMD, CC, ABMI(S); Collier's, 15 May 48, pp. 13, 15 (biographical sketch).

Int: New Bedford Morning Mercury (Maine), 30 May 35; The New Yorker, 29 Nov 47, pp. 36-37 (rept. in TRR 9, Aug 72, pp. 19-21, with notes by R. E. Briney amplifying the text).

See also: C189, C540, C541, E1516.

E2378. Avallone, Michael, and Hamilton, Frank. "Fu Manchu Revisited." MSMM, Dec 81, pp. 109-110. Illus. by Frank Hamilton.
Fu Manchu as the blueprint for oriental mastermind-villains.

E2379. Ball, John. "My Hero-Fu Manchu." TRR 11 (Dec 73):5-7.
Mystery writer Ball talks about his debt to "superhero" Fu Manchu.

E2380. Baring-Gould, William S. "I Shall Live When You Are Smoke." TAD 1 (1967/68):2-3.
Brief note on Sax Rohmer and the origin of Fu Manchu, quoting from Rohmer's article "How Fu Manchu Was Born" (E2436). Contains the assertion that Rohmer and P. G. Wodehouse once worked together in the same London banking house, but Wodehouse later said (in private correspondence) that this was not true. A biographical note on Baring-Gould by Allen J. Hubin accompanies the article (p. 3). (REB)

E2381. Biggers, Julian L. "A Walking Tour of Sax Rohmer's London." TRR 18 (Spring/Summer 81):13-15.
A report of a visit--in 1979--to sites of places figuring in Rohmer's novels.

E2382. Braveman, David. "Good Old Petrie." TRR 3 (Aug 69):18-22.
A Petrie chronology based on information in the novels.

E2383. Briney, Robert E. "Bibliographica Rohmeriana." Supplements to TRR 2 (Jan 69) - 7 (Aug 71). Loose pages, numbered S-1 through S-20, plus one unnumbered page. From issue 8 (Mar 72), incorporated as a department in the magazine.
These supplements represent a first attempt to list and describe all of Rohmer's books. After being incoporated into the magazine, "Bibliographica Rohmeriana" dealt with miscellaneous bibliographical topics. See also the entries under Robert Castle and Jan P. Ruiter. (REB)

E2384. ______. "Bibliographica Rohmeriana: The Paul Harley Series." TRR 17 (Aug 77):15-17.
An annotated bibliography of the Paul Harley stories.

E2385. ______. "The Early Chronicles of Fu Manchu." TRR 15 (Sept 76), pp. 9-10, 22.
Bibliography, with comments, of the U. S. and British magazine appearances of the first three Fu Manchu books. The article is accompanied by a 10-page portfolio of illustrations for these stories from Chums magazine. (REB)

E2386. ______. "Introduction." In The Wrath of Fu Manchu and Other Stories, by Sax Rohmer, pp. (vii-x). London: Tom Stacey, Feb. 1973. U.S. edition, NY: DAW Books, Inc., March 1976, pp. vii-x.

Gives the publishing history of the 12 stories in the collection, with brief comments on Rohmer's life and career. The version of the Introduction in the DAW Books paperback corrects an error in the original version, and is slightly rewritten for an American audience. (REB)

E2387. ______. "The Lost 'Eye'." TRR 6 (Feb 71), pp. 9-10, 15.
Description of Rohmer's stage melodrama "The Eye of Siva," based on Edward Shanks' review of the play. An "Addendum" in TRR 7 (Aug 71), p. 10, describes the connection between this play and Rohmer's short novel "The Voice of Kali." (REB)

E2388. ______. "Sax Rohmer: An Informal Survey." In Nevins (B290), pp. 42-77. With checklist.
This discussion of Rohmer's fiction is informal only in the sense that it is always readable with no trace of intellectual condescension toward Rohmer or his work. The readings are authoritative and constitute the best available introduction to Rohmer's fiction. Earlier versions of the essay and checklist appeared as follows: "Sax," Xero 10 (May 63):17-33; and "An Informal Survey of the Works of Sax Rohmer," TRR 1 (July 68):3-26.

E2389. ______. "Sax Rohmer, George Robey, and 'Round in Fifty'." TRR 8 (Mar 72), pp. 11-13. Illus.
Rohmer's connections with British comedian George Robey, who starred in a musical review for which Rohmer provided some of the music and lyrics. Robey's own account of this revue, "Looking Back on 'Round in Fifty'", appears in the same issue (pp. 15-17, reprinted from Robey's book Looking Back on Life, London: Constable, 1933, pp. 213-19). (REB)

E2390. ______. "Sax Rohmer Revisited." Views and Reviews Magazine 3:2 (Fall 71):52-57; 3:3 (Winter 72):56-62; 3:4 (1972):64-71.
A revised version of the survey in Nevins (B290). This version omits the checklist, and contains some textual and typographical errors introduced by the editors.

E2391. ______. "Sax Rohmer: A Short Survey of His Fantasy Works." Grotesque 2 (Nov 52):10-23.
This survey covers the book-length work of Rohmer which have elements of fantasy, including those which mix fantasy with a crime/detective framework.

E2392. ______. "U. S. Paperback Editions of Sax Rohmer." CP? 4:2 (Sept 82):24-27. Illus.
Checklist of all known printings of U. S. mass market paperback editions of books by Sax Rohmer, giving publisher's stock number, publication date, cover artist, pagination, and price. Some Canadian printings are also noted. Supersedes the list by Hall (E2404) in an earlier issue. (REB)

E2393. Briney, Robert E.; and W. O. G. Lofts. "Musette, Max and Sumuru." TRR 15 (Sept 76), pp. 5-8, 21. Illus.
Three BBC radio serials by Rohmer in the 1940s, based on his stories; includes cast lists and episode logs. (REB)

E2394. Burg, Gary. "Kathulos vs. Fu Manchu." Wayfarer II (Aug 65), pp. 8-10.
Comparison of Fu Manchu with Robert E. Howard's Skull Face. (REB)

E2395. (Castel, Robert, et al.) "Bibliographica Rohmeriana: Sax Rohmer in

French." TRR 12 (Sept 74):17-19.
Novels and short stories published in French translation.

E2396. Christopher, J. R. "Dantean Allusions in The Trail of Fu Manchu." TRR 5 (Aug 70):27-30.

E2397. Colombo, John Robert. "Sax Rohmer and His Yellow Shadows." The Tamarack Review, Autumn 1960, pp. 44-57.
A survey of Rohmer's career together with an affectionate but clear-eyed assessment of his characteristic features and faults and the reasons for his popularity. There is some bibliographical misinformation, much of it traceable to statements by Rohmer himself in published interviews. On balance, this is one of the best treatments of the total body of Rohmer's work. (REB)

E2398. Cooper, Anice Page. "Sax Rohmer and the Art of Making Villains." In Authors and Others, pp. 181-83. Garden City: Doubleday, Page, 1927. Reprinted in TRR 5 (Aug 70), pp. 8-9.
Rohmer's brief, abortive careers as playwright and composer.

E2399. Day, Bradford M. Sax Rohmer. A Bibliography. Denver, NY: Science Fiction and Fantasy Publications, 1963. pp. 5-34. 4to, mimeographed, stapled in card covers.
A revised edition of this booklet was later incorporated into the compiler's Bibliography of Adventure (B88). (REB)

E2400. Fitzgerald, Maureen. "The Anatomy of Fu Manchu." The Count Dracula Society Quarterly 1:4 (Dec 68). Not seen. (REB)

E2401. Frayling, Christopher. "Criminal Tendencies II: Sax Rohmer and the Devil Doctor." In London Magazine (new series) 13:2 (June/July 73):65-80. Illus.
Discussion of Rohmer's attitudes toward the police and organized crime, hi use of narrators and his transferal of romantic adventure motifs to contemporary London settings.

E2402. Germeshausen, Alvin F. "The Incredible Captain O'Hagan." TRR 1 (Jly 68), pp. 27-29.
"Biography" of Rohmer's character Bernard O'Hagan, with discussion of the six O'Hagan novelettes. (REB)

E2403. Haining, Peter. "The Arch Villains." In Haining (B138), pp. 115-30. Generously captioned illustrations from the stories of Fu Manchu, Roland Daniel's Wu Fang, and Thomas Burke's Limehouse Nights.
States that after Fu Manchu, the best-known Oriental villain was Wu Fang. It is slightly misleading of Haining, however, to classify Burke's stories as tales of Oriental villainy, since they were balanced with acts of Oriental courage and humanity as well. (GG)

E2404. Hall, Richard Paul. "The Papyrocunabula of Sax Rohmer." CP? 3:4 (Sept 81):15-16.
Sax Rohmer titles in pb.

E2405. Harwood, John. "Speculations on the Origin of Fu Manchu." TRR 2 (Jan 69):6-8.
Contemporary Chinese criminal Hanoi Shan may have inspired Fu Manchu.

E2406. Herzog, Evelyn. "On Finding Petrie's Correct Name." TRR 18 (Spring/Summer 81):25-28, 24.
Dexter identified as Flinders Petrie's first name.

E2407. "Inscrutable and Indomitable." MD Medical Newsmagazine 14:8 (Aug 70):199-204. No. 5 in "Great Detectives" series. 6 photographs.
A profile of Nayland Smith, the detective from Sax Rohmer's Fu Manchu books, illustrated with movie stills. (REB)

E2408. Klein, Gérard. "Le diabolique Docteur Fu-Manchu." midi-minuit fantastique no. 14 (June 66), pp. 47-53. Illus. Also used as the Preface (pp. v-xi) to Le Docteur Fu-Manchu/Le Diabolique Fu-Manchu by Sax Rohmer, Paris: Editions Opta (Club du Livre Policier), Jan 1968, no. 47 in series "Les Classiques du Roman Policier."
Brief descriptive essay on the Fu Manchu books. (REB)

E2409. Lacassin, Francis. "Bibliographie de Sax Rohmer (Arthur Sarsfield Wade)," and "Filmographie de Fu-Manchu." In Rohmer, Fu Manchu ou le défi de l'Asie, Vol. VII, pp. xxxv-xlii and xliii-xlvi. Paris: Editions-Alta.
The bibliography lists the British and French editions of Rohmer's books, as well as the stories in various series (Fu Manchu, Paul Harley, Sumuru, etc.) which have appeared in book form. American editions and uncollected short stories are not listed. Some errors have been repeated from other sources: the incorrect spelling of Rohmer's real name (it is Ward, not Wade), the identification of "The Red Doctor" as a Fu Manchu story, and incorrect or incomplete contents lists for three of the short story collections. The filmography lists all of the British, American and Spanish films featuring Fu Manchu. (REB)

E2410. ______. "Fu-Manchu, ou la dernière incarnation de Satan |Fu-Manchu, or the last incarnation of Satan|." Preface to Rohmer, La Fiancée de Fu-Manchu, pp. vii-xxxiv. Geneva: Edito-Service S.A., 1972. Reprinted as "Fu-Manchu, ou l'Ange exterminateur de l'Occident |Fu-Manchu, or the exterminating angel of the west|," MM no. 292 (June 72), pp. 95-104 and no. 293 (July 72), pp. 97-106.
Excellent survey of the first half of the Fu Manchu saga as represented in French translation. Emphasizes the depiction of Fu Manchu as a Satanic figure: not merely a master criminal but an embodiment of evil, a foe of rationality and the natural order (exemplified, of course, by the British Empire). (REB)

E2411. ______. "Sax Rohmer ou Aladin et la lampe incendiaire |Sax Rohmer or Aladdin and the fiery lamp|." In Rohmer, La Malédiction des mille baisers, pp. 223-229. Series: Les maîtres de l'étrange et de la peur. Paris: Union générale d'éditions, 1981. With a bibliography of the stories in this collection, pp. 233-34.
A colorful, impassioned evocation of the forces of magic and the irrational in Rohmer's fiction.

E2412. Lawrenson, Helen. "Fu Manchu Strikes Again." Holiday, Feb 66, pp. 128, 130, 132ff.
Mostly concerned with the Harry Alan Towers/Christopher Lee Fu Manchu films, with background material on Rohmer and some quoted comments from Rohmer's widow. (REB)

E2413. Lofts, W. O. G. "Secret Egypt Revealed." TRR 8 (March 72), pp. 23-24.
An account of the opening night of Rohmer's unsuccessful play Secret

Egypt. The play was discussed by Rohmer in "A Tale of 'Secret Egypt'" (E2444). (REB)

E2414. ______. "Thoughts on the Master of Villainy." TRR 10 (March 73), pp. 27-28, 26.
Comments on Rohmer's childhood and schooling. (REB)

E2415. Lofts, W. O. G., and Briney, R. E. "Sh-h-h! Fu Manchu Is on the Air!" TRR 11 (Dec 73), pp. 9-10, 15-16. Illus.
An account of the 1936-37 Radio Luxembourg Fu Manchu radio serial, with complete episode log. Scripts were by Rohmer, Mrs. Rohmer, and Cay Van Ash. (REB)

E2416. Lowndes, Robert A. W. "The Immortal Enemy." TRR 7 (Aug 71):1-10. Originally published in Is 1 (April 71).
A tribute to the Rohmer Fu Manchu series, originally scheduled to be published in Startling Mystery Stories, as part of a series of essays by editor Lowndes. Lowndes makes the point that Rohmer's novels are not detective stories and should not be judged as "poor" detective fiction but as a "wonderfully entertaining series of novels."

E2417. "Master of Menace." MD Medical Newsmagazine 13:10 (Oct 69):171-76. 8 photos.
A staff-written article on Sax Rohmer and Fu Manchu, based in large part on "Sax Rohmer: An Informal Survey," by Robert E. Briney (E2388) and on the manuscript (still unpublished at that time) of the Rohmer biography, Master of Villainy (E2459). (REB)

E2418. Moskowitz, Sam. "Sax Rohmer, 'The Green Spider'." "Gaslight Detectives" series (C565). MSMM, May 73, pp. 55-56.
Introduction to reprint of early Sax Rohmer story. (REB)

E2419. Nieminski, John. "Sax Rohmer in Chicago." TRR 14 (Jly 76), pp. 5-7.
An account of Rohmer's visit to Chicago in 1932 in connection with the premiere of the CBS radio Fu Manchu program; based on contemporary newspaper articles, one of which is reproduced in full (see Quinby, Ione, E2466). (REB)

E2420. (Obituaries) New York Times, 3 June 59, p. 35; PW, 6 June 59, p. 53; Newsweek, 15 June 59, p. 44; Time, 15 June 59, p. 84; WLB, Sept 59, p. 18; Americana Annual, 1960, p. 859; Britannica Book of the Year, 1960, p. 513. (REB)

E2421. Peck, Andrew Jay. "A Case of Identity: Being a Trifling Monograph Upon the Similarities between Sir Denis Nayland Smith and Sherlock Holmes." TRR 2 (Jan 69):9-17.
A comparative study.

E2422. Pobst, Jim. "The Politics of Fu Manchu." TRR 10 (March 73), pp. 9-14. Originally appeared under the title "Fu Manchu Imprimatur Mao Tse Tung" in Wayfarer 5 (Dec 70).
Survey of Fu Manchu's changing political views and goals, based on extracts from Rohmer's novels. (REB)

E2423. Power, Charles R. L. The Journal of Fu Manchu. nd (1965 and Jan 1968).
A newsletter containing miscellaneous comments on Rohmer, his writings, and the films based on them. Issue 1 was 4 pages, photo-offset on one

side of the page. Issue 2 was 7 pages, legal size, mimeographed on both sides of the page. Issue 1 reprints an editorial by Leslie Charteris from the May 1962 Saint Mystery Magazine (also reprinted as "The Sound of Fu Manchu" in TRR 6, Feb 71, pp. 19). Issue 2 is packed with useful information: extracts of letters from Luther Norris, Elizabeth Sax Rohmer, and others, and transcriptions of a large number of newspaper clippings about Rohmer. (REB)

E2424. ______. "The Old Doctor of Limehouse." The Pontine Dossier 2:2 (Apr 69).
On "Dr. F," a Fu Manchu surrogate who appears in three of August Derleth's Solar Pons stories. (REB)

E2425. Prager, Arthur. "The Mark of Kali." In his Rascals at Large, pp. 47-69. Garden City, NY: Doubleday, 1971.
Prager's affectionate recollections of the pleasures of reading Sax Rohmer when he was young.

E2426. Quinby, Ione. "Sax Rohmer, Thrills Author, Has to Be 'Locked In' to Write." Chicago Evening Post, 24 Sept 32, p. 2. Reprinted in TRR 14 (Jly 76), pp. 7-9, as addendum to "Sax Rohmer in Chicago" by John Nieminski (E2419). (REB)

E2427. Rivière, François. "La Nuit de Chinatown, ou le fantasme générateur |The night in Chinatown, or the generative hallucination|." In Rohmer, La Colère de Fu-Manchu, pp. 7-14. Grenoble: Editions Jacques Glenat, 1976. Wraps. Series: "Marginalia."
Introduction to the French edition of Rohmer's story collection The Wrath of Fu Manchu (London: Tom Stacey, 1973). Rivière repeats an anecdote from the first chapter of the Rohmer biography Master of Villainy (E2459) concerning the origin of Fu Manchu, and then attempts to make a virtue of the routine nature of the stories by seeing them as examples of archetypal themes and patterns: the repressed and puritanic loner fighting his own personal demons, as personified by Fu Manchu's sensual female agents. ("Pour Sax Rohmer, toute femme est fatale |For Sax Rohmer, every woman is fatal|.") (REB)

E2428. ______. "Sax Rohmer et ses fantasmes |Sax Rohmer and his phantasms|." (A Suivre), no. 6-7 (Jly/Aug 78), pp. 120-21. 2 photos (film stills).
Brief biographical sketch with comments on Fu Manchu, Sumuru, and some of Rohmer's other novels. (REB)

E2429. Rohmer, Sax. "The Birth of Fu Manchu." Empire News (Manchester), 30 Jan 38, p. 11. Illus. The first of the "Pipe Dreams" articles (E2442).
This probably comes as close as anything Rohmer wrote to revealing his "true" attitudes toward the Chinese: a curious mixture of unthinking "Yellow Peril" sensationalism with slightly patronizing approval and even outright admiration. There are reminiscences of Chinese acquaintances from London's Limehouse, experiences in New York's Chinatown, a very brief mention of Fu Manchu, and comments on the distorted Western views of the Chinese. Rohmer divides the blame for the latter between Bret Harte and British colonial attitudes, without mentioning the role his own stories might have played in perpetuating the stereotypes. (REB)

E2430. ______. "The Birth of Dr. Fu Manchu." Daily Sketch (London), 24 May 34, pp. 7, 25. Photo. Reprinted in TRR 17 (Aug 77), pp. 1-5.

A quasi-interview, bylined "by Sax Rohmer in a talk with the Daily Sketch," and signed Geraint Goodwin at the end of the article. About half of the text is quoted material by Rohmer. The interview was billed on the newpaper's front page under the title "How Fu Manchu Was Born," but is entirely separate from the article of that name published more than 20 years later in This Week. It is also separate from the article "The Birth of Fu Manchu" which first appeared in Empire News in 1938 (E2429). The Daily Sketch interview ascribes the origin of Fu Manchu to an Ouija-board message about a Chinaman. The reprint in TRR has additional notes by Cay Van Ash and R. E.Briney commenting on the innaccuracies in the text. See also "Meet Dr. Fu Manchu" (E2437) and ch. 1-10 of Master of Villainy (E2459). (REB)

E2431. ______. "'Breaking the Bank' at Monte Carlo." Empire News (Manchester), 20 March 38, p. 11. Illus. Part 8 of "Pipe Dreams" (E2442).
Visits to Monte Carlo, and anecdotes concerning various roulette systems. (REB)

E2432. ______. "Dancing Girl of Egypt." TRR 15 (Sept 76), pp. 1-4.
Reprint of the first half of the 3rd installment of "Pipe Dreams" (E2442) with an added note by R. E. Briney. (REB)

E2433. ______. "Dancing Girl of Egypt/The Green Eyes of Bast." Empire News (Manchester), 13 Feb 38, p. 11. Illus. Part 3 of "Pipe Dreams" (E2442).
Supposed psychic experiences and hauntings connected with the writing of two of Rohmer's novels. (REB)

E2434. ______. "Eager Old Lady of the Atlantic." Empire News (Manchester), 3 Apr 38, p. 11. Illus. Part 10 of "Pipe Dreams" (E2442).
Ocean crossings aboard the Berengaria, the Mauretania, and other ships. (REB)

E2435. ______. "Here and There." The Sunday Referee (London), ca, 1933, in the "Mustard and Cress" column. Reprinted (slightly abridged) in TRR 11 (Dec 73), pp. 1-3.
Eleven brief autobiographical references. (REB)

E2436. ______. "How Fu Manchu Was Born." This Week, 29 Sept 57; reprinted in TRR 2 (Jan 69):3-5.
One of Rohmer's highly-coloured accounts of the genesis of Fu Manchu, this time mentioning a tall figure glimpsed one night near the London docks as the model. See also "The Birth of Fu Manchu," "Meet Dr. Fu Manchu," and Ch. 1-10 of Master of Villainy (E2429, E2437, E2459). (REB)

E2437. ______. "Meet Dr. Fu Manchu." In Madden (E253), pp. 36-41. Reprinted in TRR 10 (March 73), pp. 1-3.
Transcription of a BBC radio talk, giving a fanciful and vague account of the genesis of the Fu Manchu character. The TRR reprint is useful for the appended note on Rohmer's other printed accounts of Fu Manchu's origin; see "The Birth of Fu Manchu," "How Fu Manchu Was Born," and Ch. 1-10 of Master of Villainy (E2429, E2437, E2459). (REB)

E2438. ______. "Mysteries of Egypt/In the False Pyramid." Empire News (Manchester), 27 Feb 38, p. 11. Illus. Part 5 of "Pipe Dreams" (E2442).
An account of visits to Egypt and an expedition into the interior of the Meydum pyramid. (REB)

E2439. _____. "Nelson Keys and Captain Kettle." Empire News (Manchester), 10 Apr 38, p. 11; rpt. in TRR 18 (Spring/Summer 81), pp. 1-8. Illus. Part 11 of "Pipe Dreams" (E2442).
Reminsicences of stage and film celebrities, and a brief account of the production of Rohmer's play "Secret Egypt." (REB)

E2440. _____. "On the Red Road to Aleppo." Empire News (Manchester), 17 Apr 38, p. 11. Illus. Part 12 of "Pipe Dreams" (E2442).
Travels in Syria and Palestine. (REB)

E2441. _____. "The Phantom Hound of Holm Peel." Empire News (Manchester), 20 Feb 38, p. 11. Illus. Part 4 of "Pipe Dreams" (E2442).
The legend of the Mauthe Dhug, the phantom dog of Peel Castle on the Isle of Man, and an account of Rohmer's visit to the Castle. (An early short story, "The Secret of Holm Peel," was the result.) (REB)

E2442. _____. "Pipe Dreams." Empire News (Manchester), 30 Jan to 17 Apr 38.
A series of 12 articles, all but the last carrying the subtitle "Popular Novelist's Own Story," published in the Sunday tabloid Empire News in Manchester, England. Each article is complete on one page (always page 11) and illustrated with small photographs and drawings. The articles are rambling reminiscences of events in Rohmer's life and of people (generally famous) he had known. Each article has an individual title; some have double titles. The articles are listed separately and annotated as the following items in this bibliography: Pt. 1 (E2429); Pt. 2 (E2443); Pt. 3 (E2433); Pt. 4 (E2441); Pt. 5 (E2438); Pt. 6 (E2445); Pt. 7 (E2447); Pt. 8 (E2431); Pt. 9 (E2446); Pt. 10 (E2434); Pt. 11 (E2439); and Pt. 12 (E2440). (REB)

E2443. _____. "The Potters Bar Zeppelin/I Planned to Kill Hindenburg!" Empire News (Manchester), 6 Feb 38, p. 11. Illus. Part 2 of "Pipe Dreams" (E2442).
Rohmer's experiences in the British Army in World War I. (REB)

E2444. _____. "A Tale of 'Secret Egypt'." TRR 7 (Aug 71), pp. 11-12.
An excerpt from "Nelson Keys and Captain Kettle" (E2439). (REB)

E2445. _____. "The Voodoo Shepherd/Sign of Blue Candles." Empire News (Manchester), 6 March 38, p. 11. Illus. Part 6 of "Pipe Dreams" (E2442).
Rohmer attends a voodoo ceremony in Jamaica; this background shows up in The Island of Fu Manchu. (REB)

E2446. _____. "Were Houdini's Feats Supernatural?" Empire News (Manchester), 27 March 38, p. 11. Illus. Reprinted in TRR 5 (Aug 70), pp. 1-7. Part 9 of "Pipe Dreams" (E2442).
Reminiscences of Harry Houdini, including the story of how he supposedly helped Rohmer out of a plot difficulty with his current novel, Fire-Tongue (unnamed in the article). The latter anecdote is also told in "How Houdini Saved the Day for Sax Rohmer" by Carl Warton and "Flashback: The Day Houdini Rescued Fu Manchu" by H. Allen Smith (E2460, E2451). (REB)

E2447. _____. "When Little Tich Walked Off." Empire News (Manchester), 23 March 38, p. 11. Illus. Part 7 of "Pipe Dreams" (E2442).
Reminiscences of British music hall star Little Tich (Harry Relph), for whom Rohmer once ghost-wrote a book. (REB)

E2448. The Rohmer Review. Edited by Robert E. Briney. Published irregularly. The first issue of this magazine devoted to the life and works of Sax Rohmer--and related subjects--appeared in July 1968, under the editorship of Douglas A. Rossman. Briney assumed the editorship with issue 5 (Aug 70) and, as of 1983, 18 issues have been published. TRR is, perhaps, the most professionally edited of the fan magazines. In addition to the articles (indexed as appropriate in this bibliography), there are informative letter columns, book notes, bibliographies and other material.

E2449. Romer, Jean-Claude. "Sax Rohmer bio-bibliographie." midi-minuit fantastique no. 14, June 66, pp. 53-54. Expanded as "Biographie" (pp. xiii-xiv) and "Bibliographie" (pp. xv-xvi) in the Club du Roman Policier volume cited in Klein (E2408).
Thumbnail sketch of Rohmer's life, and checklist of the Fu Manchu books. (REB)

E2450. (Ruiter, Jan P.) "Bibliographica Rohmeriana: Sax Rohmer in Dutch." TRR 11 (Dec 73):17-20.
Chronological listing of Dutch translations.

E2451. Smith, H. Allen. "Flashback: The Day Houdini Rescued Fu Manchu." Chicago Tribune Book World, 21 Apr 68, p. 6.
How Houdini helped Rohmer out of a plot difficulty in one of his Paul Harley novels. See also "Were Houdini's Feats Supernatural?" by Sax Rohmer and "How Houdini Saved the Day for Sax Rohmer" by Carl Warton (E2446, E2451). (REB)

E2452. Squire, J. C. (Comments on Sax Rohmer) In Life and Letters, pp. 203-209. NY: George H. Doran, 1921. Reprinted as "Rohmer" in TRR 4 (March 70), pp. 3-6.
A review of The Si-Fan Mysteries, plus more general comments on the pleasures and defects of Rohmer's work. "How, I wonder again, can any man with a taste for the nightmarish and phantasmagorical, and the desire of an occasional escape from the necessity of exerting his own intellect, deny that Mr. Rohmer is as competent a merchant of shocks as exists?" (REB)

E2453. Stafford, Jean. "The Polyglot Mr. Rohmer." TRR 14 (Jly 76), pp. 1-3.
Brief memoir by Pulitizer Prize-winning novelist of her acquaintance with Rohmer. (REB)

E2454. Stanich, Ray. "Radio Fu Manchu." TRR 12 (Sept 74), pp. 11-15. Illus.
Fu Manchu on U. S. radio (three versions); the article includes transcriptions of several newspaper items on Rohmer, and an episode log for the 1939 Fu Manchu radio serial, "The Shadow of Fu Manchu." (REB)

E2455. Van Ash, Cay. "Ourselves and Gaston Max." TRR 15 (Sept 76), pp. 23-24.
Comments on writing the scripts for the "Myself and Gaston Max" radio serial, amplifying the account in Master of Villainy (E2459). (REB)

E2456. ______. "A Question of Time." TRR 17 (Aug 77), pp. 7-10, 18.
A careful attempt to straighten out the internal chronology of the Fu Manchu series, with comments on the ages of Fu and Nayland Smith. (REB)

E2457. ______. "Sax Rohmer in the 1920's: Notes on Chronology." TRR 18 (Spring/Summer 81):21-24.
Additional information on Rohmer's literary activities in the 1920s, not included in Master of Villainy.

E2458. ______. "The Search for Sax Rohmer." TRR 14 (Jly 76), pp. 13-17. Illus.
Speculations on the source of the Sax Rohmer pen-name, amplifying and correcting the account in Master of Villainy (E2459). (REB)

E2459. Van Ash, Cay, and Rohmer, Elizabeth Sax. Master of Villainy: A Biography of Sax Rohmer. Edited, with Foreword, Notes, and Bibliography, by Robert E. Briney. Bowling Green, OH: Popular Press, 1972. ix, 312pp. Photographs. Bibliography. Index. Simultaneous hardcover and paperbound editions. British Edition: Tom Stacey, December 1972. Pp. (vi-viii), 312 + frontis. and 12 pages of photographs. Bibliography. Index.
This book was begun in the mid-1950s by Sax Rohmer himself, as a volume of reminiscences in the style of the "Pipe Dreams" newspaper articles (E2442); the manuscript remained unfinished at the time of Rohmer's death, in 1959. Several years later Mrs. Rohmer revived the project and commissioned Cay Van Ash, who had been a friend and protege of Rohmer's, to complete the book. The early chapters were then revised and the entire manuscript edited by R. E. Briney at the request of the book's U. S. publisher. The book is in no sense a formal biography. There are gaps in the coverage, especially in such areas as Rohmer's schooling and early jobs and the exact circumstances under which the adopted his pseudonym; and other incidents are incompletely verified. This is due largely to Rohmer's reticence about his early life and his habit of substituting vagueness and mystery for solid fact in his interviews and publicity material. The book is, nevertheless, a lively and entertaining account of Rohmer's life and career by two people who knew him best. The chronological bibliography lists all of Rohmer's books, and includes contents lists for the short story collections. There are also checklists covering Rohmer's various series characters. Breen 204. (REB)

E2460. Warton, Carl. "Houdini Saved the Day for Sax Rohmer." Boston Sunday Herald, 8 March 31.
After Rohmer had plotted himself into a corner in his novel Fire-Tongue, Houdini helped him out of the trap. The same anecdote is recounted in items E2446 and E2451. (REB)

E2461. West, Rick. "Fu Manchu Lives." Wayfarer 3 (March 67). (REB)

E2462. Wodehouse, P. G. "Onwards and Upwards with the Fiends." Punch, 16 Feb 65.
"An analysis of Professor Moriarty as the inferior of Fu Manchu among Fiends in Human Shape." (REB)

RONBLOM, H. K.

E2463. Fagerstrom, Allan. "Med ett direkt kliv till toppen |With a direct stride to the top|!" Jury 8:2 (1980):27-35.
The novels of H. K. Rönblom. (MS)

E2464. Lundin, Bo. "Paul Kennet." Jury 8:3 (1979):33-38.
Article about Rönblom's detective. (MS)

RONNS, EDWARD. See AARONS, EDWARD S.

ROOS, KELLEY

Ref: Hubin 2, TCCMW, SN.

ROSAMUND, BABETTE

Ref: Lachman, TPP 4:2 (April 81):19-20 (also see letter from Walter and Jean Shine in TPP 4:5/6 (Dec 81):91-92).

ROSCOE, THEODORE

Ref: Hubin 2, ABMIS; Argosy, 18 Jan 30 and 29 June 35.

E2465. Clark, Bill (William J.). "Bibliography---Theodore Roscoe." The Pulp Era no. 65 (Sept/Oct 66), pp. 15-18.
Bibliography of Roscoe stories from Argosy, 1929-43, including some crime fiction.

ROSENBERGER, JOSEPH

Ref: Hubin 2, ABMIS.

Int: Skullduggery 6 (Spring 81), pp. 24-25, 39.

ROSS, ANGUS

Ref: Hubin 2, TCCMW, ABMI(S).

Int: DAST 10:4 (1976):14-17; DAST 14:6 (1981):32-33.

ROSS, BARNABY. See QUEEN, ELLERY

ROSS, JONATHAN

Ref: Hubin 2, TCCMW, ABMI.

E2466. "Jonathan Ross né John Rossiter." BMJ, 19 July 80, pp. 218-19.
Comments on medical details in Ross's four procedurals featuring Dr. Bridget Hunter, a Home Office pathologist.

ROTH, HOLLY

Ref: Hubin 2, TCCMW, EMD, CC, ABMI.

ROUDYBUSH, ALEXANDRA

Ref: Hubin 2, ABMIS.

E2467. Cook, Wister. "The Selfish World of Alexandra Roudybush." Clues 3:2 (Fall/Winter 82):1-8.
A study of the 9 Roudybush novels published to date--each of them with "a crime,...no mystery to speak of and no suspense"--to show that they are consistent in their use of similar villains, victims, multiple plots and narrative spokesmen.

E2468. Frazier, Gerie. "Introducing Alexandra Roudybush." TMF 3:3 (May/June 79):2-5.
Brief comments on novels by an expatriate author of mystery suspense novels.

ROUSE, WILLIAM MERRIAM

Ref: ABMIS; Argosy, 21 June 30.

RUD, ANTHONY

Ref: Hubin 2, ABMI(S); Argosy, 20 Sept 30.

E2469. Drew, Bernard A. "Anthony M. Rud's Weird Tales." Attic Revivals 6 (19830, pp. 1-5.
Summary of Rud's career, focusing more on his hardcover detective novels and work for Detection Fiction Weekly (the "Jigger Masters" series) than on his contributions to Weird Tales. (REB)

ROYCE, KENNETH

Ref: Hubin 2, TCCMW, ABMI(S).

RUSSELL, MARTIN

Ref: Hubin 2, TCCMW, ABMI(S).

E2470. Pettersson, Sven-Ingmar. "Martin Russell: A Profile." TAD 8 (1974/75):48-49.
A survey of the crime novels of Martin Russell, with a checklist.

RUSSELL, RAY

Ref: Hubin 2, TCCMW, ABMI(S).

RUTHERFORD, DOUGLAS

Ref: Hubin 2, TCCMW, CC, SN, ABMI(S); UN 5:1 (1950):8-9, 13 (photo).

RYCK, FRANCIS

Ref: Hubin 2, SN.

E2471. "Dossier Francis Ryck." Nuits noires 1 (Nov 81):4-7. Photos.
A critical overview and an interview with the popular French writer of thrillers.

SADLER, MARK. See COLLINS, MICHAEL

SAGE, DANA

Ref: Hubin 2; UN 2:9 (1950):4-5, 15.

SAINT VAL, VIC

Int: MM nos. 329-30, Oct and Nov 75.

SALE, RICHARD

Ref: Hubin 2, TCCMW, EMD, SN, ABMI(S).

SAN ANTONIO. See DARD, FREDERIC

SANDERS, LAWRENCE

Ref: Hubin 2, TCCMW, ABMIS.

Int: NYTBR, 5 Oct 80, p. 40 (photo).

See also: C576.

E2472. Nelson, Bill. "Expiratory Symbolism in Lawrence Sanders' The First Deadly Sin." Clues 1:2 (Fall/Winter 80):71-76.
A discussion of elements in Sanders' police procedural which Nelson thinks fall outside the usual conventions of the genre. These elements are

the imagery associated with the murderer and the detective's relationship with his wife and his frequent self-accusations for the sin of pride. His conclusion is that Sanders has written a serious novel which provides the conventional procedural with an "important thematic statement."

SAPIR, RICHARD

Ref: Hubin 2, SN, ABMIS.

E2473. Dawn, Adam (Murray, Will). "Sinanju Superman." Fantasy Mongers 7 (July 83), pp. 2-3.
A descriptive essay on the "Destroyer" series by Sapir and Warren Murphy. (WM)

"SAPPER"

Ref: Hubin 2, TCCMW, EMD, ABMI(S).

See also: B25, B303, C540.

E2474. Hibbert, R. "Bulldog's Alma Mater." In CDA 1976, pp. 19-21.
A case is made for Bulldog Drummond having attended St. Jim's School, the setting for Charles Hamilton's stories of Tom Merry & Co. (JRC)

E2476. Trewin, Ion. "Introduction." In The Black Gang (Hodder, 1927), by Sapper. Classic Thrillers Series. London: JM Dent, 1983. Paperback.

E2477. Usborne, Richard. "Introduction." In Bulldog Drummond (Hodder, 1920), by Sapper. Classic Thrillers Series. London: JM Dent, 1983. Paperback.

E2478. ______. "Sapper." In Usborne (B420), pp. 133-86.
A discussion of the typical Sapper hero--the "tall, upstanding, typical British sportsman" --and character studies of Bulldog Drummond, Carl Peterson (the "enemy"), Ronald Standish and Jim Maitland.

E2479. Watson, Colin. "The Bulldog Breed." In Watson (B426), pp. 63-71.
Watson finds the reason for Bull-dog Drummond's enormous popularity in Sapper's creation of a fantasy character perfectly tailored to the post-W. W. I British audience, and a fictional extension of the author. He also sees in the character a "family" resemblance to the British Union of Fascists.

SARSFIELD, MAUREEN

Ref: Hubin 2.

E2480. Adey, (R. C. S.). "Maureen Sarsfield." TPP 3:6 (Dec 80):6.
Notes on two of Sarsfield's three novels (as listed in Hubin) with the comment by Adey that he could not find any biographical material on her.

SAVAGE, ERNEST

E2481. Lachman, Marvin. "Department of Unknown Mystery Writers." TPP 4:3 (June 81):11-13.
A checklist of stories appearing in EQMM and AHMM with a composite "portrait" of the author based on information in the stories. A reply from Savage giving biographical and series data was published in TPP 4:5/6 (Dec 81):33-34, with introductory and concluding comments by Lachman. In the same issue, additions to the checklist were submitted by Robert Randisi (p. 83) and Edward D. Hoch (p. 99).

SAYERS, DOROTHY L.

Ref: Hubin 2, TCCMW, EMD, CC, ABMI(S).

See also: B6, B92, B241, C151, C334, C453, E686, E1536.

E2482. Amis, Kingsley. "Whodunit, Lord Peter?" Radio Times, 30 March 72, pp. 6-7.
On the eve of the first showing on TV of the adaptation of Sayers' Clouds of Witness, starring Ian Carmichael, Amis sketches the history of that "characteristically British thing," the classical detective puzzle story.

E2483. Auerbach, Nina. "Dorothy Sayers and the Amazons." Feminist Studies 3:1/2 (Fall 75):54-62.
A discussion of the way in which the Amazon (the woman in a community without men) gradually deteriorates into a "grotesque gargoyle" and corresponds to the progressive petrification of Harriet Vane. Auerbach also sees this process as related to the characters' devolving into the stereotypes on which they are based.

E2484. Bander, Elaine. "The Case for Sir Charles Grandison: A Note on Barbara Reynolds's 'The Origins of Lord Peter Wimsey.'" TSR 1:4 (July 77):3-9.
An argument for Grandison, hero of Samuel Richardson's novel, as a model for Wimsey.

E2485. ______. "Dorothy L. Sayers and the Apotheosis of Detective Fiction." TAD 10 (1977):362-65.
To demonstrate her hypothesis that in the short story, "The Wimsey Papers," Wimsey emerges from the conventions of his character to become a direct spokesman for Sayers' views, Bander traces the character's evolution through the novels.

E2486. Barzun, Jacques, and Taylor, Wendell Hertigr. "Preface" to Strong Poison. In A Book of Prefaces (B17), pp. 97-98.

E2487. Basney, Lionel. "The Nine Tailors and the Complexity of Innocence." In Hannay (E2525), pp. 23-35.
Basney sees The Nine Tailors as the novel in which Sayers most successfully integrated a detection plot with a "criticism of life." To show how the mystery plot and the social themes are integrated, Basney analyses both elements in some detail.

E2488. Boardman, John. "Lord Peter Views the World: The Whimsy of Dorothy Sayers." Unicorn 1 (Fall/Winter 69):15-16. With "A Short Sayers Bibliography," uncredited.
Brief survey of the Lord Peter novels and the social order which they reflect. The "bibliography" is simply a list of Sayers' mystery novels. (REB)

E2489. Brabazon, James. Dorothy L. Sayers: The Life of a Courageous Woman. London: Gollancz, 1981. xviii, 308pp. Illus. Index. Preface by Anthony Fleming. Foreword by P. D. James. U. S. edition - NY: Scribner's, 1981. xvi, 308pp.
The first authorized biography based on papers made available by Sayers' son, Anthony Fleming, is an able, if not imaginative job. With a wealth of biographical documents available to him, Brabazon provides more of an understanding for Sayers' life but spends very little time discussing her

detective stories and novels. Reviews: VII An Anglo-American Literary Review 2 (March 81): 132-41; TLS, 5 June 81, pp. 629-30; Choice, Oct 81, p. 234; NYTBR, 23 Aug 81, pp. 9, 20. (KLM)

E2490. Burleson, James Bernard, Jr. "A Study of the Novels of Dorothy L. Sayers." Unpublished Ph. D. dissertation. University of Texas, 1965. 238pp. DAI 26/04, p. 2204. Not seen.

E2491. Cannadine, David. "The Eternal Wimsey." New Society, 17 Apr 80, pp. 115-18.
A discussion of the reasons Cannadine finds for the continuing popularity of the Sayers' Wimsey novels.

E2492. Christopher, Joe R. "The Complexity of the Nine Tailors." TMF 7:4 (July/Aug 83):3-9.
A close reading of Sayers' The Nine Tailors which is of a complexity that Chrisopher finds allows for diverse critical interpretations. With a checklist of secondary sources referred to in the article.

E2493. ______. "The Delightful Art of Bibliography." TSR 1:4 (July 77):1-9.
A review-essay of Harmon/Burger (E2527).

E2494. ______. "Dorothy Leigh Sayers: A Chronology." TSR 1:1 (Sept 76):1-12.
Her life and works, presented as a chronology.

E2495. ______. "The Mystery of Robert Eustace." TAD 13 (1980):365-67.
Biographical information on Dr. Eustace Robert Barton, Sayers' collaborator on The Documents in the Case.

E2496. ______. "A Sayers Checklist." TSR 4:1 (Sept 80): 13-25; 4:2 (Jan 81):18-32.
An informative annotated checklist of references to Sayers and her work in books and articles where the main subject is not Sayers or where Sayers is one element in a multi-subject treatment.

E2497. ______. "Works in Progress on Dorothy L. Sayers." TSR 2:1 (May 78):22-33.
Presented at the MLA, 28 Dec 77, and revised for publication. Although many of the items have since appeared, the survey is still of interest for the intelligent commentary on the kinds of research being done on Sayers.

E2498. Christopher, Joe R.; Gregory, E. R.; Hannay, Margaret P.; and Malone, R. Russell, compilers. "Dorothy L. Sayers's Manuscripts and Letters in Public Collections in the United States." In Hannay (E2525), pp. 214-78.
Annotated listing of materials. Much important biographical, critical and bibliographical information is provided here.

E2499. Clark, S. L. "The Female Felon in Dorothy L. Sayers' Gaudy Night." Publications of the Arkansas Philological Association 3:3 (Summer 77):59-67.
The role of Annie Wilson as a catalyst as she "knots the double threads" of Harriet's merging of detection with scholarship.

E2500. ______. "Harriet Vane Goes to Oxford: Gaudy Night and the Academic Woman." TSR 2:3 (Aug 78):22-44.
A thorough examination of the way the roles of scholar, detective and

woman merge for Harriet Vane in Gaudy Night.

E2501. Dale, Alzina Stone. "Fossils in Cloud-Cuckoo Land: The Aesthetic Relationship between Real and Imagined Time in the Wimsey-Vane Chronicle and Its Effect upon the Development of Sayers' Fiction." TSR 3:2 (Dec 78):1-13.

All events in Sayers' fiction, whether they are asssimilated from the "real" world or are fictional in origin, are considered by Sayers to be esthetically real.

E2502. ______. Maker and Craftsman: The Story of Dorothy L. Sayers. Grand Rapids, Michigan: Eerdmans Publishing Co., 1978. xiv, 158pp.

A biography with no index, references or supportive critical material. Dale refers to the writer throughout as "Dorothy," and this easy familiarity is characterisic of the unscholarly and largely uncritical approach. Review: TSR 4:1 (Sept 80):26-27. Breen 205.

E2503. Dolend, Virginia. "A Passion for Explication: Dorothy L. Sayers' Art of the Footnote." TSR 3:1 (Oct 78):1-11.

Includes a discussion of the use of footnotes in Whose Body?

E2504. Donovan, Gertrude Monica. "Dorothy L. Sayers' Detective Fiction: Fable to Myth." Ph. D. dissertation. St. John's University, 191. 140pp. Dissertation Abstracts 42/03A, p. 1157.

A theological reading.

E2505. Dorothy L. Sayers Newsletter. A publication of the Dorothy L. Sayers Historical and Literary Society. Published regularly in TAD from 15:1 (1982) to the present (December 1983).

The first installment (15:168-69) contained selections from Society Bulletins nos. 34 to 38. The Newsletter publishes a variety of material, including some reviews, but it also features quizzes, puzzles and other trivia that will be of little use to the serious researcher.

E2506. Dunlap, Barbara. "A Sayers Bibliography, Part 3." Unicorn 2:2 (Spring 72):27, 31.

Lists (some of) Sayers' poetry, literary criticism, edited books, translations, and selected secondary material. (REB)

E2507. Dunn, Robert Paul. "'The Laughter of the Universe': Dorothy L. Sayers and the Whimsical Vision." In Hannay (E2525), pp. 200-12.

A discussion of Sayers' whimsical vision--defined as "a paradoxical recognition of human limitation...and human access to a transforming spiritual reality"--in her writings including the detective fiction. The reading of the Wimsey novels fits them into a Thomistic framework.

E2508. Durkin, Mary Brian, O. P. Dorothy L. Sayers. Twayne's English Author Series, No. 281. Boston: Twayne, 1980. 204pp. Index. Selective Primary and Secondary Bibliographies.

In Chapters 2-5 (pp. 27-100), Durkin discusses the detective novels and stories and Sayers' introductions and reviews. The Twayne series is uneven but Durkin's comments are intelligent and although there is some plot discussion, it is integrated into a critical overview of the work. The bibliography of secondary material is annotated. Breen 206.

E2509. Edwards, Lee. "Love and Work: Fantasies of Resolution." Frontiers 2:3 (Fall 77):31-38.

On Gaudy Night and the relationship between love and a career and the "fantasy" (i.e. novelistic) resolution for Harriet Vane.

E2510. Forbes, Cheryl. "Dorothy L. Sayers - For Good Work, For God's Work." Christianity Today 21 (4 March 77):16-18.
Christian view of Sayers and her work including detective fiction. (KLM)

E2511. Gaillard, Dawson. Dorothy L. Sayers. "Recognitions" Series. NY: Ungar, 1981. ix-xi, 123pp. Bibliography and Index.
As a literary study that examines only the detective fiction of Sayers, Gaillard's work was greatly needed--especially the early chapter on Sayers' short stories (including those about Montague Egg). Gaillard's style approaches that of a sentimental sermon at times but the book is still an adequate critical introduction to Sayers' mysteries. Reviews: TSR 4:2 (Jan 81):14-16; Choice, Sept. 81, pp. 78-79; TLS, 4 Apr 80, p. 386. (KLM)

E2512. Gielgud, Val. "Why I Killed Peter Wimsey--by Dorothy Sayers." Sunday Dispatch (England), 15 Dec 57, p. 6.
Interview with Sayers by her friend (and mystery author) Gielgud. Published two days before her death. (KLM)

E2513. Gilbert, Coleen B. A Bibliography of the Works of Dorothy L. Sayers. Hamden, CT: Archon Press, 1978; London: Macmillan Press, Ltd., 1978. 263pp. Index.
An indispensable research item, this bibliography lists, in addition to her book and magazine appearances, contributions to periodicals (including her unsigned reviews for the Sunday Times (London). Reviews: VII An Anglo-American Literary Review 1 (March 80):126-28; PBSA 74:2 (1980):171-74. Breen 207.

E2514. Green, Peter. "A Clergyman's Daughter." TLS, 28 Feb 75, pp. 223-34.
Green differs with Hitchman on the model for Peter Wimsey. (KLM)

E2515. Gilbert, Michael. "Technicalese." In Brean (B48), pp. 57-65.
In the course of a discussion of writing techniques, Gilbert uses The Nine Tailors as an example and quotes from a Sayers' letter to him in which she talks about the writing of the novel.

E2516. Gregory, E. R. "Wilkie Collins and Dorothy L. Sayers." In Hannay (E2525), pp. 51-64.
A review of the documented evidence on Sayers' interest in Collins based on research in the Sayers collection in the Humanities Research Center, Austin, Texas. Gregory also examines Collins' influence in Sayers' fiction.

E2517. Grella, George. "Dorothy Sayers and Peter Wimsey." University of Rochester Library Bulletin 28:1 (Summer 74):33-42.
Critical appraisal of Sayers/ Peter Wimsey works, inspired by the TV adaptations of Clouds of Witness and The Unpleasantness at the Bellona Club, as well as by the recent publication of Lord Peter, the collection of all the Wimsey short stories. Grella laments the transformation of the early, amusing Wimsey into the "priggish superman" of the later novels. It is argued that Unpleasantness is the most satisfying of the Wimsey novels. After attacking the novels' snobbey, ethnocentrism and upper class contempt for the British middle class, Grella articulates a lack of excitement for the return of Wimsey and criticizes Americans who mistakenly equate high culture with British culture. (GG)

E2518. Hall, Trevor H. "Atherton Fleming: A Literary Puzzle." In Hall (E2523), pp. 40-61.

A thorough examination of the hypothesis that Sayers' husband, Atherton Fleming, may have collaborated on his wife's books. Hall studies Atherton's own published writings and comes to the conclusion that, at most, he may have furnished some information on "minor matters."

E2519. ______. "The Dates of Busman's Honeymoon." In Hall (E2523), pp. 104-13.

An astute piece of literary detection in which the fine points of the dates of the performance and publication of the play, Busman's Honeymoon, a collaboration of Sayers with St. Clare Byrne, and the composition and publication of the novel with the same title are discussed. Hall does not discuss the nature of the literary relationship between the novel and play.

E2520. ______. "The Documents in the Case." In Hall (E2523), pp. 62-74.

The circumstances of the writing of The Documents in the Case with particular emphasis on the collaboration with Robert Eustace and Sayers' discomfort with the "gigantic howler" in the book.

E2521. ______. "Dorothy L. Sayers and Psychical Research." In Hall (E2523), pp. 114-23.

Speculations on the significance of the ghostly apparition in Busman's Honeymoon and Sayers' attitudes toward spritualism.

E2522. ______. "Dorothy L. Sayers and Robert Eustace." In Hall (E2523), pp. 75-103.

Patient and diligent research establishes the identity of Sayers' collaborator as Dr. Eustace Robert Barton.

E2523. ______. Dorothy L. Sayers: Nine Literary Studies. London: Duckworth, 1980; Hamden, CT: Archon, 1980. 2 plates. vii-xi, 132pp. Index.

A collection of entertaining essays on various topics related to Sayers' life and works. The table of contents listing will indicate the topic of the essay or, where appropriate, the essay will be listed separately and annotated. Contents: "Lord Peter Wimsey and Sherlock Holmes," pp. 14 (Sayers' debt to Conan Doyle); "Dorothy L. Sayers and Sir Arthur Conan Doyle," pp. 15-28 (Sayers' essays on Sherlock Holmes); "The Singular Affair of the Verso Signature," pp. 29-34 (on the dating of Sayers' essay, "Dr. Watson, Widower"); "The Nebuly Coat," pp. 35-39 (E2524); "Atherton Fleming: A Literary Puzzle," pp. 40-61 (E2518); "The Documents in the Case," pp. 62-74 (E2520); "Dorothy L. Sayers and Robert Eustace," pp. 75-103 (E2522); "The Dates of Busman's Honeymoon," pp. 104-113 (E2519); "Dorothy L. Sayers and Psychical Research," pp. 114-123 (E2521). Reviews: TLS, 14 Nov 80, p. 1304; Choice, Oct 80, p. 246; VII 2 (March 81):141-45. Breen 208.

E2524. ______. "The Nebuly Coat." In Hall (E2523), pp. 35-39.

Hall compares Meade Falkner's novel The Nebuly Coat (1903) to Sayers' The Nine Tailors and finds evidence that Sayers used certain elements from Falkner's work in her novel.

E2525. Hannay, Margaret P., ed. As Her Whimsey Took Her: Critical Essays on the Work of Dorothy L. Sayers. Kent, OH: Kent State University Press, 1979. v-xvi, 301pp. Index.

The first section of this anthology, "Detection," has essays on Sayers' detective fiction; most of the other essays refer only in passing to her fiction. Essays by the following writers are relevant to this bibliography: R. B. Reaves (E2552); R. D. and Barbara Stock (E2567); Lionel Basney (E2487); Margaret P. Hannay (E2526); E. R. Gregory (E2516); Robert Paul Dunn (E2507); and Joe R. Christopher, E. R. Gregory, Margaret P. Hannay, and R. Russell Malone, compilers (E2498). Review: VII 2 (March 81):145-47. Breen 209.

E2526. ______. "Harriet's Influence on the Characterization of Lord Peter Wimsey." TSR 2:2 (June 78):1-16; reprinted in Hannay (E2525), pp. 36-50.
After stating that a love interest and significant development of characters is foreign to detective fiction, Sayers contradicted both of her rules by introducing Harriet Vane who humanized him.

E2527. Harmon, Robert B., and Burger, Margaret A. An Annotated Guide to the Works of Dorothy L. Sayers. Garland Reference Series in the Humanities, Volume 80. NY: Garland, 1977. x, 286pp. Index.
An annotated bibliography of primary materials with a short section of secondary sources. An essential reference tool whose full annotations of Sayers' essays and introductions make this of particular value for the reader interested in her writings about detective fiction. Review: TLS, 2 Dec 77, p. 1398. Breen 210.

E2528. Harrison, Barbara Grizutti. "Dorothy L. Sayers and the Tidy Art of Detective Fiction." Ms., Nov 74, pp. 67-69, 84-86, 89.
Written without benefit of the numerous biographies of Sayers since published, this article contains some inaccuracies regarding Sayers' life. Nonetheless, it is an excellent article, full of insight on the works of Sayers and womens' relationship to mystery fiction. (KLM)

E2529. Heilbrun, Carolyn. "Sayers, Lord Peter and God." American Scholar 37 (Spring 68):324-30, 332, 334; reprinted in Sayers, Lord Peter (Harper, 1972), pp. 454-469.
A laudatory survey of the life and works of Sayers, the "Mies van der Rohe" of the detective story. Heilbrun comments on the "unattractiveness" of Harriet Vane and laments the death of the British novel of manners. There are a number of references to other critics, but with no bibliographical information provided.

E2530. Heldreth, Lillian M. "Breaking the Rules of the Game: Shattered Patterns in Dorothy L. Sayers' Gaudy Night." Clues 3:1 (Spring/Summer 82):120-27.
The familiar point is made that Sayers, in Gaudy Night, worked against genre conventions to produce a work with some claim to status as serious literature. A brief bibliography is given; only one reference to a secondary source is given and there is no acknowledgement of the considerable body of critical work on Sayers.

E2531. Hitchman, Janet. "Introduction: Lord Peter Wimsey and His Creator." In Striding Folly, by Dorothy L. Sayers, pp. 9-31. London: New English Library, May 1973.
A survey of the known biographical facts about Lord Peter Wimsey and a discussion of his development in the course of the Sayers novels, combined with a capsule biography of Miss Sayers and a good account of her views on her own work and on detective fiction in general. (REB)

E2532. ______. "On Writing Such a Strange Lady." TSR 1:4 (July 77):16-21.

An informal paper describing the research and some of the problems Hitchman encountered in writing her biography of Sayers; originally presented as a seminar paper.

E2533. ______. Such a Strange Lady: An Introduction to Dorothy L. Sayers (1893-1957). London: New English Library, 1975. Pp. 11-203. Illus. No index or bibliography; just a checklist of Sayers's books. U. S. edition: Such a Strange Lady: A Biography of Dorothy L. Sayers. NY: Harper & Row, 1975. 177pp. Checklist.

Ms. Hitchman loves Sayers for her creation of detective Peter Wimsey, but her disinterest in everything else that fired Sayers' intellectual pasions--the history of detective fiction, theology, Dante--combines with the non-cooperation of the Sayers estate to make this a disappointingly superficial biography. Review: TLS, 28 Feb 75, p. 223. Breen 211. (REB)

E2534. Hone, Ralph E. Dorothy L. Sayers: A Literary Biography. Kent, OH: Kent State University Press, 1979. ix-xvii, 217pp. Includes bibliographical references and an index. Illus.

An extensively researched biography of Sayers--the acknowledgements to individuals who were interviewed or consulted runs to almost three pages--with a good account of her writing and literary associations. Winner of an MWA Edgar in 1979. Reviews: TSR 4:2 (Jan 81):12-13; VII 2 (March 81):126-32. Breen 212.

E2535. James, P. D. "Dorothy L. Sayers: From Puzzle to Novel." In Keating (B179), pp. 64-75.

A survey of restrained admiration for Sayers as a writer of detective fiction although James understands Sayers' importance in helping to move the "sterile" puzzle novel in the direction of the novel of manners. Allingham and Marsh are also discussed.

E2537. Keller, Joseph. "Grey-Walled Paradise: The University as Symbol in Dorothy L. Sayers' Gaudy Night." TSR 3:2 (Dec 78):29-34.

An exploration of the intellectual and spiritual dimensions of the Oxford setting and its role in relation to Harriet Vane.

E2538. Keller, Katherine, and Avenick, Karen. "Wimsey, William and Work." TSR 2:3 (Apr 78):1-15.

A reading of the Wimsey mysteries as "Christian tragedies." The authors describe Sayers' concept of work as "an almost sacramental...image of God's act of creation." Some general comments on the role of the detective in mystery fiction and how Wimsey fits or does not fit into this tradition.

E2539. Klein, Kathleen Gregory. "Dorothy L. Sayers." In Bargainnier (B16), pp. 8-39.

A disjointed discussion of Sayers' detective fiction which covers a number of topics in magpie fashion.

E2540. Leavis, Q. D. "The Case of Miss Dorothy Sayers." Scrutiny 6:3 (Dec 37):334-40.

Reviews of Gaudy Night and Busman's Honeymoon which furnish the occasion for Leavis to claim that Sayers is not markedly superior to Edgar Wallace and that a fondness for her fiction by "educated" persons shows how insensitive they are to literature.

E2541. Lee, G. A. and Alzina Stone Dale. "The Wimsey Saga Chronology." TSR 3:2 (Dec 78):14-20; originally published as an enclosure with 3:1.

E2542. Lundin, Bo. "Den skarpsinnige snobben |The astute snob|." Jury 1:2 (1972):5-7.
Lord Peter Wimsey. (MS)

E2543. McMenomy, Christe. "A Glossary of Foreign Terms and Quotations in the Wimsey Novels." TSR 1:3 (Apr 77):8-20.
Terms are given chronologically, in the order they appear in each book, with translations. See TRS 2:1 (May 78):34-35 for reader replies with comments and corrections.

E2545. Merry, Bruce. "Dorothy L. Sayers: Mystery and Demystification." In Benstock (B26), pp. 18-32.
On the technical expertise and the maker of "boa-constrictor classics in the detective genre." Merry does not agree with Leavis that the novels are insipid fictions but he does comment that, although the novels are "resourceful and highly refined," they are also "long and do not age well."

E2546. Moy, Paul R. "An Unpublished 'Lost' Work by Dorothy L. Sayers Revealed." TPP 5:4 (Oct 83):24.
On DLS's contribution to a "round robin" mystery serial (No Flowers by Request), published in the Daily Sketch (London), Nov/Dec 1923.

E2547. Ohanian, Seta. "Dinner with Dorothy L. Sayers or 'As My Whimsey Feeds Me'." JPC 13:3 (Spring 80):434-46.
General comments on the conventions of detective fiction and a survey of Wimsey novels and short stories presented as courses in a formal dinner. Apart from the formal dinner conceit, a routine examination of overly familiar material.

E2548. Panek, LeRoy Lad. "Dorothy Sayers." In Panek (B304), pp. 72-110.
A chronological examination of the novels, with the conclusion that her detective stories may be her "best pieces of theology."

E2549. Patterson, Nancy-Lou. "Eve's Sharp Apple: Five Transgressing Women in the Novels of Dorothy L. Sayers." TSR 3:3 (April 80):1-24.
Not seen. For a description, see Youngren (qv), p. 157, item 7.

E2550. ______. "Images of Judaism and Anti-Semitism in the Novels of Dorothy L. Sayers." TSR 2:2 (June 78):17-24.
Not seen. For a description, see Youngberg (E2572), p. 144, item 32.

E2551. Ray, Laura Krugman. "The Mysteries of Gaudy Night: Feminism, Faith, and the Depths of Character." In Adams, MDA 1973 (B3), pp. 272-85.
A good discussion of the central problems in Sayers' penultimate Wimsey novel.

E2552. Reaves, R. B. "Crime and Punishment in the Detective Fiction of Dorothy L. Sayers." In Hannay (E2525), pp. 1-13.
Reaves sees an obsession with the punishment of crime, not just the detecting of it, as a moral obsession in Sayers' fiction. Reaves points out that in four of the Wimsey novels, the murderer commits suicide, leading him to the conclusion that even if the legal system may be incapable of dealing with the criminal, Sayers is devoted to the principle of

retribution for crimes against others. Reaves also comments that the trial is often treated farcically in Sayers.

E2553. Reynolds, Barbara. ("Epic and Romance in the Detective Fiction of Dorothy L. Sayers.") Proceedings of the Seminar, 1977. Wilham, Essex: Dorothy L. Sayers Historical and Literary Society, 1978. Achives; 6, 18, processed, pp. 33-34.
Not seen. Cited in Youngberg (E2572), p. 145, item 33.

E2554. ______. "The Origin of Lord Peter Wimsey." TSR 2:1 (May 78):1-21. Reprinted, in part, in TLS, 22 April 77, 492.
A careful argument, with frequent comparative references, for E. C. Bentley's Philip Trent as the model for Wimsey.

E2555. Reynolds, William. "Dorothy L. Sayers' Detective Short Fition." TAD 14 (1981):176-81. Photo and illustration.
A survey of the stories in Lord Peter (Harper, 1972).

E2556. Rickman, H. P. "From Detection to Theology." The Hibbert Journal 60 (July 62):290-96.
Christian analysis of Sayers' fiction. Rickman considers Gaudy Night "a crisis in its author's thinking." (KLM)

E2557. Ryan, Elizabeth Bond, and Eakins, William J. The Lord Peter Wimsey Cookbook. New Haven, CT: Ticknor & Fields, 1981. Illus.
In addition to the recipes there is assorted information about food and drink in Sayers's fiction. Not seen. (REB)

E2558. Sandoe, James. "Contribution Toward a Bibliography of Dorothy L. Sayers." BoB 18:4 (May-August 44):76-81.
Early and excellent bibliography, now outdated. Superseded by Gilbert (E2513).

E2559. ______. "Introduction," to Sayers, Lord Peter, pp. vii-xii. NY: Harper & Row, 1972; paperback edition, Avon, 1972.
A concise introduction to Sayer's writings in an anthology which contains all of the Wimsey short stories.

E2560. Sayers, Dorothy L. "Gaudy Night." In Haycraft (B142), pp. 208-21. Originally published in Titles to Fame, edited by Denys K. Roberts (London: Nelson, 1937).
Sayers discusses the Wimsey saga, its move away from its conventional beginnings, her conscious effort to approach the novel of manners and to re-invent Wimsey, and the writing and reception of Gaudy Night. She ends with character studies of Wimsey and Harriet Vane and an amused coda on the fortunes of Peter Wimsey in and out of the pages of her fiction. The essay is a model in critical writing and is both one of the most important studies of her fiction--and one that has been constantly mined since by almost every writer on the subject--and one of the most intelligent self-examinations by a writer of mystery fiction.

E2561. The Sayers Review. Vol I, no. (Sept 76) - . 11 issues published to date (December 1983). Editor: Christe McMenomy. Published under the auspices of the Studium Generale formenoriensis.
An important journal for Sayers' fiction since much of the material has been on her detective novels. Checklists, letters to the editor, information on work-in-progress.

E2562. Scott, William M. "Lord Peter Wimsey of Piccadilly: His Lordship's Life and Times." TAD (1980):17-22, 212-218.
A two-part article on Sayers' detective. A portrait based on information in the novels and short stories.

E2563. Scott-Giles, C. W. The Wimsey Family: A Fragmentary History Compiled from Correspondence with Dorothy L. Sayers. London: Gollancz, 1977; NY: Harper and Row, 1977. 88pp. Illus.
An exercise in mock genealogy. Breen 213.

E2564. ______. "The Wimsey Pedigree." TSR 1:3 (Apr 77):1-5.
A summary of the material published in The Wimsey Family.

E2565. Shibuk, Charles. "Checklist: Dorothy L. Sayers." TMRN 2:2 (Dec 68):10-11.
A listing of Sayers' detective novels, short stories and ss collections. Addenda: letter, William White in 3:1 (Oct 69):12; letter, Mary Ann Whitten in 3:3 (Feb 70):2.

E2566. Soloway, Sara. "Dorothy Sayers: Novelist." Unpublished Ph. D. dissertation. University of Kentucky, 1971. 376pp. DAI 32/04-A, p. 2105-A.
A discussion of the 11 Wimsey novels to show that "detective fiction can indeed be considered a part of mainstream literature." Not seen.

E2567. Stock, R. D., and Stock, Barbara. "The Agents of Evil and Justice in the Novels of Dorothy L. Sayers." In Hannay (E2525), pp. 14-22.
In the early works, Sayers pits an "exceptional" criminal against a "superhuman, relentless sleuth;" in the later novels the dichotomy is less melodramatic and Sayers approaches the moral position of Dante. The authors also discuss her Faust novel The Devil to Pay.

E2568. Tillinghast, Richard. "Murder and Whimsy." New Republic, 31 July 76, pp. 30-31.
After a brief survey of her detective fiction, Tillinghast comments that Harriet Vane is "obviously" an idealized portrait of Sayers and wonders who served as model for Wimsey.

E2569. Tischler, Nancy M. Dorothy L. Sayers: A Pilgrim Soul. Atlanta: John Knox Press, 1980. 167pp. Index.
A study which emphasizes the Christian dimensions of Sayers' life and work.

E2570. Watts, Joyce Lannom. "The Androgynous Aspects of Sayers in Harriet and Peter." TSR 4:2 (Jan 81):1-11.
The premise is that Sayers has written of herself as both Peter Wimsey and Harriet Vane.

E2571. Wood, Barbara. "A Sayers Bibliography, Part 2." Unicorn 2:1 (Fall 70): p. 25.
A supplement to the Sandoe bibliography (E2558). (REB)

E2572. Youngberg, Ruth Tanis. Dorothy L. Sayers: A Reference Guide. Boston: G. K. Hall, 1982. v-xxxi, 1-178. Index.
Writings about Sayers from 1917-1981. A well-edited, annotated bibliography of secondary sources.

SCHERF, MARGARET

Ref: Hubin 2, TCCMW, EMD, CC, ABMI(S); UN 2:12 (1950):10-11, 16 (photo).

SCHIER, NORMA

Ref: Hubin 2.

E2573. Ellin, Stanley. "Introduction." In The Anagram Detectives, by Norma Schier, pp. 3-9. NY: Mysterious Press, 1979.

SCHLEY, STURGES

Ref: Hubin 2. UN 3:4 (1950):10-11 (photo).

SCHOLEY, JEAN

Ref: Hubin 2, CC.

E2574. Barzun, Jacques, and Taylor, Wendell Hertig. "Introduction." In The Dead Past (NY, 1961), by Jean Scholey. "Crime Fiction 1950-1975" (B18).

SCIASCIA, LEONARDO

Ref: Hubin 2.

E2575. Blatta, Franz. "The Detective Novel Unbound: The Novels of Leonardo Sciascia." Clues 4:1 (Spring/Summer 83):3-18.

Sciascia's novels, although they use conventions of the traditional detective novel, subvert the conventions of the least likely suspect, the mystery element and the redemptive detective in favor of political and social commentary.

E2575a. Cannon, JoAnn. "The Detective Fiction of Leonardo Sciascia." MFS 29:3 (Autumn 83):523-34.

A study of Sciascia's first three detective novels to show that they increasingly depart from genre conventions as the author's faith in the "power of reason in an irrational world" diminishes.

SCOTT, JEFFRY

Ref: Hubin 2, ABMIS (as Shaun Usher).

Int: EQMM, Sept 82, pp. 87-89 and Oct 82, pp. 83-84.

SCOTT, JUSTIN

Ref: Hubin 2, SN.

Int: DAST 8:3 (1975):28-29.

SCOTT, R. T. M.

Ref: Hubin 2, TCCMW, CC.

SEELEY, MABEL

Ref: Hubin 2, TCCMW, EMD, CC, ABMI.

SELLY, GIOVA

Int: Enigmatika 20 (1982), pp. 61-63 (with bibliography).

SELWYN, FRANCIS

Ref: Hubin 2, TCCMW.

SERGUINE, JACQUES

Int: Polar 28 (Winter 83), pp. 119-121.

SHAGAN, STEVE

Ref: Hubin 2, SN, ABMI.

Int: PW 222:6 (6 Aug 82):6-8 (photo).

SHALLIT, JOSEPH

Ref: Hubin 2; UN 3:7 (1951):8-9, 16 (photo); UN 4:12 (1952):8-9 (photos).

SHANNON DELL. See LININGTON, ELIZABETH

SHATTUCK, RICHARD

Ref: Hubin 2.

E2576. Boucher, Anthony. "Introduction." In The Body in the Bridal Bed (orig. published as The Wedding Guest Sat on a Stone, Morrow, 1940), by Richard Shattuck. NY: Mercury, 1963.

E2577. ______. "Introduction." In With Blood and Kisses (orig. published as The Snark Was a Boojum, Morrow, 1941), by Richard Shattuck. NY: Mercury, 1953.

SHEARING, JOSEPH

Ref: Hubin 2, TCCMW, CC, ABMI(S).

SHELDON, RICHARD

Ref: Hubin 2; UN 3:4 (1950):8-9, 16 (photo).

SHEPHERD, NEAL. See MORLAND, NIGEL

SHERIDAN, JUANITA

Ref: Hubin 2; UN 4:8 (1952):4-5, 14-15 (photo).

SHERWOOD, JOHN

Ref: Hubin 2, CC, ABMI; Pike, TPP 2:3 (May/June 79):23, 14; UN 1:12 (1949):10-11 (photo); UN 3:5 (1951):10-11 (photo).

E2578. Boucher, Anthony. "Introduction." In Murder of a Mistress (orig. published as Ambush for Anatol, Hodder, 1952), by John Sherwood. NY: Mercury, 1954.

SHIEL, M. P.

Ref: Hubin 2, EMD, CC, ABMI(S).

E2579. Herron, Don. "The Mysteries of M. P. Shiel." In Morse (E2582), pp. 179-93.

Covers not only The Black Box and the stories based on Prince Zaleski and Cummings King Monk but also the general fiction with mystery/crime elements and the late collaborations with John Gawsworth. (EFB)

E2580. MacLaren-Ross, J. "The Strange Realm of M. P. Shiel." London Magazine, n.s. 4 (Sept 64):76-84.

A biocritical study in which the author emphasizes that Shiel "set himself to make literature out of the late Victorian romantic mystery."

E2581. Morse, A. Reynolds. The Works of M. P. Shiel: A Study in Bibliography. Los Angeles: Fantasy Publishing Company, Inc., 1948; paperback, 1971. xvii, 170pp. Illus. Index. Revised edition published as The Works of M. P. Shiel: Updated, A Study in Bibliography; Dayton, OH: The Reynolds-Morse Foundation in association with JDS Books, 1980. Part 1: pp. 12-414; Part 2: pp. 415-858. The two volumes of the revised edition were issued in hardbound form (700 copies) and in looseleaf form with binders and section tabs (200 copies). Total edition: 900 signed and numbered copies. (Volumes II and III of The Works of M. P. Shiel, edited by A. Reynolds Morse.) Profusely illustrated. Index.

An exhaustive revision and expansion of the 1948 edition and an incredible example of bibliographic scholarship and thoroughness. The work is organized into 11 sections with front matter and sections 1-6 in Part 1 and sections 7-11 in Part 2. The hundreds of illustrations include reproductions of book covers, jackets and title pages; magazine illustrations; newspaper clippings; photographs; and 7 excellent new illustrations by Robert Arrington. The various sections are: (1) Check List. Checklist of the various editions of Shiel's novels and short story collections, magazine serializations of the novels, and published plays (pp. 15-26); (2) Collations. Minutely detailed collations of all editions of Shiel's books (pp. 27-236); (3) Short Stories. Annotated checklists of all appearances of Shiel's short fiction. Includes the text of four Shiel short stories, 2 of them not previously published (pp. 237-346); (4) Miscellaneous works. Annotated listings of Shiel's short articles, verse, brochures, letters, and other miscellany (pp. 347-64); (5) Manuscripts. List of known manuscripts, typescripts, proofs, etc. (pp. 365-84); (6) Bibliography. Works about M. P. Shiel and his writings which includes a list of published reviews and obituaries (pp. 385-414); (7) Biographical Notes. Texts of an autobiographical essay, "About Myself," and various biographical articles and notes on Shiel, including Edward Shanks's address at Shiel's funeral (pp. 415-86); (8) The Shielography Update. Essay by A. Reynolds Morse on the 30-year process of reassessing Shiel's works and preparing the new version of the bibliography (pp. 487-580); (9) The Quest for Redonda. Illustrated history of Redonda, the Carribean island of which M. P. Shiel was king, and accounts of the visits there by A. Reynolds Morse and others in 1978 and 1979 (pp. 518-742; this section has also been published as a separate paperbound volume); (10) A New Appendix on Louis Tracy, 1863-1928. Biographical sketch of Louis Tracy, and bibliography of his writings, with specific attention to the 'Gordon Holmes' detective novels, three of which were collaborations with M. P. Shiel (pp. 743-848); (11) Index (pp. 848-58). (REB)

E2582. Morse, A. Reynolds, editor. Shiel in Diverse Hands: A Collection of Essays by Twenty-nine Students of M. P. Shiel, 1865-1947, "Lord of Language." Cleveland: privately printed for The Reynolds Morse Foundation, 1983. 490pp. Illustrated. Issued both in hardbound form (100 copies) and in paper wraps (400 copies). (Volume IV of The Works of M. P. Shiel, edited by A. Reynolds Morse.)

The 29 essays cover all aspects of Shiel's writings, as well as the most complete biographical information currently available. Some of the essays are reprints; others were written especially for this volume. They are interspersed with extensive and informative notes by the editor. The numerous illustrations include reproductions of dust-jackets from Shiel books, book and magazine illustrations and photographs. Those essays relating specifically to Shiel's mystery fiction, or of interest to the Shiel collector or bibliographer, are: 14. W. O. G. Lofts, "My Search for Elusive Shiel Material," pp. 147-51; "Magazines containing works by M. P. Shiel," pp. 153-57 (checklist compiled by Lofts); 15. George Locke, "The Book Collector and M. P. Shiel," pp. 159-69; 17. Stephen Wayne Foster, "Prince Zaleski and Count Stenbock," pp. 175-76; 18. Don Herron (E2579); 19. James Wade, "You Can't Get There from Here: How the Old Woman Got Home and M. P. Shiel as Thinker," pp. 195-201. Biographical material on Shiel is contained in: 5. Sam Moskowitz, "The Dark Plots of One Shiel," pp. 57-67; 6. Malcolm Ferguson, "On Digging Shiel," pp. 63-73; 8. Harold Billings, "The Shape of Shiel, 1865-1896: a biography of the early years," pp. 77-105 (2 letters from Barbara Gawsworth to Billings are also included-pp. 68, 74. These contain additional biographical notes.); A. Reynolds Morse, "M. P. Shiel: the Author--Still Unknown," pp. 331-42. (REB)

SHUTE, NEVIL

Ref: Hubin 2, TCCMW, ABMI(S).

See also: C538.

SILLER, (HILDA) VAN

Ref: Hubin 2, TCCMW, CC; UN 4:5 (1951):4-5, 16 (photo).

SILVERMAN, MARGUERITE

Ref: Hubin 2; Pike, TPP 2:4 (July/Aug 79):20.

SIMENON, GEORGES

Ref: Hubin 2, TCCMW, EMD, CC, ABMI(S).

See also: B99, B254, B366.

Interviews: Paris Review 9 (1955):71-90 (reprinted in Writers at Work, edited by Malcolm Cowley, pp. 143-160. NY: Viking Press, 1958); MM 292, June 72, pp. 121-26; Jury 6:4 (1977):8-17 (photo); NL, 16 Feb 78, pp. 3-5; NL, 8-15 Jan 81, pp. 34-35 (photo; interview excerpted from Les Ecrivains sur la sellette, Le Seuil, 1981; not seen); Sunday Times (London), 16 May 82, p. 13 (photo).

E2583. Altenheim, Hans. "Ein Traum von Maigret |Maigret's dream|." Suddeutsche Zeitung 11/12:1 (1969); reprinted in Vogt (B424), Vol I, pp. 200-205; and in Uber Simenon (E2679), pp. 113-20.
Interesting impressionistic excursion into the world of Maigret, his history, methods, and the relationship between him and creator Simenon. Altenheim's style is to absorb and communicate his subject in a dreamy manner, just as he states Maigret absorbs his surroundings, and just as Simenon does the personality of the characters he portrays. (GG)

E2584. Améry, Jean. "Das fleissige Leben des Georges Simenon |The busy life of Georges Simenon|." Westermanns Monatshefte 106 (July 65); reprinted in Uber Simenon (E2679), pp. 100-108.
Lively look at Simenon, the man, the writer and his books. Except for one dating error, Améry is well acquainted with the Simenon corpus and the critical opinions concerning it, and provides a well-rounded, interesting discussion. (GG)

E2585. Anselmi, Luciano. "Radiografia di Maigret l'infallibile |Radiogram of the infallible Maigret|." La Fiera Letteraria, 15 Aug 71, pp. 21-25.

Diffuse report on Maigret's universe, in which is mirrored "the petit-bourgeois universe of the entire Western society." Among the literary references, Dostoevsky: "holiness and madness..., goodness and cruelty are mingled in the moth-eaten man of Simenon." (RC)

E2586. ______. "Simenon e il giallo |Simenon and the giallo)." L'osservatore politico-letterario, January 1968, pp. 73-78.
The literary ancestry of Simenon, "author of spendid and well-digested readings," is attributed to Dostoevsky, Gogol and Balzac, while Faulkner would have "contributed a drily modern 'sharpness' to his narrative." (RC)

E2587. d'Astier de la Vigerie, Emmanuel. "Préface à l'édition russe du Chien jaune." In Lacassion/Sigaux (E2646), pp. 264-67.
Comments on Simenon's childhood and youth as the key to an understanding of his work with quotes from a radio interview.

E2588. Austin, Richard. "Simenon's 'Maigret' and Adler." Adam nos. 340-342 (1970), pp. 45-50; reprinted in Lacassin/Sigaux (E2646qv), pp. 197-203.
Although Austin has found only one reference to psychologist Alfred Adler in Simenon's work, he sees a similarity between Simenon's attitudes and Adler's writings. Adler's theory on the feeling of inferiority as the "starting point of neurosis" is related to Simenon's characterizations. However, in spite of the title, this is not a study of the Maigret novels.

E2589. Becker, Lucille F. Georges Simenon. Twayne World Author Series 456. Boston: Twayne Publishers, 1977. 171pp. Bibliography and Index.
A study of Simenon's work including a chapter on Pedigree, the autobiographical novel which many critics believe to be a key to Simenon's life and work. The discussion of the fiction is limited to the Maigret series and to the psychological novels with no consideration of the extensive early writings. Bibliographies of primary and secondary sources; the secondary sources are annotated and constitute an excellent basic list of references to 1977. Review: Choice 15:1 (March 78):78.

E2590. Benelli, Graziano. "La fortuna italiana di Georges Simenon |The Italian fortune of Georges Simenon|." In Critica e societa di massa, pp. 301-28. Trieste: LINT, 1983.
Documented view of the editorial and critical fortunes of Simenon in Italy, going back to 1932, year of the first Mondadorian translations of the detective novels of the Belgian writer. Among the most authoritative and significant commentaries those of Savinio (E2677, E2678), Sciascia (E2681), and Anselmi (E2585, E2586) are pointed out. (RC)

E2591. Blochman, Lawrence G. Letter, TAD 7 (1973/74):71-72.
The translator of Simenon's Trois chambres à Manhattan comments on the low quality of Simenon translations into English and gives details of some linguistic horrors he has come across.

E2592. Body, François. "Das Wunder Simenon |The wonder Simenon|." Der Monat 106 (July 57); reprinted in Uber Simenon (E2679), pp. 71-79.
Expository essay discussing Simenon's crime and non-crime novels. Body compares Simenon to Graham Greene in this respect but argues that Simenon's crime novels are better as novels than are Greene's. Body sees Simenon's novels as fitting into the tradition of "late naturalism" but hesitates to say that they deserve a place in world literature. (GG)

E2593. Boileau, Pierre. "Quelque chose de changé dans le roman policier |Something's changed in the detective novel|." In Lacassin/Sigaux (E2646), pp. 190-92; reprinted in Uber Simenon (E2679), pp. 128-31.
In the Maigret novels, Simenon shifted the focus from the solving of a puzzle to a secondary enigma, that of the personality of the criminal.

E2594. Boisdeffre, Pierre de. "A la recherche de Simenon |In search of Simenon|." Revue de Paris 69 (Sept 62):96-107. Photo.
An attempt to understand Simenon and his work which Boisdeffre sees as not addressing the "great" problems of love, politics, etc. but as functioning at a level that is, perhaps, "too low."

E2595. ______. "Le Secret de Georges Simenon." Revue de Paris 65 (Jan 58):173-74.
Reviewing Parinaud's conversations with Simenon (E2665), Boisdeffre recalls briefly his own meetings with Simenon in 1953.

E2596. Boucher, Anthony. "Introduction." In The Short Cases of Inspector Maigret, by Georges Simenon. NY: Doubleday, 1959.

E2597. ______. "On the Brink of Life Was Death." NYTBR, 5 April 1964.
A review/essay of Simenon's The Bells of Bicêtre (Harcourt, Brace, 1964).

E2598. Boverie, Dieudonne. "Georges Simenon, écrivain liégeois |G. S., writer of Liège)." In Lacassin/Sigaux (E2646), pp. 272-75. First published in the Liège newspaper L'Essai (Sept 62).
Reminiscences of Simenon by a fellow Liège native.

E2599. Bresler, Fenton. The Mystery of Georges Simenon: A Biography. London: Heinemann/Quixote Press, 1983; NY: Beaufort Books, 1983. 260pp.
This biography is based on thorough research, including interviews with Simenon's wives, children, friends, neighbors, and publishers. Some new biographical facts ae brought to light, especially those concerning the death of Simenon's brother (killed in Indochina in 1947 while serving in the French Foreign Legion) and Simenon's involvement with the Resistance during World War II. The usual attention is paid to Simenon's widespread sexual activities. On the literary side, Bresler recounts where, when, and in what circumstances various novels were written but has little of his own to say about their quality, preferring to endorse published views by French critics. The book was published to coincide with Simenon's 80th birthday and shows signs of haste. There are, of all things, numerous errors in French phrases, several misspelled proper names, and some factual errors. But as a biography of Simenon the màn ("more often naked than dressed," as a British reviewer remarked), the book is a notable accomplishment. Reviews: TLS, 1 April 83, p. 306; NYTBR, 30 Oct 83, pp. 12-13. (REB)

E2600. Brochier, Jean-Jacques. "L'anarchiste cérébral |The intellectual anarchist|." Magazine littéraire, no. 194 (April 83), pp. 32-33. Photo.
A profile that includes some interview material.

E2601. Bronne, Carlo. "Simenon académicien." La Revue des deux mondes 10 (15 May 52):272-82.
Speech on the occasion of Simenon's election to the Belgian Royal Academy of Language and Literature. Not seen.

E2602. Brophy, Brigid. "Jules et Georges." New Statesman 67, no. 1726 (10 April 52), pp. 566, 568; reprinted in Brophy, Don't Never Forget (Holt, Rinehart and Winston, 1966), pp. 145-48.
Essay-review of Simenon's The Train and Maigret's Special Case.

E2603. Cistre: Essais 10. Lausanne, Switzerland: Editions de l'homme, 1981.
Special issue devoted to Simenon. In addition to biographical and critical material, there is information on an important Simenon collection of papers (Fonds S). Contents (partial): Robert and Rosine Georgin, "Entretien," pp. 13-27 (interview); Maurice Piron, "G. Simenon et son milieu naturel |G. S. and his natural milieu|," pp. 31-41; "Le Romancier au travail: Les Anneaux de Bicêtre. I. Dossier constitué de documents extraits du Fonds S. II. Claudine Gothot-Mersch, "La Genèse des Anneaux de Bicêtre," pp. 41-75, 77-104 |The novelist at work: Les Anneaux de Bicêtre (novel). I. dossier comprising documents from the Simenon collection. II. C. Gothot-Mersch, The genesis of Les Anneaux de Bicêtre|; Jules Bedner, "Simenon et Maigret," pp. 109-30; Gilles Henry, "Comment naît un personnage (Maigret) |How a character is born|," pp. 133-54; M. Dubourg, "Filmographie de G. S.," pp. 157-200; "Textes peu connus de G. S. |Little-known texts of G. S.|," pp. 253-69; "Mémoires et thèses universitaires conservés au Fonds S |Studies and university dissertations stored in the "S" collection|," pp. 271-75; "Les Origines du Fonds S |The origins of the "S" collection|," pp. 279-95. Not seen. Annotation from PMLA listing.

E2604. Cawelti, John G. "The Art of Simenon." In Cawelti (B69), pp. 125-31.
An examination of Maigret and the Reluctant Witnesses to show how Simenon integrates the detection structure with "alternative" interests of character and atmosphere.

E2605. Cleisz, Gérard. "Correspondance Andre Gide-Georges Simenon présenté et annoté par Gérard Cleisz |The A. Gide-G. Simenon correspondance presented and annotated by Gérard Cleisz|." In Lacassin/Sigaux (E2646), pp. 387-452.
Publication of the complete Gide-Simenon correspondance with an introduction and notes by Cleisz.

E2606. Courtine, Robert J. Le Cahier de recettes de Madame Maigret (Mme Maigret's Cook Book). Paris, 1974. English translation by Mary Manheim, published as Madame Maigret's Recipes, NY: Harcourt, Brace, Jovanovich, 1975. Japanese translation by Michiko Kikuchi. Maigret Keishi wa Nani o Taberu?: France no Katei no Aji 100 no Tsukuri-kata. Tokyo: Bunka Shuppankyoku, 1979.
The Japanese translator of this book adds comments on the differences between Japan and France in ingredients and preparation of food. A collection of more than 100 recipes associated with the Maigrets, with a letter-preface by Simenon. (HS/TT)

E2607. ______. "Simenon ou l'appétit de Maigret |Simenon or Maigret's appetite|." In Lacassin/Sigaux (E2646), pp. 204-219.
Anecdotes of Maigret's and Simenon's culinary tastes based on the novels and on meetings with Simenon.

E2608. Daniel-Rops. "Les Romans policiers de M. Georges Simenon." La Nouvelle Revue des Jeunes, 15 July 32; reprinted in Lacassin/Sigaux (E2646), pp. 223-26.
Although some detective fiction may incite readers to crime, Simenon's

fiction avoids the lure of cheap and excessive violence and his only fault may be that he insists too much on psychology.

E2609. Debray-Ritzen, Pierre. Simenon: Avocat des hommes. Paris, 1961. Not seen but the author has described this book as a study of Simenon's creativity.

E2610. ______. "Mon maître Simenon." In Lacassin/Sigaux (E2646), pp. 59-68. A psychiatrist-physician explains how Simenon helped him to understand better the mysterious workings of the human mind and influenced him in changing his specialization from pediatrics to psycho-pediatrics.

E2611. Deniker, Professor (sic). "Georges Simenon, clinicien de l'âme |G. S., therapist of the soul|." In Lacassin/Sigaux (E2646), pp. 68-69. Simenon, in his use of detail and extraordinary powers of observation, is an exemplary therapist.

E2612. "Dossier Simenon." 813 no. 3 (1981). This newsletter/magazine, issued irregularly by the members of a detective fiction collective, devotes a section of its 1981 Reims Mystery Convention report to Simenon. Contents: G. Simenon, "La Naissance de Maigret," pp. 8-10 (E2687); Anne Richter, "G. S.: Faire exploser l'homme," pp. 10-12 (E2674); Robert Perrein, "Le Commissaire Maigret enquête: meurtre en coins de rue," p. 13 (imaginary interview with Maigret); Frédéric Valmain, "Comment Maigret fit ses débuts sur les planches d'un théâtre," pp. 14-15 (report on an adaptation of a Maigret story for the stage); Ralph Messac, "Une étude en 'rouque'," pp. 15-17 (E2655); Noëlle Loriot, "Simenon et ses derniers romans," pp. 17-18 (a brief report on the last Maigrets and on Simenon's career); "G. S. et les livres," p. 18 (a checklist of some of the secondary material on Simenon and his work).

E2613. "Dossier Simenon." Magazine littéraire 107 (1975):20-41. Contents: Interview with Francis Lacassin; Claude Menguy, "Le pari de Georges Sim |The wager of Georges Sim|;" Francis Lacassin, "Maigret ou la clé des coeurs |Maigret or the key to hearts|;" Gilles Costaz, "Les collègues de Maigret;" Jean-Didier Wolfrom, "Un romancier sans imagination |A novelist without imagination|;" Gilbert Sigaux, "Le dernier de ses personnages |The last of his characters|;" unpublished short story by Simenon. Not seen.

E2614. Dubois, Jacques. "Simenon et la déviance." Littérature I (Feb 71):62-72. A quasi-sociological study of the rebel who transgresses the norms of the group and flees. Dubois thinks that all detective novels are, to some extent, novels of "deviance." He examines five Simenon novels published between 1934 and 1948 to support his theory.

E2615. Dubourg, Maurice. "Géographie de Simenon." In Lacassin/Sigaux (E2646), pp. 138-56. Uses of and ideas about geographical locations in Simenon's work.

E2616. ______. "Maigret & Co.: The Detectives of the Simenon Agency." TAD 4 (1970/71):79-86. Translation by Francis M. Nevins, Jr. of an article which originally appeared in Mystère Magazine (Dec 64). Observations on Simenon's detective fiction, with notes by the translator.

E2617. Duperray, Jean. "Au nom du Père |In the Father's name|." In Lacassin/Sigaux (E2646qv), pp. 99-129.

A portentous study of the metamorphoses of the father figure in Simenon's work as a reflection of Simenon's relationship with his own father.

E2619. Eisinger, Erica M. "Maigret and Women: La Maman and La Putain." JPC 12:1 (Summer 78):52-60.

A rapid survey of French female detectives with the comment that Maigret may be the one great French woman detective since he combines both masculine and feminine qualities. There is also a portrait of Mme Maigret, "a male fantasy, created for a man," the perfect servant.

E2620. Fabre, Jean. Enquête sur un enquêteur Maigret, un essai de sociocritique |Investigation of an investigator Maigret, an essay in sociocriticism|. Montpellier: Centre d'études et de recherches sociocritiques Université Paul Valéry, 1981.

An analysis of the Maigret phenomenon using the tools of sociological criticism. Review: TLS, 1 Oct 82, p. 1058.

E2621. Fallois, Bernard de. Simenon. Bibliothèque idéale. Paris: Gallimard, 1961. 305pp. Illus.

A study that follows the standard format of this series: biography, critical survey, some excerpts from Simenon's work, critical reviews and bio-bibliographical material.

E2622. Frank, Nino. "Hypothèse à propos de Maigret |Hypothesis concerning Maigret|." In Lacassin/Sigaux (E2646), pp. 193-96.

Frank's hypothesis is that Maigret is Simenon.

E2623. Freustié, Jean. "Une petite tente au milieu du jardin |A little tent in the middle of the garden|." In Lacassin/Sigaux (E2646qv), pp. 52-58.

After not reading any Simenon for some years, Freustié reads two recent novels, La Prison and Il y a des noisetiers, and finds the novelist still in good form. Some discussion of characters in solitude and an investigation as the mainspring of the plot.

E2624. Gallant, Mavis. "Simenon in spite of himself." NYTBR, 1 July 84, pp. 1, 29-30. Photo.

Review-essay of Simenon's Mémoires intimes (E2685). Gallant describes the excisions made in the original manuscript for the English-language edition, cuts which she thinks have improved the narrative. She discusses Simenon's biography and criticizes severely the translation by Harold J. Salemson for numerous errors, commenting that the translation seems to have been a hurried one.

E2625. Galligan, Edward L. "Simenon's Mosaic of Small Novels." South Atlantic Quarterly 66 (1967):534-43.

A presentation to an English-speaking audience based on a reading of translations. Galligan finds Simenon a powerful writer and argues that the Maigret novels are superior to Simenon's "serious" works.

E2626. Gannett, Gary L. "All the Short Cases of Inspector Maigret." TAD 10 (1977):347.

Bibliography of translated and untranslated short stories and novelettes featuring Maigret.

E2627. Gide, André. "Lettres d'un ami |Letters from a friend|." Adam no. 328-330 (1969):29-48.

Letters in French from Gide to Simenon with a short postscript by Gide and a note by editor Grindea on the correspondence.

E2628. Gill, Brendan. "Profiles: Out of the Dark." New Yorker, 24 Jan 53, 35-36, 38, 40, 42-53. Portrait.

At the time Gill wrote his profile, Simenon was living in Lakeville, Connecticut and the profile incorporates considerable interview material. Mainly biography but a lengthy and important article that gives an intimate portrait on how Simenon lived, wrote, looked and talked.

E2629. Gothot-Mersch, Claudine, et al. Lire Simenon. Collection: Dossier Media. Paris: Fernand Nathan and editions Labor, 1980.

5 essays on Simenon. Not seen.

E2630. Granholm, Arne. "Kommissarie Maigret -- en av skönlitteraturens mest systematiska skildringar av en utredares vardag |Commissioner Maigret -- one of literature's most systematic depictions of an investigator's working day|." Jury 4:4 (1975):13-17. (MS)

E2631. Grella, George. "Simenon and Maigret." Adam no. 328-330 (1969):54-60.

The Maigret novels are not only admirably drawn studies of crimes but also a portrait of the artist, both observer and commentator-moralist.

E2632. Grindea, Myron. "Simenon - cet inconnu." Adam no. 328-330 (1969):2-6; reprinted in Books & Bookmen no. 328-330 (1969):2-6.

Report on a week Grindea spent with Simenon in 1966.

E2633. Grindea, Myron, editor. Simenon issue. Adam no. 328-330 (1975). Photographs.

Contents: M. Grindea, "Simenon-cet inconnu," pp. 2-6 (E2632); G. Simenon, "A novelist is a man who writers novels: I insist on the s," pp. 7-28 (E2688); André Gide, "Lettres d'un ami," pp. 29-48 (E2627); Jarold Ramsey, "A human Babylon upon the hillside (poem)," p. 49; "Other Writers on Simenon," pp. 50-53 (Agatha Christie, C. Day Lewis, C. P. Snow, Henry Miller, et al); George Grella, "Simenon and Maigret," pp. 54-60 (E2631); Gavin Ewart, "To the idiots (poem)," p. 61; Claude Menguy, "Bibliographie, filmographie et adaptations théâtrales de Georges Simenon," pp. 62-91 (in addition to the bibliography of novels and short stories published under his own name and various pseudonyms, the bibliography also lists interviews and non-fictional writing); "Views and Reviews," pp. 92-96 (reviews and commentary).

E2634. Harris, Lis. "Maigret le Flaneur." New Yorker, 2 April 1979, pp. 122-24.

An overview of Simenon's work. Harris confesses that she does not like his "so-called" psychological novels as much as the Maigrets. She talks about the Maigrets and reviews Maigret in Exile and Maigret's Pipe.

E2635. Henry, Gilles. Commissaire Maigret, qui êtes-vous |Commissaire Maigret, who are you|? Paris: Plon, 1977. 284pp. Translated into Japanese by Shigeo Oketani and published as Simenon to Maigret Keishi. Tokyo: Kawade Shobo Shinsha, 1980.

A portrait of Maigret whom Henry believes to be modeled on Simenon's father.

E2636. Hensel, Georg. "Simenon und sein Kommissar Maigret." In Uber Simenon (E2679), pp. 149-63.
Desultory essay on various aspects of Simenon's life and attitudes toward writing, on Maigret, and on the relationship between author and detective. Relies heavily on Les Mémoires de Maigret (1951) and compares this book to Simenon's own memoirs, Quand j'étais vieux (1970). (GG)

E2637. Jacobs, Jay. "Simenon's Mosaic." Reporter 32 (14 Jan 65):38-40.
Review of recent Simenon translations with ana overview of the Maigret series and Simenon's writing methods and a consideration of his non-Maigret novels.

E2638. Johnson, Douglas. "Crypto-Christian with a pipe." TLS, 1 Oct 82, pp. 1058-59. Essay-review of Fabre (E2620).
A detailed examination of the Fabre study, with particular attention to the premise that the Maigret novels are about the process of novel writing, and to the character of Maigret with his attachment to a recognizably traditional French past.

E2639. Jour, Jean. Simenon enfant de Liège |Simenon, a child of Liège). Brussels: Editions Libro Sciences, 1980. Not seen.

E2640. ______. Simenon et "Pedigree." Liège: L'essai, 1963.
A study of Simenon's work based on a reading of the autobiographical novel Pedigree as the key to his work.

E2641. Juin, Hubert. "Un roman ininterrompu |An uninterrupted novel|." In Lacassin/Sigaux (E2646), pp. 77-88.
Juin contrasts the novelistic universes of Balzac, Aragon and Simenon with those of Zola and Jules Romain to show that these writers all create novelistic worlds that characters--and readers--"live in" rather than worlds dominated by characters and a preconceived form. In the second half of this essay, Juin discusses eroticism in Simenon's novels.

E2642. Kanters, Robert. "Sur la vieillesse et sur la mort |On old age and death|." In Lacassin/Sigaux (E2646), pp. 71-76.
As Simenon ages, attitudes toward old age and death change in his work.

E2643. Koskimies, Rafael. "Novelists' Thoughts about Their Art. 3. Georges Simenon." Neuphilologische Mittellungen 57 (1956):158-59.
In Les Mémoires de Maigret (1950), a writer, Sim, talks about the relationship between life/facts and fiction. Koskimies uses this as an excuse to remind the reader that the artist "selects and arranges" and that what is not believable in life may be in art.

E2644. Lacassin, Francis. "De Georges Sim à Simenon." In Tourteau (B408), pp. 145-56.
What Simenon owes to his first incarnation as Georges Sim for his later work's themes, characters, etc. Followed by a brief general discussion of Lacassin's presentation (pp. 157-61).

E2645. ______. "Simenon et la fugue initiatique |Simenon and the initiatory flight|." In Lacassin/Sigaux (E2646), pp. 157-83.
A thematic study of characters who, one day, flee a conventional, anonymous life to a new life which they hope will be a beginning.

E2646. Lacassin, Francis, and Sigaux, Gilbert, editors. Simenon. Paris: Plon, 1973. 481pp.

An anthology of critical writings on Simenon and his work. The critical essays will be listed separately and annotated. Texts by Simenon will be briefly characterized in the table of contents listing. Contents: Gilbert Sigaux, "Lire Simenon," pp. 13-17 (E2684); Thomas Narcejac, "Le Point Oméga," pp. 18-22 (E2664); Jean Mambrino, "Le mot du coffre," pp. 23-51 (E2650); Jean Freustié, "Une petite tente au milieu du jardin," pp. 52-58 (E2623); Pierre Debray-Ritzen, "Mon maître Simenon," pp. 59-68 (E2610); Professeur Deniker, "Georges Simenon, clinicien de l'âme," pp. 69-70 (E2611); Robert Kanters, "Sur la vieillesse et sur la mort," pp. 71-78 (E2642); Hubert Juin, "Un roman ininterrompu," pp. 77-88 (E2641); Evelyne Sullerot, "Les hommes, les hommes," pp. 89-98 (E2693); Jean Duperray, "Au nom du Père," pp. 99-129 (E2617); Ralph Messac, "Georges Simenon, romancier-nez," pp. 130-38 (E2656); Maurice Dubourg, "Géographie de Simenon," pp. 139-56 (E2615); Francis Lacassin, "Simenon et la fugue initiatique," pp. 157-83 (E2645); Eleonora Schraiber, "Georges Simenon et la littérature russe," pp. 184-89 (E2680); Pierre Boileau, "Quelque chose de changé dans le roman policier," pp. 190-92 (E2593); Nino Frank, "Hypothèse à propos de Maigret," pp. 193-96 (E2622); Richard Austin, "Maigret et Adler," pp. 197-203 (E2588); R.-J. Courtine, "Simenon ou l'appétit de Maigret," pp. 204-19 (E2607); Daniel-Rops, "Les romans policiers de M. Georges Simenon," pp. 223-26 (E2608); Marcel More, "Simenon et l'enfant de choeur," pp. 227-63 (E2659); Emmanuel d'Astier de la Vigerie, "Preface à l'édition russe du Chien jaune," pp. 264-67 (E2587); Henry Miller, "Article publié dans Candide," pp. 268-71 (E2657); Dieudonne Boverie, "Georges Simenon, écrivain liégeois," pp. 272-75 (E2598); Victor Moremans, "Mon ami Simenon," pp. 276-79 (E2660); Jean Paulhan, "Les Anneaux de Bicêtre," pp. 280-82 (E2667); François Mauriac, "Article publié dans le Figaro littéraire," pp. 283-84 (E2652); G. Simenon, "La Gazette de Liège, 1920," pp.287-98 (newspaper articles on the region and local events); G. S., "La Revue sincère," pp. 299-308 (short pieces, largely on writers); G.S., "Chez Trotsky," pp. 309-29 (Interview, 1933); G. S., "Police-Secours ou les nouveaux mystères de Paris |Police squad-car or the new mysteries of Paris|," pp. 321-68 (Paris-Soir, 1937; a series of articles on the work of Parisian policemen in squad-cars); G. S., "Préface à Traqué de Arthur Orme," pp. 369-72 (preface to a novel with some comments by Simenon on novelistic qualities that he appreciates); G. S., "Sur la propriété littéraire |On literary property|," pp. 373-79 (From Arts, 1956; Simenon protests an edict limiting exclusive copyright to 50 years); G. S., "Le grand amour de Pierre Benoît," pp. 380-84 (NL, 1962; homage to a writer); G. S., "Jean Cocteau," pp. 385-86 (1961; English translation published in Adam 300 (May 1963)); "Correspondance André Gide-Georges Simenon présenté et annoté par Gérard Cleisz," pp. 387-452 (E2605); F. Lacassin, "Bibliographie sommaire de Simenon," pp. 453-79 (fiction and non-fiction published as by G. Simenon).

E2647. la Cour, Tage. "Jules Maigret's privatliv |J. Maigret's private life|." Jury 1:3-4 (1972):20-21+. (MS)

E2648. Lambert, Gavin. "Night Vision." In Lambert (B215), pp. 171-209.

An intelligent survey of the work of a novelist whom Lambert sees as dealing with solitary people driven to their limit. He reviews both the Maigret and mainstream novels and concludes with a portrait of a Simenon renouncing writing and, at last, alone with the truly "naked man," Simenon himself.

E2649. Lundin, Bo. "Jules Maigret." Jury 2:2 (1973):20-23, 49.
Biography of Maigret on his "death," as reported in February 1973. (MS)

E2650. Mambrino, Jean. "Le mot du coffre |The password to the strongbox|." In Lacassin/Sigaux (E2646), pp. 23-51.
Supporting his essay with numerous citations from Simenon's work, Mambrino discusses some "constants": the image of light, the themes of emprisonment and flight, and, finally, for the characters in Fond de la bouteille the keys to their secret desires.

E2651. Mauriac, Claude. "Georges Simenon." As published in L'alittérature contemporaine (Paris: Albin Michel, 1958). Originally published in Preuves no. 67 (1956):79-85; published in English translation in The New Literature (NY: George Braziller, 1958), pp. 133-50. It should be noted that this essay was omitted from the revised edition of L'alittérature contemporaine (Albin Michel, 1969).
A spongy, imprecise essay which begins with the statement that all Simenon's heroes resemble their author and rambles on with comments on Simenon's psychology, characterization, settings and sexual content.

E2652. Mauriac, Francois. "Bloc-Notes." le Figaro Littéraire, 11 May 1963; reprinted in Lacassin/Sigaux (E2646), pp. 283-84.
A review by Catholic novelist Mauriac of agnostic Simenon's novel Les Anneaux de Bicêtre.

E2653. Menguy, Claude. Bibliographie des éditions originales de Georges Simenon. Brussels: Le livre et l'estampe, 1967.
A bibliography of primary sources.

E2654. ______. "Bibliographie, filmographie et adaptations théâtrales de Georges Simenon." In Adam no. 328-30 (1969), pp. 62-91.
Includes the early work written under various pseudonyms and non-fiction material. The compiler acknowledges the contributions of Bernard de Fallois and Roger Stéphane. The annotations are in French.

E2655. Messac, Ralph. "Une étude en 'rouque' |A study of redheads|." In 813 3 (1981):15-17.
Simenon's frequent use of characters with red hair.

E2656. ______. "Georges Simenon, 'romancier-nez' |G. S., 'novelist with a sense of smell'|." In Lacassin/Sigaux (E2646), pp. 130-38.
The son of critic Regis Messac (B257) analyzes the importance of odors in Simenon's work.

E2657. Miller, Henry. ("Simenon.") Candide no. 4, 11 May 61; reprinted in Lacassin/Sigaux (E2646), pp. 268-71.
Miller describes a visit to Simenon at Echandens.

E2658. Mok, Michael. "Close-up: Georges Simenon. Excuse me, I think I'm about to have a novel." Life 66 (9 May 69):43-44, 46, 48-49. Photos.
A portrait of Simenon as he prowls about Paris on the verge, as he puts it, of "having a novel." His apparently extraordinary memory, his writing habits, his obsessively private life: all these aspects are graphically described by reporter Mok.

E2659. More, Marcel. "Simenon et l'enfant de choeur |Simenon and the choirboy|." In Lacassin/Sigaux (E2646), pp. 227-63. Original publication: Dieu vivant, no. 19 (1951); reprinted in his La Foudre de Dieu (Gallimard, 1969).

Intrigued by the inner mysteries of the characters in Simenon's work, More classifies him with Kafka, Georges Bernanos and Graham Greene, finding his characters involved in spiritual dramas.

E2660. Moremans, Victor. "Mon ami Simenon." In Lacassin/Sigaux (E2646), pp. 276-79. Originally published in L'Essai (Liège), Sept 62.

Moremans describes Simenon's emotional return to Liège after many years of absence.

E2661. Nagashima, Ryozo. Maigret Keishi |Inspector Maigret|. Tokyo: Yomiuri Shinbun-sha, 1978. 206pp.

A sub-reference book on Inspector Maigret, with his biography and tidbidts, mainly quoting from Simenon's Les Mémoires de Maigret (1950) and other sources. (HS/TT)

E2663. Narcejac, Thomas. Le cas Simenon |The Simenon case|. Paris: Presses de la cité, 1950; published in English translation as The Art of Simenon. London: Routledge & Kegan Paul, 1952. Bibliography.

An important and much-cited study of Simenon as a a novelist with several chapters on the Maigret stories. (REB)

E2664. ______. "Le Point Oméga." In Lacassin/Sigaux (E2646), pp. 18-22).

Narcejac sees Simenon as limited by his ambition to create a total being, "essence and existence" perceived simultaneously. Simenon's characters do not "think," they are struggling with themselves, not with the world. However, Le Petit Saint is a "rare" masterpiece in which, for once, Simenon is closest to achieving his ambition.

E2665. Parinaud, André. Connaissance de Georges Simenon. Tome I: Le secret du romancier suivi des entretiens avec Simenon |Getting acquainted with G.S. Vol. I: The novelist's secret followed by interviews with Simenon|. Paris: Presses de la cité, 1957.

A study of Simenon that is most important for the transcriptions of radio interviews. A second volume was not published.

E2666. Parsons, Luke. "Simenon and Chandler." Contemporary Review 197 (1960):56-58; reprinted in Uber Simenon (E2679), pp. 80-84.

Straightforward argument that the crime novels of both Simenon and Chandler deserve to be called Novels. Both novelists, argues Parsons, are adept at creating hard, independent, but human worlds, Chandler excelling in scenery description and Simenon in character portrayal. (GG)

E2667. Paulhan, Jean. "Les Anneaux de Bicêtre." In Lacassin/Sigaux (E2646), pp. 280-82.

An excerpt from Paulhan's complete works in which the critic declares that none of Simenon's works is indifferently written but that a true tragic dimension is impossible in the ego-centric world of Simenon's characters.

E2668. Pettersson, Sven-Ingmar. "Deckarporträtt Nr 11." DAST 8:6 (1975):25-26.

A writer's portrait of Simenon. (MS)

E2669. Piron, Maurice. L'Univers de Simenon |Simenon's universe|. Paris:

Presses de la cité, 1982. Circa 500pp.
A "repertory" of Simenon's novels: characters, settings, plot resumes, etc. Not seen.

E2670. Porter, Dennis. "The Case in Simenon." In Porter (B315), pp. 202-15.
In France, the policeman has traditionally been seen as the enemy but Simenon has drawn on Anglo-Saxon and French detective conventions to create a sympathetic character who is quintessentially French.

E2671. Poulet, Robert. "Georges Simenon." In La Lanterne magique, pp. 106-114. Paris: Nouvelles éditions Debresse, 1956.
Poulet thinks that Simenon doesn't write literature and tries to explain the reason for his disappointment after reading 62 of the novels. He inappropriately characterizes Simenon as the "Eugène Sue"--a nineteenth century writer of potboilers--of his age.

E2672. Raymond, John. Simenon in Court. London: Hamish Hamilton, 1968; NY: Harcourt, Brace & World, 1969.
The first book on Simenon to appear in the United States. Raymond argues cogently and concisely that Simenon is one of the great European novelists. The checklist of Simenon's writings was omitted from the American edition. Breen 217. (REB)

E2673. Richardson, Maurice. "Simenon and Highsmith: Into the criminal's head." In Keating (B179), pp. 100-117.
Both Simenon and Highsmith are examples of writers of crime fiction whose novels are both entertaining and serious contributions to literature. The essay is basically a well-informed introduction to the work of the two writers.

E2674. Richter, Anne. "Georges Simenon: Faire exploser l'homme |G. S.: causing man to explode|." 813 3 (1981):10-12.
On the dissolution of faith and external supports for characters in the contemporary novel. Simenon's characters find the point at which a "real" life might begin, one which could be the "reintegration" of the personality.

E2675. ______. Georges Simenon et l'homme désintégré |G. S. and the disintegrated man|. Brussels: La Renaissance du livre, 1964.
Simenon's novels in the context of contemporary "disintegration."

E2676. Rolo, Charles J. "Simenon and Spillane: The Metaphysics of Murder for the Millions." New World Writing 1 (1952):234-45; reprinted in Mass Culture, edited by Bernard Rosenberg and David Manning White, pp. 165-75. NY: The Free Press, 1957.
The modern detective story is a contemporary Passion Play in which we, like the detective, play the role of Saviour. Spillane's popularity, in spite of his artistic limitations, and Simenon's psychologically subtle novels are both seen as expressions of this phenomenon.

E2677. Savinio, Alberto. "Georges Simenon: il romanzo della verità nuda |G. S.: the novel of the naked truth|." L'Italiano, Oct/Nov 1936, pp. 259-66; excerpted in Cremante/Rambelli (B78), pp. 85-93.
Simenon has stolen from the Anglo-Saxons the detective novel formula, bringing it into the bed of the French literary tradition of Gaboriau and Flaubert where it becomes once more what it is supposed to be: "the book of the naked truth," of life at its "rawest" and most "throbbing,"

the "most pessimistic" book on man's condition. In that definition the author also includes the short novels that do not have Maigret as their protagonist. (LR)

E2678. ______. "Romanzo poliziesco |Detective fiction|." In Souvenirs, pp. 193-99. Palermo: Sellerio, 1976.
The author, one of the most original writers of Surrealist inspiration of the 20th century, states that Georges Simenon, with the character of Maigret, has created a new type of detective novel: "the bourgeois detective novel." "As Racine has made tragedy middle-class, as Ingres has made the classic form of painting middle-class," so Simenon, following in this a tendency typical of French culture, has clothed in bourgeois forms the detective novel, introducing a "modest" crime, and a police commissioner with a good-natured temperament and a moralistic spirit who "completes his work more through the duty of a functionary than the thirst of a discoverer." In Maigret the bourgeois uniform is a form of religiosity. Simenons gives to France a "rational" novel distinguished by a literary style that places him much above the common stereotyped and anonymous detective production. (LR)

E2679. Schmolders, Claudia and Christian Strich, editors. Uber Simenon |On Simenon|. Diogenes Taschenbuch 154. Zurich: Diogenes Verlag AG, 1978.
One of the series of German language critical essay collections published by Diogenes on individual writers. Uber Simenon contains a wealth of critical and bibliographical material on the creator of Maigret. All of the material not originally written in German has been translated into German. In addition to the text of a talk Simenon gave in New York City in 1945, and an interview with French critic Francis Lacassin, this volume contains extended critical quotes from such prominent figures as André Gide, Jean Cocteau, Henry Miller, C. P. Snow and Federico Fellini. Of the 16 critical essays only 7 treat significantly Simenon's detective stories. These 7 are: François Body, "Das Wunder Simenon," pp. 71-79 (E2592); Luke Parsons, "Simenon und Chandler," pp. 80-84 (E2666); Jean Améry, "Das fleissige Leben des Georges Simenon," pp. 100-108 (E2584); Hans Altenheim, "Ein Traum von Maigret," pp. 113-20 (E2583); Julian Symons, "Simenon und sein Maigret," pp. 121-127 (excerpt from Bloody Murder, B387); and Georg Hensel, "Simenon und sein Kommissar Maigret," pp. 149-63 (E2636). The bibliography of primary and secondary sources is in 9 parts, and includes the Maigret novels, the non-Maigret mysteries and non-mysteries, non-fictional pieces and interviews, a filmography and list of stage plays, a list of languages into which Simenon has been translated (43), and a multi-language bibliography of secondary sources which includes articles and monographs. (GG)

E2680. Schraiber, Eleonora. "Georges Simenon et la littérature russe |G. S. and Russian literature|." In Lacassin/Sigaux (E2646), pp. 184-89.
The relationship of Simenon's writing to Russian authors like Gogol, Chekhov and Dostoevsky. In a note, the announcement is made of the establishment of a Simenon manuscript collection at the Saltykov-Shtchedrine Library in Leningrad.

E2681. Sciascia, Leonardo. "La carriera di Maigret |Maigret's career|." Letteratura 4 (1954):73-75.
Sciascia observes that the best detective novels of Simenon are those in which Commissaire Maigret, like Chesterton's Father Brown, pursues the investigation in the heart of Protestant society: his presence as an outsider, as a Catholic then becomes a kind of "chemical agent that

arouses revelations, sudden 'precipitants,' hidden psychological substances." (LR)

E2682. Shaffer, Norman J. "A Bibliography and English Language Index to George Simenon's Maigret Novels." TAD 3 (1969/70):31-37.
A checklist of the Maigret novels published in English translation with first publication in French, and first and subsequent publications in translation. With a British and American title index.

E2683. Shutoff, Carl Lee. "Simenon's Maigret Novels." Ph. D. dissertation. Indiana University, 1980. 171pp. DAI 41, nos. 1-2, 277-A. Not seen.

E2684. Sigaux, Gilbert. "Lire Simenon |Reading Simenon|." In Lacassin/Sigaux (E2646), pp. 13-17.
An introductory essay on Simenon's work with some sketchy biographical details and brief commentary on the fiction.

E2685. Simenon, Georges. (Autobiography)
During the past decade, Simenon has published a series of autobiographical volumes. Although Simenon does not talk extensively about his writing, these volumes are essential for an understanding of this complex, devious writer. They will be listed, in order of publication, with English translation noted, where available. Unless otherwise specified, all French editions are published by Presses de la Cité (Paris). Quand j'étais vieux (1970) (tr. by Helen Eustis: When I Was Old, NY: Harcourt Brace Jovanovich, 1971); Lettre à ma mere (1974) (tr. by Ralph Manheim: Letter to My Mother, NY: Harcourt Brace Jovanovich, 1976); Des traces de pas (1975); Un Homme comme un autre (1975); Les Petits Hommes (1976); Vent du nord-Vent du sud (1976); Banc au soleil (1977); De la cave au grenier (1977); A l'abri de notre arbre (1977); Tant que je suis vivant (1978); Mémoires intimes (1981) (tr. by Harold J. Salemson: Intimate Memoirs, Harcourt Brace Jovanovich, 1984).

E2686. ______. Mes Apprentissages |My apprenticeship). I. A la découverte de la France |Discovering France|. 2. A la recherche de l'homme nu |Looking for the naked man|. Textes selected by Francis Lacassin and Gilbert Sigaux. 10/18 series. Paris: Union générale d'éditions, 1946. 446 and 443pp. Bibliography established by Lacassin. Not seen.

E2687. ______. "La Naissance de Maigret." 813 3 (1981):8-10. First published in 1966.
1927 and the birth of Maigret during the Tour of France.

E2688. ______. "A novelist is a man who writes novels: I insist on the s." Adam no. 328-330 (1969):7-28.
From the essay "Le roman de l'homme," on the novel, how Simenon writes, and the role of the novelist and storyteller.

E2689. ______. Le Roman de l'homme |The novel of man|. Lausanne: Editions de l'Aire, 1981.
A collection of essays (the title essay, "L'âge du roman |The age of the novel|," and "Le Romancier |The novelist|," an interview and a preface by Simenon.

E2690. Steinhoff, William R. "Georges Simenon: The Most Popular Novelist in the World." Michigan Quarterly Review 2;2 (25 Apr 63):85-89.
The contemporary artist has moved away from the rest of the world but

Simenon pleases both writers (like Gide, Cocteau and Faulkner) and the general reader. There are a number of quotes from Simenon which appear to be interview material; however, no source is given.

E2691. Stéphane, Roger. Le Dossier Simenon. Paris: Laffont, 1961. Not seen.

E2692. ______. Georges Simenon, portrait souvenir. Paris: Taillandier, 1963. Not seen.

E2693. Sullerot, Evelyne. "Les hommes, les hommes." In Lacassin/Sigaux (E2646), pp. 89-98.

A tribute to Simenon's maleness, which makes a woman feel more like a woman. An ironic portrait of Maigret's masculine-dominated world mixed with Sullerot's feelings of attraction toward this protective refuge tempered by the realization that Maigret, who is happy at home, does not exist.

E2694. Symons, Julian. "A View of Simenon." In Symons (B389), pp. 148-55. Essay first published in NYRB, 12 Oct 78, p. 34-37.

A psychological study of Simenon's life and work and reviews of some recently translated books of which the Maigrets are not, Symons claims, "particularly good."

E2695. Thoorens, Leon. "Georges Simenon, romancier de la fuite inutile |G. S. novelist of the useless flight|." Revue generale belge, 15 March 54, pp. 781-98.

Not seen but appears to be another study of rebels in Simenon.

E2696. ______. Qui êtes-vous, Georges Simenon |Who are you, G. S.|? Marabout Flash no. 21, 1959. Not seen.

E2697. Tillinac, Denis. Le mystère Simenon. Paris: Calmann Levy, 1980. 224pp. Not seen. Review: NL, no. 2731, p. 28. Not seen.

E2698. Tourteau, Jean-Jacques. "Georges Simenon." In Tourteau (B408), pp. 136-61.

A compact overview touching on critical attitudes toward Simenon, themes and characters, his Catholic upbringing, and the virtues and weaknesses of his work. See also the anaylses of two novels, Le charretier de la 'Providence' and Le chien jaune on pp. 284-87, 288-92.

E2699. Vandromme, Pol. Georges Simenon. Brussels: Pierre de Meyere, 1962. Not seen.

E2700. Velman, H. La Tentation de l'inaccessible: structures narratives chez Simenon |The temptation of the inaccessible: narrative structures in Simenon|. Amsterdam: Rodopi, 1982. xxii, 272pp.

"The detective novel; narrative structure." Not seen. As listed in 1982 MLA bibliography.

E2701. Weisz, Pierre. "Simenon and 'Le Commissaire'." In Benstock (B26), pp. 174-89.

A discussion of Simenon's Maigret novels. A sensible analysis that, without offering any new insights into the fiction, manages to provide an excellent introduction to the series. Although there are separate, chronological lists of Maigret novels and of English translations, there is no attempt to correlate the translations with the original versions.

E2702. Whiteley, J. Stuart. "Simenon: The Shadow and the Self. An interview with Georges Simenon." In Adams, MDA 1973 (B3), pp. 221-36.

Transcription of a television interview, 28 September 1971. The two interviewers are doctors (a forensic pathologist and a psychiatrist) and the comment is made that the interview became, very quickly, a psychiatric session. There is an attempt made to sum up the interviewers' findings but the most revealing comments are probably ones made by Simenon.

E2703. Young, Trudee. Georges Simenon: A Checklist of his "Maigret" and Other Mystery Novels and Short Stories in French and English Translations. Author Bibliographies Series: No. 29. Metuchen, N. J.: Scarecrow Press, 1975. British edition: Folkestone: Scarecrow Press, 1977.

The most complete Simenon bibliography available in English. Includes some non-mystery titles. Based on an M. A. thesis, San Jose (CA) University, 1975. Breen 219.

SIMMEL, JOHANNES MARIO

Ref: Hubin 2, ABMI(S).

E2704. Weber, Albrecht. Das Phanomen Simmel: Zur rezeption eines Bestsellerautors unter Schulern und im Literaturunterricht |The Simmel phenomenon: on the reception of a bestseller author in the schools and in the teaching of literature|. Herder Taschenbuch Band 9303. Freiburg, Germany: Herderbucherei, 1977. 189pp.

German pedagogical examination of the work of Simmel and its reception by German gymnasium (i. e. high-school) students and teachers. In spite of the statistical popularity of Simmel's novels, most teachers find Simmel not suitable to be taught in literature courses. Although there is much statistical information of no criminous interest, there is also some interesting discussion of the "popular literature vs. Literature" question, with Simmel's novels representing popular literature. Weber firmly believes in the literary merits of Simmel's work. An appendix contains plot summaries of Caviar and Love is Just a Word (1969) to aid gynmasium teachers in their teaching of Simmel. Also included is a bibliography of primary and secondary sources. (GG)

SIMON, ROGER

Ref: Hubin 2, TCCMW.

Int: Gang 1 (198-), pp. 48-51 (photo; interview, in French, held at time of opening in Paris of film version of "The Big Fix").

E2705. Geherin, David. "Roger Simon." In Geherin (B121), pp. 83-127.

In addition to discussing the three Moses Wine private-eye novels, Geherin also discusses Simon's non-series, non-mystery novels. Geherin sees Simon, in his use of foreign settings, moving away from the traditional American urban setting; modernizing the genre by putting Wine in contemporary situations; and progressively deepening his characterization of Wine.

SIMONIN, ALBERT

Ref: SN.

Int: MM 277, March 71.

SIMPSON, HELEN

Ref: Hubin 2, TCCMW, EMD, CC, ABMI(S).

E2706. Sayers, Dorothy L. "Helen Simpson." Fortnightly 149 (new series; January 41):54-59.
Remembrance of Simpson, author of three mysteries with Clemence Dane, and friend of Sayers. (KLM)

SIMS, GEORGE (1902-66). See CAIN, PAUL

SIMS, GEORGE (1923-)

Ref: Hubin 2, TCCMW, ABMI(S).

SINCLAIR, FIONA

Ref: Hubin 2, CC; Pike, TPP 4:5/6 (Dec 81):49-50.

SINIAC, PIERRE

Ref: SN.

Int: MM 290, Apr 72; Polar 14 (Oct 80):8-19 (photos).

E2707. Deloux, Jean-Pierre. "La fête des fous |Holiday for madmen|." Polar 14 (Oct 80):4-7. Photo.
An eclectic writer who characterizes himself as having a marginal relationship to detective fiction, Siniac in recent short stories has shown affinities with the demonic Catholic writers like Barbey d'Aurevilly, Villiers de L'Isle-Adam and Léon Bloy. Deloux describes in some detail Siniac's novels.

E2708. "Dossier Siniac." Polar 14 (Oct 80):4-39.
Contents: Jean-Pierre Deloux, "La fête des fous," pp. 4-7 (E2707); "Entretien avec Pierre Siniac," pp. 8-19 (interview; photos); François Guérif, "Bibliographie," p. 21; "Un chef d'oeuvre criminel," pp. 22-39 (short story).

SJOWALL, MAJ, and WAHLOO, PER

Ref: Hubin 2, TCCMW, EMD, CC, ABMI(S); Cannon, AHMM 28:2 (Feb 83):66-69.

Int: PW 200 (6 Sept 71):13-15 (photo); New Yorker 47 (22 May 71):28.

See also: E1801.

E2709. Benstock, Bernard. "The Education of Martin Beck." In Benstock (B26), pp. 190-209.
Benstock points out the social and political concerns of the Beck procedural series, describes the make-up of the investigative team, surveys each of the novels in turn, and concludes with comments on the "final phase of Beck's tenuous politicisation."

E2710. Dove, George. "Maj Sjöwall and Per Wahlöö." In Dove (B96), pp. 217-25.
A survey of the Martin Beck procedurals with comments on the relationship between the police and society and the gradual deterioration of social structure and an increasing tendency on the part of the police toward authoritarianism and secrecy.

E2711. Duffy, Martha. "Martin Beck Passes." Time 106 (11 Aug 75):58-59. Photo.

Survey of the Martin Beck series, with an emphasis on its social and political content.

E2712. Maxfield, James F. "The Collective Detective Hero: The Police Novels of Maj Sjöwall and Per Wahlöö." Clues 3:1 (Spring/Summer 82):70-79.
Maxfield believes that it is wrong to speak of the Martin Beck series since the crimes are solved by group effort and the "only possible redemption of society lies in the willingness of people to work cooperatively." The article also includes a discussion of the political underpinning of the novels and of the individual members of the detection team.

E2713. Ochiogrosso, Frank. "The Police in Society: The Novels of Maj Sjöwall and Per Wahlöö." TAD 12 (1979): 174-77.
The society and the police, and the evolving/changing nature of their relationship as chronicled in the ten novels of the series featuring Martin Beck.

E2714. Strom, Sven. "Maj Sjöwalls och Per Wahlöös realism |The realism of Maj Sjöwall and Per Wahlöö|." Jury 4:1 (1975):39-42. (MS)

E2715. Williams, Thomas E. "Martin Beck: The Swedish Version of Barney Miller without the Canned Laughter." Clues 1:1 (Spring 80):123-28.
A defensive and critical examination of the series based on a perception of the novels as similar to the popular TV situation comedy "Barney Miller" and with the attitude that the polical and social dimensions of the novels are "unrealistic and distracting." The author offers nothing substantial in support of his thesis and much of the article consists of plot summaries and comments by other critics with some imprecise formulations by Williams.

SKOVERECKY, JOSEF

Ref: Hubin 2, ABMI(S).

See also: E500.

E2716. Greene, Graham. "Preface." In Miss Silver's Past, pp. ix-xi. NY: Grove Press, 1974.
A brief survey of Skvorecký's work, with one reference to this novel as "part detective story."

E2717. Skvorecký, Josef. "Author's Foreword." In Miss Silver's Past (E2716), pp. xiii-xvii. Tr. by Peter Kussi.
Skvorecký describes how he wrote Miss Silver's Past as a detective novel, a genre he loves, although the subject matter was serious in its treatment of the esthetic "pimps" in the Communist intellectual literary community.

E2718. Zekulin, Gleb. "Miss Silver's Past: the tragedy of an intellectual." World Literature Today 54 (Autumn 80):547-51.
The discussion of a political novel by a Czech who uses detective story conventions. Zekulin comments that this formula of using a popular form for veiled political comment was frequently employed by Czech writers of the 1960s. On pp. 530-32, there is a bibliography of Skoverecký's work which gives some idea of the extent of this writer's debt to detective fiction,including a number of novels by writers like Chandler, Hammett and Christie whom he has translated.

SLESAR, HENRY

Ref: Hubin 2, TCCMW, ABMI(S).

SMALL, SIDNEY HERSCHEL

Ref: Hubin 2, ABMI(S); Argosy, 20 Feb 31.

SMITH, CARMICHAEL

Ref: Hubin 2, ABMI; UN 1:9 (1949):6-7 (photo of man in mask).

SMITH, CHARLES MERRILL

Ref: Hubin 2.

Int: People, 2 April 69, 63, 66 (photo); TPP 5:4 (Oct 83):25-28.

SMITH, ERNEST BRAMAH. See BRAMAH, ERNEST

SMITH, GARRET

Ref: Hubin 2, ABMIS; Argosy, 3 Jan 31.

SMITH, JUNIUS B.

Ref: Hubin 2.

See also: D447, D448.

E2719. "The Men Who Make the Argosy," Argosy 219:1 (21 Feb 31):139.
Superficial glimpse of Smith's writing experiences, hobbies, and family, with comprehensive astrological data. Portrait. (RS)

SMITH, MARK

Ref: Hubin 2, SN, ABMI(S).

Int: TAD 16 (1983):167-78 (reprinted in Carr B67, pp. 322-49).

SMITH, MARTIN CRUZ

Ref: Hubin 2, ABMIS.

Int: NYTBR, 3 May 81, p. 46 (photo); PW, 20 March 81, pp. 6-7 (photo).

E2720. Dove, George N. "Case in Point: Gorky Park." TMF 6:4 (July/Aug 82):9-11, 18.
The plot devices and police portrayals in this novel set in Russia are similar to those in Western procedurals.

E2721. Prescott, Peter S. "The Making of a Best Seller." Newsweek, 25 May 81, pp. 77, 79-80.
Review-essay and interview with Smith on Gorky Park. (REB)

E2722. Vespa, Mary. "A Literary Capitalist Named Martin Cruz Smith Mines Moscow in 'Gorky Park'." People, 25 May 81. 2 photos.
3 column profile. (REB)

SMITH, SHELLEY

Ref: Hubin 2, TCCMW, CC, ABMI(S).

SNOW, C. P.

Ref: Hubin 2, EMD, CC, ABMI(S).

See also: 1104a.

E2723. Barzun, Jacques, and Taylor, Wendell Hertig. "Preface" to Death under Sail (London, 1932), by C. P. Snow. In A Book of Prefaces (B17), pp. 99-100.

E2724. Borowitz, Albert. "The Snows on the Moors: C. P. Snow and Pamela Hansford on the Moors Murder Case." In Borowitz (B42), pp. 1-25; originally published in American Scholar 40:4 (1971):708-13.
Comments on the relationship between Death under Sail and Snow's "mature" novels with special note of the "significance of integrity in scientific research as a touchstone of character and reaction in crisis." Snow's novel The Sleep of Reason (1968) is based on the Moors murder case.

E2725. Cooper, William. C. P. Snow. London: Longman Group, 1971.
Cooper's comment that Snow's plot grows out of the characters has been frequently cited by other critics who have mentioned Snow's detective novel.

E2726. Mayne, Richard. "The Club Armchair." Encounter 21:5 (Nov 63):76-82.
A general study of Snow's fiction relating his later novels to the stylized conventions of Death under Sail.

E2727. Shusterman, David. "Early Novels." In his C. P. Snow, pp. 41-44. Twayne's English Authors Series, no. 179. Boston: Twayne, 1975.
A discussion of Death under Sail as a detective novel "superior" to most since plot rises out of character.

E2728. Snow, C. P. "Author's Note" to Death Under Sail, pp. vii-viii. London: Heinemann, 1959; also in Avon reprint (NY, 1970).
This note for a new edition of Snow's 1932 detective novel emphasises his belief that no author, "not even Simenon," has done what he would like to see done to bring detective fiction closer to the realistic novel.

SOUVESTRE, PIERRE. See ALLAIN, MARCEL

SPENCER, ROSS H.

Ref: Hubin 2.

E2730. Bargainnier, Earl F. "The First Five Capers of Ross H. Spencer." TAD 16 (83):323-29.
Comic devices in the Chance Purdue novels.

SPICER, BART

Ref: Hubin 2, TCCMW, CC, ABMI; UN 2:2 (1949):12-13, 16 (photos); UN 3:3 (1950):8-9 (as "Jay Barbette;" photo).

SPILLANE, MICKEY

Ref: Hubin 2, TCCMW, EMD, CC, SN, ABMI(S).

Int: Books & Bookmen (1967), reprinted in TM(R)N 1:2 (Dec 67):9-10; DAST 6:2 (1973):3-5 (in Swedish); Writer's Digest, Sept 76, pp. 18-20 (photo); PQ 2:3 (Fall 79):13-15; TAD 12 (1979):292-99 (photos).

See also: C747, E395, E2676.

E2731. Banks, R. Jeff. "Spillane and the Critics." TAD 12 (1979):300-307.
Banks cites what he feels are misleading statements about Spillane's work made by several critics and refutes them in the text of the article and in the extensive notes. A defensive but useful discussion.

E2732. ______. "Spillane's Anti-Establishmentarian Heroes." In Landrum (B216), pp. 124-39.
A discussion of the heroes' distrust of the establishment authorities in Spillane's fiction. Banks includes Spillane's post-1960 novels in his discussion.

E2733. Blom, K. Arne. "Hämndens anglar |Angels of revenge|." DAST 10:1 (1977):17-20.
Covers five of Spillane's novels. (MS)

E2734. ______. "Mike Hammer -- ett forsok till analys |Mike Hammer -- an attempt at analysis|." DAST 9:5 (1976):17-23. (MS)

E2735. ______. "Olyckligt lottade |Unfortunately situated|." DAST 10:2 (1976):17-19.
Spillane's short stories. (MS)

E2736. ______. "Världens frälsare |Saviour of the world|." DAST 10:3 (1976):15-16.
Spillane's Tiger Mann novels. (MS)

E2737. Cawelti, John. "The Spillane Phenomenon." University of Chicago Magazine 61:5 (March/April 69); reprinted in JPC 3:1 (Summer 69):9-22; and in Cawelti (B69), pp. 183-91.
Cawelti shows how Spillane's work is related to the hard-boiled writers like Chandler and Hammett but also how he is closest, of these writers, to the "popular evangelical tradition" with its hostility to the city and its archetypes like the corrupt politician and the "scarlet" woman.

E2738. Collins, Max. "Dat's Mike Ham-muh?" TAD 12 (1979):308-19. Illus.
Film, TV and comic strip adaptations of Hammer. Includes three pages of daily strips drawn by Ed Robbins and written by Spillane.

E2739. Fetterly, Judith. "Beauty as the Beast: Fantasy and Fear in I, the Jury." JPC 8:4 (Spring 75):775-82.
A psychocritical study of the emotional conflicts in Spillane/Hammer as they affect the characterization of the ideal woman/murderer.

E2740. Funghi, Franco. "Io ti ucciderò |I'll kill you|." Il Calendario del Popolo, July 53.
The title of the article is that of the first Italian translation of Mickey Spillane's I, the Jury (1948). The author quotes frequently from Spillane's novels to show the excesses of violence and sadism and the anti-Communist propaganda (One Lonely Night, 1951). To the disorderly "asphalt jungle" of Spillane and Peter Cheyney, the author opposes the Blue City (1947) of Kenneth Millar in which are courageously revealed the relationships between the world of crime, the interests of the great capitalists and the complicity of the legal authorities. (LR)

E2741. Johnston, Richard W. "Death's Fair-Haired Boy." Life 32 (23 June 52):79-80, 82-3, 86, 89-90, 92, 95. Photos.
A portrait of Spillane and an attempt to explain the popularity of the

paradoxical, soft-spoken writer of an extravagantly violent fiction.

E2742. Jones, Robert F. "Mickey Spillane Chucks His Shamuses and Molls to Write for a Tougher Audience: Kids." People, 27 July 81, pp. 52-54, 56, 59. Photos by Thomas E. England.
Interview/profile; bio sketch, early writing for comics starting at age 17, current life-style--one anecdote on the ending of Vengeance Is Mine, not much else on the Hammer books. (REB)

E2743. La Farge, Christopher. "Mickey Spillane and His Bloody Hammer." Saturday Review, 6 Nov 54, pp. 11-12, 54-9; reprinted in Mass Culture (NY: The Free Press, 1957), edited by Barnard Rosenberg and David Manning White, pp. 176-85.
A moralistic essay equating Hammer's personal vendettas with McCarthy witch-hunting.

E2744. Nevins, Francis, M., Jr. "Department of Unmitigated Mishmosh." TMRN 3:1 (Oct 69):21-22.
Plot improbabilities in I, the Jury.

E2745. Ruehlmann, William. "The Kid from Cyanide Gulch." In Ruehlmann (B350), pp. 90-99.
A survey of Hammer's vendettas.

E2746. "A Short Psychological Portrait of Mike Hammer." DAST 15:3 (1982):18-20. (MS)

E2747. Traylor, James L. "Characternyms in Mickey Spillane's Mike Hammer Novels." TAD 16 (1983):293-95.
Humor in names and names indicative of character in Spillane's fiction.

E2748. ______. "The Violent World of Mike Hammer." TMF 7:6 (Nov/Dec 83):13-20.
A narrative catalogue of scenes of violence in the Hammer series.

E2749. Weibel, Kay. "Mickey Spillane as a Fifties Phenomenon." In Landrum (B216), pp. 114-23.
Cultural phenomena of the fifties as reflected in the early Spillane novels. With a chronology of Spillane's best-sellers (1947-65) listing copies sold.

E2750. Wylie, Philip. "The Crime of Mickey Spillane." Good Housekeeping 130:2 (Feb 55):54-55, 207-209. Photo.
Education not censorship is the remedy for Spillane's assaults on people, institutions, the English language, and law and ethics.

SPRIGG, CHRISTOPHER ST. JOHN

Ref: Hubin 2, TCCMW, EMD, ABMI(S); Pike, TPP 2:5 (Sept/Oct 79):23-24.

STADLEY, PAT

Ref: Hubin 2; Lachman, TPP 3:1 (Jan/Feb 80):23-24.

STAGGE, JONATHAN

Hubin 2, ABMI(S); Pike, TPP 3:3 (May/June 80):20-21, 19.

See also: Quentin, Patrick.

STALLWORTH, LYN

Ref: Hubin 2.

E2751. "Death, Double-dealing, and the Deep Sea." Library Journal 93 (1 Oct 68):3594-95. Photo.
Includes profile of Stallworth and her first mystery. (KLM)

STANLEY, FAY GRISSOM

Ref: Hubin 2; UN 3:6 (1951):8-9, 11 (photo).

STARK, RICHARD. See WESTLAKE, DONALD

STARNES, RICHARD

Ref: Hubin 2; UN 2:8 (1950):10-11 (photo); UN 3:3 (1950):10-11 (photo); UN 4:2 (1951):4-5 (photo).

STARRETT, VINCENT

Ref: Hubin 2, TCCMW, EMD, CC, ABMI(S).

See also: E185.

E2752. Bleiler, E. F. "Vincent Starrett vs. Arthur Machen: or, How not to Communicate over Eight Years of Correspondence." TMF 3:6 (Nov/Dec 79):11-14.
Review- essay of Starrett vs. Machen (E2754). Bleiler discusses the texts of the letters and the extent to which the correspondence was an exchange between two men who did not understand one another.

E2753. Honce, Charles. A Vincent Starrett Library: The Astonishing Results of Twenty-Three Years of Literary Activity. Mt. Vernon, NY: The Golden Eagle Press, 1941. 83pp. Edition limited to 100 copies.
Bibliography of Starrett's work, with notes by Starrett. (REB)

E2754. Murphy, Michael, editor. Starrett vs. Machen: A Record of Discovery and Correspondence. St. Louis: Autolycus Press, 1979. Not seen.

E2755. Murphy, Michael, and others. Vincent Starrett: In Memoriam. Culver City, CA: The Pontine Press, Aug 1974. 28pp. (unnumbered). Chapbook, stapled in card covers. Edition limited to 400 numbered copies. Illus.
This chapbook preserves the "words and order of the service" of the memorial service for Vincent Starrett held at Graceland Cemetary, Chicago, on January 9, 1974. The bulk of the chapbook is taken up by a greatly expanded version of Michael Murphy's eulogy of Starrett, which includes an account of his life and career. The illustrations include photographs and pen-and-ink portraits of Starrett. (Starrett's Sherlockian writings are mentioned, but not his other crime fiction.) (REB)

E2756. Ruber, Peter, editor. The Last Bookman. Introduction by Christopher Morley. NY: The Candlelight Press, 1968. 115pp. Illustrated.
An anthology of tributes to Vincent Starrett. There is only passing mention of his crime fiction (other than his Sherlockian interests) but the volume includes a long biographical study by editor Ruber, reminiscences by his friends and acquaintances in the book world on his interests as a bibliophile and writer, and a bibliography of primary sources compiled by Esther Longfellow. There are also some excerpts from letters and a number of photographs. Longfellow includes a handful of secondary

sources in her bibliography and although editor Ruber refers to the critical material that he has researched for the book, there is no specific information on its nature or extent.

E2757. Starrett, Vincent. Born in a Bookshop: Chapters from the Chicago Renascence. Norman: University of Oklahoma Press, 1965.
Autobiography.

STEEL, KURT

Ref: Hubin 2, ABMI; The Writer 52:3 (March 39):69-71.

STEEMAN, STANISLAS-ANDRE

Ref: Hubin 2.

Int: Enigmatika 6 (1977), pp. 49-54.

E2758. Baudou, Jacques. "Alias Mr. Twistelthrough." Enigmatika 6 (1977):25-31.
Steeman's use of protean powers of disguise for his detective Mr. Wens.

E2758a. ______. "Stanislas-André Steeman et le cinéma." Cahiers de la cinémathèque, no. 25 (Spring/Summer 78):17-23.
A dossier of commentary, by Steeman and other writers, on the film adaptations of his novels. With a filmography. Of particular interest for the comments of Steeman on two adaptations directed by Henri-Georges Clouzot.

E2759. Bordillon, Henri. "L'air du soupçon (à propos de Une veuve dort seule) |An air of suspicion (with reference to une veuve dort seule)|." Enigmatika 6 (1977):35-41.
An analysis of Steeman's novel Une veuve dort seule to show that the detective novel has always been a fiction that both affirms and questions its own reality. The title of the essay is a pun on the title of a famous essay by contemporary writer Nathalie Sarraute in which she announced that the new novel would contest its own role as Literature.

E2760. "Dossier St.-A. Steeman." Enigmatika 6 (1977). 72pp. Illus.
An issue devoted to the life and work of the Belgian writer St.-A. Steeman, born at Liège in 1908. The illustrations consist of drawings by Steeman. Contents: Krisha Steeman, "Stanislas-André Steeman," pp. 4-8 (biography by Steeman's wife); Maurice-Bernard Endrèbe, "Première rencontre |First meeting|," pp. 9-13 (biography); "George Jamin parle d'un ami |G. Jamin talks about a friend|," pp. 14-17 (biography; Steeman and the cinema); Paul Gayot, "Impasse des boiteux," p. 18 (book review); J. C. Dinguirard, "Duplicité et Triplicité de St.-A. Steeman dans L'Assassin habite au 21 (+) |Duplicity and triplicity of St.-A. S. in l'assassin habite au 21+|," pp. 19-20 (Binary and triplicate systems in his novel); Yves Olivier-Martin, "Démarrages en tous genres," pp. 21-24 (E2761); Jacques Baudou, ""Alias Mr. Twistelthrough," pp. 25-31 (E2758); Michel Lebrun, "Emprunt Digital |Digital borrowing|," pp. 32-34 (plagiarisms of Steeman novels); Henri Bordillon, "L'air du soupçon," pp. 35-41 (E2759); St.-A. Steeman, "Conan Doyle et son oeuvre |Conan Doyle and his work|," pp. 42-43; St.-A. S.,"Portrait: Monsieur Wens," pp. 44-45 (portrait of Steeman character by author); St.-A. S., "Les Policiers à lire |Must-read detective novels|," pp. 46-48; "Stanislas-André Steeman nous parle du Jury," pp. 49-54 (interview in which Steeman talks of Jury, a collection of original novels and reprints which he founded and supervised; a bibliography of titles is appended, pp. 55-58); Philippe Van

Hooland, "Bibliographie des éditions françaises des oeuvres de Stanislas-André Steeman |Bibliography of French editions of St-A. Steeman's works|, pp. 61-70; Jacques Baudou, "Filmographie," pp. 71-72.

E2761. Olivier-Martin, Yves. "Démarrages en tous genres |'Starts' of all kinds|." Enigmatika 6 (1977), pp. 21-24.
An analysis of the various plot devices Steeman has used to initiate the action of his novels.

E2762. Steeman, S.-A. "Le cinéma, école de la modestie |Film, the school of modesty|." MM 30 (July 1950). Not seen. (JB)

STEIN, AARON MARC

Ref: Hubin 2, TCCMW, EMD, CC, ABMIS; UN 1:1 (1948):3 (photo); UN 1:11 (1949):6-7 (as George Bagby; photo); UN 1:11 (1949):14-14 (as Hampton Stone; rear-view photo); UN 2:3 (1949):4-5 (photo); UN 3:1 (1950):6-7, 9 (photo); UN 3:9 (1951):8-9, 15 (photo); UN 4:10 (1952):12-13, 16 (as Hampton Stone; tongue-in-cheek interview; photo); UN 4:11 (1952):4-5, 15-16 (photo); UN 5:1 (1952):10-11 (photo).

Int: EQMM, April 79, pp. 115-116; Mystery 1:2 (March/April 80):23-25 (photo); DAST 14:2 (1981):32-35 (photo).

See also: B309, C781, C782.

STEIN, GERTRUDE

Ref: Hubin 2, ABMI(S).

E2764. Bartlett, Ronald, editor. A Primer for the Gradual Understanding of Gertrude Stein. Los Angeles: Black Sparrow, 1971.
On pp. 21-22, Stein comments briefly on detective stories. This material was originally published in "Gertrude Stein Talking--A Transatlantic Interview," in UCLAN Review, in three parts: Summer 62, Spring 63, and Winter 64.

E2765. Landon, Brooks. "'Not solve it but be in it': Gertrude Stein's Detective Stories and the Mystery of Creativity." American Literature 53 (Nov 81):487-98.
After describing Stein's interest in detective fiction and noting the refusal of earlier critics to relate it to her other work, Landon analyzes Blood on the Dining-Room Floor for clues to its importance in the beginning of an important phase in her career. His focus is not generic but in Stein's interest in "detection," compared to Poe's Dupin method, "as a mode of thinking and writing."

E2766. Stewart, Lawrence D. "Gertrude Stein and the Vital Dead." In Adams, MDA 1972 (B2), pp. 102-24.
A convoluted examination of Gertrude Stein's interest in detective fiction. Extensive notes.

STERLING, STEWART

Ref: Hubin 2, CC, SN; UN 1:6 (1948):6-7, 14 (photo); UN 2:4 (1949):6-7 (photo); UN 3:11 (1951):6-7, 14 (photo).

See also: D334.

E2767. "About the Detective: Gil Vine." UN 3:4 (1950):6-7, 11.
A portrait of Sterling's detective character Gil Vine.

STERN, RICHARD MARTIN

Ref: Hubin 2, TCCMW, CC, SN, ABMI(S); The Writer 28:3 (March 75):11-13.

See also: B42.

STEVENS, SHANE

Ref: Hubin 2, ABMI(S); The Writer 81:12 (Dec 68):27-29, 46 (analysis of Go Down Dead; Morrow, 1947).

STEVENSON, ROBERT LOUIS

Ref: Hubin 2, TCCMW, CC, ABMI(S).

See also: B42.

E2768. Lacassin, Francis. "Mystère maritime et roman policier |Maritime mystery and detective novel|." In Lacassin (B202), pp. 189-92. Paris: Union générale d'éditions, 1979.
Lacassin sees the technique in Stevenson's The Wrecker of having a mystery solved by a witness rather than a detective as innovative and traces briefly its literary heritage. There is also a passing reference to a similar technique in Dr. Jekyll and Mr. Hyde.

E2769. Stevenson, R. L., and Osbourne, Lloyd. "Epilogue: To Will H. Low." In The Wrecker, pp. 551-53. NY: Scribners, 1905 (first published 1891).
Passim for comments on the writing of The Wrecker as an attempt to counter the detective novel's "insincerity, shallowness of tone, and lack of realism." The authors finally realize that Dickens--in The Mystery of Edwin Drood--has already done what they set out to do.

STEWARD, DWIGHT, and STEWARD, BARBARA

Ref: Hubin 2.

Int: Delaware Today 14:3 (March 76):49-53.

STEWART, J. I. M. See INNES, MICHAEL

STEWART, MARY

Ref: Hubin 2, TCCMW, EMD, CC, ABMI(S).

See also: E1104a.

STOKER, BRAM

Ref: Hubin 2, TCCMW, EMD, CC, ABMIS).

E2770. Roth, Phyllis A. Bram Stoker. Twayne's English Author Series 343. Boston: Twayne Publishers, 1982. 167pp. Index. Bibliography of primary and secondary sources.
Although Roth makes many references to "mystery" in her discussion of Stoker's life and works, she does not use it in terms of detection or detective fiction. The ample critical literature on Dracula and the vampire in literature has taken some note of the relationship of Stoker's work to Gothic fiction but the relationship of this novel and other works of Stoker to detection elements in Gothic fiction is largely an unexplored subject. Roth is very good on the ambivalent role of women in Stoker's

novels and stories and she sees far more literary interest in the work than most critics. This is the best existing introduction to Stoker's fiction and the excellent annotated bibliography of secondary sources gives a useful overview of the subject. Stoker's fiction is a wonderful blending of the adventure/quest tale and the supernatural while in Dracula the pursuit of the vampire and the uncovering of his multiple secrets has many of the elements of a Victorian novel of detection. Although Stoker was included in TCCMW (A143), the essay makes no attempt to discuss him as a writer of detective fiction and, on the basis of that commentary, there seemed to be no justification for including him in a volume focusing on crime and mystery writers.

STONE, HAMPTON. See STEIN, AARON MARC

STOUT, REX

Ref: Hubin 2, TCCMW, EMD, CC, ABMI(S).

Int: For a comprehensive listing of interviews, see Townsend (E2822), pp. 133-47.

See also: B6, B170, B310, B366, C747, E2535.

E2771. Anderson, David R. "'As Far As I'm Concerned, You're Out of it!': Wolfe and Archie Apart." The Gazette 1:2 (Spring 79):28-31.
Novels (In the Best Families and A Family Affair) whose structure is conditioned by the separation of Wolfe and Archie.

E2772. ______. "Creative Order in Rex Stout." TMN 9 (Aug 76):Al-A6.
The sense of order that Archie and Wolfe possess makes them fit naturally into the larger world of order that Stout saw as the bedrock structure of detective fiction.

E2773. ______. "Crime and Character: Notes on Rex Stout's Early Fiction." TAD 13 (1980):169-71.
In early stories, preceding the Wolfe series by many years, Stout was already establishing relationships between crime and character and arriving at the belief that crime-solving is only possible through the acute observation of human nature.

E2774. Baker, John F. "Rex Stout: No Man My Age Writes Books." PW, 29 Oct 73, pp. 28-29. Photographs by Jill Krementz.
5 photo-portraits of Rex Stout, with brief, pungent Stouticisms as captions.

E2775. Baring-Gould, William S. Nero Wolfe of West Thirty-Fifth Street: The Life and Times of America's Largest Private Detective. NY: Viking Press, 1969. Pp. vii-xviii, 1-203. NY: Bantam Books, 1970; corrected edition, paperback, NY: Penguin Books, 1982. Pp. vii-xviii, 1-203.
A biography of Wolfe in the Baker Street Irregular manner, complete with hypothetical reconstructions of Wolfe's and Archie Goodwin's backgrounds based on discrepancies in the Rex Stout novels. Contains a floor plan of the ground floor of Wolfe's house and a chronology which attempts to assign specific dates to Wolfe's cases. Omissions in the Chronology (Bitter End, The Second Confession and "Murder's No Joke") were repaired and other corrections were made by John McAleer for the Penguin Books reprint. Corrections were also published in TMRN 3:4 (1970):16 and 3:5 (1970):35-36. The coverage still stops with the 1968

Nero Wolfe novel, The Father Hunt. Reviews: JPC 3 (Summer 69): 170-2; TAD 2 (1968/69):121-122. Breen 220. CC 2891. (REB)

E2776. Barzun, Jacques, and Taylor, Wendell Hertig. Preface to Too Many Cooks (New York, 1938), by Rex Stout. In A Book of Prefaces (B17), pp. 101-102.

E2777. Barzun, Jacques. "Rex Stout and His Two Lives." The Gazette 2:3 (Summer 83):41-43.
Text of an after-dinner talk given in 1981 at the Wolfe Pack Black Orchid Banquet. A tribute to Rex Stout who created, in Nero Wolfe and Archie, an "ideal American"; i.e., a "man or woman who can think straight...while pursuing practical ends with a social conscience." Barzun also notes that high intelligence and common habits can be combined, as they were in Rex Stout, in one person.

E2778. A Birthday Tribute to Rex Stout. NY: Viking, 1965. 15pp.
Includes a biography of Stout (by Judith I. Churnus) and Jacques Barzun's essay "About Rex Stout." Not seen.

E2789. Brooks, Lawrence F. "Nero Wolfe: Logomachizer." The Gazette (Winter 79):21-27.
Wolfe's fondness for words, his reading habits and his library.

E2780. Clark, John D. "Some Notes Relating to a Preliminary Investigation into the Paternity of Nero Wolfe." The Gazette 2:4 (Autumn 83):12-16.
Sherlock Holmes and Irene Adler proposed as Wolfe's parents.

E2781. Crystal, Tamar. "Which Doorbell Rang?" The Gazette 1:1 (Winter 79):38-40.
The shifting location of Wolfe's brownstone.

E2782. Darby, Ken. The Brownstone House of Nero Wolfe. NY: Little, Brown, 1983. 178pp.
Illus. A tour of Wolfe's brownstone with Archie Goodwin as guide, in an unfortunate attempt to imitate Archie's narrative style. Darby also "appropriates" Stout's characters to comment on contemporary social issues in a way that is both offensive and unintelligent. (Art Scott).

E2783. DeVoto, Bernard. "The Easy Chair: Alias Nero Wolfe." Harper 209 (July 54):8-9, 12-15; reprinted in The Gazette 1:2 (Spring 79):37-44.
Speculations on Nero Wolfe's biography.

E2784. Edel, Leon. "The Figure in the Carpet." In Telling Lies: The Biographer's Art, edited by Marc Pachter, pp. 23, 30-32. Washington, D. C.: New Republic Books, 1979.
Passim for comments on Rex Stout and on McAleer's biography (E2802): 600 pages is excessive for a biography on Rex Stout; the choice of names is significant in Stout's work. This essay on biographies by a leading biographer is a plea for economy and restraint in the writing of biographies, with some commentary on Conan Doyle and Rex Stout.

E2785. Galligan, Edward L. "The Comic Art of Rex Stout." The Sewanee Review 89 Spring 81):258-64.
A rambling essay on comedy in the Nero Wolfe stories. Galligan compares Wolfe/Archie to Cervantes' Don Quixote/Sancho Panza and contrasts the methods of Holmes and Wolfe. What Galligan seems to consider a major point--that all "good comedians have a strong sense of logic and a fussy

concern for language"--is certainly not unique to comic writers.

E2786. The Gazette. The Journal of the Wolfe Pack. Published irregularly. 6 issues have appeared since 1979.
There is a wide range of material in this magazine, all of it related to Rex Stout and the Nero Wolfe saga. Much of the material concerns activities of the fan organization, the Wolfe Pack, but there are some critical studies (mainly thematical) of the fiction and some playful commentary in the Sherlockian mode. Entertaining, but the poems, spoofs and crossword puzzles will be mainly of interest to some die-hard fans.

E2787. Gerhardt, Mia I. "'Homicide West': Some Observations on the Nero Wolfe Stories of Rex Stout." English Studies (1968):107-27.
A "literary" treatment of the Nero Wolfe novels. Allusions to Proust, Cervantes, Balzac and commedia dell'arte do not disguise the elementary nature of this attempt by an European critic to present Stout's "little universe" to an academic audience.

E2788. Gotwald, Rev. Frederick G. "Of Murder and Mayhem." The Gazette 2:4 (Autumn 83):21-27.
On murder methods in Stout's Wolfe series with a listing of the victims and the means of their passing by work.

E2789. Hamilton, Robert M. "The Orchidology of Nero Wolfe." The Gazette 1:2 (Spring 79):18-27.

E2790. Harwood, John. "Nero Wolfe vs. the Master Criminal." TMRN 6:1 (July 73):15-18.
Master criminal Arnold Zeck is profiled with some comparison with Conan Doyle's Professor Moriarty.

E2791. Hertzberg, Francis (Father). "A Prelininary Study in the Literature of Nero Wolfe." TMRN 2:4 (April 69):11-13.
Suggestions for future studies on Nero Wolfe: Wolfe and Sherlock Holmes, ancestry and family of Wolfe.

E2792. Jaffe, Arnold. "Murder with Dignity: Rex Stout." The New Republic, 30 July 77, pp. 41-43.
A thoughtful essay on Wolfe's view of the world and of his place in it with examples from the fiction.

E2793. Johnston, Alva. "Alias Nero Wolfe." New Yorker 25 (19 July 49):26-28, 33-38; 25 (23 July 49):30-32, 34, 39-43.
A detailed portrait of Rex Stout with some comments on his writing and Nero Wolfe to the effect that inside fat Nero Wolfe is the thin Rex Stout. An entertaining, concise, revealing portrait, based on interviews.

E2794. Kaye, Marvin. "Some Structural Considerations in Fer-de-Lance." The Gazette 1:3 (Summer 79):44-48.
Point-of-view, characters, red herrings and the relaying of information in Fer-de-Lance.

E2795. Knight, Arden. "An Appreciation of Archie Goodwin." TAD 12 (1979):328-29. Illus.
On the important role Archie plays in the Wolfe saga.

E2796. Lachman, Marvin. "President Nero Wolfe." TMF 5:3 (May/June 81):

22-26.

Ways in which Nero Wolfe appears to have identified with U. S. Presidents.

E2797. Levine, Jonathan. "The Wines of Nero Wolfe." The Gazette 2:2 (Spring 83):42-48.

E2798. Lowndes, R. A. W. "The Editor's Page: On Nero Wolfe." SMS 3:6 (March 71):4-7, 120-22, 124, 126, 128.

An excellent general essay.

E2799. Lyles, Bill. "Rex Stout in the Dell Mapbooks." PQ 2:4 (Winter 79):13-25. Illus.

A list of titles with discussion of the art work.

E2800. McAleer, John. "Introduction." In Rex Stout, Justice Ends at Home and Other Stories, edited by John McAleer, pp. ix-xxviii. NY: Viking, 1977.

McAleer discusses the early stories by Rex Stout, published between 1914-1918 and reprinted in this collection, and surveys Stout's pre-Wolfe writing career.

E2801. ______. "Nero Wolfe's Legacy of Books." The Gazette 1:2 (Spring 79):8-16.

Comments on Wolfe's library and his reading habits.

E2802. ______. Rex Stout: A Biography. Boston: Little, Brown, 1977. xvi, 621pp. Illus. Notes. Bibliography. Index. Foreword by P. G. Wodehouse.

All aspects of Rex Stout's life, his thinking, and his work are examined in what must surely be the most thoroughly researched and carefully written biography of any author in the realm of popular fiction. And the documentation is not allowed to impede the flow of the narrative, which is consistently readable. There are extensive notes, a primary and secondary bibliography, a good index, and many photographs. When the book was finished, the author still had a filing cabinet full of material on Stout, and more continued to arrive; this material has formed the contents of the "Rex Stout Newsletter," (E2805) which has appeared for several years in The Armchair Detective. Breen 221. (REB)

E2803. ______. "Rex Stout: A Creator's World." TMN 9 (Aug 76):A7-A10.

A publicity piece for the then-unpublished biography by McAleer. McAleer lists a number of questions which he announces will be answered in the book.

E2804. ______. "Rex Stout Greets the Wolfe Pack." Views & Reviews 5:3 (Spring 74):25-27.

Brief conversation/interview with Stout. (REB)

E2805. ______. "Rex Stout Newsletter." TAD 11 (1978):257-58.

The first of a series of columns on Rex Stout that appear in each issue of TAD. A collection of miscellaneous information about Rex Stout, compiled by his biographer McAleer who also provides a running account of many of his own activities. The column is usually two pages long.

E2806. ______. Royal Decree: Conversations with Rex Stout. Ashton, MD: Pontes Press, 1983. pp. l-vii, 1-73. 8vo, wraps, illustrated.

The "conversations" are in question-and-answer form, divided into four sections: Rex Stout on his Craft (pp. 1-20), Rex Stout on his Peers (pp.

21-36), Nero and Archie (pp. 37-55), and The Wolfe Corpus (pp. 56-73). The material is drawn from McAleer's correspondence with Stout during the preparation of Rex Stout: A Biography (E2802). Some of the questions (particularly those that elicit one-word answers) seem to be space-fillers; others draw meaty comments which amply illustrate, in McAleer's words, Stout's "piquant, incisive mind, and his incomparable way with words." This small book is well worth reading, but one could wish that it were more attractively produced. (REB)

E2807. ______. "The Weiner-Stout Correspondence." The Gazette 2:3 (Summer 83):34-40.
Norbert Weiner, the celebrated MIT "father" of cybernetics, wrote to Stout, on 1 Dec 53, to point out the fraudulent credentials of a probability "expert" in Stout's "Scared to Death." This brief, but lively correspondence also includes Stout's reply and a subsequent note from Weiner. With an introduction by McAleer detailing Weiner's credentials as a reader of mystery fiction.

E2808. McSherry, Frank D., Jr. "Index: Nero Wolfe Mystery Magazine." TMN 9 (Aug 76):A25-A26.
Rex Stout is listed as the "supervising editor" of this magazine of which three issues were published in 1954. In addition to the stories, the fillers and illustrations are also listed.

E2809. ______. "Rex Stout as 'Editor.'" TMN 9 (Aug 76):A21-A23.
An index to the Rex Stout Mystery Quarterly. 9 issues described, with publication dates from 1945-47.

E2810. Miller, Don, ed. "Rex Stout Memorial Issue." TMN 9 (Aug 76).
Published as a "memorial issue," TMN 9 also contains reviews and other material that is not Stout-related. Only the Stout material will be listed in this entry. Contents: David R. Anderson, "Creative Order in Rex Stout," pp. A1-A6 (E2772); Guy M. Townsend, "Rex Stout: A Tribute," p. A6; John D. McAleer, "Rex Stout: A Creator's World," pp. A7-A10 (E2803); Frank D. McSherry, Jr., "A Few Words from the Cover Artist," p. A10; Marvin Lachman, "The Real Fourth Side of the Triangle," pp. A11-A13 (pastiche); "From the Press: Extract of Obituary from Time 10/11/75," p. A13; Art Scott, "The "Lost" Nero Wolfe Tale," p. A14 ("Bitter End," American Magazine, Nov 1940; reprinted in Corsage, Bloomington, IN: James A. Rock & Co, 1977); Art Scott, "A Quick Look at A Family Affair," p. A14 (review); Mary Groff, "For Us, a Child," pp. A15-A16 (events of 1886, the year of Stout's Birth); Frank D. McSherry, Jr., "The Meaning of the Cover Symbols," p. A16 (identification of symbols in cover portrait); Art Scott, "Wolfe on the Air," pp. A17-A19 (comments on the Wolfe radio series); Judson Sapp, "Nero Wolfe is 'On the Air,'" pp. A19-A20 (further comments on radio adaptations); "From the Press: Extract of Editorial from Washington Post 30/11/75," p. A20; Frank D. McSherry, Jr., "Index: Rex Stout as 'Editor,'" pp. A21-A23 (E2809); "Rex Stout in: EQMM," p. A24 (list compiled and updated by Don Miller from John Nieminski's EQMM: 350); "Rex Stout in Detective Book Club," p. A24; Frank D. McSherry, Jr., "Index: Nero Wolfe Mystery Magazine," pp. A25-A26 (E2808); "Nero Wolfe on Film," p. A26; Michael Cook, "Rex Stout in....: Mystery Guild Editions," pp. A27-A29; "Rex Stout in....: Ellery Queen's Anthology," p. A29; Don Miller, "Editor's Notes: Addenda, Corrigenda, & Commentary," p. A30; Guy M. Townsend, "The Nero Wolfe Saga: The Early Years," pp. A31-A41 (qv); Jo Ann Vicarel, "The Nero Wolfe Sage: The First Four," pp. A42, A62 (reviews);

"The Nero Wolfe Saga: A Chronology," pp. A43-A44 (chronolgy of saga in hardcover); "Non-Nero Wolfe Rex Stout Books: A Chronology," p. A44; "From the Press: Review Extract," p. A44 (from T. J. Binyon's TLS review of A Family Affair, 6/18/76); "A Partial Checklist of Reviews of Books by Rex Stout," pp. A45-A55 (see comments by editor Miller on p. A55 for sources); "In the Press: A Few Review Extracts of Nero Wolfe Books," p. A56; "From the Press: Review Extracts of Early Stout Non-Wolfe Books," pp. A57-A60; Andre Sennwald, "Film Note: The President Vanishes," p. A60 (from NYT, 8/12/34); Don Miller, "The Nero Wolfe Saga: Three at Random," pp. A61-A62 (reviews of If Death Ever Slept, Death of a Doxy, and The Doorbell Rang); Don Miller, "Rex Stout: A Capsule Biography," pp. A63-A64; Don Miller, "Rex Stout: A Bibliography," A65-A80 (first book and magazine publication and reprints; selected secondary sources).

E2811. Mühlenbock, Kjell. "Tun mans liv |Heavy man's life|." Jury 2:1 (1973):18-20.
On Nero Wolfe, with checklist. (MS)

E2812. Queen, Ellery. "The Great O-E Theory." In Queen (B323), pp. 4-5.
A discussion of the "significant" similarities between the vowel combinations in "Sherlock Holmes" and "Nero Wolfe."

E2813. Rauber, D. F. "Sherlock Holmes and Nero Wolfe: The Role of the 'Great Detective' in Intellectual History." JPC 6 (1972-73):483-95; reprinted in Landrum (B216), pp. 89-96.
Holmes and Wolfe as they reflect "changing cultural attitudes toward the nature and practice of science." Holmes is seen as a representative of empiricism and Wolfe as a reflection of the "processes of modern theoretical physics."

E2814. Sapp, Judson. "The Bibliophile - Sooner or Later." Age of the Unicorn 1:6 (Feb 80):31-35, 25.
Text of a talk given at the Second Annual Black Orchid Banquet. Fascinating annotated list of collectible Stout material.

E2815. Stix, Thomas L. "Six Characters in Search of an Author." Baker Street Journal 16:1 (March 66):28-29.
An analysis of the differences and similarities beween Watson and Archie Goodwin, Holmes and Wolfe, Conan Doyle and Rex Stout. Not seen. DeWaal 4046.

E2816. Schultheis, Stephen F. and Patricia A. Dreyfus. "A Chronology of Crimes." The Gazette 1:1 (Winter 79):41-46.
Corrections of Baring-Gould's dating of Wolfe's cases with a chronology established by Schultheis.

E2817. Skyette, Asbjorn. "The World of Nero Wolfe." TMF 7:2 (March/April 83):11-12, 26. Originally published in Pinkerton, a Danish magazine. Translated by E. F. Bleiler.
An overview of the series.

E2818. Smith, Robert M. and Rozella B. "Nero Wolfe: Herpetologist." The Gazette 1:3 (Summer 79):1-7.
On Fer-de-Lance.

E2819. Taylor, Bruce. "Rare Books Are Getting Scarcer." CP? 2:2 (May 1980):27-29. Illus.
Preliminary checklist of Rex Stout fiction in pb.

E2820. Townsend, Guy M. "The Nero Wolfe Saga: The Early Years." TMN 9 (Aug 76):A31-A41.
The first installment of a survey of the Nero Wolfe saga. The survey consists of detailed reviews of the series, presented in chronolgical order. This installment also includes a non-series novel, Red Threads.

E2821. ______. "The Nero Wolfe Saga." Appearing serially in TMF 1:3 (May 77) through 4:3 (May/June 80).
The entire Wolfe series is surveyed by an intelligent reader. The material on the earlier novels appeared originally in TMN 9 (E2810).

E2822. Townsend, Guy M., editor. Rex Stout: An Annotated Primary and Secondary Bibliography. NY: Garland, 1980. xxvi, 199pp. Frontis. Index. Associate editors: John J. McAleer, Judson C. Sapp, Arriean Schemer.
This is the very model of an author bibliography, both in scope and in organization. The coverage includes all English-language editions of Stout's works produced in the U. S., Great Britain, and Canada. All reprint appearances are noted, and the major reviews of each item are cited. Annotations are copious and intelligent. In addition to Stout's fiction and articles, there are sections on his book introductions, reviews, jacket blurbs, poetry, and transcripts of radio broadcasts. The Nero Wolfe movies and radio series are listed, as well as pastiches of Stout's work by other writers. 74 interviews and 112 critical pieces on Stout are listed and annotated. A general introduction surveys Stout's life and discusses the wide popularity of his work. (REB)

E2823. Tuska, Jon. "Rex Stout and the Detective Story." Views & Reviews 5:3 (Spring 74):28-35. Illus.
Tuska's responses to John McAleer's questionnaire on Rex Stout (sent to a large number of people during the preparation of the Rex Stout biography), with additional comments more concerned with Tuska's reading habits than with Stout or mystery fiction. (REB)

E2824. Van Gelder, Robert. "An Interview with Rex Stout." In Writers and Writing, pp. 216-23. NY: Scribner's, 1946.

E2825. Waugh, Thomas D. "The Missing Years of Nero Wolfe." TAD 5:1 (1971/72):16-18.
Biographical speculations in the tradition of the Sherlockian waggeries.

E2826. Whitman, Alden. "Rex Stout, the Creator of Nero Wolfe, is Dead at 88." NYT, 28 Oct 75, 1, 36.
Obituary.

E2827. Wilcox, Marion. "A Meeting of Minds." The Gazette 1:3 (Summer 79):57-63; 1:4 (Autumn 79):27-32.
A correspondent of Rex Stout talks about their exchange of letters.

STRAHAN, KAY CLEAVER

Ref: Hubin 2, CC, ABMI.

E2828. DeMarr, Mary Jean. "Kay Cleaver Strahan: A Forgotten Detective Novelist." Clues 2;1 (Spring/summer 81):53-61.

A study of the seven mysteries written between 1928 and 1936 by novelist Strahan. Demarr attempts to show that Strahan was an "original creator of character and plot" and still interesting for some of her experiments with the conventions.

STRAKER, J. F.

Ref: Hubin 2, TCCMW, ABMI(S).

STRANGE, JOHN STEPHEN

Ref: Hubin 2, TCCMW, CC.

STRATTON-PORTER, GENE

Ref: Hubin 2, ABMI(S).

E2829. Bakerman, Jane S. "Gene Stratton-Porter: Mistress of the Mini-Mystery." TMF 3:1 (March/April 79):3-9.
Crime elements in Stratton-Porter's fiction which Bakerman classifies as "crime tales" and "mini-mysteries."

STRIBLING, T. S.

Ref: Hubin 2, TCCMW, EMD, CC, ABMI(S); Argosy, 4 Jan 30.

E2830. McSherry, Frank D., Jr. "Rare Vintages from the Tropics: T. S. Stribling's Clues of the Carribees." TAD 6 (1972/73):172-78.
McSherry reviews the Dr. Poggioli stories in Clues of the Carribees and speculates on the reasons for the obscurity of this collection. It is his opinion the stories are mainstream fiction with detection elements and that readers with a limited concept of the form may be put off by this combination.

E2831. Nieminski, John, and Clark, Bill. (First Appearances of Professor Poggioli Stories.) Letter, TAD 6 (1972/73):55-56.
A checklist.

E2832. Sampson, Robert. "Life as a Series of Abstract Analyses." Clues 2:2 (Fall/Winter 81):61-76. Illustrated.
A survey of Stribling's psychologist-criminologist, Dr. Henry Poggioli, and his career in the pulps and in EQMM. With a checklist of the stories in their original appearance and in selected anthology and book reprintings.

E2833. Stribling, T(homas) S(igismund). Laughing Stock. The Posthumous Autobiography of T. S. Stribling, edited by Randy K. Cross and John T. McMillan. Memphis: St. Luke's Press, 1982.
A very amusing document, written with Stribling's usual wit and mild cynicism. It does not say much about the Poggioli stories, but gives a good account of personalities and practices in the pulp world of the 1920's, notably for Adventure magazine. (EFB)

STRONG, L. A. G.

Ref: Hubin 2, CC, ABMI(S); Lachman, TPP 2:4 (July/Aug 79):13-14, 12.

STUBBS, JEAN

Ref: Hubin 2, TCCMW, ABMI(S).

Int: Books & Bookmen 18:7 (April 73):39.

STURROCK, JEREMY

Ref: Hubin 2, TCCMW, ABMIS.

STYLES, FRANK SHOWELL. See CARR, GLYN

SUE, EUGENE

Ref: Hubin 2, EMD, CC, ABMI(S)

See also: E2103.

E2834. Bory, Jean-Louis. Eugène Sue, le roi du roman populaire |Eugene Sue, king of the popular novel|. 1962.
A somewhat romanticized biography.

E2835. Olivier-Martin, Yves. "Structures de la fiction policière |Structures of detective fiction|." Europe no. 643/44 (Nov/Dec 82), pp. 47-55.
On early (19th century) detective fiction in French and detection elements in the work of Eugène Sue. Some comparison of Poe and Sue. Olivier-Martin also observes that the modern detective novel is not a descendent of the French serial novel.

SUMMERTON, MARGARET

Ref: Hubin 2, TCCMW, ABMI.

SUNESON, VICTOR

E2836. Larsson, Kerstin. "Sveriges meste deckarförfattare |Sweden's most productive detective author|." Jury 1:3/4 (1972):4-6, 13. (MS)

SWAN, PHYLLIS

Ref: Hubin 2.

E2837. Sayre, Anne. "Meet Anastasia Jugedinski, Private Eye--and Meet Phyllis Swan, Author and Creator of Anna." Equal Times, 6 Jan 80, p. 14. Photo.
Profile with interview material included. (KLM)

SWINNERTON, FRANK

Ref: Hubin 2, CC, ABMI(S).

E2838. Barzun, Jacques, and Taylor, Wendell Hertig. "Introduction." In On the Shady Side (NY, 1970), by Frank Swinnerton. "Crime Fiction 1950-1975" (B18).

SYMONS, JULIAN

Ref: Hubin 2, TCCMW, EMD, CC, ABMI(S); UN 2:5 (1950):4-5 (photo).

Int: TMRN 3:4 (April 70):24-26; EQMM, Apr 77, pp. 97-98; Cooper-Clark (B75), pp. 173-85 (photo); PW 222:1 (2 July 82):12-13 (photo).

E2839. Barzun, Jacques, and Taylor, Wendell Hertig. "Introduction." In The Narrowing Circle (NY, 1954), by Julian Symons. "Crime Fiction 1950-1975" (B18).

E2840. Carter, Steven R. "Julian Symons and Civilization's Discontents." TAD 12 (1979):57-62.
Using a comment by Symons that he uses "an act of violence to point up (his) feelings about the pressures of urban living," Carter discusses the

effects of this concept on Symons' detective fiction. Carter quotes from his correspondence with Symons.

E2841. Pettersson, Sven-Ingmar. "Deckar-portratt 6." DAST 8:1 (1975):10-13. Life and works of Julian Symons. (MS)

E2842. Queen, Ellery. "Introduction." In How To Trap a Crook and 12 Other Mysteries, by Julian Symons, pp. 7-9. NY: Davis Publications, Inc., Feb 77.

E2843. Symons, Julian. "Progress of a Crime Writer." In Adams, MDA 1973 (B3), pp. 238-44.
Symons talks about the books and authors he read when he was young, his early acquaintanceship with other writers, and his intent, in his crime novels, to express his feelings about the "pressures of urban living."

TALBOT, HAKE

Ref: Hubin 2.

E2844. Boucher, Anthony. "Introduction." In Rim of the Pit (Simon & Schuster, 1944), by Hake Talbot. NY: Bantam, 1965.

TANUGI, GILBERT

E2845. Rieben, Georges. "Fiche Technique: Gilbert Tanugi." MM 293 (July 72):107-109.
Material on the Tunisian writer, winner of the Grand Prix de Littérature policière in 1972. Not seen. (REB)

TAYLOR, PHOEBE ATWOOD

Ref: Hubin 2, TCCMW, EMD, CC, ABMI(S); UN 3:9 (1951):4-5.

E2846. Dueren, Fred. "Asey Mayo: 'The Hayseed Sherlock.'" TAD 10 (1977):21-24, 83. Photo.
A portrait of Taylor's detective Asey Mayo and the way in which he develops from "simplicity to a sophistication concealed by simplicity."

E2847. Kneeland, Paul F. "Obituary." Boston Evening Globe, 14 Jan 76, p. 43. Photo.

E2848. Nehr, Ellen. "Phoebe Atwood Taylor's Other Pseudonym." TPP 5:3 (May/June 83):36.
"Freeman Dana," author of Murder at the New York World's Fair, is identified as Phoebe Atwood Taylor.

E2849. Tilton, Rafael. "Little Known Author Previews 'World of Tomorrow'." TAD 16 (1983):305-309.
By the analysis of internal evidence and Taylor's diary, Tilton establishes a reasonable case for the authorship of Murder at the World's Fair (Random House, 1938) by Taylor, writing under the pseudonym of Freeman Dana. Tilton also points out that Freeman Dana, like Taylor's other pseudonym, Alice Tilton, is derived from family names.

TAYLOR, SAMUEL W.

Ref: Hubin 2, SN, ABMIS; UN 1:4 (1948):4-5 (photo).

TEILHET, DARWIN, and TEILHET, HILDEGARDE

Ref: Hubin 2, SN, ABMI(S); UN 2:7 (1950):4-5 (photo; on Hildegarde Teilhet).

E2850. Boucher, Anthony. "Introduction." In The Screaming Bride (orig. published as A Private Understanding, Coward, 1952), by Hildegarde Tolman Teilhet. NY: Mercury, 1954.

E2851. Greene, Douglas G. "The Demonical St. Amand and the Brave Baron von Kaz." TAD (1982):219-26, 228-33. Photos and illustrations.
Acknowledgement of Hildegarde Teilhet's assistance for biographical information. A biography of Darwin Teilhet and a detailed study of his novels written up to the outbreak of W. W. II. Greene also discusses the contributions of Hildegarde Teilhet and their method of collaboration.

TEPPERMAN, EMILE C.

E2852. Carr, Nick. "The Tepperman Quest." Age of the Unicorn 1:4 (Oct 79):28-29.
Narrative of Carr's search for information about pulp writer Emile C. Tepperman.

TERHUNE, ALBERT PAYSON

Ref: Hubin 2, ABMI(S); Argosy, 7 Oct 33.

E2853. Moskowitz, Sam. "Albert Payson Terhune, 'The Spindle Club'." "Gaslight Detectives" series (C565). MSMM, Aug 73.

E2854. Unkelbach, Kurt. Albert Payson Terhune: The Master of Sunnybank. NY: Charterhouse Press, 1972.
The first reaction is "Terhune=dogs," but the Hubin bibliography lists 13 crime novels by this author. (REB)

TERMAN, DOUGLAS

Ref: Hubin 2.

Int: PW, 29 Aug 80, pp. 276-78 (photo).

TERRALL, ROBERT

Ref: Hubin 2; UN 1:5 (1948):12-13 (photo).

Int: PQ 3:1 (Spring 80):51-56 (photo; Terrall discusses his ghost-writing of Mike Shayne novels under the house name of "Brett Halliday").

TEY, JOSEPHINE

Ref: Hubin 2, TCCMW, EMD, CC, ABMI(S); UN 2:10 (1950):4-5, 15 (photo); UN 3:10 (1951):6-7 (photo); UN 4:9 (1952):10-11, 15 (photo).

See also: B241.

E2855. Aird, Catherine. "Josephine Tey." TAD 2 (1968/69):156-57.
Brief comments on Tey's work and a checklist of the Tey/Gordon Daviot books. Correction by James Sandoe in a letter, TAD 2:280.

E2856. Barzun, Jacques, and Taylor, Wendell Hertig. "Introduction." In The Singing Sands (NY, 1953), by Josephine Tey. "Crime Fiction 1950-1975" (B18).

E2857. Boucher, Anthony. "Introduction." In Killer in the Crowd (orig. published as The Man in the Queue, by Gordon Daviot, Methuen, 1929), by Josephine Tey. NY: Mercury, 1954.

E2858. Davis, Dorothy Salisbury. "On Josephine Tey." New Republic 131 (20 Sep 54):17-18.
Review of Three by Tey as a tribute to a writer who, perhaps, "spirited" the mystery back to the "vicar's garden" after Hammett had taken it out.

E2860. Roy, Sandra. Josephine Tey. Boston: Twayne Publishers, 1980. 199pp. Index and bibliography of primary and secondary sources.
Roy concentrates on Tey's detective fiction and sees her as a writer whose work drew on both the classic puzzle mystery and the hard-boiled novels of Hammett and Chandler. Unfortunately, she offers almost no evidence in support of her theory about the Hammett-Chandler influence and much of the book consists of studies of the Tey plots and other devices which link her more closely to the Golden Age than to the Mean Streets. The secondary sources largely consist of references to book reviews, and an extensive Daughter of Time controversy (by Townsend and others) in TAD is not listed. Review: Choice, Nov 80, p. 398.

E2861. Sandoe, James. "Introduction." In Three by Tey, pp. v-x. NY: Macmillan, 1954.
A tribute to Tey's artistry with concise, perceptive comments on the novels.

E2862. Talburt, Nancy Ellen. "Josephine Tey." In Bargainnier (B16), pp. 40-77.
A discussion of the series detectives (professional and amateur), the plots, criminals and crimes, and the victims. There is some attempt to examine Tey within the conventions of the genre, and she is seen as an above-average writer with distinctive qualities that give her a "secure" place in detective fiction.

E2863. Townsend, Guy M. "Richard III and Josephine Tey: Partners in Crime." TAD 10 (1977):211-224.
A discussion of Tey's The Daughter of Time which Townsend maintains is not a detective novel and whose portrayal of the historical events surrounding the murder of the two young princes in the Tower of London during the reign of Richard III, Townsend labels as "patently false." In an exchange of letters, Myrna J. Smith vigorously responded in defense of Tey and Towsend replied in continuing support of his own position. A letter from an Egyptologist, Edmund S. Meltzer, argued for a judgment of historical fiction as literature rather than as history. The sequence of letters is as follows: Smith, 10:317-19; Meltzer, 11 (1978):5, 98; Townsend, 11:130-31; Smith, 11:237.

THACKERAY, WILLIAM M.

E2864. Cabot, Frederick C. "The Two Voices in Thackeray's Catherine." 19th Century Fiction 28 (March 1974):404-16.
Thackeray's first novel with the criminal as hero, with which he intended to expose the sham of Newgate fiction and in which realistic detail triumphs over moralizing. A brief comparison with modern fictionalized treatment of criminals.

THAYER, LEE

Ref: Hubin 2, TCCMW, EMD, CC, ABMI(S); UN 4:2 (1951):6-7, 16 (photo); Pike, TPP 3:5 (Oct 80):25-30.

E2865. Breen, Jon L. "On Lee Thayer." TAD 5 (1971/72):148-50.
A chronological bibliography of Thayer's detective novels with a biographical introduction incorporating material from an interview.

E2866. Nevins, Francis M., Jr. "Death Inside the Cow: A Few Notes on the Novels of Lee Thayer." TAD 5 (1971/72):151, 155.
Brief comments on one dozen of Thayer's several dozen novels. Nevins finds that her novels proceed at the pace of an "arthritic snail" and none of his other comments is any more flattering.

THAYER, TIFFANY

Ref: Hubin 2, ABMI(S).

E2867. Stone, Edward. "Whodunit? Moby Dick!" JPC 8 (Fall 74):280-85.
A breezy discussion of Thayer's Thirteen Men (1930) in which this ostensible murder mystery is seen as a parody of Thornton Wilder's The Bridge of San Luis Rey and an iconoclastic guide to the "twelve most subversive books ever written."

THOMAS, LOUIS-CHARLES

Ref: Hubin 2.

Int: MM 278, Apr 71.

THOMAS, ROSS

Ref: Hubin 2, TCCMW, EMD, SN, ABMI.

THOMPSON, ARTHUR LEONARD BELL. See CLIFFORD, FRANCIS

THOMPSON, JIM

Ref: Hubin 2, SN, ABMI.

E2868. "Aller Retour: Alain Cormeau - Jim Thompson |Round trip: Alain Corneau - Jim Thompson|." Gang 2 (circa 1980), pp. 64-68. Photos.
Interview with Alain Corneau who adapted a Thompson's novel Pop. 1280 (fr. title: 1275 ames) for the screen and traveled to the States to work with Thompson on the project. This film was not completed but Corneau subsequently directed Série noire based on Thompson's A Hell of a Woman.

E2869. Cassill, R. V. "The Killer Inside Me: Fear, Purgation and the Sophoclean Light." In Madden (B239), pp. 230-38.
In spite of its origin as a hastily written paperback original, Cassill finds The Killer Inside Me to be a powerful novel of ideas in which Thompson makes a "hard, scarey, Sophoclean statement on American success."

E2870. Collins, Max Allan, and Gorman, Ed, editors. Jim Thompson: The Killers Inside Him. Cedar Rapids, Iowa: Fedora Press, 1983. 104pp. Wraps. Frontispiece photos of Thompson and his widow, Alberta.
First publication of a short novel by Jim Thompson, This World, Then the Fireworks with biographical and critical material, as follows: Ed Gorman, "Introduction," pp. 5-8 (a tribute to an underrated and misunderstood writer); Arnold Hano, "Jim Thompson," pp. 9-11 (E2873); "Alberta," pp. 12-16 (an interview with Thompson's wife); "Arnold Hano," pp. 17-22 (an interview with Thompson's Lion Books editor); Max Allan Collins, "Jim Thompson: The Killers Inside Him," pp. 89-103 (E2871); "Bibliography of Fiction," p. 104 (checklist of Thompson's 29 books).

E2871. Collins, Max Allan. "Jim Thompson: The Killers Inside Him." In Collins/Gorman (E2870), pp. 89-103.

A sympathetic view of Thompson's fiction. Collins says that Thompson is to Cain as Chandler is to Hammett and proceeds to discuss Thompson's dark world, with its psychopaths and, at times, black humor, and some of the characteristics of his writing.

E2872. "Dossier Jim Thompson." Polar 2 (May 79):4-38.
Francois Guérif, in his lead editorial (p. 4), describes Thompson as the most important of the série noire writers after Hammett and Chandler. Contents; Jean-Pierre Deloux, "Mr. Zéro & l'infini |Mr. Zero and the infinite|," pp. 4-8 (photo; discussion of the 9 novels published in the série noire); Jean-Jacques Schleret, "Entretien avec Alberta Hunter," pp. 9-12 (Interview with Thompson's widow, Alberta); François Guérif and Pascal Merigeau, "Entretien avec Pierre Rissient," pp. 13-16 (reminiscences of Thompson); "Filmographie," pp. 18-19 (does not inclued French film versions of Thompson's work); F. Guérif and Jean-Paul Gratias, "Entretien avec Georges Pérec," pp. 20-21 (interview with screenwriter Pérec who adapted, with director Alain Corneau, Thompson's A Hell of a Woman for the screen as Série noire); J. Thompson, "Le défaut du système," pp. 22-27 (fiction); "Bibliographie," pp. 28-30 (American first publications and French translations); F. Guérif and Pascal Merigeau, "Entretien avec Alain Corneau," pp. 31-38 (lengthy interview with director Corneau who discusses his association with Thompson including the aborted Pop. 1780 project and the successfully completed Série noire).

E2873. Hano, Arnold. "Jim Thompson." In Collins/Gorman (E2870), pp. 9-11.
Some personal memories of Thompson whose accuracy is questioned by Thompson's family.

E2874. O'Brien, Geoffrey. "Les Thompson inédits |The unpublished Thompsons|." Polar 27 (Spring 83):43-55.
A survey of Thompson's writing with some biographical data.

THOMPSON, JULIAN F.

Ref: Lachman, TPP 1:4 (July 78):15-16.

THOMSON, (SIR) BASIL

Ref: Hubin 2, TCCMW, CC, ABMIS; Pike, TPP 3:6 (Dec 80):18-20.

THOMSON, JUNE

Ref: Hubin 2, TCCMW, ABMIS; Pike, TPP 3:4 (Jly/Aug 80):17-18.

E2875. Hedman, Iwan. "June Thomson, England." DAST 13:3 (1980):7, 16.
Brief presentation of her life and works. (MS)

E2876. Larsson, Nils. "Forsätt skriva, June |Keep on writing, June|!" Jury 11:1 (1982):44-51.
Thomson's life and novels. (MS)

THORNDIKE, RUSSELL

Ref: Hubin 2, ABMI.

E2877. Carr, Nick. "The Chronicle of Christopher Syn." Xenophile 7 (Oct 74), pp. 7-8, 73-74; 9 (Dec 74), pp. 5-6, 15-16; 10 (Jan 75), pp. 8-9.
A study of Thorndike's adventurer/hero, Syn's allies, a biography of the author and a checklist of the novels.

TIDYMAN, ERNEST

Ref: Hubin 2, TCCMW, SN, ABMI(S).

Int: PW 221:22 (28 May 82):8-10 (photo).

See also: B310.

TILTON, ALICE. See TAYLOR, PHOEBE ATWOOD

TOWNE, STUART. See RAWSON, CLAYTON

TRAIN, ARThUR

Ref: Hubin 2, TCCMW, EMD, CC, ABMI(S); The Writer 53:1 (Jan 40) and 53:4 (Apr 40) (excerpts from Train's My Day in Court, Scribner's).

Int: Robert van Gelder, Writers and Writing (NY: Scribner's, 1956), pp.169-72.

E2878. Overton, Grant. "The Documents in the Case of Arthur Train." In his Authors of the Day, pp. 57-65. NY: George H. Doran, 1921. Reprinted in his American Nights Entertainment, pp. 91-101. NY: D. Appleton/George H. Doran/Doubleday, Page/Charles Scribner's Sons, 1923. Photo.
A checklist, a review of His Children's Children and a biography. No discussion of the Mr. Tutt series.

E2878a. Train, Arthur C. Yankee Lawyer: The Autobiography of Ephraim Tutt. NY: Charles Scribner's Sons, 1943. 451pp.
A biography of Train's fictional character, Ephraim Tutt, lawyer and problem-solver.

TREAT, LAWRENCE

Ref: Hubin 2, TCCMW, CC, ABMI(S); Writer's Digest 48:1 (Jan 68):17-21, 92-95.

Int: EQMM, July 76, p. 116.; PW, 7 Aug 81, pp. 6-7 (photo).

E2879. Queen, Ellery. "Introduction." In P As in Police, by Lawrence Treat, pp. 7-10. NY: Davis Publ., Oct 1970.

TRENCH, JOHN

Ref: Hubin 2, TCCMW, CC, ABMI(S); Pike, TPP 4:1 (Feb 81):19-20.

TRENTER, STIEG

E2880. Olsson, Sven-Erik, and Unaeus, Per-Ake. Analys av en detektivförfattare |Analysis of a mystery writer|. Boras: Bibliotekshögskolan, 1978.
A critical study of the writer's works, with a bibliography. (IH)

TREVANIAN

Ref: Hubin 2, TCCMW, ABMIS.

Int: NYTBR, 10 June 79, p. 48 (photo).

TREVOR, ELLESTON. See HALL, ADAM

TREVOR, GLEN. See HILTON, JAMES

TRIPP, MILES

Ref: Hubin 2, TCCMW, ABMI(S).

TROY, SIMON

Ref: Hubin 2, TCCMW, CC, SN; UN 4:7 (1952):6-7 (photo).

E2881. Barzun, Jacques, and Taylor, Wendell Hertig. "Introduction." In Swift to Its Close (NY, 1969), by Simon Troy. "Crime Fiction 1950-1975" (B18).

TRUMAN, MARGARET

Ref: Hubin 2.

E2882. Browne, Ray B., and Browne, Alicia R. "Bad Blood on the Potomac: Margaret Truman's Washington Novels." Clues 3:2 (Fall/Winter 82):100-103.

A survey of her three detective novels.

TSUNODA, KIKUO

E2883. Henshu Iinkai, ed. Tsunoda Kikuo-shi Kako Kinen Bunshu |Mr. Kikuo Tsunoda: memorial book for the age of 61|. Tokyo: Henshu Iinkai, 1986. Privately printed edition limited to 500 copies. 283pp. Illustrated. Bibliography.

A collection of articles contributed by 39 people, in commemoration of the sixtieth birthday of writer Kikuo Tsunoda. It includes his chronology and a detailed bibliography. (HS/TT)

TSUZUKI, MICHIO

E2884. Tsuzuki Michio no Sekai |The world of Tsuzuki Michio|. Shinpyo-sha series (B367). July 1981. 216pp.

TUCKER, WILSON

Ref: Hubin 2, SN, ABMI(S).

E2885. Banks, R. Jeff. "Mystery Plus: the 'Best' of Wilson Tucker." TPP 5:4 (Oct 83):39-40, 43.

SF/mystery cross-overs in stories in The Best of Wilson Tucker (Timescape, 1982).

TWAIN, MARK

Ref: Hubin 2, EMD, CC, ABMI(S).

E2886. Baetzhold, Howard. "Of Detectives and their Derring-do: The Genesis of Mark Twain's 'The Stolen White Elephant.'" Studies in American Humor 2 (1976):183-95.

In spite of Twain's apparent contempt for real-life detectives and detective fiction, from the 1870s he used detection as a major element in his fiction. Here, Baetzhold examines the use of contemporary material, including Pinkerton's detective tales, in his burlesque treatment of detectives in "The Stolen White Elephant."

E2887. ______. "Postscript III." In his Mark Twain and John Bull: The British Connection, pp. 298-304. Bloomington: Indiana University Press, 1970.

Comments on Twain's "A Double-Barreled Detective Story," showing that it was intended as a burlesque of Conan Doyle's A Study in Scarlet.

E2888. Banks, R. Jeff. "Mark Twain: Detective Story Writer. An Appreciation." TAD 7 (1973/74):176-77.

Cursory comments on detective story elements in Twain's fiction. For further comments see R. W. Hays' letter, TAD 7:4:298.

E2889. Bay, J. Christian. "Tom Sawyer, Detective: The Origin of the Plot." In Essays Offered to Herbert Putnam by His Colleagues and Friends on His Thirtieth Anniversary as Librarian of Congress, 5 April 29, edited by William Warner Bishop and Andrew Keogh, pp. 80-88. New Haven: Yale Univ. Press, 1929.
On Danish writer S. Blicher's novel The Minster of Veilby (1829) as the source for Tom Sawyer, Detective.

E2890. Brand, John M. "The Incipient Wilderness: A Study of Pudd'nhead Wilson." Western American Literature 7 (1972):125-34.
Wilson as a patient researcher, a "hero of his time," and, potentially, of ours. An ambivalent portrait of Twain's detective as a man of limited vision who cannot see beyond his case or challenge the bases of the wrongs he finds.

E2891. Brodwin, Stanley. "Blackness and the Adamic Myth in Mark Twain's Pudd'nhead Wilson." Texas Studies in Literature and Language (1973):167-76.
Discussion, among other subjects, of the use of fingerprints as a narrative device. In contrast to other critics, Brodwin finds the thematic and structural materials, including elements of dection, well integrated in this novel.

E2892. Cook, Doris E. "Sherlock Holmes and Much More; or, Some of the Facts about William Gillette." Hartford: Connecticut Historical Society, 1970.
Discusses Mark Twain's role in bringing the play The Professor to the New York stage. Not seen.

E2893. Gerber, John C.; Baender, Paul; and Firkins, Terry, editors. Tom Sawyer, Detective. In The Works of Mark Twain, Vol. IV, pp. 345-415, 675-717. Published for The Iowa Center for Textual Studies. Berkeley, CA: University of California Press, 1980.
A critical edition of the text with extensive notes, an introduction with some discussion of detection elements in Twain's fiction, and other materials.

E2894. Honce, Charles. "Detective Stories as Literature." In Mark Twain's Associated Press Speech and Other News Stories, pp. 47-57. NY: privately printed, 1940. Not seen.

E2895. Jeffries, William B. "The Montesquiou Murder Case: A Possible Source for Some Incidents in Pudd'nhead Wilson." American Literature 31 (Jan 60):488-90; reprinted in Twainian 19 (Nov/Dec 60):1-3.
An 1849 St. Louis murder case appears to have served as a source for the development of the Capello brothers in Pudd'nhead Wilson.

E2896. Johnson, Merle. A Bibliography of the Works of Mark Twain, Samuel Langhorne Clemens: A List of First Editions in Book Form and of First Printings in Periodicals and Occasional Publications of His Varied Literary Activities. Revised and Enlarged. NY & London: Harper & Bros., 1935. Reprinted by Greenwood Press, Westport, CT, 1972.
According to Tenney (E2910), only superseded in part by Jacob Blanck's Bibliography of American Literature, Vol. II (1957), pp. 173-254.

E2897. Kolin, Philip C. "Mark Twain's Pudd'nhead Wilson: A Selected Checklist." BoB 28:2 (April/June 71):58-59.

E2898. Kraus, W. Keith. "Mark Twain's 'A Double-Barreled Detective Story': A Source for the Solitary Oesophagus." MTJ 16:2 (Summer 72):10-12.
Kraus traces the burlesque in Twain's story to Doyle's A Study in Scarlet whose elaborate structure Twain tried "unsuccessfully" to imitate.

E2899. la Cour, Tage. "The Scandinavian Crime-Detective Story." American Book Collector 9 (May 59):22-23; reprinted, in abstract, in Twainian 19 (Jan/Feb 60):2-3.
Twain's secretary denied that Twain had read Blicher's The Vicar of Veilby or that he had used it as a source for Tom Sawyer, Detective.

E2900. McKeithan, D. M. "Mark Twain's Tom Sawyer, Detective." Studia Neophilologica 25 (1953):161-79. Reprinted in his Court Trials in Mark Twain and Other Essays, pp. 169-78. The Hague: Martinus Nijhoff, 1958.
McKeithan identifies the source for Tom Sawyer, Detective as Blicher's The Minister of Veilby, and supports his claim with a close comparison of the two texts. It is claimed that Twain had not read the story but that it had been related to him.

E2901. Motola, Gabriel. Mark Twain and the Detective. Unpublished Ph. D. dissertation. New York University, 1969. 195pp. DAI 31/11-A (1970/71), p. 6066.

E2902. Orth, Michael. "Pudd'nhead Wilson Reconsidered: or, the Octoroon in the Villa Viviani." MTJ 14 (Summer 1969):11-15.
According to Tenney (E2910), Orth locates the source for the use of fingerprints in Pudd'nhead Wilson in Mayne Reid's The Quadroon (1856). Not seen.

E2903. Ritunnano, Jeanne. "Mark Twain vs. Arthur Conan Doyle on Detective Fiction." MTJ 16:1 (Winter 71-72):10-14.
Not seen but described in Abstract of English Studies 16:6 (Feb 73), item 1767 as claiming that although Twain satirizes the "whole body of Sherlock Homes fiction," parallels with A Study in Scarlet are unsubstantiated.

E2904. Rowlette, Robert. "Mark Twain and the Detective." In Mark Twain's "Pudd'nhead Wilson: The Development and Design," pp. 38-61. Bowling Green, OH: Popular Press, 1971.
A portrait of the detective in Mark Twain as a "transcendent figure," and one of the few exceptions to his sweeping condemnation of mankind.

E2905. Rogers, Franklin R. "Introduction." To Simon Wheeler, Detective, pp. xi-xxxviii. NY: The New York Public Library, 1963.
A discussion of Twain's burlesque of the Pinkerton methods in Simon Wheeler, Detective.

E2906. Saylor, Louise. "David (Pudd'nhead) Wilson: The Missing Figure in a Detectives' Group Portrait." TAD 13 (1980):8-11.
A discussion of Wilson as a predecessor of modern fictional detectives of both hard-boiled and "standard" mystery fiction.

E2907. Schell, Edgar T. "'Pears' and 'Is' in Pudd'nhead Wilson." MTJ 12 (Winter 64):12-15.
Characters in their relationship to structure. Appearance and Reality and the structural unity of this often criticized novel.

E2908. Smith, Henry Nash. "Pudd'nhead Wilson and After." Massachusetts Review 3 (Winter 1961/62):233-53; reprinted in Twainian 22 (Jan/Feb 63); and in Mark Twain: The Development of a Writer (Harvard Univ. Press, 1962), pp. 171-88.

A discussion of characters and their identities and role-playing in Pudd'nhead Wilson. Wilson, the detective figure, is borrowed from "the newspaper and popular novel," incarnating analytical intelligence.

E2909. Stone, Albert E. "On the Trail of Success." In The Innocent Eye, pp. 188-201. New Haven, CT: Yale University Press, 1961; reprinted by Archon Press, 1970.

On Twain's exploitation of detective fiction in Tom Sawyer, Detective and Pudd'nhead Wilson.

E2910. Tenney, Thomas Asa. Mark Twain: A Reference Guide. NY: G. K. Hall, 1977. xiv, 443pp.

Annotated bibliography of writings about Twain. Index provides title and author/name listings; the bibliography is arranged chronologically.

E2911. Wigger, Anne P. "The Source of the Fingerprint material in Mark Twain's Pudd'nhead Wilson and Those Extraordinary Twins." American Literature 28 (1956/57):517-20.

The probable source of Mark Twain's information on fingerprints in Francis Galton's Finger Prints (London, 1892).

TWOHY, ROBERT

Int: EQMM, 1 Jan 81, pp. 70-71; 28 Jan 81, pp. 95-96.

TYRE, NEDRA

Ref: Hubin 2, TCCMW, EMD, CC.

Int: EQMM, July 83, pp. 100-2 and Mid-July 83, pp. 71-3.

E2912. Boucher, Anthony. "Introduction." In Death Is a Lover (orig. published as Mouse in Eternity, Knopf, 1952), by Nedra Tyre. NY: Mercury, 1953.

TYRER, WALTER

Ref: Hubin 2, CC, ABMI.

E2913. Barzun, Jacques, and Taylor, Wendell Hertig. "Introduction." In Such Friends Are Dangerous (London, 1954), by Walter Tyrer. "Crime Fiction 1950-1975" (B18).

UHNAK, DOROThY

Ref: Hubin 2, TCCMW, EMD, SN, ABMI(S); The Writer 94:12 (Dec 81):11-13.

See also: C747.

Int: McCall's 98:10 (July 72):43; Akron Beacon Journal, 29 Apr 73 (reprinted in Authors in the News p. 476); NYTBR, 25 Sept 77, p. 48 (photo); NYTBR, 25 Oct 81, p. 50 (photo).

E2914. Mitterling, Philip I. "Dorothy Uhnak: The Development of a Novelist." JPC 16:1 (Summer 82):88-98.

An article on Uhnak, much of it based on an interview conducted in October 1977. Uhnak discusses how she views herself, her writing, and her audience.

E2915. Palme, Jacob. "Salt poliskvinna skriver romaner |Seasoned policewoman writes novels|." Jury 4:4 (1975):24.
The works of Dorothy Uhnak. (MS)

UNDERWOOD, MICHAEL

Ref: Hubin 2, TCCMW, CC, ABMI(S); The Writer 94:10 (Oct 81):13-14, 24 (on plotting).

UPFIELD, ARTHUR W.

Ref: Hubin 2, TCCMW, EMD, CC, ABMI(S); UN 1:1 (1948):5 (photo); UN 4:6 (1952):8-9 (photo).

E2916. Ball, John. "Introduction." In Upfield (E2927), pp. vi-xvi.
A biographical study with an emphasis on Upfield's writing career and a short commentary on The New Shoe.

E2917. Barzun, Jacques, and Taylor, Wendell Hertig. Preface to The Bone Is Pointed (Sydney, Australia, 1938), by Arthur Upfield. In A Book of Prefaces (B17), pp. 103-104.

E2918. The Bony Bulletin. Ed. by Philip T. Asdell, Frederick, MD. Published irregularly. 1st issue published in November 1981.
Specialist fanzine for enthusiasts of Upfield and his Aborigine detective, Napoleon Bonaparte. Includes articles on Australian terminology used in Upfield's novels, and on Upfield's life. Also features a letters column and Book Exchange. Illustrated with ink drawings and maps. (GG)

E2919. Cawelti, John G. "Murder in the Outback: Arthur W. Upfield." New Republic, 30 July 77, pp. 39-41.
Upfield's novels as an interesting example of the "interface" between different cultures and formulaic limitations of "deeper and more complex cultural perspectives." Cawelti considers Upfield's five or six best novels to be rich fables of cultural interaction.

E2920. Donaldson, Betty. "Arthur William Upfield: September 1, 1888 - February 13, 1964." TAD 8 (1974/75):1-11; reprinted in Upfield (B2927), pp. 233-45.
A brief biography followed by a chronological list of the novels with information on first English and American publication, the setting and a short plot resume. With a map showing where the action of the various novels is centered.

E2921. Fox, Estelle. "Arthur William Upfield, 1888-1964." TAD 3 (1969/70):89-91.
A biographical note on the author and his series character Napoleon Bonaparte, with a checklist of the fiction giving date of publication and publisher in British/Australian and American first printings. Checklist compiled by Fox, Francis M. Nevins, Jr., and Charles Shibuk. See Nevins, letter TAD 4 (1970/71):193 for correction.

E2922. Hawke, Jessica. Follow My Dust! A Biography of Arthur Upfield. London: Heinemann, 1957. xii, 238pp.
Much information on Upfield and his adventurous life, which provided the background for most of his detective novels, but little specific data or commentary on the books themselves or on Upfield as a writer. Not seen. Breen 224. (REB)

E2923. Hill, M. C. "Too Right Bony." PQ 3:2 (Summer 80):7-11. Photos and illustrations.
Upfield's novels in paperback.

E2924. Lithner, Klas. "Arthur Upfield, Napoleon Bonaparte och Australien." In Poeklubbens Arbog 1970, pp. 66-75. Copenhagen: Lademan, 1970.
Introductory article about Upfield's famous half-aborigine detective, by a Swedish crime fiction collector and member of the Swedish Academy of Detection. (GG)

E2925. Sarjeant, William Anthony S. "The Great Australian Detective." TAD 12 (1979):99-105. Illus.
A profile of Bonaporte as a detective with an "unbroken sequence of successes."

E2926. _____. "A Preliminary Chronology of the Documented Cases of Napoleon Bonaparte." TAD 12 (1979):358-59.
The chronology gives the date of the case, where possible, book, date of publication and location of action.

E2917. Upfield, Arthur W. The New Shoe. Edited by John Ball. The Mystery Library Series (B270): no. 1. 1976. iv-xvi, 245pp.
A critical edition of Upfield's 1951 novel, with illustrations by an uncredited artist. Contents: John Ball, "Introduction," pp. vi-xvi (E2916); The New Shoe, pp. 1-231; Betty Donaldson, "The Novels of Arthur W. Upfield," 233-45 (E2920).

URQUHART, MACGREGOR

Ref: Hubin 2, CC; Pike, TPP 4:4 (Aug 81):19-20.

VALIN, JONATHAN

Ref: Hubin 2, SN; The Writer 94:8 (Aug 81):19-21.

Int: St. Louis Globe-Democrat, 28-29 May 1983, p. 4E.

E2928. Lochte, Dick. "For New-Breed Detective Writer Jonathan Valin, Plots Thicken." Los Angeles Times, 9 June 83, Part V, pp. 1, 17. Photo.
A substantial interview with lengthy quotes by Valin on his writing. (JLA)

VAN ARSDALE, WIRT

Ref: Hubin 2.

E2929. Lauterbach, Ed. "The Adventure of the Purloined Red Herring." TPP 3:5 (Oct 80):3-8.
A study of references to Sherlock Holmes' stories in Van Arsdale's The Professor Knits a Shroud (Crime Club, 1951).

VANCE, JACK (JOHN HOLBROOK)

Ref: Hubin 2, TCCMW, EMD, ABMI(S).

E2930. Levack, Daniel J. H., and Underwood, Tim. Fantasms: A Bibliography of the Literature of Jack Vance. San Francisco, CA and Columbia, PA: Underwood/Miller, 1978. 92pp. Edition limited to 1000 copies: 100 clothbound, 900 paperbound. (Note: subtitle given on front cover as "A Jack Vance Bibliography.")

Although known primarily as a fantasist and science fiction writer, Jack Vance is the author of twelve published crime novels and one short story under the names John Holbrook Vance, Jack Vance, Peter Held, Alan Wade, Ellery Queen, and John Van See. This bibliography lists all of Vance's English-language work through 1978. Magazine, paperback and hardcover publications, both original and reprint are included. Information on some foreign translations is given. The covers of most hardcover and paperback books and many of the magazines are illustrated. The main listings are alphabetical by title. There is a supplementary checklist in chronological order, and lists of pseudonymous works, series, and TV scripts are given. (REB)

E2931. Squires, Roy A. Catalog 12, Science Fiction and Mystery Novels: Original Manuscripts by Jack Vance (John Holbrook Vance). Glendale, CA: Roy A. Squires, nd. 12pp. Wraps.
Roy Squires's catalogues usually deal with science fictional collectibles and fine press works. They are invariably elegant productions, with acute and informative annotations. Catalog 12 is of interest because it contains descriptions of the manuscripts of two unpublished mystery/suspense novels and the outlines for two others, one of which would have been the third in Vance's 'Sheriff Joe Bain' series. (REB)

VANCE, LOUIS JOSEPH

Ref: Hubin 2, TCCMW, EMD, CC, ABMI(S)s, 249-51, 398-9; CC, 2113.

See also: B201.

VAN DE WETERING, JANWILLEM

Ref: Hubin 2, TCCMW, ABMI; Cannon, AHMM 27:10 (Mid-Sept 82):60-62.

Int: PW, 26 Sept 77, pp. 48-49 (photo); TAD 13 (1980):98-107; EQMM, Mid-July 82, pp. 97-98 and Aug 82, pp. 80-82; Cooper-Clark (B75), pp. 149-57 (photo); Carr (B67), pp. 289-321.

E2932. Genberg, Kjell E. "Holländska mord |Dutch murder|." Jury 9:3 (1980):21-23.
Biography of van de Wetering. (MS)

E2933. White, Jean M. "Murder by Zen: Janwillem van de Wetering." New Republic, 22 July 78, pp. 34-35.
An introduction to van de Wetering's procedurals. White sees their strengths in mood, character and setting.

VAN DINE, S. S.

Ref: Hubin 2, TCCMW, EMD, CC, ABMI(S).

See also: B6, B170, B310, C535, E1060.

E2934. Beaman, Bruce R. "S. S. Van Dine: A Biographical Sketch." TAD 8 (1974-75):133-35.
Biography and a checklist of the writings of Wright/Van Dine.

E2935. Braithwaite, William Stanley. "S. S. Van Dine--Willard Huntington Wright." In Van Dine (E2952), pp. 29-45.
A profile of Van Dine/Wright by a friend based on conversations, the fiction and his non-mystery critical writings. Braithwaite says that the portrait of Philo Vance in the novels resembles Wright as he knew him.

E2936. Crawford, Walter B. "Willard Huntington Wright: Aesthete and Critic." Unpublished Master's thesis. Columbia University, 1947.

E2937. ______. "Willard Huntington Wright: A Bibliography." BoB 24 (May/August 63):11-16.
According to Crawford's introduction, this is the first Wright bibliography. Well organized, it is divided into two parts. Part I covers books, periodical and newspaper articles, introductions and dramatic adaptations by Wright, with a special section on works by "S. S. Van Dine." Included are foreign translations of Wright's books, which tend to be the Philo Vance books. Part II covers books and articles dealing with Wright. As Crawford notes, the bulk of the critical writing on Wright/Van Dine appeared before his death in 1939. (GG)

E2938. D'Amore, Bruno. "Analisi logica del romanzo poliziesco |Logical analysis of the detective novel|." Rendiconti 24 (1971), pp. 304-20.
The author, a university professor of mathematical logic, applying his own analysis to the work of S. S. Van Dine, demonstrates that "the deductive logical reasoning of the 'scientific' giallo is nothing but a series of narrative expedients to hold the reader's attention. It has no real basis in deductive logic, and rather, on many points, commits gross errors in this direction." A possibility of formalization must rather be recognized within the narrative structure, which can, for example, be reduced to a logical rationalization, according to the technico-narrative directives of Van Dine, through the application of the theory of games. (RC)

E2939. Dueren, Fred. "Philo Vance." TAD 9 (1975/76):23-24.
A profile of Vance.

E2940. Garden, Y. B. "Philo Vance: An Impressionistic Biography." In Van Dine (E2952), pp. 46-73.
A biography of Vance with privileged information about his ancestry, early life and his mature years when he was a public figure of some fame.

E2941. Hagemann, E. R. "Philo Vance's Sunday Nights at the Old Stuyvesant Club." Clues 1:2 (Fall/Winter 80):35-41.
On 8 true-crime stories published by Van Dine in Cosmospolitan in 1929 and 1930. Hagemann gives bibliographic data and discusses the narrative framework in which Philo Vance becomes increasingly prominent. Hagemann also discusses the many editorial comments by Van Dine/Vance about the judicial process.

E2942. Lowndes, R. A. W. "Dear Me, Mr. Van Dine." TAD 7 (1973/74):30-31.
A humorous checking of dates in Van Dine's novels for their accuracy.

E2943. ______. "The Editor's Page: Philo Vance." SMS 3:2 (Winter 69):4-7, 121-24, 126-27.
One of a series of surveys of important writers of detective fiction.

E2944. Penzler, Otto. "Collecting Mystery Fiction." TAD 15 (1982):350-56. Illustrated.
A discussion of Van Dine's career and of problematic areas in collecting his books and related material is followed by an annotated bibliography of books as by both Wright and Van Dine. Complete bibliographic information is given for the first editions of the mystery fiction. Penzler

also includes information on parodies of Philo Vance cases. For comments on Penzler's bibliography see Blackbeard, letter TAD 16 (1983):319-20; and R. Mitchell, letter TAD 16:322, with a reply by Penzler.

E2945. Rosenblatt, Roger. "The Back of the Book: S. S. Van Dine." New Republic, 26 July 75, pp. 32-34.
Van Dine's "great feat" is to have created a virtually unlikeable detective. Van Dine's riddle stories are clever, intricate and perfectly paced.

E2946. Thomson, H. Douglas. "The American Detective Story." In Thomson (B404), pp. 262-69.
A sympathetic view of Van Dine, with appreciative comments on his plotting and literariness.

E2947. Tomashefsky, Steven. "He Has Several Good Cases to His Credit." Studies in Scarlet 1:1 (June 65):10-13.
A comparison of Philo Vance and Sherlock Holmes. Not seen. DeWaal 4088.

E2948. Tuska, Jon, ed. Philo Vance: The Life and Times of S. S. Van Dine. Popular Writers Series, No. 1. Bowling Green, OH: Popular Press, 1971. 63pp. Illus. No index or bibliography.
A collection of essays on S. S. Van Dine's detective fiction and film adaptations of the Philo Vance novels. Contents: "Author's note," p. 5 (introduction); J. Tuska, "The Philo Vance Murder Case," pp. 5-35 (E2949); Leonard Maltin, "Philo Vance at the Movies," pp. 35-48 (excellent discussion of the films; stills); David R. Smith, "S. S. Van Dine at 20th Century Fox," pp. 48-58 (includes biographical information); "Philo Vance Film Checklist," p. 59 (rental sources for four Philo Vance films); Karl Thiede, "S. S. Van Dine Filmography," pp. 59-62; "Bibliography," p. 63 (secondary sources). The three essays in this chapbook first appeared in Tuska's Views & Reviews magazine. Breen 225. (REB)

E2949. Tuska, Jon. "The Philo Vance Murder Case." Views and Reviews 1:3 (Winter 1970):54-62; 1:4 (Spring 1970):38-46; 2:1 (Summer 1970):45-54; reprinted in Tuska (E2948).
Survey of S. S. Van Dine's detective novels, with an analysis of the Philo Vance character and biographical material on Van Dine. (REB)

E2950. Van Dine, S. S. The Benson Murder Case. The "Canary" Murder Case. The Greene Murder Case. The Bishop Murder Case. The Scarab Murder Case. The Kennel Murder Case. Boston, MA: Gregg Press, 1980. With introductions by Chris Steinbrunner. Stills.
Reissues of 6 Philo Vance titles with introductions by Chris Steinbrunner in which a general survey is presented with specific comments on each of the six novels and the film adaptations.

E2951. ______. "Introduction." In Van Dine (E2952), pp. 1-28. First published in American Magazine 106:3 (Sept 28):14-15, 118, 122, 124-29. Condensed version published as "How I Got Away with Murder," in Readers' Digest, July 36, pp. 53-55.
In the book introduction, Van Dine reveals his real name, a fact which he had carefully concealed in the magazine version. An autobiographical essay in which Van Dine describes how he came to write detective stories after a serious breakdown suffered as a result of intensive work

at his first literary career.

E2952. ______. Philo Vance Murder Cases. NY: Scribner's Sons, 1936. Illustrations by Herbert Morton Stoops and James Montgomery Flagg.
An anthology of three novels with critical material, as follows: S. S. Van Dine, "Introduction," pp. 1-28 (E2951); William Stanley Braithwaite, "S. S. Van Dine - Willard Huntington Wright," pp. 29-45 (E2935); S. S. Van Dine, "Twenty Rules for Writing Detective Stories," pp. 74-83 (C827); Introductions to The Scarab Murder Case (p. 84), The Kennel Murder Case (p. 423), and The Dragon Murder Case (p. 727). The introductions contain information on the publication history of each novel and on the film adaptation.

VAN GULIK, ROBERT

Ref: Hubin 2, TCCMW, EMD, CC, ABMI(S).

E2953. Alford, William P. "Robert van Gulik and the Judge Dee Stories." Orientations 12:11 (Nov 81):50-55. Illustrated.
Discussion of historical and legal accuracy in the Judge Dee Stories. Alford points out a few examples of poetic license, but he concludes that the stories succeed in blending entertainment with education for the broad international audience. (JLA)

E2954. Atchity, Kenneth John. "Robert van Gulik." In Adams, MDA 1972 (B2), pp. 237-45.
An overview of the Judge Dee novels seen as the work of a literary amateur whose work had several areas of strength but in which form and content were never successfully integrated. Van Gulik's powers of characterization developed slowly and his death at a time when he seemed close to achieving some artistic stature is regrettable.

E2955. Barzun, Jacques, and Taylor, Wendell Hertig. "Introduction." In The Lacquer Screen (NY, 1960), by Robert van Gulik. "Crime Fiction 1950-1975 (B18).

E2956. Chen, Chih-mai. "Sinologue Extraordinaire." Hemisphere 12:8 (Aug 68):31-36; reprinted as "Robert van Gulik and the Judge Dee Stories" in Renditions, no. 5 (Autumn 75), pp. 100-17; published in a Chinese version in Ho-lan Kao Lo-p'ei (Taipei: Biographical Literature Press, 1969). Illustrated with an uncommon photo of van Gulik, and reproductions of his illustrations.
Chronicles the varied career of Dr. van Gulik, who was a Dutch diplomat, a noted Orientalist, and the author of the Judge Dee mysteries. Emphasis is placed on his contributions to Asian studies. (JLA)

E2957. Evers, A. M. (Mrs.). Bibliography of Dr. R. H. van Gulik. Pamphlet compiled for the benefit of the Boston University Libraries, Mugar Memorial Library, "Robert van Gulik" Collection, circa 1968.
The Bibliography begins with material on van Gulik's life and continues with descriptions of all his articles, scholarly books, poems, reviews, dictionaries, and novels, including a listing of the Judge Dee books in all languages through 1967. The pamphlet also includes van Gulik's notes about the composition of the Judge Dee stories. An excellent reference work which deserves to be better known and widely used. (Douglas G. Greene)

E2958. Fitzpatrick, Al. (Letter to the editor.) TMN 13 (July 81), pp. L1-L2. A short chronology of the Judge Dee stories which is sometimes spotty, sometimes listing places of the stories without dates. Although it does not include Dee Goong An, Poets and Murder or Judge Dee at Work, it does include Necklace and Calabash which van Gulik's own chronology lacks. Fitzpatrick's letter also contains an interesting note about the two distinct series of Judge Dee stories. (GG)

E2959. Hulsewe, A. F. P. "Necrologie: R. H. van Gulik (1910-1967)." T'oung Pao 54 (1968):116-24; reprinted in Orientations 12:11 (Nov 81). Brief biographical sketch of van Gulik, accompanied by a lengthy, though incomplete, bibliography of his works. (JLA)

E2960. Lach, Donald F. "Introduction." In The Chinese Bell Murders, The Chinese Lake Murders, The Chinese Maze Murders, The Chinese Nail Murders, and The Chinese Gold Murders. Chicago: University of Chicago Press, 1977. Identical essay published as thirteen-page introduction in each of the volumes of this 1977 printing. A biography of van Gulik which emphasizes his scholarly interests and writing. Lach gives background on Chinese court fiction and van Gulik's use of it in his Judge Dee stories. With a selected bibliography of secondary sources. CC S87.

E2961. Lawton, Thomas. "Robert Hans van Gulik: Ambassador Extraordinary." Orientations 12:11 (Nov 81):12-22. Essay of appreciation for van Gulik's many talents, including his diplomatic ability, skill with 12 languages, Sinological researches, his long bibliography, and the authorship of the Judge Dee stories. One of the most detailed, informative biographical articles on van Gulik. Richly illustrated with photos and van Gulik's own drawings. (GG)

E2962. Penzler, Otto. "Collecting Mystery Fiction: Judge Dee." TAD 16 (1983):75-82. Illus. Bibliographic descriptions of first English and American editions.

E2963. Sarjeant, William Antony S. "A Detective in Seventh-Century China: Robert van Gulik and the Cases of Judge Dee." TAD 15 (1982):292-303. Photo and illustrations. An introduction to van Gulik's life and works, and a narrative chronology of Judge Dee's career as compiled from van Gulik's Judge Dee stories.

E2964. Schreiber, Mark. "Sherlock Holmes' Chinese Style." The Asia Magazine, 1 Feb 81, pp. 8-13. Informal article on van Gulik and the Judge Dee novels. States that Van Gulik's original novels were written because he could find no other writer to take over the Dee character from his translation, Dee Goong-an. Illustrated with photos. (GG)

E2965. "Summary Bibliography of the Writings of R. H. van Gulik (1910-67)." Orientations 12:11 (Nov 81):62-65; previously published in T'oung Pao 54 (1968):120-124. Seventy-two item bibliography including books, articles and crime novels. Of the 18 crime publications listed, 15 contain Dutch publication information, and many contain data on the dates of composition and pre-book publication. (GG)

E2966. van Gulik, Robert. "Translator's Preface" (pp. x-xxii) and "Translator's Postscript" (pp. 225-237). In Celebrated Cases of Judge Dee (Dee Goong An). NY: Dover, 1967. CC S89.

E2967. _____. "Judge Dee Chronology." In Judge Dee at Work, edited by Robert van Gulik, endpapers following p. 174. NY: Scribner's, 1967.
Four unnumbered pages contain a chronology of 15 novels and 8 short stories of the fictional Judge Dee. There is a running column on Dee's year, rank and place of office, to which is added a matched column of the titles of the stories for each setting, and a column with information on Dee's life and events in the stories. It is worthwhile to note that the chronology does not include Necklace and Calabash and Poets and Murder, perhaps because of the recent publication dates, nor Dee Goong An, presumably because it is a translation and not van Gulik's own creation. (GG)

VAN RJNDT, PHILIPPE

Ref: Hubin 2, ABMIS.

Int: PW, 13 Nov 78, p. 67 (photo).

VARENDE, YVES

Ref: SN.

Int: Enigmatika 20 (1982), pp. 25-30.

VAROUX, JEAN ALEX

Ref: SN.

Int: Mystère Magazine 1 (Dec 81), pp. 6-7 (photos and bibliography).

VAUTRIN, JEAN

Ref: SN.

E2968. "Dossier Jean Vautrin." Polar 5 (Sept 79):4-33.
A dossier on a screenwriter who, since 1970, has become known principally as a writer of detective novels. Contents: Richard Bocci, "Jean Vautrin: l'écrivain masqué |The masked writer|," pp. 4-5 (brief tribute); Serge Clérambault, "Entretien avec Jean Vautrin," pp. 6-13 (interview; photos); "Bibliographie," pp. 14-15 (bibliography with concise critical comments including observations by Vautrin); Jean Vautrin, "Black Monday," pp. 16-24 (short story); "Filmographie de Jean Herman dit Jean Vautrin |Filmography for Jean Herman known as Jean Vautrin|," pp. 26-33 (stills).

VEDDER, JOHN K. See GRUBER, FRANK

VERY, PIERRE

Int: MM 25 (Feb 50).

See also: B408.

E2969. Aymé, Marcel. "Pierre Véry, mon ami." NL, 8 June 61; reprinted as the preface to Un grand patron. Paris: Ronbaldi, 1964. Not seen.

E2970. Baudou, Jacques, and Caillot, Patrice. "Bibliographie critique." Enigmatika 15 (May 80):81-92.

A partial bibliography. Selected titles are listed chronologically with critical comments drawn from a variety of sources, including Véry himself.

E2971. Baudou, Jacques. "Les Héritiers de Saint-Agil." Enigmatika 15 (May 80), pp. 56-60.
A study of works by Véry that, first published as mysteries for adult readers, have been reprinted in children's series and contain fairy tale elements that have made of them childhood classics.

E2972. ______. "Jouez magie |Play magic|." Europe no. 636 (April 82):61-70.
Very's Les Métamorphoses (1931) and Le meneur de jeu (1934) as a "fusion" of mystery and poetry and as transitional works between his traditional novels and his detective fiction.

E2973. ______. "Pierre Véry, l'enchanteur assassin |Pierre Véry, the murderous enchanter|." Europe no. 636 (April 82):10-19.
A biographical and critical study of Véry which highlights his adventurous attempt to create a modern "thousand and one nights" in his detective fiction which he conceived of as one vast, continuous series novel.

E2974. Béarn, Pierre. "Mon ami, Pierre Véry." La passerelle no. 5 (Winter 70/71); no. 6 (Spring 71); no. 7 (Summer 71).
In part, a long indictment by Béarn of Véry's detective fiction. (JB)

E2975. Béarn, Pierre; Morineau, Raymond; and Ciampi, Yves. "Avec Pierre Véry." Constellation, Oct 70. Not seen.

E2976. Besnier, Patrick, and Bordillon, Henri. "Courrier vérydique." Enigmatika 15 (May 80):44-46.
Besnier, responding to Bordillon's invitation to contribute to the special issue of Enigmatika on Véry, replies that he "detests" Véry's work which fails at the "impossible" attempt to combine rigor and fantasy in fiction. Bordillon replies, sadly and vigorously, that Besnier has failed to understand Véry who has written the only poetic detective novels.

E2977. Besnick, Patrick. "Jorge Luis Borges et Pierre Véry." Enigmatika 15 (May 80), pp. 32-33.
Besnick theorizes that even if Borges used a notation from Véry's Les Métamorphoses in his Labyrinthes, which he concedes to be quite possible, Borges uses the elements much more imaginatively than Véry.

E2978. Bordillon, Henri, editor. "Dossier Pierre Véry." Enigmatika 15 (May 80), pp. 1-100. Photographs and illustrations.
A collection of articles on the life and work of Pierre Véry (1900-1960). In the listing of the contents, the subject willl be noted of material which will not be indexed separately and annotated. Contents: Pierre MacOrlan, "Pierre Véry," pp. 3-4 (reminiscences); Pierre Humbourg, "Une heure sans Pierre Véry |An hour without Pierre Véry|," pp. 5-7 (an imaginary interview); H. Bordillon, "Repères biographiques," pp. 8-9 (a biographical chronology); Jacques Baudou, "Entretien avec Mme Véry et Noël Véry," pp. 10-14 (an interview with Véry's widow and daughter); Alain Demouzon, "Chère Annie Matiquat," pp. 15-18 (E2986); H. Bordillon, "La preuve par sept," pp. 19-22 (E2981); Daniel Couegnas, "Double Assassinat au 221B Baker Street: création, innovation et imagination chez Pierre Véry," pp. 23-31 (E2983); Patrick Besnier,

"Jorge Luis Borges et Pierre Véry," pp. 32-33 (E2977); Daniel Couegnas, "Le Costume des dimanches: enquête sur les sentiers du temps perdu," pp. 34-43 (E2982); P. Besnier and H. Bordillon, "Courrier vérydique," pp. 44-46 (E2976); H. Bordillon, "Du mensonge dans le roman policier," pp. 47-49 (E2980); H. Bordillon, "Chronos assassin," pp. 50-51 (E2979); Paul Gayot, "Ronde autour du meneur de jeu," pp. 52-55 (E2990); J. Baudou, "Les héritiers de Saint-Agil," pp. 56-60 (E2971); Paul Gayot, "Pillards, billards, procédés, carambolages et séries," pp. 61-62 (E2989); P. Véry, "Textes," pp. 63-70 (critical and biographical notes by Véry); Claude Aveline, "Lettres de Pierre Véry," pp. 71-75 (Véry comments on works by Claude Aveline and related matters); Patrick Béarn, "Le grand prix du roman d'aventures a été attribué hier à Pierre Véry |The first prize for the novel of adventure was awarded yesterday to Pierre Véry)," pp. 76-78 (comments by Véry's friend on the occasion of the awarding of the prize to Véry for his Le testament de Basil Crookes in 1930); Henri Bordillon, "Prolégomènes à une bibliographie enfin complète de Pierre Véry," pp. 79-80 (Titles of works by Véry which were announced for publication but never appeared); Jacques Baudou, "Bibliographie critique," pp. 81-92 (E2970); André Pommeraud, "Véryniana," pp. 93-95 (E2995); A. Pommeraud, "Filmographie," pp. 96-99; Michel Lebrun, "Mes victoires de Marignan |My Marignan victories|," p. 100 (account of two meetings with Very).

E2979. Bordillon, Henri. "Chronos assassin |Time the assassin|." Enigmatika 15 (May 80), pp. 50-51.
On Véry's radio anecdote, "Snouk ou le rendez-vous des enfants prodiges," broadcast on June 27, 1957.

E2980. ______. "Du mensonge dans le roman policier: hypothèse à propos de L'Assassinat du Père Noël |On lying in the detective novel: a hypothesis on L'Assassinat du Père Noël|." Enigmatika 15 (May 80), pp. 47-49.
Although it is commonly accepted that the writer of detective fiction can lie only to a certain point at which he must tell the truth, one of Véry's "merits" is that he violated this convention in his novel L'Assassinat du Père Noël.

E2981. ______. "La preuve par sept |Proof by seven|." Enigmatika 15 (May 80), pp. 19-22.
A reading of Véry's novel Série de sept which is an illustration of his ambiguous relationship with the traditional detective novel.

E2982. Couegnas, Daniel. "Le costume des dimanches, enquête sur les sentiers du temps perdu |Sunday dress, an investigation along the paths of time past|." Enigmatika 15 (May 80), pp. 34-43.
Unlike other popular authors, Véry worked comfortably with the conventions of detective fiction, adapting it to his needs and creating an original form from "worn-out" materials.

E2983. ______. "Double Assassinat au 221 B, Baker Street: création, innovation et imagination chez Pierre Véry |Double murder at 221B, Baker street: creation, innovation and imagination in Pierre Véry|." Enigmatika 15 (May 80), pp. 23-31.
Véry experimented with the form of the detective novel to make of it an exercise that "enlightens" our reflexions on the nature of literary creation.

E2984. ______. "L'invention romanesque véryienne: un univers linguistique en

expansion |Véry's novelistic inventiveness: an expanding linguistic universe|." Europe no. 636 (April 82), pp. 46-52.
Examples of the way in which Véry takes apparently insignificant linguistic details and develops them in the text of his novels.

E2985. Demouzon, Alain. "L'enfant, le voyage et la mort." Europe no. 636 (April 82):53-57.
A thematic study in which Demouzon describes Very's reconciliation of childhood and maturity, of the work as an adventurous voyage, and of the basic preoccupation as an obssesion with death.

E2986. ______. "Lettre à Annie Matiquat." Enigmatika 15 (May 80), pp. 15-19.
This informal discussion of Véry consists principally of an interview with Father René Taroux who was a student at the Ecole Sainte-Marie de Meaux at the same time as Véry. Father René describes incidents which Véry used later in his fiction.

E2987. Dubourg, Maurice. "Pierre Véry et le fantastique." Europe no. 636 (April 82), pp. 32-47.
Fantastic elements in Véry's early novels in which Dubourg also finds elements that will be developed in the later work, including the detective fiction.

E2988. Gayot, Paul. "L'écriture selon Véry: essai simiologique |Style according to Véry: a simiological essay|." Europe no. 636 (April 82), pp. 57-60.
An analysis of Véry's novel Clavier universel which Gayot sees as a meditation on the creative process.

E2989. ______. "Pillards, billards, procédés, carambolages et séries |Pillaging, billiards, methods, cannons and series|." Enigmatika 15 (May 80), pp. 61-62.
A brief commentary on the method of connecting a series of crimes by a common link. Gayot finds that Véry used this technique infrequently.

E2990. ______. "Ronde autour du 'meneur de jeu' |Dance around the 'leader of the game'|." Enigmatika 15 (May 80), pp. 52-55.
In Véry's Meneur de jeu a character announces that he is aware of being a character in a novel. Gayot uses this as the point of departure for a series of other possible formulations (the novelist as character, a character as reader, etc.).

E2991. Lacassin, Francis. "Pierre Véry ou la police au pays des fées |P. Véry or police in fairyland|." In Lacassin (B201), Vol. 2, pp. 41-113.
A discussion of elements (dream, the marvellous, the unusual and childhood) that make Véry's detective novels like "no others." With a bibliography and a filmography.

E2992. Lebrun, Michel. "Dis-moi qui tu fréquentes... |Tell me with whom you associate...|." Europe no. 636 (April 82), pp. 100-102.
Lebrun lists the people to whom Véry has dedicated his novels and who constitute his "intimates."

E2993. Olivier-Martin, Yves. "L'invisible rendez-vous |The invisible rendez-vous|." Europe no. 636 (April 82), pp. 93-100.
The year 1930, a time of transition for Véry, and the date of publication of his "promenade-novel," Pont-Egaré.

E2994. "Pierre Véry." Europe no. 636 (April 82):1-138.

A collection of essays on Véry's life and work. Contents: Pierre Siniac, "Quelques petites choses sur le magicien Véry," pp. 3-9 (E2998); Jacques Baudou, "Pierre Véry, l'enchanteur assassin," pp. 10-19 (E2973); Pierre Véry, "Les enfances Léonard," pp. 21-23 (childhood reading and memories); P. Véry, "Mac Orlan sur Saint-Cyr-sur-Morin," pp. 24-29 (reminiscences); "Quelques opinions sur Pierre Véry |Some opinions about P. Véry|," pp. 30-31 (comments by writers); Maurice Dubourg, "Pierre Véry et le fantastique," pp. 32-46 (E2987); Daniel Couegnas, "L'invention romanesque véryienne: un univers linguistique en expansion," pp. 46-52 (E2984); Alain Demouzon, "L'enfant, le voyage et la mort," pp. 53-57 (E2985); Paul Gayot, "L'écriture selon Pierre Véry: essai simiologique," pp. 57-60 (E2988); Jacques Baudou, "Jouez magie," pp. 61-79 (E2972); François Raymond, "Variations sur un quatuor," pp. 70-77 (E2996); Roger Bozzetto, "Pierre Véry: une rencontre avec la science-fiction," pp. 78-86 (Véry and science-fiction); Daniel Compère, "Vision et prévision," pp. 87-92 (Véry's science-fiction works); Yves Olivier-Martin, "L'invisible rendez-vous," pp. 93-100 (E2993); Michel Lebrun, "Dis-moi qui tu fréquentes," pp. 100-102 (E2992); François Rivière, "Un garçon disparaît ou le roman de Mathieu Sorgues," pp. 103-106 (E2997); Pierre Véry, "Jacques l'enchanteur," pp. 108-17 (short story); François Guérif, "Pierre Véry et le cinéma," pp. 118-27 (annotated filmography); Claude Beylie, "Le 'cinéma imprimé' de Pierre Véry," pp. 127-130 (on Véry's film scenarios); Pierre Véry, "Esprit de Stendhal, es-tu là...?," pp. 131-34 (essay on Stendhal); Pierre Véry, "Pour m'excuser d'un article déchiré," pp. 134-38 (films and filmmakers).

E2995. Pommeraud, André. "Véryniana." Enigmatika 15 (May 80), pp. 93-95.
A bibliography listing Véry's short stories, prefaces, and articles; in addition, there is a very useful bibliography of secondary sources including interviews, and critical articles in books, journals and newspapers.

E2996. Raymond, François. "Variations sur un quatuor |Variations on a quartet|." Europe no. 636 (April 82), pp. 70-77.
Numerical variations in Véry's Les quatre vipères.

E2997. Rivière, François. "Un garçon disparaît ou le roman de Mathieu Sorgues |A boy disappears or the novel of Mathieu Sorgues|." Europe no. 636 (April 82), pp. 103-106.
The writer's apprenticeship of an adolescent protagonist in Véry's Les Disparus de Saint-Agil.

E2998. Siniac, Pierre. "Quelques petites choses sur le magicien Véry |A few little things about the magician Véry)." Europe no. 636 (April 1982), pp. 3-9.
A writer of detective novels recounts his infatuation with the work of the poet of the mystery story, Pierre Véry.

VICKERS, ROY

Ref: Hubin 2, TCCMW, EMD, CC, ABMI(S); Pike, TPP 5:1 (July 82):10-18.

E2999. Bleiler, E. F. "Introduction" to The Department of Dead Ends, pp. iii-viii. NY: Dover, 1978.
A survey of Vickers' crime fiction, concluding with a reflective note on Vickers' predilection for the use of the name "Rason."

E3000. McCarthy, Paul. "Eureka! More Stories by Roy Vickers." TPP 5:4 (Oct 83):31-32.
A listing of 18 previously unrecorded stories published in The Novel Magazine, 1914-17, under Vickers' own name and one of his pseudonyms, Sefton Kyle.

E3001. ______. "The Short Stories of Roy Vickers." TPP 5:1 (July 82):3-9.
A bibliography giving first magazine appearance and anthology/collection publication. There is also an alternate title index. See TPP 5:4 (Oct 83):32 for corrections and Pike's Profile (TPP 5:1:10-18) for additions.

E3002. Purcell, Mark. "Roy Vickers: The 'Dept. of Dead Ends' Series, A Partial Bibliography." TMRN 4:1 (Oct 70):29-31.
Collections of short stories are given with a list of contents and date of publication in EQMM. Uncollected stories from EQMM are also listed and there is some information on English anthologies and non-DDE collections.

E3003. Queen, Ellery. "Introduction" to The Department of Dead Ends, pp. 3-4. Bestseller Mystery B91. NY: Lawrence E. Spivak, 1977.
In his introduction to this first publication of a collection of "Dead Ends" stories, Queen characterizes them as "inverted" tales that so induce the "suspension of disbelief" the reader "forgets" that he is reading fiction.

E3004. Vickers, Roy. "Introduction" to Best Detective Stories of Roy Vickers. London: Faber and Faber, 1965. Not seen.

VIDAL, GORE. See BOX, EDGAR

VIDOCQ, FRANCOIS EUGENE

Ref: Hubin 2, EMD, ABMI.

See also: B179, E2182.

E3005. Edwards, Samuel. The Vidocq Dossier: The Story of the World's First Detective. Boston: Houghton Mifflin, 1977. 191pp. Bibliography.
A biography.

VILLESVIK, LINDA

Ref: Lachman, TPP 1:4 (July 78):15.

VILLIERS, GERARD DE

Ref: Hubin 2, CC.

See also: C237.

E3006. Donaldson-Evans, Lance K. "The Anatomy of a Spy Novel: Gérard de Villiers and the Modern French Roman d'espionnage." Clues 2:2 (Fall/Winter 81):28-36.
De Villiers' Prince Malko von Linge, a contemporary spy hero and descendant of Jean Bruce's OSS 117, is profiled and the structure of de Villiers' fictional world is examined.

VIVIAN, E. CHARLES. See MANN, JACK

VULLIAMY, C. E.

Ref: Hubin 2, TCCMW, EMD, CC, ABMI(S).

E3007. Shibuk, Charles. "Notes on C. E. Vulliamy." TAD 3 (1969/70):161; 5 (1971/72):145.
A brief biography and an annotated list of his novels with critical comments. For additions, see R. C. S. Adey, letter TAD 4 (1970/71):124.

WADE, HENRY

Ref: Hubin 2, TCCMW, EMD, CC, ABMI(S); Pike, TPP 4:5/6 (Dec 81):45-48.

E3008. Barzun, Jacques, and Taylor, Wendell Hertig. "Preface" to The Dying Alderman (London, 1930), by Henry Wade. In A Book of Prefaces (B17), pp. 105-106.

E3009. Shibuk, Charles. "Henry Wade." TAD 1 (1967/68):111-15; with additions by Shibuk in TAD 2 (1968/69):45 and by R. C. S. Adey in TAD 2:279. Revised and reprinted in Nevins (B290), pp. 88-97.
Shibuk compares Wade's work to that of Freeman Wills Crofts but finds his characterizations more probing than Crofts'. With an annotated bibliography.

E3010. Wade, Henry. "Murder. A Reply to Richard Keverne." Constable's Quarterly no. 3 (Autumn 1931), pp. 21-24.
Keverne had asked: "Need it always be murder?" Wade replies emphatically, in the affirmative. (RCSA)

WAGER, WALTER

Ref: Hubin 2, ABMI(S).

Int: DAST 12:1 (1979):30, 32 (photo).

E3011. Hedman, Iwan. "Walter Wager." DAST 14:4 (1981):44-47.
Descriptive article on Wager's life and works. (MS)

WAHLOO, PER. See SJOWALL, MAJ

WAINWRIGHT, JOHN

Ref: Hubin 2, TCCMW, ABMI(S).

WALLACE, EDGAR

Ref: Hubin 2, TCCMW, EMD, CC, SN, ABMI(S).

See also: B20, C183, D316, D327, E1020, E1308.

E3012. Cameron, James. "Edgar Wallace: Fiction Factory." The Listener 95 (1 April 76):403-404.
A sympathetic look at the life and times of the prolific author. (RCSA)

E3013. Curtis, Robert C. Edgar Wallace---Each Way. London: John Lane, n.d. (1932). 254pp. Illus.
"Edgar Wallace did not write his most thrilling story; he lived it...." Entertaining memoir of Wallace by his long-time secretary. Breen 226. (REB)

E3014. Doran, George H. "The Mysteryists." In Chronicles of Barrabas, pp. 272-80. NY: Harcourt & Brace, 1935.

Doran was the publisher and a friend of Wallace. He describes Wallace's prodigious energy and talks about his family and his writing.

E3015. "Dossier Edgar Wallace." Le Fulmar no. 1 (1981):5-54.
Miscellaneous material on Wallace, primarily as a writer of thrillers and adventure stories. The items will not be annotated separately but will be briefly summarized in the contents listing. Contents: Pascal Martinet, "Wallace l'épicurien," pp. 5-7 (biography); Pascal Martinet, "Edgar Wallace et la science-fiction," p. 7 (description of Wallace's Planetoid 127); Yves Olivier-Martin, "Le Fantastique chez Edgar Wallace," pp. 8-9 (fantastic elements in several novels); P. Martinet, "Wallace: imitateurs, plagiaires et continuateurs," pp. 10-12 (the posthumous publications and the Wallace imitators); P. Martinet, "Bibliographie," pp. 13-14 (a chronological listing, by year and English title, of Wallace's novels); François Ducos, "Bibliographie française," pp. 15-20 (a listing, by publisher, of Wallace's works published in French editions); P. Martinet, "Edgar Wallace au cinéma," pp. 23-36 (narrative history, principally of the Wallace German film revival that began in 1959); Pierre Charles and P. Martinet, "Filmographie," pp. 39-53 (a chronological filmography, followed by an article by P. Charles on Wallace films, with much of the discussion devoted to German adaptations); P. Charles, "Edgar Wallace et la bande dessinée," p. 54 (comic strip adaptations of Wallace's Inspector Wade stories; with two daily strips as examples).

E3016. Edgar Wallace. Boston, MA: Small, Maynard & Co., circa 1920. 11pp. Wraps.
Promotional pamphlet issued by Wallace's American publishers. (REB)

E3017. Edgar Wallace Almanach. Goldmann, 1983.
In Germany, Edgar Wallace remains the no. 1 star of the detective novel. This almanach, published by Goldmann, Wallace's German publisher, contains texts by Penelope Wallace, Graham Greene, Margaret Lane, Edgar Wallace, Wallace Haas and Kurt Seeberger. With a bibliography in English and in German. (Annie Matiquat)

E3018. Edgar Wallace Society Newsletter (EWSN). Ed/Pub: Penelope Wallace. 4 Bradmore Road, Oxford, OX2 6QW England. Quarterly newsletter; first issue, January 1969.
A prime source of biographical and critical material on Wallace. Articles include reminiscences, quotations from letters and newspapers of the 1920s, and critical reviews of Wallace material on radio, stage, and screen, as well as published material. Of particular value is research based on direct examination of early magazines and newspapers not available in the United States. Each 6-page newsletter is accompanied by a reprint of obscure Wallace work. 58 issues to May 1983. Double-column typewritten pages, reproduced and stapled. (RS)

E3019. Greene, Graham. "Edgar Wallace." In Collected Essays, pp. 226-31. NY: Viking, 1969.
Slight. On Wallace's gift of invention and the waste of his natural talent.

E3020. Haas, Willy. "Die Theologie in Kriminalroman |Theology in the crime novel|." Die literarische Welt 26, 1929, pp. 5 f.; reprinted in Vogt (B424), Vol I, pp. 116-22.
Subtitle: "A Few Notes on Edgar Wallace and Crime Fiction in General." A tongue-in-cheek look at typical plot and structural elements in Wallace's novels and likens them to theological concepts. (GG)

E3021. Hogan, John A. "Exhumation of The Tomb of Ts'in." TAD 6 (1972/73):167-71.
A discussion of the composition and publishing history of Wallace's thriller.

E3022. ______. "The Mission that Succeeded." EWSN 48 (Nov 80):4.
Discusses Edgar Wallace series fiction published in the newspapers, The Sunday Post and The Weekly News. (RS)

E3023. ______. "Seek and You Will Find." EWSN no. 26 (June 75), p. 3.
Discusses the publication history of The Adventures of Heine, The Big Four and The Brigand. (RS)

E3024. ______. "Some Bits and Pieces." EWSN no. 54 (May 82), p. 4.
Discusses little-known Wallace books and origins of The Brigand series. (RS)

E3025. ______. "Stranger than Fiction." TAD 9 (1975/76):119-21.
True crime writings by Edgar Wallace.

E3025a. Hubbard, D. C. "Popular Detective Story Writers: Edgar Wallace." Detective Story Magazine 103:2 (1 Sept 28):122-24.
A lightly romanticized biographical sketch of Wallace's childhood and young manhood to about 1906 with some detail on his military service and activities as a war correspondent during the Boer war. His mystery and detective stories are only sketchily mentioned. It would appear that Wallace provided a substantial amount of material from which this article was drawn; the anecdotal material given is of considerable interest. (RS)

E3026. Hubin, Allen et al. "Edgar Wallace: A Checklist." TAD 1 (1967-68):72-81.
A bibliography compiled by Hubin from various sources and with the assistance of Norman Donaldson and Herbert A. Smith. The books are listed chronologically with dates of first English and American publication given, although publishers are not included. Titles are given for stories in collections.

E3027. Kiddle, Charles A. A Guide to the First Editions of Edgar Wallace. Morcombe, Dorset, England: The Ivory Head Press, 1981. 88pp. Wraps. Edition limited to 1000 numbered copies. Illus.
A bibliography of first United Kingdom and American editions; no information on reprints or foreign-language editions.

E3028. Lai, Rick. "The Trail of the Feathered Serpent." Echoes 2:2 (Oct 83):26-27.
The feathered serpent motif in Wallace's The Feathered Serpent, and in Doc Savage and the Shadow novels.

E3029. Lane, Margaret. Edgar Wallace: The Biography of a Phenomenon. London: Heinemann, 1938; revised edition, 1964. Garden City, NY: Doubleday, 1939. Illustrated. Index.
Lengthy and superbly written life of one of the crime genre's most prolific and popular entertainers. The revised edition has a foreword by Graham Greene. Breen 227. (REB)

E3030. Lofts, W. O. G., and Adley, Derek. The British Bibliography of Edgar

Wallace. Preface by Leslie Charteris and Introduction by Penelope Wallace. London: Howard Baker, 1979. xv, 246pp.

British magazine and book publications of Edgar Wallace's works are listed and described in several arrangements. There are checklists of books arranged chronologically and alphabetically, with complete bibliographic details for all first editions. Then, in one of the two main portions of the bibliography (pp. 36-143), the contents of each book are listed and matched with the original periodical appearances. Opening lines of short stories and serial installments are given. In the second main portion of the bibliography (pp. 155-246), Wallace's magazine stories and serials are listed according to the magazine in which they first appeared, with cross-references to book editions. First lines are again given, as well as details of reprint appearances. There are also checklists of anthology appearances, plays, true-crime articles, and miscellanea. (REB)

E3031. Lofts, W. O. G. "Collecting Edgar Wallace." Antiquarian Book Monthly Review 4:8 (Aug 77):310-17.

Wallace looked at largely from the publishing and writing points of view. Lots of interesting facts emerge. Profusely illustrated. (RCSA)

E3032. Morland, Nigel. "The Edgar Wallace I Knew." TAD 1 (1967/68):68-70.

Biographical observations on Wallace, incorporating material from conversations.

E3033. Priestly, J. B. "A Holiday with the Bodies." The Saturday Review, 3 July 26, pp. 8-10.

On the pleasures of the "literature of sensation" so well exploited by Edgar Wallace.

E3034. Sorani, Aldo. "Edgar Wallace." Pegaso, March 1932, pp. 360-64.

The author returns to the distinction between the adventure novel (or popular novel) and the detective novel. He sees in Wallace a master of the "popular novel with a base of criminal intrigues and police problems" and he recognizes in him some fundamental innovations: the elimination from the narration of the excessive sentimentality and literary baggage of the Gothic novel of the 18th century and the serial-novel of the 19th century; understanding the plot as a close succession of actions and reducing the writing to a chronicle; taking as a model the language of the cinema and of the newspaper. The popular novelist, distancing himself from the literary writer, always resembles more closely the reporter and the popular novel assumes characteristics of a realistic genre as long as it is read like the newspaper report. (RC)

E3035. Staglieno, Marcello. "Wallace, un artigiano di emozioni |Wallace, an artisan of emotions|." Il Giornale, 16 Feb 82.

A substantial commemorative article, on the 50th anniversary of Wallace's death. "Yes, Wallace was certainly an artisan of emotions. But in his place there is today an industry which manufactures sub-products of emotion in series, scarcely manipulating its ingredients." (RC)

E3036. Stewart, J. I. M. "The Exploits of Edgar Wallace." Times (London), 6 Feb 82.

One-page article. Not seen. (REB)

E3037. Symons, Julian. "Introduction." In The Mind of Mr. J. G. Reeder (Hodder, 1925; U. S. title: The Murder Book of Mr. J. G. Reeder), by

Edgar Wallace. Classic Thrillers Series. London: J. M. Dent, 1983.

E3038. Thomson, H. Douglas. "The Wallace Collection." In Thomson (B404), pp. 222-29.
Thomson admits that he is not a Wallace fan and his essay is a run-through of the usual comments on Wallace's output and on his sacrifice of quality for quantity. Thomson groups Wallace's novels into 4 categories and discusses only the detective novels.

E3039. Touchant, Jean-Louis. "Edgar Wallace 1." Amis du crime 11 (Nov 81). 36pp. Illus.
Touchant discusses his infatuation with the work of Edgar Wallace and comments on the publication history and contents of the fiction that has been translated into French. A personal, absorbing narrative. "Edgar Wallace 2" not seen.

E3040. Usborne, Richard. "Edgar Wallace: A Voluminous Life." Radio Times 210, no. 2733 (27 March - 2 April 76), pp. 4-5.
An assessment of the popular author. Lots of photos. (RCSA)

E3041. Wallace, Edgar. My Hollywood Diary. London: Hutchinson, n.d. (1932). 259pp. Illus. Not seen. (REB)

E3042. ______. "Mystery Stories To-day and Yesterday." The Bookman 77, no. 459 (Dec 29):175-77.
Wallace sets forth some of the general principles of construction and style he used in his crime stories, with references to good (Doyle and Collins) and bad (Gaboriau) examples of the genre. Wallace concludes with an amusing example of the "least likely person" technique from his own work. (REB)

E3043. ______. People: A Short Autobiography. London: Hodder & Stoughton, 1926; reissued under the title Edgar Wallace: A Short Autobiography, 1929. xix, 234pp. No illus. or index. U. S. Edition: People: The Autobiography of a Mystery Writer. Prefatory essay, "Edgar Wallace---The Legend" (pp. ix-xix) by Anice Page Cooper. Garden City, NY: Doubleday (The Crime Club), 1929. (Note: On the U. S. edition, the subtitle appears only on the spine of the book, not inside.)
Chatty, informal reminscences covering Wallace's life and career through 1920. Breen 229. (REB)

E3044. Wallace, Ethel V. Edgar Wallace by His Wife. London: Hutchinson, (1932). 287pp. Illustrated. Index.
Reminiscences. Not seen. Breen 230.

E3045. Wallace, Penelope. Edgar Wallace (1875-1932):A Short Biography. Oxford, England: Penelope Wallace, 1965. pp. (1-4; pages not numbered). Large 4to, single folded sheet. (REB)

WALLACE, FRANCIS

Ref: Hubin 2; UN 5:2 (1952):10-11 (photo).

WALLING, R. A. J.

Ref: Hubin 2, TCCMW, EMD, CC, ABMI(S).

WALSH, THOMAS

Ref: Hubin 2, TCCMW, CC, SN; Lachman, TPP 2:1 (Jan/Feb 79):15-19.

Int: EQMM, 10 Sept 80, p. 86.

WAMBAUGH, JOSEPH

Ref: Hubin 2, TCCMW, ABMI(S).

Int: Hartford Courant, 16 Dec 73 (rpt. in Authors in the News 1, p. 490; photo); Atlanta Journal, 28 Dec 74 (rpt. in Authors in the News 1, p. 492; photo); News-American (Baltimore), 25 Sept 74 (rpt. in Authors in the News 1, p. 492); NYTBR, 15 Jan 78, p. 25; Playboy 26:7 (1979):69-70+; Pittsburgh Press, 6 June 81, p. A-10 (photo); Pittsburgh Post-Gazette, 8 June 81, p. 21 (photo).

E3046. Reed, J. D. "Those Blues in the Knights." Time, 8 June 81, pp. 76-79. Essay-review of The Glitter Dome (Morrow, 1981) and an informal look at Wambaugh's novels and career. Includes an excerpt from the novel and a photo of Wambaugh. (GG)

E3047. Roberts, Steven V. "Cop of the Year." Esquire, Dec 73, pp. 150-53, 310, 314.
A portrait of Wambaugh incorporating material from interviews with him, his friends and associates.

E3048. Ziegler, Robert E. "Freedom and Confinement: The Policeman's Experience of Public and Private in Joseph Wambaugh." Clues 3:1 (Spring/Summer 82):9-16.
The tension between the policeman's public duty and private life in the context of a theoretical discussion of the varying attractions of open space and confinement.

WARD, ARTHUR HENRY SARSFIELD. See ROHMER, SAX

WARRINER, THURMAN. See TROY, SIMON

"WATERS"

Ref: Hubin 2, TCCMW, EMD, ABMI.

E3049. Osborne, Eric. "The First Professional Detective in English Fiction." "Introduction" in Recollections of a Detective Police Officer, by "Waters" (William Russell), not paginated. London: Covent Garden Press, Ltd., 1972. Edition limited to 350 copies.
An annotated bibliographic preface, tracing the publication history of the book.

WATSON, COLIN

Ref: Hubin 2, TCCMW, EMD, CC, ABMI(S); Pike, TPP 4:2 (Apr 81):21-23.

E3050. Barzun, Jacques, and Taylor, Wendell Hertig. "Introduction." In Just What the Doctor Ordered (NY, 1969), by Colin Watson. "Crime Fiction 1950-1975" (B18).

WAUGH, HILLARY

Ref: Hubin 2, TCCMW, EMD, CC, SN, ABMI; The Writer 82:12 (Dec 69): 9-11, 28 (plotting and characterization).

Int: DAST 8:2 (1975):5-7 (photo & overview of work); EQMM, Oct 77, pp. 97-8.

See also: B96, B309.

E3051. Barzun, Jacques, and Taylor, Wendell Hertig. "Introduction." In The Missing Man (NY, 1964), by Hillary Waugh. "Crime Fiction 1950-1975" (B18).

E3052. Blom, K. Arne. "Hillary Waughs Polisrofmaner--II. Fred C. Fellows |Hillary Waugh's police novels. II. Fred C. Fellows|." DAST 9:6 (1976):3-5. (MS)

E3053. ______. "Hillary Waughs polisromaner -- Del III - Frank Sessions." DAST 10:2 (1976):41-42. (MS)

E3054. Dove, George N. "Introduction." In Waugh (E3057), pp. vii-xv.
An essay on the plot and structure of Last Seen Wearing with some concluding remarks on Waugh's other work.

E3055. "Hillary Waugh." Hard-Boiled Dicks 6 (1982).
Not seen but described in Enigmatika 25 as consisting of a bibliography and filmography, an article by George Dove, and an article by Waugh on the police procedural.

E3056. Waugh, Hillary. "Afterword." In Waugh (E3057), pp. 253-59.
Waugh describes the genesis and writing of Last Seen Wearing. For additional comments by Waugh on this novel, see also pp. 274, 277, and 279-80.

E3057. ______. Last Seen Wearing (1952). Edited by George Dove. Mystery Library Series (B270): no. 11. 1978. Illustrated by Jamie Simon. Photo. xv, 282pp.
Contents: George N. Dove, "Introduction," pp. vii-xv (E3054); Last Seen Wearing, pp. 1-251; Hillary Waugh, "Afterword," pp. 253-59 (E3056); Francis M. Nevins, Jr., "Hillary Waugh: A Checklist," pp. 262-64 (bibliography of primary sources); C. David Hellyer, "A Biographical Sketch of Hillary Waugh," pp. 265-269 (interview/biography); Reviews, illustrations, pp. 270-73; Hillary Waugh, excerpts from diary and letter, pp. 274, 277, 279-80 (on the writing of the novel).

WAYLAND, PATRICK

Ref: Hubin 2, TCCMW, ABMI.

WEBB, JACK

Ref: Hubin 2, TCCMW (E3058); The Writer 76:10 (Oct 63):17-20, 44.

E3058. Landrum, Larry N. "Jack Webb." In Reilly (A143), pp. 1452-52.
Writer Jack Webb and TV producer/actor/director Jack Webb are confused in an entry that combines their two careers.

WEBSTER, HENRY KITCHELL

Ref: Hubin 2, EMD, CC, ABMI(S).

E3059. Barzun, Jacques, and Taylor, Wendell Hertig. Preface to Who is the Next? (Indianapolis, 1931), by Henry Kitchell Webster. In A Book of Prefaces (B17), pp. 107-108.

E3060. Taylor, Wendell Hertig. "Henry Kitchell Webster: The Emergence of an American Mystery-Writer." TAD 5 (1971/72):199-201.
The effect on Webster's mystery-writing career of the "overwhelmingly

feminine control of the American mystery-genre" and an annotated list of eight of his novels.

WELCOME, JOHN

Ref: Hubin 2, TCCMW, CC, ABMI(S).

WELLMAN, MANLY WADE

Ref: Hubin 2, EMD, ABMI(S); The Writer 61:8 (Aug 48):261-64 (characterization).

E3060a. Pocsik, John. "A Man Named John." In The Conan Grimoire, edited by L. Sprague de Camp and George H. Scithers, pp. 124-29. Illus. by Roy G. Krenkel.

A brief history of psychic detectives followed by a summary of the plots of the John Thunstone series written by Wellman and published in Weird Tales in the early 1940s. Pocsik does not particularly like the English psychic detectives and states that fans of Robert E. Howard might enjoy the series character conception but dislike the "vagueness" of the style of a writer like Algernon Blackwood and the "lack of really two-fisted action." A non-academic piece that does convey some of the writer's enthusiasm for the Wellman stories. It might be noted that these stories were reprinted in Lonely Vigils (Carcosa House, 1981) in a selection of other stories including his other psychic detectives, Judge Pursuivant and Professor Nathan Enderby.

WELLS, CAROLYN

Ref: Hubin 2, TCCMW, EMD, CC, ABMI(S).

Int: Christian Science Monitor Magazine, 21 Oct 39, p. 6 (photo).

E3061. Breen, Jon. "On Carolyn Wells." TAD 3 (1969/70):77-79.

A brief survey of Wells' contributions to the field with a chronological bibliography of her detective novels giving date of publication, publisher and series detective.

E3062. Wells, Carolyn. The Rest of My Life. Philadelphia: Lippincott, 1937. 395pp. Illustrated. Index.

Informally organized commentary on many subjects, including scattered mention of detective fiction and a chapter on book collecting. Breen 231. (REB)

WELLS, TOBIAS. See FORBES, STANTON

WENTWORTH, PATRICIA

Ref: Hubin 2, TCCMW, EMD, CC, ABMI(S); Pike, TPP 5:3 (May/June 83):29-35; UN 1:5 (1948):6-7; UN 2:10 (1950):10-11.

E3063. Amelin, Michel. "Patricia Wentworth." Enigmatika 25 (Nov 83), pp. 3-9.

A biography, a bibliography, and an appreciative tribute to Wentworth and her private detective, Maud Silver.

E3064. Wynne, Nancy Blue. "Patricia Wentworth Revisited." TAD 14 (1981):90-92. Illustrations.

An overview of Wentworth's life and work with a bibliography of primary sources.

WEST, JOHN B.

Ref: Hubin 2, ABMI.

E3065. Turner, Darwin T. "The Rocky Steele Novels of John B. West." TAD 6 (1972/73):226-31; reprinted in Landrum (B216), pp. 140-48.
A paperback series by a black novelist about a white private investigator in the Mike Hammer tradition; the six novels in the series were published from 1959 to 1961.

WESTLAKE, DONALD E.

Ref: Hubin 2, TCCMW, EMD, SN, ABMI(S); Writer's Digest 39:9 (Sept 59):26-29, 80 (plotting).

Int: EQMM, Nov 76, pp. 91-2; Jury 7:4 (1978):5-11; Polar 22 (15 Jan 82):5-11 (photos).

See also: C735, E1294.

E3066. Bakerman, Jane S. "Patterns of Guilt and Isolation in Five Novels by 'Tucker Coe.'" TAD 12 (1979):118-21.
A character study of psychological patterns in the Mitch Tobin series.

E3067. Block, Lawrence. "Introduction." In The Mourner, by Richard Stark. Gregg Press Mystery Fiction Series (B134).

E3068. DeAndrea, William L. "Introduction." In The Score, by Richard Stark. Gregg Press Mystery Fiction Series (B134).

E3069. Deloux, Jean-Pierre. "Parker le voleur |Parker the thief|." Polar 22 (15 Jan 82):18-29.
A "modest" attempt to construct a psychological portrait of the enigmatic Parker.

E3070. "Dossier Donald E. Westlake." Polar 22 (15 Jan 82):5-68. Illustrated. Contents: François Guérif, "Entretien avec Donald E. Westlake," pp. 5-11 (interview; photo); Donald E. Westlake, "L'imbroglio Mulligan," pp. 13-17 (short story); Jean-Pierre Deloux, "Parker le voleur," pp. 18-29 (E3069); Westlake/Richard Stark/Tucker Coe/Timothy J. Culver, "J'entends des voix dans ma tête," pp. 30-41 (E3081); Jean-Pierre Manchette, "Notes sur l'usage du stéréotype chez Donald Westlake," pp. 42-44 (E3075); Jean-François Naudon, "Bibliographie de Donald Westlake," pp.. 45-58; Jean-Jacques Schleret, "Filmographie commentée de Donald Westlake," pp. 60-68 (stills; annotated filmography).

E3071. Garfield, Brian. "Introduction." In The Outfit, by Richard Stark. Gregg Press Mystery Fiction Series (B134).

E3072. Kennedy, Veronica S. M. Letter, TAD 6 (1972/73):127/8.
A critical note in which Kennedy points out a possible intentional borrowing by Westlake from Husymans' novel A rebours (Paris: Charpentier, 1884).

E3073. Kimball, Clay. Letter, TAD 8 (1974/75):76.
Kimball speculates that Westlake, in the Stark/Parker series, is rewriting Hammett: Killtown is based on "The Big Knockover," and The Mourner on The Maltese Falcon.

E3074. Kodaka, Nobumitsu, and Westlake, Donald E. "Donald E. Westlake: A Checklist. October 1974." TAD 8 (1974/75):203-205.
A bibliography of fiction and articles by Donald E. Westlake/Richard Stark/Tucker Coe. Addenda by Frank D. McSherry, Jr. in letter, TAD 8:319.

E3075. Manchette, Jean-Patrick. "Notes sur l'usage du stéréotype chez Donald Westlake |Notes on the use of stereotype in the work of Donald Westlake|." Polar 22 (15 Jan 82), pp. 42-44.
Manchette distinguishes 4 stages of the plot structure in the Stark novels and observes that the recent, humorous novels signed by Westlake can be considered as pastiches of the Parker capers.

E3076. Nevins, Francis M., Jr. "Walls of Guilt: Donald E. Westlake as Tucker Coe." TAD 7 (1973/74):163-64.
A survey of the Tucker Coe Mitch Tobin series.

E3077. Nussbaum, Albert F. "Introduction." In The Seventh, by Richard Stark. Gregg Press Mystery Fiction Series (B134).

E3078. The ParkerPhile. A fanzine for Westlake/Stark/Coe readers published irregularly by Coe-Stark Associates, c/o D. Kingsley Hahn, 1495 Magnolia Avenue East No. 2, St. Paul, MN 55106. 5 issues in Volume 1 appeared from December 1982 to September 1983.
Biographical, bibliographical and critical material on Westlake and his various pseudonyms is the focus of this fanzine which may have succumbed after 5 well-produced issues. The most potentially interesting item is an "Attempt at a Bibliography" of which four installments have been published.

E3079. Scott, Justin. "Introduction." In The Man with the Getaway Face, by Richard Stark. Gregg Press Mystery Fiction Series (B134).

E3080. Stark, Richard. "Introduction." In The Hunter, by Richard Stark. Gregg Press Mystery Fiction Series (B134).

E3081. Westlake, Donald E. et al. "J'entends des voix dans ma tête |I hear voices in my head|." Polar 22 (15 Jan 82):30-41. Photos.
This purports to be the transcript of a session during which Westlake and his alter egos (Stark, Coe and Culver) answer questions about their work and about the state of detective fiction. There is a certain amount of playing around but some information is furnished on the writing of the novels and on Westlake's opinion of the deplorable state of detective fiction in the last 20 years.

WESTON, CAROLYN

Ref: Hubin 2, TCCMW, SN, ABMIS.

WEYMOUTH, ANThONY

Ref: Hubin 2, CC, ABMIS; Pike, TPP 4:3 (June 81):13-14.

WHEATLEY, DENNIS

Ref: Hubin 2, TCCMW, EMD, CC, ABMI(S).

Int: Listener 97 (13 Jan 77):2491; The Writer 17:12 (Sept 37):309-10.

E3082. Gadney, Reg. "The Murder Dossiers of Dennis Wheatley and J. G.

Links." London Magazine (new series) 8:12 (March 69):41-51. Illustrated.
A discussion of the four "murder dossiers" which includes details on how they came to be written, were marketed and were received. The writer, in his own words, speculates on the implications of their form. (RCSA)

E3083. Hedman, Iwan and Jan Alexandersson. Fyra decennier med Dennis Wheatley |Five decades with Dennis Wheatley|. Dast Dossier No. 1. Strängnäs, Sweden: Dast Forlag AB, 1973. 192pp. Illustrated. N.B.: A first edition was published in an edition of 4 copies in 1963; a second edition, of 100 numbered copies, was published in January, 1973.
A biography and a critical bibliography of first editions, with numerous photos, jacket illustrations, and correspondence of Wheatley (in English).

E3084. Hedman, Iwan. "Dennis Wheatley: A Biographical Sketch and Bibliography." TAD 2 (1968/69):227-36.
The biographical introduction contains several letters by Wheatley bearing on Wheatley's work. The bibliography is arranged chronologically and covers first editions and some reprints. Additions and corrections as follows: Oswald Train, letter TAD 3 (1969/70):68; Charles Shibuk 3:136.

E3085. Wheatley, Dennis. The Time Has Come.... The Memoirs of Dennis Wheatley. (Vol. 1) The Young Man Said, 1897. London: Hutchinson, 1977. 255pp. Illus. Index. (Vol. 2) Officer and Temporary Gentleman, 1914-1919. London: Hutchinson, 1978. 254pp. Illus. Index. (Vol. 3) Drink and Ink, 1919-1977. London: Hutchinson, May 1979, 278pp. Illus. Index. Breen 233, 234, 235.
The first two volumes of Wheatley's autobiographical trilogy may tell you more than you want to know about his early life, through the end of World War I. Volume 3 carries his story from that point almost down to his death at age 80 in November 1977, although the last thirty years are somewhat sketchily covered. "Drink" covers his life while helping to run the family wine business from 1919 to 1931. "Ink" covers his career as a prolific writer of thrillers and historical adventure novels from the publication of his first book, Forbidden Territory (written in response to a casual suggestion from his second wife) in 1933. Along the way we get comments on the Bacon-Shakespeare controversy, several brushes with the occult, and hints on market gardening and bricklaying. Wheatley's work for the British government in World War II, and in particular his involvement with the strategic planning for D-Day, has been kept for a separate volume on its own, and is not covered here. (REB)

WHEELER-NICHOLSON, MALCOLM

Ref: Hubin 2, ABMI(S); Argosy, 5 July 30.

WHITE, ETHEL LINA

Ref: Hubin 2, TCCMW, EMD, CC, ABMI(S); Pike, TPP 4:5/6 (Dec 81):48-49.

WHITE, JON MANCHIP

Ref: Hubin 2, TCCMW, ABMI(S).

WHITE, LIONEL

Ref: Hubin 2, TCCMW, CC, SN, ABMIS.

WHITE, R. J.

Ref: Hubin 2, CC, ABMIS; Pike, TPP 2:2 (March/April 79):24.

WHITE, T. H.

Ref: Hubin 2, ABMI(S); Pike, TPP 4:3 (June 81):14.

E3086. Crane, John K. "Dead Mr. Nixon and Darkness at Pemberley." In T. H. White, pp. 31-42. NY: Twayne Publishers, 1974.
Discussions of White's two detective novels.

WHITE, WILLIAM ANTHONY PARKER. See BOUCHER, ANTHONY

WHITECHURCH, VICTOR L.

Ref: Hubin 2, TCCMW, EMD, CC, ABMI(S); Pike, TPP 5:2 (Nov/Dec 82):23-24.

WHITFIELD, RAOUL

Ref: Hubin 2, TCCMW, EMD, CC, SN, ABMI; Argosy, 7 March 31.

See also: D343.

E3087. Hagemann, E. R. "Ramon Dacolta, a.k.a. Raoul Whitfield, and his Diminutive Brown Man: Joe Gar, the Island Detective." TAD 14 (1981):3-8.
A portrait of the Philippine detective who appeared in 24 stories in Black Mask (1933) and in stories in Cosmopolitan (1935, 1937). With a checklist of stories giving date and place of publication. For additions to checklist, see Frank D. McSherry, Jr., letter TAD 14:382 and John Apostolou, letter TAD 14:383.

E3088. ______. "Raoul Whitfield, A Star with the Mask." TAD 13 (1980): 179-84.
A biography of pulp writer Whitfield with an annotated Black Mask checklist. For corrections and additions, see William F. Nolan, letter TAD 14 (1981):72-73 and Bill Pronzini, letter TAD 14:73-74.

E3089. Hamill, Pete. "Introduction." In Green Ice (Knopf, 1930), by Raoul Whitfield. Gregg Press Mystery Fiction Series (B134).

WHITNEY, PHYLLIS

Ref: Hubin 2, TCCMW, EMD, ABMI(S); The Writer 59:4 (April 46):107-110 (characterization); The Writer 76:4 (April 63):14-18 (juvenile mystery); The Writer 80:2 (Feb 67):9-13, 42 (modern romantic suspense novel); The Writer 92:1 (Jan 79):11-15; The Writer 93:2 (Feb 80):11-14, 46; The Writer 94:3 (March 81):7-10 (planning characters).

Int: TMRN 2:4 (April 69):3-5.

WHITTINGTON, HARRY

Ref: Hubin 2, TCCMW, SN, ABMI(S).

Int: PQ 1:1 (Spring 78):13-15; Les Amis du crime (March 80):4-9; PQ 4:2 (Summer 81):17 (cover photo; interview includes list of pb originals). Magazine littéraire no. 194 (Apr 83):30-31 (in French).

E3090. Barson, Michael S. "Fires That Create - The Versatility and Craft of Harry Whittington." PQ 4:2 (Summer 81):13-16.
A concise survey of Whittington's work.

E3091. Crider, Bill. "Paperback Writers. (Harry Whittington)." PQ 1:1 (Spring 78):9-12.
Critical comments on Whittington's plotting and characterization.

E3092. "Harry Whittington." Les Amis du crime 5 (March 80):1-35. Contents: "H. Whittington: Eléments biographiques," p. 3 (a biographical chronology); J. J. Schleret, "Entretien avec Harry Whittington," pp. 4-9 (interview; translated into French by Jean-François Naudon); J. P. Schweig, "Le Jeu du Solitaire," pp. 10-3 (E3093); "Harry Whittington vu par la critique," pp. 15-16 (reviews and critical comments on Whittington's work); "Harry Whittington: Bibliographie chronologique," pp. 17-29 (a chronological bibliography of books and short, with some information on reprints; French translations given, where available); "Harry Whittington: Filmographie," pp. 30-33 (movie and television adaptations); Harry Whittington, "Hommage à Frederick C. Davis," p. 34 (E780); "Bibliographie de Frederick Clyde Davis," p. 35.

E3093. Schweig, J. P. "Le Jeu du solitaire |The game of solitary|." Les Amis du crime 5 (March 80):10-13.
The solitary hero and the woman-puppet, dominated by an obsession with sex and money, are constants in Whittington's fiction but, in spite of this apparent limitation in characterizations, his works are ingenious variations, always different and always absorbing.

E3094. Whittington, Harry. "Baby, I Could Plot!" PQ 2:2 (Summer 79):25-27. Excerpts from the keynote address, Florida Suncoast Writers' Conference, St. Petersburg, Florida, January 27, 1978.
Whittington talks about his early writing career.

WIEGAND, WILLIAM

Ref: Hubin 2, TCCMW, CC; The Writer 89:1 (Jan 76): 20-24 (police procedural)

WILCOX, COLLIN

Ref: Hubin 2, TCCMW, CC, SN, ABMI(S).

Int: TPP 2:2 (March/April 79):15-17, 9.

E3095. Dove, George N. "Collin Wilcox." In Dove (B96), pp. 225-29.
A portrait of Lt. Frank Hastings. Dove notes that in his use of first-person narration, Wilcox has broken with procedural tradition to create a more introspective main character.

E3096. Pierce, Jeff. "The Great Mystery Series No. 1." Mystery 3:2 (Sept 81):20-23. Photos.
Wilcox's Lt. Hastings series seems to have been largely ignored by mystery fandom in spite of its attractiveness as well-written procedurals with good characterization. Pierce sees the plotting and the "under-use" of the San Francisco setting as the series' chief weakness.

WILEY, JOHN

Ref: EMD.

E3097. Harwood, John. (James Long Wong Stories: A Checklist.) Letter, TAD 7 (1973/74):239.
Some brief comments on Wiley's Wong series, with a checklist of stories, and some notes on the film versions. Additions/corrections: J. Randolph Cox, letter TAD 7:304-5; Jon Breen, letter TAD 7:306.

WILKINSON, ELLEN

Ref: Hubin 2, CC.

E3098. Barzun, Jacques, and Taylor, Wendell Hertig. Preface to The Division Bell Mystery (London, 1932), by Ellen Wilkinson. In A Book of Prefaces (B17), pp. 109-110.

WILLIAMS, CHARLES

Ref: Hubin 2, TCCMW, CC, SN.

WILLIAMS, DAVID

Ref: Hubin 2; Pike, TPP 2:4 (July/Aug 79):19-20.

WILLIAMS, JOHN B.

Ref: Hubin 2.

E3099. Bleiler, E. F. "John B. Williams, M. D., Forgotten Writer of Detective Stories." TAD 10 (1977):353.

Williams (1823-79) wrote at least one volume of short stories, based on the exploits of a professional detective, and an undetermined number of dime novels.

WILLIAMS, VALENTINE

Ref: Hubin 2, TCCMW, EMD, CC, ABMI(S); The Writer 48:5 (May 35):166-67, 198; The Writer 48:6 (June 35):210-11, 238-39.

See also: C535.

E3100. Williams, Valentine. World of Action. London: Hamish Hamilton, n. d. (1938?). 479pp. Index. Boston, MA: Houghton, Mifflin, 1938. 430pp. Index.

Autobiography; includes of the beginning of his thriller writing career. Not seen. (REB)

WILLIAMS, VINNIE

Ref: Lachman, TPP 5:1 (July 82):43-44.

WILLIAMSON, JACK

Ref: ABMI(S); UN 3:11 (1951):10-11 (photo).

WILLIAMSON, TONY

Ref: Hubin 2, ABMI,

Int: DAST 9:5 (1976):12-14 (photo).

WILLIS, (LORD) TED

Ref: Hubin 2, TCCMW, ABMI(S).

Int: DAST 13:5-6 (1980):16-19 (with checklist).

WILLOCK, COLIN

Ref: Hubin 2, CC, ABMI(S); Pike, TPP 3:2 (March/April 80):17-18.

WILLS, CECIL M.

Ref: Hubin 2, TCCMW, ABMIS.

WILSON, COLIN

Ref: Hubin 2, TCCMW, CC, ABMI(S).

See also: E1879.

E3101. Tredell, Nicolas. The Novels of Colin Wilson. London: Vision; Tolowa, N. J.: Barnes & Noble, 1982. 158pp. Bibliography. Not seen.

WILSON, MITCHELL

Ref: Hubin 2, ABMI(S); The Writer 60:1 (Jan 47):15-16.

WILSON, P. W.

Ref: Hubin 2, CC, ABMI(S); Pike, TPP 3:1 (Jan/Feb 80):28; revised biography in 3:2 (March/April 80):18.

WILSON, T. S. See CROMIE, ROBERT

WINCHELL, PRENTICE. See STERLING, STEWART

WITTING, CLIFFORD

Ref: Hubin 2, TCCMW, CC, ABMI(S); Pike, TPP 2:6 (Nov/Dec 79):25-27.

E3102. Barzun, Jacques, and Taylor, Wendell Hertig. "Preface" to Measure for Murder (London, 1945), by Clifford Witting. In A Book of Prefaces (B17), pp. 111-12.

E3103. Cole, Hubert. "He Bans Amateur 'Tecs." John Bull 84, no. 2198 (14 Aug 48):48.
The story of how Clifford Witting became a successful writer. Comments from the author himself. (RCSA)

WODEHOUSE, P. G.

Ref: Hubin 2, ABMI(S).

E3104. Asimov, Isaac. "Foreword: The Lovable Criminality of P. G. Wodehouse." In Wodehouse on Crime, pp. ix-xiii. New Haven and New York: Ticknor & Fields, 1981.
After some good-natured comments on Wodehouse's fictional world, and the mildness of the crimes committed, Asimov reflects that there is some kind of crime in almost every Wodehouse story.

E3105. Bensen, D. R. "Preface" to Wodehouse on Crime, pp. xv-xvii. New Haven and New York: Ticknor & Fields, 1981.
Brief comments on the dual influences of Conan Doyle and Dr. Thomas Arnold, "chief propagandist" of the English public-school system.

E3106. Cox, J. Randolph. "Elementary, My Dear Wooster!" Baker Street Journal 17:2 (June 67):78-83.
Comparison of elements in the Holmes/Watson stories and the Jeeves/Bertie Wooster saga. Not seen. DeWaal 4053.

E3107. Jasen, David. "The Mysterious Wodehouse." TAD 3 (1969/70):38-39.
A brief discussion of the stories and novels by Wodehouse in which there are detectives, criminals and crimes. The list of short stories gives no information on date or place of publication and only the year of publication is given for the novels.

WOLFE, ASHTON

Ref: Hubin 2,

E3108. Sanderson, Joy. ("Ashton Wolfe.") Letter, TAD 3 (1969/70):61-62.

Biographical data by Wolfe's niece, Joy Sanderson. See comments by Samuel A. Peeples in TAD 5 (1971/72):117.

WOOD, H. F.

Ref: Hubin 2, ABMI(S).

E3109. Bleiler, H. F. "Introduction." In The Passenger from Scotland Yard, pp. v-xii. NY: Dover, 1977.
According to Bleiler, The Passenger from Scotland Yard is the best detective novel between The Moonstone and The Hound of the Baskervilles. The introduction consists of the known biographical information on Wood and a discussion, with bibliographical detail, of his three detective novels.

WOOD, MRS. HENRY

Ref: Hubin 2, TCCMW, ABMI.

WOODS, SARA

Ref: Hubin 2, TCCMW, EMD, CC, ABMI(S).

E3110. Fox, Estelle. "Sara Woods." TAD 4 (1970/71):152-53.
A short biography of the writer with a checklist of her works based on information supplied by her.

WOOLRICH, CORNELL

Ref: Hubin 2, TCCMW, EMD, CC, ABMI(S).

E3111. Barbato, Joseph. "The Unknown Master of Mystery." (Amtrak) Express, March 83, pp. 26, 28, 29.
General essay on Woolrich on the occasion of the publication by Ballantine Books of a series of his novels with introductions by Francis M. Nevins, Jr.

E3112. Boucher, Anthony. "Introduction." In The Bride Wore Black (Simon & Schuster, 1940), by Cornell Woolrich. NY: Collier Books, 1964. Reprinted in Boucher (B43), pp. 125-26.

E3113. Deadline (published by the William Irish/Cornell Wollrich Fan Club). Editors: Hiromichi Iwama and Takashi Ogawa. Editorial address: 6-17-24 Sasa-shita, Konan-ku, Yokohama, Kanagawa, Japan. Quarterly. Language: mostly Japanese. (JK)

E3114. "Dossier William Irish." Polar 1 (April 79):6-45. Stills.
Contents: "Présentation des six films TV," pp. 6-8 (production credits and plot summaries of six TV films based on Irish short stories); Pascal Mérigeau, "Entretien avec Yves Boisset," pp. 9-12 (interview with director of "La Stratégie du serpent", film based on Irish's "A Death Is Caused"); Pascal Mérigeau, "Critique de la 'Stragégie du serpent'," pp. 13-14 (review); François Guérif, "William Irish et le cinéma," pp. 15-17 (critical comments on adaptations of Woolrich/Irish fiction); "Filmographie," pp. 18-19; William Irish, "Quelque chose qui s'est passé chez nous," pp. 20-38 ("Something Happened in Our House," translated by Gérard de Chergé); Jean-François Naudon, "Bibliographie: Romans et recueils de nouvelles," pp. 38-45 (a chronological bibliography, including French translations and an alphabetical listing of short stories translated into French).

E3115. Ellison, Harlan. "Introduction." In Angels of Darkness by Cornell Woolrich, pp. vii-xii. NY: The Mysterious Press, 1978.
Informal, and enthustiastic, comments on Woolrich and on the stories in this collection.

E3116. ______. "Introduction: Blood/Thoughts." In No Roses, No Windows, pp. 37-40. NY: Ace Books, 1983.
In addition to some comments about Woolrich in his introduction, Ellison also describes a meeting with Woolrich and the story ("Tired Old Man") based on that meeting.

E3117. Fisher, Steve. "Cornell Woolrich: ' - I Had Nobody'." TAD 3 (1969/70):164-65.
Personal notes on the writer that include a short, undated letter written by Woolrich to Fisher.

E3118. Guérif, François. "William Irish." In Europe no. 571/72 (Nov/Dec 76), pp. 137-41.
On film adaptations, with a filmography.

E31199 Knott, Harold; Nevins, Francis M., Jr.; and Thailing, William. "Cornell Woolrich: A Bibliography." TAD 2 (1968/69):237-50; reprinted in Nevins (E3132), pp. 478-510; and in Cornell Woolrich---Mörkrets Poet (E3126), pp. 43-46 (abridged).
American book publication and magazine appearances. With information on reprintings of short stories, a filmography and radio/TV adaptations.

E3120. Lacassin, Francis. "William Irish, le peintre intimiste du roman policier |William Irish, the intimate painter of detective fiction|." MM 287 (Jan 72); no. 288 (Feb 72). Not seen. (REB)

E3121. ______. "William Irish ou l'oeil qui voit l'intérieur des êtres |William Irish or the eye that sees inside people|." In Lacassin (B201), Vol. II, pp. 114-53.
A biography, a bibliography and a discussion of narrative patterns in his two fictional "cycles," the "tragedies in black" and the "tragedies in blue."

E3122. Malzberg, Barry N. "Afterword." In The Fantastic Stories of Cornell Woolrich, edited by Charle G. Waugh and Martin G. Greenberg, pp. 329-33. Carbondale, IL: Southern Illinois Univ. Press, 1981; reprinted in Malzberg, The Engines of the Night: Science Fiction in the Eighties (Garden City, NY: Doubleday, 1982), pp. 108-113.
A moving personal memoir by Woolrich's friend, Barry Malzberg.

E3123. Nevins, Francis M., Jr. "Afterword." In Angels of Darkness, by Cornell Woolrich, pp. 213-215. NY: Mysterious Press, 1978.

E3124. ______. "Brief Loves: The Early Short Stories of Cornell Woolrich." TAD 14 (1981):168-72.
Magazine fiction written from 1926-34.

E3125. ______. "Cornell Woolrich." TAD 2 (1968/69):25-28; 99-102; 180-82. Comments/additions/corrections: Robert E. Briney, TAD 2:126; F. M. Nevins, Jr., TAD 2:280, 280-81; Charles Shibuk, TAD 3:67; Nevins, TAD 4:193.
A study of Woolrich's fiction and a bibliography. See also Nevins, "A

Woolrich Preview," TAD 4 (1970/71):145-46, for material correcting information in series.

E3126. ______. Cornell Woolrich---Mörkrets Poet. DAST Dossier 6. Strängnäs, Sweden: DAST Forlag AB, 1980. 4-46pp.
Contents: Bertil Falk, "Cornell George Hopley-Woolrich (1903-1968)," pp. 5-7 (introduction); Kaj Ahnmen, "Cornell Woolrich Konstnaren," pp. 8-9 (tribute); K. Arne Blom, "Att Kanna," pp. 10-11 (tribute); Jan Broberg, untitled note, pp. 12; Staffan Larsson, "Cornell Woolrich," pp. 13-16 (poem); Hans Stertman, untitled note, pp. 17-18; Francis M. Nevins, Jr., "Cornell Woolrich---Mörkrets Poet," pp. 19-42 (E3129); Knott/Nevins/Thailing & Iwan Hedman, "Hopley/Irish/Woolrich - Bibliografi," pp. 43-46 (E3119); portrait of Woolrich by Jack Gaughan; 3 photos of Woolrich, reproductions of covers of 3 U. S. editions and 20 Swedish editions of Woolrich fiction. (REB)

E3127. ______. "Cornell Woolrich: The Years before Suspense." TAD 12 (1979):106-110.
A discussion of Woolrich's fiction written before 1934.

E3128. ______. "Introduction." In Manhattan Love Song (Godwin, 1932), by Cornell Woolrich. Gregg Press Mystery Fiction Series (B134).

E3129. ______. "Introduction." In Nightwebs (qv), pp. ix-xxxiv; reprinted in Nevins (E3126), pp. 19-42; and as "The Poet of the Shadows: Cornell Woolrich," in The Fantastic Stories of Cornell Woolrich (Southern Illinois Univ. Press, 1981), pp. vii-xxvi.
A substantial review of Woolrich's life and writings.

E3130. ______. Introductions to the Ballantine Books reprints of Cornell Woolrich novels, 1982-83. Titles: The Black Curtain; The Black Path of Fear; Rendezvous in Black; The Black Angel; Black Alibi; Phantom Lady; Night Has a Thousand Eyes; Deadline at Dawn; I Married a Dead Man. (REB)

E3131. ______. "Introduction." In Rendezvous in Black (Rinehart, 1938), by Cornell Woollrich, pp. v-xi. Gregg Press Mystery Fiction Series (B134).

E3132. Nevins, Francis M., ed. Nightwebs: A Collection of Stories by Cornell Woolrich. NY: Harper & Row, 1971; revised edition, pb, NY: Equinox Books (published by Avon Books), 1974.
This collection of 16 short stories by Woolrich also contains the following critical material: F. M. Nevins, Jr., "Introduction," pp. ix-xxxiv (E3129); Knotts/Nevins/Thailing, "Cornell Woolrich: A Checklist," pp. 478-510 (E3119).

E3133. Stewart, Enola. "Cornell Woolrich (William Irish, George Hopley.) A Catalogue of first and variant editions of his work, including anthology and magazine appearances." Pocono Pines, PA: Gravesend Books, 1975. v, 30pp. Stapled in pictorial covers. Illus. Edition limited to 250 numbered copies, signed by the compiler.
Detailed bibliographic listing of 157 items offered for sale, including first edition and reprint books, magazine stories, and some secondary material. Includes a portrait of Woolrich by Jack Gaughan (primarily known as a science fiction artist). (REB)

E3134. Thailing, (William). "Cornell Woolrich (1903-1968): A Memoriam." TAD 1 (1968/69):161-62.

A tribute to the writer by a reader who corresponded with him for a number of years.

E3135. Truffaut, François. "Pulp Action: dossier William Irish." Time Out, 17-23 June 1983, pp. 13-14. Illustrated. Translation by Maxim Jakubowski.
An appreciation by the noted French film director of Cornell Woolrich (William Irish), with brief mentions of David Goodis and Charles Williams. ("There is always a strong touch of despair and fatality in one who earns a lving imagining tales about crime.") In an untitled addendum (p. 14), Richard Rayner discusses Jim Thompson and David Goodis in the same vein. (REB)

WORMSER RICHARD

Ref: Hubin 2, SN, ABMIS; UN 2:6 (1950):4-5 12 (photo).

See also: C247, D172. D334.

WORSLEY-GAUGH, BARBARA

Ref: Hubin 2, CC; Pike, TPP 2:5 (Sept/Oct 79):24, 26.

WORTS, GEORGE F.

Ref: Hubin 2, ABMI(S).

E3136. Worts, George F. "The Men Who Make Good." Argosy 209:5 (25 Jan 30):718.
Crisply concentrated summary of Worts' writing career to 1930. Main series characters: Gillian Hazeltine, Peter the Brazen, Singapore Sammy. (RS)

WRIGHT, WILLARD HUNTINGTON. See VAN DINE, S.A.

WYLIE, PHILIP

Ref: Hubin 2, EMD, CC, ABMI(S).

E3137. Keefer, Truman Frederick. Philip Wylie. Twayne's United States Author Series 285. Boston: G. K. Hall, 1977.
A study of Wylie's work with discussion of fiction with detection elements on pp. 54-57, 61-62, 77-78.

E3138. Lauterbach, Edward S. "Invisible Man, U. S. A.: Some Pulp Prototypes." TAD 3 (1969/70):241-42.
A discussion of The Murderer Invisible (1932) with its use of "characters and situations that would become standard in the the pulp thrillers of the 30s." See response by Samuel Peeples, TAD 4 (1970/71):66; and reply by Lauterbach, TAD 4:133.

WYNNE, ANTHONY

Ref: Hubin 2, CC, ABMIS.

See also: B253.

E3139. Sampson, Robert. "The Fattest Man in the Medical Profession." TMF 7:3 (May/June 83):16-22.
A survey of the forgotten Anthony Wynne medical detective series featuring Dr. Eustace Hailey. With a checklist of the series. (RS)

YAMADA, FUTARO

E3141. Yamada Futaro no Sekai |The world of Futaro Yamada|. Shinpyo-sha series (B367). July, 1959. 202pp. (HS/TT)

E3142. Yamada, Futaro. Fugan Sho |The selections from Futaro's eyes|. Tokyo: Rokko Shuppan, 1979. 253pp.
The author started with mystery fiction and later swept the country with period fiction such as "ninja" (Japanese spy) stories. He is now very popular in genre fiction, rich with mystery elements, set in the Meiji Period (1868-1912). There are few references to mystery fiction in this book but the ones made are acute observations. (HS/TT)

YATES, DORNFORD

Ref: Hubin 2, EMD, CC, ABMI(S).

E3143. Cox, J. Randolph. (Dornford Yates). Letter TAD 14 (1981):185-86.
A biography with a checklist of his fiction.

E3144. Sharpe, Tom. "Introduction." In Blind Corner (Hodder, 1927), by Dornford Yates. Classic Thrillers Series. London: J. M. Dent, 1983.

E3145. ______. "Major Mercer and Mr. Yates." Radio Times 218, no. 2833 (25 Feb 78 - 3 March 78):4-5.
A brief biography of Dornford Yates, tied in with the adaptation for televison which Sharpe had done of Yates' She Fell among Thieves. (RCSA)

E3146. Smithers, A. J. Dornford Yates: A Biography. London: Hodder & Stoughton, 1982. 241pp. Not seen. Review: TLS, 19 March 82, p. 307.

E3147. Usborne, Richard. "Dornford Yates." In Usborne (B420), pp. 27-78.
Usborne's comments on Yates are a mixture of affection and recognition of his limitations. Usborne distinguishes between the style of his Berry and "Chandos" series and discusses the characters, Berry, Boy Pleydell and Jonah Mansell.

YOKOMIZO, SEISHI

E3148. "Ano Kindaichi Kosuke-san no Dojina Sosa wa Dokoka Boku-Tachi ni Niteiru no da |The Kosuke Kindaichi's stupid investigations somewhat resemble us|." Out, May 1977.
This article occupies 30 of the 168 pages of the first issue of the magazine. As Out is targeted at the young and this is the premier issue, the editorial policy is unclear. The article appears to have been hastily added as a cover story without any planning. (HS/TT)

E3149. Geneijo, ed. Yokomizo Seishi no Sekai |The world of Seishi Yokomizo|. Tokyo: Gen'eijo, 1976. 316pp. Illustrated. Bibliography.
Published as a special issue of Gen'eijo magazine in May 1976, it contains mostly original studies on and impressions of Yokomizo, including Yokomizo's memoirs, a mini-encyclopedia of his 152 works (novels and short stories) analyzed by Hirokazu Futagami, and a chronology compiled by Hiroshi Shimazaki. (HS/TT)

E3150. Kawataro, Nakajima, ed. Kindaichi Kosuke. "Meitantei Tokuhon" series (B254). 1979. vii, 219pp.
Kosuke Kindaichi, created by Yokomizo, is one of the most famous Japanese detectives. (HS/TT)

E3151. Kobayashi, Nobuhiko, ed. Yokomizo Seishi Tokuhon |The Seishi Yokomizo reader|. Tokyo: Kadokawa Shoten, 1976. 273pp. Illustrated.
This volume contains the editor's four-day interview with Yokomizo and other material such as an essay by Yokomizo, comments on his works, selections from his diary, and a chronology. The contents are very similar to those in other memorial collections. (HS/TT)

E3152. Sato, Tomoyuki. Kindaichi Kosuke-san, Anata no Suiri wa Machigai Darake |Mr. Kosuke Kindaichi, your detection is full of mistakes|! 2 vols. Tokyo: Seinen Shokan, 1978. Vol. 1: 228pp; Vol. 2: 230pp.
A summary of the contents and detection techniques of the Kindaichi series and other works by Yokomizo, with an analysis of the solutions by Sato and a presentation of the different solutions proposed by Yokomizo. Although Sato discusses 29 stories, he generally criticizes small errors and makes false accusations against Yokomizo. (HS/TT)

E3153. "Sayonara Yokomizo Seishi, Kindaichi Kosuke |Goodbye, Seishi Yokomizo and Kosuke Kindaichi|." Yasei Jidai, April 1982.
A 47 page memorial to Yokomizo. The material consists of essays by his acquaintances, as well as an analysis of his work (by Kawataro Nakajima) by character, in chronological order. The magazine's publisher, Kadokawa Shoten, has sold 55 million copies of works by Yokomizo and also devoted the April issue of another magazine, Baraetei, to Yokomizo. (HS/TT)

E3154. Yokomizo, Seishi. Tantei Shosetsu 50-nen |50 years of detective fiction|. Edited by Kawataro Nakajima. Tokyo: Kodan-sha, 1972. 444pp. Illustrated. Bibliography.
Seishi Yokomizo (1902-1981) is one of the greatest mystery Japanese mystery writers. He began writing before W. W. II, but, after reading John Dickson Carr during the war, he published, in the post-war period, good puzzle novels which the Japanese find difficult. As the "social school" gained popularity, he was forced into silence, but as editions of his works became popular in the late 70s, he resumed writing, like a phoenix. This book is the first collection of his essays, published in commemoration of his seventieth birthday. It consists largely of his memoirs but, as the author was editor-in-chief of Shin-seinen mystery magazine, there are valuable comments on little-known areas of the history of Japanese mystery fiction. (HS/TT)

E3155. ______. Tantei Shosetsu Mukashi Banashi |A legend of detective fiction|. Edited by Kawataro Nakajima. Tokyo: Kodan-sha, 1975. 332pp. Illustrated. Bibliography.
A collection of his essays, appearing in an eighteen-volume series of his works, and mostly written after Tantei (E3154). With a chronology and bibliography. (HS/TT)

E3156. ______. Yokomizo Seishi no Sekai |The world of Seishi Yokomizo|. Tokyo: Tokuma Shoten, 1976. 307pp. Illustrated.
The third collection of essays. The material is thinner than in the two previous collections, and the volume is padded with three short stories, selected by the author. (HS/TT)

E3156a. ______. Shinsetsu: Kindaichi Kosuke |The true Kosuke Kindaichi|. Tokyo: Mainichi Shinbun-sha, 1977. 262pp. Illustrated.
A collection of columns serialized, under the same title, in a newspaper. He comments not only on his famous character, Kosuke Kindaichi, but on

his other characters and works. It is not fresh, but is well-constructed. (HS/TT)

YORK, ANDREW

Ref: Hubin 2, TCCMW, CC, SN, ABMI(S); The Writer 92:2 (Feb 79):20-23.

E3157. "Christopher Nicole." DAST 11:4 (1978):51-53.
Brief biography and checklist of works. York is probably the best known of Nicole's pseudonyms.

YORKE, MARGARET

Ref: Hubin 2, TCCMW, SN, ABMI(S); Pike, TPP 3:4 (July/Aug 80):18-19, 16.

See also: E1540.

YRONDY, PIERRE

E3158. Mermet, H. Y. "Marius Pergomas." Enigmatika 25 (Nov 83), pp. 22-28.
A survey of a series (35 novels) featuring detective Marius Pergomas: characters, plot, etc.

YUILL, P. B.

Ref: Hubin 2, TCCMW, ABMI.

YUKI, SHOJI

E3159. Yuki, Shoji. Kino no Hana |Yesterday's flower|. Tokyo: Asahi Shinbunsha, 1978. 257pp.
The author is a mystery writer who has published works of high standard in many genres such as hard-boiled, spy and puzzle novel. About 100 pages deal with mystery fiction and he discusses hard-boiled writing and his favorite writers, including Raymond Chandler and E. S. Gardner. (HS/TT)

YUMENO, KYUSAKU

E3160. Karigari, Hiroshi. Dogura Magura no Yume |Dream of Dogura Mogura|. Tokyo: San'ichi Shobo, 1971. xxxiii, 264pp. Illustrated.
A commentary on Yumeno's famous work Dogura Magura from several points of view. It includes a summary of the novel in English. (HS/TT)

E3161. Nishimura, Kazumi, ed. Yumeno Kyusaku no Sekai |The world of Kyusaku Yumeno|. Tokyo: Hirakawa Shuppan, 1975. 509pp. Bibliography.
A collection of comments on Yumeno, taken from various magazines. It includes a detailed bibliography, and shows the changing evalutation of Yumeno. (HS/TT)

E3162. Sugiyama, Tatsumaru. Waga Chichi Yumeno Kyusaku |My father, Kyusaku Yumeno|. Tokyo: San'ichi Shobo, 1976. 285pp.
A biography and memoirs by Yumeno's son. (HS/TT)

E3163. Yumeno, Kyusaku. Yumeno Kyusaku no Nikki |The diary of Kyusaku Yumeno|. Edited by Tatsumaru Sugiyama. Fukuoka: Ashi Shobo, 1976. 478pp. Illustrated. Bibliography.
Yumeno's writer's diary. We can see the process by which his novel Dogura Magura was completed after long years of rewriting and polishing. (HS/TT)

E3164. ______. Yumeno Kyusaku Zenshu |The complete works of Kyusaku

Yumeno|. Vol. 7. Tokyo: San'ichi Shobo, 1970. 504pp. Illustrated. Bibliography.

A collection of essays and sketches, including several on mystery fiction. With a chronology and bibliography compiled by Kawataro Nakajima. (HS/TT)

ZANGWILL, ISRAEL

Ref: Hubin 2, TCCMW, EMD, CC, ABMI(S).

E3165. Adams, Elsie. Israel Zangwill. NY: Twayne, 1971.

See pp. 100-101 for comments on The Big Bow Mystery and the stories in The King of Schnorrers.

E3166. Bleiler, E. F. "Introduction." In Three Victorian Detective Novels, pp. xiii-xvi. NY: Dover, 1078.

Introductory comments on Zangwill's The Big Bow Mystery with a biography and a critical survey of his detective fiction.

ZAREMBA, EVE

Ref: Hubin 2.

E3167. Bearchell, Chris. "Making It in the Murder Market." Body Politic, 15 Aug 78.

Interview with and article on Eve Zaremba, Canadian author of A Reason To Kill. (KLM)

Index

Aarne-Stith Thompson, C236
Aarons, Edward S., AR, A48, D334
Abartis, Cesarea, C1
Abbé Faria (FC; A. Dumas), E1010
Abbot, Anthony, E1-E2
Aboucaya, J., E1679
Abrahams, Etta Claire, B1, E1812-E1813
Abreu, John, D112, D221, D218
Ace Books, A80
Adam Dagliesh (FC; P. D. James), E1538
Adamov, Arkadi, C420
Adams, Tom, B392
Adams, Cleve F., B62, E3
Adams, Clift, na
Adams, Donald K., B2, B3, E1286, E1358
Adams, Elsie, E3165
Adams, Eustace L., AR
Adams, Gail, C2
Adams, Harriet S., D119, D124
Adams, John, E1149
Adams, Tom, B392, E518
Adamson, Judy, E1309
Addington-Symons, Francis, B110, E4
Ade, George, D1
Adey, Robert C. S., A1, A2, A3, C3, C4, C472, E344, E272a, E1282, E2480, E3007
A. D. G., AR, A13
Adimari, Ralph, D181
Adler, Alfred, E2588, E2646
Adler, Bertha, A164
Adley, Derek J., A4, A106, D55, D256, E463, E1018, E1200, E3030
Adrian, Jack, C5, D224
Adrian, Kelly, A71, E1940
Adventure Series (Westbrook), D50
Agassi, Joseph, C6
Agent Nine (PC), D82
Agney, Stephen H., D219
AHMM. See Alfred Hitchcock's Mystery Magazine
Ahnmen, Kaj, E3126
Aiken, Albert W., D286
Aiken, Joan, AR, B64, B65
Ainslee's, D139
Ainsworth, William Harrison, E5
Ainjust, Ingmar d', E1679
Aird, Catherine, AR, B65, E2855
Aisenberg, Nadja, B4, C7, E703, E825, E1319
Aisner, Henri, E1754
Akiba, Toshitaka Cariba, E2009
Akizu, Tomoko, E2266
Akutagawa, Ryunosuke, B289
Albany, Francis, B110, E2222
Albérès, Francis Marill, E1639
Albert Campion, E27, E28, E30, E32, E33
Albert, Marvin H., B107, E6
Albert, Walter, A5, C8
Albrand, Martha, AR
Albrecht, Richard, C9
Albrecht, Wilma, C9
Albright, Donn, E201, E206
Alcott, Louisa May, E7-E13
Alderson, Martha, C10, C11
Aldine Publishing Company, D36, D80
Aldrich, Pearl G., E382
Aldridge, Howard, AR
Aldyne, Nathan, C10, C133
Alewyn, Richard, B264, B424, B451, C12, C13, C308
Alexander, David, AR, B48, B124
Alexander, Karl, C885
Alexandersson, Jan, E458, E459, E1784, E3083
Alfred Hitchcock's Mystery Magazine (AHMM), C807, D335, E65
Alford, William P., E2953
Alfu, E14, E63
Alias Dr. Death (PC), D336
All-Story Magazine (British), A103
Allain, Marcel, B107, C818
Allain (Marcel)/Souvestre (Pierre), B269, E14-E21
Allard, Yvon, A6
Allardyce, Paula. See Blackstock, Charity
Allbeury, Ted, AR, A110, C14,
All Detective Magazine, D393
Alleau, René, E1679
Allen, D. G. MacDonald, E856
Allen, Dick, B4
Allen, Grant, E22-E24
Allen, Hervey, E2167
Allen, L. David, B6, E2089
Allingham, Herbert, A106
Allingham, Joyce, E29
Allingham, Margery, A4, A106, B6, B17, B20, B48, B50, B116, B241, B304, D308, B339, B409, C76, C152, C281, C428, C488, C704, C867, E25-E33, E1539
Allison, Hughes, AR
Almanzi, Venturi, E34-E35
Almquist, C. J. L., E36
Alonso Cortés, Carolina Dafne, E519
Altenheim, Hans, B424, E2583, E2679
Alter, Jean, E2038
Altshuler, Harry, E251, E252
Ambler, Eric, A110, A158, B99, B124, B181, B215, B216, B270, B303, C72, C233, C339, C441, C494a, C541, C594, C609, E37-E50
Ambrosetti, Ronald, B216, E37, E38
Amelin, Michel, E114, E338, E1079, E3063
Améry, Jean, E2584, E2679
Ames, Delano, A106, B234
Amila, Jean, AR
Amis, Kingsley, C15, C16, C17, E2482, E1083, E1084, E51
(Les) Amis du crime, B107
Amoruso, Vito, C18, E1359
Amoury, Gloria, C265
Anastasia Jugedinski (FC; Phyllis Swan), E2837
Anders, Karl, B424, C19
Anderson, David, D2, E2771-E2773, E2810
Anderson, Frederick Irving, C410, C518, E52-E56
Anderson, Isaac, B142, C22
Anderson, James, AR
Anderson, John, E2198
Anderson, Stig, E383
Anderson, Virginia, D293
Andersson, Bernt, C20, C21
Andrew, R(ay) V(ernon), E642-E643
Andrews, Angela, E2223
Andriola, Alfred, E149
Angenot, Marc, B346, E192
Anglo, Michael, B7, D3
Anker, Jens, B8
Annie Wilson (FC; D. L. Sayers), E2499
Anonymous, C102, E57-E58
Anquêti-Turet, F., E1679

Anselmi, Luciano, E1360, E2585-E2586, E2590
Anthony, Evelyn, AR
Anton, Edoardo, C24
Antonelli, Edoardo, C24
Antonelli, George A., C853
Antonini, Fausto, E1092
Antonini, Giacomo, C25
Antony, Paul, E1086
Antony, Peter, AR
Aoki, Amenhiko, B9, B10
Apollinaire, Guillaume, E18
Apostolou, John L., C26-C28, E782, E3087
Appel, B239
Apple, A. E., D411, E59
Ara, Masahito, B280
Aragon, Louis, E2641
Aramata, Hiroshi, B11
Arbur, Rosemarie, E197
Archie Goodwin (FC; Rex Stout), E2771, E2772, E2775, E2782, E2795, E2806, E2815
Archimedes, B157
Ard, William, E60, E61
Arden, Leon, E384
Arden, William. See Collins, Michael
Ardies, Tom, AR
Argosy, D318, D438
Ariadne Oliver (FC; A. Christie), E519, E589, E596, E605
Arima, Yorichika, B183
Aristotle, B78, B424, B434, C39, C779
Arken, Albert W., D286
Arkham House, A87, E814
Arlette van der Valk (FC; Freeling), E1143
Arley, Catherine, AR
(The) Armchair Detective, A38, A163, B159
Armed Services Editions, A80
Armin, B360
Armour, Richard, B142
Armstrong, Anthony, AR
Armstrong, Charlotte, AR, B63, B64, C40
Arnaud, Noel, B12, C717
Arnaud, G.-J., E62-E63
Arnold, Armin, B13, C29, E1020, E1448
Arnold, Thomas, E3105
Arnold Zeck (FC; R. Stout), D466, E2790
Arnott, Ian, E1150
Arrington, Robert, E2581
Arsène Lupin (FC; M. Leblanc), B110, B157, B362, C148, C547, E1270, E1639-E1688, E1928
Arthur, Frank, B18, E64,
Arthur, Robert, B48
Arthur Crook (FC; Anthony Gilbert), E1273
Arthur Westbrook Company, A176, D50, D54
Artzybasheff, E2346
Arvastson, Jan Eric, B376
Arvidsson, Thomas, B386
Asarch, Joel, E2090
Asdell, Philip, E1151, E1176, E1217, E2918
Asey Mayo (FC; P. A. Taylor), E2846
Asfour, J.-C., C30
Ashdown, Clifford, E1177, E1184, E1185, E2271
Ashenden (FC; W. S. Maugham), B308
Ashley, Robert, E644-E647
Ashton-Kirk (FC; J. T. McIntyre), E1911
Ashton-Wolfe, Harry. See Wolfe, Ashton
Asimov, Isaac, B189, B366, C127, C162, C527, E65-E67, E1041, E3104
Aspen Bookhouse Catalogues, A149
Asplund, Johan, B386
Astaldi, Maria Luisa, C31
Astier, Colette, E139
Astier de la Vigerie, Emmanuel d', E2587, E2646
Atchity, Kenneth John, E2954
Atkinson, Alex, B18, E68
Atkinson, Frank, A7
Atlee, Philip, E69
Atoda, Takashi, E70
Auberjonois, Fernand, C605
Auburn, Mark S., C32
Aucott, Robert, A89, A154, C33
Audebrand, Philibert, E1674
Audemars, Pierre, AR
Auden, W. H., B5, B78, B112, B385, B396, B434, B451, C34, C773, E1311
Auerbach, Nina, E2483
August Derleth Society Newsletter, A38
Aurévilly, Barbey d', E2707
Auricoste, Véronique, B110, E1802
Austen, Jane, B237, C221, E1342
Austin, F. Britten, B41
Austin, Howard, D208
Austin, Richard, E2588, E2646
Austwick, John, AR
Avallone, Michael, A157, A158, B319, B409, C127, D450, D478, E71-E84, E636, E2378
Aveline, Claude, E85-E86, E1042, E2978
(The) Avenger (PC), D297, D337-D340, D369
(The) Avengers (TV series), A48
Avenick, Karen, E2538
Avery, Nancy, B92, C576
Avon Books, A80
Avon Classic Crime Series, A75, A114
Awasaka, Tsumao, B14
Axelson, A. E., C35
Axthelm, Pete, E1137
Aydelotte, William O., B216, B290, C36
Aylmer, Felix, E871-E873, E910, E959
Aymé, Marcel, E2969

Babcock, Henry, E1669
Babener, Liahna Klenman, B2, C37, E2091
Back, Tomas M., E1549
Backus, Jean L., AR, B64
Bacon, Peggy, E87
Baender, Paul, E2893
Baetzhold, Howard, E2886, E2887
Bagby, George, B309, E2763
Bagby, George. See also Stein, Aaron Marc
Bagley, Desmond, B65, B181, C38, C441, E88
Baig, Tara Ali, A64
Bailey, H. C., A136, B17, B253, C229, E89-E94
Bainbridge, John, E2224
Baird, Newton, C39, E252, E253, E264, E266a, E704
Baker, Isadore, E116
Baker, John F., E2774
Baker, Richard M., E95, E874-E880, E940
Baker, Robert, C587
Baker, Samm Sinclair, AR, B48
Baker, W. Howard, D248, D257
Bakerman, Jane, B16, C40, E379, E1011, E1143, E1273, E1471, E1472, E1534, E1554, E1624-E1625, E1916, E2327-E2330, E2339, E2829, E3066, E379
Bakish, David, E1490
Bales, Jack, D90
Balka, Peggy, E474
Ball, John, B15, B309, C41, C42, E37, E96, E2379, E2916, E2927
Ballard, K. G. See Roth, Holly
Ballard, W. T., C247, E97
Ballet, René, B78, C43
Ballinger, Bill S., E99
Ballinger, John, C44, E99
Ballinger, John & Emily, A8

Balmer, Edwin, AR, C638
Balow, Tom, E578, E2345
Balzac, Honoré de, B59, B257, B375, C54, C204, C585, C743, C779, E100, E2586, E2641, E2787
Bander, Elaine, C45, E2484-E2485
Bandy, Eugene Franklin, B105, B117, C46, E2092, E2093
Bankier, William, AR
Banks, R. Jeff, B216, C811, D337, E69, E785, E1343, E1353, E1694, E1772, E1810, E2036, E2731, E2731, E2885, E2888
Barbato, Joseph, C47, E1092, E3111
Barbette, Jay. See Spicer, Bart
Barbolini, Robert, C48, C49
Barbour, Ralph Henry, D4
Barde, Jacqueline, B269
Bardin, John Franklin, A12, C421, C802, 101, E102, E1428
Bargainnier, Earl F., B16, C50, C51, E193, E520-E524, E1000, E1449, E1456, E1949, E2046-E2047, E2730
Barine, J., E2978
Baring-Gould, William S., B43, B159, E2380, E2775, E2816
Barker, Dudley, E475
Barnard, Louise, E526
Barnard, Robert, B181, E525-E526, E2331
Barnes, Bruce, C52
Barnes, Dallas, E103
Barnes, Daniel R., B2, E527, E1854
Barnes, Melvin, A9, E2094
Barney Miller (TV series character), E2715
Baronian, Jean-Baptiste, E2308, E2309
Barrès, Maurice, E1928
Barry, Beatrice, D5
Barry, Charles, C53
Barry, Jerome, AR
Barson, Michael, D309, E242, E758, E769, E3090
Bart, Barry, E881
Barthes, Roland, B264, C51
Bartholomew, Cecelia, B63
Bartlett, Ronald, E2764
Bartolini, Luigi, C55
Barton, Billy, E104
Barton, Dr. Eustace Robert, E2495, E2522. See also Eustace, Robert
Barton, George, AR, E648
Bartram, George, A157
Bar-Zohar, Michael, E105
Barzun, Jacques, B93, B105, B124, B290, B434, C39, C46, C56-C65, C107, C768, C867, E385, E394, E409, E443, E777, E2777, E2778
Barzun, Jacques & Wendell Hertig Taylor, A6, A10, A11, A148, B17, B18, B322, B355, C57, E26, E64, E68, E89, E115, E118, E154, E171, E215, E254, E273, E299, E334, E341, E342, E386, E476, E528, E623, E627, E706, E721, E736, E741, E746, E765, E823, E1035, E1047, E1076, E1081, E1138, E1152, E1236, E1262, E1275, E1297, E1301, E1331, E1335, E1352, E1438, E1450a, E1457, E1473, E1477, E1514, E1517, E1525, E1526-E1527, E1535, E1550, E1581, E1592, E1615, E1617, E1620, E1626, E1766, E1779, E1814, E1855, E1903, E1907, E1950, E1984, E1990, E2005, E2013, E2018, E2024, E2039, E2066, E2081, E2083, E2086, E2095, E2213, E2216, E2332, E2372, E2486, E2574, E2723, E2776, E2838, E2839, E2856, E2881, E2913, E2917, E2955, E3008, E3050, E3051, E3059, E3102, C509
Basney, Lionel, C66, E2487, E2525
Bassett, John, E1049, E1050, E1058, E1063
Bastiani, Ange, E106
Bastid, J. P., B244
Bastos, Augusto Roa, C422
Bates, David, E1562
Bates, Susan, A12
Batman (Comic book character), B307, D319
Baudelaire, Charles, C512
Baudou, Jacques, A13, A14, B85, B110, B378, C67, C68, E1042, E1642, E1656, E1691, E1731, E1744, E1918, E1922, E1933, E2096, E2218, E2244, E2333, E2758-EE758a, E2760, E2970, E2971-E2973, E2978, E2994, E2994
Bauer, Jerry, C330
Bauer, Wolf, C69
Bauska, Barry, E1139
Bawden, Nina, AR
Baxter, A. Beverley, B364
Baxt, George, AR
Bay, J. Christian, E2889
Bayfield, William J. D246
Bazelon, David T., E1361
Bazzard (FC; Dickens), E857, E864, E873, E884, E903, E917, E975, E977, E978, E979, E982, E985, E997
Beach, Stewart, B63, B64, C69a
Beadle & Adams, D45, D54
Beadle & Co, E76. See also Dime Library and Half Dime Library
Beaman, Bruce R., E2934
Beams, David, E700
Bear, Andrew, E1128
Bearchell, Chris, E3167
Béarn, Pierre, E2974, E2975, E2978
Beattie, Anna B., C70
Beauchesne, Bernard, E1563
Beaufort, Geofrey de, E1679
Beauvais, Robert, E1934
Beck, Celia Francis, C70
Becker, Jens-Peter, B19, B20, B60, B61, B295, C71-C73, C76, C77, C137, C138, E387
Becker, Luc, E2589
Becker, May Lamberton, C77, E989
Becket, Margaret, D6
Beckett, Samuel, B338
Beckmeir, Ralph William, E1021
Beckner, Jean, B2
Bedell, Jeanne F., B16, C78, E208, E1627, E2211
Bedford-Jones, H., B21, B22, B339, E107
Bedner, Jules, E2603
Beeding, Francis, B303, E108
Beekman, E. M., E388
Beetz, Kirk H., E649, E658
Behn, Noel, AR
Behre, Frank, E529
Beineix, Jean-Jacques, B378
Belden, Henry, E2097
Bell, Eric Sinclair, A58
Bell, Jocelyn, E2014
Bell, Josephine, AR, B84, B124, B283, C79, C488
Bellairs, George, AR
Bellak, Leopold, C80
Bellem, Robert Leslie, D360, E109-E111
Belloc-Lowndes, Marie, B58, C611
Bellous, Robert Peabody, D7
Bellow, Saul, E1085
Belmont Paperbacks, D453
(Henri) Bencolin (FC; J. D. Carr), E357
Benelli, Graziano, E2590
Benét, James, AR
Benét, Stephen Vincent, C81
Benét, William Rose, C82
Bengel, Michael, C83
Bengis, Nathan L., E1470, E882, E990
Beniamino, Michel, E530

Benjamin, David A., E1815, E1816
Benners, William J., D154
Bennett, Arnold, B24, E112
Bennett, Donna, C84
Bennett, Jay, E113
Bennett, Margot, C488, E114
Bennett, Reynold, E1439
Bennich-Bjorkman, Bo, B25
Benoît, Pierre, C85, E304, E2646
Bens, Jacques, E1643, E1679, E1921, E1929
Bensen, D. R., B117, B271, E3105
Benson, Ben, AR, B48, E65
Benson, E. F., AR
Benstock, Bernard, B26, E2709
Bentley, E. C., B17, B28, B253, B270, B304, C35, C153, C183, C361, C398, C447, C567, C687, C869, E115-E123, E1362, E2554
Bentley, Phyllis, E124
Benton, Kenneth, AR
Benton, Richard, E2098
Benvenuti, Stefano, B27
Berckman, Evelyn, AR
Beresford, J. D., E125
Berger, Thomas, E126, C343
Berghaus, A., D210
Bergier, Jacques, C87
Bergler, Edmund, C88
Berg, Lillemor, E1033
Bergman, Andrew, B121, C305, E127
Bergonzi, Bernard, E1087
Berg, Ron, E605
Berg, Stanton O., C86
Berkeley, Anthony, B28, B61, B270, B289, C89, C132, C488a, C687, E128-E137
Berkett, Lord, B83
Berkley, Miriam, E1363
Bermúdez, María Elvira, B29, C90
Bernanos, Georges, A95, E139-E140, E1324, E2659
Berna, Paul, E138
Bernard, Bina, E622
Bernard, Kenneth, E245
Bernard O'Hagan (FC; S. Rohmer), E2402
Bernard, Robert, E857
Berndt, Jerry, E2074
Berns-Sobol, Leah, E468
Berry (FC; Dornford Yates), E3147
Berry, Jay, E478
Bertha Cool (FC; A. A. Fair), B29, E1252
Berthelius, Jenny, B386, AR
Bertie Wooster (FC; P. G. Wodehouse), E3106
Berto, Giuseppe, C311
Bertolucci, Attilio, C139, C311, C91
Besana, Renato, C92
Besnier, Patrick, E2976-E2978
Bessatsu, Hoseki, A90
Besses, Ona D., E2369
<u>Best Detective</u>, D351
Bester, Alfred, C162, C527, D461
Bestiault, Jacqueline, E1656
Best Seller Mystery, A115
Bettelheim, Bruno, D97
Betteredge (FC; W. Collins), E688
Beylie, Claude, E2994
Beynon, Jane. See Lewis, Lange
Bezzola, Guido, C94
Biederstadt, Lynn, C96, E2225, E2298
Bien, Guenter, B424, C95
Bierce, Ambrose, E141
Biggers, Earl Derr, A103, B201, B310, C189, C339, C450, C535, E142-E149
Biggers, Julian L., E2381
Bilesmont, E2328
Bilgewater, C. K., D84
Bilham, D. M., E883
Bilker, Audrey L., B30
Bilker, Harvey L., B30
Billings, Harold, E2582
Billy Bunter (FC; dime novel), D77
Binder, Henry, B3
Bingham, John, AR, B61, C542
Binyon, T. J., E274, E389, E409, E2811
Birch, Victor, D391
Bird, Tom, E722
Birmingham, Stephen, E1941
Birns, Margaret B., E531
Bisceglia, Jacques, A17
Bishop, John Lyman, B31
Bishop, Malden Grange, B48
Bishop, Paul, E103, E390
Black, Gavin, AR
Black, Lionel, AR
Black, Thomas B., E150
Black Bat, D341
<u>Black Book Detetive</u>, D341
<u>Black Eagle</u>, D272
Black John Smith, E1452
<u>Black Mask</u>, B2, B290, C63, C169, C298, C341, C709, C749, D309, D342-D350, E325, E332, E387, E761, E800, E804, E1240, E1391, E1805, E2026, E2085, E3088
Blackbeard, Bill, D295, D451, E2944
Blackburn, John, AR
Blackmore, Richard, C852, E151
Blackstock, Charity, E152
Blackstock, Lee. See Blackstock, Charity
Blackwood, Algernon, B41, B430, E153
Bladams (FC; Dickens), E983
Blader, Susan Roberta, B32
Blair, Allan, D246
Blair, David, E650
Blair, Walter, B424, E1364
Blaisdell, Anne, E1768
Blake, Nicholas, B17, B61, B142, B287, B385, C97, C98, C704, C789, E154-E158
Blakeney, T. S., E884
Blanc, Suzanne, AR
Blanch, Robert J., E2099
Blanchard, Robert G., E275
Blanck, Jacob, E2896
Blankfort, Michael, E159
Blassingame, Wyatt, D316
Blayn, Hugo, E1069
Bleiler, E. F., A18, B33, A102, B404, C99, C100, C101, C102, D9, E52, E57-E58, E220, E345, E886-E888, E1071, E1153, E1154, E1200, E1220, E1221, E1224, E1713-E1714, E1717, E2015, E2048, E2342, E2347, E2752, E2817, E2999, E3099, E3109, E3166
Blicher, S., E2889, E2899, E2900
Blin, Frédéric, E1733, E1744
Blinky McQuade (PC), D479
Blishen, Edward, E977
Bloch, Ernst, B283, B424, B451, C103
Blochman, Lawrence G., A64, B48, E168, E2591
Bloch, Robert, A21, A171, D499, D500, E160-E167
Block, Lawrence, A12, B34, B34a, B442, C103a, C637, E3067
Blom, K. Arne, A20, B35, B110, B386, C104-C106, E105, E1074, E2733-E2736, E3052, E3053, E3126
Bloom, Pauline, B48, B409
Bloomfield, Robert, AR
Blosser, Fred, E795
Bloy, Léon, E2707
Blue Jean Billy (PC), D351
Blumenberg, Hans C., E39
Blyth, Harry, D253, D25

Blythe, Robert, D11, E244
Boardman, John, E2488
Boardman, F. W., Jr., B35a
Bob Brooks (FC; dime novel), D42
Bocci, Richard, E1922, E2968
Bodkin, M. McDonnell, C565, E169
Body, François, E2592, E2679
Boeri, Emilio, B36
Bogan, Louise, C107, C464
Bogart, Humphrey, C746, E1256
Bogart, William, D368
Boileau, Pierre, B37, B38, B61, B201, B246, B362, B424, C107a, C260, C570, E1225, E2593, E2646
Boileau, Pierre, and Narcejac, Thomas, E170, E170a
Boisdeffre, Pierre, E2594, E2595
Boisset, Yves, E3114
Bojut, Pierre, E17
Boland, John, AR
Bolinder, Jean, B386, C389
Boll, Ernest, E2100
Boll, Heinrich, E1136
Bommart, Jean, AR, B246, C476
Bonaparte, Marie, E2101, E2129
Bond, H. M., D225-D227
Bondil, Danièle, E285
Bonett, John & Emery, B18, E171
Bonetti, Deborah, C108
Bongiovanni, Giannetto, C109
Bonn, Thomas, B39, B40, C110
Bonner, Margarie, E172
Bonnett, Hal, D296
Bonniot, Roger, B110, E1226
(The) Bony Bulletin, E2928
Booth, Bradford A., E652
Booth, Christopher, E173
Booth, Irwin, E1496
Boothby, Guy, D451, E174
Bordillon, Henri, E1644, E1645, E2759, E2760, E2976, E2978-E2981
Borgenicht, Miriam, AR
Borges, Jorge Luis, A16, A171, B78, B90, B135, B214, B219, B315, B366, B401, C145, C257, C357, C407, C416, C422, E477, E488, C596, C713, E175-E181, E1136, E1646, E2977, E2978
Borneman, Ernest. See McCabe, Cameron
Borowitz, Albert, B41, C111, E473, E889, E2724
Bory, Jean Louis, E2834
Bosetzky, Horst, C593
Bosse, Malcolm, AR
Boston Blackie (FC; Jack Boyle), B134, E196
Boucher, Anthony, A21, A47, A76, A171, B43-B45, B48, B134, B142, B154, B160, B189, B287, C112-C120, C358, C616, C714, C880, C399, E87, E150, E152, E159, E168, E182-E190, E198, E229, E339, E340, E346, E347, E479, E502, E754, E778, E781, E1046, E1075, E1080, E1155, E1263, E1274, E1336, E1440, E1458, E1528, E1546, E1550, E1595, E1614, E1616, E1633, E1773, E1785, E1796, E1851, E1951, E2019, E2037, E2082, E2200, E2201, E2206, E2226-E2229, E2234, E2276, E2299, E2323, E2576-E2578, E2596-E2596, E2844, E2850, E2857, E2912, E3112
Boulle, Pierre, AR
Bouquet, Jean-Louis, B201, E191
Bourdier, Jean, E1934
Bourget, Paul, E192
Bourgoin, Stéphane, C476
Boutell, Clarence V., C121, E532
Bouyxou, Jean-Pierre, E16, E1640
Bova, Ben, E1041
Boverie, Dieudonne, E2598, E2646
Boving, B46
Bow Street, E58
Bow Street Runners, B122
Bowery Billy (FC; dime novel), D51, D52, D171
Bowery Boy Library, D52
Bowles, Paul, B2, B3
Bowman, Barbara, B113, E1507
Bowen, Elizabeth, E1715
Box, Edgar, E193-E195
Boy Pleydell (FC; Dornford Yates), E3147
Boy Scout Series, D29
Boy Spy Series, D83
Boyd, Ann S., E1088
Boyd, Mary, E1909
Boyd, Peter, E862, E869, E890
Boyer, Alain-Michel, E2370
Boyle, Andrew, E509
Boyle, Jack, B134, E196
Boyles, John, E723
(The) Boys' Book Collector, D12
Boys Friend Library, D276, D281, D329
Boys of New York, D13, D16, 48, D204
Boysie Oakes (FC; J. Gardner), B308
Bozzetto, Roger, E2994
Brabazon, James, E2489
Brackett, Leigh, B43, C247, E203, E197-E200
Bradbrook, B. R., E480
Bradbury, Ray, E163, E200-E207, E2032
Bradd, Sid, D403
Braddon, Mary Elizabeth, B101, B163, B311, C123, C204, C533, E208-E214
Bradley, Marion Zimmer, E197
Bradley, Mary Hastings, AR
Bragin, Charles, D202
Brahce, Jack, D84
Brahms, Caryl, AR
Braithwaite, William Stanley, E2935, E2952
Bramah, Ernest, B17, C497, C605, E215-E227
Bramhall, Marion, AR
Brand, Christianna, B84, B134, B270, B309, C223, C488, E128, E228-E235, E533, E562
Brand, John, E2890
Brand, Max, A4, E2032, E236-E240
Brandon, John G., AR, A103, C272
Brandt, Bruce E., C122
Brannback, Claudia, B376
Brannon, William T., B409
Branson, H. C., AR
Brant House, D445, Ed446
Brantlinger, Patrick, C123
Brauchli, Jakob, B47
Braun, Lillian Jackson, AR
Brautigan, Richard, C343
Brave & Bold Series, D52
Braveman, David, E2382
Brean, Herbert, AR, B48, B409
Brecht, Bertolt, B78, B112, B146, B424, B451, C124, C415
Breen, Jon L., A21, A22, A148, A154, B63, B216, C125-C127, E1, E75, E142, E143, E241, E357, E481, E1082, E2230, E2865, E3061, E3097
Breit, Harvey L., E2348, E2360
Bremner, Marjorie, C128
Brend, Gavin, E891
Brentano, B360
Brengues, Frédérique, E310
Brenman, Claes, B386, C389
Bresler, Fenton, E2599
Breton, Jacques, A23
Brett, Michael, A12
Brett, Simon, AR, A12, C11, C785
Brewer, Gil, E242
Brice, Alec W., E826

Bridge, Ann, E243
Bridges, Victor, AR
Bridget Hunter (FC; Jonathan Ross), E2466
Bridgwater, John, D228-D231
Brin, Irene, C129
Briney, Robert E., A24-A26, B15, B43, B290, C130, C238, D414, D440, E182, E184, E199, E232, E233, E235, E253, E348-E350, E352, E724, E727, E1516, E1775, E1939, E2360, E2383-E2393, E2415, E2417, E2432, E2448, E2459
Briot, E2310
Brisbane, Coutts, D241, D246
Brittain, William, AR
Broadway Billy (FC; dime novel), D51, D52
Broberg, Jan, A27, B49-B57, B110, C105, C106, C131, C132, E155, E193, E1474, E2126, E2212, E2349
Brochet, Jean, E271
Brochier, Jean-Jacques, B378, E2600
Brock, Lynn, AR
Brodwin, Stanley, E2891
Brody, Howard, E1156-E1160, E1163
Brohaugh, William, B441
Bronne, Carlo, E2601
Bronner, Milton, E300
Bronski, Michael, C133
Bronson, F. W., AR
Bronte, Charlotte, E650
Brontes, C743
Brooks, Cleanth, E1051
Brooks, Edwy Searles, B58, D25, D33, D126, D222, D252, D289, E244
Brooks, Lawrence F., E2779
Brooks, Maud, A28, A85
Brooks, Van Wyck, E1879
Brophy, Bridget, C134, C188, E1464, E2602
Broset, Myrtis, E751
Brown, Carter, AR, B319
Brown, Charles Brockden, E245-E250
Brown, Elizabeth C., E252, E257, E259
Brown, Fredric, B18, B48, B134, B201, B269, B409, C39, C674, E251-E266a
Brown, May, E1052
Brown, Russell, E1856
Brown, Wray D., E2045
Browne, Alicia, E2882
Browne, G. W., E133
Browne, Howard, E267-E270
Browne, Nelson, E1716
Browne, Pat, B216
Browne, Ray B., B216, D93, E2882
Brownell, David, E1134, E1628, E1717
Broxholme, John, E1618
Bruccoli, Matthew, E391-E394, E1857-E1858
Bruce, George, AR
Bruce, Jean, C476, E271-E272, E3006
Bruce, Josette, AR
Bruce, Leo, B18, C153, E272a-E273
Bruers, Antonio, C135
Brumell, R. A., A29
Brunori, Vittorio, B59
Bruton, Eric, AR
Bryant, Edward, E1041
Bryant, Estrella S., A30
Bryson, Charles. See Barry, Charles
Buchan, John, B215, B240, B256, B270, B303, B420, C72, C146, C233, C320, C540, C541, C609, E44, E274-E298, E1087, E1311, E1356, E1712, E3147
Buch, Hans Christoph, B126, B424, E1089
Buchloh, Paul G., B295, B60, B61, C137, C138, E482, E653, E2102
Bucholtz, Herbert. See Luckless, John
Buckley, Tom, E698
Buckley, William F., Jr., C735
Bude, John, AR
Buffalo Bill, C433, D28, D79, D177
Buffalo Bill Stories, D171
Buhrer, Barbara, E1768
Buissière, François, B110, E1646
Bulldog Drummond (FC; Sapper), B253, B310, C540, E2474, E2475, E2478, E2479
Bulletin 813, B107
Bullett, Gerald, B17, E299
Bullough, Vern L., B3
Bulleseye, D19, D419
Bulwer-Lytton, Edward, C164, E5
Burack, A. S., B62-B65, B117, B124
Burack, Sylvia K., B441
Burger, Margaret A., E2493, E2527
Burgess, Gelett, AR, D131, D136, D198
Burg, Gary, E2394
Burke, John F., AR
Burke, Thomas, C492, E300-E303, E2403
Burkes, James H., B137c
Burleson, James Bernard, Jr., E2490
Burley, W. J., AR
Burnett, William Riley, B73, C623, E304-E305
Burns, Rex, AR, B64
Burns, W. B., D13
Burns, William, D131, D232
Burroughs, Edgar Rice, B88
Burt, Charles, A28
Burtich, Arloine, A85
Burtis, Thomson, AR
Burton, Frederick R., D133
Burton, Miles, B17
Burton, Miles. See also Rhode, John
Busby, Roger, AR
Busch, Lloyd, E351
Busche, Jurgen, E40, E42
Bush, Christopher, AR, E701
Butler, Gwendoline, AR
Butor, Michel, B3, B102, C429, C447, E306-E307, E1017, E2038
Buxbaum, Edith, C141
Buzzati, Dino, C139, C311
B. W. S., E1161
Byerly, Ann, C140
Byfield, Barbara Ninde, C142
Byrd, Max, C143
Byrne, Donn, C520
Byrne, St. Clare, E2519

C. B. Greenfield (FC; L. Kallen), E1554
C. W. Sughrue (FC; J. Crumley), B92, E753a
Cacaret, Allain, E16
Cadogan, Mary, B77
Cahiers Jean Ray, E2311
Cahill, Tim, E753
Caillois, Roger, B78, B93, B264, B269, C48, C107, C145, C257
Caillot, Patrice, E2970
Caillou, Allain, AR, A157
Cain, James M., B73, B134, B239, B428, C37, C623, C865, D343, E1879, E242, E309-E331, E2871
Cain, Paul, E332-E333
Caird, Janet, AR
Calder, Ritchie, E534
Calendrillo, Linda T., C146
Calisi, Romano, E1092
Callendar, Newgate, C147
Camara, Caroline, E1689, E1691
Cambiaire, Célestin Pierre, E1227, E2103
Camerer, Rudi, E858
Camerino, Aldo, C148, C149, E483, E1036
Cameron, James, E3012

Cameron, Mary, C150
Cameron, Owen, AR
Campbell, Bruce, D110
Campbell, Frank, E1817
Campbell, Ian, E1090
Campbell, John Franklin, AR
Campbell, Ramsay, E163
Campbell, SueEllen, B92, C151
Campenni, Frank J., E1479
Campos, Jorge, C152
Camus, Albert, C7, E321
Canady, John. See Head, Matthew
Cancogni, Manlio, C311
Candy, Edward, AR
Cannadine, David, E2491
Cannan, Joanna, B18, E334
Cannarozzo, Franco, C263
Canning, Victor, AR, B50
Cannon, JoAnn, B92, E2575a
Cannon, Mary, C153
Canova, Gian Battista, E1218
Capek, Karel, C154, E335-E337, E480
Capote, Truman, B410
Caprettini, C48
Caproni, Giorgio, C311
Captain Dack (FC; dime novel), D245, D282
Captain Hastings (FC; A. Christie), E521
Captain Satan (PC), D312, D352
Captain of Detectives Brady (FC; Victor Maxwell), E1977
Captain Zero (PC), D354
Caradec, François, E1932
Carboni, Guido, C155, C156
Carden, Percy, E852, E892-E894, E963, E974
Cardwell, Margaret, E851, E852, E854, E855, E895-E897, E907, E955
Carey, Bernice, E338-E340
Carl Peterson (FC; Dornford Yates), E2478
Carle, C. E. See Morgan, Michael
Carleton, Marjorie, AR
Carlin, Stanley A. E75
Carling, Bjorn, B66
Carlisle, Charles R., B216, C157
Carmichael, Harry, AR
Carnac, Carol, AR
Carnacki (FC; W. H. Hodgson), E1502
Carpenter, Edward C., E1091
Carr, A. H. Z., B18, E341
Carr, Glyn, B18, E342, E343
Carr, John Dickson, A180, B24, B43, B48, B67, B70, B134, B142, B247, B269, B287, B290, B304, B336, B419, C17, C130, C158-C160, C260, C328, C437, C734, C867, E128, E129, E344-E376, E532, E910, E1042, E2219, E3154
Carr, Margaret, AR
Carr, Nick. See Carr, Wooda Nicholas
Carr, Wooda Nicholas ("Nick"), D297, D303, D313, D338-D340, D357, D359, D394, D396, D397, D403, D404, D410, D422-D426, D428, D430, D474, D479-D481, D503, E2852, E2877
Carroll, James, AR
Carroll, Lewis, B144, E2235a
Carroll, Roy, D332
Carrouges, Michel, E16
Carse, Robert, AR
Carter, John, A31, A58, B142, C161
Carter, John Franklin. See "Diplomat"
Carter, Lin, E2283
Carter, Nick, AR, B257, B107, B310. See also Nick Carter
Carter, Steven R., B3, B16, B216, C162, E1135, E1551, E1859, E2067, E2318, E2840
Cartland, Barbara, C841
Carton, Martien, C306, E378
Carvic, Heron, AR
Casey, Robert J., B142, C163
Cashman, Gerry, C757
Caspary, Vera, B309, E379-E381
Cassiday, Bruce, B65, B68, B117, B271, B272, B409, C163
Cassill, R. V., B239, E2869
Cassis, A. F., E1312
Cassola, Carlo, C311
Castle, Robert, E2382, E2395
Cataio, Joseph, A32
Catogan, Valère, E1647, E1663
Cauthen, Irby, E2107
(The) Cavalier, D407
Cave, Hugh B., D437
Cawelti, John, B69, B315, B434, C165, E395, E535, E1365, E1629, E2104, E2604, E2737, E2919
Caylor, O. P., D133
Cecil, Henry, AR
Cendrars, Blaise, E18
Cervantes, Miguel, E2785, E2787
Chabrol, Claude, E2244
Chacko, David, B5
Chadwick, Paul, D445
Chamberlain, Anne, AR, B15
Champigny, Robert, B70, E2374, E2377
Champion, D'Arcy L., D234, D434
Champlin, Charles, E1860
Chance, John Newton, AR
Chance Purdue (FC; Ross H. Spencer), E2730
Chandler, Cissy (Mrs. Raymond), E409, E439
Chandler, Frank Wadleigh, B71, C166
Chandler, Raymond, B1, B3, B5, B17, B26, B27, B61, B63, B64, B69, B73, B79, B96, B99, B110, B116, B124, B125, B129, B142, B146, B190, B201, B215, B239, B242, B264, B269, B283, B287, B306, B310, B312, B313, B362, B371, B375, B385, B389, B396, B414, B424, B428, B429, C7, C17, C25, C35, C37, C72, C95, C156, C158, C376, C682, E41, C167, C168, C169, C171, C173, C234, C267, C272a, C278, C319, C339, C341, C343, C351, C352, C369, C399, C404, C425, C488a, C496, C499, C512, C529, C543, C568, C570, C571, C601, C616, C623, C678, C736, C758, C840, C867, E324, E382-E457, E640, E788, E1101, E1365, E1406, E1426, E1428, E1445, E1464, E1478, E1486, E1804, E1859, E1861, E1889, E1913, E1991, E203, E2032, E2068, E2071, E2110, E2666, E2718, E2737, E2860, E2871, E2872, E3159
Chandos (FC; Dornford Yates), E3147
Chang, B443
Chang Apana, E147
Chang Li Ching (FC; D. Hammett), B443
Chantland, Joy, C171
Chapman, David, E1162
Chapman, Hall, E933
Charles Grandison (FC; Samuel Richardson), E2484
Charles Paris (FC; Simon Brett), C11
Charles, Pierre, E3015
Charles Stuart, C517
Charlie Chan (FC; E. D. Biggers), A59, A73, B310, B443, C535, E142, E144-E149
Charney, Hannah, B72, C172
Charteris, Leslie, B253, A106, B36, B414, C339, E458-E466, E2423
Charyn, Jerome, B351, E467-E469
Chase, Borden, AR
Chase, James Hadley, B348, C606, E470-E472
Chastain, Thomas, AR, B105, B117, C173, E1862
Chastaing, Maxime, B78, B110, C174
Chavance, Louis, E16
Chavdarian, C. G., E1163
Chekhov, Anton, E2680

Ch'en, Jerome, C175
Chen Chih-Mai, E2956
Chenu, Bob, D4, D29, D83, D101-D103
Chenu, Julius R., D107
Chergé, Gérard de, E162, E259, E3114
Chester, George, E23, E473
Chester, Gilbert, A4, D270
Chesterton, Cecil, C176
Chesterton, Gilbert Keith, A22, A171, A179, B5, B17, B41, B60, B61, B78, B90, B122, B142, B144, B146, B201, B205, B215, B248, B269, B287, B337, B338, B340, B343, B349, B385, B424, C17, C177-C183, C195, C260, C272a, C332, C342, C436, C503, C605, C649, C713, C771, C773, C825,, E118, E175, E176, E177, E179, E180, E335, E349, E474-E501, E980, E1323, E1508, E1641, E2681
Cheyney, Peter, A4, B27, B240, B303, C499, C541, E502-E507, E2740
Chianese, Robert, B3
Chichester, John Jay, E508
Chidsey, Donald Barr, AR
Chief Inspector French (FC; F. W. Crofts), B253
Child, Richard Washburn, B430
Childers, Ernest, B303, C72, E509-E516
Chin, Shunshin, E517
Chinnock, Sara D., E909
Christensen, Peter J., E246, E1502
Christie, Agatha, A4, A105-A107, A156, A171, A180, B6, B17, B26, B28, B74, B94, B107, B135, B190, B241, B248, B254, B264, B269, B287, B302, B304, B310, B337, B364, B378, B389, B391, B398, B410, B424, B434, C2, C14, C16, C35, C39, C121, C221, C240, C287, C339, C361, C375, C398, C421, C436, C465, C479, C497, C499, C507, C518, C567, C630, C687, C718, C751, C758, C777, C801, C868, C869, E192, E440, E518-E619, E1537, E1539, E1898, E1953, E1955, E2633, E2718
Christie, Sandra Miller, B272
Christopher, J. R., B159, C182, C184, C185, C187, C188, C444, C528, E182, E184, E1313, E2023, E2105, E2233-E2241, E2396, E2492-E2497, E2498, E2525
Christopher Syn (FC; R. Thorndike), E2877
Chu Lung (PC), D404
Chung, Sue, C189
Churchill, Winston, C415
Churchill, C. E., D126
Churchill, Reginald, E842
Churnus, Judith, E2778
Ciabattini, Giuseppe, E620
Ciampi, Yves, E2975
Cicero, C779
Citati, Pietro, E1219
Clark, Al, B75, E400
Clark, Alfred Gordon, E1441
Clark, Bill, D332, E236. See also Clark, William J.
Clark, Curt. See Westlake, Donald
Clark, Dorothy, AR
Clark, Douglas, E621
Clark, Hasley, E791
Clark, James D., E487
Clark, J. C. L., E942
Clark, John D., E2780
Clark, Mary Higgins, E622
Clark, Meera, E1555
Clark, Philip, B18, E623
Clark, S. L., E1536, E2499-E2500
Clark, William J., D364, D448, E3, E107, E898, E1337, E1338, E1496, E1838, E2078, E2465, E2831, E2078, E3. See also Clark, Bill
Clarke, Anna, AR
Clarke, Donald Henderson, E624
Clason, Clyde B., AR, B62
Claude Duval (FC; dime novel), D31
Clay, Bertha M., D28, D154, E1436
Clayton, Richard. See Haggard, William
Cleary, Jon, AR, C500
Cleek (FC; T. Hanshew), E1433-E1435
Cleeve, Brian, AR
Cleisz, Gerard, E2605, E2646
Clemens, Nancy, E2296, na
Clement, Hal, C527
Clerambault, Serge, E2968
Cleveland, Carol, E1818
Clifford, Boniface, D432
Clifford, Francis, B50, E625
Clinton-Baddeley, V. C., AR
Clouzot, Henri-Georges, E2758a
Clubfoot (FC; V. Williams), C535
Clues, A38
Clues Detective, D139
Clurman, Robert, D34, D133
Coatmeur, Jean François, AR
Cobb, G. Belton, AR
Cobb, Irvin S., D14
Cockroft, T. G. L., D498
Cocteau, Jean, B157, E18, E2646, E2679, E2690
Cody, Richard, E1974
Coe, Charles Francis, E626
Coe, Tucker, C381, E3066, E3070, E3074, E3076, E3081. See also Westlake, Donald
Coffey, Joseph, E724
Cohen, Octavus Roy, AR, B298
Cohen, Ralph, C190
Cohen, Stanley, AR
Cohn, Jan, B16, E2350-E2351, E2357, E2367
Colbron, Grace Isabel, C191
Colby, Victor, D233-D235
Colcombe, William, D236, D237
Coldwell, Marion, E631
Cole, Don, C192
Cole, G. D. H., A105, B17, B253, E627-E630
Cole, Hubert, E3103
Cole, Jackson, D409
Cole, Margaret, A105, B17, B251, E627-E630
Coles, Stephen L., E2055
Coles, Manning, A110, B303, E631-E633
Colin, Jean-Paul, E16, E17, E1228, E1648, E1735, E1744
Collier, John, AR
Collins, Charles Allston, E891, E896, E897, E899, E900, E938
Collins, Mary, AR
Collins, Max Allan, E634, E2738, E2870, E2871
Collins, Michael, B107, E635-E641
Collins, Philip, E843, E859, E901, E902
Collins, Wilkie, A161, B6, B60, B61, B101, B118, B163, B215, B237, B243, B289, B300, B311, B337, B362, B372, B391, C101, C123, C176, C204, C259, C356, C366, C419, C465, C607, C703, C712, C718, C755, C875, E642-E697, E840, E908, E945, E985, E2181, E2212, E2271, E2516, E3042
Collinson, Peter. See Hammett, Dashiell
Colombo, Furio, E1092
Colombo, John Robert, E153, E2397
Colonel Clay (FC; Grant Allen), E22
Colonel Gethryn (FC; P. MacDonald), E1852
Colton Wolfe (FC; T. Hillerman), E1471
Columbia Pulp Chain, D355
Coma, Javier, B73
Comber, Leon, B449
Combs, William W., E1863
Comisso, Giovanni, B116

(The) Commissar (German series character), C746
Compère, Daniel, E1649, E1736-E1737, E1744, E2994
Conant, Paul, AR
Condon, Richard, E698-E699a
Cone, Edward T., C193
Conger, Lesley, D114
Connington, J. J., B24, B340, E700-E702
Connolly, Cyril, C194
Conrad, Horst, B74
Conrad, Joseph, B4, B162, B256, B303, C146, C754, E703-E705, E1310, E1324, E1879
Conrad, Peter, E401
Consiglio, Alberto, C195
Constance, Kent, E947
Constantine, K. C., B18, C706-C709
The Continental Op (FC; Hammett), E1361, E1367, E1376, E1389, E1392, E1398, E1403, E1405, E1412, E1413, E1417, E1420, E1428
Conway, Eustace, E903
Cook, Bruce, E1864
Cook, Doris, E2892
Cook, Fred, D418
Cook, Michael L., A33-A41, A126, A156, B107, D15, E78
Cook, Robin, C330, E710-E711
Cook, Wister, E1819
Cook, William Wallace, D65
Cool Carter (FC; dime novel), D181
Coombes, Roy, B392
Cooper-Clark, Diana, B75, E1045
Cooper, Anice, E2398
Cooper, Brian, AR
Cooper, Courtney Riley, AR
Cooper, James Fenimore, B421, C95, C341, C383, C517, C585, C744, C779
Cooper, Susan, E2214
Cooper, William, E2725
Coppard, A. E., AR
Coppel, Alec, AR
Coppel, Alfred, AR
Copper, Basil, AR
Copyright Novels, A78
Cora Twyford (FC; dime novel), D282
Corbett, James, C197
Corcoran, William, AR
Cordasco, Francesco, E654
Cordelia Gray (FC; P. D. James), B354
Cordery, Garth, E904
Cordier, George H., D16, D204
Corinth/Regency, D314a
Corinth Paperbacks, C433
Corkhill, Louis, AR
Corman, Roger, C746
Comeau, Alain, E2868
Cornillon, John, E1302
Corrigan, Mark, AR
Corsaut, Aneta, B76
Cortazar, Julio, E1136
Cory, Desmond, AR, A48
Coryell, John R., D32, D74, D134-D136, D160, D164, D198, D199
Coryell, Russell M., D135, D198
Costaz, Gilles, E1738, E1744, E2613
Coster, Howard, B41
Costume, M., E1679
Cotton, John, C198
Couch, Frisco Bert, D136
Couderc, J. J., E1679
Couegnas, Daniel, E1650, E1739, E1744, E2978, E2982-E2984, E2994
Coulter, Stephen, AR
Counselman, Mary Elizabeth, E163
Count Stenbock (FC; M. P. Shiel), E2582
Courtier, S. H., AR
Courtine, Robert J., E2606, E2607, E2646
Cowdrick, George, D85
Cowen, Frances, AR
Cox, A. B., B304, C869, E129, E132-E134, E136
Cox, A. B. See also Bentley, E. C.
Cox, Arthur J., B2, E855, E905-E908
Cox, Edmund C., C565, E715
Cox, E. G., A4
Cox, J. Randolph, B260, C186, C199, C200, D2, D17, D18, D23, D137-D147, D238, D309, D362, D452, E27, E277-E280, E461, E465, E470, E718, E1433, E1992, E2221, E2319, E3097, E3106, E3143
Cox, Tom, E511
Cox, William R., D300, E716-E717
Coxe, George Harmon, B30, B62, B234, E718-E719
Craig, Jonathan, E720
Craig Kennedy (FC; Frank Packard), C638, D328, D442, E2064, E2319, E2321
Craig, Patricia, B77, E1999
Crane, Frances, AR, B63
Crane, John K., E3086
Craufurd, Ross, D200, D205, E2312
Crawford, Francis Marion, B430
Crawford, Gary, A54, A55
Crawford, Walter, E2936-E2937
Creasey, John, A4, A106, B48, B84, B96, C201, C247, C540, C541, E721-E735
Cremante, Renzo, B78
Crichton, Michael, AR
Crichton, Robert, AR
Crider, Allen B., B79, B80, B216, E759, E1073, E3091
Crime Busters, D139, D356
Crime Club, A79, B24
Crime Writers Association, B84, C128
Crimson Mask (PC), D357
Crisparkle (FC; Dickens), E951, E981
Crispin, Edmund, B17, B50, B61, B83, C76, C153, C205, C805, E537, E562, E736-E740
Crofts, Freeman Wills, B17, B28, B253, B398, C366, C567, C715, C751, E700, E741-E745, E3009
Crombie, Darrel, E2021
Cross, Amanda, B16, B18, B75, C47, C390, C453, E746-E750
Cross, J. F., E909
Cross, James, AR
Crossen, Kendell Foster, B142, D334, E751-E752
Cruickshank, E5
Crumley, James, B92, C603, E753a
Crystal, Tamar, E2781
Cullingford, Guy, AR
Culver, Timothy J., E3070, E3081. See also Westlake, Donald
Cumberland, Marten, AR, C206
Cummings, J. C., C207
Cummings, Ralph, D15, D19-D21, D158
Cummings, Ray, AR, D310
Cummings King Monk (FC; M. P. Shiel), E2579
Cunningham, A. B., E754-E755
Cunningham, Eugene, AR
Cunningham, E. V., B339, E756
Cuppy, Will, B142, C208, D414
Cure, Ray, D22, D239
Curry, Nancy, E1226, E1229
Curtis, Richard Hale. See Deming, Richard
Curtis, Robert C., E3013
Curtiss, Ursula, AR
Cushing, Charles Phelps, C209
Cussler, Clive, A158

Cuthbert, Jack, E1564

Dacolta, Roman, E3087
Dadoun, Roger, B346
Dahlin, Robert, C212
Dahl, Roald, B398, E757
Dahl, Tor Edwin, C210, C211
Dahl, Willy, B86, B87
Daiber, Hans, B424, C213
Dale, Alzina, E485, E2541
Dale, Terry, E165
Dali, Salvador, C129
Daly, Carroll John, B216, B134, C267, C299, C734, C309, C343, E758-E764, E1240
Daly, Elizabeth, B18, B364, E765-E767
Dameron, J. Lesley, E2106, E2107
D'Amore, Bruno, E2938
Dan Fortune (FC; Michael Collins), E635, E641
Dan Fowler (PC), D358
Dana, Freeman, E2848, E2849
Dane, Clemence, AR, B28, C214, C567, E2706
Danesford, Earle, D215
Daniel (Biblical), C214
Daniel, Glyn, AR
Daniel, Robert, E2108
Daniel, Roland, E768, E2403
Daniel-Rops, E2608, E2646
Daniell, David, E281-E283
Daniels, Norman, E769-E770, D319, D334
Dannay, Frederic, E22, B234, E2249, E2253, E2273. See also Queen, Ellery
Dante, E2567
Dan Turner (PC), D359, E111
Darby, Ken, E2782
Darcis, Pierre. See Pelman, Brice
Dard, Frédéric, E771-E773
Daredevil Aces, D412
Dark, Eleanor, E774
Dark, James, A48
Darling, Carolyn, B430
Darrach, Brad, E1865
D'Atagnan (FC; A. Dumas), D134
Darwin, Charles, C352
DAST Magazine, A51
Datchery (FC; Dickens), E847, E857, E864, E869, E873, E874, E876, E880, E884, E886, E892, E903, E916, E917, E923, E926, E930, E932, E933, E936, E939, E940, E945, E949, E951, E953, E957, E960, E962, E963, E968-E970, E974, E975, E977-E979, E981-E983, E985, E986, E988, E998
Daudet, Alphonse, C204
Dauphine, Claude, E16
Dave Fearless (FC; juvenile series), D84
Davenport, Basil, E2232
Davenport, Guiles, B62, C216
Davey, Jocelyn, AR
David Callan (FC; J. Mitchell), E2002
(Chief Inspector) David Madden (FC; Disney), E1004
David-Neel, Alexandra, E775
Davidson, Edward H., E2109
Davidson, Lionel, B181, E776
Davidson, M., E174
Davidson, Martha, A43
Davidson, T. L., E777
Davies, L. P., AR
Davies, Russell, B82, E402, E409
Daviot, Gordon. See Tey, Josephine
Davis, Dorothy Salisbury, B48, B272, B105, B134, B272, B409, C217, E778, E779, E2858
Davis, Earle, E1522
Davis, Frederick C., B48, B62, D334, D422, E3092
Davis, Frederick W., D150, D157, D174, D188, E780
Davis, Mildred, E781
Davis, Norbert, E782
Davis, Nuel Pharr, E655
Davis, Paxton, E41-E42
Davis, Robert, E2061
Dawn, Adam, E2473
Dawson, Harry, E1694, E1695, E785
Dawson, Harvey D., E1343
Day, A. Grove, E774
Day, Brad, B88, E2020, E2399
Day-Lewis, C., E156. See also Blake, Nicholas
Day-Lewis, Sean, E157
Dazaar (FC; dime novel), D172, D195
Deadline, E3113
Deadwood Dick (FC; dime novel), D36, D63, D77
Deadwood Dick, Jr. (FC; dime novel), D52, D85
Deal, Babs H., AR, B64
Dean, Amber, AR, B48
DeAndrea, William, AR, C637, E1634, E3068
Deane, Paul, D93
De Angelis, Augusto, C109, C218, C350, E784
Dean, Graham M., D82
Dean, Spencer. See Sterling, Stewart
Debray-Ritzen, E2609-E2610, E2646
Debrett, Hal, AR. See also Halliday, Brett
Debyser, Francis, E538
de Camp, L. Sprague, C518
De Chirico, Giorgio, C129
Decrest, Jacques, AR, B246
De Ford, Miriam Allen, AR, B63, C219
DeGaulle, Charles, E1673
Deighton, Len, A48, B181, B240, B303, C14, C72, C320, C841, E785-E788
De Laet, Danny, B213, C220
de la Mare, Walter, E666
de la Torre, Lillian, E789-E790a, E910
Delbègue, Jean-Paul, E1651
Del Buono, Oreste, C139, C311, C316, E1092, E2110, E2242
Delcourt, Xavier, E306
Dell, A24, A80, A96, 107, A108
Dell Great Mystery Library, A107
Dell Mapbacks, E1394
Del Monte, Alberto, B89, B90
Deloux, Jean-Pierre, A13, A14, B378, E62, E63, E82, E258, E259, E285, E304, E309, E310, E403, E467, E468, E756, E1279, E1367, E1368, E1445, E1518, E1635, E1690, E1691, E1811, E1922, E1933, E1936, E1937, E2217, E2218, E2243, E2244, E2707, E2708, E2872, E3069, E3070
Delving, Michael, AR
Demaris, Ovid, AR
Demarr, Mary Jean, E1004, E2198, E2828
Dembling, Merwin, E1164
Deming, Richard, B107, E791
De Morgan, William, E980
Demouzon, Alain, B378, E1922, E2978, E2984-E2986, E2994
Denbie, Roger, C834
Denevi, Marco, B214
Deniker, (Professor), E2611, E2646
Dennington, Charlotte, C220a
Dennis, Nigel, E539
Dennis, Ralph, E792-E794
Dent, Lester, B48, D309, D367, D378, D379, D382, D467, E795-E807
Dent, (Mrs.) Lester, D389
Deorad, E959
DePaolo, Rosemary, C221

Depken, Friedrich, B61, B91, C222
De Polo, Harold, AR
Department of Dead Ends (Series; R. Vickers), E3002, E3004
Deputy Parr (FC; F. I. Anderson), E55
Derby, Mark, C541
Derek Flint (Film character), A48
Derleth, August, A87, E808-E820, E2424
D'Errico, E., C315, C350, E210, E821
Derrida, Jacques, E2173
Désiré, B107
Desmond, Hugh, AR
Desnos, Robert, E18
Detective Sergeant Belford (FC; dime novel), D240
Detective Story Magazine, D139, D145, D351, D362, D363
Detective Story Monthly, D495
Detective Tales, D80
Detective Weekly (British), D19, D274, D284
Detective Fiction Weekly, D361, D309, D497, E1455
Detective Inspector Coutts (FC; dime novel), D240
Detective Novels Magazine, D357, D408
Detective Story Magazine, D139, D145, D351, D362, D363
Detective Story Monthly, D495
Detective Tales, D80
Detective Weekly (British), D19, D274, D284
Detective Sergeant Belford (FC; dime novel), D240
Devenny, Jack, D403
Devi, Shakuntala, E822
Devillers, Jean-Pierre, E1368
Devine, D. M., AR
DeVitis, A. A., E1314
DeVoto, Bernard, C867, E2783
De Waal, Ronald Burt, C230
DeWeese, Gene, A12
Dewey, Thomas B., B18, E823
Dewitt, Jack, D392
Dexter, Colin, AR
Dexter, Walter, E911
Dey, Frederick Van Renssalaer, AR, D32, D20, D133, D137, D148, D149, D151, D152, D154, D155, D168, D173, D187, D197, D199
Dey, Haryot Holt (Mrs.), D20
De Zuani, C231
Diamond Dick (FC; dime novel), D63, D153
Diaz, Cesar E., B95
Dick Barton (FC; dime novel), D77
Dick Dobbs (FC; dime novel), D86
Dick Dobbs Detective Weekly, D86, D182
Dickens, Charles, A22, B2, B4, B60, B237, B257, B300, B311, B359, B375, C255, C703, C859, E5, E100, E498, E647, E653, E657, E669, E679, E695, E705, E825-E1009, E1053, E1157, E1201, E1310, E1342, E2271, E2313, E2769
Dickens, Charles, Jr., E891, E943, E985
Dickensheet, D. W., E182, E184
Dickenson, Fred, AR
Dickinson, Peter, B309, E1000-E1002
Dickson, Carl Byron, C232
Dickson, Carter, B134. See also Carr, John Dickson
Dickstein, Morris, C233
Dick Tracy (comic strip character), B309
Dick Turpin (dime novel), B7, D3
Didelot, Francis, AR
Diebolt, Evelyne, E1740, E1744, E1518
Diehl, William, AR
Dikty, Alan, D12
Dikty, T. E., D12
Dilnot, George, D231
Di Manno, Yves, B110, B110
Dime Library (Beadle), D52
Dime Mystery Magazine, D437
Diment, Adam, AR
Dinan, John, E462
Dingeldey, Erika, B424, C234
Dinguirard, J. C., A94, E1652-E1655, E1656, E1663, E1679, E2760
Di Pirajno, Denti, C139, C311
Diplomat, E1003
Dirckx, John F., E1165-E1176
Diskin, Patrick, E2111
Disney, Doris Miles, E1004-E1005
Disney, Dorothy Cameron, AR, E2352
di Vanni, Roberto, B116
Dixon, Franklin W., D92, E791
Dixon Hawke (FC; dime novel), D87
Dixon Hawke Library, D87
Dizer, John T., D23
"DLS Newsletter," E2505
Dobbin, William James, D155
Dobie, Charles Caldwell, B430
Doc Savage (PC), A38, D297, D305,D326, D334, D364-D390, D476, E801-E803, E806, E1832, E1833, E3028
Doctor Death (PC), D314, D392, D393
Doctor Nikola (FC; Guy Boothby), E174
Doctor Norbury (FC; F. A. Freeman), E1208
Doctor Satan (PC), D314
Doctor. See also Dr.
Dodge, David, AR
Doerrer, David, A46
Do Good Boys (juvenile series), D30
Dolend, Virginia, E2503
Dolphin, Rex, D240-D241
Dolph, Jack, AR
Dolson, Hildegarde, AR
Dominic, R. B., E1628
Dömötör, Tekla, C236
Donald Lam (FC; A. A. Fair), B290, E1252
Donaldson-Evans, Lance K., C237, E3006
Donaldson, Betty, E2920, E2927
Donaldson, Norman, A47, B2, B159, B290, C583, E22, E209, E512, E1008, E1156, E1163, E1177-E1189, E1210, E1597, E1718-E1719, E1852, E3026
Don Diavolo (PC), D440, E2304
Donelson, Ken, D24
Donovan, Dick, C228, E1006
Donovan, Frank P., C238
Donovan, Gertrude Monica, E2504
Don Quixote (FC; Cervantes), E2785
Dooley, Allan, E1952
Dooley, Linda J., E1952
Doran, George, E2353, E3014
Dorian Silk (FC; Simon Harvester), A158
Dorinson, Zahava K., E1866
Dorn, Dean M. See Morgan, Michael
Dorothée (FC; M. Leblanc), E1644
Dostoevsky, Fyodor, B295, B359, C7, C308, E327, E825, E1007, E1062, E2585, E2586, E2680, E327
Double Detective, D391
Doughty, Francis, D202, D205-D209, D211, D214
Douglass, Donald MacNutt, AR
Doulis, Thomas, E1820
Dove, George, B96, B434, C239-C243, E404, E1596, E1787, E1798, E2710, E2720, E3054, E3055, E3057, E3095
Downie, R. A., E1092
Downing, Todd, AR
Doyle, Arthur Conan, A5, A22, A171, A180, B1, B2, B6, B17, B24, B60, B78, B90, B99, B115,

B118, B142, B190, B201, B205, B208, B215, B216, B237, B243, B254, B257, B261, B264, B269, B274, B275, B300, B302, B310, B337, B343, B346, B351, B352, B355, B362, B372, B384, B391, B421, B424, C17, C25, C193, C207, C222, C230, C281, C316, C518, C534, C552, C553, C605, C607, C608, C629, C638, C642, C668, C679, C703, C718, C732, C733, C740, C758, C771, C783, C825, C862, C866, C868, C875, E353, E373, E449, E482, E697, E951, E1023, E1054, E1224, E1780, E1889, E2014, E2041, E2110, E2125, E2139, E2163, E2192, E2271, E2313, E2523, E2760, E2784, E2790, E2815, E2887, E2898, E2903, E3042, E3105
Doyle, Brian, D25
Dr. Eustace Hailey (FC; A. Wynne), B253, E3139
Dr. F (FC; A. Derleth), E2424
Dr. Ferraro (FC; dime novel), D241
Dr. Huxton Rymer (FC; dime novel), D265, D279b
Dr. Jekyll (FC; R. L. Stevenson), B42, C636
Dr. Karnak (FC; dime novel), D33
Dr. Kildare (FC; Max Brand), E237, E238
Dr. Nancy Dayland (PC), D393a
Dr. Poggioli (FC; T. S. Stribling), E2830-E2833
Dr. Thorndyke (FC; R. A. Freeman), B253, B281, B310, C226, C229, C719, D328, E976, E1150, E1151, E1160, E1162, E1167, E1168, E1170, E1172-E1175, E1180, E1182, E1189, E1191, E1193-E1197, E1206, E1213-E1215, E1217
Dr. Watson (FC; A. C. Doyle), B142, C230, C279, C732, E984, E986, E987, E2815, E3106
Dr. Yen Sin (PC), D312, D314, D394, D395
Dr. See also Doctor
Drax, Peter, AR
Dresser, Davis, C247. See also Halliday, Brett
Drew, Bernard, C244, D294, D299-D302, D309, D361, E716, E1143, E1265, E2068, E2079, E2084, E2085, E2469
Dreyfus, Pat, E2816
Driscoll, Peter, AR
Droste-Hulshoff, Annette von, B444
Drummond, Ivor, AR
Drummond, June, AR
Drury, Michael, B164a
Drury Lane (FC; E. Queen), B170, B170, E2264
Duboisgobey, Fortuné, E1008
Dubois, Jacques, E2614
Dubois, Theodora, AR
Dubourg, Maurice, E16, E140, E1658, E1679, E1741, E1744, E2603, E2615, E2616, E2987, E2994
Duchateau, A. P., B213
Ducos, François, B107, E1742, E1744, E2313, E3015
Duedder, Rolf, E712
Duende, D322
Dueren, Fred, E23, E540, E1124, E2049, E2300, E2343, E2846, E2939
Duffell, Roy, B211
Duffield, Howard, E869, E894, E913, E914, E931
Duffy, Martha, E2711
Duhamel, Marcel, B97, C657, E468
Duke, Winifred, E1009
Dukeshire, Theodore, E471, E1509, E271, E286, E470, E503, E505
Duke, Winifred, E1008
Dulac, Edmund, B41
Dumas, Alexandre, B202, C332, D187, E1010, E1731
du Maurier, Daphne, E1011-E1013
Dumont, Hervé, E1640, E1744
Dumoulin, Albert J., D31
Dunae, Patrick A., C245
Duncan (Shakespeare), E914
Duncan, Robert L., E1014
Duncan, William, E1015
Duncan Maclain (FC; Kendrick), B309, E1586
Dunlap, Barbara, E2506
Dunn, Bill, E1295
Dunn, J. Allan, AR
Dunn, Robert Paul, E2507, E2525
Dunne, John Gregory, AR
Dunnett, Dorothy, C153, E1016
Duperray, Jean, E16, E17, E2617, E2646
Dupin (FC; Poe), A73, B100, B115, B122, B144, B307, B310, C226, C228, E1227, E2089, E2091, E2093, E2098, E2102, E2106, E2108, E2109, E2113, E2116, E2136, E2137, E2139-E2142, E2144, E2145, E2147, E2150, E2154, E2157, E2161, E2184, E2186, E2191, E2192, E2765
Duplin, André, E2141
Duprez, Leif, E776
Dupuy, Josée, B98
Duras, Marguerite, E1017, B102
Durbridge, Francis, E1018-E1019
Durdles (FC; Dickens), E935, E974, E981
Durgnat, Raymond, E1094
Durham, Philip, B239, B290, C247, D342, D343, E311, E315, E405, E406
Durkin, Mary, E2112, E2508
Durling, Ulf, B376
Durrant, Digby, E2297
Dürrenmatt, Friedrich, B410, B424, C570, C571, C95, E29,E178, E1020-E1030
Duse, S. A., B224, E1031
Dusty Ayres (FC; pulp), D314a, D396-D398
Dutch, Bill, E811
Duval, Claude, D31
Dyson, A. E., E915

Eakins, William, E2557
Eames, Hugh, B99, E2113, E2618
East, Andy, A48, A158, E541
Eastman, Elizabeth, AR
Easton, Robert, E237
Eaton, J. Lloyd, B88
Eberhart, Mignon, AR, B234
Ebersohn, Wiesel, E1032, E1799
Echoes, D303
Echols, Allan R., AR
Eck, Frank, A49, A138
Eckert, Otto, B424, C248
Eco, Umberto, B264, B100, B264, B424, E1092, E1095
Ed & Am Hunter (FC; F. Brown), E258
Ed Noon (FC; M. Avallone), E72, E74, E83
Eddie Parks (FC; dime novel), D1
Edel, Leon, E2784
Eden, Dorothy, AR, B65, B181, C852
Eden, Phyllis, C852
Edenbaum, Robert I., B239, B290, E1370
Edgar, Alfred, D277
Edgar Wallace Society Newsletter, E3018
Edgar(s), A132
Edogawa, Rampo. See Rampo, Edogawa
Edward Leithen (FC; J. Buchan), E296
Edward X. Delaney (FC; L. Sanders), C576
Edwards, Alberto, C642
Edwards, J. Hamilton, C556
Edwards, John, D453, E635
Edwards, Lee, E2509
Edwards, Leo, D81, D101-D107
Edwards, P. D.. B101

Edwards, Samuel, E3005
Edwin Drood (FC; Dickens), B42, B58, E827, E842-E1009, E1157, E1179
Egan, Lesley, E1768. See also Linington, Elizabeth
Egleton, Clive, AR
Ehrlich, Max, D461
Eighty-Seventh Precinct (series; McBain), B309, E1787, E1788e, E1791, E1792
Eisenstein, Sergei, B78
Eisenzweig, Uri, B346, E2114
Eisgruber, Frank, Jr., D403, D454-D456, D467
Eisinger, Erica M., B102, E1017, E2619
Ekholm, Jan Olof, B376, B386, C389
Ekman, Kirstin, E1033-E1034
Ekström, Jan, B376, B386
Elgström, Jörgen E., B103, B104
Eliot, T. S., B61, C745, E657, E687, E1879
Elisabeth D'Andreville (FC; Leblanc), E1668
Ellery Queen (FC; E. Queen), B170, B310, B392
Ellery Queen's Anthology, A127
Ellery Queen's Mystery Magazine (EQMM), A128, D399-D401, E2255
Ellery Queen's Mystery Magazine (Japan), D400
Ellin, Stanley, B18, B48, B65, B124, B134, B181, B409, C441, C735, E1035-E1040, E2573
Elliott, Jeanne B., E210
Ellis, Edward S., D27, D71
Ellis, M. A., E916
Ellison, Harlan, E163, E312, E1041, E3115, E3116
Ellis, Peter, E2021
Ellis, Stewart Marsh, E5, E1720
Ellis, Stuart, E658
Ellman, Neil, E144
Elston, Allan Vaughan, AR
Elwin, Malcolm, E659
Emery, Richard, A50
Emperor Rudolph (PC), D424
Endrèbe, Maurice-Bernard, B110, B246, B269, E8d5, E355, E1042-E1044, E1922, E1934, E2281, E2282, E2760
Engel, Howard, B75, E1045
Engel, Leonard, E2115
Engle, William, D82
Enigmatika, B107
Enright, John M., D91, D123
Epstein, Roger, D220
Epstein, Samuel, D110
EQMM. See Ellery Queen's Mystery Magazine
Erben, Vaclac, C797
Erdman, Paul, AR
Erhardt, Pat, C473, E99
Erichsson, Iwan, A51
Erickson, Byron, D89
Ericson, Carol, E1696
Ericson, Walter. See Cunningham, E. V.
Eriksson, B46
Erisman, Fred, E786, E1340, E1354, E2301
Ernst, Paul, AR, D316, D337, D437
Errer, Emmanuel, E1978
Erskine, Margaret, AR
Eshleman, John, E1046
Esteven, John, B339
Estleman, Loren D., C267, C267a
Eustace, Robert, AR, B289, E2520, E2522, E2523. See also Barton, Dr. Robert Eustace
Eustis, Helen, B17, E1047, E2685
Evans, Gwyn, D22, D246, D275
Evans, John. See Browne, Howard
Evans, Robley, E1476
Evans, T. Jeffrey, E2069
Evelyn, John, E1151
Everett, Edward S., E917
Evernden, Margery, E1048
Evers, A. M. (Mrs.), E2957
Everson, William K., B290
Ewart, Gavin, E2633
Exbrayat, E1048
Eyre, Anthony, B27
Ezra Quirk (FC; dime novel), D33

Fabre, Dominique, AR
Fabre, Jean, E2620
Fagerström, Allan, E2463
Fair, A. A., B62, B63. See also Gardner, Erle Stanley
Fairbairn, Roger, E361. See also Carr, John Dickson
Fairlie, Gerard, AR
Faivre, Jean-Paul, E1659
Falk, Bertil, E822, E1497
Falkner, John Meade, E2524
Fallois, Bernard de, E2621, E2654
Fallon, Martin. See Higgins, Jack
Fandor (FC; Allain/Souvestre), E14
Fang Wu (PC), D419
Fantômas (FC; Allain/Souvestre), B157, B362, E14-E21, E1685, E1686, E191
Farah, Dave, D115, D116
Farmer, Philip José, D366, E806
Farren, Jonathan, E1786, E1789
Farrer, Katherine, AR
Fast, Howard, B339. See also Cunningham, E. V.
Father Bredder (FC; L. Holton), B309, E1508
Father Brown (FC; Chesterton), A73, B122, B144, B337, C16, C17, C471, C577, E474, E475, E477, E479, E480, E484, E487-E493, E495, E498-E501, E1508, E1584, E2116, E2681
Father Roger (FC; R. McInerny), E1908
Faulkner, William, B125, B216, B397, C397, C570, C606, E55, E197, E314, E1049-E1065, E2586, E2690
Faust, Irvin, E332
Faust, Frederick. See Brand, Max
Fawcett, Richard H., B255
Fayne, Eric, D276
FBI, B122
Fearing, Kenneth, B17, B201, B269, E1066-E1068
Fearn, John R., E1069
Fearnley, J. B., C495
Feccheimer, David, E1366, E1371, E1372
Feiffer, Jules, C343
Feinberg, David, E1346
Feinman, Jeffrey, E542
Felix Boyd (PC), D402
Felix, Charles, C800
Fellini, Federico, E2679
Felman, Shoshana, B346, C272
Fenady, Andrew, C885
Fen, Jessica, E791
Fenisong, Ruth, AR, B48
Fenstermaker, John J., E842, E845
Fenwick, Elizabeth, AR
Ferguson, Malcolm M., E301, E2582
Fernald, Chester Bailey, E1071
Fernez, André, E1071
Ferran, André, B269
Ferrari, Giorgio, B116
Ferrars, Elizabeth X., AR, C488
Ferrers, Lord, D282
Ferrière, Jean-Pierre, AR
Ferrini, Franco, B109
Ferris, Laurana Sheldon, D28

Ferry, Jean, E1732
Fetta, Emma Lou, B48
Fetterly, Judith, E2739
Feuser, Willifred, E1480
Féval, Paul, E1224, E1234
Fiedler, Leslie, E1053, E2116
Fielding, A., AR
Fielding, Dorothy. See Fielding, A.
Fielding, K. J., E826
Fildes, Luke, E853, E891, E918, E922, E938
Filler, Louis, B111
Filstrup, Jane, E1774
Finch, G. A., C521, E761, E792, E1373, E1867
Finckh, Erkhard, B111
Findley, Ferguson, AR
Fine, David, E313
Finnegan, Robert, AR
Finney, Jack, AR
Finzel, James N., E1190-E1192
Firkins, Terry, E2893
Fischer, Bruno, B48, D316, D437, E1073
Fischer, Peter, B424, B451, C281
Fish, Robert L., B295, B309, E1074, E1075, E1077, E1078, E2302
Fisher, Benjamin F., IV, A54, A55, A174, B3, E54, E55, E56, E660-E661, E919, E2117-E2121
Fisher, Steve, AR, D303, D316, D333, D364, D412, E240, E1339, E3117, na
Fishman, Charles, E1868
Fistell, Ira J., E2248
Fitt, Mary, B124, C488, E1079-E1080
Fitzgerald, F. Scott, E413, E1888
Fitzgerald, Maureen, E2400
Fitzgerald, Nigel, B18, E1081
Fitzgibbon, Russell H., E544
Fitzhugh, Percy Keese, D29, D30, D89
Fitzpatrick, Al, E2958
Fitzsimmons, Cortland, B62-B64, E1082
Fl*m*ng, I*n, E241
Flanagan, Graeme, E163
Flanders, John, B213
Flash Casey (FC; G. H. Coxe), B309, E719
Flashman (FC; G. M. Fraser), E297
Flaubert, Gustave, E1406, E2677
Fleenor, Juliann, B113
Fleetwood, Hugh, A144
Fleissner, Robert F., E920
Fleming-Roberts, G. T., D354, D445
Fleming, Anthony, E2489
Fleming, Atherton, E2518, E2523
Fleming, Ian, A48, A171, B3, B20, B240, B264, B302, B303, B310, B413, B424, C72, C538, C766, C838, D368b, E44, E396, E1255, E1083-E1115
Fleming, Joan, AR
Fletch (FC; G. MacDonald), E1811
Fletcher, J. S., AR, A105, B41, B248, C366
Fletcher, Lucille, AR
Fletcher, Mary, AR
"Fleuve noir", C30
Flinders Petrie (FC; S. Rohmer), E2382, E2406
Flora, Fletcher, AR
Flower, Pat, AR
Flynn's Detective Fiction Weekly, D439
Flynn's Weekly, D439
Foley, Rae, AR, C530
Follett, Ken, B117, E1116
Folsom, Franklin, D292
Footner, Hulbert, B298, C611, E1117-E1122
Forbes, Cheryl, E2510
Forbes, Colin, E1123
Forbes, Stanton, AR
Ford, George, E921
Ford, Leslie, B234, E1124-E1127
Forest, G., E942
Forestier, François, E310
Forrester, Andrew, C101
Forrest, Richard, AR
Forsberg, Thomas E., B114
Forster, John, E853, E877, E882, E891, E906, E945, E946
Forsyte, Charles, E888, E975
Forsyth, Frederick, B256, B303, C841, E1128-E1142
Fosca, François, B115, B116
Fossati, Franco, B116
Foster, Brad, E2268
Foster, Jan, AR
Foster, Stephen, E2582
Foster, W. Bert, D171, D184
Fouché, C145
Fowler, Kenneth A., E1143
Fowler, Sydney, AR
Fowles, John, E1134-E1136
Fox, Estelle, E766, E2921, E3110
Fox, James, AR, E399, B116
Fox-Davies, A. C., AR
Foxx, Jack, A12
Foxx, Jack. See also Pronzini, Bill
Francis, Dick, B18, B67, B75, E1137-E1142
Frank, Frederick S., A52-A55, A174
Frank, Nino, E2622, E2646
Frank Kerrigan (FC; J. Harrington), E1444
Frank Leslie Publishing House, D76
Frank Reade (FC; dime novel), D48
Frank Reade, Jr. (FC; dime novel), D48
Frank Sessions (FC; H. Waugh), E3053
Franklin, Max, E791
Fraser, Antonia, AR
Fraser, George MacDonald, E297
Fraser, W. A., E922, E942
Frauenglas, Robert, E1453, E1454
Frayling, Christopher, E2401
Frazier, Gerie, E2468
Freas, Frank Kelly, B43
Fred Fellows (FC; H. Waugh), B309, E3052
Fred Ford (FC; H. Waugh), E3058
Fredriksson, Karl G., C287-C289, E545, E1230, E1622, E2334
Fredriksson, Lilian, C289
Freedman, Benedict, B2, E1212
Freeling, Nicholas, B26, B96, B309, C76, E388, E1143, E1145, E1147, E1148
Freeman, Jean, C403
Freeman, Lucy, B117, B187, C290
Freeman, R. Austin, B2, B17, B61, B78, B142, B253, B281, B287, B290, B310, B312, B340, B364, B700, C132, C291, C565, C605, C689, C719, E700, E925, E976, E995, E1149-E1217
Freeman, William, A56
Freemantle, Brian, AR
Fremlin, Celia, AR, E547, E562
French, George, D28, D86
French, Larry, E356, E357
French, Philip, E409
French, Warren, E1054
Freud, Sigmund, B117, B346, C290, C419, E1663, E1859
Freustié, Jean, E2623, E2646
Fridhammer, Christer, E2070
Friedburg, Maurice, B118
Friedland, Susan, A57
Friedman, Jacqueline, E1086
Friedman, Mickey, C292
Friedman, Stanley, E828
Frieman, Joel, D429, D485
Fritz, Kathlyn Ann, C293

Frohock, William M., E314
Frome, David. See Ford, Leslie
Fronval, George, D31
Frost, Barbara, B48, B409
Fruttero, Carlo, E1218-E1219
Fu Manchu (FC; S. Rohmer), A59, B443, B253, C540, C594, D503, E2378, E2379, E2380, E2385, E2386, E2394, E2396, E2400, E2403, E2405, E2408-E2410, E2412, E2415-E2417, E2419, E2422, E2424, E2427-E2430, E2436-E2437, E2454, E2456, E2461, E2462
Fugate, Francis L., E1239
Fugate, Roberta, E1239
Fujisaki, Makoto, B119
Fukanaga, Takehiko, B120, B157
Fukuoka, Takashi, E1969
Fulcher, James, E1981
Fuller, Dean, AR
Fuller, Roy, AR, C25, C542
Fuller, Samuel, AR
Funghi, Franco, C294, E2740
Furth, Pierre-Pascal, E1743, E1744
Furthman, Jules, E197
Fusco, Richard, E2122
Futagami, Hirokazu, E3149
Futrelle, Jacques, B2, B281, C601, E1220-E1223

G-8 (PC), D297, D313, D326, D403-D404
G-Man's Son (juvenile series), D82
G-Men (Juvenile series), D82
Gaboriau, Emile, A137, B24, B68, B91, B107, B110, B257, B269, B343, B362, B424, C166, C176, C204, C222, C273, C552, C607, C610, C629, C642, C673, C679, C758, C825, C860, C862, C875, D57, E840, E1009, E1224-E1234, E2103, E2271, E2677, E3042
Gadd, George, E923, E924, E942, E991
Gadd, William Laurence, E909, E925
Gadda, Carlo Emilio, B78, B116, C139, C311, C350, E1219, E1235
Gadney, Reginald, C295, E1459, E1913, E2040, E3082
Gaillard, Noë, E1924-E1926, E1929, E2511
Gainham, Sarah, AR
Gaiter, Dorothy J., E2249
Gallant, Mavis, E2624
Galligan, Edward L., E2625, E2785
Gallimard, C666
Galton, Francis, E2911
Galway, Robert C. See McCutchan, Philip
Gamarra, Pierre, B110, C296
Gancogni, Manlio, C311
Gangster Stories, D311
Gannett, Gary, E2626
Gant, Richard, E1096
Gantner, Joe, D32, D158-D160
Garasha, Robert, C238
Garden, Y. B., E2940
Gardiner, Dorothy, AR, B48, B63, E397
Gardner, Erle Stanley, B2, B17, B27, B142, B290, B310, B385, C234, C298, C299, C339, C404, C581, D302, D537, E419, E1236-E1254, E3159
Gardner, F. M., C297
Gardner, Fred, E1366
Gardner, John, A48, B181, E1255
Garfield, Brian, A12, B105, B272, C247, C300, C301, E1256-E1259, E3071
Garfield, Leon, E977
Garis, Lilian, D112
Garner, Phil, E793
Garnet, A. H., E1260
Garrett, Pat, B99
Garrett, Randall, C527, E1261
Garson, Helen, E1697
Garve, Andrew, B17, B50, E1262
Gaskell, Mrs., C204, E1342
Gaskin, Catharine, AR
Gass, Sherlock Bronson, C302
Gasson, Andrew, E662
Gatenby, Rosemary, B64
Gatsby (FC; F. Scott Fitzgerald), B3, E413
Gattegno, Jean, C303
Gaughan, Jack, E3126, E3133
Gault, William Campbell, D364, E1263, E1264
Gaute, J. H. H., C50
Gauteur, Claude, E1927, E1931
Gavrell, Kenneth, E2123
Gawsworth, Barbara, E2582
Gawsworth, John, E2579
Gay, John, E1402
Gayot, Paul, A94, B110, C304, E1660, E1661, E2244, E2250, E2988-E2990, E2994, E2760, E2978
Gayton, Gillian, E175
(The) Gazette, E2786
(The) Ghost, D405
Geherin, David, B121, C305, E127, E1821, E1869, E2705
Genberg, Kjell E., B376, B386, C306, C307, E378, E2932
George, François, E1662, E1663
George Marsden Plummer (FC; dime novel), D88
George Marsh Co, D86
George Radfoot (FC; Dickens), E828
George Smiley (FC; John le Carré), E1695, E1698, E1699, E1704
Georgin, Robert, E2603
Georgin, Rosine, E2603
Gerber, Richard, B424, C308
Gerber, John C., E2893
Gerhardt, Mia I., E2787
Germeshausen, Alvin F., E2402
Gernsback, Hugo, D442
Gerould, Katherine Fullerton, C309, C310
Gerteis, Walter, B122
Gery, R. V., AR
Geslin, Luc, C370a, E1932
"Get Smart" (TV series), A48, A157, A158
Ghiotto, Renato, C257
Giani, Renato, C312
Giardinelli, Mempo, C313, C314
Giardini, Cesare, C315
Gibson, Frank, E829
Gibson, Walter, D300, B310, D420, D421, D457-D462, D467, D469, D470, D474, E1265, E2303
Gide, André, E1269-E1270, E2605, E2627, E2633, E2646, E2679, E2690
Gideon (FC; J. J. Marric), E723
Gideon Fell (FC; J. D. Carr), B170, C16, C17, C160, E349, E357, E368
Gidley, Mark, B216, E1055
Gielgud, Val, E1271, E2512,
Giesy, J. U., D447, D448, E1212
Gifford, Thomas, AR
Giglio, Tommaso, C316
Gilbert, Anthony, B48, C488, E1272-E1274
Gilbert, Coleen, E253, E2558
Gilbert, Elliot, B123-B123a, B216, B290, C317, C318, E1223, E2375-E2377
Gilbert, Michael, B15, B17, B48, B84, B124, B181, B283, B309, C319, C320, E277, E408, E409, E549, E562, E1275-E1278, E1441, E2525
Gilbert Symes (FC; G. K. Chesterton), C342
Gill, Brendan, E2628
Gillespie, Robert, C321, E176

Gillette, William, E2892
Gillian Hazeltine (FC; G. F. Worts), E3136
Gillis, William, E1022
Gilman, Dorothy, AR
Gil Vine (FC; Stewart Sterling), E2767
Gindi, Ioan, C634, C635
Giovanni, José, E1279, E1280
"(The) Girl from U.N.C.L.E.," A48
Giron, Tage, B376, B386, C785
Glatzer, Richard Mark, B125
Glauser, Friedrich, C353
Glover, Dorothy, A58, C322, E1428
Godey, John, E1281
Godfrey, Lydia, D216
Godfrey, Peter, E1282-E1283
Godfrey, Thomas, E2251
Godfrey Usher (FC), D328
Godsave, R. J., D33, D127
Godwin, William, A9, B300, C356, C454, E1284, E1285, E2163, E2182
Godwin, William, Jr., B3, E1286
Goedshe, Herman O. F. See Retcliffe, John
Goette, Juergen-Wolfgang, B126
Gogol, Nicolai, E2586, E2680
Goimard, Jacques, E1744, E1745
Goines, Donald, E1287
Goldberg, Marshall, B256
Goldberg, Joshua, E216
Gold, Joseph, E842, E846
Golden Master (PC), D466
Golden Weekly, D48
Goldhurst, William, E2124, E2125
Goldman, William, E1870, E1877
Goldstein, Arthur, AR
Goldstone, Adrian, C323, E1775
Golino, E2590
Gonda, Manji, B127-B130
Gonzalez, Arturo, E699a
Goode, Greg, A59, C324, C325, E713
Goodis, David, B73, D437, E1288-E1290, E3135
Goodrum, Charles, E1291
Goodstone, Tony, D304
Goodyear, R. A. H., D162
Gordon, Mark, B131
Gordon Craigie (FC), B76
Gordons (Mildred & Gordon Gordon), AR, B48, B63, B64, E1104a
Gores, Joe, B64, C292, C603, E75, E1292-E1294, E1366, E1368, E1375, E1376
Gores, Robert, C238
Gorey, Edward, E396
Gorki, Ashili, C294
Gorman, Ed, E2870
Gospel Truth Mort (FC; E. Wallace), A104
Gothot-Mersch, Claudine, E2603, E2629
Gottschalk, Jane, C326-C329
Gotwald, Rev. Frederick G., E2788
Goulart, Ron, B132, B133, D34, D305, D306, D337, D463, E260, E1295, E1296
Gould, Chester, B309
Goupil, Jacky, E1679
Grace, Sherrill, E172
Grady, James, AR
Graeme, Bruce, AR, E979
Graffy, Julian, E595
Grafton, C. W., B17, E1297, E1298
Graham, Jack. See Higgins, Jack
Graham, Janis, C330
Graham, John, C481
Graham, Keith, E794
Graham, Winston, AR
Gramigna, Giuliano, C331
Gramsci, Antonio, C332
Granata, Gorgio, C333
Granbeck, Marilyn, AR
Grand Guignol, C639
Granholm, Arne, E1594, E2630
Grant, Donald, B88, E2021
Grant, E., E550
Grant, Maxwell, A4, B309, B310, E637, E638. See also Gibson, Walter
Grant, Mary L. C., E998
Gratias, Jean-Paul, E304, E1786, E2244, E2872
Gratz, Jeffrey Michael, E926
Gravely, W. H., Jr., E2126
Gray, Berkley, E244
Gray, Curme, AR, B189
Gray, Dulcie, AR
Gray, Russell, D437
Gray Seal (FC; F. L. Packard), E2063
Graydon, William Murray, D229, D267, D275, D279a
Grayson, Rupert, B253
Grebstein, Sheldon Norman, B239, C333a
Green, Anna Katherine, B16, B17, B24, B298, C176, C191, C403, C487, C503, C533, E1299-E1308
Green, F. L., C495
Green, Martin, C334
Green, Peter, E2514
Green, Robert, E2345
Green, Roger, E1958, E847
(The) Green Magazine, A103
Greene, Douglas, A60, E241, E354, E358-E364, E1434, E2851, E1163
Greene, Frederick, B430
Greene, Graham, A58, B4, B93, B157, B240, B303, B366, C14, C25, C72, C146, C233, C248, C289, C397, C494a, C541, C594, C609, C715, C750, C773, C819, E139, E677, E1468, E1309-E1333, E2592, E2659, E2716, E3017, E3019
Greene, Hugh, C335-C338
Greene, Suzanne Ellery, C339
Greenfield, Josh, E1281
Greenleaf, Stephen, AR
Greenway, H. S. D., E1698
Gregg, Hubert, E551
Gregory, E. R., E663, E687, E2498, E2516, E2525
Gregory, Linda, E1919
Grella, George, A64, B5, B216, B239, B434, C340, C340a, C341, D6, E1089, E1097, E1377, E1699, E1871, E2517, E2631, E2633
Grennell, Dean, D352, D427, D464-D465
Grewgious (FC; Dickens), E874, E932, E940, E953, E960, E977, E978, E985, E988
Gribb, Knut, C211, E1334
Gribbin, Leonore, A61, A62
Gribble, Leonard, AR
Gribbon, William Lancaster, E2021
Grieg, Maysie, AR
Grierson, Edward, AR
Grierson, Francis D., AR, B18, B253, E1335
Griffin, Lloyd, A63
Grimes, Larry, B92, C342, C343, E1822
Grindea, Myron, E2632, E2633
Griswold, Rufus, E2127
Grivel, Charles, B12, C344
Grochowski, Mary Ann, C345, E2344
Groff, Mary, A41, C346-C349, C654, E2810
Grogg, Samuel L., Jr., A41, E1872
Groner, Augusta, C191
Grosset & Dunlap Publishers, D221
Grossman, Al, D408
Gross, Miriam, E401, E409, E443
Gross, Seymour, E2128
Grossvogel, David R., B135, B264, E449, E552, E553, E2129, E2371

Grosvenor, Rita, E787
Gruber, Frank C., C247, C556, D307, D308, D316, D437, E796, E1565, E1266, E1336-E1339
Guagnini, Elvio, C350
Guasch, Gérard-Philippe, E1664
Guérif, Catherine, E2244
Guérif, François, A14, B110, B244, B378, E63, E285, E310, E403, E410, E468, E507, E637, E1093, E1264, E1279, E1368, E1518, E1635, E1691, E1786, E1922, E1933, E1937, E2244, E2333, E2708, E2872, E2994, E3070, E3114, E3118
Guetti, James, C351
Guild, Nicholas, AR
Guiterman, Arthur, E2062
Gun Cotton (FC; R. Grayson), B253
Gunn, Victor, E244
Gupta, Brijen Kishore, A64
Gurko, Leo, C352
Gurr, David, AR
Guthrie, A. B., Jr., E1340
Gutzen, Gutzen, C353
Guymon, Ned, B15, C354
Guymon Collection, A73
Gwilt, John, C355
Gwilt, Peter, C355
Gylder, Ragnvi, E1623

Haas, Willy, C356, E3017, E3020
Haber, Ruth, E1016
Hackett, Alice, B136, B137a, B137b, B137c
Hackett, A. F., C358
Hagberg, David, E1341
Hagemann, E. R., B239, D309, D344-D347, E315, E333, E2941, E3087, E3088
Hagen, Ordean, A65, A82, C56, C359
Hager, Jean, AR
Haggard, H. Rider, B88
Haggard, William, E1342
Hahn, D. K., E3078
Hahn, Robert, E185
Hailey, Arthur, C841
Haining, Peter, B138, D310, D35-D38, E2130, E2403
Hal Keen (FC; juvenile series), D89
Hale, Christopher, AR
Haley, Alex, E1128
Half Dime Library (Beadle), D52
Halkjaer, Niels, E2325
Hall, Adam, B303, B309, E37, E1343-E1345
Hall, Graham, E164, E165
Hall, Loay, E165
Hall, Max, E1630
Hall, O. M., AR
Hall, Richard, E554, E2392, E2404
Hall, Trevor, E2518-E2524
Hallahan, William H., AR
Hallas, Richard, B134, B239, C865, E1346
Halliburton, David, E2131
Halliday, Brett, A107, B309, E1347, E1349, E1350
Halperin, John, E1700
Halpern, Daniel, C170
Halte, Jean-François, C360, E1665
Hamada, Yoshiaki, B108
Hamao, Shiro, E1351
Hamblen, Abigail, E555
Hamill, Pete, AR, E3089
Hamilton, Alex, E1556
Hamilton, Bruce, B18, E1352
Hamilton, Charles, E2474
Hamilton, Cicely, C361
Hamilton, Donald, A21, A110, B234, B309, C127, C247, C594, E44, E1353, E1354, E1356
Hamilton, Edmond, D499, D500, E200, E1357
Hamilton, Franklin, D303, D403, D467, D472, D478, E2245, E2378
Hamilton, K. M., C362
Hamilton, Patrick, AR
Hamilton, Robert, E2789
Hammer, Perry, E1679
Hammett, Dashiell, A4, A70, A148, B2, B26, B69, B73, B79, B96, B99, B125, B142, B179, B201, B239, B242, B264, B290, B306, B310, B312, B313, B362, B371, B372, B375, B389, B414, B424, B429, B443, C2, C7, C17, C71, C25, C37, C145, C168, C173, C234, C267, C278, C281, C299, C310, C319, C322, C339, C341, C342, C351, C352, C398, C404, C421, C425, C433, C465, C496, C503, C512, C529, C543, C568, C570, C601, C616, C623, C637, C678, C682, C736, C758, C766, C773, C802, C868, D309, D343, D345, D347, E41, E203, E324, E388, E395, E424, E441, E443, E1240, E1292, E1358-E1431, E1464, E1478, E1828, E1859, E1888, E1889, E2032, E2068, E2110, E2204, E2718, E2737, E2860, E2871, E2872, E3073
Hammett, Josephine, E1366, E1371
Hammett, Richard, E1380
Hanan, Patrick, B139, C363, C364
Hanaud (FC; A. E. W. Mason), B253, E1960
Hancer, Kevin, A66
Handke, Peter, C451
Handley, Alan, AR
Handsome Harry (FC; dime novel), D13
Hankiss, Jean, C365
Hanna, Archibald, E275, E287
Hannay, Margaret, E2498, E2525-E2526
Hano, Arnold, E2870, E2873
Hanrahan, Rita, A67
Hans Bärlach (FC; F. Dürrenmatt), C29
Hansen, Joseph, B3, B107, C10, E1432
Hanshew, Thomas W., B319, D327, E1433-E1436
Happy Days, D48
Harbage, Alfred. See Kyd, Thomas
Harbaugh, Thomas C., D161, D199
Harbottle, Philip, E1069
Hard-Boiled Dicks, B107
Hardesty, Susan M., E556, E557
Harding, Frank, E1922
Hardin, Nils, D415, D436, E2245
Hardman (FC; R. Dennis), E792, E794
Hardy, Alfred E. Gathorne, E1231
Hardy, Thomas, C743, E1437
Hardy, Thomas John, C366
Hardy Boys (juvenile series), D24, D46, D75, D81, D90-D99
Hare, Cyril, B17, B94, B124, B283, C153, C287, C367, E1438-E1443
Hare, Ronald, C368
Hark, Ina Rae, E927
Harkins, Edwin F., E1303
Harkins, William E., E335
Harkness, Bruce, E1537
Harlequin Books, A68
Harley Quin (FC; A. Christie), E521, E545
Harling, Robert, AR
Harmon, Robert, E2493, E2527
Harper, Ralph, B140
Harriet Vane (FC; D. L. Sayers), C453, C532, E2483, E2499, E2500, E2509, E2526, E2529, E2537, E2560, E2568, E2570
Harrington, Joseph, B144, E1444
Harrington, Joyce, AR
Harris, Edwin, E928, E978
Harris, Herbert, AR
Harris, James, E2290
Harris, Lis, E2634
Harris, Robert, E277
Harris, Rosemary, AR

Harris, Timothy, C885, E1445
Harrison, Barbara, E2528
Harrison, J. E., B2, B3
Harrison, Keith, D41, D100, D184
Harrison, Michael, E357, E504, E1446
Harrowitz, Nancy, B100, E2132
Harry Dickson (FC; Jean Ray), D31, E2310, E2311, E2312, E2314, E2315, E2316, E2317
Harry Palmer (FC; Len Deighton), B308
Hart, Denis, E2002
Hart, Frances Noyes, AR
Hart, James, B141
Hartman, Geoffrey T., B264, C369, E1873
Harvester, Simon, AR, A158
Harvey, Deryk, E730-E731
Harwood, H. C., C370
Harwood, John, C472, C521, E2320, E2405, E2490, E3097
Harwood, Ronald, E1316
Haslinger, Adolf, C371
Hassell, J. Woodrow, Jr., E2132, E2175
Hastings, Macdonald, AR
Hatch, Mary R. P., E1305, E1447
Hatvary, George E., E2169
Hauff, Wilhelm, E1448
Haultain, Phil, E1366, E1416
Hauptfuhrer, Fred, E1116, E1141, E1462
Hawke, Jessica, E2922
Hawkins, John, E2134
Hawks, Howard, E440
Hawthorne, Nathaniel, E55
Hawthorne, Julian, C372
Hayakawa's Mystery Magazine, D400, B176
Hayashi, Shun'ichiro, B143
Haycraft, Howard, A47, A69-A71, A147, A154, A147, B48, B53, B62, B63, B64, B103, B127, B142, B143, B440, C88, C373, C375, C376, C423, C696, E119, E218, E224, E664, E2135-E2136, E2232, E2276
Haycraft/Queen, A47, A89, A154, B143, C374
Hayden, George, B449, C377, C378
Hayes, Aden W., E177
Hayes, Joseph, AR
Hayne, Barrie, B16, E1304
Hays, H. R., C379
Hays, Lee, AR
Hays, Rhys W., B144, C380-C385, C472, E486, E487, E1444, E2888
Hayter, Cecil, D246
Hazama, Yotaro, B145
Hazard, Johnnine Brown, E1874
Head, Matthew, B17, E1449-E1450
Heald, Tim, E558, AR
Health Knowledge, Inc., D317, D406
Heard, H. F., AR
Heberden, M. V., B18, E1450a
Hecht, Ben, B142
Hedman, Dag, E1451
Hedman, Iwan, A72-A74, C386-C388, C491, E458, E505, E732, E1098, E1115, E1123, E1129, E1618, E1914, E1917, E2053, E2875, E3011, E3083, E3084
Heenan, Michael, E1195-E1197
Heggelund, Kjell, B146
Heibon-Sha, B147
Heiji, Zenigata, E2034
Heilbrun, Carolyn, C47, C390, C391, C2529, E1277. See also Cross, Amanda
Heissembuettel, Helmut, B78, B112, B424, B451, B264, C392, E42, E44
Held, Peter, E2930
Heldreth, Lillian M., E2530
Helena Landless (FC; Dickens), E869, E879, E884, E886, E910, E916, E930, E945, E947, E970, E974, E981, E982, E998
Hellenberg, Antony, C236
Heller, Frank, E1451
Hellerstein, Marjorie H., C393
Hellman, Lillian, E1381, E1385, E1409
Hellman, Geoffrey, E2354
Hellyer, C. David, C394, E2271, E3053
Hemenway, Robert E., E247
Hemingway, Ernest, B239, C865, E314, E396, E1364, E1395, E1431
Henderson, George, E1482
Henderson, James, D219
Hendricks, Denis, C395
Hendryx, James B., E1452
Henissart, Martha, B67. See also Lathen, Emma
Henissart, Paul, AR
Hennelly, Mark M., Jr., E665
Henneman, Horst Siegfried, B148
Henry, Gilles, E2603, E2635
Henry, O., B430, E337
Henry Gamadge (FC; Elizabeth Daly), E766
(Sir) Henry Merivale (FC; Carter Dickson), B170, E344, E357
Hensel, George, R2636, E2679
Hensley, Joe L., A75, A76, B107, E1453-E1455
Hercule Poirot (FC; A. Christie), A73, B310, B392, C215, C226, E552, E562, E563, E575, E579, E596, E597, E605, E609
Herman, Jean. See Vautrin, Jean
Herman, Linda, B149
Herodotus, B68
Herrick, Daryl S., D367, D368, D502
Herrington, Lee, AR
Herr, Kay, E1023
Herron, Don, A77, E1382, E2582, E2579
Herron, Shaun, AR
Hersey, Harold, D311
Hershman, Morris, B48
Herst, Herman, Jr., C244
Hertzberg, (Father) Francis, E2791
Herzel, Roger, E365
Herzog, Evelyn, E238, E2406
Hesse, Herman, E1531
Hetherington, John R., A78
Hevener, Natalie Kaufman, C293
Hewett, Thayer, E2159
Hey, Richard, C353, C593
Heyer, Georgette, B17, E1456-E1458
Heyes, Douglas, AR
Heywood, Christopher, E211
Heywood, John, E1452
Hibbert, R. E2474
Hickman, Lynn, D312
Hicks, Granville, E2232
Higgins, Jack, A12, E1462, E1463
Higgins, George, C396, E1431, E1459-E1461
Highet, Gilbert, C397
Highsmith, Patricia, B75, B150, B179, B181, B378, B215, C295, C441, C542, C831, E409, E1428, E1464-E1469, E2673
Hikage, Jokichi, B151, B152
Hildick, Wallace, AR
Hilfer, A. C., C398
Hillerman, Tony, B18, C767, E1471-E1476
Hill, Headon, E1470
Hill, M. C., A79-A81, E138, E145, E2923
Hill, Reginald, B179, B181, AR
Hill, Thomas W., E929, E929a
Hilton, James, B17, E1477
Hilton, John Buxton, AR
Himes, Chester, B20, B73, B111, B201, B216, B242, B73, C137, C831, E1428, E1478-E1495
Hinckle, Warren, E1366
Hintze, Naomi A., AR, B64

Hipolito, Terrence, B2
Hirabayashi, Hatsunosuke, B153
Hiroshima, Setsuya, B108
Hirschberg, Edgar W., E1823, E1826
Hirschberg, Cornelius, AR
Hisao, Juran, B413
Hitchcock, Alfred, A96, B215, B385, E39, E42, E45, C233, E277
Hitchens, Dolores & Bert. See Olsen, D. B.
Hitchman, Janet, E2514, E2531-E2533
Hitler, Adolf, E358
Hobbes, Thomas, C517
Hobel, Kathy, E1775
Hobsbaum, Philip, E860
Hobsbawn, Eric, B78, B83, C399
Hobson, Robert W., E248
Hoch, Edward D., B27, B44, B64, B105, B117, B134, B154, B160, B271, B419, B409, C127, C400, C401, C402, E65, E196, E1496-E1501, E2239, E2481
Hoch, Pat, B271
Hocking, Anne, AR
Hockley, Geoff, D111
Hockley, George, D219
Hocutt, George, D436
Hodges, Carl G., B409, B48
Hodgson, William Hope, A87, A104, C565, E1502-E1506, E2313
Hoeber, Heinz Werner, E712, E713
Hoffman, Arnold, E2355
Hoffman, Carl, E2071
Hoffman, Daniel, E2137
Hoffman, Nancy Y., B216, C403
Hoffmann, E. T. A., B74, B243, B338, B360, C13, E1059, E2159
Hoftrichter, Paul, C404
Hogan, John A., E3021-E3025
Hogan, Robert, D313, D403, B443
Hogarth, Basil, B155
Hogg, James, B3
Holbrook, David, E1099
Holbrook, Don, D113, D123, D292
Holden, Jonathan, E411
Holdheim, W. Wolfgang, C406
Holding, Elizabeth Sanxay, AR, B339
Holding, James, AR
Hollis, Christopher, E488
Holman, C. Hugh, AR, C405, E353, E1056
Holman, Harriet, E2138
Holmberg, Bo, E1790
Holmberg, John-Henri, C408
Holmblad, Karin, E1033
Holmes, Elizabeth, C409
Holmes, Gordon, E2581
Holmes, H. H. See Boucher, Anthony
Holmes, Harold C., D39-D41, D163-D167, D169, D207-D209
Holquist, Michael, B264, C407, E559, E1007
Holt, Victoria, C582, E1507
Holtan, Judith, E1875
Holtan, Orley, E1024, E1875
Holton, Leonard, B309, E1508
Holtsmark, Erling B., E1824
Holzapfel, Tamara, E178
Homberger, Eric, E409, E411a
Homer, Harry, D242-D247
Homer Gavigan (FC; C. Rawson), E2300
Homes, Geoffrey, E1509
Honce, Charles, C410, E53, E2252, E2753, E2894
Hone, Ralph, E2534
Honeymoon Detective (pulp series), D407
Hoog, Armand, E1928, E1929
Hooke, Charles W., D148
Hoopes, Roy, E316-E320
Hoover, J. Edgar, B215, B216, B318, C646, C647
Hopkins, Percy, B83
Hoppenstand, Gary, D42
Hopper Taliaferro (FC; Matthew Head), E1449
Hoppin, Hector, B93, C411
Horatio Hornblower (FC; Forester), C518
Horler, Sydney, B253, B303, E1510-E1513
Horn, Pierre, E1269, E1270
Hornung, Ernest William, AR, A106, B91, B348, C222, C334, C534, C552, C606, C740
<u>Horror Stories</u>, D437
Horvath, Odon von, C371
<u>Hoseki Magazine</u>, A90, B160
Hottinger, Mary, B61, C412, C413, C414
Houdini, Harry, D420, E2446, E2451, E2460
Hough, Stanley, B18, E1514
Household, Geoffrey, B303, E513, E1515
Houseman, John, E409, E412
Hovenmark, Nils, B386, C389
Hovenot, M., E1679
Hoveyda, Fereydoun, B156, B157, B269
Howard, Clark, AR
Howard, Leon, B2, B3, E413
Howard, Richard, C816
Howard, Robert E., D328, D499, E1516, E2394
Howatch, Susan, AR, C852
Howells, William Dean, B374, E1879
Howland, Sidney, AR
Hoyt, Charles Alva, B239, E1825
Hrastnik, Franz, B415, C424
Hsun, Lu, B158
<u>Hub 10-Cent Novels</u>, D108
Hubbard, D. C., E59, E173, E508, E1606, E1621, E1925, E2088, E3025a
Hubbard, P. M., B18, E1517
Hubbell, Jay, E2139
Huber, Gordon, D418
Hubin, Allen J., A7, A10, A21, A82-A84, A143, A158, B15, B44, B88, B136, B154, B159, B160, C394, C583, C843, D416, E725, E727, E812, E1198, E2202, E2203, E2253, E2380, E2854, E3026
Hubin, Loren, A82
Hubly, Erlene, B92, E1537a
Huch, Ricarda, B444
Hudson, Gordon, D248
Hudson, H. K., D43
Huegel, Hans Otto, B161, C758
Huet, Marie-Hélène, B110, C416
Huey, Talbott, E28
Huggins, Roy, AR
Hugh North (FC; V. W. Mason), E1963
Hughes, Catherine, B162
Hughes, Dorothy B., B62, B234, C376, C767, E560, E562, E1241, E1518-E519
Hughes, Winifred, B163, E666
Hugo, Grant, C417
Hullar, Link, D313a, D358a, D368b, D476
Hulley, Katherine, E1384
Hull, Helen B., B164, B164a, E1520
Hull, Richard, AR
Hulsewe, A. F. P., E2959
Hultgren, Russell William, E1788
Humbourg, Pierre, E2978
Hume, Fergus, A58, B208, E1521
Hunger, John, D245
Hunt, E. Howard, A21, E1522-E1524
Hunter, Alan, AR
Hunter, Alberta, E2870, E2872
Hunter, Evan, A21, B65
Hunter, Evan. See also McBain, Ed
Hunter, John, D262
Hunter, Lynette, E489

Hurt, James, E1780
Hush Magazine, A105
Hutchinson, Horace G., C418
Hutchison, Don, D314, D431, E2063
Hutter, Albert D., B3, B264, C419
Huxley, Elspeth, B17, E1525
Huysmans, Joris-Karl, E3072
Hyatt, Ruth, A28, A85
Hydak, Michael G., E1100
Hyland, Stanley, AR

Iams, Jack, AR, B63
Iannuzzi, John N., AR
Ikushima, Jiro, B165-B166a
Iles, Francis, A137, B134, C421, C802, E132, E134. See also Berkeley, Anthony
Ilya Kuryakin (TV series character), B308
Ilyina, Natalia, C420
Imbert, Enrique Anderson, E179
In'naa, Torippu-sha, B167
Inner Sanctum Series, C876
Innes, Hammond, AR, C192, C541
Innes, Michael, B17, B18, B20, B43, B50, B309, C16, C40, C76, C153, C287, C542, C609, C789, E664, E689, E1526-E1533
Inspector Bucket (FC; Dickens), B122, E151, E833, E836, E902, E837
Inspector Cockrill (FC; C. Brand), B309, E229, E230,
Inspector Cuff (FC; Dickens), B122
Inspector Cutting (FC; Richard Blackmore), E151
Inspector Field (FC; Dickens), E902
Inspector Ghote (FC; Keating), A64, B76, B309, E1555, E1556, E1561
Inspector Harker (FC; dime novel), D240
Inspector Ironsides Cromwell (FC; dime novel), D289, E244
Inspector Schmidt (FC; Bagby), B309, E2763
Inspector van der Valk (FC; Freeling), B309
Inspector Wade (FC; E. Wallace), E3015
Irby, James, E180
Ireland, Donald, E1015
Irene Adler (FC; Doyle), E2780
Irish, William, A179, B110, B201, B269. See also Woolrich, Cornell
Irving, Clifford. See Luckless, John
Irving, Washington, E2099
Irwin, John T., E2140
Isaac, Frederick, C425, E1032, E1799, E2219
Isaac Sidel (FC; J. Charyn), E467
Ishigami, Mitsutoshi, B11
Ishikawa, Takashi, B168-B170, B254
Isola, Apinwumi, C426
"I Spy," A157, A158, A48
Ito, Hideo, E1608-E1610
Iwama, Hiromichi, E3113

Jack the Ripper, B42, B181a
Jack Wright (FC; dime novel), D20, D48
Jackman, Stuart, AR
Jackson, Blake, D286
Jackson, C. A. G., D168
Jackson, Henry, E930
Jackson, Lewis, D245
Jackson, Shirley, AR
Jacobs, David, C427
Jacobs, Jay, E2637
Jacobs, T. C. H., AR
Jacobson, Wendy, E913, E931
Jaffe, Arnold, E2792
Jaffery, Sheldon, A87
Jago, David, E490
Jake & Helene Justus (FC; Rice), E2343
Jakes, John, AR
Jakob Studer (FC; F. Glauser), C353
James, Al, E1575, E1578
James, Clive, E409, E414
James, Henry, B162, C515, E555, E1324, E1377
James, M. R., B41
James, P. D., B16, B18, B26, B75, B92, B179, B181, B355, C151, C428, C441, C768, E1277, E1534-E1545, E2535, E2489
James, Thomas F., E951, E981
James Bays (FC; dime novel), D203
James Bond (FC; Fleming), B20, B156, B308, B310, B424, E396, E714, E1083-E1115, E1255
James Lee Wong (FC), C189
James Long Wong (FC; John Wiley), E3097
Jameson, Fredric, B264, B346, E415, E416
Jamieson, H. W., E932
Jamin, George, E2760
Jane Eyre (FC; Bronte), C711
Janeczko, Paul B., E113
Jankelevitch, V., E1663
Janvier, Ludovic, C429
Japrisot, Sebastien, AR, B346, C272
Jarrett, Cora, AR
Jarry, Alfred, B85, C304
Jasen, David, E2345, E3107
Jasper (FC; Dickens), E857, E862, E863, E870, E871, E873, E875, E877, E879, E881-E884, E890, E898, E902, E903, E905, E908, E910, E911, E913, E916-E918, E931-E933, E942, E949, E956, E957, E960, E966, E968, E972, E974, E975, E977-E983, E985, E986, E988, E992, E996, E997
Jay, Charlotte, E1546
(The) JDM Bibliophile, A38, E1826
Jeeves (FC; P. G. Wodehouse), E3106
Jeff Clayton (FC; dime novel), D250, D50
Jefferies, Roderic, AR
Jefferson Dimarco (FC; D. M. Disney), E1004
Jeffmar, Marianne, B376
Jeffrey, David K., C430
Jeffries, Graham, E979
Jeffries, Jay, C385
Jeffries, William B., E2895
Jenkins, Geoffrey, E1547
Jenkinson, Philip, E562
Jenkins, Will F., D367. See also Leinster, Murray
Jenks, George, D44, D153
Jennes, Gail, E710, E1582
Jennings, Edith, C431
Jennings, Robert, D497
Jepson, Edgar, B41, E1669, na
Jepson, Selwyn, AR
Jerry Cotton (FC; dime novel, German), B296, B424, C746, E712-E713
Jerry Owens (FC; dime novel), D13
Jerry Todd (FC; juvenile series), D101-D107
Jerry Wade (PC), D408
Jervis (FC; R. A. Freeman), E1193
Jess Roden (FC; A. B. Cunningham), E755
Jesse, F. Tennyson, E1548
Jesse James, D48, D28
Jevons, Shirley, E988
Jiggens, Clifford, E151
Jigger Masters (FC; A. Rud), E2469
Jim Chee (FC; T. Hillerman), E1471, E1475
Jim Hatfield (PC), D409
Jim Maitland (FC; Sapper), E2478
Jim O'Neill (FC; D. M. Disney), E1004
Jimmy Christopher (PC), D426, D427, D428
Jimmy Dale (PC), E2061, E2063
Jinga, Katuso, B173
Jinka, Katuso, C432

Jobson, Hamilton, AR
Jochmans, Betty, E561
Jocko Kelly (FC; dime novel), D108
Joe Gall (FC; P. Atlee), A48
Joe Gar (FC; R. Whitfield), E3087
Joe Leaphorn (FC; T. Hillerman), E1471, E1472, E1475, E1476
Joensuu, Matti, E1549
Johanssen, Albert, D45, D85
Johansson, Hans, B174
John Appleby (FC; M. Innes), B309, E1530
John Christman (FC; dime novel), D282
John J. Malone (FC; C. Rice), E2343
John Lawless (FC; dime novel), D267
John Shaft (FC; E. Tidyman), B310
John Silence (FC; W. H. Hodgson), D328
John Sunlight (PC), D388
John Thunstone (FC; M. W. Wellman), E3060a
Johns, Veronica, E1550
Johnson, Deidre, D46
Johnson, Diane, C753, E1363, E1385
Johnson, Douglas, E1701, E2638
Johnson, Edgar, E861
Johnson, E. Richard, AR
Johnson, Ginger, D303, D354
Johnson, Julia, A88
Johnson, Merle, E2896
Johnson, Reginald, E125, E289
Johnson, Robert L., D107
Johnson, Ryerson, AR, D430
Johnson, Tim, A88
Johnson, Tom, D303, D314, D315, D397, D444, D445, E79, E1349
Johnston, Alva, E1242, E2793
Johnston, Richard, E2741
Jolly, Emily, E878
Jonah, Mansell, E3147
Jonas Sown (PC), D385
Jonathan Press, A116
Jones, Archie, C433
Jones, Buford, E2141
Jones, Everett L., C247
Jones, G. Wayland, D336
Jones, James, E1551
Jones, James P., D117, D118
Jones, Mary Jane, C434, E1019
Jones, Raymond F., AR
Jones, Robert, D316, D353, D437, D493, E2742
Jones-Evans, Eric, E982
Jordan, Peter, E1057
José Da Silva (FC; R. L. Fish), E1076
Joshua Clunk (FC; H. C. Bailey), E91
Jour, Jean, E2639, E2640
Journal of Fu Manchu, E2423
Joyce, James, C272a
Joyner, B16, E1539
J. Rufus Wallingsford (FC, Chester), E473
J & S Graphics, A86
Judge Chou (FC; Chinese), B439
Judge Crater, C521
Judge Dee (FC; van Gulik), A59, B31, B439, E2953, E2954, E2956-E2958, E2960-E2964, E2967
Judge Lynch (pseud.), B142, C435, C575
Judge Pao (FC; Chinese), A43, A59, A109, B139, B320, B449, C69, C364, C377, C378, C501, C708
Judge Peck (FC; A. Derleth), E820
Judge Peng (FC; Chinese), B320, C175
Judge Priest (FC; I. S. Cobb), C519
Judge Pursuivant (FC; M. W. Wellman), E3060a
Judge Shih (FC; Chinese), B320
Judy Bolton (FC; juvenile series), D109
Juin, Hubert, E16, E2641, E2646
Jules de Grandin (FC; S. Quinn), D328, E2282-E2288
Julian Messner, D220
Jurdant, Louis-Thomas, E1552
Just, B424, C436
Justice, Keith L., C437
Juve (FC; Allain/Souvestre), E14

Kabatchnik, Amnon, A89, C438
Kaemmel, Ernest, B126, B264, B424, B451, C439
Kafka, Franz, C7, E825, E1324, E2659
Kagami, Saburo, B175-B178, B254
Kagerman, Elisabeth, B386
Kahn, Joan, B64, C276, C366, C440
Kai-Lung (FC; E. Bramah), E218, E226
Kajiyama, Toshiyuki, B367, E1553
Kallen, Lucille, C153, E1554
Kaminsky, Stuart, AR
Kane, Frank, AR, D333, D461
Kane, Henry, AR
Kane, Patricia, E1243, E1482
Kanfer, Stefan, B105, E1702, E2642, E2646
Kankowski, Joseph, E1357
Kantor, MacKinlay, AR
Kaplan, Fred, E862
Karigari, Hiroshi, E3160
Karig, Walter, D121
Karloff, Boris, E73
Karlsberg, J. K., E1679
Kase, Yoshio, B108
Kassak, Fred, AR
Kate Edwards (FC; dime novel), D17
Kate Fansler (FC; A. Cross), C453
Katherina Ledermacher (FC; Richard Heys), C353
Katzenbach, John, AR
Kavanagh, Mary, E933, E934, E968
Kawataro, Nakajima, B148, B254, E3150
Kawerin, Benjamin Alexandrowitsch, B295
Kaye, Howard, E417
Kaye, Marvin, C40, E2794
Keating, H. R. F., E562, A64, A156, B179, B180, B181, B309, B365, C441, C767, E130, E261, E537, E562-E564, E1555-E1561, E1953
Keddie, James, C442, E29, E743, E1187
Keefer, Truman, E3137
Keeler, Harry Stephen, B48, E1069, E1562-E1574
Keene, Carolyn, AR, B309, D119-D122, D333
Keene, Day, E1575-E1580
Keith, Carlton, B18, E1581
Kelland, Clarence Buddington, AR, C519
Keller, David, E814
Keller, Dean, E247
Keller, Harry A., D32
Keller, Joseph, E2537
Keller, Katherine, E2538
Keller, Mark, E2142
Kellett, E. E., C443
Kelley, George, E69
Kelly, Alexander, B181a
Kelly, Katharine, E959
Kelly, Mary, AR
Kelly, Patrick Joseph, E830
Kelly, R. Gordon, B216, C444, E1828
Kemelman, Francis, B349
Kemelman, Harry, B61, C137, E1582-E1585
Ken Holt (FC; juvenile series), D110, D220
Kendrick, Baynard, B309, D316, E1586
Kendrick, William A., E668
Kennedy, Foster, C445
Kennedy, Janet A., B2
Kennedy, J. Gerald, E2143

Kennedy, Milward, AR, C446
Kennedy, Veronica, E1829, E3072
Kenney, William, E1386
Kenyon, Michael, E1587
Kermode, Frank, B264, C447
Kerner, Annette, C488
Kerr, Orpheus, E983, E994
Kersh, Gerald, D1588
Keshokova, Elena S., E669
Ketterer, David, E2144
Keucher, Jerry, E596
Keverne, Richard, E1589, E3010
Kewer, Eleanor D., E2153
Keyes, Edward, AR
Keyhoe, Donald, B443
Kiddle, Charles A., E3027
Kiell, N., E1876
Kienzle, William, AR
Kigi, Takataro, B182, B183, E1590, E1591
Kikuchi, Michicho, E2606
Killmaster (FC; dime novel), D147
Kim (FC; Kipling), B308
Kimball, Clay, E3073
Kimball, Miles W., C835
Kimura, Jiro, B108, B184-B187, C448,
Kimura, Ki, B188
Kinabrew, J. M., Jr., E1195, E1214
Kindon, Thomas, B17, E1592
King, C. Daly, E2271, AR
King, Daniel, C449
King, Holly, E1703-E1704
King, J. P., C523
King, Margaret, C450
King, Rufus, E1593
King Edward VII, E30
King Kull, D328
King Solomon, C69
Kingman, James, E367, E1598
Kipling, Rudyard, B308, C700, E1712, E2211
Kircher, Hartmut, B126, C451
Kirk, Michael, E1917
Kirst, Helmut, E1594
Kit Carson, D48
Kitchin, C. H. B., AR, B94, C25, E565
Kittredge, William, C452
Klein, Gerard, E2408, E244
Klein, Katharine, C453, E2539
Klein, Kathleen Gregory, B16
Kling, Bernt, C746
Klinger, Henry, AR, B48
Klopsteg, Paul, E1253
Knebel, Fletcher, AR
Kneeland, Paul F., E2847
Knepper, Marty S., E566
Knight, Arden, E2795
Knight, Clifford, AR
Knight, Damon, B189
Knight, Jack, E1366, E1372
Knight, Stephen, B190, B264, C454, E1791, E2145
Knott, Harold, C455, C456, E3119, E3126, E3132
Knowland, Helen, E1595
Knox, Bill, B96, E1596, E1917
Knox, John H., D437
Knox, Ronald B., B6, B61, B142, B372, B385, B434, C456-C459, C567, C687, C856, C878, E491, E1548, E1597-E1601
Kobayashi, Nobuhiko, B191, B367, E1602, E3151
Kodaka, Nobumitsu, B185, B192, B193, D47, E3074
Koenig, H. C., E1503
Koga, Saburo, E1603
Koike, Shigeru, E526, E831
Koizumi, Kimiko, E1604
Kojak (TV character), B307
Kolb, Bernard, E1387
Kolin, Philip C., E2897
Kollander, Rahn, A66
Kondo, Thomas M., C460
Koontz, Dan R., B194
Korinman, Michel, B346, C461
Koskimies, Rafael, E2643
Kosuke Kindaichi (FC; Yokomizo), B254, E3150, E3157
Kozakai, Fuboku, B195, B196, E1605
Kozumi, Rei, B11
Kracauer, Siegfried, B197, B424, C462
Krasner, William, AR
Kraus, W. Keith, E2898
Krautzer, Steven M., C452
Krebs, Roland, E1606
Krementz, Jill, B366, E2774, B366
Krouse, Agate, C463, C630, E567
Krutch, Joseph Wood, B61, B142, B434, C464, C867
Kuki, Shiro, B198, B199
Kukkola, Timo, E1549
Kunkel, Klaus, E714
Kurnitz, Harry. See Page, Marco
Kuroiwa, Jugo, E1607
Kuroiwa, Ruiko, E1608-E1613
Kurosawa, Akiro, B290
Kurz, Hermann, B444
Kussi, Peter, E2717
Kustel, Nick, E935
Kutak, Rosemary, E1614
Kuttner, Henry, A10, B18, B43, D437, E200, E1615, E1616
Kvam, Lorentz M., B200
Kyd, Thomas, B17, E1617
Kyle, Duncan, A157, E1618
Kyrou, Ado, E1732

Labeau, Dennis, A90a
Labern, Art, AR
Labianca, D. A., C465
Lacan, Jacques, B264, E1662, E2129, E2146, E2173
Lacassin, Francis, B12, B201, B202, B240, B269, B324, C476, E16, E42, E46, E146, E191, E262, E418, E1010, E1067, E1483, E1663, E1666, E1667, E1679, E1688, E1744, E1746, E1759, E2314, E2409-E2411, E2644-E2646, E2679, E2686, E2768, E3120, E3121
Lach, Donald F., E2960
Lachman, Marvin, A46, A91, A148, A154, A159, A160, B159, C466-C473, C520, D368, D496, E30, E75, E96, E357, E1244, E1283, E1584, E1769, E1986, E1989, E2254-E2257, E2481, E2796, E2810
Lachtman, Howard, E419
Laclos, Michel, E1732
Lacombe, Alain, B203
la Cour, Tage, A92, B103, B204-B212, C474, C475, E568, E2258, E2647, E2899
Lacourbe, Roland, C476
Lacy, Ed, AR, B63, B64
Lady Beltham (FC; Alain/Souvestre), E14
Lafarge, Christopher, B348, E2743
Lafcadio (FC; André Gide), E1270
Lafforgue, Jorge, B214, C477, C478
Lahmon, L. H., D169
Laidlaw, Bill, D369
Lain Entralgo, Pedro, C479
Laing, Alexander, E1619
Lai, Rick, E3028
Lamb, Charles, C149
Lambert, Derek, C500

Lambert, Gavin, B215, B434, E37, E47, E290, E420, E492, E670, E1317, E2648
Lamb, Margaret, E1389
Lamy, Jean-Claude, E1744, E1747, E1748
Lancer, Jack, E791
Land, Irene Stokvis, C481
Landless (FC; Dickens), E899. See also Helena Landless
Landon, Brooks, E2765
Landon, Christopher, B18, E1620
Landon, Herman, B298, E1621
Landrum, Larry, A93, B216, E3058
Lane, Lauriat, E863
Lane, Margaret, E3017, E3029
Lane, Sheldon, E1101
Lane, Thomas, E569
Lang, Andrew, E847, E936, E937, E984, E990
Lang, Maria, B386, E1622, E1623
Langton, Jane, AR, B67, C152, C153
Lanham, Cathryn, C482
Lanocita, Arturo, C350, C483, C667
Lapin, Geoffrey S., D120, D121
Lapper, Ivan, B392
Larkin, Philip, E1255, E1111
Larmoth, Jeanine, B217
Larsen, Else, B212
Larsen, Carl, E459
Larson, Charles, C481
Larson, Randall D., E163, E165
Larsson, Nils, E2335, E2836, E2876, E3126
Lascar Sal (FC; Dickens), E902, E965
Lasic, Stanko, B218
Lasky, Michael, E277
Latham, Aaron, AR
Lathen, Emma, A12, B16, B18, B67, E562, E570, C594, E1624-E1632
Latimer, Jonathan, B134, C339, C495, C623, E1633-E1637
Latimer, Leo, E1922
Latsis, Mary Jane, B67. See also Lathen, Emma
Laucou, Christian, E1668
Laughlin, Charlotte, A96, A99
Laura, Ernesto G., B219
Lauri Conti, Lucio, C484
Lauritzen, Henry, A92, B220, B221
Lauterbach, Edward, C485, C486, E1267, E1588, E1619, E2004, E2929, E3138
Lauterbach, Karen, C485
Law, Janice, AR
Lawrence, Barbara, C487, E1631
Lawrence, Hilda, AR, C153
Lawrence, John, E1638
Lawrence, Joseph Ivers, AR
Lawrence, Margery, A87
Lawrence, Tom, C488
Lawrenson, Helen, E2412
Lawson, Lewis A., E671
Lawton, Thomas, E2961
Layman, Richard, E1390, E1391
Leacock, Stephen, B142, E864, E1879
Leah, Gordon N., E1025
Leasor, James, AR
Leavis, Q. D., E2540
Lebedel, Pierre, B378
Leblanc, Claude, E1688
Leblanc, Maurice, A138, A161, B27, B115, B201, B254, B275, C642, C719, C818, E1639-E1688
Leblanc, Edward T., D42, D48, D108
Lebois, André, E1679
Lebreton, Auguste, AR
Lebrun, Michel, A94, A95, B27, B110, B269, B378, C68, E1670, E1689-E1693, E1923, E1929, E1933, E1934, E2978, E2992, E2994, E2760
le Carré, John, A48, A110, B92, B240, B264, B303, C14, C72, C146, C153, C233, C494a, E1085, E1694-E1712
Leckenby, Herbert, D49, D249, D276
Leclerc, Jean, B107, E1744, E1749
Lecoq (FC; Gaboriau), B352, C228, E1232, E1234
Lee, A. Robert, E1484, E1485
Lee, Billy C., A96, E1102
Lee, Christopher, E2412
Lee, Elsie, B65
Lee, Eugene, D105
Lee, G. A., E2541
Lee, Manfred B., B260. See also Queen, Ellery
Lee, Peter, B222
Lee, Randolph, E2259
Lee, Roberta, E1915
Le Fanu, J. Sheridan, C123, E658, E1713-E1725, E2111, E2112, E2115
Lefèvre, Frédéric, E1093, E1732, E1750
Lefty Feep (FC; R. Bloch), E164, E165
Legars, Brigitte, E571-E573
Leggett, William, C744
Legrand (FC; E. A. Poe), E1678, E2124
Lehmann-Haupt, C. F., E938, E939
Leiber, Fritz, E163, E2021
Leinster, Murray, C520, D319, E367, E1726, E1727
Leitch, Thomas M., B92, C488a
Leithead, Edward, D50-D54, D100, D170-D184, D204, D210-D212, D250
Lejeune, Anthony, AR, B83, C489
Le Lionnais, Françcois, B287
Lem, Stanislaw, B92, C162, E1136, E1727a
Lemarchand, Elizabeth, AR
Lemay, J. A. Leo, E2147
Lemmy Caution (Film detective), B156
Leonard, Elmore, E1728
Leonard, John, C490, E1877
Leonard, Charles L. See Heberden, M. V.
Leopard (PC), D423
Lépine, Leroux, E1744, E1751
Lépine, Pierre, E1734
Le Queux, William, B248, B303, E1711, E1729, E1730, E2043
Leroux, A. G., E1732
Leroux, Gaston, B27, B107, B319, B424, C668, C818, E1230, E1646, E1731-E1764, E2103
Leroux, Gaston, fils (Jr.), E1744
Leroux, Jean, E1752
Leslie, Jean, AR
Levack, Daniel J. H., E2930
Lever, Charles, D187
Leverence, John, E1392
Levie, Françoise, E2308
Levine, Jonathan, E2797
Levinger, Larry, E1366, E1393
Levin, Ira, E1765
Levinson, Richard, AR, E369
Levy, Diane, E832
Lewandowski, Frank, D395
Lew Archer (FC; Ross Macdonald), B178, B307, B309, B310, C278, C342, C493, C512, C775, E1373, E1854, E1863, E1869, E1872, E1873, E1875, E1885, E1888, E1892, E1893, E1896, E1897, E1900
Lewin, Michael, AR
Lewis, Caleb, C491, E268-E270
Lewis, C. Day, C25, E2633. See also Blake, Nicholas
Lewis, C. S., C819
Lewis, Dave, A97, D309, E2026
Lewis, Elliott, C885

Lewis, K. W., A98
Lewis, Lange, B17, E1766
Lewis, Matthew ("Monk"), C356, E838
Lewis, Paul, C492
Lewis, Roy, E1767
Lewis, Sinclair, E833, E837
Lewis, Steve, E751
Ley, J. W. T., E980, E992
Liardon, Pierre Henri, E1923, E1929, E1930
Li, Peter, B449
Liberty Boys (dime novel series), D159
Lichtenberger, Judith, E165
Lid, R. W., E421
Liebermann, Herbert, AR
Liebman, Arthur, B223
Lt. Frank Hastings (FC; C. Wilcox), E3095, E3096
Lt. Martin Marquis (FC; John Lawrence), E1638
Lt. Valcour (FC; R. King), C641
Lilli, Laura, E1092
Limat, Maurice, E1671, E1744, E1753
Lindroth, Per, B224
Lindsay, Ethel, A100
Lindsay, Jack, E865
Lindsey, David L., C330
Lindung, Yngve, B225, 226
Linebarger, Paul. See Smith, Carmichael
Lingblom, Hans E., A101
Lingeman, Richard R., C493
Linington, Elizabeth, A12, E1768-E1771
Link, William, E369. See also Levinson, Richard
Linklater, Eric, AR
Links, J. G., E3082
Lins, Alvaro, B227
Lipman, Clayre, B48
Lipman, Michael, B48
Lippit, Noriko Mizuta, E2148
Lipsky, Eleazar, AR, B48
Lish, Gordon, AR
Lister, Tommy, E1264
Lister, William, D128, D251, D252
Lithner, Klas, E370, E574, E1199, E2925
Little, Constance & Gwyneth, AR
Little Tich, E2447
Litvinov, Ivy, AR
Ljunglöf, Lennart, C494, C494a
Llewellyn, Owen, C495
Lloyd, Hugh, D89. See also Fitzhugh, Percy Keese
Locard, Edmond, B228
Lochte, Richard S., II, C496
Locke, Clinton W., D218
Locke, George, A102-A105, E2582
Lockridge, Frances & Richard, B62, B63, B164, B309, C2, E1772-E1777
Loeffler, Karl, E2190
Lofts, Norah, AR
Lofts, W. O. G., A4, A106, C521, D55, D253, D254, D255, D256, E463, E768, E1200, E1920, E1939, E2393, E2413-E2415, E2582, E3030, E3031
Lombroso, B122
London, Jack, E1778
London, Rose, E2149
Lone Wolf (FC; Louis-Joseph Vance), E1670
Longanesi, C623
Long, Frank Belknap, D499, D500
Long, Julius, B62, B63
Longfellow, Esther, E2756
Longmate, Norman, B18, E1779
Loraine, Philip, AR
Lord, Glenn, D491
Lord Darcy (FC; Randall Garrett), E1261
Lord Mountbatten, E30
Loriot, Noelle, E2612
Louit, Robert, B378
Lous, Alexandre, A13, B378
Lovecraft, H. P., E820, E1619
Lovesey, Peter, B26, B67, B75, C153, E1780
Lowder, Christopher A. J., D257-D259,
Lowndes, Marie Belloc, AR
Lowndes, R. A. W., B290, D317, D355, D406, D441, E493, E575, E576, E813, E2150, E2284, E2285, E2416, E2798, E2942, E2943
Lu, Hsun, B229
Lucas, E. V., B142, C498
Lucentini, Franco, E1218, E1219
Luckless, John, AR
Ludlum, Robert, B256, C122, C237, E1781
Ludwig, Hans-Werner, C499
Ludwig, Myles, B375, C499
Luhr, William, E422
Luis Mendoza (FC; D. Shannon/E. Linington), B309, E1769
Lundin, Bo, A164, B230-B232, C500, C500a, E371, E464, E1982, E2464, E2542, E2649
Lundquist, Ake, B233
Lundquist, James, E1486, B233
Lustgarten, Edgar, B134, E1782
Luther Trant (FC; Balmer/MacHarg), C638, D328
Lutz, John, B64, E1783
Lyall, Gavin, E1784,
Lyles, William H., A107, A108, B234, E577, E1298, E1394, E2799
Lynch, Miriam, C705
Lynds, Dennis, E635, E641, E1878. See also Collins, Michael
Lynn, Richard, A109, B449
Lyon, Dana, AR, B48, B62, B409
Lyons, Arthur, AR, C885
Lytton, Robert, E878

Ma, Yau-Woon, B235, C501
Mabbott, Maureen, E2151
Mabbott, Thomas, E2152, E2153, E2167, E2169, E2187, E2190
McAleer, John, C502, E1217, E2784, E1201-E1204, E2775, E2800-E2807, E2810, E2822, E2823
McAleer, Ruth, E1163, E1205
McAllister, Pam, E596
MacAndrew, Elizabeth, B236
McBain, Ed, B50, B65, B67, B96, B190, B295, B309, B319, C127, C137, E1785-E1794, E2219
Macbeth (Shakespeare), E914
McCabe, Brian, E164
McCabe, Bruce, E1460
McCabe, Cameron, B134, E1795
McCafferty, William Burton, D185, E2064
McCaffery, Larry, E1919
McCaffrey, Anne, E197
McCahery, James, E1908, E1636, E1637
McCall, Dan, E1318
McCardell, Roy L., E1120
McCarry, Charles, AR
McCarthy, Justin, E980
McCarthy, Mary, B78, C379, C503
McCarthy, Paul, E578, E3000, E3001
McCleary, G. F., B237, C505, E672
McCloskey, Mark, B3
McCloy, Helen, B409, C488a, C594, C705, C1350, E1796, E1797
McClure, James, B67, B96, C287, C450, E1798
McCormack, W. J., E1721
McCormick, Donald, A110
McCourt, Edward A., C506

McCoy, Horace, B2, B3, B43, B73, B239, B428, C865, E324, E330, E1802-E1808
McCulley, Johnston, D363, E1809
McCurtin, Peter, E1810
McCutchan, Philip, AR, A48
McCutcheon, John T., D1
McDade, T. M., B105, B409
MacDermott, K. A., E423
McDonald, Gregory, B181, B67, C441, E1811
McDiarmid, John F., C507
MacDonald, Charles, E75
McDonald, Gregory, B67, B181, C441, E1811
MacDonald, John D., A21, A38, A107, A171, B1, B18, B48, B111, B216, B239, B309, B409, C122, C127, C333, C334, C508, C594, C747, D364, E1085, E1812-E1850, E2219
MacDonald, Philip, B6, C240, E1851, E1852
Macdonald, Ross, A10, B2, B3, B17, B26, B73, B75, B79, B111, B134, B216, B242, B290, B306, B310, B312, B371, B396, B414, B434, C37, C137, C143, C267, C278, C295, C341, C342, C351, C369, C490, C496, C509-C512, C529, C601, C736, C750, C840, E443, E1395, E1428, E1464, E1478, E1854-E1902, E2068
MacDonald, Ruth, E7
MacDonell, A. G., C513
MacDonnell, James Edmond, A48
McDougald, Roman, AR
McDowell, Michael, AR
McElroy, Charles F., C514
McElroy, William, B15
McFadden, Steve, E711
McFarlane, Leslie, D91, D92, D99
McGerr, Patricia, B17, B234, E1903
McGill, V. J., C515
McGilligan, Pat, E305
McGirr, Edmund, AR
McGivern, William, B73, B409, E1905-E1906
MacGowan, Kenneth, B45, B238
McGregor, Herman, D370, D482
McGuire, Paul, B17, E200, E1907
McHaney, Thomas, E1058, E1063
MacHarg, William, C638
McIlvanney, William, AR, E1707
McInerny, Ralph, E1908
MacInnes, Helen, C494a, E1104a, E1908-E1910
MacInnis, James, E1366, E1396
McIntyre, John, E1911
MacIsaac, Fred, AR
MacKaye, Milton, E2352
McKeithan, D. N., E2900
MacKenzie, Donald, E1912, E1912a
McKimmey, James, AR
McKinstry, Lohn, D334
Mackintosh, Elizabeth. See Tey, Josephine
McLaren, Ross, E424, E2580
MacLean, Alistair, C494, C541, E1913-E1915
McLean, Arthur, D261
MacLeod, Charlotte, E1916
MacLeod, Robert, E1917
McLuhan, Marshall, C38, C517
McMahon, J., D87
MacMahon, Pat, E1496
McMenomy, Christe, E2543, E2561
McMillan, Dennis, E263
McMullen, Mary, AR
McNeile, H. C. See Sapper
MacOrlan, Pierre, E2978, E2994
MacShane, Mark, AR, E398, E428, E1890
MacShane, Frank, E425
McSherry, Frank D., B290, B396, C238, C472, C473, C518-C528, D466, E219, E465, E718, E1726, E2215, E2808-E2810, E2830, E3074, E3087
MacVicar, H. M., E876, E940
Machen, Arthur, E2752
Machiavelli, C504
Mack Bolan (FC; Don Pendleton), E2077
Madden, Cecil, B253
Madden, David, B239, E126, E321-E326
Mlle Miton, the Black Wolf (FC; dime novel), D127
Maekawa, Michisuke, B122
Maertens, M., E637
Magistrate Pao. See Judge Pao
Magnan, Pierre, E1918
<u>Magnet</u>, D172, D174, D178
<u>Magnet Library</u>, D100, D165, D166, D175, D181, D195
<u>Magazine of Horror</u>, D317
Magritte, René, E1929
Mahan, Floyd, AR
Mahan, Jeffrey H., C529
Maida, Patricia, E579, E596
Maigret (FC; G. Simenon), A73, B99, B157, B315, B362, B374, B392, C17, C29, C60, C310, C392, E821, E2254, E2583, E2585, E2588, E2589, E2593, E2602-E2604, E2606, E2607, E2612, E2618-E2620, E2622, E2625, E2626, E2630, E2631, E2634-E2638, E2646, E2647-E2649, E2661-E2663, E2678, E2679, E2681-E2683, E2687, E2693, E2694, E2700
Mailly, Chevalier de, C585
Mainwaring, Daniel. See Homes, Geoffrey
Maio, Kathleen L., B113, C530-C533
Maitland, Antony, E977
Major, Clarence, E1919
Makin, William J., E1920
Malcolm, Kenton, A158
Malet, Léo, A94, B107, B378, E1921-E1934
Malin, Irving, B239, E1397
Maling, Arthur, AR
Mallarmé, Stéphane, E323
Mallerin, Daniel, E1932
Malley, Louis, AR
Mallory, Arthur, E1834, E1925
Mallowan, Max, E580
Malone, H. Russell, E2498, E2525
Maloney, Martin, C534
Malosse, Jean, E514, E701, E744, E1008, E1042, E1044
Malraux, André, E1059
Maltin, Leonard, E2948
Malzberg, Barry, A12, E3122
Mambrino, Jean, E2646, E2650
<u>Mammoth Action Adventures</u>, D368
Manchester, H. F., C535
Manchette, Jean-Patrick, A94, B346, E941-E942, E1936-E1938, E3070, E3075
<u>The Man from U.N.C.L.E.</u>, A157, A158, C52
Manheim, Mary, E2606*
Manheim, Ralph, E2685
<u>Manhunt</u>, D332, D333
Mann, Jack, A12, E1939
Mann, Jessica, AR, B181, B241
Manno, D. Yves, C536
Mann, Peter, C420
Mann, Thomas, E468, E1879, E468
Mansfield, Katherine, B24
Manvey, Christian, AR
Mao, Nathan K., B449
Marchal, Gilles, E1691
Marcus, Greil, E101
Marcus, Steven, B264, E1398, E1402, E1366
Marder, Daniel, E2154
Margolies, Edward, B216, B242, C537, E1487-E1490
Marie Galante (FC; dime novel), D269
Mario Balzic (FC; K. C. Constantine), E707

Marius Pergomas (FC; Pierre Yrondy), E3158
Mark Hood (FC; James Dark), A48
Mark McPherson (FC; Caspary), B309, E380
Markham, Virgil, E1191
Marks, Alfred H., C460
Markstein, George, AR
Marling, William, E1400
Marlowe, Dan J., A48, B409, E1940
Marlowe, Derek, AR
Marlowe, Hugh. See Higgins, Jack
Marlowe, Stephen, AR, A48
Marmin, Michel, E1933
Maron, Margaret, AR, B64
Marotta, Joseph, E1835
Marquand, John, B310, E1941-E1946
Marric, J. J., B18, E721, E723. See also Creasey, John
Marsch, Edgar, B112, B243
Marsh, Howard R., AR
Marsh, Ngaio, B3, B16, B17, B26, B241, B304, B309, C500, C704, C785, C867, E1948-E1957
Marshall, Gene, D406
Marshall, Jay, D421
Marshall, Raymond, E470
Marshall, William H., E673
Marshment, Margaret, C538
Martens, Michel, B244, E469
Martenson, Jan, B386
Martensson, Bertil, B386
Martí-Ibáñez, Felix, C540, C541
Martí, Agenor, C539
Martin, A. E., AR
Martin, Bernard, E1103
Martin, Dale, D111
Martin, Ian Kennedy, AR
Martin, Patrick, E581
Martin, Robert, AR, B63
Martin, Roger, AR, B107, E6, E637-E639, E791, E1264, E1432, E1454
Martin, Troy, B179
Martin Beck (FC; Sjöwall/Wahlöö), C353, C576, E2709-E2912, E2715
Martin Hewitt (FC; A. Morrison), B281, C228, E2014, E2015, E2017
Martina, Daniel, E1754
Martinet, P., E3015
Marty, Pierre, E18, E1676, E1757
Maruya, Saiichi, B245, B120
Marx, Karl, B78, C503, E1663
Mary Finney (FC; M. Head), E1449
Maryles, Daisy, B105
Masked Detective, D410
Maslowski, Igor B., B269, B246
Mason, A. E. W., B24, B253, B343, C35, C259, E1958-E1962
Mason, Bobbie Ann, D56
Mason, F. Van Wyck, B62, E1963-E1968
Mason, Michael, E409, E427
Masur, Harold Q., AR, B48, B63, B64, B234, B409, B419, D333
Matchett, Willouby, E941, E942
Mate, Ken, E305
Mather, Berkeley, AR, A157
Matheson, Robert, E163
Mathiews, Franklin K., D24
Matsuda, Michihiro, B247
Matsumoto, Seicho, B328, C550, E1969-E1973, E1998
Matsumoto, Tai, B248-B250
Matsushima, Eiichi, E1973
Matsuura, Masato, B108
Matt Helm (FC; D. Hamilton), B309, C594, E1353
Matthews, Brander, B61, E2155
Matthews, C. G., E959
Matthews, Christopher, C542
Maturin, Charles, B69, E838
Matz, B. W., E848, E849, E943, E945
Matz, Kerstin, E1540
Matz, Winifred, E849
Maud Silver (FC; P. Wentworth), E3063
Maugham, Robin, AR
Maugham, W. Somerset, A103, B61, B303, B378, C72, C543, C544, C545, C867, E1712, E1974-E1976
Maupassant, Guy de, C195
Mauriac, Claude, E2651
Mauriac, François, E1324, E2646, E2652
Maurice, Arthur Bartlett, D57
Mawer, Randall, E428
Max Carrados (FC; E. Bramah), E216-E218, E222, E223, E227
Max Thursday (FC; Wade Miller), E1988, E1989
Maxfield, E2712
Maxwell, Victor, E1977
May, Clifford, C546
May, H. R. D., C547
May, Keith, E582
Maybury, Anne, C852
Mayflower Books, D266
Mayne, Richard, E2726
Mayo, Oliver, E1203, E1206-E1208
Mayse, Arthur, AR
Mazarin, Jean, E1978
Meade, L. T. (Mrs.), C565, C607, E1979, E1980
Meador, Ray, E429
Mealand, Richard, B142
Medeiros e Albuquerque, Paulo de, B251, B252
Meech, Shirley, E1296
Meggs, Brown, AR
Meheust, Paul Emile, E590
Meirs, Giorgio, C668
Meissner, B360
Melcer, Wanda, C316
Melchiore, Giorgio, B78, E583
Melling, John Kennedy, B255, E834
Melody Lane (juvenile series), D112
Meltzer, Edmund, E2863
Melville, Herman, B269, E1981
Melville, James, C550, E1982
Menendez, Albert J., A111
Menguy, Claude, E2613, E2633, E2653, E2654
Menon, K. R., E121
Mercier, Jean F., B105
Mercury Mystery, A117, E1418
Merigeau, Pascal, E1368, E2872, E3114
Merivale, Patricia, E181
Merlini (FC; C. Rawson), E2300, E2301
Mermet, H. Y., A112, E3158
Merrick, Stephen, E757
Merritt, Abraham C., C520, E1983
Merry, Bruce, B256, E1130, E2545
Mertz, Barbara. See Peters, Elizabeth
Mertz, Stephen, D348, E80, E81, E97, E109, E110, E2077
Mesplède, Claude, A113, A150, E1587, E1978
Messac, Ralph, E2612, E2646, E2655, E2656
Messac, Régis, B257, C405, E674, E2156
Meyer, Lynn, C453
Meyer, Nicholas, AR, C551
Meyers, Dick, D393
Meyerson, Jeffrey, A50, A114-A117
Meynell, Laurence, AR
Micha, René, E1491
Michaels, Leonard, E1401

Michaels, Barbara. See Peters, Elizabeth
Michaux, Ginette, E2310
Michel, M. Scott, AR, B62
Michel, Raymond, C360, E1665
Mierow, Charles C., C552
Mike Hammer (FC; M. Spillane), B310, C341, C616, D333, E2734, E2739, E2742, E2743, E2745-E2748, E3065
Mike Shayne (FC; Halliday), B309, E1349, E1350
Mike Shayne Mystery Magazine, E79
Miles, John, B18, E1984
Millar, (Dr.) A. M., C553
Millar, Kenneth, B1, E2740. See also Macdonald, Ross
Millar, Margaret, B16, B75, C715, C802, E1985-E1987
Miller, Anita, A118
Miller, Bill. See Miller, Wade
Miller, Claude, B378
Miller, D(avid) A., B264, C554, C555, E675
Miller, Don, A39, A41, E751, E2336, E2337, E2339, E2357, E2810
Miller, Edmund, E372
Miller, Henry, E2633, E2646, E2657, E2679
Miller, H. Hillis, E835
Miller, Joaquin, B2
Miller, Margo, D122, E1632
Miller, Marjorie M., E66
Miller, Mary W., B3
Miller, P. Schuyler, C556
Miller, Steve, D477
Miller, Susan, A57
Miller, Wade, A12, E1988, E1989
Milliken, Stephen F., E1492
Milne, A. A., B17, B304, B340, C168, C557, C558, E1990-E1995
Milner, Jay G., E430
Milward, Peter, E494
Minakami, Tsutomu, B367, E1996-E1998
Mines, Samuel, D414
Mintz, Phil, C559
Mira, Juan José, B258
Mirku, Q., E1673, E1679
Miss Blandish (FC; J. H. Chase), B348, B61, C606
Miss Marple (FC; A. Christie), A105, B310, B392, E524, E533, E562, E576, E579, E582, E596, E601, E605, E611
"Mission Impossible (TV series)," A157, A158
Mr. Chang (FC; A. E. Apple), D411, E59
Mr. Clackworthy (FC; Christopher Booth), E173
Mr. Death (PC), D412
Mr. Fortune (FC; H. C. Bailey), B253, E90-E93
Mr. Moto (FC; J. P. Marquand), A59, B310, C28, E1941-E1946
Mr. & Mrs. North (FC; Frances & Richard Lockridge), B309, E1772, E1776, E1777
Mr. Pond ((FC; Chesterton), B144, D486
Mr. Preed (FC; dime novel), D282
Mr. Reece & the Criminals' Confederation (FC; dime novel), D242
Mr. Wens (FC; S.-A. Steeman), E2758, E2760
Mrs. Crisparkle (FC; Dickens), E969
Mrs. Gideon Fell (FC: J. D. Carr), E368
Mitch Tobin (FC; Tucker Coe), E3076
Mitchell, Charles, E927, E944
Mitchell, F. James, E2002
Mitchell, Gladys, E1999-E2001
Mitchell, R., E2944
Mitgang, Herbert, E1728
Mitterling, Philip I., E2914
Miwa, Hidehiko, B156
Miyoshi, Toru, E1611, E2003
Mizutani, Jun, B445
Modesty Blaise (FC; Peter O'Donnell), B310, B308
Moebius, Hans, B259
Moffat, Gwen, AR
Moffat, Ivan, E431
Moffatt, Bryan, E409
Moffatt, Len, E1837
Moffatt, Len & June, E1826, E1838
Moffett, Cleveland, E2004
Mogens, B172
Mogensen, Harald, B210-B212, B261, B262
Mok, Michael, E2658
Moldenhauer, Joseph, Jr., E2157
Mole, William, B18, E2005
Molsner, Michael, C593
Monaghan, David, B92, E1701a
Monblatt, Bruce L., C560
Mondadori (publishing house), C756
Mondadori, Arnaldo, C559, C620
Monig, Christopher. See Crossen, Ken
Monk Mayfair (PC), D378
Monod, Sylvère, E866, E972
Monsieur Joly (FC; W. D. Howells), B374
Monsieur Teste (poetic persona; Valéry), E2186
Monsivais, Carlos, C561
Montague Egg (FC; D. L. Sayers), E2511
Montanelli, Indro, C311
Montayne, Harold, AR
Montesinos, José F., B93, C562
Montgomery, Lyna Lee, B396
Montgomery, Robert Bruce, C205, E737. See also Crispin, Edmund
Monteilhet, Hubert, E2006
Montserrat, Nicholas, C538
Mooney, Joan, B260, C186
Moorcock, Michael, D274
Moore, Harry, B239
Moore, John R., E2158
Moore, R. L., E1437
Moore, Ruth, E1245, E1247
Moore, Tim, E1104
Moran, Carlos, E432
Moran, Peggy, E1839
Moremans, Victor, E2646, E2660
More, Marcel, E2646, E2659
Moret, Julien, E1932
Moretti, Franco, C563
Morford, Henry, E985
Morgan, L., D58, D186
Morgan, Michael, E2007
Morgan, Neil, E433
Morice, Ann, AR, C11
Morimura, Seiicho, C550, E2009-E2012
Morineau, Raymond, E2975
Morino, Nick, E791
Morland, Nigel, B2, B159, B263, E2008, E3032
Morley, Christopher, E1118, E1119
Morley, Malcolm, E993
Morrah, Dermot, B17, E2013
Morris, Homer H., E1402
Morris, Terrence, B83, C564
Morris, Virginia, B92
Morris Carruthers (FC; dime novel), D170
Morris Klaw (FC; S. Rohmer), D328
Morrison, Arthur, B282, C565, E302, E390, E2014-E2017
Morse, A. Reynolds, E2581, E2582
Morse, Laurence Allan, A119
Morton, A. Q., C100

Morton, Anthony, A12. See also Creasey, John
Morton, Charles W., E1246
Moses Wine (FC; R. L. Simon), E2705
Moskowitz, Sam, C565, C566, D59, D413, E163, E165, E166, E169, E715, E814, E1209, E1504, E1505, E1979, E2016, E2056, E2159, E2373, E2418, E2582, E2853
Moss, Leonard, E1403
Most, Glenn, B264, C145, C439, E1708
Motola, Gabriel, E2901
Mottram, Eric, E1892
Mott, Walter Fenton, D210, na
Moy, Paul R., C567, E584, E131-E134, E2546
Moyes, Patricia, B18, B50, B64, B65, C153, E2018-E2019
Muddock, J. E. Preston, E1006
Mueller, Roswitna, C103
Mueller-Fraureth, Carl, B265
Muhlenbock, Kjell, E2811
Mukherji, Santosh Kumar, A64
Muller, Marcia, AR
Mulloy, John J., E499
Mulqueen, James E., E1893
Mundell, E. H., Jr., A120, E1247, E1404
Mundy, Talbot, A4, B88, E2020, E2021
Munro, George, D52, D216
Munro, Norman L., D201
Munro (PC), D487
Munro Publishing Co., D54
Munsey Co., D367
Munsey Magazine, D59, D413
Murata, Hiroo, B266
Murch, A(lma) E., B267, C511, E676, E2160, C511
Murder Ink Series, A99
Murder Mystery Monthly (series), A178
Murder Stories, D311
Murdoch, Derrick, E585
Murphy, Agnes, B265
Murphy, Michael, C568, E2245, E2754, E2755
Murphy, Warren B., AR, E2473
Murray, Andrew, D245, D267
Murray, Max, E2022
Murray, Robert, D267, D271
Murray, Will, D303, D309, D319, D322, D356, D371-D385, D428, D432, D445, D446, D467, D468, D476, D483, D501, E770, E797-E800, E806, E1268, E2473
Mussell, Kay, B113, C569
Mussolini, Benito, C886, c21
MWA. See Mystery Writers of America
Mycroft & Moran, A87
Mylett, Andrew, B24
Mystère Magazine, B269
Mysterious Wu Fang, D312-D314
Mystery & Adventure Series Review, D60
Mystery Adventure Magazine, D418
Mystery Book Magazine, D414
(The) Mystery FANcier, A38
Mystery Guild, A35, A36
(The) Mystery Hunters (juvenile series), D113
Mystery League, A123, D415, D416, E2245
Mystery Magazine, D356
Mystery Writers of America (MWA), B419, C265, C857
Mystery Writers of Japan, C660

Nabokov, Vladimir, B401, C407, C416, E181, E2023
Nach, Barbara, B131
Nagaanuma, Kiki, B273, B274, B364
Nagasaki, Hachiro, B115
Nagashima, Ryozo, B254, E2661, E2662
Nagata, Junko, B275
Nakajima, Kawataro, A121, A122, B167, B254, B276-B281, B301, E2291, E3153, E3164
Nakamura, Katsuhiko, B120, B282
Nakano, Kii, E494, E526
Nakata, Koji, B283
Nakazono, Eisuke, B284
Nakjavani, Erik, E1405
"Nameless" (FC; B. Pronzini), E2217, E2219
Nancy Drew (FC; juvenile series), B309, D24, D46, D81, D114-D125
Nanovic, John, D469, C817
Napoleon Bonaparte (FC; Upfield), E2918, E2924-E2926
Napoleon Solo (TV series character), B307
Narasimhan, R., E1210, E1214
Narcejac, Thomas, B37, B38, B61, B201, B246, B269, B285-B287, B362, B424, C107a, C296, C570, E373, E495, E586, E1211, E1212, E1225, E2262, E2646, E2663, E2664. See also Boileau, Pierre
Naremore, James, E1406
Nash, Ogden, B62, B64, B142
Nash, Simon, B18, E2024
Nathaniel Polton (FC; R. A. Freeman), E1176, E1193
Nathanson, Jacques, E1929
Natsuki, Shizuko, C550, E2025
Natty Bumpo (FC; J. F. Cooper), C744, E1893
Naudon, Jean-François, A112, E264, E285, E310, E1093, E1575, E1576, E1786, E1937, E3092, E3114
Naudon, Marie, E2333
Naumann, Dietrich, B424, B451, C570, C571
Navy Boys (dime novel series), D83
Nayland Smith (FC; Rohmer), E2406, E2421, E2456
Nebel, Frederick, B134, D302, D309, D343, E2026, E2027
Ned Kelly (FC; dime novel), D36
Nehr, Ellen A., A123, C572-C574, E2022, E2848
Nelson, Bill, E677, E2472
Nelson, Hugh Laurence, AR
Nelson, James, C575
Nelson, John, E1840
Nelson Lee (FC; dime novel), D79, D111, D126-D130, D279b
Nelson Lee Library, D11, D126, D127
Nelson, Ray, B216, E1493
Nelson, William, B92, C576
Nemours, Pierre, AR
Nero Wolfe (FC; Stout), A73, B170, B310, B392, C16, C17, D466, E2771-E2827
Nestor Burma (FC; Malet), E1921, E1923, E1924, E1928
Neuberg, Victor E., A124, B288
Neuhaus, Volker, B289, C577-C579, E1531
Neville, Barbara Alison. See Candy, Edward
Neville, Margot, AR
Neville Landless (FC; Dickens), E879, E903, E905, E908, E910, E974, E977, E978, E982
Nevins, Francis M., Jr., AR, A148, A154, A159, B15, B43, B134, B260, B264, B290, C238, C328, C385, C387, C472, C473, C521, C525, C580-C583, C654, E2, E3, E60, E61, E75, E82-E84, E186-E188, E195, E227, E373a, E387, E470, E637, E640, E734, E751, E1248, E1249, E1407, E1496, E1566-E1571, E1638, E1841, E1842, E2220, E2221, E2231, E2245, E2262-E2269, E2271, E2304, E2345, E2390, E2744, E2866, E2921, E3057, E3076, E3111, E3119, E3123-E3132
Newell, Robert H., E983

Newgate Calendar, C454
Newlin, Keith, B92, E753a
New Magnet Library, D37, D148, D166, D168, D172, D174, D175, D178, D179, D181
New Medal Library, D139
New Mystery Adventures, D418
New Nick Carter Weekly, D139
New York Detective Library, D40, D42, D203, D204
New York Weekly, D139
Newman, Bernard, ST
Newquist, Roy, E1104a
Newton, John J., E2269
Newton, Mike, E2077
Newton, Richard, E988
Newton, William, AR
Niceforo, Alfredo, C585
Nichols, Beverly, AR
Nick and Nora Charles (FC; Hammett), B310, C234
Nick Beaumont (FC; Hammett), E1361
Nick Carter (FC; dime novel), A158, B310, D5, D8, D14, D17, D20, D31, D32, D36, D46, D62, D63, D65, D68, D70, D74, D77, D131-D199, D204, D402, E1341
Nick Carter, Jr. (FC; dime novel), D158
Nick Carter Library, D133, D137, D138, D172
Nick Carter Magazine, D172, D177
Nick Carter Stories, D59, D139, D165
Nick Carter Weekly, D53, D59, D133, D137, D138, D140, D160, D167, D169, D170, D172, D180, D182, D186, D188, D362
Nick Fury (comic book character), B308
Nick Jordan (juvenile series; French), A107
Nick Kennedy (PC), D419
Nicky Welt (FC; H. Kemelman), E1583
Nicole, Christopher, E3157a
Nicoll, W. Robertson, E848, E849, E853, E869, E945
Nicolson, Marjorie, B78, B142, C584, C771
Nielsen, Bjarne, A125
Nielsen, Helen, AR
Nieminski, John, A34, A126-A129, A154, C521, C523, C586, D401, D441, E2419, E2831
Niethammer, Friedrich I., B358
Nietzel, Michael T., C587
Nilsen, Rolf, B386, C588
Nisbet, Ada, E850
Nishikawa, Kiyoyuki, B292
Nishimura, Juko, E2029, E3161
Nitta, Jiro, B367, E2030
Niven, Larry, C87, C589
Nixon, Joan, B293
Noel, Mary, D34, D61, D62
Nogueras, Luis Rogelio, B294, B326
Nolan, Jack, E1280
Nolan, Richard, E1709
Nolan, William F., D309, D321, E204-E207, E239, E240, E265, E434, E435, E763, E762, E1366, E1407-E1412, E2031-E2033, E3088
Nomura, Kodo, E2034
Nora Charles. See Nick and Nora Charles
Nordberg, Nils, B146, C591, C592, C767, E1334
Nord, Pierre, C476
Norgil (PC), D420, D421
Norman Conquest (FC; dime novel), D289, E244
Norman, Frank, E409, E436
Norman, James, AR
Norris, Luther, E815, E2423
North, Gil, AR
Norton, Charles, E2203, E2204, E2206
Norton, Ray, D262
"Not at Night" Series, A151
Noyes, Alfred, B41
Nugget Library, D219
Nugget Weekly, D274, D79
Nussbaum, Al, B64, E592a, E3077
Nusser, Peter, B295, B296, C593
Nye, Russel, C594, D63

Oates, Joyce Carol, B239, E327, E331
Oberon (Shakespeare), B337
Oboler, Arch, D437
O'Brian, Don, E1461
O'Brien, Fitz-James, B269
O'Brien, Frances Blazer, E1060
O'Brien, Frank, D187
O'Brien, George, B297
O'Brien, Geoffrey, E1290, E2874
Obstfield, Raymond, C595
Ocampo, Victoria, C596
Ochiogrosso, Frank, E1136, E1413
O'Connell, J. J., E1199
O'Connor, E1061, E496
O'Connor, Father John, E475
O'Connor, Gerard, D93
O'Connor, William Van, E1061
Ocork, Shannon, B117, E2035
(The) Octopus (PC), D312
Oda, Mitsuo, E2029
Odell, Robin, C50, C597
O'Donnell, Donat, B93, E1319
O'Donnell, Lillian, AR
O'Donnell, Peter, B310, E2036
O'Donnell, Thomas B., B3, E307
Odyssey Publications, D322
Oe, Sen'ichi, B298
O'Faolain, Sean, C598
O'Farrell, William, AR
Offord, Lenore, B234, C714, E182, E184, E189, E2037
O'Gara, Gil, D29, D81, D106, D213
Ogawa, Takashi, E3113
Ogden, George Washington, AR
Ogilvie, Elizabeth, AR, B64
Oguri, Mushitaro, B275
Ohanian, Seta, E2547
O'Hanlon, James, AR
O'Hara, John, B239
Oka, Naoki, E1612
Old Broadbrim Weekly, D100, D139
Old Broadbrim (FC; dime novel), D54
Old Cap Collier (FC; dime novel), D14, D42, D62, D63, D68, D137, D139, D200, D201, D204
Old Cap Collier Library, D54, D181, D200
Old King Brady (FC; dime novel), D13, D16, D17, D28, D40, D42, D48, D54, D63, D202-D215, E2064
Old Man in the Corner (FC; Orczy), B281, E2047-E2049
Old Sleuth (FC; dime novel), D17, D18, D42, D54, D62, D63, D68, D204, D216, D217
Old Sleuth Library, D52, D217
Old Sleuth Weekly, D50
Olden, Marc, AR
Oliver, George. See Onions, Oliver
Oliver Quade (FC; F. Gruber), D307
Olivier-Martin, Yves, B110, B299, C599, E16, E1755, E1756, E1640, E1674, 1675, E1744, E2760, E2761, E2835, E2993, E2994, E3015
Ollie, James G., C600
Ollier, Claude, E2038
Olsen, D. B., AR
Olsen, Jack, AR
Olsson, Hans-Olof, E2321, E2880
Olsson, Sven-Erik, E2880
Omerod, David, E1105

O'Neill, Eugene, E55, E2125
O'Neill, James, E1414
Onions, Oliver, B17, E2039
Oostvogels, Joe, E581
Operator 5 (PC), D314a, D326, D334, D422-D429
Opium Woman (FC; Dickens), E871, E873, E879, E883, E902, E914, E932, E939, E957, E965, E975, E981, E985, E827
Oppenheim, E. Phillips, A4, B248, B303, B430, E44, E1333, E2040-E2045
Orczy, Baroness, B204, B248, B253, B281, E2041, E2046-E2050
Ordway, Peter, AR
Orel, Harold, C601, E2161
Oriol, Laurence, AR
O'Riordan, Daniel, C602
Ormerod, Roger, AR
Ornkloo, Ulf, E1765
Orowan-Cornish, Florella, C603
Orr, Clifford, C604, E2052
Orr, Myron, B164
Orth, Michael, E2902
Orum, Poul, AR
Orwell, George, B61, B216, B348, B385, C537, C605, C606, C614
Osborn, David, E2053
Osborne, Charles, E587
Osborne, E. A., C607
Osborne, Eric, A58, E2162, E3050
Osbourne, Lloyd, E2769
Oscar Sail (FC; Lester Dent), E795
Oshikawa, Hiroshi, B254, B281
Oshita, Udara, D469, D492, E2054
Ostrom, John Ward, E2168
O'Toole, L. M., C608
Otto, Rudolph, C342
Ottolengui, Rodrigues, C565, E2055-E2058
Oulipopo, B85, C304, C651
Oursler, Fulton. See Abbot, Anthony
Ousby, Ian, B300, C303, C783, E678, E679, E836, E1284, E1285, E2163, E2164
Overton, Grant, C610, C611, E1306, E1962, E2042, E2065, E2203, E2206, E2356, E2358, E2359, E2878
Oxenberg, Jan, E596
Oyabu, Haruhiko, B367, B418, E2059, E2060
Ozaki, Milton, B301, E1607

Pachecho, Audrey I., C612
Pachon, Stanley A., D65
Pachter, Josh, B361
Packard, Frank L., C611, C638, D327, D451, E2061-E2065
Packman, Josie, D66, D222, D263-D268, D278
Packman, Len, D269-D278
Page-Jones, Robert, C666
Page, Emma, AR
Page, Marco, B17, C339, E2066
Page, Norman, E680
Page, Norvil, D293
Pain, Barry, B430
Paine, Lauran Bosworth, AR
Pakenham, Pansy, E946
Paladini, Vinicio, C613
Palme, Jacob, E2915
Palmer, Jerry, B181, B302
Palmer, Ray, E267
Palmer, Stuart, B48, AR
Panek, LeRoy L., B303, B304, E108, E134, E291, E374, E515, E588, E632, E788, E1003, E1106, E1131, E1345, E1513, E1532, E1710, E1956, E1994, E2043, E2165, E2548
Pao, Cheng, C378
Papilia, William, D293
Pargeter, Edith, A171, A171. See also Peters, Ellis
Parinaud, André, E2595, E2665
Parisot, Paul, E1929
Park Avenue Hunt Club (F. series; Pentecost), E2078
Parker (FC; R. Stark), E3069, E3073, E3075
Parker, Eric R., D25
Parker, Joan H., E2072
Parker, Lyndon, A156
Parker, Maude, AR
Parker, Patricia L., E247, E249
Parker, Robert B., B121, B306, B67, C47, C305, C425, C463, C735, E437, E750, E2067-E2074
Parker Pyne, E521, E545
Parkerphile, E3078
Parkman, Francis B., B144, C383
Parratt, C. J., D67
Parrinder, Patrick, B216, C614
Parry, Hugh Jones. See Cross, James
Parsons, Anthony, D288
Parsons, Elizabeth, E2075
Parsons, Luke, E2666, E2679
Pate, Janet, B307, B308, D188
Paterson, John, C616
Patrick, Q., A10, B62, B63, B93, C617, C688, D364, E2282. See also Quentin, Patrick
Patrick, Robert, E816
Patrick, William, C330
Patrick Petrella (FC; M. Gilbert), B309, E1276
Patrouch, Joseph F., Jr., E67
Patterson, Nancy-Lou, E2549, E2550
Patterson, Harry. See Higgins, Jack
Patterson, Sylvia, E589
Pattow, Donald J., E1415
Paul, Angus, E1260
Paul, Elliot, AR, B62, C618
Paulhan, Jean, E2646, E2667
Paul, Harley, E2384, E2409
Paul, Justus F., B144
Paul, Raymond, E2166
Paul Pine (FC; H. Browne), E268, E269
Paul Pry (FC; E. S. Gardner), E1249
Paul Shaw (FC; Mark Sadler), E640
Paul Temple (FC; Francis Durbridge), E1018
Pavett, Mike, B179
Pavolini, Corrado, C619
Payne, Alma, E8
Payne, Ronald, E1727
Peacock, Thomas Love, E2097
Pearce, Jack, C620a
Pearson, Edmund, D68, E947, E986
Pearson, John, E1107
Peck, Andrew, E2421
Peck, Harry Thurston, C620b, C629
Pederin, Ivan, C621
Pederson-Krag, Geraldine, B216, B264, C622, C712
Peek, George S., E1843, E1844
Peeples, Samuel A., E164, E165, E167, E3138, E3108
Peeters, Benoit, E590
Peeters, Frank, E581
Pegler, Westbrook, D69
Pellegrini, Giuseppe, C623
Pellizzi, Camillo, C624
Pelman, Brice, E2076
Pember, John E., C624a
Pemberton, Max, E980, AR
Pendleton, Don, E2077
Pendo, Stephen, E438
Pennell, E. N., A56

(The) Penny Popular, D235
Pentecost, Hugh, B309, C244, E2078-E2080
Penzler, Otto, A131, A159, A160, B15, B134, B272, B309, B310, C386, C625-C628, D189, E147, E148, E189a, E217, E229, E234, E235, E357, E497, E1039, E1942, E2305, E2306, E2944, E2962
Peppard, Murray B., E1026
Perdue, Virgina, B17, E2081
Perec, Georges, E2872
Perez, Florentino, B89
Perowne, Barry, A106, AR
Perrein, Robert, E2612
Perry, Anne, AR, B75
Perry, Ritchie, AR
Perry Mason (FC; E. S. Gardner), A73, B310, E1237, E1242-E1244, E1254
Perry Pierce (FC; juvenile series), D218
Persson, Gun-Britt, E2325
Persson, Lena, C761, E748, E2325
Perugini, Kate, E948
Perutz, Leo, B43, E2082
Peske, Antoinette, E18, E1676, E1757
Peter Flint (FC; dime novel), D219
Peters, A. D., C89
Peters, Elizabeth, AR, A12
Peters, Ellis, A171, B6, B18, B65, A171, C5, E2083
Peters, Jean, C110
Peters, Ludovic, AR
Peters, Margot, C463, C630, E567
Petersen, Herman, D309, E2084, E2085
Peter the Brazen (FC; Worts), E3136
Peter Wimsey (FC; Sayers), A73, B310, C334, C532, D89, E2116, E2482, E2484, E2485, E2488, E2491, E2507, E2514, E2517, E2523, E2526, E2531, E2538, E2541-E2543, E2547, E2551, E2554, E2559, E2560, E2562-E2564, E2568, E2570
Petherbridge, Margaret, C522, D414
Petievich, Gerald, AR
Petit, Jean, C360, E1665
Petrie, Rhona, AR
Petrullo, Helen, E837
Petschek, Willa, E591
Petscher, May-Brittig, E592
Pettee, Florence, D393a
Pettersson, Sven-Ingmar, E738, E1560, E1767, E1910, E2338, E2470, E2668, E2841
Phantom Detective (PC), D297, D326, D314a, D430-D435
Phèdre (French dramatic character; Racine), C61
Philip Marlowe (FC; Chandler), A73, B99, B178, B310, B392, C29, C168, C278, C493, C512, C616, C775, E383, E388, E397, E402, E403, E417, E418, E427, E430, E432, E433, E434, E442, E443, E451, E453, E1373, E1873, E1913, E2071, E2254
Philip Trent (FC; E. C. Bentley), B253, E2554
Philips, Judson, D300. See also Pentecost, Hugh
Phillips, James Atlee, A48. See also Atlee, Philip
Phillips, Louis, C631, D94
Phillips, Walter C., B311
Phillpotts, Eden, B17, E2086, E2087
Philmore, R., B142, C632
Philo Vance (FC; S. S. Van Dine), B170, B310, C226, C271, C274, C535, E1, E2935, E2937, E2939-E2941, E2943, E2947-E2950
Phineas Spinnet (FC; Andrew Soutar), B253
Phoenix Press, B319, C653
Picchi, Mario, E1232
Pickering, Samuel, Jr., D46
Pierce, Charles, B100, E2133
Pierce, Hazel, B312
Pierce, Jeff, E3096
Pierre Chambrun (FC; H. Pentecost), B309, E2080
Piglia, Ricardo, B214, C357
Pike, B. A., E2000
Pike, B. A., C137, C633, E32, E3000, E3001
Pike, Robert L., B295, C137. See also Fish, Robert
Pincher, Chapman, C500
Pini, Donatella, B36
Pinkerton, B122, E1378, E1416, E2905
Pinkerton, Nat, D31
Pintilie, Petro, C634, C635
Piovene, Guido, C636, E2590
Piper, Evelyn, AR
Piron, Maurice, E2603, E2669
Pitaval, François Gayot de, B295, B358
Pitcairn, (Dr.) John J., C565, E1177, E1184, E1209
Plass, Paul, E2341
Platts, A. Monmouth, E131
Player, Robert, AR
Pluck and Luck, D208, D211
Plummer, Bonnie C., C637
Plutarch, C315
Poate, Ernest, E2088
Pobst, Jim, E2422
Pocsik, John, E3060a
Podolsky, Edward, C638
Poe, Edgar Allan, A22, A70, A136, A144, A156, B2, B3, B6, B27, B41, B60, B61, B90, B91, B100, B115, B118, B125, B135, B190, B195, B201, B208, B219, B220, B243, B251, B257, B264, B274, B275, B290, B307, B310, B337, B338, B343, B346, B349, B362, B372, B375, B384, B397, B424, B430, C13, C35, C166, C176, C195, C199, C222, C259, C260, C281, C291, C332, C356, C365, C436, C452, C479, C497, C512, C553, C601, C607, C613, C629, C637, C673, C679, C703, C713, C733, C744, C754, C758, C766, C777, C825, C859, C862, E54, E56, E336, E353, E484, E498, E643, E659, E664, E676, E688, E690, E838, E1054, E1059, E1207, E1223, E1227, E1464, E1660, E1674, E1678, E1756, E1760, E1889, E2089-E2197, E2204, E2234, E2271, E246, E2765, E2835
Poirier, Richard, E1381
(The) Poisoned Pen, A38
Poker (FC; Dickens), E939
Polar, B107
Poli, Vincenzo, C639
Pollin, Burton R., B2, E2170
Polyphemus, E222
Pommeraud, André, E2978, D2995
Ponder, Eleanor Anne, B313
Ponsart, Pierre, E2076
(The) Pontine Dossier, A38
Popkin, Zelda, B62, E2198, E2199
Popular Library, A80, A179, C653
Popular Publications, D293, D410, D429, D436-D438, D496
Poppy Ott (FC; juvenile series), D106
Popular Magazine, D402
Porcelain, Sidney, B48
Porter, Dennis, B264, B315, C640, E2670
Porter, Joyce, AR, B64
Portugal, Eustace, C641
Portuondo, José Antonio, B316, C642, C643
Porzio, Domenico, C316
Poster, Constance Hammett, E91
Postgate, Raymond, AR, C376, E630
Post, Melville Davisson, B270, B430, C410, C518, C581, C601, C644, C645, E2130, E2200-E2209

Potts, Jean, AR
Potts, Samuel W., E801
Poulet, Robert, E2671
Poupart, Jean-Marie, B317
Powell, Anthony, E1342
Powell, Dilys, E409, E439
Powell, James, AR
Powell, Richard, AR, B63
Powell, Robert S., D309, E1417
Powell, Talmage, E2210
Power, Charles R. L., E2423, E2424
Powers, Richard Gid, B216, B318, C647
Powys, John Cowper, C648
Prager, Arthur, D95, D124, E2425
Prairie Library, D279b
Prather, Richard S., AR
Pratt, Allan, E1845
Prescott, Peter S., E2721
Prezzolini, Giuseppe, C649
Price, Anthony, B50, E2211, E2212
Priestley, J. B., B18, E2213, E2214, E3033
Prince, Jerome & Harold, E2215
Prince Abdull Omar (PC), D447. See also "Semi-Dual"
Prince Menes (PC), D259, D270
Prince Zaleski (FC; Shiel), E2579, E2582
Prior, Allan, AR
Prior, Linda T., E2171
Pritchett, V. S., E867, E1321, E1711, E2017
Procter, Maurice, B18, B96, B124, B283, C650, E2216
Proctor, Richard A., E936, E949, E984
Professor Balthazar (FC; M. Leblanc), E1644
Professor Mark Rymer (FC; dime novel), D128
Professor Móriarty (FC; Doyle), D466, E2452
Professor Nathan Enderby (FC; Wellman), 3060a
Professor Wells (FC; F. D. Grierson), B253
Proll, Harry, B424, C652
Pronzini, Bill, A10, A12, B64, A132, B107, B319, B409, C292, C653, C654, D306, D309, D323, E111, E421, E1793, E1895, E2217-E2220, E3088
Propp, Vladimir, C272a
Propper, Milton, E2221
Proust, Marcel, E2787
Provost, Dawn, E2021
Prusek, Jaroslav, B320
Pry, Elmer, B216, C199, E1896
Puck, B337
Pudd'nhead Wilson (FC; M. Twain), E2890, E2891, E2895, E2897, E2902, E2904, E2906-E2908
Pudlowski, Gilles, C657, C658
Pulp, D324
Pulp Press, D324
Pumilia, Joe, E165
Punter, David, B321
Purcell, J. M., E749, E1256, E1593
Purcell, Mark, E92, E790, E3002
Putnam Thatcher (FC; Lathen), E1629, E1630
Pynchon, Thomas, C351
Pyramid Green Door series, A167, A177
Pythian-Adams, Canon, E928, E950

Quayle, Eric, B322, E681, E2172
Queen, Ellery, A1, A9, A22, A29, A50, A60, A71, A131-A139, A154, B48, B50, B110, B123a, B142, B207, B254, B270, B287, B290, B298, B310, B323, B336, B364, B404, B414, C16, C96, C114, C240, C339, C518, C581, C594, C659, C660, C661, C718, C747, D416, E33, E357, E568, E791, E1037, E1040, E1250, E1251, E1278, E1418, E1446, E1498, E1501, E1678, E1898, E2222-E2280, E2812, E2842, E2879, E2930, E3003
(The) Queen Canon Bibliophile, E2270
Queendom, E2274
Queen's Quorum, A91, A135, C323
Queneau, Raymond, E18, E19
Quentin Compson (FC; W. Faulkner), E1052
Quentin, Patrick, C617, C785, E1042, E2281, E2282
Quiller (FC; Adam Hall), B309, E1345
Quilter, Harry, E682
Quinby, Ione, E2426
Quincunx, C662
Quinn, Seabury, A87, E2283-E2288
Quintilian, C585, C779
Quintus Quiz, C663-C665
Quiribus Brown (FC; H. S. Keeler), E1567
Quiroule, Pierre, D246

Raabe, Juliette, B12, B240, B324, C666
Raabe, William, B338
Raban, Jonathan, E1846
Rabbi Small (FC; H. Kemelman), C471, C577, E1582, E1584, E1585
Rabinowitz, Peter J., E440, E1062
Race Williams (FC; Daly), D309, E758, E759
Racine, Jean, E2678
Racketeer Stories, D311
Radcliffe, Anne, B259, C356, E838
Radcliffe, Elsa, A140
Radcliffe, Mary Ann, B2
Radford, E. & M. A., AR
Radin, Edward D., B48
Radine, Serge, B325
Radius, Emilio, C667
Rae, Hugh C., AR
Raffaelli, Raffaella, C668, E34, E35
Rafferty (PC), E59
Rafferty, S. S., AR
Raffles (FC; E. W. Hornung), B61, B348, C222, C334, C547, C606, E1670
Rainov, Bogomil, B294, B326
Ralph Pinker Agency, E224
Ralston, H. W., D198
Rambelli, Loris, B78, B327, C504, C669, E620, E784, E821
Rameil, Claude, E1923
Rampo, Edogawa, B183, B328-B336, B416, B418, B425, B446, C474, C550, E2289-E2295
Ramsey, G. C., A156, C670
Ramsey, Gordon K., E593, E594
Ramsey, Jarold, E2633
Ramsey, Roger, E1027
Randall, David, A141, E1109
Randall, Rona, 1561
Randisi, Robert J., B187, E2027, E2481
Randolph, Marion, AR, B344
Randolph, Vance, E2296
Randolph Mason (FC; M. D. Post), E2205
Ranger Calhoun (PC), D439
Rank, Claude, AR
Raskin, Richard, C671
Rathbone, Julian, AR
Rauber, D. F., B216, E2813
Rausch, Diane, C672
Rausch, G. J., A120, C672
Rausch, George J., E1943
Ravegnani, Giuseppe, C673
Raven House, A40
Ravenscroft, N. C., E112
Raven, Simon, E2297
Rawson, Clayton, B134, B271, B272, B419, B134, C121, C400, C674, D334, D440, E532, E2105, E2298-E2307

Ray, Jean, B107, B202, C220, E2308-E2317
Ray, Laura, B3, E2551
Raymond, Alex, E1366, E1390
Raymond, François, E1677, E1678, E2994, E2996
Raymond, John, E2672
Rayner, Richard, E3135
Raynor, Henry, C675
Reach, James, AR
Reade, Charles, B311, C123
Reade, Newbury Frost, E994
Reaves, R. B., E2525, E2552
Rebecca (FC; D. du Maurier), C711
Reck, Tom S., E328
Recupito, Anna Maria, C676
Red Magazine, A104
Redman, Ben Ray, C678
Redmond, Anne, A142
Redmond, Anne, A143
Red Shadow Tong (series), D419
Red Star Mystery, D440
Reed, Ishmael, B216, E2318
Reed, J. D., E3046
Reeve, Arthur B., A105, B298, C679, D442, E2319-E2322
Reeve, Clara, B259
Reeves, Robert, E2323
Reeves, W. J., C465
Refreger, Omer, E1922
Regester, Seely, B134, E2324
Reggiani, Renée, B337
Reginald, R., A66
Reginald Fortune (FC; H. C. Bailey), B253, C229
Regis, Jul, E2325
Regis, Richard, E596
Reilly, Helen, AR, C688, na
Reilly, John M., A143, A158, B16, C680-C682, E1419, E1494, E1576, E1987, E2022
Reinert, Claus, B338
Relph, Harry, E2447
Remar, Frits, E683, C684, E2326
Renaud, Michel, A94, E1918
Renault, Maurice, B269
Rendell, Ruth, B16, B18, B67, B75, C153, B378, E2327-E2340
Renéville, J. Roland de, E1679
Reno, Marie, AR
Resnais, Alain, E2314
Rest, Jaime, B214, C357
Retchko, Bob, E708
Retcliffe, John, E2341
Reuter, Florizel von, E909, E951, E981
Revell, Laura, AR
Reverend Lionel Stainer (FC; dime novel), D279a
Revesz, Etta, AR
Revue des eç127/tudes lupiniennes, E1679
Revzin, I. I., B424, E595
Rex Stout Mystery Quarterly, E2809
Rey, Alain, B346, C685
Rey, René-Charles, E1978
Reyes, Alfonso, C686
Reynolds, Barbara, E2553, E2554
Reynolds, G. W. M., E2342
Reynolds, Paul, B48, B339
Reynolds, Quentin, D182, D70
Reynolds, William, C687, C688, E1599, E2555
Rhode, John, AR, B340
Rhodes, Henry T. F., C689
Rice-Sayre, Laura Prindle, B341
Rice, Craig, B62, B142, C690, E2343-E2346
Richard, Claude, E2173
Richard, Jean-Pierre, C691
Richard, Maurice, E2673
Richard Hannay (FC; J. Buchan), B308, E282, E292, E295-E298
Richard Quintain (FC; dime novel), D248
Richard III, E2863
Richardson, Darrell, E240
Richardson, Maurice, B179, B344, B342, E2673
Richardson, Samuel, E2484
Richert, J. Gust, B343,
Richie, Donald, B290
Richler, Mordecai, E1110
Richmond, Lee J., E1803
Richter, Anne, E2612, E2674, E2675
Rickman, H. P., C692, E2556
Ricks, Beatrice, E1058, E1063
Riddell, (Mrs.) J. H., E2347, E241
Riddell, John, E241
Rieben, Georges, E2845
Rigsby, Howard, AR
Riley, Dick, E596
Rin Tin Tin, B307
Rinehart, Mary Roberts, B16, B270, B298, C530, C594, E2348-E2367
Rines, Edward, E952, E958
Ringarp, Anna Lena, B232
Riordan, Robert V., D96
Rippin, Marion, AR
Rissient, Pierre, E2872
Ritchie, Jack, AR
Ritunnano, Jeanne, E2903
Rivera, Jorge B., B214, C477, C478
Rivera, Guillermo, B294
Rivett, Edith Carol. See Carnac, Carol
Rivière, François, A144, B110, C106, C693-C695, E597, E1466, E149, E2427, E2428, E2994, E2997, E4, E598
Rix, Walter T., B60, B78, C696
Rizzoni, Gianni, B27
Roa Bastos, Augusto, B214
Roark, Anne C., C697
Robbe-Grillet, Alain, B102, B135, B346, B366, C407, C416, C429, C451, C570, E46, E1017, E2038, E2369-E2371
Robbins, Ed, E2738
Robbins, Frank E., B290, E1252
Robert & Grace Duvall (FC; pulp), D407
Roberts, Austin F., B48
Roberts, Bette B., E2075
Roberts, Daniel G., E1213
Roberts, James Hall. See Duncan, Robert L.
Roberts, Kenneth, C698
Robertson, Helen, B18, E2372
Robertson, John, B3
Robert, John M., C699
Robertson, Sandra D., E599
Roberts, R. Ellis, B41
Roberts, Ralph, E2210
Roberts, Steven V., E3047
Roberts, Willo Davis, B64
Robeson, Kenneth, D368, D382, E806
Robey, George, E2389
Robin, Christian, B110, E1758
Robin Hood, C399, D79
Robins, Alfred, E953
Robinson, B. Fletcher, C565, E2373
Robinson, Frank M., B189
Robinson, Kenneth, E683
Robinson, Warren F., D82
Robinson Crusoe (FC; D. Defoe), C517
Robison, Roselee, E954
Robson, W. W., E498
Roby, Mary Linn, C530
Robyns, Gwen, E587, E600
Rocambole, B257
Roche, Daniel-Rolland, E530

Rochlitz, Geneviève, B197
Rochlitz, Rainer, B197
Rockwell, Joan, C700
Rocky Steele (FC; John B. West), E3065
Rodell, Marie, B142, B344
Roderick Alleyn (FC; Marsh), B309, E1947, E1949
Rodker, John, E2101
Rodrian, Irene, C593
Rodriguez Joulia St. Cyr, Carlos, B345
Roeburt, John, AR, B48
Roeder, Rudolf, B424, C701
Roeg, Nicolas, E1011
Roff, William R., D191
Roger Baxter (juvenile series), D220
Roger Sheringham (FC; A. Berkeley), E128
Rogers, Cameron, C702
Rogers, Denis, D71
Rogers, Frank, E2905
Rogers, Joel Townsley, B70, B270, E2374-E2377
Rogers, Mary, E2187, E2196, E2198
Rohmer, Sax, A4, A38, A103, A138, A158, A179, B88, B253, B269, B290, B339, C130, C189, C541, C565, C594, E1516, E2041, E2378-E2462
Rohmer, Elizabeth, E2423, E2459
(The) Rohmer Review, E2448
Rollin, Jean, E1759
Rolo, Charles J., B348, E2676
Romain, Jules, E2641
Romer, Jean-Claude, E2449
Romi, E1732
Ronald Jackson (PC), D489
Ronald Standish (FC; Sapper), E2478
Rönblom, H. K., E2463, E2464
Ronns, Edward. See Aarons, Edward S.
Roos, Kelly, AR, B46
Rosa Bud (FC; Dickens), E905, E927, E939, E956, E969, E981, E988
Rosa, E899
Rosal, Juan del, B347
Rosamund, Babette, AR
Roscoe, Theodore, C520, E2465
Rosenbach, A. S. W., C703
Rosenbaum, Samuel, B386
Rosenberg, Bernard, B348
Rosenberg, Betty, A145, A146
Rosenberg, Edgar, E955
Rosenberger, Joseph, AR
Rosenblatt, Roger, E2945
Rosenhayn, Paul, B224
Rosenkrantz, Baron Palle, C191
Rosenthal, F. M. B., E932
Rosika Storey (FC; H. Footner), E1118, E1121, E1122
Ross, Angus, AR
Ross, Barbara, B398
Ross, Barnaby, E2224, E2243, E2262, E2271. See also Queen, Ellery
Ross, Helaine, C704
Ross, Jonathan, E2466
Ross, Mary B., C705
Ross Harte (FC; C. Rawson), E2300
Rossi, Alberto, C706
Rossiter, John, E2466
Rossner, Judith, C753
Rostenberg, Leona, E9
Roth, Holly, AR
Roth, Martin, B3, E2174
Roth, Phyllis, E2770
Roudaut, Jean, B424, E1760
Roudybush, Alexandra, E2467, E2468
Rougeul, Jean, E1732
Rough Rider Weekly, D139
Rouletabille (FC; Leroux), E1686, E1734, E1744, E1748, E1763
Rouse, William Merriam, AR
Roussel, Raymond, E1646
Roussel, Roy, E956
Rousselot, Jean, E1934
Routley, Erik, B349, B434, C707
Rowe, Cecil, D279
Rowe, Cyril, D88
Rowland, John, E2087
Rowlette, Robert, E2904
Roy, David T., C708
Roy, Sandra, E2860
Roy Stover (juvenile series), D221
Royce, Kenneth, AR
Ruber, Peter, E2756
Ruble, William, E1147, E2275
Rud, Anthony, E2469
Ruehlmann, William, B350, E2745
Ruggiero, Josephine A., C852
Ruhm, Herbert, B239, C709, D349
Ruiter, Jan P., E2383
Runnquist, Ake R., B103, B104, E292
Rupert Waldo (FC; dime novel), D222, D271
Ruric, Peter, E333
Ruskin, John, E935
Russ, Joanna, B113, C711, E1041
Russell, Bertrand, C415
Russell, John, B430
Russell, Luana, D109
Russell, Martin, E2470
Russell, Ray, AR
Russell, William. See Waters
Rust, S. J., E924, E957
Rutherford, Andrew, E1712
Rutherford, Douglas, AR
Ryan, Elizabeth, E2557
Ryck, Francis, E2471
Rycroft, Charles, C712
Ryley, Robert, E1068
Rysan, Josef, B372

Sacks, Sheldon, E1897
Sacred Valley of the Himmalayas (fictional series; dime novel), D172
Sadler, Mark, E640. See also Collins, Michael
Sadoul, Jacques, B351
Sage, Dana, AR
Saikaku, Ihara, C460
(The) Saint (FC; Charteris), B253, E458, E460, E462, E463, E466
St. Armand, Barton Levi, E2175
St. Augustine, C384
"(The) Saint Mystery Library," A81
(The) Saint (Mystery) Magazine, A21, A129, D441
Saint Val, Vic, AR
Saito, Masatoshi, B108, E1972
Sakabe, Goro, B352
Sakaguchi, Ango, B353
Sakakibara, Kozo, B254
Sakurai, Hajime, B354
Salemson, Harold J., E2624, E2685
Sale, Richard, D316, AR
Sales, Roger, E1420
Salter, James, E1322
Salwak, Dale, E51
Sampson, Robert, D72, D303, D309, D325-D328, D351, D363, D386-D388, D402, D405, D407, D411, D417, D433, D439, D443, D448, D467, D471-D473, D484-D485, D495, E601, E802-E804, E806, E1121, E1911, E1977, E2287, E2832, E3139
Sam Space (FC; W. F. Nolan), E2033

Sam Spade (FC; Hammett), A73, B99, B178, B310, C278, C342, C493, C512, C546, C616, C775, E1366, E1367, E1373, E1376, E1395, E1400, E1419, E1430
Samuels, Albert, E1393
Samuels, Albert, Jr., E1393
San Antonio, B59, B107, E771-E773. See also Dard, Frédéric
Sanchez Riva, Arturo, C713
Sancho Panza (FC; Cervantes), E2785
Sanders, E. L., E958, E959
Sanders, Joe, E1847
Sanders, Lawrence, C576, E2472
Sanderson (FC; J. J. Chichester), E508
Sanderson, Joy, E743, E3108
Sandoe, James, A147-A149, B15, B142, B159, B355, C395, C714, C715, C730, E37, E128, E270, E1421, E2558, E2559, E2571, E2855, E2861
Sandow, Eugene, D168
Sandy Abuthnot (FC; J. Buchan), E296
Sanguinetti, Edoardo, C716
Sannino, Laura, C717
Sano, Yo, B356, B356a
Santesson, Hans Stefan, C400
Santucci, Antonio, B78, C718
Sapir, Richard, E2473
Sapper, B253, B303, B310, B310, B420, C611, E2474-E2479, E3147
Sapp, Judson, E2810, E2814, E2822
Sapsea (FC; Dickens), E969, E986
Sarah Chayse (FC; Lynn Meyer), C453
Sarjeant, William Anthony S., E93, E343, E633, E719, E739, E740, E2925, E2926, E2963
Sarraute, Nathalie, B102, C429, E2759
Sarsfield, Maureen, E2480
Sartre, Jean-Paul, E321
Sathianandhan, Kamala, A64
Sato, Tomoyuki, B381, E3152
Sauder, Rae Norden, C720
Sault, A. P., E1732
Saunders, Montagu, E960-E963
Savage, Colonel Richard, D375
Savage, Ernest, E2481
Savi, Tullio, C721
Savinio, Alberto, B78, C722, E2590, E2677, E2678
Savonuzzi, Luca, C723
Sawyer, Eugene T., D131, D136, D156, D198, D199
Saxlund, Tyrgils, E1031
Sayer, W. W., D246
Sayers, Dorothy L., A70, A161, A171, B5, B6, B16, B17, B26, B28, B61-B64, B78, B92, B112, B142, B179, B205, B241, B289, B304, B310, B357, B357a, B357c, B362, B372, B385, B391, B424, B434, C14, C151, C16, C223, C248, C334, C361, C436, C453, C499a, C513, C567, C630, C687, C689, C704, C724-C729, C739, C799, C867, D89, E532, E535, E569, E664, E685, E686, E750, E995, E1016, E1536, E1537, E1539, E2112, E2176, E2177, E2482-E2572, E2706
(The) Sayers Review, E2561
Saylor, Louise, E2906
Sayre, Anne, E2837
S. B. W., E1161
Scanlon, C. K. M., D319
Scaramanga (FC; I. Fleming), E1085
The Scarlet Pimpernel (FC; Orczy), B253, B308
Scene of the Crime series, A99
Schaginjan, Marietta S., B295
Schantz, Tom, E986
Schantz, Tom & Enid, A149, C730, C731, E24, E1782, E2208
Scheick, William J., E499
Schell, Edgar, E2907
Schemer, Arriean, E2822
Scherf, Margaret, AR
Schickel, Richard, E1898
Schier, Norma, E2573
Schiller, Friedrich, B265, B358-B360, B368, C701
Schimmelpfennig, Arthur, B359
Schklovskij, Viktor, B424, C732, E838. See also Sklovskij, Viktor
Schlagel, Libby, E1585
Schlegov, Y. K., C732
Schleret, Jean-Jacques, A113, A150, C476, E63, E251, E257, E259, E264, E266, E266a, E285, E304, E637, E641, E756, E720, E1279, E1368, E1518, E1552, E1575, E1576, E1635, E1691, E1786, E2872, E3092
Schley, Sturges, AR
Schloss, Carol, E1148
Schmidt-Henkel, Gerhard, B126, B451, C734
Schmidt, Aurel, E42, E48
Schmidt, Josef, B13
Schmolders, Claudia, E2679
Schneider, Jack W., E1475
Schoenhaar, Rainer F., B360, C406, C578
Scholey, Jean, B18, E2574
Schonberg, Harold C., C735
Schoolcraft, John L., E240
Schopen, Bernard A., C736
Schorer, Mark, E820
Schraiber, Eleonora, E2646, E2680
Schreiber, Mark, E2964
Schreuders, Piet, B361
Schultheis, Stephen F., E2816
Schulz-Buschaus, Ulrich, B295, B362
Schwartz, Saul, B363
Schweig, J. P., E507, E1575-E1580, E3092, E3093
Schweitzer, Darrell, A151
Sciascia, Leonardo, B92, B116, B362, C737, C738, E2575, E2575a, E2590, E2681
Scientific Detective Monthly, D441
Scientific Sprague (PC), C638
Scollo, Peter A., D48
(The) Scorpion (PC), D312
Scotland Yard, D443
Scott, A. Leslie, D409
Scott, (Mrs.) A. Leslie, D409
Scott, Arthur C., E751, E791, E1264, E1572, E1573, E2810
Scott, Carolyn D., E1323
Scott, Helen, E1288
Scott, Jeffry, AR
Scott, Justin, AR, E3079
Scott, Kenneth W., E654
Scott, Maxwell, D111, D129
Scott, R. T. M., AR
Scott, Sutherland, B364, B273
Scott, Sir Walter, E2158
Scott, William M., E2562
Scott-Giles, C. W., E2563, E2564
Scott-James, R. A., C739
Scowcroft, P. L., C740, C741
Scribner's Catalogue, A31
Scura, John, E1781
Seaborne, E. A., C742
Seagle, William, C503
Searle, Ronald, B391
Searles, A. Langley, E1506
Seaton, Esta, E1052
Sebeok, Thomas, B100
Secret Agent X (PC), B443, D397, D444-D446
Secret Service, D21, D74, D186, D204, D209, D210
Secret Six, D312, D449

See, Carolyn, B239, C743a
Seeberger, Kurt, E3017
Seeley, Mabel, AR, C397, C530, C594
Seelye, John, C744
Seesslen, Georg, C746
Sehlbach, Hans, E687
Seidman, Michael, E1078
Seldes, Gilbert, C745, E303
Seldow, Michael, E1732
Selly, Giova, AR
Selneuves, Jean de, E1922
Selwyn, Francis, AR, C5
Semi-Dual (PC), D328, D447, D448
Semjonow, Julian, C767
Sempill, Ernest, D279
Senarens, Lu, D210
Sennwald, André, E2810
Sergeant Beef (FC; Leo Bruce), E272a
Sergeant Cuff (FC; Wilkie Collins), C228, E672, E678, E679, E688
Sergeant Riordan (FC; V. Maxwell), E1977
Serguine, Jacques, AR
Seç127/rie noire, A6, A113, A150, B12, B20, B157, C657, C658, C666, E468
Setogawa, Takeshi, B119
Severin, Bill, B300
Seward, Jack, A48
Sexton Blake (FC; dime novel), A4, A106, D25, D49, D77, D79, D87, D130, D175, D179, D188, D195, D196, D224-D291
Sexton Blake Library, D233, D236, D247, D254, D258, D264, D266, D267, D288
Seymour-Smith, Martin, B365
The Shadow (PC), A1, B309, B310, D139, D297, D305, D325, D326, D334, D380, D403, D420, D450-D475, E637, E638, E1265, E1268, E1833, E3028
Shaffer, Norman J., E2682
Shaffer, Peter. See Antony, Peter
Shagan, Steve, AR
Shaginyan, Marietta, C748
Shakespeare, William, B195, C34, C40, E327, E2240
Shallabarger, Samuel, B339
Shallit, Joseph, AR
Shaner, Carl, D329
Shan, Hanoi, E2405
Shanks, Edward, E2387, E2581
Shannon, Dell, A12, B309, E1768, E1770. See also Linington, Elizabeth
Shapiro, Debbie, E1253
Sharpe, Tom, E3144
Shattuck, Richard, C714, E2576, E2577
Shaver, Richard S., E267
Shaw, George Bernard, E980, E992, E997
Shaw, Joseph, B2, C749, D309, D342, D344, D346-D348, E800, E1391, E1805
Shearing, Joseph, AR
Sheed, Wilfred, C750
Sheldon, Lauranna, D28
Sheldon, Richard, AR
Shenker, Israel, B366
Shepherd, Neal. See Morland, Nigel
Sheridan, Juanita, AR
Sheridan Keene (FC; dime novel), D166
Sheriff Hyzer (FC; J. D. MacDonald), E1812
Sheriff Joe Bain (FC; Jack Vance), E2931
Sherlock Holmes (FC; Doyle), A22, A37, A73, A120, A128, A156, A161, B20, B43, B61, B68, B78, B99, B100, B115, B122, B142, B179, B190, B239, B290, B307, B310, B346, B354, B391, B392, C16, C17, C60, C69, C81, C86, C145, C166, C207, C222, C228, C230, C294, C335-C338, C361, C505, C517, C608, C638, C642, C732, C733, C771, C862, D57, D73, D402, D466, E356, E617, E702, E810, E984, E986, E987, E990, E1640, E1682, E1686, E1778, E2014, E2116, E2192, E2254, E2273, E2312, E2315, E2316, E2320, E2421, E2523, E2780, E2785, E2791, E2812, E2813, E2815, E2892, E2903, E2929, E2947, E2964, E3106
Sherwood, John, E2578
Shibuk, Charles, A152-A154, A159, A160, B290, C520, C751, E764, E119, E123, E136, E155, E465, E1187, E1442, E2565, E2921, E3007, E3009, E3084
Shiel, M. P., A87, B24, E2579-E2582
Shield Weekly, D41, D52, D100, D139, D165, D174
Shimazaki, Hiroshi, E3149
Shimizu, Shunji, E397
Shine, Walter & Jean, E1848, E1849
Shinseinen (Magazine), A122
Shiraishi, Kiyoshi, B369, B370
Showalter, Elaine, C753
Shrapnel, Norman, B61, B83, C754
Shropshire, F., E1975
Shroyer, Frederick, E1722, E1723
Shuffleton, Frank, D6
Shulman, David, A155
Shusterman, David, E2727
Shute, Nevil, AR, C538
Shutoff, Carl Lee, E2683
Shuttlebury Cobb (FC; Freeman), E1192
Siebenheller, Norma, E596, E1541
Sigaux, Gilbert, E1934, E2613, E2646, E2684, E2686
Silbersky, Leif, B386
Siller, Van, AR
Silone, Ignazio, C139
Silverberg, Robert, E1041, E1261
Silverman, Marguerite, AR
Sim, Georges, B12, E2613, E2644
Simenon, Georges, B3, B12, B26, B27, B78, B90, B99, B107, B115, B179, B213, B215, B246, B254, B310, B315, B317, B337, B348, B374, B378, B389, B410, B424, C220, C281, C295, C376, C392, C397, C570, C718, C754, C773, E388, E821, E1464, E2583-E2703, E2728
Simmel, Johannes Mario, E2704
Simon, Beth, E596
Simon, Claude, B102
Simon, Jamie, E3057
Simon, Roger, B121, C305, E2705
Simon Ark (FC, E. D. Hoch), E1500
Simon Templar, C517. See also (The) Saint
Simonin, Albert, AR, E1932, E1934
Simpson, Helen, E2706, E532
Sims, George, AR, E1111
Sinclair, Fiona, AR
Sinclair, Murray, C885
Sinda, Gregory, E1422
Singapore Sammy (FC; G. F. Worts), E3136
Singer, Muff, B76
Siniac, Pierre, A94, E2707, E2708, E2994, E2998
Sinisgalli, Leonardo, C756
Sinister Stories, D437
Sipper, Ralph Bruno, B3, E1888
Sir Henry Fairfax (FC; dime novel), D240
Sisk, John P., C757
Sissman, L. E., E441
Sjogren, Agneta, E592
Sjöwall, Maj & Per Wahlöö, B26, B96, C153, C354, C576, C593, E1801, E2709-E2715
Skenazy, Paul, B371, E442
Skene, Anthony, D246, D247
Skene Melvin, David & Ann, A156, C8

(The) Skipper (FC; pulp), D476

Sklovskij, Viktor, B78. See also Schklovskij, Viktor
Skoverecký, Josef, B372, E336, E500, E2716-E2718
Skreb, Zdenko, B451, C758
Skyette, Asbjorn, E2817
Sladen, N. St. Barbe, E1730
Slate, John, E1069
Slesar, Henry, AR
Slote, Alfred E., E1260
Slung, Michele, B15, B181, B373, C390, C759-C765, E2324
Smalley, Jack, D330
Small, Sidney Herschel, AR
Smeltzer, Robert H., D73, D195, D214, D217
Smith, A. J. M., E1324
Smith, Bill, D389
Smith, Billy G., E805
Smith, Carmichael, AR
Smith, Charles Merrill, AR
Smith, Clark Ashton, C520
Smith, David, E443
Smith, David R., E2948
Smith, Derek, D196, D223
Smith, Edgar W., E817
Smith, Ernest Bramah. See Bramah, Ernest
Smith, (Mrs.) E. V., E2178
Smith, Frank E., E720
Smith, Garret, AR
Smith, H. Allen, E2451
Smith, Harry B., E990, E987
Smith, Henry, E2908
Smith, Herbert F., B374, E3026
Smith, Janet, E277, E293, E294
Smith, Junius B., D447, D448, E2719
Smith, Lawrence Dwight, D82
Smith, Mark, AR, B67
Smith, Martin, E2720-E2722
Smith, Mary, E128, E137
Smith, Myrna J., E2863
Smith, Myron, A48, A157, A158
Smith, Robert, E1495, E2818
Smith, Rozella, E2818
Smith, Shelley, AR
Smith, Susan, E472, C764, C765
Smith, Wilbur Jordan, B3, D74, D342
Smithers, A. J., E3146
Smollett, Tobias, B259
Smuda, Manfred, B424, C766
Smyer, Richard I., E1542
Smyth, Frank, B375
Sneary, Rick, E376
Snell, Edmund, A103
Snelling, O. F., E1112
Snow, C. P., B17, B61, C768, E2633, E2679, E2723-E2728
Soderbergh, Peter A., D75
Soderman, Harry, E1199
Sokolov, Raymond A., E1899
Solar Pons (FC; Derleth), A87, A156, E810, E813, E815, E816, E820
Soldati, Mario, C311
Soler Canas, Luis, C770
Solomon Kane (FC; R. E. Howard), D328
Soloway, Sara, E2566
Sophie (FC; F. I. Anderson), E55
Sophocles, B216, B346, C143, C187, C272, C828
Sorani, Aldo, C771, C772, E3034
Sorensen, Eric, C191
Soriano, Oswaldo, E445, E446
Sormano, Elena, B377
Sörmark, Sven, B376, B386
Soutar, Andrew, AR, B253
Souvestre, Pierre, B107. See also Allain, Marcel
Spagnoletti, Giacinto, C773
Spain, M. M., E933
Spalding, Samuel, D32, D179, D190, D192, D195, D196
Spanos, William V., C774
Speaight, Robert, E1600
Speir, Hans, E1064
Speir, Jerry, E447, E1900
Spencer, David, E190
Spencer, Ross H., E2730
Spender, Natasha, E409, E448
Spengler, Oswald, E1531
Spenser(FC; R. Parker), E2067, E2068, E2071, E2074
Spicer, Bart, AR
Spicer, Christopher H., C775
Spicy Mystery Stories, D477
(The) Spider, D293, D297, D326, D363, D478-D490
Spier, Ursula, E1325
Spillane, Mickey, A148, B3, B69, B89, B216, B226, B302, B310, B348, C17, C149, C234, C267, C269, C316, C341, C352, C452, C534, C616, C678, C737, C747, C766, E242, E267, E395, E762, E1365, E2059, E2676, E2731-E2750
Spivak, Peter, E1214
Spornick, Nicholas B., E579, E596
Sprigg, Christopher St. John, AR
Spring, Howard, C121, C739, E532
Springer, Lloyd, E1204
Springheeled Jack (FC; dime novel), B7
Spy Stories, D311
Squire, J. C., E964, E2452
Squires, Roy A., E2931
Ssu Hsi Tze (PC), B443
Stadley, Pat, AR
Stafford, Jean, E2453
Stafford, William, B92
Stagge, Jonathan, AR, C617, E2282
Staglieno, Marcello, E3035
Stallworth, Lyn, E2751
Stam, James C., A158
Standish, Robert, E2044
Stanford, Ann, B2, B3
Stange, G. Robert, B93, C776
Stanich, Ray, E2267, E2454
Staniworth, John, D129
Stanley, Fay Grissom, AR
Stanley, John, E165
Stanton, Michael, E1152
Starace, Gino, E17
Stark, Richard, A21, B134, B317, C831, E3074, E1645, E3070, E3075, E3081. See also Westlake, Donald
Starkey, Lycurgus M., E1113
Starnes, Richard, AR
Starr, Kevin, E329
Starrett, Vincent, B61, B142, B449, C568, C777, C778, E185, E688, E818, E819, E1423, E1574, E2245, E2276, E2752-E2757
Startling Mystery Stories, D317, D437, D406
Stauffer, Donald, E2179
Steeger, Henry, D436, D438
Steel, Kurt, AR, B62
Steele, Curtis, D428
Steele, Timothy, B92, B379, C779, C780
Steeman, Stanislas-André, B213, B246, E2751-E2762
Steeman, Krisha, E2760
Steeves, B142
Steeves, Harrison Ross, C782
Stein, Aaron Marc, B15,,B234, B272, B15, B409, C781, C782, E119, E2180

Stein, Gertrude, B2, E2764
Stein, William, E141
Steinbrunner, Chris, A159, A160, B271, D461, E357, E2950
Steiner, George, C783, E1326
Steinert, T. R., B92, E1727a
Steinhoff, William R., E2690
Stendhal, E1928, E2994
Stéphane, Nelly, E2691, E2692, E1681
Stéphane, Roger, E2654
Sterling, Stewart, D334, E2767
Stern, Madeleine B., D76, D78, E10-E13
Stern, Peter, A161, C784, E1669
Stern, Philip Van Doren, B142
Stern, Richard Martin, AR, B64, B409
Sternberg, Jacques, E1732
Stertman, Hans, C785, E3126
"Steve and Sim" (juvenile series), E820
Stevens, R. L., E1496
Stevens, Shane, AR
Stevenson, Robert Louis, B42, B202, C703, C773, E52, E2768, E2769
Steward, Dwight & Barbara, AR
Stewart, A. W., E702. See also Connington, J. J.
Stewart, Enola, A162, E3133
Stewart, Gordon, E1254
Stewart, J. I. M., E689, E3036. See also Innes, Michael
Stewart, Lawrence D., B2, B3, E2766
Stewart, Mary, AR, B63, B65, C852, E1004a
Stewart, R. F., B380, E690, E839, E2181
Stiel, Beth, B149
Stilwell, Steven, A163, E1410
Stith-Thompson, C7
Stix, Thomas, E2815
Stock, Barbara, E2525, E2567
Stockbridge, Grant, B443
Stock, R. D., E2525, E2567
Stockton, Frank, B430
Stoker, Bram, E2770
Stone, Albert E., E2909
Stone, Alzina, E2501, E2502
Stone, Edward, E2867
Stone, Hampton. See Stein, Aaron Marc
Stone, P. M., E1204, E1215
Stoops, Herbert Morton, C826
Storm, Harrison, D437
Storm, Michael, D275, D279, D287
Storr, Anthony, B83, C786
Story, Jack, A106
Stout, Rex, B6, B17, B27, B48, B50, B216, B142, B164, B310, B337, B364, B366, B409, B50, C17, C35, C518, C734, C747, C787, C788, C868, E1023, E1898, E2068, E2235, E2238, E2771-E2827
Stowe, William W., B264, E449
Strachey, John, C789
Stragliati, Roland, E16
Strahan, Kay Cleaver, E2828
Straker, J. F., AR
Strand Magazine, A180
Strange, John Stephen, AR
Strange Detective Stories, D491
Stratemeyer, Edward, D75, D92, D99
Stratemeyer, Harriet, D122
Stratemeyer Syndicate, D24, D46
Stratford, Philip, E1309, E1327
Stratton-Porter, Gene, E2829
Street & Smith, C817, D32, D41, D52, D61, D65, D70, D74, D138, D145, D171, D175, D178, D198, D309, D362, D367, D373, D451, D469, D492, D502
Strenski, Ellen, C409, C790, E1476
Stribling, T. S., D309, E2830-E2833
Strich, Christian, E2679
Strindberg, August, E1879
Strom, Sven, C791, E2326, E2714
Strong, L. A. G., AR, B124, C792
Strout, Strout, E1443
Strunsky, Simeon, C793, C794
Stuart, Ian, E1915
Stubbs, Jean, AR, B75
Studley, Francis, E942
Sturak, Thomas, B2, B3, B230, E1804-E1808
Sturrock, Jerry, AR, C5
Styles, Frank Showell. See Carr, Glynn
Suddaby, John, E965
Sudo, Yasuo, B254, E614, E619
Sue, Eugène, C332, C818, E2097, E2103, E2671, E2834, E2835
Suerbaum, Ulrich, B126, B424, B451, C795
Sugano, Kunihiko, B151
Sugiyama, Tatsumaru, E3162
Sullerot, Evelyne, E2646, E2693
Sullivan, Eleanor, B117, B409, C212, C795a, C807, E2277, E2307
Sullivan, Hazel, C795b
Sullivan, John F., D30
Summerton, Margaret, AR
Sumuru (FC; S. Rohmer), E2428
Sunano, Kyohei, B382
Suneson, Victor, E2836
Superintendent Pibble (FC; P. Dickinson), B309, E1000, E1001
Superintendent Stevens (FC; Graeme), E979
Superintendent Venner (FC; dime novel), D240
Superintendent Wilson (FC; G. D. H. & M. Cole), B253, E629
Sussan, René, C796
Sutherland, James, E1041
Sutherland, John, B383
Suzuki, Seeichi, D335
Suzuki, Yukio, B142, B384, B385, D335
Svedelid, Olov, B376, B386, C797, C389
Svoboda, Frederic, B92, C798
Swan, Gordon, D279a-D283
Swan, Phyllis, E2837
Sweeney Todd, B7, D3, D77
Swigart, Leslie Kay, E1041
Swinburne, Algernon Charles, E691
Swinnerton, Frank, B18, C799, E2838
Symons, Julian, A119, A165, A166, B3, B18, B50, B61, B75, B83, C5, C15, C48, B105, B112, B124, B146, B179, B181, B387-B394, B434, C281, C542, C751, C800, C801, C802, C803, C804, C805, C838, E49, E102, E409, E450-E452, E518, E562, E596, E602, E603, E692, E693, E840, E1328, E1424, E1467, E1468, E2182, E2183, E2679, E2694, E2839-E2843, E3037
Szulc, Tad, E1523

Takagi, Akimitsu, B395
Talbot, David, E604
Talbot, Hake, E2844
Talburt, Nancy Ellen, B16, B396, C806, E2862
Tallack, Douglas G., B216, E1064a
Tamburini, Pico, B397
Tamura, Ryuichi, B398, E1973
Tanaka, Junji, B399, B400, E1315
Tani, Stefani, B401
Taniguchi, Takao, B11
Tanizaki, Junichiro, E2148
Tanugi, Gilbert, E2845
Tarbell, Marta, E1259
Taroux, (Father) René, E2986
Tartar (FC; Dickens), E892, E899, E923,

E927, E933, E963, E974
Tarzan (FC; E. R. Burroughs), D328
Taublieb, Paul, C807
Taylor, Bruce, A167, E2819
Taylor, F. Sherwood, B142, C808
Taylor, Isabelle, B142, C720, C809
Taylor, Phoebe Atwood, B364, E2846-E2849
Taylor, Robert Lewis, E357, E376
Taylor, Samuel W., AR
Taylor, Wendell Hertig, E2057, E3060. See also Barzun, Jacques
Tebbel, John, B40, E2365
Tedeschi, Alberto, B27
Teed, G. H., D259, D265
Teilheit, Darwin, B63, E2850, E2851
Tennenbaum, Michael, E596
Tenney, Thomas Asa, E2896, E2910
Tepperman, Emile C., E2852
Terhune, Albert Payson, C565, E611, E2853, E2854
Terman, Douglas, AR
Ternan, Ellen, E869, E884
Terrall, Robert, AR
Terrill, Roger, D293
Terror Tales, D437
Tey, Josephine, B16, B18, B141, C40, C76, E2855-E2863
Thackeray, William Makepeace, C703, E5, E2864
Thailing, William, E3119, E3126, E3132, E3134
Thaman, Stephen, C103
Thatcher Colt (FC; A. Abbot), E1
Thayer, Lee, C714, E2865, E2866
Thayer, Tiffany, E2867
Theresa Crichton (FC; A. Morice), C11
Theroux, Paul, B215
Thibeaudeau, Jean, E572, E573
Thiede, Karl, E2948
Thier, Erich, B424, C810
(The) Thinking Machine (FC; J. Futrelle), B281, D328, E1212-E1222
(The) Third Degree, C265
Thomas, Deborah, E841
Thomas, Gilbert, B403
Thomas, Louis-Charles, AR
Thomas, Martin, D274
Thomas, Ross, AR
Thompson, Arthur Leonard Bell. See Clifford, Francis
Thompson, Charles Willis, D10, E966
Thompson, George, E1425
Thompson, Jim, B73, B239, E2868-E2874, E3135
Thompson, Julian F., AR
Thompson, Leslie M., C811
Thomson, Arthur, E625
Thomson, Basil, AR
Thomson, D. L., E777
Thomson, G. M. Hollingsworth, E967
Thomson, H. Douglas, A70, B142, B403, E745, E1216, E1233, E1682, E1761, E1961, E1995, E2184, E2946, E3038, E745
Thomson, James W., E453-E455
Thomson, June, E2875, E2876
Thoorens, Leon, E2695, E2696
Thorndike, Russell, E2877
(The) Thorndyke File, A38, E1217
Thorpe, Dickson, D488, E752
Thrill Book, D493
(The) Thriller, A4, D19, D67
Thrilling Detective, D336, D494
Thrilling Mystery, D405, D437
Thrun, Wolfgang, C205
Thrush (TV series crime organization), C52
Thunderbolt (Pulp series), D495
Thurston, Harry, D420
Tidyman, Ernest, AR, B310
Tiger Mann (FC; M. Spillane), E2736
Tiger Standish (FC; S. Horler), B253
Tillinac, Denis, E2697
Tillinghast, Richard, E2568
Tillotson, Geoffrey, E694
Tillotson, Katherine, E695
Tilton, Alice, C495, E2849. See also Taylor, Phoebe Atwood
Tilton, Rafael, E2849
Ting, Nai-Tung, A168
Tinsley, Theodore, D467, D473
Tinsman, James L., A41
Tipton, Gene, D494
Tischler, Nancy M., E2569
Titone, E2590
Titta Rosa, Giovanni, C813
Tiverton, Dana, C814, E2366
Tizziani, Ruben, B214, C357
T. J. K., E996
Todd, Ruthven, B93, C815
Todorov, Tzvetan, B78, C816
Tolley, Michael J., E1850
Tollin, Anthony, D461
Toloyan, Khachib, E177
Tomashefsky, Steven, E2947
Tom Merry & Co (F. characters; C. Hamilton), E2474
Tom Sawyer (FC; M. Twain), C519
Tom Slade (juvenile series), D29
Tom Swift (juvenile series), D23
Tonic, C817
Tonik, Al(bert), C817, D331, D390, D409, D434
Tonoyama, Taiji, B406
Tornabuoni, Lietta, E1092
Tortel, Jean, B12, C818, E20
Touchant, Jean-Louis, E2278, E3039
Tournier, Marcel, B407
Tourteau, Jean-Jacques, B408, E21, E86, E170, E272, E773, E1683, E1684, E1762, E1763, E2006, E2698
Tousey, Frank, D48, D53, D54, D61, D76, D203
Towers, Harry, E2412
Towne, Stuart, D440, E2300. See also Rawson, Clayton
Townsend, Guy, E1353, E2339, E2810, E2820-E2822, E2860, E2863
Toye, Randall, E544, E605
Tozer, Alfred B., D152
Tracey Clews (FC; Orpheus Kerr), E983
Tracy, Don, B73
Tracy, Louis, E2581
Train, Arthur, C581, E2878, E2878a
Train, Oswald, E3084
Travis McGee (FC; J. D. MacDonald), C334, C594, E1813, E1816, E1817, E1819- E1822, E1824, E1839, E1840, E1845
Traylor, James L., E717, E2747, E2748
Treat, Lawrence, B48, B117, B124, B234, B409, E2879
Tree, Gregory, A12
Trench, John, AR
Trenter, Stieg, C785, E2880
Trenter, Ulla, B376, B386
Trevanian, AR, A158, C14, C122
Trevor, Elleston, A12, E37. See also Hall, Adam
Trevor, Glen. See Hilton, James
Trewin, Ion, E466, E2476
Trewin, J. C., E562, E606
Tripp, Miles, AR

Trotsky, E2646
Trott, Floyd, A170
Troy Nesbit (FC; juvenile series), D292
Troy, Simon, B18, E2881
Truchaud, François, E2315
Truesdale, David, E200
Truffaut, François, B378, E277, E1288, E3135
Truhon, Dorothy L., C244
Truman, Margaret, E2882
Tschimmel, Ira, B410
Tsuchiya, Satoru, E157
Tsuide, Ikuteru, B411
Tsukada, Yuzo, E1591
Tsunoda, Kikuo, E2883
Tsuzuki, Michio, B367, B412, B413, E2884
Tuck, Donald, A171, A172
Tuck, Jay, E1426
Tucker, Elizabeth, C236
Tucker, Wilson, E2885
Tuckett, J. E. Shum, E968
Tullberg, Sigurd, A73, A173
Tuppence & Tommy (F. characters; A. Christie), E605
Turesson, Ygnve, E592
Turgeon, Charlotte, B217
Turnbaugh, Roy, E295
Turner, Darwin T., B216, E3065
Turner, E. S., D34, D76
Turner, Robert, D332, D333
Turpin, Pierre, E63
Tuska, Jon, B414, C820, E1519, E2823, E2948, E2949
Twain, Mark, B3, B371, C341, C410, E1419, E2271, E2886-E2911
Twohy, Robert, AR
Twyman, H. W., D284
Tymm, Marshall B., A174
Tynan, Kathleen, E602
Tyre, Nedra, E2912
Tyrer, Walter, B18, E2913

Uekusa, Jun'ichi, B415-B417
Ueno, Takashi, B418
Uhnak, Dorothy, C747, E2914, E2915
Ulam, Adam, E607
Ulanov, Barry, C821
Ullman, Alan Gordon, C822
Ulysses, E222
Unaeus, Per-Ake, E2880
Uncle Abner (FC; M. D. Post), E2200-E2204, E2208
Underwood, Michael, AR, B124, B64, C823
Underworld Romances, D496
Underworld Stories, D311
Unger, Gunnar, E1533
Unicorn Mystery Book Club, A35, A41, C400
Unicorn Mystery Book Club News, B419, C400
Union Jack, C198, D66, D227, D232, D247, D260, D264, D267, D279a, D284
Union Jack Library, D139
Unkelbach, Kurt, E2854
Unwin, Frank, D285
Upfield, Arthur, B17, B270, C450, E2276, E2916-E2927
Urquhart, Fred, A56
Urquhart, MacGregor, AR
Usborne, Richard, B420, E296, E1112, E2477, E2478, E3040, E3147
Ushida, Masao, B108
Ushijima, Hidehiko, E2295

Vadieu, Georges, E16, E1679, E1685
Valencia, Michèle, E2218
Valentié, María Eugenia, C824
Valéry, Paul, E323, E2186
Valin, Jonathan, E2928
Valmain, Frédéric, E2612
Vanardy, Varick, D20, D173
Van Arsdale, Wirt, E2929
Van Ash, Cay, E2415, E2455-E2459
Vance, John Holbrook ("Jack"), A10, A12, E2930, E2931
Vance, Louis Joseph, AR, B201
Vandercook, John W., B344
Van der Valk (FC; Freeling), C17, E1144, E1146, E1147, E1148
van de Wetering, Janwillem, B75, C152, E775, E2932, E2933, E775
Van Dine, S. S., B6, B62-B64, B116, B134, B142, B298, B310, B337, B385, B404, B414, B424, C35, C63, C82, C271, C339, C433, C535, C718, C745, C771, C825-C827, C835, C878, E1, E95, E1351, E2934-E2952
Van Gelder, Robert, E2367, E2824
Van Gulik, Robert, A156, B18, B31, B439, E2953-E2967
Van Herp, Jacques, E2315, E2316
Van Hooland, Philippe, E2760
Van Meter, Jan R., B216, C828
Van Raalte, Joseph, D197
Van Rjndt, Philippe, AR
Van See, John, E2930
Van Tilburg, Walter, A175
Vandromme, Pol, E2699
Vane, Sutton, E925
Vanes, Alexander R., E969
Varaldo, Alessandro, C829
Vareille, Jean Claude, E1686, E1687, E1744, E1764
Varende, Yves, AR
Varma, Devendra P., B236, B421, E1724
Varnado, S. L., E2185
Varoux, Jean Alex, AR, A94
Vase, Gillan, E988
Vautrin (FC; Balzac), B257
Vautrin, Jean, B378, E2968
Vedder, John K., E1336. See also Gruber, Frank
Velman, H., E2700
Ven, These, D475, D489
Veraldi, Gabriel, B422, E42, E46, E50
Veraldo, C350
Vermandel, Janet Gregory, B409
Verne, Jules, B275, E1659, E2096
Véry, Mme (Mrs. Pierre), E2978
Véry, Noël, E2978
Véry, Pierre, B27, B142, B201, B246, C484, C830, E2969-E2998
Ves Losada, Alfredo, B423
Vespa, Mary, E2722
Vey, Marc, E337
Vian, Boris, E1067
Vicarel, Joann, E2340, E2810
Vickers, Roy, A4, B124, C148, E2999-E3004
Vidal, Gore, B366, E193-E195, E1524
Vidocq, François Eugène, B36, B122, B251, B257, B269, B300, B337, C303, C454, C862, E2094, E2103, E2113, E2183, E2192, E2618, E3005
Viebig, Clara, B444
Villesvik, Linda, AR
Villiers, Gérard de, C237, E3006
Villiers de l'Isle-Adam, E2707
Vincent, Harry, E308
Vines, Lois, E2186
Violet Strange (FC; A. K. Green), E1302
Virgil, B309
Virgil Tibbs (FC; Ball), B307, C473, E96

(The) Virginian (FC; Owen Wister), E1893
Vital Books, D185
Vittorini, E., C737
Vivian le Grand (PC), D497
Vivian, E. Charles, A12, E1939. See also Mann, Jack
Vladimir (FC; Allain/Souvestre), E14
Vogt, Jochen, B295, B424, B451
Volpatti, Lia, E1469
Volpe, Edmund, E1065
Voltaire, B251, B368, C585, C629, E2155, E2271
Von Shilling, James, B131
Voorhees, Richard J., E297, E298
Vormweg, Heinrich, B424, C831
Voskresensky, V. M., C832
Vuijlsteke, Marc, E2317
Vulliamy, C. E., E3007

Wade, Alan, E2930
Wade, Henry, B17, B159, B290, E3008-E3010
Wade, James, E2582
Wade, Robert. See Miller, Wade
Waedt, Carl L., D406
Wager, Walter, C832, E3011
Wagner, Elaine, C530
Wagner, Geoffrey, E1028
Wagner, Robert, B76
Wahlöö, Per, B26, B96, C152, C354, C576, C593, E388. See also Sjöwall, Maj
Wainwright, John, AR
Waite, John B., B142, C580, C834, C835
Waldmann, Guenter, B424, E1029
Waldron, Ann, E767, E1127, E1771
Walker, Dale, E1778
Walker, Katherine, E397
Walker, Vernon, E1067
Wall, Donald, E1800
Wallace, Edgar, A103-A106, A110, B20, B24, B41, B107, B204, B248, B302, B343, C183, C361, C375, C541, C605, C718, C799, C836, D327, D437, E790a, E1020, E1308, E1332, E1333, E2540, E3012-E3045
Wallace, Francis J., AR, E790a
Wallace, Penelope, B2, E3017, E3018, E3045
Wallace, Ethel V., E3044
Wallin, Lena, E1794
Walling, R. A. J., AR
Walpole, Horace, B259, C356, E2075
Walpole, Hugh, B28, C259, C567, C687
Walsh, John, E2187
Walsh, Rodolfo, C837
Walsh, Thomas, AR
Walter, Elizabeth, E562, E608
Walters, C838, E869, E980
Walters, J. Cuming, C838, C869, E934, E961, E970, E980, E984, E997-E999
Walton, James, E705
Wambaugh, Joseph, B96, C581, E3046-E3048
Wansbrough, John, E1329
Ward, Alfred C., B61, C839
Ward, Arthur Henry Sarsfield, A12, A158. See also Rohmer, Sax
Ward, Christopher, B142
Ward, David, E1105
Ward, Lock, A78
Ward, Rex E., D341
Warden, Florence, C176
Warner, Nicholas O., C840
Warren, Francis H., D275
Warriner, Thurman. See Troy, Simon
Warton, Carl, E2451, E2460
Washer, Robert, C583, E2279, E2279
Wasylyshyn, John, D97, D98
Watanabe, Ken, B425
Waterhouse, Howard, A176-A179, E1122
Waters, E3049
Watson, Colin, B18, B179, B426, C297, C841, E562, E609, E1510, E2479, E3050
Watt, John V., E971
Watts, Joyce, E2570
Waugh, Arthur, E696
Waugh, Charles, C842
Waugh, Evelyn, E1601, E1879
Waugh, Hillary, B15, B18, B48, B65, B96, B117, B181, B270, B309, B409, C843-C846, E3051-E3057
Waugh, Thomas, E94, E2824
Wayao, W. W., C286
Wayland, Patrick, AR
Weaks, Dan, E433
Wearing, F. N., D286
Weaver, William, A156, E562, E610
Webb, Jack, A143, B48, C617, E3058
Webb, Richard. See Quentin, Patrick
Webb, Walter, D287
Weber, Albrecht, E2704
Webster, Henry Kitchell, B17, E3059, E3060
Webster, Noah, E1917
Weesner, Theodore, C351
Weibel, Kay, B216, E2949
Weinberg, Robert, A174, D324, D334, D429, D485, D490, D498-D500, E163, E806, E807, E2283, E2285, E2288
Weiner, Norbert, E2807
Weinkauf, Mary S., E611
Weinstein, Arnold, E100
<u>Weird Tales</u>, A151, D314, D353, D406, D498-D500
Welch, Deshler, E1307
Welcome, John, AR
Wellershoff, Dieter, C847
Welles, Orson, C233, E46
Wellesley, Frederick, E902
Wellman, Ellen, E2045
Wellman, Manley Wade, D499, D500, E2288, E3060a
Wells, Anna Mary, B48
Wells, Carolyn, A120, B61, B427, C848-C850, E3061, E3062
Wells, Helen, B117
Wells, Tobias. See Forbes, Stanton
Wells, Walter, B428, E330, E456
Welty, Eudora, E1877, E1888, E1901
Wenders, Wim, E1368
Wennerlund, Staffan, E1794
Wentworth, Patricia, E3063, E3064
Wentworth, Richard, D293
Wentz, Walter J., E1983
Wermers, Bernie, D435
Werner, Craig, E972
Wertz, Linda L., E2188
Wertz, S. K., E2188
West, John B., B216, E3065
Westbrook, Perry, B48
Westerberg, Nils-Gunnar, E1427, E592
Western Story Library, D139
Western Writers of America, C247
Westin, Barbro, E1033
Westlake, Donald E., A13, A21, B73, B317, C735, C747, C831, E1294, E1645, E3066-E3081
Westmacott, Mary, E560, E596
Weston, Carolyn, AR
Weston, Louise E., C852
Weymouth, Anthony, AR
Whaley, Bob, C853
Wheatley, Dennis, A110, C688, C878, E532, E3082-E3085
Wheeler, Edward, D63

Wheeler, Hugh, C617. See also Quentin, Patrick
Wheeler-Nicholson, Malcolm, AR
Whicher, Jonathan, E672, E678
Whipple, Leon, C855
(The) Whisperer (PC), D326, D501
Whitaker, Rodney H., A158. See also Trevanian
White, David, B348
White, Dennis, E305
White, Diane, E1543
White, Ethel Lina, AR
White, Frederick M., A103
White, Jean M., E1801, E2933
White, Jon Manchip, AR
White, Lionel, AR
White, Percy, D215
White, Phyllis, B43
White, R. J., AR
White, T. H., E3086
White, Trentwell Mason, B62, C856
White, William Anthony Parker. See Boucher, Anthony
White, William, E501, E218-E227, E612, E1114, E1944-E1946, E2565
Whitechurch, Victor L., AR, E2271
Whitehead, John, E1976
Whiteley, J. Stuart, B3, E2702
Whiteside, Thomas, C857
Whitfield, Raoul, B134, C145, D343, D347, E3087-E3089
Whitley, John S., B429, C322, E1428
Whitman, Alden, E2826
Whitney, Phyllis A., AR, B15, B63-B65, B409, C858, E2360
Whitt, J. F., A180
Whitten, Mary, E2565
Whittington, Harry, B378, B48, B378, E780, E3090-E3094
Whitty, James H., E2189
Wieckenberg, Ernst-Peter, E1030
Wiegand, William, AR
Wigger, Anne P., E2911
Wight, H. F., B268
Wigmore, John, E2190
Wilbur, Richard, E2191
Wilcox, Collin, B64, B96, C292, E3095, E3096
Wilcox, Marion, E2827
Wilde, Geoffrey, D288
Wilder, Billy, E431
Wilder, Thornton, E2867
Wiley, Hugh, A179
Wiley, John, E3097
Wilkinson, Burke, E516
Wilkinson, Doris, E1482
Wilkinson, Ellen, B17, E3098
William Crane (FC; J. Latimer), E1637
Williams, Blanche, B430, E2209
Williams, Charles, AR, C819, E3135
Williams, David, AR
Williams, Donna Kay, D125
Williams, H. L., C860
Williams, John B., E3099
Williams, Lisa, B431
Williams, Richard, E613
Williams, Thomas, E2715
Williams, Valentine, B62, B63, C535, C861-C864, E1234, E2192, E3100
Williams, Vinnie, AR
Williamson, Jack, AR
Williamson, J. N., B432
Williamson, Adolphus, E678
Williamson, Tony, AR
Willis, Ted, AR
Willock, Colin, AR
Willoughby, Lee, E791
Wills, Cecil M., AR
Wilson, Alison, E820
Wilson, Angus, E868
Wilson, Colin, B181a, E1879, E3101
Wilson, David, E791
Wilson, Edmund, B24, B61, B78, B142, B348, B378, B385, B434, B451, C128, C147, C155, C232, C369, C379, C656, C865-C868, E330, E331, E859, E865, E869, E1054
Wilson, J. W., E942
Wilson, Mitchell, AR
Wilson, P. W., AR
Wilson, Ralph, B232
Wilson, Robert McNair. See Wynne, Anthony
Wilson, Woodrow, C81
Wilt, Judith, B433, E750
Wimsatt, W. K., E2193-E2195
Winchell, Mark, E1808
Winchell, Prentice. See Sterling, Stewart
Wingate, Nancy, C869
Wing, George, E973
Winkauf, Mary S., C870
Winks, Robin, B434-B436, C735, C871, E709, E1342, E1356, E1544
Winn, Dilys, B105, B437, B438
Winslow, Kent, D91, D123
Winters, Warrington, E870
Wirt, Mildred, D120
Witherington, Paul, E250
Wittenbourg, Jacob, C593
Witting, Clifford, B17, E3102, E3103
Wivell, Charles Joseph, B439
(The) Wizard (PC), D502
Wobbe, R. A., E1330
Wodehouse, P. G., A180, B339, C872, E3104-E3107
Woecklen, Fritz, B112, B440
Wolfe, Ashton, E3108
Wolfe, Peter, B92, C873, E697, E1132, E1902, E1331, E1332, E1429, E1430
Wolff, Robert Lee, E214
Wolfrom, Didier, E2613
Wood, Barbara, E2571
Wood, H. F., E3109
Wood, (Mrs.) Henry, B311, C123, C204
Wood, Jack, D129, D130, E735
Wood, J. F., D289
Wood, Neville, C874
Wood, Sara, E3110
Woodford, Jack, A12
Woods, Katherine, C875
Woodson, Weldon, D136, D198, D199
Woodward, Katherine, E1308
Woodworth, Fred, D60, D91, D110
Wooley, John, D360
Woolfolk, Josiah Pitts, A12
Woolf, Virginia, E468
Woolrich, Cornell, B27, B43, B134, D437, E65, E3111-E3135
World's Great Novels of Detection, A76
Wormser, Richard, AR, C247, D172, D334
Wormull, Len, D79, D419
Worpole, Ken, E1431
Worsley-Gaugh, Barbara, AR
Worthen, Samuel C., E2193, E2196, E2197
Worts, George F., E3136
Wrenn, C. L., D171
Wright, A. B., E1725
Wright, Charles, D80
Wright, Lee, B62, B142, C876
Wright, Richard, E2058, E2128, E2171
Wright, Rochelle, E1034
Wright, S. F. See Fowler, Sydney

Wright, Willard Huntington, B142, C82. See also Van Dine, S. S.
(The) Writer, B441
Writer's Digest, B442
Wrong, E. M., A70, B61, B142, C877
Wu, William, B443, C189
Wu Fang (PC), B443, D503, E2403
Wulff, Antje, B60, C878
Wulffen, Erich, B444
Wurtemberger, Thomas, B444
Wuyek, George, A181
Wyckoff, Capwell, D91, D113
Wylde, Jack, E1200
Wylie, Philip, E2750, E3137, E3138
Wyndham, Francis, E615
Wynne, Anthony, B253, E3139, E3140
Wynne, Nancy Blue, E616, E617, E3064

Xenophile, A38

Yagi, Toshio, E2183
Yamada, Futaro, B367, B418, E3141, E3142
Yamaguchi, Masaya, B170, B254
Yamamota, Sansei, B445
Yamamura, Masao, A182, A182, B446, B447
Yanagida, Tzumi, B448
Yang, Gladys, B229
Yang, Hsien-yi, B229
Yang, Winston L. Y., A109, B229, B449
Yano, Kozaburo, B254
Yates, Donald A., B15, B290, B450, C358, C583, C879-C882, E2280
Yates, Dornford, B420, E3143-E3147
Ybarra, Bob, D220
Yellow Magazine, A103
Yellowback Library, A38, D81
Yen Sin (FC; D. Keyhoe), B443
Yokomizo, Seishi, B418, C550, E3148-E3157
York, Andrew, E3157a
Yorke, Margaret, AR, E1540
York, James, D291
York, Sue Ellen, E596
Yoshino, Mieko, E600
Young, Trudee, E2703
Young King Brady (FC; dime novel), D63
Young Men of America, D48
Young Broadbrim Weekly, D52
Young Sleuth (FC; dime novel), D13, D16, D48, D204
Young Sleuth Library, D42, D52
Youngberg, Ruth Tanis, E2572
Youngden, Lama, E775
Yrondy, Pierre, E3158
Yude, Gordon, E1032
Yudkin, John, C632
Yuill, P. B., AR
Yuki, Shoji, E3159
Yumeno, Yusaku, E3160-E3164
Yvonne Cartier (FC; dime novel), D244

Zabel, Morton Dauwen, E1333
Zaccaria, Alfonso, C145
Zaccone, Pierre, E1008
Zandel, Diego, C883
Zangwill, Israel, B116, C101, E3165, E3166
Zaremba, Eve, E3167
Zbikowski, Tadeus, C99
Zed (FC; dime novel), D185
Zeiger, Henry A., E1115
Zekulin, Gleb, E2718
Zerbe, Andy, E724
Ziegler, Robert E., E3048
Zigari, B., C124
Zinsser, David Lowe, E457
Zmegac, Viktor, B78, B112, B451, C884
Zola, Emile, C195
Zone, Ray, C885
Zorzoli, G. B., E1092
Zuckerman, Ed, D99

Contributors

Adey, Robert C. S. Surveyor for H. M. Customs and Excise Department (England). Currently in the process of revising his *Locked Room Murders and Other Impossible Crimes* (Ferret, 1979). Contributor to a number of journals and fanzines.

Baudou, Jacques. Advanced degree in cellular biology. Director of Film Program, Maison de la culture, Reims, France. Editor of *Enigmatika*, member of OULIPOPO, editor (with Paul Gayot) of *Sherlock Holmes Memorial* in two volumes, and contributor to major French genre publications.

Apostolou, John L. Writes and edits technical report films for the Space Division of the United States Air Force. He has published articles and book reviews in *The Armchair Detective*, *The Poisoned Pen* and *Extrapolation*. His major areas of interest are Japanese crime fiction and the mystery writers of the pulp era.

Bleiler, Everett F. Freelance writer. Former vice president, Dover publications; editorial consultant, Charles Scribners Sons; editor of *A Treasury of Victorian Detective Stories* and other collections and anthologies. Author of *The Guide to Supernatural Fiction*. World Fantasy Award, 1978; Pilgrim Award, Science Fiction Research Association, 1984.

Briney, Robert E. Writer on a wide variety of topics in popular fiction. He was a Contributing Editor to the *Encyclopedia of Mystery & Detection* and the *Encyclopedia of Frontier & Western Fiction*. His essays have appeared in a number of collections and journals. He is editor and publisher of *The Rohmer Review*. He served on the editorial board of The Mystery Library, is a member of the new Bantam Books Mystery Classics Editorial Board, and has lectured and taught college courses in mystery fiction.

Cox, J. Randolph. Librarian and associate professor, St. Olaf College, Northfield, Minnesota. The leading authority on Nick Carter, on whom he has compiled a number of bibliographies, and contributor of numerous essays to major journals.

Cremante, Renzo. Professor of Italian Literature at the University of Bologna. Editor, with Loris Rambelli, of an anthology of essays on detective fiction, *La trama del delitto* (Parma, 1982). Member of the committee responsible for the annual Festival internazionale del giallo at Cattolica (Italy). He has also, in collaboration with the Italian Studies Department at the University of Bologna, promoted the establishment of a Center of Documentation and Study of Detective Literature.

Fisher, Benjamin F., IV. Professor of English, University of Mississippi. Past President of the Poe Studies Association of MLA, Chairman for Speakers Selection in the Edgar Allan Poe Society (Baltimore). Author and editor of a number of articles and books on Poe. He is also Editor of *The University of Mississippi Studies in English*, and on the editorial boards of *English Literature in Transition (1880-1920)*, *Poe Studies*, and the *Housman Society Journal*. He is completing a bibliography of material on the Gothic tradition, in which Poe, Collins, Dickens and other authors linked with mystery-detective writing are considered.

Goode, Greg. Graduate Student, Department of Philosophy, University of Rochester. Contributor to Twentieth Century Crime and Mystery Writers, 2nd ed., and to the Dictionary of Literary Biography: Afro-American Novelists since 1955. Author of studies and bibliographies of German critical literature, the German dime novel, ethnic aspects of the crime novel, high adventure fiction and other topics, for The Armchair Detective, The Mystery FANcier, The Poisoned Pen, Melus, and other publications.

Hedman, Iwan. Retired Swedish army medical officer. Editor/publisher of Dast, the oldest European magazine devoted to genre fiction, and the leading Scandinavian publisher of books on mystery fiction. Contributor to journals in Europe and America.

Johnson, Deidre. Doctoral candidate in American Studies at the University of Minnesota. Author of Stratemeyer Pseudonyms and Series Books: An Annotated Checklist of Stratemeyer and Stratemeyer Syndicate Publications (Greenwood Press, 1982).

Kimura, Jiro. B. A. in anthroplogy/sociology, Pace University, New York. Translator, book reviewer. Author of The Second International Crime Writers Congress Picture Book and other publications; translator (into Japanese) of books by Joseph Wambaugh, Roger L. Simon, Michael Collins, Edward D. Hoch, and others.

Maio, Kathleen L. Librarian and free-lance writer. She is a book editor and mystery reviewer for Sojourner, Boston women's newspaper, and is the mystery columnist for Wilson Library Bulletin. Her mystery-related work has appeared in reference sources like American Women Writers: A Guide to Reference and Twentieth Century Crime and Mystery Writers.

Murray, Will. Editorial director of Odyssey publications; editor, Duende; past editor of Skullduggery. Author of The Duende History of the Shadow Magazine (1980) and co-author of The Man behind Doc Savage (1974), Secret Agent X, A History (1980), and The Assassin's Handbook (1982). Contributor to Twentieth Century Crime and Mystery Writers, Twentieth Century Science Fiction Writers and Science Fiction, Fantasy and Weird Fiction Magazines (1984) and to numerous journals and fanzines. Winner of Lamont Award (for significant contributions to pulp research and writing), 1979.

Nieminski, John. Editor of the Sherlockian journal, Baker Street Miscellanea. Bibliographer of note and author of EQMM 350 (Armchair Detective Press, 1974) and The Saint Magazine Index (Cook & McDowell Publications, 1980). He is preparing for publication an index to the Alfred Hitchcock Mystery Magazine.

Rambelli, Loris. Middle school teacher (Italy). Author of a history of the Italian "giallo" (1979); co-editor, with Renzo Cremante, of La trama del delitto, and contributor to journals.

Sampson, Robert. Born in Ohio, and a graduate of Ohio State University; works with NASA in Huntsville, Alabama. He has published some fiction and many articles about the pulp magazines. He has also published three books: The Night Master (Pulp Press, 1982; on The Shadow) and two volumes of the five-volume series, Yesterday's Faces (Bowling Green State University

Press, 1983, 1984), concerning series characters in the pulps.

Seeger, Mary Anderson. Ph. D. (University of Wisconsin) in Germanic philology. Professor of German, Director of Academic Resource Center at Grand Valley State College in Allendale, Michigan, where she also teaches detective fiction occasionally. Active in "Murder by the Book," a highly civilized group of detective fiction addicts in Grand Rapids, Michigan.

Shimpo, Hirohisa. B. A. from Waseda University (Japan). Mystery reviewer and author of a collection of detective puzzles.

Stilwell, Steven A. Authority on the writings of Vincent Starrett; compiler of *The Ten-Year Index to The Armchair Detective* (1979).

Taniguchi, Toshihiko. B. A. from Waseda University (Japan). Specialist in library science and reference books. Book reviewer, bibliographer, and contributor to Japanese journals. He is working on a bibliography of Japanese translations of crime fiction.

About the Editor

WALTER ALBERT is an Associate Professor of French at the University of Pittsburgh. He has contributed to _The Armchair Detective_, _The Mystery FANcier_, _The Poisoned Pen_, _The Not So Private Eye_, _Enigmatika_ and _Europe_. He served as an advisory editor for the second edition of _Twentieth Century Crime and Mystery Writers_ and as "Correspondant USA" for the French journal, _Enigmatika_.

808.83016 A333d
Albert, Walter.
Detective and mystery
fiction